1972

This book may be kept

# STUART PLAYS

# STUART PLAYS

EDITED BY

## ARTHUR H. NETHERCOT
FRANKLYN BLISS SNYDER PROFESSOR
OF ENGLISH, EMERITUS
NORTHWESTERN UNIVERSITY

## CHARLES R. BASKERVILL
LATE PROFESSOR OF ENGLISH
UNIVERSITY OF CHICAGO

## VIRGIL B. HELTZEL
PROFESSOR OF ENGLISH, EMERITUS
NORTHWESTERN UNIVERSITY

REVISED BY
## ARTHUR H. NETHERCOT

HOLT, RINEHART AND WINSTON, INC.
New York · Chicago · San Francisco · Atlanta · Dallas
Montreal · Toronto · London · Sydney

Copyright © 1971 by Holt, Rinehart and Winston, Inc.
Library of Congress Catalog Card Number: 79-161203
**ISBN: 0-03-083029-X**
Printed in the United States of America
1 2 3 4    0 3 8    9 8 7 6 5 4 3 2 1

# PREFACE

This collection of Elizabethan and Stuart plays exclusive of Shakespeare has the advantage of a larger compass than similar anthologies for students. It opens with such plays as *Roister Doister*, *Gammer Gurton's Needle*, and *Gorboduc*, in which, through imitation of the classics, English drama broke with medieval tradition as represented in the hybrid moralities, and it extends to the closing of the theaters in 1642, when the tone of the drama was already foreshadowing the Restoration period. Enough plays are included, moreover, to show the richness and variety of the great dramatic art of the era without neglecting the various phases of its historical development. It has been possible, for example, to print five plays and a masque as representative of Jonson's work, and at the same time to give specimens of popular romantic drama like *Mucedorus* or of a hitherto neglected form like the jig. All the significant types of drama in the period are illustrated here.

The plays have been arranged in two groups as Elizabethan and Stuart for the purpose of emphasizing what is distinctive in each period. In this way the Elizabethan group may more readily be studied in connection with medieval drama or Shakespeare, and the Stuart group as a background for Restoration drama. The division is useful even when the two eras are studied together. In Shakespeare's immediate predecessors and contemporaries, the Elizabethan characteristics of boldness of conception and execution are obvious, resulting in an imaginative and emotional power which is frequently accompanied by a disregard for restraint, structure, and form. This distinctive quality survives in the final work of Shakespeare and in the two great tragedies of Webster, so that *The Duchess of Malfi*, in spite of its late date, is included with the Elizabethan plays. Already, however, Jonson had written his chief works that represent the Stuart reaction in drama, following classical ideals of restraint and unity in design; and a change of attitude, with a more searching study of manners, resulted. The centering of interest on form and technique, even in romantic plays, gives a sufficiently distinct character to the plays of the Stuart period as a whole.

The text used as a basis of the editing is indicated in the introduction to each play. For about half the plays, original early editions, photostatic copies of them, reproductions in the Farmer Facsimile Texts, or facsimile reprints of the Malone Society have been used. The rest are based on standard modern editions, in most cases recent critical editions. These have also been checked with other modern editions, or where possible with Farmer Facsimiles or the Malone Society reproductions. In whatever affects the actual content of the play, including stage directions, the principle followed has been one of strict fidelity to the original. Emendations have been avoided when any logical interpretation of the reading given seemed possible, and those adopted are duly recorded in the footnotes. Added material has been enclosed in square brackets. When no source of an emendation is stated, it has been made on the authority of the basic text, except that in stage directions the bracketed material has usually been added by the present editors. Plays with no act and scene division have been divided simply into scenes, with bracketed numbers. Likewise few liberties have been taken with the verse arrangement found in the sixteenth and seventeenth century originals, unless by a simple change in the division of lines a whole passage could be made to fall into pattern. Footnotes call attention to such revision in the plays in which it occurs. In *George a Greene* and the additions to *The Spanish Tragedy*, there are so many doubtful cases or cases in which no satisfactory arrangement of the lines is possible that no attempt has been made to change the original arrangement even in the passages where the dramatist's intention seems fairly clear.

In matters of less fundamental importance, the editing has been done with a view to aiding the student who is interested primarily in the literary and dramatic qualities of the plays. Hence spelling, punctuation, and capitalization have been modernized.

v

Where differences in spelling, however, suggest significant differences in pronunciation resulting from the survival in Elizabethan times of variant forms now obsolete (as in *hunderd, renowm, accompt,* for example), the original has been followed, at times even in doubtful cases.   On the other hand, in certain very common words where the vowel varies so frequently as to suggest that perhaps to an Elizabethan there was little distinction in sound, the modern spelling has been adopted.   Examples include the use of *than* for *then* (in the modern sense of *than*), *whither* and *hither* for *whether* and *hether* (except in dialect or consciously archaic passages or for rime), *devil* for *divel, show* for *shew, ambassador* for *embassador,* and many *in-* combinations for *en-* combinations (for instance, *increase* for *encrease*).   In such original forms as *marchant* and *clark, -er-* has regularly been substituted for *-ar-.*   The spellings *dost* and *doth,* rather than *doest* and *doeth,* are regularly used for the words as auxiliaries.   *Wive's* as a possessive singular is printed *wife's,* but in general such voicings have been retained whenever any modern justification for them could be found.   Again, obvious misprints have been silently corrected throughout.   Numerals also are written out, and a compound form like 24 is expanded into the common Elizabethan form *four-and-twenty.*   In many of the plays, speech heads vary so irrationally that they have been frankly reduced to some consistency.   The prevalent or the most logical form of each speaker's name, usually an abbreviation, has been adopted throughout a play, except that, where there are two or three different names for the same speaker, they are retained, with explanation in the notes.   As the original speech heads in *Cambises* are printed in full consistently, however, they have been left unchanged.   It is perhaps unnecessary to mention the omission of imprints, colophons, titles repeated at the head of the text proper, and running heads, or the occasional disregard of certain unusual arrangements of the material on the page of the original.

As an aid in the matter of meter, an accent has been placed over *e* in the verbal suffix *-ed* when it is pronounced as an additional syllable contrary to ordinary usage, and an apostrophe marks the omission of a vowel when a shortening in pronunciation seems to be indicated by the spelling of the original (as in *wav'ring,* for example).   For the rest, it is felt that with a little attention to Elizabethan practice, the reader will quickly fall into the rhythm of the various dramatists, representing various periods.   Especially after playwrights learned to give verse some of the flexibility of speech, blank verse was handled very freely.   Occasionally the line is as short as one foot, or as long as six.   The foot may have an extra syllable, or a syllable may be omitted, usually at the beginning of a line or after a pause.   Inverted stress is frequent in the first foot and occasionally occurs elsewhere, especially after a pause.   It is to be noted also that some Elizabethan words differ from modern usage in the position of the accent, and a much larger number seems to have been very flexible as to accent, at least in verse. *Ácademy, revénue, infámous, envý, cómplete, canónize, obdúrate, pórtray, déprive,* and *aspéct* are a few examples taken from the plays printed here.   Another large group of words, especially those with endings in *-ion, -ian, -ia, -ience, -ier,* etc., are often to be scanned as having a syllable more than is normal in modern pronunciation (as in *motion, ocean, Christian, Persia, Delia, soldier, marriage*).   Not infrequently, too, an extra syllable is developed, especially in connection with *l* and *r* (as in *fair, fire, hour, mild, sure, sworn*).

Webster's *Collegiate Dictionary* has been taken as the standard of what the reader might properly be expected to know in the matter of current vocabulary.   Old forms that are not obvious, and words and phrases that are obsolete, or have shifted meaning, or for any other reason might not be understood, have been explained in the notes for each play, but as a rule only in the first occurrence in a given play.

The editors wish to thank Professor J. C. Murley, Professor J. G. Fucilla, and Dr. N. A. Bennetton for help in translating a few difficult or corrupt passages from Latin, Italian, and Spanish, and Professor F. H. Heidbrink, Professor M. E. Prior, Dr. L. S. Wright, and Dr. Z. S. Fink for help in proof-reading the second part.

# PREFACE TO THE REVISED EDITION

Since the first publication of this anthology thirty-five years ago so many new articles and books on Elizabethan and Stuart drama and its biographical, intellectual, and artistic environment have appeared that it became obvious that a revised edition was called for to maintain the collection's appeal to the large body of students and teachers who have found it useful. In accordance with recent textbook-format trends and for ease in handling, it was decided to publish this edition in two volumes, one to be entitled *Elizabethan Plays* and the other *Stuart Plays*, rather than in the one bulky volume.

In undertaking this revision alone, since Professor Baskervill is dead and Professor Heltzel is unavailable for anything more than consultation because of his residence in Austria, I have completely rewritten and considerably expanded the introductions to the plays in order to take advantage of what I consider the most important of the new articles and books which have recently come out. To make these introductions more interesting to the student, I have given much more attention to the lives of the playwrights, in the hope that this approach will help to make the times in which they lived more vivid. While retaining the initial and elastic Elizabethan spelling and punctuation for direct quotations from documents, manuscripts, and original texts, in order to add authenticity and picturesqueness to the portrayal of Elizabethan life, I have kept the modernized spelling and punctuation of the plays themselves and the titles of the various works referred to.

For teachers I have endeavored to furnish concise digests of the most important of the published ideas and discoveries of their fellow-scholars. For the most part I have tried to present points of view impartially whenever controversies over interpretations, purposes, textual problems, datings, etc., have arisen. In this way I have attempted to raise discussion questions without giving answers, and have, I hope, cleared the ground of some bibliographical and biographical underbrush that might otherwise have to be disposed of through time-consuming lectures. The bibliographical paraphernalia which may seem to pockmark some of the pages have been inserted for the guidance and reassurance of the teacher, and may well be skimmed by the well-trained student who knows what is useful for his own purpose. In the case of books of a general nature, which deal with genres, ideas, influences, and movements, affecting many individual playwrights, I have given the imprint of publication only on their first citation. Knowing that our anthology offers a much wider range of plays to choose from than any other on the market and realizing that probably few instructors will be able to use all the plays and introductions, I suggest that when a new title turns up without an identifying imprint it may be found by looking back through earlier introductions.

The texts of the plays have remained essentially the same, since many users of the anthology have assured me that they have found them sound. I have, however, been able to correct inevitable typographical errors and to improve many footnotes and add new ones by taking advantage of the several excellent editions of individual plays that have recently been published. I take this opportunity of thanking their editors for their unwitting aid in making many of these glosses more helpful and meaningful than they might otherwise have been.

Only two changes have been made in the selection of plays to be included. In the first volume, *Elizabethan Plays*, the 1616 text of Marlowe's *Doctor Faustus* has been substituted for the former 1604 text, since the consensus of recent scholarship seems to have concluded that the later and longer version is closer to what Marlowe intended. In second volume, *Stuart Plays, The Revenger's Tragedy* has been added by popular demand. We had planned to use it in the 1934 edition, but it was forced out by lack of space. Because of the intense recent interest in the play (which I am listing as anonymous), it is now impossible to keep it out of any group of representative Jacobean dramas. I am also shifting Webster's *The Duchess of Malfi* from the first to the second volume, where it clearly belongs.

*A.H.N.*

*January, 1971*

# ABBREVIATIONS

To save space, the following abbreviations of the names of periodicals and series have been used in the introductions:

| | |
|---|---|
| AS | *Aberystwyth Studies* |
| AUL | *Annales de l'Université de Lyons* |
| BRMMLA | *Bulletin of the Rocky Mountain Modern Language Association* |
| BUW | *Bulletin of the University of Wisconsin* |
| CE | *College English* |
| DUJ | *Durham University Journal* |
| EA | *Études Anglaises* |
| ELH | *English Literary History* |
| E&S | *Essays and Studies* |
| ES | *English Studies* |
| F | *Folklore* |
| FUS | *Furman University Studies* |
| HLQ | *Huntington Library Quarterly* |
| HSNPL | *Harvard Studies and Notes in Philology and Literature* |
| HSE | *Harvard Studies in English* |
| JEGP | *Journal of English and Germanic Philology* |
| MLN | *Modern Language Notes* |
| MLQ | *Modern Language Quarterly* |
| MLR | *Modern Language Review* |
| MP | *Modern Philology* |
| NQ | *Notes and Queries* |
| PLPS | *Proceedings of the Leeds Philosophical Society* |
| PQ | *Philological Quarterly* |
| REL | *Review of English Literature* |
| RES | *Review of English Studies* |
| RLC | *Revue de la Littérature Comparée* |
| S | *Scrutiny* |
| SAB | *Shakespeare Association Bulletin* |
| SAS | *Stratford-upon-Avon Studies* |
| SJ | *Shakespeare Jahrbuch* |
| SP | *Studies in Philology* |
| TLS | *London Times Literary Supplement* |
| TRSC | *Transactions of the Royal Society of Canada* |
| UIS | *University of Illinois Studies* |
| UNS | *University of Nebraska Studies* |
| UTSE | *University of Texas Studies in English* |
| YSE | *Yale Studies in English* |
| YWES | *Year's Work in English Studies* |

# CONTENTS

Ben Jonson. . . . . . . . . . . . . . . 1
  *Every Man in His Humor* . . . . . . . . 12
  *Sejanus His Fall* . . . . . . . . . . . 65
  *Volpone*. . . . . . . . . . . . . 129
  *The Alchemist* . . . . . . . . . . . 195
  *The Sad Shepherd* . . . . . . . . . . 263
  *The Hue and Cry after Cupid* . . . . . . 291
John Webster . . . . . . . . . . . . . 303
  *The Duchess of Malfi* . . . . . . . . . 311
Thomas Middleton and William Rowley . . . . . . 363
  *A Trick to Catch the Old One*. . . . . . . 371
  *The Changeling*. . . . . . . . . . . 411
Cyril Tourneur (?) . . . . . . . . . . . 453
  *The Revenger's Tragedy* . . . . . . . . 461
Francis Beaumont and John Fletcher . . . . . . . 507
  *The Knight of the Burning Pestle* . . . . . 513
  *The Faithful Shepherdess* . . . . . . . . 557
  *Philaster* . . . . . . . . . . . 601
  *The Maid's Tragedy* . . . . . . . . . 649
Philip Massinger . . . . . . . . . . . . 699
  *A New Way to Pay Old Debts* . . . . . . 705
  *The Maid of Honor* . . . . . . . . . 749
John Ford . . . . . . . . . . . . . 795
  *The Witch of Edmonton* . . . . . . . . 805
  *The Broken Heart* . . . . . . . . . . 845
  *Perkin Warbeck* . . . . . . . . . . 899
James Shirley . . . . . . . . . . . . 951
  *The Lady of Pleasure* . . . . . . . . . 955
  *The Cardinal* . . . . . . . . . . . 1001

# STUART PLAYS

# BEN JONSON

Ben Jonson was the only one of Shakespeare's many contemporaries of high literary standing and authority who recognized in print the magnitude of his friend's accomplishment, as acknowledged in his famous poetical tribute prefacing the 1623 folio and addressed to the memory of his "Beloved, the Author Mr. William Shakespeare: and what he hath left us." He was also, in the opinion of most later critics, readers, and playgoers from the time of Dryden onward, considered the greatest Elizabethan dramatist next to Shakespeare. Nevertheless, when Jonas A. Barish published his *Ben Jonson: A Collection of Critical Essays* (New York, 1963), containing essays by T. S. Eliot, L. C. Knights, Edmund Wilson, and Harry Levin, he prefaced the volume with the statement: "Probably no major author in English has suffered such a catastrophic decline in popularity since his own day as has Ben Jonson. Certainly none·has been so punished for not being Shakespeare." Barish then defended the publication of his volume by saying that he was offering these essays by twentieth-century authors in the hope that they would redress the balance.

This estimate of the decline of interest in Jonson even into the twentieth century is somewhat surprising, in view of the stupendous eleven-volume scholarly edition of his works by C. H. Herford and Percy and Evelyn Simpson (Clarendon Press, 1925–52). There are a number of recent popular biographies of him, in addition to the scholarly treatment of his life and career in volumes I, II, and XI of the Herford-Simpson text, which followed in the general tradition of G. Gregory Smith's *Ben Jonson* in the English Men of Letters Series (London, 1919). In the light of Jonson's own reputation as the greatest scholar-author of his age, it is rather amazing that he has largely attracted the attention of the romantic and even novelistic type of biographer: the ecstatic Byron Steel (the pseudonym of Francis Steegmüller), *O Rare Ben Jonson* (New York, 1927); Eric Linklater, *Ben Jonson and King James/Biography and Portrait* (London, 1931), whose book is broader in scope than its title indicates; and John Palmer, *Ben Jonson* (London and New York, 1934), who makes more of an attempt at a critical appraisal of his subject's literary achievements than do his predecessors. Perhaps the general tenor of these enthusiastic studies is suggested by the fact that none of them deigns to furnish either a bibliography or footnotes for the inquisitive scholar. The last of the Jonson biographies for the sincere but not too academic reader is Marchette Chute's lively *Ben Jonson of Westminster* (New York, 1953), which stands midway between the two previous types: it mentions neither Steel, Linklater, nor Palmer and contains no footnotes, but it acknowledges the invaluable aid given by Herford and the Simpsons and appends a ten-page bibliography. To reassure the student of Jonson, perhaps initially overawed by the playwright's reputation for learning, it might be confessed at the outset that recent scholars have discovered that Jonson often went to secondary rather than primary sources, even in the case of classical tragedies like *Sejanus* and *Catiline*, and in his frequently profuse marginal references he sometimes faked a credit to an original without going to it himself.

Because of his pronounced and highly individualistic personality, more is known about Ben Jonson than about any other Elizabethan dramatist, great or small. F. H. Mares, in his Revels edition of *The Alchemist* (London and Harvard, 1967), cites these sources of information as follows: twenty-two surviving letters; Jonson's conversations

1

with William Drummond; books from Jonson's library, often with marginal comments; many public documents; personal references in other writers' works; and several short lives by early biographers.

Ben Jonson was born late in 1572 or early in 1573 in some unknown place—perhaps London—though definitely not in Westminster, which soon became associated with his name.  As he told his friend William Drummond, of Hawthornden, Scotland, in 1619 (*Ben Jonson's Conversations with Drummond of Hawthornden*, London, 1924): "His Grandfather came from Carlisle, and he thought from Anandale to it," Anandale being in Scotland and Carlisle just south of the border.  According to Jonson, his grandfather "served King Harry 8" in some unspecified capacity, and "was a Gentleman."  His father, however, lost all his estate under Bloody Mary, and, "having been cast in prisson and forfaitted, at last turned Minister."  But Jonson never knew his minister father, for the elder Johnson died a month before his son's birth.  The family name was thus spelled with the conventional *h*, but when the boy Benjamin grew into a young man and began to write he decided that it would be only fitting to distinguish himself from the myriads of other Johnsons in England by dropping his *h*.  He persisted in always signing himself "Jonson," but many of his contemporaries refused to accept this version, and, as Chute points out, it was not until the great Samuel Johnson came to dominate the English literary scene in the mid-eighteenth century under the conventional spelling of the name that the public came to recognize the desirability of making an orthographic distinction between the surnames of Ben and Sam.  Chute states that this differentiation had become well established by 1840.  With or without the *h*, Benjamin Jonson seems to have been the only Englishman with this particular combination of common English names at the time.

Soon after the death of her husband, the widow Johnson moved her family to what was then the village of Charing, Westminster, and it was here in Hartshorn Lane near Charing Cross that, as Jonson's first biographer, Thomas Fuller, put it, while the boy was still "a little child, . . . his mother married a bricklayer for her second husband." The stigma of being both a bricklayer's son (or stepson) as well as a bricklayer himself, for a period, afforded Jonson's enemies (and he quickly acquired many) an easy opportunity for continuous jibes during his whole career.  For the Bricklayers' Company was one of the lowliest in the hierarchy of all the trades guilds.

The boy's early schooling was probably obtained in the small school of St. Martin's parish.  Fortunately the family had a friend (unidentified by Jonson to Drummond) who placed him to be further educated at the famous Westminster School, where he was an "oppidans," or day boy.  As Chute relates, he never became one of the privileged group of Queen's Scholars, or even a pensioner; but luckily he made an impression on the young assistant headmaster, or usher, William Camden.  Camden, who was working on his first book, a Latin history of early England, *Britannia*, was to start Jonson off on his brilliant career as one of England's greatest scholars.  The wise, gentle, and understanding Camden made a scholar and a classicist out of the promising young boy, who paid his tribute to his teacher in dedications and lines such as these:

> Camden, most reverend head, to whom I owe
> All that I am in arts, all that I know . . . .

At Westminster Jonson learned his Greek and Latin, especially Cicero, Terence, Horace, and Quintilian.  He became imbued with the true spirit of the ancient classical world, with its emphasis on moral principles, discipline, and restraint, with which his own excitable temperament often conflicted.  He was also inculcated with the gentlemanly Christian virtues (though he did not always observe them later on), and set down his cullings from readings and his observations on life in the usual commonplace book.

On his graduation, although his failure to become a Queen's Scholar prevented him from becoming a competitor for one of the six school scholarships to Oxford or Cambridge, he was, as Fuller put it, "statutably admitted into St. John's College in Cambridge . . . , where he continued but few weeks for want of further maintenance." Since the St. John's records for this period are lost, no official corroboration for this statement is possible. So instead of becoming a university graduate, and therefore ipso facto a gentleman, Jonson was apprenticed to his stepfather's trade, which he told Drummond "he could not endure," though while following it he still had time to pursue his true bent as a student. As later seventeenth-century legend had it, he worked with a trowel in his hand and a book in his pocket. He probably laid bricks at Lincoln's Inn in 1588, since a large sum was expended for construction there in that year. It must have been a welcome break in his apprenticeship when he found himself in the English army in the Low Countries, perhaps as a draftee, where he boasted to Drummond that "he had, in the face of both the Campes, killed ane enemie and taken opima spolia from him." This was just the first of the occasions on which the irascible and pugnacious Jonson fought a duel which was fatal to his opponent, though it was the only one conducted publicly, a sort of vulgar imitation of the classical conflicts between rival champions.

Back in London, he not only returned to his trade, but married, though apprentices were not supposed to marry before they were twenty-four—at which age Jonson had a a son. Mark Eccles found the record of his marriage to an Anne Lewis in her parish of St. Magnus the Martyr, near London Bridge, on November 14, 1594 (Eccles, "Jonson's Marriage," *RES*, 1936). Little is known about Anne except that many years later Jonson described her to Drummond as "a shrew yet honest." Chute remarks that Jonson undoubtedly gave his wife good reason for her shrewishness, since he was, as he conceitedly admitted to Drummond, "given to venery," and graphically described some of his sexual exploits to the somewhat shocked Scotsman. He also admitted that for "5 yeeres he had not bedded with her," while he was living with one of his later patrons, Lord Albany, or Aubigny.

Within three years of his marriage, Jonson discovered in himself an affinity with the theater. At least, he was hired as an actor by the Earl of Pembroke's Men, for whom Francis Langley had recently built the most modern London playhouse, the Swan, in Paris Garden, Southwark. Jonson, however, never made a name for himself as an actor, and apparently got much of his experience on the provincial circuit, since one of his rival playwrights later tried to insult him as having been "a poor journeyman player" who had walked along beside "a play-wagon, in the highway." Fredson T. Bowers, in his conjectural account of Jonson's career as an actor ("Ben Jonson, the Actor," *SP*, 1933), concluded that Jonson was first connected with the stage in 1595–6 as an actor with Pembroke's Men, and played the part of Kyd's Hieronimo on tour. Some years later Philip Henslowe paid Jonson to write some additions to *The Spanish Tragedy*, but apparently they were never used. Jonson remained in Pembroke's company when it returned to London in February 1597.

During the summer the company asked its old hand, Thomas Nash, to write a play, now lost, called *The Isle of Dogs*. When it was acted in July, the Privy Council immediately heard about it and closed the theater because of its alleged slanders and seditious passages. Nash insisted that he had written only the first act and Jonson was suspected of having helped to complete it. Nash then escaped to Yarborough, but Jonson, who may also have acted in it, was arrested along with two of his fellow actors, Robert Shaa (or Shaw) and Gabriel Spencer, and all three were committed to the Marshalsea prison from August to October. If this was the "close imprissonment, under Elisabeth," that Jonson reported in his conversations with Drummond, the government placed "two damnd vilans to catch advantage of him"—that is, to spy on him—but the keeper of the prison tipped him off and "his judges could gett nothing of him to all their demands bot I and No." So he and his companions were released. Eccles has offered an interesting speculation on the identity of the two prison informers ("Jonson and the Spies," *RES*, 1933). In an epigram entitled "Inviting a Friend to Supper," Jonson wrote,

"And we will have no *Pooly* or *Parrot* by," and Eccles attempts to identify these two names with two officially hired government informers of the time, an unimportant man named Parrott, and the much more notorious Robert Poley, one of those present at the murder of Christopher Marlowe.  In a later letter to Lord Salisbury Jonson referred to this episode as "my first Error."  The government took revenge at first by threatening to close all the theaters but eventually compromised by refusing to renew the license of Langley at the Swan.  By this time, however, Jonson had made connection with Henslowe and his corps of actors and writers for the Admiral's Men at the Rose. Henslowe, the amusingly illiterate but shrewd business man par excellence of the Elizabethan theater, had already recorded in his invaluable diary (*Henslowe's Diary*, London, 1904–8) a loan of £4 to "Bengeman Johnson player" on July 28, 1597, and a receipt on the same day for three shillings ninepence as "Bengemenes Johnsones Share"—presumably, as Bowers thinks, of the profits of the Admiral's Men, not of Pembroke's.  All Henslowe's later payments to Jonson were made for his contributions to the company as a playwright, not as an actor.

Like many other London dramatists, Jonson did not confine his dramatic writing to Henslowe, but became a sort of free lance.  He had soon written enough plays to be listed by Francis Meres in his *Palladis Tamia* in 1598 as among the English playwrights who were "best for tragedy."  None of these scripts could have been very good, however, since none of them have survived.  From their titles in Henslowe's diary, they all seem to have been of a romantic cast, quite unlike Jonson's later work and principles. He was never proud of his writing for Henslowe, and made no attempt to preserve it in print.  But in the autumn of 1598 the Chamberlain's Men gave Jonson's first surviving play and one of his major works, *Every Man in His Humor*, at the Curtain in Shoreditch.  This satirical comedy not only introduced Jonson to Londoners for the first time in his role as the leading exponent of the comedy of humors, but it also showed how he had been influenced in his literary theories by the studying he had done in Aristotle, Horace, Sidney's new *An Apology for Poetry*, and especially the *Poetica* of Julius Caesar Scaliger.  All these confirmed the classical views on the moral functions and technical aspects of the drama to which he had been introduced by Camden. Appropriately, therefore, when he printed the play in 1601, he dedicated it to Camden "for the profession of my thankfulness."  When Jonson brought out his epoch-making first folio edition in 1616, *Every Man in His Humor* was the first play to meet the eye of the reader.

In spite of his success, Jonson's acquaintance with the London jails was soon renewed. In one of the intervals between his writing of *Every Man* and his collaborations with members of Henslowe's corps like Henry Chettle, Thomas Dekker, and George Chapman, he had fought a duel in Hog's End Fields with his recent prisonmate and fellowactor, Gabriel Spencer, and killed him—in spite of the fact that, as he told Drummond, he had been wounded in the arm and his opponent's sword was ten inches longer than his.  The cause of their quarrel is unknown, but both young men were notorious hotheads, and Spencer had recently killed a goldsmith's son with his sword, which had not even been unsheathed.  Jonson was arrested and haled to Newgate for trial.  After two weeks he was adjudged guilty of murder, but by appealing to the ancient privilege of "benefit of clergy" he was allowed to escape any severe penalty.  This meant he was permitted to show that he was a "clericus," or educated man, by reading his "neck verse" from the Bible, and consequently escaped the jurisdiction of the secular courts.  Thus, since his crime was apparently judged to be a defensible one, he was merely branded on the thumb with a "T" for "Tyburn," the normal place of execution, so that he could not make the same plea a second time and escape without punishment.

This peculiar episode was the occasion of another strange turn in the young man's career—he became a Roman Catholic and remained one for twelve years.  As phrased by Drummond, "Then he took his Religion by trust, of a priest who visited him in prisson."  Chute speculates that this priest was not a visitor from outside the prison, but an inmate himself, perhaps facing death because of trying to do missionary work among the English Roman Catholics. In view of the phraseology of Drummond's entry, however, the latter alternative does not seem very likely. Theodore A. Stroud ("Ben Jonson and Father Thomas Wright," *ELH*, 1947) has endeavored to identify this priest as the one for whose pamphlet, *The Passions of the Mind in General*, Jonson later wrote a dedicatory sonnet. Though by his conversion Jonson put himself in danger of prosecution for recusancy—that is, of not attending the services of the established Church of England—he was not yet a conspicuous enough figure to attract any such attention. This was to come later.

All these disturbing experiences apparently undermined young Jonson's self-confidence in his ability to maintain a livelihood for himself and his family, which now had several members. Four days after the duel Henslowe wrote to his son-in-law, the actor Edward Alleyn, that Spencer had been killed by Ben Jonson, "bricklayer," not "actor," and Leslie Hotson has discovered a document of a few months later referring to "Benjamin Johnson, Citizen and Bricklayer of London." (See W. G. Bell, *A Short History of the Worshipful Company of Tylers and Bricklayers of the City of London*, London, 1938.) In Michaelmas Term of 1598 or January 1599 Jonson obtained the "freedom" of the Company of Tylers and Bricklayers, and had thus completed his apprenticeship. Fortunately, even though in January of 1599 he was again locked up in the Marshalsea because he was unable to repay a loan of £10 from a fellow-actor, he found that Henslowe and others were still willing to employ him as a playmaker, and he did not need to make any further use of his trowel, hod, and mortar.

For a time, Jonson was now able to settle down to his writing with fewer interruptions. The year after *Every Man in His Humor* he wrote a sort of non-sequel to it, at least in plot and characters, if not in theme, which he entitled *Every Man out of His Humor*. This time he went to John Florio's *A World of Words* (1598) for many of the humors of his characters. These characters, though ostensibly Italians, like those in the first version of *Every Man in*, were really Englishmen moving against a London background. *Every Man out*, though not as good a play as *Every Man in*, proved a popular success when put on at the new Globe by the Chamberlain's Men, and sold well when printed in Jonson's first quarto, which he provided with a dedication to the Gentlemen of the Inns of Court, acquainting his readers with his characters, purposes, and methods.

He followed this play with one of quite a different kind, entitled *Cynthia's Revels, or The Fountain of Self-Love*, a comical satire with a mythological background in mixed verse and prose. It was well fitted for the boy actors and was therefore produced by the Children of the Chapel at the Blackfriars in 1600. Thomas Dekker and John Marston, who had been going about town aspersing Jonson for his egotism and arrogance, thought they recognized themselves in two of the characters (they were undoubtedly right), and let it be noised abroad that Dekker was working on a reply to be entitled *Satiromastix* (i.e., *The Satirist Whipped*), but before he could get it produced Jonson anticipated him by presenting his own *The Poetaster, or The Arraignment* (1601), attacking both them and the Chamberlain's Men, with whom he was temporarily at outs. Marston was obviously the would-be poet, to whom Horace, usually taken to represent Jonson himself, administered an emetic to make him vomit up all his hard words and peculiar phrases. In retaliation Dekker (with whom Jonson had collaborated in 1599 on two now lost plays) introduced a malicious caricature of Horace into his own play, in which he ridiculed Jonson's somewhat stunted size, his pockmarked skin, and his mannerism of making strange faces when reading his own verses aloud. Nor did he overlook Jonson's slowness of thought and speech, which ensuing biographers also loved to mock at by comparing his later conversational encounters with Shakespeare to the attack on a slow-moving Spanish galleon by a quickly maneuvering English man-of-war. This was all part of what came to be known as the First Players' Quarrel, or War of the Theaters, which was suppressed by the government because Jonson also attacked the army and the law in his plays. In fact, within a few months the participants were all reconciled, although Jonson always maintained a rather low opinion of Marston as both writer and man.

As another result of these satirical engagements, Jonson announced that he intended to retire from this field in order to write a classical tragedy, which turned out to be *Sejanus His Fall* (1603). This was followed by another play in the same vein, *Catiline His Conspiracy*, after an interval of several years (1611). Neither of these tragedies, however, had any popular appeal. Nevertheless, Jonson had found a patron in Sir Robert Townshend, and composed *Sejanus* while living on his hospitality. As Chute points out, Jonson was apparently the first playwright to write dedications of his plays, to such prominent persons as William Camden and Lucy Harrington, Countess of Bedford. *Sejanus* impressed cultured people like Lord D'Aubigny, or Albany, to whom it is dedicated, and at whose home Jonson lived for five years. The Herford-Simpsons disagree with Eccles on the dates involved in Jonson's remarks to Drummond, and conclude their examination of the evidence by asking, "Did Jonson pay more than one visit to Aubigny—a shorter one about 1604 and a longer one in 1613–18?"

On the death of Elizabeth in 1603 (a year in which Jonson's oldest son also died of the plague) and the accession of James I, Jonson—though not a courtier by nature—immediately began his long association with court entertainments and functions by writing little occasional poems, speeches, and divertissements in connection with the arrival of Queen Anne from Denmark, the formal entry of the King into London, his first appearance before Parliament, and so on. Jonson's first tangible sign of royal favor came in 1604 when Queen Anne commissioned him to compose his first masque for her Christmas and New Year's festivities in 1604–5. It became known as his *Masque of Blackamoors* or *Masque of Blackness*. He had as stage designer the services of the ingenious and inventive architect, Inigo Jones (see J. Alfred Gotch, *Inigo Jones*, London, 1928), and this inauguration of their long and tempestuous collaboration on thirteen masques was an auspicious one. It cost the exorbitant sum of £3000 to produce.

In 1604 Jonson collaborated with George Chapman and his erstwhile enemy Marston in writing *Eastward Ho*, a topical satire, in response to *Westward Ho* by Dekker and a new man named John Webster, for the Paul's Boys. But when *Eastward Ho* was performed at the Blackfriars in 1605, Sir James Murray complained to James about its sarcastic references to the Scots and its allusions to the many new knighthoods being created by the King. When, consequently, Chapman and Marston were sent to prison, Jonson voluntarily accompanied them. When the trio was released after personal appeals to the King and four earls, Jonson gave a banquet for his friends, including Camden and young John Selden, on his way to becoming an even greater scholar than Camden. The high point of the feast came when Jonson's elderly mother got up to drink to him and showed the guests a packet of poison, which she said she had planned to have mixed with his drink in prison if the reported sentence that all three were to have their ears and noses slit had been confirmed. She probably remembered that her son already had a branded thumb. But, as Jonson related the story to Drummond, the doughty old lady asserted that to show that "she was no churle . . . , she minded first to have drunk of it herself."

In October 1605 Jonson attended another party which might well have got him into more trouble. It was given by Robert Catesby, one of the Roman Catholic ringleaders in planning the Gunpowder Plot to blow up the Parliament meeting in the House of Lords. (See J. Leslie Hotson, *I, William Shakespeare*, London, 1937.) When the plot was discovered, Jonson was called before the Privy Council to help them get in touch with a priest who they had been told wanted to give information, but he failed in this mission. Jonson, as an obviously loyal Englishman in spite of his non-established religion, was never suspected of being a conspirator, but most of his friends in the circle were executed. The Herford-Simpson editors think that the discussion at the party went no further than the possibility of removing certain Catholic disabilities. But on January 7, 1606, a London jury accused Jonson, among many others, of being a recusant. Since he did not offer to answer the charges, he tacitly admitted that he had not been attending the Anglican church services regularly, and was therefore subject to a fine of £20 a month while he stayed away (*London Session Records*, Catholic Record Society, 1934). Though no report of the end of the case has been found, Jonson obviously never paid any such fines. Later in the year he was formally accused of being "a seducer of youth to the popish religion" by the churchwardens of St. Anne's parish. This time he appeared at the Consistory Court and swore that he and his wife had attended regularly, but that he had not taken communion, whereas, "for any thing he knoweth," his wife had "used always to receyve the Communion." From the wording of this statement, the Herford-Simpson editors conclude that Jonson and his wife were not living together at this time, whereas Eccles assumes that they were. The wardens could not prove that Jonson had seduced any young people religiously. Then at his own suggestion he was given a list of prominent Anglicans from which he was to choose one to give him religious instruction once a week. It is very unlikely that he availed himself of any such instruction (if he was not actually pulling the legs of his accusers), since for four more years he remained a Roman Catholic. Then, with no explanation, as Chute phrases it, he "suddenly returned to the Anglican fold, with such enthusiasm that he drank all the wine in the cup when he attended his first communion."

Early in 1606, while being accused of recusancy, Jonson wrote one of his greatest comedies, *Volpone, or The Fox*, which contained no representatives of religion, but, when printed in 1607, was dedicated to "the most noble and equal sisters, the two famous universities, for their love and acceptance shown to his poem in the presentation," which had been given at Oxford and Cambridge in the summer by the King's Men. During the immediately following years, he devoted most of his time to masques and entertainments for the royal family and members of the court. Not until almost four years after *Volpone* did Jonson offer a new play, *Epicoene, or The Silent Woman*, played, with applause, by the Children of the Whitefriars, successors to the Blackfriars group. In the next year *The Alchemist*, given by the King's Men at both the Blackfriars and the Globe, was a topical and satirical comedy ranking with *Volpone* at the top of his list. It was followed by *Catiline* (1611), which confirmed the opinion of most of those who had seen *Sejanus* that Jonson could not write tragedy.

As an interlude to his more serious literary labors, which included some not-so-serious contributions to his friend Thomas Coryat's *Crudities* (1611), a curious and fantastic parody of the dignified popular travel books of the period, Jonson accepted a commission from his good friend Sir Walter Raleigh. Raleigh had been a prisoner in the Tower of London since 1603 on charges of "conspiracy," and Jonson was to act as a combination of guardian and tutor to his son Wat for a year's polishing tour on the Continent. Jonson, who had been of some help to Sir Walter in writing his unfinished *History of the World*, welcomed the opportunity to visit the mainland for the first time since his military service there (though he had been writing about it, especially Italy, in most of his plays). Sir Walter wanted a man with a firm hand to manage his wild young son, who had already had trouble with one of his tutors, and he thought Jonson was the man to give it. He did not know his man as well as he thought he did. The pair left England in 1612. Echoes of some of their experiences may be found in the letters of Sir Walter's agent in Antwerp and in the correspondence of William Trumbull, the British chargé d'affaires in Brussels. There were some problems involving bills of exchange, since travelers without influence were normally allowed to take only £20 out of the country. The most notorious incident of the trip came in Paris, when young Wat, perhaps in recognition of his tutor's own propensity toward practical jokes and tricks, got Jonson dead drunk, placed him in a cart in a spread-eagle position, and exhibited his "governor" to the Parisians on several street corners as "a more lively image of a crucifix than any they had." When the story got back to England, Lady Raleigh thought it an amusing prank, but Sir Walter was more dubious. While in Paris, Jonson—now a Protestant again—also met some of the French religious leaders like Cardinal du Perron, was unimpressed, and served as a sort of referee in a Protestant-Catholic debate. As he and his young charge (who certainly could not have studied much on the trip) prepared to leave France for Belgium, a friend of Trumbull's, Jean Beaulieu, wrote a rather ambiguous warning to Brussels about Jonson's approach, mentioning the poet's "worthy parts," but adding rather ominously, "for the rest you shall soon make discovery thereof." The pair got back to London in 1613.

Jonson's last association with the Raleighs came ten years later, after both Sir Walter and his son had died. In October 1623 the Court of Chancery called him to identify the handwriting of his old friend, whose widow had brought suit against a London jeweler over the disposal of the family plate and jewels (C. J. Sisson, *TLS*, September 27, 1957). Though the outcome of the suit is unknown and unimportant, Jonson was incidentally described in the records as "Beniamin Johnson of Gresham Colledge in London" and as being of an age of "50. yeares & upwards." This identification has given rise to some debate and speculation as to what Jonson was doing at Gresham College. Sisson, supported by Herford-Simpson, suggests that Jonson was actually lecturing in Latin on English grammar, and that his unpublished *Timber, or Discoveries Made upon Men and Matter*, and the outline for a book on English grammar, found among his papers at his death, were some of his lecture notes. Sisson and Herford-Simpson theorize that Jonson may have been deputizing for Sir Henry Croke, who had been appointed Professor of Rhetoric in 1619. They think that Jonson would have become eligible for this position because of the honorary M.A. degree procured for him at Oxford by Lord Pembroke in 1619. Living in the college would have been part of his emolument, especially since he had just been burned out of his home in Westminster. Chute, however, discounts this theory, pointing out that according to Gresham's will only celibates could teach in the college, also adding that other non-academic people, like Sir Kenelm Digby, had resided there for short times. Moreover, the records of St. Giles, Cripplegate, register the marriage, in July 1623, of a "Beniamyne Johnson" to a Hester Hopkins (Eccles, "Jonson's Marriage," *RES*, 1936). If this was the playwright, as seems possible, this record would not only indicate that Ben Jonson had married again, but that Anne Lewis Jonson had died. If so, nothing more is heard of this second wife, who herself had passed silently from the scene by the time of her husband's death. Though Jonson had several children, both legitimate and illegitimate, it is difficult to trace them. Thomas Fuller wrote that Jonson "was not happy in his children, and most happy in those which died first, though none lived to survive him." (See also Eccles, Herford-Simpson, and so on.)

During the intervening decade, Jonson and his young friend, the actor-playwright-producer Nathan Field, presented Jonson's comedy, *Bartholomew Fair*, in October 1614, at the Hope and the court before the King. In it Jonson amused himself and his audiences by satirizing more London types, such as those found at the great annual cloth fair. *The Devil Is an Ass* (1616), on the shady business transactions of a group of actual speculators calling itself the New Merchant Adventurers, was not so successful. But in February of the same year Jonson had got his first important official recognition for his literary contributions when the government granted him an annual pension of a hundred marks. Although this distinction carried with it no formal title, the public accepted it as equivalent to a poet laureateship. Jonson agreed. Actually he had been scheming toward it for some time, and had influenced his antiquarian friend John Selden to include a discussion of the office of laureate in England and abroad in the second edition of his *Titles of Honor*. In England, the only previous claimant to such a title had been John Skelton, but his right applied only to an academic honor given him by Oxford.

Almost as great an event in the same year was the publication of Jonson's collected and selected works in a magnificent folio volume of over a thousand pages. Never before had an English poet offered his works for preservation to posterity in such a careful and impressive form, and some of his envious contemporaries jeered at him for his presumption in daring to call his plays "Works." He opened the volume by putting his best foot forward and printing nine of his most important plays. After this section came two groups of his poems: *Epigrams*, which are really occasional poems, and *The Forest*, a miscellany, including his most famous lyric, "To Celia," beginning, "Drink to me only with thine eyes," actually based on several prose passages by Philostratus. The final selection was his masques. Jonson himself apparently saw all the volume except the last part through the press, and the masques are carelessly proofread. He had his own system of spelling and punctuation, and treated the whole job like a scholar.

From this time until 1626 he wrote only masques. The King was so pleased with one of these, *The Gipsies Metamorphosed*, written for the Duke of Buckingham in 1621, that he presented Jonson with the reversion of the mastership of the Office of the Revels. Unfortunately for Jonson, however, Sir George Buc, who then held the position, and Sir John Astley, who held its succession, did not die in time for Jonson to show what he could do in this capacity. He and Jones continued to collaborate on many masques, but the feud between them grew more and more bitter.

In 1618 Jonson was about forty-six years old and weighed almost two hundred and eighty pounds (see R. F. Patterson, preface to *Ben Jonson's Conversations with Drummond*). In an ironical madrigal written early in the next year, telling why no woman could any longer love him, Jonson cited as reasons, along with his age, his "mountain belly," his "rocky face," and his "hundred of gray hairs." A facetious but premature epitaph maker had already written: "Here lyes honest Ben/That had not a beard on his chen." And yet in this year this unathletic, unprepossessing tun of a man decided to uproot himself from his comfortable chair in the Mermaid Tavern and make a walking tour from London to Edinburgh. Patterson speculates on his possible reasons: perhaps, since King James had revisited his old home in Scotland the year before, Jonson was stimulated to see Anandale, the home of his ancestors; perhaps James had suggested that his "servant" gather material for a book about the country, as he apparently started to do; or perhaps it was simply a case of combined wanderlust and boredom with London. It is likely, too, that some of the Scottish lords and gentry who came often to the English court had urged the famous new laureate to visit their country. At any rate, Jonson set out on foot, probably in June, and on the journey wore out at least one pair of shoes, which he had to replace at Durham. After receiving ovations all along the road, he was royally received and entertained on his arrival at Edinburgh in September: he was granted the freedom of the city, made a guild brother, and given a great banquet, which cost well over £200, Scots money. Among the leading personages he met at Edinburgh was the thirty-three year old William Drummond, laird of Hawthornden, a quondam lawyer turned student and literary dilettante, who invited him to become his guest on his estate. The two men proved to be quite incompatible, though outwardly courteous, since Jonson's manners and drinking capacity annoyed his host, and his scabrous stories and dogmatic opinions on literary matters and authors (in which he sometimes contradicted himself) were often hard to take. Drummond was nevertheless enough of a hero-worshiper to make notes on almost everything of interest Jonson said and thus anticipated in a small way the relationship of another Johnson and his much greater biographer over a century and a half later. Jonson returned to London in January, probably by coach.

Although Jonson told Drummond he was "Master of Arts in both Universities, by their favour not his studie," it was not until June 1619 that Oxford actually conferred the degree on him in full convocation. If Cambridge really conferred one too, after perhaps merely promising it, there is no record of it. As Chute puts it, "The only other known relationship between Jonson and Cambridge is that the president of St. John's College asked him to write some verses for a reception that was given King James when he visited there in March of 1625."

To confirm himself as a sort of combined dictator and patron saint of the English literary world, in 1624 Jonson organized the Apollo Club as a rival to the older and more famous Mermaid. It met in a large room at the back of a tavern in Fleet Street near St. Dunstan's church, and was known as "The Devil and St. Dunstan's." Jonson sat on a kind of dais at one end, and had a handrail built to help him get to his chair. He had composed a set of rules in Latin, which all the young members were supposed to obey. For it was a young group that he had gathered around him to perpetuate his sway and his influence on English drama and poetry, and its members were proud to have been "sealed" as the "Sons of Ben" or the "Tribe of Ben." (See Joe Lee Davis, *The Sons of Ben/Jonsonian Comedy in Caroline England*, Wayne State University Press, 1967; also Kathryn A. McEuen, *Classical Influence upon the Tribe of Ben*, Cedar Rapids, Iowa, 1939.) Davis lists eleven young poet-dramatists, none of whom ever attained major rank: Richard Brome, William Cartwright, William Cavendish, William D'avenant, Henry Glapthorne, Peter Hausted, Thomas Killigrew, Shackerley Marmion, Jasper Mayne, Thomas Nabbes, and Thomas Randolph. But there were many other authors too who "were members at one time or another of the constantly changing nondescript group of poets, playwrights, and merely conversational wits who met so regularly with the aging Jonson at various taverns of London or in his lodgings near Westminster Abbey . . . , as if they were actually a kind of institution, a combined drinking academy, literary society, and philosophical confraternity." Among these, other writers have named Sir Lucius Carey, Sir Kenelm Digby, Edward Hyde (later Earl of Clarendon), James Shirley, Thomas Carew, John Cleveland, and even Robert Herrick. Jonson had a strong appeal to the young.

When he returned to the public stage shortly after the formal coronation of Charles II in February 1626, he did so with the King's Men's production of *The Staple of News*, a satire on London journalism, freedom of the press, and monopolies, toward which he took the conservative attitude. It might have been better for his future reputation if he had been satisfied to rest on his past laurels. His last series of plays, including *The New Inn, or The Light Heart* (1629), *The Magnetic Lady, or Humors Reconciled* (1632), and *A Tale of a Tub* (1633), were all either hissed or damned, and became unkindly known as his "dotages." After *The New Inn* was booed, Jonson voiced his disappointment and indignation by writing his furious "Ode to Himself," beginning,

> Come leave the loathéd stage
> And the more loathsome age . . . .

A small poet, Owen Feltham, immediately penned an impertinent answer, which started,

> Come leave this saucy way
> Of baiting those that pay
> Dear for the sight of your declining wit . . . .

This unmannerly attack provoked three of Jonson's "children"—Randolph, Carew, and Cleveland—to counterattack, but even while defending their admired master, they had to admit that his best days were past.

Thus, having reached a great height, Ben Jonson fell into almost as great a depth. Although the new king tried to be kind to his father's laureate and changed the annual donation from marks to pounds, along with an additional gift of a cask of canary wine, Jonson was sued by many creditors for debts of from £10 to £120. In 1628 he suffered a paralytic stroke. Shortly afterward the Dean and Chapter of Westminster voted to send £5 to "Mr. Benjamin Johnson in his sickness and want," and Charles made him a gift of £100. In September the London aldermen tried to help by appointing him City Chronologer, with a salary of a hundred nobles, to replace Thomas Middleton, who had died. After six years, during which Jonson had done no work on the job, the aldermen, after temporarily canceling the stipend, generously decided to restore it and call it a pension.

In 1630 he was commissioned to write Christmas masques for both the King and the Queen, the French Henrietta Maria, who loved such shows as much as Anne had. These were given in January 1631, but when the Queen's masque, *Chloridia*, was being prepared for publication, Jonson's feud with Inigo Jones reached its peak in a quarrel over whose name should appear first on the title page, a matter which Jonson insisted would show which was the more important in a masque, the author or the designer. Jones had previously written some verses "To His False Friend, Mr. Ben Johnson," denouncing the playwright as "the best of poets, but the worst of men," and Jonson had replied in kind. He had already remarked to Drummond that he had told Prince Charles as early as 1618 that "when he wanted words to express the greatest villaine in the world, he would call him ane Inigo." (For a discussion of another aspect of this quarrel, see D. G. Gordon, "Poet and Architect: The Intellectual Setting of the Quarrel between Ben Jonson and Inigo Jones," *Journal of the Warburg and Courtauld Institutes*, Vol. XII, a discussion of the theories, principles, and terminologies of their masques.) Jones was the official victor in the conflict, and Jonson composed no more masques for the Caroline court. Aurelian Townshend was given a single trial, and Carew and Shirley also had their chances before Will D'avenant took over as Jones's permanent partner with *The Temple of Love*, or the "Queen's Masque of Indians," as Jones called it for his designs. (See Nethercot, *Sir William D'avenant/Poet Laureate and Playwright-Manager*, University of Chicago Press, 1938; rev. Russell and Russell, New York, 1967.)

Ben Jonson grew more and more depressed. He wrote to various friends asking for help, but making it clear that he could never hope to repay them. Though he regarded himself as a good Christian, the attitude he tried to take in most of his writing about life and death was more that of a Senecan Stoic, as revealed in his conversations with visitors and friends like George Morley and Nicholas Oldisworth. If he did actually marry a second time, his wife was never mentioned at the time of his death, for, as the Herford-Simpsons say, "The 'woman that govern'd him,' received his pension, and shared his sack" in his little house near St. Margaret's, Westminster, was not his wife, but "a nameless old lady with whom Jonson boarded." He died on August 6, 1637, leaving only a few scattered and unpublished manuscripts behind him. These, later prepared and published by his "son," Kenelm Digby, included his *Timber*, an outline of his unfinished English grammar (the notes for which had perished in the burning of his house), a fragment of a historical English play, *Mortimer*, and his unfinished romantic pastoral drama, *The Sad Shepherd*.

Jonson's former friends and admirers rallied to him after his death, and a great crowd of mourners followed him to his grave in the north aisle of Westminster Abbey, rather than in the famous Poets' Corner. Legend has it that when Jonson was joking one day with the Dean of Westminster about being unable to afford the honor of being buried with the other poets, he remarked: "I am too poor for that, and no one will lay out funeral charges upon me. No, sir, six feet long by two feet wide is too much for me; two feet by two feet will do." The Dean is reported to have answered that Ben could have his two by two. The story was discounted, however, till the early eighteenth century, when workmen, preparing the floor and ground next to Jonson's grave for the interment of a certain Lady Wilson, discovered that Jonson's cheap coffin had actually been set upright, and that thus he had the two by two he had asked for. According to another story, the inscription on the small stone in the abbey floor, "O rare Ben Jonson," was carved later at the request of a passerby who admired Ben and who gave a stone cutter who was working nearby a few pence to do the job. Some bad Latinists have suggested that because of the lack of spacing between the first two words the inscription should actually read: "Orare Ben Jonson"—that is, "Pray for Ben Jonson."

While Digby was readying Jonson's manuscripts for publication, the Dean of Christ Church, Oxford, Bishop Brian Duppa, prepared a collection of memorial verses, *Jonsonus Virbius, or The Memory of Ben Jonson Revived by the Friends of the Muses* (1638). But almost none of the thirty-three contributors, mostly Oxford graduates and court friends, had enough literary standing or poetic ability to do much for their cause. It remained for posterity to rehabilitate Ben Jonson and his works and regain for them the firm place in English literary history they demand.

## EVERY MAN IN HIS HUMOR

*Every Man in His Humor* can properly be said to be the play with which Ben Jonson made his first bid for the fame which was to come.  This comedy has had a long and illustrious stage history in spite of the fact that William Archer, in his King's College, London, lectures reviewing the whole history of the English drama from the viewpoint of one of England's most influential drama critics (*The Old Drama and the New/An Essay in Re-valuation*, London, 1922), asserted with his usual iconoclasm that its characters

are all broad caricatures . . . , vigorously drawn, playable . . . .  But by no reasonable canon of art can a mere array of caricatures be said to constitute a good comedy.  One other ingredient at least is essential—a clear, more or less ingenious and entertaining, story. I defy anyone to relate comprehensibly or to make credible the wholly uninspired and uningenious comings and goings and to-ings and fro-ings of which the story consists.

Regardless of these twentieth-century strictures, after the play was presented in its first version, with its Italian setting, by the Chamberlain's Men in 1598 (according to one story, on the recommendation of Will Shakespeare, who played one of the parts), and proved an immediate hit, it was soon revived at court by the King's Men in 1605, and revised about this time.  It was then revived at both the Globe and the Black-friars in 1631 as benefits for Sir Henry Herbert, Master of the Revels.  After the Restoration, Thomas Killigrew revived it occasionally at his Theatre Royal, and Christopher Rich gave it at Lincoln's Inn Fields in 1735.  The most memorable revival was inaugurated by David Garrick at the Drury Lane in 1751, after he had worked for three years in preparing his own version and perfecting his role of Kitely, which was the favorite of all the great actors.  Garrick kept the play in his repertoire until his final stage appearance in 1776.  At the rival Covent Garden, William Smith played in the original Elizabethan version from 1772 on, and again at the Drury Lane from 1778–98.  Many of the eighteenth century reviewers, however, called the play old-fashioned; nevertheless, it was revived at the Covent Garden in 1800, Edmund Kean appeared in it at the Drury Lane in 1816, the Covent Garden resuscitated it in 1825, and the great William Charles Macready played it at the Haymarket in 1838.  Charles Dickens, whose consuming interest in the stage is now scarcely remembered, gave the play several times between 1845 and 1848 with his company of amateurs in London, Manchester, and Liverpool.  The Stratford-on-Avon Memorial Theatre saw it under the direction of Frank R. Benson in 1903, and again under B. Iden Payne in 1937. Payne had previously produced it for Annie E. F. Horniman's Gaiety Theatre repertory company at Manchester in 1909.  Except for various academic and semi-professional groups, however, the comedy has had no active attention in recent years.

*Every Man in* and *Every Man out* are two of the most important plays in the history of the Elizabethan drama, if not the whole English drama.  In them Jonson became definitely committed to a theory which had a far-reaching effect on comedy not only in Jonson's own age but on later playwrights from Thomas Shadwell to Richard Brinsley Sheridan and even to Bernard Shaw.  Even the best writers of the so-called "comedy of manners" could not wholly escape the influence of the Jonsonian "comedy of humors" in their methods of characterization and in their use of type names as quick short cuts to the essence of certain characters.  In the first play of the pair Jonson attempted to define the term "humor" only rather casually (in III, iv) when he had Cash correct Cob, who has used the out-of-date term "rheum" instead of the newly fashionable one of "humor," perhaps in reference to the title of George Chapman's comedy, *An Humorous Day's Mirth*, a year or so before.  After some rather forced punning on the words "collar" and "choler" (which was, of course, one of the four basic and original humors),

Cash answers Cob's question, "What is that humor?" with the not very helpful definition: ". . . it is a gentlemanlike monster, bred in the special gallantry of our time, by
affectation, and fed by folly." But by the time Jonson came to write the induction
to the second play two years later, he put into the mouth of Asper (the "rough" or
"sharp" one, obviously representing himself) a long speech on the subject, tracing the
derivation of the term from its original physical sense of "a quality of air or water"
holding the "two properties, moisture and fluxure," to its medieval physiological sense
of the "choler, melancholy, phlegm, and blood" found in every human body, and by
their mixture and proportions determining not only a person's physical health but,
by extension, his basic character, so that

> It may, by metaphor, apply itself
> Unto the general disposition:
> As when some one peculiar quality
> Doth so possess a man that it doth draw
> All his affects, his spirits, and his powers,
> In their confluxions, all to run one way,
> This may be truly said to be a humor.

Thus a humor in this sense was the result of an obsession or preoccupation with a single
dominant idea or passion, which resulted in a one-sided character and led to eccentric
behavior. Henry L. Snuggs, in "The Comic Humors: A New Interpretation" (*PMLA*,
1947), has suggested that Jonson deliberately used the term in two different senses: a
genuinely ingrained temperament, in accordance with the current humoral psychology,
and (the prevalent extension and misconception of the word) an assumed or "temporary
characteristic, the assumption of which was itself absurd and demanded satirical treatment." John J. Enck, in *Jonson and the Comic Truth* (University of Wisconsin Press,
1957), attempted to trace the term and its applications through Jonson's plays, and
concluded that at first, as in *Every Man in*, it simply meant eccentric behavior; that in
*Every Man out, Cynthia's Revels*, and, partially, *The Poetaster*, Jonson arbitrarily confined its associations to a more limited technical meaning; that from *Sejanus* through
*The Alchemist* he improvised upon the definition without tying it down to a single
point; and finally gave up the problem by becoming indifferent to both word and
concept. James D. Redwine, Jr., writing on "The Moral Basis of Jonson's Theory
of Humor Characterization" (*ELH*, 1961), protested against the school of critics who
have attempted to define the theory of humors in terms of Elizabethan psychology
or aesthetic decorum because they have failed to notice that, for the Renaissance, both
these matters were elements of moral philosophy; Redwine therefore insisted that
Asper in his ideas should be regarded primarily as a moralist, not a psychologist. C. G.
Thayer (*Ben Jonson/Studies in the Plays*, University of Oklahoma Press, 1963) tried
to simplify the whole matter by asserting dogmatically that "what humors finally
means for Jonson is manners," and cited the prologue to *The Alchemist* and other
passages as evidence. T. S. Eliot, in his *Elizabethan Dramatists* (London, 1963),
wished to minimize the whole question by maintaining that the importance of the
humors in Jonson's work has been exaggerated because of the titles of his first notable
comedies. In any case, most critics would be inclined to agree with Percy Simpson
himself ("The Art of Ben Jonson," *E&S*, 1945) that Jonson's theory and its application
allowed for no "light and shade" in his characters; that the "cross-play" of motives is
likely to be neglected; and that since the characters are more or less determined at the
outset, in most cases there is little opportunity for dramatic development or change
from beginning to end.

Actually, in tracing the origins of Jonson's views on the humors, one must obviously
go back to the classics. Charles R. Baskervill (*English Elements in Jonson's Early
Comedy, UTSE*, 1911) traced the primary idea of castigating follies and vices in this
way to Aristotle's *Ethics*. Kathryn A. McEuen ("Jonson and Juvenal," *RES*, 1945)

discussed Jonson's debt to Juvenal and his respect for him, especially in a number of the characters in *Every Man out*.  Though it has been traditional to find a strong Plautine or Terentian influence on the comedies, Thayer—although admitting that the characters and situation in *Every Man in* are essentially Plautine—suggested that this play "is a pleasant version of New Comedy, with Aristophanic overtones" and that its social criticism more closely resembles that in Aristophanes than in Roman comedy; in *Every Man out*, he maintained, "the parallel with Aristophanes becomes really clear."

In all these matters Jonson was of course primarily a satirist, and Helena W. Baum has discussed him from this point of view in *The Satiric and the Didactic in Ben Jonson's Comedy* (University of North Carolina Press, 1947), coming to the conclusion that avarice and lust were the two major objects of his attack, followed by drunkenness, witchcraft or the pretense of supernatural powers, and Puritanism in its different varieties.   This aspect of Jonson's work obviously involves the relationship between didacticism and art, a question further discussed by Thayer, who believes that in spite of Edward Knowell's comments on poetry (almost eliminated in the second, or English, version of *Every Man in*), it is actually Brainworm who seems to represent the comic poet, though of course he is primarily the clever, intriguing servant of Roman comedy. The question of Jonson's literary style and methods in relationship to his art has naturally been thoroughly investigated.   Edward B. Partridge has discussed Jonson's use of imagery and metaphorical language, showing how his theories on such matters "reveal his sensitivity to decorum, the crucial standard for a comic dramatist," and how the satirical inversion of Christian values accounts for some of his most striking dramatic effects (*The Broken Compass: A Study of the Major Comedies of Ben Jonson*, London, 1958).   Jonas A. Barish has approached the matter from another angle and, by analyzing the syntax of Jonson's prose, has described it as "baroque," irregular on principle, but very effective in reflecting the deficiencies and deformities of Jonson's knaves, gulls, and fops according to the principles of decorum (*Ben Jonson and the Language of Prose Comedy*, Harvard University Press, 1960).

J. A. Bryant, in analyzing "Jonson's Revision of *Every Man in His Humor*" (*SP*, 1962), has not only shown the changes Jonson made in turning the Florentine background and characters of the first version into a purely London setting and cast, but has also shown how, by eliminating most of the superfluous moralizing about poetry, he has "reshaped his play to make it a humor play all over," capable of standing with *Volpone*, *The Alchemist*, and *Epicoene*.   E. K. Chambers (*The Elizabethan Stage*, Oxford, 1923) believed that this transformation was made for the 1605 performance at court, but the Herford-Simpson editors prefer a later date, nearer to the time of *The Alchemist*.   The Italian version was entered in the Stationers' Register on August 4, 1600, and printed in the next year; but the English version first saw print in the 1616 folio.   In at least one respect, however, Jonson seems to have had a genuine Italian source for one of his characters, since Bobadill, the braggart soldier, has been identified with Rocco Bonetti, a fashionable Italian master of the rapier in London (J. D. Aylward, "The Inimitable Bobadill," *NQ*, 1950; K. T. Butler, *ibid.*).

The present text is based on the Herford-Simpson edition of the 1616 folio, checked with a copy of the original in the Newberry Library in Chicago.   Arthur Sale has edited the play for the University Tutorial Press (London, 1941).   A good approach to *Every Man in* and Jonson's other plays may be found in Robert R. Knoll's *Ben Jonson's Plays/An Introduction* (University of Nebraska Press, 1964).

# EVERY MAN IN HIS HUMOR [1]

## BY

### BEN JONSON

To the Most Learned, and My Honored Friend, Mr.[2] Camden, Clarencieux [3]

Sir:

There are, no doubt, a supercilious race in the world who will esteem all office done you in this kind an injury, so solemn a vice it is with them to use the authority of their ignorance to the crying down of poetry or the professors.[4] But my gratitude must not leave [5] to correct their error, since I am none of those that can suffer the benefits conferred upon my youth to perish with my age. It is a frail memory that remembers [10] but present things, and had the favor of the times so conspired with my disposition, as it could have brought forth other or better, you had had the same proportion and number of the fruits, the first. Now I pray you to accept this, such wherein neither the confession of my manners shall make you blush, nor of my studies repent you [6] to have been the instructor; and for the profession of my thankfulness, I am sure [20] it will, with good men, find either praise or excuse.

Your true lover,

Ben. Jonson.

## THE PERSONS OF THE PLAY

KNOWELL,[7] *an old gentleman.*
ED[WARD] KNOWELL, *his son.*
BRAINWORM, *the father's man.*
MR. STEPHEN, *a country gull.*
[GEORGE] DOWNRIGHT, *a plain squire.*
WELLBRED, *his half-brother.*
JUST[ICE] CLEMENT, *an old, merry magistrate.*
ROGER FORMAL, *his clerk.*

KITELY, *a merchant.*
DAME KITELY, *his wife.*
MRS.[8] BRIDGET, *his sister.*
MR. MATTHEW, *the town gull.*
[THOMAS] CASH, *Kitely's man.*
[OLIVER] COB, *a water bearer.*
TIB, *his wife.*
CAP[TAIN] BOBADILL, *a Paul's man.*[9]
[SERVANTS, *etc.*]

THE SCENE: *London.*

[TIME: *Contemporary.*]

### PROLOGUE

Though need make many poets, and some such
As art and nature have not bettered much,
Yet ours for want hath not so loved the stage
As he dare serve th' ill customs of the age,
Or purchase your delight at such a rate,
As, for it, he himself must justly hate:
To make a child, now swaddled, to proceed
Man, and then shoot up, in one beard and weed,
Past threescore years; or, with three rusty swords,
And help of some few foot-and-half-foot words,    10
Fight over York and Lancaster's long jars,

---

[1] The title continues: "A Comedy. Acted in the Year 1598 by the Then Lord Chamberlain His Servants. The Author B. J."
[2] Master.
[3] One of the kings-of-arms in the Heralds' College.    [5] Omit.
[4] Supporters of poetry.   [6] Make you repent.
[7] Printed *Kno'well* throughout.
[8] Mistress.
[9] A lounger in the middle aisle of St. Paul's Cathedral, a social and business center.

15

And in the tiring-house [1] bring wounds to scars.

He rather prays you will be pleased to see
One such today, as other plays should be,
Where neither chorus wafts you o'er the seas,
Nor creaking throne comes down, the boys to please,
Nor nimble squib is seen, to make afeard
The gentlewomen, nor rolled bullet heard,
To say it thunders, nor tempestuous drum
Rumbles, to tell you when the storm doth come,    20
But deeds and language such as men do use,
And persons such as comedy would choose,
When she would show an image of the times,
And sport with human follies, not with crimes—
Except we make hem [2] such, by loving still
Our popular errors, when we know th' are ill.
I mean such errors as you'll all confess,
By laughing at them, they deserve no less—
Which when you heartily do, there's hope left then,
You, that have so graced [3] monsters, may like men.    30

## Act I.  Scene i.

### [A street.]

*Knowell, Brainworm, Mr. Stephen.* [4]

[Know.] A goodly day toward, and a fresh morning!—Brainworm,

### [Enter Brainworm.]

Call up your young master; bid him rise, sir.
Tell him I have some business to employ him.
Bra. I will, sir, presently. [5]
Know.            But hear you, sirrah,
If he be at [6] his book, disturb him not.
Bra. Well, sir.            [Exit.]
Know. How happy yet should I esteem myself,

Could I, by any practice, [7] wean the boy
From one vain course of study he affects.
He is a scholar, if a man may trust    10
The liberal voice of fame, in her report
Of good accompt in both our universities,
Either of which hath favored him with graces. [8]
But their indulgence must not spring in me
A fond [9] opinion that he cannot err.
Myself was once a student, and, indeed,
Fed with the selfsame humor [10] he is now,
Dreaming on naught but idle poetry,
That fruitless and unprofitable art,
Good unto none, but least to the professors,    20
Which then I thought the mistress of all knowledge;
But, since, time and the truth have waked my judgment,
And reason taught me better to distinguish
The vain from th' useful learnings.—

### [Enter Stephen.]

            Cousin [11] Stephen,
What news with you, that you are here so early?
Ste. Nothing, but e'en come to see how you do, uncle.
Know. That's kindly done; you are welcome, coz.
Ste. Ay, I know that, sir; I would not ha' come else.    30
How do my cousin Edward, uncle?
Know. O, well, coz; go in and see; I doubt he be scarce stirring yet.
Ste. Uncle, afore I go in, can you tell me, an [12] he have e'er a book of the sciences of hawking and hunting? I would fain borrow it.
Know. Why, I hope you will not a-hawking now, will you?
Ste. No, wusse; [13] but I'll practice [40 against [14] next year, uncle. I have bought me a hawk, and a hood, and bells, and all; I lack nothing but a book to keep it by.
Know. O, most ridiculous!

---

[1] Dressing room.
[2] Them.
[3] Approved.
[4] Enters later.
[5] At once.
[6] Original reads *be 'at*. Jonson and other poets often use the apostrophe thus to indicate elision, but in deference to modern practice it has been omitted in this anthology.

[7] Artifice.    [8] *I.e.*, degrees.    [9] Foolish.
[10] A dominating quality or caprice in a person's temperament.
[11] A general term of relationship or intimacy.
[12] If.
[13] Iwis, certainly.    [14] In preparation for.

STE. Nay, look you now, you are angry, uncle. Why, you know, an a man have not skill in the hawking and hunting languages nowadays, I'll not give a rush for him. They are more studied than the Greek or the Latin. He is for no gallant's company [50 without hem; and, by Gad's lid,[1] I scorn it, I, so I do, to be a consort for every humdrum;[2] hang hem, scroyles![3] There's nothing in hem i' the world. What[4] do you talk on it? Because I dwell at Hogsden, I shall keep company with none but the archers of Finsbury or the citizens that come a-ducking to Islington ponds? A fine jest, i' faith! 'Slid,[1] a gentleman mun[5] show himself like a gentleman. Uncle, [60 I pray you be not angry; I know what I have to do, I trow; I am no novice.

KNOW. You are a prodigal, absurd coxcomb; go to!
Nay, never look at me. It's I that speak.
Take 't as you will, sir, I'll not flatter you.
Ha' you not yet found means enow to waste
That which your friends have left you, but you must
Go cast away your money on a kite,
And know not how to keep it, when you ha' done?
O, it's comely! This will make you a gentleman!      70
Well, cousin, well, I see you are e'en past hope
Of all reclaim.—Ay, so, now you are told on it,
You look another way.

STE.        What would you ha' me do?
KNOW. What would I have you do? I'll tell you, kinsman;
Learn to be wise, and practice how to thrive.
That would I have you do, and not to spend
Your coin on every bable[6] that you fancy,
Or every foolish brain that humors you.
I would not have you to invade each place,
Nor thrust yourself on all societies,    80
Till men's affections, or your own desert,
Should worthily invite you to your rank.

He that is so respectless[7] in his courses
Oft sells his reputation at cheap market.
Nor would I you should melt away yourself
In flashing bravery,[8] lest, while you affect
To make a blaze of gentry to the world,
A little puff of scorn extinguish it,
And you be left like an unsavory snuff,
Whose property is only to offend.      90
I'ld ha' you sober, and contain yourself
Not that your sail be bigger than your boat;
But moderate your expenses now, at first,
As[9] you may keep the same proportion still;[10]
Nor stand so much on your gentility,
Which is an airy and mere borrowed thing
From dead men's dust and bones, and none of yours
Except you make or hold it. Who comes here?

### ACT I. SCENE ii.

*[The same.]*

*Servant, Mr. Stephen, Knowell, Brainworm.*[11]

[SERV.] Save you, gentlemen!
STE. Nay, we do not stand much on our gentility, friend; yet you are welcome; and I assure you mine uncle here is a man of a thousand a year, Middlesex land. He has but one son in all the world; I am his next heir, at the common law, Master Stephen, as simple as I stand here, if my cousin die, as there's hope he will. I have a pretty living o' mine own too, beside, hard [10 by here.
SERV. In good time,[12] sir.
STE. In good time, sir? Why, and in very good time, sir! You do not flout, friend, do you?
SERV. Not I, sir.
STE. Not you, sir? You were not best, sir; an you should, here be them can perceive it, and that quickly too. Go to! And they can give it again soundly too, [20 and[13] need be.

---

[1] God's eyelid.               [4] Why.
[2] Commonplace person.       [5] Must.
[3] Mangy fellows.             [6] Bauble.

[7] Lacking in self-respect.     [11] Enters later.
[8] Finery.                   [12] Certainly.
[9] So that.                  [13] If.
[10] Always.

Serv. Why, sir, let this satisfy you; good faith, I had no such intent.

Ste. Sir, an I thought you had, I would talk with you, and that presently.

Serv. Good Master Stephen, so you may, sir, at your pleasure.

Ste. And so I would, sir, good my saucy companion! An you were out o' mine uncle's ground, I can tell you, [30 though I do not stand upon my gentility neither in 't.

Know. Cousin, cousin, will this ne'er be left?

Ste. Whoreson,[1] base fellow! A mechanical[2] serving-man! By this cudgel, and 'twere not for shame, I would—

Know. What would you do, you peremptory gull?[3]
　　If you cannot be quiet, get you hence.
　　You see the honest man demeans himself       40
　　Modestly towards you, giving no reply
　　To your unseasoned, quarreling, rude fashion;
　　And still you huff it,[4] with a kind of carriage
　　As void of wit as of humanity.
　　Go, get you in; fore[5] heaven, I am ashamed
　　Thou hast a kinsman's interest in me.
　　　　　　　　　　　　[Exit Stephen.]

Serv. I pray you, sir, is this Master Knowell's house?

Know. Yes, marry, is it, sir.

Serv. I should inquire for a gentle- [50 man here, one Master Edward Knowell. Do you know any such, sir, I pray you?

Know. I should forget myself else, sir.

Serv. Are you the gentleman? Cry you mercy,[6] sir! I was required by a gentleman i' the city, as I rode out at this end o' the town, to deliver you this letter, sir.

Know. To me, sir! What do you mean? Pray you, remember your court'sy.[7] [Reads.] "To his most selected friend, [60 Master Edward Knowell." What might the gentleman's name be, sir, that sent it? Nay, pray you be covered.

Serv. One Master Wellbred, sir.

Know. Master Wellbred! A young gentleman, is he not?

Serv. The same, sir. Master Kitely married his sister; the rich merchant i' the Old Jewry.       69

Know. You say very true.—Brainworm!

[Enter Brainworm.]

Bra. Sir?

Know. Make this honest friend drink here.
　　Pray you, go in.—
　　　　[Exeunt Brainworm and Servant.]
　　This letter is directed to my son;
　　Yet I am Edward Knowell too, and may,
　　With the safe conscience of good manners, use
　　The fellow's error to my satisfaction.
　　Well, I will break it ope (old men are curious),
　　Be it but for the style's sake and the phrase,
　　To see if both do answer my son's praises,
　　Who is almost grown the idolater       80
　　Of this young Wellbred. What have we here? What's this?

### THE LETTER

"Why, Ned, I beseech thee, hast thou forsworn all thy friends i' the Old Jewry? Or dost thou think us all Jews that inhabit there yet? If thou dost, come over, and but see our frippery;[8] change an old shirt for a whole smock[9] with us. Do not conceive that antipathy between us and Hogsden, as was between Jews and [89 hog's flesh. Leave thy vigilant father alone, to number over his green apricots, evening and morning, o' the northwest wall. An I had been his son, I had saved him the labor long since, if taking in all the young wenches that pass by at the backdoor, and coddling[10] every kernel of the fruit for hem, would ha' served. But, prithee, come over to me quickly this morning; I have such a present for thee! Our Turkey company never sent the like to the Grand [100 Signior. One is a rimer, sir, o' your own batch, your own leaven, but doth think himself poet-major o' the town, willing to be shown, and worthy to be seen. The

---

[1] Rascally.　　　　　　　　[2] Menial.
[3] Absolute, complete fool.
[4] Swagger.　　　　[6] I beg your pardon.
[5] Before.　　　　　[7] I.e., put on your hat.
[8] Old clothes shop.
[9] I.e., wench.　　　　　　[10] Stewing.

other—I will not venter [1] his description
with you till you come, because I would ha'
you make hither with an appetite. If the
worst of hem be not worth your journey, draw your bill of charges, as uncon-
scionable as any Guildhall verdict [110
will give it you, and you shall be allowed
your viaticum. [2]
                From the Windmill." [3]
From the Burdello [4] it might come as
    well,
The Spittle, [5] or Pict-hatch. [6] Is this the
    man
My son hath sung so, for the happiest
    wit,
The choicest brain the times hath sent
    us forth?
I know not what he may be in the arts,
Nor what in schools; [7] but, surely, for
    his manners
I judge him a profane and dissolute
    wretch,
Worse by possession of such great good
    gifts,                                    120
Being the master of so loose a spirit.
Why, what unhallowed ruffian would
    have writ
In such a scurrilous manner to a friend!
Why should he think I tell [8] my apricots,
Or play th' Hesperian dragon with my
    fruit,
To watch it? Well, my son, I had thought
Y' had had more judgment t' have made
    election
Of your companions than t' have ta'en
    on trust
Such petulant, jeering gamesters, that
    can spare                                 129
No argument or subject from their jest.
But I perceive affection makes a fool
Of any man too much the father.—
    Brainworm!

[Enter Brainworm.]

Bra. Sir?
Know.    Is the fellow gone that brought
    this letter?
Bra. Yes, sir, a pretty while since.
Know. And where's your young master?

Bra. In his chamber, sir.
Know. He spake not with the fellow, did
he?
Bra. No, sir, he saw him not.            139
Know. [9] Take you this letter, and deliver
it my son, but with no notice that I have
opened it, on your life.
Bra. O Lord, sir, that were a jest indeed!
                                        [Exit.]
Know. I am resolved I will not stop his
    journey,
Nor practice any violent mean to stay
The unbridled course of youth in him,
    for that,
Restrained, grows more impatient, and
    in kind [10]
Like to the eager, but the generous, [11]
    grayhound,
Who, ne'er so little from his game with-
    held,
Turns head, and leaps up at his holder's
    throat.                                   150
There is a way of winning more by
    love
And urging of the modesty than fear;
Force works on servile natures, not the
    free.
He that's compelled to goodness may be
    good,
But 'tis but for that fit; [12] where others,
    drawn
By softness and example, get a habit.
Then, if they stray, but warn hem, and
    the same
They should for virtue have done, they'll
    do for shame.                    [Exit.]


ACT I. SCENE ii[i].

[A room in Knowell's house.]

Edw[ard]    Knowell,    Brainworm,    Mr.
                                    Stephen. [13]

[E. Know. (With a letter in his hand.)]
Did he open it, sayest thou?
Bra. Yes, o' my word, sir, and read
the contents.
E. Know. That scarce contents me.
What countenance, prithee, made he i'
the reading of it? Was he angry or pleased?

---

[1] Venture.                    [2] Traveling expenses.
[3] A tavern, formerly a synagogue.
[4] Bordello, a brothel.        [7] Lecture rooms.
[5] Hospital.                   [8] Count.
[6] A low district of London.

[9] Here and in two or three other passages the
original verse has been changed to prose.
   [10] Nature.                 [12] Moment.
   [11] Well-bred.              [13] Enters later.

BRA. Nay, sir, I saw him not read it, nor open it, I assure your worship.

E. KNOW. No! How know'st thou [10 then that he did either?

BRA. Marry, sir, because he charged me, on my life, to tell nobody that he opened it, which unless he had done, he would never fear to have it revealed.

E. KNOW. That's true; well, I thank thee, Brainworm.

[*Enter Stephen.*]

STE. O, Brainworm, didst thou not see a fellow here in a what-sha'-call-him doublet? He brought mine uncle a letter [20 e'en now.

BRA. Yes, Master Stephen. What of him?

STE. O, I ha' such a mind to beat him—where is he, canst thou tell?

BRA. Faith, he is not of that mind; he is gone, Master Stephen.

STE. Gone! Which way? When went he? How long since?

BRA. He is rid hence; he took horse [30 at the street door.

STE. And I stayed i' the fields! Whoreson Scanderbag[1] rogue! O, that I had but a horse to fetch him back again!

BRA. Why, you may ha' my m[aste]r's gelding, to save your longing, sir.

STE. But I ha' no boots—that's the spite on 't.

BRA. Why, a fine wisp of hay, rolled hard, Master Stephen.        40

STE. No, faith, it's no boot[2] to follow him now; let him e'en go and hang. Pray thee, help to truss me[3] a little. He does so vex me—

BRA. You'll be worse vexed when you are trussed,[4] Master Stephen. Best keep unbraced,[5] and walk yourself till you be cold; your choler may founder you else.

STE. By my faith, and so I will, now thou tell'st me on 't. How dost thou [50 like my leg, Brainworm?

BRA. A very good leg, Master Stephen; but the woolen stocking does not commend it so well.

STE. Foh!        The stockings be good

enough, now summer is coming on, for the dust; I'll have a pair of silk again' winter, that[6] I go to dwell i' the town. I think my leg would show in a silk hose—

BRA. Believe me, Master Stephen, [60 rarely well.

STE. In sadness,[7] I think it would; I have a reasonable good leg.

BRA. You have an excellent good leg, Master Stephen; but I cannot stay to praise it longer now, and I am very sorry for 't.

STE. Another time will serve, Brainworm; gramercy[8] for this.

[*Exit Brainworm.*]

E. KNOW. Ha, ha, ha!        70

*Knowell laughs, having read the letter.*

STE. [*Aside.*] 'Slid, I hope he laughs not at me; and he do—

E. KNOW. Here was a letter indeed, to be intercepted by a man's father, and do him good with him! He cannot but think most virtuously both of me and the sender, sure, that make the careful costermonger of him in our familiar epistles. Well, if he read this with patience I'll be gelt,[9] and troll ballads for Mr. John Trundle[10] [80 yonder the rest of my mortality.[11] It is true, and likely, my father may have as much patience as another man, for he takes much physic; and oft taking physic makes a man very patient. But would your packet, Master Wellbred, had arrived at him in such a minute of his patience! Then we had known the end of it, which now is doubtful, and threatens—[*Notices Stephen. Aside.*] What, my wise [90 cousin! Nay, then I'll furnish our feast with one gull more toward the mess.[12] He writes to me of a brace, and here's one—that's three. O, for a fourth! Fortunate, if ever thou'lt use thine eyes, I entreat thee—

STE. [*Aside.*] O, now I see who he laughed at. He laughed at somebody in that letter. By this good light, and he had laughed at me—        100

E. KNOW. How now, cousin Stephen, melancholy?

STE. Yes, a little. I thought you had laughed at me, cousin.

---

[1] *I.e.*, mighty, in reference to Iskender-beg, fifteenth century Albanian leader against the Turks.

[2] Use.

[3] Lace me up.

[4] Beaten.

[5] Unlaced.

[6] When.

[7] Seriously.

[8] Many thanks.

[9] Gelded.

[10] An actual publisher.

[11] Life.

[12] A group of four.

E. Know. Why, what an I had, coz? What would you ha' done?

Ste. By this light, I would ha' told mine uncle.

E. Know. Nay, if you would ha' told your uncle, I did laugh at you, coz.	110

Ste. Did you, indeed?

E. Know. Yes, indeed.

Ste. Why then—

E. Know. What then?

Ste. I am satisfied; it is sufficient.

E. Know. Why, be so, gentle coz. And, I pray you, let me entreat a courtesy of you. I am sent for this morning by a friend i' the Old Jewry to come to him; it's but crossing over the fields to Moor-	[120 gate. Will you bear me company? I protest it is not to draw you into bond or any plot against the state, coz.

Ste. Sir, that's all one and 'twere; you shall command me twice so far as Moorgate, to do you good in such a matter. Do you think I would leave you? I protest—

E. Know. No, no, you shall not protest, coz.

Ste. By my fackins,[1] but I will, [130 by your leave; I'll protest more to my friend than I'll speak of at this time.

E. Know. You speak very well, coz.

Ste. Nay, not so neither; you shall pardon me. But I speak to serve my turn.

E. Know. Your turn, coz? Do you know what you say? A gentleman of your sort,[2] parts, carriage, and estimation, to talk o' your "turn"[3] i' this company, and to me alone, like a tankard bearer at [140 a conduit! Fie! A wight that, hitherto, his every step hath left the stamp of a great foot behind him, as every word the savor of a strong spirit, and he, this man, so graced, gilded, or, to use a more fit metaphor, so tin-foiled by nature, as not ten housewives' pewter again' a good time shows more bright to the world than he! And he (as I said last, so I say again, and still shall say it), this man, to conceal [150 such real ornaments as these, and shadow their glory, as a milliner's wife does her wrought stomacher, with a smoky lawn or a black cyprus![4] O, coz, it cannot be answered; go not about it! Drake's old

ship at Detford[5] may sooner circle the world again. Come, wrong not the quality of your desert, with looking downward, coz; but hold up your head, so; and let the idea of what you are be portrayed i' [160 your face, that men may read i' your physnomy,[6] "Here within this place is to be seen the true, rare, and accomplished monster, or miracle of nature," which is all one. What think you of this, coz?

Ste. Why, I do think of it; and I will be more proud, and melancholy, and gentlemanlike than I have been, I'll insure you.

E. Know. Why, that's resolute,[7] [170 Master Stephen!—[Aside.] Now, if I can but hold him up to his height, as it is happily begun, it will do well for a suburb[8] humor: we may hap have a match with the city, and play him for forty pound.— Come, coz.

Ste. I'll follow you.

E. Know. Follow me! You must go before.[9]

Ste. Nay, an I must, I will. Pray [180 you, show me, good cousin.	[Exeunt.]

Act I. Scene iv.

[The lane before Cob's house.]

Mr. Matthew, Cob.[10]

[Mat.] I think this be the house. What, ho!

[Enter Cob.]

Cob. Who's there? O, Master Matthew! Gi' your worship good morrow.

Mat. What, Cob! How dost thou, good Cob? Dost thou inhabit here, Cob?

Cob. Ay, sir, I and my linage[11] ha' kept a poor house here in our days.

Mat. Thy linage, Monsieur Cob! What linage? What linage?	10

Cob. Why, sir, an ancient linage, and a princely. Mine ance'try came from a king's belly, no worse man; and yet no man neither (by your worship's leave, I did lie in that), but herring,[12] the king of

---

[1] Faith.	[2] Station.
[3] A trip, according to which water-carriers were paid.	[4] Transparent cloth.

[5] Deptford, where the *Golden Hind* was laid up.
[6] Physiognomy.	[10] Enters later.
[7] Decided.	[11] Lineage, family.
[8] Rustic.	[12] A cob is a young herring.
[9] *I.e.*, like a servant.

fish (from his belly I proceed), one o' the monarchs o' the world, I assure you. The first red herring that was broiled in Adam and Eve's kitchen do I fetch my pedigree from, by the harrot's [1] books. His cob [20 was my great-great-mighty-great grandfather.

MAT. Why mighty, why mighty, I pray thee?

COB. O, it was a mighty while ago, sir, and a mighty great cob.

MAT. How know'st thou that?

COB. How know I? Why, I smell his ghost ever and anon.

MAT. Smell a ghost? O unsavory [30 jest! And the ghost of a herring cob? [2]

COB. Ay, sir. With favor of your worship's nose, Mr. Matthew, why not the ghost of a herring cob as well as the ghost of Rasher Bacon.

MAT. Roger Bacon, thou wouldst say?

COB. I say Rasher Bacon. They were both broiled o' the coals; and a man may smell broiled meat, I hope? You are a scholar; upsolve me that now.          40

MAT. O raw ignorance!—Cob, canst thou show me of a gentleman, one Captain Bobadill, where his lodging is?

COB. O, my guest, sir, you mean.

MAT. Thy guest! Alas! Ha, ha!

COB. Why do you laugh, sir? Do you not mean Captain Bobadill?

MAT. Cob, pray thee, advise thyself well; do not wrong the gentleman, and thyself too. I dare be sworn he scorns [50 thy house. He! He lodge in such a base, obscure place as thy house! Tut, I know his disposition so well he would not lie in thy bed if thou'ldst gi' it him.

COB. I will not give it him though, sir. Mass, I thought somewhat was in 't—we could not get him to bed all night! Well, sir, though he lie not o' my bed, he lies o' my bench; an 't please you to go up, sir, you shall find him with two cushions [60 under his head, and his cloak wrapped about him, as though he had neither won nor lost, and yet, I warrant, he ne'er cast [3] better in his life than he has done tonight.[4]

MAT. Why, was he drunk?

COB. Drunk, sir? You hear not me say

so. Perhaps he swallowed a tavern token,[5] or some such device, sir; I have nothing to do withal. I deal with water and not with wine.—Gi' me my tankard there, ho!— [70 God b' w' you, sir. It's six a-clock; I should ha' carried two turns by this. What ho! My stopple! [6] Come.

MAT. Lie in a water bearer's house! A gentleman of his havings! [7] Well, I'll tell him my mind.

*[Enter Tib with a water tankard.]*

COB. What, Tib; show this gentleman up to the captain.—*[Exit Tib with Master Matthew.]* O, an my house were the Brazen Head now, faith, it would e'en speak, [80 "Mo [8] fools yet." [9] You should ha' some now would take this Mr. Matthew to be a gentleman, at the least. His father's an honest man, a worshipful fishmonger, and so forth; and now does he creep and wriggle into acquaintance with all the brave gallants about the town, such as my guest is (O, my guest is a fine man!), and they flout him invincibly.[10] He useth [11] every day to a merchant's house where I serve [90 water, one Master Kitely's, i' the Old Jewry; and here's the jest: he is in love with my master's sister, Mistress Bridget, and calls her "Mistress"; and there he will sit you a whole afternoon sometimes, reading o' these same abominable, vile (a pox on hem, I cannot abide them), rascally verses, "poyetry," "poyetry," and speaking of "interludes"; 'twill make a man burst to hear him. And the [100 wenches, they do so jeer, and tee-hee at him. Well, should they do so much to him, I'ld forswear them all, by the foot of Pharaoh! There's an oath! How many water bearers shall you hear swear such an oath? O, I have a guest—he teaches me—he does swear the legiblest of any man christened: "By St. George! The foot of Pharaoh! The body of me! As I am [a] [109 gentleman and a soldier!" Such dainty oaths! And withal he does take this same filthy, roguish tabacco,[12] the finest and cleanliest! It would do a man good to see

[1] Herald's.          [2] Here, herring's head.
[3] Pun on *cast*, to throw dice, and to vomit.
[4] *I.e.*, last night.

[5] Slang term for *got drunk*.          [7] Possessions.
[6] Stopper.          [8] More.
[9] *Cf.* Greene's *Friar Bacon and Friar Bungay.*
[10] Exceedingly.          [11] Is accustomed to go.
[12] Tobacco.

the fume come forth at 's tonnels.[1] Well, he owes me forty shillings my wife lent him out of her purse, by sixpence a time, besides his lodging; I would I had it! I shall ha' it, he says, the next action.[2] Helter-skelter, hang sorrow, care 'll kill a cat, up-tails all, and a louse for the [120 hangman!                                    [*Exit.*]

### ACT I. SCENE V.

[*A room in Cob's house.*]

*Bobadill, Tib, Matthew.*[3] *Bobad*[*ill*] *is discovered lying on his bench.*

[BOB.] Hostess, hostess!

[*Enter Tib.*]

TIB. What say you, sir?

BOB. A cup o' thy small beer, sweet hostess.

TIB. Sir, there's a gentleman below would speak with you.

BOB. A gentleman! 'Odso,[4] I am not within.

TIB. My husband told him you were, sir.                                      10

BOB. What a plague—what meant he?

MAT. [*Below.*] Captain Bobadill?

BOB. Who's there?—(Take away the basin, good hostess!) Come up, sir.

TIB. He would desire you to come up, sir.

[*Enter Matthew.*]

You come into a cleanly house, here!

MAT. Save you, sir; save you, captain!

BOB. Gentle Master Matthew! Is it you, sir? Please you, sit down.       20

MAT. Thank you, good captain; you may see I am somewhat audacious.

BOB. Not so, sir. I was requested to supper last night by a sort[5] of gallants, where you were wished for and drunk to, I assure you.

MAT. Vouchsafe me, by whom, good captain?

BOB. Marry, by young Wellbred and others.—Why, hostess, a stool here [30 for this gentleman!

MAT. No haste, sir; 'tis very well.

BOB. Body of me! It was so late ere we parted last night I can scarce open my eyes yet; I was but new risen, as you came. How passes the day abroad, sir? You can tell.

MAT. Faith, some half hour to seven. Now, trust me, you have an exceeding fine lodging here, very neat and pri- [40 vate.

BOB. Ay, sir; sit down, I pray you. Master Matthew, in any case possess no gentlemen of our acquaintance with notice of my lodging.

MAT. Who? I, sir? No.

BOB. Not that I need to care who know it, for the cabin[6] is convenient; but in regard I would not be too popular, and generally visited, as some are.       50

MAT. True, captain, I conceive you.

BOB. For, do you see, sir, by the heart of valor in me, except it be to some peculiar and choice spirits, to whom I am extraordinarily engaged, as yourself or so, I could not extend thus far.

MAT. O Lord, sir! I resolve so.[7]

BOB. I confess I love a cleanly and quiet privacy, above all the tumult and roar of fortune. What new book [60 ha' you there? What! "Go by, Hieronymo"?[8]

MAT. Ay; did you ever see it acted? Is 't not well penned?

BOB. Well penned? I would fain see all the poets of these times pen such another play as that was! They'll prate and swagger, and keep a stir of art and devices, when, as I am a gentleman, read hem, they are the most shallow, pitiful, bar- [70 ren fellows that live upon the face of the earth again.

MAT. Indeed, here are a number of fine speeches in this book. "O eyes, no eyes, but fountains fraught with tears!" There's a conceit![9] "Fountains fraught with tears!"—"O life, no life, but lively form of death!" Another!—"O world, no world, but mass of public wrongs!" A third!—"Confused and filled with mur- [80 der and misdeeds!" A fourth!—O, the muses! Is 't not excellent? Is 't not simply the best that ever you heard, captain? Ha! How do you like it?

---

[1] Tunnels, nostrils.        [4] A mild oath.
[2] *I.e.,* court action.     [5] Company.
[3] Last two enter later.

[6] Room.        [8] *I.e.,* Kyd's *Spanish Tragedy.*
[7] I am sure of it.        [9] Fanciful thought.

BOB. 'Tis good.

MAT. "To thee, the purest object to my
  sense,
  The most refinéd essence heaven covers,
  Send I these lines, wherein I do com-
    mence
  The happy state of turtle-billing lovers.
    If they prove rough, unpolished, harsh,
      and rude,                                    90
    Haste made the waste: thus mildly I
      conclude." [1]

BOB. Nay, proceed, proceed. Where's
this?

*Bobadill is making him ready all this while.*

MAT. This, sir? A toy o' mine own, in
my nonage, the infancy of my muses. But
when will you come and see my study?
Good faith, I can show you some very good
things I have done of late.—That boot
becomes your leg passing well, captain,
methinks.                                        100

BOB. So, so; it's the fashion gentlemen
now use.

MAT. Troth, captain, and now you
speak o' the fashion, Master Wellbred's
elder brother and I are fall'n out exceedingly. This other day I happened to enter
into some discourse of a hanger,[2] which,
I assure you, both for fashion and workmanship, was most peremptory[3]-beauti-
ful and gentlemanlike! Yet he con- [110
demned and cried it down for the most
pied [4] and ridiculous that ever he saw.

BOB. Squire Downright, the half brother,
was 't not?

MAT. Ay, sir, he.

BOB. Hang him, rook! [5] He! Why, he has
no more judgment than a malt horse.[6]
By S[t]. George, I wonder you'ld loose a
thought upon such an animal; the most
peremptory-absurd clown of Chris- [120
tendom this day he is holden. I protest
to you, as I am a gentleman and a soldier,
I ne'er changed words with his like. By
his discourse, he should eat nothing but
hay; he was born for the manger, pannier,
or pack-saddle. He has not so much as a
good phrase in his belly, but all old iron

and rusty proverbs! A good commodity
for some smith to make hobnails of!

MAT. Ay, and he thinks to carry [130
it away with his manhood still, where he
comes. He brags he will gi' me the *bastinado*, as I hear.

BOB. How! He the *bastinado*! How
came he by that word, trow?

MAT. Nay, indeed, he said "cudgel
me"; I termed it so, for my more grace.

BOB. That may be, for I was sure it
was none of his word. But when? When
said he so?                                      140

MAT. Faith, yesterday, they say; a
young gallant, a friend of mine, told me so.

BOB. By the foot of Pharaoh, and
'twere my case now, I should send him a
*chartel* [7] presently. The *bastinado*! A most
proper and sufficient *dependence*,[8] warranted by the great Caranza.[9] Come
hither; you shall *chartel* him; I'll show you
a trick or two you shall kill him with at
pleasure; the first *stoccata*,[10] if you [150
will, by this air.

MAT. Indeed, you have absolute knowledge i' the mystery,[11] I have heard, sir.

BOB. Of whom? Of whom? Ha' you
heard it, I beseech you?

MAT. Troth, I have heard it spoken
of divers[12] that you have very rare and
un-in-one-breath-utterable skill, sir.

BOB. By heaven, no, not I; no skill
i' the earth; some small rudiments i' [160
the science, as to know my time, distance,
or so. I have professed it more for noblemen and gentlemen's use than mine own
practice, I assure you.—Hostess, accom-
modate us with another bedstaff [13] here
quickly. Lend us another bedstaff.—The
woman does not understand the words
of action.—[*Takes the position of a fencer.*]
Look you, sir; exalt not your point above
this state, at any hand,[14] and let your [170
*poinard*[15] maintain your defense, thus.
(Give it the gentleman, and leave us.)—
[*Exit Tib.*] So, sir. Come on. O, twine
your body more about, that you may fall
to a more sweet, comely, gentlemanlike
guard; so, indifferent![16] Hollow your

---

[1] The source of these lines in unknown, although Matthew usually pilfers other poets.
[2] A belt by which a weapon was hung from the
girdle.
[3] Exceedingly.        [5] Simpleton.
[4] Variegated.         [6] Drunkard.

[7] Challenge.        [8] Ground for a duel.
[9] Author of a Spanish book on fencing.
[10] Thrust.   [11] Art, profession.   [12] By many.
[13] For preparing a feather bed.   [15] Poniard.
[14] Under any circumstances.   [16] Fairly well.

body more, sir, thus. Now, stand fast o'
your left leg, note your distance, keep
your due proportion of time. O, you disorder your point most irregularly!     180

MAT. How is the bearing of it now, sir?

BOB. O, out of measure ill. A well-
experienced hand would pass upon you
at pleasure.

MAT. How mean you, sir, pass upon
me?

BOB. Why, thus, sir: make a thrust at
me, come in upon the answer, control
your point, and make a full career [1] at the
body. The best-practiced gallants [190
of the time name it the *passada*. A most
desperate thrust, believe it!

MAT. Well, come, sir.

BOB. Why, you do not manage your
weapon with any facility or grace to invite
me. I have no spirit to play with you;
your dearth of judgment renders you
tedious.

MAT. But one *venue*,[2] sir.

BOB. "*Venue*"! Fie! Most gross [200
denomination as ever I heard. O, the
"*stoccata*," while you live, sir; note that.—
Come, put on your cloak, and we'll go
to some private place where you are acquainted—some tavern or so—and have
a bit. I'll send for one of these fencers,
and he shall breathe [3] you, by my direction; and then I will teach you your trick.
You shall kill him with it at the first, if
you please. Why, I will learn you, by [210
the true judgment of the eye, hand, and
foot, to control any enemy's point i' the
world. Should your adversary confront
you with a pistol, 'twere nothing, by this
hand! You should, by the same rule, control his bullet, in a line, except it were hail
shot, and spread. What money ha' you
about you, Mr. Matthew?

MAT. Faith, I ha' not past a two shillings or so.                                    220

BOB. 'Tis somewhat with the least.
But come; we will have a bunch of reddish [4] and salt to taste our wine, and a
pipe of tabacco to close the orifice of the
stomach; and then we'll call upon young
Wellbred. Perhaps we shall meet the
Corydon [5] his brother there, and put him
to the question.                    [*Exeunt.*]

---

[1] Lunge.    [2] Thrust.    [3] Exercise.    [4] Radish.
[5] Rustic.                    [6] Coarse silk cloth.

ACT II. SCENE i.

[*A room in Kitely's house in the Old Jewry.*]

*Kitely, Cash, Downright.*

[KITE.] Thomas, come hither.
  There lies a note within upon my desk.
  Here, take my key. It is no matter
    neither.
  Where is the boy?

CASH.                    Within, sir, i' the warehouse.

KITE. Let him tell over straight that
    Spanish gold,
  And weigh it, with th' pieces of eight.
    Do you
  See the delivery of those silver stuffs
  To Mr. Lucre; tell him, if he will,
  He shall ha' the grograns [6] at the rate
    I told him,
  And I will meet him on the Exchange
    anon.                                    10

CASH. Good, sir.                    [*Exit.*]

KITE. Do you see that fellow, brother
    Downright?

Dow. Ay, what of him?

KITE.                    He is a jewel, brother.[7]
  I took him of[8] a child up at my door.
  And christened him, gave him mine own
    name, Thomas;
  Since, bred him at the Hospital,[9] where
    proving
  A toward imp,[10] I called him home, and
    taught him
  So much as I have made him my cashier,
  And given him who had none, a surname,
    Cash,
  And find him in his place so full of
    faith                                    20
  That I durst trust my life into his hands.

Dow. So would not I in any bastard's,
    brother,
  As it is like he is, although I knew
  Myself his father. But you said yo' had
    somewhat
  To tell me, gentle brother. What is 't?
    What is 't?

KITE. Faith, I am very loath to utter it,
  As fearing it may hurt your patience;
  But that I know your judgment is of
    strength,
  Against the nearness of affection—

---

[7] Half-brother-in-law.                    [8] As.
[9] Christ's Hospital, where foundlings and
others were educated.                    [10] Apt lad.

Dow. What need this circumstance? [1]
   Pray you, be direct.                              30
Kite. I will not say how much I do ascribe
   Unto your friendship, nor in what regard
   I hold your love; but let my past be-
      havior
   And usage of your sister but confirm
   How well I've been affected to your—
Dow. You are too tedious; come to the
   matter, the matter.
Kite. Then, without further ceremony,
      thus.
   My brother Wellbred, sir, I know not how,
   Of late is much declined in what he was,
   And greatly altered in his disposi-
      tion.                                          40
   When he came first to lodge here in my
      house,
   Ne'er trust me if I were not proud of him;
   Methought he bare himself in such a
      fashion,
   So full of man [2] and sweetness in his car-
      riage,
   And, what was chief, it showed not bor-
      rowed in him,
   But all he did became him as his own,
   And seemed as perfect, proper, and pos-
      sessed
   As breath with life, or color with the
      blood.
   But now, his course is so irregular,   49
   So loose, affected, and deprived of grace,
   And he himself withal so far fall'n off
   From that first place as scarce no note
      remains
   To tell men's judgments where he lately
      stood.
   He's grown a stranger to all due respect,
   Forgetful of his friends; and, not content
   To stale himself in all societies,
   He makes my house here common as a
      mart,
   A theater, a public receptacle
   For giddy humor and diseasèd riot;
   And here, as in a tavern or a stews,   60
   He and his wild associates spend their
      hours
   In repetition of lascivious jests,
   Swear, leap, drink, dance, and revel
      night by night,
   Control my servants, and, indeed, what
      not?

Dow. 'Sdeynes,[3] I know not what I
should say to him, i' the whole world! He
values me at a cracked three farthings, for
aught I see. It will never out o' the flesh
that's bred i' the bone. I have told him
enough, one would think, if that would   [70
serve; but counsel to him is as good as a
shoulder of mutton to a sick horse. Well,
he knows what to trust to, for George.[4]
Let him spend and spend and domineer,
till his heart ache; an he think to be relieved by me, when he is got into one o'
your city pounds, the counters,[5] he has
the wrong sow by the ear, i' faith, and claps
his dish [6] at the wrong man's door. I'll
lay my hand o' my halfpenny, ere I   [80
part with 't to fetch him out, I'll assure
him.
Kite. Nay, good brother, let it not trouble
   you thus.
Dow. 'Sdeath, he mads me! I could eat
my very spur-leathers for anger! But why
are you so tame? Why do you not speak
to him, and tell him how he disquiets your
house?
Kite. O, there are divers reasons to dis-
   suade, brother.
   But, would yourself vouchsafe to travail
      in it                                          90
   (Though but with plain and easy circum-
      stance),
   It would both come much better to his
      sense,
   And savor less of stomach [7] or of passion.
   You are his elder brother, and that title
   Both gives and warrants you authority,
   Which, by your presence seconded, must
      breed
   A kind of duty in him, and regard;
   Whereas, if I should intimate the least,
   It would but add contempt to his neglect,
   Heap worse on ill, make up a pile of
      hatred,                                        100
   That in the rearing would come tott'ring
      down,
   And in the ruin bury all our love.
   Nay, more than this, brother; if I should
      speak,
   He would be ready, from his heat of
      humor [8]

[1] Circuitous narration.        [2] Manliness.

[3] By God's dignesse, i.e., dignity(?).
[4] I.e., for all I care.        [6] I.e., like a beggar.
[5] Debtors' prisons.        [7] Anger.
[8] From his temper.

And overflowing of the vapor in him,
To blow the ears of his familiars
With the false breath of telling what dis-
   graces
And low disparagements I had put upon
   him,
Whilst they, sir, to relieve him in the
   fable,[1]
Make their loose comments upon every
   word,                                     110
Gesture, or look I use; mock me all over,
From my flat cap [2] unto my shining
   shoes; [2]
And, out of their impetuous, rioting
   fant'sies,
Beget some slander that shall dwell with
   me.
And what would that be, think you?
   Marry, this:
They would give out, because my wife is
   fair,
Myself but lately married, and my sister
Here sojourning a virgin in my house,
That I were jealous—nay, as sure as
   death,
That they would say—and how that I
   had quarreled [3]                         120
My brother purposely, thereby to find
An apt pretext to banish them my
   house.
Dow. Mass, perhaps so; they are like
   enough to do it.
Kite. Brother, they would, believe it; so
   should I,
Like one of these penurious quack-
   salvers,
But set the bills [4] up to mine own dis-
   grace,
And try experiments upon myself;
Lend scorn and envy opportunity
To stab my reputation and good
   name—

### Act II. Scene ii.

[*The same.*]

*Matthew, Bobadill, Downright, Kitely.*

[Mat. (*Enters, struggling with Bobadill.*)]
I will speak to him.
Bob. Speak to him? Away! By the foot
of Pharaoh, you shall not! You shall not
do him that grace.—The time of day to
you, gentleman o' the house. Is Mr. Well-
bred stirring?
   Dow. How then? What should he do?
   Bob. Gentleman of the house, it [5] is to
you. Is he within, sir?               10
   Kite. He came not to his lodging to-
night, sir, I assure you.
   Dow. Why, do you hear? You!
   Bob. The gentleman-citizen hath satis-
fied me; I'll talk to no scavenger.
         [*Exeunt Bobadill and Matthew.*]
   Dow. How! Scavenger? Stay, sir, stay!
   Kite. Nay, brother Downright—
   Dow. Heart! Stand you away, and you
love me.
   Kite. You shall not follow him now,  [20
I pray you, brother; good faith, you shall
not. I will overrule you.
   Dow. Ha! Scavenger? Well, go to, I say
little; but, by this good day (God forgive
me I should swear), if I put it up [6] so, say
I am the rankest cow that ever pissed.
'Sdeynes, and I swallow this, I'll ne'er draw
my sword in the sight of Fleet Street again
while I live; I'll sit in a barn with madge-
howlet,[7] and catch mice first. Scaven-  [30
ger, heart!—and I'll go near to fill that
huge tumbrel-slop [8] of yours with somewhat, and I have good luck; your Gara-
gantua breech cannot carry it away so.
   Kite. O, do not fret yourself thus; never
   think on 't.
   Dow. These are my brother's consorts,
these! These are his cam'rades, his walking
mates! He's a gallant, a *cavaliero* too, right
hangman cut! [9] Let me not live, and I
could not find in my heart to swinge   [40
the whole ging [10] of hem, one after another,
and begin with him first. I am grieved it
should be said he is my brother, and take
these courses. Well, as he brews, so shall
he drink, for George, again. Yet he shall
hear on 't, and that tightly [11] too, and I
live, i' faith.
   Kite. But, brother, let your reprehension,
   then,
Run in an easy current, not o'erhigh
Carried with rashness or devouring
   choler;                                    50
But rather use the soft, persuading way,

---

[1] Narrating.                    [3] Quarreled with.
[2] Marks of the citizen.         [4] Advertisements.

[5] *I.e.*, my question.          [7] The barn owl.
[6] Endure it.                    [8] Loose breeches.
[9] In the exact form of a hangman.
[10] Beat the whole gang.         [11] Quickly.

Whose powers will work more gently, and compose

Th' imperfect thoughts you labor to reclaim,

More winning than enforcing the consent.

Dow. Ay, ay, let me alone for that, I warrant you.                    *Bell rings.*

Kite. How now!  O, the bell rings to breakfast.

Brother, I pray you go in, and bear my wife

Company till I come; I'll but give order

For some despatch of business to my servants—              [*Exit Downright.*]

### Act II. Scene iii.

#### [*The same.*]

##### [1] *Kitely, Cob, Dame Kitely.*[2]

[Kite.] What, Cob!  Our maids will have you by the back, i' faith,

For coming so late this morning.

Cob. Perhaps so, sir; take heed somebody have not them by the belly for walking so late in the evening.

*He passes by with his tankard.*

Kite. Well, yet my troubled spirit's somewhat eased,

Though not reposed in that security

As I could wish; but I must be content,

Howe'er I set a face on 't to the world.

Would I had lost this finger at a venter,

So Wellbred had ne'er lodged within my house.                                    11

Why, 't cannot be, where there is such resort

Of wanton gallants and young revelers,

That any woman should be honest[3] long.

Is 't like that factious beauty will preserve

The public weal of chastity unshaken,

When such strong motives muster and make head[4]

Against her single peace? No, no. Beware.

When mutual appetite doth meet to treat,

And spirits of one kind and quality  20

Come once to parley in the pride of blood,

It is no slow conspiracy that follows.

Well, to be plain, if I but thought the time

Had answered their affections,[5] all the world

Should not persuade me but I were a cuckold.

Marry, I hope they ha' not got that start,

For opportunity hath balked hem yet,

And shall do still, while I have eyes and ears

To attend the impositions[6] of my heart.

My presence shall be as an iron bar    30

Twixt the conspiring motions of desire;

Yea, every look or glance mine eye ejects

Shall check occasion, as one doth his slave,

When he forgets the limits of prescription.

#### [*Enter Dame Kitely.*]

Dame. [*Calling.*] Sister Bridget, pray you, fetch down the rose water above in the closet.—Sweetheart, will you come in to breakfast?

Kite. An she have overheard me now—!                                            40

Dame. I pray thee, good muss,[7] we stay for you.

Kite. By heaven, I would not for a thousand angels.[8]

Dame. What ail you, sweetheart? Are you not well? Speak, good muss.

Kite. Troth, my head aches extremely on a sudden.

Dame. [*Putting her hand to his forehead.*] O, the Lord!                                    50

Kite. How now! What?

Dame. Alas, how it burns! Muss, keep you warm; good truth, it is this new disease;[9] there's a number are troubled withal. For love's sake, sweetheart, come in out of the air.

Kite. [*Aside.*] How simple and how subtle are her answers!

A new disease, and many troubled with it?

Why, true; she heard me, all[10] the world to nothing.

Dame. I pray thee, good sweet-      [60

[1] The marginal direction *"To them"* is erroneously printed here.    [3] Virtuous.
[2] Enters later.    [4] Gather their forces.
[5] Suited their inclinations.    [7] Mouse.
[6] Promptings.    [8] Gold coins.
[9] A form of fever, probably typhoid.
[10] *I.e.,* I wager all.

heart, come in; the air will do you harm, in troth.

KITE. [*Aside.*] The air! She has me i' the wind.[1]—Sweetheart,

    I'll come to you presently; 'twill away, I hope.

DAME. Pray heaven it do.    [*Exit.*]

KITE. A new disease? I know not, new or old,

    But it may well be called poor mortals' plague,

For, like a pestilence, it doth infect

The houses of the brain.  First it begins

Solely to work upon the fantasy,    70

Filling her seat with such pestiferous air

As soon corrupts the judgment; and from thence

Sends like contagion to the memory,

Still each to other giving the infection,

Which as a subtle vapor spreads itself

Confusedly through every sensive [2] part,

Till not a thought or motion in the mind

Be free from the black poison of suspect.[3]

Ah, but what misery is it to know this!

Or, knowing it, to want the mind's erec-

    tion [4]    80

In such extremes? Well, I will once more strive,

In spite of this black cloud, myself to be,

And shake the fever off that thus shakes

    me.    [*Exit.*]

### ACT II. SCENE iv.

*[Moorfields.]*

*Brainworm, Ed[ward] Knowell, Mr. Ste-*
*    phen.[5]*

BRA. [*Disguised like a maimed soldier.*] 'Slid, I cannot choose but laugh to see myself translated thus from a poor creature to a creator; for now must I create an intolerable sort of lies, or my present profession loses the grace. And yet the lie, to a man of my coat, is as ominous a fruit as the *fico.*[6] O, sir, it holds for good polity ever, to have that outwardly in vilest estimation, that inwardly is most dear to us. So [10] much for my borrowed shape. Well, the troth is, my old master intends to follow

my young, dry-foot,[7] over Moorfields to London this morning; now I, knowing of this hunting match, or rather conspiracy, and to insinuate with my young master (for so must we that are blue waiters [8] and men of hope and service do, or perhaps we may wear motley at the year's end, and who wears motley,[9] you know—), [20] have got me afore in this disguise, determining here to lie in *ambuscado*, and intercept him in the midway. If I can but get his cloak, his purse, his hat, nay, any thing to cut him off, that is, to stay his journey, "*Veni, vidi, vici,*"[10] I may say, with Captain Cæsar, I am made forever, i' faith. Well, now must I practice to get the true garb of one of these lance-knights,[11] my arm here, and my—young master, and his [30] cousin, Mr. Stephen, as I am true counterfeit man of war, and no soldier! [*Retires.*]

*[Enter Edward Knowell and Stephen.]*

E. KNOW. So, sir! And how then, coz?

STE. 'Sfoot, I have lost my purse, I think.

E. KNOW. How?  Lost your purse? Where? When had you it?

STE. I cannot tell. Stay.

BRA. 'Slid, I am afeard they will know me. Would I could get by them!    40

E. KNOW. What, ha' you it?

STE. No; I think I was bewitched, I—
    [*Weeps.*]

E. KNOW. Nay, do not weep the loss; hang it, let it go.

STE. [*Finding his purse.*] O, it's here. No, and it had been lost, I had not cared, but for a jet ring Mistress Mary sent me.

E. KNOW. A jet ring?  O, the poesy,[12] the poesy?

STE. Fine, i' faith.—    50
    "Though Fancy [13] sleep,
      My love is deep—"
meaning that, though I did not fancy her, yet she loved me dearly.

E. KNOW. Most excellent!

STE. And then I sent her another, and my poesy was,

---

[1] She's on my scent.
[2] Sensitive.    [4] To lack elevation of mind.
[3] Suspicion.    [5] The last two enter later.
[6] Fig, an insulting gesture.

[7] By the scent.    [8] Blue-liveried servants.
[9] The fool's coat.
[10] "I came, I saw, I conquered."
[11] Mercenary footsoldiers.
[12] Posy, motto.      [13] Affection.

"The deeper, the sweeter,
I'll be judged by St. Peter."

E. Know. How, by St. Peter? I do [60
not conceive that.

Ste. Marry, St. Peter, to make up the
meter.

E. Know. Well, there the saint was
your good patron; he helped you at your
need. Thank him, thank him.

Bra. (*He is come back.*)[1] [*Aside.*] I cannot take leave on hem so; I will venture,
come what will.—Gentlemen, please you
change a few crowns for a very excel- [70
lent good blade here? I am a poor gentleman, a soldier, one that, in the better state
of my fortunes, scorned so mean a refuge;
but now it is the humor of necessity to
have it so. You seem to be gentlemen well
affected to martial men, else I should rather
die with silence than live with shame.
However, vouchsafe to remember it is my
want speaks, not myself; this condition
agrees not with my spirit—                80

E. Know. Where hast thou served?

Bra. May it please you, sir, in all the
late wars of Bohemia, Hungaria, Dalmatia,
Poland—where not, sir? I have been a poor
servitor by sea and land any time this fourteen years, and followed the fortunes of the
best commanders in Christendom. I was
twice shot at the taking of Aleppo, once
at the relief of Vienna; I have been at
Marseilles, Naples, and the Adriatic [90
gulf, a gentleman slave in the galleys thrice,
where I was most dangerously shot in the
head, through both the thighs; and yet,
being thus maimed, I am void of maintenance, nothing left me but my scars, the
noted marks of my resolution.

Ste. How will you sell this rapier,
friend?

Bra. Generous sir, I refer it to your
own judgment. You are a gentle- [100
man; give me what you please.

Ste. True, I am a gentleman, I know
that, friend; but what though? I pray you
say, what would you ask?

Bra. I assure you, the blade may become the side or thigh of the best prince
in Europe.

E. Know. Ay, with a velvet scabbard,
I think.

Ste. Nay, and 't be mine, it shall [110
have a velvet scabbard, coz, that's flat; I'd
not wear it as 'tis, and you would give me
an angel.

Bra. At your worship's pleasure, sir.
[*Stephen examines the blade.*] Nay, 'tis a
most pure Toledo.

Ste. I had rather it were a Spaniard.
But tell me, what shall I give you for it?
An it had a silver hilt—

E. Know. Come, come, you shall [120
not buy it. Hold, there's a shilling, fellow;
take thy rapier.

Ste. Why, but I will buy it now, because you say so; and there's another shilling, fellow; I scorn to be outbidden. What,
shall I walk with a cudgel, like Higgin-
bottom,[2] and may have a rapier for money?

E. Know. You may buy one in the city.

Ste. Tut! I'll buy this i' the field, so
I will; I have a mind to 't, because 'tis [130
a field rapier. Tell me your lowest price.

E. Know. You shall not buy it, I say.

Ste. By this money, but I will, though
I give more than 'tis worth.

E. Know. Come away; you are a fool.

Ste. Friend, I am a fool, that's granted;
but I'll have it, for that word's sake. Follow me for your money.

Bra. At your service, sir.        [*Exeunt.*]

### Act II. Scene v.

[*Another part of Moorfields.*]

*Knowell, Brainworm.*[3]

[Know.] I cannot lose the thought yet of
   this letter
Sent to my son; nor leave t' admire [4] the
   change
Of manners and the breeding of our
   youth
Within the kingdom, since myself was one.
When I was young, he lived not in the
   stews
Durst have conceived a scorn and ut-
   tered it
On a gray head; age was authority
Against a buffon,[5] and a man had then
A certain reverence paid unto his years,
That had none due unto his life. So much

---

[1] This direction appears opposite the preceding
line in the original.
[2] Unidentified; probably any rustic.
[3] Enters later.
[4] Wonder at.                    [5] Buffoon.

The sanctity of some prevailed for others.
But now we all are fall'n, youth from
their fear,                                              12
And age from that which bred it, good
example.[1]
Nay, would ourselves were not the first
even parents
That did destroy the hopes in our own
children,
Or they not learned our vices in their
cradles,
And sucked in our ill customs with their
milk!
Ere all their teeth be born, or they can
speak,
We make their palates cunning; the first
words
We form their tongues with are licentious
jests!                                                    20
Can it call "whore"? Cry "bastard"?
O, then, kiss it!
A witty child! Can't swear? The father's
dearling![2]
Give it two plums. Nay, rather than 't
shall learn
No bawdy song, the mother herself will
teach it!
But this is in the infancy, the days
Of the long coat; when it puts on the
breeches,
It will put off all this. Ay, it is like,
When it is gone into the bone already!
No, no; this dye goes deeper than the
coat,                                                     29
Or shirt, or skin; it stains unto the liver[3]
And heart[4] in some. And, rather than it
should not,
Note what we fathers do! Look how we
live,
What mistresses we keep, at what ex-
pense!
In our sons' eyes, where they may handle
our gifts,
Hear our lascivious courtships, see our
dalliance,
Taste of the same provoking meats with
us,
To ruin of our states! Nay, when our own
Portion[5] is fled, to prey on their re-
mainder,[5]

We call them into fellowship of vice;
Bait hem with the young chambermaid,
to seal,[6]                                               40
And teach hem all bad ways to buy af-
fiction.[7]
This is one path; but there are millions
more,
In which we spoil our own with leading
them.
Well, I thank heaven, I never yet was he
That traveled with my son, before six-
teen,
To show him the Venetian courtesans;
Nor read the grammar of cheating I had
made,
To my sharp boy, at twelve, repeating
still
The rule,[8] "Get money;" still, "Get
money, boy,                                               49
No matter by what means; money will do
More, boy, than my lord's letter." Nei-
ther have I
Dressed snails or mushrooms curiously
before him,
Perfumed my sauces, and taught him to
make hem;
Preceding still, with my gray gluttony,
At all the ordinaries,[9] and only feared
His palate should degenerate, not his
manners.
These are the trade of fathers now; how-
ever,
My son, I hope, hath met within my
threshold
None of these household precedents,
which are strong
And swift to rape youth to their preci-
pice.[10]                                                 60
But let the house at home be ne'er so
clean—
Swept, or kept sweet from filth, nay,
dust and cobwebs,
If he will live abroad with his compan-
ions
In dung and leystalls,[11] it is worth a fear;
Nor is the danger of conversing less
Than all that I have mentioned of ex-
ample.

---

[6] "Probably, to agree to the sale of family
estates" (Neilson).
[7] Affliction, from Lat. *afficio*.
[8] The following lines are based on passages
from Horace and Juvenal.   [9] Eating-houses.
[10] Carry youth off to their downfall.
[11] Laystalls, rubbish heaps.

[1] The following twenty lines are taken from
Quintilian; previous ones from Juvenal and Ovid.
[2] Darling.                    [4] Seat of knowledge.
[3] Seat of the passions.   [5] Inheritance.

*[Enter Brainworm.]*

BRA. [*Aside.*] My master! Nay, faith, have at you; I am fleshed [1] now, I have sped so well.—Worshipful sir, I beseech you, respect the estate of a poor sol- [70 dier; I am ashamed of this base course of life—God's my comfort [2]—but extremity provokes me to 't. What remedy?

KNOW. I have not for you now.

BRA. By the faith I bear unto truth, gentleman, it is no ordinary custom in me, but only to preserve manhood. I protest to you, a man I have been; a man I may be, by your sweet bounty.

KNOW. Pray thee, good friend, be [80 satisfied.

BRA. Good sir, by that hand, you may do the part of a kind gentleman in lending a poor soldier the price of two cans of beer, a matter of small value; the king of heaven shall pay you, and I shall rest thankful. Sweet worship—

KNOW. Nay, and you be so importunate—

BRA. O, tender sir, need will have [90 his course; I was not made to this vile use! Well, the edge of the enemy could not have abated me so much. It's hard when a man hath served in his prince's cause, and be thus—(*He weeps.*) Honorable worship, let me derive a small piece of silver from you; it shall not be given in the course of time.[3] By this good ground, I was fain to pawn my rapier last night for a poor supper; I had sucked the hilts long before, I [100 am a pagan else. Sweet honor—

KNOW. Believe me, I am taken with some wonder
To think a fellow of thy outward presence
Should, in the frame and fashion of his mind,
Be so degenerate and sordid-base.
Art thou a man, and sham'st thou not to beg?
To practice such a servile kind of life?
Why, were thy education ne'er so mean,
Having thy limbs, a thousand fairer courses
Offer themselves to thy election.          110

Either the wars might still supply thy wants,
Or service of some virtuous gentleman,
Or honest labor; nay, what can I name
But would become thee better than to beg?
But men of thy condition feed on sloth,
As doth the beetle on the dung she breeds in,
Not caring how the metal of your minds
Is eaten with the rust of idleness.
Now, afore me, whate'er he be that should
Relieve a person of thy quality,          120
While thou insists in this loose, desperate course,
I would esteem the sin not thine, but his.

BRA. Faith, sir, I would gladly find some other course, if so—

KNOW. Ay, you'd gladly find it, but you will not seek it.

BRA. Alas, sir, where should a man seek? In the wars there's no ascent by desert in these days; but—and, for service, would it were as soon purchased [4] as wished [130 for! The air's my comfort, I know. What I would say—

KNOW. What's thy name?

BRA.          Please you, Fitzsword, sir.

KNOW.          Fitzsword?
Say that a man should entertain thee now,
Wouldst thou be honest, humble, just, and true?

BRA. Sir, by the place and honor of a soldier—

KNOW. Nay, nay, I like not those affected oaths.
Speak plainly, man, what think'st thou of my words?

BRA. Nothing, sir, but wish my fortunes were as happy as my service [140 should be honest.

KNOW. Well, follow me; I'll prove [5] thee, if thy deeds
Will carry a proportion to thy words.

BRA. Yes, sir, straight; I'll but garter my hose.—[*Exit Knowell.*] O, that my belly were hooped now, for I am ready to burst with laughing! Never was bottle or bagpipe fuller. 'Slid, was there ever seen a fox in years to betray himself thus? Now shall

I be possessed of all his counsels, and, [150 by that conduit, my young master. Well, he is resolved to prove my honesty; faith, and I'm resolved to prove his patience. O, I shall abuse [1] him intolerably. This small piece of service will bring him clean out of love with the soldier forever. He will never come within the sign of it, the sight of a cassock,[2] or a musket rest again. He will hate the musters at Mile End for it, to his dying day. It's no matter; let the [160 world think me a bad counterfeit, if I cannot give him the slip [3] at an instant. Why, this is better than to have stayed [4] his journey. Well, I'll follow him. O, how I long to be employed!            [*Exit.*]

### Act III. Scene i.

[*A room in the Windmill Tavern.*]

*Matthew, Wellbred, Bobadill, Ed[ward] Knowell, Stephen.*[5]

[Mat.] Yes, faith, sir, we were at your lodging to seek you too.

Well. O, I came not there tonight.

Bob. Your brother delivered us as much.

Well. Who, my brother Downright?

Bob. He. Mr. Wellbred, I know not in what kind [6] you hold me, but let me say to you this: as sure as honor, I esteem it so much out of the sunshine of reputation to throw the least beam of regard upon [10 such a——

Well. Sir, I must hear no ill words of my brother.

Bob. I protest to you, as [7] I have a thing to be saved about me, I never saw any gentlemanlike part—

Well. Good captain, "faces about" [8] to some other discourse.

Bob. With your leave, sir, and there were no more men living upon the face [20 of the earth, I should not fancy him, by St. George!

Mat. Troth, nor I; he is of a rustical cut, I know not how, he doth not carry himself like a gentleman of fashion.

Well. O, Mr. Matthew, that's a grace peculiar but to a few, "*quos æquus amavit Jupiter.*" [9]

Mat. I understand you, sir.

Well. No question, you do—[*Aside.*] [30 or you do not, sir.—

*Young Knowell enters [with Stephen].*

Ned Knowell! By my soul, welcome! How doest thou, sweet spirit, my genius? 'Slid, I shall love Apollo and the mad Thespian girls [10] the better, while I live, for this, my dear Fury; now I see there's some love in thee! Sirrah, these be the two I writ to thee of. Nay, what a drowsy humor is this now! Why dost thou not speak?

E. Know. O, you are a fine gallant; [40 you sent me a rare letter!

Well. Why, was 't not rare?

E. Know. Yes, I'll be sworn, I was ne'er guilty of reading the like; match it in all Pliny, or Symmachus' epistles, and I'll have my judgment burned in the ear for a rogue.[11] Make much of thy vein, for it is inimitable. But I mar'l [12] what camel it was that had the carriage of it, for, doubtless, he was no ordinary beast that [50 brought it.

Well. Why?

E. Know. "Why?" say'st thou! Why, dost thou think that any reasonable creature, especially in the morning, the sober time of the day too, could have mista'en my father for me?

Well. 'Slid, you jest, I hope?

E. Know. Indeed, the best use we can turn it to is to make a jest on't now; [60 but, I'll assure you, my father had the full view o' your flourishing style some hour before I saw it.

Well. What a dull slave was this! But, sirrah, what said he to it, i' faith?

E. Know. Nay, I know not what he said; but I have a shrewd guess what he thought.

Well. What? What?

E. Know. Marry, that thou art [70 some strange, dissolute young fellow, and

---

[1] Deceive.            [2] A soldier's cloak.
[3] With a pun on *counterfeit coin.*
[4] Prevented.        [5] The last two enter later.
[6] Fashion, relationship.
[7] As surely as.            [8] About face.

[9] "Whom friendly Jupiter has loved" (Virgil, *Æneid*, VI, 129).
[10] The Muses.
[11] Common method of punishing criminals.
[12] Marvel.

I—a grain or two better for keeping thee company.

WELL. Tut! That thought is like the moon in her last quarter—'twill change shortly. But, sirrah, I pray thee be acquainted with my two hang-bys here; thou wilt take exceeding pleasure in hem if thou hear'st hem once go: my wind instruments. I'll wind hem up— [80 But what strange piece of silence is this? The Sign of the Dumb Man?

E. KNOW. O, sir, a kinsman of mine, one that may make your music the fuller, and he please; he has his humor, sir.

WELL. O, what is 't? What is 't?

E. KNOW. Nay, I'll neither do your judgment nor his folly that wrong as to prepare your apprehension; I'll leave him to the mercy o' your search. If you [90 can take him, so!

WELL. Well, Captain Bobadill, Mr. Matthew, pray you, know this gentleman here; he is a friend of mine, and one that will deserve your affection.—(*To Master Stephen.*) I know not your name, sir, but I shall be glad of any occasion to render me more familiar to you.

STE. My name is Mr. Stephen, sir; I am this gentleman's own cousin, sir; [100 his father is mine uncle, sir. I am somewhat melancholy, but you shall command me, sir, in whatsoever is incident to a gentleman.

BOB. (*To [E.] Knowell.*) Sir, I must tell you this, I am no general[1] man; but, for Mr. Wellbred's sake (you may embrace it at what height of favor you please), I do communicate with you, and conceive you to be a gentleman of some parts; I love [110 few words.

E. KNOW. And I fewer, sir; I have scarce enow to thank you.

MAT. (*To Master Stephen.*) But are you, indeed, sir, so given to it?

STE. Ay, truly, sir, I am mightily given to melancholy.

MAT. O, it's your only fine humor, sir; your true melancholy breeds your perfect, fine wit, sir. I am melancholy [120 myself, diver times, sir, and then do I no more but take pen and paper presently, and overflow you half a score or a dozen of sonnets at a sitting.

(²E. KNOW. Sure he utters[3] them then by the gross.)

STE. Truly, sir, and I love such things out of measure.

E. KNOW. I' faith, better than in measure, I'll undertake.　　　　　130

MAT. Why, I pray you, sir, make use of my study; it's at your service.

STE. I thank you, sir; I shall be bold, I warrant you. Have you a stool there to be melancholy upon?

MAT. That I have, sir, and some papers there of mine own doing, at idle hours, that you'll say there's some sparks of wit in hem, when you see them.

WELL. [*Aside.*] Would the sparks [140 would kindle once, and become a fire amongst hem! I might see self-love burnt for her heresy.

STE. Cousin, is it well? Am I melancholy enough?

E. KNOW. O, ay, excellent.

WELL. Captain Bobadill, why muse you so?

E. KNOW. He is melancholy too. [149

BOB. Faith, sir, I was thinking of a most honorable piece of service, was performed tomorrow, being St. Mark's Day, shall be some ten years now.

E. KNOW. In what place, captain?

BOB. Why, at the beleag'ring of Strigonium, where, in less than two hours, seven hundred resolute gentlemen as any were in Europe lost their lives upon the breach. I'll tell you, gentlemen, it was the first, but the best leaguer[4] that [160 ever I beheld with these eyes, except the taking-in of—what do you call it?—last year, by the Genoways;[5] but that, of all other, was the most fatal and dangerous exploit that ever I was ranged in, since I first bore arms before the face of the enemy, as I am a gentleman and soldier.

STE. So! I had as lief as an angel I could swear as well as that gentleman. [169

E. KNOW. Then you were a servitor at both, it seems; at Strigonium, and what do you call 't?

BOB. O Lord, sir! By S[t]. George, I was the first man that entered the breach;

---

[1] Open to general acquaintance.

² Jonson frequently encloses speeches in parenthesis to indicate an aside or a passage incidental to the main action.

[3] Puts into circulation.　　　　　[5] Genoese.

[4] Siege.

and, had I not effected it with resolution,
I had been slain if I had had a million of
lives.

E. Know. 'Twas pity you had not ten—
a cat's and your own, i' faith. But—was
it possible?                                      180

(Mat. Pray you, mark this discourse,
sir!

Ste. So I do.)

Bob. I assure you, upon my reputation,
'tis true, and yourself shall confess.

E. Know. [Aside.] You must bring me
to the rack first.

Bob. Observe me judicially, sweet sir:
they had planted me three demi-culver-
ings [1] just in the mouth of the breach;   [190
now, sir, as we were to give on, [2] their master
gunner (a man of no mean skill and mark,
you must think) confronts me with his
linstock, [3] ready to give fire; I, spying his
intendment, discharged my petronel [4] in
his bosom, and with these single arms, my
poor rapier, ran violently upon the Moors
that guarded the ordinance, and put hem
pellmell to the sword.                        199

Well. To the sword? To the rapier,
captain?

E. Know. O, it was a good figure observed, sir. But did you all this, captain,
without hurting your blade?

Bob. Without any impeach [5] o' the earth.
You shall perceive, sir. [Shows his rapier.]
It is the most fortunate weapon that
ever rid on poor gentleman's thigh. Shall
I tell you, sir? You talk of Morglay,
Excalibur, Durindana, or so. Tut!         [210
I lend no credit to that is fabled of hem.
I know the virtue of mine own, and there-
fore I dare the boldlier maintain it.

Ste. I mar'l whether it be a Toledo or
no?

Bob. A most perfect Toledo, I assure
you, sir.

Ste. I have a countryman of his here.

Mat. Pray you, let's see, sir; yes, faith,
it is!                                            220

Bob. This a Toledo? Pish!

Ste. Why do you pish, captain?

Bob. A Fleming, by heaven! I'll buy
them for a guilder [6] apiece, an I would
have a thousand of them.

E. Know. How say you, cousin?     I
told you thus much!

Well. Where bought you it, Mr.
Stephen?                                          229

Ste. Of a scurvy rogue soldier.     A
hundred of lice go with him! He swore
it was a Toledo.

Bob. A poor provant [7] rapier, no better.

Mat. Mass, I think it be indeed, now
I look on 't better.

E. Know. Nay, the longer you look
on 't, the worse. Put it up, put it up.

Ste. Well, I will put it up; but by—
I ha' forgot the captain's oath; I     [239
thought to ha' sworn by it—an e'er I meet
him—

Well. O, it is past help now, sir; you
must have patience.

Ste. Whoreson, cony-catching [8] rascal!
I could eat the very hilts for anger.

E. Know. A sign of good digestion;
you have an ostrich stomach, cousin!

Ste. A stomach? Would I had him
here, you should see an I had a stom-
ach. [9]                                          250

Well. It's better as 'tis.—Come, gentlemen, shall we go?

### Act III. Scene ii.

[The same.]

E[dward] Knowell, Brainworm, Stephen,
        Wellbred, Bobadill, Matthew.

[Enter Brainworm.]

[E. Know.] A miracle, cousin; look here,
look here!

Ste. O!—God's lid! By your leave, do
you know me, sir?

Bra. Ay, sir, I know you by sight.

Ste. You sold me a rapier, did you not?

Bra. Yes, marry, did I, sir.

Ste. You said it was a Toledo, ha?

Bra. True, I did so.

Ste. But it is none?                          10

Bra. No, sir, I confess it; it is none.

Ste. Do you confess it? Gentlemen,
bear witness, he has confessed it.—By
God's will, and you had not confessed
it—

E. Know. O, cousin, forbear, forbear!

Ste. Nay, I have done, cousin.

---

[1] Small cannon.         [4] Petronel, a large pistol.
[2] Charge.               [5] Question.
[3] A lighted match.      [6] A Dutch coin.

[7] Supplied by the government.
[8] Swindling.            [9] Courage.

WELL. Why, you have done like a gentleman; he has confessed it; what would
you more?                                    20

STE. Yet, by his leave, he is a rascal,
under his favor, do you see?

E. KNOW. [*Aside.*] Ay, by his leave,
he is, and under favor—a pretty piece of
civility! Sirrah, how dost thou like him?

WELL. [*Aside.*] O, it's a most precious
fool; make much on him. I can compare
him to nothing more happily than a
drum, for everyone may play upon him.

E. KNOW. [*Aside.*] No, no, a child's
whistle were far the fitter.                 31

BRA. Sir, shall I entreat a word with
you?

E. KNOW. With me, sir? You have
not another Toledo to sell, ha' you?

BRA. You are conceited,[1] sir. Your
name is Mr. Knowell, as I take it?

E. KNOW. You are i' the right; you
mean not to proceed in the catechism,
do you?                                      40

BRA. No, sir; I am none of that coat.[2]

E. KNOW. Of as bare a coat, though.
Well, say, sir.

BRA. [*Taking Edward Knowell aside.*]
Faith, sir, I am but servant to the drum
extraordinary, and, indeed, this smoky
varnish .being washed off, and three or
four patches removed, I appear your
worship's in reversion, after the decease
of your good father.—Brainworm!         50

E. KNOW. Brainworm! 'Slight, what
breath of a conjurer hath blown thee
hither in this shape?

BRA. The breath o' your letter, sir,
this morning, the same that blew you to
the Windmill, and your father after you.

E. KNOW. My father?

BRA. Nay, never start; 'tis true. He
has followed you over the fields by the
foot, as you would do a hare i' the [60
snow.

E. KNOW. Sirrah, Wellbred, what shall
we do, sirrah? My father is come over
after me.

WELL. Thy father? Where is he?

BRA. At Justice Clement's house here,
in Coleman Street, where he but stays my
return; and then—

WELL. Who's this? Brainworm?

BRA. The same, sir.                          70

WELL. Why, how, i' the name of wit,
com'st thou transmuted thus?

BRA. Faith, a device, a device; nay,
for the love of reason, gentlemen, and
avoiding the danger, stand not here; withdraw, and I'll tell you all.

WELL. But art thou sure he will stay
thy return?

BRA. Do I live, sir? What a question
is that!                                     80

WELL. We'll prorogue his expectation,
then, a little. Brainworm, thou shalt go
with us.—Come on, gentlemen. Nay,
I pray thee, sweet Ned,. droop not; heart,
and our wits be so wretchedly dull that
one old plodding brain can outstrip us all,
would we were e'en pressed [3] to make porters of, and serve out the remnant of our
days in Thames Street, or at Custom-
house quay, in a civil war against [90
the carmen! [4]

BRA. Amen, amen, amen, say I.

[*Exeunt.*]

ACT III. SCENE iii.

[*Kitely's shop.*]

*Kitely, Cash.*

[KITE.] What says he, Thomas? Did you
speak with him?

CASH. He will expect you, sir, within this
half hour.

KITE. Has he the money ready, can you
tell?

CASH. Yes, sir, the money was brought in
last night.

KITE. O, that's well; fetch me my cloak,
my cloak!—              [*Exit Cash.*]
Stay, let me see. An hour to go and come—
Ay, that will be the least; and then
'twill be
An hour before I can despatch with him,
Or very near; well, I will say two hours.
Two hours? Ha! Things never dreamt
of yet                                       10
May be contrived, ay, and effected too,
In two hours' absence; well, I will not go.
Two hours! No, fleering Opportunity,
I will not give your subtilty that scope.
Who will not judge him worthy to be
robbed
That sets his doors wide open to a thief,

And shows the felon where his treasure
   lies?
Again, what earthy spirit but will
   attempt
To taste the fruit of Beauty's golden
   tree,
When leaden sleep seals up the dragon's
   eyes?                                              20
I will not go. Business, go by for once.
No, beauty, no; you are of too good
   caract [1]
To be left so, without a guard, or open.
Your luster, too, 'll inflame at any dis-
   tance,
Draw courtship to you, as a jet doth
   straws,
Put motion in a stone, strike fire from
   ice,
Nay, make a porter leap you with his
   burden.
You must be then kept up, close, and
   well watched,
For, give you opportunity, no quicksand
Devours or swallows swifter! He that
   lends                                              30
His wife, if she be fair, or [2] time or place,
Compels her to be false. I will not go!
The dangers are too many—and then the
   dressing
Is a most main attractive! [3] Our great
   heads
Within the city never were in safety
Since our wives wore these little caps.
   I'll change hem;
I'll change hem straight in mine. Mine
   shall no more
Wear three-piled acorns [4] to make my
   horns ache.
Nor will I go; I am resolved for that.—

*[Enter Cash with a cloak.]*

Carry in my cloak again. Yet stay. Yet
   do, too.                                           40
I will defer going, on all occasions.
CASH. Sir, Snare, your scrivener, will be
   there with th' bonds.
KITE. That's true! "Fool" on me! I had
   clean forgot it;
I must go. What's a-clock?
CASH.                              Exchange time,[5] sir.

[1] Carat, worth.                              [2] Either.
[3] Mighty attraction.
[4] Fine velvet tags for hat cords.
[5] Time for opening the Exchange, *i.e.*, about
ten.

KITE. Heart, then will Wellbred presently
   be here too,
With one or other of his loose consorts.
I am a knave if I know what to say,
What course to take, or which way to
   resolve.
My brain, methinks, is like an hour-
   glass,
Wherein my imaginations run like sands,
Filling up time, but then are turned and
   turned,                                            51
So that I know not what to stay upon,
And less, to put in act. It shall be so.
Nay, I dare build upon his secrecy;
He knows not to deceive me.—Thomas!
CASH.                                            Sir.
KITE. Yet now I have bethought me, too,
   I will not.—
Thomas, is Cob within?
CASH.                        I think he be, sir.
KITE. [*Aside.*] But he'll prate too; there's
   no speech of him.
No, there were no man o' the earth to [6]
   Thomas,
If I durst trust him; there is all the
   doubt.                                             60
But should he have a chink in him, I were
   gone,
Lost i' my fame forever, talk for th'
   Exchange!
The manner he hath stood with, till this
   present,
Doth promise no such change. What
   should I fear then?
Well, come what will, I'll tempt my
   fortune once.—
Thomas—you may deceive me, but, I
   hope—
Your love to me is more—
CASH.                          Sir, if a servant's
   Duty, with faith, may be called love,
   you are
More than in hope—you are possessed
   of it.
KITE. I thank you heartily, Thomas; gi'
   me your hand.                                      70
With all my heart, good Thomas. I have,
   Thomas,
A secret to impart unto you—but,
When once you have it, I must seal your
   lips up;
So far I tell you, Thomas.
CASH.                              Sir, for that—

[6] Compared to.

KITE. Nay, hear me out. Think I esteem you, Thomas,

When I will let you in thus to my private.[1]

It is a thing sits nearer to my crest

Than thou art ware of, Thomas; if thou shouldst

Reveal it, but—

CASH. How? I reveal it?

KITE. Nay,

I do not think thou wouldst; but, if thou shouldst, 80

'Twere a great weakness.

CASH. A great treachery: Give it no other name.

KITE. Thou wilt not do 't, then?

CASH. Sir, if I do, mankind disclaim me ever!

KITE. [Aside.] He will not swear; he has some reservation,

Some concealed purpose, and close meaning, sure;

Else, being urged so much, how should he choose

But lend an oath to all this protestation?

H'is no Precisian;[2] that I am certain of—

Nor rigid Roman Catholic. He'll play

At fayles and ticktack;[3] I have heard him swear. 90

What should I think of it? Urge him again,

And by some other way? I will do so.—

Well, Thomas, thou hast sworn not to disclose.

Yes, you did swear?

CASH. Not yet, sir, but I will, Please you—

KITE. No, Thomas, I dare take thy word.

But, if thou wilt swear, do as thou think'st good;

I am resolved [4] without it; at thy pleasure.

CASH. By my soul's safety then, sir, I protest,

My tongue shall ne'er take knowledge of a word 99

Delivered me in nature of your trust.

KITE. It's too much; these ceremonies need not;

I know thy faith to be as firm as rock.

Thomas, come hither, near;[5] we cannot be

Too private in this business. So it is—

[Aside.] Now he has sworn, I dare the safelier venter.—

I have of late, by divers observations—

[Aside.] But whether his oath can bind him, yea, or no,

Being not taken lawfully?[6] Ha! Say you?

I will ask counsel ere I do proceed.—

Thomas, it will be now too long to stay; 110

I'll spy some fitter time soon, or tomorrow.

CASH. Sir, at your pleasure.

KITE. I will think—and, Thomas,

I pray you, search the books gainst my return

For the receipts twixt me and Traps.

CASH. I will, sir.

KITE. And hear you, if your mistress' brother, Wellbred,

Chance to bring hither any gentlemen

Ere I come back, let one straight bring me word.

CASH. Very well, sir.

KITE. To the Exchange, do you hear?

Or here in Coleman Street, to Justice Clement's.

Forget it not, nor be not out of the way. 120

CASH. I will not, sir.

KITE. I pray you have a care on 't.

Or, whether he come or no, if any other,

Stranger or else, fail not to send me word.

CASH. I shall not, sir.

KITE. Be 't your special business Now to remember it.

CASH. Sir, I warrant you.

KITE. But, Thomas, this is not the secret, Thomas,

I told you of.

CASH. No, sir; I do suppose it.

KITE. Believe me, it is not.

CASH. Sir, I do believe you.

KITE. By heaven, it is not; that's enough.

But, Thomas,

I would not you should utter it, do you see, 130

To any creature living; yet I care not.

Well, I must hence. Thomas, conceive thus much;

It was a trial of you, when I meant

So deep a secret to you; I mean not this,

---

[1] Privacy.
[2] Puritan.
[3] Varieties of backgammon.
[4] Convinced.
[5] Nearer.
[6] *I.e.*, before an officer.

But that [1] I have to tell you; this is
nothing, this.

But, Thomas, keep this from my wife,
I charge you—

Locked up in silence, midnight, buried
here.—

[*Aside.*] No greater hell than to be slave
to fear.                              [*Exit.*]

CASH. "Locked up in silence, midnight,
buried here!"

Whence should this flood of passion,
trow, take head? Ha!                    140

Best dream no longer of this running
humor,

For fear I sink; the violence of the stream

Already hath transported me so far

That I can feel no ground at all. But
soft—

O, 'tis our water bearer; somewhat has
crossed him now.

### ACT III. SCENE iv.

#### [*The same.*]

#### *Cob, Cash.*

[COB. (*To himself.*)] Fasting days! What
tell you me of fasting days? 'Slid, would
they were all on a light fire [2] for me! They
say the whole world shall be consumed
with fire one day, but would I had these
ember weeks and villainous Fridays burnt
in the meantime, and then—

CASH. Why, how now, Cob? What
moves thee to this choler, ha?

COB. Collar, Master Thomas? I    [10
scorn your collar, I, sir; I am none o' your
cart horse, though I carry and draw water.
An you offer to ride me with your collar,
or halter either, I may hap show you a
jade's trick, sir.

CASH. O, you'll slip your head out of the
collar? Why, Goodman Cob, you mistake
me.

COB. Nay, I have my rheum, and I can
be angry as well as another, sir.       20

CASH. Thy rheum, Cob! Thy humor,
thy humor—thou mistak'st. [3]

COB. Humor? Mack, [4] I think it be so indeed. What is that humor? Some rare
thing, I warrant.

CASH. Marry, I'll tell thee, Cob: it is a

gentlemanlike monster, bred in the special
gallantry of our time, by affectation, and
fed by folly.

COB. How? Must it be fed?          30

CASH. O, ay, humor is nothing if it be
not fed; didst thou never hear that? It's a
common phrase, "Feed my humor."

COB. I'll none on it. Humor, avaunt!
I know you not; begone! Let who will,
make hungry meals for your monstership,
it shall not be I. Feed you, quoth he?
'Slid, I ha' much ado to feed myself, especially on these lean rascally days too;
and 't had been any other day but a    [40
fasting day—a plague on them all for me—
by this light, one might have done the
commonwealth good service, and have
drowned them all i' the flood, two or three
hundred thousand years ago. O, I do
stomach [5] them hugely. I have a maw [6]
now, and 'twere for S[i]r Bevis his horse,
against them.

CASH. I pray thee, good Cob, what
makes thee so out of love with fasting  [50
days?

COB. Marry, that which will make any
man out of love with them, I think—their
bad conditions, and you will needs know.
First, they are of a Flemish breed, I am
sure on 't, for they raven up [7] more butter
than all the days of the week beside; next,
they stink of fish and leek porridge miserably; thirdly, they'll keep a man devoutly
hungry all day, and at night send him   [60
supperless to bed.

CASH. Indeed, these are faults, Cob.

COB. Nay, and this were all, 'twere
something; but they are the only known
enemies to my generation. A fasting day
no sooner comes but my lineage goes to
wrack. Poor cobs, they smoke for it, they
are made martyrs o' the gridiron, they melt
in passion; and your maids too know this,
and yet would have me turn Han-      [70
nibal, [8] and eat my own fish and blood.
(*He pulls out a red herring.*) My princely
coz, fear nothing; I have not the heart to
devour you, and I might be made as rich
as King Cophetua. O, that I had room for
my tears! I could weep salt water enough
now to preserve the lives of ten thousand
of my kin! But I may curse none but these

---

[1] That which.                    [2] Ablaze.
[3] *Humor* had superseded *rheum* as a fashionable term.              [4] Corruption of *Mass.*

[5] Resent.                        [7] Devour.
[6] Stomach, appetite.             [8] *I.e.,* cannibal.

filthy almanacs; for, an 'twere not for them, these days of persecution would ne'er [80 be known. I'll be hanged an some fishmonger's son do not make of [1] hem, and puts in more fasting days than he should do, because he would utter [2] his father's dried stockfish and stinking conger.[3]

CASH. 'Slight, peace! Thou'lt be beaten like a stockfish else. Here is Mr. Matthew. Now must I look out for a messenger to my master.                    [*Exeunt.*]

## ACT III. SCENE v.

### [*The same.*]

*Wellbred, Ed[ward] Knowell, Brainworm, Bobadill, Matthew, Stephen, Thomas,[4] Cob.[5]*

[WELL.] Beshrew me, but it was an absolute good jest, and exceedingly well carried!

E. KNOW. Ay, and our ignorance maintained it as well, did it not?

WELL. Yes, faith; but was 't possible thou shouldst not know him? I forgive Mr. Stephen, for he is stupidity itself.

E. KNOW. Fore God, not I, and I might have been joined patten [6] with one of [10 the seven wise masters for knowing him. He had so writhen [7] himself into the habit of one of your poor *infanterie*,[8] your decayed, ruinous, worm-eaten gentlemen of the round,[9] such as have vowed to sit on the skirts of the city—let your provost and his half dozen of halberdiers do what they can—and have translated begging out of the old hackney pace to a fine easy amble, and made it run as smooth off [20 the tongue as a shovegroat shilling.[10] Into the likeness of one of these *reformados* [11] had he molded himself so perfectly, observing every trick of their action, as varying the accent, swearing with an emphasis, indeed, all with so special and exquisite a grace, that, hadst thou seen

---

[1] Make.                    [2] Vend.
[3] "Wednesday and Friday were fast days legally enforced for the benefit of the fisheries" (Smithson).
[4] *I.e.*, Cash.              [7] Twisted.
[5] Last two enter later.     [8] Infantry.
[6] By letters patent.        [9] Military patrol.
[10] A smooth shilling used in the game of shovel-board.
[11] "Officers of a re-formed or disbanded company" (Simpson).

him, thou wouldst have sworn he might have been sergeant major,[12] if not lieutenant coronel,[13] to the regiment.                    30

WELL. Why, Brainworm, who would have thought thou hadst been such an artificer?

E. KNOW. An artificer! An architect! Except a man had studied begging all his lifetime, and been a weaver of language from his infancy for the clothing of it, I never saw his rival.

WELL. Where got'st thou this coat, I mar'l?                    40

BRA. Of a Houndsditch man, sir, one of the devil's near kinsmen, a broker.[14]

WELL. That cannot be, if the proverb hold; for "A crafty knave needs no broker."

BRA. True, sir; but I did need a broker; ergo—

WELL. Well put off—no "crafty knave," you'll say.

E. KNOW. Tut, he has more of these shifts.                    50

BRA. And yet, where I have one, the broker has ten,[15] sir.

### [*Enter Cash.*]

CASH. Francis! Martin! Ne'er a one to be found now? What a spite's this?

WELL. How now, Thomas? Is my brother Kitely within?

CASH. No, sir, my master went forth e'en now; but Master Downright is within.—Cob! What, Cob! Is he gone too?

WELL. Whither went your master? [60 Thomas, canst thou tell?

CASH. I know not. To Justice Clement's, I think, sir.—Cob!

E. KNOW. Justice Clement! What's he?

WELL. Why, dost thou not know him? He is a city magistrate, a justice here, an excellent good lawyer, and a great scholar, but the only mad, merry old fellow in Europe. I showed him you the other day.                    70

E. KNOW. O, is that he? I remember him now. Good faith, and he has a very strange presence, methinks; it shows as if he stood out of the rank from other men. I have heard many of his jests i' univer-

---

[12] A rank corresponding to the modern major.
[13] Colonel.                    [14] Pawnbroker.
[15] Punning on the meaning of *changes of clothing*.

sity. They say he will commit a man for taking the wall [1] of his horse.

WELL. Ay, or wearing his cloak of [2] one shoulder, or serving of God; anything, indeed, if it come in the way of his humor.

*Cash goes in and out calling.*

CASH. Gasper! Martin! Cob! Heart, where should they be, trow?                    82

BOB. Master Kitely's man, pray thee vouchsafe us the lighting of this match.

CASH. Fire on your match! No time but now to vouchsafe?—Francis! Cob! [*Exit.*]

BOB. Body of me! Here's the remainder of seven pound since yesterday was sevennight. 'Tis your right *Trinidado!* [3] Did you never take any, Master Stephen? [90

STE. No, truly, sir; but I'll learn to take it now, since you commend it so.

BOB. Sir, believe me upon my relation, for what I tell you the world shall not reprove. [4] I have been in the Indies, where this herb grows, where neither myself nor a dozen gentlemen more, of my knowledge, have received the taste of any other nutriment in the world for the space of one-and-twenty weeks but the fume of this simple [5] only; therefore it cannot be but 'tis [101 most divine. Further, take it in the nature, in the true kind; so, it makes an antidote, that, had you taken the most deadly poisonous plant in all Italy, it should expel it, and clarify you, with as much ease as I speak. And for your green wound, your balsamum and your St. John's wort are all mere gulleries and trash to it, especially your *Trinidado;* [110 your *Nicotian* [6] is good too. I could say what I know of the virtue of it, for the expulsion of rheums, raw humors, crudities, obstructions, with a thousand of this kind; but I profess myself no quacksalver. Only thus much: by Hercules, I do hold it, and will affirm it before any prince in Europe, to be the most sovereign and precious weed that ever the earth tendered to the use of man.                    120

E. KNOW. This speech would ha' done decently in a tobacco trader's mouth.

[*Enter Cash with Cob.*]

CASH. At Justice Clement's he is, in the middle of Coleman Street.

COB. O! O!

BOB. Where's the match I gave thee, Master Kitely's man?

CASH. Would his match and he, and pipe and all, were at Sancto Domingo! I had forgot it.                    [*Exit.*]

COB. By God's me, [7] I mar'l [131 what pleasure or felicity they have in taking this roguish tabacco! It's good for nothing but to choke a man, and fill him full of smoke and embers. There were four died out of one house last week with taking of it, and two more the bell [8] went for yesternight; one of them, they say, will ne'er scape it; he voided a bushel of soot yesterday, upward and downward. [140 By the stocks, an there were no wiser men than I, I'ld have it present whipping, man or woman, that should but deal with a tabacco pipe. Why, it will stifle them all in the end, as many as use it; it's little better than ratsbane or rosaker. [9]

*Bobadill beats him with a cudgel.*

ALL. O, good captain, hold, hold!

BOB. You base cullion, [10] you!

[*Enter Cash.*]

CASH. Sir, here's your match.—Come, thou must needs be talking too; thou'rt [150 well enough served.

COB. Nay, he will not meddle with his match, I warrant you. Well, it shall be a dear beating, and I live.

BOB. Do you prate? Do you murmur?

E. KNOW. Nay, good captain, will you regard the humor of a fool? Away, knave!

WELL. Thomas, get him away.

[*Exeunt Cash and Cob.*]

BOB. A whoreson filthy slave, a dung worm, an excrement! Body o' Cæsar, [160 but that I scorn to let forth so mean a spirit, I'ld ha' stabbed him to the earth.

WELL. Marry, the law forbid, sir!

BOB. By Pharaoh's foot, I would have done it.

STE. [*Aside.*] O, he swears admirably! "By Pharaoh's foot!" "Body of Cæsar!"

---

[1] The cleanest part of the street was nearest the wall.

[2] On.                    [4] Disprove.

[3] The best tobacco.                    [5] Herb.

[6] Tobacco, named after Jacques Nicot.

[7] A mild oath.

[8] Rung for one in mortal extremity.

[9] Poisons.                    [10] A low fellow.

—I shall never do it, sure. Upon mine honor, and by Saint George! No, I ha' not the right grace. 170

MAT. Master Stephen, will you any? By this air, the most divine tabacco that ever I drunk.[1]

STE. None, I thank you, sir. O, this gentleman does it rarely too; but nothing like the other. "By this air!" "As I am a gentleman!" "By—"

*Master Stephen is practicing to the post.*
[*Exeunt Bobadill and Matthew.*]

BRA. Master, glance, glance! Master Wellbred!

STE. As I have somewhat to be saved, I protest— 181

WELL. You are a fool; it needs no affidavit.

E. KNOW. Cousin, will you any tabacco?

STE. I, sir! Upon my reputation—

E. KNOW. How now, cousin!

STE. I protest, as I am a gentleman, but no soldier, indeed—

WELL. No, Master Stephen! As [190 I remember, your name is entered in the artillery garden.[2]

STE. Ay, sir, that's true. Cousin, may I swear "as I am a soldier" by that?

E. KNOW. O, yes, that you may; it's all you have for your money.

STE. Then, as I am a gentleman and a soldier, it is "divine tabacco"!

WELL. But soft, where's Mr. Matthew? Gone? 200

BRA. No, sir; they went in here.

WELL. O, let's follow them. Master Matthew is gone to salute his mistress in verse; we shall ha' the happiness to hear some of his poetry now; he never comes unfurnished.—Brainworm?

STE. Brainworm? Where? Is this Brainworm?

E. KNOW. Ay, cousin; no words of it, upon your gentility. 210

STE. Not I, "body of me"! "By this air"! "S[t]. George"! And "the foot of Pharaoh"!

WELL. Rare! Your cousin's discourse is simply drawn out with oaths.

E. KNOW. 'Tis larded with hem—a kind of French dressing, if you love it. [*Exeunt.*]

[1] Smoked.
[2] Practice grounds.

## ACT III. SCENE vi.

[*A room in Justice Clement's house in Coleman Street.*]

*Kitely, Cob.*

[KITE.] Ha! How many are there, sayest thou?

COB. Marry, sir, your brother, Master Wellbred—

KITE. Tut, beside him? What strangers are there, man?

COB. Strangers? Let me see, one, two; Mass,
I know not well, there are so many.

KITE. How? So many?

COB. Ay, there's some five or six of them at the most.

KITE. [*Aside.*] A swarm, a swarm!
Spite of the devil, how they sting my head
With forkéd stings, thus wide and large!—But, Cob, 10
How long hast thou been coming hither, Cob?

COB. A little while, sir.

KITE. Didst thou come running?

COB. No, sir.

KITE. [*Aside.*] Nay, then I am familiar with thy haste.
Bane to my fortunes! What meant I to marry?
I, that before was ranked in such content,
My mind at rest too, in so soft a peace,
Being free master of mine own free thoughts,
And now become a slave? What? Never sigh; 20
Be of good cheer, man, for thou art a cuckold.
'Tis done, 'tis done! Nay, when such flowing store,
Plenty itself, falls in my wife's lap,
The *cornu-copiæ*[3] will be mine, I know.—But, Cob,
What entertainment had they? I am sure
My sister and my wife would bid them welcome! Ha?

COB. Like enough, sir; yet I heard not a word of it.

KITE. [*Aside.*] No; their lips were sealed with kisses, and the voice,
Drowned in a flood of joy at their arrival,

[3] Horns of plenty, with an allusion to cuckoldry.

Had lost her motion, state. and faculty.—
Cob, which of them was 't that first
kissed my wife,                              31
My sister, I should say? My wife, alas,
I fear not her. Ha! Who was it, say'st
thou?

Cob. By my troth, sir, will you have the
truth of it?

Kite. O, ay, good Cob, I pray thee heartily.

Cob. Then I am a vagabond, and fitter
for Bridewell than your worship's company,
if I saw anybody to be kissed, unless they
would have kissed the post in the middle
of the warehouse,[1] for there I left them  [40
all at their tabacco, with a pox!

Kite. How? Were they not gone in
then ere thou cam'st?

Cob. O, no, sir.

Kite. Spite of the devil! What do I
stay here then? Cob, follow me.      [Exit.]

Cob. Nay, soft and fair, I have eggs
on the spit; I cannot go yet, sir. Now am
I, for some five-and-fifty reasons, hammering, hammering revenge. O, for three  [50
or four gallons of vinegar to sharpen my
wits! Revenge, vinegar revenge, vinegar
and mustard revenge! Nay, and he had
not lyen[2] in my house, 'twould never have
grieved me; but being my guest, one that,
I'll be sworn, my wife has lent him her
smock off her back, while his one shirt
has been at washing; pawned her necker-
chers[3] for clean bands for him; sold almost all my platters to buy him ta-  [60
bacco; and he to turn monster of ingratitude, and strike his lawful host! Well, I
hope to raise up an host of fury for 't! Here
comes Justice Clement.

### Act III. Scene vii.

*[The same.]*

*Clement, Knowell, Formal, Cob.*

[Clem.] What, 's Master Kitely gone,
Roger?

For. Ay, sir.

Clem. Heart of me! What made him
leave us so abruptly?—How now, sirrah!
What make[4] you here? What would you
have, ha?

Cob. And 't please your worship, I am
a poor neighbor of your worship's—

Clem. A poor neighbor of mine?  [10
Why, speak, poor neighbor.

Cob. I dwell, sir, at the sign of the
Water Tankard, hard by the Green Lattice;[5] I have paid scot and lot[6] there any
time this eighteen years.

Clem. To the Green Lattice?

Cob. No, sir, to the parish. Marry, I
have seldom scaped scot-free[7] at the Lattice.

Clem. O, well; what business has  [20
my poor neighbor with me?

Cob. And 't like your worship, I am
come to crave the peace of your worship.

Clem. Of me, knave? Peace of me,
knave? Did I e'er hurt thee? Or threaten
thee? Or wrong thee, ha?

Cob. No, sir; but your worship's warrant for one that has wronged me, sir. His
arms are at too much liberty; I would fain
have them bound to a treaty of peace,  [30
an my credit could compass it with your
worship.

Clem. Thou goest far enough about
for 't, I am sure.

Know. Why, dost thou go in danger of
thy life for him, friend?

Cob. No, sir; but I go in danger of my
death every hour, by his means; an I die
within a twelvemonth and a day,[8] I may
swear by the law of the land that he  [40
killed me.

Clem. How? How, knave? Swear he
killed thee? And by the law? What pretense? What color[9] hast thou for that?

Cob. Marry, and 't please your worship, both black and blue; color enough,
I warrant you. I have it here to show your
worship.            [Shows his bruises.]

Clem. What is he that gave you this,
sirrah?                                     50

Cob. A gentleman and a soldier, he
says he is, o' the city here.

Clem. A soldier o' the city? What call
you him?

Cob. Captain Bobadill.

Clem. Bobadill? And why did he bob[10]

---

[1] Shop.                    [3] Neckerchiefs.
[2] Lain.                    [4] Do.

[5] A tavern.  [7] Without paying a tavern bill.
[6] Parish taxes.
[8] A twelvemonth and a day was the legal time
for determining the cause of death from bodily
injury.
[9] Reason.                    [10] Strike.

and beat you, sirrah? How began the quarrel betwixt you, ha? Speak truly, knave, I advise you.

Cob. Marry, indeed, and please [60 your worship, only because I spake against their vagrant tabacco, as I came by hem when they were taking on 't; for nothing else.

Clem. Ha! You speak against tabacco?—Formal, his name.

For. What's your name, sirrah?

Cob. Oliver, sir; Oliver Cob, sir.

Clem. Tell Oliver Cob he shall go to the jail, Formal.          70

For. Oliver Cob, my master, Justice Clement, says you shall go to the jail.

Cob. O, I beseech your worship, for God's sake, dear master justice!

Clem. Nay, God's precious![1] And such drunkards and tankards as you are come to dispute of tabacco once, I have done. Away with him!

Cob. O, good master justice!—[To Knowell.] Sweet old gentleman!          80

Know. Sweet Oliver, would I could do thee any good!—Justice Clement, let me entreat you, sir.

Clem. What? A threadbare rascal, a beggar, a slave that never drunk out of better than pisspot metal[2] in his life! And he to deprave[3] and abuse the virtue of an herb so generally received in the courts of princes, the chambers of nobles, the bowers of sweet ladies, the cabins[4] [90 of soldiers!—Roger, away with him! By God's precious—I say, go to.

Cob. Dear master justice, let me be beaten again; I have deserved it; but not the prison, I beseech you.

Know. Alas, poor Oliver!

Clem. Roger, make him a warrant.—[Aside.] He shall not go; I but fear[5] the knave.

For. [Aside.] Do not stink, sweet [100 Oliver; you shall not go.—My master will give you a warrant.

Cob. O, the Lord maintain his worship, his worthy worship!

Clem. Away, despatch him.—[Exeunt Formal and Cob.] How now, Master Knowell, in dumps? In dumps? Come, this becomes not.

Know. Sir, would I could not feel my cares.          110

Clem. Your cares are nothing; they are like my cap, soon put on, and as soon put off. What? Your son is old enough to govern himself. Let him run his course; it's the only way to make him a staid man. If he were an unthrift,[6] a ruffian, a drunkard, or a licentious liver, then you had reason; you had reason to take care; but, being none of these, mirth's my witness, an I had twice so [120 many cares as you have, I'd drown them all in a cup of sack. Come, come, let's try it. I muse[7] your parcel[8] of a soldier returns not all this while.          [Exeunt].

Act IV. Scene i.

[A room in Kitely's house.]

Downright, Dame Kitely.

[Dow.] Well, sister, I tell you true; and you'll find it so in the end.

Dame. Alas, brother, what would you have me to do? I cannot help it; you see my brother brings hem in here; they are his friends.

Dow. His friends? His fiends! 'Slud,[9] they do nothing but haunt him up and down like a sort of unlucky sprites, and tempt him to all manner of villainy [10 that can be thought of. Well, by this light, a little thing would make me play the devil with some of hem; and 'twere not more for your husband's sake than anything else, I'd make the house too hot for the best on hem; they should say, and swear, hell were broken loose, ere they went hence. But, by God's will, 'tis nobody's fault but yours; for, an you had done as you might have done, they should have been [20 purboiled[10] and baked too, every mother's son, ere they should ha' come in, e'er a one of them.

Dame. God's my life! Did you ever hear the like? What a strange man is this! Could I keep out all them, think you? I should put myself against half a dozen men, should I? Good faith, you'ld mad the patient'st body in the world, to hear you talk so, without any sense [30 or reason.

---

[1] God's precious body.          [2] Pewter.
[3] Disparage.          [4] Tents.          [5] Frighten.
[6] Prodigal.          [8] Portion.
[7] Wonder.          [9] God's Lord.
[10] Parboiled, boiled thoroughly.

Act IV. Scene ii.

[*The same.*]

*Mrs. Bridget, Mr. Matthew, [observed by]*
*Dame Kitely, Downright, Wellbred,*
*Stephen, Ed[ward] Knowell, Bobadill,*
*Brainworm, Cash.*[1]

[Brid.] Servant,[2] in troth you are too
    prodigal
    Of your wit's treasure, thus to pour it
    forth
    Upon so mean a subject as my worth.
Mat. You say well, mistress, and I mean
    as well.
Dow. Hoyday,[3] here is stuff!
Well. O, now stand close;[4] pray heaven,
she can get him to read! He should do it
of his own natural impudency.
Brid. Servant, what is this same, I
pray you?                                    10
Mat. Marry, an elegy, an elegy, an
odd toy—
Dow. To mock an ape withal![5] O, I
could sew up his mouth now.
Dame. Sister, I pray you let's hear it.
Dow. Are you rime-given too?
Mat. Mistress, I'll read it, if you please.
Brid. Pray you do, servant.
Dow. O, here's no foppery![6] Death,
I can endure the stocks better. [*Exit.*]  20
E. Know. What ails thy brother? Can
he not hold his water at reading of a ballad?
Well. O, no; a rime to him is worse than
cheese or a bagpipe. But mark, you lose
the protestation.
Mat. Faith, I did it in an humor; I
know not how it is. But please you come
near, sir. This gentleman has judgment; he
knows how to censure of a—pray you, sir,
you can judge?                               30
Ste. Not I, sir; upon my reputation,
and by the foot of Pharaoh!
Well. O, chide your cousin for swearing.
E. Know. Not I, so long as he does
not forswear himself.
Bob. Master Matthew, you abuse the
expectation of your dear mistress and her
fair sister. Fie! While you live, avoid this
prolixity.                                   40

Mat. I shall, sir; well, *incipere dulce.*[7]
E. Know. How, *insipere dulce!* "A
sweet thing to be a fool," indeed!
Well. What, do you take *incipere* in
that sense?
E. Know. You do not, you? This was
your villainy, to gull him with a motte.[8]
Well. O, the benchers'[9] phrase! *Pauca
verba, pauca verba!*[10]
Mat. [*Reading.*] "Rare creature, let me
    speak without offense;                   50
    Would God my rude words had the in-
    fluence
    To rule thy thoughts, as thy fair looks
    do mine;
    Then shouldst thou be his prisoner, who
    is thine."
E. Know. [*Aside.*] This is in *Hero and
Leander!*
Well. [*Aside.*] O, ay! Peace, we shall
have more of this.
Mat. "Be not unkind and fair; mis-
    shapen stuff
    Is of behavior boisterous and rough."
Well. [*Aside.*] How like you that, sir?
*Master Stephen answers with shaking his
                                        head.*
E. Know. [*Aside.*] 'Slight, he shakes  [61
his head like a bottle, to feel and there be
any brain in it!
Mat. But observe the catastrophe[11] now:
    "And I in duty will exceed all other,
    As you in beauty do excel Love's
    mother."
E. Know. [*Aside.*] Well, I'll have him
free of[12] the wit brokers, for he utters noth-
ing but stol'n remnants.
Well. [*Aside.*] O, forgive it him.       70
E. Know. A filching rogue, hang him!
And from the dead? It's worse than sacri-
lege.
Well. [*Coming forward.*] Sister, what ha'
you here? Verses? Pray you, let's see.
Who made these verses? They are ex-
cellent good.
Mat. O, Master Wellbred, 'tis your
disposition to say so, sir. They were good
i' the morning; I made hem *ex tem-*  [80
*pore* this morning.
Well. How? *Ex tempore?*
Mat. Ay, would I might be hanged

---

[1] Enters later.        [3] Exclamation of surprise.
[2] Lover.               [4] Aside.
[5] To dupe a simpleton with.        [6] Deceit.

[7] It is sweet to begin.          [8] *Mot*, word.
[9] Justices', or alehouse loafers.'    [11] Climax.
[10] Few words.          [12] Made a member of.

else. Ask Captain Bobadill; he saw me write them, at the—pox on it!—the Star yonder.

BRA. [*Aside*.] Can he find in his heart to curse the stars so?

E. KNOW. [*Aside*.] Faith, his are even with him; they ha' cursed him enough [90 already.

STE. Cousin, how do you like this gentleman's verses?

E. KNOW. O, admirable! The best that ever I heard, coz.

STE. Body o' Cæsar, they are admirable! The best that ever I heard, as I am a soldier!

[*Enter Downright*.]

DOW. [*Aside*.] I am vexed; I can hold ne'er a bone of me still! Heart, I think they mean to build and breed here. 100

WELL. Sister, you have a simple servant here, that crowns your beauty with such *encomions* [1] and devices; you may see what it is to be the mistress of a wit that can make your perfections so transparent that every blear eye may look through them, and see him drowned over head and ears in the deep well of desire. Sister Kitely, I marvel you get you not a servant that can rime, and do tricks too. 110

DOW. [*Aside*.] O monster! Impudence itself! Tricks? [2]

DAME. Tricks, brother? What tricks?

BRID. Nay, speak, I pray you, what tricks?

DAME. Ay, never spare anybody here; but say, what tricks?

BRID. Passion of my heart, do tricks?

WELL. 'Slight, here's a trick vied and revied! [3] Why, you monkeys, you, [120 what a caterwauling do you keep! Has he not given you rimes and verses and tricks?

DOW. [*Aside*.] O, the fiend!

WELL. Nay, you lamp of virginity, that take it in snuff [4] so, come, and cherish this tame poetical fury in your servant; you'll be begged else shortly for a concealment. [5]

[1] Encomiums.
[2] Punning on the sense of *wantonness*.
[3] A bet made and raised. [4] Take offense at.
[5] "This is a reference to the unauthorized holding of sequestered lands, such as those which had belonged to the monasteries. Elizabeth had appointed commissions to search such holdings or 'concealments,' which her courtiers often 'begged'" (Neilson).

Go to, reward his muse. You cannot give him less than a shilling, in conscience, for the book he had it out of cost him a [130 teston [6] at least. How now, gallants? Mr. Matthew? Captain? What, all sons of silence? No spirit?

DOW. Come, you might practice your ruffian tricks somewhere else, and not here, I wusse; this is no tavern nor drinking school to vent your exploits in.

WELL. How now! Whose cow has calved? [7]

DOW. Marry, that has mine, sir. [140 Nay, boy, never look askance at me for the matter; I'll tell you of it, I, sir. You and your companions mend yourselves when I ha' done.

WELL. My companions!

DOW. Yes, sir, your companions, so I say; I am not afraid of you, nor them neither; your hang-bys here. You must have your poets and your potlings, [8] your *soldados* and *foolados* to follow you up [150 and down the city; and here they must come to domineer and swagger.—Sirrah, you ballad singer, and slops, [9] your fellow there, get you out; get you home; or, by this steel, I'll cut off your ears, and that presently.

WELL. 'Slight, stay, let's see what he dare do! Cut off his ears? Cut a whetstone! You are an ass, do you see? Touch any man here, and, by this hand, I'll [160 run my rapier to the hilts in you.

DOW. Yea, that would I fain see, boy.
*They all draw, and they of the house make out to part them.*

DAME. O Jesu! Murder! Thomas! Gasper!

BRID. Help, help! Thomas!

[*Enter Cash and Servants*.]

E. KNOW. Gentlemen, forbear, I pray you.

BOB. Well, sirrah, you Holofernes; by my hand, I will pink your flesh full of holes with my rapier for this; I will, by this [170 good heaven!—

*They offer to fight again and are parted.*
Nay, let him come, let him come, gentle-

[6] Sixpence.
[7] *I.e.*, what's the matter?
[8] Tipplers.        [9] *I.e.*, Bobadill.

men; by the body of Saint George, I'll not kill him.

CASH. Hold, hold, good gentlemen.

DOW. You whoreson, bragging coistril! [1]

### ACT IV. SCENE iii.

*[The same.]*

*To them, Kitely.*

[KITE.] Why, how now? What's the matter? What's the stir here?

Whence springs the quarrel? Thomas! Where is he?

Put up your weapons, and put off this rage.

My wife and sister, they are the cause of this.

What, Thomas! Where is this knave?

CASH. Here, sir.

WELL. Come, let's go; this is one of my brother's ancient humors, this.

STE. I am glad nobody was hurt by his ancient humor.                              10

*[Exeunt Wellbred, Stephen, Edward Knowell, Bobadill, Brainworm, and Servants.]*

KITE. Why, how now, brother, who enforced this brawl?

DOW. A sort of lewd rakehells that care neither for God nor the devil. And they must come here to read ballads, and roguery, and trash! I'll mar the knot of hem ere I sleep, perhaps—especially Bob there, he that's all manner of shapes—and *Songs and Sonnets*, his fellow.

BRID. Brother, indeed you are too violent,
  Too sudden in your humor; and you know                              20
  My brother Wellbred's temper will not bear
  Any reproof, chiefly in such a presence,
  Where every slight disgrace he should receive
  Might wound him in opinion and respect.

DOW. Respect? What talk you of respect 'mong such as ha' nor spark of manhood nor good manners? 'Sdeynes, I am ashamed to hear you! Respect! *[Exit.]*

BRID. Yes, there was one, a civil gentleman,
  And very worthily demeaned himself.  30

KITE. O, that was some love of yours, sister.

BRID. A love of mine? I would it were no worse, brother;
  You'ld pay my portion sooner than you think for.

DAME. Indeed he seemed to be a gentleman of an exceeding fair disposition, and of very excellent good parts.
  *[Exeunt Dame Kitely and Bridget.]*

KITE. *[Aside.]* Her love, by heaven! My wife's minion!
  "Fair disposition"? "Excellent good parts"?
  Death, these phrases are intolerable!
  Good parts? How should she know his parts?                              40
  His parts? Well, well, well, well, well, well!
  It is too plain, too clear.—Thomas, come hither.
  What, are they gone?

CASH.                    Ay, sir, they went in.
  My mistress and your sister—

KITE. Are any of the gallants within?

CASH. No, sir, they are all gone.

KITE.                    Art thou sure of it?

CASH. I can assure you, sir.

KITE. What gentleman was that they praised so, Thomas?

CASH. One, they call him Master [50 Knowell, a handsome young gentleman, sir.

KITE. Ay, I thought so; my mind gave me as much.
  I'll die, but they have hid him i' the house
  Somewhere; I'll go and search; go with me, Thomas.
  Be true to me, and thou shalt find me a master.                    *[Exeunt.]*

### ACT IV. SCENE iv.

*[The lane before Cob's house.]*

*Cob, Tib.* [2]

COB. *[Knocking.]* What, Tib! Tib, I say!

TIB. *[Within.]* How now, what cuckold is that knocks so hard? *[Enters.]* O husband, is 't you? What's the news?

COB. Nay, you have stonned [3] me, i' faith; you ha' giv'n me a knock o' the forehead will stick by me. Cuckold? 'Slid, cuckold?

TIB. Away, you fool! Did I know it [10 was you that knocked? Come, come, you may call me as bad when you list. [4]

[1] Knave.

[2] Enters later.      [3] Stunned.      [4] Please.

Cob. May I? Tib, you are a whore.

Tib. You lie in your throat, husband.

Cob. How, the lie? And in my throat too? Do you long to be stabbed, ha?

Tib. Why, you are no soldier, I hope?

Cob. O, must you be stabbed by a soldier? Mass, that's true! When was [20 Bobadill here, your captain? That rogue, that foist,[1] that fencing Burgullion? [2] I'll tickle him, i' faith.

Tib. Why, what's the matter, trow?

Cob. O, he has basted me rarely, sumptiously! But I have it here in black and white. [Pulls out the warrant.] For his black and blue, shall [3] pay him. O, the justice, the honestest old brave Trojan in London; I do honor the very flea of his dog. A plague on him, though, [30 he put me once in a villainous filthy fear; marry, it vanished away like the smoke of tabacco; but I was smoked [4] soundly first. I thank the devil and his good angel, my guest. Well, wife, or Tib, which you will, get you in and lock the door; I charge you let nobody in to you, wife; nobody in to you; those are my words. Not Captain Bob himself, nor the fiend in his likeness. You are a woman; you have [40 flesh and blood enough in you to be tempted; therefore keep the door shut upon all comers.

Tib. I warrant you, there shall nobody enter here without my consent.

Cob. Nor with your consent, sweet Tib; and so I leave you.

Tib. It's more than you know, whether you leave me so.

Cob. How?                                    50

Tib. Why, "sweet."

Cob. Tut, sweet or sour, thou art a flower. Keep close thy door; I ask no more.
                                    [Exeunt.]

## Act IV. Scene v.

### [A room in the Windmill.]

*Ed[ward] Knowell, Wellbred, Stephen, Brainworm.*

[E. Know.] Well, Brainworm, perform this business happily, and thou makest a purchase of my love forever.

Well. I' faith, now let thy spirits use their best faculties. But, at any hand,[5]

remember the message to my brother, for there's no other means to start him.

Bra. I warrant you, sir; fear nothing; I have a nimble soul has waked all forces of my fant'sy by this time, and put [10 hem in true motion. What you have possessed me withal,[6] I'll discharge it amply, sir; make it no question.

Well. Forth, and prosper, Brainworm.— [Exit Brainworm.] Faith, Ned, how dost thou approve of my abilities in this device?

E. Know. Troth, well, howsoever; but it will come excellent if it take.

Well. Take, man? Why, it cannot [20 choose but take, if the circumstances miscarry not. But tell me ingenuously, dost thou affect my sister Bridget as thou pretend'st?

E. Know. Friend, am I worth belief?

Well. Come, do not protest. In faith, she is a maid of good ornament and much modesty; and, except I conceived very worthily of her, thou shouldest not have her.                                    30

E. Know. Nay, that, I am afraid, will be a question yet, whether I shall have her or no.

Well. 'Slid, thou shalt have her; by this light, thou shalt.

E. Know. Nay, do not swear.

Well. By this hand, thou shalt have her; I'll go fetch her presently. Point [7] but where to meet, and as I am an honest man I'll bring her.                                    40

E. Know. Hold, hold, be temperate.

Well. Why, by—what shall I swear by? Thou shalt have her, as I am—

E. Know. Pray thee, be at peace; I am satisfied, and do believe thou wilt omit no offered occasion to make my desires complete.

Well. Thou shalt see and know I will not.                                    [Exeunt.]

## Act IV. Scene vi.

### [A street in the Old Jewry.]

*Formal, Knowell, Brainworm.[8]*

[For.] Was your man a soldier, sir?

Know. Ay, a knave; I took him begging o' the way,
      This morning as I came over Moorfields.

---

[1] Pickpocket.                 [3] I.e., I shall.
[2] Bully.        [4] Beaten.   [5] Rate.
[6] Informed me of.   [7] Appoint.   [8] Enters later.

*[Enter Brainworm.]*

O, here he is!—Yo' have made fair speed,
   believe me.
Where, i' the name of sloth, could you
   be thus—
BRA. Marry, peace be my comfort,
where I thought I should have had little
comfort of your worship's service.
KNOW. How so?
BRA. O, sir, your coming to the   [10
city, your entertainment of me, and your
sending me to watch—indeed all the circumstances either of your charge or my
employment are as open to your son as to
yourself.
KNOW. How should that be, unless that
   villain, Brainworm,
Have told him of the letter, and discovered [1]
All that I strictly charged him to conceal? 'Tis so.
BRA. I am partly o' the faith, 'tis so,
indeed.
KNOW. But how should he know thee
to be my man?                             21
BRA. Nay, sir, I cannot tell, unless it
be by the black art. Is not your son a
scholar, sir?
KNOW. Yes, but I hope his soul is not
   allied
Unto such hellish practice; if it were,
I had just cause to weep my part in him,
And curse the time of his creation.
But where didst thou find them, Fitzsword?
BRA. You should rather ask where   [30
they found me, sir, for, I'll be sworn, I
was going along in the street, thinking
nothing, when, of a sudden, a voice calls,
"Mr. Knowell's man!" another cries,
"Soldier!" and thus half a dozen of hem,
till they had called me within a house,
where I no sooner came but they seemed
men, and out flew all their rapiers at my
bosom, with some three or four score
oaths to accompany hem; and all to   [40
tell me I was but a dead man if I did not
confess where you were, and how I was
employed, and about what; which when
they could not get out of me (as, I protest,
they must ha' dissected and made an
anatomy [2] o' me first, and so I told hem),

they locked me up into a room i' the top
of a high house, whence by great miracle
(having a light heart) I slid down by a
bottom [3] of packthread into the   [50
street, and so scaped. But, sir, thus much
I can assure you, for I heard it while I
was locked up: there were a great many
rich merchants and brave [4] citizens' wives
with hem at a feast; and your son, Mr. Edward, withdrew with one of hem, and has
pointed to meet her anon at one Cob's
house, a water bearer that dwells by the
Wall. Now there your worship shall be sure
to take him, for there he preys, and fail
he will not.                             61
KNOW. Nor will I fail to break his match,
   I doubt not.
Go thou along with Justice Clement's
   man,
And stay there for me. At one Cob's
   house, say'st thou?
BRA. Ay, sir, there you shall have him.—
*[Exit Knowell.—Aside.]*   Yes—invisible!
Much wench, or much son! 'Slight, when he
has stayed there three or four hours, travail-
ing with the expectation of wonders, and
at length be delivered of air, O, the   [70
sport that I should then take to look on him,
if I durst! But now I mean to appear no
more afore him in this shape. I have another trick to act yet. O, that I were so
happy as to light on a nupson [5] now of [6]
this justice's novice!—Sir, I make you
stay somewhat long.
FOR. Not a whit, sir. Pray you, what
do you mean, sir?
BRA. I was putting up some papers—
FOR. You ha' been lately in the   [81
wars, sir, it seems.
BRA. Marry, have I, sir, to my loss, and
expense of all, almost—
FOR. Troth, sir, I would be glad to bestow a pottle [7] of wine o' you, if it please
you to accept it—
BRA. O, sir—
FOR. But to hear the manner of your
services, and your devices in the wars,   [90
they say they be very strange, and not like
those a man reads in the Roman histories,
or sees at Mile End.
BRA. No, I assure you, sir; why, at any

[1] Revealed.                    [2] Skeleton.

[3] Ball.
[4] Finely dressed.              [6] In.
[5] Simpleton.                   [7] Bottle.

time when it please you, I shall be ready to discourse to you all I know.—[*Aside.*] And more too somewhat.

For. No better time than now, sir. We'll go to the Windmill; there we shall have a cup of neat grist,[1] we call it. [100 I pray you, sir, let me request you to the Windmill.

Bra. I'll follow you, sir.—[*Aside.*] And make grist o' you, if I have good luck.

[*Exeunt.*]

## Act IV. Scene vii.

### [*The same.*]

[2] *Matthew, Ed[ward] Knowell, Bobadill, Stephen, Downright.*[3]

[Mat.] Sir, did your eyes ever taste the like clown of him where we were to-day, Mr. Wellbred's half brother? I think the whole earth cannot show his parallel, by this daylight.

E. Know. We were now speaking of him; Captain Bobadill tells me he is fall'n foul o' you too.

Mat. O, ay, sir, he threatened me with the *bastinado*.                    10

Bob. Ay, but I think I taught you prevention this morning for that. You shall kill him beyond question, if you be so generously [4] minded.

Mat. Indeed, it is a most excellent trick.                    [*Fences.*]

Bob. O, you do not give spirit enough to your motion; you are too tardy, too heavy! O, it must be done like lightning. Hay! [5]

*He practices at a post.*

Mat. Rare, captain!                    20

Bob. Tut! 'Tis nothing, and 't be not done in a—*punto*.[6]

E. Know. Captain, did you ever prove yourself upon any of our masters of defense here?

Mat. O good sir! Yes, I hope he has.

Bob. I will tell you, sir. Upon my first coming to the city, after my long travel [7]

for knowledge in that mystery only, there came three or four of hem to me, at [30 a gentleman's house where it was my chance to be resident at that time, to entreat my presence at their schools, and withal so much importuned me that, I protest to you as I am a gentleman, I was ashamed of their rude demeanor out of all measure. Well, I told hem that to come to a public school, they should pardon me, it was opposite, in diameter,[8] to my humor; but, if so they would [40 give their attendance at my lodging, I protested to do them what right or favor I could, as I was a gentleman, and so forth.

E. Know. So, sir, then you tried their skill?

Bob. Alas, soon tried! You shall hear, sir. Within two or three days after, they came; and, by honesty, fair sir, believe me, I graced them exceedingly, showed them some two or three tricks of pre- [50 vention have purchased hem, since, a credit—to admiration. They cannot deny this; and yet now they hate me; and why? Because I am excellent; and for no other vile reason on the earth.

E. Know. This is strange and barbarous, as ever I heard.

Bob. Nay, for a more instance of their preposterous natures, but note, sir. They have assaulted me some three, four, [60 five, six of them together, as I have walked alone in divers skirts i' the town, as Turnbull, Whitechapel, Shoreditch,[9] which were then my quarters, and since, upon the Exchange, at my lodging, and at my ordinary, where I have driven them afore me the whole length of a street, in the open view of all our gallants, pitying to hurt them, believe me. Yet all this lenity will not o'ercome their spleen; they [70 will be doing with the pismire,[10] raising a hill a man may spurn abroad with his foot at pleasure. By myself, I could have slain them all, but I delight not in murder. I am loath to bear any other than this *bastinado* for hem; yet I hold it good polity not to go disarmed, for, though I be skillful, I may be oppressed with multitudes.

E. Know. Ay, believe me, may you, sir; and, in my conceit,[11] our whole [80

---

[1] Liquor sold at the Windmill.

[2] The marginal direction *To them* is erroneously printed here.

[3] Enters later.                    [4] Gentlemanly.

[5] A fencer's cry, meaning "a hit!"—"you have it!"

[6] Instant, with a pun on *thrust with a point.*

[7] With a pun on *travail.*

[8] *I.e.*, diametrically.                    [10] Ant.

[9] Disreputable districts of London.    [11] Opinion.

nation should sustain the loss by it, if it were so.

BOB. Alas, no! What's a peculiar [1] man to a nation? Not seen.

E. KNOW. O, but your skill, sir!

BOB. Indeed, that might be some loss; but who respects it? I will tell you, sir, by the way of private, and under seal; I am a gentleman, and live here obscure, and to myself; but were I known to her [90 majesty and the lords, observe me, I would undertake, upon this poor head and life, for the public benefit of the state, not only to spare the entire lives of her subjects in general, but to save the one half, nay, three parts of her yearly charge in holding war, and against what enemy soever. And how would I do it, think you?

E. KNOW. Nay, I know not, nor [100 can I conceive.

BOB. Why thus, sir. I would select nineteen more to [2] myself throughout the land; gentlemen they should be of good spirit, strong and able constitution; I would choose them by an instinct, a character, that I have; and I would teach these nineteen the special rules, as your *punto*, your *reverso*, your *stoccata*, your *imbroccata*, your *passada*, your *mon-* [110 *tanto* [3]—till they could all play very near, or altogether, as well as myself. This done, say the enemy were forty thousand strong, we twenty would come into the field the tenth of March, or thereabouts; and we would challenge twenty of the enemy; they could not in their honor refuse us. Well, we would kill them; challenge twenty more, kill them; twenty more, kill them; twenty more, kill them too; and thus [120 would we kill every man his twenty a day—that's twenty score; twenty score, that's two hundreth; two hundreth a day, five days a thousand; forty thousand; forty times five, five times forty, two hundreth days kills them all up, by computation. And this will I venture my poor gentlemanlike carcass to perform, provided there be no treason practiced upon us, by fair and discreet manhood; [130 that is, civilly by the sword.

[1] Individual.
[2] In addition to.
[3] Italian fencing terms.

E. KNOW. Why, are you so sure of your hand, captain, at all times?

BOB. Tut! Never miss [4] thrust, upon my reputation with you.

E. KNOW. I would not stand in Downright's state then, an you meet him, for the wealth of any one street in London.

BOB. Why, sir, you mistake me. If he were here now, by this welkin, I would [140 not draw my weapon on him. Let this gentleman do his mind; but I will *bastinado* him, by the bright sun, wherever I meet him.

MAT. Faith, and I'll have a fling at him, at my distance.

*Downright walks over the stage.*

E. KNOW. God's so, look where he is! Yonder he goes.

DOW. What peevish luck have I, I cannot meet with these bragging [150 rascals?

BOB. It's not he, is it?

E. KNOW. Yes, faith, it is he.

MAT. I'll be hanged, then, if that were he.

E. KNOW. Sir, keep your hanging good for some greater matter, for I assure you that was he.

STE. Upon my reputation, it was he.

BOB. Had I thought it had been [160 he, he must not have gone so; but I can hardly be induced to believe it was he yet.

E. KNOW. That I think, sir.

[*Enter Downright.*]

But see, he is come again!

DOW. O, Pharaoh's foot, have I found you? Come, draw, to your tools; draw, gipsy, or I'll thresh you.

BOB. Gentleman of valor, I do believe in thee; hear me—                          170

DOW. Draw your weapon then.

BOB. Tall [5] man, I never thought on it till now: body of me, I had a warrant of the peace served on me, even now as I came along, by a water bearer; this gentleman saw it, Mr. Matthew.

DOW. 'Sdeath, you will not draw then?

*He beats him and disarms him; Matthew*
*runs away.*

BOB. Hold, hold! Under thy favor, forbear!

[4] *I.e.*, I never miss.                    [5] Bold.

Dow. Prate again, as you like [180 this, you whoreson foist, you! You'll "control ¹ the point," you! Your consort is gone; had he stayed, he had shared with you, sir.                    [Exit.]

Bob. Well, gentlemen, bear witness I was bound to the peace, by this good day.

E. Know. No, faith, it's an ill day, captain—never reckon it other; but, say you were bound to the peace, the law allows you to defend yourself. That'll prove [190 but a poor excuse.

Bob. I cannot tell, sir; I desire good construction in fair sort. I never sustained the like disgrace, by heaven! Sure I was strook ² with a planet thence, for I had no power to touch my weapon.

E. Know. Ay, like enough; I have heard of many that have been beaten under a planet; go, get you to a surgeon. 'Slid, an these be your tricks, your pas- [200 sadas and your montantos, I'll none of them.—[Exit Bobadill.] O, manners! That this age should bring forth such creatures! That nature should be at leisure to make hem! Come, coz.

Ste. Mass, I'll ha' this cloak.

E. Know. God's will, 'tis Downright's.

Ste. Nay, it's mine now. Another might have ta'en up as well as I. I'll wear it, so I will.                             210

E. Know. How an he see it? He'll challenge it, assure yourself.

Ste. Ay, but he shall not ha' it; I'll say I bought it.

E. Know. Take heed you buy it not too dear, coz.                    [Exeunt.]

Act IV. Scene viii.

[A room in Kitely's house.]

Kitely, Wellbred, Dame Kit[ely], Bridget, Brainworm, Cash.³

[Kite.] Now, trust me, brother, you were much to blame,
T' incense his anger, and disturb the peace
Of my poor house, where there are sentinels
That every minute watch to give alarms
Of civil war, without adjection ⁴
Of your assistance or occasion.

Well. No harm done, brother, I warrant you. Since there is no harm done, anger costs a man nothing; and a tall man is never his own man till he be angry.   [10 To keep his valure ⁵ in obscurity is to keep himself as it were in a cloak bag. What's a musician, unless he play? What's a tall man, unless he fight? For, indeed, all this my wise brother stands upon absolutely; and that made me fall in with him so resolutely.

Dame. Ay, but what harm might have come of it, brother?

Well. "Might," sister? So might [20 the good warm clothes your husband wears be poisoned, for anything he knows; or the wholesome wine he drunk, even now at the table—

Kite. [Aside.] Now, God forbid! O me! Now I remember
My wife drunk to me last, and changed the cup,
And bade me wear this cursèd suit today.
See, if heaven suffer murder undiscovered!—
I feel me ill; give me some mithridate; ⁶
Some mithridate and oil, good sister, fetch me.                             30
O, I am sick at heart; I burn, I burn.
If you will save my life, go fetch it me.

Well. O strange humor! My very breath has poisoned him.

Brid. Good brother, be content. What do you mean?
The strength of these extreme conceits ⁷ will kill you.

Dame. Beshrew your heart-blood, brother Wellbred, now, for putting such a toy ⁸ into his head!

Well. Is a fit simile a "toy"? Will [40 he be poisoned with a simile? Brother Kitely, what a strange and idle ⁹ imagination is this! For shame, be wiser. O' my soul, there's no such matter.

Kite. Am I not sick? How am I then not poisoned?
Am I not poisoned? How am I then so sick?

Dame. If you be sick, your own thoughts make you sick.

---

¹ Beat down.                    ³ Last two enter later.
² Struck, bewitched.       ⁴ Addition.

⁵ Worth; 1640 edn. has valor.
⁶ Antidote to poisons.                    ⁸ Whim.
⁷ Fancies.                                          ⁹ Foolish.

WELL. [*Aside.*] His jealousy is the poison he has taken.

BRA. (*He comes disguised like Justice Clement's man.*) Mr. Kitely, my master, [50 Justice Clement, salutes you, and desires to speak with you with all possible speed.

KITE. No time but now? When I think I am sick? Very sick! Well, I will wait upon his worship. Thomas! Cob! I must seek them out, and set hem sentinels till I return. Thomas! Cob! Thomas! [*Exit.*]

WELL. This is perfectly rare, Brainworm. [*Takes him aside.*] But how got'st thou this apparel of the justice's man?    60

BRA. [*Aside.*] Marry, sir, my proper fine penman would needs bestow the grist o' me at the Windmill, to hear some martial discourse, where so I marshaled him that I made him drunk—with admiration—and, because too much heat was the cause of his distemper, I stripped him stark naked as he lay along asleep, and borrowed his suit to deliver this counterfeit message in, leaving a rusty armor and [70 an old brown bill [1] to watch him till my return—which shall be when I ha' pawned his apparel, and spent the better part o' the money, perhaps.

WELL. [*Aside.*] Well, thou art a successful, merry knave, Brainworm; his absence will be a good subject for more mirth. I pray thee, return to thy young master, and will him to meet me and my sister Bridget at the Tower [2] instantly, for here, tell [80 him, the house is so stored with jealousy there is no room for love to stand upright in. We must get our fortunes committed to some larger prison, say, and than the Tower I know no better air, nor where the liberty of the house may do us more present service. Away!

[*Exit Brainworm.    Enter Kitely, talking aside to Cash.*]

KITE. Come hither, Thomas. Now my secret's ripe,
And thou shalt have it; lay to both thine ears.
Hark what I say to thee. I must go forth, Thomas;    90
Be careful of thy promise, keep good watch,

[1] Pike.
[2] Since the Tower was in no parish, a marriage might be performed there immediately.

Note every gallant, and observe him well,
That enters in my absence to thy mistress.
If she would show him rooms—the jest is stale[3]—
Follow hem, Thomas, or else hang on him,
And let him not go after. Mark their looks;
Note if she offer but to see his band,
Or any other amorous toy about him;
But praise his leg, or foot; or if she say
The day is hot, and bid him feel her hand,
How hot it is—O, that's a monstrous thing!    101
Note me all this, good Thomas; mark their sighs,
And, if they do but whisper, break hem off.
I'll bear thee out in it. Wilt thou do this?
Wilt thou be true, my Thomas?

CASH.                    As truth's self, sir.

KITE. Why, I believe thee. Where is Cob, now? Cob!    [*Exit.*]

DAME. He's ever calling for Cob! I wonder how he employs Cob so.

WELL. Indeed, sister, to ask how he employs Cob is a necessary question for [110 you that are his wife, and a thing not very easy for you to be satisfied in; but this I'll assure you, Cob's wife is an excellent bawd, sister, and oftentimes your husband haunts her house—marry, to what end I cannot altogether accuse him; imagine you what you think convenient. But I have known fair hides have foul hearts ere now, sister.

DAME. Never said you truer than [120 that, brother; so much I can tell you for your learning. Thomas, fetch your cloak and go with me. I'll after him presently; I would to fortune I could take him there, i' faith. I'ld return him his own, I warrant him!    [*Exeunt Dame and Cash.*]

WELL. So, let hem go; this may make sport anon. Now, my fair sister-in-law, that you knew but how happy a thing it were to be fair and beautiful!    130

BRID. That touches not me, brother.

WELL. That's true; that's even the fault of it; for, indeed, beauty stands a woman in no stead, unless it procure her

[3] With a pun on the meaning *harlot.*

touching. But, sister, whether it touch you or no, it touches your beauties; and I am sure they will abide the touch. An they do not, a plague of all ceruse,¹ say I! And it touches me too in part, though not in the—Well, there's a dear and re- [140 spected friend of mine, sister, stands very strongly and worthily affected toward you, and hath vowed to inflame whole bonefires ² of zeal at his heart, in honor of your perfections. I have already engaged my promise to bring you where you shall hear him confirm much more. Ned Knowell is the man, sister; there's no exception against the party. You are ripe for a husband; and a minute's loss to such an [150 occasion is a great trespass in a wise beauty. What say you, sister? On my soul, he loves you. Will you give him the meeting?

BRID. Faith, I had very little confidence in mine own constancy, brother, if I durst not meet a man; but this motion of yours savors of an old knight-adventurer's servant a little too much, methinks.

WELL. What's that, sister?

BRID. Marry, of the squire.³        160

WELL. No matter if it did, I would be such an one for my friend. But see who is returned to hinder us.

*[Enter Kitely.]*

KITE. What villainy is this? Called out on a false message?
   This was some plot; I was not sent for.—
      Bridget,
   Where's your sister?

BRID.        I think she be gone forth, sir.

KITE. How! Is my wife gone forth?
   Whither, for God's sake?

BRID. She's gone abroad with Thomas.

KITE. Abroad with Thomas? O, that villain dors ⁴ me.        169
   He hath discovered all unto my wife.
   Beast that I was, to trust him! Whither,
      I pray you,
   Went she?

BRID.        I know not, sir.

WELL.        I'll tell you, brother,
   Whither I suspect she's gone.

KITE.        Whither, good brother?

WELL. To Cob's house, I believe; but keep my counsel.

KITE. I will, I will. To Cob's house? Doth she haunt Cob's?
   She's gone a purpose now to cuckold me
   With that lewd rascal, who, to win her favor,
   Hath told her all.        *[Exit.]*

WELL.        Come, he's once more gone;
   Sister, let's lose no time; th' affair is worth it.        *[Exeunt.]*

ACT IV. SCENE ix.

*[Another street in the Old Jewry.]*

⁵ *Matthew, Bobadill, Brainworm.*

[MAT.] I wonder, captain, what they will say of my going away, ha?

BOB. Why, what should they say, but as of a discreet gentleman, quick, wary, respectful of nature's fair lineaments? And that's all.

MAT. Why, so! But what can they say of your beating?

BOB. A rude part, a touch with soft wood, a kind of gross battery used, [10 laid on strongly, borne most patiently; and that's all.

MAT. Ay, but would any man have offered it in Venice, as you say?

BOB. Tut! I assure you, no; you shall have there your *nobilis*,⁶ your *gentilezza*,⁷ come in bravely upon your *reverse*, stand you close, stand you firm, stand you fair, save your *retricato* with his left leg, come to the *assalto* with the right, thrust [20 with brave steel, defy your base wood! But wherefore do I awake this remembrance? I was fascinated,⁸ by Jupiter—fascinated. But I will be unwitched and revenged by law.

MAT. Do you hear? Is 't not best to get a warrant, and have him arrested and brought before Justice Clement?

BOB. It were not amiss. Would we had it!        30

*[Enter Brainworm, disguised as Formal.]*

MAT. Why, here comes his man; let's speak to him.

BOB. Agreed, do you speak.

MAT. Save you, sir.

---

¹ Cosmetic of white lead.        ² Bonfires.
³ Implying the meaning *pander*.        ⁴ Cheats.
⁵ The marginal direction *To them* is erroneously printed here. The name of Downright also appears by mistake in the list of characters.
⁶ Nobility.        ⁷ Gentility.        ⁸ Bewitched.

BRA. With all my heart, sir.

MAT. Sir, there is one Downright hath abused this gentleman and myself, and we determine to make our amends by law. Now, if you would do us the favor to procure a warrant to bring him afore your [40 master, you shall be well considered, I assure you, sir.

BRA. Sir, you know my service is my living; such favors as these, gotten of my master, is his only preferment,[1] and therefore you must consider me as I may make benefit of my place.

MAT. How is that, sir?

BRA. Faith, sir, the thing is extraordinary, and the gentleman may be of [50 great accompt; yet, be what he will, if you will lay me down a brace of angels in my hand, you shall have it; otherwise not.

MAT. How shall we do, captain? He asks a brace of angels; you have no money?

BOB. Not a cross,[2] by Fortune.

MAT. Nor I, as I am a gentleman, but twopence left of my two shillings in the morning for wine and reddish. Let's find him some pawn.                              60

BOB. Pawn? We have none to the value of his demand.

MAT. O, yes. I'll pawn this jewel in my ear, and you may pawn your silk stockings, and pull up your boots; they will ne'er be missed. It must be done now.

BOB. Well, an there be no remedy, I'll step aside and pull hem off.  [Withdraws.]

MAT. Do you hear, sir? We have no store of money at this time, but you [70 shall have good pawns. Look you, sir, this jewel, and that gentleman's silk stockings, because we would have it despatched ere we went to our chambers.

BRA. I am content, sir; I will get you the warrant presently. What's his name, say you? Downright?

MAT. Ay, ay, George Downright.

BRA. What manner of man is he?

MAT. A tall, big man, sir; he goes in [80 a cloak most commonly of silk russet, laid about with russet lace.

BRA. 'Tis very good, sir.

MAT. Here, sir, here's my jewel.

BOB. [Returning.] And here are stockings.

BRA. Well, gentlemen, I'll procure you this warrant presently. But who will you have to serve it?

MAT. That's true, captain; that [90 must be considered.

BOB. Body o' me, I know not; 'tis service of danger.

BRA. Why, you were best get one o' the varlets o' the city,[3] a serjeant. I'll appoint you one, if you please.

MAT. Will you, sir? Why, we can wish no better.

BOB. We'll leave it to you, sir.
       [Exeunt Bobadill and Matthew.]

BRA. This is rare! Now will I go [100 pawn this cloak of the justice's man's at the broker's for a varlet's suit, and be the varlet myself, and get either more pawns, or more money of Downright, for the arrest.                              [Exit.]

## ACT IV. SCENE X.

[The lane before Cob's house.]

Knowell, Tib, Cash, Dame Kitely, Kitely,
                                    Cob.[4]

[KNOW.] O, here it is; I am glad. I have
     found it now.
Ho! Who is within here?

TIB. [Within.] I am within, sir. What's
     your pleasure?

KNOW. To know who is within besides
     yourself.

TIB. Why, sir, you are no constable, I
     hope?

KNOW. O, fear you the constable? Then I
     doubt not
You have some guests within deserve
     that fear.
I'll fetch him straight.

[Enter Tib.]

TIB.                    O' God's name, sir!
KNOW. Go to; come tell me, is not young
     Knowell here?
TIB. Young Knowell? I know none such,
     sir, o' mine honesty.                     10
KNOW. Your honesty? Dame, it flies too
     lightly from you.
There is no way but fetch the constable.
TIB. The constable? The man is mad, I
     think.                            [Exit.]

[1] I.e., the only reward he gives me.
[2] A small coin.
[3] Bailiffs.        [4] The last five enter later.

*[Enter Dame Kitely and Cash.]*

CASH. Ho! Who keeps house here?

KNOW. O, this is the female copesmate [1]
of my son?

Now shall I meet him straight.

DAME.                    Knock, Thomas, hard.

CASH. Ho, goodwife!

*[Enter Tib.]*

TIB.    Why, what's the matter with you?

DAME. Why, woman, grieves it you to ope
your door?

Belike you get something to keep it shut.

TIB. What mean these questions, pray
ye?                                                          20

DAME. So strange you make it? Is not my
husband here?

KNOW. Her husband!

DAME.            My tried husband, Master
Kitely.

TIB. I hope he needs not to be triéd here.

DAME. No, dame, he does it not for need,
but pleasure.

TIB. Neither for need nor pleasure is he
here.

KNOW. This is but a device to balk me
withal—

*[Enter Kitely with his face covered.]*

Soft, who is this? 'Tis not my son disguised?

DAME. *(She spies her husband come, and
runs to him.)* O, sir, have I forestalled
your honest market?

Found your close [2] walks? You stand
amazed now, do you?

I' faith, I am glad I have smoked [3] you
yet at last.                                                30

What is your jewel, trow? In, come, let's
see her.

Fetch forth your huswife, dame; if she
be fairer,

In any honest judgment, than myself,

I'll be content with it; but she is change,

She feeds you fat, she soothes your appetite,

And you are well? Your wife, an honest
woman,

Is meat twice sod [4] to you, sir? O, you
treachor! [5]

---

KNOW. *[Aside.]* She cannot counterfeit
thus palpably.

KITE. Out on thy more than strumpet's
impudence!

Steal'st thou thus to thy haunts? And
have I taken                                          40

Thy bawd and thee, and thy companion,
                    *(Pointing to old Knowell.)*

This hoary-headed lecher, this old goat,

Close at your villainy, and wouldst thou
scuse [6] it

With this stale harlot's jest, accusing
me?—

*(To him.)* O, old incontinent, dost not
thou shame,

When all thy powers in chastity is spent,

To have a mind so hot, and to entice,

And feed th' enticements of a lustful
woman?

DAME. Out, I defy thee, I, dissembling
wretch!

KITE. Defy me, strumpet? *(By [7] Thomas.)*
Ask thy pander here,                              50

Can he deny it? Or that wicked elder?

KNOW. Why, hear you, sir—

KITE.            Tut, tut, tut; never speak.

Thy guilty conscience will discover thee.

KNOW. What lunacy is this that haunts
this man?

KITE. Well, good wife Bad,[8] Cob's wife,
and you,

That make your husband such a hoddy-
doddy; [9]

And you, young apple-squire; [10] and old
cuckold-maker—

I'll ha' you every one before a justice.

Nay, you shall answer it; I charge you
go.

KNOW. Marry, with all my heart, sir, I go
willingly,                                                60

Though I do taste this as a trick put on
me,

To punish my impertinent search, and
justly,

And half forgive my son for the device.

KITE. Come, will you go?

DAME.        Go? To thy shame, believe it.

*[Enter Cob.]*

COB. Why, what's the matter here?
What's here to do?

---

[1] Companion.
[2] Secret.
[3] Found.
[4] Boiled.
[5] Traitor.

[6] Excuse.
[7] *I. e.*, referring to.
[8] With a pun on *bawd*.
[9] Dupe, cuckold.
[10] Pimp.

KITE. O, Cob, art thou come? I have been abused,
And i' thy house; never was man so wronged!
COB. 'Slid, in my house? My master, Kitely? Who wrongs you in my house? [70
KITE. Marry, young lust in old, and old in young here;
Thy wife's their bawd; here have I taken hem.
COB. How? Bawd? (*He falls upon his Wife and beats her.*) Is my house come to that? Am I preferred thither? Did I charge you to keep your doors shut, Isbel? And do you let hem lie open for all comers?
KNOW. Friend, know some cause before thou beat'st thy wife.
This's madness in thee.
COB.                    Why, is there no cause?
KITE. Yes, I'll show cause before the justice, Cob.                                          80
Come, let her go with me.
COB.                    Nay, she shall go.
TIB. Nay, I will go. I'll see an you may be allowed to make a bundle o' hemp o' [1] your right and lawful wife thus at every cuckoldly knave's pleasure. Why do you not go?
KITE. A bitter quean![2] Come, we'll ha' you tamed.                              [*Exeunt.*]

## ACT IV. SCENE xi.

[*A street near Justice Clement's house.*]

*Brainworm, Matthew, Bobadill, Stephen, Downright.*[3]

[BRA.] Well, of all my disguises yet, now am I most like myself, being in this serjeant's gown. A man of my present profession never counterfeits, till he lays hold upon a debtor and says he rests[4] him; for then he brings him to all manner of unrest. A kind of little kings we are, bearing the diminutive of a mace, made like a young artichock,[5] that always carries pepper and salt in itself.[6] Well, I know not [10 what danger I undergo by this exploit; pray heaven I come well off!

[*Enter Matthew and Bobadill.*]

MAT. See, I think, yonder is the varlet, by his gown.

BOB. Let's go in quest of him.
MAT. Save you, friend! Are not you here by appointment of Justice Clement's man?
BRA. Yes, an 't please you, sir; he told me two gentlemen had willed him to [20 procure a warrant from his master, which I have about me, to be served on one Downright.
MAT. It is honestly done of you both; and see where the party comes you must arrest. Serve it upon him quickly, afore he be aware.
BOB. Bear back, Master Matthew.

[*Enter Stephen, in Downright's cloak.*]

BRA. Master Downright, I arrest you i' the queen's name, and must carry [30 you afore a justice by virtue of this warrant.
STE. Me, friend? I am no Downright, I; I am Master Stephen. You do not well to arrest me, I tell you truly; I am in nobody's bonds nor books, I would you should know it. A plague on you heartily, for making me thus afraid afore my time!
BRA. Why, now are you deceived, gentlemen?
BOB. He wears such a cloak, and [40 that deceived us. But see, here a[7] comes indeed; this is he, officer.

[*Enter Downright.*]

DOW. Why, how now, signior gull! Are you turned filcher of late? Come, deliver my cloak.
STE. Your cloak, sir? I bought it even now in open market.
BRA. Master Downright, I have a warrant I must serve upon you, procured by these two gentlemen.                              50
DOW. These gentlemen? These rascals?                    [*Offers to beat them.*]
BRA. Keep the peace, I charge you in her majesty's name.
DOW. I obey thee. What must I do, officer?
BRA. Go before Master Justice Clement, to answer what they can object against you, sir. I will use you kindly, sir.        59
MAT. Come, let's before, and make[8] the justice, captain.

---

[1] *I.e.*, beat.    [2] Whore.    [3] Last four enter later.
[4] Arrests.                              [5] Artichoke.
[6] Punning on *mace*, the spice.

[7] He.                              [8] Prepare.

Bob. The varlet's a tall man, afore heaven! [*Exeunt Bobadill and Matthew.*]

Dow. Gull, you'll gi' me my cloak?

Ste. Sir, I bought it, and I'll keep it.

Dow. You will?

Ste. Ay, that I will.

Dow. Officer, there's thy fee; arrest him.

Bra. Master Stephen, I must arrest you.

Ste. Arrest me? I scorn it. There, take your cloak; I'll none on 't.        71

Dow. Nay, that shall not serve your turn now, sir. Officer, I'll go with thee to the justice's; bring him along.

Ste. Why, is not here your cloak? What would you have?

Dow. I'll ha' you answer it, sir.

Bra. Sir, I'll take your word, and this gentleman's too, for his appearance.        79

Dow. I'll ha' no words taken. Bring him along.

Bra. Sir, I may choose to do that; I may take bail.

Dow. 'Tis true, you may take bail, and choose at another time; but you shall not now, varlet. Bring him along, or I'll swinge you.

Bra. Sir, I pity the gentleman's case; here's your money again.        89

Dow. 'Sdeynes, tell not me of my money; bring him away, I say.

Bra. I warrant you he will go with you of himself, sir.

Dow. Yet more ado?

Bra. [*Aside.*] I have made a fair mash on 't.

Ste. Must I go?

Bra. I know no remedy, Master Stephen.        99

Dow. Come along afore me here; I do not love your hanging look behind.

Ste. Why, sir, I hope you cannot hang me for it. Can he, fellow?

Bra. I think not, sir; it is but a whipping matter, sure!

Ste. Why, then let him do his worst; I am resolute.        [*Exeunt.*]

## Act V. Scene i.

[*A hall in Justice Clement's house.*]

*Clement, Knowell, Kitely, Dame Kitely,
Tib, Cash, Cob, Servants.*

[Clem.] Nay, but stay, stay, give me leave. My chair, sirrah.—You, Master Knowell, say you went thither to meet your son?

Know. Ay, sir.

Clem. But who directed you thither?

Know. That did mine own man, sir.

Clem. Where is he?

Know. Nay, I know not now; I left him with your clerk and appointed [10 him to stay here for me.

Clem. My clerk?    About what time was this?

Know. Marry, between one and two, as I take it.

Clem. And what time came my man with the false message to you, Master Kitely?

Kite. After two, sir.

Clem. Very good; but, Mistress [20 Kitely, how that you were at Cob's, ha?

Dame. An please you, sir, I'll tell you: my brother Wellbred told me that Cob's house was a suspected place—

Clem. So it appears, methinks; but on.

Dame. And that my husband used thither daily.

Clem. No matter, so he used himself well, mistress.        30

Dame. True, sir, but you know what grows by such haunts oftentimes.

Clem. I see rank fruits of a jealous brain, Mistress Kitely; but did you find your husband there in that case as you suspected?

Kite. I found her there, sir.

Clem. Did you so? That alters the case. Who gave you knowledge of your wife's being there?        40

Kite. Marry, that did my brother Wellbred.

Clem. How? Wellbred first tell her? Then tell you after? Where is Wellbred?

Kite. Gone with my sister, sir, I know not whither.

Clem. Why, this is a mere trick, a device; you are gulled in this most grossly, all. Alas, poor wench, wert thou beaten for this?        50

Tib. Yes, most pitifully, and 't please you.

Cob. And worthily, I hope, if it shall prove so.

Clem. Ay, that's like, and a piece of a sentence.—

[*Enter a Servant.*]

How now, sir? What's the matter?

SER. Sir, there's a gentleman i' the court without, desires to speak with your worship.                                    60

CLEM. A gentleman? What's he?

SER. A soldier, sir, he says.

CLEM. A soldier? Take down my armor, my sword, quickly. A soldier speak with me! Why, when, knaves? Come on, come on. (*He arms himself.*) Hold my cap there, so; give me my gorget, my sword. Stand by. I will end your matters anon. Let the soldier enter. [*Exit Servant.*]— Now, sir,[1] what ha' you to say to me?

### ACT V. SCENE ii.

#### [*The same.*]

[*To them,*] *Bobadill, Matthew.*

[BOB.] By your worship's favor—

CLEM. Nay, keep out, sir; I know not your pretense.[2] You send me word, sir, you are a soldier. Why, sir, you shall be answered here; here be them have been amongst soldiers. Sir, your pleasure.

BOB. Faith, sir, so it is, this gentleman and myself have been most uncivilly wronged and beaten by one Downright, a coarse fellow about the town here; [10 and, for mine own part, I protest, being a man in no sort given to this filthy humor of quarreling, he hath assaulted me in the way of my peace, despoiled me of mine honor, disarmed me of my weapons, and rudely laid me along in the open streets, when I not so much as once offered to resist him.

CLEM. O, God's precious! Is this the soldier? Here, take my armor off [20 quickly. 'Twill make him swoon, I fear; he is not fit to look on 't, that will put up[3] a blow.

MAT. An 't please your worship, he was bound to the peace.

CLEM. Why, and he were, sir, his hands were not bound, were they?

#### [*Enter Servant.*]

SER. There's one of the varlets of the city, sir, has brought two gentlemen here, one, upon your worship's warrant.      30

---

[1] Notice that here and in the rest of the act Jonson does not indicate a formal scene division until the new characters actually speak.

[2] Intention.                    [3] Put up with.

CLEM. My warrant!

SER. Yes, sir; the officer says, procured by these two.

CLEM. Bid him come in. [*Exit Servant.*] Set by this picture.[4]—What, Mr. Downright! Are you brought at Mr. Freshwater's[5] suit here?

### ACT V. SCENE iii.

#### [*The same.*]

[*To them,*] *Downright, Stephen, Brainworm.*

[Dow.] I' faith, sir, and here's another brought at my suit.

CLEM. What are you, sir?

STE. A gentleman, sir—O, uncle!

CLEM. Uncle? Who? Master Knowell?

KNOW. Ay, sir; this is a wise kinsman of mine.

STE. God's my witness, uncle, I am wronged here monstrously; he charges me with stealing of his cloak, and would [10 I might never stir, if I did not find it in the street by chance.

Dow. O, did you find it now? You said you bought it erewhile.

STE. And you said I stole it. Nay, now my uncle is here, I'll do well enough with you.

CLEM. Well, let this breathe awhile. You that have cause to complain there, stand forth. Had you my warrant for [20 this gentleman's apprehension?

BOB. Ay, an 't please your worship.

CLEM. Nay, do not speak in passion[6] so. Where had you it?

BOB. Of your clerk, sir.

CLEM. That's well! An my clerk can make warrants, and my hand not at hem! Where is the warrant—officer, have you it?

BRA. No, sir. Your worship's man, Master Formal, bid me do it for these [30 gentlemen, and he would be my discharge.[7]

CLEM. Why, Master Downright, are you such a novice, to be served and never see the warrant?

Dow. Sir, he did not serve it on me.

CLEM. No? How then?

Dow. Marry, sir, he came to me, and said he must serve it, and he would use me kindly, and so—

---

[4] Put aside this imitation of a soldier.

[5] A soldier who had seen no service abroad.

[6] Feeling.                    [7] Guarantee.

CLEM. O, God's pity, was it so, sir? [40 "He must serve it"? Give me my long sword there, and help me off. So, come on, Sir Varlet. (*He flourishes over him with his long sword.*) I "must" cut off your legs, sirrah. [*Brainworm kneels.*] Nay, stand up! I'll "use you kindly"; I *must* cut off your legs, I say.

BRA. O, good sir, I beseech you; nay, good Master Justice!

CLEM. I "must" do it; there is no [50 remedy. I "must" cut off your legs, sirrah; I "must" cut off your ears, you rascal; I "must" do it. I "must" cut off your nose; I "must" cut off your head.

BRA. O, good your worship!

CLEM. Well, rise; how dost thou do now? Dost thou feel thyself well? Hast thou no harm?

BRA. No, I thank your good worship, sir.                                              60

CLEM. Why, so! I said I must cut off thy legs, and I must cut off thy arms, and I must cut off thy head; but I did not do it. So you said you must serve this gentleman with my warrant, but you did not serve him. You knave, you slave, you rogue, do you say you "must," sirrah! Away with him to the jail; I'll teach you a trick for your "must," sir.

BRA. Good sir, I beseech you, be [70 good to me.

CLEM. Tell him he shall to the jail; away with him, I say.

BRA. Nay, sir, if you will commit me, it shall be for committing more than this; I will not lose, by my travail, any grain of my fame, certain.        [*Reveals himself.*]

CLEM. How is this?

KNOW. My man Brainworm!

STE. O, yes, uncle; Brainworm has [80 been with my cousin Edward and I all this day.

CLEM. I told you all there was some device.

BRA. Nay, excellent justice, since I have laid myself thus open to you, now stand strong for me—both with your sword and your balance.

CLEM. Body o' me, a merry knave! Give me a bowl of sack. If he belong [90 to you, Master Knowell, I bespeak your patience.

BRA. That is it I have most need of.

Sir, if you'll pardon me only, I'll glory in all the rest of my exploits.

KNOW. Sir, you know I love not to have my favors come hard from me. You have your pardon, though I suspect you shrewdly for being of counsel with my son against me.                                    100

BRA. Yes, faith, I have, sir, though you retained me doubly this morning for yourself: first, as Brainworm; after, as Fitzsword. I was your reformed soldier, sir. 'Twas I sent you to Cob's upon the errand without end.

KNOW. Is it possible? Or that thou shouldst disguise thy language so as I should not know thee?

BRA. O, sir, this has been the day [110 of my metamorphosis. It is not that shape alone that I have run through today. I brought this gentleman, Master Kitely, a message too, in the form of Master Justice's man here, to draw him out o' the way, as well as your worship, while Master Wellbred might make a conveyance of Mistress Bridget to my young master.

KITE. How! My sister stol'n away?

KNOW. My son is not married, I [120 hope.

BRA. Faith, sir, they are both as sure as love, a priest, and three thousand pound, which is her portion, can make hem, and by this time are ready to bespeak their wedding supper at the Windmill, except some friend here prevent [1] hem, and invite hem home.

CLEM. Marry, that will I; I thank thee for putting me in mind on 't.—Sirrah, [130 go you and fetch hem hither upon my warrant.—[*Exit Servant.*] Neither's friends have cause to be sorry, if I know the young couple aright. Here, I drink to thee for thy good news. But, I pray thee, what hast thou done with my man Formal?

BRA. Faith, sir, after some ceremony past, as making him drunk, first with story, and then with wine (but all in kindness), and stripping him to his shirt, I left [140 him in that cool vein, departed, sold your worship's warrant to these two, pawned his livery for that varlet's gown to serve it in, and thus have brought myself by my activity to your worship's consideration.

[1] Forestall.

CLEM. And I will consider thee in another cup of sack. Here's to thee, which having drunk off, this is my sentence: Pledge me. Thou hast done, or assisted to, nothing, in my judgment, but de- [151 serves to be pardoned for the wit o' the offense. If thy master, or any man here, be angry with thee, I shall suspect his ingine,[1] while I know him, for 't. How now, what noise is that?

*[Enter Servant.]*

SER. Sir, it is Roger is come home.

CLEM. Bring him in, bring him in.— What! Drunk in arms against me? Your reason, your reason for this?      160

### ACT V. SCENE iv.

*[The same.]*

*To them, Formal [in armor].*

[FOR.] I beseech your worship to pardon me; I happened into ill company by chance, that cast me into a sleep, and stripped me of all my clothes.

CLEM. Well, tell him I am Justice Clement, and do pardon him. But what is this to your armor? What may that signify?

FOR. And 't please you, sir, it hung up i' the room where I was stripped, and I borrowed it of one o' the drawers[2] to [10 come home in, because I was loath to do penance through the street i' my shirt.

CLEM. Well, stand by a while.—Who be these? O, the young company; welcome, welcome! Gi' you joy. Nay, Mistress Bridget, blush not, you are not so fresh a bride, but the news of it is come hither afore you. Master Bridegroom, I ha' made your peace, give me your hand. So will I for all the rest ere you forsake [20 my roof.

### ACT V. SCENE v.

*[The same.]*

*To them Ed[ward] Knowell, Wellbred, Bridget.*

[E. KNOW.] We are the more bound to your humanity, sir.

CLEM. Only these two have so little

---

[1] Ingenuity, wit.        [2] Waiters.

of man in hem, they are no part of my care.

WELL. Yes, sir, let me pray you for this gentleman; he belongs to my sister, the bride.

CLEM. In what place, sir?      9

WELL. Of her delight, sir, below the stairs, and in public: her poet, sir.

CLEM. A poet? I will challenge him myself presently at extempore.

> Mount up thy Phlegon,[3] Muse, and testify
>> How Saturn, sitting in an ebon cloud,
> Disrobed his podex,[4] white as ivory,
>> And through the welkin thundered all aloud.

WELL. He is not for extempore, sir; he is all for the pocket muse. Please you command a sight of it.      20

CLEM. Yes, yes, search him for a taste of his vein.      *[They search Matthew.]*

WELL. You must not deny the queen's justice, sir, under a writ o' rebellion.

CLEM. What! All this verse? Body o' me, he carries a whole realm,[5] a commonwealth of paper, in 's hose. Let's see some of his subjects.      *[Reads.]*

> Unto the boundless ocean of thy face,
> Runs this poor river, charged with streams
>> of eyes.      30

How? This is stol'n!

E. KNOW. A parody![6] A parody! With a kind of miraculous gift to make it absurder than it was!

CLEM. Is all the rest of this batch? Bring me a torch, lay it together, and give fire. Cleanse the air. *[Sets the papers on fire.]* Here was enough to have infected the whole city, if it had not been taken in time. See, see how our poet's glory shines! Brighter and brighter! Still it increases! [41 O, now it's at the highest; and now it declines as fast. You may see, *sic transit gloria mundi!*[7]

KNOW. There's an emblem[8] for you, son, and your studies.

---

[3] One of the Sun's horses.
[4] Fundament.
[5] Pronounced *ream*.
[6] Of the opening lines of Daniel's *Delia*.
[7] Thus passes the glory of the world.
[8] Motto.

CLEM. Nay, no speech or act of mine be drawn against such as profess it worthily. They are not born every year, as an alderman. There goes more to the making of a good poet than a sheriff, Master [51 Kitely. You look upon me! Though I live i' the city here amongst you, I will do more reverence to him, when I meet him, than I will to the mayor out of his year.[1] But these paper-peddlers! These ink-dabblers! They cannot expect reprehension or reproach; they have it with the fact.[2]                                    59

E. KNOW. Sir, you have saved me the labor of a defense.[3]

CLEM. It shall be discourse for supper between your father and me, if he dare undertake me. But to despatch away these: you sign o' the soldier, and picture o' the poet (but both so false I will not ha' you hanged out at my door till midnight), while we are at supper, you two shall penitently fast it out in my court

---

[1] When his term is expired.   [2] Deed, crime.
[3] At approximately this point in the Italian version the following passage, based on Sidney's *Defense of Poesy*, occurs:

If it may stand with your most wished content,
I can refel *a* opinion and approve
The state of poesy, such as it is,
Blessed, eternal, and most true divine.
Indeed, if you will look on poesy
As she appears in many, poor and lame,
Patched up in remnants and old worn rags,
Half starved for want of her peculiar food,
Sacred invention, then I must confirm
Both your conceit and censure of her merit.
But view her in her glorious ornaments,
Attired in the majesty of art,
Set high in spirit with the precious taste
Of sweet philosophy, and, which is most,
Crowned with the rich traditions of a soul
That hates to have her dignity profaned
With any relish of an earthly thought—
O, then how proud a presence doth she bear!
Then is she like herself, fit to be seen
Of none but grave and consecrated eyes.
Nor is it any blemish to her fame
That such lean, ignorant, and blasted wits,
Such brainless gulls, should utter their stol'n wares
With such applauses in our vulgar ears,
Or that their slubbered lines have current pass
From the fat judgments of the multitude.
But that this barren and infected age
Should set no difference twixt these empty spirits
And a true poet, than which reverend name
Nothing can more adorn humanity!

---

*a* Refute.

without; and, if you will, you may [70 pray there that we may be so merry within as to forgive or forget you when we come out. Here's a third,[4] because we tender your safety, shall watch you; he is provided for the purpose.—Look to your charge, sir.

STE. And what shall I do?

CLEM. O! I had lost a sheep an he had not bleated. Why, sir, you shall give Mr. Downright his cloak; and I will entreat him to take it. A trencher and a nap- [81 kin you shall have i' the butt'ry, and keep Cob and his wife company here, whom I will entreat first to be reconciled, and you to endeavor with your wit to keep hem so.

STE. I'll do my best.

COB. Why, now I see thou art honest, Tib, I receive thee as my dear and mortal wife again.                                       90

TIB. And I you, as my loving and obedient husband.

CLEM. Good complement! It will be their bridal night too. They are married anew. Come, I conjure the rest to put off all discontent. You, Mr. Downright, your anger; you, Master Knowell, your cares; Master Kitely and his wife, their jealousy.

For, I must tell you both, while that is fed,
Horns i' the mind are worse than o' the head.                                            100

KITE. Sir, thus they go from me; kiss me, sweetheart.

See what a drove of horns fly in the air,
Winged with my cleanséd and my credulous breath!
Watch hem, suspicious eyes, watch where they fall.
See, see! On heads that think th' have none at all!
O, what a plenteous world of this will come!
When air rains horns, all may be sure of some.

I ha' learned so much verse out of a jealous man's part in a play.[5]                              110

CLEM. 'Tis well, 'tis well! This night we'll dedicate to friendship, love, and laughter. Master Bridegroom, take your bride and lead, everyone, a fellow. Here

---

[4] *I.e.*, Formal in his armor.
[5] The play has not been traced.

is my mistress, Brainworm, to whom all my addresses of courtship shall have their reference—whose adventures this day, when our grandchildren shall hear to be made a fable, I doubt not but it shall find both spectators and applause.          [*Exeunt.*]

THE END.

This comedy was first acted in the year 1598 by the then L[ord] Chamberlain his Servants.  The principal comedians were:

| | |
|---|---|
| *Will. Shakespeare* | *Ric. Burbadge* |
| *Aug. Philips* | *Joh. Hemings* |
| *Hen. Condell* | *Tho. Pope* |
| *Will. Sly* | *Chr. Beeston* |
| *Will. Kemp* | *Joh. Duke* |

With the allowance of the Master of Revels.

# BEN JONSON

## SEJANUS HIS FALL

*Sejanus His Fall* (that is, *Sejanus's Fall*) was first acted by the King's Men in 1603, perhaps at court on account of the plague (Chambers, *Elizabethan Stage*). When the theaters reopened in March 1604, it was offered at the Globe, but was hissed. Chute points out that Jonson believed the play was responsible for one of his not infrequent appearances before the Privy Council, and assigned the cause to the Earl of Northampton, because one day in April the poet had had a quarrel with one of the Earl's retainers. Chute, however, feels that references in the play to the burning of books, to the relations between subjects and kings, and to the fact that it dealt with a conspiracy would have been enough to make it suspect. When Jonson printed his tragedy in 1605, after entering it in the Stationers' Register on November 2, 1604, he ended his address "To the Readers" with an emphatic statement that the ending of the play was actually a warning to traitors, and apparently this explanation placated the government. Jonson saw this quarto through the press with his usual care, since the corrections and minor alterations made in the process suggest his personal supervision. Of course the play occupied a prominent place in the 1616 folio, a text which Evelyn May Simpson defended vigorously against the attack of Henry de Vocht, who, in his edition of it in 1936, used the 1605 version, maintaining that Jonson "had no part in the 1616 edition, which was entirely at the mercy of the printer and his staff." Nevertheless, the stage history of *Sejanus* was short. According to the *Roscius Anglicanus* of John Downes, the prompter at Thomas Killigrew's Theatre Royal during the Restoration, it became one of Killigrew's repertoire, but he gave no dates. A Francis Gentleman made what Herford-Simpson call a "worthless" adaptation of it in 1752, but Garrick, though an admirer of Jonson, rejected it. The only modern revival of the play was given by William Poel in London on February 12, 1928, but it attracted little attention.

Perhaps as a natural reaction against the unanimously harsh treatment given the tragedy by earlier critics, who regarded it as cold, stiff, and labored, a few modern scholars like Enck (who calls it "a purer work than the English stage deserves") and Thayer have defended both it and *Catiline*. T. S. Eliot went against popular opinion in another way when, in recommending half a dozen of Jonson's plays as typical of his powers, he chose *Catiline* in preference to *Sejanus*. Here, perhaps without knowing it, he followed Felix E. Schelling, who had taken the same position in his *Elizabethan Drama, 1558–1642* (Boston and New York, 1908). Even Archer admitted that there is "undoubted dignity and strength" in *Sejanus*, and added, "Relieved of some of its verbosity, it might even produce a certain effect on the modern stage." But he ended by contrasting *Sejanus* with *Julius Caesar* and *Antony and Cleopatra* to Jonson's great disfavor and quoted an article in the *Times Literary Supplement* in 1919, which pontificated: "For some generations . . . no critic has succeeded in making him appear pleasurable or even interesting."

It is noteworthy that Shakespeare also acted in this play and that for a time many critics identified him with the "so happy a genius" who Jonson admitted in his preface had aided him considerably in the original stage production, but for whose contribution he had substituted his own "weaker, and no doubt less pleasing" passages in the printed text. Other speculations as to this collaborator also included either Middleton, Fletcher, or Chapman, with recent opinion veering toward Chapman, in spite of the fact that

Sydney A. Cockrell, in "Ben Jonson on Chapman" (*TLS*, March 3, 1932) printed a number of derisive marginal comments by Jonson found in his copy of Chapman's *Homer* (1616); these, using such phrases as "profanè et putidè" and "scurriliter," include four protests against Chapman's sneers against J. C. Scaliger, whom Jonson always admired.

In accordance with his strong sense of scholarly responsibility, Jonson made no attempt to conceal the classical sources for his two Roman plays, and in his preface to *Sejanus*, as well as in his marginal notes, acknowledged his major indebtedness to the 1600 quarto edition of the works of Tacitus, published at Antwerp by Lipsius, as well as to supplementary works by Suetonius, Seneca, and so forth. Ellen M. T. Duffy, however, in "Ben Jonson's Debt to Renaissance Scholarship in *Sejanus* and *Catiline*" (*MLR*, 1947), pointed out a number of passages in which Jonson failed to confess his debt to Tacitus. Daniel C. Boughner supplemented this article in "Jonson's Use of Lipsius in *Sejanus*" (*MLN*, 1958), in which he showed that many of Jonson's own notes were taken from Lipsius or resulted from Jonson's consulting the additional references given by him. Joseph A. Bryant, in "*Catiline* and the Nature of Jonson's Tragic Fable" (*PMLA*, 1954), stated his belief that not enough serious consideration had been given to Jonson's manipulation of his source material in his two Roman tragedies, but dealt especially with his use of Sallust's *Bellum Catilinae* in *Catiline*. Boughner, in *The Devil's Disciple/Ben Jonson's Debt to Machiavelli* (New York, 1968), has of course placed most of his emphasis on the Roman tragedies in his investigation of the influence of Machiavelli.

But these tragedies are also history plays, and Jonson had unusual ideas about the integrity of the dramatist in presenting accurate and authentic events and characters in transferring history to the stage. In these views, so unlike those of Shakespeare and most of the other authors of chronicle plays of the time (and, if the truth were stated, of all time), Jonson was a disciple of Scaliger. Jonson's particular and peculiar role in preserving the history play in England is discussed by Irving Ribner in *The English History Play in the Age of Shakespeare* (Princeton University Press, 1957), though only briefly since his study is primarily concerned with English history alone. Ribner points out that apparently Jonson's first interest in dramatizing history was in British history, as shown by Henslowe's references to Jonson's share in plays with titles like *Richard Crookback* and *Robert II, King of Scots*. These, however, were probably done in the accepted vein of the romaticized historical tragedy. Moreover, found among Jonson's papers at his death was the fragment, *Mortimer His Fall*, consisting of the "arguments," or plots, for five acts and the completed text of one whole scene and part of another. As a student of Camden's he had also probably become acquainted with the antiquarian school of history, influenced by Italian humanists like Flavio Biondi of Forli, and thus accepted the value of historical fact for its own sake. Joseph A. Bryant, Jr., in two articles ("The Significance of Ben Jonson's First Requirement for Tragedy: 'Truth of "Argument," ' " *SP*, 1952, and "*Catiline* and the Nature of Jonson's Tragic Fable," *PMLA*, 1954), has discussed Jonson's insistence on fidelity to historical sources which can be readily verified.

At the same time, this attitude did not imply a lessened interest in the didactic value of lessons from history, since both *Sejanus* and *Catiline* teach such political lessons for Englishmen (see also Geoffrey Hill, "The World's Proportion: Jonson's Dramatic Poetry in *Sejanus* and *Catiline*," *Jacobean Theatre*, *SAS*, 1960). The most significant difference, perhaps, between Jonson's and Shakespeare's historical tragedies is that, as Ribner puts it (*Jacobean Tragedy: The Quest for Moral Order*, London, 1962), Jonson's plays "do not use the events of Rome to reflect, as Shakespeare always does in his Roman tragedies, upon the larger questions of mankind in general. Roman history is used for the parallels it may afford to the specific political vices of Jonson's own day." Thayer states the contrast in slightly different words: ". . . the battleground in Jonsonian tragedy is the state, not the universe; and history is the guiding and shaping force. For Jonson the tragic muse is really the muse of history, and the tragic poet becomes the poet of history." In this matter, K. M. Burton has drawn an interesting comparison between Jonson and Chapman ("The Political Tragedies of Chapman and Jonson," *Essays in Criticism*, 1952), saying that in neither case are their plays to be judged by Aristotelian standards, since both authors are concerned with the tragic flaw within the social order, not the individual. But Chapman usually focuses the problem in the fate of one man, Jonson in that of a number of men. Chapman holds the rulers responsible when they fail to govern themselves by reason and the moral law, and thus pass down their corruption to their subjects. Jonson shows that the general body of Rome's citizens was basically responsible for its decadence, and that "a Sejanus, a Tiberius, a Catiline" is the legitimate offspring of such a society.

In *Sejanus* Jonson makes many other departures from traditional tragedy, some of them even in the application of presumably basic classical rules. He himself called attention to his violation of the unity of time, insisting that modern writers should be allowed to treat the rule liberally and still compose a "true poem" in spite of the violation. Second, he omitted the classical chorus, since his "chorus of musicians" hardly fulfills the same function. These things, he asserts, are too difficult for a modern dramatist to handle successfully and still delight his audience. As Thayer puts it, there is no "recognition scene," in which the protagonist realizes his mistakes or weakness, and thereby becomes a better person before his death. In fact, the play is unique because its central character never evokes any sympathy from the audience, except perhaps for the comments made at the end on his death. He is largely responsible for his own destruction, although the way in which the goddess Fortuna turns her face away from his sacrifice suggests for a moment that Fate will take control. But, as Thayer says, "Sejanus is brought down by Tiberius through Macro and is never represented as being engaged in any kind of cosmic or universal struggle." The only pity in the play is not for any of the men, but for Sejanus's wife and children. The ending is not only ambiguous but ironical to anyone who was familiar with what was to happen next in Roman history. Though the villain-protagonist was dead, Tiberius and Macro —almost equally villainous—were not, and seemed to triumph. Jonson counted on his audience to remember "that the nightmare reign of Tiberius was to be followed by the unspeakable reign of Caligula, which began when that amiable young man helped murder the old gentleman," even if the spectators did not recall that after a few years Arruntius himself would be accused and would commit suicide.

But in other ways Jonson composed his tragedy in the classical tradition, and maintained that he observed the more fundamental "offices of a tragic writer" in his choice of persons and events and in the elevated tone of his dialogue and its sententiousness. In its picture of Roman life, with its all-Roman cast, it is classical; its spirit, as modern historians say, is much nearer reality than anything Shakespeare ever wrote, with the possible exception of *Coriolanus*. There is a conventional Nuntius, or messenger, at the end to describe the horrible deaths of Sejanus and his innocent family. Unity of tone is preserved in the almost complete lack of humor, unlike the method of Shakespeare in introducing comic scenes for contrast. The only even mildly humorous scene is the one in which Eudemus helps Livia primp, and even this seems somewhat out of place. The elevation of style which Jonson himself proclaimed has been analyzed at some length by Moody E. Prior in *The Language of Tragedy* (Columbia University Press, 1947). Jonson is above such rhetorical tricks as practiced by Kyd in his patterning of lines. His blank verse is "designed with the rhythms of well-phrased, even somewhat formal, discourse as its basis," as in the senate scene; but there are more long speeches than the purpose seems to demand. Surprisingly, Jonson "shows the same zest in the use of figurative language and the same fecundity in the creation of striking images which is characteristic of the Elizabethan dramatist generally." Nevertheless, Prior feels that in the end the elaborate and profuse development of the style does not really add up to much since "the imagery cannot be made integral to the play in the sense

that it is closely related to the features which provide necessity and probability."
Consequently, Jonson's "attempts to endow the play with the quality of magnitude
by the customary devices of figurative language led, on occasion, to the very extrava-
gance he deplored." Alexander H. Sackton has supplemented this analysis by a discussion of *The Rhymed Couplet in Ben Jonson's Plays* (*UTSE*, 1951). Whereas the
couplet was Jonson's favorite measure for non-dramatic verse, he used it prominently
in only *The Poetaster*, *Sejanus*, and *The Sad Shepherd* among his plays. Though the
amount of rhyme in *Sejanus* is partly due to the translation of Latin texts, it also
becomes a convention of dramatic speech used for a variety of effects, usually in contrast with blank verse. Only in this play, thinks Sackton, did Jonson use the couplet
"with a mature sureness of dramatic purpose."

The present text is based on the Herford-Simpson edition of the 1616 folio, checked
with a copy of the original in the Newberry Library, Chicago. In 1965 Jonas A. Barish
edited the play as Volume III of the Yale edition of Ben Jonson.

# SEJANUS HIS FALL[1]

BY

## BEN JONSON

To the No Less Noble by Virtue Than Blood, Esme, L[ord] Aubigny

My Lord:

If ever any ruin were so great as to survive, I think this be one I send you, *The Fall of Sejanus.* It is a poem, that, if I well remember, in your lo[rdship's] sight, suffered no less violence from our people here than the subject of it did from the rage of the people of Rome—but with a different fate as, I hope, merit; for this hath outlived their malice, and begot [10 itself a greater favor than he lost, the love of good men. Amongst whom, if I make your lo[rdship] the first it thanks, it is not without a just confession of the bond your benefits have, and ever shall hold, upon me.

Your lo[rdship's] most faithful honorer,

BEN. JONSON.

[2]To the Readers

The following and voluntary labors [3] of my friends, prefixed to my book, have relieved me in much whereat, without them, I should necessarily have touched. Now I will only use three or four short and needful notes, and so rest.

First, if it be objected that what I publish is no true poem, in the strict laws of time, I confess it, as also in the want of a proper chorus, whose habit and moods [10 are such and so difficult as not any whom I have seen since the ancients—no, not they who have most presently affected laws [4] —have yet come in the way of. Nor is it needful, or almost possible in these our times, and to such auditors as commonly things are presented, to observe the old state and splendor of dramatic poems, with preservation of any popular delight. But of this I shall take more seasonable [20 cause to speak, in my observations upon Horace his *Art of Poetry*, which, with the text translated, I intend shortly to publish.[5] In the meantime, if in truth of argument,[6] dignity of persons, gravity and height of elocution, fullness and frequency of sentence,[7] I have discharged the other offices of a tragic writer, let not the absence of these forms be imputed to[8] me, wherein I shall give you occasion here- [30 after, and without my boast, to think I could better prescribe than omit the due use for want of a convenient knowledge.

The next is, lest in some nice nostril the quotations might savor affected, I do let you know that I abhor nothing more, and have only done it to show my integrity in the story, and save myself in those common torturers that bring all wit to the rack, whose noses are ever like swine [40 spoiling and rooting up the Muses' gardens, and their whole bodies like moles, as blindly working under earth to cast any, the least, hills upon virtue.

Whereas they are in Latin, and the work in English, it was presupposed none but the learned would take the pains to confer[9] them, the authors themselves being all in the learned tongues, save one,[10] with whose

---

[1] The title continues: "A Tragedy, Acted in the Year 1603 by the K. Majesty's Servants. The Author, B. J. Mart[ial]. *Non hic centauros, non Gorgonas, Harpyiasque invenies; hominem pagina nostra sapit.*" ("You will not find centaurs, nor Gorgons, nor Harpies here; our page deals with man.")

[2] This address occurs only in the 1605 edn.

[3] Commendatory verses by George Chapman, Hugh Holland, John Marston, etc., printed in the 1605 edn.

[4] Most recently favored the rules of dramatic composition.

[5] This commentary, but not the translation, was destroyed in the burning of his library.

[6] Plot.       [7] Sententious statement.

[8] Charged against.

[9] Compare.

[10] Tacitus, translated by Richard Greenwey in 1598.

English side I have had little to do. [50
To which it may be required, since I have
quoted the page, to name what edition
I followed: *Tacit. Lips. in 4.º, Antverp. edit.*
[1]600. *Dio. folio Hen. Step.* [15]92. For
the rest, as *Sueton., Seneca, etc.*, the chapter doth sufficiently direct, or the edition
is not varied.[1]

Lastly, I would inform you that this
book, in all numbers,[2] is not the same with
that which was acted on the public [60
stage, wherein a second pen[3] had good share,
in place of which I have rather chosen to
put weaker, and, no doubt, less pleasing,
of mine own than to defraud so happy a
genius of his right by my loathed usurpa-
tion.

Fare you well. And if you read farder[4]
of me, and like, I shall not be afraid of it,
though you praise me out.      69

*Neque enim mihi cornea fibra est.*[5]

But that I should plant my felicity in
your general saying, "good," or "well," etc.,
were a weakness which the better sort of
you might worthily contemn, if not absolutely hate me for.

BEN. JONSON, and no such,

*Quem*

*Palma negata macrum, donata reducit
opimum.*[6]

## THE ARGUMENT

Ælius Sejanus, son to Sejus Strabo, a
gentleman of Rome, and born at Vul-
sinium, after his long service in court—
first under Augustus, afterward, Tiberius—
grew into that favor with the latter, and
won him by those arts, as there wanted
nothing but the name to make him a co-
partner of the empire. Which greatness
of his, Drusus, the emperor's son, not brooking, after many smothered dislikes, [10
it one day breaking out, the prince strook[7]

[1] The hundreds of marginal notes referring to
Jonson's sources appeared only in the 1605 edn.

[2] Verses.

[3] Probably Chapman.

[4] Farther.

[5] "For my fiber is not of cornel wood"
(Persius' *Satires*, I, 47); *i.e.*, I am not hardened
to praise.

[6] "Whom denied applause makes lean, but
bestowed applause makes happy" (Horace,
*Epist.*, II, i, 181).

[7] Struck.

him publicly on the face. To revenge
which disgrace, Livia, the wife of Drusus
(being before corrupted by him to her dishonor, and the discovery of her husband's
counsels), Sejanus practiceth[8] with, together with her physician, called Eudemus,
and one Lygdus, an eunuch, to poison
Drusus. This their inhuman act having
successful and unsuspected passage,[9] [20
it emboldeneth Sejanus to farther and more
insolent projects, even the ambition of
the empire; where finding the lets[10] he
must encounter to be many and hard, in respect of the issue of Germanicus, who
were next in hope for the succession, he
deviseth to make Tiberius' self his means,
and instills into his ears many doubts and
suspicions, both against the princes, and
their mother Agrippina, which Cæsar [30,
jealously[11] heark'ning to, as covetously
consenteth to their ruin, and their friends'.
In this time, the better to mature and
strengthen his design, Sejanus labors to
marry Livia, and worketh with all his
ingine[12] to remove Tiberius from the
knowledge of public business, with al-
lurements of a quiet and retired life; the
latter of which, Tiberius, out of a proneness to lust, and a desire to hide those [40
unnatural pleasures which he could not
so publicly practice, embraceth; the former
enkindleth his fears, and there gives him
first cause of doubt or suspect towards
Sejanus. Against whom he raiseth in
private a new instrument, one Sertorius
Macro, and by him underworketh, discovers the other's counsels, his means, his
ends, sounds the affections of the senators,
divides, distracts them; at last, when [50
Sejanus least looketh, and is most secure,
with pretext of doing him an unwonted
honor in the senate, he trains[13] him from
his guards, and with a long doubtful letter
in one day hath him suspected, accused,
condemned, and torn in pieces by the rage
of the people.[14]

[8] Conspires.      [11] Suspiciously.
[9] Outcome.      [12] Ingenuity.
[10] Obstacles.      [13] Tricks.

[14] The following passage, apparently alluding
to the Gunpowder Plot, occurs only in the 1605
edn.: "This do we advance as a mark of terror
to all traitors and treasons, to show how just
the heavens are in pouring and thund'ring down
a weighty vengeance on their unnatural intents."

## THE PERSONS OF THE PLAY

TIBERIUS [, *the emperor*].
DRUSUS SE[NIOR, *his son*].
NERO ⎫ [, *sons of Germanicus*
DRUSUS JU[NIOR] ⎬ *and grandnephews*
CALIGULA ⎭ *of Tiberius*].
[LUCIUS] ARRUNTIUS ⎫
[CAIUS] SILIUS ⎪ [, *gentlemen*
[TITIUS] SABINUS ⎪ *opposed*
[MARCUS] LEPIDUS ⎬ *to*
[CREMUTIUS] CORDUS ⎪ *Sejanus*].
[ASINIUS] GALLUS ⎭
REGULUS [, *consul*].
TERENTIUS.
[GRACINUS] LACO.
EUDEMUS [, *a physician*].
RUFUS.
SEJANUS.
LATIARIS.
VARRO [, *consul*].
[SERTORIUS] MACRO.
COTTA.
[DOMITIUS] AFER.

HATERIUS.
SANQUINIUS.
POMPONIUS.
[JULIUS] POSTHUMUS.
[FULCINUS] TRIO, *consul*.
MINUTIUS.
SATRIUS [SECUNDUS].
[PINNARIUS] NATTA.
OPSIUS.

AGRIPPINA [, *widow of Germanicus*].
LIVIA [, *wife of Drusus Senior*].
SOSIA [, *wife of Caius Silius*].

TRIBUNI.
PRÆCONES.
FLAMEN.
TUBICINES.
NUNTIUS.
LICTORES.
MINISTRI.
TIBICINES.
SERVUS [, *etc.*]

THE SCENE: *Rome.*

[TIME: *23–31 A.D.*]

ACT I. [SCENE i.

*A room of state in the palace.*]

*Sabinus, Silius, Natta, Latiaris, Cordus,*
*Satrius, Arruntius, Eudemus, Haterius, etc.*

[SAB.] Hail, Caius Silius!
SIL.                    Titius Sabinus, hail!
   Yo' are rarely met in court!
SAB.                    Therefore, well met.
SIL. 'Tis true; indeed, this place is not our
   sphere.
SAB. No, Silius, we are no good inginers.[1]
   We want the fine arts, and their thriving
      use
   Should make us graced or favored of the
      times;
   We have no shift of faces, no cleft
      tongues,
   No soft and glutinous bodies that can
      stick

even to the worst princes—much more to those,
for guard of whose piety and virtue the angels
are in continual watch, and God himself mi-
raculously working."
   [1] Plotters.

Like snails on painted walls, or on our
   breasts
Creep up, to fall from that proud height
   to which                              10
We did by slavery, not by service, climb.
We are no guilty men, and then no great;
We have nor place in court, office in state,
That we can say we owe unto our crimes;
We burn with no black secrets, which
   can make
Us dear to the [pale] [2] authors; or live
   feared
Of their still waking jealousies, to raise
Ourselves a fortune by subverting theirs.
We stand not in the lines that do advance
To that so courted point.
SIL. [*Pointing to Satrius and Natta.*]    But
   yonder lean                          20
   A pair that do.
([3]SAB.                    Good cousin Latiaris.)

   [2] Supplied from the Newberry Library copy
of the 1616 folio.
   [3] Jonson frequently encloses speeches in parenthesis to indicate an aside or a passage incidental to the main action.

SIL. Satrius Secundus and Pinnarius
    Natta,
The great Sejanus' clients.[1]  There be
    two
Know more than honest counsels, whose
    close [2] breasts,
Were they ripped up to light, it would
    be found
A poor and idle [3] sin to which their
    trunks
Had not been made fit organs.  These
    can lie,
Flatter, and swear, forswear, deprave,
    inform,
Smile, and betray; make guilty men;
    then beg
The forfeit lives, to get the livings;
    cut                                        30
Men's throats with whisp'rings; sell to
    gaping suitors
The empty smoke that flies about the
    palace;
Laugh when their patron laughs; sweat
    when he sweats;
Be hot and cold with him; change every
    mood,
Habit, and garb as often as he varies;
Observe him, as his watch observes [4] his
    clock;
And, true as turkis [5] in the dear lord's
    ring,
Look well or ill with him; [6] ready to
    praise
His lordship, if he spit, or but piss
    fair,
Have an indifferent stool, or break wind
    well;                                      40
Nothing can scape their catch.
SAB.                    Alas! These things
    Deserve no note, conferred with other
    vile
And filthier flatteries that corrupt the
    times,
When, not alone our gentries chief are
    fain
To make their safety from such sordid
    acts,
But all our consuls, and no little part
Of such as have been prætors, yea, the
    most

Of senators, that else not use their
    voices,[7]
Start up in public senate, and there
    strive
Who shall propound most abject things
    and base,                                  50
So much as oft Tiberius hath been heard,
Leaving the court, to cry, "O race of men,
Prepared for servitude!"—which showed
    that he,
Who least the public liberty could like,
As loathly brooked their flat servility.
SIL. Well, all is worthy of us, were it more,
Who with our riots, pride, and civil hate
Have so provoked the justice of the
    gods—
We, that within these fourscore years
    were born
Free, equal lords of the triumphéd[8]
    world,                                     60
And knew no masters but affections,
To which, betraying first our liberties,
We since became the slaves to one man's
    lusts,
And now to many; every minist'ring
    spy
That will accuse and swear is lord of you,
Of me, of all, our fortunes and our lives.
Our looks are called to question, and our
    words,
How innocent soever, are made crimes;
We shall not shortly dare to tell our
    dreams,
Or think, but 'twill be treason.
SAB.                    "Tyrans'[9] arts  [70
Are to give flatterers grace, accusers
    power,
That those may seem to kill whom they
    devour."[10]—
[Turns to Cordus.]  Now, good Cremutius
    Cordus.
COR.               Hail to your lordship!
NAT. [To Latiaris.]  Who's that salutes
    your cousin?
        They whisper. [Exeunt Satrius and
                            Eudemus.]
LAT.                    'Tis one Cordus,
A gentleman of Rome, one that has writ
Annals of late, they say, and very well.

[1] Dependents of a patrician family.
[2] Secret.                    [4] Is set by.
[3] Empty.                    [5] Turquoise.
[6] A common superstition.
[7] Jonson's marginal note reads *Pedarii* (i.e.,
senators who could speak only when called upon
by the presiding officer.         [8] Conquered.
[9] Tyrants'.
[10] Sententious passages were commonly set in
quotation marks.

NAT. Annals? Of what times?

LAT.                    I think of Pompey's
And Caius Cæsar's; and so down to
these.

NAT. How stands h' affected to the pres-
ent state?
Is he or [1] Drusian or Germanican?    80
Or ours or neutral?

LAT.                    I know him not so far.

NAT. Those times are somewhat queasy to
be touched.
Have you or seen or heard part of his
work?

LAT. Not I; he means they shall be public shortly.

NAT. O, Cordus do you call him?

LAT.            Ay.

SAB.                    But these our times
Are not the same, Arruntius.

ARR.                    Times? The men,
The men are not the same! 'Tis we are
base,
Poor, and degenerate from th' exalted
strain
Of our great fathers. Where is now the
soul
Of godlike Cato—he that durst be
good                                        90
When Cæsar durst be evil, and had
power,
As not to live his slave, to die his master?
Or where the constant Brutus, that,
being proof
Against all charm of benefits, did strike
So brave a blow into the monster's heart
That sought unkindly to captive [2] his
country?
O, they are fled the light! Those mighty
spirits
Lie raked up with their ashes in their
urns,
And not a spark of their eternal fire
Glows in a present bosom. All's but
blaze,                                      100
Flashes, and smoke, wherewith we
labor so;
There's nothing Roman in us, nothing
good,
Gallant, or great. 'Tis true that Cordus
says,
"Brave Cassius was the last of all that
race."

_____
[1] Either.
[2] Unnaturally to capture.

*Drusus [Senior] passeth by.*

SAB. Stand by! Lord Drusus!

HAT.            Th' emp'ror's son! Give place.

SIL. I like the prince well.

ARR.                    A riotous youth;
There's little hope of him.

SAB.                    That fault his age
Will, as it grows, correct. Methinks he
bears
Himself each day more nobly than other,
And wins no less on men's affections    110
Than doth his father lose. Believe me, I
love him,
And chiefly for opposing to Sejanus.

SIL. And I, for gracing his young kinsmen
so,
The sons of Prince Germanicus; it shows
A gallant clearness in him, a straight
mind
That envies not, in them, their father's
name.

ARR. His name was, while he lived, above
all envy,
And, being dead, without it. O, that man!
If there were seeds of the old virtue left,
They lived in him.

SIL.            He had the fruits, Arruntius,    120
More than the seeds; Sabinus and my-
self
Had means to know him within, and
can report him.
We were his followers (he would call us
friends).
He was a man most like to virtue; in all,
And every action, nearer to the gods
Than men, in nature; of a body as fair
As was his mind; and no less reverend
In face than fame. He could so use his
state,
Temp'ring his greatness with his gravity,
As it avoided all self-love in him        130
And spite in others. What his funerals
lacked
In images and pomp, they had supplied
With honorable sorrow, soldiers' sad-
ness,
A kind of silent mourning, such as men,
Who know no tears but from their cap-
tives, use
To show in so great losses.

COR.                    I thought once,
Considering their forms, age, manner of
deaths,

The nearness of the places where they
fell,
T' have paralleled him with great Alex-
ander;
For both were of best feature, of high
race,                                          140
Yeared [1] but to thirty, and, in foreign
lands,
By their own people alike made away.
SAB. I know not, for his death, how you
might wrest [2] it;
But, for his life, it did as much disdain
Comparison with that voluptuous, rash,
Giddy, and drunken Macedon's as mine
Doth with my bondman's. All the good
in him,
His valor, and his fortune, he made his;
But he had other touches of late Romans,
That more did speak [3] him: Pompey's
dignity,                                       150
The innocence of Cato, Cæsar's spirit,
Wise Brutus' temperance, and every
virtue,
Which, parted unto others, gave them
name,
Flowed mixed in him. He was the soul
of goodness;
And all our praises of him are like
streams
Drawn from a spring, that still rise
full, and leave
The part remaining greatest.
ARR.                          I am sure
He was too great for us, and that they
knew
Who did remove him hence.
SAB.               When men grow fast [4]
Honored and loved, there is a trick in
state                                          160
(Which jealous princes never fail to use)
How to decline [5] that growth, with fair
pretext,
And honorable colors [6] of employment,
Either by embassy, the war, or such,
To shift them forth into another air
Where they may purge and lessen. So
was he,
And had his seconds there, sent by
Tiberius
And his more subtile dam, to discontent
him,

To breed and cherish mutinies, detract
His greatest actions, give audacious
check                                          170
To his commands, and work to put him
out
In open act of treason. All which
snares
When his wise cares prevented, a fine
poison
Was thought on to mature their prac-
tices.
COR. Here comes Sejanus.
SIL.               Now observe the stoops,
The bendings, and the falls.
ARR.               Most creeping base!

[Enter] Sejanus, Satrius, Terentius, etc.
                    They pass over the stage.

[SEJ.] I note hem [7] well; no more. Say
you?
SAT.     My lord,
There is a gentleman of Rome would
buy—
SEJ. How call you him you talked with?
SAT.               Please your lordship,
It is Eudemus, the physician       180
To Livia, Drusus' wife.
SEJ.               On with your suit.
Would buy, you said—
SAT.          A tribune's place, my lord.
SEJ. What will he give?
SAT.               Fifty sestertia.
SEJ. Livia's physician, say you, is that
fellow?
SAT. It is, my lord. Your lordship's
answer?
SEJ.          To what?
SAT. The place, my lord. 'Tis for a gen-
tleman
Your lordship will well like of, when
you see him,
And one you may make yours by the
grant.
SEJ. Well, let him bring his money, and his
name.
SAT. Thank your lordship. He shall, my
lord.
SEJ.          Come hither.       190
Know you this same Eudemus? Is he
learned?
SAT. Reputed so, my lord, and of deep
practice.
SEJ. Bring him in to me in the gallery,

[1] Aged.
[2] Interpret.
[3] Celebrate.
[4] Greatly.
[5] Lower.
[6] Pretenses.
[7] Them.

And take you cause to leave us there
    together;
I would confer with him, about a
    grief.¹—On!
[*Exit Sejanus with Satrius, Terentius, and
                                Attendants.*]
ARR. So, yet! Another? Yet? O desperate
    state
Of grov'ling honor! Seest thou this, O
    sun,
And do we see thee after? Methinks,
    day
Should lose his light when men do lose
    their shames,
And for the empty circumstance of
    life                                    200
Betray their cause of living.
SIL.                        Nothing so.
Sejanus can repair, if Jove should ruin.
He is the now court-god; and, well ap-
    plied
With sacrifice of knees, of crooks, and
    cringe,
He will do more than all the house of
    heav'n
Can for a thousand hecatombs. 'Tis
    he
Makes us our day or night; hell and
    Elysium
Are in his look. We talk of Radamanth,
Furies, and firebrands; but 'tis his frown
That is all these, where, on the adverse
    part,                                   210
His smile is more than e'er yet poets
    feigned
Of bliss, and shades, nectar—
ARR.                        A serving boy!
I knew him at Caius' trencher, when for
    hire
He prostituted his abuséd body
To that great gourmand, fat Apicius,
And was the noted pathic² of the time.
SAB. And, now, the second face of the
    whole world,
The partner of the empire—hath his
    image
Reared equal with Tiberius, borne in
    ensigns;
Commands, disposes every dignity.   220
Centurions, tribunes, heads of prov-
    inces,
Prætors, and consuls, all that hereto-
    fore

¹ Ailment.              ² A male prostitute.

Rome's general suffrage gave, is now his
    sale.³
The gain, or rather spoil of all the earth,
One, and his house, receives.
SIL.                        He hath of late
Made him a strength too, strangely, by
    reducing
All the prætorian bands into one camp,
Which he commands, pretending that
    the soldiers,
By living loose and scattered, fell to riot;
And that, if any sudden enterprise   230
Should be attempted, their united
    strength
Would be far more than severed; and
    their life
More strict, if from the city more re-
    moved—
SAB. Where now he builds what kind of
    forts he please,
Is heard to court the soldier by his name,
Woos, feasts the chiefest men of action,
Whose wants, not loves, compel them
    to be his.
And, though he ne'er were liberal by
    kind,⁴
Yet, to his own dark ends, he's most
    profuse,
Lavish, and letting fly he cares not
    what                                    240
To his ambition.
ARR.                Yet hath he ambition?
Is there that step in state can make
    him higher,
Or more, or anything he is, but less?
SIL. Nothing but emp'ror.
ARR.                The name Tiberius,
I hope, will keep, howe'er he hath for-
    gone
The dignity and power.
SIL.                Sure, while he lives.
ARR. And dead, it comes to Drusus.⁵
    Should he fail,
To the brave issue of Germanicus;
And they are three: too many—ha?—for
    him
To have a plot upon?
SAB.                I do not know   250
The heart of his designs, but sure their
    face
Looks farther than the present.

³ At his disposal for sale.
⁴ Nature.
⁵ *I.e.*, Drusus Senior.

ARR.                By the gods,
   If I could guess he had but such a
     thought,
   My sword should cleave him down from
     head to heart
   But I would find it out; and with my
     hand
   I'ld hurl his panting brain about the
     air
   In mites as small as *atomi* [1] to undo
   The knotted bed—
SAB.          You are observed, Arruntius!
ARR. *(He turns to Sejanus' Clients.)* Death!
   I dare tell him so, and all his spies.
   You, sir, I would—do you look?—and
   you.
SAB.      Forbear!              260

*[Enter] Satrius, Eudemus, Sejanus* [2] *[in the
                 gallery above].*

SAT. Here he will instant be; let's walk a
   turn;
   Yo' are in a muse, Eudemus?
EUD.              Not I, sir.—
   *[Aside.]* I wonder he should mark me
     out so. Well,
   Jove and Apollo form it for the best!
SAT. Your fortune's made unto you now,
     Eudemus,
   If you can but lay hold upon the means;
   Do but observe his humor, and—believe
     it—
   He's the noblest Roman, where he
     takes—
   Here comes his lordship.

*[Enter Sejanus.]*

SEJ.            Now, good Satrius.
SAT. This is the gentleman, my lord.
SEJ.            Is this?    270
   Give me your hand; we must be more ac-
     quainted.
   Report, sir, hath spoke out your art and
     learning,
   And I am glad I have so needful cause,
   However in itself painful and hard,
   To make me known to so great virtue.
     Look,
   Who's that? Satrius—*[He motions and
     Satrius leaves.]* I have a grief, sir,
   That will desire your help. Your name's
   Eudemus?

EUD. Yes.
SEJ.        Sir?
EUD.           It is, my lord.
SEJ.               I hear you are
   Physician to Livia, the princess.    279
EUD. I minister unto her, my good lord.
SEJ. You minister to a royal lady, then.
EUD. She is, my lord, and fair.
SEJ.            That's understood
   Of all their sex, who are or would be so;
   And those that would be, physic soon
     can make hem;
   For those that are, their beauties fear
     no colors. [3]
EUD. Your lordship is conceited. [4]
SEJ.            Sir, you know it,
   And can, if need be, read a learned lec-
     ture
   On this, and other secrets. Pray you,
     tell me,
   What more of ladies, besides Livia,
   Have you your patients?
EUD.         Many, my good lord:   290
   The great Augusta, Urgulania,
   Mutilia Prisca, and Plancina; divers—
SEJ. And all these tell you the particulars
   Of every several grief: how first it grew,
   And then increased; what action caused
     that;
   What passion that; and answer to each
     point
   That you will put hem?
EUD.          Else, my lord, we know not
   How to prescribe the remedies.
SEJ.               Go to,
   Yo' are a subtile nation, you physicians,
   And grown the only cabinets in court 300
   To ladies' privacies! Faith, which of
     these
   Is the most pleasant lady in her physic?
   Come, you are modest now.
EUD.            'Tis fit, my lord.
SEJ. Why, sir, I do not ask you of their
     urines,
   Whose smell's most violet, or whose
     siege [5] is best,
   Or who makes hardest faces on her
     stool,
   Which lady sleeps with her own face
     a-nights,
   Which puts her teeth off, with her
     clothes, in court,

---

[1] Atoms.          [2] Actually enters later.
[3] With a punning reference to *fear no enemy.*
[4] Witty.                     [5] Defecation.

Or which her hair, which her com-
plexion,
And in which box she puts it.  These
were questions                          310
That might, perhaps, have put your
gravity
To some defense of blush.  But I in-
quired
Which was the wittiest, merriest, wan-
tonest?
Harmless intergatories,[1] but conceits.[2]
Methinks Augusta should be most per-
verse,
And froward in her fit?
EUD.                          She's so, my lord.
SEJ. I knew it; and Mutilia the most
jocund?
EUD. 'Tis very true, my lord.
SEJ.                          And why would you
Conceal this from me, now?  Come,
what's Livia?
I know she's quick and quaintly[3] spir-
ited,                          320
And will have strange thoughts, when
she's at leisure.
She tells hem all to you?
EUD.                          My noblest lord,
He breathes not in the empire, or on
earth,
Whom I would be ambitious to serve
(In any act that may preserve mine
honor)
Before your lordship.
SEJ.                          Sir, you can lose no honor
By trusting aught to me.  The coarsest
act
Done to my service I can so requite
As all the world shall style it honorable.
"Your idle, virtuous definitions          330
Keep honor poor, and are as scorned as
vain;
Those deeds breathe honor that do suck
in gain."
EUD. But, good my lord, if I should thus
betray
The counsels of my patient, and a lady's
Of her high place and worth, what might
your lordship
(Who presently are to trust me with
your own)
Judge of my faith?

SEJ.                          Only the best, I swear.
Say now that I should utter you my
grief—
And with it the true cause—that it were
love,
And love to Livia—you should tell her
this?                          340
Should she suspect your faith?  I would
you could
Tell me as much from her; see if my
brain
Could be turned jealous.[4]
EUD.                          Happily,[5] my lord,
I could in time tell you as much and
more,
So I might safely promise but the first
To her from you.
SEJ.                          As safely, my Eudemus
(I now dare call thee so), as I have put
The secret into thee.
EUD.                          My lord—
SEJ.                          Protest not;
Thy looks are vows to me; use only
speed;                          349
And but affect her with Sejanus' love,
Thou art a man made to make consuls.
Go!
EUD. My lord, I'll promise you a private
meeting
This day together.
SEJ.                          Canst thou?
EUD.                          Yes.
SEJ.                          The place?
EUD. My gardens, whither I shall fetch
your lordship.
SEJ. Let me adore my Æsculapius![6]
Why, this indeed is physic, and out-
speaks
The knowledge of cheap drugs, or any
use
Can be made out of it!  More comfort-
ing
Than all your opiates, *julebes*,[7] *apozems*,[8]
Magistral[9]  syrups, or—begone,  my
friend,                          360
Not barely styléd, but created so;
Expect things greater than thy largest
hopes
To overtake thee.  Fortune shall be
taught

---

[1] Interrogatories.
[2] Merely fancies.
[3] Pleasingly.

[4] Suspicious.                          [5] Haply, perhaps.
[6] God of medicine, used here in reference to
Venus.                          [8] Decoctions.
[7] Juleps.                          [9] Sovereign.

To know how ill she hath deserved thus
   long,
To come behind thy wishes.  Go, and
   speed.                    [*Exit Eudemus.*]
"Ambition makes more trusty slaves
   than need."
These fellows, by the favor of their art,
Have still the means to tempt, ofttimes
   the power.
If Livia will be now corrupted, then
Thou hast the way, Sejanus, to work
   out                                    370
His secrets, who, thou knowest, endures
   thee not,
Her husband, Drusus; and to work
   against them.
Prosper it, Pallas, thou that better'st
   wit;
For Venus hath the smallest share in it.

[*Enter*] *Tiberius; Sejanus* [*from the gallery*];
           *Drusus* [*Senior*].

[Tib.]  (*One kneels to him.*)  We not endure
   these flatteries; let him stand.
Our empire, ensigns, axes, rods, and state
Take not away our human nature from
   us.
Look up on us, and fall before the gods.
Sej.  How like a god speaks Cæsar!
Arr.  [*Aside to Cordus.*]           There,
   observe!
He can endure that second [1]—that's no
   flattery.                              380
O, what is it proud slime will not believe
Of his own worth, to hear it equal
   praised
Thus with the gods?
Cor.  [*Aside.*]       He did not hear it, sir.
Arr.  [*Aside.*]  He did not?  Tut, he must
   not; we think meanly.
'Tis your most courtly known confed-
   eracy,
To have your private parasite redeem
What he, in public subtilty, will lose
To making him a name.
Hat.                    Right mighty lord—
           [*Gives him letters.*]
Tib.  We must make up our ears gainst
   these assaults
Of charming tongues.  We pray you use
   no more                                390
These contumelies to us; style not us

[1] Disciple.

Or "lord" or "mighty," who profess
   ourself
The servant of the senate, and are proud
T' enjoy them our good, just, and favor-
   ing lords.
Cor.  [*Aside.*]  Rarely dissembled!
Arr.  [*Aside.*]           Princelike to the life.
Sab.  "When power that may command,
   so much descends,
Their bondage, whom it stoops to, it
   intends."
Tib.  Whence are these letters?
Hat.                    From the senate.
Tib.                                    So.
        [*Latiaris gives him letters.*]
Whence these?
Lat.                    From thence too.
        [*Tiberius reads the letters.*]
Tib.        Are they sitting now?
Lat.  They stay [2] thy answer, Cæsar.
Sil.  [*Aside.*]           If this man   400
Had but a mind allied unto his words,
How blessed a fate were it to us, and
   Rome!
We could not think [3] that state for
   which to change, [4]
Although the aim were our old liberty;
The ghosts of those that fell for that
   would grieve
Their bodies lived not now, again to
   serve.
"Men are deceived, who think there can
   be thrall
Beneath a virtuous prince.  Wished
   liberty
Ne'er lovelier looks than under such a
   crown."
But, when his grace is merely but lip-
   good,                                  410
And that no longer than he airs himself
Abroad in public, there to seem to shun
The strokes and stripes of flatterers,
   which within
Are lechery unto him, and so feed
His brutish sense with their afflicting
   sound,
As, dead to virtue, he permits himself
Be carried like a pitcher by the ears,
To every act of vice—this is a case
Deserves our fear, and doth presage the
   nigh
And close approach of blood and tyr-
   anny.                                  420

[2] Await.        [3] Imagine.        [4] Exchange.

"Flattery is midwife unto prince's rage;
And nothing sooner doth help forth a
    tyran
Than that and whisperers' grace, who
    have the time,
The place, the power to make all men
    offenders."
ARR. [*Aside.*] He should be told this; and
    be bid dissemble
With fools and blind men. We that know
    the evil
Should hunt the palace rats, or give them
    bane;
Fright hence these worse than ravens,
    that devour
The quick, where they but prey upon
    the dead.
He shall be told it.
SAB. [*Aside.*]            Stay, Arruntius,  430
We must abide our opportunity,
And practice what is fit, as what is
    needful.
"It is not safe t' enforce a sovereign's
    ear;
Princes hear well, if they at all will
    hear."
ARR. [*Aside.*]  Ha, say you so?  Well!
    In the meantime, Jove
(Say not but I do call upon thee now),
Of all wild beasts preserve me from a
    tyran;
And of all tame, a flatterer.
SIL. [*Aside.*]              'Tis well prayed.
TIB. Return the lords this voice: We are
    their creature,
And it is fit a good and honest prince, 440
Whom they, out of their bounty, have
    instructed
With so dilate [1] and absolute a power,
Should owe the office of it to their service
And good of all and every citizen.
Nor shall it e'er repent us to have
    wished
The senate just and fav'ring lords unto
    us,
"Since their free loves do yield no less
    defense
T' a prince's state than his own inno-
    cence."
Say then, there can be nothing in their
    thought
Shall want to please us, that hath
    pleaséd them;                          450

[1] Extended.

Our suffrage rather shall prevent [2] than
    stay
Behind their wills; 'tis empire to obey,
Where such, so great, so grave, so good,
    determine.
Yet, for the suit of Spain t' erect a
    temple
In honor of our mother and ourself,
We must, with pardon of the senate, not
Assent thereto. Their lordships may ob-
    ject
Our not denying the same late request
Unto the Asian cities. We desire
That our defense for suffering that be
    known                                  460
In these brief reasons, with our after-
    purpose.
Since deified Augustus hindered not
A temple to be built at Pergamum,
In honor of himself and sacred Rome,
We, that have all his deeds and words
    observed
Ever, in place of laws, the rather followed
That pleasing precedent, because with
    ours
The senate's reverence, also, there was
    joined.
But as,[3] t' have once received it, may
    deserve
The gain of pardon, so to be adored  470
With the continued style and note [4]
    of gods,
Through all the provinces, were wild am-
    bition,
And no less pride. Yea, ev'n Augustus'
    name
Would early vanish, should it be pro-
    faned
With such promiscuous flatteries. For
    our part,
We here protest it, and are covetous
Posterity should know it: we are mortal,
And can [5] but deeds of men. 'Twere
    glory enough,
Could we be truly a prince. And they
    shall add
Abounding grace unto our memory,  480
That shall report us worthy our fore-
    fathers,
Careful of your affairs, constant in
    dangers,
And not afraid of any private frown

[2] Anticipate.          [4] Manner of address.
[3] *I.e.*, as one.        [5] Can do.

For public good.  These things shall be to
 us
Temples and statues, rearéd in your
 minds,
The fairest and most during imag'ry;
For those of stone or brass, if they be-
 come
Odious in judgment of posterity,
Are more contemned[1] as dying sepulchers
Than ta'en for living monuments.  We
 then         490
Make here our suit alike to gods and men:
The one, until the period of our race,
T' inspire us with a free and quiet mind,
Discerning both divine and human laws;
The other, to vouchsafe us after death
An honorable mention and fair praise
T' accompany our actions and our name.
The rest of greatness princes may com-
 mand,
And, therefore, may neglect; only, a long,
A lasting, high, and happy memory 500
They should, without being satisfied,
 pursue.
Contempt of fame begets contempt of
 virtue.
NAT. Rare!
SAT.   Most divine!
SEJ.     The oracles are ceased
That only Cæsar, with their tongue,
 might speak.
ARR. [*Aside.*] Let me be gone!  Most
 felt and open this!
COR. [*Aside.*] Stay.
ARR. [*Aside.*]  What?  To hear more
 cunning and fine words,
With their sound flattered, ere their
 sense be meant?
TIB. Their choice of Antium, there to
 place the gift,
Vowed to the goddess for our mother's
 health,
We will the senate know we fairly
 like,        510
As also of their grant[2] to Lepidus
For his repairing the Æmilian place
And restoration of those monuments.
Their grace, too, in confining of Silanus
To th' other isle Cithera, at the suit
Of his religious sister, much commends
Their policy, so tempered with their
 mercy.

[1] Disdained.
[2] Permission.

But for the honors which they have
 decreed
To our Sejanus, to advance [3] his statue
In Pompey's theater (whose ruining
 fire        520
His vigilance and labor kept restrained
In that one loss), they have therein
 outgone
Their own great wisdoms, by their
 skillful choice
And placing of their bounties on a man
Whose merit more adorns the dignity
Than that can him, and gives a benefit
In taking greater than it can receive.
Blush not, Sejanus, thou great aid of
 Rome,
Associate of our labors, our chief helper;
Let us not force thy simple modesty 530
With off'ring at [4] thy praise, for more
 we cannot,
Since there's no voice can take [5] it.  No
 man here
Receive our speeches as hyperboles,
For we are far from flattering our
 friend,
Let envy know, as from the need to
 flatter.
Nor let them ask the causes of our
 praise;
Princes have still their grounds reared
 with themselves,
Above the poor low flats of common men;
And who will search the reasons of their
 acts,
Must stand on equal bases.  Lead,
 away.      540
Our loves unto the senate.
ARR.    Cæsar!—
SAB.     Peace!—
[*Exeunt Tiberius, Sejanus, and Attendants.*]
COR. Great Pompey's theater was never
 ruined
Till now that proud Sejanus hath a
 statue
Reared on his ashes.
ARR.   Place the shame of soldiers
Above the best of generals?  Crack the
 world,
And bruise the name of Romans into
 dust,
Ere we behold it!
SIL.    Check your passion;
Lord Drusus tarries.

[3] Set up. [4] Attempting. [5] Accomplish.

DRU.                    Is my father mad,
Weary of life and rule, lords, thus to
heave
An idol up with praise? Make him his
mate,                                        550
His rival in the empire?
ARR.                    O, good prince!
DRU. Allow him statues, titles, honors,
such
As he himself refuseth?
ARR.                    Brave, brave Drusus!
DRU. The first ascents to sovereignty are
hard;
But, entered once, there never wants or
means
Or ministers to help th' aspirer on.
ARR. True, gallant Drusus.
DRU.                We must shortly pray
To Modesty, that he will rest con-
tented—
ARR. Ay, where he is, and not write em-
p'ror.

*Sejanus,*[1] *etc.; he enters, followed with Clients.*

[SEJ.] There is your bill, and yours.—[*To
Satrius.*] Bring you your man.    560
I have moved for you, too, Latiaris.
DRU.                                What?
Is your vast greatness grown so blindly
bold
That you will over us?
SEJ.                Why, then give way!
DRU. Give way, Colossus? Do you lift?
Advance you?
Take that!            *Drusus strikes him.*
ARR.            Good! Brave! Excellent
brave prince!
DRU. Nay, come, approach. [*Draws his
sword.*] What, stand you off?    At
gaze?
It looks too full of death for thy cold
spirits.
Avoid mine eye, dull camel, or my sword
Shall make thy brav'ry fitter for a grave
Than for a triumph.    I'll advance a
statue                                        570
O' your own bulk; but 't shall be on the
cross,
Where I will nail your pride at breadth
and length,

---

[1] The fact that the names, *Drusus, Arruntius,*
are repeated at this point in the original would
perhaps indicate that Jonson conceived of his
act as being divided into scenes in classical fashion.

And crack those sinews, which are yet
but stretched
With your swol'n fortune's rage.
ARR.                    A noble prince!
ALL. A Castor, a Castor, a Castor, a
Castor!        [*Exeunt All but Sejanus.*]
SEJ. He that, with such wrong moved,
can bear it through
With patience and an even mind, knows
how
To turn it back. Wrath, covered, carries
fate;
Revenge is lost if I profess my hate.
What was my practice [2] late, I'll now
pursue                                        580
As my fell justice. This hath styled it
new.                                    [*Exit.*]
        CHORUS—*of Musicians.*

        ACT II. [SCENE i.

        *The garden of Eudemus.*]

        *Sejanus, Livia, Eudemus.*

[SEJ.] Physician, thou art worthy of a
province
For the great favors done unto our loves,
And, but that greatest Livia bears a
part
In the requital of thy services,
I should alone despair of aught like
means
To give them worthy satisfaction.
LIV. Eudemus, I will see it, shall receive
A fit and full reward for his large merit.
But for this potion we intend to Drusus
(No more our husband now), whom
shall we choose                            10
As the most apt and abled instrument
To minister it to him?
EUD.                    I say, Lygdus.
SEJ. Lygdus? What's he?
LIV.                    An eunuch Drusus loves.
EUD. Ay, and his cupbearer.
SEJ.                Name not a second.
If Drusus love him, and he have that
place,
We cannot think a fitter.
EUD.                    True, my lord;
For free access and trust are two main
aids.
SEJ. Skillful physician!
LIV.                But he must be wrought
To th' undertaking with some labored art.

---

[2] Trickery.

SEJ. Is he ambitious?

LIV.                    No.

SEJ.                          Or covetous?   20

LIV. Neither.

EUD.     Yet gold is a good general charm.

SEJ. What is he, then?

LIV.               Faith, only wanton, light.

SEJ. How! Is he young and fair?

EUD.                          A delicate youth.

SEJ. Send him to me; I'll work him.—
   Royal lady,
Though I have loved you long, and with
   that height
Of zeal and duty, like the fire, which
   more
It mounts it trembles, thinking naught
   could add
Unto the fervor which your eye had
   kindled,
Yet, now I see your wisdom, judgment,
   strength,
Quickness, and will to apprehend the
   means                          30
To your own good and greatness, I
   protest
Myself through rarefied, and turned all
   flame
In your affection. Such a spirit as yours
Was not created for the idle second
To a poor flash, as Drusus, but to shine
Bright as the moon among the lesser
   lights,
And share the sov'reignty of all the
   world.
Then Livia triumphs in her proper
   sphere,
When she and her Sejanus shall divide
The name of Cæsar, and Augusta's star
Be dimmed with glory of a brighter
   beam,                          41
When Agrippina's fires are quite ex-
   tinct,
And the scarce-seen Tiberius borrows
   all
As little light from us, whose folded
   arms
Shall make one perfect orb! [*Knocking
   within.*] Who's that? Eudemus,
Look 'tis not Drusus.—[*Exit Eudemus.*]
   Lady, do not fear.

LIV. Not I, my lord. My fear and love
   of him
Left me at once.[1]

[1] Simultaneously.

SEJ.                    Illustr'ous lady, stay—

EUD. [*Within.*] I'll tell his lordship.

[*Enter Eudemus.*]

SEJ.               Who is 't, Eudemus?

EUD. One of your lordship's servants
   brings you word                          50
The emp'ror hath sent for you.

SEJ.               O! Where is he?—
With your fair leave, dear princess, I'll
   but ask
A question, and return.     *He goes out.*

EUD.               Fortunate princess!
How are you blessed in the fruition
Of this unequaled man, this soul of
   Rome,
The empire's life, and voice of Cæsar's
   world!

LIV. So blessed, my Eudemus, as to know
The bliss I have, with what I ought to
   owe
The means that wrought it. How do I
   look today?

EUD. Excellent clear, believe it.   This
   same fucus [2]                          60
Was well laid on.

LIV.               Methinks 'tis here not white.

EUD. Lend me your scarlet, lady. 'Tis
   the sun
Hath giv'n some little taint unto the
   ceruse; [3]
You should have used of the white oil
   I gave you.
Sejanus for your love! His very name
Commandeth above Cupid or his shafts—
     [*Paints her cheek.*]

(LIV. Nay, now yo' have made it worse.

EUD.               I'll help it straight.)
—And, but pronounced, is a sufficient
   charm
Against all rumor, and of absolute power
To satisfy for any lady's honor.          70

(LIV. What do you now, Eudemus?

EUD.               Make a light fucus,
To touch you o'er withal.) Honored
   Sejanus!
What act, though ne'er so strange and
   insolent,
But that addition [4] will at least bear out,
If 't do not expiate?

LIV.               Here, good physician.

[2] Cosmetic.

[3] Cosmetic containing white lead.

[4] Title.

EUD. I like this study to preserve the love
   Of such a man, that comes not every
      hour
   To greet the world. ('Tis now well, lady;
      you should
   Use of the dentifrice I prescribed you,
      too,
   To clear your teeth, and the prepared
      pomatum,                              80
   To smooth the skin.) A lady cannot be
   Too curious [1] of her form, that still
      would hold
   The heart of such a person, made her
      captive,
   As you have his; who, to endear him
      more
   In your clear eye, hath put away his
      wife,
   The trouble of his bed and your delights,
   Fair Apicata, and made spacious room
   To your new pleasures.
LIV.                    Have not we returned
   That with our hate of Drusus, and dis-
      covery
   Of all his counsels?
EUD.                    Yes, and wisely, lady.  90
   The ages that succeed, and stand far off
   To gaze at your high prudence, shall
      admire,
   And reckon it an act without [2] your sex;
   It hath that rare appearance. Some will
      think
   Your fortune could not yield a deeper
      sound
   Than mixed with Drusus'; but, when
      they shall hear
   That and the thunder of Sejanus meet,
   Sejanus, whose high name doth strike
      the stars,
   And rings about the concave—great
      Sejanus,
   Whose glories, style, and titles are him-
      self,                                 100
   The often iterating of Sejanus—
   They then will lose their thoughts, and
      be ashamed
   To take acquaintance of them.

              [*Enter Sejanus.*]

SEJ.                    I must make
   A rude departure, lady; Cæsar sends
   With all his haste both of command and
      prayer.

Be resolute in our plot; you have my
   soul,
As certain yours as it is my body's.
And, wise physician, so prepare the
   poison
As you may lay the subtile operation
Upon some natural disease of his.     110
Your eunuch send to me. I kiss your
   hands,
Glory of ladies, and commend my love
To your best faith and memory.
LIV.                              My lord,
   I shall but change [3] your words. Fare-
      well. Yet, this
   Remember for your heed, he loves you
      not;
   You know what I have told you. His
      designs
   Are full of grudge and danger; we must
      use
   More than a common speed.
SEJ.                    Excellent lady,
   How you do fire my blood!
LIV.                    Well, you must go?
   The thoughts be best, are least set forth
      to show.        [*Exit Sejanus.*]  120
EUD. When will you take some physic,
   lady?
LIV.          When
   I shall, Eudemus; but let Drusus' drug
   Be first prepared.
EUD.          Were Lygdus made,[4] that's done;
   I have it ready. And tomorrow morning
   I'll send you a perfume, first to resolve
   And procure sweat, and then prepare
      a bath
   To cleanse and clear the cutis;[5] against
      when
   I'll have an excellent new fucus made,
   Resistive gainst the sun, the rain, or
      wind,
   Which you shall lay on with a breath,
      or oil,                              130
   As you best like, and last some fourteen
      hours.
   This change came timely, lady, for your
      health,
   And the restoring your complexion,
   Which Drusus' choler had almost burnt
      up,
   Wherein your fortune hath prescribed
      you better
   Than art could do.

---

[1] Careful.                    [2] Beyond.

[3] Reciprocate.   [4] Won to our purpose.   [5] Skin.

Liv.                    Thanks, good physician;
I'll use my fortune, you shall see, with
    reverence.
Is my coach ready?
Eud.                    It attends your highness.
                                        [*Exeunt.*]


[Scene ii.

*A room in the palace.*]

*Sejanus.*

[Sej.] If this be not revenge, when I have
    done
And made it perfect, let Egyptian slaves,
Parthians, and barefoot Hebrews brand
    my face,
And print my body full of injuries.
Thou lost thyself, childe [1] Drusus, when
    thou thought'st
Thou couldst outskip my vengeance,
    or outstand [2]
The power I had to crush thee into air.
Thy follies now shall taste what kind
    of man
They have provoked, and this thy
    father's house                            9
Crack in the flame of my incenséd rage,
Whose fury shall admit no shame or
    mean.
Adultery? It is the lightest ill
I will commit. A race of wicked acts
Shall flow out of my anger, and o'er-
    spread
The world's wide face, which no pos-
    terity
Shall e'er approve, nor yet keep silent—
    things
That, for their cunning, close, and cruel
    mark,
Thy father would wish his, and shall,
    perhaps,
Carry the empty name, but we the prize.
On, then, my soul, and start not in thy
    course;                                    20
Though heav'n drop sulphur, and hell
    belch out fire,
Laugh at the idle terrors. Tell proud
    Jove,
Between his power and thine there is
    no odds.
'Twas only fear first in the world made
    gods.

[Tib.] Is yet Sejanus come?
Sej.                    He's here, dread Cæsar.
Tib. Let all depart that chamber, and the
    next.—            [*Exeunt Attendants.*]
Sit down, my comfort. When the master-
    prince
Of all the world, Sejanus, saith he fears,
Is it not fatal?
Sej.                    Yes, to those are feared.
Tib. And not to him?
Sej.                    Not if he wisely turn    30
That part of fate he holdeth, first on
    them.
Tib. That nature, blood, and laws of
    kind forbid.
Sej. Do policy and state forbid it?
Tib.                                        No.
Sej. The rest of poor respects, then, let
    go by;
State [4] is enough to make th' act just,
    them guilty.
Tib. Long hate pursues such acts.
Sej.                    Whom hatred frights,
Let him not dream on sov'reignty.
Tib.                                Are rites
Of faith, love, piety, to be trod down,
Forgotten, and made vain?
Sej.                    All for a crown.
The prince who shames a tyran's name
    to bear                                    40
Shall never dare do anything but fear;
All the command of scepters quite doth
    perish,
If it begin religious thoughts to cherish;
Whole empires fall, swayed by those
    nice respects;
It is the license of dark deeds protects
Ev'n states most hated, when no laws
    resist
The sword, but that it acteth what it
    list.
Tib. Yet so, we may do all things cruelly,
Not safely.
Sej.            Yes, and do them thoroughly.
Tib. Knows yet Sejanus whom we point
    at?
Sej.        Ay,                                50
Or else my thought, my sense, or both
    do err:
'Tis Agrippina?
Tib.                    She, and her proud race.

SEJ. Proud? Dangerous, Cæsar; for in them apace
The father's spirit shoots up. Germanicus
Lives in their looks, their gait, their form, t' upbraid us
With his close death, if not revenge the same.
TIB. The act's not known.
SEJ.  Not proved; but whisp'ring Fame [1]
Knowledge and proof doth to the jealous give,
Who, than to fail, would their own thought believe.
It is not safe the children draw long breath, 60
That are provokéd by a parent's death.
TIB. It is as dangerous to make them hence,
If nothing but their birth be their offense.
SEJ. Stay till they strike at Cæsar; then their crime
Will be enough; but late and out of time
For him to punish.
TIB.  Do they purpose it?
SEJ. You know, sir, thunder speaks not till it hit.
Be not secure; [2] none swiftlier are oppressed
Than they whom confidence betrays to rest.
Let not your daring make your danger such; 70
All power's to be feared, where 'tis too much.
The youths are of themselves hot, violent,
Full of great thought; and that male-spirited dame,
Their mother, slacks no means to put them on,
By large allowance, popular presentings,
Increase of train and state, suing for titles;
Hath them commended with like prayers, like vows,
To the same gods, with Caesar; days and nights
She spends in banquets and ambitious feasts
For the nobility, where Caius Silius, 80
Titius Sabinus, old Arruntius,

Asinius Gallus, Furnius, Regulus,
And others of that discontented list
Are the prime guests. There, and to these, she tells
Whose niece [3] she was, whose daughter, and whose wife.
And then must they compare her with Augusta,
Ay, and prefer her too, commend her form,
Extol her fruitfulness, at which a shower
Falls for the memory of Germanicus,
Which they blow over straight with windy praise 90
And puffing hopes of her aspiring sons,
Who, with these hourly ticklings, grow so pleased
And wantonly conceited of themselves
As now they stick not to believe they're such
As these do give hem out, and would be thought
More than competitors, [4] immediate heirs,
Whilest to their thirst of rule they win the rout
(That's still the friend of novelty) with hope
Of future freedom, which on every change 99
That greedily, though emptily, expects. [5]
Cæsar, 'tis age in all things breeds neglects,
And princes that will keep old dignity
Must not admit too youthful heirs stand by—
Not their own issue—but so darkly set
As shadows are in picture, to give height
And luster to themselves.
TIB.  We will command
Their rank thoughts down, and with a stricter hand
Than we have yet put forth; their trains must bate,
Their titles, feasts, and factions.
SEJ.  Or your state.
But how, sir, will you work?
TIB.  Confine hem.
SEJ.  No. 110
They are too great, and that too faint a blow

[1] Rumor.  [2] Overconfident.  [3] Granddaughter.  [4] Partners.  [5] Awaits.

To give them now; it would have served
  at first,
When with the weakest touch their
  knot had burst.
But now your care must be, not to de-
  tect[1]
The smallest cord or line of your suspect,
For such, who know the weight of
  princes' fear,
Will, when they find themselves dis-
  covered, rear
Their forces, like seen snakes, that else
  would lie
Rolled in their circles, close.  Naught is
  more high,
Daring, or desperate than offenders
  found;                              120
Where guilt is, rage and courage doth
  abound.
The course must be, to let hem still
  swell up,
Riot, and surfeit on blind Fortune's cup;
Give hem more place, more dignities,
  more style,
Call hem to court, to senate; in the while,
Take from their strength some one or
  twain or more
Of the main fautors[2] (it will fright the
  store[3]),
And by some by-occasion.  Thus, with
  sleight
You shall disarm first, and they, in
  night                              129
Of their ambition, not perceive the train,
Till in the ingine[4] they are caught and
  slain.
Tib. We would not kill, if we knew how
  to save;
  Yet, than a throne, 'tis cheaper give a
  grave.
  Is there no way to bind them by deserts?
Sej. Sir, wolves do change their hair, but
  not their hearts.
  While thus your thought unto a mean
  is tied,
  You neither dare enough, nor do provide.
  All modesty is fond,[5] and chiefly where
  The subject is no less compelled to bear,
  Than praise, his sov'reign's acts.
Tib.                We can no longer  140
  Keep on our mask to thee, our dear
  Sejanus;

Thy thoughts are ours, in all, and we
  but proved
Their voice, in our designs, which by as-
  senting
Hath more confirmed us than if heart'n-
  ing Jove
Had, from his hundred statues, bid us
  strike,
And at the stroke clicked all his marble
  thumbs.
But who shall first be strook?
Sej.                First, Caius Silius;
  He is the most of mark, and most of
  danger—
  In power and reputation equal strong,
  Having commanded an imperial army
  Seven years together, vanquished Sa-
  crovir                            151
  In Germany, and thence obtained to
  wear
  The ornaments triumphal.  His steep
  fall,
  By how much it doth give the weightier
  crack,
  Will send more wounding terror to the
  rest,
  Command them stand aloof, and give
  more way
  To our surprising of the principal.
Tib. But what, Sabinus?
Sej.                Let him grow awhile;
  His fate is not yet ripe.  We must not
  pluck                             159
  At all together, lest we catch ourselves.
  And there's Arruntius too; he only talks.
  But Sosia, Silius' wife, would be wound
  in
  Now, for she hath a fury in her breast
  More than hell ever knew, and would
  be sent
  Thither in time.  Then is there one Cre-
  mutius
  Cordus, a writing fellow, they have got
  To gather notes of the precedent times,
  And make them into annals—a most
  tart
  And bitter spirit, I hear, who, under
  color
  Of praising those, doth tax[6] the present
  state,                            170
  Censures[7] the men, the actions, leaves
  no trick,
  No practice unexamined, parallels

The times, the governments—a professed champion
For the old liberty—

TIB.            A perishing wretch!
As if there were that chaos bred in things,
That laws and liberty would not rather
choose
To be quite broken and ta'en hence by
us
Than have the stain to be preserved by
such.
Have we the means to make these guilty
first?

SEJ. Trust that to me. Let Cæsar, by
his power,                  180
But cause a formal meeting of the senate,
I will have matter and accusers ready.

TIB. But how? Let us consult.

SEJ.            We shall misspend
The time of action. Counsels are unfit
In business where all rest is more per-
nicious
Than rashness can be. Acts of this close
kind
Thrive more by execution than advice.
There is no ling'ring in that work be-
gun,
Which cannot praiséd be, until through
done.

TIB. Our edict shall forthwith command
a court.                   190
While I can live, I will prevent earth's
fury:
Ἐμοῦ θανόντος γαῖα μιχθήτω πυρί.[1]
                     [Exit.]

[Enter] Posthumus.[2]

[Pos.] My Lord Sejanus—

SEJ.           Julius Posthumus,
Come with my wish! What news from
Agrippina's?

Pos. Faith, none. They all lock up them-
selves alate,
Or talk in character;[3] I have not seen
A company so changed. Except they
had
Intelligence by augury of our practice—

SEJ. When were you there?

Pos.     Last night.

SEJ.        And what guests found you?

Pos. Sabinus, Silius (the old list), Arruntius,                   200
Furnius, and Gallus.

SEJ.        Would not these talk?

Pos.                  Little.
And yet we offered choice of argument.[4]
Satrius was with me.

SEJ.       Well. 'Tis guilt enough,
Their often meeting. You forgot t'
extol
The hospitable lady?

Pos.           No; that trick
Was well put home, and had succeeded
too,
But that Sabinus coughed a caution
out;
For she began to swell—

SEJ.         And may she burst!
Julius, I would have you go instantly
Unto the palace of the great Augusta, 210
And, by your kindest friend,[5] get swift
access;
Acquaint her with these meetings. Tell
the words
You brought me, th' other day, of Silius;
Add somewhat to hem. Make her under-
stand
The danger of Sabinus, and the times,
Out of his closeness. Give Arruntius'
words
Of malice against Cæsar; so, to Gallus;
But, above all, to Agrippina. Say,
As you may truly, that her infinite
pride,
Propped with the hopes of her too fruit-
ful womb,             220
With popular studies [6] gapes for sover-
eignty,
And threatens Cæsar. Pray Augusta
then
That for her own, great Cæsar's, and
the pub-
Lic safety, she be pleased to urge these
dangers.
Cæsar is too secure; he must be told,
And best he'll take it from a mother's
tongue.
Alas! What is 't for us to sound, t' ex-
plore,

---

[1] When I am dead, let the earth be overwhelmed with fire.

[2] The name Sejanus is repeated here.

[3] Cipher.

[4] Subject.

[5] Marginal note reads "Mutilia Prisca."

[6] Jonson's questionable rendering of populari-
bus studiis, i.e., "The zeal and devotion of the
people" (Briggs).

To watch, oppose, plot, practice, or pre-
vent,
If he, for whom it is so strongly labored,
Shall, out of greatness and free spirit,
be                                            230
Supinely negligent?   Our city's now
Divided as in time o' th' civil war,
And men forbear not to declare them-
selves
Of Agrippina's party.   Every day
The faction multiplies, and will do more
If not resisted; you can best enlarge it,
As you find audience.   Noble Posthumus,
Commend me to your Prisca, and pray
her
She will solicit this great business
To earnest and most present execu-
tion,                                         240
With all her utmost credit with Augusta.
Pos. I shall not fail in my instructions.
                                    [*Exit.*]
Sej. This second, from his mother, will
well urge
Our late design, and spur on Cæsar's
rage,
Which else might grow remiss.   The way
to put
A prince in blood [1] is to present the
shapes
Of dangers greater than they are, like
late
Or early shadows, and, sometimes, to
feign
Where there are none, only to make him
fear.
His fear will make him cruel, and, once
entered,                                      250
He doth not easily learn to stop, or
spare
Where he may doubt.   This have I
made my rule
To thrust Tiberius into tyranny,
And make him toil to turn aside those
blocks
Which I alone could not remove with
safety.
Drusus once gone, Germanicus' three
sons
Would clog my way, whose guards have
too much faith
To be corrupted, and their mother known
Of too-too unreproved [2] a chastity

[1] *I.e.*, make him angry.
[2] Too completely blameless.

To be attempted as light Livia was.   260
Work then, my art, on Cæsar's fears,
as they
On those they fear, till all my lets [3] be
cleared,
And he in ruins of his house, and hate
Of all his subjects, bury his own state,
When with my peace and safety I will
rise
By making him the public sacrifice.
                                    [*Exit.*]

[SCENE iii.

*A room in Agrippina's house.*]

*Satrius, Natta.*

[Sat.] They are grown exceeding circum-
spect and wary.
Nat.  They have us in the wind; [4] and yet
Arruntius
Cannot contain himself.
Sat.                     Tut, he's not yet
Looked after; there are others more
desired
That are more silent.
Nat.       Here he comes.   Away! [*Exeunt.*]

[*Enter*] *Sabinus, Arruntius, Cordus.*

[Sab.] How is it that these beagles haunt
the house
Of Agrippina?
Arr.               O, they hunt, they hunt!
There is some game here lodged, which
they must rouse,
To make the great ones sport.
Cor.                        Did you observe
How they inveighed gainst Cæsar?
Arr.                             Ay, baits, baits
For us to bite at; would I have my
flesh                                          11
Torn by the public hook, [5] these qualified
hangmen
Should be my company.
Cor.                     Here comes another.
                              [*After passes by.*]

Arr. Ay, there's a man, After the orator!
One that háth phrases, figures, and fine
flowers
To strew his rethoric [6] with, and doth
make haste

[3] From 1605 edn.; original reads *betts.*
[4] They are on our scent.       [6] Rhetoric.
[5] The hangman's hook, used on executed
criminals.

To get him note or name by any offer
Where blood or gain be objects; steeps
   his words,
When he would kill, in artificial tears—
The crocodile of Tiber! Him I love,   20
That man is mine.   He hath my heart
   and voice
When I would curse—he, he.
SAB.                        Contemn the slaves;
Their present lives will be their future
   graves.                        [*Exeunt.*]

[*Enter*] *Silius, Agrippina, Nero, Sosia.*

[SIL.] May 't please your highness not
   forget yourself;
I dare not, with my manners, to attempt
Your trouble farder.
AGR.                        Farewell, noble Silius!
SIL. Most royal princess!
AGR.                        Sosia stays with us?
SIL. She is your servant, and doth owe
   your grace
An honest, but unprofitable love.
AGR. How can that be, when there's no
   gain but virtue's?               30
SIL. You take the moral, not the politic
   sense.
I meant, as she is bold, and free of
   speech,
Earnest to utter what her zealous
   thought
Travails withal, in honor of your house—
Which act, as it is simply borne in her,
Partakes of love and honesty, but may,
By th' over-often and unseasoned use,
Turn to your loss and danger; for your
   state
Is waited on by envies, as by eyes;
And every second guest your tables take
Is a fee'd spy, t' observe who goes, who
   comes,                          41
What conference you have, with whom,
   where, when,
What the discourse is, what the looks,
   the thoughts
Of ev'ry person there, they do extract
And make into a substance.
AGR.                        Hear me, Silius.
Were all Tiberius' body stuck with
   eyes,
And ev'ry wall and hanging in my house
Transparent, as this lawn I wear, or air,
Yea, had Sejanus both his ears as long
As to my inmost closet, I would hate   50

To whisper any thought, or change an
   act,
To be made Juno's rival.   Virtue's forces
Show ever noblest in conspicuous
   courses.
SIL. 'Tis great, and bravely spoken, like
   the spirit
Of Agrippina; yet, your highness knows,
There is nor loss nor shame in provi-
   dence;[1]
Few can, what all should do, beware
   enough.
You may perceive with what officious
   face
Satrius and Natta, Afer and the rest
Visit your house of late, t' inquire the
   secrets,                        60
And with what bold and privileged art
   they rail
Against Augusta, yea, and at Tiberius;
Tell tricks of Livia, and Sejanus—all
T' excite, and call your indignation on,
That they might hear it at more liberty.
AGR. Yo' are too suspicious, Silius.
SIL.                        Pray the gods
I be so, Agrippina; but I fear
Some subtile practice.   They that durst
   to strike
At so exampless [2] and unblamed a life
As that of the renowned Germanicus,   70
Will not sit down with that exploit alone.
"He threatens many that hath injured
   one."
NERO. 'Twere best rip forth their tongues,
   sear out their eyes,
When next they come.
SOS.                        A fit reward for spies.

[*Enter*] *Drusus Ju[nior].*[3]

DRU. Hear you the rumor?
AGR.                        What?
DRU.                        Drusus is dying.
AGR. Dying?
NERO.        That's strange!
AGR.                        Yo' were with him yesternight.
DRU. One met Eudemus the physician,
Sent for but now, who thinks he can-
   not live.
SIL. Thinks?   If 't be arrived at that, he
   knows,
Or none.

_____
[1] Prudence.   [2] Example-less, unexampled.
[3] The names *Agrippina, Nero,* and *Silius* are
here repeated.

AGR.        This 's quick!  What should
   be his disease?                              80
SIL.  Poison, poison—
AGR.                       How, Silius!
NERO.                          What's that?
SIL.  Nay, nothing.   There was late a
   certain blow
   Giv'n o' the face.
NERO.               Ay, to Sejanus?
SIL.                              True.
DRU.  And what of that?
SIL.               I am glad I gave it not.
NERO.  But there is somewhat else?
SIL.                  Yes, private meetings,
   With a great lady at a physician's,
   And a wife turned away—
NERO.          Ha!
SIL.                        Toys, mere toys!
   What wisdom's now i' th' streets?  I'
   th' common mouth?
DRU.  Fears, whisp'rings, tumults, noise,
   I know not what;
   They say the senate sit.
SIL.               I'll thither straight,   90
   And see what's in the forge.
AGR.                       Good Silius, do;
   Sosia and I will in.
SIL.                     Haste you, my lords,
   To visit the sick prince; tender your
   loves
   And sorrows to the people.  This Sejanus,
   Trust my divining soul, hath plots on
   all;
   No tree that stops his prospect but must
   fall.                              [Exeunt.]
     CHORUS—of Musicians.


           ACT III.  [SCENE i.]

              The Senate.

Sejanus, Varro, Latiaris.  Cotta, Afer.
   [Sabinus,] Gallus, Lepidus, Arruntius.
        Præcones,[1] Lictores.[2]
[SEJ.] 'Tis only you must urge against him,
   Varro;
   Nor I nor Cæsar may appear therein,
   Except in your defense, who are the
   consul,
   And, under color of late enmity
   Between your father and his, may better
   do it,
   As free from all suspicion of a practice.

Here be your notes, what points to touch
   at.  Read;
   Be cunning in them.  Afer has them too.
VAR.  But is he summoned?
SEJ.                No.  It was debated
   By Cæsar, and concluded as most fit   10
   To take him unprepared.
AFER.                     And prosecute
   All under name of treason.
VAR.                          I conceive.
SAB.  Drusus being dead, Cæsar will not be
   here.
GAL.  What should the business of this
   senate be?
ARR.  That can my subtile whisperers tell
   you: we
   That are the good-dull-noble lookers-on
   Are only called to keep the marble
   warm.
   What should we do with those deep
   mysteries,
   Proper to these fine heads?  Let them
   alone.
   Our ignorance may, perchance, help us
   be saved                              20
   From whips and Furies.
GAL.               See, see, see their action!
ARR.  Ay, now their heads do travail, now
   they work;
   Their faces run like shittles;[3] they are
   weaving
   Some curious[4] cobweb to catch flies.
SAB.                              Observe,
   They take their places.
ARR.               What, so low?
GAL.                              O, yes,
   They must be seen to flatter Cæsar's
   grief,
   Though but in sitting.
VAR.               Bid us silence.
PRÆ,                              Silence!
VAR.  "Fathers conscript, may this our
   present meeting
   Turn fair and fortunate to the common-
   wealth!"


           [Enter] Silius.[5]

SEJ.  See, Silius enters.
SIL.               Hail, grave fathers!
LIC.                          Stand.   30
   Silius, forbear thy place!
SEN[ATE].                     How!

---

[1] Public criers.     [2] Magistrates' assistants.

[3] Shuttles.          [4] Carefully made.
[5] The word Senate is repeated here.

PRÆ.              Silius, stand forth;
The consul hath to charge thee.

LIC.               Room for Cæsar!

ARR. Is he come too? Nay, then, expect a
trick.

SAB. Silius accused? Sure he will answer
nobly.

*[Enter] Tiberius* [1] *[with Attendants].*

[TIB.] We stand amazéd, fathers, to be-
hold
This general dejection. Wherefore sit
Rome's consuls thus dissolved,[2] as they
had lost
All the remembrance both of style and
place?
It not becomes. No woes are of fit weight
To make the honor of the empire stoop,
Though I, in my peculiar self, may
meet            41
Just reprehension, that so suddenly,
And in so fresh a grief, would greet the
senate,
When private tongues of kinsmen and
allies,
Inspired with comforts, loathly are en-
dured,
The face of men not seen, and scarce the
day,
To thousands that communicate [3] our
loss.
Nor can I argue these of weakness, since
They take but natural ways; yet I must
seek
For stronger aids, and those fair helps
draw out          50
From warm embraces of the common-
wealth.
Our mother, great Augusta, is strook
with time,
Our self impressed with agéd characters,
Drusus is gone, his children young and
babes.
Our aims must now reflect on those that
may
Give timely succor to these present ills,
And are our only glad-surviving hopes,
The noble issue of Germanicus,
Nero and Drusus. Might it please the
consul
Honor them in; they both attend with-
out.          60

I would present them to the senate's
care,
And raise those suns of joy that should
drink up
These floods of sorrow in your drownéd
eyes.

ARR. By Jove, I am not Œdipus enough
To understand this Sphinx.

SAB.         The princes come.

*[Enter]* [4] *Nero, Drusus Junior.*

[TIB.] Approach you, noble Nero, noble
Drusus.
These princes, fathers, when their parent
died,
I gave unto their uncle, with this prayer,
That though h' had proper issue of his
own,
He would no less bring up and foster
these         70
Than that self-blood, and by that act
confirm
Their worths to him and to posterity.
Drusus ta'en hence, I turn my prayers to
you,
And, fore [5] our country and our gods, be-
seech
You take and rule Augustus' nephew's
sons,
Sprung of the noblest ancestors, and so
Accomplish both my duty and your own.
Nero and Drusus, these shall be to you
In place of parents, these your fathers,
these;
And not unfitly, for you are so born    80
As all your good or ill's the common-
wealth's.
Receive them, you strong guardians, and,
blessed gods,
Make all their actions answer to their
bloods;
Let their great titles find increase by
them,
Not they by titles. Set them, as in place,
So in example, above all the Romans;
And may they know no rivals but them-
selves.
Let Fortune give them nothing, but
attend
Upon their virtue, and that still come
forth

[1] The word *Senate* is repeated here.
[2] Discomposed.            [3] Share.
[4] The name of *Tiberius* is repeated here.
[5] Before.

Greater than hope, and better than their
    fame..        90
Relieve me, fathers, with your general
    voice.
SEN. "May all the gods consent to Cæsar's
    wish,
And add to any honors that may crown
The hopeful issue of Germanicus!" [1]
TIB. We thank you, reverend fathers, in
    their right.
ARR. [Aside.] If this were true now! But
    the space, the space
Between the breast and lips! Tiberius'
    heart
Lies a thought farder than another
    man's.
TIB. My comforts are so flowing in my
    joys,
As, in them, all my streams of grief are
    lost,        100
No less than are land-waters in the sea,
Or showers in rivers, though their cause
    was such
As might have sprinkled ev'n the gods
    with tears;
Yet, since the greater doth embrace the
    less,
We covetously obey.
(ARR.          Well acted, Cæsar.)
TIB. And, now I am the happy witness
    made
Of your so much desired affections
To this great issue, I could wish the
    Fates
Would here set peaceful period to my
    days;
However, to my labors I entreat—    110
And beg it of this senate—some fit ease.
(ARR. Laugh, fathers, laugh! Ha' you no
    spleens [2] about you?)
TIB. The burden is too heavy I sustain
On my unwilling shoulders; and I pray
It may be taken off, and reconferred
Upon the consuls, or some other Roman,
More able and more worthy.
(ARR.          Laugh on still!
SAB. Why, this doth render all the rest
    suspected!
GAL. It poisons all.
ARR.         O, do you taste it then?

SAB. It takes away my faith to anything
He shall hereafter speak.
ARR.         Ay, to pray that,   121
Which would be to his head as hot as
    thunder,
Gainst which he wears that charm,[3]
    should but the court
Receive him at his word.
GAL.           Hear!)
TIB.           For myself
I know my weakness, and so little covet,
Like some gone past, the weight that will
    oppress me,
As my ambition is the counterpoint.[4]
(ARR. Finely maintained; good still!)
SEJ.         But Rome, whose blood,
Whose nerves, whose life, whose very
    frame relies
On Cæsar's strength, no less than heaven
    on Atlas,    130
Cannot admit it but with general ruin.
(ARR. Ah, are you there to bring him off?)
SEJ.          Let Cæsar
No more then urge a point so contrary
To Cæsar's greatness, the grieved sen-
    ate's vows,
Or Rome's necessity.
(GAL.          He comes about.
ARR. More nimbly than Vertumnus.)
TIB.          For the public,
I may be drawn to show I can neglect
All private aims, though I affect my
    rest;
But, if the senate still command me
    serve,
I must be glad to practice my obedience.
(ARR. You must and will, sir. We do
    know it.)
SEN.         "Cæsar,   141
Live long and happy, great and royal
    Cæsar;
The gods preserve thee and thy modesty,
Thy wisdom and thy innocence!" [5]
(ARR.         Where is 't?
The prayer is made before the subject.)
SEN.          "Guard
His meekness, Jove, his piety, his care,
His bounty—"
ARR. [Aside.]    And his subtilty, I'll put
    in;

---

[1] Jonson's marginal note reads, "A form of
speaking they had."
[2] Supposed seat of the emotions such as
laughter.

[3] Jonson's marginal note reads, "A wreath
of laurel."    [4] Opposite.
[5] Jonson's marginal note reads, "Another
form."

Yet he'll keep that himself, without the
gods.
All prayers are vain for him.

TIB.                            We will not hold
Your patience, fathers, with long answer,
but                                                       150
Shall still contend [1] to be what you de-
sire,
And work to satisfy so great a hope.
Proceed to your affairs.

ARR. [*Aside.*]      Now, Silius, guard thee;
The curtain's drawing. Afer advanceth.

PRÆ.                                       Silence!

AFER. Cite Caius Silius.

PRÆ.                            Caius Silius!

SIL.                                          Here.

AFER. The triumph that thou hadst in
Germany
For thy late victory on Sacrovir,
Thou hast enjoyed so freely, Caius Silius,
As no man it envied thee; nor would
Cæsar
Or Rome admit that thou wert then de-
frauded                                                160
Of any honors thy deserts could claim
In the fair service of the commonwealth;
But now, if after all their loves and
graces
(Thy actions and their courses being dis-
covered)
It shall appear to Cæsar and this senate,
Thou hast defiled those glories with thy
crimes—

SIL. Crimes?

AFER.            Patience, Silius.

SIL.                    Tell thy moil [2] of patience;
I am a Roman. What are my crimes?
Proclaim them.
Am I too rich, too honest for the times?
Have I or treasure, jewels, land, or
houses                                                  170
That some informer gapes for?  Is my
strength
Too much to be admitted, or my knowl-
edge?
These now are crimes.

AFER.                    Nay, Silius, if the name
Of crime so touch thee, with what impotence
Wilt thou endure the matter to be
searched?

SIL. I tell thee, Afer, with more scorn than
fear:

Employ your mercenary tongue and art.
Where's my accuser?

VAR.                            Here.

ARR. [*Aside.*]            Varro? The consul?
Is he thrust in?

VAR.                    'Tis I accuse thee, Silius.
Against the majesty of Rome and
Cæsar,                                                  180
I do pronounce thee here a guilty cause,
First, of beginning and occasioning,
Next, drawing out the war in Gallia,
For which thou late triumph'st; dissem-
bling long
That Sacrovir to be an enemy,
Only to make thy entertainment [3] more,
Whilst thou and thy wife Sosia polled [4]
the province—
Wherein, with sordid-base desire of gain,
Thou hast discredited thy actions' worth,
And been a traitor to the state.

SIL.                            Thou liest!  190

ARR. [*Aside.*] I thank thee, Silius; speak
so still and often.

VAR. If I not prove it, Cæsar, but injustly
Have called him into trial, here I bind
Myself to suffer what I claim gainst him,
And yield to have what I have spoke,
confirmed
By judgment of the court and all good
men.

SIL. Cæsar, I crave to have my cause
deferred,
Till this man's consulship be out.

TIB.                            We cannot,
Nor may we grant it.

SIL.                    Why?  Shall he design [5]
My day of trial?  Is he my accuser?  200
And must he be my judge?

TIB.                            It hath been usual,
And is a right that custom hath allowed
The magistrate, to call forth private men
And to appoint their day, which privilege
We may not in the consul see infringed,
By whose deep watches and industrious
care
It is so labored, as the commonwealth
Receive no loss, by any oblique course.

SIL. Cæsar, thy fraud is worse than violence.

TIB. Silius, mistake us not; we dare not
use                                                      210

[1] Strive.                    [2] Mule.

[3] Reward, proceeds.
[4] Plundered by extortion.
[5] Designate.

The credit of the consul to thy wrong,
But only do preserve his place and power
So far as it concerns the dignity
And honor of the state.

ARR.                 Believe him, Silius.

COT. Why, so he may, Arruntius.

ARR.                 I say so;
And he may choose too.

TIB.                By the Capitol
And all our gods, but that the dear
    republic,
Our sacred laws, and just authority
Are interested [1] therein, I should be
    silent.

AFER. Please Cæsar to give way unto his
    trial.                        220
He shall have justice.

SIL.           Nay, I shall have law;
Shall I not, Afer? Speak!

AFER.        Would you have mo[re?] [2]

SIL. No, my well-spoken man, I would no
    more;
Nor less, might I enjoy it natural,
Not taught to speak unto your present
    ends,
Free from thine, his, and all your unkind
    handling,
Furious enforcing, most unjust pre-
    suming,
Malicious and manifold applying,
Foul wresting, and impossible construc-
    tion.

AFER. He raves, he raves!

SIL.         Thou durst not tell me so,    230
Hadst thou not Cæsar's warrant. I can
    see
Whose power condemns me.

VAR.           This betrays his spirit;
This doth enough declare him what he is.

SIL. What am I? Speak.

VAR.          An enemy to the state.

SIL. Because I am an enemy to thee,
And such corrupted ministers o' the
    state,
That here art made a present instru-
    ment
To gratify it with thine own disgrace.

SEJ. This, to the consul, is most insolent,
And impious!

SIL.      Ay, take part. Reveal yourselves.
Alas! I scent not your confed'racies,   241

Your plots, and combinations? I not
    know
Minion Sejanus hates me, and that all
This boast of law and law is but a form,
A net of Vulcan's filing, a mere ingine
To take that life by a pretext of justice,
Which you pursue in malice? I want
    brain
Or nostril to persuade me that your ends
And purposes are made to what they are,
Before my answer? O, you equal gods,
Whose justice not a world of wolf-turned
    men                             251
Shall make me to accuse (howe'er pro-
    voke[d]),
Have I for this so oft engaged myself?
Stood in the heat and fervor of a fight,
When Phœbus sooner hath forsook the
    day
Than I the field, against the blue-eyed
    Gauls,
And crispéd [3] Germans, when our Roman
    eagles
Have fanned the fire with their laboring
    wings,
And no blow dealt that left not death
    behind it;
When I have charged, alone, into the
    troops                           260
Of curled Sicambrians, routed them, and
    came
Not off with backward ensigns of a slave,
But forward marks, wounds on my breast
    and face,
Were meant to thee, O Cæsar, and thy
    Rome?
And have I this return? Did I, for this,
Perform so noble and so brave defeat
On Sacrovir? O Jove, let it become me
To boast my deeds, when he whom they
    concern
Shall thus forget them.

AFER.           Silius, Silius,
These are the common customs of thy
    blood                          270
When it is high with wine, as now with
    rage.
This well agrees with that intemperate
    vaunt
Thou lately mad'st at Agrippina's table
That, when all other of the troops were
    prone
To fall into rebellion, only yours

---

[1] Concerned.
[2] Remainder of the word is dropped out in the original.
[3] Curled-haired.

Remained in their obedience. You were
   he
That saved the empire, which had then
   been lost
Had but your legions there rebelled or
   mutined; [1]
Your virtue met and fronted every peril.
You gave to Cæsar and to Rome their
   surety.            280
Their name, their strength, their spirit,
   and their state,
Their being was a donative from you.
ARR. [*Aside.*] Well worded, and most like
   an orator.
TIB. Is this true, Silius?
SIL.          Save thy question, Cæsar;
   Thy spy of famous credit hath affirmed
   it.
ARR. [*Aside.*] Excellent Roman!
SAB. [*Aside.*]     He doth answer stoutly.
SEJ. If this be so, there needs no farder
   cause
Of crime against him.
VAR.         What can more impeach
   The royal dignity and state of Cæsar
   Than to be urgéd with a benefit   290
He cannot pay?
COT.       In this, all Cæsar's fortune
   Is made unequal to the courtesy.
LAT. His means are clean destroyed that
   should requite.
GAL. [*Ironically.*] Nothing is great enough
   for Silius' merit.
ARR. [*Aside.*] Gallus on that side too?
SIL.          Come, do not hunt
   And labor so about for circumstance
To make him guilty whom you have
   foredoomed.
Take shorter ways; I'll meet your pur-
   poses.
The words were mine, and more I now
   will say:
Since I have done thee that great service,
   Cæsar,           300
Thou still hast feared me; and, in place
   of grace,
Returned me hatred; so soon all best
   turns,
With doubtful [2] princes, turn deep in-
   juries
In estimation, when they greater rise
Than can be answered. Benefits, with
   you,

Are of no longer pleasure than you can
With ease restore them; that transcended
   once,
Your studies are not how to thank, but
   kill.
It is your nature to have all men slaves
To you, but you acknowledging to none.
The means that makes your greatness
   must not come       311
In mention of it; if it do, it takes
So much away, you think; and that
   which helped
Shall soonest perish, if it stand in eye,
Where it may front [3] or but upbraid the
   high.
COT. Suffer him speak no more.
VAR.          Note but his spirit.
AFER. This shows him in the rest.
LAT.         Let him be censured.[4]
SEJ. He hath spoke enough to prove him
   Cæsar's foe.
COT. His thoughts look through his words.
SEJ.         A censure!
SIL.               Stay,
   Stay, most officious senate, I shall
     straight         320
Delude thy fury. Silius hath not placed
His guards within him, against Fortune's
   spite,
So weakly but he can escape your gripe
That are but hands of Fortune. She
   herself,
When Virtue doth oppose, must lose her
   threats.
All that can happen in humanity,
The frown of Cæsar, proud Sejanus'
   hatred,
Base Varro's spleen, and Afer's bloodying
   tongue,
The senate's servile flattery, and these
Mustered to kill, I am fortified against,
And can look down upon; they are be-
   neath me.         331
It is not life whereof I stand enamored,
Nor shall my end make me accuse my
   fate.
The coward and the valiant man must
   fall;
Only the cause, and manner how, dis-
   cerns them[5]—
Which then are gladdest, when they cost
   us dearest.

[1] Mutinied.      [2] Suspicious.
[3] Affront.                   [4] Judged.
[5] Distinguishes them from each other.

Romans, if any here be in this senate,
Would know to mock Tiberius' tyranny,
Look upon Silius, and so learn to die.
                   [*Stabs himself.*] [1]

VAR. O desperate act!
ARR. [*Aside.*]     An honorable hand!   340
TIB. Look, is he dead?
SAB. [*Aside.*]        'Twas nobly strook, and
    home.
ARR. [*Aside.*] My thought did prompt him
    to it. Farewell, Silius!
Be famous ever for thy great example.
TIB. We are not pleased in this sad acci-
    dent,
That thus hath stalléd,[2] and abused our
    mercy,
Intended to preserve thee, noble Roman,
And to prevent thy hopes.
ARR. [*Aside.*]         Excellent wolf!
Now he is full, he howls.
SEJ.          Cæsar doth wrong
His dignity and safety thus to mourn
The deserved end of so professed a
    traitor,                       350
And doth, by this his lenity, instruct
Others as factious to the like offense.
TIB. The confiscation merely of his state
Had been enough.
ARR. [*Aside.*]      O, that was gaped for
    then?
VAR. Remove the body.
SEJ.          Let citation
Go out for Sosia.
GAL.         Let her be proscribed;
And for the goods, I think it fit that half
Go to the treasure,[3] half unto the chil-
    dren.
LEP. With leave of Cæsar, I would think
    that fourth
Part, which the law doth cast on the
    informers,                      360
Should be enough; the rest go to the
    children—
Wherein the prince shall show humanity
And bounty, not to force them by their
    want,
Which in their parent's trespass they
    deserved,
To take ill courses.
TIB.          It shall please us.
ARR. [*Aside.*]            Ay,
Out of necessity. This Lepidus

Is grave and honest, and I have observed
A moderation still in all his censures.
SAB. [*Aside.*] And bending to the better.—
    Stay, who's this?
Cremutius Cordus? What? Is he brought
    in?                            370
ARR. [*Aside.*] More blood unto the ban-
    quet? Noble Cordus,
    I wish thee good; be as thy writings, free
And honest.
TIB.        What is he?
SEJ.             For th' annals, Cæsar.

[*Enter*] *Præco*[*nes*], *Cordus* [*with Guards*],
                      *Satrius, Natta.*

[PRÆ.] Cremutius Cordus!
COR.        Here.
PRÆ.           Satrius Secundus,
Pinnarius Natta, you are his accusers.
ARR. [*Aside.*] Two of Sejanus' blood-
    hounds, whom he breeds
With human flesh, to bay at citizens.
AFER. Stand forth before the senate, and
    confront him.
SAT. I do accuse thee here, Cremutius
    Cordus,
To be a man factious and dangerous, 380
A sower of sedition in the state,
A turbulent and discontented spirit,
Which I will prove from thine own writ-
    ings here,
The annals thou hast published, where
    thou bit'st
The present age, and with a viper's
    tooth,
Being a member of it, dar'st that ill
Which never yet degenerous [4] bastard
    did
Upon his parent.
NAT.        To this I subscribe,
And, forth [5] a world of more particu-
    lars,
Instance in only one: comparing men
And times, thou praisest Brutus, and
    affirm'st                      391
That Cassius was the last of all the
    Romans.
COT. How! What are we then?
VAR.         What is Cæsar? Nothing?
AFER. My lords, this strikes at every
    Roman's private,[6]

---

[1] From 1692 edn.            [3] Treasury.
[2] Forestalled.                 [4] Degenerate.        [6] Private interest.
                                       [5] From.

In whom reigns gentry and estate of
  spirit,[1]
To have a Brutus brought in parallel,
A parricide, an enemy of his country,
Ranked, and preferred to any real worth
That Rome now holds.  This is most
  strangely invective,
Most full of spite, and insolent up-
  braiding.                                    400
Nor is 't the time alone is here disprized,[2]
But the whole man of time, yea, Cæsar's
  self,
Brought in disvalue; and he aimed at
  most
By oblique glance of his licentious pen.
Cæsar, if Cassius were the last of Ro-
  mans,
Thou hast no name.
TIB.    Let's hear him answer.  Silence!
COR.  So innocent I am of fact,[3] my lords,
As but my words are argued, yet those
  words
Not reaching either prince or prince's
  parent—
The which your law of treason compre-
  hends.                                       410
Brutus and Cassius I am charged t' have
  praised,
Whose deeds, when many more besides
  myself
Have writ, not one hath mentioned with-
  out honor.
Great Titus Livius, great for eloquence
And faith amongst us, in his history
With so great praises Pompey did extol,
As oft Augustus called him a Pompeian:
Yet this not hurt their friendship.  In his
  book
He often names Scipio, Afranius,
Yea, the same Cassius, and this Brutus
  too,                                         420
As worthi'st men—not thieves and par-
  ricides,
Which notes upon their fames are now
  imposed.
Asinius Pollio's writings quite throughout
Give them a noble memory; so Messala
Renowned his general, Cassius; yet both
  these
Lived with Augustus, full of wealth and
  honors.

To Cicero's book, where Cato was heaved
  up
Equal with heaven, what else did Cæsar
  answer,
Being then dictator, but with a penned
  oration,
As if before the judges?  Do but see    430
Antonius' letters; read but Brutus'
  pleadings—
What vile reproach they hold against
  Augustus,
False, I confess, but with much bitter-
  ness.
The epigrams of Bibaculus and Catullus
Are read, full stuffed with spite of both
  the Cæsars;
Yet deified Julius, and no less Augustus,
Both bore them, and contemned them.
  I not know,
Promptly to speak it, whether done with
  more
Temper, or wisdom; for such obloquies
If they despiséd be, they die suppressed;
But, if with rage acknowledged, they are
  confessed.                                   441
The Greeks I slip,[4] whose license not
  alone
But also lust did scape unpunishéd,
Or where someone, by chance, exception
  took,
He words with words revenged.  But in
  my work
What could be aimed more free,[5] or
  farder off
From the time's scandal, than to write of
  those
Whom death from grace or hatred had
  exempted?
Did I, with Brutus and with Cassius,
Armed and possessed of the Philippi
  fields,                                       450
Incense the people in the civil cause,
With dangerous speeches?  Or do they,
  being slain
Seventy years since, as by their images,
Which not the conqueror hath defaced,
  appears,
Retain that guilty memory with writers?
Posterity pays every man his honor.
Nor shall there want, though I con-
  demnéd am,
That [6] will not only Cassius well approve,

---

[1] Gentle blood and spirit befitting one of rank.
[2] Contemptuously depreciated.
[3] Deed.

[4] Pass over.                    [6] Those who.
[5] Innocently.

And of great Brutus' honor mindful be,
But that will also mention make of
    me.                                    460
ARR. [*Aside.*] Freely and nobly spoken!
SAB. [*Aside.*]       With good temper;
    I like him, that he is not moved with
    passion.
ARR. [*Aside.*] He puts hem to their whis-
    per.
TIB.      Take him hence;
    We shall determine of him at next sit-
    ting.
              [*Exeunt Guards with Cordus.*]
COT. Meantime, give order that his books
    be burnt,
    To the ædiles.
SEJ.      You have well advised.
AFER. It fits not such licentious things
    should live
    T' upbraid the age.
ARR.      If th' age were good, they might.
LAT. Let hem be burnt.
GAL.      All sought and burnt today.
PRÆ. The court is up; lictors, resume the
    fasces.                                    470
[*Exeunt All but*] *Arruntius, Sabinus, Lepidus.*
[ARR.] Let hem be burnt! O, how ridic-
    ulous
    Appears the senate's brainless diligence,
    Who think they can, with present power,
    extinguish
    The memory of all succeeding times!
SAB. 'Tis true, when, contrary, the punish-
    ment
    Of wit doth make th' authority in-
    crease.
    Nor do they aught, that use this cruelty
    Of interdiction, and this rage of burn-
    ing,
    But purchase to themselves rebuke and
    shame,
    And to the writers an eternal name.  480
LEP. It is an argument the times are
    sore,
    When virtue cannot safely be advanced,
    Nor vice reproved.
ARR.        Ay, noble Lepidus;
    Augustus well foresaw what we should
    suffer
    Under Tiberius, when he did pronounce
    The Roman race most wretched, that
    should live
    Between so slow jaws, and so long
    a-bruising.               [*Exeunt.*]

[SCENE ii.

*A room in the palace.*]

*Tiberius, Sejanus.*

[TIB.] This business hath succeeded well,
    Sejanus,
    And quite removed all jealousy of prac-
    tice
    Gainst Agrippina and our nephews. Now
    We must bethink us how to plant our in-
    gines
    For th' other pair, Sabinus and Arrun-
    tius,
    And Gallus too; howe'er he flatter us,
    His heart we know.
SEJ.      Give it some respite, Cæsar.
    Time shall mature and bring to perfect
    crown
    What we, with so good vultures,[1] have
    begun;
    Sabinus shall be next.
TIB.        Rather Arruntius.  10
SEJ. By any means, preserve him. His
    frank tongue,
    Being lent the reins, will take away all
    thought
    Of malice, in your course against the
    rest.
    We must keep him to stalk with.
TIB.        Dearest head,
    To thy most fortunate design I yield it.
SEJ. Sir, I have been so long trained up
    in grace,
    First with your father, great Augustus,
    since
    With your most happy bounties so
    familiar,
    As I not sooner would commit my
    hopes
    Or wishes to the gods than to your
    ears.                                    20
    Nor have I ever yet been covetous
    Of overbright and dazzling honors—
    rather
    To watch and travail in great Cæsar's
    safety,
    With the most common soldier.
TIB.         'Tis confessed.
SEJ. The only gain, and which I count
    most fair
    Of all my fortunes, is that mighty Cæsar

---

[1] *I.e.*, auspiciously, with reference to augury
by means of birds.

Hath thought me worthy his alliance.[1]
Hence
Begin my hopes.
TIB.            H'mh?
SEJ.                      I have heard Augustus,
In the bestowing of his daughter, thought
But even [2] of gentlemen of Rome; if
    so—                                          30
I know not how to hope so great a favor—
But, if a husband should be sought for
    Livia,
And I be had in mind, as Cæsar's friend,
I would but use the glory of the kindred.
It should not make me slothful, or less
    caring
For Cæsar's state; it were enough to me
It did confirm and strengthen my weak
    house
Against the now-unequal opposition
Of Agrippina; and for dear regard
Unto my children, this I wish. Myself 40
Have no ambition farder than to end
My days in service of so dear a master.
TIB. We cannot but commend thy piety,
Most loved Sejanus, in acknowledging
Those bounties, which we, faintly, such
    remember.
But to thy suit. The rest of mortal men,
In all their drifts and counsels, pursue
    profit;
Princes alone are of a different sort,
Directing their main actions still to
    fame.
We therefore will take time to think and
    answer.                                       50
For Livia she can best, herself, resolve
If she will marry, after Drusus, or
Continue in the family; besides,
She hath a mother, and a grandame yet,
Whose nearer counsels she may guide
    her by;
But I will simply deal. That enmity
Thou fear'st in Agrippina would burn
    more,
If Livia's marriage should, as 'twere in
    parts,
Divide th' imperial house; an emulation
Between the women might break forth,
    and discord                                   60
Ruin the sons and nephews on both
    hands.

What if it cause some present difference?
Thou art not safe, Sejanus, if thou
    prove [3] it.
Canst thou believe that Livia, first the
    wife
To Caius Cæsar, then my Drusus, now
Will be contented to grow old with thee,
Born but a private gentleman of Rome,
And raise thee with her loss, if not her
    shame?
Or, say that I should wish it, cans't
    thou think
The senate or the people (who have
    seen                                          70
Her brother, father, and our ancestors
In highest place of empire) will endure it?
The state thou hold'st already, is in
    talk;
Men murmur at thy greatness; and the
    nobles
Stick not, in public, to upbraid thy
    climbing
Above our father's favors, or thy scale,
And dare accuse me, from their hate to
    thee.
Be wise, dear friend. We would not hide
    these things,
For friendship's dear respect. Nor will
    we stand
Adverse to thine or Livia's design-
    ments.                                        80
What we have purposed to thee, in our
    thought,
And with what near degrees of love to
    bind thee,
And make thee equal to us, for the pres-
    ent
We will forbear to speak. Only, thus
    much
Believe, our loved Sejanus, we not know
That height in blood or honor, which
    thy virtue
And mind to us may not aspire [4] with
    merit.
And this we'll publish on all watched
    occasion
The senate or the people shall present.
SEJ. I am restored, and to my sense
    again.,                                       90
Which I had lost in this so blinding suit.
Cæsar hath taught me better to refuse
Than I knew how to ask. How pleaseth
    Cæsar

---

[1] Jonson's marginal note reads, "His daughter
was betrothed to Claudius his son."
[2] Without impartiality.

[3] Try, attempt.                    [4] Aspire to.

T' embrace my late advice for leaving
    Rome?

TIB.  We are resolved.

SEJ.          Here are some motives more,
                            [Gives him a paper.]
Which I have thought on since, may
    more confirm.

TIB. Careful Sejanus!  We will straight
    peruse them.
Go forward in our main design, and
    prosper.                     [Exit.]

SEJ. If those but take, I shall.  Dull, heavy
    Cæsar!
Wouldst thou tell me tby favors were
    made crimes,                          100
And that my fortunes were esteemed thy
    faults,
That thou for me wert hated, and not
    think
I would with wingéd haste prevent that
    change,
When thou might'st win all to thyself
    again
By forfeiture of me?  Did those fond
    words
Fly swifter from thy lips than this my
    brain,
This sparkling forge, created me an
    armor
T' encounter chance and thee?  Well,
    read my charms,
And may they lay that hold upon thy
    senses,
As thou hadst snuffed up hemlock, or
    ta'en down                          110
The juice of poppy and of mandrakes.
    Sleep,
Voluptuous Cæsar, and security
Seize on thy stupid powers, and leave
    them dead
To public cares; awake but to thy
    lusts,
The strength of which makes thy li-
    bidinous soul
Itch to leave Rome—and I have thrust
    it on,
With blaming of the city business,
The multitude of suits, the confluence
Of suitors, then their importunacies,
The manifold distractions he must
    suffer,                          120
Besides ill-rumors, envies, and re-
    proaches,
All which a quiet and retiréd life,

Larded with ease and pleasure, did
    avoid,
And yet for any weighty and great
    affair,
The fittest place to give the soundest
    counsels.
By this shall I remove him both from
    thought
And knowledge of his own most dear
    affairs;
Draw all despatches through my private
    hands;
Know his designments, and pursue mine
    own;
Make mine own strengths by giving suits
    and places,                          130
Conferring dignities and offices;
And these that hate me now, wanting
    access
To him, will make their envy none, or
    less;
For, when they see me arbiter of all,
They must observe, or else with Cæsar
    fall.                          [Exit.]

[SCENE iii.

*Another room in the palace.*]

*Tiberius, Servus.*[1]

[TIB.] To marry Livia?  Will no less,
    Sejanus,
Content thy aims?  No lower object?
    Well!
Thou know'st how thou art wrought into
    our trust,
Woven in our design, and think'st we
    must
Now use thee, whatso'er thy projects
    are.
'Tis true—but yet with caution and fit
    care.
And, now we better think—who's there
    within?

[*Enter Servus.*]

SER. Cæsar?

TIB. [*Aside.*]     To leave our journey off
    were sin
Gainst our decreed delights, and would
    appear
Doubt, or, what less becomes a prince,
    low fear.                          20

_____
[1] *I.e.,* a servant, who enters later.

Yet doubt hath law, and fears have their
   excuse,
Where princes' states plead necessary
   use,
As ours doth now more in Sejanus'
   pride
Than all fell[1] Agrippina's hates beside.
Those are the dreadful enemies we raise
With favors and make dangerous with
   praise;
The injured by us may have will alike,
But 'tis the favorite hath the power to
   strike;
And fury ever boils more high and
   strong,
Heat'[2] with ambition, than revenge of
   wrong.                                     20
'Tis then a part of supreme skill, to
   grace
No man too much, but hold a certain
   space
Between th' ascender's rise and thine
   own flat,[3]
Lest, when all rounds[4] be reached, his
   aim be that.
'Tis thought—[To Servus.]  Is Macro in
   the palace?  See.
If not, go seek him, to come to us.—[Exit
   Servus.]  He
Must be the organ we must work by
   now,
Though none less apt for trust; need
   doth allow
What choice would not.  I have heard
   that aconite,
Being timely taken, hath a healing
   might                                      30
Against the scorpion's stroke; the proof
   we'll give,
That, while two poisons wrastle, we may
   live.
He hath a spirit too working[5] to be
   used
But to th' encounter of his like; ex-
   cused
Are wiser sov'reigns then, that raise
   one ill
Against another, and both safely kill.
The prince that feeds great natures,
   they will sway him;
Who nourisheth a lion, must obey him.—

[Enter Servus with] Macro.[6]

Macro, we sent for you.
MAC.                    I heard so, Cæsar.   39
TIB. Leave us awhile.—        [Exit Servus.]
       When you shall know, good Macro,
The causes of our sending and the ends,
You will then hearken nearer, and be
   pleased
You stand so high both in our choice and
   trust.
MAC. The humblest place in Cæsar's
   choice or trust
May make glad Macro proud, with-
   out ambition
Save to do Cæsar service.
TIB.                    Leave our courtings.
We are in purpose, Macro, to depart
The city for a time, and see Campania,
Not for our pleasures, but to dedicate
A pair of temples, one to Jupiter    50
At Capua, th' other at Nola to Augustus,
In which great work, perhaps, our stay
   will be
Beyond our will produced.[7]  Now, since
   we are
Not ignorant what danger may be born
Out of our shortest absence, in a state
So subject unto envy, and embroiled
With hate and faction, we have thought
   on thee,
Amongst a field of Romans, worthiest
   Macro,
To be our eye and ear, to keep strict
   watch
On Agrippina, Nero, Drusus, ay,    60
And on Sejanus—not that we distrust
His loyalty, or do repent one grace
Of all that heap we have conferred on
   him
(For that were to disparage our elec-
   tion,[8]
And call that judgment now in doubt,
   which then
Seemed as unquestioned as an oracle);
But greatness hath his cankers.  Worms
   and moths
Breed out of too fit matter, in the things
Which after they consume, transferring
   quite
The substance of their makers int'
   themselves.                               70

---

[1] Fierce.                    [4] I.e., of the ladder.
[2] Heated.                    [5] Active.
[3] Level.

[6] The name Tiberius is repeated here.
[7] Prolonged.                    [8] Selection.

Macro is sharp, and apprehends.  Besides,
I know him subtile, close, wise, and well-read
In man, and his large nature; he hath studied
Affections, passions, knows their springs, their ends,
Which way and whether they will work; 'tis proof
Enough of his great merit that we trust him.
Then to a point (because our conference
Cannot be long without suspicion):
Here, Macro, we assign thee both to spy,
Inform, and chastise; think, and use thy means,          80
Thy ministers, what, where, on whom thou wilt;
Explore, plot, practice.  All thou dost in this
Shall be, as if the senate or the laws
Had giv'n it privilege, and thou thence styled
The savior both of Cæsar and of Rome,
We will not take thy answer but in act,
Whereto, as thou proceed'st, we hope to hear
By trusted messengers.  If 't be inquired
Wherefore we called you, say you have in charge
To see our chariots ready, and our horse.          90
Be still our loved and, shortly, honored
Macro.          [*Exit.*]
MAC. I will not ask why Cæsar bids do this,
But joy that he bids me.  It is the bliss
Of courts to be employed, no matter how;
A prince's power makes all his actions virtue.
We whom he works by are dumb instruments,
To do, but not inquire; his great intents
Are to be served, not searched.  Yet, as that bow
Is most in hand whose owner best doth know
T' affect [1] his aims, so let that statesman hope          100
Most use, most price, can hit his prince's scope.[2]

Nor must he look at what or whom to strike,
But loose [3] at all; each mark must be alike.
Were it to plot against the fame, the life
Of one with whom I twinned; remove a wife
From my warm side, as loved as is the air;
Practice away each parent; draw mine heir
In compass,[4] though but one; work all my kin
To swift perdition; leave no untrained engine [5]
For friendship, or for innocence; nay, make          110
The gods all guilty; I would undertake
This, being imposed me, both with gain and ease.
The way to rise is to obey and please.
He that will thrive in state, he must neglect
The trodden paths that truth and right respect,
And prove new, wilder ways; for virtue there
Is not that narrow thing she is elsewhere.
Men's fortune there is virtue; reason, their will;
Their license, law; and their observance, skill.
Occasion is their foil; conscience, their stain;          120
Profit, their luster; and what else is, vain.
If then it be the lust of Cæsar's power
T' have raised Sejanus up, and in an hour
O'erturn him, tumbling, down from height of all,
We are his ready engine, and his fall
May be our rise.  It is no uncouth [6] thing
To see fresh buildings from old ruins spring.          [*Exit.*]

CHORUS—*of Musicians.*

---

[1] Know how to effect.          [2] Mark.

[3] Shoot.
[4] Into a trap.
[5] Instrument.
[6] Unknown.

Act IV. [Scene i.

*A room in Agrippina's house.*]

*Gallus, Agrippina, Nero, Drusus, Caligula.*[1]

[Gal.] You must have patience, royal Agrippina.

Agr. I must have vengeance first; and that were nectar
  Unto my famished spirits. O, my fortune,
  Let it be sudden thou prepar'st against me;
  Strike all my powers of understanding blind,
  And ignorant of destiny to come!
  Let me not fear, that cannot hope.

Gal.                       Dear princess,
  These tyrannies[2] on yourself are worse than Cæsar's.

Agr. Is this the happiness of being born great?
  Still to be aimed at? Still to be suspected?                                    10
  To live the subject of all jealousies?
  At least the color[3] made, if not the ground,
  To every painted danger? Who would not
  Choose once to fall than thus to hang forever?

Gal. You might be safe if you would—

Agr.               What, my Gallus?
  Be lewd Sejanus' strumpet? Or the bawd
  To Cæsar's lusts he now is gone to practice?
  Not these are safe, where nothing is. Yourself,
  While thus you stand but by me, are not safe.
  Was Silius safe? Or the good Sosia safe?                                        20
  Or was my niece, dear Claudia Pulchra, safe?
  Or innocent Furnius? They that latest have
  (By being made guilty) added reputation
  To Afer's eloquence? O, foolish friends,
  Could not so fresh example warn your loves,
  But you must buy my favors with that loss

Unto yourselves, and when you might perceive
  That Cæsar's cause of raging must forsake him
  Before his will? Away, good Gallus, leave me.
  Here to be seen is danger; to speak, treason;                                    30
  To do me least observance is called faction.
  You are unhappy in me, and I in all.
  Where are my sons, Nero and Drusus? We
  Are they be shot at; let us fall apart,
  Not in our ruins sepulcher our friends.
  Or shall we do some action, like offense,[4]
  To mock their studies that would make us faulty,
  And frustrate practice by preventing[5] it?
  The danger's like; for what they can contrive
  They will make good. No innocence is safe                                        40
  When power contests; nor can they trespass more,
  Whose only being was all crime before.

[*Enter Nero, Drusus, and Caligula.*]

Nero. You hear Sejanus is come back from Cæsar?

Gal. No. How? Disgraced?

Dru.               More gracéd now than ever.

Gal. By what mischance?

Cal.               A fortune like enough
  Once to be bad.

Dru.               But turned too good to both.

Gal. What was 't?

Nero.               Tiberius sitting at his meat,
  In a farmhouse they call Spelunca, sited
  By the seaside, among the Fundane hills,
  Within a natural cave, part of the grot   50
  About the entry fell and overwhelmed
  Some of the waiters; others ran away;
  Only Sejanus with his knees, hands, face,
  O'erhanging Cæsar, did oppose himself
  To the remaining ruins, and was found
  In that so laboring posture by the soldiers
  That came to succor him. With which adventure

---

[1] Last three enter later.        [2] Cruelties.
[3] Pretext, although double meanings run through the sentence.

[4] Like what we are charged with.
[5] Anticipating.

He hath so fixed himself in Cæsar's trust
As thunder cannot move him, and is
  come
With all the height of Cæsar's praise to
  Rome.                60
AGR. And power to turn those ruins all
  on us,
And bury whole posterities beneath
  them.
Nero and Drusus and Caligula,
Your places are the next, and therefore
  most
In their offense.  Think on your birth
  and blood,
Awake your spirits, meet their violence;
'Tis princely when a tyran doth oppose,
And is a fortune sent to exercise
Your virtue, as the wind doth try strong
  trees,
Who by vexation [1] grow more sound and
  firm.                70
After your father's fall, and uncle's fate,
What can you hope, but all the change
  of stroke
That force or sleight can give?  Then
  stand upright;
And, though you do not act, yet suffer
  nobly.
Be worthy of my womb, and take strong
  cheer;
What we do know will come, we should
  not fear.        [*Exeunt.*]

[SCENE ii.

*A room in the palace.*]

*Macro.*

[MAC.] Returned so soon?  Renewed in
  trust and grace?
Is Cæsar then so weak, or hath the
  place
But wrought this alteration with the
  air,
And he, on next remove, will all repair?
Macro, thou art engaged,[2] and what
  before
Was public, now must be thy private
  more.
The weal of Cæsar, fitness did imply;
But thine own fate confers necessity
On thy employment; and the thoughts
  borne nearest

Unto ourselves, move swiftest still and
  dearest.             10
If he recover, thou art lost; yea, all
The weight of preparation to his fall
Will turn on thee, and crush thee.  There-
  fore strike
Before he settle, to prevent the like
Upon thyself.  He doth his vantage
  know,
That makes [3] it home, and gives the
  foremost blow.      [*Exit.*]

[SCENE iii.

*An upper room in Agrippina's house.*]

*Latiaris, Rufus, Opsius.*

[LAT.] It is a service great Sejanus will
See well requited, and accept of nobly.
Here place yourselves between the roof
  and ceiling,
And, when I bring him to his words of
  danger,
Reveal yourselves, and take him.
RUF.              Is he come?
LAT. I'll now go fetch him.    [*Exit.*]
OPS.        With good speed.—I long
To merit from the state in such an action.
RUF. I hope it will obtain the consulship
For one of us.
OPS.        We cannot think of less,
To bring in one so dangerous as Sa-
  binus.             10
RUF. He was a follower of Germanicus,
And still is an observer of [4] his wife
And children, though they be declined
  in grace—
A daily visitant, keeps them company
In private and in public, and is noted
To be the only client of the house.
Pray Jove, he will be free [5] to Latiaris.
OPS. H' is allied to him, and doth trust
  him well.
RUF. And he'll requite his trust?
OPS.          To do an office  19
So grateful to the state, I know no man
But would strain nearer bands than
  kindred—
RUF.        List!
I hear them come.
OPS.      Shift to our holes with silence.
               [*They retire.*]

[1] Shaking.        [2] Entangled.

[3] Strikes.
[4] One who shows respectful attentions to.
[5] Outspoken.

*[Enter] Latiaris, Sabinus.*

[LAT.] It is a noble constancy you show
  To this afflicted house, that not like
    others,
  The friends of season, you do follow
    fortune,
  And, in the winter of their fate, forsake
  The place whose glories warmed you.
    You are just,
  And worthy such a princely patron's
    love,
  As was the world's-renowned Germani-
    cus,
  Whose ample merit when I call to
    thought,                                    30
  And see his wife and issue objects made
  To so much envy, jealousy, and hate,
  It makes me ready to accuse the gods
  Of negligence, as men of tyranny.
SAB. They must be patient; so must we.
LAT.                                        O Jove,
  What will become of us or of the times,
  When to be high or noble are made
    crimes,
  When land and treasure are most dan-
    gerous faults?
SAB. Nay, when our table, yea, our bed
    assaults
  Our peace and safety? When our writ-
    ings are,                                   40
  By any envious instruments that dare
  Apply them to the guilty, made to speak
  What they will have to fit their tyran-
    nous wreak? [1]
  When ignorance is scarcely innocence,
  And knowledge made a capital offense?
  When not so much but the bare empty
    shade
  Of liberty is reft us, and we made
  The prey to greedy vultures and vile
    spies,
  That first transfix us with their murder-
    ing eyes?
LAT. Methinks the genius of the Roman
    race                                        50
  Should not be so extinct, but that bright
    flame
  Of liberty might be revived again
  (Which no good man but with his life
    should lose)
  And we not sit like spent and patient
    fools,

[1] Vengeance.

Still puffing in the dark at one poor coal,
Held on by hope, till the last spark is
  out.
The cause is public, and the honor,
  name,
The immortality of every soul
That is not bastard or a slave in Rome
Therein concerned; whereto, if men
  would change                                 60
The wearied arm, and for the weighty
  shield
So long sustained employ the ready
  sword,
We might have some assurance of our
  vows.
This ass's fortitude doth tire us all;
It must be active valor must redeem
Our loss, or none. The rock and our hard
  steel
Should meet t' enforce those glorious
  fires again,
Whose splendor cheered the world, and
  heat gave life
No less than doth the sun's.
SAB.                                    'Twere better stay
  In lasting darkness and despair of day. 70
  No ill should force the subject undertake
  Against the sovereign, more than hell
    should make
  The gods do wrong. A good man should
    and must
  Sit rather down with loss than rise un-
    just,
  Though, when the Romans first did yield
    themselves
  To one man's power, they did not mean
    their lives,
  Their fortunes, and their liberties should
    be
  His absolute spoil, as purchased by the
    sword.
LAT. Why, we are worse, if to be slaves,
    and bond
  To Cæsar's slave, be such, the proud
    Sejanus!                                    80
  He that is all, does all, gives Cæsar leave
  To hide his ulcerous and anointed face,
  With his bald crown at Rhodes, while
    he here stalks
  Upon the heads of Romans and their
    princes,
  Familiarly to empire. [2]

[2] *I.e.*, as if accustomed to the state of an
emperor.

SAB.                    Now you touch
A point indeed, wherein he shows his art
As well as power.
LAT.                    And villainy in both.
Do you observe where Livia lodges? How
Drusus came dead? What men have been cut off?
SAB. Yes, those are things removed. I nearer looked                    90
Into his later practice, where he stands
Declared a master in his mystery.[1]
First, ere Tiberius went, he wrought his fear
To think that Agrippina sought his death;
Then put those doubts in her; sent her oft word,
Under the show of friendship, to beware
Of Cæsar, for he laid to poison her;
Drave them to frowns, to mutual jealousies,
Which now in visible hatred are burst out.
Since, he hath had his hired instruments                    100
To work on Nero, and to heave him up;
To tell him Cæsar's old, that all the people,
Yea, all the army have their eyes on him;
That both do long to have him undertake
Something of worth, to give the world a hope;
Bids him to court their grace. The easy youth
Perhaps gives ear, which straight he writes to Cæsar,
And with this comment: "See yon dangerous boy;
Note but the practice of the mother there;
She's tying him for purposes at hand, 110
With men of sword." Here's Cæsar put in fright
Gainst son and mother. Yet he leaves not thus.
The second brother, Drusus, a fierce nature
And fitter for his snares, because ambitious
And full of envy, him he clasps and hugs,

Poisons with praise, tells him what hearts he wears,
How bright he stands in popular expectance,
That Rome doth suffer with him in the wrong
His mother does him, by preferring Nero.
Thus sets he them asunder, each gainst other,                    120
Projects the course that serves him to condemn,
Keeps in opinion of a friend to all,
And all drives on to ruin.
LAT.                    Cæsar sleeps,
And nods at this?
SAB.                    Would he might ever sleep,
Bogged in his filthy lusts!
                    [Opsius and Rufus rush in.]
OPS.                    Treason to Cæsar!
RUF. Lay hands upon the traitor, Latiaris,
Or take the name thyself.
LAT.                    I am for Cæsar.
SAB. Am I then catched?
RUF.                    How think you, sir? You are.
SAB. Spies of this head, so white, so full of years!
Well, my most reverend monsters, you may live                    130
To see yourselves thus snared.
OPS.                    Away with him!
LAT. Hale him away!
RUF.                    To be a spy for traitors
Is honorable vigilance.
SAB.                    You do well,
My most officious instruments of state,
Men of all uses. Drag me hence, away.
The year is well begun, and I fall fit
To be an off'ring to Sejanus. Go!
OPS. Cover him with his garments; hide his face.
SAB. It shall not need. Forbear your rude assault.
The fault's not shameful, villainy makes a fault.                    [Exeunt.]    140

[SCENE iv.

A street before Agrippina's house.]

Macro, Caligula.

[MAC.] Sir, but observe how thick your dangers meet
In his clear drifts! Your mother and your brothers,

[1] Profession. art.

Now cited to the senate; their friend
    Gallus,
Feasted today by Cæsar, since com-
    mitted!
Sabinus here we met, hurried to fetters!
The senators all strook with fear and
    silence,
Save those whose hopes depend not on
    good means,
But force their private prey from public
    spoil.
And you must know, if here you stay,
    your state
Is sure to be the subject of his hate,    10
As now the object.

CAL.          What would you advise me?

MAC. To go for Capreæ presently,[1] and
    there
Give up yourself entirely to your uncle.
Tell Cæsar (since your mother is accused
To fly for succors [2] to Augustus' statue,
And to the army, with your brethren)
    you
Have rather chose to place your aids in
    him
Than live suspected, or in hourly fear
To be thrust out by bold Sejanus' plots—
Which you shall confidently urge to be    20
Most full of peril to the state and Cæsar,
As being laid to his peculiar ends,
And not to be let run with common
    safety.
All which, upon the second,[3] I'll make
    plain,
So both shall love and trust with Cæsar
    gain.

CAL. Away then; let's prepare us for our
    journey.              [*Exeunt.*]

[SCENE V.

*Another street.*]

*Arruntius.*

[ARR.] Still dost thou suffer, heaven?
    Will no flame,
No heat of sin, make thy just wrath to
    boil
In thy distempered bosom, and o'er-
    flow
The pitchy blazes of impiety,
Kindled beneath thy throne? Still canst
    thou sleep,

Patient, while vice doth make an antic
    face
At thy drad[4] power, and blow dust and
    smoke
Into thy nostrils? Jove, will nothing
    wake thee?
Must vile Sejanus pull thee by the beard
Ere thou wilt open thy black-lidded
    eye    10
And look him dead? Well! Snore on,
    dreaming gods,
And let this last of that proud giant race
Heave mountain upon mountain gainst
    your state.
Be good unto me, Fortune, and you
    powers
Whom I, expostulating, have profaned;
I see (what's equal with a prodigy)
A great, a noble Roman, and an honest,
Live an old man!—O Marcus Lepidus,
When is our turn to bleed? Thyself
    and I,
Without our boast, are a'most all the
    few    20
Left to be honest in these impious times.

*[Enter] Lepidus.*[5]

[LEP.] What we are left to be, we will be,
    Lucius,
Though tyranny did stare as wide as
    death
To fright us from it.

ARR.            'T hath so on Sabinus.

LEP. I saw him now drawn from the Gem-
    onies,[6]
And, what increased the direness of
    the fact,
His faithful dog, upbraiding all us Ro-
    mans,
Never forsook the corpse, but, seeing it
    thrown
Into the stream, leaped in, and drownéd
    with it.    29

ARR. O act, to be envied him of[7] us men!
We are the next the hook lays hold on,
    Marcus.
What are thy arts (good patriot, teach
    them me)

---

[1] At once.          [3] In your support.
[2] Accused of flying for the right of asylum.

[4] Dread.
[5] The name *Arruntius* is repeated here.
[6] Steps on the Aventine, down which corpses
of criminals were dragged by the executioner's
hook and thrown into the river.
[7] By.

That have preserved thy hairs to this
    white dye,
And kept so reverend and so dear a head
Safe on his comely shoulders?

LEP.                    Arts, Arruntius?
    None but the plain and passive fortitude
    To suffer and be silent, never stretch
    These arms against the torrent, live at
        home
    With my own thoughts and innocence
        about me,
    Not tempting the wolves' jaws—these
        are my arts.                            40

ARR. I would begin to study hem, if I
        thought
    They would secure me. May I pray to
        Jove
    In secret and be safe? Ay, or aloud?
    With open wishes? So I do not mention
    Tiberius or Sejanus? Yes, I must,
    If I speak out. 'Tis hard, that. May I
        think,
    And not be racked? What danger is 't
        to dream?
    Talk in one's sleep, or cough? Who
        knows the law?
    May I shake my head without a com-
        ment? Say
    It rains, or it holds up, and not be
        thrown                                    50
    Upon the Gemonies? These now are
        things
    Whereon men's fortune, yea, their fate
        depends.
    Nothing hath privilege gainst the violent
        ear.
    No place, no day, no hour, we see, is
        free
    (Not our religious and most sacred
        times)
    From some one kind of cruelty; all
        matter,
    Nay, all occasion pleaseth. Madmen's
        rage,
    The idleness of drunkards, women's
        nothing,
    Jester's simplicity, all, all is good
    That can be catched at. Nor is now th'
        event [1]                                 60
    Of any person, or for any crime,
    To be expected,[2] for 'tis always one:
    Death, with some little difference of
        place,

[1] Fate.                    [2] Dreaded.

Or time—what's this? Prince Nero?
    Guarded?

[Enter] Laco, Nero [, with Guards].[3]

[LAC.] On, lictors, keep your way. My
        lords, forbear.
    On pain of Cæsar's wrath, no man at-
        tempt
    Speech with the prisoner.

NERO.                Noble friends, be safe;
    To lose yourselves for words were as
        vain hazard
    As unto me small comfort. Fare you
        well!
    Would all Rome's suff'rings in my fate
        did dwell!                               70

LAC. Lictors, away!

LEP.                Where goes he, Laco?

LAC.                                      Sir,
    H' is banished into Pontia by the
        senate.

ARR. Do I see, and hear, and feel? May
    I trust sense?
    Or doth my phant'sy form it?

LEP.                    Where's his brother?

LAC. Drusus is prisoner in the palace.

ARR.                                    Ha!
    I smell it now; 'tis rank. Where's Agrip-
        pina?

LAC. The princess is confined to Panda-
        taria.

ARR. Bolts, Vulcan, bolts for Jove! Phœ-
        bus, thy bow;
    Stern Mars, thy sword; and, blue-eyed
        Maid, thy spear;
    Thy club, Alcides—all the armory     80
    Of heaven is too little!—Ha! To guard
    The gods, I meant. Fine, rare despatch!
        This same
    Was swiftly borne! Confined? Im-
        prisoned? Banished?
    Most tripartite! The cause, sir?

LAC.                    Treason.

ARR.                                      O!
    The complement of all accusings? That
    Will hit, when all else fails.

LEP.                    This turn is strange!
    But yesterday the people would not
        hear,
    Far less objected, but cried Cæsar's
        letters

[3] The names Lepidus and Arruntius are repeated here.

Were false and forged, that all these
   plots were malice,
And that the ruin of the prince's house 90
Was practiced gainst his knowledge.
   Where are now
Their voices, now that they behold his
   heirs
Locked up, disgraced, led into exile?
ARR.                              Hushed.
   Drowned in their bellies. Wild Sejanus'
   breath
Hath, like a whirlwind, scattered that
   poor dust
With this rude blast.—(*He turns to Laco
   and the Rest.*) We'll talk no treason, sir,
If that be it you stand for. Fare you well.
We have no need of horse-leeches. Good
   spy,
Now you are spied, begone.
     [*Exeunt Laco, Nero, and Guards.*]
LEP.                    I fear you wrong him.
   He has the voice to be an honest Ro-
   man.                                    100
ARR. And trusted to this office? Lepidus,
   I'ld sooner trust Greek Sinon than a
   man
Our state employs. He's gone; and be-
   ing gone,
I dare tell you, whom I dare better
   trust,
That our night-eyed Tiberius doth not
   see
His minion's drifts; or, if he do, h' is not
So arrant subtile as we fools do take
   him.
To breed a mungrel [1] up in his own house,
With his own blood, and, if the good
   gods please,
At his own throat flesh [2] him to take a
   leap!                                    110
I do not beg it, heav'n; but, if the fates
Grant it these eyes, they must not wink.
LEP.                              They must
   Not see it, Lucius.
ARR.              Who should let [3] hem?
LEP.                                  Zeal
   And duty; with the thought he is our
   prince.
ARR. He is our monster, forfeited to vice
   So far as no racked virtue can redeem
   him;
His loathéd person fouler than all crimes;
An emp'ror only in his lusts. Retired,

From all regard of his own fame or
   Rome's,
Into an obscure island, where he lives, 120
Acting his tragedies with a comic face,
Amidst his rout of Chaldees,[4] spending
   hours,
Days, weeks, and months in the unkind [5]
   abuse
Of grave astrology, to the bane of men,
Casting the scope of men's nativities,
And, having found aught worthy in
   their fortune,
Kill, or precipitate them in the sea,
And boast he can mock fate. Nay,
   muse not; these
Are far from ends of evil, scarce de-
   grees.
He hath his slaughterhouse at Capreæ,
Where he doth study murder as an art;
And they are dearest in his grace that
   can                                    132
Devise the deepest tortures. Thither,
   too,
He hath his boys and beauteous girls
   ta'en up
Out of our noblest houses, the best
   formed,
Best nurtured, and most modest; what's
   their good
Serves to provoke his bad. Some are
   allured,
Some threatened; others, by their friends
   detained,
Are ravished hence like captives, and,
   in sight
Of their most grievéd parents, dealt
   away                                    140
Unto his spintries,[6] sellaries,[7] and slaves,
Masters of strange and new-com-
   mented [8] lusts,
For which wise nature hath not left a
   name.
To this (what most strikes us and bleed-
   ing Rome)
He is, with all his craft, become the
   ward
To his own vassal, a stale catamite [9]
Whom he, upon our low and suffering
   necks,

[1] Mongrel.        [2] Incite.        [3] Hinder.

[4] Chaldeans, astrologers.
[5] Unnatural.
[6] Male prostitutes.
[7] Lewd persons.
[8] New-invented.
[9] Male prostitute.

Hath raised from excrement to side [1]
the gods
And have his proper sacrifice in Rome,
Which Jove beholds, and yet will sooner
rive                                        150
A senseless oak with thunder than his
trunk!

*Laco, Pomponius, Minutius, Terentius, to
them.*

[LAC.] These letters make men doubtful
what t' expect,
Whether his coming or his death.
POM.                              Troth, both;
And which comes soonest, thank the
gods for.
(ARR.                                List!
Their talk is Cæsar; I would hear all
voices.)
       [*Arruntius and Lepidus withdraw.*]
MIN. One day he's well and will return
to Rome;
The next day, sick, and knows not when
to hope it.
LAC. True; and today one of Sejanus'
friends
Honored by special writ, and on the
morrow
Another punished—
POM.        By more special writ.  160
MIN.  This man receives his praises of
Sejanus;
A second, but slight mention; a third,
none;
A fourth, rebukes.   And thus he leaves
the senate
Divided and suspended, all uncertain.
LAC. These forkéd tricks, I understand
hem not;
Would he would tell us whom he·loves
or hates,
That we might follow, without fear or
doubt.
(ARR. Good Heliotrope! [2]  Is this your
honest man?
Let him be yours so still; he is my knave.)
POM. I cannot tell; Sejanus still goes
on,                                        170
And mounts, we see; new statues are
advanced,
Fresh leaves of titles, large inscriptions
read,

[1] Match.
[2] Because he keeps turning toward the sun.

His fortune sworn by, himself new gone
out
Cæsar's colleague in the fifth consulship;
More altars smoke to him than all the
gods.
What would we more?
(ARR.        That the dear smoke would
choke him,
That would I more!
LEP.              Peace, good Arruntius.)
LAC. But there are letters come, they
say, ev'n now,
Which do forbid that last.
MIN.              Do you hear so?
LAC.                            Yes.
POM. By Pollux, that's the worst.
(ARR.              By Hercules, best.)
MIN. I did not like the sign, when Regu-
lus,                                       181
Whom all we know no friend unto Se-
janus,
Did, by Tiberius' so precise command,
Succeed a fellow in the consulship;
It boded somewhat.
POM.              Not a mote. His partner,
Fulcinius Trio, is his own, and sure.—
Here comes Terentius. He can give us
more.

[*Enter Terentius.*]    *They whisper with
Terentius.*

LEP. I'll ne'er believe but Cæsar hath
some scent
Of bold Sejanus' footing.  These cross-
points
Of varying letters and opposing con-
suls,                                      190
Mingling his honors and his punish-
ments,
Feigning now ill, now well, raising Se-
janus,
And then depressing him, as now of late
In all reports we have it, cannot be
Empty of practice; 'tis Tiberius' art,
For (having found his favorite grown
too great,
And with his greatness strong, that all
the soldiers
Are, with their leaders, made at his de-
votion,
That almost all the senate are his crea-
tures,
Or hold on him their main dependen-
cies,                                      200

Either for benefit, or hope, or fear,
And that himself hath lost much of his
    own,
By parting unto him, and, by th' in-
    crease
Of his rank lusts and rages, quite dis-
    armed
Himself of love or other public means
To dare an open contestation)
His subtilty hath chose this doubling
    line,
To hold him even in, not so to fear him,
As wholly put him out, and yet give
    check                                       209
Unto his farder boldness; in meantime,
By his employments, makes him odious
Unto the staggering rout,[1] whose aid,
    in fine,
He hopes to use, as sure, who, when
    they sway,
Bear down, o'erturn all objects in their
    way.
ARR. You may be a Lynceus, Lepidus;
    yet I
See no such cause but that a politic
    tyran,
Who can so well disguise it, should
    have ta'en
A nearer way: feigned honest, and come
    home
To cut his throat, by law.
LEP.                          Ay, but his fear
Would ne'er be masked, allbe[2] his vices
    were.                                       220
POM. His lordship then is still in grace?
TER.                          Assure you,
Never in more, either of grace or power.
POM. The gods are wise and just.
(ARR.                    The fiends they are,
To suffer thee belie hem!)
TER.                          I have here
His last and present letters, where he
    writes him,
The "partner of his cares," and "his
    Sejanus"—
LAC. But is that true, it is[3] prohibited
To sacrifice unto him?
TER.                    Some such thing
Cæsar makes scruple of, but forbids it
    not,
No more than to himself; says he could
    wish                                        230

It were forborne to all.
LAC.                          Is it no other?
TER. No other, on my trust.  For your
    more surety,
Here is that letter too.
(ARR.                    How easily
Do wretched men believe what they
    would have!
Looks this like plot?
LEP.                    Noble Arruntius, stay.)
LAC. He names him here without his
    titles.
(LEP.               Note!
ARR. Yes, and come off[4] your notable
    fool.  I will.)
LAC. No other than Sejanus.
POM.                    That's but haste
In him that writes.  Here he gives large
    amends.                                     239
MIN. And with his own hand written?
POM.                          Yes.
LAC.                          Indeed?
TER. Believe. it, gentlemen, Sejanus'
    breast
Never received more full contentments
    in
Than at this present.
POM.               Takes he well th' escape
Of young Caligula with Macro?
TER.                          Faith,
At the first air it somewhat troubled
    him.
(LEP. Observe you?
ARR.               Nothing; riddles.  Till I see
Sejanus strook, no sound thereof strikes
    me.)
POM. I like it not.  I muse h' would not
    attempt
Somewhat against him in the consul-
    ship,
Seeing the people gin[5] to favor him.   250
TER. He doth repent it now; but h' has
    employed
Pagònianus after him; and he holds
That correspondence there, with all
    that are
Near about Cæsar,[6] as no thought can
    pass
Without his knowledge thence, in act
    to front[7] him.
POM. I gratulate[8] the news.

---

[1] Changeable mob.              [2] Although.
[3] From 1640 edn.  Original reads 'tis.

[4] Turn out to be.              [7] Oppose.
[5] Begin.                        [8] Welcome.
[6] I.e., Caligula.

LAC.                    But how comes Macro
So in trust and favor with Caligula?
POM. O, sir, he has a wife, and the young
    prince
An appetite.  He can look up and spy
Flies in the roof, when there are fleas
    i' bed,                                    260
And hath a learned nose to assure his
    sleeps.
Who, to be favored of the rising sun,
Would not lend little of his waning moon?
'Tis the saf'st ambition.  Noble Teren-
    tius!
TER. The night grows fast upon us.  At
    your service.                    [*Exeunt.*]

CHORUS—of *Musicians.*

ACT V. [SCENE i.

*An apartment in Sejanus' house.*]

*Sejanus.*

[SEJ.] Swell, swell, my joys, and faint not
    to declare
Yourselves as ample as your causes are.
I did not live till now—this my first
    hour,
Wherein I see my thoughts reached by
    my power.
But this, and gripe my wishes.[1]  Great
    and high,
The world knows only two, that's Rome
    and I.
My roof receives me not; 'tis air I
    tread;
And at each step I feel my advancéd
    head
Knock out a star in heaven!  Reared to
    this height,
All my desires seem modest, poor, and
    slight,                                    10
That did before sound impudent; 'tis
    place,
Not blood, discerns the noble and the
    base.
Is there not something more than to
    be Cæsar?
Must we rest there?  It irks t' have come
    so far,
To be so near a stay.  Caligula,
Would thou stood'st stiff and many in
    our way!

Winds lose their strength, when they
    do empty fly,
Unmet of woods or buildings; great
    fires die,
That want their matter to withstand
    them; so,
It is our grief, and will be our loss, to
    know                                      20
Our power shall want opposites, unless
The gods, by mixing in the cause, would
    bless
Our fortune with their conquest.  That
    were worth
Sejanus' strife, durst fates but bring it
    forth.

*[Enter] Terentius.*[2]

[TER.] Safety to great Sejanus!
SEJ.                    Now, Terentius?
TER. Hears not my lord the wonder?
SEJ.                    Speak it; no.
TER. I meet it violent in the people's
    mouths,
Who run in routs to Pompey's theater
To view your statue, which, they say,
    sends forth
A smoke, as from a fornace,[3] black and
    dreadful.                                  30
SEJ. Some traitor hath put fire in; you
    go see,
And let the head be taken off, to look
What 'tis.  Some slave hath practiced
    an imposture
To stir the people.—[*Terentius starts to
    go.*]  How now!  Why return you?

*Satrius, Natta, to them.*

SAT. The head, my lord, already is ta'en
    off;
I saw it; and, at op'ning, there leaped
    out
A great and monstrous serpent.
SEJ.                    Monstrous!  Why?
Had it a beard and horns, no heart, a
    tongue
Forkéd as flattery?  Looked it of the
    hue
To such as live in great men's bosoms?
    Was                                        40
The spirit of it Macro's?
NAT.                    May it please

---

² The name *Sejanus* is repeated here.
³ Furnace.

The most divine Sejanus, in my days
(And by his sacred fortune I affirm it)
I have not seen a more extended, grown,
Foul, spotted, venomous, ugly—
SEJ.                    O, the Fates!
What a wild muster's here of attributes
T' express a worm, a snake?
TER.                    But how that should
Come there, my lord?
SEJ.          What, and you too, Terentius?
I think you mean to make 't a prodigy
In your reporting!
TER.               Can the wise Sejanus  50
Think heav'n hath meant it less?
SEJ.                    O, superstition!
Why, then the falling of our bed, that
     brake
This morning, burdened with the popu-
     lous weight
Of our expecting clients, to salute us,
Or running of the cat bewixt our legs,
As we set forth unto the Capitol,
Were prodigies.
TER.               I think them ominous,
And would they had not happened—
     as, today,
The fate of some your servants, who,
     declining
Their way, not able, for the throng, to
     follow,                              60
Slipped down the Gemonies, and brake
     their necks!
Besides, in taking your last augury,
No prosperous bird appeared, but croak-
     ing ravens
Flagged up and down, and from the
     sacrifice
Flew to the prison, where they sat all
     night,
Beating the air with their obstreperous
     beaks!
I dare not counsel, but I could entreat
That great Sejanus would attempt the
     gods
Once more with sacrifice.
SEJ.               What excellent fools
Religion makes of men!     Believes
     Terentius,                          70
If these were dangers, as I shame to
     think them,
The gods could change the certain
     course of fate?
Or, if they could, they would, now in a
     moment,

For a beeve's fat, or less, be bribed t'
     invert
Those long decrees?     Then think the
     gods, like flies,
Are to be taken with the steam of flesh,
Or blood, diffused about their altars:
     think
Their power as cheap as I esteem it
     small.
Of all the throng that fill th' Olympian
     hall,
And, without pity, lade poor Atlas'
     back,                               80
I know not that one deity, but Fortune,
To whom I would throw up, in begging
     smoke,
One grain of incense, or whose ear I'ld
     buy
With thus much oil. Her I indeed adore,
And keep her grateful image in my
     house,
Sometimes belonging to a Roman king,
But now called mine, as by the better
     style;
To her I care not, if, for satisfying
Your scrupulous phant'sies, I go offer.
     Bid
Our priest prepare us honey, milk, and
     poppy,                              90
His masculine odors and night vest-
     ments; say
Our rites are instant, which performed,
     you'll see
How vain, and worthy laughter, your
     fears be.               [Exeunt.]

[SCENE ii.

A street.]

Cotta, Pomponius.

[COT.] Pomponius, whither in such speed?
POM.                    I go
To give my lord Sejanus notice—
COT.                    What?
POM. Of Macro.
COT.          Is he come?
POM.                    Entered but now
The house of Regulus.
COT.               The opposite consul?
POM. Some half hour since.
COT.          And by night too! Stay, sir;
I'll bear you company.
POM.               Along then. [Exeunt.]

[SCENE iii.

*A room in Regulus' house.*]

*Macro, Regulus, Laco*[1] [*, and Attendant*].

[MAC.] 'Tis Cæsar's will to have a frequent [2] senate;
And therefore must your edict lay deep mulct
On such as shall be absent.

REG.                                    So it doth.
Bear it my fellow consul to adscribe.[3]

MAC. And tell him it must early be proclaimed;
The place Apollo's temple.
                              [*Exit Attendant.*]

REG.                    That's remembered.

MAC. And at what hour?

REG.                    Yes.

MAC.                    You do forget
To send one for the provost of the watch?

REG. I have not; here he comes.


[*Enter Laco.*]

MAC.                    Gracinus Laco,
You are a friend most welcome; by-and-by                                    10
I'll speak with you.—[*Aside.*] You must procure this list
Of the prætorian cohorts, with the names
Of the centurions and the tribunes.

REG. [*Aside.*]                    Ay.

MAC. I bring you letters, and a health from Cæsar.

LAC. Sir, both come well.

(MAC.        And, hear you, with your note,
Which are the eminent men, and most of action.

REG. That shall be done you too.)
                    *The Consul goes out.*

MAC.                    Most worthy Laco,
Cæsar salutes you.—[*Aside.*] Consul!
Death and furies!
Gone now?—The argument will please you, sir.—
[*Aside.*] Ho! Regulus? The anger of the gods                                    20
Follow his diligent legs, and overtake hem,
In likeness of the gout!—

---

[1] Enters later.        [2] Full.        [3] Sign.

[*Regulus*] *returns.*

                                    O, good my lord,
We lacked you present; I would pray you send
Another to Fulcinius Trio straight,
To tell him you will come and speak with him;
The matter we'll devise, to stay him there,
While I with Laco do survey the watch.—
                    [*Regulus*] *goes out again.*
What are your strengths, Gracinus?

LAC.                    Seven cohorts.

MAC. You see what Cæsar writes; and
    —[*Aside.*] Gone again?
H' has sure a vein of mercury in his feet.—                                    30
Knew you what store of the prætorian soldiers
Sejanus holds about him for his guard?

LAC. I cannot the just number, but I think
Three centuries.

MAC.        Three? Good.

LAC.                    At most not four.

MAC. And who be those centurions?

LAC.                    That the consul
Can best deliver you.

(MAC.                    When h' is away?
Spite on his nimble industry!)—Gracinus,
You find what place you hold, there, in the trust
Of royal Cæsar?

LAC.                    Ay, and I am—

MAC.                    Sir,
The honors there proposed are but beginnings                                    40
Of his great favors.

LAC.        They are more—

MAC.                    I heard him
When he did study what to add.

LAC.                    My life,
And all I hold—

MAC.        You were his own first choice,
Which doth confirm as much as you can speak,
And will, if we succeed, make more—
    Your guards
Are seven cohorts, you say?

LAC.                    Yes.

MAC.                    Those we must

Hold still in readiness and undis-
charged.
LAC. I understand so much.  But how it
can—
MAC. Be done without suspicion, you'll
object?

*[Regulus] returns.*

REG. What's that?
LAC.        The keeping of the watch in
arms,                                        50
When morning comes.
MAC.            The senate shall be met, and
set
So early in the temple, as all mark
Of that will be avoided.
REG.                        If we need,
We have commission to possess the pal-
ace,
Enlarge ¹ Prince Drusus, and make him
our chief.
(MAC. That secret would have burnt his
reverend mouth,
Had he not spit it out now.)—By the
gods,
You carry things too.  Let me borrow a
man
Or two to bear these.  That of freeing
Drusus,
Cæsar projected as the last and ut-
most—                                        60
Not else to be remembered.
REG. *[Beckoning to Servants.]*    Here are
servants.
MAC. These to Arruntius, these to Lepi-
dus.
This bear to Cotta, this to Latiaris.
If they demand you of me, say I have
ta'en
Fresh horse and am departed.—*[Exeunt
Servants.]* You, my lord,
To your colleague, and be you sure to
hold him
With long narration of the new fresh
favors,
Meant to Sejanus, his great patron; I,
With trusted Laco here, are for the
guards;
Then, to divide.  For night hath many
eyes,                                        70
Whereof, though most do sleep, yet some
are spies.                          *[Exeunt.]*

¹ Free.

*[SCENE iv.*

*A chapel in Sejanus' house.]*

*Præcones, Flamen,² Ministri,³ Sejanus, Te-
rentius, Satrius, [Natta,] etc.*

*[PRÆ.]  Be all profane far hence; fly, fly far
off.
Be absent far; far hence be all profane!*
Tub[icines], Tib[icines] ⁴ sound while the
Flamen washeth.
FLA. *We have been faulty, but repent us
now,
And bring pure hands, pure vestments, and
pure minds.*
[1] MIN. *Pure vessels.*
[2] MIN.                    *And pure off'rings.*
[3] MIN.                        *Garlands pure.*
FLA. *Bestow your garlands; and, with reverence, place
The vervine ⁵ on the altar.*
PRÆ.                    *Favor ⁶ your tongues.*
While they sound again, the Flamen takes
of the honey with his finger, and tastes,
then ministers to all the rest; so of the
milk, in an earthen vessel, he deals
about; which done, he sprinkleth upon
the altar, milk; then imposeth the
honey, and kindleth his gums, and
after censing about the altar, placeth
his censer thereon, into which they
put several branches of poppy, and,
        the music ceasing, proceed.
FLA. *Great mother Fortune, queen of human
state,
Rectress ⁷ of action, arbitress of fate,
To whom all sway, all power, all empire
bows,                                        10
Be present, and propitious to our vows!*
PRÆ. *Favor it with your tongues.*⁸
MIN. *Be present, and propitious to our
vows!
Accept our off'ring, and be pleased, great
goddess.*
TER. *See, see, the image stirs!*
SAT.                    *And turns away!*
NAT. *Fortune averts her face!*
FLA.                    *Avert, you gods,
The prodigy! Still! Still! Some pious rite
We have neglected.   Yet, heav'n, be
appeased,*

² Priest.                              ³ Servitors.
⁴ Trumpeters, flute-players.
⁵ Vervain, verbena.              ⁷ Governess.
⁶ Silence.              ⁸ Speak the good words.

And be all tokens false or void that speak
Thy present wrath!
SEJ.      Be thou dumb, scrupulous¹ priest,
And gather up thyself, with these thy
    wares,                                          21
Which I, in spite of thy blind mistress, or
Thy juggling mystery, religion, throw
Thus scornéd on the earth.
        [*Overturns the statue and the altar.*]
                    Nay, hold thy look
Averted till I woo thee turn again;
And thou shalt stand, to all posterity,
Th' eternal game and laughter, with thy
    neck
Writhed to thy tail, like a ridiculous cat.
Avoid ² these fumes, these superstitious
    lights,                                         29
And all these coz'ning ceremonies—you,
Your pure and spicéd ³ conscience!
        [*Exit Flamen with his Attendants.*]
                    I, the slave
And mock of fools (scorn on my worthy
    head!),
That have been titled and adored a god,
Yea, sacrificed unto, myself, in Rome,
No less than Jove—and I be brought
    to do
A peevish giglot rites! ⁴  Perhaps the
    thought
And shame of that made Fortune turn
    her face,
Knowing herself the lesser deity,
And but my servant.—Bashful queen,
    if so,
Sejanus thanks thy modesty.—Who's
    that?                                            40

[*Enter*] *Pomponius,*⁵ *Minutius, etc.*

[POM.] His fortune suffers till he hears my
    news;
I have waited here too long.  Macro, my
    lord—
SEJ. Speak lower and withdraw.
                    [*Draws him aside.*]
TER.               Are these things true?
MIN. Thousands are gazing at it in the
    streets.
SEJ. What's that?
TER.        Minutius tells us here, my lord,

¹ Doubtful, untrustworthy.
² Remove.
³ Overscrupulous.
⁴ Do rites to a crazy wanton (*i.e.*, to Fortune).
⁵ The name *Sejanus* is repeated here.

That, a new head being set upon your
    statue,
A rope is since found wreathed about it,
    and
But now a fiery meteor in the form
Of a great ball was seen to roll along
The troubled air, where yet it hangs un-
    perfect,                                         50
The amazing wonder of the multitude!
SEJ. No more.  That Macro's come, is more
    than all!
TER. Is Macro come?
POM.        I saw him.
TER.               Where?  With whom?
POM. With Regulus.
SEJ.               Terentius!
TER.                    My lord?
SEJ. Send for the tribunes; we will straight
    have up
More of the soldiers for our guard.—[*Exit
    Terentius.*]  Minutius,
We pray you go for Cotta, Latiaris,
Trio the consul, or what senators
You know are sure, and ours.—[*Exit
    Minutius.*]  You, my good Natta,
For Laco, provost of the watch.—[*Exit
    Natta.*]  Now, Satrius,                         60
The time of proof comes on; arm all our
    servants,
And without tumult.—[*Exit Satrius.*]
    You, Pomponius,
Hold some good correspondence with the
    consul;
Attempt him, noble friend.—[*Exit Pom-
    ponius.*]  These things begin
To look like dangers, now, worthy my
    fates.
Fortune, I see thy worst.  Let doubtful
    states
And things uncertain hang upon thy will;
Me surest death shall render certain still.
Yet why is now my thought turned
    toward death,
Whom fates have let go on so far in
    breath,                                          70
Unchecked or unreproved?  I, that did
    help
To fell the lofty cedar of the world,
Germanicus; that at one stroke cut down
Drusus, that upright elm; withered his
    vine;
Laid Silius and Sabinus, two strong oaks,
Flat on the earth; besides those other
    shrubs,

Cordus and Sosia, Claudia Pulchra,
Furnius and Gallus, which I have
    grubbed up;
And since, have set my ax so strong
    and deep
Into the root of spreading Agrippine;   80
Lopped off and scattered her proud
    branches, Nero,
Drusus, and Caius too, although re-
    planted;
If you will, Destinies, that, after all,
I faint now ere I touch my period,
You are but cruel; and I already have
    done
Things great enough.   All Rome hath
    been my slave;
The senate sate an idle looker-on
And witness of my power, when I have
    blushed
More to command than it to suffer; [1] all
The fathers have sat ready and pre-
    pared   90
To give me empire, temples, or their
    throats,
When I would ask hem; and, what crowns
    the top,
Rome, senate, people, all the world have
    seen
Jove but my equal, Cæsar but my second.
'Tis then your malice, Fates, who, but
    your own,
Envy and fear t' have any power long
    known.                        [*Exit.*]

[SCENE v.

*A room in the same.*]

*Terentius, Tribunes.*

[TER.] Stay here; I'll give [2] his lordship you
    are come.

[*Enter*] *Minutius, Cotta, Latiaris.*

[MIN.] Marcus Terentius, pray you, tell
    my lord
Here's Cotta and Latiaris.
TER.                            Sir, I shall.
        [*Exit.*] *They confer their letters.*
COT. My letter is the very same with
    yours,
    Only requires me to be present there,
    And give my voice to strengthen his
        design.

[1] *I.e.*, than it has blushed to permit me to
command.        [2] *I.e.*, tell.        [3] Ready.

LAT. Names he not what it is?
COT.                        No, nor to you.
LAT. 'Tis strange and singular doubtful!
COT.                            So it is.
    It may be all is left to Lord Sejanus.

*Natta, Laco, to them.*

[NAT.] Gentlemen, where's my lord?
TRI.                    We wait him here.   10
COT. The provost Laco?   What's the
    news?
LAT.        My lord—

*Sejanus, to them.*

[SEJ.] Now, my right dear, noble, and
    trusted friends,
    How much I am a captive to your kind-
        ness!
    Most worthy Cotta, Latiaris, Laco,
    Your valiant hand; and, gentlemen, your
        loves.
    I wish I could divide myself unto you,
    Or that it lay within our narrow powers
    To satisfy for so enlargéd bounty.
    Gracinus, we must pray you, hold your
        guards
    Unquit[3] when morning comes.   Saw you
        the consul?                    20
MIN. Trio will presently be here, my lord.
COT. They are but giving order for the
    edict,
    To warn the senate?
SEJ.                How! The senate?
LAT.                            Yes.
    This morning in Apollo's temple—
COT.                            We
    Are charged by letter to be there, my
        lord.
SEJ. By letter?   Pray you, let's see.
LAT.                Knows not his lordship?
COT. It seems so!
SEJ.            A senate warned?   Without
    my knowledge?
    And on this sudden?   Senators by letters
    Required to be there!   Who brought
        these?
COT.        Macro.
SEJ. Mine enemy!   And when?
COT.                        This midnight.
SEJ.                            Time,   30
    With ev'ry other circumstance, doth give
    It hath some strain of ingine in 't!—How
    now?

[*Enter*] *Satrius*.[1]

[Sat.] My lord, Sertorius Macro is without,
Alone, and prays t' have private conference
In business of high nature with your
lordship,
He says to me, and which regards you
much.

Sej. Let him come here.

Sat.            Better, my lord, withdraw;
You will betray what store and strength
of friends
Are now about you, which he comes to
spy.

Sej. Is he not armed?

Sat.            We'll search him.

Sej.            No; but take    40
And lead him to some room, where you
concealed
May keep a guard upon us.—[*Exit
Satrius*.] Noble Laco,
You are our trust; and, till our own co-
horts
Can be brought up, your strengths must
be our guard.
Now, good Minutius, honored Latiaris.
            *He salutes them humbly.*
Most worthy and my most unwearied
friends,
I return instantly.            [*Exit*.]

Lat.            Most worthy lord!

Cot. His lordship is turned instant kind,
methinks;
I have not observed it in him heretofore.

Tri. 1. 'Tis true, and it becomes him
nobly.

Min.        I                50
Am rapt withal.

Tri. 2.        By Mars, he has my lives,
Were they a million, for this only
grace.

Lac. Ay, and to name a man!

Lat.            As he did me!

Min. And me!

Lat.        Who would not spend his life
and fortunes
To purchase but the look of such a
lord?

Lac. [*Aside*.] He that would nor be lord's
fool nor the world's.        [*Exeunt*.]

[1] The words *Sejanus*, etc., are repeated here.

*Another room in the same.*]

*Sejanus, Macro* [, *Satrius*].

[Sej.] Macro, most welcome as most
coveted friend!
Let me enjoy my longings.    When arrived you?

Mac. About the noon of night.

Sej.        Satrius, give leave. [*Exit Satrius*.]

Mac. I have been, since I came, with both
the consuls,
On a particular design from Cæsar.

Sej. How fares it with our great and royal
master?

Mac. Right plentifully well, as with a
prince
That still holds out the great proportion
Of his large favors, where his judgment
hath                9
Made once divine election, like the god
That wants not, nor is wearied to be-
stow
Where merit meets his bounty, as it doth
In you, already the most happy, and, ere
The sun shall climb the south, most high
Sejanus.
Let not my lord be amused.[2]    For to this
end
Was I by Cæsar sent for to the isle,
With special caution to conceal my
journey,
And thence had my despatch as privately
Again to Rome, charged to come here by
night,                19
And only to the consuls make narration
Of his great purpose, that the benefit
Might come more full and striking, by
how much
It was less looked for, or aspired by you,
Or least informéd to the common
thought.

Sej. What may this be?    Part of myself,
dear Macro,
If good, speak out, and share with your
Sejanus.

Mac. If bad, I should forever loathe my-
self
To be the messenger to so good a lord.
I do exceed m' instructions to acquaint
Your lordship with thus much; but 'tis
my venture                30

[2] Amazed.

On your retentive wisdom, and because
I would no jealous scruple should molest
Or rack your peace of thought.  For I
   assure
My noble lord, no senator yet knows
The business meant, though all by sev-
   eral letters
Are warnéd to be there, and give their
   voices,
Only to add unto the state and grace
Of what is purposed.
SEJ.            You take pleasure, Macro,
   Like a coy wench, in torturing your
      lover.
   What can be worth this suffering?
MAC.            That which follows,  40
   The tribunitial dignity and power—
   Both which Sejanus is to have this day
   Conferred upon him, and by public
      senate.
SEJ. [Aside.] Fortune, be mine again! Thou
      hast satisfied
   For thy suspected loyalty.
MAC.                        My lord,
   I have no longer time; the day approach-
      eth,
   And I must back to Cæsar.
SEJ.                    Where's Caligula?
MAC. That I forgot to tell your lordship.
      Why,
   He lingers yonder about Capreæ,
   Disgraced; Tiberius hath not seen him
      yet.                                50
   He needs would thrust himself to go with
      me,
   Against my wish or will; but I have
      quitted
   His forward trouble,[1] with as tardy note
   As my neglect or silence could afford
      him.
   Your lordship cannot now command me
      aught,
   Because I take no knowledge that I saw
      you;
   But I shall boast to live to serve your
      lordship;
   And so take leave.
SEJ.              Honest and worthy Macro,
   Your love and friendship.—[Exit Macro.]
      Who's there? Satrius,                59
   Attend my honorable friend forth.—O!
   How vain and vile a passion is this
      fear!

[1] Troublesome forwardness.

What base uncomely things it makes
   men do:
Suspect their noblest friends, as I did
   this,
Flatter poor enemies, entreat their ser-
   vants,
Stoop, court, and catch at the benevo-
   lence
Of creatures unto whom, within this hour,
I would not have vouchsafed a quarter-
   look,
Or piece of face!  By you that fools call
   gods,
Hang all the sky with your prodigious
   signs,
Fill earth with monsters, drop the scor-
   pion down                              70
Out of the zodiac, or the fiercer lion,
Shake off the loosened globe from her
   long henge,[2]
Roll all the world in darkness, and let
   loose
Th' enragéd winds to turn up groves and
   towns!
When I do fear again, let me be strook
With forkéd fire, and unpitied die;
Who fears, is worthy of calamity.  [Exit.]

[SCENE vii.

*Another room in the same.*]

*Pomponius, Regulus, Trio, to the Rest.*[3]

P[OM.]  Is not my lord here?
TER.                    Sir, he will be straight.
COT. What news, Fulcinius Trio?
TRIO.                    Good, good tidings;
   But keep it to yourself.  My lord Sejanus
   Is to receive this day in open senate
   The tribunitial dignity.
COT.              Is 't true?
TRIO. No words, not to your thought; but,
   sir, believe it.
LAT. What says the consul?
COT. [Aside.]        Speak it not again.—
   He tells me that today my lord Seja-
   nus—
(TRIO. I must entreat you, Cotta, on your
   honor
   Not to reveal it.
COT.              On my life, sir.)
LAT.                        Say.  10

[2] Hinge, axis.
[3] *I.e.*, Terentius, Minutius, Laco, Cotta,
Latiaris, and Tribunes.

Cot. Is to receive the tribunitial power.
　But, as you are an honorable man,
　Let me conjure you not to utter it;
　For it is trusted to me with that bond.
Lat. I am Harpocrates.
Ter. 　　　　　　　　Can you assure it?
Pom. The consul told it me; but keep it
　close.
Min. Lord Latiaris, what's the news?
Lat. 　　　　　　　　I'll tell you;
　But you must swear to keep it secret.

*To them, Sejanus.*

[Sej.] I knew the Fates had on their distaff
　left
　More of our thread than so.
Reg. 　　　　　Hail, great Sejanus!　20
Trio. Hail, the most honored—!
Cot. 　　　　　　　　Happy—!
Lat. 　　　　　　　　High Sejanus!
Sej. Do you bring prodigies too?
Trio. 　　　　　　May all presage
　Turn to those fair effects whereof we
　bring
　Your lordship news.
Reg. 　　May 't please my lord withdraw.
Sej. Yes.—(*To Some that stand by.*)　I
　will speak with you anon.
Ter. 　　　　　　　　My lord,
　What is your pleasure for the tribunes?
Sej. 　　　　　　　　Why,
　Let hem be thanked and sent away.
Min. 　　　　　　　My lord—
Lac. Will 't please your lordship to
　command me—
Sej. 　　　　No.
　You are troublesome.
Min. 　　　　The mood is changed.
Tri.[1.] 　　　　　　Not speak?
Tri.[2.] Nor look?
Lac. 　　　Ay, he is wise, will
　make him friends　　　　30
Of such who never love but for their
　ends. 　　　　　　　[*Exeunt.*]

[Scene viii.

*Before the Temple of Apollo.*]

*Arruntius, Lepidus, divers other Senators
　　　　　　　passing by them.*

[Arr.] Ay, go, make haste; take heed you
　be not last
　To tender your "All hail" in the wide
　hall

Of huge Sejanus; run a lictor's pace;
Stay not to put your robes on, but
　away
With the pale troubled ensigns of great
　friendship
Stamped i' your face!　Now, Marcus
　Lepidus,
You still believe your former augury?
Sejanus must go downward?　You per-
　ceive
His wane approaching fast?
Lep. 　　　　　Believe me, Lucius,
I wonder at this rising.
Arr. 　　　　Ay, and that we　10
　Must give our suffrage to it?　You will
　say,
It is to make his fall more steep and
　grievous?
It may be so.　But think it, they that
　can
With idle wishes 'ssay to bring back
　time;
In cases desperate, all hope is crime.
See, see!　What troops of his officious
　friends
Flock to salute my lord, and start before
My great proud lord, to get a lordlike
　nod!
Attend my lord unto the Senate House!
Bring back my lord!　Like servile
　huishers,[1] make　　　　20
Way for my lord!　Proclaim his idol
　lordship,
More than ten criers, or six noise of
　trumpets![2]
Make legs,[3] kiss hands, and take a scat-
　tered hair
From my lord's eminent shoulder!　See,
　Sanquinius,
With his slow belly, and his dropsy!
　Look,
What toiling haste he makes!　Yet here's
　another
Retarded with the gout, will be afore
　him.
Get thee Liburnian porters, thou gross
　fool,
To bear thy obsequious fatness, like
　thy peers.
They are met!　The gout returns, and
　his great carriage.　　　　30

[1] Ushers.
[2] Companies of trumpeters.
[3] *I.e.,* bow.

*Lictors, Consuls, Sejanus, etc., pass over*
*the stage.*

Lic. Give way, make place, room for the
consul!

San.            Hail,
Hail, great Sejanus!

Hat.            Hail, my honored lord!

Arr. [*Aside.*] We shall be marked anon
for our not "Hail."

Lep. [*Aside.*] That is already done.

Arr. [*Aside.*]                    It is a note
Of upstart greatness to observe and
watch
For these poor trifles, which the noble
mind
Neglects and scorns.

Lep. [*Aside.*]    Ay, and they think them-
selves
Deeply dishonored where they are
omitted,
As if they were necessities that helped
To the perfection of their dignities,    40
And hate the men that but refrain hem.

Arr. [*Aside.*]                            O!
There is a farder cause of hate. Their
breasts
Are guilty that we know their obscure
springs
And base beginnings; thence the anger
grows. On! Follow!            [*Exeunt.*]

[Scene ix.

*The same.*]

*Macro, Laco.*

[Mac.] When all are entered, shut the
temple doors,
And bring your guards up to the gate.

Lac.                            I will.

Mac. If you shall hear commotion in the
senate,
Present yourself, and charge on any man
Shall offer to come forth.

Lac.            I am instructed. [*Exeunt.*]

[Scene x.

*The Temple of Apollo.*]    *The Senate.*

*Haterius, Trio, Sanquinius, Cotta, Regulus,*
*Sejanus, Pomponius, Latiaris, Lepidus,*
*Arruntius, Præcones, Lictores, [etc.]*

[Hat.] How well his lordship looks today!

Trio.                            As if
He had been born or made for this
hour's state.

Cot. Your fellow consul's come about,
methinks?

Trio. Ay, he is wise.

San.            Sejanus trusts him well.

Trio. Sejanus is a noble, bounteous lord.

Hat. He is so, and most valiant.

Lat.                    And most wise.

[1] Sen. He's everything.

Lat.            Worthy of all, and more
Than bounty can bestow.

Trio.                        This dignity
Will make him worthy.

Pom.            Above Cæsar.

San.                            Tut,
Cæsar is but the rector of an isle,    10
He of the empire.

Trio.            Now he will have power
More to reward than ever.

Cot.                    Let us look
We be not slack in giving him our
voices.

Lat. Not I.

San.        Nor I.

Cot.            The readier we seem
To propagate his honors, will more bind
His thought to ours.

Hat.    I think right with your lordship;
It is the way to have us hold our places.

San. Ay, and get more.

Lat.            More office and more titles.

Pom. I will not lose the part I hope to
share
In these his fortunes, for my patrimony.    20

Lat. See how Arruntius sits, and Lepidus!

Trio. Let hem alone; they will be marked
anon.

[1] Sen. I'll do with others.

[2] Sen.            So will I.

[3] Sen.                    And I.
Men grow not in the state but as they
are planted
Warm in his favors.

Cot.            Noble Sejanus!

Hat. Honored Sejanus!

Lat.            Worthy and great Sejanus!

Arr. [*Aside.*] Gods! How the sponges
open and take in
And shut again! Look, look! Is not he
blessed
That gets a seat in eye-reach of him?
More
That comes in ear- or tongue-reach? O,
but most    30

Can claw his subtile elbow, or with a
    buzz
Flyblow his ears?
Præt[or].    Proclaim the senate's peace,
And give last summons by the edict.
Præ.                              Silence!
    In name of Cæsar and the senate! Si-
    lence!
"Memmius Regulus, and Fulcinius Trio,
consuls, these present kalends of June, with
the first light, shall hold a senate in the
Temple of Apollo Palatine; all that are
fathers, and are registered fathers,[1] that
have right of ent'ring the senate, we    [40
warn or command you be frequently present; take knowledge the business is the
commonwealth's.    Whosoever is absent,
his fine or mulct will be taken, his excuse
will not be taken."
Trio.  Note who are absent, and record
    their names.
Reg.  Fathers conscript, may what I am
    to utter
    Turn good and happy for the common-
        wealth!
    And thou, Apollo, in whose holy house
    We here are met, inspire us all with
        truth,                            50
    And liberty of censure to our thought!
    The majesty of great Tiberius Cæsar
    Propounds to this grave senate the
        bestowing
    Upon the man he loves, honored Sejanus,
    The tribunitial dignity and power.
    Here are his letters, signéd with his
        signet.
    What pleaseth now the fathers to be
        done?
Sen.  Read, read hem, open, publicly read
    hem.
Cot.  Cæsar hath honored his own great-
    ness much
    In thinking of this act.
Trio.                    It was a thought  60
    Happy, and worthy Cæsar.
Lat.                          And the lord
    As worthy it, on whom it is directed!
Hat.  Most worthy!
San.      Rome did never boast the virtue
    That could give envy bounds, but his;
        Sejanus—
[1] Sen.  Honored and noble!
[2] Sen.            Good and great Sejanus!

_____
[1] *I.e.*, conscript fathers.

Arr.  [*Aside.*]  O, most tame slavery, and
    fierce flattery!
Præ.        Silence!    *The epistle is read.*
"Tiberius Cæsar to the senate, greeting.
If you, conscript fathers, with your children, be in health, it is abundantly well;
we with our friends here are so.  The  [70
care of the commonwealth, howsoever we
are removed in person, cannot be absent
to our thought, although oftentimes, even
to princes most present, the truth of their
own affairs is hid; than which nothing
falls out more miserable to a state, or
makes the art of governing more difficult.
But, since it hath been our easeful happiness to enjoy both the aids and industry
of so vigilant a senate, we profess to  [80
have been the more indulgent to our
pleasures, not as being careless of our office,
but rather secure of the necessity.  Neither
do these common rumors of many and infamous libels published against our retirement, at all afflict us, being born more
out of men's ignorance than their malice,
and will, neglected, find their own grave
quickly; whereas, too sensibly acknowledged, it would make their obloquy  [90
ours.    Nor do we desire their authors,
though found, be censured, since in a free
state, as ours, all men ought to enjoy their
minds and tongues free."
(Arr.  The lapwing, the lapwing!)
"Yet in things which shall worthily and
more near concern the majesty of a prince,
we shall fear to be so unnaturally cruel
to our own fame, as to neglect them.  True
it is, conscript fathers, that we have  [100
raised Sejanus from obscure and almost
unknown gentry"—
(Sen.  How, how!)
"to the highest and most conspicuous
point of greatness, and, we hope, deserv-
ingly; yet not without danger, it being a
most bold hazard in that sov'reign who,
by his particular love to one, dares adventure the hatred of all his other subjects."
(Arr.  This touches; the blood turns.)
"But we affy [2] in your loves and un-  [111
derstandings, and do no way suspect the
merit of our Sejanus to make our favors
offensive to any."
(Sen.  O, good, good!)
"Though we could have wished his zeal

_____
[2] Trust.

had run a calmer course against Agrippina
and our nephews, howsoever the openness
of their actions declared them delinquents,
and that he would have remembered   [120
no innocence is so safe but it rejoiceth
to stand in the sight of mercy—the use
of which in us he hath so quite taken away
toward them, by his loyal fury, as now our
clemency would be thought but wearied
cruelty, if we should offer to exercise it."
(ARR.   I thank him; there I looked for 't.
    A good fox!)
"Some there be that would interpret this
his public severity to be particular ambition, and that, under a pretext of   [130
service to us, he doth but remove his own
lets, alleging the strengths he hath made to
himself, by the prætorian soldiers, by his
faction in court and senate, by the offices
he holds himself, and confers on others,
his popularity and dependents, his urging
and almost driving us to this our unwilling
retirement, and, lastly, his aspiring to be
our son-in-law."
(SEN.   This 's strange!                        140
ARR.   I shall anon believe your vultures,
    Marcus.)
"Your wisdoms, conscript fathers, are
able to examine and censure these suggestions.   But were they left to our absolving
voice, we durst pronounce them, as we
think them, most malicious."
(SEN.   O, he has restored all; list!)
"Yet are they offered to be averred, and
on the lives of the informers.   What we
should say, or rather what we should   [150
not say, lords of the senate, if this be
true, our gods and goddesses confound
us if we know!   Only we must think,
we have placed our benefits ill, and conclude that, in our choice, either we were
wanting to the gods, or the gods to us."
        *The Senators shift their places.*
(ARR.   The place grows hot; they shift.)
"We have not been covetous, honorable
fathers, to change; neither is it now any
new lust that alters our affection,   [160
or old loathing, but those needful jealousies
of state, that warn wiser princes hourly
to provide their safety, and do teach them
how learned a thing it is to beware of the
humblest enemy—much more of those
great ones whom their own employed
favors have made fit for their fears."

([1] SEN.   Away!
[2] SEN.                    Sit farder.
COT.                                Let's remove—
ARR.   Gods!   How the leaves drop off,
    this little wind!)
"We therefore desire that the offices   [170
he holds be first seized by the senate, and
himself suspended from all exercise of
place or power—"
(SEN.   How!
SAN.   [*Pushing through.*]   By your leave!
ARR.   Come, porcpisce.[1]—Where's Hate-
    rius?
    His gout keeps him most miserably
        constant!—
    Your dancing shows a tempest.)
SEJ.                             Read no more!
REG.   Lords of the senate, hold your
    seats; read on.
SEJ.   These letters, they are forged.

REG.                    A guard! Sit still.   180

        *Laco enters with the Guards.*

ARR.   There's change!
REG.                    Bid silence, and read forward.
    PRÆ.   Silence!—"and himself suspended
from all exercise of place or power but
till due and mature trial be made of his
innocency, which yet we can faintly apprehend the necessity to doubt.   If, conscript fathers, to your more searching wisdoms there shall appear farther cause
—or of farder proceeding, either to seizure
of lands, goods, or more—it is not our   [190
power that shall limit your authority, or
our favor that must corrupt your justice;
either were dishonorable in you, and
both uncharitable to ourself.   We would
willingly be present with your counsels in
this business; but the danger of so potent
a faction, if it should prove so, forbids
our attempting it, except one of the consuls
would be entreated for our safety, to undertake the guard of us home; then we   [200
should most readily adventure.   In the
meantime, it shall not be fit for us to importune so judicious a senate, who know
how much they hurt the innocent that
spare the guilty, and how grateful a
sacrifice to the gods is the life of an ingrateful person.   We reflect not in this on Sejanus (notwithstanding, if you keep an

---

[1] Porpoise, which was supposed to portend
storms.

eye upon him—and there is Latiaris, a
senator, and Pinnarius Natta, two [210
of his most trusted ministers, and so professed, whom we desire not to have apprehended) but as the necessity of the cause
exacts it.''

Reg. A guard on Latiaris!

Arr.                    O, the spy,
The reverend spy is caught! Who pities
him?
Reward, sir, for your service.    Now
you ha' done
Your property,[1] you see what use is
made?
   [Exeunt Latiaris and Natta, guarded.]
Hang up the instrument.

Sej.               Give leave.

Lac.               Stand, stand!
He comes upon his death, that doth
advance                    220
An inch toward my point.

Sej.          Have we no friends here?

Arr. Hush't!    Where now are all the
hails and acclamations?


### [Enter] Macro.[2]

[Mac.] Hail to the consuls, and this noble
senate!

Sej. [Aside.] Is Macro here? O, thou art
lost, Sejanus!

Mac. Sit still and unaffrighted, reverend
fathers;
Macro, by Cæsar's grace the new-made
provost,
And now possessed of the prætorian
bands,
An honor late belonged to that proud
man,
Bids you be safe, and, to your constant
doom [3]                    229
Of his deservings, offers you the surety
Of all the soldiers, tribunes, and cen-
turions
Received in our command.

Reg.               Sejanus, Sejanus,
Stand forth, Sejanus!

Sej.          Am I called?

Mac.               Ay, thou,
Thou insolent monster, art bid stand.

Sej.               Why, Macro,

It hath been otherwise between you
and I;
This court, that knows us both, hath
seen a difference,
And can, if it be pleased to speak, confirm
Whose insolence is most.

Mac.          Come down, Typhœus!
If mine be most, lo, thus I make it more;
Kick up thy heels in air, tear off thy
robe,                    240
Play with thy beard and nostrils. Thus
'tis fit
(And no man take compassion of thy
state)
To use th' ingrateful viper, tread his
brains
Into the earth.

Reg.               Forbear!

Mac.               If I could lose
All my humanity now, 'twere well to
torture
So meriting a traitor.—Wherefore, fa-
thers,
Sit you amazed and silent, and not
censure
This wretch, who, in the hour he first
rebelled
Gainst Cæsar's bounty, did condemn
himself?
Phlegra, the field where all the sons of
earth                    250
Mustered against the gods, did ne'er
acknowledge
So proud and huge a monster.

Reg.               Take him hence;
And all the gods guard Cæsar!

Trio.               Take him hence.

Hat. Hence.

Cot.          To the dungeon with him.

San.               He deserves it.

Sen. Crown all our doors with bays.

San.               And let an ox,
With gilded horns and garlands, straight
be led
Unto the Capitol.

Hat.          And sacrificed
To Jove, for Cæsar's safety.

Trio.               All our gods
Be present still to Cæsar!

Cot.               Phœbus.

San.               Mars.

Hat. Diana.

San.          Pallas.

---

[1] Performed your office.
[2] The word Senate is repeated here.
[3] Firm judgment.

SEN.            Juno, Mercury,    260
All guard him!
MAC.    Forth, thou prodigy of men.
            [*Exit Sejanus, guarded.*]
COT. Let all the traitor's titles be de-
faced.
TRIO. His images and statues be pulled
down.
HAT. His chariot-wheels be broken.
ARR.            And the legs
Of the poor horses, that deserved naught,
Let them be broken too!
LEP.            O violent change,
And whirl of men's affections!
ARR.            Like as both
Their bulks and souls were bound on
Fortune's wheel,
And must act only with her motion.
     [*Exeunt All but*] *Lepidus, Arruntius.*
[LEP.] Who would depend upon the popu-
lar air,            270
Or voice of men, that have today
beheld
(That which, if all the gods had fore-
declared,
Would not have been believed) Sejanus'
fall?
He that this morn rose proudly as the
sun,
And, breaking through a mist of clients'
breath,
Came on as gazed at and admired as
he
When superstitious Moors salute his
light!
That had our servile nobles waiting
him
As common grooms, and hanging on
his look            279
No less than human life on destiny!
That had men's knees as frequent as the
gods,
And sacrifices more than Rome had
altars!
And this man fall! Fall? Ay, without
a look
That durst appear his friend, or lend
so much
Of vain relief, to his changed state, as
pity!
ARR. They that before, like gnats, played
in his beams,
And thronged to circumscribe him, now
not seen,

Nor deign to hold a common seat with
him!
Others, that waited him unto the
senate,            289
Now inhumanely ravish him to prison,
Whom but this morn they followed as
their lord;
Guard through the streets, bound like
a fugitive;
Instead of wreaths give fetters, strokes
for stoops,
Blind shame for honors, and black taunts
for titles!
Who would trust slippery Chance?
LEP.           They that would make
Themselves her spoil, and foolishly
forget,
When she doth flatter, that she comes
to prey.
Fortune, thou hadst no deity, if men
Had wisdom; we have placéd thee so
high
By fond belief in thy felicity.      300
SEN. (*Shout within.*) The gods guard Cæ-
sar! All the gods guard Cæsar!

      [*Enter*] *Macro, Regulus, Senators.*

[MAC.] Now, great Sejanus, you that awed
the state,
And sought to bring the nobles to your
whip;
That would be Cæsar's tutor, and dis-
pose
Of dignities and offices; that had
The public head still bare to your de-
signs,
And made the general voice to echo
yours;
That looked for salutations twelve
score off,
And would have pyramids, yea, temples,
reared
To your huge greatness—now you lie
as flat           310
As was your pride advanced!
REG.          Thanks to the gods!
SEN. And praise to Macro, that hath
savéd Rome!
Liberty, liberty, liberty! Lead on,
And praise to Macro, that hath savéd
Rome!
[*Exeunt All but*] *Arruntius, Lepidus.* [*Enter*]
                *Terentius.*

[ARR.] I prophesy, out of this senate's flattery,
That this new fellow, Macro, will become
A greater prodigy in Rome than he
That now is fall'n.
TER.        O you whose minds are good,
And have not forced all mankind[1] from your breasts,
That yet have so much stock of virtue left        320
To pity guilty states, when they are wretched,
Lend your soft ears to hear, and eyes to weep,
Deeds done by men beyond the acts of Furies.
The eager multitude (who never yet
Knew why to love or hate, but only pleased
T' express their rage of power) no sooner heard
The murmur of Sejanus in decline,
But with that speed and heat of appetite
With which they greedily devour the way
To some great sports or a new theater,        330
They filled the Capitol and Pompey's Cirque[2]
Where, like so many mastives[3] biting stones,
As if his statues now were sensive[4] grown
Of their wild fury, first, they tear them down,
Then, fast'ning ropes, drag them along the streets,
Crying in scorn, "This, this was that rich head
Was crowned with girlands[5] and with odors, this
That was in Rome so reverencéd! Now
The fornace and the bellows shall to work,
The great Sejanus crack, and piece by piece        340
Drop in the founder's pit."
LEP.        O popular rage!
TER. The whilst the senate at the Temple of Concord

Make haste to meet again, and thronging cry,
"Let us condemn him, tread him down in water,
While he doth lie upon the bank. Away!"
Where some, more tardy, cry unto their bearers,
"He will be censured ere we come; run, knaves,"
And use that furious diligence, for fear
Their bondmen should inform against their slackness,
And bring their quaking flesh unto the hook.        350
The rout, they follow with confuséd voice,
Crying they are glad; say they could ne'er abide him;
Inquire what man he was, what kind of face,
What beard he had, what nose, what lips; protest
They ever did presage h' would come to this,
They never thought him wise, nor valiant, ask
After his garments, when he dies; what death.
And not a beast of all the herd demands
What was his crime, or who were his accusers,        359
Under what proof or testimony he fell.
There came, says one, a huge long-worded letter
From Capreæ against him. Did there so?
O, they are satisfied; no more.
LEP.        Alas!
They follow Fortune, and hate men condemned,
Guilty or not.
ARR.        But had Sejanus thrived
In his design, and prosperously oppressed
The old Tiberius, then, in that same minute,
These very rascals, that now rage like Furies,
Would have proclaimed Sejanus emperor.
LEP. But what hath followed?
TER.        Sentence by the senate,
To lose his head, which was no sooner off        371
But that and th' unfortunate trunk were seized

---

[1] Humanity.        [2] Circus, stadium.
[3] Mastiffs.        [4] Sensitive.        [5] Garlands.

By the rude multitude, who, not content
With what the forward justice of the
    state
Officiously[1] had done, with violent rage
Have rent it limb from limb.  A thousand
    heads,
A thousand hands, ten thousand tongues
    and voices,
Employed at once in several acts of
    malice!
Old men not staid with age, virgins with
    shame,
Late wives with loss of husbands, moth-
    ers of children,                380
Losing all grief in joy of his sad fall, .
Run quite transported with their cruelty!
These mounting at his head, these at
    his face,
These digging out his eyes, those with
    his brain
Sprinkling themselves, their houses, and
    their friends;
Others are met, have ravished thence
    an arm,
And deal small pieces of the flesh for
    favors;
These with a thigh, this hath cut off
    his hands,
And this his feet; these fingers, and
    these toes;
That hath his liver, he his heart; there
    wants                           390
Nothing but room for wrath, and place
    for hatred!
What cannot oft be done, is now o'er-
    done.
The whole, and all of what was great
    Sejanus,
And, next to Cæsar, did possess the world,
Now torn and scattered, as he needs
    no grave;
Each little dust covers a little part.
So lies he nowhere, and yet often buried!

            *[Enter] Nuntius.*[2]

[ARR.] More of Sejanus?
NUN.            Yes.
LEP.               What can be added?
    We know him dead.
NUN.         Then there begin your pity.
    There is enough behind to melt ev'n
    Rome                           400

[1] Officially.
[2] The names *Arruntius, Lepidus,* and *Terentius*
are repeated here.

And Cæsar into tears; since never
    slave
Could yet so highly offend, but tyranny,
In torturing him, would make him worth
    lamenting.
A son and daughter to the dead Se-
    janus
(Of whom there is not now so much
    remaining
As would give fast'ning to the hang-
    man's hook)
Have they drawn forth for farder sac-
    rifice;
Whose tenderness of knowledge, unripe
    years,
And childish silly[3] innocence was such
As scarce would lend them feeling of
    their danger;               410
The girl so simple, as she often asked
Where they would lead her, for what
    cause they dragged her,
Cried she would do no more, that she
    could take
Warning with beating.  And, because
    our laws
Admit no virgin immature to die,
The wittily and strangely cruel Macro
Delivered her to be deflowered and
    spoiled
By the rude lust of the licentious hang-
    man,
Then to be strangled with her harmless
    brother.
LEP.   O, act most worthy hell and lasting
    night                        420
    To hide it from the world!
NUN.                Their bodies thrown
    Into the Gemonies (I know not how,
    Or by what accident returned), the
        mother,
    Th' expulséd Apicata, finds them there,
    Whom when she saw lie spread on the
        degrees,[4]
    After a world of fury on herself,
    Tearing her hair, defacing of her face,
    Beating her breasts and womb, kneeling
        amazed,
    Crying to heaven, then to them, at
        last
    Her drownéd voice gat up above her
        woes,                    430
    And with such black and bitter execra-
        tions

[3] Simple.                           [4] Steps.

As might affright the gods, and force
the sun
Run backward to the east, nay, make the
old
Deforméd chaos rise again, t' o'erwhelm
Them, us, and all the world, she fills
the air,
Upbraids the heavens with their partial
dooms,[1]
Defies their tyrannous powers, and de-
mands
What she and those poor innocents have
transgressed,
That they must suffer such a share in
vengeance,
Whilst Livia, Lygdus, and Eudemus
live,      440
Who, as she says, and firmly vows to
prove it
To Cæsar and the senate, poisoned
Drusus.
LEP. Confederates with her husband?
NUN.            Ay.
LEP.               Strange act!
ARR. And strangely opened. What says
now my monster,
The multitude? They reel now, do they
not?
NUN. Their gall is gone, and now they
gin to weep
The mischief they have done.
ARR.        I thank hem, rogues.
NUN. Part are so stupid, or so flexible,
As they believe him innocent; all
grieve;

[1] Unfair judgments.

And some whose hands yet reek with
his warm blood,      450
And gripe the part which they did tear
of him,
Wish him collected and created new.
LEP. How Fortune plies her sports, when
she begins
To practice hem! Pursues, continues,
adds,
Confounds with varying her impassioned
moods!
ARR. Dost thou hope, Fortune, to redeem
thy crimes,
To make amends for thy ill-placéd
favors
With these strange punishments? For-
bear, you things
That stand upon the pinnacles of state,
To boast your slippery height; when you
do fall,      460
You pash [2] yourselves in pieces, ne'er to
rise;
And he that lends you pity is not wise.
TER. Let this example move th' insolent
man
Not to grow proud and careless of the
gods.
It is an odious wisdom to blaspheme,
Much more to slighten or deny their
powers;
For whom the morning saw so great
and high,
Thus low and little, fore the even doth
lie.            [Exeunt.]

[2] Dash.

THE END.

This tragedy was first acted in the year 1603 by the King's Majesty's Servants. The
principal tragedians were:

     *Ric. Burbadge*                          *Will. Shakespeare*
     *Aug. Philips*                             *Joh. Hemings*
     *Will. Sly*                                *Hen. Condell*
     *Joh. Lowin*                            *Alex. Cooke*

With the allowance of the Master of Revels.

# BEN JONSON

## VOLPONE

*Volpone, or The Fox*, perhaps the best of Jonson's plays, has undoubtedly remained his most popular with the playgoing public. As Jonson admitted in his prologue, it was "fully penned" in five weeks early in 1606, and acted by the King's Men at the Globe soon afterward, although the date 1605 is given on the title page. This, however, was according to the Old Calendar, and the Herford-Simpson editors believe that the topical references to the whale in the Thames and other remarkable events in II, i, confirm the date 1606. Later in the year or early in 1607 the company took the play to Oxford and Cambridge, where Jonson always had friends. It was published in quarto in 1608 and appeared in the 1616 folio. The King's Men kept it in their repertoire for many years. Performances were given at court in 1624, 1630, and 1638, and also at the Blackfriars in 1638. During the Restoration it was one of the stock plays at Killigrew's Theatre Royal from 1662 onward, and was still in vogue at Dorset Garden as late as 1691. Oxford students gave amateur performances twice in January 1663, and court performances were given in 1667 and 1676. During the eighteenth century all three theaters—the Drury Lane, the Covent Garden, and the Haymarket—kept it actively alive on the stage until 1785. Then it disappeared until the Phoenix Society in London resuscitated it in 1921 and 1923. In 1935 the Malvern Festival gave it as part of its program to keep the older English dramatic classics alive, and was imitated by the Shakespeare Memorial Theatre at Stratford in 1944. London commercial theaters like the Westminster and the St. James's followed suit, as did college organizations at Oxford, Cambridge, Harvard, and many other schools. It was adapted into German by Ludwig Tieck in 1793, and translated into French in 1835, 1863, and 1934. In 1928 an adaptation by Stefan Zweig, aided by Jules Romains, proved highly popular in Paris, and was equally so when translated back again into English in the same year by Ruth Langner and played all over the United States by the New York Theatre Guild. There has recently even been a musical version.

Jonson himself furnished a full explanation of his purposes, methods, and critical opinions of the current English stage in his prologue and his long address to the two universities, calling attention to his observance of every "needful rule" and swearing, somewhat inaccurately, that

> All gall and copp'ras from his ink he draineth;
> Only a little salt remaineth. . . .

This observation immediately raises one of the cruxes of the play for those critics who like classifications: can a play with such an atmosphere, such characters, and such an ending be regarded as a genuine comedy? Even the incipient love affair between Bonario and Celia is not sufficiently developed to give the play any air of romantic comedy. The problem has worried critics for centuries, nor have recent commentators neglected it. Archer is inclined to regard the play, "without doubt the greatest of Jonson's works," as almost a farce because of its exaggerations of human folly, if not of human cupidity ("which would perhaps be difficult"); the preternatural gullibility of the gulls; the exclusive emphasis on imposture and cozenage; and the caricaturing (though a "spirited" one) of all the characters. To Archer, all these things consign *Volpone*, like most Elizabethan comedy, to "a low stage of dramatic development." The Elizabethan dramatists, he repeats, were working in "too soft a medium."

129

Ralph Nash, however, in "The Comic Intent in *Volpone*" (*SP*, 1947), has insisted that, in view of Jonson's remarks quoted above, the critics have seen the play in much darker colors than Jonson intended, and that "throughout the play the ruling spirit of master and parasite is that of delight in their own cleverness and malicious pleasure in gulling the stupid legacy hunters." Thus when the play ends with the discomfiture of both the legacy hunters and their cozeners, who have overreached themselves, the near-tragic catastrophe is the result of what Jonson in his dedication has warned of as his "special aim," that of putting the "snaffle" in the mouths of those who object that playwrights "never punish vice" in their "interludes." S. L. Greenberg, in "Folly into Crime: The Catastrophe of *Volpone*" (*MLQ*, 1959), has attacked the problem from a somewhat different angle. He has emphasized the view that from the opening scene onward for some time the desire of the audience is to be attracted to the "villains," often because of "imaginative delight" in the poetry they speak, which is at the same time balanced by the realization of their corruption. This early sympathy on the audience's part remains strong enough so that at the end it finds the grim catastrophe too severe a moral catharsis; "our judgment may assent, but our feelings are still lagging." But from Act IV on, the theme is broadened from "private folly" to "public folly," and the question becomes not only that of "poetic justice" but of "civic justice," for which the early acts have not been a sufficient preparation. As a result, the audience is not ready for the necessary simplification when it is demanded. Arthur Sale, in the introduction to his edition of the play for the University Tutorial Press in 1951, had dissented from Gregory Smith's "too narrow" concept of the play as presenting so black a picture of human depravity that it practically removes itself from the realm of comedy. Nevertheless, Sale found in it an influence carrying over from its tragic predecessor, *Sejanus*, pointing the way to a comedy in which the distinguishing feature is power. Thayer also disagrees with those critics who feel that classification of the play is difficult because it "seems to move perilously close to tragedy" and reminds his readers that *Volpone* "contains no scenes that are even remotely tragic." He joins with Rufus Putney ("Jonson's Poetic Comedy," *PQ*, 1962) in expressing his appreciation of the play as comedy. P. H. Davidson agrees that it is a comedy, but one of a special type, "the ultimate source of which is to be found in the Old Comedy" of Aristophanes, with which Jonson was quite familiar ("*Volpone* and the Old Comedy," *MLQ*, 1963).

The naming of the theme of the play has also occasioned some slight falling out among the critics. Greed, as illustrated in legacy hunting, is certainly prominent. Robert Ornstein, in "*Volpone* and Renaissance Psychology" (*NQ*, 1956), trying to see the play as it would have appeared to its contemporaries, considered that the Elizabethans did not see in *Volpone* the "near-tragic grandeur" that some modern critics have detected, but were impressed only by the conventional vices and vanities of the rich man. To substantiate his point, Ornstein called attention to the very similar portrait, or "character," of a rich man as described in F. N. Coffeteau's *Table of Human Passions*, though this was not translated by Edward Grimestone till 1621. R. P. Draper also perceived the same theme in "The Golden Age and Volpone's Address to His Gold" (*NQ*, 1956), and suggested that Jonson had had Ovid's account of the Golden Age in the *Metamorphoses* ironically in mind when he wrote Volpone's opening speech on his gold. For the same situation John S. Weld ("Christian Comedy: *Volpone*," *SP*, 1954) concluded that from the deceiver-deceived plot Jonson intended to make the wisdom of the world seem foolish, and that from his depiction of Volpone as a foolish worldling worshiping gold and his introduction of various passages drawn from popular sermons, emblem books, and didactic verse Jonson was leading up to his Christian unifying theme: the folly of worldliness.

J. D. Rae, in his edition of the play (Yale University Press, 1919), stated, in discussing its sources, such as Erasmus's *Praise of Folly*, Lucian's dialogues, Horace's satires, and Libanius's orations and speeches, that the play had little originality and that "the sources are almost the play itself." But later scholars have discovered further sources which come even closer to Jonson's allegory and setting, without actually paralleling specific situations and episodes. Notably in this respect D. A. Sheve, in "Jonson's *Volpone* and Traditional Fox Lore" (*RES*, 1950), drew attention to Konrad von Gesner's *Historia Animalium* (1551–8), which was in Jonson's library. In this great work, the basis of modern zoology, Jonson found a statement of the tradition of how the fox often feigned death in order to catch birds, especially "ravens, crows, and other birds," which light near the supposed carcass and are seized. With this allegorical hint Jonson interwove his episodes of the lengths to which his legacy hunters would go, and gave to his leading characters the Italian names of some bird, animal, or insect.

Barish, in defending what he calls "The Double Plot in *Volpone*" (*MP*, 1953), not only challenged the usual opinion that Jonson's introduction of the three English visitors, Sir Politic Would-Be, Lady Would-Be, and Peregrine, into his Italian scene was an irrelevant excrescence, but extended Rae's suggestion that Sir Pol had his roots in the popular beast fable: ". . . he is Sir Pol, the chattering poll parrot, and his wife is a deadlier specimen of the same species." Barish adds that parrots not only chatter, but they mimic. To him this points to the complex thematic structure of the play, in the way in which the trio try to italianize themselves in manners, costumes, reading, seductions, political plots, etc., as well as in their caricaturing of the actors in the main plot. Alvin B. Kernan, in his edition of the play for the new Yale edition of Jonson (Yale University Press, 1962), has also stressed the recurrence of symbolical animal imagery throughout the play.

At least two scholars have discussed Jonson's choice of Venice as the setting for *Volpone*. In "*Volpone* and the Reputation of Venetian Justice" (*MLR*, 1940), R. H. Parkinson argued that Jonson needed a locale "with a legal code disinterested enough to make the punishment of the patrician Volpone plausible and rigorous enough to be identifiable with Jonson's own stern moral sense." This he probably found in Cardinal Gasparo Contarini's *De Magistratibus et Republica Venetorum*, referred to in the play (IV, i) and translated by Lewis Lewkenor in 1599 as *The Commonwealth and Government of Venice*. Boughner has worked out in much greater detail Jonson's debt to Lewkenor ("Lewkenor and *Volpone*," *NQ*, 1962). Jonson's use of an Italian setting and Italian names in this play led Baskervill to place the English version of *Every Man in His Humor* after it. For a discussion of the type of Italian interlude introduced into the play, see Winifred Smith, *Commedia dell'Arte* (Columbia University Press, 1912). Harry Levin, in "Jonson's Metempsychosis" (*PQ*, 1943), has dealt in some detail with Mosca's interlude in Act I, and traced the "jingling speech" by Nano on the transmigration of souls to Lucian's dialogue, "Gallus," known to Jonson in the translation by Erasmus. The idea for Volpone's song, "Come, my Celia," in III, vii, was drawn from Catullus, and shows Jonson again in his lyric role as love poet. (See John P. Cutts, "Volpone's Song: A Note on the Source and Jonson's Translation," *NQ*, 1959; and T. W. Sternfeld, "Song in Jonson's Comedy: A Gloss on *Volpone*," *Studies in English Renaissance Drama in Honor of Karl J. Holtzknecht*, New York University Press, 1959, which also discusses the larger subject of Jonson's attitude toward music and his use of it in his plays.)

The present text is based on the Herford-Simpson edition of the 1616 folio, checked with a copy of the original in the Newberry Library. In addition to the several modern editions of the play referred to above, the editions by Philip Brockbank in the New Mermaids series (London, 1968) and Jay L. Halio in the old spelling Fountainwell Drama Texts (Edinburgh and the University of California Press, 1968) have been consulted.

# VOLPONE, OR THE FOX[1]

## BY

## BEN JONSON

*To the most noble and most equal sisters, the two famous universities, for their love and acceptance shown to his poem in the presentation, Ben Jonson, the grateful acknowledger, dedicates both it and himself.*

Never, most equal sisters, had any man a wit so presently[2] excellent as that it could raise itself, but there must come both matter, occasion, commenders, and favorers to it. If this be true, and that [10 the fortune of all writers doth daily prove it, it behooves the careful to provide well toward these accidents, and, having acquired them, to preserve that part of reputation most tenderly wherein the benefit of a friend is also defended. Hence it is that I now render myself grateful and am studious to justify the bounty of your act, to which, though your mere authority were satisfying, yet, it being an [20 age wherein poetry and the professors[3] of it hear so ill[4] on all sides, there will a reason be looked for in the subject. It is certain, nor can it with any forehead[5] be opposed, that the too much license of poetasters in this time hath much deformed their mistress, that every day their manifold and manifest ignorance doth stick unnatural reproaches upon her. But for their petulancy it were an act of the [30 greatest injustice either to let the learned suffer, or so divine a skill, which indeed should not be attempted with unclean hands, to fall under the least contempt. For, if men will impartially and not asquint look toward the offices and function of a poet, they will easily conclude to themselves the impossibility of any man's being the good poet without first being a good man. He that is said [40

to be able to inform young men to all good disciplines, inflame grown men to all great virtues, keep old men in their best and supreme state or, as they decline to childhood, recover them to their first strength; that comes forth the interpreter and arbiter of nature, a teacher of things divine no less than human, a master in manners, and can alone, or with a few, effect the business of mankind— [50 this, I take him, is no subject for pride and ignorance to exercise their railing rhetoric upon. But it will here be hastily answered that the writers of these days are other things; that not only their manners but their natures' are inverted, and nothing remaining with them of the dignity of poet but the abused name, which every scribe usurps; that now, especially in dramatic or, as they term it, stage [60 poetry, nothing but ribaldry, profanation, blasphemy, all license of offense to God and man is practiced. I dare not deny a great part of this, and am sorry I dare not, because in some men's abortive features (and would they had never boasted the light) it is overtrue; but that all are embarked in this bold adventure for hell is a most uncharitable thought and, uttered, a more malicious slander. For my par- [70 ticular[6] I can, and from a most clear conscience, affirm that I have ever trembled to think toward the least profaneness, have loathed the use of such foul and unwashed bawdry as is now made the food of the scene;[7] and, howsoever I cannot escape from some the imputation of sharpness but that they will say I have taken a pride or lust to be bitter, and not my youngest infant[8] but hath come [80 into the world with all his teeth, I would ask of these supercilious politics[9] what

---

[1] The title continues: "A Comedy, Acted in the Year 1605, by the K[ing's] Majesty's Servants."   [2] Actually.   [3] Practitioners.
[4] Are so ill spoken of.   [5] Impudence.
[6] In my own case.   [8] *I.e., Sejanus.*
[7] Stage.   [9] Politicians, intriguers.

nation, society, or general order or state I have provoked?—what public person?— whether I have not in all these preserved their dignity, as mine own person, safe? My works are read, allowed [1] (I speak of those that are entirely mine); look into them. What broad reproofs have I used? Where have I been particular, where [90 personal, except to a mimic, cheater, bawd, or buffoon—creatures for their insolencies worthy to be taxed? Yet to which of these so pointingly as he might not either ingenuously have confessed or wisely dissembled his disease? But it is not rumor can make men guilty, much less entitle me to other men's crimes. I know that nothing can be so innocently writ or carried but may be made obnoxious to con- [100 struction; [2] marry, whilst I bear mine innocence about me I fear it not. Application [3] is now grown a trade with many; and there are that profess to have a key for the deciphering of everything. But let wise and noble persons take heed how they be too credulous or give leave to these invading interpreters to be overfamiliar with their fames, who cunningly and often utter their own virulent malice under [110 other men's simplest meanings. As for those that will (by faults which charity hath raked [4] up or common honesty concealed) make themselves a name with the multitude, or, to draw their rude and beastly claps, care not whose living faces they intrench with their petulant styles, may they do it without a rival, for me! I choose rather to live graved [5] in obscurity than share with them in so prepos- [120 terous a fame. Nor can I blame the wishes of those severe and wiser patriots, who, providing [6] the hurts these licentious spirits may do in a state, desire rather to see fools and devils and those antique relics of barbarism retrieved, with all other ridiculous and exploded follies, than behold the wounds of private men, of princes and nations, for, as Horace makes Trebatius speak among these, 130

*Sibi quisque timet, quanquam est intactus, et odit.*[7]

And men may justly impute such rages, if continued, to the writer as his sports. The increase of which lust in liberty, together with the present trade of the stage in all their misc'line [8] interludes, what learned or liberal soul doth not already abhor, where nothing but the filth of the time is uttered, and that with such impropriety of phrase, such [140 plenty of solecisms, such dearth of sense, so bold prolepses, so racked metaphors, with brothelry able to violate the ear of a pagan, and blasphemy to turn the blood of a Christian to water? I cannot but be serious in a cause of this nature, wherein my fame and the reputations of divers honest and learned are the question, when a name so full of authority, antiquity, and all great mark is through [150 their insolence become the lowest scorn of the age, and those men subject to the petulancy of every vernaculous [9] orator, that were wont to be the care of kings and happiest monarchs. This it is that hath not only rapt [10] me to present indignation, but made me studious heretofore, and, by all my actions, to stand off from them, which may most appear in this my latest work, which you, most [160 learned arbitresses, have seen, judged, and to my crown approved, wherein I have labored for their instruction and amendment, to reduce not only the ancient forms but manners of the scene, the easiness, the propriety, the innocence, and, last, the doctrine, which is the principal end of poesy, to inform men in the best reason of living. And, though my catastrophe may, in the strict rigor of comic law, [170 meet with censure, as turning back to my promise, I desire the learned and charitable critic to have so much faith in me to think it was done of industry, for with what ease I could have varied it nearer his scale (but that I fear to boast my own faculty) I could here insert. But my special aim being to put the snaffle in their mouths that cry out, "We never

---

[1] *I.e.*, passed by the censor.
[2] Through interpretation.
[3] Reading of cloaked allusions.
[4] Covered.
[5] Buried.
[6] Foreseeing.

[7] "Everybody fears for himself and is vexed, although he is untouched" (*Sermones*, II, i, 23).
[8] Miscelline, miscellaneous.
[9] Scurrilous.     [10] Transported.

punish vice in our interludes," etc., [180 I took the more liberty, though not without some lines of example, drawn even in the ancients themselves, the goings out [1] of whose comedies are not always joyful, but ofttimes the bawds, the servants, the rivals, yea, and the masters are mulcted —and fitly, it being the office of a comic poet to imitate justice and instruct to life as well as purity of language, or stir up gentle affections,[2] to which I shall [190 take the occasion elsewhere to speak.

For the present, most reverenced sisters, as I have cared to be thankful for your affections past, and here made the understanding acquainted with some ground of your favors, let me not despair their continuance to the maturing of some worthier fruits, wherein, if my muses be true to me, I shall raise the despised head of poetry again, and, stripping her out [200 of those rotten and base rags wherewith the times have adulterated her form, restore her to her primitive habit, feature, and majesty, and render her worthy to be embraced and kissed of all the great and master spirits of our world. As for the vile and slothful, who never affected an act worthy of celebration, or are so inward [3] with their own vicious natures as they worthily fear her and think it [210 a high point of policy to keep her in contempt with their declamatory and windy invectives, she shall out of just rage incite her servants (who are *"genus irritabile"* [4]) to spout ink in their faces, that shall eat farder [5] than their marrow, into their fames; and not Cinnamus the barber,[6] with his art, shall be able to take out the brands; but they shall live and be read till the wretches die, as things worst deserving [220 of themselves in chief and then of all mankind.

[From my house in the Blackfriars, this 11th day of February, 1607.][7]

## THE PERSONS OF THE PLAY

VOLPONE [*the Fox*], a *magnifico* [*nobleman*].
MOSCA [*the Gadfly*], *his parasite.*
VOLTORE [*the Vulture*], *an advocate.*
CORBACCIO [*the Crow*], *an old gentleman.*
CORVINO [*the Raven*], *a merchant.*
AVOCATORI, *four magistrates.*
NOTARIO, *the register.*
NANO, *a dwarf.*
CASTRONE, *an eunuch.*
GREGE [*or* MOB].

POLITIC WOULD-BE, *a knight.*
PEREGRINE, *a gent[leman] traveler.*
BONARIO, *a young gentleman.*

FINE MADAME WOULD-BE, *the knight's wife.*
CELIA, *the merchant's wife.*

COMMANDADORI, *officers [of justice].*
MERCATORI, *three merchants.*
ANDROGYNO, *a hermaphrodite.*
SERVITORE, *a servant;* WOMEN [SERVANTS].

THE SCENE: *Venice.*

[TIME: *Contemporary.*]

## THE ARGUMENT

V olpone, childless, rich, feigns sick, despairs,
O ffers his state to hopes of several heirs,
L ies languishing; his parasite receives
P resents of all, assures, deludes, then weaves
O ther cross plots, which ope themselves, are told.
N ew tricks for safety are sought; they thrive, when, bold,
E ach tempts th' other again, and all are sold.

## PROLOGUE

Now, luck yet send us, and a little wit
     Will serve to make our play hit;
According to the palates of the season,
     Here is rhyme, not empty of reason.
This we were bid to credit from our poet,
     Whose true scope, if you would know it,
In all his poems still hath been this measure:
     To mix profit with your pleasure;

[3] Familiar.
[4] *"Genus irritabile vatum"* (Horace, *Epistles*, II, 2, 102): "The excitable race of poets."
[5] Farther.
[6] The barber was also a surgeon.
[7] From 1607 edn.

[1] Conclusions.          [2] Feelings.

And not as some, whose throats their envy
    failing,      9
Cry hoarsely, "All he writes is railing,"
And, when his plays come forth, think
    they can flout them,
With saying he was a year about them.
To these there needs no lie, but this his
    creature,[1]
Which was two months since no feature;
And, though he dares give them five lives
    to mend it,
'Tis known five weeks fully penned it,
From his own hand, without a coadjutor,
Novice, journeyman, or tutor.
Yet thus much I can give you as a token
Of his play's worth: no eggs are broken,
Nor quaking custards [2] with fierce teeth
    affrighted,      21
Wherewith your rout are so delighted;
Nor hales he in a gull, old ends reciting,
To stop gaps in his loose writing;
With such a deal of monstrous and forced
    action,
As might make Bet'lem a faction; [3]
Nor made he his play for jests stol'n from
    each table,
But makes jests to fit his fable;[4]
And so presents quick[5] comedy refined
As best critics have designed.    30
The laws of time, place, persons he observ-
    eth;
From no needful rule he swerveth.
All gall and copp'ras from his ink he drain-
    eth;
Only a little salt remaineth,
Wherewith he'll rub your cheeks till, red
    with laughter,
They shall look fresh a week after.

### ACT I. SCENE i.

*[A room in Volpone's house.]*[6]

*Volpone, Mosca.*

VOLP. Good morning to the day; and next
    my gold!
Open the shrine that I may see my saint.

[1] Creation, *i.e.*, the play.
[2] An allusion to the tricks sometimes played
with immense custards at the lord mayors' and
other official feasts, and apparently later transferred to the theater (Gifford).
[3] Make Bedlam, the madhouse, more confused.
[4] Plot.    [5] Living, lively.
[6] The scene remains the same throughout the
act, and the action is continuous.

*[Mosca opens the curtain, revealing Vol-*
*    pone's treasure.]*
Hail, the world's soul and mine!  More
    glad than is
The teeming earth to see the longed-for
    sun
Peep through the horns of the celestial
    Ram,
Am I, to view thy splendor darkening
    his,
That, lying here amongst my other
    hoards,
Show'st like a flame by night, or like
    the day
Strook[7] out of chaos, when all darkness
    fled
Unto the center.[8] O, thou son of Sol,    [10
But brighter than thy father, let me
    kiss
With adoration thee and every relic
Of sacred treasure in this blessèd room.
Well did wise poets, by thy glorious
    name,
Title that age which they would have
    the best,
Thou being the best of things, and far
    transcending
All style of joy in children, parents,
    friends,
Or any other waking dream on earth.
Thy looks when they to Venus did as-
    cribe,
They should have given her twenty
    thousand Cupids;    20
Such are thy beauties and our loves!
    Dear saint,
Riches, the dumb god, that giv'st all
    men tongues,
That canst do naught, and yet mak'st
    men do all things,
The price of souls, even hell, with thee
    to boot,
Is made worth heaven! Thou art virtue,
    fame,
Honor, and all things else. Who can
    get thee,
He shall be noble, valiant, honest, wise—
MOS. And what he will, sir. Riches are
    in fortune
A greater good than wisdom is in na-
    ture.
VOLP. True, my belovèd Mosca. Yet I
    glory    30
[7] Struck.    [8] *I.e.*, of the earth.

More in the cunning purchase[1] of my
    wealth
Than in the glad possession, since I gain
No common way: I use no trade, no
    venter;[2]
I wound no earth with plowshares; I
    fat no beasts
To feed the shambles, have no mills
    for iron,
Oil, corn, or men to grind hem[3] into
    poulder;[4]
I blow no subtle glass, expose no ships
To threat'nings of the furrow-facéd sea;
I turn no moneys in the public bank,
Nor usure[5] private.
Mos.            No, sir, nor devour  40
    Soft prodigals. You shall ha' some will
        swallow
A melting heir as glibly as your Dutch
Will pills of butter, and ne'er purge for 't;
Tear forth the fathers of poor families
Out of their beds, and coffin them alive
In some kind, clasping prison, where
    their bones
May be forthcoming when the flesh is
    rotten.
But your sweet nature doth abhor these
    courses;
You loathe the widow's or the orphan's
    tears
Should wash your pavements, or their
    piteous cries               50
Ring in your roofs, and beat the air for
    vengeance.
Volp.  Right, Mosca; I do loathe it.
Mos.            And besides, sir,
You are not like a thresher that doth
    stand
With a huge flail, watching a heap of corn,
And, hungry, dares not taste the small-
    est grain,
But feeds on mallows and such bitter
    herbs,
Nor like the merchant, who hath filled
    his vaults
With Romagnia and rich Candian wines,
Yet drinks the lees of Lombard's vinegar.
You will not lie in straw, whilst moths
    and worms             60
Feed on your sumptuous hangings and
    soft beds;

You know the use of riches, and dare
    give now
From that bright heap, to me, your
    poor observer,[6]
Or to your dwarf, or your hermaphrodite,
Your eunuch, or what other household
    trifle
Your pleasure allows maint'nance—
Volp.            Hold thee, Mosca;
Take of my hand; thou strik'st on truth
    in all,
And they are envious term thee parasite.
Call forth my dwarf, my eunuch, and
    my fool,
And let hem make me sport. [Exit
    Mosca.] What should I do    70
But cocker up[7] my genius, and live free
To all delights my fortune calls me to?
I have no wife, no parent, child, ally,
To give my substance to; but whom I
    make
Must be my heir; and this makes men
    observe[8] me.
This draws new clients daily to my
    house,
Women and men of every sex and age,
That bring me presents, send me plate,
    coin, jewels,
With hope that when I die (which they
    expect
Each greedy minute) it shall then re-
    turn                80
Tenfold upon them, whilst some, cov-
    etous
Above the rest, seek to engross[9] me
    whole,
And counterwork the one unto the other,
Contend in gifts, as they would seem in
    love—
All which I suffer, playing with their
    hopes,
And am content to coin hem into profit,
And look upon their kindness, and take
    more,
And look on that, still bearing them in
    hand,[10]
Letting the cherry knock against their
    lips,
And draw it by their mouths, and back
    again.—           90
How now!

---

[1] Gain by underhand methods.    [4] Powder.
[2] Venture.    [5] Usury.
[3] Them.

[6] Dutiful attendant.    [8] Take notice of.
[7] Indulge.    [9] Absorb.
[10] Deceiving them.

ACT I. SCENE ii.

*Nano, Androgyno, Castrone, Volpone, Mosca.*

[NAN.] Now, room for fresh gamesters,
    who do will you to know
They do bring you neither play nor
    university show,
And therefore do entreat you that what-
    soever they rehearse
May not fare a whit the worse for the
    false pace of the verse.[1]
If you wonder at this, you will wonder
    more ere we pass,
For know, here [*Points to Androgyno.*]
    is enclosed the soul of Pythagoras,
That juggler divine, as hereafter shall
    follow—
Which soul, fast and loose, sir, came
    first from Apollo,
And was breathed into Æthalides, Mer-
    curius his son,
Where it had the gift to remember all
    that ever was done.     10
From thence it fled forth, and made
    quick transmigration
To goldilocked Euphorbus, who was
    killed in good fashion
At the siege of old Troy, by the cuck-
    old of Sparta.
Hermotimus was next (I find it in my
    charta [2]),
To whom it did pass, where no sooner
    it was missing
But with one Pyrrhus of Delos it learned
    to go a-fishing;
And thence did it enter the sophist of
    Greece.
From Pythagore, she went into a beauti-
    ful piece,
Hight [3] Aspasia, the meretrix; [4] and the
    next toss of her
Was again of [5] a whore she became a
    philosopher,     20
Crates the Cynic, as itself doth relate it.
Since, kings, knights, and beggars,
    knaves, lords, and fools gat it,
Besides ox and ass, camel, mule, goat,
    and brock,[6]

In all which it hath spoke, as in the cob-
    bler's cock.
But I come not here to discourse of that
    matter,
Or his "one," "two," or "three," or his
    great oath, "by quater," [7]
His musics, his trigon,[8] his golden thigh,[9]
Or his telling how elements shift; but I
Would ask how of late thou hast suffered
    translation,
And shifted thy coat in these days of
    reformation.     30
AND. Like one of the reformed, a fool, as
    you see,
Counting all old doctrine heresy.
NAN. But not on thine own forbid meats [10]
    hast thou ventered?
AND. On fish, when first a Carthusian I
    entered.
NAN. Why, then thy dogmatical silence
    hath left thee?
AND. Of that an obstreperous lawyer be-
    reft me.
NAN. O wonderful change, when Sir
    Lawyer forsook thee!
For Pythagore's sake, what body then
    took thee?
AND. A good dull moil.[11]
NAN.     And how! By that means
    Thou wert brought to allow of the eat-
    ing of beans?     40
AND. Yes.
NAN.     But from the moil into whom
    didst thou pass?
AND. Into a very strange beast, by some
    writers called an ass;
By others, a precise, pure, illuminate
    brother [12]
Of those devour flesh, and sometimes
    one another,
And will drop you forth a libel or a
    sanctified lie
Betwixt every spoonful of a Nativity pie.
NAN. Now quit thee, for heaven, of that
    profane nation,
And gently report thy next transmigra-
    tion.
AND. To the same that I am.

[1] The verse of this interlude or debate based
on Lucian's dialogue of a cobbler and a cock is
in the old-fashioned tumbling meter. In the
original the sixty-two lines of the passage are
printed in italics.      [4] Courtesan.
  [2] Paper.                  [5] From being.
  [3] Called.                 [6] Badger.

[7] By four.
[8] Triangular harp.
[9] According to legend, Pythagoras actually
showed his golden thigh to Abaris, priest of the
Hyperboreans, and also exhibited it once at the
Olympic games.     [11] Mule.
[10] Forbidden foods.     [12] *I.e.,* Puritan.

NAN.                    A creature of delight?
And, what is more than a fool, an her-
    maphrodite?                                50
Now, pray thee, sweet soul, in all thy
    variation,
Which body wouldst thou choose to
    take up thy station?
AND.  Troth, this I am in; even here would
    I tarry.
NAN.  Cause [1] here the delight of each sex
    thou canst vary?
AND.  Alas, those pleasures be stale and
    forsaken;
No, 'tis your fool wherewith I am so
    taken,
The only one creature that I can call
    blessed,
For all other forms I have proved most
    distressed.
NAN.  Spoke true, as thou wert in Pythag-
    oras still.
This learnéd opinion we celebrate will,  [60
Fellow eunuch, as behooves us, with all
    our wit and art,
To dignify that whereof ourselves are
    so great and special a part.—

VOLP.  Now, very, very pretty!  Mosca,
    this
Was thy invention?
MOS.                    If it please my patron;
    Not else.
VOLP.    It doth, good Mosca.
MOS.                        Then it was, sir.

### SONG

Fools, they are the only nation
Worth men's envy or admiration,
Free from care or sorrow-taking,
Selves and others merry making;
All they speak or do is sterling.        70
Your fool he is your great man's dearling [2]
And your ladies' sport and pleasure;
Tongue and bable [3] are his treasure.
E'en his face begetteth laughter,
And he speaks truth free from slaughter; [4]
He's the grace of every feast,
And sometimes the chiefest guest,
Hath his trencher and his stool,
When wit waits upon the fool.
    O, who would not be              80
    He, he, he?

[1] Because.                          [2] Darling.
[3] Babble; also the fool's bauble, or scepter.
[4] I.e., with safety.

*One knocks without.*
VOLP.  Who's that?  Away!  Look, Mosca.
MOS.                            Fool, begone!—
[*Exeunt Nano, Castrone, and Androgyno.*]
'Tis Signior Voltore, the advocate;
I know him by his knock.
VOLP.                    Fetch me my gown,
My furs, and nightcaps.  Say my couch
    is changing,
And let him entertain himself awhile
Without i' th' gallery.—[*Exit Mosca.*]
    Now, now, my clients
Begin their visitation!  Vulture, kite,
Raven, and gorcrow, [5] all my birds of
    prey,
That think me turning carcass, now they
    come.                                  90
I am not for hem yet.—

[*Enter Mosca, with the gown, etc.*]
                    How now!  The news?
MOS.  A piece of plate, sir.
VOLP.                    Of what bigness?
MOS.                            Huge,
Massy, and antique, with your name
    inscribed
And arms engraven.
VOLP.              Good!  And not a fox
Stretched on the earth, with fine delusive
    sleights
Mocking a gaping crow?  Ha, Mosca?
MOS.                        Sharp, sir.
VOLP.  Give me my furs. [*Puts on his dress-
    ing gown.*]  Why dost thou laugh so,
    man?
MOS.  I cannot choose, sir, when I appre-
    hend
What thoughts he has without now, as he
    walks:
That this might be the last gift he should
    give;                                  100
That this would fetch you; if you died
    today,
And gave him all, what he should be
    tomorrow;
What large return would come of all
    his venters;
How he should worshiped be and rever-
    enced,
Ride with his furs and footcloths, [6]
    waited on
By herds of fools and clients, have clear
    way

[5] Carrion crow.      [6] A caparison of a horse.

Made for his moil, as lettered as him-
     self,
Be called the great and learnéd advocate,
And then concludes there's naught im-
     possible.
VOLP. Yes, to be learnéd, Mosca.
MOS.                    O, no. Rich [110
     Implies it.  Hood an ass with reverend
          purple,
     So you can hide his two ambitious [1] ears,
     And he shall pass for a cathedral doctor.[2]
VOLP. My caps, my caps, good Mosca.
     Fetch him in.
MOS. Stay, sir; your ointment for your
     eyes.
VOLP.          That's true;
     Despatch, despatch!  I long to have pos-
          session
     Of my new present.
MOS.               That, and thousands more,
     I hope to see you lord of.
VOLP.               Thanks, kind Mosca.
MOS. And that, when I am lost in blended
     dust,
     And hundred such as I am, in succes-
          sion—                              120
VOLP. Nay, that were too much, Mosca.
MOS.                    You shall live
     Still to delude these harpies.
VOLP.               Loving Mosca,
     'Tis well!  My pillow now, and let him
          enter.—                    [Exit Mosca.]
     Now, my feigned cough, my phthisic,
          and my gout,
     My apoplexy, palsy, and catarrhs,
     Help, with your forcéd functions, this
          my posture,
     Wherein this three year I have milked
          their hopes.
     He comes; I hear him—Uh! uh! uh! uh!
     O—

ACT I. SCENE iii.

*Mosca, Voltore, Volpone.*

[MOS. (*To Voltore.*)]  You still are what you
     were, sir.  Only you,
     Of all the rest, are he commands his love,
     And you do wisely to preserve it thus,
     With early visitation and kind notes
     Of your good meaning to him, which I
          know

[1] Towering.
[2] One who holds a university chair.

Cannot but come most grateful.—Pa-
     tron! Sir!
     Here's Signior Voltore is come—
VOLP.               What say you?
MOS. Sir, Signior Voltore is come this
     morning
     To visit you.
VOLP.               I thank him.
MOS.               And hath brought
     A piece of antique plate, bought of S[t].
          Mark,[3]                              10
     With which he here presents you.
VOLP.               He is welcome.
     Pray him to come more often.
MOS.          Yes.
VOLP.               What says he?
MOS. He thanks you, and desires you see
     him often.
VOLP. Mosca!
MOS.     My patron?
VOLP.     Bring him near.  Where is he?
     I long to feel his hand.
MOS.               The plate is here, sir.
VOLT. How fare you, sir?
VOLP.               I thank you, Signior Voltore.
     Where is the plate?  Mine eyes are bad.
VOLT. [*Giving the plate to him.*]     I'm sorry
     To see you still thus weak.
MOS. [*Aside.*]          That he is not weaker.
VOLP. You are too munificent.
VOLT.               No, sir; would to heaven
     I could as well give health to you as
          that plate!                         20
VOLP. You give, sir, what you can; I
     thank you.  Your love
     Hath taste in this, and shall not be un-
          answered.
     I pray you see me often.
VOLT.               Yes, I shall, sir.
VOLP. Be not far from me.
MOS.               Do you observe that, sir?
VOLT. Hearken unto me still; it will con-
     cern you.
MOS. You are a happy man, sir; know
     your good.
VOLP. I cannot now last long—
[4] (MOS.               You are his heir, sir.
VOLT. Am I?)
VOLP.     I feel me going.  Uh! uh! uh! uh!
     I am sailing to my port.  Uh! uh! uh! uh!

[3] *I.e.*, at a shop in St. Mark's Place.
[4] Jonson frequently uses parentheses to indicate asides and other passages incidental to
the main action.

And I am glad I am so near my haven. 30
Mos. Alas, kind gentleman!  Well, we
     must all go—
Volt. But, Mosca—
Mos.               Age will conquer.
Volt.                    Pray thee, hear me.
Am I inscribed his heir for certain?
Mos.                         Are you?
I do beseech you, sir, you will vouchsafe
To write me i' your family.  All my hopes
Depend upon your worship.  I am lost
Except the rising sun do shine on me.
Volt. It shall both shine and warm thee,
     Mosca.
Mos.          Sir,
I am a man that hath not done your
     love
All the worst offices; here I wear your
     keys,                                    40
See all your coffers and your caskets
     locked,
Keep the poor inventory of your jewels,
Your plate, and moneys, am your stew-
     ard, sir,
Husband your goods here.
Volt.                    But am I sole heir?
Mos. Without a partner, sir—confirmed
     this morning.
The wax is warm yet, and the ink scarce
     dry
Upon the parchment.
Volt.                    Happy, happy me!
By what good chance, sweet Mosca?
Mos.               Your desert, sir;
I know no second cause.
Volt.                    Thy modesty
Is loath to know it; well, we shall requite
     it.                                       50
Mos. He ever liked your course, sir; that
     first took him.
I oft have heard him say how he admired
Men of your large profession, that could
     speak
To every cause, and things mere con-
     traries,
Till they were hoarse again, yet all be
     law;
That with most quick agility could turn,
And re-turn, make knots and undo them,
Give forkéd counsel, take provoking gold
On either hand, and put it up—these
     men,
He knew, would thrive with their hu-
     mility.                                   60

And, for his part, he thought he should
     be blessed
To have his heir of such a suffering spirit,
So wise, so grave, of so perplexed a
     tongue,
And loud withal, that would not wag, nor
     scarce
Lie still, without a fee, when every word
Your worship but lets fall is a cecchine![1]—
                    *Another knocks.*
Who's that?  One knocks; I would not
     have you seen, sir.
And yet—pretend you came and went
     in haste;
I'll fashion an excuse.  And, gentle sir,
When you do come to swim in golden
     lard,                                     70
Up to the arms in honey, that your chin
Is borne up stiff with fatness of the flood,
Think on your vassal; but remember me.
I ha' not been your worst of clients.
Volt.                    Mosca!—
Mos. When will you have your inventory
     brought, sir?
Or see a copy of the will?  (Anon!)
I'll bring hem to you, sir.  Away, begone;
Put business i' your face. [*Exit Voltore.*]
Volp.                    Excellent Mosca!
Come hither; let me kiss thee.
Mos.                    Keep you still, sir.
Here is Corbaccio.
Volp.               Set the plate away. 80
The vulture's gone, and the old raven's
     come.

### Act I. Scene iv.

*Mosca, Corbaccio,[2] Volpone.*

[Mos.] Betake you to your silence and
     your sleep.—
     [*Puts the plate among the treasures.*]
Stand there and multiply.—Now we
     shall see
A wretch who is indeed more impotent
Than this can feign to be, yet hopes to
     hop
Over his grave.

     [*Enter Corbaccio.*]
               Signior Corbaccio!
Yo' are very welcome, sir.
Corb.               How does your patron?
Mos. Troth, as he did, sir; no amends.

[1] Sequin, a gold coin.        [2] Enters later.

CORB.                    What? Mends he?
Mos. No, sir; he is rather worse.
CORB.                    That's well. Where is he?
Mos. Upon his couch, sir, newly fall'n
    asleep.
CORB. Does he sleep well?
Mos.        No wink, sir, all this night, 10
    Nor yesterday; but slumbers.
CORB.                    Good! He should take
    Some counsel of physicians.  I have
    brought him
    An opiate here from mine own doctor—
Mos. He will not hear of drugs.
CORB.                    Why? I myself
    Stood by while 'twas made, saw all th'
        ingredients,
    And know it cannot but most gently
        work.
    My life for his, 'tis but to make him
        sleep.
VOLP. [Aside.] Ay, his last sleep, if he
    would take it.
Mos.                    Sir,
    He has no faith in physic.
CORB.                    Say you, say you?
Mos. He has no faith in physic. He does
    think                                    20
    Most of your doctors are the greater
        danger,
    And worse disease, t' escape.  I often
        have
    Heard him protest that your physician
    Should never be his heir.
CORB.                    Not I his heir?
Mos. Not your physician, sir.
CORB.                    O, no, no, no,
    I do not mean it.
Mos.                    No, sir, nor their fees
    He cannot brook; he says they flay a
        man
    Before they kill him.
CORB.                    Right, I do conceive you.
Mos. And then they do it by experiment,
    For which the law not only doth absolve
        hem,                                    30
    But gives them great reward; and he is
        loath
    To hire his death so.
CORB.                    It is true, they kill
    With as much license as a judge.
Mos.                    Nay, more,
    For he but kills, sir, where the law con-
        demns,
    And these can kill him too.

CORB.                    Ay, or me,
    Or any man.  How does his apoplex?[1]
    Is that strong on him still?
Mos.                    Most violent.
    His speech is broken, and his eyes are
        set,
    His face drawn longer than 'twas wont—
CORB.                    How? How?
    Stronger than he was wont?
Mos.                    No, sir; his face    40
    Drawn longer than 'twas wont.
CORB.                    O, good!
Mos.                    His mouth
    Is ever gaping, and his eyelids hang.
CORB.                                    Good.
Mos. A freezing numbness stiffens all his
        joints,
    And makes the color of his flesh like lead.
CORB.                                    'Tis good.
Mos. His pulse beats slow and dull.
CORB.                    Good symptoms still.
Mos. And from his brain—
CORB.        Ha? How? Not from his brain?
Mos. Yes, sir, and from his brain—
(CORB.                    I conceive you; good.)
Mos. Flows a cold sweat, with a continual
        rheum,[2]
    Forth the resolvéd[3] corners of his eyes.
CORB. Is 't possible? Yet I am better, ha!
    How does he with the swimming of his
        head?                                    51
Mos. O, sir, 'tis past the scotomy;[4] he
        now
    Hath lost his feeling, and hath left[5] to
        snort;
    You hardly can perceive him, that he
        breathes.
CORB. Excellent, excellent!  Sure I shall
        outlast him.
    This makes me young again, a score of
        years.
Mos. I was a-coming for you, sir.
CORB.                    Has he made his will?
    What has he given me?
Mos.                    No, sir.
CORB.                    Nothing? Ha?
Mos. He has not made his will, sir.
CORB.                    O, O, O!    59
    What then did Voltore, the lawyer, here?
Mos. He smelt a carcass, sir, when he
        but heard

[1] Apoplexy.        [2] Discharge.        [3] Loosened.
[4] Dizziness, with dimness of sight.
[5] Ceased.

My master was about his testament;
As I did urge him to it for your good—
CORB. He came unto him, did he?    I
    thought so.
MOS. Yes, and presented him this piece
    of plate.
CORB. To be his heir?
MOS.                    I do not know, sir.
CORB.                              True;
    I know it too.
MOS. [*Aside.*]    By your own scale, sir.
CORB.                              Well,
    I shall prevent him yet. See, Mosca,
    look!
    Here I have brought a bag of bright
    cecchines
    Will quite weigh down his plate.
MOS.                    Yea, marry, sir.  70
    This is true physic, this your sacred
    medicine;
    No talk of opiates to this great elixir!
CORB. 'Tis *aurum palpabile*, if not *pota-
    bile*.[1]
MOS. It shall be ministered to him in his
    bowl?
CORB. Ay, do, do, do.
MOS.                    Most blessed cordial!
    This will recover him.
CORB.                    Yes, do, do, do.
MOS. I think it were not best, sir.
CORB.            What?
MOS.                    To recover him.
CORB. O, no, no, no; by no means.
MOS.                    Why, sir, this
    Will work some strange effect, if he but
    feel it.
CORB. 'Tis true; therefore forbear.  I'll
    take my venter;                    80
    Give me 't again.
MOS.                    At no hand;[2] pardon me.
    You shall not do yourself that wrong,
    sir.  I
    Will so advise you, you shall have it all.
CORB. How?
MOS.            All, sir; 'tis your right, your
    own; no man
    Can claim a part. 'Tis yours without a
    rival,
    Decreed by destiny.
CORB.            How, how, good Mosca?
MOS. I'll tell you, sir. This fit he shall
    recover—

CORB. I do conceive you.
MOS.                    And, on first advantage
    Of his gained sense, will I reimportune
    him
    Unto the making of his testament,  90
    And show him this.
CORB.            Good, good.
MOS.                    'Tis better yet,
    If you will hear, sir.
CORB.            Yes, with all my heart.
MOS. Now would I counsel you, make
    home with speed;
    There, frame a will, whereto you shall
    inscribe
    My master your sole heir.
CORB.                    And disinherit
    My son?
MOS. O, sir, the better, for that color[3]
    Shall make it much more taking.
CORB.                    O, but[4] color?
MOS. This will, sir, you shall send it unto
    me.
    Now, when I come to enforce, as I will
    do,
    Your cares, your watchings, and your
    many prayers,                    100
    Your more than many gifts, your this
    day's present,
    And, last, produce your will, where
    without thought
    Or least regard unto your proper issue,
    A son so brave and highly meriting,
    The stream of your diverted love hath
    thrown you
    Upon my master, and made him your
    heir,
    He cannot be so stupid or stone dead
    But out of conscience and mere grati-
    tude—
CORB. He must pronounce me his?
MOS.                    'Tis true.
CORB.                    This plot
    Did I think on before.
MOS.            I do believe it.  110
CORB. Do you not believe it?
MOS.            Yes, sir.
CORB.                    Mine own project.
MOS. Which when he hath done, sir—
CORB.            Published me his heir?
MOS. And you so certain to survive him—
CORB.                              Ay.
MOS. Being so lusty a man—
CORB.            'Tis true.

<hr>

[1] Palpable gold, if not potable.—"Potable gold" was a medicine.    [2] By no means.

[3] Pretense.    [4] Merely.

Mos.                              Yes, sir—

Corb. I thought on that too.  See, how
    he should be
The very organ to express my thoughts!

Mos. You have not only done yourself a
    good—

Corb. But multiplied it on my son?

Mos.                              'Tis right, sir.

Corb. Still, my invention.

Mos.                    'Las, sir!  Heaven knows
It hath been all my study, all my care  120
    (I e'en grow gray withal) how to work
    things—

Corb. I do conceive, sweet Mosca.

Mos.                              You are he
For whom I labor here.

Corb.                    Ay, do, do, do.
    I'll straight about it.

Mos. [Aside.]     Rook go with you,[1] raven!

Corb. I know thee honest.

Mos. [Aside.]              You do lie, sir!

Corb.                              And—

Mos. [Aside.] Your knowledge is no better
    than your ears, sir.

Corb. I do not doubt to be a father to
    thee.

Mos. [Aside.] Nor I to gull my brother
    of his blessing.

Corb. I may ha' my youth restored to
    me; why not?

Mos. [Aside.] Your worship is a precious
    ass!

Corb.    What say'st thou?          130

Mos. I do desire your worship to make
    haste, sir.

Corb. 'Tis done, 'tis done; I go.     [Exit.]

Volp. [Springing from his bed.]    O, I
    shall burst!
Let out my sides, let out my sides—

Mos.                              Contain
    Your flux of laughter, sir.  You know
    this hope
Is such a bait it covers any hook.

Volp. O, but thy working, and thy plac-
    ing it!
I cannot hold; good rascal, let me kiss
    thee.
I never knew thee in so rare a humor.

Mos. Alas, sir, I but do as I am taught—
    Follow your grave instructions, give
        hem words,          140
    Pour oil into their ears, and send them
        hence.

May you be rooked.

Volp. 'Tis true, 'tis true.  What a rare
    punishment
Is avarice to itself!

Mos.                    Ay, with our help, sir.

Volp. So many cares, so many maladies,
So many fears attending on old age,
Yea, death so often called on, as no wish
Can be more frequent with hem, their
    limbs faint,
Their senses dull, their seeing, hearing,
    going,
All dead before them, yea, their very
    teeth,
Their instruments of eating, failing
    them—          150
Yet this is reckoned life!  Nay, here was
    one,
Is now gone home, that wishes to live
    longer—
Feels not his gout nor palsy, feigns him-
    self
Younger by scores of years, flatters his
    age
With confident belying it, hopes he may
With charms like Æson have his youth
    restored,
And with these thoughts so battens, as
    if fate
Would be as easily cheated on as he,
And all turns air!  Who's that there,
    now?  A third?     Another knocks.

Mos. Close, to your couch again; I hear
    his voice.          160
It is Corvino, our spruce merchant.

Volp. [Lying on his bed.]          Dead!

Mos. Another bout, sir, with your eyes.—
    Who's there?


Act I.  Scene v.

_Mosca, Corvino, Volpone._

[Mos.] Signior Corvino!  Come most
    wished for! O,
    How happy were you, if you knew it,
        now!

Corv. Why?  What?  Wherein?

Mos.              The tardy hour is come, sir.

Corv. He is not dead?

Mos.              Not dead, sir, but as good;
He knows no man.

Corv.              How shall I do then?

Mos.                              Why, sir?

Corv. I have brought him here a pearl.

Mos.                              Perhaps he has

So much remembrance left as to know
    you, sir;
He still [1] calls on you; nothing but your
    name
Is in his mouth. Is your pearl orient,[2]
    sir?

CORV. Venice was never owner of the
    like.    10

VOLP. Signior Corvino!

MOS.             Hark!

VOLP.                  Signior Corvino!

MOS. He calls you; step and give it him.—
    H' is here, sir,
And he has brought you a rich pearl.

CORV.            How do you, sir?—
    Tell him it, doubles the twelve caract.[3]

MOS.                    Sir,
    He cannot understand; his hearing's
    gone;
And yet it comforts him to see you—

CORV.                 Say
    I have a diamant [4] for him, too.

MOS.           Best show 't, sir;
    Put it into his hand—'tis only there
He apprehends. He has his feeling yet.
See how he grasps it!

CORV.        'Las, good gentleman!  20
    How pitiful the sight is!

MOS.            Tut, forget, sir.
    The weeping of an heir should still be
    laughter
Under a visor.[5]

CORV.        Why, am I his heir?

MOS. Sir, I am sworn; I may not show
    the will
Till he be dead. But here has been Cor-
    baccio,
Here has been Voltore, here were others
    too;
I cannot number hem, they were so
    many,
All gaping here for legacies; but I,
Taking the vantage of his naming you,
    "Signior Corvino, Signior Corvino,"
    took  30
Paper and pen and ink and there I
    asked him
Whom he would have his heir. "Cor-
    vino." Who
Should be executor? "Corvino." And

To any question he was silent to,
I still interpreted the nods he made,
Through weakness, for consent, and
    sent home th' others,
Nothing bequeathed them, but to cry
    and curse.

CORV. O, my dear Mosca! (*They embrace.*)
    Does he not perceive us?

MOS. No more than a blind harper. He
    knows no man,
No face of friend, nor name of any serv-
    ant,  40
Who 'twas that fed him last, or gave
    him drink—
Not those he hath begotten or brought up
Can he remember.

CORV.          Has he children?

MOS.                 Bastards,
    Some dozen or more, that he begot on
    beggars,
Gypsies and Jews and blackmoors,
    when he was drunk.
Knew you not that, sir? 'Tis the com-
    mon fable.
The dwarf, the fool, the eunuch are all
    his;
H' is the true father of his family,
In all save me; but he has given hem
    nothing.

CORV. That's well, that's well! Art sure
    he does not hear us?  50

MOS. Sure, sir? Why, look you, credit
    your own sense.—[*Shouts at Volpone.*]
The pox approach, and add to your
    diseases,
If it would send you hence the sooner, sir.
For your incontinence, it hath deserved
    it
Throughly [6] and throughly, and the
    plague to boot!—
(You may come near, sir.) Would you
    would once close
Those filthy eyes of yours, that flow
    with slime
Like two frog-pits; [7] and those same
    hanging cheeks,
Covered with hide instead of skin—
    (Nay, help, sir!)
That look like frozen dishclouts set on
    end!  60

CORV. Or like an old smoked wall, on
    which the rain
Ran down in streaks!

---

[1] Continually.
[2] Lustrous.
[3] Carat.
[4] Diamond.
[5] *I.e.*, an heir's sorrow is actually disguised
happiness.
[6] Thoroughly.
[7] Stagnant puddles.

Mos.          Excellent, sir! Speak out.
You may be louder yet. A culvering [1]
Discharg&#233;d in his ear would hardly bore
it.

Corv. His nose is like a common sewer,
still running.

Mos. 'Tis good! And what his mouth?

Corv.                    A very draught.

Mos. O, stop it up—

Corv.               By no means.

Mos.                    Pray you, let me.
Faith, I could stifle him rarely with a
pillow
As well as any woman that should keep [2]
him.

Corv. Do as you will; but I'll be gone.

Mos.                    Be so; 70
It is your presence makes him last so
long.

Corv. I pray you use no violence.

Mos.                No, sir? Why?
Why should you be thus scrupulous,
pray you, sir?

Corv. Nay, at your discretion.

Mos.          Well, good sir, begone.

Corv. I will not trouble him now to take [3]
my pearl?

Mos. Pooh! Nor your diamant. What
a needless care
Is this afflicts you? Is not all here yours?
Am not I here, whom you have made?
Your creature
That owe my being to you?

Corv.               Grateful Mosca!
Thou art my friend, my fellow, my companion,                    80
My partner, and shalt share in all my
fortunes.

Mos. Excepting one.

Corv.          What's that?

Mos.               Your gallant wife,
sir.—     [Exit Corvino precipitately.]
Now is he gone. We had no other means
To shoot him hence but this.

Volp.               My divine Mosca!
Thou hast today outgone thyself.—
(Another knocks.)          Who's there?
I will be troubled with no more. Pre-
pare
Me music, dances, banquets, all delights;
The Turk is not more sensual in his
pleasures

<hr/>

[1] Culverin, a small cannon.
[2] Care for.          [3] Take away (from Volpone).

Than will Volpone. [Exit Mosca.] Let
me see. A pearl?
A diamant? Plate? Cecchines? [4] Good
morning's purchase.               90
Why, this is better than rob churches,
yet;
Or fat by eating once a month a man—

[Enter Mosca.]

Who is 't?

Mos.          The beauteous Lady Would-be,
sir,
Wife to the English knight, Sir Politic
Would-be
(This is the style, sir, is directed me),
Hath sent to know how you have slept
tonight,
And if you would be visited.

Volp.               Not now.
Some three hours hence—

Mos.          I told the squire [5] so much.

Volp. When I am high with mirth and
wine, then, then!
Fore heaven, I wonder at the desperate
valure [6]                    100
Of the bold English, that they dare
let loose
Their wives to all encounters!

Mos.               Sir, this knight
Had not his name for nothing; he is
politic,
And knows, howe'er his wife affect
strange airs,
She hath not yet the face to be dishonest. [7]
But, had she Signior Corvino's wife's
face—

Volp. Has she so rare a face?

Mos.               O, sir, the wonder,
The blazing star of Italy! A wench
O' the first year, a beauty ripe as har-
vest!
Whose skin is whiter than a swan all
over,                    110
Than silver, snow, or lilies! A soft lip
Would tempt you to eternity of kissing!
And flesh that melteth in the touch to
blood!
Bright as your gold, and lovely as your
gold!

Volp. Why had not I known this before?

Mos.               Alas, sir,
Myself but yesterday discovered it.

<hr/>

[4] Sequins.  [5] Messenger.  [6] Valor.  [7] Unchaste.

VOLP.  How might I see her?

Mos.                              O, not possible;
She's kept as warily as is your gold;
Never does come abroad, never takes
    air
But at a windore.[1]  All her looks are
    sweet,                                    120
As the first grapes or cherries, and are
    watched
As near as they are.

VOLP.                    I must see her—

Mos.                                    Sir,
There is a guard of ten spies thick upon
    her,
All his whole household, each of which
    is set
Upon his fellow, and have all their
    charge,
When he goes out, when he comes in,
    examined.

VOLP.  I will go see her, though but at her
    windore.

Mos.  In some disguise then.

VOLP.                    That is true; I must
Maintain mine own shape still the same.
We'll think.                    [Exeunt.]


### ACT II. SCENE i.

[Before Corvino's house on St. Mark's
                                    Place.]

*Politic Would-be, Peregrine.*

[POL.]  Sir, to a wise man all the world's his
    soil:
It is not Italy nor France nor Europe
That must bound me, if my fates call me
    forth.
Yet I protest it is no salt [2] desire
Of seeing countries, shifting a religion,
Nor any disaffection to the state
Where I was bred, and unto which I owe
My dearest plots,[3] hath brought me out,
    much less
That idle, antique, stale, gray-headed
    project
Of knowing men's minds and manners,
    with Ulysses,                            10
But a peculiar humor of my wife's,
Laid for this height [4] of Venice, to ob-
    serve,

To quote, [5] to learn the language, and so
    forth—
I hope you travel, sir, with license? [6]

PER.                                    Yes.

POL.  I dare the safelier converse.  How
    long, sir,
Since you left England?

PER.                    Seven weeks.

POL.                                    So lately!
You ha' not been with my lord ambassa-
    dor?

PER.  Not yet, sir.

POL.          Pray you, what news, sir, vents
    our climate? [7]
I heard last night a most strange thing
    reported
By some of my lord's followers, and I
    long                                        20
To hear how 'twill be seconded.[8]

PER.                    What was 't, sir?

POL.  Marry, sir, of a raven that should
    build
In a ship royal of the king's.[9]

PER.  [Aside.]                    This fellow,
Does he gull me, trow? [10]  Or is gulled?—
    Your name, sir?

POL.  My name is Politic Would-be.

PER.  [Aside.]          O, that speaks him.—
    A knight, sir?

POL.          A poor knight, sir.

PER.                                Your lady
Lies here in Venice, for intelligence
Of tires [11] and fashions and behavior
Among the courtesans?  The fine Lady
    Would-be?

POL.  Yes, sir; the spider and the bee oft-
    times                                        30
Suck from one flower.

PER.                    Good Sir Politic,
I cry you mercy; I have heard much of
    you.
'Tis true, sir, of your raven.

POL.                    On your knowledge?

PER.  Yes, and your lion's whelping in the
    Tower.

[5] Make notes.
[6] Required of men of rank by the English
government.
[7] *I.e.*, does our country give forth?
[8] Followed up.
[9] Probably a reference to an actual event of
the day, like the following allusions to the lion's
whelping, the Woolwich whale, etc.
[10] Do you suppose?
[11] Attires.

[1] Window.                    [3] Plans.
[2] Wanton.                    [4] Latitude.

POL. Another whelp!

PER.          Another, sir.

POL.             Now, heaven!
What prodigies be these? The fires at
    Berwick!
And the new star! These things concur-
    ring, strange,
And full of omen! Saw you those
    meteors?

PER. I did, sir.

POL.     Fearful! Pray you, sir, confirm me.
Were there three porcpisces [1] seen above
    the bridge,                 40
As they give out?

PER.         Six, and a sturgeon, sir.

POL. I am astonished.

PER.          Nay, sir, be not so;
I'll tell you a greater prodigy than these.

POL. What should these things portend!

PER.          The very day
(Let me be sure) that I put forth from
    London,
There was a whale discovered in the
    river,
As high as Woolwich, that had waited
    there,
Few know how many months, for the
    subversion
Of the Stode fleet.

POL.      Is 't possible? Believe it,
'Twas either sent from Spain, or the
    archduke's—             50
Spinola's whale, upon my life, my credit!
Will they not leave these projects?
    Worthy sir,
Some other news.

PER.     Faith, Stone the fool is dead,
And they do lack a tavern fool extremely.

POL. Is Mas' Stone dead?

PER.      H' is dead, sir; why, I hope
You thought him not immortal?—
    [Aside.] O, this knight,
Were he well-known, would be a precious
    thing
To fit our English stage; he that should
    write
But such a fellow, should be thought to
    feign
Extremely, if not maliciously.

POL.         Stone dead! 60

PER. Dead. Lord! How deeply, sir, you
    apprehend it!
He was no kinsman to you?

[1] Porpoises.

POL.             That I know of.
Well, that same fellow was an unknown
    fool.

PER. And yet you knew him, it seems?

POL.          I did so. Sir,
I knew him one of the most dangerous
    heads
Living within the state, and so I held
    him.

PER. Indeed, sir?

POL.       While he lived, in action,
He has received weekly intelligence,
Upon my knowledge, out of the Low
    Countries,              69
For all parts of the world, in cabbages,
And those dispensed again to ambas-
    sadors,
In oranges, muskmelons, apricots,
Limons,[2] pome-citrons,[3] and suchlike—
    sometimes
In Colchester oysters, and your Selsey
    cockles.

PER. You make me wonder.

POL.       Sir, upon my knowledge.
Nay, I've observed him, at your public
    ordinary,
Take his advertisement [4] from a traveler,
A concealed statesman, in a trencher of
    meat,
And instantly, before the meal was done,
Convey an answer in a toothpick.

PER.         Strange! 80
How could this be, sir?

POL.       Why, the meat was cut
So like his character, and so laid as he
Must easily read the cipher.

PER.          I have heard
He could not read, sir.

POL.       So 'twas given out,
In polity, by those that did employ him;
But he could read, and had your lan-
    guages,
And to 't as sound a noddle—

PER.       I have heard, sir,
That your babions [5] were spies, and that
    they were
A kind of subtle nation near to China.

POL. Ay, ay, your Mamuluchi.[6] Faith,
    they had            90
Their hand in a French plot or two; but
    they

[2] Lemons.                [4] Information.
[3] Citrons.               [5] Baboons.
[6] Mamelukes, a kind of Islamite soldier.

Were so extremely given to women as
They made discovery of all; yet I
Had my advices here, on Wednesday
    last,
From one of their own coat, they were
    returned,
Made their relations,[1] as the fashion is,
And now stand fair for fresh employ-
    ment.
PER. [*Aside.*]        Heart!
This Sir Pol will be ignorant of noth-
    ing.—
It seems, sir, you know all.
POL.                    Not all, sir; but
I have some general notions.  I do
    love                                    100
To note and to observe.  Though I live
    out,
Free from the active torrent, yet I'ld
    mark
The currents and the passages of things
For mine own private use, and know the
    ebbs
And flows of state.
PER.                    Believe it, sir, I hold
Myself in no small tie [2] unto my fortunes
For casting me thus luckily upon you,
Whose knowledge, if your bounty equal it,
May do me great assistance in instruction
For my behavior and my bearing,
    which                                   110
Is yet so rude and raw—
POL.                    Why?  Came you forth
Empty of rules for travel?
PER.                    Faith, I had
Some common ones, from out that vulgar
    grammar,
Which he that cried Italian to me taught
    me.
POL. Why, this it is that spoils all our
    brave bloods,
Trusting our hopeful gentry unto ped-
    ants,
Fellows of outside, and mere bark.  You
    seem
To be a gentleman of ingenuous race—
I not profess it, but my fate hath been
To be where I have been consulted
    with,                                   120
In this high kind, touching some great
    men's sons,
Persons of blood and honor.
PER.                    Who be these, sir?

¹ Reports.                    ² Obligation.

ACT II.  SCENE ii.

[*The same.*]

*Mosca [with Assistants carrying material for
    a platform], Politic, Peregrine, Volpone,
                    Nano, Grege.*[3]

[Mos.] Under that windore, there 't must
    be.  The same.
POL. Fellows, to mount a bank.[4]  Did your
    instructor
In the dear tongues [5] never discourse to
    you
Of the Italian mountebanks?
PER.                    Yes, sir.
POL.                              Why,
Here shall you see one.
PER.                    They are quacksalvers,
Fellows that live by venting [6] oils and
    drugs.
POL. Was that the character he gave you
    of them?
PER. As I remember.
POL.                    Pity his ignorance.
They are the only knowing men of
    Europe!
Great general scholars, excellent physi-
    cians,                                  10
Most admired statesmen, professed fa-
    vorites
And cabinet counselors to the greatest
    princes—
The only languaged men of all the world!
PER. And, I have heard, they are most
    lewd [7] impostors,
Made all of terms and shreds, no less be-
    liers
Of great men's favors than their own vile
    med'cines,
Which they will utter[8] upon monstrous
    oaths,
Selling that drug for twopence ere they
    part,
Which they have valued at twelve crowns
    before.
POL. Sir, calumnies are answered best with
    silence.                               20
Yourself shall judge.—Who is it mounts,
    my friends?
Mos. Scoto of Mantua,[9] sir.

³ Last three enter later.        ⁶ Vending.
⁴ Bench, platform.              ⁷ Ignorant.
⁵ Modern languages.            ⁸ Vend.
⁹ An actual Italian juggler who was then in
England.

Pol.                    Is 't he? Nay, then
I'll proudly promise, sir, you shall behold
Another man than has been fant'sied [1]
    to you.
I wonder yet that he should mount his
    bank
Here in this nook, that has been wont t'
    appear
In face of the Piazza!—Here he comes.

[*Enter Volpone, disguised as a mountebank,
    followed by Nano, also disguised, and
                                    Grege.*]

Volp. Mount, zany.[2]
Gre. Follow, follow, follow, follow, follow!
Pol. See how the people follow him! H' is
    a man                                        30
May write ten thousand crowns in bank
    here. Note,
        [*Volpone mounts the platform.*]
Mark but his gesture; I do use to observe
The state he keeps in getting up.
Per.                    'Tis worth it, sir.
Volp. Most noble gentlemen and my
worthy patrons! It may seem strange that
I, your Scoto Mantuano, who was ever
wont to fix my bank in face of the public
Piazza, near the shelter of the Portico to the
Procuratia, should now, after eight months'
absence from this illustrous city of  [40
Venice, humbly retire myself into an obscure nook of the Piazza.
Pol. [*Aside.*] Did not I now object the
    same?
Per. [*Aside.*]         Peace, sir.
Volp. Let me tell you I am not, as your
Lombard proverb saith, cold on my feet, or
content to part with my commodities at a
cheaper rate than I accustomed—look not
for it; nor that the calumnious reports of
that impudent detractor and shame to
our profession (Alessandro Buttone, I  [50
mean), who gave out, in public, I was condemned *a' sforzato* [3] to the galleys for
poisoning the Cardinal Bembo's—cook,
hath at all attached,[4] much less dejected
me. No, no, worthy gentlemen! To tell you
true, I cannot endure to see the rabble of
these ground *ciarlitani*,[5] that spread their
cloaks on the pavement as if they meant to
do feats of activity, and then come in

lamely with their moldy tales out of  [60
Boccaccio, like stale Tabarine,[6] the fabu-
list,[7] some of them discoursing their travels,
and of their tedious captivity in the Turks'
galleys, when indeed, were the truth known,
they were the Christians' galleys, where
very temperately they eat bread and drunk
water as a wholesome penance, enjoined
them by their confessors, for base pilferies.
Pol. [*Aside.*] Note but his bearing, and
    contempt of these.
Volp. These turdy-facey-nasty-  [70
patey-lousy-fartical rogues, with one poor
groatsworth of unprepared antimony,
finely wrapped up in several *scartoccios*,[8] are
able, very well, to kill their twenty a week,
and play; yet these meager, starved spirits,
who have half stopped the organs of their
minds with earthy oppilations, [9] want not
their favorers among your shriveled, salad-
eating artisans, who are overjoyed that they
may have their half-pe'rth of physic;  [80
though it purge hem into another world, 't
makes no matter.
Pol. [*Aside.*] Excellent! Ha' you heard
    better language, sir?
Volp. Well, let hem go. And, gentlemen, honorable gentlemen, know that for
this time our bank, being thus removed
from the clamors of the *canaglia*,[10] shall
be the scene of pleasure and delight, for
I have nothing to sell, little or nothing to
sell.                                          90
Pol. [*Aside.*] I told you, sir, his end.
Per. [*Aside.*]              You did so, sir.
Volp. I protest I and my six servants
are not able to make of this precious liquor
so fast as it is fetched away from my lodging by gentlemen of your city, strangers of
the *terrafirma*,[11] worshipful merchants, ay,
and senators too, who ever since my arrival
have detained me to their uses by their
splendidous liberalities—and worthily. For
what avails your rich man to have his  [100
magazines stuffed with *moscadelli*,[12] or of the
purest grape, when his physicians prescribe
him, on pain of death, to drink nothing but
water cocted [13] with anis seeds? O health,
health! The blessing of the rich! The riches

---

[1] Represented.                    [4] Attacked.
[2] A subordinate buffoon.    [5] Trivial charlatans.
[3] To hard labor.

[6] Tabarin, a popular French mountebank.
[7] A professional teller of tales.
[8] Twists of paper.               [11] Mainland.
[9] Obstructions.                    [12] Muscatel.
[10] Canaille, mob.               [13] Boiled.

of the poor! Who can buy thee at too dear a rate, since there is no enjoying this world without thee? Be not then so sparing of your purses, honorable gentlemen, as to abridge the natural course of life—    [110

PER. [*Aside*.] You see his end?

POL. [*Aside*.]                    Ay, is 't not good?

VOLP. For, when a humid flux, or catarrh, by the mutability of air, falls from your head into an arm or shoulder, or any other part, take you a ducat, or your cecchine of gold, and apply to the place affected; see what good effect it can work. No, no, 'tis this blessed *unguento*,[1] this rare extraction, that hath only power to disperse all malignant humors[2] that    [120 proceed either of hot, cold, moist, or windy causes—

PER. [*Aside*.] I would he had put in dry too.

POL. [*Aside*.]             Pray you, observe.

VOLP. To fortify the most indigest[3] and crude stomach, ay, were it of one that, through extreme weakness, vomited blood, applying only a warm napkin to the place, after the unction and fricace;[4] for the *vertigine*[5] in the head, putting but a drop into your nostrils, likewise behind the    [130 ears, a most sovereign and approved remedy, the *mal caduco*,[6] cramps, convulsions, paralyses, epilepsies, *tremorcordia*,[7] retired[8] nerves, ill vapors of the spleen, stoppings of the liver, the stone, the strangury, *hernia ventosa*, *iliaca passio;*[9] stops a *dysenteria* immediately; easeth the torsion of the small guts; and cures *melancholia hypocondriaca*, being taken and applied according to my printed receipt.    [140 (*Pointing to his bill and his glass.*) For this is the physician, this the medicine; this counsels, this cures; this gives the direction, this works the effect; and, in sum, both together may be termed an abstract of the theoric and practic in the Æsculapian art.[10] 'Twill cost you eight crowns. And, Zan Fritada, pray thee, sing a verse extempore in honor of it.                          149

POL. [*Aside*.] How do you like him, sir?

PER. [*Aside*.]                    Most strangely, I!

POL. [*Aside*.] Is not his language rare?

PER. [*Aside*.]                    But [11] alchemy, I never heard the like—or Broughton's [12] books.

### SONG

Had old Hippocrates or Galen,
That to their books put med'cines all in,
But known this secret, they had never
(Of which they will be guilty ever)
Been murderers of so much paper,
Or wasted many a hurtless taper;
No Indian drug had e'er been famed,
Tabacco,[13] sassafras not named;          160
Ne [14] yet of guacum [15] one small stick, sir,
Nor Raymond Lully's [16] great elixir;
Ne had been known the Danish Gonswart,[17]
Or Paracelsus, with his long sword.[18]

PER. [*Aside*.]  All this, yet, will not do; eight crowns is high.

VOLP. No more.—Gentlemen, if I had but time to discourse to you the miraculous effects of this my oil, surnamed Oglio del Scoto, with the countless catalogue of those I have cured of th' aforesaid and    [170 many more diseases, the patents and privileges of all the princes and commonwealths of Christendom, or but the depositions of those that appeared on my part before the signiory of the Sanita and most learned College of Physicians, where I was authorized, upon notice taken of the admirable virtues of my medicaments, and mine own excellency in matter of rare and unknown secrets, not only to disperse them    [180 publicly in this famous city, but in all the territories that happily joy under the government of the most pious and magnificent states of Italy! But may some other gallant fellow say, "O, there be divers that make profession to have as good and as experimented receipts as yours." Indeed, very many have assayed, like apes, in imitation of that which is really and essentially in me, to make of this oil,    [190 bestowed great cost in furnaces, stills, alembics, continual fires, and preparation

---

[1] Ointment.
[2] Fluids.
[3] Disordered.
[4] Salve.
[5] Vertigo.
[6] Epilepsy.
[7] Palpitating heart.
[8] Overtired.
[9] Varieties of colic.
[10] The theory and practice of medicine.
[11] Except for.
[12] Hugh Broughton was a fanatical commentator on the Old Testament.
[13] Tobacco.    [15] Guaiacum, a kind of resin.
[14] Nor.    [16] Fourteenth century alchemist.
[17] Johan Gansfort, or Wessel, a fifteenth century scholar.
[18] In the hollow handle of which his familiar spirit was supposed to reside.

of the ingredients (as indeed there goes to it six hundred several simples, besides some quantity of human fat, for the conglutination, which we buy of the anatomists), but, when these practitioners come to the last decoction, blow, blow, puff, puff, and all flies *in fumo*.[1] Ha, ha, ha! Poor wretches! I rather pity their folly and in- [200 discretion than their loss of time and money, for those may be recovered by industry, but to be a fool born is a disease incurable. For myself I always from my youth have endeavored to get the rarest secrets, and book them, either in exchange or for money; I spared nor cost nor labor, where anything was worthy to be learned. And, gentlemen, honorable gentlemen, I will undertake, by virtue of chymi- [210 cal[2] art, out of the honorable hat that covers your head, to extract the four elements; that is to say, the fire, air, water, and earth, and return you your felt without burn or stain. For, whilst others have been at the balloo,[3] I have been at my book, and am now past the craggy paths of study, and come to the flowery plains of honor and reputation.

POL. [*Aside.*] I do assure you, sir, that is his aim. 220

VOLP. But to our price—

PER. [*Aside.*]    And that withal, Sir Pol.

VOLP. You all know, honorable gentlemen, I never valued this *ampulla*, or vial, at less than eight crowns; but for this time I am content to be deprived of it for six; six crowns is the price, and less in courtesy I know you cannot offer me. Take it or leave it; howsoever, both it and I am at your service. I ask you not as the value of the thing, for then I should de- [230 mand of you a thousand crowns; so the Cardinals Montalto, Fernese, the great Duke of Tuscany, my gossip,[4] with divers other princes, have given me; but I despise money. Only to show my affection to you, honorable gentlemen, and your illustrous state here, I have neglected the messages of these princes, mine own offices, framed my journey hither, only to present you with the fruits of my travels.—Tune [240 your voices once more to the touch of your

instruments, and give the honorable assembly some delightful recreation.

PER. What monstrous and most painful circumstance
Is here, to get some three or four gazettes,[5]
Some threepence i' th' whole, for that 'twill come to.

### SONG

You that would last long, list to my song;
Make no more coil,[6] but buy of this oil.
Would you be ever fair and young?
Stout of teeth, and strong of tongue?    250
Tart of palate? Quick of ear?
Sharp of sight? Of nostril clear?
Moist of hand? And light of foot?
Or, I will come nearer to 't,
Would you live free from all diseases?
Do the act your mistress pleases?
Yet fright all aches[7] from your bones?
Here's a med'cine for the nones.[8]

VOLP. Well, I am in a humor at this time to make a present of the small [260 quantity my coffer contains—to the rich in courtesy, and to the poor for God's sake. Wherefore now mark: I asked you six crowns; and six crowns at other times you have paid me; you shall not give me six crowns, nor five, nor four, nor three, nor two, nor one; nor half a ducat; no, nor a muccinigo.[9] Six—pence it will cost you, or six hundred pound—expect no lower price, for, by the banner of my front, I will [270 not bate a bagatine[10]—that I will have, only, a pledge of your loves, to carry something from amongst you, to show I am not contemned by you. Therefore, now, toss your handkerchiefs[11] cheerfully, cheerfully; and be advertised that the first heroic spirit that deigns to grace me with a handkerchief, I will give it a little remembrance of something beside, shall please it better than if I had presented it with a [280 double pistolet.[12]

PER. [*Aside.*]    Will you be that heroic spark, Sir Pol?

*Celia, at the windo', throws down her handkerchief.*

O, see! The windore has prevented[13] you.

[1] In smoke.        [2] Chemical.
[3] More correctly, *balloon;* a Venetian game of ball.    [4] Intimate friend.
[5] Small Italian coins.
[6] Fuss.    [7] Pronounced *aitches.*    [8] Occasion.
[9] Moccinigo, an Italian coin.
[10] An Italian coin.
[11] With money tied in them.
[12] A Spanish gold coin.    [13] Anticipated.

VOLP. Lady, I kiss your bounty; and for this timely grace you have done your poor Scoto of Mantua I will return you, over and above my oil, a secret of that high and inestimable nature shall make you forever enamored on that minute wherein your eye first descended on so mean, [290 yet not altogether to be despised, an object. Here is a poulder concealed in this paper, of which, if I should speak to the worth, nine thousand volumes were but as one page, that page as a line, that line as a word, so short is this pilgrimage of man (which some call life) to the expressing of it. Would I reflect on the price? Why, the whole world were but as an empire, that empire as a province, that province as [300 a bank, that bank as a private purse to the purchase of it. I will only tell you it is the poulder that made Venus a goddess (given her by Apollo), that kept her perpetually young, cleared her wrinkles, firmed her gums, filled her skin, colored her hair; from her derived [1] to Helen, and at the sack of Troy unfortunately lost; till now, in this our age, it was as happily recovered, by a studious antiquary, out of some ruins [310 of Asia, who sent a moiety of it to the court of France (but much sophisticated[2]), wherewith the ladies there now color their hair. The rest, at this present, remains with me, extracted to a quintessence, so that, wherever it but touches, in youth it perpetually preserves, in age restores, the complexion; seats your teeth, did they dance like virginal jacks,[3] firm as a wall; makes them white as ivory, that were black as— [320

### ACT II. SCENE iii.

#### [The same.]

##### Corvino, Politic, Peregrine.

[CORV.] Spite o' the devil, and my shame! Come down here;
Come down! No house but mine to make your scene?
Signior Flaminio,[4] will you down, sir? Down?

[1] Transmitted.
[2] Adulterated.
[3] Attachments to the keys of a virginal.
[4] This name. like the following ones, is associated with the Italian *commedia dell' arte* of the day.

What, is my wife your Franciscina, sir?
No windores on the whole Piazza here
To make your properties but mine? But mine?
*He beats away the Mountebank, etc.*[5]
Heart! Ere tomorrow I shall be new christened,
And called the Pantalone di Besogniosi [6]
About the town.
PER.        What should this mean, Sir Pol?
POL. Some trick of state, believe it; I will home.                                              10
PER. It may be some design on you.
POL.                                   I know not.
I'll stand upon my guard.
PER.                          It is your best, sir.
POL. This three weeks, all my advices, all my letters,
They have been intercepted.
PER.                          Indeed, sir?
Best have a care.
POL.                Nay, so I will.
PER.                                This knight,
I may not lose him, for my mirth, till night.                              [*Exeunt.*]

### ACT II. SCENE iv.

#### [A room in Volpone's house.]

##### Volpone, Mosca.

VOLP. O, I am wounded!
MOS.                    Where, sir?
VOLP.                                Not without;
Those blows were nothing—I could bear them ever.
But angry Cupid, bolting from her eyes,
Hath shot himself into me like a flame,
Where now he flings about his burning heat,
As in a fornace [7] an ambitious fire,
Whose vent is stopped. The fight is all within me.
I cannot live except thou help me, Mosca;
My liver melts, and I, without the hope
Of some soft air from her refreshing breath,                                              10
Am but a heap of cinders.
MOS.                        'Las, good sir,

[5] This stage direction appears as a marginal note opposite the first line of the scene.
[6] Fool of Beggars.
[7] Furnace.

Would you had never seen her!

VOLP.                    Nay, would thou
Hadst never told me of her!

Mos.                    Sir, 'tis true;
I do confess I was unfortunate,
And you unhappy; but I'm bound in
conscience,
No less than duty, to effect my best
To your release of torment, and I will,
sir.

VOLP. Dear Mosca, shall I hope?

Mos.                    Sir, more than dear,
I will not bid you to despair of aught
Within a human compass.

VOLP.                    O, there spoke  20
My better angel. Mosca, take my
keys,
Gold, plate, and jewels—all 's at thy de-
votion;
Employ them how thou wilt. Nay, coin
me too,
So thou in this but crown my longings,
Mosca.

Mos. Use but your patience.

VOLP.                    So I have.

Mos.                    I doubt not
To bring success to your desires.

VOLP.                    Nay, then,
I not repent me of my late disguise.

Mos. If you can horn [1] him, sir, you need
not.

VOLP.        True.
Besides, I never meant him for my heir.
Is not the color o' my beard and eye-
brows                    30
To make me known?

Mos.                    No jot.

VOLP.                    I did it well.

Mos. So well, would I could follow you
in mine
With half the happiness! And yet I
would
Escape your epilogue.[2]

VOLP.                    But were they gulled
With a belief that I was Scoto?

Mos.                    Sir,
Scoto himself could hardly have dis-
tinguished!
I have not time to flatter you now; we'll
part,
And, as I prosper, so applaud my art.
                    [Exeunt.]

[1] Cuckold.
[2] I.e., a similar beating from Corvino.

ACT II. SCENE v.

[A room in Corvino's house.]

Corvino, Celia, Servatore.[3]

[CORV.] Death of mine honor, with the
city's fool?
A juggling, tooth-drawing, prating
mountebank?
And at a public windore? Where, whilst
he,
With his strained action and his dole of
faces,[4]
To his drug-lecture draws your itching
ears,
A crew of old, unmarried, noted lechers
Stood leering up like satyrs; and you
smile
Most graciously, and fan your favors
forth,
To give your hot spectators satisfaction!
What, was your mountebank their call?
Their whistle?                    10
Or were you enamored on his copper
rings,
His saffron jewel, with the toadstone [5]
in 't,
Or his embroidered suit, with the cope
stitch,
Made of a hearse cloth? Or his old tilt [6]
feather?
Or his starched beard? Well, you shall
have him, yes!
He shall come home, and minister unto
you
The fricace for the mother.[7] Or, let me
see,
I think you had rather mount; would
you not mount?
Why, if you'll mount, you may; yes,
truly, you may!
And so you may be seen, down to th'
foot.                    20
Get you a cittern, Lady Vanity,
And be a dealer with the virtuous man;
Make one. I'll but protest myself a cuck-
old,
And save your dowry. I'm a Dutch-
man, I!
For, if you thought me an Italian,

[3] Enters later.        [4] Grimaces.
[5] A fossil or semi-precious stone, popularly
supposed to have come from the head of a toad.
[6] Tilted.                    [7] Hysteria.

You would be damned ere you did this,
you whore!
Thou'ldst tremble to imagine that the
murder
Of father, mother, brother, all thy race,
Should follow as the subject of my jus-
tice.
CEL. Good sir, have patience.
CORV. [*Drawing his dagger.*]  What
couldst thou propose [1]  30
Less to thyself than, in this heat of wrath
And stung with my dishonor, I should
strike
This steel unto thee, with as many stabs
As thou wert gazed upon with goatish
eyes?
CEL. Alas, sir, be appeased! I could not
think
My being at the windore should more now
Move your impatience than at other
times.
CORV. No? Not to seek and entertain a
parley
With a known knave, before a multi-
tude?
You were an actor with your handker-
chief,  40
Which he most sweetly kissed in the re-
ceipt,
And might, no doubt, return it with a
letter,
And point the place where you might
meet; your sister's,
Your mother's, or your aunt's might
serve the turn.
CEL. Why, dear sir, when do I make these
excuses,
Or ever stir abroad but to the church?
And that so seldom—
CORV.  Well, it shall be less;
And thy restraint before was liberty
To what I now decree; and therefore
mark me.
First, I will have this bawdy light
dammed up,  50
And, till 't be done, some two or three
yards off
I'll chalk a line, o'er which if thou but
chance
To set thy desp'rate foot, more hell,
more horror,
More wild, remorseless rage shall seize
on thee

[1] Expect.

Than on a conjuror that had heedless
left
His circle's safety ere, his devil was laid.
Then here's a lock which I will hang upon
thee,
And, now I think on 't, I will keep thee
backwards; [2]
Thy lodging shall be backwards; thy
walks backwards;
Thy prospect, all be backwards; and no
pleasure  60
That thou shalt know but backwards.
Nay, since you force
My honest nature, know it is your own,
Being too open, makes me use you thus.
Since you will not contain your subtle
nostrils
In a sweet room, but they must snuff
the air
Of rank and sweaty passengers—(*Knock
within.*) One knocks.
Away, and be not seen, pain of thy life;
Not look toward the windore; if thou
dost—
Nay, stay, hear this—let me not pros-
per, whore,
But I will make thee an anatomy, [3]  70
Dissect thee mine own self, and read a
lecture
Upon thee to the city, and in public.
Away!—  [*Exit Celia.*

*Enter Servitore.*]

Who's there?
SER.  'Tis Signior Mosca, sir.

ACT II. SCENE vi.

[*The same.*]

*Corvino, Mosca.*

[CORV.] Let him come in. His master's
dead; there's yet
Some good to help the bad.—My Mosca,
welcome!
I guess your news.
MOS.  I fear you cannot, sir.
CORV. Is 't not his death?
MOS.  Rather the contrary.
CORV. Not his recovery?
MOS.  Yes, sir.
CORV.  I am cursed,

[2] In the rear of the house.  [3] Cadaver.

I am bewitched, my crosses meet to
   vex me.
   How? How? How? How?
Mos.            Why, sir, with Scoto's oil;
   Corbaccio and Voltore brought of it,
   Whilst I was busy in an inner room—
Corv. Death!    That damned mounte-
   bank! But for the law         10
   Now, I could kill the rascal. 'T cannot be
   His oil should have that virtue. Ha'
   not I
   Known him a common rogue, come fid-
   dling in
   To th' *osteria*,[1] with a tumbling whore,
   And, when he has done all his forced
   tricks, been glad
   Of a poor spoonful of dead wine, with
   flies in 't?
   It cannot be. All his ingredients
   Are a sheep's gall, a roasted bitch's
   marrow,
   Some few sod[2] earwigs, pounded cater-
   pillars,
   A little capon's grease, and fasting
   spittle—                  20
   I know hem to a dram.
Mos.              I know not, sir;
   But some on 't, there, they poured into
   his ears,
   Some in his nostrils, and recovered him,
   Applying but the fricace.
Corv.           Pox o' that fricace!
Mos. And since, to seem the more officious
   And flatt'ring of his health, there they
   have had,
   At extreme fees, the College of Physicians
   Consulting on him, how they might
   restore him,
   Where one would have a cataplasm[3]
   of spices,
   Another a flayed ape clapped to his
   breast,                 30
   A third would ha' it a dog, a fourth an
   oil,
   With wild cats' skins. At last, they all
   resolved
   That to preserve him was no other means
   But some young woman must be straight
   sought out,
   Lusty, and full of juice, to sleep by him;
   And to this service most unhappily,
   And most unwillingly, am I now em-
   ployed,

Which here I thought to preacquaint
   you with,
For your advice, since it concerns you
   most,
Because I would not do that thing might
   cross                40
Your ends, on whom I have my whole
   dependence, sir.
Yet, if I do it not, they may delate[4]
My slackness to my patron, work me
   out
Of his opinion, and there all your hopes,
Venters, or whatsoever are all frustrate!
I do but tell you, sir. Besides, they are
   all
Now striving who shall first present him;
   therefore,
I could entreat you, briefly conclude
   somewhat;
Prevent hem if you can.
Corv.           Death to my hopes!
   This is my villainous fortune! Best to
   hire                 50
   Some common courtesan.
Mos.         Ay, I thought on that, sir;
   But they are all so subtle, full of art—
   And age again doting and flexible,
   So as—I cannot tell—we may, per-
   chance,
   Light on a quean[5] may cheat us all.
Corv.                'Tis true.
Mos. No, no. It must be one that has no
   tricks, sir,
   Some simple thing, a creature made[6]
   unto it—
   Some wench you may command. Ha'
   you no kinswoman?
   Godso[7]—think, think, think, think,
   think, think, think, sir.
   One o' the doctors offered there his
   daughter.             60
Corv. How!
Mos.    Yes, Signior Lupo,[8] the physician.
Corv. His daughter?
Mos.        And a virgin, sir. Why, alas,
   He knows the state of 's body, what it is—
   That naught can warm his blood, sir,
   but a fever,
   Nor any incantation raise his spirit.
   A long forgetfulness hath seized that
   part.

---

[1] Hostelry.   [2] Sodden, boiled.   [3] Poultice.
[4] Blame, denounce.         [5] Strumpet.
[6] Prepared beforehand.     [8] Wolf.
[7] Gadso, catso, a term of impatience.

Besides, sir, who shall know it? Some
    one or two—
Corv. I pray thee give me leave. [*Walks
    aside.*] If any man
But I had had this luck—the thing in
    'tself,
I know, is nothing.—Wherefore should
    not I                                     70
As well command my blood and my af-
    fections
As this dull doctor? In the point of
    honor,
The cases are all one of wife and daugh-
    ter.
Mos. [*Aside.*] I hear him coming.[1]
Corv.            She shall do 't; 'tis done.
'Slight! If this doctor, who is not en-
    gaged,
Unless 't be for his counsel, which is
    nothing,
Offer his daughter, what should I, that
    am
So deeply in? I will prevent him. Wretch!
Covetous wretch!—Mosca, I have de-
    termined.
Mos. How, sir?
Corv. We 'll make all sure. The party
    you wot [2] of                            80
Shall be mine own wife, Mosca.
Mos.               Sir, the thing,
But that I would not seem to counsel
    you,
I should have motioned [3] to you at the
    first;
And, make your count,[4] you have cut
    all their throats.[5]
Why, 'tis directly taking a possession!
And in his next fit we may let him go.
'Tis but to pull the pillow from his
    head,
And he is thratled.[6] 'T had been done
    before
But for your scrupulous doubts.
Corv.               Ay, a plague on 't,
My conscience fools my wit! Well, I'll
    be brief,                                 90
And so be thou, lest they should be be-
    fore us.
Go home, prepare him, tell him with
    what zeal
And willingness I do it; swear it was

On the first hearing, as thou mayst do
    truly,
Mine own free motion.
Mos.               Sir, I warrant you,
I'll so possess him with it that the rest
Of his starved clients shall be banished
    all,
And only you received. But come not,
    sir,
Until I send, for I have something else
To ripen for your good—you must not
    know 't.                                  100
Corv. But do not you forget to send now.
Mos.               Fear not. [*Exit.*]

## Act II. Scene vii.

### [*The same.*]

*Corvino, Celia.*

Corv. Where are you, wife? My Celia!
    Wife!

### [*Enter Celia.*]

               What, blubbering?
Come, dry those tears. I think thou
    thought'st me in earnest?
Ha! By this light, I talked so but to
    try thee.
Methinks the lightness of the occasion
Should ha' confirmed thee. Come, I am
    not jealous.
Cel. No?
Corv. Faith, I am not, I, nor never was;
It is a poor, unprofitable humor.
Do not I know, if women have a will,
They'll do gainst all the watches o' the
    world,
And that the fiercest spies are tamed
    with gold?                                10
Tut, I am confident in thee; thou shalt
    see 't.
And see I'll give thee cause, too, to
    believe it.
Come, kiss me. Go, and make thee ready
    straight,
In all thy best attire, thy choicest jewels;
Put hem all on, and with hem thy best
    looks;
We are invited to a solemn feast,
At old Volpone's, where it shall appear
How far I am free from jealousy or fear.
                              [*Exeunt.*]

---

[1] *I.e.,* into my trap.       [4] Count on it.
[2] Know.                       [5] Worsted them all.
[3] Suggested.                  [6] Throttled.

## ACT III. SCENE i.

### [A street.]

#### Mosca.

[Mos.] I fear I shall begin to grow in love
With my dear self and my most pros-
p'rous parts,
They do so spring and burgeon; I can feel
A whimsy i' my blood. I know not how,
Success hath made me wanton. I could
skip
Out of my skin now, like a subtle snake,
I am so limber. O! Your parasite
Is a most precious thing, dropped from
above,
Not bred 'mongst clods and clotpolls [1]
here on earth.
I muse the mystery [2] was not made a
science,                                        10
It is so liberally professed! Almost
All the wise world is little else, in nature,
But parasites or sub-parasites. And yet
I mean not those that have your bare
town-art,
To know who's fit to feed hem, have no
house,
No family, no care, and therefore mold
Tales for men's ears to bait that sense,
or get
Kitchen invention and some stale re-
ceipts
To please the belly and the groin, nor
those,
With their court-dog tricks, that can
fawn and fleer,                                20
Make their revenue out of legs and
faces, [3]
Echo my lord, and lick [4] away a moth—
But your fine, elegant rascal, that can
rise
And stoop, almost together, like an ar-
row,
Shoot through the air as nimbly as a
star,
Turn short as doth a swallow, and be
here,
And there, and here, and yonder, all
at once,
Present to any humor, all occasion,
And change a visor [5] swifter than a
thought!

---

[1] Clodpolls, blockheads.      [4] Flick.
[2] I wonder that the profession.
[3] Bows and smiles.            [5] Facial expression.

This is the creature had the art born
with him,                                       30
Toils not to learn it, but doth practice it
Out of most excellent nature, and such
sparks
Are the true parasites, others but their
zanies.

## ACT III. SCENE ii.

### [The same.]

#### Mosca, Bonario.

[Mos. (Aside.)] Who's this? Bonario, old
Corbaccio's son?
The person I was bound to seek.—Fair
sir,
You are happ'ly met.
Bon.                    That cannot be by thee.
Mos. Why, sir?
Bon.            Nay, pray thee, know thy way,
and leave me;
I would be loath to interchange discourse
With such a mate [6] as thou art.
Mos.                          Courteous sir,
Scorn not my poverty.
Bon.                    Not I, by heaven;
But thou shalt give me leave to hate thy
baseness.
Mos. Baseness?
Bon.        Ay; answer me, is not thy sloth
Sufficient argument? Thy flattery?      10
Thy means of feeding?
Mos.                Heaven be good to me!
These imputations are too common, sir,
And easily stuck on virtue when she's
poor.
You are unequal [7] to me, and howe'er
Your sentence may be righteous, yet you
are not,
That, ere you know me, thus proceed in
censure.
St. Mark bear witness gainst you, 'tis
inhuman.                              [Weeps.]
Bon. [Aside.] What! Does he weep? The
sign is soft and good!
I do repent me that I was so harsh.
Mos. 'Tis true that, swayed by strong
necessity,                                      20
I am enforced to eat my careful bread
With too much obsequy; [8] 'tis true, be-
side,
That I am fain to spin mine own poor
raiment

---

[6] Fellow.      [7] Unfair.      [8] Obsequiousness.

Out of my mere observance,[1] being not
    born
To a free fortune; but that I have done
Base offices, in rending friends asunder,
Dividing families, betraying counsels,
Whispering false lies, or mining men
    with praises,
Trained [2] their credulity with perjuries,
Corrupted chastity, or am in love        30
With mine own tender ease, but would
    not rather
Prove the most rugged and laborious
    course,
That might redeem my present estima-
    tion,
Let me here perish, in all hope of good-
    ness.
Bon. [*Aside.*] This cannot be a personated
    passion.—
I was to blame, so to mistake thy nature;
Pray thee, forgive me, and speak out thy
    business.
Mos. Sir, it concerns you; and, though I
    may seem
At first to make a main offense in man-
    ners,
And in my gratitude unto my master,   40
Yet for the pure love which I bear all
    right,
And hatred of the wrong, I must reveal
    it.
This very hour your father is in purpose
To disinherit you—
Bon.              How!
Mos.                    And thrust you forth
As a mere stranger to his blood; 'tis true,
    sir.
The work no way engageth me but as
I claim an interest in the general state
Of goodness and true virtue, which I hear
T' abound in you, and for which mere
    respect,
Without a second aim, sir, I have done
    it.                                       50
Bon. This tale hath lost thee much of the
    late trust
Thou hadst with me; it is impossible.
I know not how to lend it any thought
My father should be so unnatural.
Mos. It is a confidence that well becomes
Your piety;[3] and formed, no doubt, it is
From your own simple innocence, which
    makes

[1] Service.    [2] Enticed, led on.    [3] Filial love.

Your wrong more monstrous and ab-
    horred. But, sir,
I now will tell you more. This very
    minute
It is or will be doing; and, if you        60
Shall be but pleased to go with me, I'll
    bring you,
I dare not say where you shall see, but
    where
Your ear shall be a witness of the deed,
Hear yourself written bastard, and pro-
    fessed
The common issue of the earth.
Bon.                              I'm mazed!
Mos. Sir, if I do it not, draw your just
    sword,
And score[4] your vengeance on my front
    and face;
Mark me your villain. You have too
    much wrong,
And I do suffer for you, sir. My heart   69
Weeps blood in anguish—
Bon.          Lead; I follow thee. [*Exeunt.*]

Act III. Scene iii.
Act III. Scene iii.

[*A room in Volpone's house.*][5]

*Volpone, Nano, Androgyno, Castrone.*
[Volp.][6] Mosca stays long, methinks.—
    Bring forth your sports,
And help to make the wretched time
    more sweet.
Nan. Dwarf, fool, and eunuch, well met
    here we be.
A question it were now, whether[7] of us
    three,
Being all the known delicates of a rich
    man,
In pleasing him, claim the precedency
    can?
Cas. I claim for myself.
And.                    And so doth the fool.
Nan. 'Tis foolish indeed; let me set you
    both to school.
First, for your dwarf, he's little and
    witty,                                    9
And everything, as it is little, is pretty;
Else why do men say to a creature of my
    shape,

[4] Cut, mark.
[5] The scene remains the same to the end of the
act.
[6] The following short debate through line 20
is printed in italics in the original.
[7] Which.

So soon as they see him, "It's a pretty
  little ape"?
And why a pretty ape but for pleasing
  imitation
Of greater men's action in a ridiculous
  fashion?
Beside, this feat [1] body of mine doth not
  crave
Half the meat, drink, and cloth one of
  your bulks will have.
Admit your fool's face be the mother of
  laughter,
Yet, for his brain, it must always come
  after;
And, though that do feed him, it's a
  pitiful case,
His body is beholding [2] to such a bad
  face.        *One knocks.*   20
VOLP. Who's there? My couch! Away!
  Look, Nano, see!
      [*Exeunt Androgyno and Castrone.*]
Give me my caps first—go, inquire. [*Exit
  Nano.*] Now, Cupid
Send it be Mosca, and with fair return!
NAN. [*Within.*] It is the beauteous Mad-
  am—
VOLP.        Would-be—is it?
NAN. The same.
VOLP. Now torment on me! Squire her in,
For she will enter, or dwell here forever.
Nay, quickly. [*Lies down on his couch.*]
  That my fit were past! I fear
A second hell too, that my loathing this
Will quite expel my appetite to the other.
Would she were taking now her tedious
  leave.        30
Lord, how it threats me what I am to
  suffer!

## ACT III. SCENE iv.

*Lady* [*Politic Would-be*], *Volpone, Nano,
Women 2.* [3]

[LADY.] I thank you, good sir. Pray you
  signify
Unto your patron I am here.—This band
Shows not my neck enough.—(I trouble
  you, sir;
Let me request you bid one of my women
Come hither to me.) In good faith, I am
  dressed
Most favorably today! It is no matter;
'Tis well enough.

---

[1] Delicate, dainty.        [2] Beholden.
[3] The waiting-women enter later.

[*Enter 1 Waiting-woman.*]

      Look, see these petulant things,
How they have done this!
VOLP. [*Aside.*]        I do feel the fever
Ent'ring in at mine ears. O, for a
  charm        9
To fright it hence!
LADY.        Come nearer. Is this curl
In his right place, or this? Why is this
  higher
Than all the rest? You ha' not washed
  your eyes yet?
Or do they not stand even i' your head?
Where's your fellow? Call her.
                [*Exit 1 Woman.*]
NAN. [*Aside.*]        Now St. Mark
Deliver us! Anon she'll beat her women
Because her nose is red.

[*Enter 1 and 2 Women.*]

LADY.        I pray you view
This tire,[4] forsooth. Are all things apt,
  or no?
[1] WOM. One hair a little here sticks out,
  forsooth.
LADY. Does 't so, forsooth? And where was
  your dear sight
When it did so, forsooth? What now!
  Bird-eyed? [5]        20
And you, too? Pray you, both approach
  and mend it.
Now, by that light, I muse yo' are not
  ashamed!
I, that have preached these things so oft
  unto you,
Read you the principles, argued all the
  grounds,
Disputed every fitness, every grace,
Called you to counsel of so frequent
  dressings—
(NAN. More carefully than of your fame
  or honor.)
LADY. Made you acquainted what an
  ample dowry
The knowledge of these things would be
  unto you,
Able alone to get you noble husbands 30
At your return—and you thus to neglect
  it!
Besides, you seeing what a curious [6]
  nation

---

[4] Headdress.        [6] Fastidious.
[5] Sharp-eyed.

Th' Italians are, what will they say of
me?
"The English lady cannot dress herself."
Here's a fine imputation to our country!
Well, go your ways, and stay i' the next
room.
This fucus [1] was too coarse too; it's no
matter.—
Good sir, you 'll give hem entertainment?
[*Exeunt Nano and Waiting-women.*]
VOLP. [*Aside.*] The storm comes toward
me.

LADY.          How does my Volp[one]?
VOLP. Troubled with noise, I cannot sleep;
I dreamt                                    40
That a strange fury entered now my
house,
And with the dreadful tempest of her
breath
Did cleave my roof asunder.
LADY.                Believe me, and I
Had the most fearful dream, could I
remember 't—
VOLP. [*Aside.*] Out on my fate! I ha'
given her the occasion
How to torment me; she will tell me hers.
LADY. Methought the golden mediocrity, [2]
Polite and delicate—
VOLP.               O, if you do love me,
No more! I sweat and suffer at the
mention                                     49
Of any dream; feel how I tremble yet.
LADY. Alas, good soul! The passion of the
heart.
Seed pearl were good now, boiled with
syrup of apples,
Tincture of gold, and coral, citron pills, [3]
Your elecampane [4] root, myrobalans [5]—
VOLP. Ay me, I have ta'en a grasshopper
by the wing!
LADY. Burnt silk and amber. You have
muscadel
Good i' the house—
VOLP.     You will not drink, and part?
LADY. No, fear not that. I doubt we shall
not get
Some English saffron (half a dram would
serve),
Your sixteen cloves, a little musk, dried
mints,                                      60
Bugloss, and barley meal—

[1] Cosmetic.          [3] Peels.
[2] Golden mean.      [4] A herb used as a tonic.
[5] A dried fruit, once used as a medicine.

VOLP. [*Aside.*]          She's in again!
Before, I feigned diseases; now I have
one.
LADY. And these applied with a right
scarlet cloth—
VOLP. [*Aside.*] Another flood of words! A
very torrent!
LADY. Shall I, sir, make you a poultice?
VOLP.               No, no, no!
I am very well; you need prescribe no
more.
LADY. I have a little studied physic; but
now
I am all for music, save, i' the forenoons,
An hour or two for painting. I would
have
A lady, indeed, t' have all—letters and
arts,                                       70
Be able to discourse, to write, to paint,
But principal, as Plato holds, your music
(And so does wise Pythagoras, I take it)
Is your true rapture, when there is con-
cent [6]
In face, in voice, and clothes, and is,
indeed,
Our sex's chiefest ornament.
VOLP.               The poet
As old in time as Plato, and as knowing,
Says that your highest female grace is
silence.
LADY. Which of your poets? Petrarch?
Or Tasso? Or Dante?
Guarini? Ariosto? Aretine?          80
Cieco di Hadria? I have read them all.
VOLP. [*Aside.*] Is everything a cause to
my destruction?
LADY. I think I ha' two or three of hem
about me.
VOLP. [*Aside.*] The sun, the sea will sooner
both stand still
Than her eternal tongue! Nothing can
scape it.
LADY. Here's *Pastor Fido*[7]—
VOLP. [*Aside.*] Profess obstinate silence;
That's now my safest.
LADY.               All our English writers,
I mean such as are happy in th' Italian,
Will deign to steal out of this author,
mainly,
Almost as much as from Montagnié. [90
He has so modern and facile a vein,
Fitting the time, and catching the court
ear!

[6] Harmony, agreement.
[7] Guarini's *Faithful Shepherd.*

Your Petrarch is more passionate, yet
    he,
In days of sonneting, trusted hem with
    much;
Dante is hard, and few can understand
    him.
But for a desperate wit there's Aretine;
Only his pictures are a little obscene—
You mark me not?
VOLP.            Alas, my mind's perturbed.
LADY. Why, in such cases, we must cure
    ourselves,
Make use of our philosophy—
VOLP.                Oi me!  100
LADY. And, as we find our passions do
    rebel,
Encounter hem with reason, or divert
    hem
By giving scope unto some other humor
Of lesser danger, as, in politic bodies,
There's nothing more doth overwhelm
    the judgment
And cloud the understanding than too
    much
Settling and fixing, and, as 'twere, sub-
    siding
Upon one object. For the incorporating
Of these same outward things into that
    part
Which we call mental, leaves some cer-
    tain fæces            110
That stop the organs, and, as Plato says,
Assassinates our knowledge.
VOLP. [Aside.]            Now, the spirit
Of patience help me!
LADY.            Come, in faith, I must
Visit you more a-days, and make you
    well.
Laugh and be lusty.
VOLP. [Aside.]  My good angel save me!
LADY. There was but one sole man in all
    the world
With whom I e'er could sympathize, and
    he
Would lie you, often, three, four hours
    together
To hear me speak, and be sometime so
    rapt
As he would answer me quite from the
    purpose,            120
Like you; and you are like him, just. I'll
    discourse,
And 't be but only, sir, to bring you
    asleep,

How we did spend our time and loves
    together
For some six years.
VOLP.            O, O, O, O, O, O!
LADY. For we were coætanei,[1] and brought
    up—
VOLP. [Aside.] Some power, some fate,
    some fortune rescue me!

## ACT III. SCENE V.

### Mosca, Lady, Volpone.

[MOS.] God save you, madam!
LADY.            Good sir.
VOLP.            Mosca, welcome,
    Welcome to my redemption!
MOS.                Why, sir?
VOLP. [Aside.]                O,
    Rid me of this my torture, quickly,
    there—
My madam with the everlasting voice.
The bells, in time of pestilence, ne'er
    made
Like noise, or were in that perpetual
    motion!
The Cockpit[2] comes not near it. All
    my house,
But now, steamed like a bath with her
    thick breath;
A lawyer could not have been heard, nor
    scarce
Another woman, such a hail of words  10
She has let fall. For hell's sake, rid her
    hence.
MOS. [Aside.] Has she presented?
VOLP. [Aside.]            O, I do not care;
    I'll take her absence upon any price,
With any loss.
MOS.        Madam—
LADY.            I ha' brought your patron
A toy, a cap here, of mine own work.
MOS.                'Tis well.
    I had forgot to tell you I saw your knight
Where you'ld little think it.
LADY.                Where?
MOS.                Marry,
Where yet, if you make haste, you may
    apprehend him,
Rowing upon the water in a gondole,
With the most cunning courtesan of
    Venice.            20
LADY. Is 't true?

[1] Of the same age.
[2] Where cockfighting and other noisy entertainments were held.

Mos.    Pursue hem, and believe your eyes;
Leave me to make your gift.—
                              [*Exit Lady.*]
                    I knew 'twould take,
For, lightly,[1] they that use themselves
    most license
Are still most jealous.
Volp.                    Mosca, hearty thanks
For thy quick fiction and delivery of
    me.
Now to my hopes, what say'st thou?

                    [*Enter Lady.*]

Lady.                    But do you hear, sir?
Volp. [*Aside.*] Again! I fear a paroxysm.
Lady.                    Which way
Rowed they together?
Mos.                    Toward the Rialto.
Lady. I pray you lend me your dwarf.
Mos.    I pray you take him.—[*Exit Lady.*]
Your hopes, sir, are like happy blossoms,
    fair,                    30
And promise timely fruit, if you will
    stay
But the maturing; keep you at your
    couch.
Corbaccio will arrive straight with the
    will;
When he is gone, I'll tell you more.
                              [*Exit.*]
Volp.                    My blood,
My spirits are returned; I am alive,
And, like your wanton gamester at
    primero,[2]
Whose thought had whispered to him,
    "Not go less,"
Methinks I lie, and draw [3]—[*Draws the
    curtains across his bed.*] for an en-
    counter.[3]

### Act III. Scene vi.

*Mosca, Bonario.*

[Mos.] Sir, here concealed you may hear
    all. [*Shows Bonario the hiding place.*]
    But, pray you,
Have patience, sir. (*One knocks.*) The
    same's your father knocks;
I am compelled to leave you.    [*Exit.*]
Bon.                    Do so.—Yet
Cannot my thought imagine this a truth.
                    [*Hides himself.*]

[1] Generally.            [2] A card game.
[3] Terms in primero, used punningly.

### Act III. Scene vii.

*Mosca, Corvino, Celia, Bonario, Volpone.*

[Mos.] Death on me! You are come too
    soon. What meant you?
Did not I say I would send?
Corv.                    Yes, but I feared
You might forget it, and then they pre-
    vent us.
Mos. Prevent?—[*Aside.*]    Did e'er man
    haste so for his horns?
A courtier would not ply it so for a
    place.—
Well, now there's no helping it, stay
    here;
I'll presently return.            [*Exit.*]
Corv.                    Where are you, Celia?
You know not wherefore I have brought
    you hither?
Cel.  Not well, except you told me.
Corv.                    Now I will:
Hark hither.            [*They step aside.*]

                    *Enter Mosca.*]

Mos. (*To Bonario.*)    Sir, your father
    hath sent word                    10
It will be half an hour ere he come;
And therefore, if you please to walk the
    while
Into that gallery—at the upper end,
There are some books to entertain the
    time;
And I'll take care no man shall come
    unto you, sir.
Bon. Yes, I will stay there.—[*Aside.*]  I
    do doubt this fellow.            [*Exit.*]
Mos. There! He is far enough; he can
    hear nothing.
And, for his father, I can keep him off.
                    [*Draws Volpone's curtains.*]
Corv. Nay, now, there is no starting back,
    and therefore
Resolve upon it. I have so decreed.   20
It must be done. Nor would I move 't
    afore,
Because I would avoid all shifts and
    tricks
That might deny me.
Cel.                    Sir, let me beseech you,
Affect not these strange trials; if you
    doubt
My chastity, why, lock me up forever;
Make me the heir of darkness. Let me
    live

Where I may please your fears, if not
   your trust.
Corv. Believe it, I have no such humor, I.
   All that I speak I mean; yet I am not
   mad—
   Not horn-mad,[1] see you?  Go to, show
   yourself                                                    30
   Obedient, and a wife.
Cel.                                    O heaven!
Corv.                                              I say it,
   Do so.
Cel.        Was this the train?[2]
Corv.                          I have told you reasons:
   What the physicians have set down,
   how much
   It may concern me, what my engage-
   ments are,
   My means, and the necessity of those
   means
   For my recovery; wherefore, if you be
   Loyal and mine, be won; respect my
   venture.
Cel. Before your honor?
Corv.                          Honor?  Tut, a breath!
   There's no such thing in nature—a mere
   term                                                         39
   Invented to awe fools.  What is my gold
   The worse for touching, clothes for be-
   ing looked on?
   Why, this 's no more.  An old decrepit
   wretch
   That has no sense, no sinew; takes his
   meat
   With others' fingers; only knows to gape
   When you do scald his gums; a voice, a
   shadow;
   And what can this man hurt you?
Cel. [Aside.]                    Lord!  What spirit
   Is this hath entered him?
Corv.                          And, for your fame,
   That's such a jig.[3]  As if I would go tell it,
   Cry it on the Piazza!  Who shall know it
   But he that cannot speak it, and this
   fellow,                                                     50
   Whose lips are i' my pocket?  Save
   yourself
   (If you'll proclaim 't, you may), I know
   no other
   Should come to know it.
Cel.                          Are heaven and saints then
   nothing?
   Will they be blind or stupid?

[1] Raving mad, with a reference to cuckoldry.
[2] Trick.                                    [3] Trifle.

Corv.                                              How!
Cel.                                              Good sir,
   Be jealous still, emulate them, and think
   What hate they burn with toward every
   sin.
Corv. I grant you; if I thought it were a
   sin,
   I would not urge you.  Should I offer
   this
   To some young Frenchman, or hot
   Tuscan blood
   That had read Aretine, conned all his
   prints,                                                     60
   Knew every quirk within lust's laby-
   rinth,
   And were professed critic in lechery,
   And I would look upon him and applaud
   him,
   This were a sin; but here, 'tis contrary,
   A pious work, mere charity for physic,
   And honest polity to assure mine own.
Cel. O heaven!  Canst thou suffer such
   a change?
Volp. [Aside.] Thou art mine honor,
   Mosca, and my pride,
   My joy, my tickling, my delight!  Go
   bring hem.
Mos.  Please you draw near, sir.
Corv.                          Come on!  What?  70
   You will not be rebellious?  By that
   light—
Mos. Sir, Signior Corvino, here, is come
   to see you.
Volp. O!
Mos.        And, hearing of the consultation
   had
   So lately for your health, is come to
   offer,
   Or rather, sir, to prostitute—
Corv.                          Thanks, sweet Mosca.
Mos. Freely, unasked, or unentreated—
Corv.                                              Well.
Mos. As the true, fervent instance of his
   love,
   His own most fair and proper wife, the
   beauty
   Only of price in Venice—
Corv.                                    'Tis well urged.
Mos. To be your comfortress, and to pre-
   serve you.                                                80
Volp. Alas, I am past already!  Pray you,
   thank him
   For his good care and promptness; but
   for that,

'Tis a vain labor e'en to fight gainst
  heaven—
Applying fire to a stone—uh, uh, uh,
  uh!—
Making a dead leaf grow again. I take
His wishes gently, though; and you may
  tell him
What I have done for him. Marry, my
  state is hopeless.
Will him to pray for me, and t' use his
  fortune
With reverence when he comes to 't.
Mos.           Do you hear, sir?
  Go to him with your wife.
Corv.        Heart of my father! 90
  Wilt thou persist thus? Come, I pray
    thee, come.
  Thou seest 'tis nothing, Celia. By this
    hand,
I shall grow violent. Come, do 't, I say.
Cel. Sir, kill me father; I will take down
  poison,
  Eat burning coals, do anything—
Corv.           Be damned!
  Heart, I will drag thee hence home by
    the hair;
  Cry thee a strumpet through the streets;
    rip up
  Thy mouth unto thine ears; and slit
    thy nose,
  Like a raw rochet![1] Do not tempt me;
    come.
  Yield, I am loath—Death! I will buy
    some slave              100
  Whom I will kill, and bind thee to him
    alive,
  And at my windore hang you forth,
    devising
  Some monstrous crime, which I, in cap-
    ital letters,
  Will eat into thy flesh with aqua fortis
  And burning corsives[2] on this stubborn
    breast.
  Now, by the blood thou hast incensed,
    I'll do 't!
Cel. Sir, what you please, you may; I
  am your martyr.
Corv. Be not thus obstinate; I ha' not
  deserved it.
  Think who it is entreats you. Pray thee,
    sweet—
  Good faith, thou shalt have jewels,
    gowns, attires,          110

[1] A fish.           [2] Corrosives.

What thou wilt think and ask. Do but
  go kiss him.
Or touch him but. For my sake. At my
  suit—
This once. No? Not? I shall remember
  this.
Will you disgrace me thus? Do you
  thirst my undoing?
Mos. Nay, gentle lady, be advised.
Corv.               No, no.
  She has watched her time. God's pre-
    cious, this is scurvy,
  'Tis very scurvy; and you are—
Mos.            Nay, good sir.
Corv. An arrant locust—by heaven, a
  locust!—
  Whore, crocodile, that hast thy tears
    prepared,
  Expecting how thou'lt bid hem flow—
Mos.      Nay, pray you, sir! 120
  She will consider.
Cel.      Would my life would serve
  To satisfy.
Corv.      'Sdeath! If she would but
    speak to him,
  And save my reputation, 'twere some-
    what;
  But spitefully to affect my utter ruin—
Mos. Ay, now you have put your fortune
  in her hands.
  Why, i' faith, it is her modesty; I must
    quit [3] her.
  If you were absent, she would be more
    coming;
  I know it, and dare undertake for her.
  What woman can before her husband?
    Pray you,
  Let us depart and leave her here.
Corv.           Sweet Celia, 130
  Thou mayst redeem all yet; I'll say no
    more.
  If not, esteem yourself as lost. Nay,
    stay there.
          [Exeunt Corvino and Mosca.]
Cel. O God and his good angels! Whither,
  whither
  Is shame fled human breasts, that with
    such ease
  Men dare put off your honors and their
    own?
  Is that, which ever was a cause of life,[4]
  Now placed beneath the basest circum-
    stance,

[3] Acquit, excuse.    [4] I.e., wedlock.

And modesty an exile made for money?
VOLP. (*He leaps off from his couch.*) Ay,
    in Corvino, and such earth-fed minds,
That never tasted the true heaven of
    love.          140
Assure thee, Celia, he that would sell
    thee
Only for hope of gain, and that uncertain,
He would have sold his part of Paradise
For ready money, had he met a cope-
    man.[1]
Why art thou mazed to see me thus re-
    vived?
Rather applaud thy beauty's miracle;
'Tis thy great work, that hath, not now
    alone,
But sundry times, raised me in several
    shapes,
And but this morning, like a mounte-
    bank,        149
To see thee at thy windore. Ay, before
I would have left my practice,[2] for thy
    love,
In varying figures I would have con-
    tended
With the blue Proteus or the hornéd
    flood.[3]
Now art thou welcome.
CEL.               Sir!
VOLP.             Nay, fly me not,
    Nor let thy false imagination
That I was bedrid make thee think I
    am so;
Thou shalt not find it. I am now as
    fresh,
As hot, as high, and in as jovial plight
As when, in that so celebrated scene
At recitation of our comedy    160
For entertainment of the great Valois,[4]
I acted young Antinous, and attracted
The eyes and ears of all the ladies pres-
    ent
To admire each graceful gesture, note,
    and footing.

SONG

Come, my Celia, let us prove,
While we can, the sports of love.
Time will not be ours forever;
He, at length, our good will sever.

[1] Chapman, dealer.    [2] Plotting.
[3] A reference to the story of Acheloüs, god of
the Grecian river.
[4] Henry VI was entertained at Venice in 1574.

Spend not then his gifts in vain.
Suns that set may rise again;    170
But, if once we lose this light,
'Tis with us perpetual night.
Why should we defer our joys?
Fame and rumor are but toys.
Cannot we delude the eyes
Of a few poor household spies,
Or his easier ears beguile,
Thus removéd by our wile?
'Tis no sin love's fruits to steal,
But the sweet thefts to reveal,    180
To be taken, to be seen,
These have crimes accounted been.

CEL. Some serene [5] blast me, or dire light-
    ning strike
    This my offending face!
VOLP.           Why droops my Celia?
Thou hast in place of a base husband
    found
A worthy lover; use thy fortune well,
With secrecy and pleasure. See, behold,
What thou art queen of—not in expec-
    tation,
As I feed others, but possessed and
    crowned.
See here a rope of pearl, and each more
    orient    190
Than that the brave Egyptian queen
    caroused;[6]
Dissolve and drink hem. See, a car-
    buncle,
May put out both the eyes of our St.
    Mark;
A diamant, would have bought Lollia
    Paulina,[7]
When she came in like starlight, hid
    with jewels
That were the spoils of provinces. Take
    these,
And wear and lose hem; yet remains
    an earring
To purchase them again, and this whole
    state.
A gem but worth a private patrimony
Is nothing; we will eat such at a meal. 200
The heads of parrots, tongues of night-
    ingales,
The brains of peacocks and of estriches[8]
Shall be our food, and, could we get the
    phœnix,

[5] The damp evening air.
[6] *I.e.*, Cleopatra drank.
[7] Mistress of Emperor Claudius.
[8] Ostriches.

Though nature lost her kind, she were
    our dish.
CEL.  Good sir, these things might move a
    mind affected
With such delights; but I, whose inno-
    cence
Is all I can think wealthy, or worth th'
    enjoying,
And which, once lost, I have naught to
    lose beyond it,
Cannot be taken with these sensual
    baits.                                      209
If you have conscience—
VOLP.                    'Tis the beggar's virtue;
If thou hast wisdom, hear me, Celia.
Thy baths shall be the juice of July-
    flowers,[1]
Spirit of roses and of violets,
The milk of unicorns, and panthers'
    breath [2]
Gathered in bags and mixed with Cre-
    tan wines.
Our drink shall be preparéd gold and
    amber,
Which we will take until my roof whirl
    round
With the vertigo, and my dwarf shall
    dance,
My eunuch sing, my fool make up the
    antic,[3]
Whilst we, in changéd shapes, act Ovid's
    tales,                                      220
Thou, like Europa now, and I like Jove,
Then I like Mars, and thou like Erycine;
So of the rest, till we have quite run
    through
And wearied all the fables of the gods.
Then will I have thee in more modern
    forms,
Attired like some sprightly dame of
    France,
Brave Tuscan lady, or proud Spanish
    beauty,
Sometimes unto the Persian sophy's
    wife,
Or the grand signior's mistress, and,
    for change,
To one of our most artful courtesans, 230
Or some quick Negro, or cold Russian;

And I will meet thee in as many shapes,
Where we may so transfuse our wan-
    d'ring souls
Out at our lips, and score up sums of
    pleasures,

    That the curious shall not know
    How to tell [4] them as they flow,
    And the envious, when they find
    What their number is, be pined.[5]

CEL.  If you have ears that will be pierced,
    or eyes
That can be opened, a heart may be
    touched,                                    240
Or any part that yet sounds man about
    you,
If you have touch of holy saints or
    heaven,
Do me the grace to let me scape. If not,
Be bountiful and kill me. You do know
I am a creature, hither ill betrayed,
By one whose shame I would forget it
    were;
If you will deign me neither of these
    graces,
Yet feed your wrath, sir, rather than
    your lust
(It is a vice comes nearer manliness),
And punish that unhappy crime of
    nature,                                     250
Which you miscall my beauty. Flay my
    face,
Or poison it with ointments, for seducing
Your blood to this rebellion. Rub these
    hands
With what may cause an eating leprosy,
E'en to my bones and marrow—anything
That may disfavor me, save in my honor.
And I will kneel to you, pray for you,
    pay down
A thousand hourly vows, sir, for your
    health,
Report and think you virtuous—
VOLP.                    Think me cold,
Frozen, and impotent, and so report
    me?                                        260
That I had Nestor's hernia, thou wouldst
    think.
I do degenerate, and abuse my nation,
To play with opportunity thus long;
I should have done the act, and then
    have parleyed.
Yield, or I'll force thee.        [Seizes her.]

[1] Gillyflowers.
[2] It was a common belief that panthers had
fragrant breaths. Panther was also the name
of a sweet-smelling drug.
[3] Buffoonery.
[4] Count.                    [5] Pained.

CEL.        O! Just God!

VOLP.        In vain—

BON. (*He leaps out from where Mosca had placed him.*) Forbear, foul ravisher! Libidinous swine!

Free the forced lady, or thou di'st, impostor.

But that I am loath to snatch thy punishment

Out of the hand of justice, thou shouldst yet

Be made the timely sacrifice of vengeance        270

Before this altar and this dross, thy idol.—

Lady, let's quit the place; it is the den

Of villainy. Fear naught; you have a guard.

And he ere long shall meet his just reward.     [*Exeunt Bonario and Celia.*]

VOLP. Fall on me, roof, and bury me in ruin!

Become my grave, that wert my shelter! O!

I am unmasked, unspirited, undone,

Betrayed to beggary, to infamy—

## ACT III. SCENE viii.

### *Mosca, Volpone.*

[MOS.] Where shall I run, most wretched shame of men,

To beat out my unlucky brains?

VOLP.        Here, here.

What! Dost thou bleed?

MOS.     O, that his well-driv'n sword

Had been so courteous to have cleft me down

Unto the navel, ere I lived to see

My life, my hopes, my spirits, my patron, all

Thus desperately engagéd by my error!

VOLP. Woe on thy fortune!

MOS.        And my follies, sir.

VOLP. Th' hast made me miserable.

MOS.        And myself, sir.

Who would have thought he would have hearkened so?        10

VOLP. What shall we do?

MOS.     I know not; if my heart

Could expiate the mischance, I'ld pluck it out.

Will you be pleased to hang me, or cut my throat?

And I'll requite you, sir. Let's die like Romans,[1]

Since we have lived like Grecians.[2]

       *They knock without.*

VOLP.     Hark! Who's there?

I hear some footing; officers, the *saffi*,[3]

Come to apprehend us! I do feel the brand

Hissing already at my forehead; now

Mine ears are boring.

MOS.     To your couch, sir; you

Make that place good, however. [*Volpone lies down.*] Guilty men    20

Suspect what they deserve still.—Signior Corbaccio!

## ACT III. SCENE ix.

### *Corbaccio, Mosca, Voltore,[4] Volpone.*

[CORB.] Why, how now, Mosca?

MOS.     O, undone, amazed, sir.

Your son, I know not by what accident,

Acquainted with your purpose to my patron,

Touching your will and making him your heir,

Entered our house with violence, his sword drawn,

Sought for you, called you wretch, unnatural,

Vowed he would kill you.

CORB.        Me?

MOS.        Yes, and my patron.

CORB. This act shall disinherit him indeed;

Here is the will.

MOS.        'Tis well, sir.

CORB.        Right and well.

Be you as careful now for me.

### [*Enter Voltore behind.*]

MOS.        My life, sir,    10

Is not more tendered;[5] I am only yours.

CORB. How does he? Will he die shortly, think'st thou?

MOS.        I fear

He'll outlast May.

CORB.        Today?

MOS.     No, last out May, sir.

CORB. Couldst thou not gi' him a dram?

MOS.        O, by no means, sir.

CORB. Nay, I'll not bid you.

---

[1] *I.e.*, commit suicide.

[2] Greeks, roisterers.

[3] Police.

[4] Enters later.

[5] Attended to.

VOLT. [*Coming forward.*]      This is a
knave, I see.

MOS. [*Aside.*] How! Signior Voltore! Did
he hear me?

VOLT.          Parasite!

MOS. Who's that?—O, sir, most timely
welcome—

VOLT.          Scarce
To the discovery of your tricks, I fear.
You are his, "only"? And mine also,
are you not?

MOS. Who? I, sir?

VOLT. You, sir. What devise is this   20
About a will?

MOS.        A plot for you, sir.

VOLT.           Come,
Put not your foists [1] upon me; I shall
scent hem.

MOS. Did you not hear it?

VOLT.       Yes, I hear Corbaccio
Hath made your patron there his heir.

MOS.       'Tis true,
By my device, drawn to it by my plot,
With hope—

VOLT.    Your patron should reciprocate?
And you have promised?

MOS.      For your good I did, sir.
Nay, more, I told his son, brought, hid
him here,
Where he might hear his father pass the
deed,
Being persuaded to it by this thought,
sir,          30
That the unnaturalness, first, of the act,
And then his father's oft disclaiming in
him
(Which I did mean t' help on), would
sure enrage him
To do some violence upon his parent,
On which the law should take sufficient
hold,
And you be stated in a double hope.
Truth be my comfort and my conscience,
My only aim was to dig you a fortune
Out of these two old rotten sepulchers—

VOLT. I cry thee mercy, Mosca.

MOS.       Worth your patience  40
And your great merit, sir. And see the
change!

VOLT. Why, what success?

MOS.     Most hapless! You must help, sir.
Whilst we expected th' old raven, in
comes

Corvino's wife, sent hither by her
husband—

VOLT. What, with a present?

MOS.            No, sir, on visitation
(I'll tell you how anon), and, staying long,
The youth he grows impatient, rushes
forth,
Seizeth the lady, wounds me, makes her
swear
(Or he would murder her, that was his
vow)
T' affirm my patron to have done her
rape—          50
Which how unlike it is, you see!—and
hence,
With that pretext he's gone, t' accuse his
father,
Defame my patron, defeat you—

VOLT.        Where's her husband?
Let him be sent for straight.

MOS.         Sir, I'll go fetch him.

VOLT. Bring him to the Scrutineo. [2]

MOS.            Sir, I will.

VOLT. This must be stopped.

MOS.        O, you do nobly, sir.
Alas, 'twas labored all, sir, for your good;
Nor was there want of counsel in the
plot;
But Fortune can at any time o'erthrow
The projects of a hundred learned clerks,
sir.          60

CORB. [*Cupping his ear.*] What's that?

VOLT.    Wilt please you, sir, to go along?
                 [*Exit with Corbaccio.*]

MOS. Patron, go in, and pray for our success.

VOLP. [*Rising.*] Need makes devotion;
heaven your labor bless!    [*Exeunt.*]

### ACT IV. SCENE i.

#### [*A street.*]

*Politic, Peregrine.*

[POL.] I told you, sir, it was a plot; you see
What observation is! You mentioned me
For some instructions; I will tell you, sir
(Since we are met here in this height of
Venice),
Some few particulars I have set down,
Only for this meridian, [3] fit to be known
Of your crude [4] traveler; and they are
these.

[1] Tricks.

[2] Senate House.            [4] Inexperienced.
[3] Special locality.

I will not touch, sir, at your phrase, or
    clothes,
For they are old.
PER.           Sir, I have better.
POL.                 Pardon;
    I meant, as they are themes.
PER.         O, sir, proceed.    10
    I'll slander you no more of wit, good sir.
POL. First, for your garb, [1] it must be
    grave and serious,
Very reserved and locked; not tell a secret
On any terms, not to your father; scarce
A fable, but with caution; make sure
    choice
Both of your company and discourse;
    beware
You never speak [2] a truth—
PER.        How!
POL.             Not to strangers,
    For those be they you must converse [3]
    with most;
Others I would not know, sir, but at
    distance,
So as I still might be a saver in hem; [4]  20
You shall have tricks else passed upon
    you hourly.
And then, for your religion, profess none,
But wonder at the diversity of all;
And, for your part, protest, were there
    no other
But simply the laws o' th' land, you
    could content you.
Nic. Machiavel and Monsieur Bodine [5]
    both
Were of this mind. Then must you learn
    the use
And handling of your silver fork at meals,
The metal of your glass (these are main
    matters
With your Italian), and to know the
    hour    30
When you must eat your melons and
    your figs.
PER. Is that a point of state too?
POL.               Here it is.
    For your Venetian, if he see a man
Preposterous in the least, he has him
    straight;

He has; he strips him. I'll acquaint you,
    sir.
I now have lived here 'tis some fourteen
    months.
Within the first week of my landing here
All took me for a citizen of Venice,
I knew the forms so well.
PER. [*Aside.*]        And nothing else.
POL. I had read Contarene, [6] took me a
    house,    40
Dealt with my Jews to furnish it with
    movables—
Well, if I could but find one man, one
    man
To mine own heart, whom I durst trust,
    I would—
PER. What, what, sir?
POL.        Make him rich, make him a
    fortune.
He should not think again. I would
    command it.
PER. As how?
POL.    With certain projects that I have,
    Which I may not discover.
PER. [*Aside.*]        If I had
    But one to wager with, I would lay odds
    now
He tells me instantly.
POL.            One is, and that
    I care not greatly who knows, to serve
    the state    50
Of Venice with red herrings for three
    years,
And at a certain rate from Rotterdam,
Where I have correspondence. There's
    a letter,
Sent me from one o' th' states, and to
    that purpose.
He cannot write his name, but that's his
    mark.
PER. He is a chaundler? [7]
POL.           No, a cheesemonger.
    There are some other too with whom I
    treat
About the same negotiation;
And I will undertake it. For 'tis thus
(I'll do 't with ease; I have cast [8] it all):
    your hoy [9]    60
Carries but three men in her, and a boy;

---

[1] Demeanor.
[2] Original reads *spake*.
[3] Associate.
[4] *I.e.*, so that I might not lose any money
through them.
[5] Jean Bodin, a sixteenth century French political philosopher.

[6] Cardinal Gasparo Contarini, author of a
work on Venice.
[7] Chandler, dealer in candles, which were
greasy.
[8] Calculated.    [9] A small coasting vessel.

And she shall make me three returns a
    year;
So, if there come but one of three, I save;
If two, I can defalk.[1] But this is, now,
If my main project fail.
PER.                    Then you have others?
POL. I should be loath to draw the subtle
    air
Of such a place without my thousand
    aims.
I'll not dissemble, sir; where'er I come,
I love to be considerative; and, 'tis true,
I have at my free hours thought upon    70
Some certain goods unto the state of
    Venice,
Which I do call my cautions, and, sir,
    which
I mean, in hope of pension, to propound
To the Great Council, then unto the
    Forty,
So to the Ten. My means are made al-
    ready—
PER. By whom?
POL.         Sir, one that, though his place
    b' obscure,
Yet he can sway, and they will hear him.
    H'is
A *commandadore.*
PER.         What! A common sergeant?
POL. Sir, such as they are, put it in their
    mouths,
What they should say, sometimes; as
    well as greater.                    80
I think I have my notes to show you—
PER.                    Good sir.
POL. But you shall swear unto me, on your
    gentry,
Not to anticipate—
PER.                    I, sir?
POL.                    Nor reveal
A circumstance—My paper is not with
    me.
PER. O, but you can remember, sir.
POL.                    My first is
Concerning tinder boxes. You must
    know
No family is here without its box.
Now, sir, it being so portable a thing,
Put case that you or I were ill affected
Unto the state, sir; with it in our pockets,
Might not I go into the Arsenal,    91
Or you come out again, and none the
    wiser?

[1] Cut off, reduce.

PER. Except yourself, sir.
POL.                    Go to, then. I therefore
Advertise to the state how fit it were
That none but such as were known
    patriots,
Sound lovers of their country, should be
    suffered
T' enjoy them in their houses, and even
    those
Sealed at some office, and at such a
    bigness
As might not lurk in pockets.
PER.                    Admirable!
POL. My next is, how t' inquire, and be re-
    solved                    100
By present demonstration, whether a
    ship,
Newly arrived from Soria [2] or from
Any suspected part of all the Levant,
Be guilty of the plague; and, where they
    use
To lie out forty, fifty days sometimes,
About the Lazaretto, for their trial,
I'll save that charge and loss unto the
    merchant,
And in an hour clear the doubt.
PER.                    Indeed, sir?
POL. Or—I will lose my labor.
PER.                    My faith, that's much.
POL. Nay, sir, conceive [3] me. 'Twill cost
    me, in onions,                    110
Some thirty livres—
PER.         Which is one pound sterling.
POL. Beside my waterworks; for this I do,
    sir:
First, I bring in your ship twixt two brick
    walls
(But those the state shall venter); on the
    one
I strain me a fair tarpauling, and in that
I stick my onions, cut in halves; the
    other
Is full of loopholes, out at which I thrust
The noses of my bellows; and those
    bellows
I keep, with waterworks, in perpetual
    motion,                    119
Which is the easi'st matter of a hundred.
Now, sir, your onion, which doth nat-
    urally
Attract th' infection, and your bellows
    blowing
The air upon him, will show instantly,

[2] Syria.                    [3] Understand.

By his changed color, if there be con-
　tagion,
Or else remain as fair as at the first.
Now 'tis known, 'tis nothing.
PER.　　　　　　　　You are right, sir.
POL. I would I had my note.
PER.　　　　　　　　Faith, so would I;
　But you ha' done well for once, sir.
POL.　　　　　　　　Were I false,
　Or would be made so, I could show you
　reasons
　How I could sell this state now to the
　　Turk,　　　　　　　　　　　　130
　Spite of their galleys or their—
　　　　　　　　　　[Examines his notes.]
PER.　　　　　　　　Pray you, Sir Pol.
POL. I have hem not about me.
PER. [Aside.]　　　　That I feared.—
　They are there, sir?
POL.　　　　　　No, this is my diary,
　Wherein I note my actions of the day.
PER. Pray you, let's see, sir. What is here?
　Notandum,[1]　　　　　　　　[Reads.]
　"A rat had gnawn my spur leathers;
　　notwithstanding,
　I put on new, and did go forth; but first
　I threw three beans over the threshold.
　　Item,
　I went and bought two toothpicks,
　　whereof one
　I burst immediately, in a discourse　140
　With a Dutch merchant, 'bout ragion'
　　del stato.[2]
　From him I went and paid a moccinigo
　For piecing my silk stockings; by the way
　I cheapened [3] sprats; and at St. Mark's I
　　urined."
　Faith, these are politic notes!
POL.　　　　　　　　Sir, I do slip
　No action of my life, thus but I quote it.
PER. Believe me, it is wise!
POL.　　　　　Nay, sir, read forth.

### ACT IV. SCENE ii.

*[The same.]*

*[Enter, at a distance,] Lady, Nano, Women,
　　　　　　　　　　Politic, Peregrine.*

[LADY.] Where should this loose knight be,
　trow? Sure, h' is housed.
NAN. Why, then he's fast.

LADY.　　　Ay, he plays both [4] with me.
　I pray you stay. This heat will do more
　　harm
　To my complexion than his heart is
　　worth.
　(I do not care to hinder, but to take
　　him.) [Rubs her cheeks.]
　How it comes off!
[1] WOM.　　　My master's yonder.
LADY.　　　　　　　　　Where?
[2] WOM. With a young gentleman.
LADY.　　　　　　That same's the party—
　In man's apparel! Pray you, sir, jog my
　　knight;
　I will be tender to his reputation,
　However he demerit.
POL. [Spying his Wife at a distance.]　My
　lady!
PER.　　Where?　　　　　　　　10
POL. 'Tis she indeed, sir; you shall know
　her. She is,
　Were she not mine, a lady of that merit,
　For fashion and behavior; and for beauty
　I durst compare—
PER.　　　　It seems you are not jealous,
　That dare commend her.
POL.　　　　　Nay, and for discourse—
PER. Being your wife, she cannot miss
　that.
POL. [Approaching his Wife.]　　Madam,
　Here is a gentleman; pray you, use him
　　fairly;
　He seems a youth, but he is—
LADY.　　　　　　　　None?
POL.　　　　　　　　　Yes, one
　Has put his face as soon into the
　　world—
LADY. You mean, as early? But today?
POL.　　　　　　　How's this?　　20
LADY. Why, in this habit, sir; you appre-
　hend me.
　Well, Master Would-be, this doth not
　　become you;
　I had thought the odor, sir, of your good
　　name
　Had been more precious to you; that you
　　would not
　Have done this dire massacre on your
　　honor.
　One of your gravity and rank besides!
　But knights, I see, care little for the oath
　They make to ladies—chiefly their own
　　ladies.

---

[1] Let it be noted; take notice.
[2] Politics.　　　　　　　　　[3] Bargained for.
[4] I.e., both fast and loose.

Pol. Now, by my spurs, the symbol of my
      knighthood—
(Per. Lord, how his brain is humbled for
      an oath!)                                    30
Pol. I reach [1] you not.
Lady.                    Right, sir, your polity
   May bear it through thus.—[*To Pere-
      grine.*] Sir, a word with you.
   I would be loath to contest publicly
   With any gentlewoman, or to seem
   Froward or violent, as the courtier says;
   It comes too near rusticity in a lady,
   Which I would shun by all means. And
      however
   I may deserve from Master Would-be,
      yet
   T' have one fair gentlewoman thus be
      made
   Th' unkind instrument to wrong an-
      other,                                       40
   And one she knows not, ay, and to
      persever,[2]
   In my poor judgment, is not warranted
   From being a solecism in [3] our sex,
   If not in manners.
Per.                    How is this!
Pol.                              Sweet madam,
   Come nearer to your aim.
Lady.                         Marry, and will, sir.
   Since you provoke me with your im-
      pudence
   And laughter of your light land-siren
      here,
   Your Sporus, your hermaphrodite—
Per.                         What's here?
   Poetic fury and historic storms! [4]
Pol. The gentleman, believe it, is of
      worth                                        50
   And of our nation.
Lady.          Ay, your Whitefriars [5] nation.
   Come, I blush for you, Master Would-be,
      I,
   And am ashamed you should ha' no more
      forehead [6]
   Than thus to be the patron, or St.
      George,
   To a lewd harlot, a base fricatrice,[7]
   A female devil, in a male outside.
Pol.                              Nay,

And you be such a one, I must bid adieu
To your delights. The case appears too
   liquid.[8]                              [*Exit.*]
Lady. Ay, you may carry 't clear, with
   your state face!                               59
   But, for your carnival concupiscence,[9]
   Who here is fled for liberty of con-
      science,
   From furious persecution of the marshal,
   Her will I disc'ple.[10]
Per.                    This is fine, i' faith!
   And do you use this often? Is this part
   Of your wit's exercise gainst you have
      occasion?
   Madam—
Lady.          Go to, sir.
Per.                    Do you hear me, lady?
   Why, if your knight have set you to beg
      shirts,
   Or to invite me home, you might have
      done it
   A nearer way by far.
Lady.                    This cannot work you
   Out of my snare.
Per.                    Why, am I in it, then?  70
   Indeed, your husband told me you were
      fair,
   And so you are, only your nose inclines,
   That side that's next the sun, to the
      queenapple.[11]
Lady. This cannot be endured by any
   patience.

### Act IV.  Scene iii.

### [*The same.*]

*Mosca, Lady, Peregrine* [*, Nano, Women*].

[Mos.] What's the matter, madam?
Lady.                         If the senate
   Right not my quest in this, I will protest
      hem
   To all the world no aristocracy.
Mos. What is the injury, lady?
Lady.                    Why, the callet [12]
   You told me of, here I have ta'en dis-
      guised.
Mos. Who? This? What means your
   ladyship? The creature

---

[1] Comprehend.          [3] Crime against.
[2] Persevere.           [4] Dramatic stormings.
[5] Disreputable district in London where evil-
doers were not followed by the law.
[6] Modesty.             [7] Prostitute.

[8] Clear.
[9] The object of your carnal desire.
[10] Disciple, discipline.
[11] A particularly red apple.
[12] Wench.

I mentioned to you is apprehended now
Before the senate; you shall see her—
LADY.             Where?
Mos. I'll bring you to her. This young
   gentleman,
I saw him land this morning at the
   port.                       10
LADY. Is 't possible! How has my judg-
   ment wandered!
Sir, I must, blushing, say to you I have
   erred
And plead your pardon.
PER.        What, more changes yet?
LADY. I hope yo' ha' not the malice to
   remember
A gentlewoman's passion. If you stay
In Venice here, please you to use me,
   sir—
Mos. Will you go, madam?
LADY.     Pray you, sir, use me; in faith,
The more you see me, the more I shall
   conceive
You have forgot our quarrel.
              [Exeunt All but Peregrine.]
PER.            This is rare!
Sir Politic Would-be? No, Sir Politic
   Bawd,                      20
To bring me thus acquainted with his
   wife!
Well, wise Sir Pol, since you have prac-
   ticed thus
Upon my freshmanship, I'll try your
   salthead,[1]
What proof it is against a counterplot.
                     [Exit.]

### ACT IV. SCENE iv.

[The Senate.]

*Voltore, Corbaccio, Corvino, Mosca.*

[VOLT.] Well, now you know the carriage
   of the business,
Your constancy is all that is required
Unto the safety of it.
Mos.            Is the lie
Safely conveyed[2] amongst us? Is that
   sure?
Knows every man his burden?[3]
CORV.       Yes.
Mos.          Then shrink not.
CORV. But knows the advocate the truth?
Mos.              O, sir,

By no means; I devised a formal tale
That salved your reputation. But be
   valiant, sir.
CORV. I fear no one but him, that this his
   pleading
Should make him stand for a co-heir—
Mos.            Co-halter!   10
Hang him; we will but use his tongue,
   his noise,
As we do Croaker's[4] here.
CORV.       Ay, what shall he do?
Mos. When we ha' done, you mean?
CORV.       Yes.
Mos.           Why, we'll think—
Sell him for mummia![5] He's half dust
   already.—
(To Voltore.) Do not you smile to see
   this buffalo,[6]
How he doth sport it with his head?—
[Aside.] I should,
If all were well and past.—(To Corbaccio.)
   Sir, only you
Are he that shall enjoy the crop of all,
And these not know for whom they toil.
CORB.           Ay, peace.
Mos. (To Corvino.) But you shall eat it.—
[Aside.] Much!—(Then to Voltore
   again.) Worshipful sir,        20
Mercury sit upon your thund'ring tongue,
Or the French Hercules,[7] and make your
   language
As conquering as his club, to beat along,
As with a tempest, flat, our adversaries;
But much more yours, sir.
VOLT.      Here they come; ha' done.
Mos. I have another witness, if you need,
   sir,
I can produce.
VOLT.         Who is it?
Mos.           Sir, I have her.

### ACT IV. SCENE v.

[The same.]

*Avocatori 4, Bonario, Celia, Voltore, Cor-
baccio, Corvino, Mosca, Notario, Commandadori.*

[Avoc. 1.] The like of this the senate
   never heard of.

---

[1] Salthood, lechery.
[2] Arranged.     [3] Refrain of a song: part.
[4] Corbaccio's.
[5] Mummy, a medicine.
[6] A horned animal; i.e., a cuckold.
[7] I.e., Ognius, regarded as the symbol of eloquence. See Lucian.

Avoc. 2. 'Twill come most strange to them when we report it.

Avoc. 4. The gentlewoman has been ever held
Of unreprovéd name.

Avoc. 3.                    So the young man.

Avoc. 4. The more unnatural part, that of his father.

Avoc. 2. More of the husband.

Avoc. 1.                    I not know to give
His act a name, it is so monstrous!

Avoc. 4. But the impostor, he is a thing created
    T' exceed example!

Avoc. [1.]                    And all aftertimes! 9

Avoc. 2. I never heard a true voluptuary
Described but him.

Avoc. 3.        Appear yet those were cited?

Not. All but the old magnifico, Volpone.

Avoc. 1. Why is not he here ?

Mos.                    Please your fatherhoods,
Here is his advocate. Himself's so weak,
So feeble—

Avoc. 4.        What are you?

Bon.                    His parasite,
His knave, his pander. I beseech the court
He may be forced to come, that your grave eyes
May bear strong witness of his strange impostures.

Volt. Upon my faith and credit with your virtues,
He is not able to endure the air.    20

Avoc. 2. Bring him, however.

Avoc. 3.        We will see him.

Avoc. 4.                    Fetch him.

Volt. Your fatherhoods' fit pleasures be obeyed;    [Exeunt Commandadori.]
But sure, the sight will rather move your pities
Than indignation. May it please the court,
In the meantime, he may be heard in me.
I know this place most void of prejudice,
And therefore crave it, since we have no reason
To fear our truth should hurt our cause.

Avoc. 3.                    Speak free.

Volt. Then know, most honored fathers,
I must now    29
Discover to your strangely abuséd ears,

The most prodigious and most frontless [1] piece
Of solid impudence and treachery
That ever vicious nature yet brought forth
To shame the state of Venice. This lewd woman,
That wants no artificial looks or tears
To help the visor she has now put on,
Hath long been known a close [2] adulteress
To that lascivious youth there; not suspected,
I say, but known, and taken in the act
With him, and by this man, the easy husband,    40
Pardoned, whose timeless [3] bounty makes him now
Stand here, the most unhappy, innocent person
That ever man's own goodness made accused.
For these not knowing how to owe [4] a gift
Of that dear grace, but with their shame, being placed
So above all powers of their gratitude,
Began to hate the benefit, and, in place
Of thanks, devise t'extirp [5] the memory
Of such an act, wherein I pray your fatherhoods
To observe the malice, yea, the rage of creatures    50
Discovered in their evils, and what heart
Such take, even from their crimes. But that anon
Will more appear. This gentleman, the father,
Hearing of this foul fact,[6] with many others,
Which daily strook at his too tender ears,
And, grieved in nothing more than that he could not
Preserve himself a parent (his son's ills
Growing to that strange flood), at last decreed
To disinherit him.

Avoc. 1.                    These be strange turns!

[1] Shameless.
[2] Secret.
[3] Untimely.
[4] Own.
[5] Extirpate.
[6] Deed.

Avoc. 2. The young man's fame was ever
   fair and honest.                        60
Volt. So much more full of danger is his
   vice,
   That can beguile so, under shade of
      virtue.
   But, as I said, my honored sires, his
      father
   Having this settled purpose, by what
      means
   To him betrayed we know not, and this
      day
   Appointed for the deed, that parricide—
   I cannot style him better—by confeder-
      acy
   Preparing this his paramour to be there,
   Entered Volpone's house (who was the
      man,
   Your fatherhoods must understand,
      designed                             70
   For the inheritance), there sought his
      father—
   But with what purpose sought he him,
      my lords?
   I tremble to pronounce it, that a son
   Unto a father, and to such a father,
   Should have so foul, felonious intent!
   It was to murder him—when, being pre-
      vented
   By his more happy absence, what then
      did he?
   Not check his wicked thoughts; no, now
      new deeds!
   (Mischief doth ever end where it begins.)
   An act of horror, fathers! He dragged
      forth                               80
   The aged gentleman that had there
      lyen [1] bedrid
   Three years and more, out of his inno-
      cent couch,
   Naked upon the floor; there left him;
      wounded
   His servant in the face; and with this
      strumpet,
   The stale to his forged practice,[2] who
      was glad
   To be so active (I shall here desire
   Your fatherhoods to note but my col-
      lections [3]
   As most remarkable), thought at once
      to stop

[1] Lain.
[2] Decoy to his invented plot.
[3] Inferences, conclusions.

His father's ends, discredit his free choice
In the old gentleman, redeem them-
   selves                                  90
By laying infamy upon this man,
To whom, with blushing, they should
   owe their lives.
Avoc. 1. What proofs have you of this?
Bon.                  Most honored fathers,
   I humbly crave there be no credit given
   To this man's mercenary tongue.
Avoc. 2.                          Forbear.
Bon. His soul moves in his fee.
Avoc. 3.               O, sir!
Bon.                          This fellow
   For six sols [4] more would plead against
      his Maker.
Avoc. 1. You do forget yourself.
Volt.                  Nay, nay, grave fathers,
   Let him have scope. Can any man im-
      agine
   That he will spare his accuser, that
      would not                           100
   Have spared his parent?
Avoc. 1.         Well, produce your proofs.
Cel. I would I could forget I were a
   creature.
Volt. Signior Corbaccio!
                  [Corbaccio advances.]
Avoc. 4.               What is he?
Volt.                        The father.
Avoc. 2. Has he had an oath?
Not.        Yes.
Corb.                 What must I do now?
Not. Your testimony's craved.
Corb.                 Speak to the knave?
   I'll ha' my mouth first stopped with
      earth; my heart
   Abhors his knowledge. I disclaim in [5]
      him.
Avoc. 1. But for what cause?
Corb.               The mere portent of nature!
   He is an utter stranger to my loins.
Bon. Have they made [6] you to this?
Corb.                 I will not hear thee,
   Monster of men, swine, goat, wolf, par-
      ricide!                             111
   Speak not, thou viper.
Bon.                 Sir, I will sit down,
   And rather wish my innocence should
      suffer
   Than I resist the authority of a father.
Volt. Signior Corvino!
                  [Corvino advances.]

[4] Small coins.   [5] Disown.   [6] Worked, wrought.

Avoc. 2.          This is strange.

Avoc. 1.              Who's this?

Not. The husband.

Avoc. 4.      Is he sworn?

Not.           He is.

Avoc. 3.            Speak then.

Corv. This woman, please your fatherhoods, is a whore,

Of most hot exercise, more than a partrich,[1]

Upon record—

Avoc. 1.       No more.

Corv.          Neighs like a jennet.

Not. Preserve the honor of the court.

Corv.           I shall, 120

And modesty of your most reverend
ears.

And yet I hope that I may say these
eyes

Have seen her glued unto that piece of
cedar,

That fine, well-timbered gallant, and
that here     [*Points to Celia's face.*]

The letters may be read, thorough[2] the
horn,[3]

That make the story perfect.

Mos.          Excellent, sir!

Corv. [*Aside to Mosca.*] There is no shame
in this now, is there?

Mos. [*Aside.*]       None.

Corv. Or, if I said I hoped that she were
onward

To her damnation, if there be a hell

Greater than whore and woman, a good
Catholic         130

May make the doubt.

Avoc. 3.       His grief hath made him
frantic.

Avoc. 1. Remove him hence.  *She swoons.*

Avoc. 2.       Look to the woman!

Corv.           Rare!

Prettily feigned again!

Avoc. 4.      Stand from about her!

Avoc. 1. Give her the air.

Avoc. 3. [*To Mosca.*]    What can you say?

Mos.          My wound,

May 't please your wisdoms, speaks for
me, received

In aid of my good patron, when he
missed

His sought-for father, when that well-
taught dame

Had her cue given her to cry out a rape.

Bon. O most laid[4] impudence! Fathers—

Avoc. 3.         Sir, be silent.

You had your hearing free; so must they
theirs.         140

Avoc. 2. I do begin to doubt th' imposture
here.

Avoc. 4. This woman has too many
moods.

Volt.        Grave fathers,

She is a creature of a most professed

And prostituted lewdness.

Corv.          Most impetuous,

Unsatisfied—grave fathers!

Volt.        May her feignings

Not take your wisdoms; but this day
she baited

A stranger, a grave knight, with her
loose eyes

And more lascivious kisses. This man
saw hem

Together on the water in a gondola.

Mos. Here is the lady herself that saw
hem too,        150

Without, who then had in the open
streets

Pursued them but for saving her knight's
honor.

Avoc. 1. Produce that lady.

Avoc. 2.      Let her come. [*Exit Mosca.*]

Avoc. 4.          These things,

They strike with wonder.

Avoc. 3.      I am turned a stone.

### Act IV. Scene vi.

[*The same.*]

*Mosca, Lady, Avocatori, etc.*

[Mos.] Be resolute, madam.

Lady.         Ay, this same is she.

Out, thou chameleon harlot! Now thine
eyes

Vie tears with the hyena. Dar'st thou
look

Upon my wrongéd face? I cry your
pardons.

I fear I have forgettingly transgressed

Against the dignity of the court—

Avoc. 2.         No, madam.

Lady. And been exorbitant—

---

[1] Partridge.            [2] Through.

[3] The child's A B C card, or hornbook, had a
thin covering of horn. The inevitable allusion
to cuckoldry is also present.

[4] Carefully plotted.

Avoc. 2.                    You have not, lady.
Avoc. 4. These proofs are strong.
LADY.                Surely, I had no purpose
   To scandalize your honors or my sex's.
Avoc. 3. We do believe it.
LADY.          Surely you may believe it.   10
Avoc. 2. Madam, we do.
LADY.          Indeed you may; my breeding
   Is not so coarse—
Avoc. 4.               We know it.
LADY.                        To offend
   With pertinacy[1]—
Avoc. 3.               Lady—
LADY.                  Such a presence!
   No, surely.
Avoc. 1,     We well think it.
LADY.                You may think it.
Avoc. 1. Let her o'ercome.—What wit-
   nesses have you,
   To make good your report?
BON.                    Our consciences.
CEL. And heaven, that never fails the
   innocent.
Avoc. 4. These are no testimonies.
BON.                    Not in your courts,
   Where multitude and clamor overcomes.
Avoc. 1. Nay, then you do wax insolent.


*Volpone is brought in, as impotent.* [*Lady*
                *Would-be kisses him.*]

VOLT.                        Here, here,   20
   The testimony comes that will convince
   And put to utter dumbness their bold
   tongues!
   See here, grave fathers, here's the rav-
   isher,
   The rider on men's wives, the great im-
   postor,
   The grand voluptuary! Do you not think
   These limbs should affect venery?[2] Or
   these eyes
   Covet a concubine? Pray you, mark
   these hands.
   Are they not fit to stroke a lady's breasts?
   Perhaps he doth dissemble?
BON.                    So he does.
VOLT. Would you ha' him tortured?
BON.     I would have him proved.     30
VOLT. Best try him then with goads, or
   burning irons;
   Put him to the strappado.[3] I have heard

The rack hath cured the gout; faith,
   give it him,
And help him of a malady. Be courteous.
I'll undertake, before these honored
   fathers,
He shall have yet as many left diseases
As she has known adulterers, or thou
   strumpets.
O, my most equal[4] hearers, if these deeds,
Acts of this bold and most exorbitant
   strain,                         39
May pass with suffrance, what one citizen
But owes the forfeit of his life, yea, fame,
To him that dares traduce him? Which
   of you
Are safe, my honored fathers? I would
   ask,
With leave of your grave fatherhoods, if
   their plot
Have any face or color like to truth?
Or if, unto the dullest nostril here,
It smell not rank, and most abhorréd
   slander?
I crave your care of this good gentleman,
Whose life is much endangered by their
   fable;
And, as for them, I will conclude with
   this,                          50
That vicious persons, when they are
   hot and fleshed
In impious acts, their constancy abounds.
Damned deeds are done with greatest
   confidence.
Avoc. 1. Take hem to custody, and sever
   them.
Avoc. 2. 'Tis pity two such prodigies
   should live.
Avoc. 1. Let the old gentleman be re-
   turned with care.
      [*Exeunt Commandadori with Volpone.*]
   I am sorry our credulity wronged him.
Avoc. 4. These are two creatures!
Avoc. 3.        I have an earthquake in me.
Avoc. 2. Their shame, even in their
   cradles, fled their faces.
Avoc. 4. [*To Voltore.*] You have done a
   worthy service to the state, sir,   60
   In their discovery.
Avoc. 1.          You shall hear, ere night,
   What punishment the court decrees
   upon hem.
[*Exeunt Avocatori, Notario, and Command-
      adori with Bonario and Celia.*]

---

[1] Pertinacity.   [2] Lust.   [3] A kind of torture.       [4] Impartial.

VOLT. We thank your fatherhoods. How like you it?

MOS. Rare!
I'ld ha' your tongue, sir, tipped with gold for this;
I'ld ha' you be the heir to the whole city;
The earth I'ld have want men ere you want living.
They are bound to erect your statue in St. Mark's.
Signior Corvino, I would have you go
And show yourself, that you have conquered.

CORV. Yes.

MOS. It was much better that you should profess 70
Yourself a cuckold thus than that the other
Should have been proved.

CORV. Nay, I considered that;
Now it is her fault.

MOS. Then it had been yours.

CORV. True. I do doubt this advocate still.

MOS. I' faith,
You need not; I dare ease you of that care.

CORV. I trust thee, Mosca.

MOS. As your own soul, sir.
[Exit Corvino.]

CORB. Mosca!

MOS. Now for your business, sir.

CORB. How! Ha' you business?

MOS. Yes, yours, sir.

CORB. O, none else?

MOS. None else, not I.

CORB. Be careful then.

MOS. Rest you with both your eyes, sir.

CORB. Despatch it.

MOS. Instantly.

CORB. And look that all, 80
Whatever, be put in, jewels, plate, moneys,
Household stuff, bedding, cortines.[1]

MOS. Cortine rings, sir;
Only the advocate's fee must be deducted.

CORB. I'll pay him now; you'll be too prodigal.

MOS. Sir, I must tender it.

CORB. Two cecchines is well?

MOS. No, six, sir.

CORB. 'Tis too much.

[1] Curtains.

MOS. He talked a great while;
You must consider that, sir.

CORB. Well, there's three—

MOS. I'll give it him.

CORB. Do so, and there's for thee. [Exit.]

MOS. [Aside.] Bountiful bones! What horrid, strange offense
Did he commit gainst nature, in his youth, 90
Worthy this age?—You see, sir, how I work
Unto your ends; take you no notice.

VOLT. No;
I'll leave you.

MOS. All is yours, the devil and all,
Good advocate!—[Exit Voltore.] Madam, I'll bring you home.

LADY. No, I'll go see your patron.

MOS. That you shall not;
I'll tell you why. My purpose is to urge
My patron to reform his will, and for
The zeal you have shown today, whereas before
You were but third or fourth, you shall be now
Put in the first, which would appear as begged 100
If you were present. Therefore—

LADY. You shall sway me. [Exeunt.]

### ACT V. SCENE i.

*[A room in Volpone's house.]*

*Volpone.*

[VOLP.] Well, I am here, and all this brunt is past.
I ne'er was in dislike with my disguise
Till this fled moment; here 'twas good, in private;
But in your public—*cave*[2] whilst I breathe.
Fore God, my left leg gan[3] to have the cramp,
And I apprehended straight some power had strook me
With a dead palsy. Well, I must be merry,
And shake it off. A many of these fears
Would put me into some villainous disease,
Should they come thick upon me; I'll prevent hem. 10

[2] Beware.     [3] Began.

Give me a bowl of lusty wine to fright
This humor from my heart. (*He drinks.*)
　　Hum, hum, hum!
'Tis almost gone already; I shall con-
　　quer.
Any device now of rare, ingenious knav-
　　ery,
That would possess me with a violent
　　laughter,
Would make me up again.　(*Drinks
　　again.*) So, so, so, so!
This heat is life; 'tis blood by this time.—
　　Mosca!

### ACT V. SCENE ii.

#### [*The same.*]

*Mosca, Volpone, Nano, Castrone.*[1]

[Mos.] How now, sir? Does the day look
　　clear again?
Are we recovered, and wrought out of
　　error,
Into our way, to see our path before us?
Is our trade free once more?
VOLP.　　　　　　　　Exquisite Mosca!
MOS. Was it not carried learnedly?
VOLP.　　　　　　　　And stoutly.
Good wits are greatest in extremities.
MOS. It were a folly beyond thought to
　　trust
Any grand act unto a cowardly spirit.
You are not taken with it enough, me-
　　thinks?
VOLP. O, more than if I had enjoyed the
　　wench;　　　　　　　　　　　　10
The pleasure of all womankind's not like
　　it.
MOS. Why, now you speak, sir. We must
　　here be fixed;
Here we must rest. This is our master-
　　piece;
We cannot think to go beyond this.
VOLP.　　　　　　　　　　　　True,
Thou hast played thy prize, my precious
　　Mosca.
MOS.　　　　Nay, sir,
To gull the court—
VOLP.　　　And quite divert the torrent
Upon the innocent.
MOS.　　　　　　Yes, and to make
So rare a music out of discords—
VOLP.　　　　　　　　　　Right.

That yet to me 's the strangest (how th'
　　hast borne it!),
That these, being so divided mongst
　　themselves,　　　　　　　　　20
Should not scent somewhat or [2] in me or
　　thee,
Or doubt their own side.
MOS.　　　　True, they will not see 't.
Too much light blinds hem, I think.
　　Each of hem
Is so possessed and stuffed with his own
　　hopes
That anything unto the contrary,
Never so true, or never so apparent,
Never so palpable, they will resist it—
VOLP. Like a temptation of the devil.
MOS.　　　　　　　　Right, sir.
Merchants may talk of trade, and your
　　great signiors
Of land that yields well; but, if Italy　30
Have any glebe [3] more fruitful than these
　　fellows,
I am deceived. Did not your advocate
　　rare?
VOLP. O—"My most honored fathers, my
　　grave fathers,
Under correction of your fatherhoods,
What face of truth is here? If these
　　strange deeds
May pass, most honored fathers"—I had
　　much ado
To forbear laughing.
MOS.　　'T seemed to me you sweat, sir.
VOLP. In troth, I did a little.
MOS.　　　　　　　But confess, sir,
Were you not daunted?
VOLP.　　　　　　In good faith, I was
A little in a mist, but not dejected;　40
Never but still myself.
MOS.　　　　　　　I think it, sir.
Now, so truth help me, I must needs
　　say this, sir,
And out of conscience for your advocate,
He has taken pains, in faith, sir, and
　　deserved,
In my poor judgment, I speak it under
　　favor,
Not to contrary you, sir, very richly—
Well—to be cozened.
VOLP.　　　　Troth, and I think so too,
By that I heard him in the latter end.
MOS. O, but before, sir. Had you heard
　　him first

---

[1] Last two enter later.　　　[2] Either.　　　[3] Cultivated ground.

Draw it to certain heads, then ag-
gravate,[1]                                            50
Then use his vehement figures—I looked
still
When he would shift a shirt; and doing
this
Out of pure love, no hope of gain—
VOLP.                                      'Tis right.
I cannot answer him, Mosca, as I would,
Not yet; but for thy sake, at thy en-
treaty,
I will begin even now—to vex hem all,
This very instant.
MOS.                        Good sir.
VOLP.                              Call the dwarf
And eunuch forth.
MOS.                        Castrone, Nano!

[*Enter Castrone and Nano.*]

NANO.                                      Here.
VOLP. Shall we have a jig[2] now?
MOS.                        What you please, sir.
VOLP.                                      Go,
Straight give out about the streets, you
two,                                              60
That I am dead. Do it with constancy,
Sadly,[3] do you hear? Impute it to the
grief
Of this late slander.
                [*Exeunt Castrone and Nano.*]
MOS.                    What do you mean, sir?
VOLP.                                      O,
I shall have instantly my vulture, crow,
Raven, come flying hither, on the news,
To peck for carrion, my she-wolf, and all,
Greedy, and full of expectation—
MOS. And then to have it ravished from
their mouths?
VOLP. 'Tis true. I will ha' thee put on a
gown,
And take upon thee, as thou wert mine
heir;                                             70
Show hem a will. Open that chest, and
reach
Forth one of those that has the blanks;
I'll straight
Put in thy name.
MOS.                    It will be rare, sir.
                [*Gives him a paper.*]
VOLP.                                      Ay,
When they e'en gape, and find themselves
deluded—

MOS. Yes.
VOLP.                    And thou use them scurvily!
Despatch;
Get on thy gown.
MOS. [*Putting on a gown.*]        But what,
sir, if they ask
After the body?
VOLP.                    Say it was corrupted.
MOS. I'll say it stunk, sir, and was fain t'
have it
Coffined up instantly, and sent away.
VOLP. Anything; what thou wilt. Hold,
here's my will.                                   80
Get thee a cap, a count-book, pen and
ink,
Papers afore thee; sit as thou wert taking
An inventory of parcels. I'll get up
Behind the cortine, on a stool, and
harken;
Sometime peep over; see how they do
look,
With what degrees their blood doth leave
their faces.
O, 'twill afford me a rare meal of laugh-
ter!
MOS. [*Following Volpone's directions.*] Your
advocate will turn stark dull upon it.
VOLP. It will take off his oratory's edge.
MOS. But your clarissimo,[4] old round-
back, he                                          90
Will crump you[5] like a hog louse, with
the touch.
VOLP. And what Corvino?
MOS.                        O, sir, look for him
Tomorrow morning with a rope and a
dagger
To visit all the streets; he must run mad.
My lady, too, that came into the court
To bear false witness for your wor-
ship—
VOLP.                    Yes,
And kissed me fore the fathers, when my
face
Flowed all with oils—
MOS.        And sweat, sir. Why, your gold
Is such another med'cine, it dries up
All those offensive savors; it trans-
forms                                             100
The most deforméd, and restores hem
lovely,
As 'twere the strange poetical girdle.[6]
Jove

---

[1] Make his accusations.
[2] Entertainment, jest.                [3] Seriously.
[4] Grandee.                        [5] Curl up.
[6] Jonson's marginal note reads: "Cestus."

Could not invent t' himself a shroud more
  subtile
To pass Acrisius' [1] guards. It is the thing
Makes all the world her grace, her youth,
  her beauty.
VOLP. I think she loves me.
MOS.       Who? The lady, sir?
  She's jealous of you.
VOLP.       Dost thou say so?
              [Knocking within.]
MOS.             Hark!
  There's some already.
VOLP.     Look.
MOS.         It is the vulture;
  He has the quickest scent.
VOLP.       I'll to my place;
  Thou to thy posture.
          [Goes behind the curtain.]
MOS.      I am set.
VOLP.       But, Mosca, 110
  Play the artificer now; torture hem
  rarely.

       ACT V. SCENE iii.

        [The same.]

*Voltore, Mosca, Corbaccio,*[2] *Corvino,*[2] *Lady,*[2]
                  *Volpone.*

[VOLT.] How now, my Mosca?
MOS. [Writing.]   "Turkey carpets,
  nine—"
VOLT. Taking an inventory? That is well.
MOS. "Two suits of bedding, tissue—"
VOLT.       Where's the will?
  Let me read that the while.

[Enter Servants with Corbaccio in a chair.]

CORB.       So, set me down,
  And get you home.   [Exeunt Servants.]
VOLT.   Is he come now to trouble us?
MOS. "Of cloth of gold, two more—"
CORB.       Is it done, Mosca?
MOS. "Of several vellets,[3] eight—"
VOLT.       I like his care.
CORB. Dost thou not hear?

      [Enter Corvino.]

CORV.    Ha! Is the hour come, Mosca?
  *Volpone peeps from behind a traverse.*
VOLP. [Aside.] Ay, now they muster.

[1] Danaë's father's.
[2] Enters later.         [3] Velvets.

CORV.    What does the advocate here,
  Or this Corbaccio?
CORB.       What do these here?

   [Enter Lady Would-be.]

LADY.          Mosca! 10
  Is his thread spun?
MOS.     "Eight chests of linen—"
VOLP. [Aside.]         O,
  My fine Dame Would-be, too!
CORV.      Mosca, the will,
  That I may show it these, and rid hem
  hence.
MOS. "Six chests of diaper,[4] four of dam-
  ask."—There! [Gives them the will.]
CORB. Is that the will?
MOS.    "Down beds, and bolsters—"
VOLP. [Aside.]       Rare!
  Be busy still. Now they begin to flut-
  ter;
  They never think of me. Look, see, see,
  see!
  How their swift eyes run over the long
  deed,
  Unto the name, and to the legacies, 19
  What is bequeathed them there—
MOS.     "Ten suits of hangings—"
VOLP. [Aside.] Ay, i' their garters, Mosca.
  Now their hopes
  Are at the gasp.
VOLT.      Mosca the heir!
CORB.       What's that?
VOLP. [Aside.] My advocate is dumb.
  Look to my merchant;
  He has heard of some strange storm—
  a ship is lost;
  He faints. My lady will swoon. Old
  glazen-eyes,
  He hath not reached his despair yet.
CORB.       All these
  Are out of hope; I am, sure, the man.
           [Takes the will.]
CORV.       But, Mosca—
MOS. "Two cabinets—"
CORV.      Is this in earnest?
MOS.         "One
  Of ebony—"
CORV.    Or do you but delude me?
MOS. "The other, mother of pearl."—I'm
  very busy. 30
  Good faith, it is a fortune thrown upon
  me—

[4] Fine linen.

"Item, one salt [1] of agate"—not my seeking.

LADY. Do you hear, sir?

MOS.            "A perfumed box"—pray you, forbear;

You see I am troubled—"made of an onyx—"

LADY.        How!

MOS. Tomorrow or next day, I shall be at leisure

To talk with you all.

CORV.        Is this my large hope's issue?

LADY. Sir, I must have a fairer answer.

MOS.               Madam!

Marry, and shall. Pray you, fairly quit my house.

Nay, raise no tempest with your looks; but, hark you,      39

Remember what your ladyship offered me

To put you in an heir; go to, think on 't,

And what you said e'en your best madams did

For maintenance; and why not you? Enough.

Go home, and use the poor Sir Pol, your knight, well,

For fear I tell some riddles. Go, be melancholic.     [Exit Lady Would-be.]

VOLP. [Aside.] O, my fine devil!

CORV.        Mosca, pray you a word.

MOS. Lord! Will not you take your despatch hence yet?

Methinks, of all, you should have been th' example.

Why should you stay here? With what thought, what promise?

Hear you! Do not you know I know you an ass?      50

And that you would most fain have been a wittol [2]

If fortune would have let you? That you are

A declared cuckold, on good terms? This pearl,

You'll say, was yours? Right. This diamant?

I'll not deny 't, but thank you. Much here else?

It may be so. Why, think that these good works

May help to hide your [3] bad. I'll not betray you;

Although you be but extraordinary,

And have it only in title, it sufficeth.

Go home; be melancholy too, or mad.    60
                     [Exit Corvino.]

VOLP. [Aside.] Rare Mosca! How his villainy becomes him!

VOLT. Certain he doth delude all these for me.

CORB. Mosca the heir?

VOLP. [Aside.]        O, his four eyes have found it.

CORB. I am cozened, cheated, by a parasite-slave;

Harlot,[4] t' hast gulled me.

MOS.       Yes, sir. Stop your mouth,

Or I shall draw the only tooth is left.

Are not you he, that filthy, covetous wretch,

With the three legs,[5] that here, in hope of prey,

Have, any time this three year, snuffed about

With your most grov'ling nose, and would have hired      70

Me to the pois'ning of my patron, sir?

Are not you he that have today in court

Professed the disinheriting of your son?

Perjured yourself? Go home, and die, and stink;

If you but croak a syllable, all comes out.

Away, and call your porters! Go, go, stink!      [Exit Corbaccio.]

VOLP. [Aside.] Excellent varlet!

VOLT.        Now, my faithful Mosca,

I find thy constancy—

MOS.        Sir?

VOLT.        Sincere.

MOS. [Writing.]        "A table

Of porphyry"—I marl [6] you'll be thus troublesome.

VOLT. Nay, leave off now; they are gone.

MOS.        Why, who are you?    80

What? Who did send for you? O, cry you mercy,

Reverend sir! Good faith, I am grieved for you,

That any chance of mine should thus defeat

Your (I must needs say) most deserving travails;

But I protest, sir, it was cast upon me,

And I could almost wish to be without it,

But that the will o' th' dead must be
  observed.
Marry, my joy is that you need it not;
You have a gift, sir (thank your educa-
  tion),
Will never let you want, while there are
  men                   90
And malice to breed causes.[1]   Would I
  had
But half the like, for all my fortune, sir!
If I have any suits (as I do hope,
Things being so easy and direct, I shall
  not),
I will make bold with your obstreperous
  aid,
Conceive me—for your fee, sir. In mean-
  time,
You that have so much law, I know ha'
  the conscience
Not to be covetous of what is mine.
Good sir, I thank you for my plate;
  'twill help
To set up a young man. Good faith, you
  look                   100
As you were costive; best go home and
  purge, sir.         [*Exit Voltore.*]
VOLP. [*Coming from behind the curtain.*]
  Bid him eat lettuce well.[2] My witty
  mischief,
Let me embrace thee. O, that I could
  now
Transform thee to a Venus!—Mosca, go,
Straight take my habit of clarissimo,
And walk the streets. Be seen; torment
  hem more.
We must pursue as well as plot. Who
  would
Have lost this feast?
Mos.         I doubt it will lose them.
VOLP. O, my recovery shall recover all.
  That I could now but think on some dis-
  guise                 110
To meet hem in, and ask hem questions!
How I would vex hem still at every turn!
Mos. Sir, I can fit you.
VOLP.            Canst thou?
Mos.             Yes, I know
  One o' the *commandadori*,[3] sir, so like
  you;
Him will I straight make drunk, and
  bring you his habit.

[1] Lawsuits.
[2] *I.e.*, as a soporific.
[3] Original has *commandatori*.

VOLP. A rare disguise, and answering thy
  brain!
O, I will be a sharp disease unto hem.
Mos. Sir, you must look for curses—
VOLP.            Till they burst;
The fox fares ever best when he is curst.
                  [*Exeunt.*]

## ACT V. SCENE iv.

[*A room in Politic's house.*]

*Peregrine,* [*disguised,*] *Mercatori 3, Woman,
Politic.*[4]

[PER.] Am I enough disguised?
MER. 1.           I warrant you.
PER. All my ambition is to fright him
  only.
MER. 2. If you could ship him away,
  'twere excellent.
MER. 3. To Zant or to Aleppo!
PER.         Yes, and ha' his
  Adventures put i' th' *Book of Voyages*,[5]
And his gulled story registered for truth.
Well, gentlemen, when I am in a while,
And that you think us warm in our dis-
  course,
Know your approaches.
MER. 1.       Trust it to our care.
               [*Exeunt Mercatori.*]

*Enter Woman.*]

PER. Save you, fair lady!   Is Sir Pol
  within?                 10
WOM. I do not know, sir.
PER.         Pray you, say unto him
  Here is a merchant, upon earnest busi-
  ness,
Desires to speak with him.
WOM.         I will see, sir. [*Exit.*]
PER.            Pray you.
  I see the family is all female here.

*[Enter Woman.]*

WOM. He says, sir, he has weighty affairs
  of state
That now require him whole; some other
  time
You may possess him.
PER.         Pray you, say again,
  If those require him whole, these will
  exact[6] him,

[4] Last two enter later.
[5] Such as Hakluyt's.       [6] Finish off.

Whereof I bring him tidings.— [*Exit
   Woman.*] What might be
His grave affair of state now?  How to
   make                                    20
Bolognian sausages here in Venice, spar-
   ing
One o' th' ingredients!

*[Enter Woman.]*

Wom.                     Sir, he says he knows
   By your word "tidings" that you are
      no statesman,
   And therefore wills you stay.
Per.        Sweet, pray you, return [1] him:
   I have not read so many proclamations,
   And studied them for words as he has
      done,
   But—here he deigns to come.
                                 [*Exit Woman.*

*Enter Sir Politic.]*

Pol.                     Sir, I must crave
   Your courteous pardon.  There hath
      chanced today
   Unkind disaster twixt my lady and me;
   And I was penning my apology         30
   To give her satisfaction, as you came
      now.
Per.  Sir, I am grieved I bring you worse
      disaster.
   The gentleman you met at th' port to-
      day,
   That told you he was newly arrived—
Pol.                             Ay, was
   A fugitive punk? [2]
Per.           No, sir, a spy set on you;
   And he has made relation to the senate
   That you professed to him to have a
      plot
   To sell the state of Venice to the Turk.
Pol.  O me!
Per.       For which warrants are signed by
      this time,
   To apprehend you, and to search your
      study                              40
   For papers—
Pol.       Alas, sir, I have none but notes
   Drawn out of playbooks—
Per.                     All the better, sir.
Pol.  And some essays.  What shall I do?
Per.                             Sir, best
   Convey yourself into a sugar chest,

[1] Answer.                    [2] Prostitute.

Or, if you could lie round, a frail [3] were
   rare,
   And I could send you aboard.
Pol.                     Sir, I but talked so
   For discourse' sake merely.
                        *They knock without.*
Per.                     Hark!  They are there.
Pol.  I am a wretch, a wretch!
Per.                     What will you do, sir?
   Ha' you ne'er a curran-butt [4] to leap
      into?
   They'll put you to the rack; you must
      be sudden.                          50
Pol.  Sir, I have an engine [5]—
Mer. 3. [*Within.*]     Sir Politic Would-be?
Mer. 2. [*Within.*]     Where is he?
Pol.                     That I have
   thought upon before time.
Per.  What is it?
Pol.       (I shall ne'er endure the torture.)
   Marry, it is, sir, of a tortoise shell.
   Fitted for these extremities; pray you,
      sir, help me. [*Brings out his contrivance.*]
   Here I have a place, sir, to put back my
      legs
   (Please you to lay it on, sir), with this cap
   And my black gloves.  I'll lie, sir, like
      a tortoise,
   Till they are gone.
Per.       And call you this an engine?
Pol.  Mine own device.—Good sir, bid my
      wife's women                        60
   To burn my papers.       [*Exit Peregrine.*]

*They rush in.*

Mer. 1.               Where's he hid?
Mer. 3.                     We must
   And will sure find him.
Mer. 2.               Which is his study?

*[Enter Peregrine.]*

Mer. 1.                          What
   Are you, sir?
Per.       I am a merchant that came here
   To look upon this tortoise.
Mer. 3.               How?
Mer. 1.                     St. Mark!
   What beast is this?
Per.               It is a fish.
Mer. 2.                     Come out here!

[3] A basket made of rushes.
[4] Wine cask.
[5] Contrivance.

PER. Nay, you may strike him, sir, and tread upon him;
He'll bear a cart.
MER. 1. What, to run over him?
PER. Yes.
MER. 3. Let's jump upon him.
MER. 2. Can he not go?
PER. He creeps, sir.
MER. 1. [Drawing a weapon.] Let's see him creep.
PER. No, good sir, you will hurt him.
MER. 2. Heart, I'll see him creep, or prick his guts. 70
MER. 3. Come out here!
PER. Pray you, sir.—(Creep a little!)
MER. 1. Forth.
MER. 2. Yet furder.
PER. Good sir!—(Creep!)
MER. 2. We'll see his legs.
*They pull off the shell and discover him.*
MER. 3. Godso, he has garters!
MER. 1. Ay, and gloves!
MER. 2. Is this Your fearful tortoise?
PER. [*Discovering himself.*] Now, Sir Pol, we're even;
For your next project I shall be prepared.
I am sorry for the funeral of your notes, sir.
MER. 1. 'Twere a rare motion [1] to be seen in Fleet Street.
MER. 2. Ay, i' the term.
MER. 1. Or Smithfield, in the fair.
MER. 3. Methinks 'tis but a melancholic sight.
PER. Farewell, most politic tortoise!
[*Exeunt Peregrine and Merchants.*

*Enter Woman.*]

POL. Where's my lady? 80
Knows she of this?
WOM. I know not, sir.
POL. Inquire.—
O, I shall be the fable of all feasts,
The freight of the *gazetti*,[2] ship boys' tale,
And, which is worst, even talk for ordinaries.
WOM. My lady's come most melancholic home,

[1] Puppet show.
[2] The theme of the newspapers.

And says, sir, she will straight to sea for physic.
POL. And I, to shun this place and clime forever,
Creeping with house on back, and think it well
To shrink my poor head in my politic shell. [*Exeunt* ]

ACT V. SCENE v.

[*A room in Volpone's house.*]

*Volpone, Mosca, the first in the habit of a commandadore, the other of a clarissimo.*

[VOLP.] Am I then like him?
MOS. O, sir, you are he;
No man can sever you.
VOLP. Good.
MOS. But what am I?
VOLP. Fore heaven, a brave clarissimo; thou becom'st it!
Pity thou wert not born one.
MOS. [*Aside.*] If I hold
My made one, 'twill be well.
VOLP. I'll go and see
What news first at the court. [*Exit.*]
MOS. Do so. My fox
Is out on his hole, and, ere he shall re-enter,
I'll make him languish in his borrowed case,[3]
Except he come to composition [4] with me.—
Androgyno, Castrone, Nano!

[*Enter Androgyno, Castrone, and Nano.*]

ALL. Here! 10
MOS. Go, recreate yourselves abroad; go, sport.— [*Exeunt.*]
So, now I have the keys, and am possessed.
Since he will needs be dead afore his time,
I'll bury him, or gain by him. I am his heir,
And so will keep me till he share at least.
To cozen him of all were but a cheat
Well placed; no man would construe it a sin.
Let his sport pay for 't. This is called the Fox Trap. [*Exit.*]

[3] Disguise. [4] Agreement, terms.

## Act V. Scene vi.

[*A street.*]

*Corbaccio, Corvino, Volpone.*[1]

[Corb.] They say the court is set.

Corv.                          We must maintain
Our first tale good, for both our reputations.

Corb.  Why, mine's no tale; my son would
there have killed me.

Corv.  That's true; I had forgot.  Mine is,
I am sure.

But for your will, sir—

Corb.               Ay, I'll come upon him
For that hereafter, now his patron's dead.

[*Enter Volpone.*]

Volp.  Signior Corvino!  And Corbaccio!
Sir,

Much joy unto you.

Corv.           Of what?

Volp.                     The sudden good
Dropped down upon you—

Corb.           Where?

Volp.                (And none knows how.)
From old Volpone, sir.

Corb.               Out, arrant knave!  10

Volp.  Let not your too much wealth, sir,
make you furious.

Corb.  Away, thou varlet!

Volp.           Why, sir?

Corb.               Dost thou mock me?

Volp.  You mock the world, sir.  Did you
not change wills?

Corb.  Out, harlot!

Volp.           O! Belike you are the man,
Signior Corvino?  Faith, you carry it
well;

You grow not mad withal.  I love your
spirit.

You are not overleavened with your
fortune.

You should ha' some would swell now,
like a wine fat,[2]

With such an autumn.—Did he gi' you
all, sir?

Corv.  Avoid, you rascal!

Volp.           Troth, your wife has shown  20
Herself a very woman; but you are
well.

You need not care; you have a good
estate

To bear it out, sir, better by this
chance—

Except Corbaccio have a share?

Corb.                     Hence, varlet!

Volp.  You will not be a'known,[3] sir; why,
'tis wise.

Thus do all gamesters, at all games, dissemble;

No man will seem to win.—[*Exeunt Corvino and Corbaccio.*]  Here comes my
vulture,

Heaving his beak up i' the air, and snuff-
ing.

## Act V. Scene vii.

[*The same.*]

*Voltore, Volpone.*

[Volt.] Outstripped thus by a parasite?
A slave?

Would run on errands?  And make legs[4]
for crumbs?

Well, what I'll do—

Volp.           The court stays for your[5]
worship.

I e'en rejoice, sir, at your worship's
happiness,

And that it fell into so learnéd hands,
That understand the fingering.

Volt.                     What do you mean?

Volp.  I mean to be a suitor to your worship,

For the small tenement out of repara-
tions[6]—

That at the end of your long row of
houses,

By the Piscaria.  It was, in Volpone's
time,                                    10

Your predecessor, ere he grew diseased,
A handsome, pretty, customed[7] bawdyhouse

As any was in Venice, none dispraised,
But fell with him; his body and that
house

Decayed together.

Volt.           Come, sir, leave your prating.

Volp.  Why, if your worship give me but
your hand

That I may ha' the refusal, I have done.
'Tis a mere toy to you, sir—candle-
rents.[8]

[1] Enters later.                    [2] Vat.

[3] Acknown, recognized.        [6] Out of repair.
[4] Bows.                       [7] Well patronized.
[5] Original reads *you*.        [8] Pin money.

As your learned worship knows—
VOLT.                    What do I know?
VOLP. Marry, no end of your wealth, sir;
    God decrease it!                    20
VOLT. Mistaking knave! What, mock'st
    thou my misfortune?
VOLP. His blessing on your heart, sir;
    would 'twere more!—    [*Exit Voltore.*]
    Now to my first again, at the next corner.
                                    [*Exit.*]


ACT V. SCENE viii.

[*The Senate.*]

*Corbaccio, Corvino, (Mosca    passant,)*[1]
                            *Volpone.*

[CORB.] See, in our habit![2] See the impu-
    dent varlet!
CORV. That I could shoot mine eyes at
    him, like gunstones![3]

[*Enter Volpone.*]

VOLP. But is this true, sir, of the parasite?
CORB. Again, t' afflict us? Monster!
VOLP.                    In good faith, sir,
    I am heartily grieved a beard of your
        grave length
    Should be so overreached.    I never
        brooked[4]
    That parasite's hair; methought his nose
        should cozen;
    There still was somewhat in his look
        did promise
    The bane of a clarissimo.
CORB.                    Knave—
VOLP. [*To Corvino.*]        Methinks    9
    Yet you, that are so traded i' the world,
    A witty merchant, the fine bird, Corvino,
    That have such moral emblems[5] on
        your name,
    Should not have sung your[6] shame,
        and dropped your cheese
    To let the fox laugh at your emptiness.
CORV. Sirrah, you think the privilege of
    the place
    And your red, saucy cap, that seems to
        me

[1] *I.e.,* passing over the stage.
[2] *I.e.,* of a clarissimo.
[3] Cannon balls.
[4] Could endure.
[5] Allegorical pictures with mottoes.
[6] Original reads *you.*

Nailed to your jolthead[7] with those
    two cecchines,[8]
Can warrant your abuses.    Come you
    hither;
You shall perceive, sir, I dare beat you.
    Approach!
VOLP. No haste, sir; I do know your valure
    well,                            29
    Since you durst publish what you are,
        sir.
CORV.    Tarry;
    I'ld speak with you.
VOLP.                Sir, sir, another time—
CORV. Nay, now.
VOLP.        O God, sir! I were a wise man,
    Would stand the fury of a distracted
        cuckold.            *Mosca walks by hem.*
CORB. What, come again?
VOLP. [*Aside.*]        Upon hem, Mosca;
    save me.
CORB. The    air's    infected    where    he
    breathes.
CORV.        Let's fly him.
            [*Exeunt Corvino and Corbaccio.*]
VOLP. Excellent basilisk! Turn upon the
    vulture.


ACT V. SCENE ix.

[*The same.*]

*Voltore, Mosca, Volpone.*

[VOLT.] Well, flesh fly, it is summer with
    you now;
    Your winter will come on.
MOS.                        Good advocate,
    Pray thee not rail, nor threaten out of
        place thus;
    Thou'lt make a solecism, as madam
        says.
    Get you a biggin[9] more; your brain
        breaks loose.                [*Exit.*]
VOLT. Well, sir.
VOLP.        Would you ha' me beat the inso-
    lent slave?
    Throw dirt upon his first good clothes?
VOLT.                            This same
    Is doubtless some familiar.[10]
VOLP.                    Sir, the court,
    In troth, stays for you.    I am mad, a
        mule
    That never read Justinian should get
        up                            10

[7] Blockhead.                [9] Lawyer's coif.
[8] *I.e.,* gold buttons.    [10] Familiar spirit.

And ride an advocate. Had you no quirk
To avoid gullage, sir, by such a creature?
I hope you do but jest; he has not done 't.
This 's but confederacy to blind the rest.
You are the heir?
VOLT. A strange, officious,
Troublesome knave! Thou dost torment me.
VOLP. I know—
It cannot be, sir, that you should be cozened.
'Tis not within the wit of man to do it;
You are so wise, so prudent; and 'tis fit
That wealth and wisdom still should go together. [*Exeunt.*] 20

ACT V. SCENE X.

[*The same.*]

*Avocatori 4, Notario, Commandadore, Bonario, Celia, Corbaccio, Corvino, Voltore, Volpone.*

[AVOC. 1.] Are all the parties here?
NOT. All but the advocate.
AVOC. 2. And here he comes.

[*Enter Voltore and Volpone.*]

AVOC. [1.] Then bring hem forth to sentence.
VOLT. O, my most honored fathers, let your mercy
Once win upon your justice, to forgive—
I am distracted—
(VOLP. What will he do now?)
VOLT.[1] O,
I know not which t' address myself to first,
Whether your fatherhoods or these innocents—
(CORV. Will he betray himself?)
VOLT. Whom equally
I have abused, out of most covetous ends—
(CORV. The man is mad!
CORB. What's that?
CORV. He is possessed.) 10
VOLT. For which, now strook in conscience, here I prostrate
Myself at your offended feet for pardon.
AVOC. 1, 2. Arise.

[1] Original reads *Volp.*

CEL. O heaven, how just thou art!
VOLP. [*Aside.*] I am caught
I' mine own noose—
CORV. [*To Corbaccio.*] Be constant, sir; naught now
Can help but impudence.
AVOC. 1. Speak forward.
COM. Silence!
VOLT. It is not passion in me, reverend fathers,
But only conscience, conscience, my good sires,
That makes me now tell truth. That parasite,
That knave, hath been the instrument of all.
AVOC. [1.] Where is that knave? Fetch him.
VOLP. I go. [*Exit.*]
CORV. Grave fathers, 20
This man's distracted; he confessed it now;
For, hoping to be old Volpone's heir,
Who now is dead—
AVOC. 3. How?
AVOC. 2. Is Volpone dead?
CORV. Dead since, grave fathers—
BON. O sure vengeance!
AVOC. 1. Stay!
Then he was no deceiver?
VOLT. O, no, none;
The parasite, grave fathers.
CORV. He does speak
Out of mere envy, cause the servant's made
The thing he gaped for. Please your fatherhoods,
This is the truth, though I'll not justify
The other, but he may be somedeal[2] faulty. 30
VOLT. Ay, to your hopes as well as mine, Corvino;
But I'll use modesty.[3] Pleaseth your wisdoms
To view these certain notes, and but confer[4] them;
As I hope favor, they shall speak clear truth.
CORV. The devil has entered him!
BON. Or bides in you.
AVOC. 4. We have done ill, by a public officer
To send for him, if he be heir.

[2] Somewhat. [3] Moderation. [4] Compare.

Avoc. 2.                              For whom?

Avoc. 4. Him that they call the parasite.

Avoc. 3.                              'Tis true;
He is a man of great estate, now left.

Avoc. 4. Go you, and learn his name, and
   say the court                              40
   Entreats his presence here, but to the
   clearing
   Of some few doubts.        [Exit Notario.]

Avoc. 2.                    This same's a labyrinth!

Avoc. 1. Stand you unto your first report?

Corv.                              My state,
   My life, my fame—

(Bon.                              Where is 't?)

Corv.                              Are at the stake.

Avoc. 1. Is yours so too?

Corb.                    The advocate's a knave,
   And has a forkéd tongue—

Avoc. 2.                    Speak to the point.[1]

Corb. So is the parasite too.

Avoc. 1.                    This is confusion.

Volt. I do beseech your fatherhoods,
   read but those—   [Gives them papers.]

Corv. And credit nothing the false spirit
   hath writ.
   It cannot be but he is possessed, grave
   fathers.   [Exeunt.]                              50

## Act V.  Scene xi.

### [A street.]

*Volpone, Nano, Androgyno, Castrone.*[2]

[Volp.] To make a snare for mine own
   neck, and run
My head into it willfully, with laughter,
When I had newly scaped, was free and
   clear!
Out of mere wantonness! O, the dull
   devil
Was in this brain of mine when I de-
   vised it,
And Mosca gave it second; he must now
Help to sear up this vein, or we bleed
   dead.—

[Enter Nano, Androgyno, and Castrone.]

How now! Who let you loose? Whither
   go you now?
What, to buy gingerbread, or to drown
   kittlings? [3]

[1] This speech is printed in parenthesis in the
original.

[2] Last three enter later.

[3] Kittens.

Nan. Sir, Master Mosca called us out of
   doors,                              10
   And bid us all go play, and took the keys.

And. Yes.

Volp.    Did Master Mosca take the keys?
   Why, so!
I am farder in. These are my fine con-
   ceits!
I must be merry, with a mischief to me!
What a vile wretch was I, that could
   not bear
My fortune soberly? I must ha' my
   crotchets
And my conundrums! Well, go you,
   and seek him;
His meaning may be truer than my fear.
Bid him, he straight come to me to the
   court;
Thither will I, and, if 't be possible,  20
Unscrew my advocate, upon new hopes.
When I provoked him, then I lost my-
   self.                              [Exeunt.]

## Act V.  Scene xii.

### [The Senate.]

*Avocatori, etc.*

[Avoc. 1.] These things can ne'er be
   reconciled.   He here
               [Points to the papers.]
Professeth that the gentleman was
   wronged,
And that the gentlewoman was brought
   thither,
Forced by her husband, and there left.

Volt.                              Most true.

Cel. How ready is heaven to those that
   pray!

Avoc. 1.        But that
   Volpone would have ravished her, he
   holds
   Utterly false, knowing his impotence.

Corv. Grave fathers, he is possessed;
   again, I say,
Possessed; nay, if there be possession
And obsession, he has both.

Avoc. 3.        Here comes our officer.  10

[Enter Volpone.]

Volp. The parasite will straight be here,
   grave fathers.

Avoc. 4. You might invent some other
   name, Sir Varlet.

Avoc. 3. Did not the notary meet him?

VOLP.                    Not that I know.

Avoc. 4.  His coming will clear all.

Avoc. 2.                    Yet it is misty.

VOLT. May 't please your fatherhoods—
*Volpone whispers the Advocate.*

VOLP.                    Sir, the parasite
Willed me to tell you that his master
lives;
That you are still the man; your hopes
the same;
And this was only a jest—

VOLT.                    How?

VOLP.                    Sir, to try
If you were firm, and how you stood
affected.

VOLT.  Art sure he lives?

VOLP.                    Do I live, sir?

VOLT.                    O me! 20
I was too violent.

VOLP.            Sir, you may redeem it.
They said you were possessed; fall
down, and seem so.
I'll help to make it good.—(*Voltore falls.*)
God bless the man!—
(Stop your wind hard, and swell.) See,
see, see, see!
He vomits crooked pins!  His eyes are
set,
Like a dead hare's hung in a poulter's
shop!
His mouth's running away!  Do you
see, signior?
Now 'tis in his belly.

(CORV.                    Ay, the devil!)

VOLP. Now in his throat.

(CORV.            Ay, I perceive it plain.)

VOLP. 'Twill out, 'twill out!  Stand clear.
See where it flies,                    30
In shape of a blue toad, with a bat's
wings!
Do not you see it, sir?

CORB.            What?  I think I do.

CORV. 'Tis too manifest.

VOLP.            Look!  He comes t' himself!

VOLT. Where am I?

VOLP.            Take good heart; the worst
is past, sir.
You're dispossessed.

Avoc. 1.            What accident is
this?

Avoc. [2.] Sudden and full of wonder!

Avoc. 3.                    If he were
Possessed, as it appears, all this is
nothing.

CORV. He has been often subject to
these fits.

Avoc. 1. Show him that writing.—Do
you know it, sir?

VOLP. [*Whispering to Voltore.*]  Deny it,
sir; forswear it; know it not.        40

VOLT. Yes, I do know it well; it is my hand
But all that it contains is false.

BON.                    O, practice! [1]

Avoc. 2.  What maze is this!

Avoc. 1.            Is he not guilty then
Whom you there name the parasite?

VOLT.                    Grave fathers,
No more than his good patron, old
Volpone.

Avoc. 4.  Why, he is dead.

VOLT.            O, no, my honored fathers,
He lives—

Avoc. 1.            How! Lives?

VOLT.            Lives.

Avoc. 2.                    This is subtler yet!

Avoc. 3.  You said he was dead.

VOLT.            Never.

Avoc. 3.                    You said so.

CORV.                    I heard so.

Avoc. 4.  Here comes the gentleman; make
him way.

[*Enter Mosca.*]

Avoc. 3.            A stool!

Avoc. 4. [*Aside.*]  A proper man; and,
were Volpone dead,                    50
A fit match for my daughter.

Avoc. 3.                    Give him way.

VOLP. [*Aside to Mosca.*]  Mosca, I was
a'most lost; the advocate
Had betrayed all; but now it is recovered.
All's o' the hinge again.—Say I am
living.

Mos. What busy knave is this!—Most
reverend fathers,
I sooner had attended your grave pleas-
ures,
But that my order for the funeral
Of my dear patron did require me—

(VOLP.                    Mosca!)

Mos. Whom I intend to bury like a
gentleman.

VOLP. [*Aside.*]  Ay, quick,[2] and cozen me
of all.

Avoc. 2.    Still stranger!            60
More intricate!

[1] Deceit.                    [2] Alive.

Avoc. 1.          And come about again!

Avoc. 4. [*Aside.*] It is a match; my daughter is bestowed.

(Mos. Will you gi' me half?

Volp.          First I'll be hanged.

Mos.          I know Your voice is good; cry not so loud.)

Avoc. 1.          Demand The advocate.—Sir, did you not affirm Volpone was alive?

Volp.          Yes, and he is; This gent'man told me so.—(Thou shalt have half.)

Mos. Whose drunkard is· this same? Speak, some that know him; I never saw his face.—(I cannot now Afford it you so cheap.

Volp.          No?)

Avoc. 1.          What say you?          70

Volt. The officer told me.

Volp.          I did, grave fathers, And will maintain he lives, with mine own life, And that this creature [*Points to Mosca.*] told me.—(I was born With all good stars my enemies.)

Mos.          Most grave fathers, If such an insolence as this must pass Upon me, I am silent; 'twas not this For which you sent, I hope.

Avoc. 2.          Take him away.

(Volp. Mosca!)

Avoc. 3.          Let him be whipped.

(Volp.          Wilt thou betray me? Cozen me?)

Avoc. 3.          And taught to bear himself Toward a person of his rank

Avoc. 4.          Away!          80
          [*Commendadore seizes Volpone.*]

Mos. I humbly thank your fatherhoods.

Volp.          Soft, soft!— [*Aside.*] Whipped? And lose all that I have? If I confess, It cannot be much more.

Avoc. 4. [*To Mosca.*] Sir, are you married?

Volp. They'll be allied anon; I must be resolute. The fox shall here uncase.
          *He puts off his disguise.*

(Mos.          Patron!)

Volp.          Nay, now

My ruins shall not come alone; your match I'll hinder sure. My substance shall not glue you, Nor screw you, into a family.

(Mos.          Why, patron!)

Volp. I am Volpone, and this is my knave;          [*Points to Mosca.*] This [*To Voltore.*] his own knave; this [*To Corbaccio.*] avarice's fool;          90 This [*To Corvino.*] a chimera of wittol, fool, and knave; And, reverend fathers, since we all can hope Naught but a sentence, let's not now despair it. You hear me brief.

Corv.          May it please your fatherhoods—

Com.          Silence!

Avoc. 1. The knot is now undone by miracle.

Avoc. 2. Nothing can be more clear.

Avoc. 3.          Or can more prove These innocent.

Avoc. 1.          Give hem their liberty.
          [*Bonario and Celia are released.*]

Bon. Heaven could not long let such gross crimes be hid.

Avoc. 1. If this be held the highway to get riches, May I be poor!

Avoc. 3.          This 's not the gain, but torment.          100

Avoc. 1. These possess wealth, as sick men possess fevers, Which trulier may be said to possess them.

Avoc. 2. Disrobe that parasite.

Corv. ⎫
Mos. ⎭          Most honored fathers—

Avoc. 1. Can you plead aught to stay the course of justice? If you can, speak.

Corv. ⎫
Volt. ⎭          We beg favor.

Cel.          And mercy.

Avoc. 1. You hurt your innocence, suing for the guilty. Stand forth; and first the parasite. You appear T' have been the chiefest minister, if not plotter, In all these lewd impostures, and now, lastly,

Have with your impudence abused [1]
the court,                                        110
And habit of a gentleman of Venice,
Being a fellow of no birth or blood—
For which our sentence is, first, thou be
whipped,
Then live perpetual prisoner in our
galleys.
VOLP. I thank you for him.
MOS.            Bane to thy wolvish nature!
AVOC. 1. Deliver him to the saffi.— [*Mosca
is led away.*] Thou, Volpone,
By blood and rank a gentleman, canst
not fall
Under like censure; but our judgment
on thee
Is that thy substance all be straight
confiscate
To the hospital of the Incurabili;  120
And, since the most was gotten by
imposture,
By feigning lame, gout, palsy, and
such diseases,
Thou art to lie in prison, cramped with
irons,
Till thou beest sick and lame indeed.
Remove him!
        [*Volpone is removed from the bar.*]
VOLP. This is called mortifying of a
fox.
AVOC. 1. Thou, Voltore, to take away the
scandal
Thou hast giv'n all worthy men of thy
profession,
Art banished from their fellowship and
our state.—
Corbaccio!—Bring him near.—We here
possess                                          129
Thy son of all thy state,[2] and confine
thee
To the monastery of San Spirito,
Where, since thou knew'st not how to
live well here,
Thou shalt be learned to die well.
CORB.               Ha! What said he?
COM. You shall know anon, sir.
AVOC. [1.]          Thou, Corvino, shalt
[1] Imposed on.          [2] Estate.

Be straight embarked from thine own
house, and rowed
Round about Venice, through the Grand
Canal,
Wearing a cap, with fair, long ass's ears,
Instead of horns, and so to mount, a
paper
Pinned on thy breast, to the *berlino!*[3]
CORV.                                    Yes,
And have mine eyes beat out with stink-
ing fish,                                        140
Bruised fruit, and rotten eggs—'tis well.
I am glad
I shall not see my shame yet.
AVOC. 1.                    And, to expiate
Thy wrongs done to thy wife, thou art
to send her
Home to her father, with her dowry
trebled.
And these are all your judgments—
(ALL.                        Honored fathers—)
AVOC. 1. Which may not be revoked.
Now you begin,
When crimes are done and past, and
to be punished,
To think what your crimes are. Away
with them!
Let all that see these vices thus re-
warded,
Take heart, and love to study hem.
Mischiefs feed                                   150
Like beasts, till they be fat, and then
they bleed.                        [*Exeunt.*]

*Volpone [comes forward].*

The seasoning of a play is the applause.
Now, though the fox be punished by
the laws,
He yet doth hope there is no suff'ring due
For any fact which he hath done gainst
you.
If there be, censure him; here he doubt-
ful stands.
If not, fare jovially, and clap your
hands.                              [*Exit.*]

THE END.

[3] Pillory.

This comedy was first acted in the year 1605 by the King's Majesty's Servants.
The principal comedians were:

|  |  |  |
|---|---|---|
| *Ric. Burbadge* | *Will. Sly* | *Joh. Lowin* |
| *Hen. Condell* | *Joh. Hemings* | *Alex. Cooke* |

With the allowance of the Master of Revels.

# BEN JONSON

## THE ALCHEMIST

So far as stage popularity and general critical opinion have been concerned, the only play from Jonson's pen to dispute the place of preëminence among his works with *Volpone* is *The Alchemist*. Coleridge considered it Jonson's unqualified masterpiece and said that it possesses one of the three "most perfect plots ever planned." Thayer stated dogmatically, "Unquestionably *The Alchemist* is one of the great triumphs of comic art," and called it "superior to *Volpone* in construction, to *Epicoene* in conception; indeed, there is nothing quite like it." Even Archer's standard complaint was tinctured with grudging but still warm admiration: "*The Alchemist* is a comedy of cozenage carried to its highest power, a carnival of rampant rascality on the one hand and grotesque gullibility on the other," and dependent "upon the free use of impenetrable disguise." Nevertheless, he had to admit, "It eludes criticism by dint of its luxuriant audacity."

This unique comedy was apparently written sometime in the first half of 1610, although for some unknown reason Jonson took considerable care to set its action in the near future, probably late in September of the same year, as Ananias's meticulous datings of the progress of the alchemical experiment he has commissioned would indicate (see III, ii, 131–2; V, v, 102–3). In addition, references to the age of Dame Pliant (II, vi, 31; IV, iv, 29–30) set the year as 1610. Thus the performance itself anticipated the outbreak of the plague which necessitated the closing of the theaters in July, though the situation in the play prophesied a contingency in which a master who had betaken himself to the country to escape the contagion would return home unannounced after it was over, only to find that the house had been taken over by his butler and two cheating confederates. Though the Herford-Simpson commentary states domatically that the performance by the King's Men named on the title page took place at the Globe, F. H. Mares, in his introduction to the Revels edition (London, 1967), finds no support for this conclusion and believes that all the references in the play itself indicate the Blackfriars. The suggestion that Jonson was commissioned by the King's Men to write a play for the private indoor theater at this time was first made by Gerald E. Bentley ("Shakespeare and the Blackfriars Theatre," *Theatre Survey*, no. 1, Cambridge, 1948).

The play was registered in the Stationers' Register on October 3, 1610, but was not actually published till 1612. It was given at Oxford late in 1610 and in court in 1612 or 1613 and in 1623. It was then revived in London in 1631 and 1639, and performed in Dublin about 1636, when James Shirley opened his theater there. Immediately after the Restoration it was given at the Theatre Royal every year from 1660 to 1664, and again in 1674 and 1675. It was then played with considerable regularity during the eighteenth century at both the Drury Lane and the Covent Garden, always with leading actors like Garrick as stars, but was unrevived in the nineteenth century until the Elizabethan Stage Society gave it in London in 1899. Similar revivals by devotees of the older dramatic classics were offered by the Birmingham Repertory Company in 1916, the Phoenix in 1923, the Malvern Festival in 1932, and the Old Vic in 1947. Performances by college groups on both sides of the Atlantic in the twentieth century have been too numerous and widespread to list. The latest professional organization to undertake a revival has been the Stratford Festival of Canada, which has also brought the play to the United States (1969).

As usual, Jonson's plot, although essentially original, had various contributories. Harold H. Child's suggestion of Giordano Bruno's *Il Gandelaio* (*The Candlemaker;* 1582) has not won general acceptance, but from Plautus's *Mostellaria* Jonson may have derived the idea of the quarrel scene at the opening of the play and the idea of the unexpected return of Lovewit to discover the rogues in his house (Herford-Simpson and Douglas Brown, in the New Mermaids edition, London, 1966). He may also have taken certain minor suggestions from Plautus's *Poenulus* and Erasmus's colloquy on alchemy. In addition, the ludicrous episode of Dapper and his credulous efforts to enlist the help of his "aunt," the "Queen of Fairy," in his gambling ventures may well have been based on an actual event of the time in which a wealthy and "phantastical" young man was similarly gulled out of a good sum of money (C. J. Sisson, "A Topical Reference in *The Alchemist*," *J. Q. Adams Memorial Studies*, Washington, 1948). In a more general way attempts have been made to identify the major characters with actual charlatans of the time. As Herford-Simpson points out, these began with Margaret of Newcastle in her *The Description of a New World, Called the Blazing World* (1666 and 1668), and continued to William Gifford in his edition of Jonson in 1816, who "was inclined to accept the 'indenture tripartite' of Subtle, Face, and Doll" as representing the famous astrologer John Dee and his collaboration with Edward Kelley. Kelley claimed he had discovered the philosopher's stone and could also raise spirits. The patronage of both Dee and Kelly was not only by Queen Elizabeth but especially by Albert Laski, the young Polish palatine of Siradez, who may have been transformed into Doll, since in their seances he played the part of an angel.

In a category of source material more general than plot and characters, Jonson obviously owed a huge debt to his researches in all sorts of occult studies, both alchemical and non-alchemical. His extensive reading in the subject of alchemy, still widely believed in during the Renaissance, has been discussed by Herford-Simpson and Edgar H. Duncan ("Jonson's *Alchemist* and the Literature of Alchemy," *PMLA*, 1946), as well as by Mares in his introduction, which contains a useful section on the history and nature of alchemy. Jonson's knowledge of the hypothetical methods in the search for the "philosopher's stone" and the process of turning base metals into gold was derived partly from such literary sources as Chaucer's "Canon's Yeoman's Tale" and the dialogue "Alcumista" in the *Colloquies* of Erasmus, but chiefly from the technical works of Martin Delrio, Lazarus Zetzner, Arnold of Villa Nova, the Arabian Geber or Jabir, Paracelsus, and Robertus Vellensis, passages from which are often worked into the dialogue of the play. Duncan had already written on Jonson's use of alchemy in one of his masques ("The Alchemy in Jonson's *Mercury Vindicated*," *SP*, 1942), in which his satirical attack on this pseudo-science was even more direct than in his play. As for his use of many of the non-alchemical occult studies, Johnstone Parr has dealt with Subtle's parade of a superficial knowledge of metoposcopy, physiognomy, chiromancy, and astrology to convince Abel Drugger that he can help him to a great success as a tobacconist. Parr has pointed out that in his astrological lore, however, Jonson is less accurate than in his use of the other pseudo-sciences. (See Herford-Simpson and Parr, "Non-Alchemical Pseudo-Sciences in *The Alchemist*," *PQ*, 1945, and *Tamburlaine's Malady and Other Essays on Astrology in Elizabethan Drama*, University of Alabama Press, 1953.)

As many critics have pointed out, however (such as Herford-Simpson, Mares), Jonson is really not so much concerned with ridiculing these "sciences" and their pretensions as he is in exposing human greed and credulity, which are his chief general themes. Another favorite object of his continuing attacks was religious dogmatism and hypocrisy, especially as they appeared in the various Puritan and Anabapist sects of the time, such as Tribulation Wholesome and Ananias of *The Alchemist* and Zeal-of-the-Land Busy of *Bartholomew Fair*. (See, especially, Maurice Hussey, "Ananias the Deacon: A Study in Jonson's *The Alchemist*," *English*, 1953.) Jonson's references to Hugh Broughton, Puritan divine and rabbinical scholar, and to his visionary and fanatical writings on the prophets, are part of the religious satire in the play. Similarly, Alan C. Dessen, in *"The Alchemist:* Jonson's 'Estates' Play" (*Renaissance Drama*, 1964), has suggested that such late morality plays as *The Three Ladies of London* and *A Knack to Know a Knave* help one to understand Jonson's "highly realistic exposé of London folly and knavery."

Nevertheless, in spite of Jonson's announced didacticism in his satire and his desire to follow Horace in his program of instructing as well as delighting, the moral conclusions to be drawn from the ending of *The Alchemist* have bewildered many readers and alienated others. For this time, unlike the ending of *Volpone*, there is no poetic justice, or, as Thayer states it, "there is a lack of a clearly-defined moral norm," since the two subordinate rogues are let off pretty easily and Face himself is praised for his cleverness by his master Lovewit, who is himself willing to profit by his servant's swindles. Though Surly has been proposed as this "moral norm," since he immediately sees through the rogues and tries to expose them, he too is governed by rather base motives and tries to profit shadily from the situation which he has unearthed. Thayer even suggests that, in the interpretation of the title, "in Subtle's long speech about alchemy, in his quip about the inferior works, and in his analogy of the choicest fables of the poets, alchemy has been made a metaphor for art." Thayer therefore concludes that Subtle is both "an alchemist of sorts" and also "the symbolic comic alchemist." Consequently he may be supposed to stand, by implication, for "the other artist alchemist, Ben Jonson."

The present text is based on C. H. Hathaway's reprint of the 1616 folio, checked with a copy of the original in the Newberry Library. Occasional reference has also been made to the Noel Douglas replica of the 1612 quarto in the British Museum. The following modern editions have also been consulted: H. C. Hart in the King's Library (London, 1903); R. L. J. Kingsford (Cambridge, 1952); Douglas Brown, the New Mermaids (London, 1966); F. H. Mares, the Revels Plays (London and Harvard, 1967); and S. Musgrove, the Fountainwell Drama Texts (Edinburgh and the University of California Press, 1968).

# THE ALCHEMIST[1]

## BY

## BEN JONSON

[TO THE READER[2]

If thou beest more, thou art an understander, and then I trust thee. If thou art one that tak'st up,[3] and but a pretender, beware at what hands thou receiv'st thy commodity, for thou wert never more fair in the way to be cozened than in this age in poetry, especially in plays—wherein now the concupiscence of jigs and dances[4] so reigneth, as to run away from nature and be afraid of her is the only point of art [10 that tickles the spectators. But how out of purpose and place do I name art, when the professors[5] are grown so obstinate contemners of it, and presumers on their own naturals,[6] as they are deriders of all diligence that way, and, by simple mocking at the terms when they understand not the things, think to get off wittily with their ignorance? Nay, they are esteemed the more learned and sufficient for this by [20 the multitude,[7] through their excellent vice[8] of judgment, for they commend writers as they do fencers or wrastlers, who, if they come in robustuously[9] and put for it with a great deal of violence, are received for the braver fellows, when many times their own rudeness is the cause of their disgrace, and a little touch of their adversary gives all that boisterous force the foil.[10] I deny not but that these men who always seek to [30 do more than enough may sometime happen on something that is good and great, but very seldom. And, when it comes, it doth not recompense the rest of their ill. It sticks out, perhaps, and is more eminent, because all is sordid and vile about it, as lights are more discerned in a thick darkness than a faint shadow. I speak not this out of a hope to do good on any man against his will, for I know, if it were put to the question of [40 theirs and mine. the worse would find more suffrages, because the most favor common errors. But I give thee this warning, that there is a great difference between those that (to gain the opinion of copy[11]) utter[12] all they can, however unfitly, and those that use election and a mean.[13] For it is only the disease of the unskillful to think rude things greater than polished, or scattered more numerous than composed.] 50

## THE PERSONS OF THE PLAY

SUBTLE, *the alchemist*.
FACE, *the housekeeper*.
DOLL COMMON, *their colleague*.
DAPPER, *a [lawyer's] clerk*.

DRUGGER, *a tabacco-man*.[14]
LOVEWIT, *master of the house*.
EPICURE MAMMON, *a knight*.
[PERTINAX] SURLY, *a gamester*.
TRIBULATION [WHOLESOME], *a pastor of Amsterdam*.
ANANIAS, *a deacon there*.
KASTRIL, *the angry boy*.
DA[ME] PLIANT, *his sister, a widow*.
NEIGHBORS.
OFFICERS.
MUTES.

[1] The title continues: "A Comedy, Acted in the Year 1610 by the King's Majesty's Servants." After the title-page appears a dedication to Mary, Lady Wroth.
[2] This address appears in the 1612 edn. only.
[3] *I.e.*, a person who accepts other peoples' judgments on faith.
[4] The Hoe copy reads *dances and antics*.
[5] Practitioners.
[6] Natural endowments; also fools.
[7] The Hoe copy reads *many*.
[8] Surpassing corruption.
[9] Robustuously.
[10] An incomplete fall in wrestling.
[11] Copious supply, abundance of wit.
[12] Publish.
[13] Selection and moderation.   [14] Tobacconist.

THE SCENE: [*A house in the Blackfriars district,*] *London.*

[TIME: *A single day in the autumn of 1610.*]

### THE ARGUMENT [1]

T he sickness [2] hot, a master quit, for fear,
H is house in town and left one servant
    there.
E ase him corrupted, and gave means to
    know
A cheater and his punk, [3] who, now brought
    low,
L eaving their narrow practice, were be-
    come
C oz'ners at large, and, only wanting some
H ouse to set up, with him they here con-
    tract
E ach for a share, and all begin to act.
M uch company they draw and much
    abuse, [4]                   9
I n casting figures, [5] telling fortunes, news,
S elling of flies, [6] flat bawdry, with the
    stone, [7]
T ill it and they and all in fume are gone.

### PROLOGUE

Fortune, that favors fools, these two short
    hours
    We wish away, both for your sakes and
       ours,
Judging spectators; and desire in place,
    To th' author justice, to ourselves but
       grace.
Our scene is London, cause we would make
    known
    No country's mirth is better than our
       own;
No clime breeds better matter for your
    whore,
    Bawd, squire, impostor, many persons
       more,
Whose manners, now called humors, feed
    the stage,
    And which have still [8] been subject for
       the rage                    10
Or spleen of comic writers. Though, this
    pen
    Did never aim to grieve, but better, men,
Howe'er the age he lives in doth endure

The vices that she breeds, above their
    cure.
But, when the wholesome remedies are
    sweet
    And in their working gain and profit
       meet,
He hopes to find no spirit so much diseased
    But will with such fair correctives be
       pleased;
For here he doth not fear who can apply.
    If there be any that will sit so nigh     20
Unto the stream, to look what it doth run,
    They shall find things they'ld think or
       wish were done;
They are so natural follies, but so shown,
    As even the doers may see, and yet not
       own.

### ACT I. SCENE i.

[*A room in Lovewit's house.*] [9]

*Face, Subtle, Doll Common.*

[FACE.] Believe 't, I will.
SUB.            Thy worst. I fart at thee!
DOLL. Ha' you your wits? Why, gentle-
    men! For love—
FACE. Sirrah, I'll strip you—
SUB.            What to do? Lick figs [10]
    Out at my—
FACE.        Rogue, rogue, out of all your
    sleights! [11]
DOLL. Nay, look ye! Sovereign, general,
    are you madmen?
SUB. O, let the wild sheep loose. I'll gum
    your silks
    With good strong water, [12] an [13] you come.
DOLL.            Will you have
    The neighbors hear you? Will you betray
    all?
    Hark! I hear somebody.
FACE.            Sirrah—
SUB.            I shall mar
    All that the tailor has made, if you
    approach.                      10

[9] The scene and the action are continuous
throughout the act.
[10] For this vulgar allusion, *cf.* Rabelais, bk. IV,
ch. 45. But Mares suggests *ficus morbus; i.e.,*
piles.
[11] Cease your tricks!
[12] *I.e.,* some chemical preparation which he
carries in his hand.                [13] If.

[1] Summary of the plot.       [5] Horoscopes.
[2] The plague.                  [6] Familiar spirits.
[3] Mistress.                    [7] Philosophers' stone.
[1] Deceive.                    [8] Always.

FACE. You most notorious whelp, you in-
    solent slave,
  Dare you do this?
SUB.           Yes, faith; yes, faith.
FACE.                           Why, who
Am I, my mungril? [1] Who am I?
SUB.                     I'll tell you,
  Since you know not yourself.
FACE.               Speak lower, rogue.
SUB. Yes. You were once (time's not long
    past) the good,
  Honest, plain, livery-three-pound-thrum [2]
    that kept
  Your master's worship's house here in the
    Friars [3]
  For the vacations [4]—
FACE.           Will you be so loud?
SUB. Since, by my means, translated sub-
    urb-captain. [5]
FACE. By your means, Doctor Dog?
SUB.           Within man's memory,   20
  All this I speak of.
FACE.           Why, I pray you, have I
  Been countenanced by you, or you by
    me?
  Do but collect, [6] sir, where I met you
    first.
SUB. I do not hear well.
FACE.                 Not of this, I think it.
  But I shall put you in mind, sir—at Pie
    Corner,
  Taking your meal of steam in from cooks'
    stalls,
  Where, like the father of hunger, you did
    walk
  Piteously costive, with your pinched
    horn-nose
  And your complexion of the Roman
    wash, [7]
  Stuck full of black and melancholic
    worms,                             30
  Like poulder corns [8] shot at th' artillery
    yard.
SUB. I wish you could advance your voice
    a little.

FACE. When you went pinned up in the
    several rags
  Yo' had raked and picked from dunghills
    before day,
  Your feet in moldy slippers for your
    kibes, [9]
  A felt of rug, [10] and a thin-threaden cloak
  That scarce would cover your no-
    buttocks—
SUB.           So, sir!
FACE. When all your *alchemy* and your
    *algebra*,
  Your *minerals, vegetals,* and *animals,* [11]
  Your conjuring, coz'ning, and your dozen
    of trades                          40
  Could not relieve your corpse with so
    much linen
  Would make you tinder but to see a
    fire, [12]
  I ga' you count'nance, credit for your
    coals,
  Your stills, your glasses, your *materials,*
  Built you a fornace, [13] drew you cus-
    tomers,
  Advanced all your black arts, lent you,
    beside,
  A house to practice in—
SUB.           Your master's house?
FACE. Where you have studied the more
    thriving skill
  Of bawdry since.
SUB.           Yes, in your master's house.
  You and the rats here kept possession.
  Make it not strange. [14] I know yo' were
    one could keep                     51
  The butt'ry-hatch still locked and save
    the chippings, [15]
  Sell the dole-beer [16] to aqua-vitæ-men, [17]
  The which, together with your Christ-
    mas vails [18]
  At post-and-pair, [19] your letting out of
    counters, [20]
  Made you a pretty stock, some twenty
    marks,

[1] Mongrel.
[2] An inferior servant wearing a livery made out
of weaver's warp.
[3] The Blackfriars, a district in London.
[4] *I.e.,* between the terms of court.
[5] Pander, since the stews were generally located in the suburbs.
[6] Recollect.
[7] *I.e.,* swarthy (?).
[8] Powder corns, grains of powder.

[9] Chilblains.        [10] A hat of coarse cloth.
[11] Throughout the play Jonson italicizes terms
associated with alchemy. The present editors
have not glossed these except where intelligi-
bility demands.
[12] *I.e.,* as would make you sufficient tinder to
provide a fire.                    [13] Furnace.
[14] Do not counterfeit ignorance.
[15] Scraps of bread.
[16] Beer intended to be given to the poor.
[17] Liquor-dealers.        [19] A game of cards.
[18] Tips.        [20] *I.e.,* to the gamesters.

And gave you credit to converse with
  cobwebs
Here since your mistress' death hath
  broke up house.
FACE. You might talk softlier, rascal.
SUB.             No, you scarab,
  I'll thunder you in pieces. I will teach
  you                    60
  How to beware to tempt a Fury again
  That carries tempest in his hand and
  voice.
FACE. The place has made you valiant.
SUB.           No, your clothes.
  Thou vermin, have I ta'en thee out of
  dung,
  So poor, so wretched, when no living
  thing
  Would keep thee company but a spider
  or worse?
  Raised thee from brooms, and dust, and
  wat'ring-pots,
  *Sublimed* thee, and *exalted* thee, and
  *fixed* thee
  I' the *third region*, called our *state of
  grace?*
  Wrought thee to *spirit*, to *quintessence*,
  with pains          70
  Would twice have won me the *philos-
  ophers' work?*
  Put thee in words and fashion? Made
  thee fit
  For more than ordinary fellowships?
  Giv'n thee thy oaths, thy quarreling
  dimensions?
  Thy rules to cheat at horse race, cockpit,
  cards,
  Dice, or whatever gallant tincture [1] else?
  Made thee a second in mine own great
  art?
  And have I this for thank? Do you
  rebel?
  Do you fly out i' the *projection?* [2]
  Would you be gone now?
DOLL.    Gentlemen, what mean you?  80
  Will you mar all?
SUB.    Slave, thou hadst had no name—
DOLL. Will you undo yourselves with
  civil war?
SUB. Never been known, past *equi cliba-
  num,*
  The heat of horse dung, under ground,
  in cellars,

[1] Inclination to gallantry.
[2] On the completion of the experiment.

Or an alehouse darker than deaf John's—
  been lost
To all mankind but laundresses and
  tapsters,
Had not I been.
DOLL.    Do you know who hears you,
  sovereign?
FACE. Sirrah—
DOLL.      Nay, general, I thought you
  were civil.
FACE. I shall turn desperate, if you grow
  thus loud.
SUB. And hang thyself, I care not.
FACE.      Hang thee, collier,  90
  And all thy pots and pans! In picture
  I will,
  Since thou hast moved me—
[3] (DOLL.    O, this'll o'erthrow all.)
FACE. Write thee up bawd in Paul's,[4] have
  all thy tricks
  Of coz'ning with a hollow coal, dust,
  scrapings,
  Searching for things lost, with a sieve and
  shears,
  Erecting *figures* in your rows of *houses*,
  And taking in of shadows with a glass,[5]
  Told [6] in red letters, and a face cut for
  thee
  Worse than Gamaliel Ratsey's.[7]
DOLL.      Are you sound?
  Ha' you your senses, masters?
FACE.      I will have  100
  A book, but barely reckoning thy im-
  postures,
  Shall prove a true *philosophers' stone* to
  printers.
SUB. Away, you trencher-rascal!
FACE.      Out, you dog leech!
  The vomit of all prisons—
DOLL.      Will you be
  Your own destructions, gentlemen?
FACE.      Still spewed out
  For lying too heavy o' the basket.[8]
SUB.      Cheater!
FACE. Bawd!

[3] Jonson frequently encloses in parenthesis
passages that are aside or are incidental to the
main action.
[4] St. Paul's Cathedral, a common meeting
place for all London.
[5] A method of divination.
[6] Written.
[7] A highwayman hanged in 1605.
[8] Taking more than his share of the prisoners
food.

SUB.        Cowherd!
FACE.            Conjurer!
SUB.                Cutpurse!
FACE.                    Witch!
DOLL.                        O me!
We are ruined, lost! Ha' you no more regard
To your reputations? Where's your judgment? 'Slight,[1]
Have yet some care of me, o' your republic—                                    110
FACE. Away, this brach![2] I'll bring thee, rogue, within
The statute of sorcery, tricesimo tertio
Of Harry the Eight,[3] ay, and perhaps thy neck
Within a noose, for laund'ring[4] gold and barbing[5] it.
DOLL. You'll bring your head within a coxcomb,[6] will you?

*She catcheth out Face his sword, and breaks Subtle's glass.*

And you, sir, with your *menstrue!*[7]
Gather it up.
'Sdeath, you abominable pair of stinkards,
Leave off your barking, and grow one again,
Or, by the light that shines, I'll cut your throats.
I'll not be made a prey unto the marshal[8]                                    120
For ne'er a snarling dogbolt[9] o' you both.
Ha' you together cozened all this while
And all the world, and shall it now be said
Yo' have made most courteous shift to cozen yourselves?—
[*To Face.*] You will accuse him? You will bring him in
Within the statute? Who shall take your word—
A whoreson, upstart, apocryphal captain,
Whom not a Puritan in Blackfriars will trust

So much as for a feather?—[*To Subtle.*]
And you too
Will give the cause, forsooth? You will insult,[10]                            130
And claim a primacy in the divisions?
You must be chief, as if you only had
The poulder to project[11] with, and the work
Were not begun out of equality?
The venter[12] tripartite? All things in common?
Without priority? 'Sdeath, you perpetual curs,
Fall to your couples again, and cozen kindly
And heartily and lovingly, as you should,
And lose not the beginning of a term,[13]
Or, by this hand, I shall grow factious too                                    140
And take my part and quit you.
FACE.                    'Tis his fault;
He ever murmurs, and objects his pains,
And says the weight of all lies upon him.
SUB. Why, so it does.
DOLL.                How does it? Do not we
Sustain our parts?
SUB.                Yes, but they are not equal.
DOLL. Why, if your part exceed today, I hope
Ours may tomorrow match it.
SUB.                    Ay, they *may.*
DOLL. "May," murmuring mastiff? Ay, and do. Death on me!
Help me to thrattle[14] him.
                    [*Strives to choke him.*]
SUB.            Dorothy! Mistress Dorothy!
Od's precious, I'll do anything. What do you mean?                            150
DOLL. Because o' your *fermentation* and *cibation?*
SUB. Not I, by heaven—
DOLL.    Your *Sol* and *Luna*—[*To Face.*]
Help me!
SUB. Would I were hanged then! I'll conform myself.
DOLL. Will you, sir? Do so then, and quickly. Swear.
SUB. What should I swear?

---

[1] By God's light, a mild oath. *Cf.* also *Od's precious, 'Slid,* etc.        [2] Bitch.
[3] In the thirty-third year of Henry the Eighth, *i.e.,* 1541.
[4] "Sweating," *i.e.,* washing in acid.
[5] Clipping.                [7] Solvent.
[6] Fool's cap.                [8] Prison warden.
[9] Useless arrow; hence, a worthless thing.

[10] Behave insolently.
[11] Apply the elixir to the metal to be transmuted.                [12] Venture.
[13] A term of court, when London was crowded with visitors.                [14] Throttle.

DOLL. To leave your faction, sir,
And labor kindly in the commune [1] work.
SUB. Let me not breathe if I meant aught
beside.
I only used those speeches as a spur
To him.
DOLL. I hope we need no spurs, sir.
Do we?
FACE. 'Slid, prove today who shall shark [2]
best.
SUB. Agreed. 160
DOLL. Yes, and work close and friendly.
SUB. 'Slight, the knot
Shall grow the stronger for this breach,
with me. [*They shake hands.*]
DOLL. Why, so, my good baboons! Shall
we go make
A sort [3] of sober, scurvy, precise neigh-
bors,[4]
That scarce have smiled twice sin' the
king came in,[5]
A feast of laughter at our follies? Rascals,
Would run themselves from breath to see
me ride,[6]
Or you t' have but a hole to thrust your
heads in,
For which you should pay ear-rent.[7] No,
agree.
And may Don Provost [8] ride a-feasting [9]
long 170
In his old velvet jerkin and stained
scarfs,
My noble sovereign and worthy general,
Ere we contribute a new crewel [10] garter
To his most worsted worship.
SUB. Royal Doll!
Spoken like Claridiana,[11] and thyself.
FACE. For which at supper thou shalt sit
in triumph,
And not be styled Doll Common, but
Doll Proper,
Doll Singular. The longest cut at
night
Shall draw thee for his Doll Particular.
[*A bell rings.*]

SUB. Who's that? One rings. To the
window, Doll. Pray heaven 180
The master do not trouble us this
quarter.
FACE. O, fear not him. While there dies
one a week
O' the plague, he's safe from thinking
toward London.
Beside, he's busy at his hopyards now;
I had a letter from him. If he do,
He'll send such word for airing o' the
house
As you shall have sufficient time to quit
it.
Though we break up a fortnight, 'tis no
matter.
SUB. Who is it, Doll?
DOLL. A fine young quodling.[12]
FACE. O,
My lawyer's clerk I lighted on last
night 190
In Holborn at the Dagger. He would
have
(I told you of him) a familiar,[13]
To rifle [14] with at horses and win cups.
DOLL. O, let him in.
SUB. Stay. Who shall do 't?
FACE. Get you
Your robes on; I will meet him, as [15]
going out.
DOLL. And what shall I do?
FACE. Not be seen; away!—[*Exit Doll*]
Seem you very reserved.
SUB. Enough. [*Exit.*]
FACE. [*Shouting to Subtle.*] God be
w' you, sir.
I pray you let him know that I was here.
His name is Dapper.—[*Pretends to leave.*]
I would gladly have stayed, but—

ACT I. SCENE ii.

*Dapper, Face, Subtle.*

[DAP.] Captain, I am here.
FACE. Who's that?—He's come, I think,
doctor.—
Good faith, sir, I was going away.
DAP. In truth,
I am very sorry, captain.
FACE. But I thought
Sure I should meet you.

[1] Common.
[2] Swindle, cozen.
[3] Crowd.
[4] *I.e.*, the Puritans.
[5] In 1603.
[6] *I.e.*, carted as a bawd.
[7] *I.e.*, lose your ears in the pillory.
[8] *I.e.* the hangman, part of whose perquisites
was the clothes of the criminal.
[9] Thriving.
[10] A worsted yarn, with a pun on *cruel*.
[11] Heroine of the romance, *The Mirror of
Knighthood.*

[12] Codling, a green apple; here an immature
young man. [14] Raffle, hold a lottery
[13] Familiar spirit. [15] As if.

DAP.                    Ay, I am very glad.
I had a scurvy writ or two to make,
And I had lent my watch last night to
one
That dines today at the shrief's,[1] and
so was robbed
Of my pass-time.

[*Enter Subtle in his robes.*]

                    Is this the cunning [2] man?
FACE. This is his worship.
DAP.                    Is he a doctor?
FACE.                    Yes.
DAP. And ha' you broke [3] with him, cap-
tain?
FACE.          Ay.
DAP.                    And how?  10
FACE. Faith, he does make the matter,
sir, so dainty [4]
I know not what to say.
DAP.               Not so, good captain.
FACE. Would I were fairly rid on 't, be-
lieve me.
DAP. Nay, now you grieve me, sir. Why
should you wish so?
I dare assure you, I'll not be ungrate-
ful.
FACE. I cannot think you will, sir. But
the law
Is such a thing—and then he says Read's
matter
Falling so lately [5]—
DAP.               Read? He was an ass,
And dealt, sir, with a fool.
FACE.               It was a clerk, sir.
DAP. A clerk?
FACE.     Nay, hear me, sir. You know the
law     20
Better, I think—
DAP.          I should, sir, and the danger.
You know I showed the statute to
you?
FACE.               You did so.
DAP. And will I tell then? By this hand
of flesh,
Would it might never write good court-
hand [6] more,

If I discover.[7] What do you think of me,
That I am a chiaus? [8]
FACE.          What's that?
DAP.               The Turk was here.
As one would say, do you think I am a
Turk?
FACE. I'll tell the doctor so.
DAP.               Do, good sweet captain.
FACE. Come, noble doctor, pray thee, let's
prevail;
This is the gentleman, and he is no
chiaus.     30
SUB. Captain, I have returned you all my
answer.
I would do much, sir, for your love—
but this
I neither may, nor can.
FACE.               Tut, do not say so.
You deal now with a noble fellow, doctor,
One that will thank you richly; and
h' is no chiaus.
Let that, sir, move you.
SUB.               Pray you, forbear.
FACE.                    He has
Four angels [9] here.
SUB.          You do me wrong, good sir.
FACE. Doctor, wherein? To tempt you
with these spirits?
SUB. To tempt my art and love, sir, to my
peril.
Fore [10] heav'n, I scarce can think you
are my friend,     40
That so would draw me to apparent
danger.
FACE. I draw you? A horse draw you,
and a halter,
You and your flies together—
DAP.               Nay, good captain.
FACE. That know no difference of men.
SUB.               Good words, sir.
FACE. Good deeds, sir, Doctor Dogs'-
meat. 'Slight, I bring you
No cheating Clim o' the Cloughs or
Claribels,[11]
That look as big as five-and-fifty and
flush,[12]
And spit out secrets like hot custard—
DAP.               Captain!

[1] Sheriff's.
[2] Learned, especially in magic.
[3] Broached the question.
[4] *I.e.*, he has so many scruples.
[5] Dr. Simon Read had been recently convicted
as a magician.
[6] Handwriting of the law courts.
[7] Reveal.
[8] Chouse, a Turkish messenger, like the one
who had recently cheated some London merchants.
[9] Gold coins.          [10] Before.
[11] Heroes of romantic tales.
[12] The highest hand at primero, a card game.

FACE. Nor any melancholic underscribe,
Shall tell the vicar; but a special gentle,[1]
That is the heir to forty marks a year,  51
Consorts with the small poets of the time,
Is the sole hope of his old grandmother;
That knows the law and writes you six fair hands,
Is a fine clerk and has his ciph'ring perfect,
Will take his oath o' the Greek Xenophon,
If need be, in his pocket, and can court
His mistress out of Ovid.

DAP.                          Nay, dear captain—
FACE. Did you not tell me so?
DAP.                          Yes; but I'ld ha' you
Use Master Doctor with some more respect.  60
FACE. Hang him, proud stag, with his broad velvet head!
But for your sake I'ld choke ere I would change
An article of breath with such a puckfist! [2]
Come, let's be gone.
SUB.        Pray you, le' me speak with you.
DAP. His worship calls you, captain.
FACE.                          I am sorry
I e'er embarked myself in such a business.
DAP. Nay, good sir; he did call you.
FACE.                          Will he take then?
SUB. First, hear me—
FACE.        Not a syllable, 'less you take.
SUB. Pray ye, sir—
FACE.        Upon no terms but an *assumpsit*.[3]
SUB. Your humor must be law.
                          *He takes the money.*
FACE.                Why now, sir, talk.  [70
Now I dare hear you with mine honor. Speak.
So may this gentleman too.
SUB. [*Pretending to whisper to Face.*]  Why, sir—
FACE.        No whisp'ring.
SUB. Fore heav'n, you do not apprehend the loss
You do yourself in this.
FACE.                Wherein? For what?

<hr>

[1] Gentleman.
[2] Puffball, a worthless person.
[3] Legal term for a contract involving an initial payment.

SUB. Marry, to be so importunate for one
That, when he has it, will undo you all;
He'll win up all the money i' the town.
FACE. How!
SUB.        Yes, and blow up gamester after gamester,
As they do crackers in a puppet play.
If I do give him a familiar,        80
Give you him all you play for; never set [4] him,
For he will have it.
FACE.                Y' are mistaken, doctor.
Why, he does ask one but for cups and horses,
A rifling fly—none o' your great familiars.
DAP. Yes, captain, I would have it for all games.
SUB. I told you so.
FACE. [*Drawing Dapper aside.*]        'Slight, that's a new business!
I understood you, a tame bird,[5] to fly
Twice in a term or so, on Friday nights
When you had left the office, for a nag
Of forty or fifty shillings.
DAP.                Ay, 'tis true, sir;  90
But I do think now I shall leave the law,
And therefore—
FACE.        Why, this changes quite the case.
Do you think that I dare move him?
DAP.                If you please, sir;
All's one to him, I see.
FACE.                What? For that money?
I cannot with my conscience, nor should you
Make the request, methinks.
DAP.                No, sir, I mean
To add consideration.
FACE.                Why, then, sir,
I'll try.—[*To Subtle.*]  Say that it were for all games, doctor?
SUB. I say then not a mouth shall eat for[6] him
At any ordinary[7] but o' the score;[8]  100
That is a gaming mouth, conceive me.
FACE.                          Indeed!
SUB. He'll draw you all the treasure of the realm,
If it be set him.
FACE.                Speak you this from art?
SUB. Ay, sir, and reason too, the ground of art.

<hr>

[4] Stake against.        [5] A familiar spirit.
[6] On account of.    [7] Inn.    [8] On credit.

H' is o' the only best complexion
The Queen of Fairy loves.
FACE.          What! Is he?
SUB.               Peace!
He'll overhear you. Sir, should she but
    see him—
FACE. What?
SUB.        Do not you tell him.
FACE.          Will he win at cards too?
SUB. The spirits of dead Holland, living
    Isaac,[1]
You'ld swear, were in him—such a
    vigorous luck               110
As cannot be resisted. 'Slight, he'll put
Six o' your gallants to a cloak,[2] indeed.
FACE. A strange success, that some man
    shall be born to!
SUB.        He hears you, man—
DAP.        Sir, I'll not be ingrateful.
FACE. Faith, I have a confidence in his
    good nature.
You hear, he says he will not be ingrate-
    ful.
SUB. Why, as you please; my venture
    follows yours.
FACE. Troth, do it, doctor; think him
    trusty, and make him.
He may make us both happy in an
    hour—
Win some five thousand pound, and send
    us two on 't.             120
DAP. Believe it, and I will, sir.
FACE.          And you shall, sir.
You have heard all?
                *Face takes him aside.*
DAP.     No, what was 't? Nothing, I, sir.
FACE. Nothing?
DAP.        A little, sir.
FACE.          Well, a rare star
Reigned at your birth.
DAP.        At mine, sir? No!
FACE.          The doctor
Swears that you are—
SUB.     Nay, captain, yo'll tell all now.
FACE. Allied to the Queen of Fairy.
DAP.         Who? That I am?
Believe it, no such matter.
FACE.          Yes, and that
Yo' were born with a caul o' your head.[3]

DAP.          Who says so?
FACE.             Come,
You know it well enough, though you
    dissemble it.
DAP. I' fac,[4] I do not; you are mistaken.
FACE.            How! 130
Swear by your fac, and in a thing so
    known
Unto the doctor? How shall we, sir,
    trust you
I' the other matter? Can we ever think,
When you have won five or six thousand
    pound,
You'll send us shares in 't, by this rate?
DAP.          By Jove, sir,
I'll win ten thousand pound, and send
    you half.
I' fac 's no oath.
SUB.        No, no, he did but jest.
FACE. Go to. Go thank the doctor. He's
    your friend,
To take it so.
DAP.       I thank his worship.
FACE.            So?
Another angel.
DAP.       Must I?
FACE.         Must you? 'Slight, 140
What else is thanks? Will you be triv-
    ial?—[*Dapper gives Subtle money.*]
    Doctor,
When must he come for his familiar?
DAP. Shall I not ha' it with me?
SUB.          O, good sir,
There must a world of ceremonies pass;
You must be bathed and fumigated
    first;
Besides, the Queen of Fairy does not
    rise
Till it be noon.
FACE.      Not if she danced tonight.[5]
SUB. And she must bless it.
FACE.         Did you never see
Her royal grace yet?
DAP.      Whom?
FACE.         Your aunt of Fairy?
SUB. Not since she kissed him in the cra-
    dle, captain;            150
I can resolve[6] you that.
FACE.         Well, see her grace,
Whate'er it cost you, for a thing that I
    know.
It will be somewhat hard to compass
    but,

---

[1] Dutch alchemists.
[2] *I.e.*, strip them to a single cloak for all.
[3] An old superstition connected with good
luck.
[4] In faith.        [5] Last night.        [6] Tell.

However, see her.  You are made, be-
lieve it,
If you can see her.  Her grace is a lone
woman,
And very rich; and, if she take a fancy,
She will do strange things.  See her, at
any hand.[1]
'Slid, she may hap to leave you all she
has!
It is the doctor's fear.
DAP.          How will 't be done, then?
FACE.  Let me alone; take you no thought.
Do you                                            160
But say to me, "Captain, I'll see her
grace."
DAP.  Captain, I'll see her grace.
FACE.          Enough.     *One knocks without.*
SUB.                              Who's there?
Anon.—(Conduct him forth by the back
way.)
Sir, against one a-clock prepare your-
self;
Till when, you must be fasting; only
take
Three drops of vinegar in at your nose,
Two at your mouth, and one at either
ear;
Then bath [2] your fingers' ends and wash
your eyes,
To sharpen your five senses, and cry
"hum"
Thrice, and then "buzz" as often; and
then come.               *[Exit.]*   170
FACE.  Can you remember this?
DAP.                              I warrant you.
FACE.  Well then, away.  'Tis but your be-
stowing
Some twenty nobles 'mong her grace's
servants,
And put on a clean shirt.  You do not
know
What grace her grace may do you in
clean linen.               *[Exeunt.]*

### ACT I.  SCENE iii.

*Subtle, Drugger, Face.*[3]

[SUB. (*Within.*)]  Come in!  (Good wives,
I pray you forbear me now;
Troth, I can do you no good till after-
noon.)

[Enter Subtle and Drugger.]

SUB.  What is your name, say you?  Abel
Drugger?
DRUG.          Yes, sir.
SUB.  A seller of tobacco?
DRUG.                              Yes, sir.
SUB.                              Umh!
Free of the Grocers? [4]
DRUG.               Ay, and [5] 't please you.
SUB.                              Well.
Your business, Abel?
DRUG.  This, and 't please your worship:
I am a young beginner, and am building
Of a new shop, and 't like your worship,
just
At corner of a street.     (Here's the plot [6]
on 't.)
And I would know by art, sir, of your
worship,                                            10
Which way I should make my door, by
necromancy,
And where my shelves, and which should
be for boxes,
And which for pots.  I would be glad to
thrive, sir.
And I was wished [7] to your worship by
a gentleman,
One Captain Face, that says you know
men's planets,
And their good angels, and their bad.
SUB.                              I do,
If I do see hem.[8]—

[Enter Face.]

FACE.               What!  My honest Abel?
Thou art well met here.
DRUG.          Troth, sir, I was speaking,
Just as your worship came here, of your
worship.
I pray you speak for me to Master
Doctor.                                            20
FACE.  He shall do anything.  Doctor, do
you hear?
This is my friend, Abel, an honest
fellow;
He lets me have good tobacco, and he
does not
Sophisticate [9] it with sack lees or oil,
Nor washes it in muscadel and grains,[10]

---

[1] Rate.                    [3] All actually enter later.
[2] Bathe.

[4] *I.e.*, a member of the Grocers' Guild.
[5] If it.                          [7] Recommended.
[6] Plat, diagram.          [8] Them.
[9] Adulterate.
[10] Grains of paradise, a spice.

Nor buries it in gravel under ground,
Wrapped up in greasy leather or pissed
    clouts,
But keeps it in fine lily pots,[1] that,
    opened,
Smell like conserve of roses, or French
    beans.                                    29
He has his maple block,[2] his silver tongs,
Winchester pipes, and fire of juniper [3]—
A neat, spruce, honest fellow, and no
    goldsmith.[4]
SUB. H' is a fortunate fellow; that I am
    sure on.
FACE. Already, sir, ha' you found it?
    Lo thee,[5] Abel!
SUB. And in right way toward riches.
FACE.                    Sir!
SUB.                    This summer
He will be of the clothing [6] of his com-
    pany,
And next spring called to the scarlet;[7]
    spend what he can—
FACE. What, and so little beard?
SUB.                    Sir, you must think
He may have a receipt to make hair
    come.
But he'll be wise, preserve his youth,
    and fine [8] for 't;                      40
His fortune looks for him another way.
FACE. 'Slid, doctor, how canst thou know
    this so soon?
I am amused [9] at that.
SUB.                    By a rule, captain,
In metoposcopy,[10] which I do work by—
A certain star i' the forehead, which
    you see not.
Your chestnut- or your olive-colored
    face
Does never fail, and your long ear doth
    promise.
I knew 't by certain spots too in his
    teeth
And on the nail of his mercurial finger.
FACE. Which finger's that?
SUB.                    His little finger. Look.  50
Yo' were born upon a Wednesday?
DRUG.                    Yes, indeed, sir.

SUB. The thumb, in chiromanty [11] we give
    Venus,
The forefinger to Jove, the midst to
    Saturn,
The ring to Sol, the least to Mercury,
Who was the lord, sir, of his horoscope,
His house of life being Libra, which fore-
    showed
He should be a merchant, and should
    trade with balance.
FACE. Why, this is strange! Is 't not,
    honest Nab?
SUB. There is a ship now coming from
    Ormus,
That shall yield him such a commodity 60
Of drugs—[Points to the plan.]    This
    is the west, and this the south?
DRUG. Yes, sir.
SUB.                    And those are your two sides?
DRUG.                    Ay, sir.
SUB. Make me your door then, south;
    your broad side, west;
And on the east side of your shop, aloft,
Write Mathlai, Tarmiel, and Baraborat;
Upon the north part, Rael, Velel, Thiel.
They are the names of those Mercurial
    spirits
That do fright flies from boxes.
DRUG.                    Yes, sir.
SUB.                    And
Beneath your threshold bury me a load-
    stone
To draw in gallants that wear spurs;
    the rest,                                 70
They'll seem [12] to follow.
FACE.                    That's a secret, Nab!
SUB. And on your stall a puppet, with a
    vise [13]
And a court-fucus,[14] to call city dames;
You shall deal much with minerals.
DRUG.                    Sir, I have,
At home, already—
SUB.                    Ay, I know you have ars'nic,
Vitriol, sal tartar, argaile,[15] alkali,
Cinoper.[16] I know all.—This fellow, cap-
    tain,
Will come, in time, to be a great distiller,
And give a say [17]—I will not say directly,
But very fair—at the philosophers'
    stone.                                    80

---

[1] Ornamental jars.
[2] For shredding tobacco.
[3] At which customers could light their pipes.
[4] Usurer.                    [7] Become alderman.
[5] Behold thyself.           [8] Pay a fine.
[6] Wear the livery.          [9] Amazed.
[10] Divination by observing the forehead.
Original reads *metaposcopy*.

[11] Chiromancy.              [13] Screw, clamp.
[12] Be seen.                 [14] A cosmetic used at court.
[15] Argol, tartar deposited by wine.
[16] Cinnabar.               [17] An assay, attempt.

FACE. Why, how now, Abel! Is this true?

DRUG. [*Drawing Face aside.*]     Good captain,

What must I give?

FACE.     Nay, I'll not counsel thee.

Thou hear'st what wealth (he says, spend what thou canst)

Thou 'rt like to come to.

DRUG.     I would gi' him a crown.

FACE. A crown? And toward such a fortune? Heart,

Thou shalt rather gi' him thy shop. No gold about thee?

DRUG. Yes, I have a portague [1] I ha' kept this half year.

FACE. Out on thee, Nab! 'Slight, there was such an offer.

Shalt keep 't no longer. I'll gi' it him for thee?—Doctor,

Nab prays your worship to drink this, and swears                    90

He will appear more grateful, as your skill

Does raise him in the world.

DRUG.     I would entreat

Another favor of his worship.

FACE.     What is 't, Nab?

DRUG. But to look over, sir, my almanac,

And cross out my ill-days, that I may neither

Bargain, nor trust upon them.

FACE.     That he shall, Nab.

Leave it; it shall be done gainst afternoon.

SUB. And a direction for his shelves.

FACE.     Now, Nab,

Art thou well pleased, Nab?

DRUG.     Thank, sir, both your worships.

FACE.     Away! [*Exit Drugger.*]

Why, now, you smoky persecutor of nature!                    100

Now do you see that something's to be done

Beside your beech-coal and your corsive [2] waters,

Your crosslets, [3] crucibles, and cucurbites? [4]

You must have stuff brought home to you, to work on?

And yet you think I am at no expense

In searching out these veins, then following hem,

[1] A gold coin.
[2] Corrosive.
[3] Vessels.
[4] Retorts.

Then trying hem out. Fore God, my intelligence

Costs me more money than my share oft comes to

In these rare works.

SUB.     You are pleasant, sir.—How now?

## ACT I. SCENE iv.

*Face, Doll, Subtle.*

[SUB.] What says my dainty Dolkin?

DOLL.     Yonder fishwife

Will not away. And there's your giantess,

The bawd of Lambeth.

SUB.     Heart, I cannot speak with hem.

DOLL. Not afore night, I have told hem in a voice

Thorough the trunk, [5] like one of your familiars.

But I have spied Sir Epicure Mammon.

SUB.     Where?

DOLL. Coming along, at far end of the lane,

Slow of his feet, but earnest of his tongue

To one that's with him.

SUB.     Face, go you and shift. [6]—

[*Exit Face.*]

Doll, you must presently [7] make ready too.                    10

DOLL. Why, what's the matter?

SUB.     O, I did look for him

With the sun's rising. Marvel, he could sleep!

This is the day I am to perfect for him

The *magisterium*, our *great work*, the *stone*,

And yield it, made, into his hands—of which

He has this month talked as he were possessed. [8]

And now he's dealing pieces on 't away.

Methinks I see him ent'ring ordinaries,

Dispensing for the pox, and plaguy houses, [9]

Reaching [10] his dose, walking Moorfields for lepers,                    20

And off'ring citizens' wives pomander bracelets [11]

[5] Through the speaking tube.
[6] Change your clothes.     [7] At once.
[8] *I.e.*, as if he owned it.
[9] Houses infested with the plague.
[10] Offering.
[11] As a protection against disease.

As his preservative, made of the *elixir;*
Searching the spital [1] to make old bawds
    young,
And the highways for beggars to make
    rich.
I see no end of his labors.  He will make
Nature ashamed of her long sleep,
    when art,
Who's but a stepdame, shall do more
    than she
In her best love to mankind ever could.
If his dream last, he'll turn the age to
    gold.                              [*Exeunt.*]

### Act II. Scene i.

*[The same.]* [2]

*Mammon, Surly.*

[Mam.]  Come on, sir.  Now you set your
    foot on shore
In *Novo Orbe;* [3] here's the rich Peru,
And there within, sir, are the golden
    mines,
Great Salomon's [4] Ophir!    He was
    sailing to 't
Three years, but we have reached it in
    ten months.
This is the day wherein to all my
    friends
I will pronounce the happy word, "Be
    rich;
This day you shall be *spectatissimi.*" [5]
You shall no more deal with the hollow [6]
    die
Or the frail card; no more be at charge
    of keeping                              10
The livery-punk [7] for the young heir
    that must
Seal at all hours in his shirt; no more,
If he deny, ha' him beaten to 't, as he is
That brings him the commodity.  No
    more
Shall thirst of satin, or the covetous
    hunger
Of velvet entrails [8] for [9] a rude-spun cloak,

To be displayed at Madam Augusta's, [16]
    make
The sons of sword and hazard fall
    before
The golden calf, and on their knees,
    whole nights,
Commit idolatry with wine and trump-
    ets,                                   20
Or go a-feasting after drum and en-
    sign.
No more of this.  You shall start up
    young viceroys,
And have your punks and punkettees, [11]
    my Surly.
And unto thee I speak it first, "Be
    rich."
Where is my Subtle there?  Within, ho!
[Face.]  (*Within.*)                    Sir,
He'll come to you by-and-by.
Mam.                    That's his firedrake, [12]
His lungs, [13] his Zephyrus, he that puffs
    his coals
Till he firk [14] nature up in her own cen-
    ter.
You are not faithful, [15] sir.  This night
    I'll change
All that is metal in my [16] house to
    gold,                                 30
And early in the morning will I send
To all the plumbers and the pewter-
    ers,
And buy their tin and lead up, and to
    Lothbury
For all the copper.
Sur.                    What, and turn that too?
Mam.  Yes, and I'll purchase Devonshire
    and Cornwall,
And make them perfect Indies!    You
    admire [17] now?
Sur.  No, faith.
Mam.              But, when you see th' effects
    of the great med'cine,
Of which one part projected on a hun
    dred
Of Mercury, or Venus, or the Moon    3
Shall turn it to as many of the Sun [18]—
Nay, to a thousand, so *ad infinitum*—
You will believe me.

[1] Hospital.
[2] The setting and action are continuous
throughout the act.
[3] The New World.        [5] Highly esteemed.
[4] Solomon's.            [6] *I.e.,* loaded.
[7] A prostitute used as an accomplice in ef-
fecting the commodity swindle in which a young
heir was tricked to lend money on the security
of valueless goods.
[8] Lining.                [9] In exchange for.

[10] Probably a brothel.       [13] Bellows.
[11] Young prostitutes.        [14] Stir.
[12] Dragon.                   [15] Believing.
[16] From 1612 edn.  Original reads *thy.*
[17] Wonder.
[18] Transmute quicksilver, copper, or silver
into gold.

Sur.                    Yes, when I see 't, I
    will.
But, if my eyes do cozen me so, and I
Giving hem no occasion, sure I'll have
A whore shall piss hem out next day.
Mam.                            Ha! Why?
    Do you think I fable with you?   I
        assure you,
    He that has once the *Flower of the
        Sun,*
    The perfect *ruby,* which we call *elixir,*
    Not only can do that, but by its vir-
        tue
    Can confer honor, love, respect, long
        life;                                     50
    Give safety, valure, [1] yea, and victory
    To whom he will.  In eight-and-twenty
        days
    I'll make an old man of fourscore a
        child.
Sur.  No doubt; he's that already.
Mam.                        Nay, I mean,
    Restore his years, renew him, like an
        eagle,
    To the fifth age,[2] make him get sons and
        daughters,
    Young giants (as our philosophers have
        done,
    The ancient patriarchs afore the flood),
    But, taking once a week on a knife's
        point
    The quantity of a grain of mustard of
        it,                                       60
    Become stout Marses and beget young
        Cupids.
Sur.  The decayed vestals of Pickt-hatch [3]
    would thank you,
    That keep the fire alive there.
Mam.                        'Tis the secret
    Of nature naturized gainst all infec-
        tions,
    Cures all diseases coming of all causes,
    A month's grief in a day, a year's in
        twelve,
    And, of what age soever, in a month,
    Past all the doses of your drugging
        doctors.
    I'll undertake, withal, to fright the
        plague
    Out o' the kingdom in three months.
Sur.                        And I'll   70

Be bound, the players shall sing your
    praises then,
Without their poets.[4]
Mam.                    Sir, I'll do 't.  Meantime,
    I'll give away so much unto my man,
    Shall serve th' whole city with preserva-
        tive
    Weekly, each house his dose, and at the
        rate—
Sur.  As he that built the Waterwork
    does with water?
Mam.  You are incredulous.
Sur.                    Faith, I have a humor;
    I would not willingly be gulled.  Your
        *stone*
    Cannot transmute me.
Mam.                    Pertinax Surly,
    Will you believe antiquity?  Records?   80
    I'll show you a book where Moses and
        his sister
    And Salomon have written of the art;
    Ay, and a treatise penned by Adam—
Sur.                                     How!
Mam.  O' the *philosophers' stone,* and in
    High Dutch.
Sur.  Did Adam write, sir, in High Dutch?
Mam.                                He did,
    Which proves it was the primitive
        tongue.
Sur.            What paper?
Mam.  On cedar board.
Sur.                O, that, indeed, they say,
    Will last gainst worms.
Mam.                    'Tis like your Irish wood
    Gainst cobwebs.  I have a piece of
        Jason's fleece too,
    Which was no other than a book of
        alchemy,                                  90
    Writ in large sheepskin, a good fat ram-
        vellam.[5]
    Such was Pythagoras' thigh,[6] Pandora's
        tub,
    And all that fable of Medea's charms.
    The manner of our work: the bulls,
        our fornace,
    Still breathing fire; our *argent-vive,* [7] the
        dragon;
    The dragon's teeth, *mercury sublimate,*
    That keeps the whiteness, hardness,
        and the biting;

---

[1] Valor.
[2] *I.e.,* of the seven ages of man.
[3] A low district in London.

[4] Plays were not given when the plague was
raging.                            [7] Quicksilver.
[5] Vellum made of ram skin.
[6] *Cf.* note on *Volpone,* I, ii, 27.

And they are gathered into Jason's helm,

Th' *alembic*, and then sowed in Mars his field,

And thence sublimed so often, till they are fixed.                                        100

Both this, th' Hesperian garden, Cadmus' story,

Jove's shower, the boon of Midas, Argus' eyes,

Boccace his Demogorgon, thousands more,

All abstract riddles of our *stone*.—How now?

### Act II. Scene ii.

*Mammon, Face, Surly.*

[Mam.] Do we succeed? Is our day come? And holds it?

Face. The evening will set red upon you, sir;

You have color for it, crimson; the red *ferment*

Has done his office; three hours hence prepare you

To see projection.

Mam.                    Pertinax, my Surly,

Again I say to thee, aloud, "Be rich."

This day thou shalt have ingots, and tomorrow

Give lords th' affront.—Is it, my Zephyrus, right?

Blushes the bolt's-head? [1]

Face.          Like a wench with child, sir,

That were but now discovered to her master.                                              10

Mam. Excellent witty Lungs!—My only care is

Where to get stuff enough now to project on;

This town will not half serve me.

Face.                    No, sir? Buy

The covering off o' churches.

Mam.                    That's true.

Face.                    Yes.

Let hem stand bare, as do their auditory, [2]

Or cap hem new with shingles.

Mam.                    No, good thatch;

Thatch will lie light upo' the rafters, Lungs.

Lungs, I will manumit thee from the fornace;

I will restore thee thy complexion, Puff,

Lost in the embers, and repair this brain,                                                20

Hurt wi' the fume o' the metals.

Face.                    I have blown, sir,

Hard for your worship, thrown by many a coal,

When 'twas not beech, weighed those I put in, just, [3]

To keep your heat still even. These bleared eyes

Have waked to read your several colors, sir,

Of the *pale citron*, the *green lion*, the *crow*,

The *peacock's tail*, the *plumed swan*.

Mam.                    And lastly

Thou hast descried the *flower*, the *sanguis agni?* [4]

Face. Yes, sir.

Mam.                    Where's master?

Face.                    At 's prayers, sir, he;

Good man, he's doing his devotions          30

For the success.

Mam.                    Lungs, I will set a period

To all thy labors; thou shalt be the master

Of my seraglia. [5]

Face.                    Good, sir.

Mam.                    But do you hear?

I'll geld you, Lungs.

Face.                    Yes, sir.

Mam.                    For I do mean

To have a list of wives and concubines

Equal with Salomon, who had the *stone*

Alike with me; and I will make me a back

With the *elixir*, that shall be as tough

As Hercules, to encounter fifty a night.—

Thou'rt sure thou saw'st it *blood?*

Face.          Both *blood and spirit*, sir.    40

Mam. I will have all my beds blown up, not stuffed;

Down is too hard. And then, mine oval room

Filled with such pictures as Tiberius took

From Elephantis, and dull Aretine

But coldly imitated. Then, my glasses

---

[1] Flask.                    [2] Auditors, congregation.

[3] Exactly.                    [5] Seraglio.
[4] Blood of the Lamb.

Cut in more subtle angles to disperse
And multiply the figures, as I walk
Naked between my *succubæ*.[1] My mists
I'll have of perfume, vapored 'bout the
room,
To lose ourselves in, and my baths like
pits            50
To fall into, from whence we will come
forth,
And roll us dry in gossamer and roses.—
Is it arrived at *ruby?*—Where I spy
A wealthy citizen or rich lawyer
Have a sublimed pure wife, unto that
fellow
I'll send a thousand pound to be my
cuckold.

FACE. And I shall carry it?

MAM.                    No. I'll ha' no bawds
But fathers and mothers. They will
do it best,
Best of all others. And my flatterers
Shall be the pure and gravest of
divines            60
That I can get for money; my mere
fools
Eloquent burgesses; and then my poets
The same that writ so subtly of the
fart,
Whom I will entertain still for that
subject.
The few that would give out themselves
to be
Court- and town-stallions, and, each-
where, belie
Ladies who are known most innocent,
for them,
Those will I beg to make me eunuchs of;
And they shall fan me with ten es-
trich [2] tails
Apiece, made in a plume to gather
wind.            70
We will be brave, Puff, now we ha' the
*med'cine*.
My meat shall all come in, in Indian
shells,
Dishes of agate set in gold, and studded
With emeralds, sapphires, hyacinths,[3]
and rubies.
The tongues of carps, dormice, and
camels' heels,
Boiled i' the spirit of *Sol*, and dissolved
pearl

(Apicius' diet gainst the epilepsy)—
And I will eat these broths with spoons
of amber,
Headed with diamant [4] and carbuncle.
My footboy shall eat pheasants, calvered
salmons,[5]            80
Knots,[6] godwits,[7] lampreys; I myself
will have
The beards of barbels [8] served instead of
salads;
Oiled mushrooms; and the swelling
unctuous paps
Of a fat pregnant sow, newly cut off,
Dressed with an exquisite and poignant
sauce,
For which I'll say unto my cook,
"There's gold;
Go forth, and be a knight."

FACE.                    Sir, I'll go look
A little how it heightens.

MAM.            Do.—[*Exit Face.*] My shirts
I'll have of taffeta-sarsnet,[9] soft and
light
As cobwebs; and for all my other rai-
ment,            90
It shall be such as might provoke the
Persian,
Were he to teach the world riot anew.
My gloves of fishes' and birds' skins,
perfumed
With gums of Paradise, and Eastern
air—

SUR. And do you think to have the *stone*
with this?

MAM. No, I do think t' have all this with
the *stone*.

SUR. Why, I have heard he must be
*homo frugi*,
A pious, holy, and religious man,
One free from mortal sin, a very virgin.

MAM. That makes it, sir; he is so. But
I buy it;            100
My venter brings it me. He, honest
wretch,
A notable, superstitious, good soul,
Has worn his knees bare, and his slip-
pers bald,
With prayer and fasting for it. And,
sir, let him

[1] Paramours.    [3] An ancient precious stone.
[2] Ostrich.

[4] Diamond.
[5] Sliced while alive and perhaps pickled.
[6] Robin-snipes, a kind of sandpiper.
[7] Wading birds of the snipe family.
[8] A fresh-water fish.
[9] Fine silk.

Do it alone, for me, still. Here he comes.
Not a profane word afore him; 'tis
poison.—

### Act II. Scene iii.

*Mammon, Subtle, Surly, Face.*[1]

[Mam.] Good morrow, father.
Sub.                Gentle son, good morrow,
And to your friend there. What is he
is with you?
Mam. An heretic that I did bring along
In hope, sir, to convert him.
Sub.                Son, I doubt[2]
Yo' are covetous, that thus you meet
your time
I' the just point, prevent your day[3] at
morning.
This argues something worthy of a fear
Of importune and carnal appetite.
Take heed you do not cause the blessing
leave you,
With your ungoverned haste. I should
be sorry                              10
To see my labors, now e'en at perfection,
Got by long watching and large patience,
Not prosper where my love and zeal
hath placed hem—
Which[4] (heaven I call to witness, with
yourself,
To whom I have poured my thoughts),
in all my ends,
Have looked no way but unto public
good,
To pious uses and dear charity,
Now[5] grown a prodigy with men;
wherein
If you, my son, should now prevaricate,
And to your own particular lusts em-
ploy                                  20
So great and catholic a bliss, be sure
A curse will follow, yea, and overtake
Your subtle and most secret ways.
Mam.                I know, sir;
You shall not need to fear me; I but
come
To ha' you confute this gentleman.
Sur.                        Who is,
Indeed, sir, somewhat costive of belief
Toward your *stone*—would not be gulled.

Sub.                        Well, son,
All that I can convince him in is this:
The work is done; bright *Sol* is in his
robe.
We have a *med'cine of the triple soul*,  30
The *glorified spirit*. Thanks be to heaven,
And make us worthy of it!—Ulen
Spiegel![6]
Face. [*Within*.] Anon, sir.
Sub.                Look well to the register,
And let your heat still lessen by degrees
To the *aludels*.[7]
Face. [*Within*.] Yes, sir.
Sub.                        Did you look
O' the *bolt's-head* yet?
Face. [*Within*.] Which? On *D*, sir?
Sub.                                Ay.
What's the complexion?
Face. [*Within*.] Whitish.
Sub.                        Infuse vinegar,  40
To draw his *volatile substance* and his
*tincture;*
And let the water in *glass E* be feltered,[8]
And put into the *gripe's egg*. Lute[9]
him well,
And leave him closed *in balneo*.[10]
Face. [*Within*.]                I will, sir.
Sur. What a brave language here is!
Next to canting.[11]
Sub. I have another work you never saw,
son,
That three days since passed the *philos-
ophers' wheel*,
In the lent[12] heat of *Athanor*,[13] and 's
become
*Sulphur o' nature.*
Mam.                But 'tis for me?
Sub.                        What need you?
You have enough, in that is perfect.
Mam.                        O, but—  50
Sub. Why, this is covetise![14]
Mam.                No, I assure you,
I shall employ it all in pious uses,
Founding of colleges and grammar
schools,
Marrying young virgins, building hos-
pitals,
And now and then a church.

[6] Owl Glass, the hero of a popular German
jest book.
[7] Alchemical vessels.        [12] Mild.
[8] Filtered.                    [13] Furnace.
[9] Seal.                       [14] Covetousness.
[10] In a pan of warm water.
[11] Cant, rogues' jargon.

[1] Enters later.                    [2] Fear.
[3] Come before your time.
[4] *I.e.*, I who.
[5] From 1640 edn. Original has *no*.

*[Enter Face.]*

SUB.            How now?
FACE.                        Sir, please you,
Shall I not change the felter?
SUB.                        Marry, yes;
And bring me the complexion of *glass B.*
                        *[Exit Face.]*
MAM. Ha' you another?
SUB.            Yes, son; were I assured
Your piety were firm, we would not
    want
The means to glorify it. But I hope the
    best.                                          60
I mean to tinct *C* in *sand-heat* tomorrow,
And give him *imbibition.*
MAM.                        Of white oil?
SUB. No, sir, of red. *F* is come over the
    *helm* too,
I thank my Maker, in *S[t]. Mary's
    bath,*
And shows *lac virginis.*[1] Blessed be
    heaven!
I sent you of his *fæces* there *calcined;*
Out of that *calx* I ha' won the *salt of
    mercury.*
MAM. By pouring on your *rectified water?*
SUB. Yes, and *reverberating* in *Athanor.—*

*[Enter Face.]*

How now? What color says it?
FACE.            The ground black, sir.  70
MAM. That's your *crow's head?*
SUR. [*Aside.*]        Your coxcomb's, is 't
    not?
SUB. No, 'tis not perfect. Would it were
    the *crow!*
That work wants something..
SUR. [*Aside.*]            O, I looked for this;
The hay [2] is a-pitching.
SUB.            Are you sure you loosed hem
    I' their own *menstrue?*
FACE.      Yes, sir, and then married hem,
And put hem in a *bolt's-head* nipped to
    *digestion,*
According as you bade me, when I set
The *liquor of Mars* to *circulation*
In the same heat.
SUB.            The process then was right.
FACE. Yes, by the token, sir, the *retort*
    brake,                                        80

And what was saved was put into the
    *pelican,*
And signed with *Hermes' seal.*[3]
SUB.                        I think 'twas so.
We should have a new *amalgama.*
SUR. [*Aside.*]            O, this ferret
Is rank as any polecat.
SUB.                        But I care not;
Let him e'en die; we have enough be-
    side,
In *embryon. H* has his *white shirt* on?
FACE.                        Yes, sir,
He's ripe for *inceration;* he stands warm
In his *ash-fire.* I would not you should let
Any die now, if I might counsel, sir,
For luck's sake to the rest. It is not
    good.                                          90
MAM. He says right.
SUR. [*Aside.*]        Ay, are you bolted? [4]
FACE.                        Nay, I know 't, sir;
I have seen th' ill fortune. What is
    some three ounces
Of fresh *materials?*
MAM.                        Is 't no more?
FACE.                        No more, sir,
Of gold, t' *amalgam* with some six of
    *mercury.*
MAM. Away, here's money. What will
    serve?
FACE.      Ask him, sir.
MAM. How much?
SUB.                        Give him nine pound;
    you may gi' him ten.
SUR. [*Aside.*] Yes, twenty, and be cozened,
    do.
MAM.      There 'tis. [*Gives Face the money.*]
SUB. This needs not, but that you will
    have it so,
To see conclusions of all. For two
Of our inferior works are at *fixation;* 100
A third is in *ascension.* Go your ways.
Ha' you set the *oil of Luna* in *kemia?*
FACE. Yes, sir.
SUB.            And the *philosophers' vinegar?*
FACE.                        Ay. [*Exit.*]
SUR. [*Aside.*] We shall have a salad!
MAM.      When do you make *projection?*
SUB. Son, be not hasty. I *exalt* our
    *med'cine*
By hanging him *in balneo vaporoso,*
And giving him solution; then *congeal*
    him,

---

[1] Milk of the Virgin.
[2] Net for catching rabbits.
[3] *I.e.,* hermetically sealed.
[4] Dislodged, like a rabbit.

And then *dissolve* him; then again *con-
geal* him;
For look, how oft I iterate the work,
So many times I add unto his vir-
tue.                                          110
As, if at first one ounce convert a hun-
dred,
After his second loose, he'll turn a
thousand;
His third solution, ten; his fourth, a
hundred;
After his fifth, a thousand thousand
ounces
Of any imperfect metal, into pure
Silver or gold, in all examinations,
As good as any of the natural mine.
Get you your stuff here against after-
noon,
Your brass, your pewter, and your
andirons.
MAM. Not those of iron?
SUB.     Yes, you may bring them too; 120
We'll change all metals.
SUR. [*Aside.*]         I believe you in that.
MAM. Then I may send my spits?
SUB.                 Yes, and your racks.
SUR. And dripping pans, and pothangers,
and hooks?
Shall he not?
SUB.             If he please.
SUR.                        To be an ass.
SUB. How, sir!
MAM.        This gent'man you must bear
withal.
I told you he had no faith.
SUR.                And little hope, sir;
But much less charity, should I gull
myself.
SUB. Why, what have you observed, sir,
in our art
Seems so impossible?
SUR.       But your whole work; no more.
That you should hatch gold in a fornace,
sir,                                          130
As they do eggs in Egypt!
SUB.                Sir, do you
Believe that eggs are hatched so?
SUR.                        If I should?
SUB. Why, I think that the greater
miracle.
No egg but differs from a chicken
more
Than metals in themselves.
SUR.                    That cannot be.

The egg's ordained by nature to that
end,
And is a chicken *in potentia*.[1]
SUB. The same we say of lead and other
metals,
Which would be gold if they had time.
MAM.                        And that
Our art doth furder.[2]
SUB.             Ay, for 't were absurd  140
To think that nature in the earth bred
gold
Perfect i' the instant; something went
before.
There must be *remote matter*.
SUR.                    Ay, what is that?
SUB. Marry, we say—
MAM.     Ay, now it heats. Stand, father;
Pound him to dust.
SUB.                It is, of the one part,
A humid exhalation, which we call
*Materia liquida*, or the *unctuous water;*
On th' other part, a certain crass and
viscous
Portion of earth; both which, concor-
porate,
Do make the *elementary matter* of
gold,                                         150
Which is not yet *propria materia*,
But commune to all metals and all stones;
For, where it is forsaken of that moisture,
And hath more dryness, it becomes a
stone;
Where it retains more of the humid
fatness,
It turns to *sulphur* or to *quicksilver*,
Who are the parents of all other metals.
Nor can this *remote matter* suddenly
Progress so from extreme unto extreme
As to grow gold, and leap o'er all the
means.[3]                                     160
Nature doth first beget th' imperfect;
then
Proceeds she to the perfect.  Of that
airy
And oily water, *mercury* is engendered;
*Sulphur* o' the fat and earthy part; the
one,
Which is the last, supplying the place
of male,
The other of the female, in all metals.
Some do believe hermaphrodeity,

[1] Potentially.
[2] Further.
[3] Intermediate stages.

That both do act and suffer. But these
two
Make the rest ductile, malleable, ex-
tensive.
And even in gold they are; for we do
find                                    170
Seeds of them by our fire, and gold in
them,
And can produce the *species* of each
metal
More perfect thence than nature doth in
earth.
Beside, who doth not see in daily prac-
tice
Art can beget bees, hornets, beetles,
wasps
Out of the carcasses and dung of crea-
tures—
Yea, scorpions of an herb, being rightly
placed?
And these are living creatures, far more
perfect
And excellent than metals.
MAM.                        Well said, father!
Nay, if he take you in hand, sir, with
an argument,                            180
He'll bray [1] you in a mortar.
SUR.                        Pray you, sir, stay.
Rather than I'll be brayed, sir, I'll be-
lieve
That alchemy is a pretty kind of game,
Somewhat like tricks o' the cards, to
cheat a man
With charming.
SUB.       Sir?
SUR.            What else are all your terms,
Whereon no one o' your writers grees
with other?
Of your *elixir*, your *lac virginis*,
Your *stone*, your *med'cine*, and your
*chrysosperm*,
Your *sal*, your *sulphur*, and your *mer-
cury*,
Your *oil of height*, your *tree of life*, your
*blood*,                                190
Your *marchesite*, your *tutie*, your
*magnesia*,
Your *toad*, your *crow*, your *dragon*, and
your *panther*,
Your *sun*, your *moon*, your *firmament*,
your *adrop*,
Your *lato, azoch, zernich, chibrit, heau-
tarit*,

[1] Pulverize.

And then your *red man* and your
*white woman*,
With all your broths, your *menstrues*, and
*materials*
Of piss and eggshells, women's terms,
man's blood,
Hair o' the head, burnt clouts, chalk,
merds,[2] and clay,
Poulder of bones, scalings of iron, glass,
And worlds of other strange *ingredi-
ents*                                   200
Would burst a man to name?
SUB.                And all these, named,
Intending but one thing, which art our
writers
Used to obscure their art.
MAM.                    Sir, so I told him—
Because [3] the simple idiot should not
learn it,
And make it vulgar.
SUB.                Was not all the knowledge
Of the Egyptians writ in mystic sym-
bols?
Speak not the Scriptures oft in parables?
Are not the choicest fables of the poets,
That were the fountains and first springs
of wisdom,
Wrapped in perplexéd allegories?
MAM.                I urged that,   210
And cleared to him that Sisyphus was
damned
To roll the ceaseless stone, only because
He would have made ours common.—
(*Doll is seen.*) Who is this?
SUB. God's precious!—What do you mean?
Go in, good lady,
Let me entreat you.—[*Exit Doll.*]
Where's this varlet?

[*Enter Face.*]

FACE.                        Sir?
SUB. You very knave! Do you use me
thus?
FACE.        Wherein, sir?
SUB. Go in and see, you traitor. Go!
                            [*Exit Face.*]
MAM.                    Who is it, sir?
SUB. Nothing, sir; nothing.
MAM.            What's the matter, good sir?
I have not seen you thus distempered.
Who is 't?

[2] Fæces.
[3] In order that.

Sub. All arts have still had, sir, their
     adversaries;                              220
But ours the most ignorant.—

*Face returns.*

                              What now?
Face. 'Twas not my fault, sir; she would
     speak with you.
Sub. Would she, sir? Follow me. [*Exit.*]
Mam.                     Stay, Lungs!
Face.                    I dare not, sir.
Mam. How! Pray thee, stay.
Face.                    She's mad, sir, and
     sent hither—
Mam. Stay, man; what is she?
Face.               A lord's sister, sir.—
     (He'll be mad too.
Mam.        I warrant thee.[1])   Why sent
     hither?
Face. Sir, to be cured.
Sub. [*Within.*]              Why, rascal!
Face.                    Lo you!—Here, sir!
                              *He goes out.*
Mam. Fore God, a Bradamante,[2] a brave
     piece.
Sur. Heart, this is a bawdyhouse! I'll be
     burnt else.
Mam. O, by this light, no. Do not wrong
     him. H' is                           230
Too scrupulous that way; it is his vice.
No, h' is a rare physician (do him right),
An excellent Paracelsian, and has done
Strange cures with mineral physic. He
     deals all
With spirits, he; he will not hear a word
Of Galen or his tedious recipes.—

*Face again.*

                       How now, Lungs?
Face. Softly, sir; speak softly. I meant
To ha' told your worship all. This[3]
     must not hear.
Mam. No, he will not be gulled; let him
     alone.
Face. Y' are very right, sir; she is a most
     rare scholar,                        240
And is gone mad with studying Brough-
     ton's[4] works.
If you but name a word touching the
     Hebrew,

---

[1] *I.e.*, I guarantee to protect you against
Subtle.   [2] Heroine in Ariosto's *Orlando Furioso.*
[3] *I.e.*, Surly.
[4] A puritan and rabbinical scholar.

She falls into her fit, and will discourse
So learnedly of genealogies
As you would run mad, too, to hear her,
     sir.
Mam. How might one do t' have confer-
     ence with her, Lungs?
Face. O, divers have run mad upon the
     conference.
I do not know, sir. I am sent in haste
To fetch a vial.
Sur.              Be not gulled, Sir Mammon.
Mam. Wherein? Pray ye, be patient.
Sur.                    Yes, as you are,   250
And trust confederate knaves and bawds
     and whores.
Mam. You are too foul, believe it.—
     Come here, Ulen.
One word.
Face.             I dare not, in good faith.
Mam.                     Stay, knave.
Face. H' is extreme angry that you saw
     her, sir.
Mam. Drink that. [*Gives him money.*]
     What is she when she's out of her
     fit?
Face. O, the most affablest creature, sir!
     So merry!
So pleasant! She'll mount you up, like
     *quicksilver,*
*Over the helm,* and *circulate* like *oil;*
A very *vegetal;* discourse of state,   259
Of mathematics, bawdry, anything—
Mam. Is she no way accessible? No means,
No trick to give a man a taste of her—
     wit—
Or so?—Ulen!
Face.        I'll come to you again, sir. [*Exit.*]
Mam. Surly, I did not think one o' your
     breeding
Would traduce personages of worth.
Sur.                              Sir Epicure,
Your friend to use, yet still loath to be
     gulled.
I do not like your philosophical bawds.
Their *stone* is lechery enough to pay
     for,
Without this bait.
Mam.              Heart, you abuse yourself.
I know the lady, and her friends, and
     means,                              270
The original of this disaster. Her brother
Has told me all.
Sur.              And yet you ne'er saw her
     Till now?

MAM.          O, yes, but I forgot. I have, believe it,
One o' the treacherous'st memories, I do think,
Of all mankind.

SUR.          What call you her brother?

MAM.          My lord—
He wi' not have his name known, now I think on 't.

SUR. A very treacherous memory!

MAM.          O' my faith—

SUR. Tut, if you ha' it not about you, pass it
Till we meet next.

MAM.          Nay, by this hand, 'tis true.
He's one I honor, and my noble friend;
And I respect his house.

SUR.          Heart! Can it be     281
That a grave sir, a rich, that has no need,
A wise sir, too, at other times, should thus
With his own oaths and arguments make hard means
To gull himself?     And this be your *elixir*,
Your *lapis mineralis*, and your *lunary*,
Give me your honest trick yet at primero
Or gleek,[1] and take your *lutum sapientis*,
Your *menstruum simplex*!     I'll have gold before you,     289
And with less danger of the *quicksilver*,
Or the hot *sulphur*.

[*Enter Face*.]

FACE. (*To Surly*.)          Here's one from Captain Face, sir,
Desires you meet him i' the Temple Church
Some half hour hence, and upon earnest business.—
(*He whispers Mammon*.) Sir, if you please to quit us now, and come
Again within two hours, you shall have
My master busy examining o' the works;
And I will steal you in unto the party,
That you may see her converse.—Sir, shall I say
You'll meet the captain's worship?

SUR.          Sir, I will.—
[*Aside*.] But by attorney, and to a second purpose.     300

Now I am sure it is a bawdyhouse;
I'll swear it, were the marshal here to thank me.
The naming this commander doth confirm it.
Don Face! Why, h' is the most autentic [2] dealer
I' these commodities, the superintendent
To all the quainter [3] traffickers in town!
He is their visitor, and does appoint
Who lies with whom, and at what hour, what price,
Which gown, and in what smock, what fall,[4] what tire.[5]
Him will I prove, by a third person, to find     310
The subtleties of this dark labyrinth,
Which if I do discover, dear Sir Mammon,
You'll give your poor friend leave, though no *philosopher*,
To laugh; for you that are, 't is thought, shall weep.

FACE. Sir, he does pray you'll not forget.

SUR.          I will not, sir.
Sir Epicure, I shall leave you.     [*Exit*.]

MAM.          I follow you straight.

FACE. But do so, good sir, to avoid suspicion.
This gent'man has a parlous[6] head.

MAM.          But wilt thou, Ulen,
Be constant to thy promise?

FACE.          As my life, sir.

MAM. And wilt thou insinuate what I am, and praise me,     320
And say I am a noble fellow?

FACE.          O, what else, sir?
And that you'll make her royal with the *stone*,
An empress, and yourself King of Bantam.

MAM. Wilt thou do this?

FACE.          Will I, sir?

MAM.          Lungs, my Lungs, I love thee!

FACE.          Send your stuff, sir, that my master
May busy himself about projection.

MAM. Th' hast witched me, rogue. Take, go.          [*Gives him money*.]

---

[1] Card games.     [2] Authentic.     [3] More crafty.     [4] Collar, ruff.
[5] Headdress.          [6] Perilous, shrewd.

FACE.        Your jack [1] and all, sir.

MAM. Thou art a villain! I will send my jack,
And the weights too.  Slave, I could bite thine ear.
Away, thou dost not care for me.

FACE.                        Not I, sir?    330

MAM. Come, I was born to make thee, my good weasel,
Set thee on a bench, and ha' thee twirl a chain
With the best lord's vermin of hem all.

FACE.                        Away, sir.

MAM. A count, nay, a count palatine—

FACE.                        Good sir, go.

MAM. Shall not advance thee better; no, nor faster.                [*Exit.*]

### ACT II.  SCENE iv.

*Subtle, Face, Doll.*

[SUB.] Has he bit?  Has he bit?

FACE.                And swallowed too, my Subtle.
I ha' given him line, and now he plays, i' faith.

SUB.  And shall we twitch him?

FACE.                Thorough both the gills.
A wench is a rare bait, with which a man
No sooner 's taken, but he straight firks [2] mad.

SUB.  Doll, my Lord What's-hum's sister, you must now
Bear yourself ſtatelich.[3]

DOLL.                O, let me alone,
I'll not forget my race, I warrant you.
I'll keep my distance, laugh and talk aloud,
Have all the tricks of a proud, scurvy lady,                    10
And be as rude as her woman.

FACE.                Well said, sanguine! [4]

SUB.  But will he send his andirons?

FACE.                        His jack too,
And 's iron shoeing-horn; I ha' spoke to him.  Well,
I must not lose my wary gamester yonder.

SUB.  O, Monsieur Caution, that will not be gulled?

FACE.  Ay, if I can strike a fine hook into him now!

The Temple Church, there I have cast mine angle.
Well, pray for me.  I'll about it.
                        (*One knocks.*)

SUB.                What, more gudgeons!
Doll, scout, scout!—[*Doll goes to the window.*] Stay, Face, you must go to the door.
Pray God it be my Anabaptist.—Who is 't, Doll?                    20

DOLL. I know him not.  He looks like a gold-end man.[5]

SUB.  God's so! [6]  'Tis he, he said he would send—what call you him?—
The sanctified elder, that should deal
For Mammon's jack and andirons.  Let him in.
Stay, help me off first with my gown.—[*Exit Face with the gown.*] Away,
Madam, to your withdrawing chamber.—[*Exit Doll.*] Now,
In a new tune, new gesture, but old language.—
This fellow is sent from one negotiates with me
About the *stone* too, for the holy Brethren
Of Amsterdam, the exiled Saints, that hope                    30
To raise their discipline [7] by it.  I must use him
In some strange fashion now, to make him admire me.

### ACT II.  SCENE v.

*Subtle, Face, Ananias.*

[SUB.] Where is my drudge?

FACE. [*Entering.*]                Sir!

SUB.                        Take away the *recipient*,
And rectify your *menstrue* from the *phlegma.*
Then pour it o' the *Sol* in the *cucurbite*,
And let hem macerate together.

FACE.                        Yes, sir.
And save the ground?

SUB.                No; *terra damnata*
Must not have entrance in the *work.*—
Who are you?

ANA. A faithful Brother,[8] if it please you.

[5] One who buys odds and ends of gold.
[6] A mild oath.
[7] Form of church government.
[8] *I.e.*, a Puritan.

[1] A turnspit moved by weights.
[2] Runs.        [3] Stately.        [4] Red face.

SUB.                 What's that?
A Lullianist? A Ripley? [1] *Filius artis?* [2]
Can you *sublime* and *dulcify? Calcine?*
Know you the *sapor pontic? Sapor*
*stiptic?*                        10
Or what is *homogene* or *heterogene?*
ANA. I understand no heathen language,
truly.
SUB. Heathen, you Knipperdolling? [3] Is
*ars sacra,*
Or *chrysopœia*, or *spagyrica,*
Or the *pamphysic* or *panarchic* knowledge
A heathen language?
ANA.           Heathen Greek, I take it.
SUB. How? Heathen Greek?
ANA.          All's heathen but the Hebrew.
SUB. Sirrah, my varlet, stand you forth
and speak to him
Like a *philosopher;* answer i' the lan-
guage.
Name the vexations and the martyriza-
tions                       20
Of metals in the *work.*
FACE.          Sir, *putrefaction,*
*Solution, ablution, sublimation,*
*Cohobation, calcination, ceration,* and
*Fixation.*
SUB.        This is heathen Greek to you
now?—
And when comes *vivification?*
FACE.            After *mortification.*
SUB. What's *cohobation?*
FACE.           'Tis the pouring on
Your *aqua regis*, and then drawing him
off,
To the *trine circle* of the *seven spheres.*
SUB. What's the proper passion of metals?
FACE.               *Malleation.*
SUB. What's your *ultimum supplicium*
*auri?*
FACE.     *Antimonium.*           30
SUB. This 's heathen Greek to you?—And
what's your *mercury?*
FACE. A very *fugitive*, he will be gone, sir.
SUB. How know you him?
FACE.           By his *viscosity,*
His *oleosity*, and his *suscitability.*
SUB. How do you *sublime* him?
FACE.       With the *calce of eggshells,*
White *marble, talc.*

[1] Followers of Lully and Ripley, two earlier
alchemists.
[2] Son of the art?
[3] An Anabaptist leader.

SUB.          Your *magisterium* now,
What's that?
FACE.        Shifting, sir, your *elements*,
Dry into cold, cold into moist, moist in-
To hot, hot into dry.
SUB.        This is heathen Greek to you
still?—
Your *lapis philosophicus?*
FACE.            'Tis a *stone,*    40
And not a *stone;* a *spirit*, a *soul*, and a
*body;*
Which if you do *dissolve*, it is *dissolved;*
If you *coagulate*, it is *coagulated;*
If you make it to *fly*, it *flieth.*
SUB.          Enough.—[*Exit Face.*]
This 's heathen Greek to you? What are
you, sir?
ANA. Please you, a servant of the exiled
Brethren,
That deal with widows' and with or-
phans' goods,
And make a just account unto the
Saints—
A deacon.
SUB.        O, you are sent from Master
Wholesome,
Your teacher?
ANA.    From Tribulation Wholesome,   50
Our very zealous pastor.
SUB.          Good! I have
Some orphans' goods to come here.
ANA.          Of what kind, sir?
SUB. Pewter and brass, andirons and
kitchenware,
Metals that we must use our *med'cine*
on,
Wherein the Brethren may have a penn'-
orth
For ready money.
ANA.        Were the orphans' parents
Sincere professors?
SUB.        Why do you ask?
ANA.                Because
We then are to deal justly, and give, in
truth,
Their utmost value.
SUB.          'Slid, you'ld cozen else,
And if their parents were not of the
faithful?                      60
I will not trust you, now I think on 't,
Till I ha' talked with your pastor. Ha'
you brought money
To buy more coals?
ANA.          No, surely

SUB.                    No? How so?

ANA. The Brethren bid me say unto you, sir,

Surely they will not venter any more

Till they may see *projection*.

SUB.                    How!

ANA.                    Yo' have had

For the *instruments*, as bricks and lome,[1] and glasses,

Already thirty pound, and for *materials*,

They say, some ninety more; and they have heard since

That one at Heidelberg made it of an egg                    70

And a small paper of pin dust.[2]

SUB.                    What's your name?

ANA. My name is Ananias.

SUB.                    Out, the varlet

That cozened the apostles! Hence, away!

Flee, mischief! Had your holy consistory

No name to send me of another sound

Than wicked Ananias? Send your elders

Hither, to make atonement for you, quickly,

And gi' me satisfaction; or out goes

The fire, and down th' *alembics*, and the *fornace*,

*Piger Henricus*, or what not.    Thou wretch!                    80

Both *sericon* and *bufo* shall be lost,

Tell hem.  All hope of rooting out the bishops

Or th' antichristian hierarchy shall perish,

If they stay threescore minutes; the *aqueity*,

*Terreity*, and *sulphureity*

Shall run together again, and all be annulled,

Thou wicked Ananias!—[*Exit Ananias.*]

This will fetch hem,

And make hem haste towards their gulling more.

A man must deal like a rough nurse, and fright                    89

Those that are froward, to an appetite.

## ACT II. SCENE vi.

*Face [in his uniform], Subtle, Drugger.*

[FACE.] H' is busy with his spirits, but we'll upon him.

[1] A vessel.

[2] Dust from the manufacture of pins.

SUB. How now!    What mates,[3] what Bayards[4] ha' we here?

FACE. I told you he would be furious.—

Sir, here's Nab

Has brought yo' another piece of gold to look on

(We must appease him.  Give it me.) and prays you

You would devise—(What is it, Nab?)

DRUG.                    A sign, sir.

FACE. Ay, a good lucky one, a thriving sign, doctor.

SUB. I was devising now.

FACE. [*Aside to Subtle.*]    'Slight, do not say so;

He will repent he ga' you any more.—

What say you to his constellation, doctor, The Balance?

SUB.                    No, that way is stale and common.                    11

A townsman born in Taurus gives the Bull,

Or the bull's head; in Aries, the Ram—

A poor device! No, I will have his name

Formed in some mystic character, whose *radii*,

Striking the senses of the passers-by,

Shall, by a virtual influence,[5] breed affections[6]

That may result upon the party owns it, As thus—

FACE. Nab!

SUB.                    He first shall have *a bell*—that's *Abel;*

And by it standing one whose name is *Dee*,[7]                    20

In a *rug*[8] gown; there's D, and *rug*—that's *Drug;*

And right anenst[9] him a dog snarling *"er"*—

There's Drugger, Abel Drugger.  That's his sign.

And here's now mystery and hieroglyphic!

FACE. Abel, thou art made.

[3] Wretches.

[4] Blind fools—named from a legendary blind horse of Charlemagne.

[5] *I.e.*, an influence deriving from the virtue or power of the symbol.

[6] Inclinations.

[7] Referring to the mathematician and astrologer, Dr. John Dee, popularly regarded as a magician, who had recently died.

[8] Coarse cloth.

[9] Beside.

DRUG. [*Bowing*.]      Sir, I do thank his
worship.

FACE. Six o' thy legs [1] more will not do it,
Nab.—

He has brought you a pipe of tabacco,
doctor.

DRUG.          Yes, sir.

I have another thing I would impart—

FACE. Out with it, Nab.

DRUG.     Sir, there is lodged hard by me
A rich young widow—

FACE.               Good! A *bona roba?* [2]   31

DRUG. But nineteen at the most.

FACE.                     Very good, Abel.

DRUG. Marry, sh' is not in fashion yet; she
wears
A hood, but 't stands acop.[3]

FACE.                   No matter, Abel.

DRUG. And I do now and then give her a
fucus—

FACE. What! Dost thou deal, Nab?

SUB.               I did tell you, captain.

DRUG. And physic too sometime, sir, for
which she trusts me
With all her mind. She's come up here
of purpose
To learn the fashion.

FACE.               Good! (His match too!)
On, Nab.

DRUG. And she does strangely long to
know her fortune.                    40

FACE. God's lid, Nab, send her to the
doctor, hither.

DRUG. Yes, I have spoke to her of his
worship already;
But she's afraid it will be blown abroad,
And hurt her marriage.

FACE.                Hurt it? 'Tis the way
To heal it, if 'twere hurt—to make it
more
Followed and sought. Nab, thou shalt
tell her this.
She'll be more known, more talked of;
and your widows
Are ne'er of any price till they be famous;
Their honor is their multitude of suitors.
Send her; it may be thy good fortune.
What?                                50
Thou dost not know?

DRUG.       No, sir, she'll never marry
Under a knight; her brother has made
a vow.

FACE. What, and dost thou despair, my
little Nab,
Knowing what the doctor has set down
for thee,
And seeing so many o' the city dubbed?
One glass o' thy water, with a madam I
know,
Will have it done, Nab. What's her
brother? A knight?

DRUG. No, sir, a gentleman newly warm
in his land, sir,
Scarce cold in his one-and-twenty, that
does govern
His sister here, and is a man himself   60
Of some three thousand a year, and is
come up
To learn to quarrel, and to live by his
wits,
And will go down again, and die i' the
country.

FACE. How! To quarrel?

DRUG.          Yes, sir, to carry quarrels
As gallants do, and manage hem by line.[4]

FACE. 'Slid, Nab, the doctor is the only
man
In Christendom for him. He has made
a table,
With mathematical demonstrations,
Touching the art of quarrels. He will
give him
An instrument to quarrel by. Go, bring
hem both,                            70
Him and his sister. And, for thee, with
her
The doctor haply may persuade.[5] Go to!
Shalt give his worship a new damask suit
Upon the premises.

SUB.               O, good captain!

FACE.                     He shall;
He is the honestest fellow, doctor. Stay
not,
No offers; bring the damask and the
parties.

DRUG. I'll try my power, sir.

FACE.               And thy will too, Nab.

SUB. 'Tis good tabacco, this! What is 't an
ounce?

FACE. He'll send you a pound, doctor.

SUB.               O, no.

FACE.                     He will do 't.
It is the goodest soul!—Abel, about it.
(Thou shalt know more anon. Away, be-
gone.)—                [*Exit Abel.*]  81

---

[1] Bows.  [2] Finely dressed girl; also courtesan.
[3] On the top of her head, not tilted.
[4] Rule.                          [5] Plead.

A miserable rogue, and lives with cheese,
And has the worms. That was the cause,
   indeed,
Why he came now; he dealt with me in
   private,
To get a med'cine for hem.
SUB.       And shall, sir. This works.
FACE. A wife, a wife for one on us, my dear
   Subtle!
We'll e'en draw lots, and he that fails
   shall have
The more in goods, the other has in tail.
SUB. Rather the less, for she may be so
   light
She may want grains.[1]
FACE.      Ay; or be such a burden  90
A man would scarce endure her for the
   whole.
SUB. Faith, best let's see her first, and
   then determine.
FACE. Content, but Doll must ha' no
   breath on 't.
SUB.      Mum!
Away, you, to your Surly yonder; catch
   him.
FACE. Pray God I ha' not stayed too long.
SUB.       I fear it. [*Exeunt.*]

## ACT III. SCENE i.

[*The street before Lovewit's house.*]

*Tribulation, Ananias.*

[TRI.] These chastisements are common
   to the Saints,
And such rebukes we of the separation [2]
Must bear with willing shoulders as the
   trials
Sent forth to tempt our frailties.
ANA.       In pure zeal,
I do not like the man; he is a heathen,
And speaks the language of Canaan,
   truly.
TRI. I think him a profane person indeed.
ANA.       He bears
The visible mark of the beast in his
   forehead.
And, for his *stone*, it is a work of darkness,
And with *philosophy* blinds the eyes of
   man.                                    10
TRI. Good brother, we must bend unto all
   means
That may give furtherance to the holy
   cause.

[1] Groins, with a pun on the measure of weight.
[2] Dissenting sect.

ANA. Which his cannot. The sanctified
   cause
Should have a sanctified course.
TRI.       Not always necessary.
The children of perdition are ofttimes
Made instruments even of the greatest
   works.
Beside, we should give somewhat to [3]
   man's nature,
The place he lives in, still about the fire
And fume of metals, that intoxicate
The brain of man and make him prone
   to passion.                            20
Where have you greater atheists than
   your cooks?
Or more profane or choleric than your
   glassmen?
More antichristian than your bell-
   founders?
What makes the devil so devilish, I
   would ask you,
Sathan, our common enemy, but his
   being
Perpetually about the fire, and boiling
Brimstone and arsenic? We must give,
   I say,
Unto the motives and the stirrers-up
Of humors in the blood. It may be so.
Whenas [4] the *work* is done, the *stone* is
   made,                                  30
This heat of his may turn into a zeal,
And stand up for the beauteous discipline
Against the menstruous cloth and rag of
   Rome.
We must await his calling and the com-
   ing
Of the good spirit. You did fault t' up-
   braid him
With the Brethren's blessing of Heidel-
   berg, weighing
What need we have to hasten on the work
For the restoring of the silenced Saints,[5]
Which ne'er will be but by the *philos-
   ophers' stone.*                         39
And so a learned elder, one of Scotland,
Assured me, *aurum potabile* [6] being
The only med'cine for the civil magistrate
T' incline him to a feeling of the cause,
And must be daily used in the disease.

[3] Make allowance for.
[4] When.
[5] Non-conformist clergy not permitted to
preach.
[6] Drinkable gold, an elixir; here a bribe.

ANA. I have not edified [1] more, truly, by man,
Not since the beautiful light first shone on me;
And I am sad my zeal hath so offended.
TRI. Let us call on him then.
ANA.                     The motion's good,
And of the spirit. I will knock first.—
    [Knocks.] Peace be within!
              [Exeunt into the house.] [2]

### ACT III. SCENE ii.

*[A room in Lovewit's house.]* [3]

*Subtle, Tribulation, Ananias.*

[SUB.] O, are you come? 'Twas time. Your threescore minutes
Were at the last thread, you see; and down had gone
*Furnus acediæ, turris circulatorius;*
*Lembec,*[4] *bolt's-head, retort,* and *pelican*
Had all been cinders. Wicked Ananias!
Art thou returned? Nay, then it goes down yet.
TRI. Sir, be appeased; he is come to humble
Himself in spirit, and to ask your patience,
If too much zeal hath carried him aside
From the due path.
SUB.             Why, this doth qualify! [5]  10
TRI. The Brethren had no purpose, verily,
To give you the least grievance, but are ready
To lend their willing hands to any project
The spirit and you direct.
SUB.                     This qualifies more!
TRI. And, for the orphans' goods, let them be valued,
Or what is needful else to the holy work,
It shall be numbered; here, by me, the Saints
Throw down their purse before you.
SUB.                     This qualifies most!
Why, thus it should be, now you understand.
Have I discoursed so unto you of our stone,             20

And of the good that it shall bring your cause?
Showed you (beside the main [6] of hiring forces
Abroad, drawing the Hollanders, your friends,
From th' Indies to serve you with all their fleet)
That even the med'cinal use shall make you a faction
And party in the realm? As, put the case
That some great man in state, he have the gout,
Why, you but send three drops of your *elixir*,
You help him straight; there you have made a friend.
Another has the palsy or the dropsy;  30
He takes of your incombustible stuff,
He's young again; there you have made a friend.
A lady that is past the feat of body,
Though not of mind, and hath her face decayed
Beyond all cure of paintings, you restore
With the *oil of talc;* there you have made a friend—
And all her friends. A lord that is a leper,
A knight that has the boneache, or a squire
That hath both these, you make hem smooth and sound
With a bare *fricace* [7] of your *med'cine;* still  40
You increase your friends.
TRI.                     Ay, 'tis very pregnant.
SUB. And then the turning of this lawyer's pewter
To plate at Christmas—
ANA.                 Christ-tide, I pray you.
SUB. Yet,[8] Ananias!
ANA.                 I have done.
SUB.                     Or changing
His parcel [9] gilt to massy gold. You cannot
But raise you friends. Withal, to be of power
To pay an army in the field, to buy

---

[1] Been edified.
[2] They perhaps simply pass from the outer to the inner stage by the drawing of the traverse.
[3] The scene and action are continuous through the remainder of the act.             [5] Mollify.
[4] Alembic.

[6] Important matter.
[7] Rubbing.
[8] An exclamation of impatience.
[9] Partly.

The King of France out of his realms,
or Spain
Out of his Indies—what can you not do
Against lords spiritual or temporal 50
That shall oppone [1] you?
TRI.                        Verily, 'tis true.
We may be temporal lords ourselves, I
take it.
SUB. You may be anything, and leave off
to make
Long-winded exercises, or suck up
Your "ha!" and "hum!" in a tune. I
not deny,
But such as are not gracéd in a state,
May, for their ends, be adverse in re-
ligion,
And get a tune to call the flock together,
For, to say sooth, a tune does much with
women
And other phlegmatic people; it is your
bell.                                                60
ANA. Bells are profane; a tune may be
religious.
SUB. No warning with you? Then fare-
well my patience.
'Slight, it shall down; I will not be thus
tortured.
TRI. I pray you, sir.
SUB.        All shall perish. I have spoke it.
TRI. Let me find grace, sir, in your eyes;
the man,
He stands corrected. Neither did his
zeal,
But as yourself, allow a tune somewhere,
Which now, being toward [2] the *stone*,
we shall not need.
SUB. No, nor your holy vizard,[3] to win
widows
To give you legacies; or make zealous
wives                                              70
To rob their husbands for the common
cause;
Nor take the start of bonds broke but
one day,[4]
And say they were forfeited by provi-
dence.
Nor shall you need o'er night to eat huge
meals,
To celebrate your next day's fast the
better,

The whilst the Brethren and the Sisters,
humbled,
Abate the stiffness of the flesh. Nor cast
Before your hungry hearers scrupulous
bones,[5]
As whether a Christian may hawk or
hunt,                                              79
Or whether matrons of the holy assembly
May lay their hair out, or wear doublets,
Or have that idol, starch, about their
linen.
ANA. It is indeed an idol.
TRI.                        Mind him not, sir.
I do command thee, spirit (of zeal, but
trouble),
To peace within him! Pray you, sir, go
on.
SUB. Nor shall you need to libel gainst
the prelates,
And shorten so your ears [6] against the
hearing
Of the next wiredrawn grace;[7] nor of
necessity
Rail against plays, to please the alder-
man
Whose daily custard you devour; nor
lie                                                90
With zealous rage till you are hoarse.
Not one
Of these so singular arts! Nor call your-
selves
By names of Tribulation, Persecution,
Restraint, Long-patience, and suchlike,
affected
By the whole family or wood[8] of you,
Only for glory, and to catch the ear
Of the disciple.
TRI.                        Truly, sir, they are
Ways that the godly Brethren have in-
vented
For propagation of the glorious cause,
As very notable means, and whereby
also                                              100
Themselves grow soon and profitably
famous.
SUB. O, but the *stone*, all's idle to it! Noth-
ing!
The art of angels, nature's miracle,
The *divine secret* that doth fly in clouds
From east to west, and whose tradition
Is not from men, but *spirits*.

---

[1] Oppose.
[2] Near to owning.
[3] Mask, sanctimonious expression.
[4] *I.e.*, foreclose obligations just expired.

[5] Dry bones of discussion on small points.
[6] Lose your ears in a pillory.
[7] Drawn-out prayer.                    [8] Crowd.

Ana.                    I hate traditions;
I do not trust them——
Tri.            Peace!
Ana.                    They are popish all.
I will not peace.  I will not——
Tri.                    Ananias!
Ana. Please the profane, to grieve the
    godly; I may not.                    109
Sub. Well, Ananias, thou shalt overcome.
Tri. It is an ignorant zeal that haunts
    him, sir—
    But truly else a very faithful Brother,
    A botcher,[1] and a man by revelation
    That hath a competent knowledge of
    the truth.
Sub. Has he a competent sum there i'
    the bag
    To buy the goods within?  I am made
    guardian,
    And must, for charity and conscience'
    sake,
    Now see the most be made for my poor
    orphan,
    Though I desire the Brethren, too, good
    gainers.
    There they are within.  When you have
    viewed and bought them,        120
    And ta'en the inventory of what they
    are,
    They are ready for *projection;* there's no
    more
    To do.  Cast on the *med'cine,* so much
    silver
    As there is tin there, so much gold as
    brass,
    I'll gi' it you in by weight.
Tri.                    But how long time,
Sir, must the Saints expect[2] yet?
Sub.                    Let me see,
    How's the moon now?  Eight, nine, ten
    days hence,
    He will be *silver potate;* then three days
    Before he *citronize;* some fifteen days,
    The *magisterium* will be perfected.    130
Ana. About the second day of the third
    week
    In the ninth month?
Sub.                    Yes, my good Ananias.
Tri. What will the orphans' goods arise
    to, think you?
Sub. Some hundred marks, as much as
    filled three cars,[3]

1 Tailor, a cant term for Puritan.
2 Wait.                    3 Carts.

Unladed now; you'll make six millions
    of hem.
    But I must ha' more coals laid in.
Tri.            How!
Sub.                    Another load,
    And then we ha' finished.  We must
    now increase
    Our fire to *ignis ardens;* we are past
    *Fimus equinus, balnei, cineris,*
    And all those lenter heats.  If the holy
    purse                            140
    Should with this draught fall low, and
    that the Saints
    Do need a present sum, I have [a][4] trick
    To melt the pewter you shall buy now
    instantly,
    And with a *tincture* make you as good
    Dutch dollars
    As any are in Holland.
Tri.                    Can you so?
Sub. Ay, and shall bide the third exami-
    nation.
Ana. It will be joyful tidings to the
    Brethren.
Sub. But you must carry it secret.
Tri.                    Ay; but stay—
This act of coining, is it lawful?
Ana.                    Lawful?
We know[5] no magistrate; or, if we did,
This's foreign coin.
Sub.                    It is no coining, sir.    151
It is but casting.
Tri.            Ha!  You distinguish well.
Casting of money may be lawful.
Ana.                    'Tis, sir.
Tri. Truly, I take it so.
Sub.                    There is no scruple,
Sir, to be made of it; believe Ananias;
This case of conscience he is studied in.
Tri. I'll make a question of it to the Breth·
    ren.
Ana. The Brethren shall approve it law-
    ful, doubt not.
    Where shall 't be done?
Sub.                    For that we'll talk anon.
                    *Knock without.*
    There's some to speak with me.  Go in,
    I pray you,                        160
    And view the parcels.  That's the in-
    ventory.
    I'll come to you straight.—[*Exeunt Trib-
    ulation and Ananias.*]  Who is it?—
    Face, appear!

4 From 1640 edn.            5 Acknowledge.

ACT III. SCENE iii.

*Subtle, Face, Doll.*[1]

[SUB.] How now? Good prize?

FACE.      Good pox! Yond' costive cheater
Never came on.

SUB.          How then?

FACE.            I ha' walked the round
Till now, and no such thing.

SUB.          And ha' you quit him?

FACE. Quit him? And hell would quit
him too, he were happy.

'Slight! Would you have me stalk like
a mill jade,

All day, for one that will not yield us
grains?

I know him of old.

SUB.          O, but to ha' gulled him
Had been a maistry.[2]

FACE.           Let him go, black boy!
And turn thee, that some fresh news
may possess thee.

A noble count, a don of Spain (my
dear                        10

Delicious compeer, and my party-[3]
bawd),

Who is come hither private for his conscience

And brought munition with him, six
great slops,[4]

Bigger than three Dutch hoys,[5] beside
round trunks,[6]

Furnished with pistolets[7] and pieces of
eight,[7]

Will straight be here, my rogue, to have
thy bath

(That is the color[8]) and to make his
batt'ry

Upon our Doll, our castle, our Cinque
Port,[9]

Our Dover pier, our what thou wilt.
Where is she?

She must prepare perfumes, delicate
linen,                  20

The bath in chief, a banquet, and her
wit,

For she must milk his epididymis.

Where is the doxy?

SUB.           I'll send her to thee,

And but despatch my brace of little
John Leydens[10]

And come again myself.

FACE.           Are they within then?

SUB. Numb'ring the sum.

FACE. How much?

SUB.      A hundred marks, boy. [*Exit.*]

FACE. Why, this 's a lucky day. Ten
pounds of Mammon!

Three o' my clerk! A portague o' my
grocer!

This o' the Brethren! Beside reversions

And states to come i' the widow and
my count!             30

My share today will not be bought for
forty—

[*Enter Doll.*]

DOLL.         What?

FACE. Pounds, dainty Dorothy! Art
thou so near?

DOLL. Yes. Say, lord general, how fares
our camp?

FACE. As with the few that had entrenched
themselves

Safe, by their discipline, against a world,
Doll,

And laughed within those trenches, and
grew fat

With thinking on the booties, Doll,
brought in

Daily by their small parties. This dear
hour

A doughty don is taken with my Doll;

And thou mayst make his ransom what
thou wilt,           40

My dowsabel;[11] he shall be brought here,
fettered

With thy fair looks, before he sees thee,
and thrown

In a down bed as dark as any dungeon,

Where thou shalt keep him waking with
thy drum—

Thy drum, my Doll, thy drum—till he
be tame

As the poor blackbirds were i' the great
frost,[12]

Or bees are with a basin, and so hive
him

---

[1] Enters later.          [5] Ships.

[2] Mastery, achievement.    [6] Trunk hose.

[3] Partner.                [7] Gold coins.

[4] Loose breeches.         [8] Pretext.

[9] One of five strategic Channel towns.

[10] Puritans, so called from their leader, John
Bockholdt, or John of Leyden.

[11] Douce et belle; sweetheart.    [12] Of 1608.

I' the swan-skin coverlid and cambric
    sheets,
Till he work honey and wax, my little
    God's-gift.[1]
DOLL. What is he, general?
FACE.　　　　　　　An adalantado,[2]　　50
    A grandee, girl.　Was not my Dapper
    here yet?
DOLL. No.
FACE.　　　　Nor my Drugger?
DOLL.　　　　　　　　　　　Neither.
FACE.　　　　　　　　A pox on hem,
    They are so long a-furnishing!　Such
    stinkards
    Would not be seen upon these festival
    days.—

*[Enter Subtle.]*

How now!　Ha' you done?
SUB.　　　　Done.　They are gone; the sum
    Is here in bank, my Face.　I would we
    knew
    Another chapman[3] now would buy hem
    outright.
FACE. 'Slid, Nab shall do 't against he ha'
    the widow,
    To furnish household.
SUB.　　　　　　Excellent, well thought on.
    Pray God he come.
FACE.　　　　　　I pray he keep away　60
    Till our new business be o'erpast.
SUB.　　　　　　　　　　　But, Face,
    How cam'st thou by this secret don?
[FACE.][4]　　　　　　　　　　A spirit
    Brought me th' intelligence in a paper
    here,
    As I was conjuring yonder in my circle
    For Surly; I ha' my flies abroad.　Your
    bath
    Is famous, Subtle, by my means.　Sweet
    Doll,
    You must go tune your virginal, no los-
    ing
    O' the least time.　And—do you hear?—
    good action!
    Firk like a flounder; kiss like a scallop,
    close;
    And tickle him with thy mother-tongue.
    His great　　　　　　　　　　　70

Verdugoship[5] has not a jot of lan-
    guage[6]—
So much the easier to be cozened, my
    Dolly.
He will come here in a hired coach, ob-
    scure,
And our own coachman, whom I have
    sent, as guide,
No creature else.　(*One knocks.*)　Who's
    that?　　　　　　　　　　*[Exit Doll.]*
SUB.　　　　It i' not he?
FACE. O, no, not yet this hour.

*[Enter Doll.]*

SUB.　　　　　　　　　　Who is 't?
DOLL.　　　　　　　　　　　Dapper,
    Your clerk.
FACE.　　　God's will then, Queen of Fairy,
    On with your tire[7]—*[Exit Doll.]* and, doc-
    tor, with your robes.
    Let's despatch him for God's sake.
SUB.　　　　　　　　　　'Twill be long.
FACE. I warrant you, take but the cues
    I give you,　　　　　　　　　　80
    It shall be brief enough.　*[Goes to the*
    *window.]*　'Slight, here are more!
    Abel and, I think, the angry boy, the
    heir
    That fain would quarrel.
SUB.　　　　　　　　　　And the widow?
FACE.　　　　　　　　　　　　No,
    Not that I see.　Away!—*[Exit Subtle.]*
    O, sir, you are welcome.

## ACT III.　SCENE iv.

*Face, Dapper, Drugger, Kastril.*[8]

[FACE.] The doctor is within, a-moving for
    you.
    (I have had the most ado to win him to
    it!)
    He swears you'll be the dearling o' the
    dice;
    He never heard her highness dote till
    now, he says.
    Your aunt has giv'n you the most
    gracious words
    That can be thought on.
DAP.　　　　　　Shall I see her grace?
FACE. See her, and kiss her too.—

---

[1] Alluding to the etymological meaning of
*Dorothea.*
[2] Adelantado, a Spanish governor.
[3] Dealer.　　　　　　[4] From 1612 edn.

[5] Hangmanship; a word coined from the
Spanish.
[6] *I.e.*, he cannot speak English.
[7] Attire.　　　[8] The last two enter later.

*[Enter Drugger and Kastril.]*

What, honest Nab!
Hast brought the damask?

NAB.                    No, sir; here's tabacco.

FACE. 'Tis well done, Nab. Thou'lt bring
    the damask too?

DRUG. Yes. Here's the gentleman, cap-
    tain, Master Kastril,                    10
I have brought to see the doctor.

FACE.                    Where's the widow?

DRUG. Sir, as he likes, his sister, he says,
    shall come.

FACE. O, is it so? Good time. Is your
    name Kastril, sir?

KAS. Ay, and the best o' the Kastrils—
    I'ld be sorry else—
By fifteen hundred a year. Where is this
    doctor?
My mad tabacco-boy here tells me of
    one
That can do things. Has he any skill?

FACE.                    Wherein, sir?

KAS. To carry a business, manage a
    quarrel fairly,
Upon fit terms,

FACE     It seems, sir, yo' are but young
About the town, that can make that a
    question.                    20

KAS. Sir, not so young but I have heard
    some speech
Of the angry boys,[1] and seen hem take
    tabacco,
And in his shop; and I can take it too.
And I would fain be one of hem, and go
    down
And practice i' the country.

FACE.                    Sir, for the duello,
The doctor, I assure you, shall inform
    you
To the least shadow of a hair, and show
    you
An instrument he has of his own making,
Wherewith, no sooner shall you make
    report
Of any quarrel, but he will take the
    height on 't                    30
Most instantly, and tell in what degree
Of safety it lies in, or mortality,
And how it may be borne, whether in a
    right line
Or a half circle, or may else be cast
Into an angle blunt, if not acute—

[1] Roisterers.

All this he will demonstrate; and then,
    rules
To give and take the lie by.

KAS.                    How? To take it?

FACE. Yes, in oblique [2] he'll show you, or
    in circle; [2]
But ne'er in diameter.[3] The whole
    town
Study his theorems, and dispute them
    ordinarily                    40
At the eating academies.

KAS.                    But does he teach
Living by the wits too?

FACE.                    Anything whatever.
You cannot think that subtlety but he
    reads it.
He made me a captain. I was a stark
    pimp,
Just o' your standing, fore I met with
    him;
It i' not two months since. I'll tell you
    his method:
First, he will enter you at some ordi-
    nary.

KAS. No, I'll not come there. You shall
    pardon me.

FACE.                    For why, sir?

KAS. There's gaming there, and tricks.

FACE.                    Why, would you be
A gallant, and not game?

KAS.                    Ay, 'twill spend a man.    50

FACE. Spend you? It will repair you when
    you are spent.
How do they live by their wits there,
    that have vented
Six times your fortunes?

KAS.                    What, three thousand a year!

FACE. Ay, forty thousand.

KAS.                    Are there such?

FACE.                    Ay, sir,
And gallants yet. Here's a young gentle-
    man
Is born to nothing—*[Indicates Dapper.]*
    forty marks a year,
Which I count nothing. H' is to be
    initiated,
And have a fly o' the doctor. He will win
    you
By unresistible luck, within this fort-
    night,
Enough to buy a barony. They will set
    him                    60

[2] *I.e.*, the lie circumstantial.
[3] *I.e.*, the lie direct.

Upmost, at the groom porter's,[1] all the
　　Christmas,
And, for the whole year through at every
　　place
Where there is play, present him with the
　　chair,
The best attendance, the best drink,
　　sometimes
Two glasses of Canary—and pay noth-
　　ing—
The purest linen and the sharpest knife,
The partrich [2] next his trencher, and
　　somewhere
The dainty bed, in private, with the
　　dainty.
You shall ha' your ordinaries bid for
　　him,
As playhouses for a poet, and the mas-
　　ter　　　　　　　　　　　　　　　　70
Pray him aloud to name what dish he
　　affects,
Which must be buttered shrimps; and
　　those that drink
To no mouth else will drink to his, as
　　being
The goodly president mouth of all the
　　board.
KAS. Do you not gull one?
FACE.　　　　'Od's my life! Do you think it?
You shall have a cast [3] commander (can
　　but get
In credit with a glover or a spurrier
For some two pair of either's ware afore-
　　hand)
Will, by most swift posts, dealing with
　　him,
Arrive at competent means to keep
　　himself,　　　　　　　　　　　　　80
His punk, and naked boy in excellent
　　fashion,
And be admired for 't.
KAS.　　　　Will the doctor teach this?
FACE. He will do more, sir: when your
　　land is gone
(As men of spirit hate to keep earth
　　long),
In a vacation,[4] when small money is
　　stirring,
And ordinaries suspended till the term,

He'll show a perspective [5] where on one
　　side
You shall behold the faces and the per-
　　sons
Of all sufficient young heirs in town,　89
Whose bonds are current for commodity;
On th' other side, the merchants' forms,
　　and others
That, without help of any second broker,
Who would expect a share, will trust such
　　parcels;
In the third square, the very street and
　　sign
Where the commodity dwells, and does
　　but wait
To be delivered, be it pepper. soap,
Hops, or tabacco, oatmeal, woad,[6] or
　　cheeses—
All which you may so handle, to enjoy
To your own use, and never stand
　　obliged.
KAS. I' faith, is he such a fellow?
FACE.　　　Why, Nab here knows him.　100
And then for making matches for rich
　　widows,
Young gentlewomen, heirs, the for-
　　tunat'st man!
He's sent to, far and near, all over
　　England,
To have his counsel and to know their
　　fortunes.
KAS. God's will, my suster [7] shall see him.
FACE.　　　　　　　　　　I'll tell you, sir,
What he did tell me of Nab.　It's a
　　strange thing!
(By the way, you must eat no cheese,
　　Nab; it breeds melancholy,
And that same melancholy breeds worms
　　—but pass it.)
He told me, honest Nab here was ne'er
　　at tavern　　　　　　　　　　　109
But once in 's life.
DRUG.　　Truth, and no more I was not.
FACE. And then he was so sick—
DRUG.　　　　Could he tell you that too?
FACE. How should I know it?
DRUG.　In troth, we had been a-shooting,
And had a piece of fat ram-mutton to
　　supper,
That lay so heavy o' my stomach—

---

[1] An officer of the court who superintended
gaming.
　[2] Partridge.
　[3] Cassed, cashiered, dismissed.
　[4] Of the law courts.

[5] A picture the appearance of which changes
according to the angle of vision.
　[6] A plant which produced blue dye.
　[7] Provincial form for *sister*.

FACE.                    And he has no head
    To bear any wine; for what with the
    noise o' the fiddlers
    And care of his shop, for he dares keep
    no servants—
DRUG. My head did so ache—
FACE.            As he was fain to be brought
    home,
    The doctor told me. And then a good
    old woman—
DRUG. Yes, faith, she dwells in Seacoal
    Lane—did cure me
    With sodden [1] ale and pellitory o' the
    wall [2]—                                    120
    Cost me but twopence. I had another
    sickness
    Was worse than that.
FACE.            Ay, that was with the grief
    Thou took'st for being cessed [3] at eigh-
    teenpence
    For the waterwork.
DRUG.            In truth, and it was like
    T' have cost me almost my life.
FACE.                    Thy hair went off?
DRUG. Yes, sir; 'twas done for spite.
FACE.            Nay, so says the doctor.
KAS. Pray thee, tabacco-boy, go fetch my
    suster;
    I'll see this learnéd boy before I go;
    And so shall she.
FACE.            Sir, he is busy now;
    But, if you have a sister to fetch
    hither,                                       130
    Perhaps your own pains may command
    her sooner,
    And he by that time will be free.
KAS.                    I go. [Exit.]
FACE. Drugger, she's thine. The damask!
    —[Exit Abel.] (Subtle and I
    Must wrastle for her.) Come on, Master
    Dapper;
    You see how I turn clients here
    away,
    To give your cause despatch; ha' you
    performed
    The ceremonies were enjoined you?
DAP.                    Yes, o' the vinegar
    And the clean shirt.
FACE. 'Tis well. That shirt may do you
    More worship than you think. Your
    aunt's afire,

[1] Heated.
[2] Wall-pellitory, a herb.
[3] Assessed.

But that she will not show it, t' have a
    sight on you.                                 140
Ha' you provided for her grace's serv-
    ants?
DAP. Yes, here are sixscore Edward shil-
    lings—
FACE.            Good!
DAP. And an old Harry's sovereign—
FACE.                    Very good!
DAP. And three James shillings, and an
    Elizabeth groat—
    Just twenty nobles.
FACE.                    O, you are too just.
    I would you had had the other noble in
    Marys.
DAP. I have some Philip and Marys.
FACE.                    Ay, those same
    Are best of all. Where are they? Hark,
    the doctor.

ACT III. SCENE V.

*Subtle, Face, Dapper, Doll.[4] Subtle disguised
    like a Priest of Fairy.*

[SUB.] Is yet her grace's cousin come?
FACE.                    He is come.
SUB. And is he fasting?
FACE.            Yes.
SUB.            And hath cried "hum"?
FACE. Thrice, you must answer.
DAP.                    Thrice.
SUB.            And as oft "buzz"?
FACE. If you have, say.
DAP.            I have.
SUB.                    Then, to her coz,
    Hoping that he hath vinegared his senses,
    As he was bid, the Fairy Queen dispenses,
    By me, this robe, the petticoat of For-
    tune,
    Which that he straight put on, she doth
    importune.
    And though to Fortune near be her
    petticoat,
    Yet nearer is her smock, the queen doth
    note;                                         10
    And therefore even of that a piece she
    hath sent,
    Which, being a child, to wrap him in was
    rent,
    And prays him for a scarf he now will
    wear it
    (With as much love as then her grace
    did tear it)

[4] Enters later.

About his eyes (*They blind him with a rag.*) to show he is fortunate.

And, trusting unto her to make his state,
He'll throw away all worldly pelf about him;
Which that he will perform, she doth not doubt him.

FACE. She need not doubt him, sir. Alas, he has nothing
But what he will part withal as willingly,    20
Upon her grace's word (throw away your purse),
As she would ask it. (Handkerchiefs and all!)
She cannot bid that thing but he'll obey.
(If you have a ring about you, cast it off,
Or a silver seal at your wrist; her grace will send

*He throws away, as they bid him.*

Her fairies here to search you; therefore deal
Directly [1] with her highness. If they find
That you conceal a mite, you are undone.)

DAP. Truly, there's all.
FACE.            All what?
DAP.            My money; truly.
FACE. Keep nothing that is transitory about you.    30
(Bid Doll play music.)

*Doll enters with a cittern. They pinch him.*

              Look, the elves are come
To pinch you, if you tell not truth. Advise you.
DAP. O! I have a paper with a spur ryal [2] in 't.
FACE.        *Ti, ti.*
They knew 't, they say.
SUB.        *Ti, ti, ti, ti.* He has more yet.
FACE. *Ti, ti-ti-ti.* I' the tother [3] pocket?
SUB.                *Titi, titi, titi, titi.*
They must pinch him or he will never confess, they say.
              [*They pinch him again.*]
DAP. O, O!
FACE.    Nay, pray you, hold. He is her grace's nephew.—
*Ti, ti, ti?* What care you? Good faith, you shall care.—

---

[1] Honestly.
[2] Spur royal, a gold coin.
[3] Other.

Deal plainly, sir, and shame the fairies. Show    39
You are an innocent.
DAP.    By this good light, I ha' nothing.
SUB. *Titi, titota.* He does equivocate, she says—
*Ti, ti do ti, ti ti do, ti da*—and swears by the light when he is blinded.
DAP. By this good dark, I ha' nothing but a half crown
Of gold about my wrist, that my love gave me;
And a leaden heart I wore sin' she forsook me.
FACE. I thought 'twas something. And would you incur
Your aunt's displeasure for these trifles? Come,
I had rather you had thrown away twenty half crowns. [*Removes the coin.*]
You may wear your leaden heart still.—
How now?
SUB. [*Aside.*] What news, Doll?
DOLL. [*Aside.*]        Yonder's your knight, Sir Mammon.    50
FACE. [*Aside.*] God's lid, we never thought of him till now!
Where is he?
DOLL. [*Aside.*]        Here hard by. H' is at the door.
SUB. [*Aside.*] And you are not ready now?
Doll, get his suit.—        [*Exit Doll.*]
He must not be sent back.
FACE. [*Aside.*]        O, by no means.
What shall we do with this same puffin here,
Now he's o' the spit?
SUB. [*Aside.*]        Why, lay him back awhile
With some device.—

[*Enter Doll with Face's clothes.*]

        *Ti, titi, tititi.* Would her grace speak with me?
I come.—Help, Doll!
FACE. (*He speaks through the keyhole, the Other knocking.*)        Who's there?
Sir Epicure,
My master's i' the way. Please you to walk
Three or four turns but till his back be turned,    60
And I am for you.—Quickly, Doll!

SUB. 　　　　　　Her grace
Commends her kindly to you, Master
　Dapper.
DAP. I long to see her grace.
SUB. 　　　　　She now is set
At dinner in her bed, and she has sent you
From her own private trencher a dead
　mouse
And a piece of gingerbread, to be merry
　withal
And stay your stomach, lest you faint
　with fasting;
Yet if you could hold out till she saw
　you, she says,
It would be better for you.
FACE. 　　　　　Sir, he shall
Hold out, and 'twere this two hours, for
　her highness; 　　　　　　　　70
I can assure you that. We will not lose
All we ha' done.—
SUB. 　　　　He must not see nor speak
To anybody till then.
FACE. 　　　　For that we'll put, sir,
A stay in 'is mouth.
SUB. 　　　　　Of what?
FACE. 　　　　　Of gingerbread.
Make you it fit. He that hath pleased
　her grace
Thus far, shall not now crinkle [1] for a
　little.—
Gape, sir, and let him fit you.
　　　　　　　　　　[They gag him.]
SUB. [Aside.] 　　Where shall we now
Bestow him?
DOLL. [Aside.] 　　I' the privy.
SUB. 　　　　　Come along, sir;
I must now show you Fortune's privy
　lodgings.
FACE. Are they perfumed, and his bath
　ready?
SUB. 　　All. 　　　　　　　　80
Only the fumigation's somewhat strong.
FACE. [Through the keyhole.] Sir Epicure,
I am yours, sir, by-and-by.[2]
　　[Exeunt Subtle and Doll with Dapper.]

ACT IV. SCENE i.

[The same.]

Face, Mammon, Doll.[3]

[FACE.] O, sir, yo' are come i' the only
　finest time!
MAM. Where's master?

[1] Turn aside. 　[2] Immediately. 　[3] Enters later.

FACE. Now preparing for projection, sir.
Your stuff will b' all changed shortly.
MAM. 　　　　　　　Into gold?
FACE. To gold and silver, sir.
MAM. 　　　　　Silver I care not for.
FACE. Yes, sir, a little to give beggars.
MAM. 　　　　　Where's the lady?
FACE. At hand here. I ha' told her such
　brave things o' you,
Touching your bounty and your noble
　spirit—
MAM. 　　　　Hast thou?
FACE. As she is almost in her fit to see
　you.
But, good sir, no divinity i' your confer-
　ence,
For fear of putting her in rage.[4]
MAM. 　　　　　I warrant thee. 10
FACE. Six men will not hold her down.
　And then,
If the old man should hear or see you—
MAM. 　　　　　　　　Fear not.
FACE. The very house, sir, would run
　mad. You know it,
How scrupulous he is and violent
Gainst the least act of sin. Physic or
　mathematics,
Poetry, state,[5] or bawdry, as I told you,
She will endure, and never startle; but
No word of controversy.
MAM. 　　　I am schooled, good Ulen.
FACE. And you must praise her house,
　remember that,
And her nobility.
MAM. 　　　　Let me alone; 　20
No herald, no, nor antiquary, Lungs,
Shall do it better. Go.
FACE. [Aside.] 　　　Why, this is yet
A kind of modern[7] happiness,[8] to have
Doll Common for a great lady. [Exit.]
MAM. 　　　　　Now, Epicure.
Heighten thyself; talk to her all in gold;
Rain her as many showers as Jove did
　drops
Unto his Danaë; show the god a miser,
Compared with Mammon. What! The
　stone will do 't.
She shall feel gold, taste gold, hear gold,
　sleep gold;

[4] Insanity.
[5] Matters of state; politics.
[6] Family.
[7] With a pun on the meaning common.
[8] Fitness, appropriateness.

Nay, we will *concumbere* [1] gold. I will be
    puissant                                    30
And mighty in my talk to her.—

*[Enter Face with Doll.]*

                      Here she comes.
FACE. [*Aside.*] To him, Doll; suckle him.—
    This is the noble knight
I told your ladyship—
MAM.          Madam, with your pardon,
I kiss your vesture.
DOLL.          Sir, I were uncivil
If I would suffer that; my lip to you,
    sir.
MAM. I hope my lord your brother be in
    health, lady.
DOLL. My lord my brother is, though I
    no lady, sir.
(FACE. Well said, my Guinea bird. [2])
MAM.          Right noble madam—
(FACE. O, we shall have most fierce idola-
    try.)
MAM. 'Tis your prerogative.
DOLL.       Rather your courtesy.   40
MAM. Were there naught else t' enlarge
    your virtues to me,
These answers speak your breeding and
    your blood.
DOLL. Blood we boast none, sir; a poor
    baron's daughter.
MAM. "Poor"!—and gat you? Profane
    not. Had your father
Slept all the happy remnant of his life
After that act, lyen [3] but there still, and
    panted,
H' had done enough to make himself,
    his issue,
And his posterity noble.
DOLL.          Sir, although
We may be said to want the gilt and
    trappings,
The dress of honor, yet we strive to
    keep                                        50
The seeds and the materials.
MAM.            I do see
The old ingredient, virtue, was not lost,
Nor the drug, money, used to make your
    compound.
There is a strange nobility i' your eye,
This lip, that chin! Methinks you do
    resemble
One o' the Austriac [4] princes.

FACE. [*Aside.*]          Very like!
Her father was an Irish costermonger. [5]
MAM. The house of Valois, just, had
    such a nose,
And such a forehead yet the Medici
Of Florence boast.
DOLL.       Troth, and I have been likened 60
    To all these princes.
FACE. [*Aside.*]    I'll be sworn, I heard it.
MAM. I know not how! It is not any one,
    But e'en the very choice of all their
    features.
FACE. [*Aside.*] I'll in, and laugh. [*Exit.*]
MAM.          A certain touch, or air,
That sparkles a divinity beyond
An earthly beauty!
DOLL.        O, you play the courtier.
MAM. Good lady, gi' me leave—
DOLL.          In faith, I may not,
To mock me, sir.
MAM.        To burn i' this sweet flame;
The phœnix never knew a nobler death.
DOLL. Nay, now you court the courtier,
    and destroy                                  70
What you would build. This art, sir,
    i' your words,
Calls your whole faith in question.
MAM.            By my soul—
DOLL. Nay, oaths are made o' the same
    air, sir.
MAM.       Nature
Never bestowed upon mortality
A more unblamed, [6] a more harmonious
    feature;
She played the stepdame in all faces else.
Sweet madam, le' me be particular—
DOLL. Particular, [7] sir? I pray you, know
    your distance.
MAM. In no ill sense, sweet lady, but to
    ask
How your fair graces pass the hours.
    I see                                        80
Yo' are lodged here i' the house of a rare
    man,
An excellent artist—but what's that
    to you?
DOLL. Yes, sir; I study here the mathe-
    matics,
And distillation.
MAM.          O, I cry your pardon.
H' is a divine instructor, can extract
The souls of all things by his art, call all

---

[1] Lie with.                [3] Lain.
[2] Prostitute.          [4] Austrian.
[5] Apple seller.         [7] Personal.
[6] Unblemished.

The virtues and the miracles of the sun
Into a temperate fornace, teach dull na-
   ture
What her own forces are—a man the
   emp'ror
Has courted above Kelly,[1] sent his
   medals                90
And chains t' invite him.
DOLL.        Ay, and for his physic, sir—
MAM. Above the art of Esculapius,
That drew the envy of the Thunderer!
I know all this, and more.
DOLL.         Troth, I am taken, sir,
Whole with these studies that con-
   template nature.
MAM. It is a noble humor; but this form
Was not intended to so dark a use.
Had you been crooked, foul, of some
   coarse mold,
A cloister had done well; but such a
   feature,
That might stand up the glory of a
   kingdom,             100
To live recluse is a mere solecism,
Though in a nunnery. It must not be.
I muse [2] my lord your brother will per-
   mit it!
You should spend half my land first,
   were I he.
Does not this diamant better on my
   finger
Than i' the quarry?
DOLL.   Yes.
MAM.         Why, you are like it.
You were created, lady, for the light.
Here, you shall wear it; take it, the first
   pledge
Of what I speak, to bind you to believe
   me.
DOLL. In chains of adamant?
MAM.    Yes, the strongest bands.  110
And take a secret too—here, by your
   side,
Doth stand this hour the happiest man
   in Europe.
DOLL. You are contented, sir?
MAM.        Nay, in true being,
The envy of princes and the fear of
   states.
DOLL. Say you so, Sir Epicure?
MAM.   Yes, and thou shalt prove it,
Daughter of honor. I have cast mine
   eye

Upon thy form, and I will rear this
   beauty
Above all styles.
DOLL.      You mean no treason, sir?
MAM. No, I will take away that jealousy.[3]
I am the lord of the *philosophers' stone*,
And thou the lady.
DOLL.   How, sir! Ha' you that?  121
MAM. I am the master of the *maistry*.
This day the good old wretch here o'
   the house
Has made it for us; now he's at *projec-
   tion*.
Think therefore thy first wish now; let
   me hear it,
And it shall rain into thy lap—no shower,
But floods of gold, whole cataracts, a
   deluge,
To get a nation on thee.
DOLL.        You are pleased, sir,
To work on the ambition of our sex.
MAM. I am pleased the glory of her sex
   should know           130
This nook here of the Friars is no climate
For her to live obscurely in, to learn
Physic and surgery for the constable's
   wife
Of some odd hundred [4] in Essex; but
   come forth,
And taste the air of palaces; eat, drink
The toils of emp'rics,[5] and their boasted
   practice—
Tincture of pearl and coral, gold and
   amber;
Be seen at feasts and triumphs;[6] have
   it asked
What miracle she is; set all the eyes
Of court afire, like a burning glass,  140
And work hem into cinders, when the
   jewels
Of twenty states adorn thee, and the
   light
Strikes out the stars that,[7] when thy
   name is mentioned,
Queens may look pale, and, we but show-
   ing our love,
Nero's Poppæa may be lost in story!
Thus will we have it.
DOLL.      I could well consent, sir.
But in a monarchy how will this be?

---

[1] The partner of Dee.    [2] Am astonished.
[3] Suspicion.
[4] A division of a county.
[5] The results of the toil of experimenters.
[6] Festivities.             [7] So that.

The prince will soon take notice, and
    both seize
You and your *stone*, it being a wealth
    unfit
For any private subject.
MAM.                            If he knew it.    150
DOLL. Yourself do boast it, sir.
MAM.                            To thee, my life.
DOLL. O, but beware, sir! You may come
    to end
The remnant of your days in a loathed
    prison
By speaking of it.
MAM.                        'Tis no idle fear.
We'll therefore go with all, my girl, and
    live
In a free state, where we will eat our
    mullets,
Soused in high-country wines, sup pheas-
    ants' eggs,
And have our cockles boiled in silver
    shells,
Our shrimps to swim again, as when
    they lived,
In a rare butter made of dolphins'
    milk,                              160
Whose cream does look like opals, and
    with these
Delicate meats set ourselves high for
    pleasure,
And take us down again, and then renew
Our youth and strength with drinking
    the *elixir*,
And so enjoy a perpetuity
Of life and lust! And thou shalt ha'
    thy wardrobe
Richer than Nature's, still to change
    thyself,
And vary oft'ner, for thy pride, than
    she,
Or Art, her wise and almost equal serv-
    ant.

[*Enter Face.*]

FACE. Sir, you are too loud. I hear you
    every word                        170
Into the laboratory. Some fitter place;
The garden, or great chamber above.—
    [*Aside.*] How like you her?
MAM. [*Aside.*] Excellent, Lungs. There's
    for thee.              [*Gives him money.*]
FACE. [*Aside.*]      But do you hear?
Good sir, beware, no mention of the
    rabbins.

MAM. [*Aside.*] We think not on hem.
FACE.          O, it is well, sir.—[*Exeunt
Mammon and Doll.*] Subtle!

ACT IV. SCENE ii.

[*The same.*]

*Face, Subtle, Kastril, Dame Pliant.*[1]

[FACE.] Dost thou not laugh?
SUB.                    Yes. Are they gone?
FACE.                        All's clear.
SUB. The widow is come.
FACE.        And your quarreling disciple?
SUB. Ay.
FACE.        I must to my captainship again
    then.
SUB. Stay, bring hem in first.
FACE.            So I meant. What is she?
    A bonnibel?[2]
SUB.              I know not.
FACE.                    We'll draw lots.
You'll stand to that?
SUB.              What else?
FACE.                    O, for a suit,
To fall now like a cortine[3]— flap!
SUB.                    To th' door, man.
FACE You'll ha' the first kiss, cause[4] I
    am not ready.                    [*Exit.*]
SUB. Yes, and perhaps hit you through
    both the nostrils.[5]
FACE. [*Within.*] Who would you speak
    with?
KAS. [*Within.*]        Where's the captain?
FACE. [*Within.*]            Gone, sir,    10
    About some business.
KAS. [*Within.*]      Gone?
FACE. [*Within.*]          He'll return straight.
But Master Doctor, his lieutenant, is
    here.

[*Enter Kastril and Dame Pliant.*]

SUB. Come near, my worshipful boy, my
    *terræ fili,*
That is, my boy of land; make thy ap-
    proaches.
Welcome. I know thy lusts and thy de-
    sires,
And I will serve and satisfy hem. Begin;

[1] Last two enter later.        [3] Curtain.
[2] Bonne et belle; fair lass.    [4] Because.
[5] "Put your nose out of joint."

Charge me from thence, or thence, or
    in this line.
Here is my center; ground thy quarrel.
KAS.                              You lie!
SUB.  How, child of wrath and anger! The
    loud lie?
For what, my sudden boy?
KAS.            Nay, that look you to;  20
    I am aforehand.
SUB.            O, this 's no true grammar,
    And as ill logic! You must render causes,[1]
        child,
    Your first and second intentions, know
        your canons
    And your divisions, moods, degrees, and
        differences,
    Your predicaments, substance, and ac-
        cident,
    Series extern and intern, with their
        causes,
    Efficient, material, formal, final,
    And ha' your elements perfect.
KAS.                       What is this?
    The angry [2] tongue he talks in?
SUB.                    That false precept
    Of being aforehand has deceived a
        number,                            30
    And made hem enter quarrels often-
        times
    Before they were aware, and afterward
    Against their wills.
KAS.            How must I do then, sir?
SUB.  I cry this lady mercy; she should
        first
    Have been saluted.  I do call you lady,
    Because you are to be one ere 't be long,
                            *He kisses her.*
    My soft and buxom widow.
KAS.                    Is she, i' faith?
SUB.  Yes, or my art is an egregious liar.
KAS.  How know you?
SUB.            By inspection on her forehead,
    And subtlety of her lip, which must be
        tasted                            40
    Often to make a judgment.  (*He kisses
        her again.*)—[*Aside.*] 'Slight, she melts
    Like a myrobalan![3]— Here is yet a line
    In *rivo frontis* [4] tells me he is no knight.
PLI.  What is he then, sir?
SUB.            Let me see your hand.

O, your *linea Fortunæ* [5] makes it plain,
And *stella* [6] here in *monte Veneris*,[7]
But, most of all, *junctura annularis*.[8]
He is a soldier, or a man of art, lady,
But shall have some great honor shortly.
PLI.                            Brother,
He's a rare man, believe me!

[*Enter Face, in his uniform.*]

KAS.                    Hold your peace!  50
Here comes the tother rare man.—Save
    you, captain.
FACE.  Good Master Kastril!  Is this your
    sister?
KAS.            Ay, sir.
Please you to kuss [9] her, and be proud
    to know her?
FACE.  I shall be proud to know you, lady.
                            [*Kisses her.*]
PLI.                            Brother,
    He calls me lady, too.
KAS.            Ay, peace.  I heard it.
FACE.  [*Taking Subtle aside.*]  The count is
    come.
SUB.            Where is he?
FACE.                    At the door.
SUB.  Why, you must entertain him.
FACE.                    What'll you do
    With these the while?
SUB.  Why, have hem up, and show hem
    Some fustian book, or the dark glass.[10]
FACE.                            Fore God,
    She is a delicate dabchick! [11]  I must have
        her.                        [*Exit.*]  60
SUB.  [*Aside.*]  Must you?    Ay, if your
    fortune will, you must.—
    Come, sir, the captain will come to us
        presently.
I'll ha' you to my chamber of demon-
    strations,
Where I'll show you both the grammar
    and logic
And rhetoric of quarreling; my whole
    method
Drawn out in tables; and my instrument
That hath the several scale[12] upon 't
    shall make you
Able to quarrel at a straw's breadth by
    moonlight.

---

[1] The following terms are from scholastic logic.
[2] Quarrel-provoking.
[3] A kind of dried plum.
[4] The vein of the forehead.
[5] Line of Fortune.        [6] The star.
[7] Mount of Venus.    [8] The ring joint.    [9] Kiss.
[10] Polished black stone into which astrologers
gazed.
[11] Water hen.        [12] With various divisions.

And, lady, I'll have you look in a glass,
Some half an hour, but to clear your
eyesight                                    70
Against you see [1] your fortune, which
is greater
Than I may judge upon the sudden,
trust me.                       [*Exeunt.*]


Act IV. Scene iii.

[*The same.*]

*Face, Subtle, Surly.* [2]

[Face.] Where are you, doctor?
Sub. [*Within.*]            I'll come to you
presently.
Face. I will ha' this same widow, now I
ha' seen her,
On any composition. [3]


[*Enter Subtle.*]

Sub.                    What do you say?
Face. Ha' you disposed of them?
Sub.                    I ha' sent hem up.
Face. Subtle, in troth, I needs must have
this widow.
Sub. Is that the matter?
Face.                    Nay, but hear me.
Sub.                    Go to!
If you rebel once, Doll shall know it
all;
Therefore be quiet, and obey your
chance.
Face. Nay, thou art so violent now. Do
but conceive:
Thou art old, and canst not serve—
Sub.               Who cannot? I? 10
'Slight, I will serve her with thee, for a—
Face.                    Nay,
But understand; I'll gi' you composi-
tion.
Sub. I will not treat with thee. What!
Sell my fortune?
'Tis better than my birthright. Do not
murmur.
Win her, and carry her. If you grumble,
Doll
Knows it directly.
Face.               Well, sir, I am silent.
Will you go help to fetch in Don in state?

Sub. I follow you, sir.—[*Exit Face.*] We
must keep Face in awe,
Or he will overlook [4] us like a tyran. [5]


[*Enter Face with*] *Surly like a Spaniard.*

Brain of a tailor! Who comes here?
Don John!                       20
Sur. *Senores, beso las manos á vuestras
mercedes.* [6]
Sub. Would you had stooped a little, and
kissed our *anos.*
Face. Peace, Subtle!
Sub.        Stab me; I shall never hold, man.
He looks in that deep ruff like a head in
a platter,
Served in by a short cloak upon two
trestles. [7]
Face. Or what do you say to a collar of
brawn, [8] cut down
Beneath the souse, [9] and wriggled [10]
with a knife?
Sub. 'Slud, [11] he does look too fat to be a
Spaniard.
Face. Perhaps some Fleming or some
Hollander got him
In d'Alva's time—Count Egmont's bas-
tard.
Sub.        Don,                       30
Your scurvy, yellow, Madrid face is
welcome.
Sur. *Gratia.* [12]
Sub.        He speaks out of a fortification.
Pray God he ha' no squibs in those deep
sets. [13]
Sur. *Por dios, senores, muy linda casa!* [14]
Sub. What says he?
Face.               Praises the house, I think;
I know no more but's action.
Sub.                    Yes, the *casa,*
My precious Diego, will prove fair
enough
To cozen you in. Do you mark? You
shall
Be cozened, Diego.

[4] Domineer over.
[5] Tyrant.
[6] Gentlemen, I kiss your worships' hands.
[7] Stilts.
[8] Roll of boar's flesh.
[9] Ear.
[10] Cut into wrinkles, like a ruff.
[11] God's Lord, a mild oath.
[12] Thanks.
[13] Plaits of the ruff.
[14] By Jove, sirs, a very fine house!

[1] In preparation for seeing.
[2] Last two enter later.
[3] Terms.

Face. Cozened, do you see,
My worthy Donzel,[1] cozened.

Sur. *Entiendo.*[2] 40

Sub. Do you intend it? So do we, dear
Don.
Have you brought pistolets or porta-
gues,[3]
My solemn Don?—(*He [, i.e., Face,] feels
his pockets.*) Dost thou feel any?

Face. Full.

Sub. You shall be emptied, Don, pumped
and drawn
Dry, as they say.

Face. Milked, in troth, sweet Don.

Sub. See all the monsters[4]—the great
lion of all, Don.

Sur. *Con licencia, se puede ver á esta senora?* [5]

Sub. What talks he now?

Face. O' the *senora*.

Sub. O, Don,
That is the lioness, which you shall see
Also, my Don.

Face. 'Slid, Subtle, how shall we do? 50

Sub. For what?

Face. Why, Doll's employed, you know.

Sub. That's true.
Fore heav'n, I know not. He must stay,
that's all.

Face. Stay? That he must not, by no
means.

Sub. No? Why?

Face. Unless you'll mar all. 'Slight, he'll
suspect it;
And then he will not pay, not half so
well.
This is a traveled punk-master, and
does know
All the delays—a notable hot rascal,
And looks already rampant.

Sub. 'Sdeath, and Mammon
Must not be troubled.

Face. Mammon, in no case!

Sub. What shall we do then?

Face. Think; you must be sudden. 60

Sur. *Entiendo que la senora es tan hermosa,
que codicio tan
Á verla como la bien aventuranza de mi
vida.*[6]

Face. *Mi vida?* 'Slid, Subtle, he puts me
in mind o' the widow.
What dost thou say to draw her to 't—
ha!—
And tell her it is her fortune? All our
venter
Now lies upon 't. It is but one man
more,
Which on 's chance[7] to have her; and
beside,
There is no maidenhead to be feared
or lost.
What dost thou think on 't, Subtle?

Sub. Who, I? Why—

Face. The credit of our house too is engaged. 70

Sub. You made me an offer for my share
erewhile.
What wilt thou gi' me, i' faith?

Face. O, by that light,
I'll not buy now. You know your doom[8]
to me.
E'en take your lot; obey your chance,
sir; win her,
And wear her—out for me.

Sub. 'Slight, I'll not work her then.

Face. It is the common cause; therefore
bethink you.
Doll else must know it, as you said.

Sub. I care not.

Sur. *Senores, porque se tarda tanta?* [9]

Sub. Faith, I am not fit; I am old.

Face. That's now no reason, sir.

Sur. *Puede ser de hazer burla de mi
amor?* [10] 80

Face. You hear the Don too? By this air
I call,
And loose the hinges—Doll!

Sub. A plague of hell—

Face. Will you then do?

Sub. Yo' are a terrible rogue!
I'll think of this. Will you, sir, call the
widow?

Face. Yes, and I'll take her too with all
her faults,
Now I do think on 't better.

Sub. With all my heart, sir.
Am I discharged o' the lot?

Face. As you please.

Sub. Hands. [*They shake hands.*]

---

[1] Little Don.
[2] I understand.
[3] Gold coins.
[4] *I.e.*, see the sights.
[5] By your leave, may I see this lady?
[6] I understand that the lady is so beautiful that I desire to see her as much as the good fortune of my life.
[7] Whichever of us should chance.
[8] Decision.
[9] Sirs, why so much delay?
[10] Can it be you are making a jest of my love?

FACE. Remember now, that upon any change
You never claim her.
SUB.    Much good joy and health to you, sir.
Marry a whore?  Fate, let me wed a witch first.                        90
SUR. *Por estas honradas barbas* [1]—
SUB.            He swears by his beard.
Despatch, and call the brother too.
                                        [*Exit Face.*]
SUR. *Tengo duda, senores, que no me hagan alguna traycion.* [2]
SUB. How, *issue on?* Yes, *præsto, senor.* [3]
Please you
*Enthratha* the *chambratha*, worthy Don,
Where, if it please the Fates, in your *bathada*,
You shall be soaked, and stroked, and tubbed, and rubbed,
And scrubbed, and fubbed, [4] dear Don, before you go.
You shall, in faith, my scurvy babion [5] Don,
Be curried, clawed, and flawed, [6] and tawed, [7] indeed.                100
I will the heartlier go about it now,
And make the widow a punk so much the sooner,
To be revenged on this impetuous Face;
The quickly doing of it is the grace.
                                        [*Exeunt.*]

ACT IV. SCENE iv.

[*Another room in the same.*]

*Face, Kastril, Da[me] Pliant, Subtle, Surly.* [8]

[FACE.] Come, lady.  I knew the doctor would not leave
Till he had found the very nick of her fortune.
KAS. To be a countess, say you?
[FACE.] [9]        A Spanish countess, sir.
PLI. Why, is that better than an English countess?
FACE. Better?  'Slight, make you that a question, lady?

KAS. Nay, she is a fool, captain; you must pardon her.
FACE. Ask from your courtier to your Inns of Court man,
To your mere milaner; [10] they will tell you all
Your Spanish jennet is the best horse; your Spanish
Stoop is the best garb; [11] your Spanish beard                        10
Is the best cut; your Spanish ruffs are the best
Wear; your Spanish pavin the best dance;
Your Spanish titillation in a glove
The best perfume; and for your Spanish pike,
And Spanish blade, let your poor captain speak.—
Here comes the doctor.

[*Enter Subtle with a paper.*]

SUB.            My most honored lady,
For so I am now to style you, having found,
By this my scheme, [12] you are to undergo
An honorable fortune very shortly,
What will you say now, if some—
FACE.            I ha' told her all, sir,   20
And her right worshipful brother here, that she shall be
A countess; do not delay hem, sir.  A Spanish countess!
SUB. Still, my scarce-worshipful captain, you can keep
No secret! Well, since he has told you, madam,
Do you forgive him, and I do.
KAS.            She shall do that, sir.
I'll look to 't; 'tis my charge.
SUB.            Well then, naught rests
But that she fit her love now to her fortune.
PLI. Truly, I shall never brook a Spaniard.
SUB.                        No?
PLI. Never sin' eighty-eight [13] could I abide hem,
And that was some three year afore I was born, in truth.                30

[1] By these honored hairs—
[2] I fear, sirs, that you are playing me some trick.
[3] Quickly, sir.        [5] Baboon.
[4] Cheated.        [6] Flayed.
[7] Soaked in preparation for tanning.
[8] Last two enter later.
[9] From 1612 edn.

[10] Milliner, dealer in fancy articles.
[11] Bearing.
[12] Horoscope.
[13] 1588, the date of the destruction of the Armada.

Sub. Come, you must love him, or be miserable;
Choose which you will.

Face.      By this good rush, persuade her,
She will cry[1] strawberries else within this twelvemonth.

Sub. Nay, shads and mack'rel, which is worse.

Face.      Indeed, sir?

Kas. God's lid, you shall love him, or I'll kick you.

Pli.      Why,
I'll do as you will ha' me, brother.

Kas.                              Do,
Or by this hand I'll maul you.

Face.                    Nay, good sir,
Be not so fierce.

Sub.            No, my enragéd child;
She will be ruled. What, when she comes to taste
The pleasures of a countess! To be courted—                            40

Face. And kissed and ruffled!

Sub.            Ay, behind the hangings.

Face. And then come forth in pomp!

Sub.                        And know her state!

Face. Of keeping all th' idolators o' the chamber
Barer to her than at their prayers!

Sub.                        Is served
Upon the knee!

Face.      And has her pages, huishers,[2]
Footmen, and coaches—

Sub.            Her six mares—

Face.                        Nay, eight!

Sub. To hurry her through London to th' Exchange,[3]
Bet'lem,[4] the China-houses[5]—

Face.                  Yes, and have
The citizens gape at her, and praise her tires,
And my lord's goose-turd bands,[6] that rides with her!                          50

Kas. Most brave![7] By this hand, you are not my suster
If you refuse.

Pli.      I will not refuse, brother.

---

[1] Hawk on the street.
[2] Ushers.
[3] Where shops were located.
[4] Bethlehem Hospital, where people visited the insane for amusement.
[5] Where ware from China was shown.
[6] Green-colored collars.
[7] Fine.

*[Enter Surly.]*

Sur. *Que es esto, senores, que non se venga? Esta tardanza me mata!* [8]

Face.            It is the count come;
The doctor knew he would be here, by his art.

Sub. *En gallanta madama, Don, gallantissima!*

Sur. *Por todos los dioses, la mas acabada Hermosura, que he visto en mi vida!* [9]

Face. Is 't not a gallant language that they speak?

Kas. An admirable language! Is 't not French?                            60

Face. No, Spanish, sir.

Kas.            It goes like law French,
And that, they say, is the court-liest language.

Face.            List, sir.

Sur. *El sol ha perdido su lumbre, con el Resplandor que træ esta dama! Valgame dios!* [10]

Face. He admires your sister.

Kas.            Must not she make court'sy?

Sub. 'Od's will, she must go to him, man, and kiss him!
It is the Spanish fashion for the women
To make first court.

Face.            'Tis true he tells you, sir;
His art knows all.

Sur.            *Porque no se acude?* [11]

Kas. He speaks to her, I think?

Face.            That he does, sir.  70

Sur. *Por el amor de dios, que es esto que se tarda?* [12]

Kas. Nay, see; she will not understand him!—Gull!
Noddy!

Pli.      What say you, brother?

Kas.                  Ass, my suster,
Go kuss him, as the cunning man would ha' you;
I'll thrust a pin i' your buttocks else.

Face.                  O, no, sir.

---

[8] What's the matter, sirs, that nobody comes? This delay is killing me.
[9] By all the gods, the most finished beauty that I have seen in my life.
[10] The sun has lost his light in comparison with the splendor which this lady brings! God bless me!
[11] Why don't you draw near?
[12] For the love of God, why this delay?

Sur. *Senora mia, mi persona muy indigna esta*
*Á llegar á tanta hermosura.*[1] [*Kisses her.*]
Face. Does he not use her bravely?
Kas.                          Bravely, i' faith!
Face. Nay, he will use her better.
Kas.                          Do you think so?
Sur. *Senora, si sera servida, entremos.*[2] 80
                          [*Exit with Dame Pliant.*]
Kas. Where does he carry her?
Face.                          Into the garden, sir.
    Take you no thought; I must interpret
    for her.
Sub. [*Aside to Face.*] Give Doll the word.—
                          [*Exit Face*].
    Come, my fierce child, advance;
    We'll to our quarreling lesson again.
Kas.                          Agreed.
    I love a Spanish boy with all my heart.
Sub. Nay, and by this means, sir, you shall
    be brother
    To a great count.
Kas.                    Ay, I knew that at first.
    This match will advance the house of
    the Kastrils.
Sub. Pray God your sister prove but
    pliant!
Kas.          Why,
    Her name is so, by her other husband.
Sub.                          How! 90
Kas. The Widow Pliant. Knew you not
    that?
Sub.          No, faith, sir;
    Yet, by erection of her figure,[3] I guessed it.
    Come, let's go practice.
Kas.          Yes, but do you think, doctor,
    I e'er shall quarrel well?
Sub.                          I warrant you. [*Exeunt.*]

### Act IV. Scene v.

[*Another room in the same.*]

*Doll, Mammon, Face, Subtle.*[4]

[Doll.] (*In her fit of talking.*) For after
    Alexander's death [5]—
Mam.                          Good lady—

Doll. That Perdiccas and Antigonus were
    slain,
    The two that stood, Seleuc' and Ptol-
    omy—
Mam. Madam—
Doll.          Made up the two legs, and the
    fourth beast,
    That was Gog-north and Egypt-south,
    which after
    Was called Gog-iron-leg and South-iron-
    leg—
Mam.          Lady—
Doll. And then Gog-horned. So was
    Egypt, too.
    Then Egypt-clay-leg, and Gog-clay-leg—
Mam.                          Sweet madam –
Doll. And last Gog-dust, and Egypt-dust,
    which fall
    In the last link of the fourth chain. And
    these                          10
    Be stars in story, which none see, or look
    at—
Mam. What shall I do?
Doll.          For, as he says, except
    We call the rabbins and the heathen
    Greeks—
Mam. Dear lady—
Doll.          To come from Salem, and from
    Athens,
    And teach the people of Great Britain—

[*Enter Face, in his livery.*]

Face.                          What's the matter, sir?
Doll. To speak the tongue of Eber and
    Javan [6]—
Mam.                          O,
    Sh' is in her fit.
Doll.          We shall know nothing—
Face.                          Death, sir,
    We are undone!
Doll.          Where then a learned linguist
    Shall see the ancient used communion
    Of vowels and consonants—
Face.          My master will hear! 20
Doll. A wisdom which Pythagoras held
    most high—
Mam. Sweet honorable lady!
Doll.                          To comprise
    All sounds of voices, in few marks of
    letters—
Face. Nay, you must never hope to lay
    her now.          *They* [all] *speak together.*

---

[1] Madam, my person is entirely unworthy to
come near to such beauty.
[2] Madam, if you will, let us go in.
[3] Casting of her horoscope, with an obvious
double meaning.
[4] Last two enter later.
[5] The following speeches by Doll are inco-
herent extracts from Hugh Broughton's *Concent
of Scripture.*
[6] *I.e.*, of the Hebrews and the Greeks.

Doll. And so we may arrive by Talmud
    skill [1]
And profane Greek to raise the building
    up
Of Helen's house against the Ismaelite,
King of Thogarma, and his habergeons
Brimstony, blue, and fiery; and the force
Of King Abaddon, and the beast of
    Cittim,                        30
Which Rabbi David Kimchi, Onkelos,
And Aben Ezra do interpret Rome.

Face. How did you put her into 't?

Mam.                  Alas, I talked
Of a fift [2] monarchy I would erect
With the *philosophers' stone*, by chance,
    and she
Falls on the other four straight.

Face.            Out of Broughton!
I told you so. 'Slid, stop her mouth.

Mam.                  Is 't best?

Face. She'll never leave else. If the old
    man hear her,
We are but fæces, ashes.

Sub. [*Within.*]        What's to do there?

Face. O, we are lost! Now she hears him,
    she is quiet.                  40

Mam. Where shall I hide me?

Sub.          How! What sight is here?
        *Upon Subtle's entry they disperse.*
Close [3] deeds of darkness, and that shun
    the light!
Bring him again. Who is he? What, my
    son!
O, I have lived too long.

Mam.           Nay, good, dear father,
There was no unchaste purpose.

Sub.              Not? And flee me
When I come in?

Mam.          That was my error.

Sub.                   Error?
Guilt, guilt, my son; give it the right
    name. No marvel
If I found check in our *great work* within,
When such affairs as these were managing!

Mam. Why, have you so?

Sub.       It has stood still this half hour,
And all the rest of our *less works* gone
    back.                         51
Where is the instrument of wickedness,
My lewd, false drudge?

Mam.          Nay, good sir, blame not him;
Believe me, 'twas against his will or
    knowledge.
I saw her by chance.

Sub.          Will you commit more sin,
T' excuse a varlet?

Mam.          By my hope, 'tis true, sir.

Sub. Nay, then I wonder less, if you, for
    whom
The blessing was prepared, would so
    tempt heaven,
And lose your fortunes.

Mam.         Why, sir?

Sub.               This 'll retard
The *work* a month at least.

Mam.          Why, if it do,   60
What remedy? But think it not, good
    father.
Our purposes were honest. [4]

Sub.             As they were,
So the reward will prove. (*A great crack
    and noise within.*)—How now! Ay me!
God and all saints be good to us.—

[*Enter Face.*]

                         What's that?

Face. O, sir, we are defeated! All the
    *works*
Are flown *in fumo;* every glass is burst;
Fornace and all rent down, as if a bolt
Of thunder had been driven through the
    house.
*Retorts, receivers, pelicans, boltheads,*
All strook [5] in shivers!
         *Subtle falls down as in a swoon.*
               Help, good sir! Alas,   70
Coldness and death invades him. Nay,
    Sir Mammon,
Do the fair offices of a man! You stand,
As you were readier to depart than he.—
                     *One knocks.*
Who's there?—My lord her brother is
    come.

Mam.          Ha, Lungs?

Face. His coach is at the door. Avoid his
    sight,
For he's as furious as his sister is mad.

Mam. Alas!

Face.         My brain is quite undone with
    the fume, sir;
I ne'er must hope to be mine own man
    again.

---

[1] In the original this speech and the following
dialogue including Face's final speech are
printed in parallel columns.
[2] Fifth.                         [3] Secret.               [4] Chaste.               [5] Struck.

MAM. Is all lost, Lungs? Will nothing be preserved
Of all our cost?
FACE.         Faith, very little, sir;   80
A peck of coals or so, which is cold comfort, sir.
MAM. O, my voluptuous mind! I am justly punished.
FACE. And so am I, sir.
MAM.       Cast from all my hopes—
FACE. Nay, certainties, sir.
MAM.      By mine own base affections.
*Subtle seems come to himself.*
SUB. O, the cursed fruits of vice and lust!
MAM.          Good father,
It was my sin. Forgive it.
SUB.         Hangs my roof
Over us still, and will not fall, O justice,
Upon us for this wicked man?
FACE.         Nay, look, sir;
You grieve him now with staying in his sight.
Good sir, the nobleman will come too, and take you,   90
And that may breed a tragedy.
MAM.         I'll go.
FACE. Ay, and repent at home, sir. It may be
For some good penance you may ha' it yet;
A hundred pound to the box at Bet'lem—
MAM.           Yes.
FACE. For the restoring such as—ha' their wits.
MAM.    I'll do 't.
FACE. I'll send one to you to receive it.
MAM.            Do.
Is no *projection* left?
FACE.       All flown, or stinks, sir.
MAM. Will naught be saved that's good for *med'cine*, think'st thou?
FACE. I cannot tell, sir. There will be perhaps
Something about the scraping of the shards   100
Will cure the itch—[*Aside.*] though not your itch of mind, sir.—
It shall be saved for you, and sent home. Good sir,
This way, for fear the lord should meet you.     [*Exit Mammon.*]
SUB.    Face!
FACE. Ay.
SUB.    Is he gone?

FACE.           Yes, and as heavily
As all the gold he hoped for were in his blood.
Let us be light though.
SUB.         Ay, as balls, and bound
And hit our heads against the roof for joy;
There's so much of our care now cast away.
FACE. Now to our Don.
SUB.    Yes, your young widow by this time
Is made a countess, Face; sh' has been in travail   110
Of a young heir for you.
FACE.          Good, sir.
SUB.         Off with your case,[1]
And greet her kindly, as a bridegroom should,
After these common hazards.
FACE.         Very well, sir.
Will you go fetch Don Diego off the while?
SUB. And fetch him over too, if you'll be pleased, sir.
Would Doll were in her place, to pick his pockets now!
FACE. Why, you can do it as well, if you would set to 't.
I pray you, prove your virtue.[2]
SUB.     For your sake, sir.    [*Exeunt.*]

## ACT IV. SCENE vi.

[*Another room in the same.*]

*Surly, Da[me] Pliant, Subtle, Face.*[3]

[SUR.] Lady, you see into what hands you are fall'n,
'Mongst what a nest of villains, and how near
Your honor was t' have catched a certain clap,
Through your credulity, had I but been
So punctually forward, as place, time,
And other circumstance would ha' made a man;
For yo' are a handsome woman—would yo' were wise too!
I am a gentleman come here disguised,
Only to find the knaveries of this citadel·

---

[1] *I.e.,* his present costume.
[2] Power.
[3] Last two enter later.

And where I might have wronged your
    honor, and have not,         10
I claim some interest in your love.  You
    are,
They say, a widow, rich; and I'm a
    bachelor,
Worth naught; your fortunes may make
    me a man,
As mine ha' preserved you a woman.
    Think upon it,
And whether I have deserved you or no.
PLI.                  I will, sir.
SUR. And for these household-rogues, let
    me alone
To treat with them.

*[Enter Subtle.]*

SUB.          How doth my noble Diego,
And my dear madam countess? Hath the
    count                18
Been courteous, lady, liberal and open?
Donzel, methinks you look melancholic
After your *coitum*,[1] and scurvy! Truly,
I do not like the dullness of your eye;
It hath a heavy cast—'tis upsee Dutch,[2]
And says you are a lumpish whoremaster.
Be lighter; I will make your pockets so.
          *He falls to picking of them.*
SUR. [*Disclosing himself.*] Will you, Don
    bawd and pickpurse?  [*Beats him.*]
    How now? Reel you?
Stand up, sir; you shall find, since I am
    so heavy,
I'll gi' you equal weight.
SUB.          Help! Murder!
SUR.                No, sir,
There's no such thing intended.  A good
    cart[3]
And a clean whip shall ease you of that
    fear.                30
I am the Spanish Don that should be
    cozened,
Do you see?  Cozened?  Where's your
    Captain Face,
That parcel[4] broker, and whole bawd,
    all rascal?

*[Enter Face in his uniform.]*

FACE. How, Surly!
SUR.          O, make your approach,
    good captain.

I have found from whence your copper
    rings and spoons
Come now, wherewith you cheat abroad
    in taverns.
'Twas here you learned t' anoint your
    boot with brimstone,
Then rub men's gold on 't for a kind of
    touch,
And say, 'twas naught, when you had
    changed the color,
That you might ha't for nothing?  And
    this doctor,          40
Your sooty, smoky-bearded compeer,
    he
Will close you so much gold, in a *bolt's-
    head*,
And, on a turn, convey i' the stead an-
    other
With *sublimed mercury*, that shall burst
    i' the heat,
And fly out all *in fumo!*  Then weeps
    Mammon;
Then swoons his worship.  [*Exit Face.*]
    Or he is the Faustus,
That casteth figures and can conjure,
    cures
Plague, piles, and pox, by the ephemer-
    ides,[5]
And holds intelligence with all the bawds
And midwives of three shires, while you
    send in            50
(Captain!—What!  Is he gone?) damsels
    with child,
Wives that are barren, or the waiting-
    maid
With the green sickness? [*Seizes Subtle
    as he attempts to escape.*]  Nay, sir,
    you must tarry,
Though he be scaped, and answer by the
    ears,[6] sir.

### ACT IV. SCENE vii.

*[The same.]*

*Face, Kastril, Surly, Subtle, Drugger,[7]
    Ananias,[7] Da[me] Pliant, Doll.[7]*

[FACE. (*To Kastril.*)] Why, now's the
    time, if ever you will quarrel
Well, as they say, and be a true-born
    child.
The doctor and your sister both are
    abused.

---

[1] Coition.      [2] In the Dutch fashion.
[3] Bawds were "carted" through the city as a
punishment.    [4] Partial, part.
[5] Astrological almanacs.    [7] Enters later.
[6] Referring to punishment in the pillory.

KAS. Where is he? Which is he? He is a slave,
Whate'er he is, and the son of a whore.—
Are you
The man, sir, I would know?

SUR. I should be loath, sir,
To confess so much.

KAS. Then you lie i' your throat.

SUR. How!

FACE. [To Kastril.] A very arrant rogue, sir, and a cheater,
Employed here by another conjurer
That does not love the doctor, and would cross him 10
If he knew how.

SUR. Sir, you are abused.

KAS. You lie—
And 'tis no matter.

FACE. Well said, sir! He is
The impudent'st rascal—

SUR. You are indeed. Will you hear me, sir?

FACE. By no means. Bid him be gone.

KAS. Begone, sir, quickly!

SUR. This 's strange!—Lady, do you inform your brother.
                    [Dame Pliant whispers to Kastril.]

FACE. There is not such a foist [1] in all the town.
The doctor had him [2] presently,[3] and finds yet
The Spanish count will come here.—
[Aside.] Bear up, Subtle.

SUB. Yes, sir, he must appear within this hour.

FACE. And yet this rogue would come in a disguise, 20
By the temptation of another spirit,
To trouble our art, though he could not hurt it!

KAS. Ay,
I know.—[To Pliant.] Away, you talk like a foolish mauther.[4]

SUR. Sir, all is truth she says.

FACE. Do not believe him, sir.
He is the lying'st swabber! Come your ways, sir.

SUR. You are valiant out of company!

KAS. Yes, how then, sir?

[Enter Drugger with a piece of cloth.]

FACE. Nay, here's an honest fellow too that knows him
And all his tricks. (Make good what I say, Abel.
This cheater would ha' cozened thee o' the widow.)
He owes this honest Drugger here seven pound 30
He has had [5] on him in twopenny'orths of tabacco.

DRUG. Yes, sir. And h' has damned himself [6] three terms to pay me.

FACE. And what does he owe for lotium? [7]

DRUG. Thirty shillings, sir;
And for six syringes.

SUR. Hydra of villainy!

FACE. [To Kastril.] Nay, sir, you must quarrel him out o' the house.

KAS. I will.—
Sir, if you get not out o' doors, you lie;
And you are a pimp.

SUR. Why, this is madness, sir,
Not valure in you; I must laugh at this.

KAS. It is my humor; you are a pimp and a trig,[8]
And an Amadis de Gaul, or a Don Quixote. 40

DRUG. Or a Knight o' the Curious Coxcomb, do you see?

[Enter Ananias.]

ANA. Peace to the household!

KAS. I'll keep peace for no man.

ANA. Casting of dollars is concluded lawful.

KAS. Is he the constable?

SUB. Peace, Ananias.

FACE. No, sir.

KAS. Then you are an otter, and a shad, a whit,
A very tim.[9]

SUR. You'll hear me, sir?

KAS. I will not.

ANA. What is the motive?

SUB. Zeal in the young gentleman
Against his Spanish slops—

ANA. They are profane,
Lewd, superstitious, and idolatrous breeches.

---

[1] Rogue.
[2] I.e., the count(?).
[3] In actual presence.
[4] Awkward girl.
[5] Charged.
[6] I.e., sworn.
[7] Lotion.
[8] Coxcomb.
[9] A term of abuse which has baffled the editors.

Sur. New rascals!

Kas.                    Will you be gone, sir?

Ana.                          Avoid, Sathan! 50
Thou art not of the light! That ruff of
    pride
About thy neck betrays thee, and is
    the same
With that which the unclean birds, in
    seventy-seven,[1]
Were seen to prank it with on divers
    coasts.
Thou look'st like antichrist, in that lewd
    hat.

Sur. I must give way.

Kas.                          Begone, sir.

Sur.                          But I'll take
A course with you—

Ana.          Depart, proud Spanish fiend!

Sur. Captain and doctor—

Ana.          Child of perdition!

Kas.                    Hence, sir!—[Exit Surly.]
Did I not quarrel bravely?

Face.                          Yes, indeed, sir.

Kas. Nay, and I give my mind to 't, I
    shall do 't.                          60

Face. O, you must follow, sir, and
    threaten him tame.
He'll turn again else.

Kas.          I'll re-turn him then. [Exit.]

Face. Drugger, this rogue prevented[2] us
    for thee;
We had determined that thou shouldst
    ha' come
In a Spanish suit, and ha' carried her so;
    and he,
A brokerly slave, goes, puts it on him-
    self.
Hast brought the damask?

Drug.          Yes, sir.

Face.                          Thou must borrow
A Spanish suit. Hast thou no credit
    with the players?

Drug. Yes, sir; did you never see me play
    the Fool?

Face. I know not, Nab.—[Aside.] Thou
    shalt, if I can help it.—              70
Hieronimo's[3] old cloak, ruff, and hat
    will serve;
I'll tell thee more when thou bring'st
    hem.                    [Exit Drugger]

[1] An occurrence in 1577 which has not been
explained.
[2] Forestalled.
[3] Referring to Kyd's Spanish Tragedy.

Ana. (Subtle hath whispered with him this
    while.)          Sir, I know
The Spaniard hates the Brethren, and
    hath spies
Upon their actions; and that this was
    one
I make no scruple.—But the holy Synod
Have been in prayer and meditation
    for it;
And 'tis revealed no less to them than me
That casting of money is most lawful.

Sub.                          True.
But here I cannot do it; if the house
Should chance to be suspected, all
    would out,                          80
And we be locked up in the Tower for-
    ever,
To make gold there for th' state, never
    come out;
And then are you defeated.

Ana.                          I will tell
This to the elders and the weaker
    Brethren,
That the whole company of the sepa-
    ration
May join in humble prayer again.

(Sub.                          And fasting.)

Ana. Yea, for some fitter place. The peace
    of mind
Rest with these walls!

Sub.          Thanks, courteous Ananias.
                              [Exit Ananias.]

Face. What did he come for?

Sub.                          About casting dollars,
Presently out of hand. And so I told
    him                                  90
A Spanish minister came here to spy
Against the faithful—

Face.          I conceive. Come, Subtle,
Thou art so down upon the least disaster!
How wouldst thou ha' done, if I had not
    helped thee out?

Sub. I thank thee, Face, for the angry
    boy, i' faith.

Face. Who would ha' looked[4] it should
    ha' been that rascal
Surly? He had dyed his beard and all.
    Well, sir,
Here's damask come to make you a suit.

Sub.                          Where's Drugger?

Face. He is gone to borrow me a Spanish
    habit;
I'll be the count now.

[4] Expected.

SUB.          But where's the widow?  100
FACE. Within, with my lord's sister;
    Madam Doll
  Is entertaining her.
SUB.          By your favor, Face,
  Now she is honest, I will stand again.
FACE. You will not offer it?
SUB.          Why?
FACE.          Stand to your word,
  Or—here comes Doll.  She knows—
SUB.          Yo' are tyrannous still.
FACE. Strict for my right.—

*[Enter Doll.]*

          How now, Doll?  Hast told her
  The Spanish count will come?
DOLL.          Yes; but another is come
  You little looked for!
FACE.          Who's that?
DOLL.          Your master;
  The master of the house.
SUB.          How, Doll!
FACE.          She lies.
  This is some trick.  Come, leave your
    quiblins,[1] Dorothy.          110
DOLL. Look out and see.
          *[Face goes to the window.]*
SUB.          Art thou in earnest?
DOLL.          'Slight,
  Forty o' the neighbors are about him,
    talking.
FACE. 'Tis he, by this good day.
DOLL.          'Twill prove ill day
  For some on us.
FACE.  We are undone, and taken.
DOLL. Lost, I am afraid.
SUB.          You said he would not come,
  While there died one a week within the
    liberties.[2]
FACE. No; 'twas within the walls.
SUB.          Was 't so?  Cry you mercy.
  I thought the liberties.  What shall we
    do now, Face?
FACE. Be silent; not a word, if he call or
    knock.
  I'll into mine old shape again, and meet
    him,          120
  Of Jeremy, the butler.  I' the meantime,
  Do you two pack up all the goods and
    purchase [3]

[1] Quibbles, equivocations.
[2] Slum district just outside the walls of the
city.
[3] Plunder, booty.

That we can carry i' the two trunks
    I'll keep him
Off for today, if I cannot longer; and
    then
At night I'll ship you both away to
    Ratcliff,
Where we'll meet tomorrow, and there
    we'll share.
Let Mammon's brass and pewter keep
    the cellar;
We'll have another time for that.  But,
    Doll,
Pray thee, go heat a little water quickly;
Subtle must shave me.  All my captain's
    beard          130
Must off, to make me appear smooth
    Jeremy.
You'll do 't?
SUB.          Yes, I'll shave you as well as
  I can.
FACE. And not cut my throat, but trim
  me?
SUB.          You shall see, sir.          *[Exeunt.]*

ACT V.  SCENE i.

*[The street before Lovewit's house.]*
*Lovewit, Neighbors.*

[LOVE.] Has there been such resort, say
    you?
NEI. 1.  Daily, sir.
NEI. 2. And nightly, too.
NEI. 3.          Ay, some as brave as lords.
NEI. 4. Ladies and gentlewomen.
NEI. 5.          Citizens' wives.
NEI. 1. And knights.
NEI. 6.  In coaches.
NEI. 2.          Yes, and oyster women.
NEI. 1. Beside other gallants.
NEI. 3.          Sailors' wives.
NEI. 4.          Tabacco men.
NEI. 5. Another Pimlico! [4]
LOVE.  What should my knave advance
  To draw this company?  He hung out
    no banners
  Of a strange calf with five legs to be seen,
  Or a huge lobster with six claws?
NEI. 6.          No, sir.
NEI. 3. We had gone in then, sir.
LOVE.          He has no gift  10
  Of teaching i' the nose [5] that e'er I
    knew of.

[4] A popular summer resort.
[5] *I.e.*, like a Puritan.

You saw no bills set up that promised
cure
Of agues or the toothache?

NEI. 2.           No such thing, sir!

LOVE. Nor heard a drum strook for
babions or puppets?

NEI. 5. Neither, sir.

LOVE.       What device should he bring
forth now?
I love a teeming wit as I love my nour-
ishment.
Pray God he ha' not kept such open
house
That he hath sold my hangings and my
bedding!
I left him nothing else. If he have
eat hem,
A plague o' the moth, say I! Sure he
has got           20
Some bawdy pictures to call all this
ging: [1]
The Friar and the Nun; or the new
motion [2]
Of the knight's courser covering the
parson's mare;
The boy of six year old with the great
thing.
Or 't may be he has the fleas that run
at tilt
Upon a table, or some dog to dance?
When saw you him?

NEI. 1.         Who, sir, Jeremy?

NEI. 2.         Jeremy butler?
We saw him not this month.

LOVE.     How!

NEI. 4.        Not these five weeks, sir.

NEI. [6.] [3] These six weeks, at the least.

LOVE.       Yo' amaze me, neighbors!

NEI. 5. Sure, if your worship know not
where he is,         30
He's slipped away.

NEI. 6.   Pray God he be not made away.
                      *He knocks.*

LOVE. Ha! It's no time to question, then.

NEI. 6.            About
Some three weeks since I heard a doleful cry,
As I sat up a-mending my wife's stockings.

LOVE. This 's strange that none will
answer! Didst thou hear
A cry, say'st thou?

NEI. 6.          Yes, sir, like unto a man
That had been strangled an hour, and
could not speak.

NEI. 2. I heard it, too, just this day three
  weeks, at two a-clock
Next morning.

LOVE.     These be miracles, or you make
hem so!
A man an hour strangled, and could
not speak,          40
And both you heard him cry?

NEI. 3.         Yes, downward,[4] sir.

LOVE. Thou art a wise fellow. Give me
thy hand, I pray thee.
What trade art thou on?

NEI. 3.       A smith and 't please your
worship.

LOVE. A smith? Then lend me thy help
to get this door open.

NEI. 3. That I will presently, sir; but
fetch my tools—        *[Exit.]*

NEI. 1. Sir, best to knock again afore
you break it.

## ACT V. SCENE ii.

### [*The same.*]

*Lovewit, Face, Neighbors.*

[LOVE. (*Knocking again.*)] I will.

### [*Enter Face dressed as a butler.*]

FACE.         What mean you, sir?

NEI. 1, 2, 4.        O, here's Jeremy!

FACE. Good sir, come from the door.

LOVE.        Why, what's the matter?

FACE. Yet farder;[5] you are too near yet.

LOVE.        I' the name of wonder,
What means the fellow?

FACE.     The house, sir, has been visited.

LOVE. What, with the plague? Stand thou
then farder.

FACE.          No, sir,
I had it not.

LOVE.       Who had it then? I left
None else but thee i' the house.

FACE.         Yes, sir, my fellow,
The cat that kept [6] the butt'ry, had it
on her
A week before I spied it; but I got her

---

[1] Gang.
[2] Puppet show.
[3] From 1640 edn.
[4] Hathaway suggests that this is a slang term
of negation.
[5] Farther.
[6] Guarded.

Conveyed away i' the night. And so I
shut                                    10
The house up for a month—
LOVE.                    How!
FACE.                    Purposing then, sir,
T' have burnt rose-vinegar, treacle, and
tar,
And ha' made it sweet, that you should
ne'er ha' known it,
Because I knew the news would but
afflict you, sir.
LOVE. Breathe less, and farder off! Why,
this is stranger!
The neighbors tell me all here that the
doors
Have still been open—
FACE.        How, sir!
LOVE.                Gallants, men and women,
And of all sorts, tag-rag, been seen to
flock here
In threaves [1] these ten weeks, as to a
second Hogsden,
In days of Pimlico and Eye-bright.[2]
FACE.                        Sir,    20
Their wisdoms will not say so.
LOVE.                    Today they speak
Of coaches and gallants; one in a French
hood
Went in, they tell me; and another
was seen
In a velvet gown at the windore;[3]
divers more
Pass in and out.
FACE.        They did pass through the doors
then,
Or walls, I assure their eyesights and
their spectacles;
For here, sir, are the keys, and here
have been,
In this my pocket, now above twenty
days!
And for before, I kept the fort alone
there.
But that 'tis yet not deep i' the after-
noon,                                    30
I should believe my neighbors had seen
double
Through the black pot, and made these
apparitions!
For, on my faith to your worship, for
these three weeks
And upwards, the door has not been
opened.

[1] Droves.        [2] A tavern.        [3] Window.

LOVE.            Strange!
NEI. 1. Good faith, I think I saw a coach.
NEI. 2.                        And I too,
I'ld ha' been sworn.
LOVE.            Do you but think it now?
And but one coach?
NEI. 4.            We cannot tell, sir; Jeremy
Is a very honest fellow.
FACE.            Did you see me at all?
NEI. 1. No; that we are sure on.
NEI. 2.            I'll be sworn o' that.
LOVE. Fine rogues to have your testi-
monies built on!                        40

[*Enter Third Neighbor, with his tools.*]

NEI. 3. Is Jeremy come?
NEI. 1.            O, yes; you may leave your
tools;
We were deceived, he says.
NEI. 2.            He has had the keys,
And the door has been shut these three
weeks.
NEI. 3.        Like enough!
LOVE. Peace, and get hence, you change-
lings.

[*Enter Surly and Mammon.*]

FACE. [*Aside.*]        Surly come!
And Mammon made acquainted! They'll
tell all.
How shall I beat them off? What shall
I do?
Nothing's more wretched than a guilty
conscience.

ACT V. SCENE iii.

[*The same.*]

*Surly, Mammon, Lovewit, Face, Neigh-
bors, Kastril, Ananias, Tribulation,
Dapper, Subtle.*[4]

[SUR.] No, sir, he was a great physician.
This,
It was no bawdyhouse, but a mere[5]
chancel!
You knew the lord and his sister.
MAM.                Nay, good Surly—
SUR. The happy word, "Be rich"—
MAM.                Play not the tyran—
SUR. Should be today pronounced to all
your friends.

[4] The last five enter later.        [5] Absolute.

And where be your andirons now, and
your brass pots,
That should ha' been golden flagons
and great wedges?
MAM. Let me but breathe. What, they
ha' shut their doors,
Methinks!    *Mammon and Surly knock.*
SUR.      Ay, now 'tis holiday with them.
MAM.                          Rogues,
Cozeners, impostors, bawds!
FACE.          What mean you, sir?    10
MAM. To enter if we can.
FACE.              Another man's house?
Here is the owner, sir; turn you to
him,
And speak your business.
MAM.              Are you, sir, the owner?
LOVE. Yes, sir.
MAM.      And are those knaves within,
your cheaters?
LOVE. What knaves? What cheaters?
MAM.              Subtle and his Lungs.
FACE. The gentleman is distracted, sir!
No lungs
Nor lights[1] ha' been seen here these
three weeks, sir,
Within these doors, upon my word.
SUR.                      Your word,
Groom arrogant?
FACE.          Yes, sir, I am the housekeeper,
And know the keys ha' not been out o'
my hands.                          20
SUR. This 's a new Face?
FACE.                  You do mistake the
house, sir.
What sign was 't at?
SUR.              You rascal! This is one
O' the confederacy. Come, let's get
officers,
And force the door.
LOVE.          Pray you, stay, gentle-
men.
SUR. No, sir, we'll come with warrant.
MAM.                      Ay, and then
We shall ha' your doors open.
                  *[Exeunt Mammon and Surly.]*
LOVE.              What means this?
FACE. I cannot tell, sir.
NEI. 1.      These are two o' the gallants
That we do think we saw.
FACE.              Two o' the fools?
You talk as idly as they. Good faith,
sir,
I think the moon has crazed hem all.

*[Enter Kastril.]*

(O me,                                    30
The angry boy come too? He'll make a
noise,
And ne'er away till he have betrayed us
all.)                      *Kastril knocks.*
KAS. What, rogues, bawds, slaves, you'll
open the door anon!
Punk, cockatrice,[2] my suster! By this
light,
I'll fetch the marshal to you. You are
a whore
To keep your castle—
FACE.      Who would you speak with, sir?
KAS. The bawdy doctor, and the cozen-
ing captain,
And Puss, my suster.
LOVE.              This is something, sure.
FACE. Upon my trust, the doors were
never open, sir.
KAS. I have heard all their tricks told me
twice over                          40
By the fat knight and the lean gentle-
man.
LOVE. Here comes another.

*[Enter Ananias and Tribulation.]*

FACE. *[Aside.]*              Ananias too?
And his pastor?
TRI.          The doors are shut against us.
                  *They beat, too, at the door.*
ANA. Come forth, you seed of sulphur,
sons of fire!
Your stench, it is broke forth; abomina-
tion
Is in the house.
KAS.          Ay, my suster's there.
ANA.                      The place,
It is become a cage of unclean birds.
KAS. Yes, I will fetch the scavenger and
the constable.
TRI. You shall do well.
ANA.          We'll join to weed them out.
KAS. You will not come then, punk de-
vice,[3] my suster!                    50
ANA. Call her not sister; she is a harlot
verily.
KAS. I'll raise the street.
LOVE.              Good gentlemen, a word.
ANA. Sathan avoid, and hinder not our
zeal!

[1] Lungs of a slaughtered animal.
[2] Here, a prostitute.
[3] Perfect harlot, possibly with a pun on *point-
device.*

[*Exeunt Ananias, Tribulation, and Kastril.*]

LOVE. The world's turned Bet'lem.

FACE.                These are all broke loose

Out of S[t]. Kather'ne's, where they use to keep

The better sort of madfolks.

NEI. 1.                All these persons

We saw go in and out here.

NEI. 2.                Yes, indeed, sir.

NEI. 3. These were the parties.

FACE.                Peace, you drunk-

ards! Sir,

I wonder at it. Please you to give me leave

To touch the door; I'll try an the lock be changed.                60

LOVE. It mazes me!

FACE. [*Going to the door.*]    Good faith, sir, I believe

There's no such thing. 'Tis all *deceptio visus.*[1]—

[*Aside.*] Would I could get him away.

*Dapper cries out within.*

DAP.        Master Captain! Master Doc-

tor!

LOVE. Who's that?

FACE.                (Our clerk within, that I

forgot!)—I know not, sir.

DAP. For God's sake, when will her grace be at leisure?

FACE.                Ha!

Illusions, some spirit o' the air!—(His gag is melted,

And now he sets out the throat.[2])

DAP.                I am almost stifled—

(FACE. Would you were altogether.)

LOVE.                'Tis i' the house.

Ha! List!

FACE.        Believe it, sir, i' the air.

LOVE.                Peace, you—

DAP. Mine aunt's grace does not use me well.

SUB. [*Within.*]        You fool,        70

Peace; you'll mar all.

FACE. [*Through the keyhole, but is overheard by Lovewit.*]        Or you will else, you rogue.

LOVE. O, is it so? Then you converse with spirits!—

Come, sir. No more o' your tricks, good Jeremy.

The truth, the shortest way.

[1] Optical illusion.
[2] "Lets off his mouth."

FACE.        Dismiss this rabble, sir.—

[*Aside.*] What shall I do? I am catched.

LOVE.                Good neighbors,

I thank you all. You may depart.—

[*Exeunt Neighbors.*] Come, sir,

You know that I am an indulgent master;

And therefore conceal nothing. What's your med'cine,

To draw so many several sorts of wild fowl?

FACE. Sir, you were wont to affect mirth and wit—                80

But here's no place to talk on 't i' the street.

Give me but leave to make the best of my fortune,

And only pardon me th' abuse of your house;

It's all I beg. I'll help you to a widow,

In recompense, that you shall gi' me thanks for,

Will make you seven years younger, and a rich one.

'Tis but your putting on a Spanish cloak.

I have her within. You need not fear the house;

It was not visited.

LOVE.                But by me, who came

Sooner than you expected.

FACE.                It is true, sir.   90

Pray you, forgive me.

LOVE.        Well; let's see your widow.

[*Exeunt.*]

ACT V. SCENE iv.

[*A room in Lovewit's house.*]

*Subtle, Dapper* [*blindfolded*], *Face, Doll.*[3]

[SUB.] How! Ha' you eaten your gag?

DAP.                Yes, faith, it crumbled

Away i' my mouth.

SUB.                You ha' spoiled all then.

DAP.                No!

I hope my aunt of Fairy will forgive me.

SUB. Your aunt's a gracious lady; but in troth

You were to blame.

DAP.        The fume did overcome me,

And I did do 't to stay my stomach. Pray you

So satisfy her grace.

[3] Last two enter later.

[*Enter Face in his uniform.*]

Here comes the captain.

FACE. How now! Is his mouth down?

SUB.                    Ay, he has spoken!

FACE. (A pox, I heard him, and you too.)
He's undone then.—
(I have been fain to say the house is
        haunted                              10
With spirits, to keep churl back.

SUB.                    And hast thou done it?

FACE. Sure, for this night.

SUB.                    Why, then triumph and sing
Of Face so famous, the precious king
Of present wits.

FACE.                    Did you not hear the coil [1]
About the door?

SUB.            Yes, and I dwindled with it.)

FACE. Show him his aunt, and let him be
        despatched;
I'll send her to you.                    [*Exit.*]

SUB.                    Well, sir, your aunt her
        grace
Will give you audience presently, on
        my suit,
And the captain's word that you did
        not eat your gag
In any contempt of her highness.
        [*Removes the blindfold from his eyes.*]

DAP.                    Not I, in troth, sir.    20

[*Enter*] Doll *like the Queen of Fairy.*

SUB. Here she is come.   Down o' your
        knees and wriggle;
She has a stately presence.
                        [*Dapper kneels.*]
Good!  Yet nearer,
And bid, "God save you!"

DAP.                    Madam!

SUB.                    And your aunt.

DAP. And my most gracious aunt, God
        save your grace.

DOLL. Nephew, we thought to have been
        angry with you;
But that sweet face of yours hath
        turned the tide,
And made it flow with joy, that ebbed
        of love.
Arise, and touch our velvet gown.

SUB.                    The skirts,
And kiss hem.  So!

DOLL.        Let me now stroke that head.

[1] Disturbance.

Much, nephew, shalt thou win; much shalt
        thou spend.                          30
Much shalt thou give away; much shalt
        thou lend.

SUB. (Ay, much, indeed.)—Why do you
        not thank her grace?

DAP. I cannot speak for joy.

SUB.                    See, the kind wretch!
Your grace's kinsman right.

DOLL.                    Give me the bird.—
Here is your fly in a purse, about your
        neck, cousin;
Wear it, and feed it about this day
        sev'night,
On your right wrist—

SUB.                    Open a vein with a pin
And let it suck but once a week; till then,
You must not look on 't.

DOLL.            No.  And, kinsman,
Bear yourself worthy of the blood you
        come on.                             40

SUB. Her grace would ha' you eat no
        more Woolsack [2] pies
Nor Dagger [2] frume'ty. [3]

DOLL.            Nor break his fast
In Heaven [2] and Hell. [2]

SUB.                    She's with you everywhere!
Nor play with costermongers, at mum-
        chance, [4] traytrip, [4]
God-make-you-rich [4] (whenas your aunt
        has done it); but keep
The gallant'st company and the best
        games—

DAP.            Yes, sir.

SUB. Gleek [4] and primero; [4] and what you
        get, be true to us.

DAP. By this hand, I will.

SUB. You may bring 's a thousand pound
Before tomorrow night (if but three
        thousand
Be stirring), [5] an you will.

DAP.            I swear I will then.    50

SUB. Your fly will learn you all games.

FACE. [*Within.*]        Ha' you done there?

SUB. Your grace will command him no
        more duties?

DOLL.                    No;
But come and see me often.   I may
        chance
To leave him three or four hundred
        chests of treasure,

[2] Name of a tavern.        [4] A game of chance.

[3] Frumenty, wheat boiled in milk, etc.

[5] *I.e.*, if this is the whole wager.

And some twelve thousand acres of fairy land,
If he game well and comely with good gamesters.

SUB. There's a kind aunt! Kiss her departing part.—
But you must sell your forty mark a year now.

DAP. Ay, sir, I mean.

SUB.                  Or gi't away; pox on 't!

DAP. I'll gi't mine aunt. I'll go and fetch the writings.                                        60

SUB. 'Tis well; away.               [Exit Dapper.

*Enter Face.*]

FACE.                  Where's Subtle?

SUB.                  Here. What news?

FACE. Drugger is at the door; go take his suit,
And bid him fetch a parson presently.
Say he shall marry the widow. Thou shalt spend
A hundred pound by the service!—
                              [Exit Subtle.]
                  Now, Queen Doll,
Ha' you packed up all?

DOLL.          Yes.

FACE.                  And how do you like
The Lady Pliant?

DOLL.                  A good, dull innocent.

[Enter Subtle.]

SUB. Here's your Hieronimo's cloak and hat.

FACE.          Give me hem.

SUB. And the ruff too?

FACE.          Yes; I'll come to you presently.
                                        [Exit.]

SUB. Now he is gone about his project, Doll,                                      70
I told you of, for the widow.

DOLL.                          'Tis direct
Against our articles.

SUB.          Well, we'll fit him, wench.
Hast thou gulled her of her jewels or her bracelets?

DOLL. No; but I will do 't.

SUB.                  Soon at night, my Dolly,
When we are shipped, and all our goods aboard,
Eastward for Ratcliff, we will turn our course

To Brainford, westward, if thou say'st the word,
And take our leaves of this o'erweening rascal,
This peremptory Face.

DOLL.          Content; I am weary of him.

SUB. Thou hast cause, when the slave will run a-wiving, Doll,                    80
Against the instrument[1] that was drawn between us.

DOLL. I'll pluck his bird as bare as I can.

SUB.                          Yes, tell her
She must by any means address some present
To th' cunning man, make him amends for wronging
His art with her suspicion, send a ring,
Or chain of pearl; she will be tortured else
Extremely in her sleep, say, and ha' strange things
Come to her. Wilt thou?

DOLL.          Yes.

SUB.                  My fine flittermouse,[2]
My bird o' the night! We'll tickle it at the Pigeons,[3]
When we have all, and may unlock the trunks,          *They kiss.*   90
And say this 's mine and thine, and thine and mine—

[Enter Face.]

FACE. What now! A-billing?

SUB.                  Yes, a little exalted
In the good passage of our stock-affairs.

FACE. Drugger has brought his parson; take him in, Subtle,
And send Nab back again to wash his face.

SUB. I will—and shave himself?

FACE.                  If you can get him.
                              [Exit Subtle.]

DOLL. You are hot upon it, Face, whate'er it is!

FACE. A trick that Doll shall spend ten pound a month by.

[Enter Subtle.]

Is he gone?

SUB.          The chaplain waits you i' the hall, sir.                            99

---

[1] Agreement.                              [2] Bat.
[3] An inn at Brainford, or Brentford.

FACE. I'll go bestow him.                    [*Exit.*]
DOLL.       He'll now marry her instantly.
SUB. He cannot yet; he is not ready.
    Dear Doll,
    Cozen her of all thou canst. To deceive
    him
    Is no deceit, but justice, that would
    break
    Such an inextricable tie as ours was.
DOLL. Let me alone to fit him.

[*Enter Face.*]

FACE.                Come, my venturers;
    You ha' packed up all? Where be the
    trunks? Bring forth.
SUB. Here.
FACE.          Let 's see hem. Where's the
    money?
SUB.             Here.
    In this.
FACE.        Mammon's ten pound; eight
    score before;
    The Brethren's money this; Drugger's
    and Dapper's.                                 109
    What paper's that?
DOLL.       The jewel of the waiting-maid's,
    That stole it from her lady, to know
    certain—
FACE. If she should have precedence of
    her mistress?
DOLL.               Yes.
FACE. What box is that?
SUB.          The fishwife's rings, I think,
    And th' alewife's single money.[1] Is 't
    not, Doll?
DOLL. Yes; and the whistle that the sail-
    or's wife
    Brought you, to know and her husband
    were with Ward.[2]
FACE. We'll wet it tomorrow; and our
    silver beakers
    And tavern cups. Where be the French
    petticoats
    And girdles and hangers?[3]
SUB.             Here, i' the trunk,
    And the bolts of lawn.
FACE.      Is Drugger's damask there,     120
    And the tabacco?
SUB.       Yes.
FACE.             Give me the keys.
DOLL. Why you the keys?

[1] Small change.
[2] A notorious pirate.
[3] Loops from which swords were hung.

SUB.               No matter, Doll; because
    We shall not open hem before he comes.
FACE. 'Tis true, you shall not open them,
    indeed;
    Nor have hem forth. Do you see? Not
    forth, Doll.
DOLL.        No!
FACE. No, my smock-rampant. The right
    is, my master
    Knows all, has pardoned me, and he
    will keep hem.
    Doctor, 'tis true—you look [4]—for [5] all
    your figures;
    I sent for him, indeed. Wherefore, good
    partners,
    Both he and she, be satisfied, for here  130
    Determines [6] the indenture tripartite
    Twixt Subtle, Doll, and Face. All I
    can do
    Is to help you over the wall, o' the back
    side,
    Or lend you a sheet to save your velvet
    gown, Doll.
    Here will be officers presently; bethink
    you
    Of some course suddenly to scape the
    dock,
    For thither you'll come else. (*Some
    knock.*) Hark you, thunder!
SUB. You are a precious fiend!
OFFICERS. [*Without.*]       Open the door!
FACE. Doll, I am sorry for thee, i' faith;
    but hear'st thou?
    It shall go hard but I will place thee
    somewhere;                                    140
    Thou shalt ha' my letter to Mistress
    Amo—
DOLL.             Hang you—
FACE. Or Madam Cæsarean.
DOLL.               Pox upon you, rogue!
    Would I had but time to beat thee!
FACE.                Subtle,
    Let 's know where you set up next; I'll
    send you
    A customer now and then, for old ac-
    quaintance.
    What new course ha' you?
SUB.               Rogue, I'll hang myself,
    That I may walk a greater devil than
    thou,
    And haunt thee i' the flockbed [7] and the
    buttery.                              [*Exeunt.*]

[4] Stare.     [5] In spite of.     [6] Terminates.
[7] A bed stuffed with pieces of wool or cloth.

Act V. Scene v.

[*Another room in the same.*]

*Lovewit* [*in Spanish costume, Parson*], *Officers, Mammon, Surly, Face, Kastril, Ananias, Tribulation, Drugger, Da*[*me*] *Pliant.*[1]

[Love.] What do you mean, my masters?
Mam. [*Without.*]          Open your door,
   Cheaters, bawds, conjurers.
Off. [*Without.*]     Or we'll break it open.
Love. What warrant have you?
Off. [*Without.*]          Warrant enough, sir,
   doubt not,
If you'll not open it.
Love.               Is there an officer there?
Off. [*Without.*] Yes, two or three for [2]
   failing.
Love.          Háve but patience,
And I will open it straight.

[*Enter Face, as butler.*]

Face.                    Sir, ha' you done?
   Is it a marriage? Perfect?
Love.                    Yes, my brain.
Face. Off with your ruff and cloak then;
   be yourself, sir.
                    [*Lovewit takes off his disguise.*]
Sur. [*Without.*] Down with the door!
Kas. [*Without.*]     'Slight, ding [3] it open.
Love. [*Opening the door.*]          Hold,
   Hold, gentlemen, what means this vio-
   lence?                          10

[*Enter Mammon, Surly, Kastril, Ananias,
              Tribulation, and Officers.*]

Mam. Where is this collier?
Sur.               And my Captain Face?
Mam. These day-owls.
Sur.     That are birding [4] in men's purses.
Mam. Madam Suppository.
Kas.               Doxy, my sister.
Ana.                    Locusts
   Of the foul pit.
Tri.          Profane as Bel and the Dragon.
Ana. Worse than the grasshoppers, or the
   lice of Egypt.

Love. Good gentlemen, hear me. Are you
   officers,
And cannot stay this violence?
Off. [1.]                    Keep the peace.
Love. Gentlemen, what is the matter?
   Whom do you seek?
Mam. The chymical [5] cozener.
Sur.               And the captain pander.
Kas. The nun my suster.
Mam.               Madam Rabbi.
Ana.                    Scorpions   20
   And caterpillars.
Love.          Fewer at once, I pray you.
Off. [1.] One after another, gentlemen, I
   charge you,
By virtue of my staff—
Ana.               They are the vessels
   Of pride, lust, and the cart.
Love.               Good zeal, lie still
A little while.
Tri.          Peace, Deacon Ananias.
Love. The house is mine here, and the
   doors are open;
If there be any such persons as you seek
   for,
Use your authority; search on, o' God's
   name.
I am but newly come to town, and, find-
   ing
This tumult 'bout my door, to tell you
   true,                          30
It somewhat mazed me, till my man here,
   fearing
My more displeasure, told me he had
   done
Somewhat an insolent part, let out my
   house
(Belike presuming on my known aversion
From any air o' the town while there was
   sickness)
To a doctor and a captain, who, what
   they are
Or where they be, he knows not.

*They enter.*[6]

Mam.                    Are they gone?
Love. You may go in and search, sir.—
   [*Exit Mammon.*] Here I find
The empty walls worse than I left hem,
   smoked,

---

[1] All except Lovewit and the Parson are without or enter later.
[2] For fear of.     [3] Break.     [4] Thieving.

[5] Chemical.
[6] *I.e.*, the Officers, Tribulation, and Ananias
start their search.

A few cracked pots, and glasses, and a
  fornace;  40
The ceiling filled with poesies of the
  candle,
And "Madam with a dildo" [1] writ o' the
  walls.
Only one gentlewoman I met here,
That is within, that said she was a
  widow—

KAS. Ay, that's my suster; I'll go thump
  her. Where is she?  [*Exit.*]

LOVE. And should ha' married a Spanish
  count, but he,
When he came to 't, neglected her so
  grossly
That I, a widower, am gone through with
  her.

SUR. How! Have I lost her then?

LOVE.  Were you the Don, sir?
Good faith, now she does blame yo'
  extremely, and says  50
You swore and told her you had ta'en the
  pains
To dye your beard, and umber o'er your
  face,
Borrowed a suit and ruff, all for her
  love—
And then did nothing. What an over-
  sight
And want of putting forward, sir, was
  this!
Well tare an old hargubuzier [2] yet,
Could prime his poulder, and give fire,
  and hit,
All in a twinkling!

*Mammon comes forth.*

MAM.  The whole nest are fled!

LOVE. What sort of birds were they?

MAM.  A kind of choughs,
Or thievish daws, sir, that have picked
  my purse  60
Of eight score and ten pounds within
  these five weeks,
Beside my first materials, and my goods
That lie i' the cellar, which I am glad
  they ha' left.
I may have home yet.

LOVE.  Think you so, sir?

MAM.  Ay.

LOVE. By order of law, sir, but not otherwise.

MAM. Not mine own stuff?

LOVE.  Sir, I can take no knowledge
That they are yours, but by public
  means.
If you can bring certificate that you were
  gulled of hem,
Or any formal writ out of a court
That you did cozen yourself, I will not
  hold them.  70

MAM. I'll rather lose hem.

LOVE.  That you shall not, sir,
By me, in troth; upon these terms, they
  are yours.
What, should they ha' been, sir, turned
  into gold, all?

MAM.  No.
I cannot tell. It may be they should.
  What then?

LOVE. What a great loss in hope have you
  sustained!

MAM. Not I; the commonwealth has.

FACE.  Ay, he would ha' built
The city new, and made a ditch about it
Of silver, should have run with cream
  from Hogsden,
That every Sunday in Moorfields the
  younkers [3]
And tits [4] and tomboys should have fed
  on, gratis.  80

MAM. I will go mount a turnip-cart, and
  preach
The end o' the world within these two
  months.—Surly,
What! In a dream?

SUR.  Must I needs cheat myself
With that same foolish vice of honesty?
Come, let us go and hearken [5] out the
  rogues.
That Face I'll mark for mine, if e'er I
  meet him.

FACE. If I can hear of him, sir, I'll bring
  you word
Unto your lodging; for, in troth, they
  were strangers
To me. I thought hem honest as myself,
  sir.

*They come forth.*

TRI. 'Tis well, the Saints shall not lose all
  yet. Go  90
And get some carts—

LOVE.  For what, my zealous friends?

---

[1] Fragment of a ballad.
[2] Harquebusier, musketeer.
[3] Youths.
[4] Wenches.
[5] Inquire, search.

ANA. To bear away the portion of the righteous
Out of this den of thieves.

LOVE.                    What is that portion?

ANA. The goods sometimes the orphans', that the Brethren
Bought with their silver pence.

LOVE.          What, those i' the cellar
The knight Sir Mammon claims?

ANA.                    I do defy
The wicked Mammon; so do all the Brethren,
Thou profane man! I ask thee with what conscience
Thou canst advance that idol against us,
That have the seal? [1]  Were not the shillings numbered          100
That made the pounds? Were not the pounds told out
Upon the second day of the fourth week
In the eighth month, upon the table dormant, [2]
The year of the last patience of the Saints,
Six hundred and ten?

LOVE.     Mine earnest, vehement botcher,
And deacon also, I cannot dispute with you;
But, if you get you not away the sooner,
I shall confute you with a cudgel.

ANA.                    Sir!

TRI. Be patient, Ananias.

ANA.                    I am strong,
And will stand up, well girt, against an host          110
That threaten Gad in exile.

LOVE.               I shall send you
To Amsterdam, to your cellar.

ANA.               I will pray there,
Against thy house. May dogs defile thy walls,
And wasps and hornets breed beneath thy roof,
This seat of falsehood, and this cave of coz'nage!
          [*Exeunt Ananias and Tribulation.*]

*Drugger enters, and he beats him away.*

LOVE. Another too?

DRUG.          Not I, sir; I am no Brother.

LOVE. Away, you Harry Nicholas! [3]  Do you talk?          [*Exit Drugger.*]

[1] *I.e.*, of the chosen of God.
[2] Fixed, stationary.          [3] A notorious fanatic.

FACE. No, this was Abel Drugger.—(*To the Parson.*) Good sir, go,
And satisfy him; tell him all is done.
He stayed too long a-washing of his face.          120
The doctor, he shall hear of him at Westchester,
And of the captain, tell him, at Yarmouth, or
Some good port-town else, lying for a wind.—          [*Exit Parson.*]
If you [can] [4] get off the angry child now, sir—

[*Enter Kastril and Dame Pliant.*]

KAS. (*To his sister.*) Come on, you ewe; you have matched most sweetly, ha' you not?
Did not I say I would never ha' you tupped
But by a dubbed boy, [5] to make you a lady-tom?
'Slight, you are a mammet! [6] O, I could touse you now.
Death, mun [7] you marry, with a pox!

LOVE.               You lie, boy;
As sound as you; and I'm aforehand with you.

KAS. [*To Pliant.*]          Anon!          130

LOVE. Come, will you quarrel? I will feeze [8] you, sirrah;
Why do you not buckle to your tools?

KAS.               God's light,
This is a fine old boy as e'er I saw!

LOVE. What, do you change your copy [9] now? Proceed;
Here stands my dove. Stoop [10] at her if you dare.

KAS. 'Slight, I must love him! I cannot choose, i' faith,
And I should be hanged for 't! Suster, I protest
I honor thee for this match.

LOVE.               O, do you so, sir?

KAS. Yes, and thou canst take tabacco and drink, old boy,
I'll give her five hundred pound more to her marriage          140
Than her own state.

[4] From 1612 edn.          [7] Must.
[5] *I.e.*, a knight.          [8] Flog.
[6] Puppet.          [9] Theme, " tune."
[10] Swoop (a term of falconry). The name Kastril meant a hawk.

Love.                    Fill a pipeful, Jeremy.
Face. Yes; but go in and take it, sir.
Love.                    We will.
    I will be ruled by thee in anything,
    Jeremy.
Kas. 'Slight, thou art not hidebound; thou
    art a jovy [1] boy!
    Come, let 's in, I pray thee, and take our
    whiffs.
Love. Whiff in with your sister, brother
    boy.—[*Exeunt Kastril and Dame
                            Pliant.*]
                            That master
    That had received such happiness by a
    servant,
    In such a widow, and with so much
    wealth,
    Were very ungrateful if he would not
    be
    A little indulgent to that servant's
    wit,                                    150
    And help his fortune, though with some
    small strain
    Of his own candor.[2]—[*To the audience.*]
    Therefore, gentlemen

And kind spectators, if I have out-
    stripped
An old man's gravity or strict canon,
    think
What a young wife and a good brain may
    do—
Stretch age's truth sometimes, and crack
    it too.—
Speak for thyself, knave.
Face.                    So I will, sir.—Gentlemen,
    My part a little fell in this last scene,
    Yet 'twas decorum.[3]  And though I am
    clean
    Got off from Subtle, Surly, Mammon,
    Doll,                                    160
    Hot Ananias, Dapper, Drugger, all
    With whom I traded, yet I put myself
    On you, that are my country; [4] and this
    pelf
    Which I have got, if you do quit [5] me,
    rests
    To feast you often and invite new guests.
                            [*Exeunt.*]
                    The End.

[1] Jovial.                    [2] Integrity.

[3] Dramatic propriety.
[4] Jury.                    [5] Acquit.

This comedy was first acted in the year 1610 by the King's Majesty's Servants.  The
principal comedians were:

|  |  |
|---|---|
| *Ric. Burbadge* | *Joh. Hemings* |
| *Joh. Lowin* | *Will. Ostler* |
| *Hen. Condell* | *Joh. Underwood* |
| *Alex. Cooke* | *Nic. Tooly* |
| *Rob. Armin* | *Will. Eglestone* |

With the allowance of the Master of Revels.

# BEN JONSON

## THE SAD SHEPHERD

Among the papers found in Jonson's desk on his death was an unfinished pastoral drama, *The Sad Shepherd, or A Tale of Robin Hood*, his only extant attempt at this romantic genre, though some writers have thought that it may have grown from, or incorporated fragments from, his early lost entertainment, *The May Lord*. For many years after Sir Kenelm Digby printed it in Jonson's second folio, dated 1641 on its title page, scholars wrangled over whether it was to be considered as an early or late work, since there is no real evidence for assigning it a date, except for certain implications in its prologue. It is now the consensus that Jonson was actually working on it up to the time of his death, and that it therefore, like Shakespeare's *The Tempest*, represents a new and happier turn in the mind of the pessimistic and misanthropic old poet. Chute points out that just two years before Jonson's death Joseph Rutter, one of his young admirers, if not actually one of his "sons," had published a pastoral tragicomedy, *The Shepherds' Holiday*, had had it produced successfully at Whitehall, and had been honored with a commendatory poem by Jonson. A quarter of a century earlier still, Jonson had written a similar poem for Fletcher's *The Faithful Shepherdess*, which had also been recently revived at Whitehall. The two poems show Jonson's continuing interest in the type. Since he began his prologue with a reference to himself as "He who hath feasted you these forty years"—a time when he was writing the lost *Isle of Dogs*—the implication is that his pastoral was still in progress at the time of his death. Chute also reminds her readers that the setting of the play is Sherwood Forest, that the Lord Warden of Sherwood Forest was the Earl of Newcastle, Jonson's patron, and that when Jonson wrote his "Entertainment at Welbeck" in 1633, he mentioned the

> odd tales
> Of our outlaw, Robin Hood,
> That reveled here in Sherwood.

Could *The Sad Shepherd* be regarded as one of these "odd tales"?

The play obviously had no stage history in its own time, although Herford-Simpson say that a private performance was apparently given at some noble's house during the reign of Charles II. The pastoral was then forgotten till William Poel revived it at Fulham Palace for the Elizabethan Stage Society in 1898. However, in the meantime Francis Waldron had written and published his completion of the play in 1783. When Alan Porter did the same thing in 1935, his version was produced at Vassar in that year and again in 1947; so *The Sad Shepherd* has retained some modern appeal.

The three chief modern discussions of the play are Freda L. Townsend's "Ben Jonson's 'Censure' of Rutter's *Shepheards Holy-Day*" (*MP*, 1947), John Leon Lievsay's "Italian *Favole Boscarecce* and Jacobean Pastoralism" (*Essays on Shakespeare and the Elizabethan Drama in Honor of Hardin Craig*, University of Missouri Press, 1962), and a long section in Thayer's studies. By examining Jonson's poem to Rutter primarily and his verses to Fletcher secondarily, Townsend attempted to arrive at Jonson's conception of a good pastoral play. Through his approval of his two predecessors he committed himself to a dramatic type which was non-existent in classical times, although pastoral poetry was well-known and popular. When Giovanni Battista

Guarini published his *Il Pastor Fido* in 1590, he argued that in spite of Aristotle, it was proper to draw what was useful from both tragedy and comedy and combine them into a new form of pastoral tragicomedy. Since both Rutter's and Fletcher's plays neglect the unity of action, while conforming in other respects to Guarini's principles, Jonson when praising them "was not even classical in the Renaissance sense." His own liberal principles are stated in several lines in the prologue in which he criticizes those who believe that "all poesy" should have only "one character." Lievsay, admitting that he was using the Italian term *boscareccia* as a synonym for "the pastoral drama in general, exclusive of simple dramatic eclogue," also remarked that some Italian pastoral writers, like Guarini and Francesco Partini, deliberately tried to make their readers or spectators "aware of any resemblances between their plays and those of the ancient tragic poets." Accepting W. W. Greg's thesis (*Pastoral Poetry and Pastoral Drama*, London, 1906) that the pastoral drama of England descended directly from the pastoral drama of Italy, Lievsay stressed the surprisingly un-Italian and unclassical aspects of Jonson's play—that is, the purely English elements—and concluded that, however Jonson may have planned to end his play, it "was not headed in the direction of the *favole boscareccia*." All "the outworn machinery of regular pastoral tradition"—the oracles, satyrs, masquelike *intermedii*, dependence on a *deus ex machina*, echo scenes, stock names for characters, and so on—is gone, and Jonson has produced a purely English and, in its way, realistic pastoral drama.

Thayer feels that the play, although its masquelike single setting is "stylized, ideal, inclusive," moves not so much in the world of Marlowe's passionate shepherd or even Spenser's *The Shepherd's Calendar* as in that of *The Faery Queen* or even *Comus*. But Thayer stresses particularly his speculations on Jonson's intended theme, his interpretation of his characters, and his probable ending. Admitting his admiration for both Waldron's and Porter's continuations, he rejects their final reformation of Maudlin, the Witch of Papplewick, and insists that she is not only "the envious," as Jonson described her, but a real witch and "a real evil, as are her daughter, Douce the proud, her son, Lorel the rude, and Puck-Hairy, their servant." Projecting the unfinished last two acts from the completed three, Thayer speculates that Jonson would have rendered Maudlin and Puck-Hairy incapable of future evil by stripping them of their magic powers; that Earine, through the agency of Alken the sage, would "experience the ritual rebirth implicit in her escape from the tree;" that Aeglamour would be reunited with Earine after being restored to his senses through the agency of Alken and probably Reuben, the "devout hermit" and "the Reconciler," who has not appeared in the completed three acts but is named in the cast; and that Robin Hood and Maid Marian would be left to rule "henceforth over an undisturbed and ideal pastoral world." Thayer would emphasize the theme of reconciliation throughout, which he regards as the essence of tragicomedy. The theme or pattern is that of love deprived of life by envy and restored by love. In the symbolic value of Alken and in some of his speeches, Thayer regards the sage as an autobiographical version of Jonson himself and thus as a poetic figure.

Thayer's explanation of Jonson's intention in the figures of the rustic or sylvan plot as opposed to the pastoral—that is, of Maudlin and Puck-Hairy, Robin Hood and Marian—is based largely on the teasingly speculative theories of Robert Graves in *The White Goddess*. These are founded on the belief that Maid Marian in English folklore was a "Lady of Misrule" at the Christmas revels, and that in this guise she deserts Robin, the chief deity of the Robin Hood religion, for his rival, "apparently a rather elaborate combination of Chronos-Saturn-Bran." This theory, involving ritual murder and the confusion of Maid Marian with Maud Marian—that is, Mary Magdalene (which of course the English pronounce "Maudlin")—becomes extremely complex and is best read in its full development by Graves. The same advice applies to Robin Hood and Puck-Hairy, in which case it would appear that "Jonson's Puck-Hairy is a real agent of the devil, while his Robin Hood is the other aspect of the hero of folklore, tidied up considerably . . . ." It is somewhat questionable that Jonson was sufficiently acquainted with this phase of native and classical folklore to have had these relationships and interpretations in mind when writing his rather simple and easily intelligible play.   Thayer apparently shares this feeling, since he ends his account by summarizing: "But we can say with certainty, I think, that Maudlin and her train represent forces of genuine evil, not comic vice; that Earine [meaning "the beautiful," or, in Greek, "maiden of spring"] and Aeglamour represent innocence upset and tempted by evil; that Robin and Marian represent virtue separated from evil; that Alken represents the wisdom which can defeat evil; and that the hermit will represent the holiness which overcomes evil by reconciling those who have been tempted by it.   Robin and Marian are the most potent characters in the play of the sad shepherd, because they represent the rational and moral ideal. . . ."   Any play which can combine these elements and maintain the interest of readers for long over three centuries deserves its niche in the history of English literature.

Alexander H. Sackton, in *The Rhymed Couplet in Ben Jonson's Plays* (*UTSE*, 1951), while concluding that it was in *Sejanus* that Jonson used the couplet to the best effect, added that its frequency in *The Sad Shepherd* arises naturally from the pastoral character of the piece.   On the other hand, the Herford-Simpson editors question Jonson's use of dialect, which they think may have been an afterthought, after he had written the dialogue first in "plain English."   At any rate, although it is intended for northern English, the treatment, they think, is amateurish.

The present text is based on a copy of the second folio in the Newberry Library.

# THE SAD SHEPHERD
## OR
# A TALE OF ROBIN HOOD

BY

BEN JONSON

### THE PERSONS OF THE PLAY

ROBIN HOOD, *the chief woodman,*[1] *master of the feast.*
MARIAN, *his lady, the mistress.*

#### THEIR FAMILY [2]

FRIAR TUCK, *the chaplain and steward.*
LITTLE JOHN, *bow bearer.*[3]
SCARLET } *two brothers, huntsmen.*
SCATHLOCK }
GEORGE A GREENE, *huisher* [4] *of the bower.*[5]
MUCH, *Robin Hood's bailiff or acater.*[6]

#### THE GUESTS INVITED

CLARION, *the rich*
LIONEL, *the courteous*
ALKEN, *the sage* } *shepherds.*
EGLAMOUR, *the sad*
KAROLIN, *the kind*

MELLIFLEUR, *the sweet*
AMIE, *the gentle* } *shepherdesses.*
EARINE, *the beautiful*

#### THE TROUBLES UNEXPECTED

MAUDLIN, *the envious, the Witch of Papplewick.*
DOUCE, *the proud, her daughter.*
LOREL, *the rude, a swine'ard,* [7] *the witch's son.*
PUCK-HAIRY, *or Robin Goodfellow, their hine.*[8]

#### THE RECONCILER

REUBEN, *a devout hermit.*

*The scene is Sherwood, consisting of a landtshape* [9] *of forest, hills, valleys, cottages, a castle, a river, pastures, herds, flocks, all full of country simplicity. Robin Hood's bower; his well; the witch's dimble;* [10] *the swine'ard's oak; the hermit's cell.*

[TIME: *Late Middle Ages.*]

### PROLOGUE [11]

He that hath feasted you these forty years,
And fitted fables for your finer ears,
Although at first he scarce could hit the bore,[12]

Yet you, with patience heark'ning more and more,
At length have grown up to him, and made known
The working of his pen is now your own.
He prays you would vouchsafe, for your own sake,
To hear him this once more, but sit awake.
And, though he now present you with such wool
As from mere [13] English flocks his muse can pull, 10
He hopes when it is made up into cloth,

---

[1] Huntsman.  [2] Household.
[3] An under officer charged with the prevention of trespassing.
[4] Usher, doorkeeper.  [5] Rustic cottage.
[6] Caterer, purchaser of provisions.
[7] Swineherd.  [9] Landscape.
[8] Hind, servant.  [10] Dingle, narrow valley.
[11] In the original the prologue follows the argument of the first act.
[12] *I.e.*, suit the caliber of your intelligence.
[13] Pure.

267

Not the most curious head here will be
    loath
To wear a hood of it, it being a fleece
To match or [1] those of Sicily or Greece.
His scene is Sherwood, and his play a tale
Of Robin Hood's inviting from the Vale
Of Be'voir [2] all the shepherds to a feast,
Where by the casual absence of one guest
The mirth is troubled much, and in one
    man                                    19
As much of sadness shown as passion can—
The sad young shepherd, whom we here
    present,

*The Sad Shepherd passeth silently over the*
                      *stage.*

Like his woes' figure, dark and discontent
For his lost love, who in the Trent is said
To have miscarried. 'Las! What knows the
    head
Of a calm river whom the feet have
    drowned?
Hear what his sorrows are, and, if they
    wound
Your gentle breasts, so that the end crown
    all,
Which in the scope of one day's chance
    may fall,
Old Trent will send you more such tales
    as these,
And shall grow young again as one doth
    please.                                    30

*Here the Prologue, thinking to end, returns*
    *upon a new purpose and speaks on.*

But here's an heresy of late let fall,
That mirth by no means fits a pastoral.
Such say so, who can make none, he pre-
    sumes;
Else there's no scene more properly as-
    sumes
The sock. [3] For whence can sport in kind [4]
    arise
But from the rural routs and families?
Safe on this ground then, we not fear today
To tempt your laughter by our rustic play;
Wherein if we distaste, [5] or be cried down,
We think we therefore shall not leave the
    town,                                    40

[1] Either.
[2] Belvoir, the seat of the Earls of Rutland.
[3] Shoe worn by actors of classical comedy.
[4] In nature, naturally.   [5] Disgust, displease.

Nor that the forewits, [6] that would draw
    the rest
Unto their liking, always like the best.
The wise and knowing critic will not say,
This worst, or better is, before he weigh
Where [7] every piece be perfect in the kind, [8]
And then, though in themselves he differ-
    ence find,
Yet, if the place require it where they stood,
The equal fitting makes them equal good.
You shall have love and hate and jealousy,
As well as mirth and rage and melancholy,
Or whatsoever else may either move   51
Or stir affections, [9] and your likings prove.
But that no style for pastoral should go
Current but what is stamped with "Ah"
    and "O,"
Who judgeth so, may singularly err,
As if all poesy had one character
In which what were not written, were not
    right,
Or that the man who made such one poor
    flight
In his whole life, had with his wingèd skill
Advanced him upmost on the muses' hill, 60
When he like poet yet remains, as those
Are painters who can only make a rose.
From such your wits redeem you, or your
    chance,
Lest to a greater height you do advance
Of folly, to contemn those that are known
Artificers, and trust such as are none.

### THE ARGUMENT[10] OF THE FIRST ACT

Robin Hood, having invited all the
shepherds and shepherdesses of the Vale
of Be'voir to a feast in the Forest of Sherwood, and, trusting to his mistress, Maid
Marian, with her woodmen, to kill him
venison against[11] the day, having left the
like charge with Friar Tuck, his chaplain
and steward, to command the rest of his
merry men to see the bower made ready
and all things in order for the enter-   [10
tainment, meeting with his guests at their
entrance into the wood, welcomes and
conducts them to his bower, where, by
the way, he receives the relation of the
Sad Shepherd, Eglamour, who is fallen
into a deep melancholy for the loss of his
beloved Earine, reported to have been
drowned in passing over the Trent some

[6] Critics.        [7] Whether.        [8] Type.
[9] Emotions.   [10] Plot.   [11] In preparation for.

few days before. They endeavor in what
they can to comfort him, but, his dis-  [20
ease having taken so strong root, all is in
vain, and they are forced to leave him.
In the meantime Marian is come from
hunting with the huntsmen, where the
lovers interchangeably express their loves.
Robin Hood inquires if she hunted the
deer at force [1] and what sport he made,
how long he stood, and what head [2] he
bore; all which is briefly answered with a
relation of breaking him up,[3] and the  [30
raven and her bone, the suspect [4] had of
that raven to be Maudlin, the Witch of
Papplewick, whom one of the huntsmen
met i' the morning at the rousing of the
deer, and is confirmed by her, being then
in Robin Hood's kitchen, i' the chimney
corner broiling the same bit which was
thrown to the raven at the quarry [5] or fall
of the deer. Marian, being gone in to show
the deer to some of the shepherdesses,  [40
returns instantly to the scene discontented,
sends away the venison she had killed to
her they call the Witch, quarrels with
her love, Robin Hood, abuseth him and
his guests, the shepherds, and so departs,
leaving them all in wonder and perplexity.

### Act I. Scene i.

[*Robin Hood's bower.*] [6]

*Eglamour.*

EG. Here she was wont to go, and here,
   and here—
   Just where those daisies, pinks, and
      violets grow!
   The world may find the spring by fol-
      lowing her,
   For other print her airy steps ne'er
      left.
   Her treading would not bend a blade
      of grass,
   Or shake the downy blowball [7] from his
      stalk!
   But like the soft west wind she shot
      along,

And, where she went, the flowers took
   thickest root,
As she had sowed hem [8] with her odorous
   foot.

### Act I. Scene ii.

[*To him,*] *Marian, Tuck, John, Woodmen,*
                                      *etc.*

MAR. Know you, or can you guess, my
   merry men,
   What 'tis that keeps your master Robin
      Hood
   So long both from his Marian and the
      wood?
TUCK. Forsooth, madam, he will be here
   by noon,
   And prays it of your bounty, as a boon,
   That you by then have killed him veni-
      son some
   To feast his jolly friends, who hither
      come
   In threaves [9] to frolic with him and make
      cheer.
   Here's Little John hath harbored [10] you
      a deer,
   I see by his tackling.[11]
JOHN.               And a hart of ten,[12]   10
   I trow he be, madam, or blame your
      men,
   For by his slot,[13] his entries,[14] and his
      port,[15]
   His frayings,[16] fewmets [17] he doth prom-
      ise sport
   And standing fore [18] the dogs; he bears
      a head
   Large and well-beamed, with all rights
      summed [19] and spread.
MAR. Let's rouse him quickly, and lay
   on the hounds.
JOHN. Scathlock is ready with them on
   the grounds;
   So is his brother Scarlet.  Now they
      'ave found
   His lair, they have him sure within the
      pound.[20]

[1] Ran the deer down with dogs instead of
slaying it with weapons.
[2] Horns.                    [4] Suspicion.
[3] *I.e.*, cutting up the deer.   [5] Cutting up.
[6] The scene remains the same throughout the
act.
[7] Dandelion's head gone to seed.

[8] Them.            [11] Equipment.
[9] Numbers.         [12] *I.e.*, ten-pronged horns.
[10] Tracked down.   [13] Track.
[14] Openings made in the thickets by the deer.
[15] Weight indicated by the depth of his foot-
prints.
[16] Velvet rubbed from his antlers.
[17] Dung of a deer.              [18] Before.
[19] With all tines completed.
[20] *I.e.*, in a hopeless position.

MAR. Away then! When my Robin bids
    a feast,    20
'Twere sin in Marian to defraud a guest.
[*Exeunt Marian and John with the Wood-
              men.*]

### ACT I. SCENE iii.

*Tuck, George a Greene, Much, Eglamour.*[1]

TUCK. And I, the chaplain, here am left
    to be
Steward today, and charge you all in fee [2]
To don your liveries, see the bower
    dressed,
And fit the fine devices for the feast.
You, George, must care to make the
    baldric [3] trim,
And garland that must crown or her or
    him
Whose flock this year hath brought the
    earliest lamb.
GEORGE. Good Father Tuck, at your com-
    mands I am
To cut the table out o' the greensward,
Or any other service for my lord,   10
To carve the guests large seats and these
    laid in
With turf as soft and smooth as the
    mole's skin,
And hang the bulléd [4] nosegays 'bove
    their heads . . . .[5]
The piper's bank whereon to sit and
    play,
And a fair dial to mete out the day.
Our master's feast shall want no just
    delights;
His entertainments must have all the
    rites.
MUCH. Ay, and all choice that plenty
    can send in—
Bread, wine, acates,[6] fowl, feather, fish,
    or fin,
For which my father's nets have swept
    the Trent.    20

*Eglamour falls in with them.*

EG. And ha' you found her?
MUCH.          Whom?
EG.            My drownéd love,
    Earine! The sweet Earine!

The bright and beautiful Earine!
Have you not heard of my Earine?
Just by your father's mills (I think I am
    right—
Are not you Much the Miller's son?)—
MUCH.              I am.
EG. And baily [7] to brave Robin Hood?
MUCH.           The same.
EG. Close by your father's mills, Earine,
Earine was drowned! O my Earine!
(Old Maudlin tells me so, and Douce, her
    daughter.)    30
Ha' you swept the river, say you, and
    not found her?
MUCH. For fowl and fish we have.
EG.             O, not for her?
    You are goodly friends, right charita-
    ble men!
    Nay, keep your way and leave me; make
    your toys,
    Your tales, your poesies, that you talked
    of—all
    Your entertainments. You not injure me.
    Only if I may enjoy my cypress wreath,
    And you will let me weep, 'tis all I ask,
    Till I be turned to water as was she!
    And, troth, what less suit can you grant
    a man?    40
TUCK. His fantasy [8] is hurt; let us now
    leave him;
    The wound is yet too fresh to admit
    searching.    [*Exit.*]
EG. Searching? Where should I search,
    or on what track?
    Can my slow drop of tears or this dark
    shade
    About my brows enough describe her
    loss?
    Earine! O, my Earine's loss!
    No, no, no, no; this heart will break first.
GEORGE. How will this sad disaster strike
    the ears
    Of bounteous Robin Hood, our gentle
    master!    [*Exit.*]
MUCH. How will it mar his mirth, abate
    his feast,    50
    And strike a horror into every guest!
                    [*Exit.*]
EG. If I could knit whole clouds about
    my brows,
    And weep like Swithin [9] or those wat'ry
    signs,

---

[1] Enters later.        [3] Belt.
[2] Fealty.           [4] Swollen, budding.
[5] The rime and sense indicate that at least one
line has here dropped out.    [6] Cates, dainties.
[7] Bailiff.                      [8] Imagination.
[9] Patron saint of rainy weather.

The Kids [1] that rise then, and drown all
   the flocks
Of those rich shepherds dwelling in this
   vale,
Those careless shepherds that did let
   her drown,
Then I did something; or could make old
   Trent
Drunk with my sorrow, to start out in
   breaches
To drown their herds, their cattle, and
   their corn,
Break down their mills, their dams, o'er-
   turn their weirs,                          60
And see their houses and whole liveli-
   hood
Wrought into water with her, all were
   good—
I'ld kiss the torrent and those whirls of
   Trent
That sucked her in, my sweet Earine!
When they have cast their body [2] on
   the shore,
And it comes up as tainted as them-
   selves,
All pale and bloodless, I will love it still,
For all that they can do, and make hem
   mad
To see how I will hug it in mine arms,
And hang upon the looks, dwell on her
   eyes,                                       70
Feed round about her lips, and eat her
   kisses,
Suck of her drownéd flesh!—and where's
   their malice? [3]
Not all their envious sousing can change
   that.
But I will study some revenge past this!
I pray you, give me leave, for I will study,
Though all the bells, pipes, tabors, tim-
   burines [4] ring,
That you can plant about me; I will study.

ACT I. SCENE iv.

*To him, Robin Hood, Clarion, Mellifleur,
   Lionel, Amie, Alken, Tuck, Servants,
              with music of all sorts.*

ROB. Welcome, bright Clarion and sweet
   Mellifleur,
The courteous Lionel, fair Amie, all

My friends and neighbors, to the jolly
   bower
Of Robin Hood and to the greenwood
   walks!
Now that the shearing of your sheep is
   done,
And the washed flocks are lighted [5] of
   their wool,
The smoother ewes are ready to receive
The mounting rams again; and both do
   feed,
As either promised, to increase your
   breed
At eaning [6] time, and bring you lusty
   twins.                                       10
Why should or you or we so much forget
The season in ourselves as not to make
Use of our youth and spirits to awake
The nimble hornpipe [7] and the timbu-
   rine,
And mix our songs and dances in the
   wood,
And each of us cut down a triumph
   bough?
Such were the rites the youthful June
   allow.
CLA. They were, gay Robin; but the sourer
   sort
Of shepherds [8] now disclaim in [9] all such
   sport,
And say our flocks the while are poorly
   fed,                                         20
When with such vanities the swains are
   led.
TUCK. Would they, wise Clarion, were
   not hurried more
With covetise [10] and rage, when to their
   store
They add the poor man's eanling,[11] and
   dare sell
Both fleece and carcass, not gi'ing him
   the fell,[12]
When to one goat they reach that prickly
   weed,
Which maketh all the rest forbear to
   feed,
Or strew tods'[13] hairs, or with their tails
   do sweep
The dewy grass, to doff the simpler
   sheep,

[1] A group of stars supposed to influence hur-
ricanes.
[2] *I.e.*, the body held by the waters.
[3] Power to harm.          [4] Tambourines.

[5] Lightened.          [7] A musical instrument.
[6] Yeaning, lambing.
[8] Satirical allusion to the Puritans.
[9] Declaim against.          [11] Yeanling, lamb.
[10] Covetousness.          [12] Hide.          [13] Foxes'.

Or dig deep pits their neighbor's neat [1]
to vex,　　　　　　　　　　　　30
To drown the calves and crack the heifers' necks,
Or with pretense of chasing thence the brock [2]
Send in a cur to worry the whole flock!

Lio. O friar, those are faults that are not seen;
Ours open and of worst example been. [3]
They call ours pagan pastimes, that infect
Our blood with ease, our youth with all neglect,
Our tongues with wantonness, our thoughts with lust;
And what they censure [4] ill, all others must.

Rob. I do not know what their sharp sight may see　　　　　　　　　　40
Of late, but I should think it still might be,
As 'twas, a happy age, when on the plains
The woodmen met the damsels, and the swains,
The neat'ards, [5] plowmen, and the pipers loud,
And each did dance, some to the kit or crowd, [6]
Some to the bagpipe; some the tabret [7] moved,
And all did either love or were beloved.

Lio. The dextrous shepherd then would try his sling,
Then dart his hook at daisies, then would sing,
Sometimes would wrastle.

Cla.　　　　　　　　Ay, and with a lass,　50
And give her a new garment on the grass [8]
After a course [9] at barleybreak or base. [10]

Lio. And all these deeds were seen without offense,
Or the least hazard o' their innocence.

Rob. Those charitable times had no mistrust;
Shepherds knew how to love and not to lust.

Cla. Each minute that we lose thus, I confess,
Deserves a censure on us, more or less,
But that a sadder chance hath given allay [11]
Both to the mirth and music of this day.　　　　　　　　　　60
Our fairest shepherdess we had of late,
Here upon Trent, is drowned, for whom her mate,
Young Eglamour, a swain, who best could tread
Our country dances, and our games did lead,
Lives like the melancholy turtle, [12] drowned
Deeper in woe than she in water, crowned
With yew and cypress, and will scarce admit
The physic of our presence to his fit.

Lio. Sometimes he sits, and thinks all day, then walks,
Then thinks again, and sighs, weeps, laughs, and talks,　　　　　　70
And twixt his pleasing frenzy [13] and sad grief
Is so distracted as [14] no sought relief
By all our studies can procure his peace.

Cla. The passion finds in him that [15] large increase
As we doubt hourly we shall lose him too.

Rob. You should not cross him then, whate'er you do,
For fant'sy stopped will soon take fire and burn
Into an anger, or to a frenzy turn.

Cla. Nay, so we are advised by Alken here,
A good sage shepherd, who, although he wear　　　　　　　　　　80
An old worn hat and cloak, can tell us more
Than all the forward fry that boast their lore.

Lio. See, yonder comes the brother of the maid,
Young Karolin! How curious and afraid
He is at once, willing to find him out,
And loath to offend him.

Alk.　　　　　　　Sure he's here about.

---

[1] Cattle.
[2] Badger.
[3] Are.
[4] Judge.
[5] Neatherds.

[6] Two varieties of fiddle.
[7] Taboret, a small drum.
[8] Stain her dress green.
[9] Round.
[10] Varieties of boys' games.

[11] Abatement, check.
[12] Turtledove.
[13] Happy delirium.

[14] That.
[15] Such.

## Act I. Scene v.

*Robin Hood, Clarion, Mellifleur, Lionel,*
*Amie, Alken, Karolin; Eglamour, sit-*
*ting upon a bank by.*

Cla. See where he sits.

Eg.                    It will be rare, rare, rare!
An exquisite revenge! But peace, no
    words—
Not for the fairest fleece of all the flock!
If it be known afore, 'tis all worth noth-
    ing.
I'll carve it on the trees and in the turf,
On every greensworth [1] and in every path,
Just to the margin of the cruel Trent.
There will I knock the story in the
    ground,
In smooth great pebble and moss fill it
    round,
Till the whole country read how she
    was drowned,                              10
And with the plenty of salt tears there
    shed
Quite alter the complexion of the spring.
Or I will get some old, old grandam
    thither,
Whose rigid foot, but dipped into the
    water,
Shall strike that sharp and sudden cold
    throughout
As it shall lose all virtue; and those
    nymphs,
Those treacherous nymphs, pulled in
    Earine,
Shall stand curled up like images of ice,
And never thaw. Mark, never! A sharp
    justice!
Or, stay, a better! When the year's at
    hottest,                                  20
And that the Dog Star foams, and the
    streams boils
And curls and works and swells ready
    to sparkle,
To fling a fellow with a fever in,
To set it all on fire till it burn
Blue as Scamander fore the walls of Troy
When Vulcan leaped into him to con-
    sume him!

Rob. A deep-hurt fant'sy!
                                *[They approach him.]*

Eg.                    Do you not approve it?

Rob. Yes, gentle Eglamour, we all ap-
    prove,

And come to gratulate your just revenge,
Which, since it is so perfect, we now
    hope                                      30
You'll leave all care thereof and mix
    with us
In all the proffered solace of the spring.

Eg. A spring, now she is dead! Of what?
    Of thorns?
Briars and brambles? Thistles? Burs
    and docks?
Cold hemlock? Yew? The mandrake
    or the box?
These may grow still; but what can
    spring beside?
Did not the whole earth sicken when she
    died?
As if there since did fall one drop of dew
But what was wept for her, or any stalk
Did bear a flower, or any branch a
    bloom,                                    40
After her wreath was made! In faith, in
    faith,
You do not fair to put these things upon
    me,
Which can in no sort be. Earine,
Who had her very being and her name
With the first knots [2] or buddings of
    the spring,
Born with the primrose and the violet,
Or earliest roses blown, when Cupid
    smiled,
And Venus led the Graces out to dance,
And all the flowers and sweets in na-
    ture's lap
Leaped out, and made their solemn con-
    juration                                  50
To last but while she lived! Do not I
    know
How the vale withered the same day,
    how Dove,
Dean, Eye, and Erwash, Idel, Snite,
    and Soare
Each broke his urn,[3] and twenty waters
    more
That swelled proud Trent shrunk them-
    selves dry? That, since,
No sun or moon or other cheerful star
Looked out of heaven, but all the cope [4]
    was dark,
As it were hung so for her exequies!
And not a voice or sound to ring her
    knell

[1] Greensward.

[2] Swellings.
[3] Flow(?).                    [4] Vault of the sky.

But of that dismal pair, the scritching
  owl [1]                                    60
And buzzing hornet! Hark, hark, hark,
  the foul
Bird! How she flutters with her wicker [2]
  wings!
Peace! You shall hear her scritch.
CLA.                    Good Karolin, sing.
  Help to divert this fant'sy.
KAR.                          All I can.

*The Song, which while Karolin sings, Egla-*
*                          mour reads.*

Though I am young and cannot tell
Either what Death or Love is well,
Yet I have heard they both bear darts,
And both do aim at human hearts.
And then again I have been told,
Love wounds with heat,[3] as Death with
  cold,                                      70
So that I fear they do but bring
Extremes to touch, and mean one thing.

As in a ruin we it call
One thing to be blown up or fall,
Or to our end like way may have
By a flash of lightning or a wave,
So Love's inflaméd shaft or brand
May kill as soon as Death's cold hand,
Except Love's fires the virtue have
To fright the frost out of the grave.        80

EG. Do you think so? Are you in that
  good heresy,
I mean opinion? If you be, say nothing.
I'll study it as a new philosophy,
But by myself alone. Now you shall
  leave me.
Some of these nymphs here will reward
  you—this,
This pretty maid, although but with a
  kiss. *He forces Amie to kiss him.*[4]
Lived my Earine, you should have
  twenty;
For every line here, one I would allow
  hem
From mine own store, the treasure I
  had in her.
Now I am as poor as you.
KAR.                    And I a wretch!    90
CLA. Yet keep an eye upon him, Karolin.
*Eglamour goes out and Karolin follows him.*

MEL. Alas, that ever such a generous spirit
  As Eglamour's should sink by such a loss!
CLA. The truest lovers are least fortunate:
  Look 't [5] all their lives and legends, what
    they call
  The lovers' scriptures, Heliodore's or
    Tatii,
  Longi, Eustathii, Prodomi,[6] you'll find it!
  What think you, father?
ALK.              I have known some few,
  And read of more, wh' have had their
    dose, and deep,
  Of these sharp bittersweets.
LIO.                But what is this    100
  To jolly Robin, who the story [7] is
  Of all beatitude in love?
CLA.                    And told
  Here every day with wonder on the
    wold.[8]
LIO. And with Fame's voice.
ALK.          Save that some folk delight
  To blend all good of others with some
    spite.
CLA. He and his Marian are the sum and
  talk
  Of all that breathe here in the green-
    wood walk.
MEL. Or Be'voir Vale.
LIO.              The turtles of the wood.
CLA. The billing pair.
ALK.              And so are understood
  For simple loves, and sampled [9] lives
    beside.                                  110
MEL. Faith, so much virtue should not
  be envied.
ALK. Better be so than pitied, Mellifleur,
  For gainst all envy virtue is a cure,
  But wretched pity ever calls on scorns.—
                          [*Horns within.*]
  The deer's brought home; I hear it by
    their horns.

ACT I. SCENE vi.

*To Robin, etc., Marian, John, Scarlet,*
*                          Scathlock.*[10]

ROB. My Marian, and my mistress!
MAR.                    My loved Robin!
MEL. The moon's at full; the happy pair
  are met.

[5] Original reads *looks.*
[6] Authors of late Greek romances, the last four
names being Latin genitives.
[7] Example.        [9] Exemplary.
[8] Original reads *world.*   [10] Enters later.

[1] Screech owl.    [4] *I.e.*, Karolin, the singer.
[2] Pliant(?), ominous(?).
[3] Original reads *heart.*

MAR. How hath this morning paid me for
    my rising—
    First, with my sports, but most with
      meeting you.
    I did not half so well reward my hounds
    As she hath me today, although I gave
      them
    All the sweet morsels called tongue, ears,
      and dowcets! [1]
ROB. What, and the inchpin? [2]
MAR. Yes.
ROB.       Your sports then pleased you?
MAR. You are a wanton.
ROB.           *One*, I do confess,
    I *want*ed till you came; but now I have
      you     10
    I'll grow to your embraces, till two souls,
    Distilléd into kisses through our lips,
    Do make one spirit of love. [*Kisses her.*]
MAR.          O Robin, Robin!
ROB. Breathe, breathe awhile. What says
    my gentle Marian?
MAR. Could you so long be absent?
ROB.          What, a week?
    Was that so long?
MAR.      How long are lovers' weeks,
    Do you think, Robin, when they are
      asunder?
    Are they not pris'ners' years?
ROB.       To some they seem so,
    But, being met again, they are school-
      boys' hours—
MAR. That have got leave to play, and
    so we use them.     20
ROB. Had you good sport i' your chase
    today?
JOHN.     O, prime!
MAR. A lusty stag.
ROB.       And hunted ye at force?
MAR. In a full cry.
JOHN.       And never hunted change! [3]
ROB. You had stanch hounds then?
MAR.       Old and sure; I love
    No young rash dogs, no more than chang-
      ing friends.
ROB. What relays set you?
JOHN.       None at all; we laid not
    In one fresh dog.
ROB.     He stood not long then?
SCAR.          Yes,
    Five hours and more. A great, large deer!
ROB.     What head?

JOHN. Forkéd! A hart of ten.
MAR.          He is good venison,
    According to the season i' the blood,   30
    I'll promise all your friends for whom he
      fell.
JOHN. But at his fall there happed a
    chance.
MAR.     Worth mark.
ROB. Ay, what was that, sweet Marian?
                  *He kisses her.*
MAR.          You'll not hear?
ROB. I love these interruptions in a story;
                  *He kisses her again.*
    They make it sweeter.
MAR.         You do know as soon
    As the assay [4] is taken.
                  *He kisses her again.*
ROB.         On, my Marian.
    I did but take the assay.
MAR.         You stop one's mouth,
    And yet you bid hem speak!—When the
      arbor's [5] made—
ROB. Pulled down, and paunch turned
    out—
MAR.         He that undoes him [6]
    Doth cleave the brisket bone, upon the
      spoon     40
    Of which a little gristle grows; you call
      it—
ROB. The raven's bone.[7]
MAR.         Now o'erhead sat a raven
    On a sere bough—a grown, great bird,
      and hoarse,
    Who, all the while the deer was breaking
      up,
    So croaked and cried for 't as all the
      huntsmen,
    Especially old Scathlock, thought it omi-
      nous,
    Swore it was mother Maudlin, whom he
      met
    At the day-dawn just as he roused the deer
    Out of his lair; but we made shift to run
      him
    Off his four legs, and sunk him ere we
      left.     50

            [*Enter Scathlock.*]
    Is the deer come?
SCATH.     He lies within o' the dresser.[8]
MAR. Will you go see him, Mellifleur?

    [4] Test of quality.         [6] Cuts him up.
    [5] Disemboweling is.
    [7] Because it was given to the ravens.
    [8] Block on which meat is dressed.

    [1] Doucets, testicles.
    [2] Sweetbread.     [3] Followed a cross scent.

MEL.　　　　　　　　　　I attend you.
MAR. Come, Amie, you'll go with us?
AMIE.　　　　　　　　I am not well.
LIO. She's sick o' the young shepherd that
　　bekissed her.
MAR. Friend, cheer your friends up; we
　　will eat him merrily.
　　[*Exeunt Marian, Mellifleur, and Amie.*]
ALK. Saw you the raven, friend?
SCATH.　　　　　　Ay, quha suld let me? [1]
　　I suld be afraid o' you, sir, suld I?
CLAR.　　　　　　　　　Huntsman,
　　A dram more of civility would not hurt
　　you.
ROB. Nay, you must give [2] them all their
　　rudenesses;
　　They are not else themselves without
　　their language.　　　　　　　60
ALK. And what do you think of her?
SCATH.　　　　　　As of a witch.
　　They call her a wise woman, but I think
　　her
　　An arrant witch.
CLAR.　　　And wherefore think you so?
SCATH. Because I saw her since, broiling
　　the bone
　　Was cast her at the quarry.
ALK.　　　　　　Where saw you her?
SCATH. I' the chimley nuik, [3] within; she's
　　there now.
ROB.　　　Marian!

## ACT I. SCENE vii.

### *To them, Marian.*

[ROB.] Your hunt holds in [4] his tale still,
　　and tells more.
MAR. My hunt? What tale?
ROB.　　　　　　How! Cloudy, Marian!
　　What look is this?
MAR.　　　　　　A fit one, sir, for you.
　　Hand off, rude ranger!—(*To Scathlock.*)
　　Sirrah, get you in,
　　And bear the venison hence. It is too
　　good
　　For these coarse, rustic mouths that
　　cannot open,
　　Or spend a thank for 't. A starved mut-
　　ton's carcass
　　Would better fit their palates. See it
　　carried

To mother Maudlin's, whom you call
　　the witch, sir.
　　Tell her I sent it to make merry with.　10
　　She'll turn [5] us thanks at least! Why
　　stand'st thou, groom?
ROB. I wonder he can move, that he's not
　　fixed,
　　If that his feeling be the same with
　　mine!
　　I dare not trust the faith of mine own
　　senses;
　　I fear [6] mine eyes and ears. This is not
　　Marian!
　　Nor am I Robin Hood! I pray you ask
　　her,
　　Ask her, good shepherds, ask her all for
　　me—
　　Or rather ask yourselves—if she be she,
　　Or I be I.
MAR.　　　　Yes, and you are the spy,
　　And the spied spy that watch upon my
　　walks　　　　　　　　　　20
　　To inform what deer I kill or give away!
　　Where! When! To whom! But spy your
　　worst, good spy.
　　I will dispose of this where least you like!
　　Fall to your cheesecakes, curds, and
　　clawted [7] cream,
　　Your fools, [8] your flauns, [9] and of ale a
　　stream
　　To wash it from your livers. Strain ewes'
　　milk
　　Into your cider sillabubs, and be drunk
　　To [10] him whose fleece hath brought the
　　earliest lamb
　　This year, and wears the baudric [11] at your
　　board,
　　Where you may all go whistle, and
　　record　　　　　　　　　　30
　　This i' your dance, and foot it lustily.
　　　　　　　　　　　*She leaves them.*
ROB. I pray you, friends, do you hear and
　　see as I do?
　　Did the same accents strike your ears,
　　and objects
　　Your eyes, as mine?
ALK.　　　We taste the same reproaches.
LIO. Have seen the changes.
ROB.　　　　　　Are we not all changed,
　　Transforméd from ourselves?

---

[1] Who should stop me?　[3] Chimney nook.
[2] Grant, allow.　　　　[4] Huntsman holds to.

[5] Return.　　　　　　　[9] Pancakes.
[6] Doubt.　　　　　　　[10] In honor of.
[7] Clouted, clotted.　　[11] Baldric.
[8] Custards.

Lıo.                          I do not know.
   The best is silence.
Alk.                    And to await the issue.
Rob. The dead or lazy wait for 't! I will
   find it.                        [*Exeunt.*]

The Argument of the Second Act

The Witch Maudlin, having taken the
shape of Marian to abuse Robin Hood and
perplex his guests, cometh forth with her
daughter, Douce, reporting in what confusion she hath left them, defrauded them
of their venison, made them suspicious each
of the other, but most of all Robin Hood so
jealous of his Marian as she hopes no effect
of love would ever reconcile them, glorying
so far in the extent of her mischief as   [10
she confesseth to have surprised Earine,
stripped her of her garments to make her
daughter appear fine at this feast in them,
and to have shut the maiden up in a tree
as her son's prize, if he could win her, or his
prey, if he would force her. Her son, a rude,
bragging swine'ard, comes to the tree to
woo her (his mother and sister stepping
aside to overhear him) and first boasts his
wealth to her and his possessions—   [20
which move not. Then he presents her
gifts such as himself is taken with, but she
utterly shows a scorn and loathing both of
him and them. His mother is angry, rates
him, instructs him what to do the next time,
and persuades her daughter to show herself
about the bower, tells how she shall know
her mother, when she is transformed, by
her broidered belt. Meanwhile the young
shepherdess Amie, being kissed by   [30
Karolin, Earine's brother, before, falls in
love, but knows not what love is, but describes her disease so innocently that
Marian pities her. When Robin Hood and
the rest of his guests, invited, enter to
Marian, upbraiding her with sending away
their venison to mother Maudlin by Scathlock, which she denies, Scathlock affirms
it, but, seeing his mistress weep and to
forswear it, begins to doubt his own   [40
understanding rather than affront her
farder,[1] which makes Robin Hood and
the rest to examine themselves better. But
Maudlin, entering like herself, the witch,
comes to thank her for her bounty, at

[1] Farther.

which Marian is more angry, and more
denies the deed. Scathlock enters, tells he
has brought it again, and delivered it to the
cook. The witch is inwardly vexed the
venison is so recovered from her by   [50
the rude huntsman, and murmurs and
curses, bewitches the cook, mocks poor
Amie and the rest, discovereth her ill nature, and is a mean of reconciling them all.
For the Sage Shepherd suspecteth her mischief, if she be not prevented,[2] and so
persuadeth to seize on her. Whereupon
Robin Hood despatcheth out his woodmen
to hunt and take her, which ends the act.

Act II. Scene i.

[*The witch's dimble, with the swineherd's
                            oak at one side.*]

*Maudlin, Douce* [*dressed in Earine's clothes*].

Maud. Have I not left 'em in a brave
      confusion,
   Amazed their expectation, got their veni-
      son,
   Troubled their mirth and meeting, made
      them doubtful
   And jealous of each other, all distracted,
   And, i' the close, uncertain of themselves?
   This can your mother do, my dainty
      Douce:
   Take any shape upon her, and delude
   The senses best acquainted with their
      owners!
   The jolly Robin, who hath bid this feast,
   And made this solemn invitation,       10
   I ha' possesséd so with syke [3] dislikes
   Of his own Marian that, albee [4] he know
      her
   As doth the vauting [5] hart his venting [6]
      hind,
   He ne'er fra hence sall nase [7] her i' the
      wind,
   To his first liking.
Douce.            Did you so distaste him?
Maud. As far as her proud scorning him
      could bate
   Or blunt the edge of any lover's temper.
Douce. But were ye like her, mother?
Maud.                    So like, Douce,
   As, had she seen me her sel', her sel' had
      doubted                              19

[2] Anticipated.          [5] Vaulting.
[3] Sic, such.            [6] Scenting, smelling.
[4] Albeit, although.
[7] From hence shall nose (smell).

Whether had been the liker of the twa!
This can your mother do, I tell you,
　daughter!
I ha' but dight [1] ye yet i' the outdress [2]
And parel [3] of Earine; but this raiment,
These very weeds, sall make ye as, but
　coming
In view or ken of Eglamour, your form
Shall show too slippery [4] to be looked
　upon,
And all the forests swear you to be she!
They shall rin [5] after ye, and wage the
　odds,
Upo' their own deceivéd sights, ye are
　her,
Whilst she, poor lass, is stocked up [6] in a
　tree—　　　　　　　　　　　　　　30
Your brother Lorel's prize! For so my
　largess
Hath lotted her to be your brother's mis-
　tress,
Gif [7] she can be reclaimed [8]—gif not, his
　prey!
And here he comes new claithéd, [9] like a
　prince
Of swine'ards. Syke he seems, dight i'
　the spoils
Of those he feeds—a mighty lord of
　swine!
He is comand [10] now to woo. Let's step
　aside,
And hear his lovecraft. See, he opes the
　door,
And takes her by the hand, and helps her
　forth.
This is true courtship, and becomes his
　ray. [11]　　　　　　　　　　　　　40

### Act II. Scene ii.

#### [The same.]·

*Lorel, Earine, Maudlin, Douce.*

Lor. Ye kind to others, but ye coy to me,
Deft mistress, whiter than the cheese new
　pressed,
Smoother than cream, and softer than
　the curds,

Why start ye from me ere ye hear me tell
My wooing errand and what rents I
　have?
Large herds and pastures! Swine and
　ky [12] mine own!
And though my nase be camused, [13] my
　lips thick,
And my chin bristled, Pan, great Pan,
　was such,
Who was the chief of herdsmen, and our
　sire!　　　　　　　　　　　　　　9
I am na [14] fay, na incubus, na changelin',
But a good man that lives o' my awn
　gear. [15]
This house, these grounds, this stock is
　all mine awn.
Ear. How better 'twere to me, this were
　not known!
Maud. [*Aside.*] She likes it not; but it is
　boasted well.
Lor. An hundred udders for the pail I
　have,
That gi' me milk and curds, that make
　me cheese
To cloy the markets! Twenty swarm of
　bees,
Whilk [16] all the summer hum about the
　hive,
And bring me wax and honey in bilive. [17]
An agéd oak, the king of all the field,　[20
With a broad beech there grows afore my
　dur, [18]
That mickle mast [19] unto the farm doth
　yield.
A chestnut, whilk hath larded mony [20] a
　swine,
Whose skins I wear to fend [21] me fra the
　cold;
A poplar green, and with a carvéd seat,
Under whose shade I solace in the heat,
And thence can see gang [22] out and in my
　neat.
Twa trilland [23] brooks each from his
　spring doth meet
And make a river to refresh my feet,
In which each morning, ere the sun doth
　rise,　　　　　　　　　　　　　　30
I look myself, and clear my pleasant eyes,
Before I pipe, for therein I have skill

---

[1] Dressed.
[2] Outer dress.
[3] Apparel.
[4] Uncertain.
[5] Run.
[6] Imprisoned.
[7] If.
[8] Tamed, as a hawk.
[9] Clothed.
[10] Coming. In many later words in this play the northern ending *-and* is used for participles in *-ing*.
[11] Array, dress.
[12] Kine.
[13] Flat.
[14] No.
[15] Own property.
[16] Which.
[17] Belive, quickly.
[18] Before my door.
[19] Much food (nuts).
[20] Fattened many.
[21] Defend, protect.
[22] Go.
[23] Trickling.

'Bove other swine'ards. Bid me, and I
    will
Straight play to you, and make you
    melody.
EAR. By no means. Ah, to me all min-
    strelsy
Is irksome, as are you.
LOR.                    Why scorn you me?
Because I am a herdsman, and feed
    swine!    *He draws out other presents.*
I am a lord of other gear. This fine,
Smooth bauson's [1] cub, the young grice
    of a gray,[2]                                    39
Twa tiny urshins,[3] and this ferret gay.
EAR. Out on hem! What are these?
LOR.                    I give hem ye
As presents, Mrs.[4]—
EAR.            O, the fiend and thee!
Gar [5] take them hence; they fewmand [6]
    all the claithes,
And prick my coats.[7] Hence with hem,
    limmer lown,[8]
Thy vermin and thyself; thyself art one!
Ay, lock me up—all's well when thou art
    gone.
        [*Lorel shuts her in the tree again.*]

### ACT II. SCENE iii.

[*The same.*]

*Lorel, Maudlin, Douce.*

LOR. Did you hear this? She wished me at
    the fiend
With all my presents!
MAUD.                    A too lucky end
She wishend [9] thee, foul limmer, dritty [10]
    lown!
Gude [11] faith, it dules [12] me that I am thy
    mother.
And see, thy sister scorns thee for her
    brother.
Thou woo thy love, thy mistress, with
    twa hedgehogs,
A stinkand brock, a polecat? Out, thou
    howlet! [13]
Thou shouldst ha' given her a madge-
    owl,[14] and then

Tho' hadst made a present o' thyself,
    owlspiegle! [15]
DOUCE. Why, mother, I have heard ye bid
    to give,                                    10
And often as the cause calls.
MAUD.                    I know well,
It is a witty [16] part sometimes to give;
But what? To wham? [17] No monsters,
    nor to maidens.
He suld present them with mare [18]
    pleasand things,
Things natural, and what all women
    covet
To see: the common parent of us all,
Which maids will twire [19] at tween their
    fingers thus;
With which [20] his sire gat him, he s' [21]
    get another,
And so beget posterity upon her.
This he should do! False gelden,[22] gang
    thy gait,                                    20
And do thy turns betimes; or I s' gar
    take
Thy new breikes [23] fra thee, and thy
    duiblet [24] too.
The talleur [25] and the souter [26] sall
    undo
All they ha' made, except thou manlier
    woo!                    *Lorel goes out.*
DOUCE. Gud mother, gif you chide him,
    he'll do wairs.[27]
MAUD. Hang him! I geif [28] him to the
    devil's erse.[29]
But ye, my Douce, I charge ye, show
    yoursel'
To all the shepherds baudly.[30] Gang
    amang hem,
Be mickel i' their eye, frequent and
    fugeand,[31]
And, gif they ask ye of Earine,          30
Or of these claithes, say that I ga' hem
    ye,
And say no more. I ha' that wark [32] in
    hand,

[15] Mirror of an owl, a term of contempt derived
from *Eulenspiegel*, the hero of certain medieval
German jest books.          [18] More.
[16] Clever.                          [19] Peer.
[17] Whom.                          [20] That which.
[21] Shall. Put later in the original the first person
of this form reads '*is*.          [27] Worse.
[22] Gelding.                          [28] Give.
[23] Breeks, breeches.          [29] Arse.
[24] Doublet.                          [30] Joyously.
[25] Tailor.                          [31] Figent, lively.
[26] Cobbler.                          [32] Work.

[1] Badger's.                          [4] *I.e.*, mistress.
[2] Cub of a badger.          [5] Cause to.
[3] Hedgehogs.
[6] Soil—a form perhaps invented by Jonson.
[7] Make holes in my petticoats.   [11] Good.
[8] Rascally loon.                    [12] Grieves.
[9] Wished.                            [13] Owl.
[10] Dirty.                              [14] Barn owl.

That web upo' the luime,[1] shall gar hem think

By then, they feelin' their own frights and fears,

I s' pu' [2] the world or nature 'bout their ears.

But hear ye, Douce, bycause [3] ye may meet me

In mony shapes today, where'er you spy

This brodered [4] belt with characters, 'tis I.

A Gypsan [5] lady, and a right beldame,

Wrought it by moonshine for me, and starlight,          40

Upo' your grannam's [6] grave, that very night

We earthed her in the shades, when our dame Hecate

Made it her gang-night [7] over the kirk-yard,

With all the barkand parish-tikes set at her,

While I sat whirland of my brazen spindle.

At every twisted thrid [8] my rock [9] let fly

Unto the sewster,[10] who did sit me nigh,

Under the town turnpike,[11] which ran each spell

She stitchéd in the work, and knit it well.

See ye take tent[12] to this, and ken your mother.          [*Exeunt.*]          50

### Act II. Scene iv.

[*Before Robin Hood's bower.*]

*Marian, Mellifleur, Amie.*

MAR. How do you, sweet Amie? Yet?

MEL.                    She cannot tell;

If she could sleep, she says, she should do well.

She feels a hurt, but where, she cannot show

Any least sign that she is hurt or no.

Her pain's not doubtful to her, but the seat

Of her pain is. Her thoughts, too, work and beat,

Oppressed with cares, but why she cannot say.

All matter of her care is quite away.

MAR. Hath any vermin[13] broke into your fold?

Or any rot seized on your flock, or cold?          10

Or hath your fighting ram burst his hard horn,

Or any ewe her fleece or bag hath torn,

My gentle Amie?

AMIE.                    Marian, none of these.

MAR. Ha' you been stung by wasps or angry bees,

Or rased [14] with some rude bramble or rough brier?

AMIE. No, Marian, my disease is some-what nigher.

I weep, and boil away myself in tears;

And then my panting heart would dry those fears.

I burn, though all the forest lend a shade,

And freeze, though the whole wood one fire were made.

MAR.                    Alas!          20

AMIE. I often have been torn with thorn and brier,

Both in the leg and foot, and somewhat higher,

Yet gave not then such fearful shrieks as these. Ah!

I often have been stung too with curst [15] bees,

Yet not remember that I then did quit

Either my company or mirth for it. Ah!

And therefore what it is that I feel now,

And know no cause of it, nor where, nor how

It entered in me, nor least print can see,

I feel, afflicts me more than brier or bee. O!          30

How often when the sun, heaven's brightest birth,

Hath with his burning fervor cleft the earth,

Under a spreading elm or oak hard by

A cool, clear fountain could I sleeping lie,

Safe from the heat! But now no shady tree

Nor purling brook can my refreshing be.

---

[1] Loom.
[2] Pull.
[3] Because.
[7] **Night when spirits walk.**
[8] **Thread.**
[9] **Spindle.**
[4] Embroidered.
[5] Egyptian, gipsy.
[6] Grandam's, grandmother's.
[10] Sempstress.
[11] Turnstile.
[12] Attention.
[13] Obnoxious animal.          [15] Angry.
[14] Scratched.

Oft when the meadows were grown rough with frost,
The rivers ice-bound, and their currents lost,
My thick, warm fleece I wore was my defense;
Or large, good fires I made drave [1] winter thence.  40
But now my whole flock's fells, nor this thick grove,
Enflamed to ashes, can my cold remove.
It is a cold and heat that doth outgo.
All sense of winter's and of summer's so.

## Act II. Scene v.

### [The same.]

[To them,] *Robin Hood, Clarion, Lionel, Alken.*

Rob. O, are you here, my mistress?
Mar.                                Ay, my love!
*She, seeing him, runs to embrace him. He puts her back.*
Where should I be but in my Robin's arms,
The sphere which I delight in so to move?
Rob. What, "the rude ranger" and "spied spy"? Hand off!
You are "for no such rustics."
Mar.                                What means this?
Thrice worthy Clarion, or wise Alken, know ye?
Rob. 'Las, no, not they! "A poor, starved mutton's carcass
Would better fit their palates than your venison."
Mar. What riddle is this? Unfold yourself, dear Robin.
Rob. You ha' not sent your venison hence by Scathlock  10
To mother Maudlin?
Mar.                    I to mother Maudlin!
Will Scathlock say so?
Rob.                    Nay, we will all swear so.
For all did hear it when you gave the charge so,
Both Clarion, Alken, Lionel, myself.
Mar. Good honest shepherds, masters of your flocks,
Simple and virtuous men, no others' hirelings,

[1] Drove.

Be not you made to speak against your conscience
That which may soil the truth. I send the venison
Away? By Scathlock, and to mother Maudlin?
I came to show it here to Mellifleur,  20
I do confess; but Amie's falling ill
Did put us off it. Since, we employed ourselves
In comforting of her.

*Scathlock enters.*

                        O, here he is!—
Did I, sir, bid you bear away the venison
To mother Maudlin?
Scath.                    Ay, gude faith, madam,
Did you, and I ha' done it.
Mar.                    What ha' you done?
Scath. Obeyed your hests,[2] madam, done your commands.
Mar. Done my commands, dull groom? Fetch it again,
Or kennel with the hounds.—Are these the arts,
Robin, you rede [3] your rude ones o' the wood  30
To countenance your quarrels and mistakings?
Or are the sports to entertain your friends
Those forméd jealousies? [4]     Ask of Mellifleur
If I were ever from her here, or Amie,
Since I came in with them, or saw this Scathlock
Since I related to you his tale o' the raven.
Scath. Ay, say you so? *Scathlock goes out.*
Mel.                    She never left my side
Since I came in here, nor I hers.
Cla.                                This 's strange!
Our best of senses were deceived, our eyes, then!
Lio. And ears too.
Mar. What you have concluded on,  40
Make good, I pray you.
Amie.                    O my heart, my heart!
Mar. My heart it is, is wounded, pretty Amie.
Report not you your griefs; I'll tell for all.

[2] Behests.     [4] I.e., suspicions of those kinds.
[3] Counsel.

MEL. Somebody is to blame there is a fault.

MAR. Try if you can take rest. A little slumber

Will much refresh you, Amie.

[*Amie sleeps.*]

ALK.                    What's her grief?

MAR. She does not know, and therein she is happy.

## ACT II. SCENE vi.

[*The same.*]

*To them, John, Maudlin, and Scathlock after.*

JOHN. Here's mother Maudlin come to give you thanks,

Madam, for some late gift she hath received—

Which she's not worthy of, she says, but crakes [1]

And wonders of it, hops about the house,

Transported with the joy.

MAUD.                    Send me a stag,

(*She danceth.*)

A whole stag, madam, and so fat a deer!

So fairly hunted, and at such a time too,

When all your friends were here!

ROB.                    Do you mark this, Clarion?

Her own acknowledgment?

MAUD.                    'Twas such a bounty

And honor done to your poor beads-woman,                    10

I know not how to owe [2] it but to thank you;

And that I come to do. I shall go round

And giddy with the toy [3] of the good turn.

|        | Look out, look out, |    |
|--------|---------------------|----|
|        | Gay folk about,     |    |
| *She*  | And see me spin     |    |
| *turns*| The ring I am in    |    |
| *round*| Of mirth and glee,  |    |
|        | With thanks for fee |    |
|        | The heart puts on,  | 20 |
|        | For th' venison     |    |
|        | My lady sent.       |    |
|        | Which shall be spent|    |
|        | In draughts of wine,|    |
|        | To fume up fine     |    |
|        | Into the brain,     |    |
| *till* | And down again      |    |
| *she*  | Fall in a swoun,[4] |    |
| *falls.*| Upo' the groun'.   | 29 |

[1] Cracks, chatters.   [3] Surprising thought.
[2] Own, acknowledge.   [4] Swoon.

ROB. Look to her; she is mad.

MAUD. [*Rising.*]    My son hath sent you

A pot of strawberries gathered i' the wood

(His hogs would else have rooted up or trod);

With a choice dish of wildings [5] here to scald

And mingle with your cream.

MAR.                    Thank you, good Maudlin,

And thank your son. Go, bear hem in to Much,

Th' acater; let him thank her. Surely, mother,

Your were mistaken, or my woodmen more,

Or most myself, to send you all our store

Of venison, hunted for ourselves this day.

You will not take it, mother, I dare say,                    40

If we'ld entreat you, when you know our guests;

Red deer is head still of the forest feasts.

MAUD. But I knaw [6] ye, a right free-hearted lady,

Can spare it out of superfluity.

I have departit [7] it 'mong my poor neighbors,

To speak your largess.

MAR.                    I not gave it, mother;

You have done wrong then. I know how to place

My gifts, and where; and when to find my seasons

To give, not throw away my courtesies.

MAUD. Count you this thrown away?

MAR.                    What's ravished from me    50

I count it worse, as stolen; I lose my thanks.

But leave this quest. They fit not you nor me,

Maudlin, contentions of this quality.—

*Scathlock enters.*

                    How now?

SCATH. Your stag's returned upon my shoulders;

He has found his way into the kitchen again

With his two legs, if now your cook can dress him.

[5] Crab apples.   [6] Know.   [7] Divided.

'Slid,[1] I thought the swine'ard would ha'
    beat me,
He looks so big, [2] the sturdy karl,[3]
    lewd [4] Lorel!
MAR. There, Scathlock, for thy pains;
    thou hast deserved it.
              *Marian gives him gold.*
MAUD. Do you give a thing, and take a
    thing, madam?             60
MAR. No, Maudlin, "you had imparted
    to your neighbors;"
As much good do 't them!  I ha' done
    no wrong.

### THE FIRST CHARM

MAUD.
    The spit stand still, no broaches turn
    Before the fire, but let it burn
    Both sides and haunches till the whole
    Converted be into one coal!

CLA. What devil's paternoster mumbles
    she?
ALK. Stay, you will hear more of her
    witchery.

MAUD.
    The swilland [5] dropsy enter in
    The lazy cuke [6] and swell his skin;   70
    And the old mortmal [7] on his shin
    Now prick and itch withouten blin.[8]

CLA. Speak out, hag, we may hear your
    devil's matins.

MAUD.
    The pain we call S[t]. Anton's fire,
    The gout, or what we can desire,
    To cramp a cuke in every limb,
    Before they dine yet, seize on him.

ALK. A foul, ill spirit hath possesséd
    her.
AMIE. [*From her sleep.*]  O Karol, Karol,
    call him back again!
LIO. Her thoughts do work upon her in
    her slumber,             80
And may express some part of her
    disease.
ROB. Observe and mark, but trouble not
    her ease.

[1] By God's lid, a mild oath.
[2] Menacing.
[3] Churl, fellow.
[4] Rude.
[5] Swelling.
[6] Cuckold(?).
[7] Mormal, ulcer.
[8] Without stopping.

AMIE. O, O!
MAR.           How is 't, Amie?
MEL.           Wherefore start you?
AMIE. [*Awakening.*]  O Karol! He is fair
    and sweet.
MAUD.          What then?
Are there not flowers as sweet and fair
    as men?
The lily is fair, and rose is sweet.
AMIE.                Ay, so!
Let all the roses and the lilies go.
Karol is only fair to me.
MAR.           And why?
AMIE. Alas, for Karol, Marian, I could
    die!
Karol, he singeth sweetly too.
MAUD.         What then? 9C
Are there not birds sing sweeter far than
    men?
AMIE. I grant the linnet, lark, and bull-
    finch sing,
But best the dear, good angel [9] of the
    spring,
The nightingale.
MAUD.       Then why, then why, alone,
Should his notes please you?
AMIE.          I not long agone [10]
Took a delight with wanton kids to
    play,
And sport with little lambs a summer's
    day,
And view their frisks.  Methought it
    was a sight
Of joy to see my two brave rams to
    fight!                99
Now Karol only all delight doth move;
All that is Karol, Karol I approve!
This very morning but,[11] I did bestow
(It was a little gainst my will, I know)
A single kiss upon the seely [12] swain,
And now I wish that very kiss again.
His lip is softer, sweeter than the rose;
His mouth and tongue with dropping
    honey flows;
The relish of it was a pleasing thing.
MAUD. Yet, like the bees, it had a little
    sting.
AMIE. And sunk, and sticks yet in my
    marrow deep;           110
And what doth hurt me I now wish to
    keep.
MAR. Alas, how innocent her story is!

[9] Messenger.
[10] Ago.
[11] Just this morning.
[12] Simple.

AMIE. I do remember, Marian, I have oft
With pleasure kissed my lambs and puppies soft;
And once a dainty, fine roe-fawn I had,
Of whose outskipping bounds I was as glad
As of my health, and him I oft would kiss;
Yet had his no such sting or pain as this.
They never pricked or hurt my heart; and, for
They were so blunt and dull, I wish no more.                                    120
But this, that hurts and pricks, doth please; this sweet
Mingled with sour I wish again to meet;
And that delay, methinks, most tedious is
That keeps or hinders me of Karol's kiss.
MAR. We'll send for him, sweet Amie, to come to you.
MAUD. But I will keep him off, if charms will do it.        *She goes murmuring out.*
CLA. Do you mark the murmuring hag, how she doth mutter?
ROB. I like her not; and less her manners now.
ALK. She is a shrewd, deforméd piece, I vow.
LIO. As crooked as her body.
ROB.                        I believe        130
She can take any shape, as Scathlock says.
ALK. She may deceive the sense, but really
She cannot change herself.
ROB.                        Would I could see her
Once more in Marian's form, for I am certain
Now it was she abused us, as I think
My Marian. and my love, now innocent—
Which faith I seal unto her with this kiss,
And call you all to witness of my penance.        *[Kisses Marian.]*
ALK. It was believed before, but now confirmed,
That we have seen the monster.        140

## ACT II. SCENE vii.

### [*The same.*]

*To them, Tuck, John, Much, Scarlet.*

TUCK.                        Hear you how
Poor Tom, the cook, is taken![1] All his joints
Do crack, as if his limbs were tied with points;[2]
His whole frame slackens; and a kind of rack
Runs down along the spondils[3] of his back;
A gout or cramp now seizeth on his head,
Then falls into his feet; his knees are lead;
And he can stir his either hand no more
Than a dead stump, to his office, as before.
ALK. He is bewitched.
CLA.                        This is an argument        10
Both of her malice and her power, we see.
ALK. She must by some device restrainéd be,
Or she'll go far in mischief.
ROB.                        Advise how,
Sage Shepherd, we shall put it straight in practice.
ALK. Send forth your woodmen then into the walks,
Or let 'em prick[4] her footing hence; a witch
Is sure a creature of melancholy,
And will be found or sitting in her fourm,[5]
Or else at relief,[6] like a hare.
CLA.                        You speak,
Alken, as if you knew the sport of witch-hunting,        20
Or starting of a hag.

*Enter George to the Huntsmen, who by themselves continue the scene, the Rest going off.*

ROB.                        Go, sirs, about it.
Take George here with you; he can help to find her.

---

[1] Bewitched.
[2] Laces.
[3] Vertebræ.
[4] Track.
[5] Form, bed of a hare.
[6] Feeding.

Leave Tuck and Much behind to dress
the dinner
I' the cook's stead.

MUCH.  We'll care to get that done.

ROB. Come, Marian, let's withdraw into
the bower.

ACT II. SCENE viii.

[*The same.*]

*John, Scarlet, Scathlock, George, Alken.*[1]

JOHN. Rare sport, I swear, this hunting
of the witch
Will make us.

SCAR.  Let's advise upon 't like
huntsmen.

GEORGE. And [2] we can spy her once, she
is our own.

SCATH. First, think which way she four-
meth,[3] on what wind—
Or north or south.

GEORGE.  For, as the shepherd said,
A witch is a kind of hare.

SCATH.  And marks the weather,
As the hare does.

JOHN.  Where shall we hope to find her?
*Alken returns.*

ALK. I have asked leave to assist you,
jolly huntsmen,
If an old shepherd may be heard among
you,
Not jeered or laughed at.

JOHN.  Father, you will see  10
Robin Hood's household know more
courtesy.

SCATH. Who scorns at eld,[4] peels off his
own young hairs.

ALK. Ye say right well.  Know ye the
Witch's Dell?

SCATH. No more than I do know the walks
of hell.

ALK. Within a gloomy dimble she doth
dwell
Down in a pit, o'ergrown with brakes
and briers,
Close by the ruins of a shaken abbey,
Torn with an earthquake down unto the
ground,
'Mongst graves and grots, near an old
charnel house,
Where you shall find her sitting in her
fourm  20

As fearful and melancholic as that
She is about, with caterpillars' kells [5]
And knotty cobwebs, rounded in with
spells.
Thence she steals forth to relief, in the
fogs
And rotten mists, upon the fens and
bogs,
Down to the drownéd lands of Lincoln
shire,
To make ewes cast their lambs, swine
eat their farrow,
The housewife's tun not work,[6] nor the
milk churn!
Writhe children's wrists, and suck their
breath in sleep,
Get vials of their blood!  And, where
the sea  30
Casts up his slimy owze,[7] search for a
weed
To open locks with, and to rivet charms,
Planted about her in the wicked feat [8]
Of all her mischiefs, which are mani-
fold.

JOHN. I wonder such a story could be
told
Of her dire deeds.

GEORGE.  I thought a witch's banks [9]
Had enclosed nothing but the merry
pranks
Of some old woman.

SCAR.  Yes, her malice more.

SCATH. As it would quickly appear had
we the store
Of his collects.[10]

GEORGE.  Ay, this gude, learnéd man  40
Can speak her right.

SCAR.  He knows her shifts and haunts.

ALK. And all her wiles and turns; the
venomed plants
Wherewith she kills; where the sad mandrake grows,
Whose groans are deathful; the dead-
numbing nightshade,
The stupefying hemlock, adder's tongue,
And martagan;[11] the shrieks of luckless [12]
owls
We hear, and croaking night crows in
the air;

[5] Cauls, cocoons.  [7] Ooze.
[6] Ferment.  [8] Performance.
[9] *I.e.,* the banks of the dimble.
[10] Collections of information.
[11] Martagon, a kind of lily.
[12] Ominous of ill luck.

[1] Enters later.  [3] Crouches.
[2] If.  [4] Age.

Green-bellied snakes; blue firedrakes [1]
in the sky,
And giddy flittermice [2] with leather wings;
The scaly beetles, with their haber-
geons,                                    50
That make a humming murmur as they fly!
There in the stocks [3] of trees white fays
do dwell,
And span-long elves that dance about
a pool,
With each a little changeling in their
arms!
The airy spirits play with falling stars,
And mount the sphere of fire to kiss the
moon,
While she sits reading by the glowworm's
light
Or rotten wood, o'er which the worm
hath crept,
The baneful schedule of her nocent [4]
charms,
And binding characters through which
she wounds                                60
Her puppets, [5] the sigilla [6] of her witch-
craft.
All this I know, and I will find her for you,
And show you her sitting in her fourm.
I'll lay
My hand upon her, make her throw her
scut
Along her back, when she doth start be-
fore us.
But you must give her law; [7] and you
shall see her
Make twenty leaps and doubles, cross
the paths,
And then squat down beside us.
JOHN.                          Crafty crone!
I long to be at the sport, and to report it.
SCAR.  We'll make this hunting of the witch
as famous                                 70
As any other blast of venery. [8]
SCATH.  Hang her, foul hag!  She'll be a
stinking chase.
I had rather ha' the hunting of her heir.
GEORGE.  If we could come to see her, cry
"so haw" [9] once.
ALK.  That I do promise, or I am no good
hag-finder.                    [Exeunt.]

---

[1] Firedragons.        [5] I.e., images in wax or cloth.
[2] Bats.               [6] Signatures.
[3] Trunks.             [7] A fair start.
[4] Hurtful.            [8] Famous story of hunting.
[9] A huntsman's cry of discovery.

## THE ARGUMENT OF THE THIRD ACT

Puck-Hairy discovers himself in the
forest, and discourseth his offices, with
their necessities, briefly; after which,
Douce, entering in the habit of Earine, is
pursued by Karol, who, mistaking her at
first to be his sister, questions her how she
came by those garments.  She answers, by
her mother's gift.  The Sad Shepherd coming in the while, she runs away affrighted,
and leaves Karol suddenly; Eglamour,  [10
thinking it to be Earine's ghost he saw, falls
into a melancholic expression of his fant'sy
to Karol, and questions him sadly about
that point, which moves compassion in
Karol of his mistake still.  When Clarion
and Lionel enter to call Karol to Amie,
Karol reports to them Eglamour's passion with much regret.  Clarion resolves
to seek him, Karol to return with Lionel.
By the way, Douce and her mother,  [20
in the shape of Marian, meet them, and
would divert them, affirming Amie to be
recovered, which Lionel wondered at to
be so soon.  Robin Hood enters; they tell
him the relation of the witch, thinking
her to be Marian; Robin, suspecting her
to be Maudlin, lays hold of her girdle
suddenly, but, she striving to get free,
they both run out, and he returns with
the belt broken.  She, following in her  [30
own shape, demanding it, but at a distance, as fearing to be seized upon again,
and seeing she cannot recover it, falls into
a rage and cursing, resolving to trust to
her old arts, which she calls her daughter
to assist in.  The shepherds, content with
this discovery, go home triumphing, make
the relation to Marian.  Amie is gladded [10]
with the sight of Karol, etc.  In the meantime, enters Lorel, with purpose to  [40
ravish Earine, and, calling her forth to
that lewd end, he, by the hearing of Clarion's footing, [11] is stayed and forced to commit her hastily to the tree again, where
Clarion, coming by and hearing a voice
singing, draws near unto it; but Eglamour,
hearing it also and knowing it to be Earine's, falls into a superstitious commendation of it, as being an angel's, and in the
air; when Clarion espies a hand put  [50
forth from the tree, and makes towards it,

---

[10] Gladdened.                    [11] Footsteps.

leaving Eglamour to his wild fant'sy, who
quitteth the place; and, Clarion beginning
to court the hand and make love to it,
there ariseth a mist suddenly, which darkening all the place, Clarion loseth himself
and the tree where Earine is enclosed,
lamenting his misfortune, with the unknown nymph's misery. The air clearing,
enters the witch with her son and [60
daughter, tells them how she had caused
that late darkness, to free Lorel from surprisal, and his prey from being rescued
from him, bids him look to her, and lock
her up more carefully, and follow her to
assist a work she hath in hand of recover-
ing her lost girdle, which she laments the
loss of, with cursings, execrations, wishing confusion to their feast and meeting;
sends her son and daughter to gather [70
certain simples for her purpose, and bring
them to her dell. This Puck, hearing, prevents, and shows her error still. The huntsmen, having found her footing, follow the
tract,[1] and prick after her. She gets to
her dell, and takes her form.[2] Enter [the
huntsmen]. Alken has spied her sitting
with her spindle, threads, and images.
They are eager to seize her presently,[3] but
Alken persuades them to let her begin [80
her charms, which they do. Her son and
daughter come to her; the huntsmen are
affrighted as they see her work go forward;
and, overhasty to apprehend her, she es-
capeth them all by the help and delusions
of Puck.

### Act III. Scene i.

*[The forest.]*[4]

*Puck-Hairy.*

[Puck.] The fiend hath much to do that
    keeps a school,
  Or is the father of a family,
  Or governs but a country academy.
  His labors must be great, as are his cares,
  To watch all turns, and cast[5] how to
    prevent hem.
  This dame of mine here, Maud, grows
    high in evil,
  And thinks she does all, when 'tis I,
    her devil,

---

[1] Track.
[2] *I.e.* her human figure.    [3] Immediately.
[4] The scene remains the same through the act.
[5] Plan.

That both delude her and must yet pro-
  tect her.
She's confident in mischief, and pre-
  sumes
The changing of her shape will still[6]
  secure her;                10
But that may fail, and divers hazards
  meet
Of other consequence, which I must
  look to—
Not let her be surprised on the first
  catch.
I must go dance about the forest now,
And firk[7] it like a goblin till I find her.
Then will my service come worth ac-
  ceptation,
When not expected of her; when the
  help
Meets the necessity, and both do kiss,
'Tis called the timing of a duty, this.
                        *[Exit.]*

### Act III. Scene ii.

*Karol, Douce [in the dress of Earine]. To
them, Eglamour.*

Kar. Sure, you are very like her! I con-
  ceived
  You had been she, seeing you run afore
    me,
  For such a suit she made her gainst this
    feast,
  In all resemblance, or the very same;
  I saw her in it. Had she lived t' enjoy it,
  She had been there an acceptable guest
  To Marian and the gentle Robin Hood,
  Who are the crown and girlond[8] of the
    wood.
Douce. I cannot tell; my mother gave it
  me,
  And bade me wear it.
Kar.      Who, the wise, good woman,  10
  Old Maud of Papplewick?
Douce.      Yes.—*[Aside.]* This sullen man,
  I cannot like him.—I must take my
    leave.

*Eglamour enters and Douce goes out.*

Eg. What said she to you?
Kar.                Who?
Eg.                      Earine.
  I saw her talking with you, or her ghost,

---

[6] Always.        [7] Frisk.        [8] Garland.

For she indeed is drowned in old Trent's
    bottom.
Did she not tell who would ha' pulled her
    in,
And had her maidenhead upon the place,
The river's brim, the margin of the
    flood?
No ground is holy enough (you know my
    meaning);
Lust is committed in kings' palaces,   20
And yet their majesty's not violated!
No words!
KAR.        How sad and wild his thoughts
    are! Gone?
    *Eglamour goes out, but comes in again.*
EG. But she, as chaste as was her name,
    Earine,
Died undeflowered; and now her sweet
    soul hovers
Here in the air above us, and doth haste
To get up to the moon and Mercury,
And whisper Venus in her orb; then
    spring
Up to old Saturn, and come down by
    Mars,
Consulting Jupiter, and seat herself
Just in the midst with Phœbus, temp'ring
    all         30
The jarring spheres, and giving to the
    world
Again his first and tuneful planeting.[1]
O, what an age will here be of new con-
    cords!
Delightful harmony, to rock old sages,
Twice infants, in the cradle o' specula-
    tion,
And throw a silence upon all the crea-
    tures!
*He goes out again but returns as soon as*
    *before.*
KAR. A cogitation of the highest rapture!
EG. The loudest seas and most enragéd
    winds
Shall lose their clangor; tempest shall
    grow hoarse,
Loud thunder dumb, and every spece[2] of
    storm,     40
Laid in the lap of list'ning nature, hushed
To hear the changéd chime of this eighth
    sphere.
Take tent, and hearken for it; lose it not.
    *Eglamour departs.*

[1] An allusion to the music of the spheres.
[2] Species.

## ACT III. SCENE iii.

*Clarion, Lionel, Karol.*

CLA. O, here is Karol! Was not that the
    Sad
Shepherd slipped from him?
LIO.            Yes, I guess it was.—
Who was that left you, Karol?
KAR.                 The lost[3] man,
Whom we shall never see himself again,
Or ours, I fear; he starts away from hand
    so,
And all the touches or soft stroke of rea-
    son
Ye can apply! No colt is so unbroken,
Or hawk yet half so haggard or un-
    manned![4]
He takes all toys that his wild fant'sy
    proffers,
And flies away with them. He now con-
    ceives     10
That my lost sister, his Earine,
Is lately turned a sphere amid the seven,
And reads a music lecture to the planets!
And with this thought he's run to call
    hem hearers.
CLA. Alas, this is a strained but innocent
    fant'sy!
I'll follow him. and find him if I can.
Meantime, go you with Lionel, sweet
    Karol;
He will acquaint you with an accident,[5]
Which much desires your presence on the
    place.               *[Exit.]*

## ACT III. SCENE iv.

*Karol, Lionel.*

KAR. What is it, Lionel, wherein I may
    serve you?
Why do you so survey and circumscribe
    me,
As if you stuck one eye into my breast,
And with the other took my whole dimen-
    sions?
LIO. I wish you had a window i' your
    bosom,
Or i' your back, I might look thorough
    you,
And see your in-parts, Karol, liver, heart;
For there the seat of Love is, whence the
    boy,

[3] Original reads *last*.
[4] Untamed or unmastered.     [5] Happening.

The wingéd archer, hath shot home a
  shaft
Into my sister's breast, the innocent
  Amie,                                    10
Who now cries out, upon her bed, on
  Karol,
Sweet-singing Karol, the delicious Karol,
That kissed her like a Cupid! In your
  eyes,
She says, his stand is, and between your
  lips
He runs forth his divisions [1] to her ears,
But will not bide there, 'less yourself do
  bring him.
Go with me, Karol, and bestow a visit
In charity upon the afflicted maid,
Who pineth with the languor of your
  love.

*To them, Maud and Douce, but Maud ap-*
*pearing like Marian.*

Mar.[2] Whither intend you? Amie is re-
  covered,                                 20
  Feels no such grief as she complained of
    lately.
  This maiden hath been with her from her
    mother
  Maudlin, the cunning woman, who hath
    sent her
  Herbs for her head, and simples of that
    nature
  Have wrought upon her a miraculous
    cure,
  Settled her brain to all our wish and
    wonder.
Lio. So instantly? You know I now but
  left her,
  Possessed with such a fit almost to a
    frenzy;
  Yourself, too, feared her,[3] Marian, and
    did urge
  My haste to seek out Karol and to bring
    him.                                    30
Mar. I did so. But the skill of that wise
  woman,
  And her great charity of doing good,
  Hath by the ready hand of this deft
    lass,
  Her daughter, wrought effects beyond
    belief,

And to astonishment; we can but thank,
And praise, and be amazed, while we tell
  it.                          *They go out.*
Lio. 'Tis strange that any art should so
  help nature
In her extremes.
Kar.                Then it appears most real,
When th' other is deficient.

*Enter Robin Hood.*

Rob.                     Wherefore stay you
  Discoursing here, and haste not with
    your succors                            40
  To poor afflicted Amie, that so needs
    them?
Lio. She is recovered well, your Marian
  told us
  But now here. See, she is returned t' af-
    firm it!

*Enter Maudl[in] like Marian. Maudl[in],*
*espying Robin Hood, would run out,*
*but he stays her by the girdle, and runs*
*in with her.*

Rob. My Marian?
Mar.                Robin Hood! Is he here?
Rob.                                    Stay;
  What was 't you ha' told my friend?
*He returns with the girdle broken and she in*
*her own shape.*
Maud.                Help, murder, help!
  You will not rob me, outlaw? Thief,
    restore
  My belt that ye have broken!
Rob.                          Yes, come near.
Maud. Not i' your gripe.
Rob.            Was this the charméd circle,[4]
  The copy [5] that so cozened and deceived
    us?
  I'll carry hence the trophy of your
    spoils.                                  50
  My men shall hunt you too upon the
    start,[6]
  And course [7] you soundly.
Maud.                I shall make hem sport,
  And send some home without their legs
    or arms.
  I'll teach hem to climb stiles, leap ditches,
    ponds,
  And lie i' the waters, if they follow me.

---

[1] Melodies.
[2] While Maudlin is still undiscovered she is
referred to as Marian.          [3] For her.

[4] Spell.
[5] Disguise, assumed shape.
[6] Without a fair start.          [7] Pursue.

Rob.  Out, murmuring hag!
                    [*Exeunt All but Maudlin.*]
Maud.               I must use all my powers,
    Lay all my wits to piecing of this loss.
    Things run unluckily.  Where's my
        Puck-Hairy?

### Act III.  Scene v.

*Maud, Puck.*

[Maud.]  Hath he forsook me?
Puck.                    At your beck, madam.
Maud.  O Puck, my goblin!  I have lost
        my belt;
    The strong thief, Robin Outlaw, forced
        it from me.
Puck.  They are other clouds and blacker
        threat you, dame;
    You must be wary, and pull in your
        sails,
    And yield unto the weather of the tem-
        pest.
    You think your power's infinite as your
        malice,
    And would do all your anger prompts you
        to;
    But you must wait occasions, and obey
        them.

Sail in an eggshel[1], make a straw your
        mast,                              10
    A cobweb all your cloth,[1] and pass un-
        seen,
    Till you have scaped the rocks that are
        about you.
Maud.  What rocks about me?
Puck.                    I do love, madam,
    To show you all your dangers, when you
        are past hem!
    Come, follow me; I'll once more be your
        pilot,
    And you shall thank me.        [*Exit.*]
Maud.               Lucky, my loved goblin!

*Lorel meets her.*

Where are you gaang [2] now?
Lor.                    Unto my tree,
    To see my maistress.
Maud.               Gang thy gait, and try
    Thy turns with better luck, or hang
        thysel'.

### The End.[3]

[1] Sail.                    [2] Going(?).
[3] The play, of course, is actually unfinished,
but F. G. Waldron published a completion of it
in 1783, reprinted by W. W. Greg in his edition
of the play (Bang's *Materialen*, 1905).

# BEN JONSON

## THE HUE AND CRY AFTER CUPID

Although the masque was a minor form in the history of the English theater, it bulked very large in the work of Ben Jonson, as shown by the fact that he devoted at least as much time and attention to the composition and preparation of such entertainments as he did to his plays and other works. In "The Jonsonian Masque as a Literary Form" (*ELH*, 1955), D. Cunningham complained that the masque has seldom been accorded the respect it deserves and that Jonson's comments on his contributions to this genre show that he felt himself to be working in accordance with the serious historical and aesthetic principles of decorum, hierarchical unity, and ethical purpose that are to be found in most Elizabethan literature.

The English masque (the word with this spelling was first used in Edward Hall's *Chronicle* in 1548) of course did not begin with Ben Jonson, although he and Inigo Jones raised it to its greatest height of perfection. It goes back well into the Middle Ages, with its fondness for pageantry, for the sensuous in color, sound, and movement, and especially for the dance, which was the germ of it all. As early as 1377 "mumming" or "disguising" was held in honor of Richard II, in which the mummers rode through London in costume, with masks over their faces, entered the palace, performed their dance, and then left—all without speaking, since the original masques were all done in dumb show. Then pageants or wagons (or, as we would say, "floats") were added as stages for street presentation. The next step allowed the mummers to mingle with the spectators and dance with them after their show was completed; this was done in imitation of the Italian masque, which was the origin of the whole form. Since these masquers, however, still retained their masks while dancing, as in a masquerade, the element of intrigue now began to enter in. The final step toward drama came in the addition of words in verse form, both as dialogue and as lyrics. Since these masques were usually allegorical, as in the morality plays, and the allegory often, as in the case of Jonson, became very elaborate and scholarly, words were clearly necessary to help the spectators to an understanding of the meaning. The mythological element also contributed to both the spectacularity and the difficulty of interpretation of the masque.

The English masque has been examined and analyzed in great detail, historically and theoretically, by many writers in English, French, and German. The chief of these works, which of course devote considerable space to Jonson, are: H. A. Evans, *English Masques* (London, 1897); Ashley H. Thorndike, "The Influence of the Court-Masques on the Drama, 1608–15," *PMLA*, 1900; Rudolf Brotanek, *Die Englischen Maskenspiele* (Vienna, 1902); John W. Cunliffe, "Italian Prototypes of the Masque and the Dumb Show," *PMLA*, 1907; Paul Reyher, *Les Masques Anglais* (Paris, 1909); W. J. Lawrence, "The Mounting of the Carolan Masques," *The Elizabethan Playhouse* (Stratford, 1912); Mary Sullivan, *The Court Masques of James I* (New York, 1913); Lily B. Campbell, *Scenes and Machines on the English Stage during the Renaissance* (Cambridge University Press, 1923); Herford-Simpson, 1925; Mary S. Steele, *Plays and Masques at Court* (Yale University Press, 1926); Enid Welsford, *The Court Masque* (Harvard University Press, 1927); J. Alfred Gotch, *Inigo Jones* (London, 1928); Edward J. Dent, *The Foundations of English Opera* (Cambridge, 1928); and Allardyce Nicoll, *Stuart Masques and the Renaissance Stage* (New York, 1938).

The Haddington masque, named *The Hue and Cry after Cupid* by William Gifford and reprinted in this anthology, is one of the shorter and less elaborate of Jonson's masques, but is nevertheless quite representative of his work and quite charming in its own right. It was given at court on February 9, 1608, to help celebrate the marriage of one of James's young Scotch favorites, John Ramsey, Viscount Haddington, to Elizabeth Ratcliffe, or Radcliffe, daughter of the Earl of Sussex, and cost each of the five English and seven Scottish gentlemen who participated some £300 a man. Ramsey had been in the so-called "Gowrie conspiracy" in 1600, had been knighted, and then raised to a peerage by the King. At the wedding the King himself drank the health of the bride and groom in a gold cup, which he then sent to them, inside which was the grant of a pension of £600 a year to them both and to the survivor of the pair. The Lady Elizabeth died of smallpox ten years later, but "died wonderful religious, and most well-prepared for heaven," as one pious commentator phrased it. Several letter writers of the day commented on the great success of the masque, but unfortunately none of Inigo Jones's drawings survive in the famous Chatsworth Collection. *The Hue and Cry after Cupid* was revived in a shortened form by the Mermaid Society in London in 1902, and was given at Bryn Mawr College in 1906, 1910, and 1920.

Jonson's chief sources for this masque were Italian works by Vincenzo Cartari and Natale Conti (D. J. Gordon, "*The Haddington Masque:* The Story and the Fable," *MLR*, 1947). Several studies of his use of mythological material for his masques, including of course *The Hue and Cry*, have thrown considerable light on his reading habits and his use of sources. The masques have thus proved a treasure trove for source researchers in comparative literature. In 1938 Charles F. Wheeler provided a sort of handbook, *Classical Mythology in the Plays, Masques, and Poems of Ben Jonson*, in which, in his discussion of Jonson's use of myth for ornamentation, character portrayal, and criticism of life, he analyzed *The Hue and Cry* from these viewpoints. Five years later Ernest W. Talbert, in an article, "New Light on Ben Jonson's Workmanship" (*SP*, 1943), proved that, as a matter of fact, a number of the classical references cited by Wheeler had not actually been directly used by Jonson, who had really relied considerably on two very popular handbooks, *Dictionarum Historicum, Geographicum, Poeticum* by Charles Stephanus and *Thesaurus Linguae Latinae* by Robert Stephanus. F. S. Boas, in his review of these articles in *The Year's Work in English Studies*, accepted Jonson's use of the books, but added that, in his opinion, Talbert had ignored Jonson's debt to Conti, Valeriano, Pico, Ficino, and other Italian humanists. In any case, Jonson's familiarity with a considerable body of Italian literature is indubitable.

In 1946 Talbert added to his contribution to the general subject with his article, "The Interpretation of Jonson's Courtly Spectacles" (*PMLA*, 1946,) and in 1958 W. Todd Furniss supplemented Talbert further in "Ben Jonson's Masques" (*Three Studies in the Renaissance: Sidney, Jonson, Milton, YSE*). Gordon studied "The Imagery of Ben Jonson's *The Masque of Blackness* and *The Masque of Beauty*" for *The Journal of the Warburg and Courtauld Institutes* (1943), and added more to the knowledge of Jonson's sources and the inner meaning of his masques. Allan H. Gilbert approached the same matter from a somewhat different angle in *The Symbolic Personages in the Masques of Ben Jonson* (Duke University Press, 1948), adding further Italian, English, and Latin sources, and maintaining that if Jonson has recently been found to be less erudite than was formerly believed, this was because he "was primarily a poet, not a scholar." Gilbert also suggested once more that the basic cause of Jonson's breach with Inigo Jones may have been that he believed that the masque should not be regarded as a mere spectacular amusement but rather as an entertainment of moral and intellectual profit. But at the same time Jonson, as a writer of comedy, was primarily responsible for the addition of the element of comedy to the masque in the form of the antimasque and the frequent introduction of lively comic dialogue (Thomas M. Parrott, "Comedy in the Court Masque: A Study of Ben Jonson's Contribution," *Essays on Shakespeare and the Elizabethan Drama in Honor of Hardin*

*Craig,* University of Missouri Press, 1962).   W. A. Armstrong went so far in 1960 ("Ben Jonson and Jacobean Stagecraft," *The Jacobean Theatre, SAS*) as to suggest that many of Jonson's attacks on the stagecraft of Inigo Jones "are better understood when they are related to Inigo's innovations in the staging of court masques," since "it is clear that from the outset of their collaboration he regarded the art of designing the settings and costumes as vastly inferior to that of writing the texts of the masques."   Finally, the general subject of music in the masques has received the recent attention of Ernst Ulrich in "Die Musik in Ben Jonsons Maskenspielen und Entertainments" (*SJ*, 1937), a digest of his longer work in 1933, and of John P. Cutts in his description of his discovery of the manuscripts for the musical settings of several masques or songs in them in a college library (*NQ*, 1954).

The present text is based on that in a copy of the 1641 folio in the Newberry Library.

# THE HUE AND CRY AFTER CUPID[1]

BY

BEN JONSON

[DRAMATIS PERSONÆ

| | |
|---|---|
| CUPID. | PYRACMON ⎫ |
| VULCAN. | BRONTES ⎬ Cyclopes. |
| HYMEN. | STEROPES ⎭ |
| VENUS. | GRACES 1, 2, and 3. |

SCENE: *Imaginary.*

TIME: *Contemporary.*]

*The worthy custom of honoring worthy marriages with these noble solemnities hath of late years advanced itself frequently with us, to the reputation no less of our court than nobles, expressing besides (through the difficulties of expense and travel, with the cheerfulness of undertaking) a most real affection in the personators, to those for whose sake they would sustain these persons. It behoves then us, that are trusted with a part of their honor in these celebrations, to do nothing in them beneath the dignity of either. With this proposed part of judgment, I adventure to give that abroad, which in my first conception I intended honorably fit; and, though it hath labored since, under censure, I, that know truth to be always of one stature and so like a rule as [2] who bends it the least way must needs do an injury to the right, cannot but smile at their tyrannous ignorance, that will offer to slight me (in these things being an artificer) and give themselves a peremptory license to judge, who have never touched so much as to the bark or utter [3] shell of any knowl-edge. But their daring dwell with them. They have found a place to pour out their follies, and I a seat to sleep out the passage.*

*The scene to this masque was a high, steep, red cliff, advancing itself into the clouds, figuring the place from whence (as I have been, not fabulously, informed) the honorable family of the Radcliffes first took their name, a clivo rubro,[4] and is to be written with that orthography, as I have observed out of M[aster] Camden in his mention of the Earls of Sussex. This cliff was also a note of height, greatness, and antiquity, before which, on the two sides, were erected two pilasters, charged with spoils and trophies of Love and his mother, consecrate to marriage; amongst which were old and young persons figured, bound with roses, the wedding garments, rocks and spindles, hearts transfixed with arrows, others flaming, virgins' girdles, girlonds, [5] and worlds of suchlike, all wrought round and bold; and overhead two personages, Triumph and Victory, in flying postures, and twice so big as the life, in place of the arch, and holding a girlond of myrtle for the key— all which, with the pillars, seemed to be of burnished gold, and embossed out of the metal. Beyond the cliff was seen nothing but clouds, thick and obscure, till on the sudden, with a solemn music, a bright sky breaking forth, there were discovered first two doves,*

[1] This title was assigned to the masque by Gifford. The title in the 1616 folio reads: "The Description of the Masque, with the Nuptial Songs, at the Lord Viscount Haddington's Marriage at Court on the Shrove Tuesday at Night. 1608." On this occasion the bride was Lady Elizabeth Ratcliffe, or Radcliffe, daughter of Robert Earl of Sussex.

[2] That.

[3] Outer.

[4] From a red cliff.

[5] Garlands.

295

*then two swans,[1] with silver gears,[2] drawing forth a triumphant chariot, in which Venus sat, crowned with her star, and beneath her the three Graces, or* Charites, *Aglaia, Thalia, Euphrosyne, all attired according to their antique figures. These from their chariot alighted on the top of the cliff, and, descending by certain abrupt and winding passages, Venus having left her star only flaming in her seat, came to the earth, the Graces throwing girlonds all the way, and began to speak.*

VENUS. It is no common cause, ye will conceive,
  My lovely Graces, makes your goddess leave
  Her state in heaven, tonight to visit earth.
  Love late is fled away, my eldest birth,
  Cupid, whom I did joy to call my son;
  And, whom long absent, Venus is undone.
  Spy, if you can, his footsteps on this green,
  For here, as I am told, he late hath been,
  With divers of his brethren,[3] lending light
  From their best flames to gild a glorious night,          10
  Which I not grudge at, being done for her
  Whose honors to mine own I still prefer.
  But he not yet returning, I am in fear
  Some gentle Grace or innocent Beauty here
  Be taken with him, or he hath surprised
  A second Psyche, and lives here disguised.
  Find ye no tract [4] of his strayed feet?
1 GRACE.                                    Not I.
2 GRACE. Nor I.
3 GRACE.          Nor I.

VENUS.                              Stay, nymphs,
  we then will try
  A nearer way.  Look [5] all these ladies' eyes,
  And see if there he not concealéd lies,          20
  Or in their bosoms twixt their swelling breasts
  (The wag affects to make himself such nests).
  Perchance he hath got some simple heart to hide
  His subtle shape in.  I will have him cried,[6]
  And all his virtues told, that, when they know
  What sprite he is, she soon may let him go,
  That guards him now, and think herself right blessed
  To be so timely rid of such a guest.
  Begin, soft Graces, and proclaim reward
  To her that brings him in.  Speak to be heard.          30
1 GRACE. Beauties, have ye seen this toy,
  Calléd Love, a little boy,
  Almost naked, wanton, blind,
  Cruel now, and then as kind?
  If he be amongst ye, say.
  He is Venus' runaway.
2 GRACE. She that will but now discover
  Where the wingéd wag doth hover,
  Shall tonight receive a kiss,
  How or where herself would wish;          40
  But who brings him to his mother,
  Shall have that kiss, and another.
3 GRACE. H' hath of marks about him plenty;
  You shall know him among twenty.
  All his body is a fire,
  And his breath a flame entire,
  That being shot, like lightning, in,
  Wounds the heart, but not the skin.
1 GRACE. At his sight, the sun hath turned;
  Neptune in the waters burned;          50
  Hell hath felt a greater heat;
  Jove himself forsook his seat.
  From the center [7] to the sky
  Are his trophies reeréd high.
2 GRACE. Wings he hath, which though ye clip,
  He will leap from lip to lip,

---

[1] Jonson's note runs: "Both doves and swans were sacred to this goddess, and as well with the one as the other; her chariot is induced by Ovid, L. x and xi, *Metamor.*" The editors of the present text omit most of Jonson's notes on this masque and a small amount of similar material incorporated in the stage directions.
  [2] Trappings.
  [3] "Alluding to the Loves in the Queen's Masque before" (Jonson's note referring to his *Masque of Beauty*).
  [4] Track, trace.

[5] Look at, examine.
[6] Proclaimed by the public crier.
[7] Center of the world.

Over liver, lights, and heart,
But not stay in any part;
And, if chance his arrow misses,
He will shoot himself in kisses.          60
3 GRACE.  He doth bear a golden bow,
And a quiver, hanging low,
Full of arrows that outbrave
Dian's shafts, where, if he have
Any head more sharp than other,
With that first he strikes his mother.
1 GRACE.  Still the fairest are his fuel.
When his days are to be cruel,
Lovers' hearts are all his food,
And his baths their warmest blood.     70
Naught but wounds his hand doth
      season,
And he hates none like to Reason.
2 GRACE.  Trust him not; his words, though
      sweet,
Seldom with his heart do meet.
All his practice is deceit,
Every gift it is a bait,
Not a kiss but poison bears,
And most treason in his tears.
3 GRACE.  Idle minutes are his reign;
Then the straggler makes his gain     80
By presenting maids with toys,
And would have ye think hem joys;
'Tis the ambition of the elf
To have all childish as himself.
1 GRACE.  If by these ye please to know
      him,
Beauties, be not nice,[1] but show him.
2 GRACE.  Though ye had a will to hide
      him,
Now, we hope, ye'll not abide him—
3 GRACE.  Since ye hear his falser play,
And that he is Venus' runaway.          90

*At this, from behind the trophies, Cupid
discovered himself and came forth
armed, attended with twelve Boys, most
anticly attired, that represented the
Sports and pretty Lightnesses that accompany Love, under the titles of Joci
and Risus, and are said to wait on
Venus, as she is Prefect of Marriage.*

CUPID.  Come, my little jocund Sports,
Come away; the time now sorts [2]
With your pastime.  This same night
Is Cupid's day.  Advance your light.
With your revel fill the room,
That our triumphs be not dumb.

[1] Scrupulous.        [2] Agrees.        [3] Heated.

*Wherewith they fell into a subtle, capricious
dance, to as odd a music, each of them
bearing two torches, and nodding with
their antic faces, with other variety of
ridiculous gesture, which gave much
occasion of mirth and delight to the
spectators.  The dance ended, Cupid
went forward.*

CUPID.  Well done, antics!  Now my bow
And my quiver bear to show
That these Beauties here may know
By what arms this feat was done,     100
That hath so much honor won
Unto Venus and her son.

*At which his Mother apprehended him and,
circling him in with the Graces, began
to demand.*

VENUS.  What feat, what honor is it that
      you boast,
My little straggler?  I had given you
      lost,
With all your games here.
CUPID.                    Mother?
VENUS.                            Yes, sir, she.
What might your glorious cause of
      triumph be?
Ha' you shot Minerva or the Thespian
      dames?
Heat[3] agéd Ops[4] again with youthful
      flames?
Or have you made the colder Moon to
      visit
Once more a sheepcote?  Say, what con-
      quest is it                          110
Can make you hope such a renown to
      win?
Is there a second Hercules brought to
      spin?
Or, for some new disguise, leaves Jove
      his thunder?
CUPID.  Nor that, nor those, and yet no
      less a wonder—
Which to tell, I may not stay.
                    *And there slips from her.*

*Here Hymen, the God of Marriage, entered,
and was so induced here as you have
him described in my* Hymenæi.

Hymen's presence bids away;
'Tis already at his night;

[4] Goddess of the harvest and fertility.

He can give you farther light.
You, my Sports, may here abide
Till I call to light the bride.          120
HYMEN. Venus, is this a time to quit your car?
To stoop to earth, to leave alone your star,
Without your influence, and, on such a night,
Which should be crowned with your most cheering sight,
As [1] you were ignorant of what were done
By Cupid's hand, your all-triumphing son?
Look on this state, [2] and, if you yet not know
What crown there shines, whose scepter here doth grow,
Think on thy loved Æneas; and what name
Maro, the golden trumpet [3] of his fame,          130
Gave him, read thou in this: a prince that draws
By example more than others do by laws,
That is so just to his great act and thought,
To do, not what kings may, but what kings ought;
Who, out of piety, unto peace is vowed,
To spare his subjects, yet to quell the proud,
And dares esteem it the first fortitude
To have his passions, foes at home, subdued;
That was reserved, until the Parcæ spun
Their whitest wool and then his thread begun,          140
Which thread, when treason would have burst, [4] a soul
(Today renowned and added to my roll)
Opposed; and, by that act, to his name did bring
The honor to be saver of his king—
This king, whose worth, if gods for virtue love,
Should Venus with the same affections move

As her Æneas, and no less endear
Her love to his safety than when she did cheer,
After a tempest, long-afflicted Troy,
Upon the Lybian shore, and brought them joy.          150
VENUS. I love, and know his virtues, and do boast
Mine own renown when I renown him most.
My Cupid's absence I forgive and praise,
That me to such a present grace could raise.
His champion shall hereafter be my care
But speak his bride, and what her virtues are.
HYMEN. She is a noble virgin, styled the Maid
Of the Red Cliff, and hath her dowry weighed
No less in virtue, blood, and form than gold;
Thence, where my pillar's reared (you may behold)          160
Filled with Love's trophies, doth she take her name.
Those pillars did uxorious Vulcan frame
Against [5] this day; and underneath that hill
He and his Cyclopes are forging still
Some strange and curious piece t' adorn the night,
And give these gracéd nuptials greater light.

*Here Vulcan presented himself, as over-hearing Hymen, attired in a cassock girt to him, with bare arms, his hair and beard rough, his hat of blue and ending in a cone, in his hand a hammer and tongs, as coming from the forge.*

VULCAN. Which I have done—the best of all my life—
And have my end, if it but please my wife,
And she commend it, to the labored worth.
Cleave, solid rock, and bring the wonder forth!          170

*At which, with a loud and full music, the cliff parted in the midst and dis-*

---

[1] As if.   [2] Canopied throne.   [3] Trumpeter.
[4] Jonson's note runs: "In that monstrous conspiracy of E[arl] Gowry." Haddington aided the future James I to put down the conspiracy in 1600.

[5] In preparation for.

*covered an illustrious [1] concave, filled
with an ample and glistering light, in
which an artificial sphere was made of
silver, eighteen foot in the diameter,
that turned perpetually; the* coluri [2]
*were heightened with gold; so were the
arctic and antarctic circles, the tropics,
the equinoctial, the meridian and hori-
zon; only the zodiac was of pure gold,
in which the Masquers, under the characters of the twelve signs, were placed,
answering them in number, whose offices, with the whole frame, as it turned,
Vulcan went forward to describe.*

VULCAN. It is a sphere I have formed
  round and even,
In due proportion to the sphere of
  heaven,
With all his [3] lines and circles that compose
The perfect'st form, and aptly do disclose
The heaven of marriage (which I title it),
Within whose zodiac I have made to sit,
In order of the signs, twelve sacred
  powers
That are presiding at all nuptial hours:
  1. The first, in Aries' place, respecteth
    pride
    Of youth and beauty, graces in
      the bride.                    180
  2. In Taurus, he loves strength and
    manliness,
    The virtues which the bridegroom
      should profess.
  3. In Gemini, that noble power is
    shown,
    That twins their hearts, and doth
      of two make one.
  4. In Cancer, he that bids the wife
    give way
    With backward yielding to her
      husband's sway.
  5. In Leo, he that doth instill the heat
    Into the man, which from the follow-
      ing seat
  6. Is tempered so as he that looks
    from thence
    Sees yet they keep a Virgin in-
      nocence.                    190

[1] Brilliantly lighted.
[2] The great circles of the celestial sphere in-
tersecting at the poles.                    [3] Its.

  7. In Libra's room, rules he that doth
    supply
    All happy beds with sweet equality.
  8. The Scorpion's place he fills, that
    makes the jars,
    And stings in wedlock little strifes
      and wars,
  9. Which he in th' Archer's throne
    doth soon remove
    By making with his shafts new
      wounds of love.
  10. And those the follower with more
    heat inspires,
    As in the Goat the sun renews his
      fires.
  11. In wet Aquarius' stead, reigns he
    that showers
    Fertility upon the genial bowers.  200
  12. Last, in the Fishes' place, sits he
    doth say,
    "In married joys all should be dumb
      as they."
And this hath Vulcan for his Venus done,
To grace the chaster triumph of her
  son.
VENUS. And for this gift will I to heaven
  return,
And vow forever that my lamp shall
  burn
With pure and chastest fire, or never
  shine
But when it mixeth with thy sphere and
  mine.

*Here Venus returned to her chariot with
the Graces, while Vulcan, calling out
the Priests of Hymen, who were the
musicians, was interrupted by Pyracmon (one of the Cyclopes), . . .
Brontes, and Steropes. . . .*

VULCAN. Sing then, ye priests.
PYRACMON.          Stay, Vulcan, shall not
  these                    209
Come forth and dance?
VULCAN.          Yes, my Pyracmon, please
The eyes of these spectators with our
  art.
PYRACMON. Come here, then, Brontes;
  bear a Cyclops' part,
And Steropes; both with your sledges
  stand,
And strike a time unto them as they
  land,

And, as they forwards come, still guide
their paces
In musical and sweet proportioned
graces,
While I upon the work and frame attend,
And Hymen's priests forth, at their
seasons, send
To chaunt their hymns, and make this
square admire
Our great artificer, the god of fire.     220

*Here the Musicians, attired in yellow,
with wreaths of marjoram, and veils like
Hymen's priests, sung the first staff of the
following epithalamion, which, because it
was sung in pieces between the dances,
showed to be so many several songs, but
was made to be read an entire poem. After
the song, they came forth (descending in
an oblique motion) from the zodiac, and
danced their first dance; then, music inter-
posed (but varied with voices, only keeping
the same chorus), they danced their second
dance. So after, their third and fourth
dances, which were all full of elegancy and
curious device. The two latter were made
by M[aster] Tho. Giles,[1] the two first by
M[aster] Hie. Herne,[2] who, in the persons
of the two Cyclopes, beat a time to them with
their hammers. The tunes were M[aster]
Alphonso Ferrabosco's.[3] The device and act
of the scene M[aster] Inigo Jones [4] his, with
addition of the trophies. For the invention
of the whole and the verses,* Assertor qui
dicat esse meos, imponet plagiario pu-
dorem.[5]

*The attire of the Masquers throughout
was most graceful and noble, partaking of
the best both ancient and later figure; the
colors carnation and silver, enriched both
with embroidery [6] and lace; the dressing of
their heads, feathers and jewels; and so*

---

[1] Formerly Master of the Children of Paul's
and later instructor in music to the princes
royal.
[2] Hierome Herne, a minor musician and
dancing master.
[3] A well-known Italian dancing master.
[4] The most famous architect of the day and
inventor of scenery and costumes for court
masques. He was on constantly shifting terms
of enmity and friendship with Jonson.
[5] The declarer who calls them mine will bring
shame upon the plagiarist.
[6] Embroidery.

*excellently ordered to the rest of the habit
as all would suffer under any description
after the show. Their performance of all, so
magnificent and illustrous that nothing can
add to the seal of it but the subscription of
their names:* [7]

| | |
|---|---|
| *The Duke of Lennox* | *Lord Hay* |
| *Earl of Arundel* | *Lord Sankre* |
| *Earl of Pembroke* | *Sir Ro. Riche* |
| *Earl of Montgomery* | *Sir Jo. Kennethie* |
| *Lord D'Aubigny* | *[Master of Mar]*[8] |
| *Lord of Walden* | *Mr. Ersskins* |

## EPITHALAMION

Up, youths and virgins, up, and praise
The god whose nights outshine his days—
Hymen, whose hallowed rites
Could never boast of brighter lights;
Whose bands pass liberty.
Two of your troop, that with the morn were
free,
Are now waged to his war.
And what they are,
If you'll perfection see,
Yourselves must be.                          10
Shine, Hesperus, shine forth, thou wisnéd
star!

What joy or honors can compare
With holy nuptials, when they are
Made out of equal parts
Of years, of states, of hands, of hearts,
When, in the happy choice,
The spouse and spouséd have the fore-
most voice?
Such, glad of Hymen's war,
Live what they are,
And long perfection see;                     20
And such ours be.
Shine, Hesperus, shine forth, thou wishéd
star!

The solemn state of this one night
Were fit to last an age's light;

---

[7] Gifford in his 1816 edn. of Jonson, VII, 94,
quotes a letter from Rowland White to the Earl
of Shrewsbury: "The great masque intended for
my L. Haddington's marriage is now *the only
thing thought upon* at court, by 5 English: L.
Arundel, L. Pemb., L. Montgomery, L. Theoph.
Howard, and Sir Robt. Rich; and by 7 Scots:
D. Lennox, D'Aubigny, Hay, Mr. of Mar, young
Erskine, Sankier, and Kennedy. It will cost
them about 300 *l.* a man."
[8] Supplied from White's letter above.

But there are rites behind
Have less of state, but more of kind: [1]
Love's wealthy crop of kisses,
And fruitful harvest of his mother's blisses.
Sound then to Hymen's war—
That what these are,                    30
Who will perfection see,
May haste to be.
Shine, Hesperus, shine forth, thou wishéd
    star!

Love's commonwealth consists of toys;
His council are those antic boys,
Games, Laughter, Sports, Delights,
That triumph with him on these nights,
To whom we must give way,
For now their reign begins, and lasts till
    day.
They sweeten Hymen's war,                40
And, in that jar,
Make all that married be,
Perfection see.
Shine, Hesperus, shine forth, thou wishéd
    star!

Why stays the bridegroom to invade
Her that would be a matron made?
Good night, whilst yet we may
Good night, to you a virgin, say;
Tomorrow rise the same                   49
Your mother is, and use a nobler name.
Speed well in Hymen's war

    Nature.

That what you are,
By your perfection we
And all may see.
Shine, Hesperus, shine forth, thou wishéd
    star!

Tonight is Venus' vigil kept.
This night no bridegroom ever slept;
And, if the fair bride do,
The married say, 'tis his fault, too.
Wake then, and let your lights           60
Wake too; for they'll tell nothing of your
    nights
But that in Hymen's war
You perfect are.
And such perfection we
Do pray should be.
Shine, Hesperus, shine forth, thou wishéd
    star!

That, ere the rosy-fingered morn
Behold nine moons, there may be born
A babe, t' uphold the fame               69
Of Radcliffe's blood and Ramsey's [2] name,
That may, in his great seed,
Wear the long honors of his father's deed.
Such fruits of Hymen's war
Most perfect are;
And all perfection we
Wish you should see.
Shine, Hesperus, shine forth, thou wishéd
    star!

[2] The family name of Viscount Haddington.

# JOHN WEBSTER

It is astonishing that practically nothing is known about the life of a writer like John Webster. Critic after critic has ranked him next to Shakespeare on the basis of two of his tragedies, in spite of the fact that other well qualified critics have denounced him as a dramatic bungler, and a blackener and blasphemer of human life. There are no clear parish records of his birth, marriage, or death, no clear school records of his education, no court records of his being sued, imprisoned for debt, or tried for brawling or fighting. His history is almost entirely that of the acting of his plays and the publication of his various works. And yet he collaborated with most of the major and minor playwrights of his time—with Heywood, Dekker, Marston, Middleton, Ford, Munday, Drayton, William Rowley, and perhaps Massinger—and wrote commendatory verses for some of his friends' works and was the subject of other verses, not always commendatory.

The only things of importance discovered about Webster's life since F. L. Lucas summed up the little which was known about him in his introduction to *The Complete Works of John Webster* (London, 1927; revised 1958) concern his probable parentage and his connection with the Merchant Taylors' Company. In 1968 T. W. Howarth published "Two Notes on John Webster" (*MLR*), both based on new and more thorough examinations of the records of that company. In the first, entitled "John Webster, Merchant Taylor," he recalled the statement on the title page of Webster's Lord Mayor's show, *Monuments of Honor* (1624), that it was "Invented and Written by John Webster Merchant-Taylor," and added it to another statement in the dedication to the Lord Mayor, himself a Merchant Taylor, in which Webster proclaimed himself "one born free of your Company." This phrase meant that his father was already a member of the guild. After comparing the data in the records concerning the many members named Webster in the 1570s and 1580s, Howarth decided that John Webster the poet-dramatist was probably the eldest son of a similarly named John Webster who became "free" of the company in 1577 and was therefore probably in a position to marry. Thus Howarth concluded that the boy could not have been born earlier than that year. There is no evidence, however, that he attended the famous Merchant Taylors' School, as he might have done. In fact, since in his early writings he showed little or no knowledge of Latin, Howarth hazarded the guess that he did not even receive the usual grammar school education ("John Webster's Classical Nescience," *The Sydney University Union Recorder*, 1954), though his father should have been able to afford one, since he lent money in 1591. In an attempt to find a reason for such a situation, Howarth even went so far as to speculate that the boy "may have had some physical deficiency such as weakness of sight or malformation of body." On June 19, 1615, nevertheless, John Webster, Jr., took out his own freedom in the company "by patrimony" rather than apprenticeship. His payment of the fee of three shillings fourpence was apparently not only to gain such privileges as membership in the company would confer but to qualify as official poet to it, as he later became by writing shows and pageants. At the time of his first membership, guessed Howarth, "he was no doubt at least in his thirties." Howarth also quoted some of the minutes and accounts for 1623-5 showing Webster's name.

In the second "Note" ("John Webster, Sr., and Edward Webster, Tailors and Undertakers?") Howarth presented some speculative evidence that John Webster had a brother Edward, and that their father "plied the two trades of tailor and livery-stable keeper or jobmaster," and in the latter capacity "furnished coaches for funerals and doubtless undertook burials." Howarth even found a possible connection between tailoring and undertaking in the making of shrouds, although he admitted that this specialty was usually that of the linen drapers, and ended with the comment: "Little wonder, then, that the dramatist, perhaps from early acquaintance with mortuary activities, was, in T. S. Eliot's term, 'much possessed by death.' "

If Howarth's evidence and his conclusions can be accepted, then the earlier suggestion that Webster was the Johannes Webster, son and heir of Johannes Webster of London, who was admitted to the Middle Temple on August 1, 1598, must be discarded. A hundred years later, the hack writer, Charles Gildon, in his *Lives and Characters of the English Dramatic Poets*, stated without evidence that Webster became parish clerk of St. Andrew's, Holborn, but his statement is discredited as unlikely and unsupported. Other even less likely speculations have been summarily rejected. Since Thomas Heywood's *The Hierarchy of the Blessed Angels*, licensed on November 7, 1634, referred to Webster in the past tense, he seems to have been dead by that time; but C. J. Sisson has suggested that the John Webster who was buried at St. James's, Clerkenwell, on March 3, 1638, may well have been the poet-dramatist (*Lost Plays of Shakespeare's Age*, Cambridge University Press, 1936; Sisson was echoed by R. G. Howarth in "John Webster's Burial," *NQ*, 1954). The first certain record of him occurs in 1602, when Henslowe's diary shows that in that one year he had a part in several plays, now lost under the titles given, in which he collaborated in different combinations with Dekker, Heywood, Middleton, Drayton, and others. In other words, Webster began his career as a hack playwright, helping out other playwrights in Henslowe's organization when he could get an assignment.

Clifford Leech, in his monograph, *John Webster/A Critical Study* (London, 1951), proposes the following canon for Webster's works. I. Plays wholly by him: (1) *The White Devil, or, The Tragedy of Paulo Giordano Ursini, Duke of Brachiano, with the Life and Death of Vittoria Corombona the Famous Venetian Courtesan* (published in 1612; written probably later than February 2, 1609; acted by the Queen's Men at the Red Bull in the winter, but at first not well received). (2) *The Tragedy of the Duchess of Malfi* (published in 1623; performed before December 16, 1614, since William Ostler, the actor of Antonio, died on that date; presented by the "King's Majesty's Servants" at both the Blackfriars and the Globe; revived in 1617; and reprinted in 1640, about 1664, 1678, and 1708). (3) *The Devil's Law Case*, a comedy (published in 1623, and probably acted about 1620 by "Her Majesty's Servants" at the Red Bull). II. Plays partly by Webster: (1) The Induction to Marston's *The Malcontent*. (2) *The Famous History of Sir Thomas Wyatt*, with Dekker, probably a revised form of one of the otherwise titled plays in 1602 (published in 1607, but probably acted in 1602 by the Queen's Men). (3) *Westward Ho*, with Dekker (published in 1607, and acted by the Children of Paul's, probably in 1604). (4) *Northward Ho*, again with Dekker (published in 1607, and acted by the Children of Paul's, probably in 1605. For Webster's share in the *Ho* plays, see also Peter B. Murray, *Papers of the Bibliographical Society of America*, 1962). (5) *A Cure for a Cuckold*, with William Rowley (published in 1661, and probably acted about 1625). (6) *Appius and Virginia* (published in 1654 and probably collaborated on by Heywood). III. Several conjectural collaborated plays, some extant and some lost. IV. A few nondramatic works, mostly verses. Especially interesting are the thirty-two prose "New Characters" added to the sixth edition of Sir Thomas Overbury's famous collection of *Characters* (1615), and assigned to Webster on the basis of style and parallel passages in some of his plays. But of the total output from Webster's pen, covering a period of perhaps a quarter of a century, only his two unaided tragedies, *The White Devil* and *The Duchess of Malfi*, written in the middle of his career, bear the burden of preserving his name for posterity. What he wrote before and after them is deservedly forgotten, and what caused the blossoming of his genius in them is unknown.

Of the few extant comments on Webster in his own day, only one—a sardonic picture of the man drawn by the otherwise forgotten Henry Fitzjeffrey and printed in *Certain Elegies Done by Sundry Excellent Wits* in 1618—reveals anything of his character and manner of writing. To Fitzjeffrey he is "crabbed Websterio," as he asks:

> . . . Lord! Who would know him?
> Was ever man so mangled with a poem?
> See how he draws his mouth awry of late,
> How he scrubs: wrings his wrists: scratches his pate.

It is as if "Some Centaur strange, some huge Bucephalus, or Pallas," were engendering in his brain. And Fitzjeffrey says he does not fear Webster as a critic because, although he will "industriously examine" what has been written and take twelve months to report on its errors, no one will understand his criticism because "it will be so obscure."

This portrait of Webster at work, however, accords perfectly with that drawn by R. W. Dent in his *Webster's Borrowings* (University of California Press, 1960; see also P. F. Whitman, "Webster's *Duchess of Malfi*," *NQ*, 1957, and G. P. V. Akrigg, "John Webster and *The Book of Homilies*," *ibid.*). Building on the evidence produced by earlier scholars, such as Alexander Dyce and William Hazlitt in their nineteenth-century editions of Webster, John Addington Symonds in his Mermaid edition (London, 1888), and Charles Crawford in his *Collectanea* (Stratford, 1906–7), that Webster was in the habit of echoing phrases and ideas from other authors, Dent conducted an exhaustive investigation of Webster's compositional and creative habits, based mostly on the major tragedies, and concluded that if one only had access to all the works the playwright consulted, it would be found that at least three-quarters of what he wrote could be traced to other sources. Not only did Webster keep a commonplace book in which he entered notable and useful passages from his reading and listening, but he placed this close to his elbow when writing and made lavish use of it. As was the habit of most cultured Europeans of the time, he arranged this notebook by both author and subject. He also included thoughts that he had heard in conversations, sermons, trials, and so forth. Sometimes he apparently worked directly from his sources, many of which are probably now lost. Webster's reading habits can thus be deduced from his writings. Although he read widely, he apparently browsed or skimmed much. He certainly knew Sidney, Montaigne, Guazzo, Sir William Alexander, and Pierre Matthieu thoroughly, and Camden, Donne, Hall, Nicolas de Montreux, Nash, and Whetstone almost as thoroughly. Strangely enough, there are scarcely any reminscences of or references to the Bible, to classical literature, or to Renaissance works not available in English translation, such as the translations of North, Pettie, Painter, Florio, Grimestone, and Tofte. In other words, Webster was not a linguist, and apparently had had no linguistic training in school. He was also not much interested in nondramatic poetry, and even in the drama there are few clear signs of direct verbal borrowing. It was English prose, then, that he chiefly depended on. He used continental history and semi-history, "especially such as provide colorful accounts of individual men," prose narrative, books on the governor, courtier, and civil behavior generally, topical satire, religio-ethical works in the *nosce teipsum* and *memento mori* tradition, and collections of apothegms and *sententiae*. Out of these sources Webster wove a pattern that was both complex and original. Nor did he have a guilty conscience, since until fairly recent modern times such a practice was not regarded as plagiarism, but was admired as a proof of a writer's learning, taste, and discrimination. (See Harold O. White, *Plagiarism and Imitation during the English Renaissance*, *HSE*, 1935.) This pervasive practice of borrowing, however, probably contributed to Webster's tendency to stress the smaller units in his dramatic composition more than the overall design.

The *criticomachia* over Webster's right to occupy a preeminent position in the English drama has focused in modern times, as might be expected, on William Archer's savage onslaught in *The Old Drama and the New*—a position which Bernard Shaw had already taken up in his critiques in *The Saturday Review* between 1895 and 1898. Archer's attack is given a prominent place by Dan D. Moore, in *John Webster and His Critics 1617–1964* (Louisiana State University Press, 1966), by Travis Bogard, in *The Tragic Satire of John Webster* (University of California Press, 1955), by Moody E. Prior, in *The Language of Tragedy*, and by Lucas in his introduction. Archer had begun by referring to Charles Lamb's ecstatic eulogy in his *Specimens of the English Dramatic Poets Who Lived about the Time of Shakespeare* (1808): "To move a horror skilfully, to touch a soul to the quick, to lay upon fear as much as it can bear, to wean and weary a life till it is ready to drop, and then to step in with mortal instruments to make its last forfeit: this only a Webster can do." Archer then went on to quote Swinburne's essay on Webster in *The Nineteenth Century* for June 1886: "Except in Aeschylus, in Dante, and in Shakespeare, I, at least, know not where to seek for passages which in sheer force of tragic and noble horror . . . may be set against the subtlest, the deepest, the sublimest passages of Webster." Finally, Archer allowed the young and "lamented" poet Rupert Brooke to give his own bald synopsis of the plot of *The Duchess of Malfi* (*John Webster and the Elizabethan Drama*, London, 1916), and then added his own comments: "To this concisely accurate argument of the play I will only add that the butcher's bill is by no means complete. Brooke tells of only five corpses: to these we must add the Cardinal's mistress, Julia, the Duchess's maid, Cariola, two of her children and a servant, making ten in all. The murders in *Hamlet* amount to only half that number." Archer then proceeded to dissect the most famous scenes of the play in his most scathingly ironical style, and ended by recording his conviction that in Lamb's "rhapsodic" praise of the strangling scene in Act IV "a more topsy-turvy criticism . . . was never penned." Bosola's "dirge," he admitted, is "haunting poetry; but it is as inappropriate, dramatically, as any aria by Donizetti. It is only one instance out of a thousand to prove that a fine poet may be a bad dramatist." Webster's work, to Archer, was only a further proof of the thesis of his lectures: that true and genuine drama cannot exist until it has divested itself of the lyric element. Prior, in evaluating the diagnoses of Webster by Muriel C. Bradbrook (*Themes and Conventions of Elizabethan Tragedy*, Cambridge, 1952) and by Una M. Ellis-Fermor (*The Jacobean Drama*, London, 1936), both of whom shift their approaches away from the dramatic to the "spatial" and the "musical," decides that "Archer somehow seems to have come off the winner," and concludes judiciously that, "though *The Duchess of Malfi* might have been improved if Webster could have had the advantage of Archer's suggestions, it would have been utterly ruined if he had followed all of them." Prior proceeds to an illuminating analysis of Webster's "intense and figurative language, and skill in adapting this language to dramatic dialogue," a gift in which he was next to Shakespeare himself. (See also J. R. Mulryne, *The Jacobean Theatre*, SAS, 1960.) Leech, however, comments on the more naturalistic style of the two plays.

Whatever the judgment of the modern student may be in this dispute, all critics agree that Webster's genius, however it may be constituted, rose to its height in his two uncollaborated plays, *The White Devil* and *The Duchess of Malfi*. Critics prefer one or the other according as they are impressed by the greater plausibility and dramatic effectiveness of the former or the greater poetry and pathos of the latter. Both plays are concerned with actual events that occurred in Italy. *The White Devil* dramatizes a murder committed in 1585. (For a full study of Webster's sources, see Gunnar Boklund, *The Sources of "The White Devil,"* *Essays and Studies on English Language and Literature*, Upsala, 1957; also J. R. Brown, "The Papal Election in John Webster's *The White Devil*," NQ, 1957.) *The Duchess of Malfi* came ultimately from a story of Bandello, translated into French by Belleforest in his *Histoires Tragiques*, and from the French version into English in Painter's *The Palace of Pleasure* (1556–7), which was

Webster's direct source. Bandello claimed to have known intimately those involved in the tragedy, and he may even have been the original of the character Delio. (See Boklund, *The Duchess of Malfi: Sources, Themes, Characters*, Cambridge, 1962.) To some extent, facts have been altered in both plays to meet the needs of drama, and have been overlaid with conventions of the Elizabethan tragedy of blood. In the treatment of revenge for honor, features of the older revenge plays have been used. But the tool-villain in each case is of the malcontent type, and the Italian characters breathe a spirit only less fraught with deadly passions than those in *The Spanish Tragedy*, *Antonio's Revenge*, and *The Revenger's Tragedy*. In *The Duchess* it is chiefly on the characters and the appropriateness and poetic power of their speech that Webster fixed his attention. His interest in humanizing his characters is suggested in a note printed at the end of *The White Devil* praising the actors for their "true imitation of life, without striving to make nature a monster."

Nevertheless, to some critics Webster's motivation of his major characters is one of the chief weaknesses of *The Duchess*. For example, as Leech and others point out, Webster never attempts to give any real explanation for the implacable opposition of Duke Ferdinand and the Cardinal to the marriage of their sister, except as a sort of afterthought on Ferdinand's part in IV, ii. Leech also makes a long examination of the Duchess's conduct as compared with the "Rules for Widows, or Vidual Chastity," as laid down by Jeremy Taylor in *The Rule and Exercises of Holy Living*. Although Taylor did not enunciate his principles till 1650, Leech decides that the Duchess breaks practically all of them, and that "the more we consider the Duchess, the more hints of guilt seem to appear;" however, when we come to the fourth act "questions of innocence or guilt seem irrelevant. We have here a long ecstasy of pain which gives its own cosmic vision." Frank W. Wadsworth, on the other hand, took issue with Leech, and quoted several contemporary documents to prove that the Jacobean audience would not have condemned the Duchess's motives or conduct and concluded that Webster himself did not regard her as guilty ("Webster's *The Duchess of Malfi* and Some Contemporary Ideas on Marriage and Re-marriage," *PQ*, 1956; replied to by Leech in "Addendum on Webster's Duchess," *ibid.*, 1958). P. F. Vernon analyzes the opposing opinions of both Leech and Wadsworth in "The Duchess of Malfi's Guilt" (*NQ*, 1963) and reached his own conclusion that the play is mainly concerned with "how good and noble people ought to behave in a society dominated by the values of 'Machiavellian' policy, as the early seventeenth century understood it," and that the tragic error of both the Duchess and Antonio is that they have ignored this dictum in their consideration of the ends rather than the means, though eventually they gain increased stature as they learn from their errors.

The character and role of Bosola have also bothered many readers. The title of C. G. Thayer's article, "The Ambiguity of Bosola" (*SP*, 1957), is symptomatic, even though Thayer concludes that Webster intended Bosola to emerge as "a major tragic protagonist" rather than as the sub-antagonist, or villain, that he had been through most of the play. This had been the opinion of Clarence V. Boyer many years before, in his book, *The Villain as Hero in Elizabethan Tragedy* (London, 1914). Moore, not long after Thayer, was somewhat dubious about this interpretation. In 1951 Leech had found that "Despite all his activity in the play, he is less a character than a chorus. We cannot put his features together and make a living man out of them." Ribner, however, in *Jacobean Tragedy: The Quest for Moral Order* (London, 1962), preferred to regard Antonio as "a kind of choral commentator," and explained Bosola's transformation by suggesting that he had been educated through the example of the Duchess and thus had become "the agent through which the spirit of the Duchess is made to permeate the world." Nevertheless, although Ribner stoutly maintained that this transformation of Bosola remained a "symbol of Webster's moral argument," he had to admit that it still "may defy logical probability." To Ribner, Bosola is the "most important unifying element in the play."

The structure of the play has also come under considerable fire, especially the "anti-climax" of the fifth act after the death of the protagonist of the title (e.g., Leech; Bogard; Ribner; Prior; Robert Ornstein, *The Moral Vision of Jacobean Tragedy*, University of Wisconsin Press, 1960; F. L. Lucas, edition of *The Duchess of Malfi*, London, 1958). Minor structural flaws include the casual revelation that the Duchess has already had a child by her first husband, the overlooking of the fact that this young "Duke of Malfi" should have been the heir to her estate (III, iii), the ease with which she and Antonio conceal the births of their own children, the Duchess's absent-minded-ness about what has happened to these children in the death scene, the failure of the prediction in the horoscope of a "violent death" for the first son to come true, and the reduction of the *scene à faire* of the banishment of the Duchess and her family to a mere dumb show (III, iv). The whole subject is examined by Cecil W. Davies in "The Structure of *The Duchess of Malfi*" (*English*, 1958), with the conclusion that the play nevertheless has more assets than defects. The scene of the invasion of the Duchess's house by the madmen has also been both attacked and defended, not as mere sensation-alism but, in its presentation of the various types of mad people to be found there, as a microcosmic mirror reflecting the madness in the macrocosm of the outside world (Leech, Ribner). S. I. Hayakawa, opposing the views of Lucas and Louis B. Wright that the scene has strong elements of comic intent, insisted that it is "an episode in a carefully calculated series of increasingly horrible events—to wit, the dead hand, the waxworks, the madman, the dirge, and the strangling" ("A Note on the Madman's Scene in Webster's *The Duchess of Malfi*," *PMLA*, 1932). Inga-Stina Ekeblad, building on T. S. Eliot's assertion (*Elizabethan Dramatists*) that "The art of the Elizabethans is an impure art," which aims to "attain complete realism without surrendering any of the advantages which as artists they observed in unrealistic conventions," pro-posed the idea that the madmen's masque was actually intended as a sort of grotesque antimasque within the larger structural unit of the whole play, conceived and presented as a formalized masque of the Duchess's love and death, marriage and murder ("The 'Impure' Art of John Webster," *RES*, 1958).

Should Webster's attitude toward life be regarded as moral, immoral, or amoral? This is one of the main problems examined by Moore in his study of Webster's critics, and becomes of special interest in his chapters concerned with twentieth-century criticism. The titles of Chapter Six, "The Gray World of Webster," and of Chapter Seven, "The Moral Vision," are particularly apropos. Moore cites Leech and Ornstein as generally belonging to the school of Eliot and Ellis-Fermor in seeing Webster as a writer "with little hope and a tenuous moral vision," whose oral focus is "dim or non-existent." Bogard, with his special approach to the plays as a combination of tragedy and satire, falls essentially into this school, although he is inclined toward a moral phi-losophy, at least by implication. Gunnar Boklund, too, in his studies of the sources of *The White Devil* and *The Duchess of Malfi*, "admits the importance of the theme of integrity of life, but also sees an amoral world of shadows where virtue may not long live." The question had been inadvertently focused earlier when Lord David Cecil had included a study of John Webster in his volume of critical essays, *Poets and Story-Tellers* (London, 1949). In this he maintained that Webster's vision was a moral one, seeing life as a struggle between right and wrong, or rather between good and evil, with each play presenting its audience with an act of sin and its consequences. But Ian Jack, not knowing of Cecil's essay, had written in *Scrutiny* that there was no coherent moral unity in Webster's plays, in which the doctrines of Machiavelli supplanted the normal Elizabethan concept of unity and degree as the basis of the universe and of human society ("The Case of John Webster," *Scrutiny*, 1949). This would agree in general with Archer's attitude. In 1957 S. L. Gross published an article ("A Note on Webster's Tragic Attitude," *NQ*) in which he called attention to a number of remarks and situations in *The Duchess* which show an awareness on the part of the characters that "integrity of life is essentially bound up with some kind of possible moral value."

But in 1963 Elizabeth Brennan brought up a new aspect of the problem in "The Relationship between Brother and Sister in the Plays of John Webster" (*MLR*), in which she traced the shift in the social code of revenge which governed the behavior of a large part of the playgoing audience from revenge for murder to revenge for honor. In the case of Webster, however, especially in *The Duchess*, she concluded that "revenge for honor was only a cloak to cover a passion which was, in Ferdinand at least, more horrible and unnatural." But it was Irving Ribner, in his *Jacobean Tragedy* and a preliminary article ("Webster's Italian Tragedies," *Tulane Drama Review*, 1961), who sustained most positively and thoroughly the thesis that Webster's two powerful tragedies represent his indubitable "search for moral order in the uncertain and chaotic world of Jacobean skepticism," and that in the last act of *The Duchess* "we see a new morality emerging out of evils more chilling in their horror than those of the earlier play." The secret of these plays, to Ribner, is that they must be regarded as symbolic rather than realistic works, in both their good and their evil characters, and in this light even the play's impossibilities become part of the symbolism. Ribner finds support for this position and optimistic interpretation in F. P. Wilson's *Elizabethan and Jacobean* (Oxford, 1945), W. R. Edwards's "John Webster" (*Scrutiny*, 1933), and David Cecil, who even tried to define Webster's morality in Calvinistic and deterministic terms. Ribner concluded that Webster was, in spite of his skepticism, a moralist and humanist who did not preach, and that the nobility of his characters and of human life is revealed in their deaths.

Like most of his contemporaries, Webster—or at least his characters—subscribed to a belief in all forms of the occult: astrology and horoscopes, the power of different forms of curses, the Black Art, and the agencies of Fortune or Chance vs. Fate. These matters, of course, had some bearing on his moral views. (See Bradbrook, "Fate and Chance in *The Duchess of Malfi*," *MLR*, 1947, and Johnstone Parr, "The Horoscope in Webster's *The Duchess of Malfi*," *PMLA*, 1945, and *Tamburlaine's Malady and Other Essays on Astrology in Elizabethan Drama*.)

In the second installment of "The Printing of John Webster's Plays" (*Studies in Bibliography*, 1956), John Russell Brown developed his subject as applied to Webster's three unaided plays. He carried his analysis further in 1962 (*ibid.*), as applied to *The Duchess*, and decided that the 1623 text must have been set from a scribal transcript and that Webster may have added some of the stage directions while printing was in progress. W. R. Todd discovered an apparent echo from *Don Quixote*, and deduced that this must have been added to the original text sometime during the revival of the play between 1619 and 1623 ("*The White Devil*, *The Duchess of Malfi*, and *The Devil's Law Case*: Webster and Cervantes," *MLR*, 1956). But on the evidence of Webster's general borrowings, Dent concluded that in spite of Todd, the play was probably completed about 1613. G. P. V. Akrigg also concluded that the many allusions to "Heaven" in the play and the almost complete absence of the word "God" indicate a phraseological revision just before publication in order to avoid the danger of trouble with the censorship, which had become severe about what was considered blasphemy (*NQ*, 1950).

Elizabeth Brennan edited *The Duchess* for the New Mermaids in 1964, praising its virtues but not minimizing its weaknesses. John Russell Brown edited it for the Revels Plays in the same year, and described its "fitful" stage history down to the present, even to its adaptation by W. H. Auden in 1945. Simultaneously with this production a de luxe edition of the play was brought out by George Rylands and Charles Williams. The best account of the professional and semiprofessional performances of the play from its first production to the present is that of Moore, but it has had many academic revivals which he would not have been able to list. Most of the journalistic reviews of the revivals have been either savage or sarcastic. Although Leech has attempted to outline the acting qualities of the play, Moore has pointed out that since the middle of the nineteenth century its audiences, unlike those of earlier times, have been inclined to laugh instead of being terrified.   He suggests that in our day the power of the play seems greater when it is read in the study than when seen on the stage.

Thus Webster remains—in his thought as well as in his life—an enigma, but an enigma which has provoked and challenged the playgoers, readers, and critics of the English drama for over three and a half centuries.   Perhaps, like Shakespeare's Hamlet, this is one of the reasons for his survival as one of England's most unforgettable dramatists.

The present text is based on the critical edition of the quarto of 1623 as printed by Sampson in the Belles-Lettres Series.   The edition of the play published by Lucas in *The Complete Works of John Webster* has also been consulted.

# THE DUCHESS OF MALFI[1]

## BY

## JOHN WEBSTER

### THE ACTORS' NAMES

[DANIEL DE] BOSOLA [, *gentleman of the horse to the Duchess*]: *J. Lowin.*

FERDINAND [, *Duke of Calabria*]: 1. *R. Burbadge;* 2. *J. Taylor.*

CARDINAL [, *his brother*]: 1. *H. Condell;* 2. *R. Robinson.*

ANTONIO [BOLOGNA, *the Duchess' steward*]: 1. *W. Ostler;* 2. *R. Benfield.*

DELIO [, *his friend*]: *J. Underwood.*

FOROBOSCO[2] [, *an attendant*]: *N. Tooley.*

MALATESTE [, *a count*].

THE MARQUIS OF PESCARA: *J. Rice.*

SILVIO [, *a lord*]: *T. Pollard.*

[CASTRUCHIO, *an old lord*.]

[RODERIGO, *a lord*.]

[GRISOLAN, *a lord*.]

THE SEVERAL MADMEN: *N. Tooley, J. Underwood, etc.*

THE DUCHESS [, *sister to Ferdinand and Cardinal*]: *R. Sharp.*

[JULIA, *Castruchio's wife and*] *the Cardinal's* mis[*tress*]: *J. Thompson.*

DOCTOR ⎫
CARIOLA ⎬ : *R. Pallant.*

COURT OFFICERS.

[OLD LADY.]

THREE YOUNG CHILDREN.

TWO PILGRIMS.

[LADIES, EXECUTIONERS, *and* ATTENDANTS.]

[SCENE: *Italy.*

TIME: *Early sixteenth century.*][3]

### ACTUS I. SCENA i.

[*The presence chamber of the Duchess' palace at Amalfi.*]

*Antonio and Delio; Bosola, Cardinal.*[4]

DEL. You are welcome to your country, dear Antonio;
You have been long in France, and you return

A very formal Frenchman in your habit.
How do you like the French court?

ANT.                    I admire it.
In seeking to reduce both state and people
To a fixed order, their judicious king
Begins at home, quits[5] first his royal palace
Of flatt'ring sycophants, of dissolute
And infamous persons, which he sweetly terms
His master's masterpiece, the work of heaven,                    10
Consid'ring duly that a prince's court
Is like a common fountain, whence should flow
Pure silver drops in general,[6] but, if 't chance
Some cursed example poison 't near the head,

---

[1] The complete title reads: "The Tragedy of the Duchess of Malfi. As It Was Presented Privately at the Blackfriars, and Publicly at the Globe, by the King's Majesty's Servants. The Perfect and Exact Copy, with Divers Things Printed That the Length of the Play Would not Bear in the Presentment. Written by John Webster."

[2] In the printed version of the play this character does not speak.

[3] A dedication to George Harding, Baron Berkeley, and commendatory verses by Thomas Middleton, William Rowley, and John Ford are omitted in the present edition.

[4] Last two enter later.

[5] Clears.

[6] Without exception.

"Death and diseases through the whole
land spread." [1]
And what is 't makes this blessed govern-
ment
But a most provident council, who dare
freely
Inform him the corruption of the times?
Though some o' th' court hold it pre-
sumption
To instruct princes what they ought to
do,                                              20
It is a noble duty to inform them
What they ought to foresee.—Here
comes Bosola,
The only court-gall.

*[Enter Bosola.]*

                    Yet I observe his railing
Is not for simple love of piety.
Indeed, he rails at those things which he
wants,
Would be as lecherous, covetous, or
proud,
Bloody, or envious as any man,
If he had means to be so.—Here's the
cardinal.

*[Enter Cardinal.]*

Bos. I do haunt you still.
Card. So.                                        30
Bos.[2] I have done you better service
than to be slighted thus. Miserable age,
where only the reward of doing well is the
doing of it!
Card. You enforce your merit too much.
Bos. I fell into the galleys in your service, where, for two years together, I wore
two towels instead of a shirt, with a knot on
the shoulder, after the fashion of a Roman
mantle. Slighted thus! I will thrive [40
some way. Blackbirds fatten best in
hard weather; why not I in these dog
days?
Card. Would you could become honest!
Bos. With all your divinity, do but
direct me the way to it. I have known many
travel far for it, and yet return as arrant
knaves as they went forth, because they

carried themselves always along with them.
*[Exit Cardinal.]* Are you gone? Some [50
fellows, they say, are possessed with the
devil, but this great fellow were able to
possess the greatest devil, and make him
worse.
Ant. He hath denied thee some suit?
Bos. He and his brother are like plum
trees that grow crooked over standing
pools; they are rich and o'erladen with
fruit, but none but crows, pies, and caterpillars feed on them. Could I be one [60
of their flatt'ring panders, I would hang
on their ears like a horseleech, till I were
full, and then drop off. I pray, leave me.
Who would rely upon these miserable
dependences, in expectation to be advanced tomorrow? What creature ever
fed worse than hoping Tantalus? Nor
ever died [3] any man more fearfully than
he that hoped for a pardon.[3] There are
rewards for hawks and dogs when [4] [70
they have done us service; but, for a soldier
that hazards his limbs in a battle, nothing
but a kind of geometry is his last supporta-
tion.
Del. Geometry?
Bos. Ay, to hang in a fair pair of slings,
take his latter swing in the world upon
an honorable pair of crutches, from hospital to hospital. Fare ye well, sir. And
yet do not you scorn us, for places in [80
the court are but like beds in the hospital,
where this man's head lies at that man's
foot, and so lower and lower.     *[Exit.]*
Del. I knew this fellow seven years in
the galleys
For a notorious murther; and 'twas
thought
The cardinal suborned it. He was released
By the French general, Gaston de Foix,[5]
When he recovered Naples.
Ant.                                'Tis great pity
He should be thus neglected  I have
heard
He's very valiant. This foul melan-
choly                                            90
Will poison all his goodness; for, I'll
tell you,

---

[1] Sententious passages set off in the original
with quotation marks or italics are here indicated throughout by quotation marks.
[2] All prose passages in the play were originally
printed as irregular verse.

[3] Readings from 1640 edn. Original reads *did*
and *pleadon*.
[4] From 1640 edn. Earlier edns. read *and when.*
[5] Original reads *Foux*.

If too immoderate sleep be truly said
To be an inward rust unto the soul,
It then doth follow want of action
Breeds all black malcontents; and their
　close rearing,
Like moths in cloth, do hurt for want of
　wearing.[1]

SCENA ii.

[The same.]

*Antonio,　Delio,　Ferdinand,*[2]　*Cardinal,*[2]
*Duchess,*[2]　*Castruchio,　Silvio,　Roderigo,
　Grisolan,　Bosola,　Julia,*[2]　*Cariola.*[2]

DEL. The presence gins [3] to fill. You prom-
　ised me
To make me the partaker of the natures
Of some of your great courtiers.
ANT.　　　　　　The lord cardinal's
And other strangers' that are now in
　court?
I shall.—Here comes the great Calabrian
　duke.

[Enter Ferdinand and Attendants.]

FERD. Who took the ring oft'nest? [4]
SIL. Antonio Bologna, my lord.
FERD. Our sister duchess' great master
of her household? Give him the jewel.—
When shall we leave this sportive ac- [10
tion, and fall to action indeed?
CAST. Methinks, my lord, you should
not desire to go to war in person.
FERD. [*Aside.*] Now for some gravity.—
Why, my lord?
CAST. It is fitting a soldier arise to be a
prince, but not necessary a prince descend
to be a captain.
FERD. No?
CAST. No, my lord; he were far bet- [20
ter do it by a deputy.
FERD. Why should he not as well sleep
or eat by a deputy? This might take idle,
offensive, and base office from him, whereas
the other deprives him of honor.
CAST. Believe my experience: that realm
is never long in quiet where the ruler is a
soldier.
FERD. Thou told'st me thy wife could
not endure fighting—　　　　　　　30

CAST. True, my lord.
FERD. And of a jest she broke [5] of a captain she met full of wounds—I have forgot
it.
CAST. She told him, my lord, he was a
pitiful fellow, to lie, like the children of
Ismael, all in tents.[6]
FERD. Why, there's a wit were able to
undo all the chirurgeons [7] o' the city, for,
although gallants should quarrel, and [40
had drawn their weapons, and were ready
to go to it, yet her persuasions would make
them put up.
CAST. That she would, my lord.—How
do you like my Spanish jennet?
ROD. He is all fire.
FERD. I am of Pliny's opinion; I think
he was begot by the wind; he runs as if he
were ballast with quicksilver.
SIL. True, my lord, he reels from [50
the tilt often.
ROD. }
GRIS. } Ha, ha, ha!
FERD. Why do you laugh? Methinks you
that are courtiers should be my touchwood—
take fire when I give fire; that is, laugh when
I laugh, were the subject never so witty.
CAST. True, my lord; I myself have
heard a very good jest, and have scorned to
seem to have so silly [8] a wit as to understand
it.　　　　　　　60
FERD. But I can laugh at your fool, my
lord.
CAST. He cannot speak, you know, but
he makes faces. My lady cannot abide him.
FERD. No?
CAST. Nor endure to be in merry company; for she says too much laughing and
too much company fills her too full of the
wrinkle.
FERD. I would, then, have a mathe- [70
matical instrument made for her face, that
she might not laugh out of compass.—I
shall shortly visit you at Milan, Lord
Silvio.
SIL. Your grace shall arrive most welcome.
FERD. You are a good horseman, Antonio; you have excellent riders in France.
What do you think of good horsemanship?
ANT. Nobly, my lord. As out of [80

---

[1] The scene division throughout appears to be purely artificial, since the action continues without pause.　　[3] Begins.
[2] Enters later.　[4] *I.e.*, in the tilting at the ring.

[5] Told.
[6] With a pun on the meaning *lint*, for dressing wounds.　　[7] Surgeons.　　[8] Simple.

the Grecian horse issued many famous princes, so out of brave horsemanship arise the first sparks of growing resolution, that raise the mind to noble action.

FERD. You have bespoke it worthily.

SIL. Your brother, the lord cardinal, and sister duchess.

[*Enter Cardinal, Duchess, Cariola, and Julia.*]

CARD. Are the galleys come about?

GRIS.                    They are, my lord.

FERD. Here's the Lord Silvio, is come to take his leave.

DEL. [*Aside to Antonio.*] Now, sir, your promise. What's that cardinal?     90
I mean his temper. They say he's a brave fellow,
Will play his five thousand crowns at tennis, dance,
Court ladies, and one that hath fought single combats.

ANT. Some such flashes superficially hang on him for form, but, observe his inward character, he is a melancholy churchman. The spring in his face is nothing but the engend'ring of toads; where he is jealous of any man, he lays worse plots for them than ever was imposed [100 on Hercules, for he strews in his way flatter[er]s, panders, intelligencers,[1] atheists, and a thousand such political monsters. He should have been pope; but, instead of coming to it by the primitive decency of the church, he did bestow bribes so largely and so impudently as if he would have carried it away without heaven's knowledge. Some good he hath done—

DEL. You have given too much of him. What's his brother?     110

ANT. The duke there? A most perverse and turbulent nature.
What appears in him mirth is merely outside;
If he laugh heartily, it is to laugh
All honesty out of fashion.

DEL.               Twins?

ANT.                    In quality.
He speaks with others' tongues, and hears men's suits
With others' ears; will seem to sleep o' th' bench
Only to entrap offenders in their answers;

[1] Spies.

Dooms men to death by information;[2]
Rewards by hearsay.

DEL.               Then the law to him
Is like a foul, black cobweb to a spider—     120
He makes it his dwelling and a prison
To entangle those shall feed him.

ANT.                    Most true.
He never pays debts unless they be shrewd turns,[3]
And those he will confess that he doth owe.
Last, for his brother there, the cardinal,
They that do flatter him most say oracles
Hang at his lips; and verily I believe them,
For the devil speaks in them.
But for their sister, the right noble duchess,
You never fixed your eye on three fair medals     130
Cast in one figure,[4] of so different temper.
For her discourse, it is so full of rapture,
You only will begin then to be sorry
When she doth end her speech, and wish, in wonder,
She held it less vainglory to talk much
Than your penance to hear her. Whilst she speaks,
She throws upon a man so sweet a look
That it were able raise one to a galliard
That lay in a dead palsy, and to dote
On that sweet countenance; but in that look     140
There speaketh so divine a continence
As cuts off all lascivious and vain hope.
Her days are practiced in such noble virtue
That sure her nights, nay, more, her very sleeps,
Are more in heaven than other ladies' shrifts.[5]
Let all sweet ladies break their flatt'ring glasses,
And dress themselves in her.

DEL.                    Fie, Antonio,
You play the wire-drawer with her commendations.[6]

ANT. I'll case the picture up only thus much—

[2] Informer's evidence.
[3] Evil deeds. From 1640 edn. Original has *shewed.*     [4] Mold.     [5] Confessions.
[6] You draw her praises out at great length.

All her particular worth grows to this
sum:                                                   150
She stains [1] the time past, lights the time
to come.

CARI. You must attend my lady in the gallery
Some half an hour hence.

ANT. I shall.
                          [*Exeunt Antonio and Delio.*]

FERD. Sister, I have a suit to you.

DUCH.                              To me, sir?

FERD. A gentlemen here, Daniel de
Bosola,
One that was in the galleys—

DUCH.                     Yes, I know him.

FERD. A worthy fellow h' is; pray, let me
entreat for
The provisorship [2] of your horse.

DUCH.      Your knowledge of him
Commends him and prefers him.

FERD.                        Call him hither.
                          [*Exeunt Attendants.*]
We now upon [3] parting, good Lord
Silvio,                                                161
Do us commend to all our noble friends
At the leaguer.[4]

SIL.            Sir, I shall.

FERD.[5]              You are for Milan?

SIL. I am.

DUCH. Bring the caroches.[6]—We'll bring
you down to the haven.

[*Exeunt all except Cardinal and Ferdinand.*]

CARD. Be sure you entertain that Bosola
For your intelligence.[7] I would not be
seen in 't;
And therefore many times I have slighted
him
When he did court our furtherance, as
this morning.

FERD. Antonio, the great master of her
household,                                        170
Had been far fitter.

CARD.    You are deceived in him.
His nature is too honest for such busi-
ness.—
He comes; I'll leave you.            [*Exit.*]

[1] Dims, eclipses.
[2] Office of purveyor.
[3] At the point of.
[4] Camp. From 1640 edn.; original reads
*leagues.*
[5] Sampson assigns this speech to the Duchess.
[6] Coaches.
[7] Information from spies.

[*Enter Bosola.*]

BOS.              I was lured [8] to you.

FERD. My brother here, the cardinal,
could never
Abide you.

BOS.      Never since he was in my debt.

FERD. May be some oblique character in
your face
Made him suspect you.

BOS.          Doth he study physiognomy?
There's no more credit to be given to th'
face
Than to a sick man's urine, which some
call
The physician's whore, because she
cozens him.                                    180
He did suspect me wrongfully.

FERD.                        For that
You must give great men leave to take
their times.
Distrust doth cause us seldom be de-
ceived.
You see, the oft shaking of the cedar tree
Fastens it more at root.

BOS.                    Yet take heed,
For to suspect a friend unworthily
Instructs him the next way to suspect
you,
And prompts him to deceive you.

FERD.                        There's gold.

BOS.                                    So!
What follows? Never rained such
showers as these
Without thunderbolts i' th' tail of
them. Whose throat must I cut?

FERD. Your inclination to shed blood rides
post [9]                                        191
Before my occasion to use you. I give
you that
To live i' th' court here, and observe the
duchess;
To note all the particulars of her havior,
What suitors do solicit her for marriage,
And whom she best affects.[10] She's a
young widow;
I would not have her marry again.

BOS.                              No, sir?

FERD. Do not you ask the reason, but be
satisfied.
I say I would not.

BOS.        It seems you would create me
One of your familiars.

[8] Called, like a falcon.    [9] At full speed.
[10] Likes.

FERD.                    Familiar! What's that?

Bos. Why, a very quaint invisible devil in
　　flesh—                                      201
　　An intelligencer.

FERD.        Such a kind of thriving thing
　　I would wish thee; and ere long thou
　　mayst arrive
　　At a higher place by 't.

Bos.                    Take your devils,
　　Which hell calls angels! [1]  These cursed
　　gifts would make
　　You a corrupter, me an impudent traitor;
　　And, should I take these, they'ld take
　　me [to][2] hell.

FERD. Sir, I'll take nothing from you that
　　I have given.
　　There is a place that I procured for you
　　This morning, the provisorship o' th'
　　horse.                                      210
　　Have you heard on 't?

Bos.        No.

FERD.                    'Tis yours. Is 't not
　　worth thanks?

Bos. I would have you curse yourself now,
　　that your bounty
　　(Which makes men truly noble) e'er
　　should make me
　　A villain. O, that to avoid ingratitude
　　For the good deed you have done me, I
　　must do
　　All the ill man can invent! Thus the
　　devil
　　Candies all sins o'er; [3] and what heaven
　　terms vild,[4]
　　That names he complimental.

FERD.                    Be yourself;
　　Keep your old garb of melancholy. 'Twill
　　express
　　You envy those that stand above your
　　reach,                                      220
　　Yet strive not to come near 'em. This
　　will gain
　　Access to private lodgings, where yourself
　　May, like a politic dormouse—

Bos.                    As I have seen some
　　Feed in a lord's dish, half asleep, not
　　seeming
　　To listen to any talk; and yet these
　　rogues
　　Have cut his throat in a dream. What's
　　my place?

The provisorship o' th' horse? Say, then,
　　my corruption
Grew out of horse dung. I am your
　　creature.

FERD.        Away!

Bos. [Aside.] Let good men, for good
　　deeds, covet good fame,
　　Since place and riches oft are bribes of
　　shame.                                      230
　　Sometimes the devil doth preach.
　　　　　　　　　　　　　　　Exit Bosola.[5]

[Enter Duchess, Cardinal, and Cariola.]

CARD. We are to part from you, and your
　　own discretion
　　Must now be your director.

FERD.                    You are a widow:
　　You know already what man is; and
　　therefore
　　Let not youth, high promotion, elo-
　　quence—

CARD. No, nor anything without the addi-
　　tion,[6] Honor,
　　Sway your high blood.

FERD.                    Marry! They
　　are most luxurious [7]
　　Will wed twice.

CARD.        O, fie!

FERD.                    Their livers [8] are
　　more spotted
　　Than Laban's sheep.

DUCH.        Diamonds are of most value,
　　They say, that have passed through most
　　jewelers' hands.                            240

FERD. Whores by that rule are pre-
　　cious.

DUCH.        Will you hear me?
　　I'll never marry.

CARD.                    So most widows say;
　　But commonly that motion [9] lasts no
　　longer
　　Than the turning of an hourglass—the
　　funeral sermon
　　And it end both together.

FERD.                    Now hear me:
　　You live in a rank pasture, here, i' th'
　　court.
　　There is a kind of honeydew that's
　　deadly;

---

[1] Gold coins.　　　　[2] From 1708 edn.
[3] From 1640 edn. Original reads are.
[4] Vile.

[5] With no indication of scene division the
scene apparently shifts slowly to the gallery of
the palace.
[6] Title.　　　　　　[8] Seat of love.
[7] Lecherous.　　　　[9] Intention.

'Twill poison your fame; look to 't. Be
not cunning,
For they whose faces do belie their
hearts
Are witches ere they arrive at twenty
years—        250
Ay, and give the devil suck.
DUCH. This is terrible good counsel.
FERD. Hypocrisy is woven of a fine, small
thread,
Subtler than Vulcan's engine; [1] yet, be-
lieve 't,
Your darkest actions, nay, your privat'st
thoughts,
Will come to light.
CARD.        You may flatter yourself,
And take your own choice; privately be
married
Under the eaves of night—
FERD.        Think 't the best voyage
That e'er you made, like the irregular
crab,
Which, though 't goes backward, thinks
that it goes right        260
Because it goes its own way. But ob-
serve,
Such weddings may more properly be
said
To be executed than celebrated.
CARD.        The marriage night
Is the entrance into some prison.
FERD.        And those joys,
Those lustful pleasures, are like heavy
sleeps
Which do forerun man's mischief.
CARD.        Fare you well.
Wisdom begins at the end; remember it.
[Exit.]
DUCH. I think this speech between you
both was studied,
It came so roundly off.
FERD.        You are my sister.
This was my father's poniard, do you
see?        270
I'ld be loath to see 't look rusty, cause
'twas his.
I would have you to give o'er these
chargeable [2] revels;
A visor and a mask are whispering-
rooms [3]
That were never built for goodness—
fare ye well—

And women like that part which, like the
lamprey,
Hath never a bone in 't.
DUCH.        Fie, sir!
FERD.        Nay,
I mean the tongue—variety of courtship.
What cannot a neat knave with a smooth
tale
Make a woman believe? Farewell, lusty
widow.        [Exit.]
DUCH. Shall this move me? If all my royal
kindred        280
Lay in my way unto this marriage,
I'ld make them my low footsteps. [4] And
even now,
Even in this hate, as men in some great
battles,
By apprehending [5] danger, have achieved
Almost impossible actions (I have heard
soldiers say so),
So I through frights and threat'nings will
assay
This dangerous venture. Let old wives
report
I winked [6] and chose a husband.—
Cariola,
To thy known secrecy I have given up
More than my life—my fame.
CARI.        Both shall be safe,  290
For I'll conceal this secret from the world
As warily as those that trade in poison
Keep poison from their children.
DUCH.        Thy protestation
Is ingenious and hearty; [7] I believe it.
Is Antonio come?
CARI.        He attends [8] you.
DUCH.        Good dear soul,
Leave me, but place thyself behind the
arras,
Where thou mayst overhear us. Wish
me good speed,
[Cariola hides behind the arras.]
For I am going into a wilderness
Where I shall find nor path nor friendly
clew        299
To be my guide.—

[Enter Antonio.]

        I sent for you; sit down.
Take pen and ink, and write. Are you
ready?

[1] Device; here, a net.        [2] Costly.
[3] Private chambers.

[4] Rungs of a ladder.
[5] Grasping.        [6] Shut my eyes.
[7] Ingenuous and from the heart.        [8] Awaits.

ANT.        Yes.

DUCH. What did I say?

ANT. That I should write somewhat.

DUCH.        O, I remember.
  After these triumphs [1] and this large expense
  It's fit, like thrifty husbands,[2] we inquire
  What's laid up for tomorrow.

ANT. So please your beauteous excellence.

DUCH. Beauteous?  Indeed, I thank you.
    I look young for your sake;
  You have ta'en my cares upon you.

ANT.        I'll fetch your grace [3]
  The particulars of your revenue and
    expense.        310

DUCH. O, you are an upright treasurer,
    but you mistook;
  For, when I said I meant to make inquiry
  What's laid up for tomorrow, I did mean
  What's laid up yonder for me.

ANT.        Where?

DUCH.        In heaven.
  I am making my will (as 'tis fit princes
    should,
  In perfect memory), and, I pray, sir, tell
    me,
  Were not one better make it smiling,
    thus,
  Than in deep groans and terrible ghastly
    looks,
  As if the gifts we parted with procured [4]
  That violent destruction? [5]

ANT.        O, much better.

DUCH. If I had a husband now, this care
    were quit.        321
  But I intend to make you overseer.[6]
  What good deed shall we first remember?
    Say.

ANT. Begin with that first good deed began
    i' th' world
  After man's creation, the sacrament of
    marriage.
  I'ld have you first provide for a good
    husband;
  Give him all.

DUCH.    All?

ANT.        Yes, your excellent self.

DUCH. In a winding sheet?

ANT.        In a couple.

DUCH. Saint Winfrid, that were a strange
    will!

ANT.        'Twere strange
  If there were no will in you to marry
    again.        330

DUCH. What do you think of marriage?

ANT. I take 't, as those that deny purgatory,
  It locally contains or heaven or hell;
  There's no third place in 't.

DUCH.        How do you affect it?

ANT. My banishment, feeding my melancholy,
  Would often reason thus:—

DUCH.        Pray, let's hear it.

ANT. Say a man never marry nor have
    children,
  What takes that from him?  Only the
    bare name
  Of being a father, or the weak delight
  To see the little wanton ride a cockhorse
  Upon a painted stick, or hear him
    chatter        341
  Like a taught starling.

DUCH.        Fie, fie, what's all this?
  One of your eyes is bloodshot.  Use my
    ring to 't;
  They say 'tis very sovereign.  'Twas my
    wedding ring,
  And I did vow never to part with it
  But to my second husband.

ANT. You have parted with it now.

DUCH. Yes, to help your eyesight.

ANT. You have made me stark blind.

DUCH. How?        350

ANT. There is a saucy and ambitious
    devil
  Is dancing in this circle.

DUCH.        Remove him.

ANT.        How?

DUCH. There needs small conjuration
    when your finger
  May do it: thus. [*She puts the ring upon
    his finger.*]  Is it fit?

ANT.        What said you? *He kneels.*

DUCH.        Sir,
  This goodly roof of yours is too low built;
  I cannot stand upright in 't nor discourse,
  Without I raise it higher.  Raise yourself;
  Or, if you please, my hand to help you—so.
        [*Raises him.*]

Ant. Ambition, madam, is a great man's
    madness,
    That is not kept in chains and close-pent
        rooms,                                    360
    But in fair, lightsome lodgings, and is
        girt
    With the wild noise of prattling visitants,
    Which makes it lunatic beyond all cure.
    Conceive not I am so stupid but I aim [1]
    Whereto your favors tend; but he's a
        fool
    That, being acold, would thrust his hands
        i' th' fire
    To warm them.
Duch.        So, now the ground's broke,
    You may discover what a wealthy mine
    I make you lord of.
Ant.                    O, my unworthiness!
Duch. You were ill to sell yourself.    370
    This dark'ning of your worth is not like
        that
    Which tradesmen use i' th' city; their
        false lights
    Are to rid bad wares off; and I must tell
        you,
    If you will know where breathes a com-
        plete man
    (I speak it without flattery), turn your
        eyes,
    And progress through yourself.
Ant. Were there nor heaven nor hell,
    I should be honest. I have long served
        virtue,
    And never ta'en wages of her.
Duch.                    Now she pays it.
    The misery of us that are born great!
    We are forced to woo,[2] because none dare
        woo [2] us;                              381
    And, as a tyrant doubles with his words
    And fearfully equivocates, so we
    Are forced to express our violent pas-
        sions
    In riddles and in dreams, and leave the
        path
    Of simple virtue, which was never made
    To seem the thing it is not. Go, go brag
    You have left me heartless; mine is in
        your bosom.
    I hope 'twill multiply love there. You do
        tremble.
    Make not your heart so dead a piece of
        flesh,                                    390

To fear more than to love me. Sir, be
    confident.
What is 't distracts you? This is flesh and
    blood, sir;
'Tis not the figure cut in alablaster [3]
Kneels at my husband's tomb. Awake,
    awake, man!
I do here put off all vain ceremony,
And only do appear to you a young
    widow
That claims you for her husband, and,
    like a widow,
I use but half a blush in 't.
Ant.                    Truth speak for me;
    I will remain the constant sanctuary
    Of your good name.
Duch.        I thank you, gentle love,    400
    And, cause you shall not come to me in
        debt,
    Being now my steward, here upon your
        lips
    I sign your *Quietus est.*[4] This you should
        have begged now.
    I have seen children oft eat sweetmeats
        thus,
    As fearful to devour them too soon.
Ant. But for your brothers?
Duch.                    Do not think of them.
    All discord without this circumference
                    [*Puts her arms about him.*]
    Is only to be pitied, and not feared.
    Yet, should they know it, time will easily
    Scatter the tempest.
Ant.                    These words should be mine,
    And all the parts you have spoke, if some
        part of it                               411
    Would not have savored flattery.
Duch.                    Kneel!
                    [*Cariola discloses herself.*]
Ant.                    Ha!
Duch. Be not amazed. This woman's of
    my counsel.
    I have heard lawyers say a contract in a
        chamber
    *Per verba* [*de*] *presenti*[5] is absolute
        marriage. [*She and Antonio kneel.*]
    Bless, heaven, this sacred Gordian,[6]
        which let violence
    Never untwine.        [*They rise.*]

[1] Guess.
[2] Original spelling is *woe* with double meaning.
[3] Common corrupt pronunciation of *alabaster.*
[4] He is acquitted of his obligations (an ac-
countant's term).
[5] Using words (*i.e.,* vows) in the present tense:
I take thee. etc.                        [6] Knot.

ANT. And may our sweet affections, like
the spheres,
Be still [1] in motion!
DUCH.                Quick'ning, and make
The like soft music!                    420
ANT. That we may imitate the loving palms,
Best emblem of a peaceful marriage,
That never bore fruit, divided!
DUCH. What can the church force more?
ANT. That fortune may not know an acci-
dent,
Either of joy or sorrow, to divide
Our fixéd wishes!
DUCH.    How can the church build faster?[2]
We now are man and wife, and 'tis the
church
That must but echo this.[3]—Maid, stand
apart.—
I now am blind.
ANT.        What's your conceit [4] in this?
DUCH. I would have you lead your fortune
by the hand                          431
Unto your marriage bed.
(You speak in me this, for we now are one.)
We'll only lie and talk together, and plot
T' appease my humorous [5] kindred; and,
if you please,
Like the old tale in *Alexander and Lodo-
wick*,
Lay a naked sword between us, keep us
chaste.
O, let me shroud my blushes in your
bosom,
Since 'tis the treasury of all my secrets!
CARI. [*Aside.*] Whether the spirit of great-
ness or of woman              440
Reign most in her, I know not; but it
shows
A fearful madness. I owe her much of
pity.                          *Exeunt.*

### ACTUS II. SCENA i.

[*An apartment in the Duchess' palace.*]

*Bosola, Castruchio, an Old Lady, Antonio,
Delio, Duchess, Roderigo, Grisolan.*[6]

BOS. You say you would fain be taken
for an eminent courtier? [7]

CAST. 'Tis the very main [8] of my ambition.
BOS. Let me see. You have a reasonable good face for 't already, and your
nightcap [9] expresses your ears sufficient
largely. I would have you learn to twirl
the strings of your band with a good grace,
and in a set speech, at th' end of every
sentence, to hum three or four times, [11
or blow your nose till it smart again, to
recover your memory. When you come
to be a president in criminal causes, if
you smile upon a prisoner, hang him; but,
if you frown upon him and threaten
him, let him be sure to scape the gallows.
CAST. I would be a very merry president.                              20
BOS. Do not sup a-nights; 'twill beget
you an admirable wit.
CAST. Rather it would make me have
a good stomach to quarrel; for they say
your roaring boys [10] eat meat seldom, and
that makes them so valiant. But how shall
I know whether the people take me for an
eminent fellow?                    28
BOS. I will teach a trick to know it.
Give out you lie a-dying, and, if you hear
the common people curse you, be sure you
are taken for one of the prime nightcaps.—

[*Enter an Old Lady.*]

You come from painting now?
OLD LADY. From what?
BOS. Why, from your scurvy face-
physic. To behold thee not painted inclines somewhat near a miracle. These in
thy face here were deep ruts and foul
sloughs the last progress.[11]    There was
a lady in France that, having had the [40
small-pox, flayed the skin off her face to
make it more level; and, whereas before
she looked like a nutmeg-grater, after
she resembled an abortive hedgehog.
OLD LADY. Do you call this painting?
BOS. No, no, but you call [it] [12] careen-
ing [13] of an old morphewed [14] lady, to make
her disembogue [15] again. There's rough-cast
phrase to your plastic.[16]

---

[1] Always.        [2] More firmly.
[3] Ordinarily it was expected that the church
ceremony should follow such a marriage.
[4] Idea.          [5] Temperamental.
[6] All but the first two enter later.
[7] Member of a law court.

[8] Goal.
[9] Lawyer's coif.    [11] Royal journey.
[10] Rowdies.        [12] Supplied from 1678 edn.
[13] Turning a boat on its side for repairs.
[14] Scabbed.  [15] Put to sea.  [16] Modeling.

OLD LADY. It seems you are well ac- [50 quainted with my closet.

BOS. One would suspect it for a shop of witchcraft, to find in it the fat of serpents, spawn of snakes, Jews' spittle, and their young children['s] ordures; and all these for the face. I would sooner eat a dead pigeon taken from the soles of the feet of one sick of the plague than kiss one of you fasting. Here are two of you whose sin of your youth is the very patrimony [60 of the physician; makes him renew his footcloth[1] with the spring, and change his highpriced courtesan with the fall of the leaf. I do wonder you do not loathe yourselves. Observe my meditation now.

What thing is in this outward form of man
To be beloved? We account it ominous
If nature do produce a colt, or lamb,
A fawn, or goat, in any limb resembling
A man, and fly from 't as a prodigy.
Man stands amazed to see his deformity
In any other creature but himself. 72
But in our own flesh, though we bear diseases
Which have their true names only ta'en from beasts,
As the most ulcerous wolf[2] and swinish measle;
Though we are eaten up of lice and worms;
And though continually we bear about us
A rotten and dead body, we delight
To hide it in rich tissue. All our fear,
Nay, all our terror, is lest our physician
Should put us in the ground to be made sweet.— 81
Your wife's gone to Rome; you two couple; and get you
To the wells at Lucca to recover your aches.
I have other work on foot.
     [Exeunt Castruchio and Old Lady.]
I observe our duchess
Is sick a-days. She pukes, her stomach seethes,
The fins[3] of her eyelids look most teeming blue,[4]

She wanes i' th' cheek, and waxes fat i' th' flank,
And, contrary to our Italian fashion,
Wears a loose-bodied gown. There's somewhat in 't. 90
I have a trick may chance discover it,
A pretty one; I have bought some apricocks,
The first our spring yields.

*[Enter Antonio and Delio.]*

DEL. [Aside to Antonio.]      And so long since married?
You amaze me.
ANT. [Aside to Delio.]      Let me seal your lips forever,
For, did I think that anything but th' air
Could carry these words from you, I should wish
You had no breath at all.—[To Bosola.]
Now, sir, in your contemplation?
You are studying to become a great wise fellow?
BOS. O, sir, the opinion of wisdom is a foul tetter that runs all over a man's [100 body. If simplicity direct us to have no evil, it directs us to a happy being, for the subtlest folly proceeds from the subtlest wisdom. Let me be simply honest.
ANT. I do understand your inside.
BOS.      Do you so?
ANT. Because you would not seem to appear to th' world
Puffed up with your preferment, you continue
This out-of-fashion melancholy. Leave it, leave it!
BOS. Give me leave to be honest in any phrase, in any compliment whatsoever. [110 Shall I confess myself to you? I look no higher than I can reach. They are the gods that must ride on winged horses; a lawyer's mule of a slow pace will both suit my disposition and business; for, mark me, when a man's mind rides faster than his horse can gallop, they quickly both tire.
ANT. You would look up to heaven, but I think
The devil, that rules i' th' air, stands in your light. 119
BOS. O, sir, you are lord of the ascendant,[5] chief man with the duchess; a duke was

[1] Ornamental cloth for a horse.
[2] Lupus (Lat. for *wolf*) is a medical term for ulcer.      [3] Rims.
[4] Blue like those of a pregnant woman.
[5] Person of the highest influence (an astrological term).

your cousin-german removed. Say you
were lineally descended from King Pepin,
or he himself, what of this? Search the
heads of the greatest rivers in the world,
you shall find them but bubbles of water.
Some would think the souls of princes
were brought forth by some more weighty
cause than those of meaner persons. They
are deceived; there's the same hand to    [130
them. The like passions sway them; the
same reason that makes a vicar go to law
for a tithe-pig and undo his neighbors,
makes them spoil a whole province, and
batter down goodly cities with the cannon.

*[Enter Duchess and Ladies.]*

Duch. Your arm, Antonio. Do I not grow
    fat?
I am exceeding short-winded.—Bosola,
I would have you, sir, provide for me a
    litter,
Such a one as the Duchess of Florence
    rode in.
Bos. The duchess used one when she was
    great with child.                      140
Duch. I think she did.—Come hither;
    mend my ruff.
Here, when? Thou art such a tedious
    lady, and
Thy breath smells of lemon pills.[1]
    Would thou hadst done!
Shall I sound[2] under thy fingers? I am
So troubled with the mother![3]
Bos. [*Aside.*]              I fear, too much.
Duch. I have heard you say that the
    French courtiers
Wear their hats on fore the king.
Ant. I have seen it.
Duch.                  In the presence?
Ant.                                Yes.
[Duch.] Why should not we bring up that
    fashion?
'Tis ceremony more than duty that con-
    sists                                 150
In the removing of a piece of felt.
Be you the example to the rest o' th'
    court;
Put on your hat first.
Ant.              You must pardon me.
I have seen, in colder countries than in
    France,

---

Nobles stand bare to th' prince; and the
    distinction
Methought showed reverently.
Bos. I have a present for your grace.
Duch.                    For me, sir?
Bos. Apricocks, madam.
Duch.              O, sir, where are they?
I have heard of none to-year.[4]
Bos. [*Aside.*]        Good; her color rises!
Duch. Indeed, I thank you; they are won-
    drous fair ones.                       160
What an unskillful fellow is our gardener!
We shall have none this month.
Bos. Will not your grace pare them?
Duch. No. They taste of musk, methinks;
    indeed they do.
Bos. I know not; yet I wish your grace
    had pared 'em.
Duch. Why?
Bos.          I forgot to tell you, the
    knave gard'ner,
Only to raise his profit by them the sooner,
Did ripen them in horse dung.
Duch.              O, you jest!—
You shall judge. Pray, taste one.
Ant.              Indeed, madam,
I do not love the fruit.
Duch.              Sir, you are loath
To rob us of our dainties. 'Tis a delicate
    fruit;                                 171
They say they are restorative.
Bos.              'Tis a pretty
Art, this grafting.
Duch.        'Tis so; a bett'ring of nature.
Bos. To make a pippin grow upon a crab,
A damson on a blackthorn.—[*Aside.*]
    How greedily she eats them!
A whirlwind strike off these bawd-
    farthingales!
For, but for that and the loose-bodied
    gown,
I should have discovered apparently[5]
The young springal[6] cutting a caper in
    her belly.
Duch. I thank you, Bosola. They were
    right good ones,                       180
If they do not make me sick.
Ant.              How now, madam?
Duch. This green fruit and my stomach
    are not friends.
How they swell me!
Bos. [*Aside.*] Nay, you are too much
    swelled already.

---

[1] Lemon peels.          [2] Swoon.
[3] Hysteria, with a double meaning.
[4] This year.    [5] Clearly.    [6] Youngster.

DUCH. O, I am in an extreme cold sweat!
Bos. I am very sorry.          [*Exit.*]
DUCH. Lights to my chamber!—O good
    Antonio,
I fear I am undone!
                    *Exit Duchess [with Ladies].*
DEL.                    Lights there, lights!
ANT. O my most trusty Delio, we are lost!
I fear she's fall'n in labor; and there's left
No time for her remove.
DEL.                    Have you prepared    191
Those ladies to attend her, and procured
That politic safe conveyance for the
    midwife
Your duchess plotted?
ANT. I have.
DEL. Make use, then, of this forced occa-
    sion.
Give out that Bosola hath poisoned her
With these apricocks; that will give some
    color
For her keeping close.
ANT.                    Fie, fie, the physicians
Will then flock to her.
DEL.        For that you may pretend    200
She'll use some prepared antidote of her
    own,
Lest the physicians should repoison her.
ANT. I am lost in amazement. I know not
what to think on 't.          *Ex[eunt].*

SCENA ii.

[*A hall in the palace.*]

*Bosola,   Old   Lady,   Antonio,   Roderigo,
    Grisolan, Servants, Delio, Cariola.*[1]

Bos. So, so, there's no question but her
techiness and most vulturous eating of the
apricocks are apparent signs of breeding.—

[*Enter Old Lady.*]

Now?
OLD LADY. I am in haste, sir.
Bos. There was a young waiting-woman
had a monstrous desire to see the Glass
House [2]—
OLD LADY. Nay, pray, let me go.
Bos. And it was only to know what    [10
strange instrument it was should swell up
a glass to the fashion of a woman's belly.
OLD LADY. I will hear no more of the
Glass House. You are still abusing women!

[1] All except the first enter later.
[2] A London glass factory.

Bos. Who? I? No, only, by the way
now and then, mention your frailties. The
orange tree bear[s] ripe and green fruit
and blossoms all together; and some of
you give entertainment for pure love, but
more for more precious reward. The    [20
lusty spring smells well, but drooping autumn tastes well. If we have the same
golden showers that rained in the time of
Jupiter the thunderer, you have the same
Dan[ä]es [3] still, to hold up their laps to
receive them. Didst thou never study the
mathematics?
OLD LADY. What's that, sir?
Bos. Why, to know the trick how to
make a many lines meet in one center.    [30
Go, go, give your foster daughters good
counsel. Tell them the devil takes delight to hang at a woman's girdle, like a
false, rusty watch, that she cannot dis-
cern how the time passes. [*Exit Old Lady.*

*Enter   Antonio,   Delio,   Roderigo,   and
                    Grisolan.*]

ANT. Shut up the court gates!
ROD.        Why, sir? What's the danger?
ANT. Shut up the posterns presently,[4] and
    call
All the officers o' th' court.
GRIS.                    I shall instantly. [*Exit.*]
ANT. Who keeps the key o' th' park gate?
ROD.                    Forobosco.
ANT. Let him bring 't presently.        40

[*Enter Grisolan with Servants.*]

[1] SER. O, gentleman o' th' court, the
    foulest treason!
Bos. [*Aside.*] If that these apricocks should
    be poisoned now,
Without my knowledge!
[1] SER. There was taken even now a
    Switzer
In the duchess' bedchamber—
2 SER.                    A Switzer?
[1] SER. With a pistol in his great codpiece.
Bos. Ha, ha, ha!
[1] SER. The codpiece was the case for 't.
2 SER. There was a cunning traitor.    [50
Who would have searched his codpiece?
[1] SER. True, if he had kept out of the
ladies' chambers. And all the molds of his
buttons were leaden bullets.

[3] Correction from 1708 edn.        [4] At once.

2 SER. O wicked cannibal! A firelock in 's codpiece?

[1] SER. 'Twas a French plot, upon my life.

2 SER. To see what the devil can do!

ANT. All the officers[1] here?          60

[1] SER. We are.

ANT. Gentlemen,
We have lost much plate, you know; and but this evening
Jewels, to the value of four thousand ducats,
Are missing in the duchess' cabinet.
Are the gates shut?

[1] SER.          Yes.

ANT.          'Tis the duchess' pleasure
Each officer be locked into his chamber
Till the sun-rising, and to send the keys
Of all their chests and of their outward doors          69
Into her bedchamber. She is very sick.

ROD. At her pleasure.

ANT. She entreats you take 't not ill. The innocent
Shall be the more approved[2] by it.

BOS. Gentlemen o' th' woodyard, where's your Switzer now?

[1] SER. By this hand, 'twas credibly reported by one o' th' black guard.[3]

*[Exeunt all except Antonio and Delio.]*

DEL. How fares it with the duchess?

ANT.          She's exposed
Unto the worst of torture—pain and fear.

DEL. Speak to her all happy comfort.          80

ANT. How I do play the fool with mine own danger!
You are this night, dear friend, to post to Rome.
My life lies in your service.

DEL.          Do not doubt me.

ANT. O, 'tis far from me; and yet fear presents me
Somewhat that look[s] like danger.

DEL.          Believe it,
'Tis but the shadow of your fear, no more.
How superstitiously we mind our evils!
The throwing down salt, or crossing of a hare,
Bleeding at nose, the stumbling of a horse,

Or singing of a cricket are of power          90
To daunt whole man in us. Sir, fare you well.
I wish you all the joys of a blessed father;
And, for my faith, lay this unto your breast:
Old friends, like old swords, still are trusted best.          *[Exit.]*

*[Enter Cariola with a Child.]*[4]

CARI. Sir, you are the happy father of a son.
Your wife commends him to you.

ANT.          Blessed comfort!—
For heaven sake, tend her well. I'll presently
Go set a figure for 's nativity.[5]          *Exeunt.*

SCENA iii.

*[The courtyard of the palace.]*

*Bosola, Antonio.*[6]

BOS. Sure I did hear a woman shriek. List, ha!
And the sound came, if I received it right,
From the duchess' lodgings. There's some stratagem
In the confining all our courtiers
To their several wards. I must have part of it;
My intelligence will freeze else. List, again!
It may be 'twas the melancholy bird,
Best friend of silence and of solitariness,
The owl, that screamed so.—Ha! Antonio?

*[Enter Antonio with a candle, his sword drawn.]*[7]

ANT. I heard some noise.—Who's there? What art thou? Speak.          10

BOS. Antonio, put not your face nor body
To such a forced expression of fear;
I am Bosola, your friend.

ANT.          Bosola!—
*[Aside.]* This mole does undermine me.—
Heard you not
A noise even now?

---

[1] From 1640 edn. Original reads *offices*.
[2] Proved.
[3] Scullions.
[4] From 1708 edn.          [5] Cast his horoscope.
[6] Antonio enters later. 1708 edn. reads *Enter Bosola with a dark lanthorn.*
[7] From 1708 edn.

Bos.       From whence?
Ant.               From the duchess' lodging.
Bos.  Not I.  Did you?
Ant.               I did, or else I dreamed.
Bos.  Let's walk towards it.
Ant.               No; it may be 'twas
But the rising of the wind.
Bos.                       Very likely.
Methinks 'tis very cold, and yet you
  sweat.
You look wildly.
Ant.       I have been setting a figure   20
For the duchess' jewels.
Bos.       Ah, and how falls your question?
Do you find it radical? [1]
Ant.               What's that to you?
'Tis rather to be questioned what design,
When all men were commanded to their
  lodgings,
Makes you a night-walker.
Bos.               In sooth, I'll tell you.
Now all the court's asleep, I thought the
  devil
Had least to do here; I came to say my
  prayers;
And, if it do offend you I do so,
You are a fine courtier.
Ant.  [Aside.]           This fellow will undo
  me.—
You gave the duchess apricocks to-
  day.                                    30
Pray heaven they were not poisoned!
Bos.               Poisoned?  A Spanish fig
For the imputation!
Ant.               Traitors are ever confident
Till they are discovered.   There were
  jewels stol'n too—
In my conceit, none are to be suspected
More than yourself.
Bos.               You are a false steward!
Ant.  Saucy slave, I'll pull thee up by the
  roots!
Bos.  May be the ruin will crush you to
  pieces.
Ant.  You are an impudent snake indeed,
  sir.
Are you scarce warm, and do you show
  your sting?
[Bos.] [2] . . . .                       40
Ant.  You libel [3] well, sir?

Bos.                       No, sir; copy it out,
And I will set my hand to 't.
Ant.               My nose bleeds.—
[Aside, taking out his handkerchief and care-
       lessly dropping a paper.]  One that were
       superstitious would count
This ominous, when it merely comes by
  chance.
Two letters, that are wrought[4] here for
  my name,
Are drowned in blood!
Mere accident!—For you, sir, I'll take
  order;
I' th' morn you shall be safe.—[Aside.]
  'Tis that must color
Her lying-in.—Sir, this door you pass not.
I do not hold it fit that you come near
The duchess' lodgings till you have
  quite[5] yourself.—                    51
[Aside.]  "The great are like the base,
  nay, they are the same.
When they seek shameful ways to avoid
  shame."               Ex[it].
Bos.  Antonio hereabout did drop a paper.
Some of your help, false friend[6]—O,
  here it is.
What's here?  A child's nativity calculated!               [Reads.]
"The duchess ·was delivered of a son,
tween the hours twelve and one in the
night, Anno Dom. 1504"—that's this
year—"decimo nono Decembris"[7]—that's
this night—"taken according to the  [61
meridian of Malfi"—that's our duchess.
Happy discovery!—"The lord of the first
house being combust in the ascendant
signifies short life; and Mars being in a
human sign, joined to the tail of the
Dragon, in the eight house, doth threaten a
violent death.  Cætera non scrutantur."[8]
Why, now 'tis most apparent; this precise fellow
Is the duchess' bawd.  I have it to my
  wish!                                  70
This is a parcel of intelligence[9]
Our courtiers were cased up for!  It needs
  must follow
That I must be committed on pretense
Of poisoning her, which I'll endure, and
  laugh at.

---

[1] Fit to be decided (astrological term).
[2] The passage is obscure.  Lucas suggests that
a speech by Bosola seems to have been omitted.
[3] Draw up a document, with a double meaning.

[4] Embroidered.        [6] I.e., his dark lantern.
[5] Acquitted.          [7] December 19.
                        [8] Other things are not investigated.
                        [9] News.

If one could find the father now! But
  that
Time will discover. Old Castruchio
I' th' morning posts to Rome; by him
  I'll send
A letter that shall make her brothers'
  galls
O'erflow their livers. This was a thrifty
  way!
"Though Lust do mask in ne'er so
  strange disguise.        80
She's oft found witty, but is never
  wise."            [*Exit.*]

SCENA iv.

[*An apartment in the Cardinal's palace at
Rome.*]

*Cardinal and Julia; Servant and Delio.*[1]

CARD. Sit; thou art my best of wishes.
  Prithee, tell me
What trick didst thou invent to come
  to Rome
Without thy husband?
JUL.        Why, my lord, I told him
I came to visit an old anchorite
Here, for devotion.
CARD.       Thou art a witty false one—
I mean, to him.
JUL.       You have prevailed with me
Beyond my strongest thoughts; I would
  not now
Find you inconstant.
CARD.         Do not put thyself
To such a voluntary torture, which pro-
  ceeds
Out of your own guilt.
JUL.     How, my lord!
CARD.        You fear  10
My constancy, because you have ap-
  proved [2]
Those giddy and wild turning[s] in
  yourself.
JUL. Did you e'er find them?
CARD.     Sooth, generally for women;
A man might strive to make glass mal-
  leable
Ere he should make them fixéd.
JUL.        So, my lord!
CARD. We had need go borrow that fan-
  tastic glass
Invented by Galileo the Florentine

To view another spacious world i' th'
  moon,
And look to find a constant woman
  there.
JUL. [*Weeping.*] This is very well, my lord.
CARD.      Why do you weep?  20
Are tears your justification? The self-
  same tears
Will fall into your husband's bosom,
  lady,
With a loud protestation that you love
  him
Above the world. Come, I'll love you
  wisely—
That's jealously, since I am very cer-
  tain
You cannot me make cuckold.
JUL.          I'll go home
To my husband.
CARD.     You may thank me, lady,
I have taken you off your melancholy
  perch,
Bore you upon my fist, and showed you
  game,
And let you fly at it. I pray thee, kiss
  me.         30
When thou wast with thy husband, thou
  wast watched
Like a tame elephant. (Still you are to
  thank me.)
Thou hadst only kisses from him, and
  high feeding;
But what delight was that? 'Twas just
  like one
That hath a little fing'ring on the lute,
Yet cannot tune it. (Still you are to
  thank me.)
JUL. You told me of a piteous wound i'
  th' heart
And a sick liver when you wooed me
  first,
And spake like one in physic.[3]
CARD.        Who's that?—

[*Enter Servant.*]

Rest firm; for my affection to thee,  40
Lightning moves slow to 't.
SER.       Madam, a gentleman
That's comes post from Malfi desires
  to see you.
CARD. Let him enter; I'll withdraw. *Exit.*
SER.          He says

---

[1] Last two enter later.    [2] Experienced.    [3] *I.e.,* sick.

Your husband, old Castruchio, is come
to Rome,
Most pitifully tired with riding post.
                                    [*Exit.*

*Enter Delio.*]

JUL. Signior Delio?—[*Aside.*] 'Tis one of
my old suitors.
DEL. I was bold to come and see you.
JUL.                    Sir, you are welcome.
DEL. Do you lie here?
JUL.                    Sure, your own experience
Will satisfy you no—our Roman prel-
ates
Do not keep lodging for ladies.
DEL.                    Very well.    50
I have brought you no commendations
from your husband,
For I know none by him.
JUL.                    I hear he's come to Rome.
DEL. I never knew man and beast, of a
horse and a knight,
So weary of each other. If he had had
a good back,
He would have undertook to have borne
his horse,
His breech was so pitifully sore.
JUL.                    Your laughter
Is my pity.
DEL.                    Lady, I know not whether
You want money, but I have brought
you some.
JUL. From my husband?
DEL.    No, from mine own allowance.
JUL. I must hear the condition, ere I
be bound to take it.                    60
DEL. Look on 't; 'tis gold. Hath it not a
fine color?
JUL. I have a bird more beautiful.
DEL.                    Try the sound on 't.
JUL. A lutestring far exceeds it.
It hath no smell, like cassia or civet;
Nor is it physical,[1] though some fond [2]
doctors
Persuade us seethe 't [3] in cullises.[4] I'll
tell you,
This is a creature bred by—

[*Enter Servant.*]

SER.                    Your husband's come,
Hath delivered a letter to the Duke of
Calabria

---

[1] Medicinal.                    [2] Foolish.
[3] Boil it. Dyce's emendation. Original reads
*seeth's.*        [4] Strong broths.        [5] Chastity.

That, to my thinking, hath put him out
of his wits.                    [*Exit.*]
JUL. Sir, you hear.                    70
Pray, let me know your business and
your suit
As briefly as can be.
DEL.                    With good speed.
I would wish you
(At such time as you are non-resident
With your husband) my mistress.
JUL. Sir, I'll go ask my husband if I shall,
And straight return your answer.    *Exit.*
DEL.                    Very fine!
Is this her wit, or honesty,[5] that speaks
thus?
I heard one say the duke was highly
moved
With a letter sent from Malfi. I do fear
Antonio is betrayed. How fearfully    80
Shows his ambition now! Unfortunate
fortune!
"They pass through whirlpools, and
deep woes do shun,
Who the event weigh ere the action's
done."                    *Exit.*

SCENA V.

[*The same.*]

*Cardinal and Ferdinand, with a letter.*

FERD. I have this night digged up a man-
drake.[6]
CARD.        Say you?
FERD. And I am grown mad with 't.
CARD.                    What's the prodigy?
FERD. Read there—a sister damned! She's
loose i' th' hilts,
Grown a notorious strumpet.
CARD.                    Speak lower.
FERD.                    Lower?
Rogues do not whisper 't now, but seek
to publish 't
(As servants do the bounty of their
lords)
Aloud, and with a covetous, searching
eye,
To mark who note them. O, confusion
seize her!
She hath had most cunning bawds to
serve her turn,                    9
And more secure conveyances for lust
Than towns of garrison for service.

---

[6] The mandrake, when dug up, supposedly
gave forth shrieks which drove the hearer mad.

CARD.                            Is 't possible?
Can this be certain?
FERD.                    Rhubarb, O, for rhubarb
To purge this choler! [*Points to the
horoscope.*] Here's the cursed day
To prompt my memory; and here 't
shall stick
Till of her bleeding heart I make a
sponge
To wipe it out.
CARD.        Why do you make yourself
So wild a tempest?
FERD.                    Would I could be one,
That I might toss her palace 'bout her ears,
Root up her goodly forests, blast her
meads,
And lay her general territory as waste    20
As she hath done her honors.
CARD.                        Shall our blood,
The royal blood of Aragon and Castile,
Be thus attainted?
FERD.                    Apply desperate physic.
We must not now use balsamum, but
fire—
The smarting cupping glass, for that's
the mean
To purge infected blood, such blood as
hers.
There is a kind of pity in mine eye;
I'll give it to my handkercher, and, now
'tis here,
I'll bequeath this to her bastard.
CARD.                        What to do?
FERD. Why, to make soft lint for his
mother's [1] wounds,                    30
When I have hewed her to pieces.
CARD.                        Cursed creature!
Unequal nature, to place women's
hearts
So far upon the left side! [2]
FERD.                    Foolish men,
That e'er will trust their honor in a bark
Made of so slight, weak bulrush as is
woman,
Apt every minute to sink it!
CARD.                        Thus
Ignorance, when it hath purchased
honor,
It cannot wield it.
FERD.        Methinks I see her laughing—
Excellent hyena! Talk to me some-
what, quickly,

Or my imagination will carry me    40
To see her in the shameful act of sin.
CARD. With whom?
FERD.                    Happily [3] with some
strong-thighed bargeman,
Or one [o'] [4] th' woodyard that can quoit
the sledge [5]
Or toss the bar, or else some lovely
squire
That carries coals up to her privy lodg-
ings.
CARD. You fly beyond your reason.
FERD.                        Go to, mistress!
'Tis not your whore's milk that shall
quench my wildfire,
But your whore's blood.
CARD. How idly [6] shows this rage, which
carries you,
As men conveyed by witches through
the air,                    50
On violent whirlwinds! This intemper-
ate noise
Fitly resembles deaf men's shrill dis-
course,
Who talk aloud, thinking all other
men
To have their imperfection.
FERD.                        Have not you
My palsy?
CARD.        Yes. I can be angry
Without this rupture. There is not in
nature
A thing that makes man so deformed,
so beastly,
As doth intemperate anger. Chide your-
self.
You have divers men who never yet
expressed
Their strong desire of rest but by un-
rest,                    60
By vexing of themselves. Come, put
yourself
In tune.
FERD.        So! I will only study to seem
The thing I am not. I could kill her
now,
In you, or in myself; for I do think
It is some sin in us heaven doth re-
venge
By her.
CARD.        Are you stark mad?
FERD.                    I would have their bodies

<hr>

[1] From 1640 edn. Original reads *mother.*
[2] *I.e.,* to make women so perverse.

[3] Haply, perhaps.        [5] Throw the hammer.
[4] From 1678 edn.        [6] Madly.

Burnt in a coalpit with the ventage
   stopped,
That their cursed smoke might not as-
   cend to heaven;
Or dip the sheets they lie in in pitch or
   sulphur,
Wrap them in 't, and then light them
   like a match;                                              70
Or else to boil their bastard to a cullis,
And give 't his lecherous father to re-
   new
The sin of his back.
CARD.      I'll leave you.
FERD.               Nay, I have done.
I am confident, had I been damned in
   hell,
And should have heard of this, it would
   have put me
Into a cold sweat. In, in! I'll go sleep.
Till I know who leaps my sister, I'll not
   stir.
That known, I'll find scorpions to string
   my whips,
And fix her in a general eclipse.    *Exeunt.*

### ACTUS III. SCENA i.

[*An apartment in the Duchess' palace.*]

*Antonio and Delio; Duchess, Ferdinand,*
*Bosola.*[1]

ANT. Our noble friend, my most beloved
   Delio!
O, you have been a stranger long at
   court.
Came you along with the Lord Ferdi-
   nand?
DEL. I did, sir. And how fares your noble
   duchess?
ANT. Right fortunately well. She's an
   excellent
Feeder of pedigrees; since you last saw
   her,
She hath had two children more, a son
   and daughter.
DEL. Methinks 'twas yesterday. Let me
   but wink,
And not behold your face, which to mine
   eye
Is somewhat leaner, verily I should
   dream                                                       10
It were within this half hour.
ANT. You have not been in law, friend
   Delio,

[1] Last three enter later.

Nor in prison, nor a suitor at the court,
Nor begged the reversion of some great
   man's place,
Nor troubled with an old wife, which
   doth make
Your time so insensibly hasten.
DEL.             Pray, sir, tell me,
Hath not this news arrived yet to the ear
Of the lord cardinal?
ANT.            I fear it hath.
The Lord Ferdinand, that's newly come
   to court,
Doth bear himself right dangerously.
DEL.             Pray, why?  20
ANT. He is so quiet that he seems to sleep
The tempest out, as dormice do in winter.
Those houses that are haunted are most
   still
Till the devil be up.
DEL.      What say the common people?
ANT. The common rabble do directly say
She is a strumpet.
DEL.          And your graver heads
Which would be politic, what censure [2]
   they?
ANT. They do observe I grow to infinite
   purchase [3]
The left-hand way; and all suppose the
   duchess
Would amend it, if she could; for, say
   they,                      30
Great princes, though they grudge their
   officers
Should have such large and unconfinéd
   means
To get wealth under them, will not com-
   plain,
Lest thereby they should make them
   odious
Unto the people. For other obligation
Of love or marriage between her and me,
They never dream of.

[*Enter Duchess, Ferdinand, Bosola, and*
*Attendants.*]

DEL. [*Aside.*]        The Lord Ferdinand
Is going to bed.
FERD.          I'll instantly to bed,
For I am weary.—I am to bespeak
A husband for you.
DUCH.   For me, sir? Pray, who is 't?  40
FERD. The great Count Malateste.
DUCH.             Fie upon him!

[2] Judge.                                 [3] Wealth.

A count?  He's a mere stick of sugar
  candy;
You may look quite thorough him.
  When I choose
A husband, I will marry for your honor.
FERD.  You shall do well in 't.—How is 't,
  worthy Antonio?
DUCH.  But, sir, I am to have private con-
  ference with you
About a scandalous report is spread
Touching mine honor.
FERD.           Let me be ever deaf to 't—
One of Pasquil's paper bullets,[1] court
  calumny,
A pestilent air which princes' palaces  50
Are seldom purged of.  Yet, say that it
  were true,
I pour it in your bosom, my fixed love
Would strongly excuse, extenuate, nay,
  deny
Faults, were they apparent in you.  Go,
  be safe
In your own innocency.
DUCH.  [Aside.]      O blessed comfort!
This deadly air is purged.
Exeunt [all except Ferdinand and Bosola].
FERD.           Her guilt treads on
Hot, burning cultures.[2]  Now, Bosola,
How thrives our intelligence?
BOS.          Sir, uncertainly.
'Tis rumored she hath had three bas-
  tards, but
By whom we may go read i' th' stars.
FERD.          Why, some  60
Hold opinion all things are written there.
BOS.  Yes, if we could find spectacles to
  read them.
I do suspect there hath been some sorcery
Used on the duchess.
FERD.        Sorcery!  To what purpose?
BOS.  To make her dote on some desertless
  fellow
She shames to acknowledge.
FERD.        Can your faith give way
To think there's power in potions or in
  charms,
To make us love whether we will or no?
BOS.  Most certainly.
FERD.  Away!  These are mere gulleries,[3]
  horrid things,          70
Invented by some cheating mountebanks
To abuse us.  Do you think that herbs or
  charms

Can force the will?  Some trials have
  been made
In this foolish practice, but the ingredi-
  ents
Were lenitive poisons, such as are of
  force
To make the patient mad; and straight
  the witch
Swears by equivocation they are in
  love.
The witchcraft lies in her rank blood.
  This night
I will force confession from her.  You told
  me
You had got, within these two days, a
  false key        80
Into her bedchamber.
BOS.        I have.
FERD.           As I would wish.
BOS.  What do you intend to do?
FERD.          Can you guess?
BOS.          No.
FERD.  Do not ask, then.
He that can compass me, and know my
  drifts,
May say he hath put a girdle 'bout the
  world,
And sounded all her quicksands.
BOS.          I do not
  Think so.
FERD.    What do you think, then, pray?
BOS.          That you are
Your own chronicle too much, and grossly
Flatter yourself.
FERD.    Give me thy hand; I thank thee.
I never gave pension but to flatterers  90
Till I entertainéd thee.  Farewell.
"That friend a great man's ruin strongly
  checks,
Who rails into his belief all his defects."
                    Exeunt.

SCENA ii.

[The Duchess' bedchamber.]

Duchess, Antonio, Cariola, Ferdinand,
Bosola, Officers.[4]

DUCH.  Bring me the casket hither, and the
  glass.—
You get no lodging here tonight, my lord.
ANT.  Indeed, I must persuade one.
DUCH.          Very good!
I hope in time 'twill grow into a custom

---

[1] Pasquinades.    [2] Plowshares.    [3] Deceptions.

[4] Ferdinand, Bosola, and Officers enter later.

That noblemen shall come with cap and
knee
To purchase a night's lodging of their
wives.
ANT. I must lie here.
DUCH.   Must? You are a lord of misrule.
ANT. Indeed, my rule is only in the night.
DUCH. To what use will you put me?
ANT.                    We'll sleep together.
DUCH. Alas, what pleasure can two lovers
find in sleep?                              10
CARI. My lord, I lie with her often, and I
know
She'll much disquiet you.
ANT.          See, you are complained of.
CARI. For she's the sprawling'st bedfellow.
ANT. I shall like her the better for that.
CARI. Sir, shall I ask you a question?
ANT. I pray thee, Cariola.
CARI. Wherefore still when you lie with my
lady
Do you rise so early?
ANT.                    Laboring men
Count the clock oft'nest, Cariola,
Are glad when their task's ended.
DUCH.               I'll stop your mouth.  20
                              [Kisses him.]
ANT. Nay, that's but one; Venus had two
soft doves
To draw her chariot; I must have
another.—                    [Another kiss.]
When wilt thou marry, Cariola?
CARI.                    Never, my lord.
ANT. O, fie upon this single life! Forgo it.
We read how Daphne, for her peevish
slight,[1]
Became a fruitless bay tree, Syrinx
turned
To the pale, empty reed, Anaxarete
Was frozen into marble; whereas those
Which married or proved kind unto their
friends
Were by a gracious influence trans-
shaped                                     30
Into the olive, pomegranate, mulberry,
Became flowers, precious stones, or
eminent stars.
CARI. This is a vain poetry   But I pray
you, tell me,
If there were proposed me wisdom,
riches, and beauty,
In three several young men, which should
I choose?

[1] I.e., of Apollo. Mod. edns. print flight.

ANT. 'Tis a hard question. This was Paris'
case,
And he was blind in 't, and there was a
great cause.
For how was 't possible he could judge
right,
Having three amorous goddesses in view,
And they stark naked? 'Twas a motion[2]
Were able to benight the apprehension
Of the severest counselor of Europe.   42
Now I look on both your faces so well
formed,
It puts me in mind of a question I would
ask.
CARI. What is 't?
ANT.               I do wonder why hard-
favored ladies
For the most part keep worse-favored
waiting-women
To attend them, and cannot endure fair
ones.
DUCH. O, that's soon answered.
Did you ever in your life know an ill
painter
Desire to have his dwelling next door to
the shop                                   50
Of an excellent picture maker? 'Twould
disgrace
His face-making, and undo him. I prithee,
When were we so merry?—My hair
tangles.
ANT. [Aside.]   Pray thee, Cariola, let's
steal forth the room,
And let her talk to herself. I have divers
times
Served her the like, when she hath
chafed extremely.
I love to see her angry. Softly, Cariola.
              Exeunt [Antonio and Cariola].
DUCH. Doth not the color of my hair gin
to change?
When I wax gray, I shall have all the
court
Powder their hair with arras,[3] to be like
me.                                        60
You have cause to love me; I entered you
into my heart

[Enter Ferdinand unseen.] [4]

Before you would vouchsafe to call for
the keys.

[2] Spectacle, show.      [3] Powder of orris-root.
[4] Stage direction from 1708 edn.

We shall one day have my brothers take
  you napping.
Methinks his presence, being now in court,
Should make you keep your own bed;
  but you'll say
Love mixed with fear is sweetest. I'll
  assure you,
You shall get no more children till my
  brothers
Consent to be your gossips.[1] Have you
  lost your tongue?—[*Sees Ferdinand
  with a poniard.*] 'Tis welcome;
For know, whether I am doomed to live
  or die,
I can do both like a prince.

*Ferdinand gives her a poniard.*

FERD.           Die, then, quickly. 70
  Virtue, where art thou hid? What hid-
    eous thing
  Is it that doth eclipse [2] thee?
DUCH.           Pray, sir, hear me!
FERD. Or is it true thou art but a bare
  name,
And no essential thing?
DUCH.         Sir—
FERD.           Do not speak.
DUCH. No, sir!
  I will plant my soul in mine ears, to hear
    you.
FERD. O most imperfect light of human
  reason,
That mak'st [us] [3] so unhappy to foresee
What we can least prevent! Pursue thy
  wishes,
And glory in them; there's in shame no
  comfort           80
But to be past all bounds and sense of
  shame.
DUCH. I pray, sir, hear me. I am married!
FERD.           So!
DUCH. Happily, not to your liking. But
  for that,
Alas, your shears do come untimely now
To clip the bird's wings that's already
  flown!
Will you see my husband?
FERD.           Yes, if I
  Could change eyes with a basilisk.
DUCH.        Sure, you came hither
  By his confideracy.[4]

[1] Godparents to your children.
[2] Perhaps with a pun on *clip*, to embrace.
[3] From 1708 edn.
[4] Confederacy. It is not clear in the original
whether the word is *consideracy* or *confideracy*.

FERD.         The howling of a wolf
  Is music to thee, screech owl! Prithee,
    peace!—
  Whate'er thou art that hast enjoyed my
    sister,         90
  For I am sure thou hear'st me, for thine
    own sake
  Let me not know thee. I came hither
    prepared
  To work thy discovery, yet am now per-
    suaded
  It would beget such violent effects
  As would damn us both. I would not for
    ten millions
  I had beheld thee; therefore use all
    means
  I never may have knowledge of thy
    name;
  Enjoy thy lust still, and a wretched life,
  On that condition.—And for thee, vild
    woman,
  If thou do wish thy lecher may grow
    old         100
  In thy embracements, I would have thee
    build
  Such a room for him as our anchorites
  To holier use inhabit. Let not the sun
  Shine on him till he's dead; let dogs and
    monkeys
  Only converse with him, and such dumb
    things
  To whom nature denies use to sound his
    name;
  Do not keep a paraquito, lest she learn it;
  If thou do love him, cut out thine own
    tongue,
  Lest it bewray him.
DUCH.      Why might not I marry? 109
  I have not gone about in this to create
  Any new world or custom.
FERD.          Thou art undone;
  And thou hast ta'en that massy sheet of
    lead
  That hid thy husband's bones, and folded
    it
  About my heart.
DUCH.      Mine bleeds for 't.
FERD.         Thine? Thy heart?
  What should I name 't, unless a hollow
    bullet
  Filled with unquenchable wildfire?
DUCH.         You are in this
  Too strict, and, were you not my princely
    brother,

I would say, too willful. My reputation
Is safe.
FERD.        Dost thou know what reputa-
tion is?
I'll tell thee—to small purpose, since th'
instruction                                          120
Comes now too late.
Upon a time Reputation, Love, and
Death
Would travel o'er the world; and it was
concluded
That they should part, and take three
several ways.
Death told them they should find him in
great battles,
Or cities plagued with plagues.  Love
gives them counsel
To inquire for him 'mongst unambitious
shepherds,
Where dowries were not talked of and
sometimes
'Mongst quiet kindred that had nothing
left
By their dead parents.  "Stay," quoth
Reputation,                                          130
"Do not forsake me; for it is my nature,
If once I part from any man I meet,
I am never found again."  And so, for
you.
You have shook hands with Reputation,
And made him invisible.  So, fare you
well;
I will never see you more.
DUCH.                Why should only I,
Of all the other princes of the world,
Be cased up, like a holy relic?  I have
youth
And a little beauty.
FERD.        So you have some virgins
That are witches.  I will never see thee
more.                        *Exit.* 140

*Enter Antonio with a pistol [, and Cariola].*[1]

DUCH.  You saw this apparition?
ANT.                          Yes; we are
Betrayed.  How came he hither?  [*Points
the pistol at Cariola.*]  I should turn
This to thee, for that.
CARI.              Pray, sir, do; and, when
That you have cleft my heart, you shall
read there
Mine innocence.
DUCH.        That gallery gave him entrance.

[1] Direction in original follows next speech.

ANT.  I would this terrible thing would
come again
That, standing on my guard, I might
relate
My warrantable love.—Ha! what means
this?              *She shows the poniard.*
DUCH.  He left this with me.
ANT.                And it seems did wish
You would use it on yourself?
DUCH.                His action seemed  150
To intend so much.
ANT.                This hath a handle to 't,
As well as a point—turn it towards him,
and
So fasten the keen edge in his rank gall.
                        [*Knocking within.*]
How now!  Who knocks?  More earth-
quakes?
DUCH.        I stand
As if a mine beneath my feet were ready
To be blown up.
CARI.              'Tis Bosola.
DUCH.                          Away!
O misery!  Methinks unjust actions
Should wear these masks and curtains,
and not we.
You must instantly part hence; I have
fashioned it already.  *Ex[it] Ant[onio].*

[*Enter Bosola.*]

BOS.  The duke your brother is ta'en up
in a whirlwind,                                      160
Hath took horse, and 's rid post to
Rome.
DUCH.                          So late?
BOS.  He told me, as he mounted into th'
saddle,
You were undone.
DUCH.              Indeed I am very near it.
BOS.  What's the matter?
DUCH.  Antonio, the master of our house-
hold,
Hath dealt so falsely with me in 's
accounts.
My brother stood engaged with me for
money
Ta'en up of certain Neapolitan Jews,
And Antonio lets the bonds be forfeit.
BOS.  Strange!—[*Aside.*]  This is cunning.
DUCH.                And hereupon  170
My brother's bills at Naples are pro-
tested
Against.—Call up our officers.
BOS.                          I shall.  *Exit.*

[*Enter Antonio.*]

DUCH. The place that you must fly to is Ancona.

Hire a house there; I'll send after you

My treasure and my jewels. Our weak safety

Runs upon enginous [1] wheels; short syllables

Must stand for periods. I must now accuse you

Of such a feignéd crime as Tasso calls

*Magnanima menzogna,* "a noble lie,"

Cause it must shield our honors.—Hark! they are coming.          180

[*Enter Bosola and Officers.*]

ANT. Will your grace hear me?

DUCH. I have got well by you; you have yielded me

A million of loss. I am like to inherit

The people's curses for your stewardship.

You had the trick in audit-time to be sick,

Till I had signed your *Quietus;* and that cured you

Without help of a doctor.—Gentlemen,

I would have this man be an example to you all;

So shall you hold my favor. I pray, let him, [2]

For h'as done that, alas, you would not think of,          190

And, because I intend to be rid of him,

I mean not to publish.—Use your fortune elsewhere.

ANT. I am strongly armed to brook my overthrow,

As commonly men bear with a hard year.

I will not blame the cause on 't; but do think

The necessity of my malevolent star

Procures this, not her humor. O, the inconstant

And rotten ground of service! You may see,

'Tis even like him that in a winter night

Takes a long slumber o'er a dying fire,          200

As loath [3] to part from 't, yet parts thence as cold

As when he first sat down.

[1] Ingenious, intricate.          [2] Let him go.

[3] Some apparently uncorrected copies of 1623 edn. read *a-loth.*

DUCH.               We do confiscate,

Towards the satisfying of your accounts,

All that you have.

ANT.          I am all yours; and 'tis very fit

All mine should be so.

DUCH.          So, sir, you have your pass.

ANT. You may see, gentlemen, what 'tis to serve

A prince with body and soul.          *Exit.*

BOS. Here's an example for extortion; what moisture is drawn out of the sea, when foul weather comes, pours down, and [210 runs into the sea again.

DUCH. I would know what are your opinions of this Antonio.

2 OFF. He could not abide to see a pig's head gaping; [4] I thought your grace would find him a Jew.

3 OFF. I would you had been his officer, for your own sake.

4 OFF. You would have had more money.          220

1 OFF. He stopped his ears with black wool, and to those came to him for money said he was thick of hearing.

2 OFF. Some said he was an hermaphrodite, for he could not abide a woman.

4 OFF. How scurvy proud he would look when the treasury was full! Well, let him go.

1 OFF. Yes, and the chippings [5] of the butt'ry fly after him, to scour his gold [230 chain. [6]

DUCH. Leave us.—     (*Exeunt* [*Officers*].)

What do you think of these?

BOS. That these are rogues that, in 's prosperity,

But to have waited on his fortune could have wished

His dirty stirrup riveted through their noses,

And followed after 's mule, like a bear in a ring;

Would have prostituted their daughters to his lust;

Made their first-born intelligencers; thought none happy

But such as were born under his blessed planet,          240

And wore his livery—and do these lice drop off now?

Well, never look to have the like again.

[4] A roasted pig with an apple in its mouth.

[5] Crumbs.     [6] Symbol of a steward's office.

He hath left a sort [1] of flatt'ring rogues
  behind him;
Their doom must follow.  Princes pay
  flatterers
In their own money; flatterers dissemble
  their vices,
And they dissemble their lies.  That's
  justice.
Alas, poor gentleman!
Duch.  Poor?  He hath amply filled his
  coffers.
Bos.  Sure, he was too honest.  Pluto, the
  god of riches,
When he's sent by Jupiter to any
  man,                                        250
He goes limping, to signify that wealth
That comes on God's name comes slowly;
  but, when he's sent
On the devil's errand, he rides post and
  comes in by scuttles.[2]
Let me show you what a most unvalued
  jewel
You have in a wanton humor thrown
  away,
To bless the man shall find him.  He was
  an excellent
Courtier and most faithful; a soldier that
  thought it
As beastly to know his own value too
  little
As devilish to acknowledge it too much.
Both his virtue and form deserved a far
  better fortune;                             260
His discourse rather delighted to judge
  itself than show itself;
His breast was filled with all perfec-
  tion,
And yet it seemed a private whisp'ring-
  room,
It made so little noise of 't.
Duch.  But he was basely descended.
Bos.  Will you make yourself a mercenary
  herald,
Rather to examine men's pedigrees than
  virtues?
You shall want him;
For know an honest statesman to a
  prince
Is like a cedar planted by a spring;      270
The spring bathes the tree's root; the
  grateful tree
Rewards it with his shadow.  You have
  not done so.

I would sooner swim to the Bermoothes [3]
  on two politicians'[4]
Rotten bladders, tied together with an
  intelligencer's heartstring,
Than depend on so changeable a prince's
  favor.
Fare thee well, Antonio!  Since the malice
  of the world
Would needs down with thee, it cannot
  be said yet
That any ill happened unto thee, con-
  sidering thy fall
Was accompanied with virtue.
Duch.  O, you render me excellent music!
Bos.                              Say you?  280
Duch.  This good one that you speak of is
  my husband.
Bos.  Do I not dream?  Can this ambitious
  age
Have so much goodness in 't as to prefer
A man merely for worth, without these
  shadows
Of wealth and painted honors?  Possible?
Duch.  I have had three children by him.
Bos.                          Fortunate lady!
For you have made your private nuptial
  bed
The humble and fair seminary [5] of peace—
No question but.  Many an unbeneficed
  scholar
Shall pray for you for this deed, and
  rejoice                                     290
That some preferment in the world can
  yet
Arise from merit.  The virgins of your
  land
That have no dowries shall hope your
  example
Will raise them to rich husbands.  Should
  you want
Soldiers, 'twould make the very Turks
  and Moors
Turn Christians, and serve you for this
  act.
Last, the neglected poets of your time,
In honor of this trophy of a man,
Raised by that curious engine, your white
  hand,
Shall thank you in your grave for 't, and
  make that                                   300
More reverend than all the cabinets[6]
Of living princes.  For Antonio,

[1] Crowd.                    [2] Quick steps.

[3] Bermudas.               [5] Seedbed.
[4] Intriguers'.            [6] Museums.

His fame shall likewise flow from many a
   pen,
When heralds shall want coats to sell to
   men.
DUCH. As I taste comfort in this friendly
   speech,
So would I find concealment.
Bos. O, the secret of my prince,
   Which I will wear on th' inside of my
   heart!
DUCH. You shall take charge of all my
   coin and jewels,
   And follow him, for he retires himself   310
   To Ancona.
Bos.        Sc!
DUCH.        Whither, within few days,
   I mean to follow thee.
Bos.        Let me think.
   I would wish your grace to feign a pil-
   grimage
   To our Lady of Loretto, scarce seven
   leagues
   From fair Ancona; so may you depart
   Your country with more honor, and your
   flight
   Will seem a princely progress, retaining
   Your usual train about you.
DUCH.        Sir, your direction
   Shall lead me by the hand.
CARI.        In my opinion,
   She were better progress to the baths   320
   At Lucca, or go visit the Spa
   In Germany, for, if you will believe me,
   I do not like this jesting with religion,
   This feignéd pilgrimage.
DUCH. Thou art a superstitious fool!
   Prepare us instantly for our departure.
   Past sorrows, let us moderately lament
   them,
   For those to come, seek wisely to prevent
   them.
            *Exit [Duchess with Cariola].*
Bos. A politician is the devil's quilted
   anvil;
   He fashions all sins on him, and the
   blows        330
   Are never heard.  He may work in a
   lady's chamber,
   As here for proof.  What rests [1] but I
   reveal
   All to my lord? O, this base quality [2]
   Of intelligencer! Why, every quality i'
   th' world

[1] Remains.        [2] Profession.

Prefers but gain or commendation.
Now, for this act I am certain to be
   raised,
"And men that paint weeds to the life
   are praised."        *Exit.*

SCENA iii.

*[An apartment in the Cardinal's palace at
                    Rome.]*

*Cardinal, Ferdinand, Malateste, Pescara,
           Silvio, Delio, Bosola.*[3]

CARD. Must we turn soldier, then?
MAL.        The emperor,
   Hearing your worth that way ere you
   attained
   This reverend garment, joins you in
   commission
   With the right fortunate soldier, the
   Marquis of Pescara,
   And the famous Lannoy.
CARD.        He that had the honor
   Of taking the French king prisoner?
MAL.        The same.
   Here's a plot drawn for a new fortifica-
   tion
   At Naples.

*[Cardinal and Malateste stand aside con-
                 versing.]*

FERD.        This great Count Mala-
   [teste], I perceive,
   Hath got employment?
DEL.        No employment, my lord;
   A marginal note in the muster book that
   he is        10
   A voluntary [4] lord.
FERD.        He's no soldier?
DEL. He has worn gunpowder in 's hollow
   tooth for the toothache.
SIL. He comes to the leaguer with a full
   intent
   To eat fresh beef and garlic, means to
   stay
   Till the scent be gone, and straight re-
   turn to court.
DEL. He hath read all the late service
   As the city chronicle relates it;
   And keep[s] two painters [5] going, only to
   express
   Battles in model.

[3] Enters later.        [4] *I.e.,* a volunteer.
[5] Some apparently uncorrected copies of 1623
edn. read *pewterers.*

SIL.            Then he'll fight by the book.
DEL.  By the almanac, I think,            20
  To choose good days and shun the
    critical.
  That's his mistress' scarf.
SIL.                    Yes, he protests
  He would do much for that taffeta.
DEL.  I think he would run away from a
    battle
  To save it from taking prisoner.
SIL.            He is horribly afraid
  Gunpowder will spoil the perfume on 't.
DEL.  I saw a Dutchman break his pate
    once
  For calling him potgun;[1] he made his
    head
  Have a bore in 't like a musket.
SIL.  I would he had made a touchhole
    to 't.                    30
  He is indeed a garded sumpter cloth,[2]
  Only for the remove of the court.[3]

*[Enter Bosola.]*

PES.  Bosola arrived?  What should be the
    business?
  Some falling out amongst the cardinals.
  These factions amongst great men, they
    are like
  Foxes; when their heads are divided,
  They carry fire in their tails, and all
    the country
  About them goes to wrack for 't.
SIL.                    What's that Bosola?
DEL.  I knew him in Padua—a fan-
tastical scholar, like such who study to  [40
know how many knots was in Hercules'
club, of what color Achilles' beard was, or
whether Hector were not troubled with the
toothache.  He hath studied himself half
blear-eyed to know the true symmetry of
Cæsar's nose by a shoeinghorn; and this
he did to gain the name of a speculative
man.
PES.  Mark Prince Ferdinand.
  A very salamander lives in 's eye,   50
  To mock the eager violence of fire.
SIL.  That cardinal hath made more bad
faces with his oppression than ever Michael
Angelo made good ones.  He lifts up 's nose
like a foul porpoise before a storm.
PES.  The Lord Ferdinand laughs.

DEL.                    Like a deadly cannon
  That lightens ere it smokes.
PES.  These are your true pangs of death,
  The pangs of life, that struggle with
    great statesmen.
DEL.  In such a deformed silence, witches
  whisper their charms.            60
*[Silvio, Pescara, and Delio stand aside.]*
CARD.  Doth she make religion her riding
    hood
  To keep her from the sun and tempest?
FERD.  That, that damns her.  Methinks
    her fault and beauty,
  Blended together, show like leprosy—
  The whiter the fouler.  I make it a ques-
    tion
  Whether her beggarly brats were ever
    christened.
CARD.  I will instantly solicit the state of
    Ancona
  To have them banished.
FERD.                    You are for Loretto?
  I shall not be at your ceremony.  Fare
    you well.—
  Write to the Duke of Malfi, my young
    nephew                    70
  She had by her first husband, and ac-
    quaint him
  With 's mother's honesty.[4]
BOS.                    I will.
FERD.                    Antonio!
  A slave that only smelled of ink and
    compters,[5]
  And never in 's life looked like a gentle-
    man
  But in the audit-time.—Go, go pres-
    ently;
  Draw me out an hundreth and fifty of
    our horse,
  And meet me at the fort-bridge.
                    *Exeunt.*

SCENA iv.

*Two Pilgrims to the Shrine of Our Lady of
                    Loretto.*

1 PIL.  I have not seen a goodlier shrine
    than this;
  Yet I have visited many.
2 PIL.            The Cardinal of Aragon
  Is this day to resign his cardinal's hat;
  His sister duchess likewise is arrived

---

[1] Popgun.
[2] Ornamented horse cloth.
[3] When the court moves from place to place.

[4] Chastity.            [5] Counters.

To pay her vow of pilgrimage. I expect
A noble ceremony.

1 PIL.                No question.—They come.

*Here the ceremony of the Cardinal's in-*
*stallment in the habit [of]* [1] *a soldier,*
*performed in delivering up his cross, hat,*
*robes, and ring at the shrine, and in-*
*vesting him with sword, helmet, shield,*
*and spurs.   Then Antonio, the Duch-*
*ess, and their Children, having presented*
*themselves at the shrine, are, by a form*
*of banishment in dumb show, expressed*
*towards them by the Cardinal and the*
*state of Ancona, banished.   During all*
*which ceremony, this ditty is sung, to*
*very solemn music, by divers Church-*
*men; and then exeunt.*

Arms and honors deck thy story
To thy fame's eternal glory!
Adverse fortune ever fly thee;
No disastrous fate come nigh
    thee!
I alone will sing thy praises,     ⎡ *The author*
Whom to honor virtue raises,      ⎢ *disclaims this*
And thy study, that divine is,    ⎣ *ditty to be his.*
Bent to martial discipline is,
Lay aside all those robes lie by thee.
Crown thy arts with arms; they'll beautify
    thee.

O worthy of worthiest name, adorned in
    this manner,
Lead bravely thy forces on under war's
    warlike banner!
O, mayst thou prove fortunate in all mar-
    tial courses!                           19
Guide thou still by skill in arts and forces!
Victory attend thee nigh, whilst fame sings
    loud thy powers;
Triumphant conquest crown thy head, and
    blessings pour down showers!

1 PIL. Here's a strange turn of state! Who
    would have thought
So great a lady would have matched
    herself
Unto so mean a person? Yet the cardinal
Bears himself much too cruel.

2 PIL.                They are banished.

1 PIL. But I would ask what power hath
    this state
Of Ancona to determine of a free prince?

2 PIL. They are a free state, sir, and her
    brother showed

[1] Supplied from 1640 edn.

How that the pope, forehearing of her
    looseness,                              30
Hath seized into th' protection of the
    church
The dukedom which she held as dowager.

1 PIL. But by what justice?

2 PIL.                Sure, I think by none,
Only her brother's instigation.

1 PIL. What was it with such violence he
    took
Off from her finger?

2 PIL.                'Twas her wedding ring,
Which he vowed shortly he would
    sacrifice
To his revenge.

1 PIL.                Alas, Antonio!
If that a man be thrust into a well,
No matter who sets hand to 't, his own
    weight                                  40
Will bring him sooner to th' bottom.
Come, let's hence.
Fortune makes this conclusion general,
"All things do help th' unhappy man to
    fall."                          *Exeunt.*

SCENA V.

*[A road near Loretto.]*

*Antonio, Duchess, Children, Cariola, Serv-*
*ants; Bosola, Soldiers with vizards.* [2]

DUCH. Banished Ancona!

ANT.                Yes, you see what power
Lightens in great men's breath.

DUCH.                Is all our train
Shrunk to this poor remainder?

ANT.                These poor men,
Which have got little in your service,
    vow
To take your fortune. But your wiser
    buntings,
Now they are fledged, are gone.

DUCH.                They have done wisely.
This puts me in mind of death; physi-
    cians thus,
With their hands full of money, use to
    give o'er
Their patients.

ANT.    Right the fashion of the world—
From decayed fortunes every flatterer
    shrinks;                                10
Men cease to build where the founda-
    tion sinks.

[2] Bosola and Soldiers enter later.

Duch. I had a very strange dream tonight.

Ant.                 What was 't?

Duch. Methought I wore my coronet of
    state,
And on a sudden all the diamonds
Were changed to pearls.

Ant.            My interpretation
Is, you'll weep shortly, for to me the
    pearls
Do signify your tears.

Duch.        The birds, that live i' th' field
On the wild benefit of nature, live
Happier than we, for they may choose
    their mates,
And carol their sweet pleasures to the
    spring.                   20

*[Enter Bosola with a letter.]*

Bos. You are happily o'erta'en.

Duch.              From my brother?

Bos. Yes, from the Lord Ferdinand your
    brother
All love and safety.

Duch.        Thou dost blanch mischief,
Wouldst make it white. See, see, like to
    calm weather
At sea before a tempest, false hearts
    speak fair
To those they intend most mischief.

A Letter:

"Send Antonio to me; I want his head in
    a business."

A politic equivocation!

He doth not want your counsel, but your
    head;

That is, he cannot sleep till you be
    dead.                      30

And here's another pitfall that's strewed
    o'er

With roses. Mark it; 'tis a cunning one:
"I stand engaged for your husband
for several debts at Naples. Let not
that trouble him; I had rather have his
heart than his money."

And I believe so too.

Bos.             What do you believe?

Duch. That he so much distrusts my
    husband's love,
He will by no means believe his heart
    is with him
Until he see it. The devil is not cunning
    enough                 40
To circumvent us in riddles.

Bos. Will you reject that noble and free
    league
Of amity and love which I present you?

Duch. Their league is like that of some
    politic kings,
Only to make themselves of strength and
    power
To be our after-ruin. Tell them so.

Bos. And what from you?

Ant.        Thus tell him: I will not come.

Bos. And what of this?

Ant.           My brothers have dispersed
Bloodhounds abroad, which till I hear
    are muzzled,
No truce, though hatched with ne'er
    such politic skill,            50
Is safe, that hangs upon our enemies'
    will.
I'll not come at them.

Bos.          This proclaims your breeding.
Every small thing draws a base mind to
    fear
As the adamant [1] draws iron. Fare you
    well, sir;
You shall shortly hear from 's. *Exit.*

Duch.          I suspect some ambush;
Therefore by all my love I do conjure
    you
To take your eldest son, and fly to-
    wards Milan.
Let us not venture all this poor re-
    mainder
In one unlucky bottom.

Ant.              You counsel safely.
Best of my life, farewell. Since we must
    part,                     60
Heaven hath a hand in 't; but no other-
    wise
Than as some curious artist takes in
    sunder
A clock or watch, when it is out of
    frame,
To bring 't in better order.

Duch. I know not which is best,
To see you dead or part with you.
    Farewell, boy.
Thou art happy that thou hast not
    understanding
To know thy misery, for all our wit
And reading brings us to a truer sense
Of sorrow.—In the eternal church, sir,
I do hope we shall not part thus.

Ant.            O, be of comfort!    71

[1] Magnet.

Make patience a noble fortitude,
And think not how unkindly we are
used.
"Man, like to cassia, is proved best,
being bruised."
DUCH. Must I, like to a slave-born
Russian,
Account it praise to suffer tyranny?
And yet, O heaven, thy heavy hand is
in 't!
I have seen my little boy oft scourge [1]
his top,
And compared myself to 't. Naught
made me e'er
Go right but heaven's scourge-stick.
ANT.                    Do not weep. 80
Heaven fashioned us of nothing, and
we strive
To bring ourselves to nothing.—Fare-
well, Cariola,
And thy sweet armful.—If I do never see
thee more,
Be a good mother to your little ones,
And save them from the tiger. Fare
you well.
DUCH. Let me look upon you once more,
for that speech
Came from a dying father. Your kiss is
colder
Than that I have seen an holy anchorite
Give to a dead man's skull.
ANT. My heart is turned to a heavy lump
of lead,                              90
With which I sound my danger. Fare
you well.              *Exit [with his Son].*
DUCH. My laurel is all withered.
CARI. Look, madam, what a troop of
armèd men
Make toward us!

*Enter Bosola with a Guard.*

DUCH.          O, they are very welcome.
When Fortune's wheel is overcharged
with princes,
The weight makes it move swift. I
would have my ruin
Be sudden.—I am your adventure,[2] am
I not?
BOS. You are. You must see your hus-
band no more.
DUCH. What devil art thou that counter-
feits heaven's thunder?

[1] Whip, to keep in motion.
[2] Object of your quest.

BOS. Is that terrible? I would have you
tell me whether              100
Is that note worse that frights the silly
birds
Out of the corn, or that which doth al-
lure them
To the nets? You have hearkened to
the last too much.
DUCH. O misery! Like to a rusty o'er-
charged [3] cannon,
Shall I never fly in pieces? Come, to
what prison?
BOS. To none.
DUCH.          Whither, then?
BOS.                    To your palace.
DUCH.                              I have heard
That Charon's boat serves to convey
all o'er
The dismal lake, but brings none back
again.
BOS. Your brothers mean you safety and
pity.
DUCH. Pity! With such a pity men pre-
serve alive              110
Pheasants and quails, when they are
not fat enough
To be eaten.
BOS.      These are your children?
DUCH.          Yes.
BOS.                    Can they prattle?
DUCH. No.
But I intend, since they were born ac-
cursed,
Curses shall be their first language.
BOS.                    Fie, madam!
Forget this base, low fellow!
DUCH.                    Were I a man,
I'd beat that counterfeit face [4] into thy
other.
BOS. One of no birth.
DUCH.          Say that he was born mean,
Man is most happy when 's own actions
Be arguments and examples of his vir-
tue.                              120
BOS. A barren, beggarly virtue!
DUCH. I prithee, who is greatest? Can
you tell?
Sad tales befit my woe; I'll tell you one.
A salmon, as she swam unto the sea,
Met with a dogfish, who encounters her
With this rough language, "Why art
thou so bold

[3] From 1640 edn. Original reads *o'erchar'd.*
[4] His vizard.

To mix thyself with our high state of
    floods,
Being no eminent courtier, but one
That for the calmest and fresh time o' th'
    year
Dost live in shallow rivers, rank'st thy-
    self                                          130
With silly smelts and shrimps?    And
    darest thou
Pass by our dogship without reverence?"
"O," quoth the salmon, "sister, be at
    peace.
Thank Jupiter we both have passed the
    net!
Our value never can be truly known
Till in the fisher's basket we be shown;
I' th' market then my price may be the
    higher,
Even when I am nearest to the cook and
    fire."
So to great men the moral may be
    stretched,
"Men oft are valued high, when they're
    most wretch'd."                               140
But come, whither you please.    I am
    armed gainst misery,
Bent to all sways of the oppressor's will.
"There's no deep valley but near some
    great hill."                      *Ex[eunt]*.

### Actus IV.  Scena i.

*[The place of the Duchess' imprisonment.]*

*Ferdinand,   Bosola,   Duchess,   Cariola,
                              Servants.*[1]

FERD.  How doth our sister duchess bear
    herself
In her imprisonment?
BOS.                    Nobly.  I'll describe her.
    She's sad, as one long used to 't, and
        she seems
    Rather to welcome the end of misery
    Than shun it, a behavior so noble
    As gives a majesty to adversity;
    You may discern the shape of loveli-
        ness
    More perfect in her tears than in her
        smiles.
    She will muse four hours together, and
        her silence,
    Methinks, expresseth more than if she
        spake.                                     10

[1] All but first two enter later.

FERD.  Her melancholy seems to be forti-
    fied
With a strange disdain.
BOS.                    'Tis so; and this restraint,
    Like English mastiffs that grow fierce
        with tying,
    Makes her too passionately apprehend
    Those pleasures she's kept from.
FERD.                    Curse upon her!
    I will no longer study in the book
    Of another's heart.  Inform her what I
        told you.                    *Exit.*

*[Enter Duchess and Attendants.]*

BOS.  All comfort to your grace!
DUCH.                    I will have none.
    Pray thee, why dost thou wrap thy
        poisoned pills
    In gold and sugar?                             20
BOS.  Your elder brother, the Lord Ferdi-
    nand,
    Is come to visit you, and sends you
        word,
    Cause once he rashly made a solemn
        vow
    Never to see you more, he comes i' th'
        night;
    And prays you gently neither torch nor
        taper
    Shine in your chamber.  He will kiss
        your hand,
    And reconcile himself; but for his vow
    He dares not see you.
DUCH.                    At his pleasure.—
    Take hence the lights.—He's come.
                *[Exeunt Attendants with lights.*

*Enter Ferdinand.]*

FERD.                    Where are you?
DUCH.                    Here, sir.
FERD.  This darkness suits you well.
DUCH.            I would ask you pardon.    30
FERD.  You have it;
    For I account it the honorabl'st revenge,
    Where I may kill, to pardon.—Where
        are your cubs?
DUCH.  Whom?
FERD.  Call them your children;
    For, though our national law distinguish
        bastards
    From true legitimate issue, compassion-
        ate nature
    Makes them all equal.

DUCH.          Do you visit me for this?
You violate a sacrament o' th' church
Shall make you howl in hell for 't.
FERD.          It had been well
Could you have lived thus always; for
indeed          41
You were too much i' th' light. But
no more;
I come to seal my peace with you. Here's
a hand          *Gives her a dead man's hand.*
To which you have vowed much love;
the ring upon 't
You gave.
DUCH.          I affectionately kiss it.
FERD. Pray do, and bury the print of it
in your heart.
I will leave this ring with you for a love
token;
And the hand as sure as the ring; and
do not doubt
But you shall have the heart too. When
you need a friend,
Send it to him that owed [1] it; you shall
see          50
Whether he can aid you.
DUCH.          You are very cold.
I fear you are not well after your
travel.—
Ha! Lights!—O, horrible!
FERD.          Let her have lights enough.
          *Exit.*
DUCH. What witchcraft doth he practice,
that he hath left
A dead man's hand here?

[*By Servants who enter,*] *here is discovered,
behind a traverse,*[2] *the artificial figures
of Antonio and his Children, appearing as if they were dead.*

BOS. Look you, here's the piece from
which 'twas ta'en.
He doth present you this sad spectacle,
That, now you know directly they are
dead,
Hereafter you may wisely cease to
grieve
For that which cannot be recoveréd.
DUCH. There is not between heaven and
earth one wish          61
I stay for after this. It wastes me more
Than were 't my picture, fashioned out
of wax,

Stuck with a magical needle, and then
buried
In some foul dunghill; and yon's an ex-
cellent property
For a tyrant, which I would account
mercy.
BOS.          What's that?
DUCH. If they would bind me to that
lifeless trunk,
And let me freeze to death.
BOS.          Come, you must live.
DUCH. That's the greatest torture souls
feel in hell—
In hell, that they must live, and cannot
die.          70
Portia, I'll new kindle thy coals again,
And revive the rare and almost dead
example
Of a loving wife.
BOS.          O, fie! Despair? Remember
You are a Christian.
DUCH.          The church enjoins fasting.
I'll starve myself to death.
BOS.          Leave this vain sorrow.
Things being at the worst begin to mend.
The bee, when he hath shot his sting
into your hand,
May then play with your eyelid.
DUCH.          Good comfortable fellow,
Persuade a wretch that's broke upon
the wheel
To have all his bones new set; entreat
him live          80
To be executed again! Who must des-
patch me?
I account this world a tedious theater,
For I do play a part in 't gainst my
will.
BOS. Come, be of comfort; I will save
your life.
DUCH. Indeed, I have not leisure to tend
so small a business.
BOS. Now, by my life, I pity you.
DUCH.          Thou art a fool, then,
To waste thy pity on a thing so wretched
As cannot pity it.[3] I am full of daggers.
Puff, let me blow these vipers from me.—
[*To a Servant.*] What are you?
SER.          One that wishes you long life.'
DUCH. I would thou wert hanged for the
horrible curse          91
Thou hast given me. I shall shortly
grow one

---

[1] Owned.          [2] Curtain.          [3] *I.e.,* itself.

Of the miracles of pity. I'll go pray.—
No,
I'll go curse.
Bos.            O, fie!
Duch.            I could curse the stars—
Bos.                    O, fearful!
Duch. And those three smiling seasons
of the year
Into a Russian winter; nay, the world
To its first chaos.
Bos.        Look you, the stars shine still.
Duch. O, but you must remember my
curse hath a great way to go.—
Plagues, that make lanes through larg-
est families,
Consume them!
Bos.        Fie, lady!
Duch.            Let them, like tyrants, 100
Never be remembered but for the ill
they have done;
Let all the zealous prayers of mortified
Churchmen forget them!
Bos.                    O, uncharitable!
Duch. Let heaven a little while cease
crowning martyrs, to punish them!
Go, howl them this, and say I long to
bleed:
"It is some mercy when men kill with
speed."            Exit [with Servants.

*Enter Ferdinand.]*

Ferd. Excellent, as I would wish; she's
plagued in art.
These presentations are but framed in
wax
By the curious master in that quality,
Vincentio Lauriola, and she takes
them            110
For true substantial bodies.
Bos.                    Why do you do this?
Ferd. To bring her to despair.
Bos.                    Faith, end here,
And go no farther in your cruelty.
Send her a penitential garment to put on
Next to her delicate skin, and furnish
her
With beads and prayer books.
Ferd.            Damn her! That body of hers,
While that my blood ran pure in 't, was
more worth
Than that which thou wouldst comfort,
called a soul.
I will send her masques of common
courtesans,

Have her meat served up by bawds and
ruffians,            120
And, cause she'll needs be mad, I am
resolved
To remove forth [1] the common hospital
All the mad folk, and place them near
her lodging;
There let them practice together, sing
and dance,
And act their gambols to the full o' th'
moon.
If she can sleep the better for it, let her.
Your work is almost ended.
Bos.                    Must I see her again?
Ferd. Yes.
Bos.        Never.
Ferd.        You must.
Bos.                    Never in mine own shape;
That's forfeited by my intelligence
And this last cruel lie. When you send
me next,            130
The business shall be comfort.
Ferd.                    Very likely!
Thy pity is nothing of kin to thee. An-
tonio
Lurks about Milan; thou shalt shortly
thither
To feed a fire as great as my revenge,
Which never will slack till it hath
spent his fuel.
"Intemperate agues make physicians
cruel."            *Exeunt*

## Scena ii.

*[The same.]*

*Duchess, Cariola, Servant, Madmen, Bosola,
Executioners, Ferdinand.[2]*

Duch. What hideous noise was that?
Cari.            'Tis the wild consort [3]
Of madmen, lady, which your tyrant
brother
Hath placed about your lodging. This
tyranny,
I think, was never practiced till this hour.
Duch. Indeed, I thank him. Nothing
but noise and folly
Can keep me in my right wits, whereas
reason
And silence make me stark mad. Sit
down;
Discourse to me some dismal tragedy.

[1] From.    [2] All but the first two enter later.
[3] Company, especially of musicians.

Cari. O, 'twill increase your melancholy!
Duch.                Thou art deceived;
To hear of greater grief would lessen
mine.                                    10
This is a prison?
Cari.            Yes, but you shall live
To shake this durance off.
Duch.            Thou art a fool.
The robin redbreast and the nightin-
gale
Never live long in cages.
Cari.        Pray, dry your eyes.—
What think you of, madam?
Duch.            Of nothing;
When I muse thus, I sleep.
Cari. Like a madman, with your eyes
open?
Duch. Dost thou think we shall know
one another
In th' other world?
Cari.        Yes, out of question.  19
Duch. O, that it were possible we might
But hold some two days' conference with
the dead!
From them I should learn somewhat, I
am sure,
I never shall know here. I'll tell thee a
miracle:
I am not mad yet, to my cause of sorrow.
Th' heaven o'er my head seems made of
molten brass,
The earth of flaming sulphur, yet I am
not mad.
I am acquainted with sad misery
As the tanned galley slave is with his
oar.
Necessity makes me suffer constantly,
And custom makes it easy. Who do I
look like now?                          30
Cari. Like to your picture in the gallery,
A deal of life in show, but none in prac-
tice;
Or rather like some reverend monument
Whose ruins are even pitied.
Duch.            Very proper;
And Fortune seems only to have her
eyesight
To behold my tragedy.—How now!
What noise is that?

*[Enter Servant.]*

Ser.            I am come to tell you
Your brother hath intended you some
sport.

A great physician, when the pope was
sick
Of a deep melancholy, presented him   40
With several sorts of madmen, which
wild object,
Being full of change and sport, forced
him to laugh,
And so th' imposthume [1] broke. The
selfsame cure
The duke intends on you.
Duch.            Let them come in.
Ser. There's a mad lawyer and a secular
priest;
A doctor that hath forfeited his wits
By jealousy; an astrologian
That in his works said such a day o' th'
month
Should be the day of doom, and, failing
of 't,
Ran mad; an English tailor crazed i' th'
brain                                   50
With the study of new fashion; a gentle-
man usher
Quite beside himself with care to keep
in mind
The number of his lady's salutations
(Or "How do you") she employed him
in each morning;
A farmer, too, an excellent knave in
grain,[2]
Mad cause he was hindered transporta-
tion.[3]
And let one broker [4] that's mad loose to
these,
You'd think the devil were among them.
Duch. Sit, Cariola.—Let them loose when
you please,
For I am chained to endure all your tyr-
anny.                                   60

*[Enter Madmen.]*

*Here by a Madman this song is sung to a
dismal kind of music.*

O, let us howl some heavy note,
Some deadly dogged howl,
Sounding as from the threat'ning throat
Of beasts and fatal fowl!
As ravens, scritch owls, bulls, and bears,
We'll bill [5] and bawl our parts,

[1] Abscess.
[2] A pun on (1) in dye, *i.e.*, incorrigible, and (2) in the grain trade.
[3] *I.e.*, forbidden to export his produce.
[4] Pawnbroker.
[5] Bell, bellow.

Till yerksome [1] noise have cloyed your ears
　And corrasived [2] your hearts.
At last, whenas our choir wants breath,
　Our bodies being blessed,　　　　70
We'll sing, like swans, to welcome death,
　And die in love and rest.

1 Mad. Doomsday not come yet? I'll draw it nearer by a perspective,[3] or make a glass that shall set all the world on fire upon an instant. I cannot sleep; my pillow is stuffed with a litter of porcupines.

2 Mad. Hell is a mere glass house, where the devils are continually blowing up women's souls on hollow irons, and [80 the fire never goes out.

3 Mad. I will lie with every woman in my parish the tenth night. I will tithe them over like haycocks.

4 Mad. Shall my pothecary outgo me, because I am a cuckold? I have found out his roguery: he makes alum of his wife's urine, and sells it to Puritans that have sore throats with overstraining.

1 [Mad.] I have skill in heraldry.　90

2 [Mad.] Hast?

1 [Mad.] You do give for your crest a woodcock's head with the brains picked out on 't; you are a very ancient gentleman.

3 [Mad.] Greek is turned Turk; we are only to be saved by the Helvetian translation.[4]

1 [Mad.] Come on, sir, I will lay [5] the law to you.

2 [Mad.] O, rather lay a corrasive; [100 the law will eat to the bone.

3 [Mad.] He that drinks but to satisfy nature is damned.

4 [Mad.] If I had my glass here, I would show a sight should make all the women here call me mad doctor.

1 [Mad. (Pointing at 3 Madman.)] What's he? A rope maker?

2 [Mad.] No, no, no; a snuffling knave that, while he shows the tombs, will [110 have his hand in a wench's placket.[6]

3 [Mad.] Woe to the caroche that brought home my wife from the masque at three a-clock in the morning! It had a large feather bed in it.

4 [Mad.] I have pared the devil's nails

forty times, roasted them in raven's eggs, and cured agues with them.

3 [Mad.] Get me three hundred milch-bats, to make possets to procure sleep. [120

4 [Mad.] All the college may throw their caps at me—I have made a soap boiler costive; it was my masterpiece.

*Here the dance, consisting of eight Madmen, with music answerable thereunto, after which Bosola, like an old man, enters.*

Duch. Is he mad too?

Ser. Pray, question him. I'll leave you.
　　　　　　[*Exeunt Servant and Madmen.*]

Bos. I am come to make thy tomb.

Duch.　　　　　　　　　Ha! My tomb?
Thou speak'st as if I lay upon my death-bed,
Gasping for breath. Dost thou perceive me sick?

Bos. Yes, and the more dangerously since thy sickness is insensible.　　　130

Duch. Thou art not mad, sure. Dost know me?

Bos.　　　　　Yes.

Duch.　　　　　　　Who am I?

Bos. Thou art a box of worm-seed, at best but a salvatory of green mummy.[7] What's this flesh? A little crudded [8] milk, fantastical puff paste. Our bodies are weaker than those paper prisons boys use to keep flies in; more contemptible, since ours is to preserve earthworms. Didst thou ever see a lark in a cage? Such is the soul in the body; this world is like [140 her little turf of grass, and the heaven o'er our heads, like her looking-glass, only gives us a miserable knowledge of the small compass of our prison.

Duch. Am not I thy duchess?

Bos. Thou art some great woman, sure, for riot begins to sit on thy forehead (clad in gray hairs) twenty years sooner than on a merry milkmaid's. Thou sleep'st worse than if a mouse should be forced to [150 take up her lodging in a cat's ear; a little infant that breeds its teeth, should it lie with thee, would cry out, as if thou wert the more unquiet bedfellow.

Duch. I am Duchess of Malfi still!

Bos. That makes thy sleep so broken,

---

[1] Irksome.　　[2] Corroded.　　[3] Telescope.
[4] The Geneva Bible, prohibited in England because of its Puritan tone.
[5] Expound.　　[6] Opening in petticoat.
[7] Ointment box filled with dried flesh, widely used as a medicine.
[8] Curdled.

Glories, like glowworms, afar off shine
    bright,
But, looked to near, have neither heat
    nor light.
Duch. Thou art very plain.    159
Bos. My trade is to flatter the dead,
not the living; I am a tomb-maker.
Duch. And thou com'st to make my
tomb?
Bos. Yes.
Duch. Let me be a little merry.    Of
what stuff wilt thou make it?
Bos. Nay, resolve [1] me first, of what
fashion?
Duch. Why, do we grow fantastical in
    our deathbed?
Do we affect fashion in the grave?    170
Bos. Most ambitiously.    Princes' images
    on their tombs
Do not lie, as they were wont, seeming
    to pray
Up to heaven, but with their hands under
    their cheeks,
As if they died of the toothache.    They
    are not carved
With their eyes fixed upon the stars,
    but, as their
Minds were wholly bent upon the world,
The selfsame way they seem to turn
    their faces.
Duch. Let me know fully therefore the
    effect
Of this thy dismal preparation,
This talk fit for a charnel.
Bos.    Now I shall.—

[Enter Executioners, with] a coffin, cords,
    and a bell.

Here is a present from your princely
    brothers;    181
And may it arrive welcome, for it brings
Last benefit, last sorrow.
Duch.    Let me see it.
    I have so much obedience in my blood,
I wish it in their veins to do them good.
Bos. This is your last presence chamber.
Cari. O, my sweet lady!
Duch.    Peace; it affrights not me.
Bos. I am the common bellman
    That usually is sent to condemned per-
    sons
The night before they suffer.

[1] Satisfy.

Duch.    Even now thou said'st    190
    Thou wast a tomb-maker.
Bos.    'Twas to bring you
By degrees to mortification.    Listen.
    [Rings his bell.][2]

Hark, now everything is still;
The scritch owl and the whistler shrill
Call upon our dame aloud,
And bid her quickly don her shroud!
Much you had of land and rent;
Your length in clay's now competent.
A long war disturbed your mind;
Here your perfect peace is signed.    200
Of what is 't fools make such vain keeping?
Sin their conception, their birth weeping,
Their life a general mist of error,
Their death a hideous storm of terror.
Strew your hair with powders sweet,
Don clean linen, bathe your feet,
And (the foul fiend more to check)
A crucifix let bless your neck.
'Tis now full tide tween night and day;
End your groan, and come away.    210

Cari. Hence, villains, tyrants, murderers!
    Alas!
What will you do with my lady?—Call
    for help!
Duch. To whom?    To our next neighbors?
    They are madfolks.
Bos. Remove that noise!
Duch.    Farewell, Cariola.
    In my last will I have not much to give—
A many hungry guests have fed upon
    me;
Thine will be a poor reversion.[3]
Cari.    I will die with her.
Duch. I pray thee, look thou giv'st my
    little boy
Some syrup for his cold, and let the girl
Say her prayers ere she sleep.
    [Cariola is forced off.] [4]
    Now what you please—
What death?
Bos.    Strangling; here are your
    executioners.    221
Duch. I forgive them.
    The apoplexy, cathar,[5] or cough o' th'
    lungs
Would do as much as they do.
Bos. Doth not death fright you?

[2] From 1708 edn.
[3] Right of future possession.
[4] From 1708 edn.
[5] Catarrh; here, cerebral hemorrhage.

DUCH.         Who would be afraid on 't,
Knowing to meet such excellent company
In th' other world?
BOS. Yet, methinks,
The manner of your death should much afflict you—
This cord should terrify you!
DUCH.             Not a whit.
What would it pleasure me to have my
throat cut            231
With diamonds? Or to be smotheréd
With cassia? Or to be shot to death
with pearls?
I know death hath ten thousand several
doors
For men to take their exits; and 'tis
found
They go on such strange geometrical
hinges,
You may open them both ways. Any
way, for heaven sake,
So I were out of your whispering. Tell
my brothers
That I perceive death, now I am well
awake,
Best gift is they can give or I can
take.               240
I would fain put off my last woman's
fault:
I'ld not be tedious to you.
[1] EXEC.          We are ready.
DUCH. Dispose my breath how please
you; but my body
Bestow upon my women, will you?
[1] EXEC.             Yes.
DUCH. Pull, and pull strongly, for your
able strength
Must pull down heaven upon me.—
Yet stay. Heaven-gates are not so
highly arched
As princes' palaces; they that enter
there
Must go upon their knees.—[*Kneels.*]
Come, violent death;
Serve for mandragora to make me
sleep!—           250
Go tell my brothers, when I am laid
out,
They then may feed in quiet.
                 *They strangle her.*
BOS. Where's the waiting-woman?
Fetch her. [*Exeunt Executioners.*] Some
other strangle the children.

[*Enter Cariola.*]

Look you, there sleeps your mistress.
CARI.           O, you are damned
Perpetually for this! My turn is next.
Is 't not so ordered?
BOS.           Yes, and I am glad
You are so well prepared for 't.
CARI.          You are deceived, sir;
I am not prepared for 't. I will not die;
I will first come to my answer,[1] and
know              260
How I have offended.
    BOS.        Come, despatch her.—
You kept her counsel; now you shall
keep ours.
CARI. I will not die; I must not! I am
contracted
To a young gentleman.
[1] EXEC.      Here's your wedding ring.
CARI. Let me but speak with the duke.
I'll discover
Treason to his person.
BOS.       Delays!—Throttle her!
[1] EXEC. She bites and scratches.
CARI.          If you kill me now,
I am damned; I have not been at confession
This two years.
BOS. [*To Executioners.*]      When![2]
CARI.       I am quick with child.
BOS.             Why, then,
Your credit's saved. [*Executioners
strangle Cariola.*] Bear her into th'
next room;          270
Let this lie still.
[*Exeunt Executioners with body of Cariola.*

*Enter Ferdinand.*]

FERD.           Is she dead?
BOS.            She is what
You'ld have her. But here begin your
pity! *Shows the Children strangled.*
Alas, how have these offended?
FERD.           The death
Of young wolves is never to be pitied.
BOS. Fix your eye here.
FERD.       Constantly.
BOS.          Do you not weep?
Other sins only speak; murther shrieks
out.
The element of water moistens the earth,

---

[1] Opportunity for defense.
[2] Exclamation of impatience.

But blood flies upwards and bedews the
  heavens.
FERD. Cover her face! Mine eyes dazzle;
  she died young.
Bos. I think not so; her infelicity          280
  Seemed to have years too many.
FERD. She and I were twins;
  And, should I die this instant, I had
    lived
  Her time to a minute.
Bos.          It seems she was born first.
  You have bloodily approved the ancient
    truth
  That kindred commonly do worse agree
  Than remote strangers.
FERD.          Let me see her face
  Again. Why didst thou not pity her? What
  An excellent, honest man mightst thou
    have been,
  If thou hadst borne her to some sanc-
    tuary,          290
  Or, bold in a good cause, opposed thy-
    self
  With thy advancéd sword above thy
    head
  Between her innocence and my revenge!
  I bade thee, when I was distracted of my
    wits,
  Go kill my dearest friend, and thou hast
    done 't.
  For let me but examine well the cause.
  What was the meanness of her match
    to me?
  Only I must confess I had a hope,
  Had she continued widow, to have
    gained
  An infinite mass of treasure by her
    death,          300
  And that was the main cause. Her mar-
    riage—
  That drew a stream of gall quite through
    my heart.
  For thee (as we observe in tragedies
  That a good actor many times is cursed
  For playing a villain's part), I hate thee
    for 't.
  And, for my sake, say thou hast done
    much ill well.
Bos. Let me quicken your memory, for
  I perceive
  You are falling into ingratitude. I chal-
    lenge
  The reward due to my service.

FERD.          I'll tell thee
  What I'll give thee.
Bos.          Do.
FERD.          I'll give thee a pardon          310
  For this murther.
Bos.          Ha!
FERD.          Yes, and 'tis
  The largest bounty I can study to do
    thee.
  By what authority didst thou execute
  This bloody sentence?
Bos. By yours.
FERD. Mine? Was I her judge?
  Did any ceremonial form of law
  Doom her to not-being? Did a complete
    jury
  Deliver her conviction up i' th' court?
  Where shalt thou find this judgment
    registered,          320
  Unless in hell? See, like a bloody fool,
  Th' hast forfeited thy life, and thou shalt
    die for 't.
Bos. The office of justice is perverted quite
  When one thief hangs another. Who
    shall dare
  To reveal this?
FERD.          O, I'll tell thee;
  The wolf shall find her grave, and scrape
    it up,
  Not to devour the corpse, but to dis-
    cover
  The horrid murther.
Bos.          You, not I, shall quake for 't.
FERD. Leave me.
Bos.          I will first receive my pension.
FERD. You are a villain!
Bos.          When your ingratitude          330
  Is judge, I am so.
FERD. O horror,
  That not the fear of him which binds
    the devils
  Can prescribe man obedience!—
  Never look upon me more.
Bos.          Why, fare thee well.
  Your brother and yourself are worthy
    men!
  You have a pair of hearts are hollow
    graves,
  Rotten, and rotting others; and your
    vengeance,
  Like two chained-bullets, still goes arm
    in arm.
  You may be brothers, for treason, like
    the plague,          340

Doth take much in a blood. I stand
like one
That long hath ta'en a sweet and golden
dream.
I am angry with myself, now that I
wake.

FERD. Get thee into some unknown part
o' th' world,
That I may never see thee.

BOS.              Let me know
Wherefore I should be thus neglected.
Sir,
I served your tyranny, and rather strove
To satisfy yourself than all the world;
And, though I loathed the evil, yet I
loved
You that did counsel it, and rather
sought          350
To appear a true servant than an honest
man.

FERD. I'll go hunt the badger by owl-
light;
'Tis a deed of darkness.       *Exit.*

BOS. He's much distracted.    Off, my
painted honor!
While with vain hopes our faculties we
tire,
We seem to sweat in ice and freeze in
fire.
What would I do, were this to do again?
I would not change my peace of con-
science
For all the wealth of Europe. She stirs;
here's life!
Return, fair soul, from darkness, and
lead mine        360
Out of this sensible hell! She's warm;
she breathes!
Upon thy pale lips I will melt my heart,
To store them with fresh color.—Who's
there?
Some cordial drink!—Alas! I dare not
call.
So pity would destroy pity. Her eye
opes,
And heaven in it seems to ope, that late
was shut,
To take me up to mercy.

DUCH. Antonio!

BOS.        Yes, madam, he is living;
The dead bodies you saw were but
feigned statues.
He's reconciled to your brothers; the
pope hath wrought      370

The atonement.[1]

DUCH. Mercy!            *She dies.*

BOS. O, she's gone again! There the cords
of life broke.
O sacred Innocence, that sweetly sleeps
On turtles'[2] feathers, whilst a guilty
conscience
Is a black register wherein is writ
All our good deeds and bad, a perspec-
tive
That shows us hell! That we cannot be
suffered
To do good when we have a mind to it!
This is manly sorrow;         380
These tears, I am very certain, never
grew
In my mother's milk. My estate is sunk
Below the degree of fear. Where were
These penitent fountains while she was
living?
O, they were frozen up! Here is a sight
As direful to my soul as is the sword
Unto a wretch hath slain his father.
Come, I'll bear thee hence,
And execute thy last will—that's de-
liver
Thy body to the reverend dispose
Of some good women. That the cruel
tyrant        390
Shall not deny me. Then I'll post to
Milan,
Where somewhat I will speedily enact
Worth my dejection.

            *Exit [with the body].*[3]

## ACTUS V. SCENA i.

### [A public place in Milan.]

*Antonio, Delio, Pescara, Julia.*[4]

ANT. What think you of my hope of reconcilement
To the Aragonian brethren?

DELIO.            I misdoubt it;
For, though they have sent their letters
of safe-conduct
For your repair to Milan, they appear
But nets to entrap you. The Marquis of
Pescara,
Under whom you hold certain land in
cheat,[5]

[1] Reconciliation.
[2] Turtledoves'.
[3] From 1708 edn.
[4] Last two enter later.
[5] Escheat.

Much gainst his noble nature hath been
     moved
To seize those lands; and some of his
     dependants
ᴬre at this instant making it their suit
To be invested in your revenues.     10
I cannot think they mean well to your
     life
That do deprive you of your means of
     life,
Your living.
ANT.               You are still an heretic
To any safety I can shape myself.
DEL.  Here comes the marquis.  I will make
     myself
Petitioner for some part of your land,
To know whither it is flying.
ANT.               I pray, do.  [*Withdraws.*

*Enter Pescara.*]

DEL.  Sir, I have a suit to you.
PES.               To me?
DEL.               An easy one.
There is the Citadel of Saint Bennet,
With some demesnes, of late in the
     possession                         20
Of Antonio Bologna—please you bestow
     them on me.
PES.  You are my friend; but this is such a
     suit
Nor fit for me to give nor you to take.
DEL.  No, sir?
PES.     I will give you ample reason for 't
Soon in private.—Here's the cardinal's
     mistress.

[*Enter Julia.*]

JUL.  My lord, I am grown your poor peti-
     tioner,
And should be an ill beggar, had I not
A great man's letter here, the cardinal's,
To court you in my favor. [*Gives a letter.*]
PES. [*After reading.*]     He entreats
     for you
The Citadel of Saint Bennet, that be-
     longed                             30
To the banishéd Bologna.
JUL.               Yes.
PES.  I could not have thought of a friend I
     could
Rather pleasure with it. 'Tis yours.
JUL.               Sir, I thank you;
And he shall know how doubly I am
     engaged

Both in your gift and speediness ọ
     giving,
Which makes your grant the greater.
                                        *Exit.*
ANT. [*Aside.*]          How they fortify
Themselves with my ruin!
DEL.               Sir, I am
Little bound to you.
PES.  Why?
DEL.  Because you denied this suit to me,
     and gave 't                        40
To such a creature.
PES.               Do you know what it was?
It was Antonio's land, not forfeited
By course of law, but ravished from his
     throat
By the cardinal's entreaty.  It were not
     fit
I should bestow so main a piece of wrong
Upon my friend; 'tis a gratification
Only due to a strumpet, for it is injustice.
Shall I sprinkle the pure blood of in-
     nocents
To make those followers I call my friends
Look ruddier [1] upon me?  I am glad   50
This land, ta'en from the owner by such
     wrong,
Returns again unto so foul an use
As salary for his lust.  Learn, good Delio,
To ask noble things of me, and you shall
     find
I'll be a noble giver.
DEL.               You instruct me well.
ANT. [*Aside.*]  Why, here's a man now
     would fright impudence
From sauciest beggars.
PES.               Prince Ferdi-
     nand's come to Milan,
Sick, as they give out, of an apoplexy;
But some say 'tis a frenzy.  I am going
To visit him.               *Exit.*
ANT.               'Tis a noble old fellow!
DEL.  What course do you mean to take,
     António?                           61
ANT.  This night I mean to venture all my
     fortune,
Which is no more than a poor ling'ring
     life,
To the cardinal's worst of malice.  I have
     got
Private access to his chamber, and in-
     tend
To visit him about the mid of night,
[1] More favorably.

As once his brother did our noble
duchess.

It may be that the sudden apprehension
Of danger (for I'll go in mine own shape),
When he shall see it fraight [1] with love
and duty,                                     70
May draw the poison out of him, and
work
A friendly reconcilement. If it fail,
Yet it shall rid me of this infamous
calling;
For better fall once than be ever falling.
DEL. I'll second you in all danger; and,
howe'er,
My life keeps rank with yours.
ANT. You are still my lovéd and best
friend.                                *Exeunt.*

SCENA ii.

[*A gallery in the palace of the Cardinal and
Ferdinand at Milan.*]

*Pescara, a Doctor, Ferdinand, Cardinal,
Malateste, Bosola, Julia.* [2]

PES. Now, doctor, may I visit your pa-
tient?
DOC. If 't please your lordship; but he's
instantly
To take the air here in the gallery
By my direction.
PES.            Pray thee, what's his disease?
DOC. A very pestilent disease, my lord,
They call lycanthropia.
PES.                    What's that?
I need a dictionary to 't.
DOC.                    I'll tell you.
In those that are possessed with 't there
o'erflows
Such melancholy humor they imagine
Themselves to be transforméd into
wolves,                                       10
Steal forth to churchyards in the dead
of night,
And dig dead bodies up; as two nights
since
One met the duke 'bout midnight in a
lane
Behind Saint Mark's Church, with the
leg of a man
Upon his shoulder; and he howled fear-
fully;
Said he was a wolf, only the difference

<hr>

[1] Fraught.        [2] Last five enter later.

Was, a wolf's skin was hairy on the out-
side,
His on the inside; bade them take their
swords,
Rip up his flesh, and try. Straight I was
sent for,
And, having ministered to him, found his
grace                                         20
Very well recovered.
PES. I am glad on 't.
DOC.            Yet not without some fear
Of a relapse. If he grow to his fit again,
I'll go a nearer way to work with him
Than ever Paracelsus dreamed of. If
They'll give me leave, I'll buffet his
madness out of him.
Stand aside; he comes.

[*Enter  Ferdinand,  Cardinal,  Malateste,
and Bosola.*]

FERD. Leave me.
MAL. Why doth your lordship love this
solitariness?                                 30
FERD. Eagles commonly fly alone; they
are crows, daws, and starlings that flock
together.      Look, what's that follows
me?
MAL. Nothing, my lord.
FERD. Yes.
MAL. 'Tis your shadow.
FERD. Stay it; let it not haunt me.
MAL. Impossible, if you move, and the
sun shine.                                    40
FERD. I will throttle it.
[*Throws  himself  down  on  his  shadow.*]
MAL. O, my lord, you are angry with
nothing.
FERD. You are a fool. How is 't possible
I should catch my shadow unless I fall
upon 't? When I go to hell, I mean to carry
a bribe, for, look you, good gifts evermore
make way for the worst persons.
PES. Rise, good my lord.                      49
FERD. I am studying the art of patience.
PES. 'Tis a noble virtue.
FERD. To drive six snails before me
from this town to Moscow; neither use
goad nor whip to them, but let them take
their own time (the patient'st man i' th'
world match me for an experiment!), and
I'll crawl after like a sheepbiter. [3]
CARD. Force him up. [*They raise him.*]
FERD. Use me well, you were best.
[3] A dog which worries sheep; a sneak-thief.

What I have done, I have done; I'll [60
confess nothing.

Doc. Now let me come to him.—Are you
mad, my lord?

Are you out of your princely wits?

Ferd.          What's he?

Pes.          Your doctor.

Ferd. Let me have his beard sawed off,
and his eyebrows filed more civil.

Doc. I must do mad tricks with him, for
that's the only way on 't.—I have brought
your grace a salamander's skin to keep you
from sunburning.

Ferd. I have cruel sore eyes.    70

Doc. The white of a cockatrix's egg is
present remedy.

Ferd. Let it be a new-laid one, you were
best.

Hide me from him! Physicians are like
kings—

They brook no contradiction.

Doc. Now he begins to fear me; now let
me alone with him.

[*Puts off his four cloaks one after another.*][1]

Card. How now! Put off your gown?

Doc. Let me have some forty urinals
filled with rose water. He and I'll go [80
pelt one another with them.—Now he begins
to fear me.—Can you fetch a frisk,[2] sir?—
Let him go, let him go, upon my peril!
I find by his eye he stands in awe of me;
I'll make him as tame as a dormouse.

Ferd. Can you fetch your frisks, sir?—
I will stamp him into a cullis, flay off his
skin to cover one of the anatomies[3] this
rogue hath set i' th' cold yonder in Barber-
Chirurgeons'[4] Hall.—Hence, hence! [90
You are all of you like beasts for sacrifice.
[*Throws the Doctor down and beats him.*][5]
There's nothing left of you but tongue
and belly, flattery and lechery.    [*Exit.*]

Pes. Doctor, he did not fear you
throughly!

Doc. True; I was somewhat too forward.

Bos. Mercy upon me, what a fatal judgment
Hath fall'n upon this Ferdinand!

Pes.          Knows your grace
What accident hath brought unto the
prince

[1] From 1708 edn.   [2] Cut a caper.   [3] Skeletons.
[4] Barber-Surgeons'.  Barbers often performed
some of the duties of the physician.
[5] From 1708 edn.

This strange distraction?    100

Card. [*Aside.*] I must feign somewhat.—
Thus they say it grew:

You have heard it rumored, for these
many years,

None of our family dies but there is seen

The shape of an old woman, which is
given

By tradition to us to have been murthered

By her nephews for her riches. Such a
figure

One night, as the prince sat up late at 's
book,

Appeared to him, when, crying out for
help,

The gentleman of 's chamber found his
grace    109

All on a cold sweat, altered much in face

And language; since which apparition,

He hath grown worse and worse, and I
much fear

He cannot live.

Bos.          Sir, I would speak with you.

Pes. We'll leave your grace,
Wishing to the sick prince, our noble
lord,

All health of mind and body.

Card.          You are most welcome.

[*Exeunt. Manent[6] Cardinal and Bosola.*][7]

Are you come? So.—[*Aside.*] This fellow
must not know

By any means I had intelligence

In our duchess' death; for, though I
counseled it,

The full of all th' engagement seemed to
grow    120

From Ferdinand.—Now, sir, how fares
our sister?

I do not think but sorrow makes her
look

Like to an oft-dyed garment. She shall
now

Taste comfort from me. Why do you
look so wildly?

O, the fortune of your master here, the
prince,

Dejects you; but be you of happy comfort.

If you'll do one thing for me I'll entreat,

Though he had a cold tombstone o'er his
bones,

I'ld make you what you would be.

[6] Remain.        [7] From 1708 edn.

Bos.                              Anything;
  Give it me in a breath, and let me fly
    to 't.                              130
  They that think long, small expedition
    win,
  For musing much o' th' end, cannot
    begin.

          *[Enter Julia.]*

Jul. Sir, will you come in to supper?
Card. I am busy; leave me.
Jul. [*Aside.*]  What an excellent shape
  hath that fellow!               *Exit.*
Card. 'Tis thus. Antonio lurks here in
  Milan;
  Inquire him out, and kill him. While he
    lives,
  Our sister cannot marry; and I have
    thought
  Of an excellent match for her. Do this,
    and style me
  Thy advancement.                140
Bos. But by what means shall I find him
  out?
Card. There is a gentleman called Delio
  Here in the camp, that hath been long
    approved
  His loyal friend.  Set eye upon that
    fellow;
  Follow him to mass; may be Antonio,
  Although he do account religion
  But a school-name, for fashion of the
    world
  May accompany him; or else go inquire
    out
  Delio's confessor, and see if you can bribe
  Him to reveal it.  There are a thousand
    ways                          150
  A man might find to trace him—as to
    know
  What fellows haunt the Jews for taking up
  Great sums of money, for sure he's in
    want;
  Or else to go to th' picture makers, and
    learn
  Who bought [1] her picture lately. Some
    of these
  Happily may take.
Bos.    Well, I'll not freeze i' th' business;
  I would see that wretched thing, An-
    tonio,
  Above all sights i' th' world.
Card.            Do, and be happy. *Exit.*

[1] Dyce's emendation for *brought.*

Bos. This fellow doth breed basilisks in 's
  eyes;
  He's nothing else but murder; yet he
    seems                           160
  Not to have notice of the duchess' death.
  'Tis his cunning; I must follow his
    example.
  There cannot be a surer way to trace
  Than that of an old fox.

     *[Enter Julia, with a pistol.]*

Jul. So, sir, you are well met.
Bos. How now!
Jul. Nay, the doors are fast enough.
Now, sir, I will make you confess your
treachery.
  Bos.  Treachery?              170
Jul. Yes, confess to me
  Which of my women 'twas you hired to
    put
  Love powder into my drink.
Bos.  Love powder!
Jul.                Yes, when I was at Malfi.
  Why should I fall in love with such a
    face else?
  I have already suffered for thee so much
    pain,
  The only remedy to do me good
  Is to kill my longing.
Bos.              Sure, your pistol holds
  Nothing but perfumes or kissing-comfits.[2]
  Excellent lady,                179
  You have a pretty way on 't to discover
  Your longing.  Come, come, I'll disarm
    you,
  And arm [3] you thus. Yet this is wondrous
    strange.
Jul. Compare thy form and my eyes to-
  gether,
  You'll find my love no such great miracle.
  Now you'll say
  I am wanton.  This nice modesty in ladies
  Is but a troublesome familiar [4]
  That haunts them.
Bos. Know you me; I am a blunt soldier.
Jul.                        The better.
  Sure, there wants fire where there are no
    lively sparks
  Of roughness.                    190
Bos. And I want compliment.
Jul.                    Why, ignorance

[2] Sweetmeats for the breath.
[3] Embrace.                    [4] Spirit.

In courtship cannot make you do amiss,
If you have a heart to do well.

Bos.                    You are very fair.

Jul. Nay, if you lay beauty to my charge,
I must plead unguilty.

Bos.                    Your bright eyes
Carry a quiver of darts in them, sharper
Than sunbeams.

Jul.                    You will mar me with
commendation;
Put yourself to the charge of courting me,
Whereas now I woo you.

Bos. [*Aside*.] I have it; I will work upon
this creature.—                    200
Let us grow most amorously familiar.
If the great cardinal now should see me
thus,
Would he not count me a villain?

Jul. No; he might count me a wanton,
Not lay a scruple of offense on you;
For, if I see and steal a diamond,
The fault is not i' th' stone, but in me,
the thief
That purloins it. I am sudden with you.
We that are great women of pleasure use
to cut off
These uncertain wishes and unquiet long-
ings,                    210
And in an instant join the sweet delight
And the pretty excuse together. Had you
been i' th' street,
Under my chamber window, even
. there
I should have courted you.

Bos. O, you are an excellent lady!

Jul. Bid me do somewhat for you presently
To express I love you.

Bos. I will; and, if you love me, fail not to
effect it.
The cardinal is grown wondrous melancholy;
Demand the cause; let him not put you
off                    220
With feigned excuse; discover the main
ground on 't.

Jul. Why would you know this?

Bos.                    I have depended on him,
And I hear that he is fall'n in some dis-
grace
With the emperor. If he be, like the
mice
That forsake falling houses, I would shift
To other dependence.

Jul.                    You shall not need follow the
wars—
I'll be your maintenance.

Bos.                    And I your loyal servant;
But I cannot leave my calling.

Jul.                    Not leave an
Ungrateful general for the love of a sweet
lady!
You are like some cannot sleep in feather
beds,                    230
But must have blocks for their pillows.

Bos.                    Will you do this?

Jul. Cunningly.

Bos. Tomorrow I'll expect th' intelligence.

Jul. Tomorrow! Get you into my cabinet;
You shall have it with you. Do not delay
me,
No more than I do you. I am like one
That is condemned; I have my pardon
promised,
But I would see it sealed. Go, get you in;
You shall see me wind my tongue about
his heart
Like a skein of silk.          [*Exit Bosola.*

*Enter Cardinal.*]

Card.                    Where are you?

[*Enter Servants.*]

Servants.                    Here.

Card. Let none, upon your lives,          241
Have conference with the Prince Fer-
dinand,
Unless I know it. [*Exeunt Servants.*]—
[*Aside.*] In this distraction
He may reveal the murther.
Yond's my lingering consumption.
I am weary of her, and by any means
Would be quit of.

Jul. How now, my lord! What ails you?

Card. Nothing.

Jul.                    O, you are much altered.
Come, I must be your secretary,[1] and
remove
This lead from off your bosom. What's
the matter?                    250

Card. I may not tell you.

Jul. Are you so far in love with sorrow
You cannot part with part of it? Or
think you

---

[1] Sharer of secrets.

I cannot love your grace when you are sad
As well as merry? Or do you suspect
I, that have been a secret to your heart
These many winters, cannot be the same
Unto your tongue?

CARD.                        Satisfy thy longing—
The only way to make thee keep my counsel                    259
Is not to tell thee.

JUL.                        Tell your echo this,
Or flatterers, that like echoes still report
What they hear, though most imperfect, and not me;
For, if that you be true unto yourself, I'll know.

CARD.        Will you rack me?

JUL.                        No, judgment shall
Draw it from you. It is an equal fault
To tell one's secrets unto all or none.

CARD. The first argues folly.

JUL. But the last tyranny.

CARD. Very well; why, imagine I have committed
Some secret deed which I desire the world                    270
May never hear of.

JUL.                Therefore may not I know it?
You have concealed for me as great a sin
As adultery. Sir, never was occasion
For perfect trial of my constancy
Till now. Sir, I beseech you—

CARD.                        You'll repent it.

JUL. Never.

CARD. It hurries thee to ruin. I'll not tell thee.
Be well advised, and think what danger 'tis
To receive a prince's secrets. They that do,
Had need have their breasts hooped with adamant                    280
To contain them. I pray thee, yet be satisfied;
Examine thine own frailty; 'tis more easy
To tie knots than unloose them. 'Tis a secret
That, like a ling'ring poison, may chance lie
Spread in thy veins, and kill thee seven year hence.

JUL. Now you dally with me.

CARD. No more; thou shalt know it.

By my appointment, the great Duchess of Malfi
And two of her young children, four nights since,
Were strangled.

JUL.                        O heaven! Sir, what have you done?                    290

CARD. How now? How settles this? Think you your
Bosom will be a grave, dark and obscure enough
For such a secret?

JUL.                You have undone yourself, sir.

CARD. Why?

JUL.        It lies not in me to conceal it.

CARD. No? Come, I will swear you to 't upon this book.

JUL. Most religiously.

CARD. Kiss it.                [She kisses the book.]
Now you shall never utter it; thy curiosity
Hath undone thee; thou'rt poisoned with that book.
Because I knew thou couldst not keep my counsel,                    300
I have bound thee to 't by death.

[Enter Bosola.]

BOS. For pity sake, hold!

CARD.                        Ha, Bosola?

JUL.                        I forgive you
This equal piece of justice you have done;
For I betrayed your counsel to that fellow.
He overheard it; that was the cause I said
It lay not in me to conceal it.

BOS. O foolish woman,
Couldst not thou have poisoned him?

JUL.                        'Tis weakness
Too much to think what should have been done.                    309
I go, I know not whither.                [Dies.]

CARD. Wherefore com'st thou hither?

BOS. That I might find a great man like yourself,
Not out of his wits, as the Lord Ferdinand,
To remember my service.

CARD.        I'll have thee hewed in pieces.

BOS. Make not yourself such a promise of that life
Which is not yours to dispose of.

CARD.                        Who placed thee here?

Bos. Her lust, as she intended.

Card. Very well;
Now you know me for your fellow-murderer.

Bos. And wherefore should you lay fair marble colors
Upon your rotten purposes to me,          320
Unless you imitate some that do plot great treasons,
And, when they have done, go hide themselves i' th' graves
Of those were actors in 't?

Card. No more; there is
A fortune attends thee.

Bos. Shall I go sue to Fortune any longer?
'Tis the fool's pilgrimage.

Card. I have honors in store for thee.

Bos. There are a many ways that conduct to seeming
Honor, and some of them very dirty ones.

Card. Throw to the devil          330
Thy melancholy. The fire burns well;
What need we keep a-stirring of 't, and make
A greater smoother? [1] Thou wilt kill Antonio?

Bos. Yes.

Card. Take up that body.

Bos. I think I shall
Shortly grow the common bier for churchyards!

Card. I will allow thee some dozen of attendants
To aid thee in the murther.

Bos. O, by no means. Physicians that apply horseleeches to any rank swelling use to cut off their tails, that the blood     [340 may run through them the faster. Let me have no train when I go to shed blood, lest it make me have a greater when I ride to the gallows.

Card. Come to me after midnight, to help to remove
That body to her own lodging. I'll give out She died o' th' plague;
'Twill breed the less inquiry after her death.

Bos. Where's Castruchio her husband?

Card. He's rode to Naples, to take possession          350
Of Antonio's citadel.

Bos. Believe me, you have done a very happy turn.

[1] Smother, smoke.

Card. Fail not to come. There is the master key
Of our lodgings; and by that you may conceive
What trust I plant in you.          Exit.

Bos. You shall find me ready.—
O poor Antonio, though nothing be so needful
To thy estate as pity, yet I find
Nothing so dangerous! I must look to my footing;
In such slippery ice-pavements men had need
To be frost-nailed well—they may break their necks else.          360
The precedent's here afore me. How this man
Bears up in blood, seems fearless! Why, 'tis well.
Security some men call the suburbs of hell,
Only a dead wall between. Well, good Antonio,
I'll seek thee out; and all my care shall be
To put thee into safety from the reach
Of these most cruel biters that have got
Some of thy blood already. It may be,
I'll join with thee in a most just revenge.
The weakest arm is strong enough that strikes          370
With the sword of justice. Still methinks the duchess
Haunts me. There, there!—'Tis nothing but my melancholy.
O Penitence, let me truly taste thy cup,
That throws men down only to raise them up!          Exit.

## Scena iii.

[A fortification in Milan.]

Antonio, Delio. Echo (from the Duchess' grave).

Del. Yond's the cardinal's window. This fortification
Grew from the ruins of an ancient abbey;
And to yond side o' th' river lies a wall,
Piece of a cloister, which in my opinion
Gives the best echo that you ever heard,
So hollow and so dismal, and withal
So plain in the distinction of our words
That many have supposed it is a spirit
That answers.

Ant. I do love these ancient ruins.
We never tread upon them but we set 10
Our foot upon some reverend history;
And, questionless, here in this open
court,
Which now lies naked to the injuries
Of stormy weather, some men lie interred
Loved the church so well, and gave so
largely to 't,
They thought it should have canopied
their bones
Till doomsday. But all things have their
end;
Churches and cities, which have diseases
like to men,
Must have like death that we have.
Echo.                    *Like death that we have.*
Del. Now the echo hath caught you. 20
Ant. It groaned, methought, and gave
A very deadly accent.
Echo.                        *Deadly accent.*
Del. I told you 'twas a pretty one. You
may make it
A huntsman, or a falconer, a musician,
Or a thing of sorrow.
Echo.                        *A thing of sorrow.*
Ant. Ay, sure, that suits it best.
Echo.                          *That suits it best.*
Ant. 'Tis very like my wife's voice.
Echo.                          *Ay, wife's voice.*
Del. Come, let's us walk farther from 't.
I would not have you go to th' cardinal's
tonight.
Do not.                                    30
Echo. *Do not.*
Del. Wisdom doth not more moderate
wasting sorrow
Than time. Take time for 't; be mindful
of thy safety.
Echo. *Be mindful of thy safety.*
Ant. Necessity compels me.
Make scrutiny throughout the passes
Of your own life, you'll find it impossible
To fly your fate.
[Echo.] *O, fly your fate!*
Del. Hark! The dead stones seem to
have pity on you,                      40
And give you good counsel.
Ant. Echo, I will not talk with thee,
For thou art a dead thing.
Echo. *Thou art a dead thing.*
Ant. My duchess is asleep now,
And her little ones, I hope sweetly. O
heaven,

Shall I never see her more?
Echo. *Never see her more.*
Ant. I marked not one repetition of the
echo
But that; and on the sudden a clear
light                                    50
Presented me a face folded in sorrow.
Del. Your fancy merely.
Ant.        Come, I'll be out of this ague.
For to live thus is not indeed to live;
It is a mockery and abuse of life.
I will not henceforth save myself by
halves;
Lose all, or nothing.
Del.            Your own virtue save you!
I'll fetch your eldest son, and second you.
It may be that the sight of his own blood
Spread in so sweet a figure may beget
The more compassion. However, fare
you well.                                60
Though in our miseries Fortune have a
part,
Yet in our noble suff'rings she hath none.
Contempt of pain, that we may call our
own.                          *Exe[unt].*

SCENA iv.

[*An apartment in the palace of the Cardinal
and Ferdinand at Milan.*]

*Cardinal, Pescara, Malateste, Roderigo,
Grisolan, Bosola, Ferdinand, Antonio,
Servant.*[1]

Card. You shall not watch tonight by the
sick prince;
His grace is very well recovered.
Mal. Good my lord, suffer us.
Card.                    O, by no means;
The noise, and change of object in his
eye,
Doth more distract him. I pray, all to
bed;
And, though you hear him in his violent
fit,
Do not rise, I entreat you.
Pes. So, sir; we shall not.
Card.        Nay, I must have you promise
Upon your honors, for I was enjoined
to 't
By himself; and he seemed to urge it
sensibly.                                10
Pes. Let our honors bind this trifle.
Card. Nor any of your followers.

[1] Last four enter later.

MAL. Neither.

CARD. It may be, to make trial of your promise,

When he's asleep, myself will rise and feign

Some of his mad tricks, and cry out for help,

And feign myself in danger.

MAL. If your throat were cutting,

I'ld not come at you, now I have protested against it.

CARD. Why, I thank you.

GRIS. 'Twas a foul storm tonight.  20

ROD. The Lord Ferdinand's chamber shook like an osier.

MAL. [Aside.] 'Twas nothing but pure kindness in the devil

To rock his own child.

Exeunt [all except the Cardinal].

CARD. The reason why I would not suffer these

About my brother is because at midnight

I may with better privacy convey

Julia's body to her own lodging. O, my conscience!

I would pray now, but the devil takes away my heart

For having any confidence in prayer.

About this hour I appointed Bosola  30

To fetch the body. When he hath served my turn,

He dies.          Exit.

[Enter Bosola.]

BOS. Ha! 'Twas the cardinal's voice; I heard him name

Bosola and my death.  Listen; I hear one's footing.

[Enter Ferdinand.]

FERD. Strangling is a very quiet death.

BOS. [Aside.] Nay, then, I see I must stand upon my guard.

FERD. What say to that?  Whisper softly.  Do you agree to 't?  So; it must be done i' th' dark; the cardinal would not for a thousand pounds the doctor should  [40 see it.          Exit.

BOS. My death is plotted; here's the consequence of murther.

"We value not desert nor Christian breath,

When we know black deeds must be cured with death."

[Enter Antonio and Servant.]

SER. Here stay, sir, and be confident, I pray;

I'll fetch you a dark lanthorn.          Exit.

ANT.          Could I take

Him at his prayers, there were hope of pardon.

BOS. Fall right, my sword! [Stabs him.]—

I'll not give thee so much leisure as to pray.

ANT. O, I am gone!  Thou hast ended a long suit          50

In a minute.

BOS.          What art thou?

ANT.          A most wretched thing,

That only have thy benefit [1] in death,

To appear myself.

[Enter Servant with a lantern.]

SER. Where are you, sir?

ANT. Very near my home!—Bosola!

SER.          O, misfortune!

BOS. [To Servant.] Smother thy pity; thou art dead else.—Antonio!

The man I would have saved 'bove mine own life!

We are merely the stars' tennis balls, strook [2] and banded [3]

Which way please them.—O good Antonio,

I'll whisper one thing in thy dying ear          60

Shall make thy heart break quickly!

Thy fair duchess

And two sweet children—

ANT.          Their very names

Kindle a little life in me.

BOS.          Are murdered!

ANT. Some men have wished to die

At the hearing of sad tidings; I am glad

That I shall do 't in sadness. [4]  I would not now

Wish my wounds balmed nor healed, for I have no use

To put my life to.  In all our quest of greatness,

Like wanton boys whose pastime is their care,

We follow after bubbles blown in th' air.          70

Pleasure of life, what is 't?  Only the good hours

[1] Assistance.          [3] Bandied.
[2] Struck.          [4] Seriousness, reality.

Of an ague; merely a preparative to rest,
To endure vexation. I do not ask
The process¹ of my death; only com-
mend me
To Delio.
Bos. Break, heart!
Ant. And let my son fly the courts of
princes.  [*Dies.*]
Bos. Thou seem'st to have loved An-
tonio?
Ser. I brought him hither,  79
To have reconciled him to the cardinal.
Bos. I do not ask thee that.
Take him up, if thou tender² thine own
life,
And bear him where the lady Julia
Was wont to lodge.—O, my fate moves
swift!
I have this cardinal in the forge al-
ready;
Now I'll bring him to th' hammer. O
direful misprision!³
I will not imitate things glorious,
No more than base; I'll be mine own
example.—
On, on, and look thou represent, for
silence,
The thing thou bear'st.  *Exeunt.*  90

### Scena v.

[*A hall and gallery of the same.*]

*Cardinal, with a book. Bosola, Pescara,
Malateste, Roderigo, Ferdinand, Delio,
Servant with Antonio's body.*⁴

Card. I am puzzled in a question about
hell.
He says in hell there's one material fire,
And yet it shall not burn all men alike,
Lay him by. How tedious is a guilty
conscience!
When I look into the fish ponds in my
garden,
Methinks I see a thing armed with a
rake,
That seems to strike at me.

[*Enter Bosola, and Servant bearing Antonio's
body.*]

Now, art thou come? Thou look'st
ghastly;

¹ Account, story.  ² Care for.  ³ Mistake.
⁴ All but the first enter later.

There sits in thy face some great deter-
mination,
Mixed with some fear.
Bos.  Thus it lightens into action;  10
I am come to kill thee.
Card.  Ha!—Help! Our guard!
Bos. Thou art deceived; they are out of
thy howling.
Card. Hold, and I will faithfully divide
Revenues with thee.
Bos.  Thy prayers and proffers
Are both unseasonable.
Card.  Raise the watch!
We are betrayed!
Bos.  I have confined your flight.
I'll suffer your retreat to Julia's chamber,
But no further.
Card.  Help! We are betrayed!

[*Enter, above, Pescara, Malateste, Roderigo,
and Grisolan.*]

Mal. Listen!
Card. My dukedom for rescue!  20
Rod. Fie upon his counterfeiting!
Mal. Why, 'tis not the cardinal.
Rod. Yes, yes, 'tis he.
But I'll see him hanged ere I'll go down
to him.
Card. Here's a plot upon me. I am as-
saulted! I am lost,
Unless some rescue!
Gris.  He doth this pretty well;
But it will not serve to laugh me out of
mine honor.
Card. The sword's at my throat!
Rod.  You would not bawl so loud then.
Mal. Come, come, lets 's go to bed. He
told us this much aforehand.  30
Pes. He wished you should not come at
him; but, believe 't,
The accent of the voice sounds not in
jest.
I'll down to him, howsoever, and with
engines
Force ope the doors.  [*Exit above.*]
Rod.  Let's follow him aloof,
And note how the cardinal will laugh
at him.

[*Exeunt, above, Malateste, Roderigo, and
Grisolan.*]

Bos. There's for you first, cause you shall
not unbarricade the door
To let in rescue.  *He kills the Servant.*

CARD. What cause hast thou to pursue my life?

Bos.        Look there.

CARD. Antonio?

Bos.        Slain by my hand unwittingly.
Pray, and be sudden.  When thou killedst thy sister,        40
Thou took'st from Justice her most equal balance,
And left her naught but her sword.

CARD.        O, mercy!

Bos. Now it seems thy greatness was only outward;
For thou fall'st faster of thyself than calamity
Can drive thee.  I'll not waste longer time.  There!        [*Wounds him.*]

CARD. Thou hast hurt me!

Bos.        Again!

CARD.        Shall I die like a leveret,
Without any resistance?—Help, help, help!
I am slain!

[*Enter Ferdinand.*]

FERD.        Th' alarum!  Give me a fresh horse;
Rally the vaunt-guard,[1] or the day is lost.
Yield, yield!  I give you the honor of arms,        50
Shake my sword over you.  Will you yield?

CARD. Help me; I am your brother!

FERD. The devil!
My brother fight upon the adverse party?

*He wounds the Cardinal, and, in the scuffle, gives Bosola his death wound.*

There flies your ransom.

CARD. O justice!
I suffer now for what hath former been.
"Sorrow is held the eldest child of sin."

FERD. Now you're brave fellows.  Cæsar's fortune was harder than Pompey's;  [60
Cæsar died in the arms of prosperity, Pompey at the feet of disgrace.  You both died in the field.  The pain's nothing; pain many times is taken away with the apprehension of greater, as the toothache with the sight of a barber that comes to pull it out.  There's philosophy for you.

Bos. Now my revenge is perfect.—Sink, thou main cause
Of my undoing!—The last part of my life
Hath done me best service.        70
        *He kills Ferdinand.*

FERD. Give me some wet hay; I am broken-winded.
I do account this world but a dog kennel.
I will vault credit[2] and affect[3] high pleasures
Beyond death.

Bos. He seems to come to himself, now he's so near the bottom.

FERD. My sister, O my sister!  There's the cause on 't.
"Whether we fall by ambition, blood, or lust,
Like diamonds, we are cut with our own dust."        [*Dies.*]

CARD. Thou hast thy payment too.

Bos. Yes, I hold my weary soul in my teeth;        80
'Tis ready to part from me.  I do glory
That thou, which stood'st like a huge pyramid
Begun upon a large and ample base,
Shalt end in a little point, a kind of nothing.

[*Enter, below, Pescara, Malateste, Roderigo, and Grisolan.*]

PES. How now, my lord!

MAL.        O sad disaster!

ROD.        How comes this?

Bos. Revenge for the Duchess of Malfi, murdered
By th' Aragonian brethren; for Antonio
Slain by this[4] hand; for lustful Julia
Poisoned by this man; and lastly for myself,
That was an actor in the main of all        90
Much gainst mine own good nature, yet i' th' end
Neglected.

PES.        How now, my lord!

CARD.        Look to my brother.
He gave us these large wounds, as we were struggling

---

[1] Vanguard.

[2] "Overleap rational expectation" (Lucas).

[3] Aspire to.

[4] From 1708 edn.  Original has *his*.

Here i' th' rushes. And now, I pray, let me
Be laid by and never thought of. [*Dies.*]
PES. How fatally, it seems, he did with-
stand
His own rescue!
MAL.        Thou wretched thing of blood,
How came Antonio by his death?
BOS. In a mist; I know not how;
Such a mistake as I have often seen    100
In a play. O, I am gone!
We are only like dead walls or vaulted
graves,
That, ruined, yields no echo. Fare you
well!
It may be pain, but no harm, to me to
die
In so good a quarrel. O, this gloomy
world!'
In what a shadow, or deep pit of dark-
ness,
Doth womanish and fearful mankind
live!
Let worthy minds ne'er stagger in dis-
trust
To suffer death or shame for what is
just.
Mine is another voyage.    [*Dies.*] 110
PES. The noble Delio, as I came to th'
palace.

Told me of Antonio's being here, and
showed me
A pretty gentleman, his son and heir.

[*Enter Delio, and Antonio's Son.*]

MAL. O, sir, you come too late!
DEL.                    I heard so, and
Was armed for 't, ere I came. Let us
make noble use
Of this great ruin, and join all our force
To establish this young hopeful gentle-
man
In 's mother's right. These wretched
eminent things
Leave no more fame •behind 'em than
should one
Fall in a frost, and leave his print in
snow.    120
As soon as the sun shines, it ever melts,
Both form and matter. I have ever
thought
Nature doth nothing so great for great
men
As when she's pleased to make them
lords of truth.
"Integrity of life is fame's best friend,
Which nobly, beyond death, shall crown
the end."                    *Exeunt.*

**FINIS.**

# THOMAS MIDDLETON AND WILLIAM ROWLEY

Richard Hindry Barker, in *Thomas Middleton*, the only full-length study of this dramatist (Columbia University Press, 1958), ends his book with this unequivocal statement: "He is not indeed another Shakespeare or another Jonson, but he stands above his other contemporaries. He is the third great dramatist of the Jacobean stage." Samuel Schoenbaum, once a student under Barker, had already asserted with almost equal confidence at the end of the first part of his *Middleton's Tragedies/A Critical Study* (Columbia University Press, 1955): "And yet, for all their defects, these five tragedies have, I feel, sufficient merit to entitle Middleton to the foremost place after Shakespeare in the hierarchy of Jacobean writers of tragedy—a place superior to that of Ford and Chapman, and also of Webster, the author of two great plays." These are the verdicts of two of the leading scholarly authorities on Middleton, but they are backed by such non-academic critics as T. S. Eliot, who wrote (*Elizabethan Dramatists*): "In some respects in which Elizabethan tragedy can be compared to French or Greek tragedy, *The Changeling* stands above every tragic play of its time, except those of Shakespeare." It is, thought Eliot, the poetic and romantic masterpiece of Middleton's mature style. Nevertheless, Schoenbaum has cast a slight shadow across the unquestioning acceptance of the critical verdict of Eliot ("the most highly esteemed man of letters of our time") simply because he himself is a great poet by pointing out that the passage that Eliot chose to prove that Middleton is on occasion "a great master of versification" is now considered, "according to all the evidence and all the reputable authorities," to be the work of Middleton's collaborator, William Rowley.

Although Barker raises the old problem of "how little we know about the lives of the early English dramatists," he slightly qualifies the application of this generalization to Middleton by adding, "We can follow the general outlines of Middleton's career, but we know nothing or next to nothing about the man himself." As a matter of fact, we know considerably more about the life of Middleton than we do about the lives of a great many of his colleagues. Barker's own account is based largely on the recent discoveries of research scholars like Mark Eccles ("Middleton's Birth and Education," *RES*, 1931, and "Thomas Middleton/A Poett," *SP*, 1957), Mildred G. Christian ("An Autobiographical Note by Thomas Middleton," *NQ*, 1938; "Middleton's Residence at Oxford," *MLR*, 1946; and "A Sidelight on the Family History of Thomas Middleton," *SP*, 1948), Peter J. Phialas ("Middleton's Early Contact with the Law," *SP*, 1955), R. C. Bald ("Middleton's Civic Employments," *MP*, 1933, and "The Chronology of Middleton's Plays," *MLR*, 1937), Joseph Quincy Adams (in his edition of *The Ghost of Lucrece*, New York and London, 1937), and Gerald E. Bentley (*The Jacobean and Caroline Stage*, Oxford, 1941 ff.). These works have supplemented or corrected the earlier accounts provided by Middleton's first editors, like Alexander Dyce (London, 1840) and A. H. Bullen (London, 1885–6).

Thomas Middleton's father, William, was a rather remarkable London bricklayer who achieved a coat-of-arms and a crest; his mother Anne was the daughter of another Londoner, William Snow. The two were married in the church of St. Lawrence in the Old Jewry on February 17, 1574, but Thomas was not born until six years later, since he was christened in the same church on April 18, 1580. A sister, Avice or Alice, was born two years later. When their father made his oral will on January 20, 1586, very shortly before his death, he owned or leased two substantial pieces of property, one in Limehouse with a "tenement" and a wharf on it and the other of some four acres next to the Curtain theater, on which were several tenements, at least some of which had been built or remodeled by their owner. (Incidentally, this theater was called the Curtain because that was the name of its owner, not because of any theatrical equipment.) The latter property, known as the "Curtain garden," was not only to bring Thomas Middleton into a theatrical atmosphere from his babyhood, but was to be the occasion of some bitter family disputes and lawsuits which may have helped to shape his cynical outlook on life in later years. According to the father's will, a third of the total estate of a little over £335, as valued in the Guild Hall Record Office estimate, was to be divided between the children, this amount to be brought up by the mother to a hundred marks apiece.

Though Anne Middleton thus seemed to have been prudently looking after the welfare of her two small children, her next step, taken in less than ten months, showed her unfortunate lack of good judgment: she married again, a certain Thomas Harvey, a grocer who had invested his small fortune in an expedition to Roanoke Island, Virginia, organized by Sir Walter Raleigh and led by Sir Richard Grenville, soon to be the hero of the last fight of his ship, the little *Revenge*, against the whole Spanish fleet off the Azores in 1591. But the Roanoke expedition proved to be neither heroic nor successful, and after a year of starving and fighting Indians, it had to be rescued by Sir Francis Drake. Thus, when the would-be grocer-colonist Harvey found himself back in London, he was so poor that he could not pay his creditors, and must have thought himself lucky when he persuaded the widow Middleton to marry him. The marriage, obviously not a love match, turned out to be disastrous to all concerned, since by November 1586 both husband and wife began to try to trick one another out of the income from the property, and in order to meet the terms of the will Harvey had to sell what few possessions he had at an "outcrye at his doore"—that is, at public auction. His reaction to the whole situation was to spend the remaining family income riotously, so that three years later the tenants of the Curtain property complained that there was practically nothing left "for the releyeffe of his Wieffe & her children." His best solution was to get out of the country, and he found some sort of job "on Her Majesty's service" in Portugal and the Low Countries. These measures also proved abortive, and on his return he asked his wife for £30. But she gave him only fifty shillings and threatened to have him arrested if he bothered her. In 1595 she charged in court that he had tried to poison her, and so he apparently disappeared abroad again to escape his creditors.

During this absence Avice or Alice married a cloth-worker named Allan Waterer, who soon entered into the family feud by claiming his wife's share of the inheritance and moving in with his mother-in-law. By the middle of 1598 matters had reached such a state that Waterer also entered the courts to sue for a writ of attachment calling for sureties of the peace against Thomas Harvey, Anne Harvey, Thomas Middleton, and a fourth party who had somehow got mixed up in the family affairs. At one point Waterer swore that his mother-in-law "went about by develishe and subtell practizes . . . to deceave all the world and then lastlie her owne Children." Mistress Harvey then tried to enlist the help of another friend, Philip Bond, telling him that her son-in-law "went about to thruste her out of her house: and forbade her tenants to paye her any rent;" but Bond refused to be drawn into the squabble. By this time it is no wonder that Mistress Harvey impressed Bond as being "very sycke," but she was not so ill that she could not pretend a reconcilement with her husband, who by this time was back in London. Nevertheless, after a day or two, when Harvey, accompanied by Bond, came to the house again, she slammed the door in his face, and told Bond, " 'Tis no matter, nowe I have other Counselle to doe soe." What the other counsel was never transpired, but on June 10, 1600, Harvey came to the end of his patience and started suit to regain control of the property.  In his bill he named both his wife and Waterer, who had already once attacked him and, he said, nearly killed him.

Unfortunately, the full outcome of this family row is unknown, except that in June 1600 young Thomas Middleton was able to sell his share in the property to his sister's husband.  But the affair must have made a deep impression on him, and its inevitable effects would seem to appear in his later works, especially in his so-called "city comedies," like *A Trick to Catch the Old One*, with their chicaneries, cheatings, quarrels over money, materialistic characters, and general pictures of the meanness and baseness of human nature.

Young Middleton sold his rights to the family property because he needed money to continue his education.  As he put it, he exchanged his half share in the Limehouse and Curtain properties for money "paid disbursed for my advauncement & p[re]ferment in the Vniu[er]sity of Oxford where I am now a student and for my maintenance with meat drinke and apparrell and other necessaries."  In April 1598, at the rather late age of eighteen, he had matriculated at Queen's College, as a "pleb. fil."—that is, the son of a commoner.  One of the many legal documents concerning the family litigations said that his stepfather, Harvey, had obtained a fellowship for him, but Barker discounts this possibility, in view of Harvey's antecedents and actions.  The same document stated that the young man lost this appointment when he came home "to ayde his mother against his brother in lawe in the absence of his Father in Lawe."  Just what Middleton learned or accomplished in his three years at Oxford is unknown, but Barker speculates that perhaps he had himself in mind in one of his pamphlets, *Father Hubburd's Tales* (1604).  He described the life of a poor young man, with a library of only four books, who went up to Oxford and attached himself as a poor scholar and servant to a well-to-do Londoner's son, "a pure cockney," who spent most of his time "in the tennis-court, tossing of balls instead of books," while he himself "kept his study warm, and sucked the honey of wit from the flowers of Aristotle."  But with all his hard work he accomplished very little until he was "unfruitfully led to the lickerish study of poetry, that sweet honey-poison . . . ."  There is no evidence that Middleton ever took his degree.  Thus, as Eccles pointed out, Middleton did not get his knowledge of the law from any of the Inns of Court, as Dyce once thought.  As for his education before he got to college, the only evidence so far produced is that offered by John D. Reeves, who in "Thomas Middleton and Lily's Grammar" (*NQ*, 1952) showed that Middleton was familiar with this authorized Latin grammar by discussing parallels between it and five passages from his plays, *A Chaste Maid in Cheapside* and *The Family of Love*.

Perhaps Middleton's preoccupation with "that sweet honey-poison," poetry, may account for the next recorded event in his life, for on February 8, 1601, a witness in the continuous family lawsuit deposed that the son "nowe remayneth heare in London daylie accompaninge the players."  Barker surmises that perhaps this "tantalizingly vague" final phrase implies that Middleton was already writing or trying to write for the theaters, near one of which he had lived for so many years.  From either prosperity or rashness he now also decided to get married.  His wife, Mary Marbeck or Merbeck, came from a rather distinguished family, her paternal grandfather having been organist of St. George's Chapel, Windsor, after 1541.  Since he was also a devoted Calvinist, he was saved from the stake only at the last moment by a royal pardon because of his musicianship, but was nevertheless listed temporarily in Foxe's *Book of Martyrs*.  Later, John Marbeck published the first English concordance to the Bible, as well as a number of musical and theological works.  Mary's uncle, Dr. Roger Marbeck, was, first, Provost of Oriel College, Oxford, and later chief physician to Queen Elizabeth and registrar for life of the London College of Physicians.  Roger's brother Edward had a much less distinguished career, becoming only one of the six clerks in Chancery, but through his daughter Mary he became Thomas Middleton's father-in-law.  One of her brothers was Thomas Marbeck, an actor for a time with the Admiral's Men, through whom Mary may have met Tom Middleton. The couple had a son, Edward, born in 1603 or 1604, and still living twenty years later.

Although Middleton's name does not appear in Philip Henslowe's diary of his theater activities till 1602, when it is mentioned five times, Phialas believes that Middleton started writing for the stage as early as 1600. By this time, as a rather precocious lad, he had already published a rhetorical versified paraphrase, *The Wisdom of Solomon* (1597), based on the Apocrypha; *Micro-Cynicon, Six Snarling Satires* (1599), imitating Persius, Juvenal, and Bishop John Hall; and *The Ghost of Lucrece* (1600), a retelling of the old Roman story. His record with Henslowe shows that he was receiving payments for two now lost plays, *Two Shapes* (also called *Caesar's Fall*) and *The Chester Tragedy* (also called *Randal, Earl of Chester*), the pair showing his early diversity of subject matter. According to Henslowe's usual method, Middleton worked on the first with Dekker, Drayton, Webster, and Munday, but the second he wrote alone, receiving the normal £6 for his work. On December 14, 1602, he got five shillings for a prologue and epilogue for a court performance of Greene's *Friar Bacon and Friar Bungay*. He was also advanced a pound for an unnamed play for the Earl of Worcester's Men, the second of Henslowe's companies, the first being the Lord Admiral's Men, for whom Middleton was also writing. Neither of these companies had a very high rating with the best London audiences, being noted for generally rather crude, unpolished, popular productions, though occasionally they turned out plays of a higher quality. But Middleton did not stay with Henslowe alone, and was soon writing both for him and for the more fashionable and respectable children's companies at the two "private" theaters—the Children of Paul's and the Children of the Chapel. Before the theaters were temporarily closed in April 1604, he was writing *The Phoenix* for the Children of Paul's, was collaborating in a minor way with Dekker on *The Honest Whore* for the Admiral's Men (now Lord Henry's Men), and turning out a couple of prose pamphlets. On the reopening of the theaters in a few months he wrote at least three comedies for the Children of Paul's: *Michaelmas Term* (about 1604–6), *A Mad World, My Masters* (about 1604–6), and his comic masterpiece, *A Trick to Catch the Old One* (also 1604–6). At the same time he wrote a lost play which involved him in a lawsuit with the Master of the Blackfriars, *The Viper and Her Brood*, for the Children of the Chapel (now the Children of Blackfriars), and, says Barker, "was almost certainly" the author of *The Revenger's Tragedy*, acted by the King's Men. Although in his preface Barker asserts that, so far as *The Revenger's Tragedy* is concerned, he feels that he has "given new evidence that will, I think, settle the controversy about the authorship once and for all," the scholarly world has been far from agreeing with him, and the whole problem of *The Revenger's Tragedy* and its authorship will be dealt with separately in this anthology.

After the Paul's Boys disbanded in 1606, several of Middleton's plays were published, Barker thinks because the company could not make money from them in any other way. He also thinks that in most cases Middleton had nothing to do with the publication himself, since apparently he did not believe his plays had any literary interest. Four, including *The Revenger's Tragedy*, were printed with no name attached, two had his initials on the title pages, and only one had his name, or at least his surname, spelled out. In fact, during the last twenty years of his life, only three more plays with which his name is associated were published, and two of these were collaborations. The one which has a signed preface, *The Roaring Girl, or Moll Cut-Purse*, admits that he is offering his work to the reader not as art but as "venery and laughter"—at least sixpence worth of the former and enough of the latter "to keep you in an afternoon from dice at home in your chambers." Barker concludes that, so far as the booksellers and Middleton himself were concerned, "Thomas Middleton" was not as yet a "name to conjure with." The passage of over three hundred and fifty years has made a considerable difference in that situation.

After leaving the boys Middleton transferred his services to the adult companies, for most of which he wrote in the next few years—first for Prince Henry's Men and Lady Elizabeth's Men, and finally for the best of them all, the King's Men, for whom Shakespeare and Fletcher also wrote. In the last dozen years of his life he supplemented his income from his legitimate plays with a series of masques and pageants. The masques began with one, now lost, on the trite subject, *The Masque of Cupid* (1614), and continued with *The Inner Temple Masque, or Masque of Heroes* (1619). The pageants, or "entertainments," were inaugurated on the celebration of the completion of a new public water system, *The Opening of the New River* (1613), which was notable not because of any originality or stage devices but because it was designed to honor two men of Middleton's own name, apparently unrelated to him, Sir Thomas Middleton, the incoming Lord Mayor, and Hugh Middleton, the engineer who had executed the construction. Middleton's most popular work of this general type, however, consisted of his series of Lord Mayor's shows, beginning with *The Triumphs of Truth* (1613). The scenes of this moved from the Guild Hall to the wharves, then to Westminster by barge, then to St. Paul's churchyard, and finally to its climax at the Little Conduit in Cheapside. During all of this time the Mayor, his attendants, and the public were regaled with flattering allegorical speeches delivered by properly costumed figures personifying the Five Senses, Truth, Zeal, Religion, Liberality, and Perfect Love, who had been opposed by Error, Barbarism, Ignorance, Impudence, and Falsehood. From this time on to *The Triumphs of Wealth and Prosperity* in 1626, Middleton was the favorite purveyor of these civic shows. For *The Triumphs of Honor and Industry* in 1617 he received the highest sum ever paid for "ordering, overseeing and wryting of the whole devyce." (See David H. Horne, *The Life and Minor Works of George Peele*, Yale University Press, 1952. For a full account of this phase of Middleton's dramatic activities, see R. C. Bald, "Middleton's Civic Employments," *MP*, 1933.)

On September 6, 1620, Middleton was also made City Chronologer, a post, says Barker, "which was probably intended to include that of Inventor of the City's Honorable Entertainments" (see Bald, as above). For these jobs he eventually received an annual stipend of £10, but this sum was frequently supplemented by extra fees for additional services, speeches, and interludes. Part of his duties as Chronologer necessitated keeping a journal of important events in municipal history, some of the manuscripts of which were seen and summarized by the antiquarian William Oldys a century later (see Dyce's edition of Middleton). Middleton was thus thoroughly qualified to reflect London life, manners, and mores in his plays. In the latter part of his career these plays continued to be in various genres: realistic comedies like *The Roaring Girl* with Dekker (1604–8), *A Chaste Maid in Cheapside* (1611), *No Wit, No Help Like a Woman's* (about 1610), *The Widow* (about 1616), *Wit at Several Weapons* (about 1612?), and *Anything for a Quiet Life* (about 1621), in all of which he exploited the seamier sides of the London life of sharpers, loose women, and gulls; tragicomedies in the Beaumont and Fletcher school like *The Witch* (about 1610–16), *More Dissemblers besides Women* (before 1623), *The Old Law* (about 1618), and *A Fair Quarrel*, with Rowley (about 1615–17); and tragedies like *Hengist, King of Kent*, also called *The Mayor of Quinborough* (about 1616), *Women Beware Women*, his second greatest tragedy (before 1627), and *The Changeling* (1622), with Rowley, his greatest and one of the best of the period. Several anonymous plays, like *Blurt, Master Constable, The Puritan*, and *The Second Maiden's Tragedy*, have also been ascribed to Middleton. (For the canon and chronology of his plays, see Mark Eccles, "Middleton's Birth and Education," *RES*, 1931, and R. C. Bald, "The Chronology of Middleton's Plays," *MLR*, 1937; but their speculations should be compared with Bentley's listings.)

Middleton's last significant play, *A Game at Chess* (1624), is really unclassifiable, since it belongs to a genre of its own, a combination of fantasy, allegory, and politics. It was the outgrowth of the renewed anti-Spanish, anti-Catholic feeling which resulted from the failure of the negotiations between King James and Spain to bring about international peace by marrying his son Charles to the Infanta Maria. When the negotiations conducted by Buckingham and the Spanish ambassador Gondomar failed, there was great rejoicing among the people of England, whose old hatred and distrust of Spain had not been dispelled by James's diplomacy.  Middleton made full use of this situation, but hid the real persons involved in the affair under the disguise of a chess game, peopled with characters named the White Duke, the Black Knight, the Black King, the White Queen's Pawn, the Black Bishop's Pawn, and the Fat Bishop. Though the play was hastily thrown together, it proved to be a tremendous success for nine performances, when it experienced the natural and inevitable closing down by the government.  The Privy Council reprimanded the actors and forbade them ever to give the play again, even though it had been licensed by the Master of the Revels. Middleton's own punishment is uncertain, though one story has it that after he had twice failed to appear before the Council he was committed to prison, from which he was released only after petitioning the King.  (See Bald's edition of *A Game at Chess*, Cambridge, 1929; also Samuel A. Tannenbaum, "A Middleton Forgery," *PQ*, 1933, and Bernard Wagner's reply in July.  For the whole story of Middleton's relations with King James from the beginning of his writing career to its culmination in *A Game at Chess*, see William Power, "Thomas Middleton vs. King James I," *NQ*, 1957.)

Two years later Middleton found himself in trouble again with the government, this time of the city rather than of the nation.  There were complaints about the "ill" performance of his 1626 pageant, but, even worse, about a special pageant that he and his chief assistant, Garret Christmas, designer of costumes and scenes, had prepared to welcome the new King Charles and his French queen, Henrietta Maria.  This revealed "abuses and badd workmanshipp in and about the contrivings and payntings" of the wagons, as the City Records put it.  However, if Middleton had jeopardized his municipal position through these failures, his career was not affected, because on July 4, 1627, he was buried at the parish church of Newington Butts, where he had apparently lived since as early as 1609.  His first wife, Mary, seems to have died sometime before him, since seven months after his death his widow Magdalen petitioned the city for financial help and was granted a gift of twenty nobles.  Within five months, however, she too was buried in the same parish church.  Middleton's death seems to have occasioned no particular attention on the part of his contemporaries, for no printed comments or elegies survive.  Not until 1640 did an anonymous epigrammatist in *Wit's Recreations* devote three couplets to him, calling him "Facetious Middleton" and praising his "witty Muse."  Although John Cotgrave used a surprising number of quotations from him in his *English Treasury of Wit and Language* in 1655 (G. E. Bentley, "John Cotgrave's *English Treasury of Wit and Language* and the Elizabethan Drama," *SP*, 1943), references to Middleton practically disappeared from the literary scene until the nineteenth century, when he was discovered by critics like Lamb and Swinburne and editors like Dyce and Bullen.

A few more facts about the life of William Rowley, one of Middleton's favorite collaborators, have been discovered since C. W. Stork published his introduction to Rowley's *All's Lost by Lust* and *A Shoemaker, a Gentleman* (Philadelphia, 1910).  Rowley is known chiefly through his stage connections.  He was probably born about 1580 and died in 1626.  So far as is known, he was not related to Samuel Rowley, also a playwright, none of whose plays are extant except one about Henry VIII, *When You See Me, You Know Me;* but in 1602 he and Samuel Bird were paid £4 by Henslowe for making additions to *Doctor Faustus*.  Thus he and William Rowley were both attached to Henslowe's organization.  William, however, was also a popular actor of comic roles such as clowns and yokels in Prince Charles's Company and the King's Company from about 1610 on, acting in the London public theaters, in the provinces, and at court. (See Edwin Nungezer, *A Dictionary of Actors and of Other Persons Associated with the Public Representation of Plays in England before 1642*, Yale University Press,, 1929.) His name is found on several financial and organizational agreements made by these companies, and he was involved in the evidence given in a lawsuit concerning a lost play by himself, Ford, Webster, and Dekker, *Keep the Widow Waking, or The Late Murder in Whitechapel*, licensed in September 1624 (Charles J. Sisson, *Library*, 1927, and *Lost Plays of Shakespeare's Age*). He wrote at least four plays alone, and at least eleven others in collaboration, with Dekker, Day, Webster, and others, but was especially successful with Middleton, since the two men seemed to stimulate and supplement one another. From Dekker's deposition in the law case, Rowley died before March 24, 1626, and the parish register of St. James's, Clerkenwell, records the burial of a "William Rowley, householder," on February 11, 1626. Five days later, "Grace, relict of William Rowley," renounced administration of his estate before a notary. (M. J. Dickson, "William Rowley," *TLS*, March 28, 1929. See also Bentley; Schoenbaum; E. K. Chambers, *The Elizabethan Stage*, Oxford, 1923; N. W. Bawcutt, edition of *The Changeling* for the Revels Plays, London, 1958; and D. M. Robb, "The Canon of William Rowley's Plays," *MLR*, 1950.)

# THOMAS MIDDLETON

## A TRICK TO CATCH THE OLD ONE

As for the position of *A Trick* among Middleton's plays, it and *A Chaste Maid* are usually named as his most successful comedies. Dyce considered it one of his most perfect, and Bullen agreed with Gerard Langbaine's "brief but emphatic judgement that 'this is an excellent old play'" (*An Account of the English Dramatic Poets*, 1691). Swinburne said it was "by far the best play Middleton had yet written, and one of the best he ever wrote" (Mermaid edition of *Plays*, London, 1887). Eliot went even further and called it one of the greatest comedies of a "great comic writer." William Archer's praises are perhaps the most flattering of all, in view of his animadversions on most of the Elizabethan drama. As might be expected, it was the "more modern note" of the play's realism that impressed him (*The Old Drama and the New*). To him, *A Trick* and *Michaelmas Term* were "spirited transcriptions of contemporary life, full of coarseness and gross exaggeration . . . , but realistic in spirit and aim, and not without a certain power of characterization." Archer reached this conclusion in spite of his realization that the whole action of the play turned upon the favorite Elizabethan comic theme of "cozenage"—i.e., rascality vs. credulity. Other critics, admitting the same central situation, have come to different conclusions about Middleton himself and his attitude toward the life around him. George F. Watson, in his New Mermaids edition of the play (London, 1968), brought together a rather miscellaneous "school of critics who are uneasy about the absence of conventional moral signposts." These included Arthur Symons, who complained that Middleton is "no more careful of his ethical than of his other improbabilities;" Louis B. Wright, who objected to the absence of any good or admirable characters in the play; L. C. Knights, who felt that the "ambition of Hoard is not set in the light of a possible ideal of citizen conduct;" Alfred Harbage, who objected to Middleton's failure to punish Witgood at the end of the play and complained that the Courtesan "orates in favor of harlotry;" C. M. Gayley, who considered Middleton's comedies to be nothing but "cinematography of immorality, . . . the apotheosis of irreverence, wantonness, and filth;" and M. L. Hunt, who lamented that Middleton "concentrated his great gifts upon the evil and the unclean" and "carried the comedy of mud to the greatest length." Watson admitted that Middleton's so-called "realism" had an important function in his "attempt to subdue the note of moral seriousness and to disguise the ethical bent of the play" and that he tried to convince his hearers that his villains were after all "perfectly ordinary London business men," without exaggerating "their acquisitive drive to make a moral point." But Watson, agreeing with Muriel C. Bradbrook (*Themes and Conventions of Elizabethan Tragedy*), also emphasized his feeling that "in Middleton the silent judgement is provided by weight of irony—by all that is left unsaid," and insisted that the satiric element should not be overlooked. R. B. Parker recognized the presence of both points of view in the play, but reconciled them by suggesting that at the heart of Middleton's comic style is "a tension between skill in the presentation of manners and a desire to denounce immorality," concealed by the ingenious intrigue, the verbal wit, and the vivid representation of contemporary London scenes and behavior, which tended to obscure his concern with deprecation and which played down moral judgment ("Middleton's Experiments with Comedy and Judgement," *The Jacobean Theatre, SAS*, 1960). Charles L. Barber, in his old spelling edition of the play for the Fountainwell

Drama Texts (Edinburgh and Berkeley, 1968), maintained that Middleton's realism went beyond the usual conventional "minute depiction of contemporary habits and manners, a surface verisimilitude," to a clear and unsentimental presentation of "some of the social tensions of Jacobean England," especially those having to do with the fluid social boundary now being set between, first, citizen shopkeepers, second, money-lenders and capitalists, and third, the landed gentry. Barber implied that Middleton also recognized this element and illustrated it through the presence of a great deal of dramatic irony in the play, but he diagnosed the attitude taken toward the play by one school of critics as resulting from the author's apparent "detachment," his refusal to take sides with either the gentry or the citizenry, and pointed out that in the play there is no retribution, that Hoard and Lucre, although overreaching themselves, are not seriously damaged, and that Witgood, the protagonist, "the cleverest scoundrel of the lot," gets away with everything. "Events," he says, "are consistently seen in an ironic light, and even the conventional moral speeches that end the play undermine themselves by their own knowingness." Readers have always tended to discount the sincerity of the final promises of reform by both Witgood and the Courtesan after they each have found the kind of mate they most desire—one who has plenty of money and who will relieve them of the necessity of worrying about their futures.

In working out his general theme of greed and gullibility, Middleton has been widely praised for his skill in construction and his clever manipulation and development of a basically conventional and unoriginal situation, the passing off of a propertyless and undesirable woman as an heiress to help the younger generation dupe its elders. (See, in general, Wilbur D. Dunkel, *The Dramatic Technique of Thomas Middleton in His Comedies of London Life*, University of Chicago Press, 1925.) The scenes involving the usurers Dampit and Gulf in *The Trick*, however, have somewhat impaired this opinion, though in themselves they furnish both audiences and actors with some of the best comic and satiric material in the play. Various explanations have been offered for what seem like excrescences, since they certainly do not form anything like a sub-plot and could easily be omitted. Some critics have felt that Middleton must have had in mind some actual person on whom he wished to get revenge; others, that he was simply pillorying and caricaturing the heartless and depraved moneylender in general. (See R. Levin, "The Dampit Scenes in *A Trick to Catch the Old One*," *MLQ*, 1964; M. W. Sampson, edition of *Thomas Middleton*, New York, 1915.) The gusto with which Dampit is portrayed and the torrent of his highly original vocabulary, however, almost alone justify his inclusion; but Watson suggests that his presence "serves to emphasise by contrast the normality and even, in a curious way, the respectability, of Lucre and Hoard."

Middleton's language is always one of his strongest features, with its easy and rich colloquialism, its natural speed and rhythm, and its raciness. Though he probably shows little of his ability as a poet in this sort of comedy, he also at times uses verse, both unrhymed and rhymed, with considerable effectiveness, even in its irregularities. Watson points out that these verse passages are generally used as a way of "under-cutting any heavily moral response" and of burlesquing many of the things being said.

Middleton has also named most of his characters with considerable care, according to the humors technique. William Power ("Middleton's Way with Names," *NQ*, 1960) has discussed the names Middleton used in his entire literary output, showing how he often repeated certain ones from work to work, and giving the origins and interpretations of many of them; and various editors have added their own contributions. Most of the purely English names, such as Witgood, Hoard, Pecunius Lucre, Limber, Sam Freedom, and Moneylove, are self-explanatory, but others deserve further annotation. Kix, in addition to the obvious pun, Middleton probably took from the dialectal *kex*, meaning a dried, hollow stalk. Hoard's remark in V, ii, that the fathers of himself, Lamprey, and Spichcock "were all free a th' Fishmongers," calls attention to the watery ancestry of their names, a lamprey of course being a kind of eellike fish with a suckerlike mouth and a spichcock being a split and broiled eel.  The Courtesan is given the name Mistress Medler not only because of the obvious implication but also because a medlar was a favorite Elizabethan fruit which was ready to eat only after it had begun to rot.  As Audrey's song to Dampit at the opening of IV, v, suggests, "There's pits enow to damn" the usurers' victim all over London "before he comes to hell;" and Gulf is an appropriate name for his associate.  Witgood not only possesses sharp wits but he has been christened Theodorus, which means a "gift of God;" but the name was unusual in Jacobean times.  Onesiphorus and Walkadine were also unusual names, but were not invented by Middleton, both being known at the time. An Onesiphorus is mentioned twice in Paul's second epistle to Timothy as a man of Ephesus who "oft refreshed me, and was not ashamed of my chain; but, when he was in Rome, he sought me out very diligently, and found me."  The name was therefore clearly ironical, as well as funny to English ears.  No derivation of the name Walkadine, however, has been turned up.  The applicability of the name Foxtone is also uncertain. In her somewhat dubious Ladyship's brief appearance at Hoard's celebration in V, ii, it is spelled in two ways in the original text: Foxestone and Foxtone.  The first syllable of the word could well imply that Lady Foxtone has achieved her social position by cunningness and foxiness; the second might be derived from the French ton, or style, breeding.  However this may be, there is no doubt that Middleton, like most of his colleagues in the drama, was much preoccupied with names.

The search for sources of the play has commanded some attention, though with few results so far as the main plot is concerned, since most of it seems to have been original. Such a search has been undertaken by R. C. Bald ("The Sources of Middleton's City Comedies," *JEGP*, 1934), Margery Fisher ("Notes on the Sources of Some of Middleton's London Plays," *RES*, 1939), Mildred C. Christian ("Middleton's Acquaintance with the *Merrie Conceited Jests of George Peele*," *PMLA*, 1935, and *Non-Dramatic Sources for the Rogues in Middleton's Plays*, University of Chicago Press, 1936), A. B. Stonex ("The Usurer in Elizabethan Drama," *PMLA*, 1916), and Signi Falk ("Plautus' *Persa* and Middleton's *Trick to Catch the Old One*," *MLN*, 1951), but positive results have been slight.  The general conclusion is that the printed sources for most of Middleton's comedies should be regarded with suspicion, and that he was probably mostly indebted to his own invention and oral gossip with friends and neighbors—if not his own experience—concerning crooks, sharpers, avaricious business men, lawsuits, lawyers, and fast-living young gentlemen, all driven by greed, lust, or desire for social advancement.

The play itself was entered anonymously in the Stationers' Register on October 7, 1607, by George Elde, along with another anonymous play, *The Revenger's Tragedy*. Since almost no other cases exist in which a single publisher entered two plays simultaneously, some scholars have argued that this entry is presumptive evidence that the same man wrote both, and have concluded that when Middleton's authorship of *A Trick* was established his claim on the other play was strengthened.  This sort of argument, however, has not proved very convincing.  At any rate, *A Trick* was published as a quarto by Elde in 1608, with two variant title pages, one with no indication of authorship, but with the statement that it had "been lately acted by the Children of Paul's," the other signed with the initials "T. M." and carrying the statement that it "hath been often in action, both at Paul's and at the Blackfriars," and also had been "Presented before His Majesty on New Year's Night Last."  The early stage history is thus fairly clear, though the first performances must have come at least as early as 1606, since the Children of Paul's were dissolved in the summer of that year.  The reference to "Povey's new buildings" in III, iv, tends to confirm such a date (Charles Barber, ed. of *A Trick;* Sampson).  In 1616 Elde republished the same text, mentioning the two boys' companies and the court performance, and giving the name of the playwright as "T. Middleton."  Both Watson and Barber accept the 1608 text as authoritative, the former writing that "It is most probable that the copy for Q1 was the author's foul papers or a fair copy of these which Middleton made for sale to the company.

It is at any rate unlikely that the play was printed from an acting copy." Barber also states that there is nothing in the 1608 quarto "to suggest that it was a prompt-copy or was marked for playhouse use—no instructions or advance warnings to actors or effects-men. On the contrary, there are positive signs that it was not . . . ." G. R. Price has discussed the whole problem in "The Early Editions of *A Trick to Catch the Old One*" (*The Library*, 1967). The play was still alive as an acting play during the early years of the Restoration, since John Downes, the prompter at the Duke's Playhouse, recorded that it was one of a group of old plays given between 1662 and 1665 at D'avenant's theater in Lincoln's-Inn-Fields (*Roscius Anglicanus*, 1708). This is the last heard of it on the stage until it was revived at the Mermaid Theater in London in October 1952.

The present text is based on photostats of the copy of the 1608 quarto, with readings from a photostat of the 1616 text—both in the possession of the Huntington Library in San Marino, California.

# A TRICK TO CATCH THE OLD ONE

BY

THOMAS MIDDLETON

*[DRAMATIS PERSONÆ*

Theodorus Witgood.
Pecunius Lucre, *his uncle.*
Walkadine Hoard.
Onesiphorus Hoard, *his brother.*
Limber
Kix
Lamprey            } *friends of Hoard.*
Spichcock
Harry Dampit    } *usurers.*
Gulf
Sam Freedom, *son of Mistress Lucre.*
Moneylove.

Sir Lancelot.
Host.
George, *Lucre's servant.*
Arthur, *Hoard's servant.*
Creditors, Gentlemen, Drawer, Boy
    Scrivener, Servants, *etc.*

Courtesan.
Mistress Lucre.
Joyce, *Hoard's niece.*
Lady Foxstone.
Audrey, *Dampit's servant.*

Scene: *Leicestershire and London.*

Time: *Contemporary.*

Actus I. Scena i.

*A street in a town in Leicestershire.]*

*Enter Witgood, a gentleman, solus.*

Wit. All's gone! Still thou'rt a gentleman—that's all; but a poor one—that's nothing. What milk brings thy meadows forth now? Where are thy goodly uplands and thy downlands? All sunk into that little pit, lechery. Why should a gallant pay but two shillings for his ordinary[2] that nourishes him, and twenty times two for his brothel that consumes him? But where's Longacre?[3] In my uncle's conscience, [10 which is three years' voyage about. He that sets out upon his conscience ne'er finds the way home again; he is either swallowed in the quicksands of law quillets,[4] or splits upon the piles of a præmunire. Yet these old fox-brained and ox-browed uncles have still defenses for their avarice, and apologies for their practices, and will thus greet our follies:

He that doth his youth expose        20
    To brothel, drink, and danger,
Let him that is his nearest kin
    Cheat him before a stranger—

and that's his uncle; 'tis a principle in usury. I dare not visit the city; there I should be too soon visited by that horrible plague, my debts, and by that means I lose a virgin's love, her portion, and her virtues. Well, how should a man live now that has no living—hum? Why, are there not [30 a million of men in the world that only sojourn upon their brain, and make their wits their mercers; and am I but one amongst that million, and cannot thrive upon 't? Any trick, out of the compass of law, now would come happily to me.

*Enter Courtesan.*

Cour. My love!
Wit. My loathing! Hast thou been the secret consumption of my purse, and now

---

[1] The title continues: "As It Hath Been Often in Action, Both at Paul's and the Blackfriars. Presented before His Majesty on New Year's Night Last. Composed by T. M." [2] Inn.
[3] A general name for an estate. [4] Quibbles.

375

com'st to undo my last means, my [40
wits? Wilt leave no virtue in me, and yet
thou ne'er the better?

　　Hence, courtesan, round-webbed taran-
　　　tula,[1]
　　That dryest the roses in the cheeks of
　　　youth!

Cour. I have been true unto your
pleasure; and all your lands thrice racked [2]
was never worth the jewel which I prodigally gave you, my virginity.

　　Lands mortgaged may return, and more
　　　esteemed,
　　But honesty,[3] once pawned, is ne'er re-
　　　deemed.                                     50

Wit. Forgive; I do thee wrong

　　To make thee sin, and then to chide thee
　　　for 't.

Cour. I know I am your loathing now.
Farewell.

Wit. Stay, best invention,[4] stay!

Cour. I that have been the secret consumption of your purse, shall I stay now to
undo your last means, your wits? Hence,
courtesan, away!

Wit. I prithee, make me not mad at my
own weapon.  Stay (a thing few [60
women can do, I know that, and therefore
they had need wear stays); be not contrary.
Dost love me? Fate has so cast [5] it that all
my means I must derive from thee.

Cour. From me? Be happy then;

　　What lies within the power of my per-
　　　formance
　　Shall be commanded of thee.

Wit.                                Spoke like
　　An honest drab, i' faith! It may prove
　　　something.
　　What trick is not an embryon at first,
　　Until a perfect shape come over it?       70

Cour. Come, I must help you.  Whereabouts left you?

　　I'll proceed.
　　Though you beget, 'tis I must help to
　　　breed.
　　Speak, what is 't? I'd fain conceive it.

Wit. So, so, so.  Thou shalt presently
take the name and form upon thee of a rich

---

country widow, four hundred a year valiant [6] in woods, in bullocks, in barns, and
in rye stacks. We'll to London, and to my
covetous uncle.                                80

Cour. I begin to applaud thee; our
states being both desperate, they are soon
resolute. But how for horses?

Wit. Mass, that's true; the jest will be
of some continuance.  Let me see; horses
now, a bots [7] on 'em!  Stay, I have acquaintance with a mad host, never yet
bawd to thee.  I have rinsed the whoreson's
gums in mull-sack [8] many a time and often.
Put but a good tale into his ear now,  [90
so it come off cleanly, and there's horse
and man for us, I dare warrant thee.

Cour. Arm your wits then speedily;

　　There shall want nothing in me, either in
　　　behavior, discourse, or fashion,
　　That shall discredit your intended pur-
　　　pose.
　　I will so artfully disguise my wants,
　　And set so good a courage on my state,
　　That I will be believed.

Wit. Why, then, all's furnished.  [100
I shall go nigh to catch that old fox, mine
uncle, though he make but some amends
for my undoing.  Yet there's some comfort
in 't: he cannot otherwise choose (though
it be but in hope to cozen me again) but
supply any hasty want that I bring to town
with me.  The device well and cunningly
carried, the name of a rich widow and four
hundred a year in good earth will so conjure up a kind of usurer's love in him  [110
to me that he will not only desire my
presence—which at first shall scarce be
granted him; I'll keep off a [9] purpose—but
I shall find him so officious to deserve, so
ready to supply! I know the state of an old
man's affection so well: if his nephew be
poor indeed, why, he lets God alone with
him;[10] but, if he be once rich, then he'll be
the first man that helps him.

Cour. 'Tis right the world;[11] for,  [120
in these days, an old man's love to his
kindred is like his kindness to his wife—
'tis always done before he comes at it.

Wit. I owe thee for that jest.  Begone!
Here's all my wealth; prepare thyself.
Away! I'll to mine host with all possible

---

[1] Here and in a few other passages the original
prose has been changed into verse. Later, some
line divisions have also been regularized.
[2] Rented at excessively high rates.
[3] Chastity.
[4] Referring to her as the instrument for his
plan described below.        [5] Planned.

[6] Worth.     [9] On.     [10] Leaves him to God.
[7] Plague.   [11] Exactly the way of the world.
[8] Spiced and heated wine.

haste, and, with the best art and most profitable form, pour the sweet circumstance into his ear, which shall have the gift to turn all the wax to honey.—[*Exit* [130 *Courtesan.*] How now? O, the right worshipful seniors of our country!

[*Enter Onesiphorus Hoard, Limber, and Kix.*] [1]

O. Hoa. Who's that?

Lim. O, the common rioter; take no note of him.

Wit. [*Aside.*] You will not see me now; the comfort is,

Ere it be long you will scarce see yourselves.     [*Exit.*]

O. Hoa. I wonder how he breathes; h'as consumed all

Upon that courtesan.

Lim.     We have heard so much.

O. Hoa. You have heard all truth. His uncle and my brother     140

Have been these three years mortal adversaries.

Two old, tough spirits, they seldom meet but fight,

Or quarrel when 'tis calmest. I think their anger

Be the very fire that keeps their age alive.

Lim. What was the quarrel, sir?

O. Hoa. Faith, about a purchase,[2] fetching over a young heir. Master Hoard, my brother, having wasted much time in beating the bargain, what did me old Lucre, but, as his conscience moved him, knowing [150 the poor gentleman, stepped in between 'em and cozened him himself.

Lim. And was this all, sir?

O. Hoa. This was e'en it, sir; yet for all this I know no reason but the match might go forward betwixt his wife's son and my niece. What though there be a dissension between the two old men? I see no reason it should put a difference between the two younger; 'tis as natural for old folks [160 to fall out as for young to fall in. A scholar comes a-wooing to my niece; well, he's wise, but he's poor. Her son comes a-wooing to my niece; well, he's a fool, but he's rich.

Lim. Ay, marry, sir?

O. Hoa. Pray now, is not a rich fool better than a poor philosopher?

Lim. One would think so, i' faith.

O. Hoa. She now remains at London with my brother, her second uncle, [170 to learn fashions, practice music; the voice between her lips, and the viol between her legs, she'll be fit for a consort [3] very speedily. A thousand good pound is her portion; if she marry, we'll ride up and be merry.

Kix. A match, if it be a match. *Exeunt.*

[Scena ii.

*Another street in the same town.*]

*Enter at one door, Witgood; at the other, Host.*

Wit. Mine host!

Host. Young Master Witgood.

Wit. I have been laying[4] all the town for thee.

Host. Why, what's the news, bully[5] Hadland?

Wit. What geldings are in the house, of thine own? Answer me to that first.

Host. Why, man, why?

Wit. Mark me what I say. I'll [10 tell thee such a tale in thine ear that thou shalt trust me spite of thy teeth, furnish me with some money willy-nilly, and ride up with me thyself *contra voluntatem et professionem.*[6]

Host. How? Let me see this trick, and I'll say thou hast more art than a conjuror.

Wit. Dost thou joy in my advancement?     20

Host. Do I love sack and ginger?

Wit. Comes my prosperity desiredly to thee?

Host. Come forfeitures to a usurer, fees to an officer, punks[7] to an host, and pigs to a parson desiredly? Why, then, la![8]

Wit. Will the report of a widow of four hundred a year, boy, make thee leap and sing and dance, and come to thy place again?     30

Host. Wilt thou command me now? I am thy spirit; conjure me into any shape.

Wit. I ha' brought her from her friends, turned back the horses by a sleight; not

---

[1] These characters, represented in the speech heads of the original by the numbers 1, 2, and 3 only, were first identified by Dyce. The following speech heads have been altered accordingly.     [2] Assignation of property.

[3] With the double meaning, *band of musicians* and *husband.*     [4] Searching.     [5] A fine fellow.
[6] Contrary to your wish and profession.
[7] Whores.     [8] Lo, look.

378    A TRICK TO CATCH THE OLD ONE    I, iii.

so much as one amongst her six men, goodly, large, yeomanly fellows, will she trust with this her purpose—by this light, all unmanned,[1] regardless of her state, neglectful of vainglorious ceremony, all for my love. O, 'tis a fine little vol- [40 uble tongue, mine host, that wins a widow!

Host. No, 'tis a tongue with a great T, my boy, that wins a widow.

Wit. Now, sir, the case stands thus. Good mine host, if thou lov'st my happiness, assist me.

Host. Command all my beasts i' th' house.

Wit. Nay, that's not all neither. Prithee, take truce with thy joy, and listen to me. Thou know'st I have a wealthy [50 uncle i' th' city, somewhat the wealthier by my follies. The report of this fortune, well and cunningly carried, might be a means to draw some goodness from the usuring rascal, for I have put her in hope already of some estate that I have either in land or money. Now, if I be found true in neither, what may I expect but a sudden breach of our love, utter dissolution of the match, and confusion [60 of my fortunes forever?

Host. Wilt thou but trust the managing of thy business with me?

Wit. With thee? Why, will I desire to thrive in my purpose? Will I hug four hundred a year, I that know the misery of nothing? Will that man wish a rich widow, that has ne'er a hole to put his head in? With thee, mine host? Why, believe it, sooner with thee than with a [70 covey of counselors.

Host. Thank you for your good report, i' faith, sir; and, if I stand you not in stead, why, then, let an host come off *hic et hæc hostis*,[2] a deadly enemy to dice, drink, and venery. Come, where's this widow?

Wit. Hard at Park End.

Host. I'll be her serving-man for once.

Wit. Why, there we let off together, keep full time; my thoughts were strik- [80 ing then just the same number.

Host. I knew 't. Shall we then see our merry days again?

Wit. Our merry nights—[*Aside.*] which ne'er shall be more seen.    *Exeunt.*

[1] Without attendants.
[2] A pun on the meaning *host* and *enemy* is intended.

[Scena iii.

*A street in London.*]

*Enter at several doors old Lucre and old Hoard, Gentlemen [, i.e., Lamprey, Spichcock, Freedom, and Moneylove,] coming between them to pacify 'em.*

Lamp. Nay, good Master Lucre, and you, Master Hoard, anger is the wind which you're both too much troubled withal.

Hoard. Shall my adversary thus daily affront me, ripping up the old wound of our malice, which three summers could not close up, into which wound the very sight of him drops scalding lead instead of balsamum?    10

Luc. Why, Hoard, Hoard, Hoard, Hoard, Hoard! May I not pass in the state of quietness to mine own house? Answer me to that, before witness, and why? I'll refer the cause to honest, even-minded gentlemen, or require the mere indifferences[3] of the law to decide this matter. I got the purchase, true. Was 't not any man's case? Yes. Will a wise man stand as a bawd, whilst another wipes [20 his nose[4] of the bargain? No; I answer no in that case.

Lamp. Nay, sweet Master Lucre.

Hoard. Was it the part of a friend? No, rather of a Jew. Mark what I say— when I had beaten the bush to the last bird, or, as I may term it, the price to a pound, then, like a cunning usurer, to come in the evening of the bargain and glean all my hopes in a minute, to en- [30 ter, as it were, at the back door of the purchase? For thou ne'er cam'st the right way by it.

Luc. Hast thou the conscience to tell me so without any impeachment to thyself?

Hoard. Thou that canst defeat thy own nephew, Lucre, lap his lands into bonds, and take the extremity of thy kindred's forfeitures, because he's a [40 rioter, a wastethrift, a brothel-master, and so forth—what may a stranger expect from thee but *vulnera dilacerata*,[5] as the poet says, dilacerate dealing?

[3] Impartialities.    [5] Lacerated wounds.
[4] *I.e.*, cheats him.

Luc. Upbraidest thou me with nephew? Is all imputation laid upon me? What acquaintance have I with his follies? If he riot, 'tis he must want it; if he surfeit, 'tis he must feel it; if he drab it, 'tis he must lie by 't. What's this to me? 50

Hoard. What's all to thee? Nothing, nothing; such is the gulf of thy desire and the wolf of thy conscience. But be assured, old Pecunius Lucre, if ever fortune so bless me that I may be at leisure to vex thee, or any means so favor me that I may have opportunity to mad thee, I will pursue it with that flame of hate, spirit of malice, unrepressed wrath, that I will blast thy comforts. 60

Luc. Ha, ha, ha!

Lamp. Nay, Master Hoard, you're a wise gentleman—

Hoard. I will so cross thee—

Luc. And I thee.

Hoard. So without mercy fret thee—

Luc. So monstrously oppose thee—

Hoard. Dost scoff at my just anger? O, that I had as much power as usury has over thee! 70

Luc. Then thou wouldst have as much power as the devil has over thee.

Hoard. Toad!

Luc. Aspic!

Hoard. Serpent!

Luc. Viper!

Spi. Nay, gentlemen, then we must divide you perforce.

Lamp. When the fire grows too unreasonable hot, there's no better way [80 than to take off the wood.

*Exeunt. Mane[n]t* [1] *Sam* [Freedom] *and Moneylove.*

Sam. A word, good signior.

Mon. How now, what's the news?

Sam. 'Tis given me to understand that you are a rival of mine in the love of Mistress Joyce, Master Hoard's niece. Say me ay, say me no?

Mon. Yes, 'tis so.

Sam. Then look to yourself. You cannot live long; I'm practicing every [90 morning. A month hence I'll challenge you.

Mon. Give me your hand upon 't; there's my pledge I'll meet you.

*Strikes him. Exit.*

Sam. O, O! What reason had you for that, sir, to strike before the month? You knew I was not ready for you, and that made you so crank.[2] I am not such a coward to strike again, I warrant you. My ear has the law of her side, for it burns [100 horribly. I will teach him to strike a naked face, the longest day of his life. 'Slid,[3] it shall cost me some money, but I'll bring this box into the chancery. *Exit.*

[Scena iv.

*Another street in London.*]

*Enter Witgood and the Host.*

Host. Fear you nothing, sir; I have lodged her in a house of credit, I warrant you.

Wit. Hast thou the writings?

Host. Firm, sir.

Wit. Prithee, stay, and behold two the most prodigious rascals that ever slipped into the shape of men—Dampit, sirrah, and young Gulf, his fellow caterpillar. 10

Host. Dampit? Sure, I have heard of that Dampit.

Wit. Heard of him? Why, man, he that has lost both his ears may hear of him—a famous, infamous trampler of time:[4] his own phrase. Note him well. That Dampit, sirrah, he in the uneven beard and the serge cloak, is the most notorious, usuring, blasphemous, atheistical, brothel-vomiting rascal that we [20 have in these latter times now extant, whose first beginning was the stealing of a masty[5] dog from a farmer's house.

Host. He looked as if he would obey the commandment well, when he began first with stealing.

Wit. True. The next town he came at, he set the dogs together by th' ears.

Host. A sign he should follow the law, by my faith. 30

Wit. So it followed, indeed; and, being destitute of all fortunes, staked his masty against a noble,[6] and by great fortune his dog had the day. How he made it up ten shillings, I know not, but his own boast is that he came to town with but

---

[1] Remain.

[2] Lively.     [3] God's eyelid, a mild oath.
[4] Lawyer.     [5] Mastiff.     [6] Gold coin.

ten shillings in his purse, and now is credibly worth ten thousand pound.

HOST. How the devil came he by it?

*[Enter Dampit and Gulf.]*

WIT. [*Aside.*] How the devil came [40 he not by it? If you put in the devil once, riches come with a vengeance. H'as been a trampler of the law, sir; and the devil has a care of his footmen. The rogue has spied me now; he nibbled me finely once, too.—A pox search you!—[*Turns to Dampit.*] O, Master Dampit!—[*Aside.*] The very loins of thee!—Cry you mercy,[1] Master Gulf; you walk so low I promise you I saw you not, sir.                              50

GULF. He that walks low walks safe, the poets tell us.

WIT. [*Aside.*] And nigher hell by a foot and a half than the rest of his fellows.— But, my old Harry!

DAMP. My sweet Theodorus!

WIT. 'Twas a merry world when thou cam'st to town with ten shillings in thy purse.

DAMP. And now worth ten thou- [60 sand pound, my boy. Report it. Harry Dampit, a trampler of time, say, he would be up in a morning, and be here with his serge gown, dashed up to the hams in a cause, have his feet stink about Westminster Hall and come home again, see the galleons, the galleasses. the great armadoes [2] of the law; then there be hoys and petty vessels, oars [3] and scullers of the time. There be picklocks of the [70 time too. Then would I be here; I would trample up and down like a mule. Now to the judges: "May it please your reverend-honorable fatherhoods!" Then to my counselor: "May it please your worshipful patience!" Then to the examiner's office: "May it please your mastership's gentleness!" Then to one of the clerks: "May it please your worshipful lousiness!"—for I find him scrubbing in [80 his codpiece. Then to the hall again, then to the chamber again—

WIT. And when to the cellar again?

DAMP. E'en when thou wilt again. Tramplers of time, motions [4] of Fleet Street, and visions of Holborn! Here I have fees of one, there I have fees of another; my clients come about me, the fooliaminy [5] and coxcombry of the country. I still trashed [6] and trotted for [90 other men's causes. Thus was poor Harry Dampit made rich by others' laziness, who though they would not follow their own suits, I made 'em follow me with their purses.

WIT. Didst thou so, old Harry?

DAMP. Ay, and I soused 'em with bills of charges, i' faith; twenty pound a year have I brought in for boat hire, and I ne'er stepped into boat in my life.        100

WIT. Tramplers of time!

DAMP. Ay, tramplers of time, rascals of time, bull-beggars! [7]

WIT. Ah, thou'rt a mad old Harry!— Kind Master Gulf, I am bold to renew my acquaintance.

GULF. I embrace it, sir.        *Exeunt.*

MUSIC.

*Incipit* [8]

ACT[US] II. [SCENA i.

*A room in Lucre's house.*]

*Enter Lucre.*

LUC. My adversary evermore twits me with my nephew, forsooth, my nephew. Why may not a virtuous uncle have a dissolute nephew? What though he be a brotheler, a wastethrift, a common surfeiter, and, to conclude, a beggar? Must sin in him call up shame in me? Since we have no part in their follies, why should we have part in their infamies? For my strict hand toward his mortgage, that I deny not; [10 I confess I had an uncle's pen'worth. Let me see, half in half; true. I saw neither hope of his reclaiming nor comfort in his being, and was it not then better bestowed upon his uncle than upon one of his aunts? —I need not say bawd, for everyone knows what "aunt" stands for in the last translation.[9]—

---

[1] I beg your pardon.
[2] Armadas, large warships.
[3] Rowboats.
[4] Puppet shows.

[5] One of Dampit's coinages.
[6] Tramped.
[7] Hobgoblins.
[8] Begins.
[9] Tralation, metaphor.

*[Enter Servant.]*

Now, sir?

SER.[1] There's a country serving- [20 man, sir, attends to speak with your worship.

Luc. I'm at best leisure now; send him in to me.                    *[Exit Servant.]*

*Enter Host like a serving-man.*

HOST. Bless your venerable worship.

Luc. Welcome, good fellow.

HOST. [*Aside.*] He calls me thief[2] at first sight, yet he little thinks I am an host.

Luc. What's thy business with me?

HOST. Faith, sir, I am sent from [30 my mistress to any sufficient gentleman indeed, to ask advice upon a doubtful point. 'Tis indifferent, sir, to whom I come, for I know none, nor did my mistress direct me to any particular man, for she's as mere[3] a stranger here as myself; only I found your worship within, and 'tis a thing I ever loved, sir, to be despatched as soon as I can.

Luc. [*Aside.*] A good, blunt honesty; I like him well.—What is thy mistress? [40

HOST. Faith, a country gentlewoman, and a widow, sir. Yesterday was the first flight of us; but now she intends to stay till a little term[4] business be ended.

Luc. Her name, I prithee?

HOST. It runs there in the writings, sir, among her lands: Widow Medler.

Luc. Medler? Mass, have I ne'er heard of that widow?

HOST. Yes, I warrant you, have [50 you, sir; not the rich widow in Staffordshire?

Luc. Cud's[5] me, there 'tis indeed; thou hast put me into memory. There's a widow indeed; ah, that I were a bachelor again!

HOST. No doubt your worship might do much then; but she's fairly promised to a bachelor already.

Luc. Ah, what is he, I prithee?

HOST. A country gentleman too, [60 one whom your worship knows not, I'm sure; h'as spent some few follies in his youth, but marriage, by my faith, begins to call him home. My mistress loves him,

sir, and love covers faults, you know: one Master Witgood, if ever you have heard of the gentleman.

Luc. Ha! Witgood, say'st thou?

HOST. That's his name indeed, sir my mistress is like to bring him to a goodly [70 seat yonder—four hundred a year, by my faith.

Luc. But, I pray, take me with you.[6]

HOST. Ay, sir.

Luc. What countryman might this young Witgood be?

HOST. A Leicestershire gentleman, sir.

Luc. [*Aside.*] My nephew, by th' Mass, my nephew! I'll fetch out more of this, i' faith. A simple country fellow! I'll [80 work 't out of him.—And is that gentleman, say'st thou, presently[7] to marry her?

HOST. Faith, he brought her up to town, sir; h'as the best card in all the bunch for 't, her heart; and I know my mistress will be married ere she go down.[8] Nay, I'll swear that, for she's none of those widows that will go down first, and be married after; she hates that, I can tell you, sir.

Luc. By my faith, sir, she is like to [90 have a proper gentleman and a comely; I'll give her that gift.

HOST. Why, does your worship know him, sir?

Luc. I know him? Does not all the world know him? Can a man of such exquisite qualities be hid under a bushel?

HOST. Then your worship may save me a labor, for I had charge given me to inquire after him.                    100

Luc. Inquire of him? If I might counsel thee, thou shouldst ne'er trouble thyself further; inquire of him no more but of me; I'll fit thee. I grant he has been youthful, but is he not now reclaimed? Mark you that, sir. Has not your mistress, think you, been wanton in her youth? If men be wags, are there not women wagtails?

HOST. No doubt, sir.

Luc. Does not he return wisest [110 that comes home whipped with his own follies?

HOST. Why, very true, sir.

Luc. The worst report you can hear of him, I can tell you, is that he has been a kind gentleman, a liberal, and a worthy.

---

[1] Original reads *Ser. 2.*
[2] *Good fellow* was a cant phrase for *thief.*
[3] Absolute.                    [5] God's.
[4] Pertaining to court sessions.

[6] Tell me your meaning.
[7] Immediately.        [8] *I.e.,* to the country.

Who but lusty Witgood, thrice-noble Witgood!

Host. Since your worship has so much knowledge in him, can you resolve [120 me, sir, what his living might be? My duty binds me, sir, to have a care of my mistress' estate; she has been ever a good mistress to me, though I say it. Many wealthy suitors has she nonsuited for his sake; yet, though her love be so fixed, a man cannot tell whether his non-performance may help to remove it, sir; he makes us believe he has lands and living.

Luc. Who, young Master Wit- [130 good? Why, believe it, he has as goodly a fine living out yonder—what do you call the place?

Host. Nay, I know not, i' faith.

Luc. Hum—see, like a beast, if I have not forgot the name—pooh! And out yonder again, goodly grown woods and fair meadows—pax [1] on 't, I can ne'er hit of that place neither. He? Why, he's Witgood of Witgood Hall. He an un- [140 known thing?

Host. Is he so, sir? To see how rumor will alter! Trust me, sir, we heard once he had no lands, but all lay mortgaged to an uncle he has in town here.

Luc. Push! [2] 'Tis a tale, 'tis a tale.

Host. I can assure you, sir, 'twas credibly reported to my mistress.

Luc. Why, do you think, i' faith, he was ever so simple to mortgage his lands [150 to his uncle, or his uncle so unnatural to take the extremity of such a mortgage?

Host. That was my saying still, sir.

Luc. Pooh, ne'er think it.

Host. Yet that report goes current.

Luc. Nay, then you urge me. Cannot I tell that best that am his uncle?

Host. How, sir? What have I done!

Luc. Why, how now! In a sown, [3] man?

Host. Is your worship his uncle, [160 sir?

Luc. Can that be any harm to you, sir?

Host. I do beseech you, sir, do me the favor to conceal it. What a beast was I to utter so much! Pray, sir, do me the kindness to keep it in; I shall have my coat pulled o'er my ears, an 't [4] should be known; for the truth is, an 't please your worship, to prevent much rumor and many suitors,

they intend to be married very sud- [170 denly and privately.

Luc. And dost thou think it stands with my judgment to do them injury? Must I needs say the knowledge of this marriage comes from thee? Am I a fool at fifty-four? Do I lack subtilty now, that have got all my wealth by it? There's a leash of angels [5] for thee. Come, let me woo thee; speak, where lie they?

Host. So I might have no anger, [180 sir—

Luc. Passion of me, not a jot. Prithee, come.

Host. I would not have it known it came by my means.

Luc. Why, am I a man of wisdom?

Host. I dare trust your worship, sir; but I'm a stranger to your house; and to avoid all intelligencers, [6] I desire your worship's ear. 190

Luc. [Aside.] This fellow's worth a matter of trust.—Come, sir. [Host whispers to him.] Why, now, thou'rt an honest lad.— [Aside.] Ah, Sirrah Nephew!

Host. Please you, sir, now I have begun with your worship, when shall I attend for your advice upon that doubtful point? I must come warily now.

Luc. Tut, fear thou nothing; tomorrow's evening shall resolve the doubt. 200

Host. The time shall cause my attendance. *Exit.*

Luc. Fare thee well.—There's more true honesty in such a country serving-man than in a hundred of our cloak companions; [7] I may well call 'em companions, for, since blue coats [8] have been turned into cloaks, we can scarce know the man from the master.—George!

[*Enter George.*]

Geo. Anon, [8] sir? 210

Luc. List hither. [*Whispers.*] Keep the place secret. Commend me to my nephew; I know no cause, tell him, but he might see his uncle.

Geo. I will, sir.

Luc. And, do you hear, sir, take heed you use him with respect and duty.

Geo. [*Aside.*] Here's a strange alteration! One day he must be turned out like

[5] Three gold coins.    [8] Servants' livery.
[6] Informers.    [9] At once.
[7] Servants, knaves.

---

[1] Pox.    [2] Pish!    [3] Swoon.    [4] If it.

a beggar, and now he must be called [220
in like a knight. *Exit.*

Luc. Ah, sirrah, that rich widow! Four
hundred a year! Beside, I hear she lays
claim to a title of a hundred more. This
falls unhappily that he should bear a
grudge to me now, being likely to prove so
rich. What is 't, trow,[1] that he makes me a
stranger for? Hum—I hope he has not so
much wit to apprehend that I cozened him.
He deceives me then? Good heaven, [230
who would have thought it would ever
have come to this pass! Yet he's a proper
gentleman, i' faith, give him his due—
marry, that's his mortgage; but that I
ne'er mean to give him. I'll make him rich
enough in words, if that be good, and, if it
come to a piece of money, I will not greatly
stick for 't. There may be hope some of
the widow's lands, too, may one day fall
upon me, if things be carried wisely.—[240

*[Enter George.]*

Now, sir, where is he?

Geo. He desires your worship to hold
him excused; he has such weighty business it commands him wholly from all men.

Luc. Were those my nephew's words?

Geo. Yes, indeed, sir.

Luc. [*Aside.*] When men grow rich,
they grow proud too, I perceive that. He
would not have sent me such an answer
once within this twelvemonth. See [250
what 'tis when a man comes to his lands!—
Return to him again, sir; tell him his uncle
desires his company for an hour. I'll trouble him but an hour, say; 'tis for his own
good, tell him. And, do you hear, sir, put
"worship" upon him. Go to, do as I bid
you; he's like to be a gentleman of worship
very shortly.

Geo. [*Aside.*] This is good sport, i'
faith. *Exit.* 260

Luc. Troth, he uses his uncle discour-
teously now. Can he tell what I may do
for him? Goodness may come from me
in a minute, that comes not in seven year
again. He knows my humor; I am not so
usually good. 'Tis no small thing that
draws kindness from me; he may know
that and[2] he will. The chief cause that
invites me to do him most good is the

[1] An exclamation of indignant surprise.   [2] If.

sudden astonishing of old Hoard, [270
my adversary. How pale his malice will
look at my nephew's advancement! With
what a dejected spirit he will behold his
fortunes, whom but last day he proclaimed
rioter, penurious makeshift, despised brothel-master! Ha, ha! 'Twill do me more
secret joy than my last purchase, more
precious comfort than all these widow's
revenues.—Now, sir—

*Enter Witgood [, shown in by George].*

Geo. With much entreaty he's at [280
length come, sir. *[Exit.]*

Luc. O, nephew, let me salute you, sir!
You're welcome, nephew.

Wit. Uncle, I thank you.

Luc. Y'ave a fault, nephew; you're a
stranger here. Well, heaven give you
joy!

Wit. Of what, sir?

Luc. Hah, we can hear!
   You might have known your uncle's
      house, i' faith,                      290
   You and your widow. Go to, you were
      to blame,
   If I may tell you so without offense.

Wit. How could you hear of that, sir?

Luc.                        O, pardon me!
   It was your will to have kept it from me,
      I perceive now.

Wit. Not for any defect of love, I protest, uncle.

Luc. O, 'twas unkindness,[3] nephew! Fie,
fie, fie!

Wit. I am sorry you take it in that
sense, sir.                                 300

Luc. Pooh, you cannot color it, i' faith,
nephew.

Wit. Will you but hear what I can say
in my just excuse, sir?

Luc. Yes, faith, will I, and welcome.

Wit. You that know my danger i' th'
city, sir, so well, how great my debts are,
and how extreme my creditors, could not
out of your pure judgment, sir, have
wished us hither.                           310

Luc. Mass, a firm reason indeed.

Wit. Else, my uncle's house, why, 't 'ad
been the only make-match—

Luc. Nay, and thy credit.

Wit. My credit? Nay, my counte-

[3] Perhaps *unnaturalness*, forgetfulness of the
relationship due a relative.

nance. Push, nay, I know, uncle, you would have wrought it so by your wit you would have made her believe in time the whole house had been mine. 319

Luc. Ay, and most of the goods too—

Wit. La, you there! Well, let 'em all prate what they will, there's nothing like the bringing of a widow to one's uncle's house.

Luc. Nay, let nephews be ruled as they list, they shall find their uncle's house the most natural place when all's done.

Wit. There they may be bold.

Luc. Life, they may do anything there, man, and fear neither beadle nor som- [330 ner.[1] An uncle's house! A very Cole Harbor.[2] Sirrah, I'll touch thee near now. Hast thou so much interest in thy widow that by a token thou couldst presently send for her?

Wit. Troth, I think I can, uncle.

Luc. Go to, let me see that.

Wit. Pray, command one of your men hither, uncle.

Luc. George! 340

*[Enter George.]*

Geo. Here, sir.

Luc. Attend my nephew.—[*Witgood whispers to George, who goes out.—Aside.*] I love a' life [3] to prattle with a rich widow; 'tis pretty, methinks, when our tongues go together—and then to promise much and perform little. I love that sport a' life, i' faith; yet I am in the mood now to do my nephew some good, if he take me handsomely.—What, have you despatched? 350

Wit. I ha' sent, sir.

Luc. Yet I must condemn you of un- kindness, nephew.

Wit. Heaven forbid, uncle!

Luc. Yes, faith, must I. Say your debts be many, your creditors importunate, yet the kindness of a thing is all, nephew. You might have sent me close [4] word on 't with- out the least danger or prejudice to your fortunes. 360

Wit. Troth, I confess it, uncle; I was to blame there; but, indeed, my intent was to have clapped it up suddenly, and

so have broke forth like a joy to my friends, and a wonder to the world. Beside, there's a trifle of a forty pound matter toward the setting of me forth; my friends should ne'er have known on 't; I meant to make shift for that myself.

Luc. How, nephew? Let me not [370 hear such a word again, I beseech you. Shall I be beholding [5] to you?

Wit. To me? Alas, what do you mean, uncle?

Luc. I charge you, upon my love, you trouble nobody but myself.

Wit. Y'ave no reason for that, uncle.

Luc. Troth, I'll ne'er be friends with you while you live, and you do.

Wit. Nay, and you say so, uncle, [380 here's my hand; I will not do 't—

Luc. Why, well said! There's some hope in thee when thou wilt be ruled. I'll make it up fifty, faith, because I see thee so re- claimed. Peace; here comes my wife with Sam, her tother [6] husband's son.

*[Enter Mistress Lucre and Sam Freedom.]*

Wit. Good aunt—

Sam. Cousin Witgood! I rejoice in my salute; you're most welcome to this noble city, governed with the sword in the [390 scabbard.

Wit. [*Aside.*] And the wit in the pom- mel.[7]—Good Master Sam Freedom, I re- turn the salute.

Luc. By the Mass, she's coming, wife; let me see now how thou wilt entertain her.

Wife. I hope I am not to learn, sir, to entertain a widow; 'tis not so long ago since I was one myself.

*[Enter Courtesan.]*

Wit. Uncle— 400

Luc. She's come indeed.

Wit. My uncle was desirous to see you, widow, and I presumed to invite you.

Cour. The presumption was nothing, Master Witgood. Is this your uncle, sir?

Luc. Marry am I, sweet widow; and his good uncle he shall find me; ay, by this smack that I give thee [*Kisses her.*], thou'rt welcome.—Wife, bid the widow welcome the same way again. 410

---

[1] Summoner.
[2] Cold Harbor, where debtors found sanctuary.
[3] As life, dearly.  [4] Secret.

[5] Beholden.  [6] Other.
[7] The amount of wit in the knob on the hilt of a sword; *i.e.*, no wit at all.

SAM. [*Aside.*] I am a gentleman now too by my father's occupation, and I see no reason but I may kiss a widow by my father's copy;[1] truly, I think the charter[2] is not against it. Surely these are the words, "The son, once a gentleman, may revel it, though his father were a dauber"[3] —'tis about the fifteen page. I'll to her. [*Attempts to kiss the Courtesan, who rebuffs him.*]

LUC. Y' are not very busy now; a word with thee, sweet widow—      420

SAM. [*Aside.*] Coad's nigs![4] I was never so disgraced since the hour my mother whipped me.

LUC. Beside, I have no child of mine own to care for; she's my second wife, old, past bearing. Clap sure to him, widow; he's like to be my heir, I can tell you.

COUR. Is he so, sir?

LUC. He knows it already, and the knave's proud on 't; jolly rich widows [430 have been offered him here i' th' city, great merchants' wives; and do you think he will once look upon 'em? Forsooth, he'll none. You are beholding to him i' th' country, then, ere we could be; nay, I'll hold a wager, widow, if he were once known to be in town, he would be presently sought after; nay, and happy were they that could catch him first.

COUR. I think so.      440

LUC. O, there would be such running to and fro, widow! He should not pass the streets for 'em; he'd be took up in one great house or other presently. Fah! They know he has it, and must have it. You see this house here, widow; this house and all comes to him, goodly rooms, ready furnished, ceiled with plaster of Paris, and all hung about with cloth of arras.—Nephew!

WIT. Sir.      450

LUC. Show the widow your house; carry her into all the rooms, and bid her welcome.—You shall see, widow.—[*Aside to Witgood.*] Nephew, strike all sure above and thou beest a good boy—ah!

WIT. Alas, sir, I know not how she would take it!

LUC. The right way, I warrant t'ee. A pox, art an ass? Would I were in thy stead! Get you up; I am ashamed of you.— [460

[*Exeunt Witgood and Courtesan.*] So, let 'em agree as they will now. Many a match has been struck up in my house a[5] this fashion. Let 'em try all manner of ways, still there's nothing like an uncle's house to strike the stroke in. I'll hold my wife in talk a little. —Now, 'Ginny, your son there goes a-wooing to a poor gentlewoman but of a thousand portion. See my nephew, a lad of less hope, strikes at four hundred [470 a year in good rubbish.[6]

WIFE. Well, we must do as we may, sir.

LUC. I'll have his money ready told[7] for him again[8] he come down. Let me see, too. By th' Mass, I must present the widow with some jewel, a good piece a[9] plate, or such a device; 'twill hearten her on well. I have a very fair standing cup; and a good high standing cup will please a widow above all other pieces.      *Exit.*    480

WIFE. Do you mock us with your nephew?—I have a plot in my head, son— i' faith, husband, to cross you.

SAM. Is it a tragedy plot, or a comedy plot, good mother?

WIFE. 'Tis a plot shall vex him. I charge you, of my blessing, son Sam, that you presently withdraw the action of your love from Master Hoard's niece.

SAM. How, mother!      490

WIFE. Nay, I have a plot in my head, i' faith. Here, take this chain of gold and this fair diamond. Dog me the widow home to her lodging, and at thy best opportunity fasten 'em both upon her. Nay, I have a reach;[10] I can tell you thou art known what thou art, son, among the right worshipful, all the twelve companies.[11]

SAM. Truly, I thank 'em for it.

WIFE. He? He's a scab to thee— [500 and so certify her thou hast two hundred a year of thyself, besides thy good parts—a proper person and a lovely. If I were a widow, I could find in my heart to have thee myself, son; ay, from 'em all.

SAM. Thank you for your good will, mother; but, indeed, I had rather have a stranger. And, if I woo her not in that violent fashion, that I will make her be glad to take these gifts ere I leave [510

---

[1] Property rights.      [2] *I.e.*, of a trade guild.
[3] Plasterer.    [4] God's nigs, a meaningless oath.
[5] In.                  [9] Of.
[6] Money.            [10] Scheme.
[7] Counted.          [11] *I.e.*, of the trade guilds.
[8] Against, by the time that.

her, let me never be called the heir of your body.

WIFE. Nay, I know there's enough in you, son, if you once come to put it forth.

SAM. I'll quickly make a bolt or a shaft on 't.[1]                          *Exeunt.*

[SCENA ii.

*A street in London.*]

*Enter Hoard and Moneylove.*

MON. Faith, Master Hoard, I have bestowed many months in the suit of your niece, such was the dear love I ever bore to her virtues; but, since she hath so extremely denied me, I am to lay out for my fortunes elsewhere.

HOARD. Heaven forbid but you should, sir! I ever told you my niece stood otherwise affected.[2]

MON. I must confess you did, sir; [10 yet, in regard of my great loss of time, and the zeal with which I sought your niece, shall I desire one favor of your worship.

HOARD. In regard of those two, 'tis hard but you shall, sir.

MON. I shall rest grateful. 'Tis not full three hours, sir, since the happy rumor of a rich country widow came to my hearing.

HOARD. How? A rich country widow?

MON. Four hundred a year landed.   20

HOARD. Yea?

MON. Most firm, sir; and I have learnt her lodging. Here my suit begins, sir; if I might but entreat your worship to be a countenance for me, and speak a good word (for your words will pass), I nothing doubt but I might set fair for the widow; nor shall your labor, sir, end altogether in thanks; two hundred angels—

HOARD. So, so. What suitors has [30 she?

MON. There lies the comfort, sir; the report of her is yet but a whisper, and only solicited by young riotous Witgood, nephew to your mortal adversary.

HOARD. Ha! Art certain he's her suitor?

MON. Most certain, sir; and his uncle very industrious to beguile the widow, and make up the match.

HOARD. So? Very good.        40

MON. Now, sir, you know this young

Witgood is a spendthrift, dissolute fellow.

HOARD. A very rascal.

MON. A midnight surfeiter.

HOARD. The spume of a brothel house.

MON. True, sir; which, being well told in your worship's phrase, may both heave him out of her mind, and drive a fair way for me to the widow's affections.

HOARD. Attend me about five.       50

MON. With my best care, sir.      *Exit.*

HOARD. Fool, thou hast left thy treasure with a thief,

To trust a widower with a suit in love! Happy revenge, I hug thee! I have not only the means laid before me, extremely to cross my adversary, and confound the last hopes of his nephew, but thereby to enrich my state, augment my revenues, and build mine own fortunes greater. Ha, ha!

I'll mar your phrase, o'erturn your
        flatteries,                60
Undo your windings, policies, and plots,
Fall like a secret and despatchful plague
On your securéd comforts. Why, I am
        able
To buy three of Lucre, thrice outbid him,
Let my outmonies[3] be reckonéd and all.

*Enter three Creditors.*

1 [CRED.] I am glad of this news.

2 [CRED.] So are we, by my faith.

3 [CRED.] Young Witgood will be a gallant again now.

HOARD. [*Aside.*] Peace!         70

1 [CRED.] I promise you, Master Cockpit, she's a mighty rich widow.

2 [CRED.] Why, have you ever heard of her?

1 [CRED.] Who? Widow Medler? She lies open to much rumor.

3 [CRED.] Four hundred a year, they say, in very good land.

1 [CRED.] Nay, take 't of my word, if you believe that, you believe the least. [80

2 [CRED.] And to see how close he keeps it!

1 [CRED.] O, sir, there's policy in that to prevent better suitors.

3 [CRED.] He owes me a hundred pound, and I protest I ne'er looked for a penny.

1 [CRED.] He little dreams of our coming; he'll wonder to see his creditors upon him.               *Exeunt* [*Creditors*].

---

[1] A proverb meaning *to succeed or fail.*
[2] Was in love with another.
[3] Money put out in loans.

HOARD. Good! His creditors! I'll follow.
    This makes for me.                    90
    All know the widow's wealth; and 'tis
        well known
    I can estate her fairly, ay, and will.
    In this one chance shines a twice happy
        fate;
    I both deject my foe and raise my state.
                                        *Exit.*

MUSIC.

*Incipit*

ACT[US] III. [SCENA i.

*Witgood's room.]*

*Witgood with his Creditors.*

WIT. Why, alas, my creditors, could you
find no other time to undo me but now?
Rather your malice appears in this than the
justness of the debt.

1 [CRED.] Master Witgood, I have forborne my money long.

WIT. I pray, speak low, sir. What do
you mean?

2 [CRED.] We hear you are to be married
suddenly to a rich country widow.      10

WIT. What can be kept so close but you
creditors hear on 't! Well, 'tis a lamentable
state that our chiefest afflictors should first
hear of our fortunes. Why, this is no good
course, i' faith, sirs. If ever you have hope
to be satisfied, why do you seek to confound
the means that should work it? There's
neither piety,[1] no, nor policy in that. Shine
favorably now, why, I may rise and spread
again to your great comforts.          20

1 [CRED.] He says true, i' faith.

WIT. Remove me now, and I consume for-
    ever.

2 [CRED.] Sweet gentleman!

WIT. How can it thrive which from the sun
    you sever?

3 [CRED.] It cannot, indeed.

WIT. O, then, show patience! I shall have
    enough
    To satisfy you all.

1 [CRED.]                Ay, if we could
    Be content, a shame take us!

WIT.                        For, look you,
    I am but newly sure[2] yet to the widow,
    And what a rend might this discredit
        make!                          30

[1] Pity.                    [2] Engaged.

Within these three days will I bind you
    lands
For your securities.

1 [CRED.]        No, good Master Witgood.
    Would 'twere as much as we dare trust
        you with!

WIT. I know you have been kind; how-
    ever, now,
    Either by wrong report or false incite-
        ment
    Your gentleness is injured. In such
    A state as this a man cannot want
        foes.
    If on the sudden he begin to rise,
    No man that lives can count his enemies.
    You had some intelligence, I warrant
        ye,                            40
    From an ill-willer.

2 [CRED.] Faith, we heard you brought
up a rich widow, sir, and were suddenly to
marry her.

WIT. Ay, why, there it was; I knew 'twas
so; but, since you are so well resolved[3] of
my faith toward you, let me be so much
favored of you, I beseech you all—

ALL. O, it shall not need, i' faith,
sir!—                                  50

WIT. As to lie still awhile, and bury my
debts in silence, till I be fully possessed of
the widow; for the truth is—I may tell you
as my friends—

ALL. O—O—O!—

WIT. I am to raise a little money in the
city, toward the setting forth of myself, for
my own credit and your comfort. Now, if
my former debts should be divulged, all
hope of my proceedings were quite  [60
extinguished.

1 [CRED.] Do you hear, sir? I may deserve your custom hereafter. Pray, let my
money be accepted before a stranger's.
Here's forty pound I received as I came to
you. If that may stand you in any stead,
make use on 't. [*Offers money, which Witgood at first refuses.*] Nay, pray, sir; 'tis at
your service.

WIT. You do so ravish me with kindness
    that                               70
    I'm constrained to play the maid, and
        take it.

1 [CRED. (*Aside to Witgood.*)] Let none
of them see it, I beseech you.

WIT. [*Taking money. (Aside.*)] Fah!

[3] Satisfied.

1 [CRED. (*Aside*.)] I hope I shall be first in
    your remembrance
After the marriage rites.
WIT. [*Aside*.]                    Believe it firmly.
    1 [CRED.] So.—What, do you walk, sirs?
    2 [CRED.] I go.—[*Aside to Witgood*.]
Take no care, sir, for money to furnish you;
within this hour I'll send you suffi-  [80
cient.—Come, Master Cockpit, we both
stay for you.
    3 [CRED.] I ha' lost a ring, i' faith; I'll
follow you presently.—[*Exeunt 1 and 2
Creditors*.] But you shall find it, sir. I
know your youth and expenses have dis-
furnished you of all jewels. There's a ruby
of twenty pound price, sir; bestow it upon
your widow. [*Offers a ring, which Witgood
at first refuses*.] What, man! 'Twill  [90
call up her blood to you; beside, if I might
so much work with you, I would not have
you beholding to those bloodsuckers for
any money.
    WIT. [*Taking ring*.] Not I, believe it.
    3 [CRED.] They're a brace of cutthroats.
    WIT. I know 'em.
    3 [CRED.] Send a note of all your wants
to my shop, and I'll supply you instantly.
    WIT. Say you so? Why, here's my  [100
hand then; no man living shall do 't but
thyself.
    3 [CRED.] Shall I carry it away from 'em
both, then?
    WIT. I' faith, shalt thou.
    3 [CRED.] Troth, then, I thank you, sir.
    WIT. Welcome, good Master Cockpit.
—(*Exit* [*3 Creditor*].) Ha, ha, ha! Why, is
not this better now than lying abed? I perceive there's nothing conjures up wit  [110
sooner than poverty, and nothing lays it
down sooner than wealth and lechery! This
has some savor yet. O, that I had the
mortgage from mine uncle as sure in possession as these trifles! I would forswear
brothel at noonday, and muscadine and
eggs [1] at midnight.

*Enter Courtesan.*

    COUR. Master Witgood, where are you?
    WIT. Holla!
    COUR. Rich news!                    120
    WIT. Would 'twere all in plate!
    COUR. There's some in chains and jew-
els. I am so haunted with suitors, Master

[1] A concoction used as an aphrodisiac.

Witgood, I know not which to despatch
first.
    WIT. You have the better term,[2] by my
faith.
    COUR. Among the number one Master
Hoard, an ancient gentleman.
    WIT. Upon my life, my uncle's  [130
adversary.
    COUR. It may well hold so, for he rails on
    you,
Speaks shamefully of him.
    WIT.                    As I could wish it.
    COUR. I first denied him, but so cunningly
It rather promised him assuréd hopes
Than any loss of labor.
    WIT.                    Excellent!
    COUR. I expect him every hour with gen-
        tlemen,
With whom he labors to make good his
        words,
To approve [3] you riotous, your state con-
        sumed,
Your uncle—                                140
    WIT. Wench, make up thy own fortunes
now; do thyself a good turn once in thy
days. He's rich in money, movables, and
lands. Marry him. He's an old, doting
fool, and that's worth all. Marry him.
'Twould be a great comfort to me to see
thee do well, i' faith. Marry him. 'Twould
ease my conscience well to see thee well
bestowed; I have a care of thee, i' faith.
    COUR. Thanks, sweet Master Wit-  [150
good.
    WIT. I reach at farder happiness. First, I
am sure it can be no harm to thee, and there
may happen goodness to me by it. Prosecute it well; let's send up for our [4] wits, now
we require their best and most pregnant
assistance.
    COUR. Step in; I think I hear 'em.
                            *Exit* [*with Witgood*].

*Enter Hoard and Gentlemen with the Host
[as] serving-man.*

    HOARD. Art thou the widow's man? By
my faith, sh'as a company of proper [5]  [160
men then.
    HOST. I am the worst of six, sir; good
enough for bluecoats.

[2] The time for lawsuits, at which many dissolute people came to London.
[3] Prove.                    [5] Handsome.
[4] From 1616 edn. Original reads *out*.

HOARD. Hark hither. I hear say thou art in most credit with her.

HOST. Not so, sir.

HOARD. Come, come, thou'rt modest. There's a brace of royals;[1] prithee, help me to th' speech of her. [*Gives him money.*]

HOST. I'll do what I may, sir, al- [170 ways saving myself harmless.

HOARD. Go to, do 't, I say; thou shalt hear better from me.

HOST. [*Aside.*] Is not this a better place than five mark a year standing wages? Say a man had but three such clients in a day, methinks he might make a poor living on 't. Beside, I was never brought up with so little honesty to refuse any man's money; never. What gulls there are a this side the [180 world! Now know I the widow's mind, none but my young master comes in her clutches. Ha, ha, ha!	*Exit.*

HOARD. Now, my dear gentlemen, stand firmly to me;
You know his follies and my worth.

1 [GENT.]	We do, sir.

2 [GENT.] But, Master Hoard, are you sure he is not i' th' house now?

HOARD. Upon my honesty, I chose this time
A purpose, fit; the spendthrift is abroad.
Assist me; here she comes.—

[*Enter Courtesan.*]

Now, my sweet widow. 190

COUR. Y' are welcome, Master Hoard.

HOARD. Despatch, sweet gentlemen, despatch.—
I am come, widow, to prove those my words
Neither of envy[2] sprung nor of false tongues,
But such as their[3] deserts and actions
Do merit and bring forth, all which these gentlemen,
Well known and better reputed, will confess.

COUR. I cannot tell
How my affections may dispose of me;
But surely, if they find him so desertless,	200
They'll have that reason to withdraw themselves;

And therefore, gentlemen, I do entreat you,
As you are fair in reputation
And in appearing form, so shine in truth.
I am a widow, and, alas, you know,
Soon overthrown! 'Tis a very small thing
That we withstand, our weakness is so great.
Be partial unto neither, but deliver,
Without affection,[4] your opinion.

HOARD. And that will drive it home.	210

COUR. Nay, I beseech your silence, Master Hoard;
You are a party.

HOARD.	Widow, not a word.

1 [GENT.] The better first to work you to belief,
Know neither of us owe him flattery,
Nor tother[5] malice, but unbribéd censure[6]—
So help us our best fortunes!

COUR.	It suffices.

1 [GENT.] That Witgood is a riotous, undone man,
Imperfect both in fame and in estate,
His debts wealthier than he, and executions
In wait for his due body, we'll maintain	220
With our best credit and our dearest blood.

COUR. Nor land nor living, say you? Pray, take heed
You do not wrong the gentleman.

1 [GENT.]	What we speak
Our lives and means are ready to make good.

COUR. Alas, how soon are we poor souls beguiled!

2 [GENT.] And for his uncle—

HOARD.	Let that come to me.
His uncle, a severe extortioner;
A tyrant at a forfeiture; greedy of others' Miseries; one that would undo his brother,	229
Nay, swallow up his father, if he can,
Within the fadoms[7] of his conscience.

1 [GENT.] Nay, believe it, widow,
You had not only matched yourself to wants,
But in an evil and unnatural stock.

[1] Gold pieces.	[3] *I.e.*, Lucre's and Witgood's.
[2] Malice.

[4] Prejudice.	[6] Judgment.
[5] *I.e.*, Witgood.	[7] Fathoms.

HOARD. [*Aside to Gentlemen.*] Follow hard, gentlemen, follow hard.

COUR. Is my love so deceived? Before you all
I do renounce him; on my knees I vow
He ne'er shall marry me.

WIT. [*Looking in. (Aside.)*] Heaven knows he never meant it!

HOARD. [*Aside to Gentlemen.*] There take her at the bound.                     240

1 [GENT.] Then, with a new and pure affection,
Behold yon gentleman, grave, kind, and rich,
A match worthy yourself; esteeming him,
You do regard your state.

HOARD. [*Aside to Gentlemen.*] I'll make her a jointure, say.

1 [GENT.] He can join land to land, and will possess you
Of what you can desire.

2 [GENT.]                     Come, widow, come.

COUR. The world is so deceitful!

1 [GENT.]                     There, 'tis deceitful
Where flattery, want, and imperfection lies;
But none of these in him. Push!

COUR.                     Pray, sir—     250

1 [GENT.] Come, you widows are ever most backward when you should do yourselves most good; but, were it to marry a chin not worth a hair now, then you would be forward enough. Come, clap hands! A match!

HOARD. With all my heart, widow.— Thanks, gentlemen.
I will deserve [1] your labor and thy love.

COUR. Alas, you love not widows but for wealth!
I promise you I ha' nothing, sir.

HOARD.                     Well said, widow,     260
Well said; thy love is all I seek, before
These gentlemen.

COUR.                     Now I must hope the best.

HOARD. My joys are such they want to be expressed.

COUR. But, Master Hoard, one thing I must remember you of, before these gentlemen, your friends: how shall I suddenly avoid the loathed soliciting of that perjured Witgood, and his tedious, dissembling uncle, who this very day hath appointed a meeting for the same     [270

[1] Reward.

purpose too, where, had not truth come forth, I had been undone, utterly undone?

HOARD. What think you of that, gentlemen?

1 [GENT.] 'Twas well devised.

HOARD. Hark thee, widow. Train [2] out young Witgood single; hasten him thither with thee, somewhat before the hour, where, at the place appointed, these gentlemen and myself will wait the oppor-     [280
tunity, when, by some slight removing him from thee, we'll suddenly enter and surprise thee, carry thee away by boat to Cole Harbor, have a priest ready, and there clap it up instantly. How lik'st it, widow?

COUR. In that it pleaseth you, it likes me well.

HOARD. I'll kiss thee for those words.
Come, gentlemen;
Still must I live a suitor to your favors,
Still to your aid beholding.

1 [GENT.]                     We're engaged, sir;
'Tis for our credits now to see 't well ended.     290

HOARD. 'Tis for your honors, gentlemen; nay, look to 't.
Not only in joy, but I in wealth excel.
No more sweet widow, but, sweet wife, farewell.

COUR. Farewell, sir.
                    *Exeunt* [*Hoard and Gentlemen*].

*Enter Witgood.*

WIT O, for more scope! I could laugh eternally!
Give you joy, Mistress Hoard. I promise your fortune was good, forsooth. Y'ave fell upon wealth enough, and there's young gentlemen enow can help you to the rest. Now it requires our wits. Carry thy-     [300
self but heedfully now, and we are both—

[*Enter Host.*]

HOST. Master Witgood, your uncle.

*Enter Lucre.*

WIT. [*Aside.*] Cud's me! Remove thyself awhile; I'll serve for him.
                    [*Exeunt Courtesan and Host.*]

LUC. Nephew, good morrow, nephew.

WIT. The same to you, kind uncle.

[2] Lure.

Luc. How fares the widow? Does the meeting hold?

Wit. O, no question of that, sir.

Luc. I'll strike the stroke, then, for thee; no more days.[1]  309

Wit. The sooner the better, uncle. O, she's mightily followed!

Luc. And yet so little rumored!

Wit. Mightily! Here comes one old gentleman, and he'll make her a jointure of three hundred a year, forsooth; another wealthy suitor will estate his son in his lifetime, and make him weigh down the widow; here a merchant's son will possess her with no less than three goodly lordships[2] at once, which were all pawns to his father.  320

Luc. Peace, nephew, let me hear no more of 'em; it mads me. Thou shalt prevent[3] 'em all. No words to the widow of my coming hither. Let me see—'tis now upon nine. Before twelve, nephew, we will have the bargain struck, we will, faith, boy.

Wit. O, my precious uncle!

*Exit [with Lucre].*

[Scena ii.

*A room in Hoard's house.]*

*Hoard and his Niece.*

Hoard. Niece, sweet niece, prithee, have a care to my house; I leave all to thy discretion. Be content to dream awhile. I'll have a husband for thee shortly; put that care upon me, wench, for in choosing wives and husbands I am only fortunate; I have that gift given me.  *Exit.*

Niece. But 'tis not likely you should choose for me,
Since nephew to your chiefest enemy  9
Is he whom I affect. But, O, forgetful!
Why dost thou flatter thy affections so,
With name of him that for a widow's bed
Neglects thy purer love? Can it be so,
Or does report dissemble?—

[*Enter George.]*

How now, sir?

Geo. A letter, with which came a private charge.

Niece. Therein I thank your care.—
[*Exit George.]*
I know this hand—(*Reads.*)
"Dearer than sight,

---

What the world reports of me, yet believe not; rumor will alter shortly. Be thou constant; I am still the same that I was in  [20 love, and I hope to be the same in fortunes.
THEODORUS WITGOOD."

I am resolved. No more shall fear or doubt
Raise their pale powers to keep affection out.  *Exit.*

[Scena iii.

*A room in a tavern.]*

*Enter, with a Drawer, Hoard and two Gentlemen.*

Dra. You're very welcome, gentlemen.—Dick, show those gentlemen the Pomegranate[4] there.

Hoard. Hist!

Dra. Up those stairs, gentlemen.

Hoard. Pist,[5] drawer!

Dra. Anon, sir.

Hoard. Prithee, ask at the bar if a gentlewoman came not in lately.

Dra. William, at the bar, did you  [10 see any gentlewoman come in lately? Speak you ay, speak you no?

[William.] (*Within.*) No, none came in yet but Mistress Florence.

Dra. He says none came in yet, sir, but one Mistress Florence.

Hoard. What is that Florence? A widow?

Dra. Yes, a Dutch widow.

Hoard. How?  20

Dra. That's an English drab, sir—give your worship good morrow.  [*Exit.*]

Hoard. A merry knave, i' faith! I shall remember a Dutch widow the longest day of my life.

1 [Gent.] Did not I use most art to win the widow?

2 [Gent.] You shall pardon me for that, sir; Master Hoard knows I took her at best vantage.  30

Hoard. What's that, sweet gentlemen, what's that?

2 [Gent.] He will needs bear me down, that his art only wrought with the widow most.

Hoard. O, you did both well, gentlemen, you did both well, I thank you.

1 [Gent.] I was the first that moved her.

---

[1] Delays.  [2] Manors.  [3] Anticipate.

[4] The name of one of the rooms.  [5] Hist!

HOARD.                    You were, i' faith.

.2 [GENT.] But it was I that took her at the bound.

HOARD. Ay, that was you. Faith, gentlemen, 'tis right.                    40

1 [GENT.] I boasted least, but 'twas I joined their hands.

HOARD. By th' Mass, I think he did. You did all well,

Gentlemen, you did all well. Contend no more.

1 [GENT.] Come, yon room's fittest.

HOARD.                    True, 'tis next the door.
                    *Exit [with Gentlemen].*

*Enter [Drawer,] Witg[ood], Court[esan], and Host.*

DRA. You're very welcome. Please you to walk upstairs; cloth's laid, sir.

COUR. Upstairs? Troth, I am weary. Master Witgood.

WIT. Rest yourself here awhile, widow; we'll have a cup of muscadine in this [50 little room.

DRA. A cup of muscadine? You shall have the best, sir.

WIT. But do you hear, sirrah?

DRA. Do you call? Anon, sir.

WIT. What is there provided for dinner?

DRA. I cannot readily tell you, sir. If you please, you may go into the kitchen and see yourself, sir; many gentlemen of worship do use to do it, I assure you, [60 sir.                    *[Exit.]*

HOST. A pretty, familiar, prigging [2] rascal; he has his part without book.

WIT. Against you are ready to drink to me, widow, I'll be present to pledge you.

COUR. Nay, I commend your care; 'tis done well of you.—*[Exit Witgood.]* 'Las,[3] what have I forgot!

HOST. What, mistress?

COUR. I slipped my wedding ring off [70 when I washed, and left it at my lodging. Prithee, run; I shall be sad without it.— *[Exit Host.]* So, he's gone.—Boy!

*[Enter Boy.]*

BOY. Anon, forsooth.

COUR. Come hither, sirrah.    Learn

secretly if one Master Hoard, an ancient gentleman, be about house.

BOY. I heard such a one named.

COUR. Commend me to him.

*Enter Hoard with Gentlemen.*

HOARD.                    I'll do thy commendations!

COUR. O, you come well. Away, to boat, begone!                    80

HOARD. Thus wise men are revenged, give two for one.                    *Exeunt.*

*Enter Witgood and Vintner.*

WIT. I must request
You, sir, to show extraordinary care.
My uncle comes with gentlemen, his friends,
And 'tis upon a making.[4]

VIN.                    Is it so?
I'll give a special charge, good Master Witgood.
May I be bold to see her?

WIT.                    Who? The widow?
With all my heart, i' faith; I'll bring you to her.

VIN. If she be a Staffordshire gentlewoman, 'tis much if I know her not.    90

WIT. How now? Boy! Drawer!

VIN. Hie!

*[Enter Boy.]*

BOY. Do you call, sir?

WIT. Went the gentlewoman up that was here?

BOY. Up, sir? She went out, sir.

WIT. Out, sir?

BOY. Out, sir. One Master Hoard, with a guard of gentlemen, carried her out at back door, a pretty while since, sir.    100

WIT. Hoard?    Death and darkness! Hoard?

*Enter Host.*

HOST. The devil of ring I can find.

WIT. How now? What news? Where's the widow?

HOST. My mistress? Is she not here, sir?

WIT. More madness yet!

HOST.                    She sent me for a ring.

WIT. A plot, a plot!—To boat! She's stole away.

HOST. What?                    109

---

[1] Original reads *3*, but see III, i, 251-6.

[2] Prigging; usually *thieving*, here *smart*.

[3] Emended by Bullen. Early edns. read *asse,* but apparently a letter has dropped out.

[4] Mating.

*Enter Lucre with Gentlemen.*

Wit. Follow! Inquire! Old Hoard, my
uncle's adversary—        [*Exit Host.*]
Luc. Nephew, what's that?
Wit.        Thrice-miserable wretch!
Luc. Why, what's the matter?
Vin.        The widow's borne away, sir.
Luc. Ha, passion of me!—A heavy wel-
    come, gentlemen.
1 [Gent.] The widow gone?
Luc. Who durst attempt it?
Wit. Who but old Hoard, my uncle's
    adversary?
Luc. How?
Wit. With his confederates.
Luc. Hoard, my deadly enemy?—Gentle-
    men, stand to me;        120
    I will not bear it; 'tis in hate of me;
    That villain seeks my shame, nay,
        thirsts [1] my blood.
    He owes me mortal malice.
    I'll spend my wealth on this despiteful
        plot,
    Ere he shall cross me and my nephew
        thus.
Wit. So maliciously!

*Enter Host.*

Luc. How now, you treacherous rascal?
Host. That's none of my name, sir.
Wit. Poor soul, he knew not on 't!
Luc. I'm sorry. I see then 'twas a mere
    plot.        130
Host. I traced 'em nearly—
Luc.        Well?
Host.        And hear for certain
    They have took Cole Harbor.
Luc.        The devil's sanctuary!
    They shall not rest, I'll pluck her from
        his arms—
    Kind and dear gentlemen,
    If ever I had seat within your breasts—
1 [Gent.] No more, good sir; it is a wrong
    to us
    To see you injured in a cause so just.
    We'll spend our lives but we will right
        our friends.
Luc. Honest and kind! Come, we have
    delayed too long.        139
    Nephew, take comfort; a just cause is
        strong.        *Exeunt* [*All but Witgood*].

Wit. That's all my comfort, uncle. Ha,
    ha, ha!
    Now may events fall luckily and well;
    He that ne'er strives, says wit, shall ne'er
        excel.        *Exit.*

[Scena iv.

*A room in Dampit's house.*]

*Enter Dampit, the usurer, drunk.*

Damp. When did I say my prayers?
In *anno* '88, when the great armado was
coming; and in *anno* '99, when the great
thunder and lightning was, I prayed heartily then, i' faith, to overthrow Poovies'
new buildings; I kneeled by my great iron
chest, I remember.

[*Enter Audrey.*]

Aud. Master Dampit, one may hear
you before they see you. You keep sweet
hours, Master Dampit; we were all [10
abed three hours ago.
Damp. Audrey?
Aud. O, y' are a fine gentleman!
Damp. So I am, i' faith, and a fine
scholar. Do you use to go to bed so early,
Audrey?
Aud. Call you this early, Master Dam-
pit?
Damp. Why, is 't not one of clock i' th'
morning? Is not that early enough? [20
Fetch me a glass of fresh beer.
Aud. Here, I have warmed your night-
cap for you, Master Dampit.
Damp. Draw it on then. I am very weak,
truly. I have not eaten so much as the
bulk of an egg these three days.
Aud. You have drunk the more, Master
Dampit.
Damp. What's that?
Aud. You mought,[3] and you would, [30
Master Dampit.
Damp. I answer you, I cannot. Hold
your prating; you prate too much, and
understand too little. Are you answered?
Give me a glass of beer.
Aud. May I ask you how you do, Mas-
ter Dampit?
Damp. How do I? I' faith, naught.
Aud. I ne'er knew you do otherwise.
Damp. I eat not one pennort[4] of [40

---

[1] Early edns. read *thrifts*.        [2] Closely.        [3] Might.        [4] Pennyworth.

bread these two years. Give me a glass of fresh beer. I am not sick, nor I am not well.

AUD. Take this warm napkin about your neck, sir, whilst I help to make you unready.[1]

DAMP. How now, Audrey-prater, with your scurvy devices, what say you now?

AUD. What say I, Master Dampit? I say nothing but that you are very weak. [50

DAMP. Faith, thou hast more cunny-catching [2] devices than all London.

AUD. Why, Master Dampit, I never deceived you in all my life.

DAMP. Why was that? Because I never did trust thee.

AUD. I care not what you say, Master Dampit.

DAMP. Hold thy prating. I answer thee, thou art a beggar, a quean, and a bawd. [60 Are you answered?

AUD. Fie, Master Dampit! A gentleman, and have such words!

DAMP. Why, thou base drudge of infortunity, thou kitchen-stuff drab of beggary, roguery, and coxcombry, thou cavernesed [3] quean of foolery, knavery, and bawdreaminy, I'll tell thee what, I will not give a louse for thy fortunes.

AUD. No, Master Dampit? And [70 there's a gentleman comes a-wooing to me, and he doubts [4] nothing but that you will get me from him.

DAMP. I? If I would either have thee or lie with thee for two thousand pound, would I might be damned! Why, thou base, impudent quean of foolery, flattery, and coxcombry, are you answered?

AUD. Come, will you rise and go to bed, sir? 80

DAMP. Rise, and go to bed too, Audrey? How does Mistress Proserpine?

AUD. Fooh!

DAMP. She's as fine a philosopher of a stinkard's wife as any within the liberties.[5] Fah, fah, Audrey!

AUD. How now, Master Dampit?

DAMP. Fie upon 't, what a choice of stinks here is! What hast thou done, Au-

drey? Fie upon 't, here's a choice of [90 stinks indeed! Give me a glass of fresh beer, and then I will to bed.

AUD. It waits for you above, sir.

DAMP. Foh! I think they burn horns in Barnard's Inn.[6] If ever I smelt such an adominable stink, usury forsake me. [Exit.]

AUD. They be the stinking nails of his trampling feet, and he talks of burning horns. Exit.

*Incipit*
ACT[US] IV. [SCENA i.]

*Enter at Cole Harbor, Hoard, the Widow,*
*[Lamprey, Spichcock,] and Gentlemen,*
*he married now.*

1 [GENT.] Join hearts, join hands,
In wedlock's bands,
Never to part
Till death cleave your heart.
[*To Hoard.*] You shall forsake all other women;
[*To Courtesan.*] You lords, knights, gentlemen, and yeomen.
What my tongue slips
Make up with your lips.

HOARD. Give you joy, Mistress Hoard; let the kiss come about.—[*One knocks.*]
Who knocks? Convey my little pig-eater[7] out. 10

LUC. [*Within.*] Hoard!

HOARD. Upon my life, my adversary, gentlemen!

LUC. [*Within.*] Hoard, open the door, or we will force it ope.
Give us the widow.

HOARD. Gentlemen, keep 'em out.

LAMP. He comes upon his death that enters here.

LUC. [*Within.*] My friends, assist me!

HOARD. He has assistants, gentlemen.

LAMP. Tut, nor him nor them we in this action fear.

LUC. [*Within.*] Shall I, in peace, speak one word with the widow?

COUR. Husband and gentlemen, hear me but a word.

HOARD. Freely, sweet wife.

COUR. Let him in peaceably; 20
You know we're sure from any act of his.

HOARD. Most true.

---

[1] Undress you. [2] Cheating.
[3] Another of Dampit's coinages, of doubtful meaning. [4] Fears.
[5] The slum district just outside the walls of the city. [6] Hostel for law students.
[7] Term of endearment.

Cour. [1] You may stand by and smile at his old weakness.

Let me alone to answer him.

Hoard.                        Content;
'Twill be good mirth, i' faith.  How think you, gentlemen?

Lamp.  Good gullery!

Hoard.  Upon calm conditions let him in.

Luc. [*Within.*] All spite and malice!

Lamp.                Hear me, Master Lucre.
So you will vow a peaceful entrance
With those your friends, and only exercise
Calm conference with the widow, without fury,                        30
The passage shall receive you.

*Enter Lucre [, Gentlemen, and Host].*

Luc.                        I do vow it.

Lamp.  Then enter and talk freely.  Here she stands.

Luc.  O, Master Hoard, your spite has watched [2] the hour!
You're excellent at vengeance, Master Hoard.

Hoard.  Ha, ha, ha!

Luc.                I am the fool you laugh at.
You are wise, sir, and know the seasons well.—
Come hither, widow.  Why is it thus?
O, you have done me infinite disgrace,
And your own credit no small injury!
Suffer mine enemy so despitefully  40
To bear you from my nephew?  O, I had rather
Half my substance had been forfeit and begged by some
Starved rascal!

Cour.                Why, what would you wish me do, sir?
I must not overthrow my state for love.
We have too many presidents [3] for that;
From thousands of our wealthy undone widows
One may derive some wit.  I do confess
I loved your nephew, nay, I did affect him
Against the mind and liking of my friends,[4]
Believed his promises, lay here in hope  50
Of flattered living and the boast of lands.

[1] Early edns. read *Luc.*        [3] Precedents.
[2] Awaited.
[4] From 1616 edn.  Original reads *friend.*

Coming to touch his wealth and state indeed,
It appears dross; I find him not the man,
Imperfect, mean, scarce furnished of his needs—
In words, fair lordships; in performance, hovels.
Can any woman love the thing that is not?

Luc.  Broke you for this?

Cour.        Was it not cause too much?
Send to inquire his state; most part of it
Lay two years mortgaged in his uncle's hands.

Luc.  Why, say it did; you might have known my mind.                        60
I could have soon restored it.

Cour.  Ay, had I but seen any such thing performed,
Why, 'twould have tied my affection, and contained
Me in my first desires.  Do you think, i' faith,
That I could twine such a dry oak as this,
Had promise in your nephew took effect?

Luc.  Why, and there's no time past; and rather than
My adversary should thus thwart my hopes,
I would—

Cour.  Tut, y'ave been ever full of golden speech.                        70
If words were lands, your nephew would be rich.

Luc.  Widow, believe it, I vow by my best bliss,
Before these gentlemen, I will give in
The mortgage to my nephew instantly,
Before I sleep or eat.

1 [Gent.] [5]                We'll pawn our credits,
Widow, what he speaks shall be performed
In fullness.

Luc.        Nay, more.  I will estate him
In farther blessings; he shall be my heir;
I have no son;
I'll bind myself to that condition.  80

[5] Of Lucre's party.

Cour. When I shall hear this done, I
shall soon yield
To reasonable terms.
Luc.                In the mean season,
Will you protest, before these gentle-
men,
To keep yourself as you are now at this
present?
Cour. I do protest, before these gentle-
men,
I will be as clear then as I am now.
Luc. I do believe you. Here's your own
honest servant;
I'll take him along with me.
Cour.                Ay, with all my heart.
Luc. He shall see all performed, and
bring you word.
Cour. That's all I wait for.        90
Hoard. What, have you finished, Master
Lucre? Ha, ha, ha, ha!
Luc. So laugh, Hoard, laugh at your
poor enemy, do;
The wind may turn; you may be laughed
at too.
Yes, marry, may you, sir.—Ha, ha, ha!
    *Exeunt [Lucre, Gentlemen, and Host].*
Hoard. Ha, ha, ha! If every man that
swells in malice
Could be revenged as happily as I,
He would choose hate, and forswear
amity.—
What did he say, wife, prithee?
Cour. Faith, spoke to ease his mind.
Hoard. O—O—O!
Cour.            You know now, little to
any purpose.        100
Hoard. True, true, true!
Cour.        He would do mountains now.
Hoard. Ay, ay, ay, ay.
Lamp.        Y'ave struck him dead, Master
Hoard.
Spi. And his nephew desperate.
Hoard.            I know 't, sirs, I.
Never did man so crush his enemy.
                    *Exeunt.*

[Scena ii.

*A room in Lucre's house.*]

*Enter Lucre with Gentlemen, [and Host,]
        meeting Sam Freedom.*

Luc. My   son-in-law,   Sam   Freedom,
where's my nephew?
Sam. O, man in lamentation, father!

Luc.                        How!
Sam. He thumps his breast like a gallant dicer that has lost his doublet, and
stands in 's shirt to do penance.
Luc. Alas, poor gentleman!
Sam. I warrant you may hear him sigh
in a still evening to your house at High-
gate.
Luc. I prithee, send him in.        10
Sam. Were it to do a greater matter,
I will not stick with you, sir, in regard you
married my mother.        [*Exit.*]
Luc. Sweet gentlemen, cheer him up;
I will but fetch the mortgage and return
to you instantly.        *Exit.*
1 [Gent.] We'll do our best, sir.—See
where he comes,
E'en joyless and regardless of all form.

[*Enter Witgood.*]

2 [Gent.] Why, how now, Master Witgood? Fie! You a firm scholar, and    [20
an understanding gentleman, and give
your best parts to passion?
1 [Gent.] Come, fie!
Wit. O, gentlemen—
1 [Gent.] Sorrow of me, what a sigh was
there, sir!
Nine such widows are not worth it.
Wit. To be borne from me by that lecher,
Hoard!
1 [Gent.] That vengeance is your uncle's,
being done
More in despite to him than wrong to
you.
But we bring comfort now.
Wit.    I beseech you, gentlemen—    30
2 [Gent.] Cheer thyself, man; there's
hope of her, i' faith.
Wit. Too gladsome to be true.

*Enter Lucre.*

Luc.                Nephew, what cheer?
Alas, poor gentleman, how art thou
changed!
Call thy fresh blood into thy cheeks
again.
She comes.
Wit.        Nothing afflicts me so much,
But that it is your adversary, uncle,
And merely plotted in despite of you.
Luc. Ay, that's it mads me, spites me!
I'll spend my wealth ere he shall carry her

so, because I know 'tis only to spite me. [40
Ay, this is it.    Here, nephew.    [*Gives a
paper.*]    Before these kind gentlemen, I
deliver in your mortgage my promise to
the widow. See, 'tis done. Be wise; you're
once more master of your own. The widow
shall perceive now you are not altogether
such a beggar as the world reputes you;
you can make shift to bring her to three
hundred a year, sir.
1 [GENT.]  Berlady,[1] and that's no toy,
    sir.
LUC.        A word, nephew.                50
1 [GENT. (*To Host*.)] Now you may certify
    the widow.
LUC.  You must conceive it aright, nephew,
    now;
    To do you good I am content to do this.
WIT.  I know it, sir.
LUC.  But your own conscience can tell I
    had it
    Dearly enough of you.
WIT.                Ay, that's most certain.
LUC.  Much money laid out, beside many
    a journey
    To fetch the rent; I hope you'll think
    on 't, nephew.
WIT.  I were worse than a beast else, i'
    faith.
LUC.  Although to blind the widow and
    the world,                              60
    I out of policy do 't, yet there's a con-
    science, nephew.
WIT.  Heaven forbid else!
LUC.        When you are full possessed,
    'Tis nothing to return it.
WIT.  Alas, a thing quickly done, uncle!
LUC.  Well said! You know I give it you
    but in trust.
WIT.  Pray, let me understand you rightly,
    uncle:
    You give it me but in trust?
LUC.  No.
WIT.  That is, you trust me with it?
LUC.  True, true.                          70
WIT.  [*Aside*.] But, if ever I trust you with
    it again,
    Would I might be trussed up for my
    labor!
LUC.  You can all witness, gentlemen,
and you, Sir Yeoman?
HOST.  My life for yours, sir, now, I
know my mistress's mind too well toward

your nephew; let things be in preparation,
and I'll train her hither in most excellent
fashion.                        *Exit.*  79
LUC.  A good old boy!—Wife! 'Ginny!

### *Enter Wife.*

WIFE.  What's the news, sir?
LUC.  The wedding day's at hand.
Prithee, sweet wife, express thy house-
wifery.  Thou'rt a fine cook, I know 't;
thy first husband married thee out of an
alderman's kitchen; go to, he raised thee
for raising of paste. What! Here's none
but friends; most of our beginnings must
be winked at.—Gentlemen, I invite you
all to my nephew's wedding against  [90
Thursday morning.
1 [GENT.]  With all our hearts, and we
shall joy to see your enemy so mocked.
LUC.  He laughed at me, gentlemen;
ha, ha, ha!      *Exeunt* [*All but Witgood*].
WIT.  He has no conscience, faith,
would laugh at them. They laugh at one
another.
    Who then can be so cruel?  Troth,
    not I;
    I rather pity now than aught envy.  100
    I do conceive such joy in mine own
    happiness I have no leisure yet to laugh
    at their follies.—
    [*To the mortgage.*] Thou soul of my es-
    tate, I kiss thee!
    I miss life's comfort when I miss thee
    O, never will we part again,
    Until I leave the sight of men!
    We'll ne'er trust conscience of our kin,
    Since cozenage brings that title in. [*Exit.*]

### [SCENA iii.

### *A street in London.*]

### *Enter three Creditors.*

1 [CRED.]  I'll wait these seven hours but
I'll see him caught.
2 [CRED.]  Faith, so will I.
3 [CRED.]  Hang him, prodigal!  He's
stripped of the widow.
1 [CRED.]  A my troth, she's the wiser; she
has made the happier choice. And I wonder
of what stuff those widows' hearts are made
of, that will marry unfledged boys before
comely thrum-chinned[2] gentlemen.        10

---

[1] By our Lady

[2] Fringe-chinned.

*Enter a Boy.*

BOY. News, news, news!

1 [CRED.] What, boy?

BOY. The rioter is caught.

1 [CRED.] So, so, so, so! It warms me at the heart; I love a' life to see dogs upon men. O, here he comes.

*Enter Witgood, with Serjeants.*

WIT. My last joy was so great it took away the sense of all future afflictions. What a day is here o'ercast! How soon a black tempest rises!          20

1 [CRED.] O, we may speak with you now, sir! What's become of your rich widow? I think you may cast your cap at [1] the widow, may you not, sir?

2 [CRED.] He a rich widow? Who, a prodigal, a daily rioter, and a nightly vomiter? He a widow of account? He a hole i' th' Counter! [2]

WIT. You do well, my masters, to tyrannize over misery, to afflict the afflicted; [30] 'tis a custom you have here amongst you. I would wish you never leave it, and I hope you'll do as I bid you.

1 [CRED.] Come, come, sir, what say you extempore now to your bill of a hundred pound? A sweet debt for froating [3] your doublets.

2 [CRED.] Here's mine of forty.

3 [CRED.] Here's mine of fifty.          39

WIT. Pray, sirs—you'll give me breath?

1 [CRED.] No, sir, we'll keep you out of breath still; then we shall be sure you will not run away from us.

WIT. Will you but hear me speak?

2 [CRED.] You shall pardon us for that, sir. We know you have too fair a tongue of your own. You overcame us too lately, a shame take you! We are like to lose all that for want of witnesses. We dealt in policy then; always when we strive to be [50] most politic we prove most coxcombs—*non plus ultra*.[4] I perceive by us we're not ordained to thrive by wisdom, and therefore we must be content to be tradesmen.

WIT. Give me but reasonable time, and I protest I'll make you ample satisfaction.

1 [CRED.] Do you talk of reasonable time to us?

WIT. 'Tis true, beasts know no reasonable time.          60

2 [CRED.] We must have either money or carcass.

WIT. Alas, what good will my carcass do you?

3 [CRED.] O, 'tis a secret delight we have amongst us! We that are used to keep birds in cages have the heart to keep men in prison, I warrant you.

WIT. [*Aside.*] I perceive I must crave a little more aid from my wits. Do but [70] make shift for me this once, and I'll forswear ever to trouble you in the like fashion hereafter; I'll have better employment for you, and I live.—You'll give me leave, my masters, to make trial of my friends, and raise all means I can?

1 [CRED.] That's our desires, sir.

*Enter Host.*

HOST. Master Witgood.

WIT. O, art thou come?

HOST. May I speak one word with [80] you in private, sir?

WIT. No, by my faith, canst thou; I am in hell here, and the devils will not let me come to thee.

CIT.[5] Do you call us devils? You shall find us Puritans.—Bear him away; let 'em talk as they go. We'll not stand to hear 'em.—Ah, sir, am I a devil? I shall think the better of myself as long as I live. A devil, i' faith!          *Exeunt.*  90

[SCENA iv.

*A room in Hoard's house.*]

*Enter Hoard.*

HOARD. What a sweet blessing hast thou, Master Hoard, above a multitude! Wilt thou never be thankful? How dost thou think to be blessed another time? Or dost thou count this the full measure of thy happiness? By my troth, I think thou dost. Not only a wife large in possessions, but spacious in content; she's rich, she's young, she's fair, she's wise.[6] When I wake, I think of her lands—that revives me;  [10

---

[1] Give up.

[2] London prison for debtors.

[3] Rubbing, probably with perfume.

[4] *I.e.*, go no further.

[5] Probably meaning *citizens, i.e., creditors.*

[6] From 1616 edn. Original reads *wife.*

when I go to bed, I dream of her beauty—
and that's enough for me. She's worth four
hundred a year in her very smock, if a man
knew how to use it. But the journey will
be all, in troth, into the country, to ride to
her lands in state and order following—my
brother and other worshipful gentlemen,
whose companies I ha' sent down for
already, to ride along with us in their goodly
decorum beards, their broad velvet [20
chashocks,[1] and chains of gold twice or
thrice double, against which time I'll entertain some ten men of mine own into liveries, all of occupations or qualities; I will
not keep an idle man about me, the sight
of which will so vex my adversary Lucre—
for we'll pass by his door a purpose, make
a little stand for [the][2] nonce, and have our
horses curvet before the window—certainly
he will never endure it, but run up [30
and hang himself presently.—

*[Enter Servant.]*

How now, sirrah, what news? Any that
offer their service to me yet?

SER. Yes, sir, there are some i' th' hall
that wait for your worship's liking, and
desire to be entertained.

HOARD. Are they of occupation?

SER. They are men fit for your worship,
sir.                                          39

HOARD. Say'st so? Send 'em all in.—
*[Exit Servant.]* To see ten men ride after
me in watchet[3] liveries, with orange-
tawny capes—'twill cut his comb, i' faith.

*Enter All[4] [, i.e., Tailor, Barber, Perfumer,
Falconer, and Huntsman].*

How now? Of what occupation are you,
sir?

TAIL. A tailor, an 't please your worship

HOARD. A tailor? O, very good. You
shall serve to make all the liveries.—What
are you, sir?

BAR. A barber, sir.                          50

HOARD. A barber? Very needful. You
shall shave all the house, and, if need
require, stand for a reaper i' th' summer
time.—You, sir?

PER. A perfumer.

HOARD. I smelt you before. Perfumers,
of all men, had need carry themselves
uprightly; for if they were once knaves
they would be smelt out quickly.—To you,
sir?                                          60

FAL. A falc'ner, an 't please your worship.

HOARD. Sa ho, sa ho, sa ho![5]—And
you, sir?

HUNT. A huntsman, sir.

HOARD. There, boy, there, boy, there,
boy![6] I am not so old but I have pleasant
days to come. I promise you, my masters,
I take such a good liking to you that I entertain you all. I put you already [70
into my countenance, and you shall be
shortly in my livery. But especially you
two, my jolly falc'ner and my bonny huntsman, we shall have most need of you at my
wife's manor-houses i' th' country. There's
goodly parks and champion[7] grounds for
you; we shall have all our sports within ourselves; all the gentlemen a th' country shall
be beholding to us and our pastimes.

FAL. And we'll make your[8] worship [80
admire, sir.

HOARD. Say'st thou so? Do but make
me admire, and thou shall want for nothing.—My tailor.

TAIL. Anon, sir.

HOARD. Go presently in hand with the
liveries.

TAIL. I will, sir.

HOARD. My barber.

BAR. Here, sir.                              90

HOARD. Make 'em all trim fellows,
louse 'em well—especially my huntsman—
and cut all their beards of the Polonian[9]
fashion.—My perfumer.

PER. Under your nose, sir.

HOARD. Cast a better savor upon the
knaves, to take away the scent of my
tailor's feet, and my barber's lotium
water.[10]

PER. It shall be carefully per- [100
formed, sir.

HOARD. But you, my falc'ner and
huntsman, the welcom'st men alive, i'
faith!

---

[1] Cassocks.   [2] Added by Dyce.   [3] Pale blue.
[4] This direction appears at the end of the speech
in the original.

[5] A hawking cry.          [7] Champaign.
[6] A hunting cry.
[8] From 1616 edn. Original reads *you*.
[9] Polish.
[10] A preparation of urine used as a cosmetic.

HUNT. And we'll show you that, sir, shall deserve your worship's favor.

HOARD. I prithee, show me that.—Go, you knaves all, and wash your lungs i' th' buttery, go.—[Exeunt Tailor, Barber, etc.] By th' Mass, and well remembered! [110 I'll ask my wife that question.—Wife, Mistress Jane Hoard!

*Enter Courtesan, altered in apparel.*

COUR. Sir, would you with me?

HOARD. I would but know, sweet wife, which might stand best to thy liking, to have the wedding dinner kept here or i' th' country?

COUR. Hum! Faith, sir, 'twould like me better here; here you were married, here let all rites be ended.          120

HOARD. Could a marquesse [1] give a better answer? Hoard, bear thy head aloft; thou'st a wife will advance it.—

*[Enter Host with a letter.]*

What haste comes here now? Yea, a letter? Some dreg of my adversary's malice. Come hither; what's the news?

HOST. A thing that concerns my mistress, sir.          [Gives letter to Courtesan.]

HOARD. Why, then it concerns me, knave.          130

HOST. Ay, and you, knave, too (cry your worship mercy). You are both like to come into trouble, I promise you, sir; a precontract. [2]

HOARD. How? A precontract, say'st thou?

HOST. I fear they have too much proof on 't, sir. Old Lucre, he runs mad up and down, and will to law as fast as he can; young Witgood laid hold on [140 by his creditors, he exclaims upon you a tother side, says you have wrought his undoing by the injurious detaining of his contract.

HOARD. Body a me!

HOST. He will have utmost satisfaction; The law shall give him recompense, he says.

COUR. [Aside.] Alas, his creditors so

[1] Marchioness.
[2] "A pre-contract of marriage could not be set aside without the mutual consent of the parties" (Bullen).

merciless! My state being yet uncertain, I deem it not unconscionable to fur-  [150 der him.

HOST. True, sir.

HOARD. Wife, what says that letter? Let me construe it.

COUR. Cursed be my rash and unadviséd words!
    [Tears and stamps upon the letter.]
I'll set my foot upon my tongue,
And tread my inconsiderate grant to dust.

HOARD. Wife—

HOST. [Aside.] A pretty shift, i' faith! I commend a woman when she can [160 make away a letter from her husband handsomely, and this was cleanly done, by my troth.

COUR. I did, sir;
    Some foolish words I must confess did pass,
Which now litigiously he fastens on me.

HOARD. Of what force? Let me examine 'em.

COUR. Too strong, I fear; would I were well freed of him!          170

HOARD. Shall I compound?

COUR. No, sir, I'd have it done some nobler way
Of your side; I'd have you come off with honor;
Let baseness keep with them. Why, have you not
The means, sir? The occasion's offered you.

HOARD. Where, how, dear wife?

COUR. He is now caught by his creditors; the slave's needy; his debts petty. He'll rather bind himself to all inconveniences than rot in prison; by this only [180 means you may get a release from him. 'Tis not yet come to his uncle's hearing. Send speedily for the creditors. By this time he's desperate; he'll set his hand to anything. Take order for his debts, or discharge 'em quite. A pax on him, let's be rid of a rascal!

HOARD. Excellent!
    Thou dost astonish me.—Go, run, make haste;
    Bring both the creditors and Witgood hither.          190

HOST. [Aside.] This will be some revenge yet.          [Exit.]

HOARD. In the mean space I'll have a release drawn.—
Within there!

[*Enter Servant.*]

SER. [1] Sir?

HOARD. Sirrah, come, take directions; go to my scrivener.

COUR. [*Aside.*] I'm yet like those whose riches lie in dreams;
If I be waked, they're false. Such is my fate,
Who ventures deeper than the desperate state.
Though I have sinned, yet could I become new,                              199
For, where I once vow, I am ever true.

HOARD. Away, despatch! On my displeasure, quickly.—[*Exit Servant.*] Happy occasion! Pray heaven he be in the right vein now to set his hand to 't, that nothing alter him; grant that all his follies may meet in him at once, to besot him enough! I pray for him, i' faith, and here he comes.

[*Enter Witgood and Creditors.*]

WIT. What would you with me now, my uncle's spiteful adversary?                      210

HOARD. Nay, I am friends.

WIT.          Ay, when your mischief's spent.

HOARD. I heard you were arrested.

WIT.                    Well, what then?
You will pay none of my debts, I am sure.

HOARD. A wise man cannot tell;
There may be those conditions 'greed upon
May move me to do much.

WIT.                    Ay, when?—'Tis thou,
Perjuréd woman! (O, no name is vild [2]
Enough to match thy treachery!) That art
The cause of my confusion.

COUR.                    Out, you
Penurious slave!

HOARD.          Nay, wife, you are too forward;                                    220
Let him alone; give losers leave to talk.

WIT. Shall I remember thee of another promise
Far stronger than the first?

[1] Original reads *1.*          [2] Vile.

COUR.                    I'd fain know that.

WIT. 'Twould call shame to thy cheeks.

COUR.          Shame!

WIT.                    Hark in your ear.—
[*Draws Courtesan aside.*]
Will he come off, think'st thou, and pay my debts roundly?

COUR. Doubt nothing; there's a release a-drawing and all, to which you must set your hand.

WIT. Excellent!                                    230

COUR. But methinks, i' faith, you might have made some shift to discharge this yourself, having in the mortgage, and never have burdened my conscience with it.

WIT. A my troth, I could not, for my creditors' cruelties extend to the present.

COUR. No more.—[*Aloud.*] Why, do your worst for that. I defy you.

WIT. Y' are impudent. I'll call up witnesses.

COUR. Call up thy wits, for thou hast been devoted                                    240
To follies a long time.

HOARD.          Wife, y' are too bitter.—
Master Witgood, and you, my masters, you shall hear a mild speech come from me now, and this it is: 't 'as been my fortune, gentlemen, to have an extraordinary blessing poured upon me alate, and here she stands; I have wedded her, and bedded her, and yet she is little the worse. Some foolish words she hath passed to you in the country, and some peevish [3] debts you owe [250 here in the city. Set the hare's head to the goose-giblet [4]—release you her of her words, and I'll release you of your debts, sir.

WIT. Would you so? I thank you for that, sir; I cannot blame you, i' faith.

HOARD. Why, are not debts better than words, sir?

WIT. Are not words promises, and are not promises debts, sir?

HOARD. [*Aside.*] He plays at [260 backracket with me.[5]

1 [CRED.] Come hither, Master Witgood, come hither; be ruled by fools once.
[*Creditors take Witgood aside.*]

2 [CRED.] We are citizens, and know what belong to 't.

1 [CRED.] Take hold of his offer. Pax

[3] Small.
[4] *I.e.*, let equivalents balance each other.
[5] *I.e.*, he hits the ball back at me.

on her, let her go. If your debts were once discharged, I would help you to a widow myself worth ten of her.

3 [CRED.] Mass, partner, and now [270 you remember me on 't, there's Master Mulgrave's sister newly fallen a widow.

1 [CRED.] Cud's me, as pat as can be! There's a widow left for you, ten thousand in money, beside plate, jewels, *et cetera*. I warrant it a match; we can do all in all with her. Prithee, despatch; we'll carry thee to her presently.

WIT. My uncle will ne'er endure me when he shall hear I set my hand to a [280 release.

2 [CRED.] Hark, I'll tell thee a trick for that. I have spent five hundred pound in suits in my time; I should be wise. Thou'rt now a prisoner; make a release; take 't of my word, whatsoever a man makes as long as he is in durance, 'tis nothing in law, not thus much.

WIT. Say you so, sir? 289

3 [CRED.] I have paid for 't; I know 't.

WIT. Proceed then; I consent.

3 [CRED.] Why, well said.

HOARD. How now, my masters, what have you done with him?

1 [CRED.] With much ado, sir, we have got him to consent.

HOARD. Ah—a—a! And what came his debts to now?

1 [CRED.] Some eightscore odd pounds, sir. 300

HOARD. Naw, naw, naw, naw, naw! Tell me the second time; give me a lighter sum. They are but desperate debts, you know, ne'er called in but upon such an accident. A poor, needy knave, he would starve and rot in prison. Come, come, you shall have ten shillings in the pound, and the sum down roundly.

1 [CRED.] You must make it a mark, sir.

HOARD. Go to then; tell your money [310 in the meantime; you shall find little less there.—[*Gives money.*] Come, Master Witgood, you are so unwilling to do yourself good now!—

[*Enter Scrivener.*]

Welcome, honest scrivener.—Now you shall hear the release read.

SCRI. [*Reading.*] "Be it known to all men, by these presents, that I, Theodorus Witgood, gentleman, sole nephew to Pecunius Lucre, having unjustly made [320 title and claim to one Jane Medler, late widow of Anthony Medler, and now wife to Walkadine Hoard, in consideration of a competent sum of money to discharge my debts, do forever hereafter disclaim any title, right, estate, or interest in or to the said widow, late in the occupation of said Anthony Medler, and now in the occupation of Walkadine Hoard; as also neither to lay claim by virtue of any former [330 contract, grant, promise, or demise, to any of her manor[s], manor houses, parks, groves, meadow grounds, arable lands, barns, stacks, stables, dove holes, and cunny borrows,[1] together with all her cattle, money, plate, jewels, borders, chains, bracelets, furnitures, hangings, movables or immovables. In witness whereof, I, the said Theodorus Witgood, have interchangeably set to my hand and seal before [340 these presents, the day and date above written."

WIT. What a precious fortune hast thou slipped here, like a beast as thou art!

HOARD. Come, unwilling heart, come.

WIT. Well, Master Hoard, give me the pen; I see
'Tis vain to quarrel with our destiny. [*Signs.*]

HOARD. O, as vain a thing as can be! You cannot commit a greater absurdity, sir. So, so; give me that hand now; before [350 all these presents, I am friends forever with thee.

WIT. Troth, and it were pity of my heart now, if I should bear you any grudge, i' faith.

HOARD. Content. I'll send for thy uncle against the wedding dinner; we will be friends once again.

WIT. I hope to bring it to pass myself, sir.

HOARD. How now? Is 't right, my [360 masters?

1 [CRED.] 'Tis something wanting, sir; yet it shall be sufficient.

HOARD. Why, well said; a good conscience makes a fine show nowadays. Come, my masters, you shall all taste of my wine ere you depart.

ALL. We follow you, sir.

[*Exeunt Hoard and Scrivener.*]

[1] Rabbit burrows.

WIT. [*Aside.*] I'll try these fellows now.
—A word, sir. What, will you carry [370
me to that widow now?

1 [CRED.] Why, do you think we were
in earnest, i' faith? Carry you to a rich
widow? We should get much credit by that.
A noted rioter! A contemptible prodigal!
'Twas a trick we have amongst us to get
in our money. Fare you well, sir.
                        *Exeunt* [*Creditors*].

WIT. Farewell, and be hanged, you short
pig-haired, ram-headed rascals! He that
believes in you shall ne'er be saved, [380
I warrant him. By this new league I shall
have some access unto my love.
                *She* [, *i.e., Niece,*] *is above.*

NIECE. Master Witgood!

WIT. My life!

NIECE. Meet me presently; that note
directs you. [*Drops him a paper.*] I would
not be suspected. Our happiness attends
us. Farewell!

WIT. A word's enough.        *Exeunt.* [1]

[SCENA v.]

*Dampit the usurer in his bed, Audrey spin-*
*ning by.* [*Boy.*]

SONG [*by Audrey*]

Let the usurer cram him, in interest that
    excel,
There's pits enow to damn him, before he
    comes to hell;
In Holborn some, in Fleet Street some,
Where'er he come there's some, there's
    some.

DAMP. *Trahe, trahito,* draw the curtain;
give me a sip of sack more.

*Enter Gentlemen* [, *i.e., Lamprey and Spich-*
*cock*].

LAMP. Look you; did not I tell you he
lay like the devil in chains, when he was
bound for a thousand year?

SPI. But I think the devil had no [10
steel bedstaffs; [2] he goes beyond him for that.

LAMP. Nay, do but mark the conceit [3] of
his drinking; one must wipe his mouth for
him with a muckinder,[4] do you see, sir?

SPI. Is this the sick trampler? Why, he
is only bedrid with drinking.

LAMP. True, sir. He spies us.

DAMP. What, Sir Tristram? You come
and see a weak man here, a very weak
man—                                    20

LAMP. If you be weak in body, you
should be strong in prayer, sir.

DAMP. O, I have prayed too much.
poor man!

LAMP. There's a taste of his soul for
you!

SPI. Fah, loathsome!

LAMP. I come to borrow a hundred
pound of you, sir.

DAMP. Alas, you come at an ill [30
time! I cannot spare it, i' faith; I ha' but
two thousand i' th' house.

AUD. Ha, ha, ha!

DAMP. Out, you gernative [5] quean, the
mullipoop[6] of villainy, the spinner of
concupiscency!

*Enter other Gentleman* [, *i.e., Sir Lancelot*].

LAN. Yea, gentlemen, are you here before us? How is he now?

LAMP. Faith, the same man still. The
tavern bitch has bit him i' the head.[7]      40

LAN. We shall have the better sport
with him. Peace!—And how cheers Master Dampit now?

DAMP. O, my bosom, Sir Lancelot, how
cheer I? Thy presence is restorative.

LAN. But I hear a great complaint of
you, Master Dampit, among gallants.

DAMP. I am glad of that, i' faith.
Prithee, what?

LAN. They say you are waxed proud [50
alate, and, if a friend visit you in the afternoon, you'll scarce know him.

DAMP. Fie, fie! Proud? I cannot remember any such thing. Sure, I was
drunk then.

LAN. Think you so, sir?

DAMP. There 'twas, i' faith; nothing
but the pride of the sack; and so certify
'em.—Fetch sack, sirrah.

BOY. A vengeance sack you once!      60
            [*Exit Boy, who returns with sack.*]

AUD. Why, Master Dampit, if you hold
on as you begin, and lie a little longer, you

---

[1] In original, stage direction appears after preceding line.

[2] For preparing a feather bed.

[3] Fancy, singularity.        [4] Handkerchief.

[5] Grinning, peevish.

[6] Moldy rump(?).

[7] *I.e.,* he is drunk.

need not take care how to dispose your wealth; you'll make the vintner your heir.

DAMP. Out, you babliaminy, you un-feathered, cremitoried quean, you culli-sance of scabiosity![1]

AUD. Good words, Master Dampit, to speak before a maid and a virgin!          69

DAMP. Hang thy virginity upon the pole of carnality!

AUD. Sweet terms! My mistress shall know 'em.

LAMP. Note but the misery of this usur-ing slave. Here he lies, like a noisome dunghill, full of the poison of his drunken blasphemies; and they to whom he be-queaths all grudge him the very meat that feeds him, the very pillow that eases him. Here may a usurer behold his [80 end. What profits it to be a slave in this world, and a devil i' th' next?

DAMP. Sir Lancelot, let me buss thee, Sir Lancelot; thou art the only friend that I honor and respect.

LAN. I thank you for that, Master Dam-pit.

DAMP. Farewell, my bosom Sir Lance-lot.

LAN. Gentlemen, and you love me, [90 let me step behind you, and one of you fall a-talking of me to him.

LAMP. Content.—Master Dampit—

DAMP. So, sir.

LAMP. Here came Sir Lancelot to see you e'en now.

DAMP. Hang him, rascal!

LAMP. Who, Sir Lancelot?

DAMP. Pythagorical rascal!

LAMP. Pythagorical?          100

DAMP. Ay, he changes his cloak when he meets a serjeant.

LAN. What a rogue's this!

LAMP. I wonder you can rail at him, sir; he comes in love to see you.

DAMP. A louse for his love! His father was a comb maker; I have no need of his crawling love. He comes to have longer day, the superlative rascal!

LAN. 'Sfoot, I can no longer en- [110 dure the rogue!—Master Dampit, I come to take my leave once again, sir.

DAMP. Who? My dear and kind Sir Lancelot, the only gentleman of England? Let me hug thee; farewell, and a thousand.

LAMP. Composed of wrongs and slav-ish flatteries!

LAN. Nay, gentlemen, he shall show you more tricks yet; I'll give you another taste of him.          120

LAMP. Is 't possible?

LAN. His memory is upon departing.

DAMP. Another cup of sack!

LAN. Mass, then 'twill be quite gone! Before he drink that, tell him there's a country client come up, and here attends for his learned advice.

LAMP. Enough.

DAMP. One cup more, and then let the bell toll. I hope I shall be weak [130 enough by that time.

LAMP. Master Dampit—

DAMP. Is the sack spouting?

LAMP. 'Tis coming forward, sir. Here's a countryman, a client of yours, waits for your deep and profound advice, sir.

DAMP. A coxcombry? Where is he? Let him approach. Set me up a peg higher.

LAMP. [To Sir Lancelot.] You must draw near, sir.          140

DAMP. Now, good man fooliaminy, what say you to me now?

LAN. Please your good worship, I am a poor man, sir—

DAMP. What make [2] you in my chamber then?

LAN. I would entreat your worship's de-vice in a just and honest cause, sir.

DAMP. I meddle with no such matters; I refer 'em to Master No-man's office.          [150

LAN. I had but one house left me in all the world, sir, which was my father's, my grandfather's, my great-grandfather's, and now a villain has unjustly wrung me out, and took possession on 't.

DAMP. Has he such feats? Thy best course is to bring thy ejectione firmæ; [3] and in seven year thou mayst shove him out by the law.

LAN. Alas, an 't please your wor- [160 ship, I have small friends and less money!

DAMP. Hoyday! This gear will fadge [4] well. Hast no money? Why, then, my advice is, thou must set fire a th' house, and so get him out.

LAMP. That will break [5] strife, indeed.

LAN. I thank your worship for your hot counsel, sir.—Altering but my voice a little, you see he knew me not. You may observe by this that a drunkard's mem- [170 ory holds longer in the voice than in the person. But, gentlemen, shall I show you a sight? Behold the little divedapper [1] of damnation, Gulf the usurer, for his time worse than tother.

*Enter Hoard with Gulf.*

LAMP. What's he comes with him?

LAN. Why, Hoard, that married lately the Widow Medler.

LAMP. O, I cry you mercy, sir.

HOARD. Now, gentlemen visitants, [180 how does Master Dampit?

LAN. Faith, here he lies, e'en drawing in, sir, good canary as fast as he can, sir; a very weak creature, truly, he is almost past memory.

HOARD. Fie, Master Dampit! You lie lazing abed here, and I come to invite you to my wedding dinner. Up, up, up!                                        189

DAMP. Who's this? Master Hoard? Who hast thou married, in the name of foolery?

HOARD. A rich widow.

DAMP. A Dutch widow?

HOARD. A rich widow; one Widow Medler.

DAMP. Medler? She keeps open house.

HOARD. She did, I can tell you, in her tother husband's days—open house for all comers; horse and man was welcome, [200 and room enough for 'em all.

DAMP. There's too much for thee, then; thou mayst let out some to thy neighbors.

GULF. What, hung alive in chains? O spectacle! Bedstaffs of steel? *"O monstrum horrendum, informe, ingens, cui lumen ademptum!"* [2] O Dampit, Dampit, here's a just judgment shown upon usury, extortion, and trampling villainy!            210

LAN. [*Aside.*] This exc'llent thief rails upon the thief!

GULF. Is this the end of cutthroat usury, brothel, and blasphemy? Now mayst thou see what race a usurer runs.

DAMP. Why, thou rogue of universal-

ity, do not I know thee? Thy sound is like the cuckoo, the Welsh ambassador; [3] thou cowardly slave, that offers to fight with a sick man when his weapon's [220 down! Rail upon me in my naked bed? Why, thou great Lucifer's little vicar, I am not so weak but I know a knave at first sight. Thou inconscionable rascal, thou that goest upon Middlesex juries, and will make haste to give up thy verdit [4] because thou wilt not lose thy dinner, are you answered?

GULF. An 't were not for shame— [22c
*Draws his dagger.*

DAMP. Thou wouldst be hanged then.

LAMP. Nay, you must exercise patience, Master Gulf, always in a sick man's chamber.

LAN. He'll quarrel with none, I warrant you, but those that are bedrid.

DAMP. Let him come, gentlemen; I am armed. Reach my close-stool [5] hither.

LAN. Here will be a sweet fray anon. I'll leave you, gentlemen.

LAMP. Nay, we'll along with [240 you.—Master Gulf—

GULF. Hang him, usuring rascal!

LAN. Push, set your strength to his, your wit to his!

AUD. Pray, gentlemen, depart; his hour's come upon him.—Sleep in my bosom, sleep.

LAN. Nay, we have enough of him, i' faith; keep him for the house.
Now make your best.                        250
For thrice his wealth I would not have his breast.

GULF. A little thing would make me beat him now he's asleep.

LAN. Mass, then 'twill be a pitiful day when he wakes. I would be loath to see that day come.

GULF. You overrule me, gentlemen, i' faith.                                  *Exeunt.*

ACTUS V. [SCENA i.
*A room in Lucre's house.*]
*Enter Lucre and Witgood.*

WIT. Nay, uncle, let me prevail with you so much. I' faith, go, now he has invited you.

---

[1] Didapper, dabchick.

[2] "O horrible monster, misshapen, huge, from whom sight is taken away!" (Virgil's *Æneid*, iii, ¡58).

[3] Nares conjectures that the cuckoo was so named because it migrated from the west.

[4] Verdict.        [5] Chamber pot.

Luc. I shall have great joy there when he has borne away the widow!

Wit. Why, la, I thought where I should find you presently. Uncle, a my troth, 'tis nothing so.

Luc. What's nothing so, sir? Is not he married to the widow?　　　10

Wit. No, by my troth, is he not, uncle.

Luc. How?

Wit. Will you have the truth on 't? He is married to a whore, i' faith.

Luc. I should laugh at that.

Wit. Uncle, let me perish in your favor if you find it not so, and that 'tis I that have married the honest woman.

Luc. Ha! I'd walk ten mile afoot to see that, i' faith.　　　20

Wit. And see 't you shall, or I'll ne'er see you again.

Luc. A quean, i' faith? Ha, ha, ha!
　　　　　　　　　　　　*Exeunt.*

[Scena ii.

*A room in Hoard's house.*]

*Enter Hoard, tasting wine, the Host following in a livery cloak.*

Hoard. Pup, pup, pup, pup! I like not this wine. Is there never a better tierce [1] in the house?

Host. Yes, sir, there are as good tierce in the house as any are in England.

Hoard. Desire your mistress, you knave, to taste 'em all over; she has better skill.

Host. [*Aside.*] Has she so? The better for her, and the worse for you.　　*Exit.*

Hoard. Arthur!　　　10

[*Enter Arthur.*]

Is the cupboard of plate set out?

Art. All's in order, sir.　　　[*Exit.*]

Hoard. I am in love with my liveries every time I think on 'em; they make a gallant show, by my troth.—Niece!

[*Enter Niece.*]

Niece. Do you call, sir?

Hoard. Prithee, show a little diligence, and overlook the knaves a little; they'll filch and steal today, and send whole pasties home to their wives; and thou beest [20 a good niece, do not see me purloined.

¹ A small cask; with a word-play on *tears.*

Niece. Fear it not, sir.—[*Aside.*] I have cause; though the feast be prepared for you, yet it serves fit for my wedding dinner too.
　　　　　　　　　　　　[*Exit.*]

*Enter two Gentlemen* [, *i.e., Lamprey and Spichcock*].

Hoard. Master Lamprey and Master Spichcock, two the most welcome gentlemen alive! Your fathers and mine were all free a th' Fishmongers.²

Lamp. They were indeed, sir. You see bold guests, sir, soon entreated.　　　30

Hoard. And that's best, sir.—

[*Enter Servant.*]

How now, sirrah?

Ser. There's a coach come to th' door, sir.　　　[*Exit.*]

Hoard. My Lady Foxstone, a my life!— Mistress Jane Hoard! Wife!—Mass, 'tis her ladyship indeed!—

[*Enter Lady Foxstone.*]

Madam, you are welcome to an unfurnished house, dearth of cheer, scarcity of attendance.　　　40

Lad. You are pleased to make the worst, sir.

Hoard. Wife!

[*Enter Courtesan.*]

Lad. Is this your bride?

Hoard. Yes, madam.—Salute my Lady Foxstone.

Cour. Please you, madam, awhile to taste the air in the garden?

Lad. 'Twill please us well.
　　　　　*Exeunt* [*Lady and Courtesan*].

Hoard. Who would not wed? The most delicious life!　　　50
No joys are like the comforts of a wife.

Lamp. So we bachelors think, that are not troubled with them.

[*Enter Servant.*]

Ser. Your worship's brother with another ancient gentleman are newly alighted, sir.　　　[*Exit.*]

Hoard. Master Onesiphorus Hoard? Why, now our company begins to come in.—

² Members of the Company of Fishmongers.

*[Enter Onesiphorus Hoard, Limber, and Kix.]*

My dear and kind brother, welcome, i' faith.

O. HOA.[1] You see we are men at an [60 hour, brother.

HOARD. Ay, I'll say that for you, brother; you keep as good an hour to come to a feast as any gentleman in the shire.—What, old Master Limber and Master Kix! Do we meet, i' faith, jolly gentlemen?

LIM. We hope you lack guess,[2] sir?

HOARD. O, welcome, welcome! We lack still such guess as your worships.

O. HOA. Ah, Sirrah Brother, have [70 you catched up Widow Medler?

HOARD. From 'em all, brother; and I may tell you I had mighty enemies, those that stuck sore; old Lucre is a sore fox, I can tell you, brother.

O. HOA. Where is she? I'll go seek her out; I long to have a smack at her lips.

HOARD. And most wishfully,[3] brother, see where she comes.

*[Enter Courtesan and Lady.]*

Give her a smack[4] now we may hear [80 it all the house over.

COUR. *[Aside.]* O heaven, I am betrayed! (*Both* [, *i.e., Courtesan and Onesiphorus Hoard,*] *turn back.*) I know that face.

HOARD. Ha, ha, ha! Why, how now? Are you both ashamed?—Come, gentlemen, we'll look another way

O. HOA. Nay, brother, hark you. Come, y' are disposed to be merry.　　90

HOARD. Why do we meet else, man?

O. HOA. That's another matter. I was ne'er so fraid in my life but that you had been in earnest.

HOARD. How mean you, brother?

O. HOA. You said she was your wife?

HOARD. Did I so? By my troth, and so she is.

O. HOA. By your troth, brother?　　99

HOARD. What reason have I to dissemble with my friends, brother? If marriage can make her mine, she is mine. Why—

O. HOA. Troth, I am not well of a sudden. I must crave pardon, brother; I came

to see you, but I cannot stay dinner, i' faith.

HOARD. I hope you will not serve me so, brother?

LIM. By your leave, Master Hoard—

HOARD. What now? What now? [110 Pray, gentlemen, you were wont to show yourselves wise men.

LIM. But you have shown your folly too much here.

HOARD. How?

KIX. Fie, fie! A man of your repute and name!

You'll feast your friends, but cloy 'em first with shame.

HOARD. This grows too deep; pray, let us reach the sense.

LIM. In your old age dote on a courtesan!

HOARD. Ha!

KIX. Marry a strumpet!　　120

HOARD. Gentlemen!

O. HOA. And Witgood's quean!

HOARD. O! Nor lands nor living?

O. HOA. Living!

HOARD. *[To Courtesan.]*　　Speak!

COUR.　　Alas, you know, at first, sir, I told you I had nothing!

HOARD. Out, out! I am cheated; infinitely cozened!

LIM. Nay, Master Hoard—

*Enter Witgood, [Niece,] and Lucre.*

HOARD. A Dutch widow! A Dutch widow! A Dutch widow!

LUC. Why, nephew, shall I trace thee still a liar?

Wilt make me mad? Is not yon thing the widow?　　130

WIT. Why, la, you are so hard a belief, uncle!

By my troth, she's a whore.

LUC.　　Then thou'rt a knave.

WIT. *Negatur argumentum,*[5] uncle.

LUC. *Probo tibi,*[6] nephew. He that knows a woman to be a quean must needs be a knave; thou say'st thou know'st her to be one; *ergo*, if she be a quean, thou'rt a knave.

WIT. *Negatur sequela majoris,*[7] uncle. He that knows a woman to be a [140 quean must needs be a knave; I deny that.

---

[1] Through the rest of this scene in the original this speech head reads *Ony.* or *On.*

[2] Guests.　　　　[4] Early edns. read *smerck.*

[3] Exactly on your wish.

[5] Proof is denied.　　[6] I'll prove it to you.

[7] The conclusion of your major premise is denied.

HOARD. Lucre and Witgood, y' are both villains; get you out of my house!

LUC. Why, didst not invite me to thy wedding dinner?

WIT. And are not you and I sworn perpetual friends before witness, sir, and were both drunk upon 't?

HOARD. Daintily abused!  Y'ave put a junt [1] upon me!    149

LUC. Ha, ha, ha!

HOARD.    A common strumpet!

WIT.    Nay, now
You wrong her, sir; if I were she, I'd have
The law on you for that; I durst depose for her
She ne'er had common use nor common thought.

COUR. Despise me, publish me, I am your wife.
What shame can I have now but you'll have part?
If in disgrace you share, I sought not you;
You pursuéd me, nay, forc[é]d me.
Had I friends would follow it,
Less than your action has been proved a rape.

O. HOA. Brother!    160

COUR. Nor did I ever boast of lands unto you,
Money, or goods; I took a plainer course,
And told you true, I'd nothing.
If error were committed, 'twas by you;
Thank your own folly.  Nor has my sin been
So odious, but worse has been forgiven;
Nor am I so deformed, but I may challenge
The utmost power of any old man's love.
She that tastes not sin before, twenty to one
but she'll taste it after.  Most of you  [170
old men are content to marry young virgins,
and take that which follows; where, marrying one of us, you both save a sinner and are
quit from a cuckold forever.
"And more, in brief, let this your best thoughts win,
She that knows sin, knows best how to hate sin." [2]

HOARD. Cursed be all malice!  Black are the fruits of spite,

And poison first their owners.  O, my friends,
I must embrace shame, to be rid of shame!
Concealed disgrace prevents a public name.    180
Ah, Witgood! Ah, Theodorus!

WIT. Alas, sir, I was pricked in conscience to see her well bestowed, and where could I bestow her better than upon your pitiful worship?  Excepting but myself, I dare swear she's a virgin; and now, by marrying your niece, I have banished myself forever from her.  She's mine aunt now, by my faith, and there's no meddling with mine aunt, you know—a sin  [190
against my nuncle. [3]

COUR. [Kneeling.] Lo, gentlemen, before you all
In true reclaiméd form I fall.
Henceforth forever I defy [4]
The glances of a sinful eye,
Waving of fans (which some suppose
Tricks of fancy [5]), treading of toes,
Wringing of fingers, biting the lip,
The wanton gait, th' alluring trip,    199
All secret friends and private meetings,
Close-borne letters and bawds' greetings,
Feigning excuse to women's labors
When we are sent for to th' next neighbor's,
Taking false physic, and ne'er start
To be let blood, though sign be at heart, [6]
Removing chambers, shifting beds,
To welcome friends in husbands' steads,
Them to enjoy, and you to marry,
They first served, while you must tarry,
They to spend, and you to gather,    210
They to get, and you to father—
These and thousand thousand more,
New reclaimed, I now abhor.

LUC. [To Witgood.] Ah, here's a lesson, rioter, for you!

WIT. I must confess my follies; I'll down too.    [Kneels.]
And here forever I disclaim
The cause of youth's undoing, game,
Chiefly dice, those true outlanders,
That shake out beggars, thieves, and panders,
Soul-wasting surfeits, sinful riots,    220

[1] Trick, fraud.
[2] Quotation marks were often used to call attention to sententious passages.
[3] Uncle.    [4] Renounce.    [5] Love.
[6] According to the almanacs a propitious time for bloodletting.

Queans' evils, doctors' diets,
Pothecaries' drugs, surgeons' glisters,
Stabbing of arms [1] for a common mis-
   tress,
Riband favors, ribald speeches,
Dear   perfumed   jackets,   penniless
   breeches,
Dutch flapdragons, [2] healths in urine,

[1] To drink off one's blood mixed with wine.
[2] Tidbits swallowed from burning brandy.

Drabs that keep a man too sure in—
I do defy you all.
Lend me each honest hand, for here I rise
A reclaimed man, loathing the general
   vice.                        230
HOARD. So, so, all friends! The wedding
   dinner cools.
Who seem most crafty prove ofttimes
   most fools.                [Exeunt.]
             FINIS.

# THOMAS MIDDLETON AND WILLIAM ROWLEY

## THE CHANGELING

*The Changeling* has exerted a sort of dreadful fascination over practically everyone who has read it. Even William Archer, blind as he was to certain aspects of the play, confessed that it was worthy of close study, and reminded his readers that its "horribly striking" power had been pointed out by Sir Walter Scott (in his edition of *Sir Tristrem* in 1806), even before Charles Lamb extolled it (in his *Specimens of English Dramatic Poets Contemporary with Shakespeare* in 1808). Admitting that the theme is "undoubtedly very tragic," Archer maintained that "the treatment affords an excellent example of the way in which the minor Elizabethans neglected verism, ignored psychology, and concentrated their whole effort on the elements of lust and horror." Focusing on the turning-point scene (III, iv) in which Beatrice-Joanna capitulates to Deflores when she finds herself in his power because she has failed to realize the full implications of the murder for which she has used him as a willing tool, Archer at one and the same time criticized her "imbecility"—almost her "comic" "simplicity"— and granted that the scene "leaves us face to face with a situation full of dramatic possibilities." *The Changeling*, he concluded, is "a good play gone wrong," written by an author who was "a real dramatist, who, in another environment, would have been capable of working up to higher standards." Barker, on the other hand, though admitting that Middleton was not always "sufficiently sure of himself—or his audience—to make the transformation complete," insisted that Middleton, through his "preoccupation with the minds of somewhat abnormal characters," was "trying to transform the melodramatic tragedy of his age into something like psychological tragedy." N. W. Bawcutt, in his edition of the play for the Revels series (London, 1958), also felt that the interest of the playwright was primarily psychological rather than philosophical. Agreeing in part with Una Ellis-Fermor (*The Jacobean Drama*) that the key to Beatrice-Joanna's character is to see her as a "spoilt" but "clever" child, and with Eliot that hers is "the tragedy of the not naturally bad but irresponsible and undeveloped nature, caught in the consequences of its own action," Bawcutt qualifies his agreement by stating that she is "not innocent in any worthy sense. It is the innocence of selfishness, of ignorance, of one who has failed to realize that she is as much subject to the laws of morality as anyone else. But it would not be right to say that she is unaware of morality," to judge from many of her speeches. To him, "the tragedy of Beatrice is that at the decisive moment in her life, the testing of her character, she comes to discover that she is evil, that she belongs with the wicked." Samuel Schoenbaum, too, describes Beatrice-Joanna as "a pampered, irresponsible child who has been deluded into regarding herself as an adult." In her willful but ingenuous desire to order the lives of those around her to suit her own cravings, in her naive inability to "understand the pathology" of a man like Deflores, she finds that her projects never work out according to plan, and brings destruction on many of those about her, including Deflores, whose sinister ingenuity which has so attracted her to him finally overreaches itself. Deflores himself, according to Schoenbaum, is "clearly a pathological type, a study in abnormal psychology," whose intense morbid passion for the girl overcomes the loathing which his repulsive appearance has inspired in her. Both he and she are used by Middleton to make "the most powerful statement of the . . . self-destructive nature of evil." Irving Ribner, too (*Jacobean Tragedy: The Search for Moral Order*), takes the position that "Middleton is concerned not so much with the complexities of human nature as with the nature of evil in the world." He maintains that Middleton's point of view was basically Christian, even Calvinistic in its attitude toward sin and redemption, and that his tragedies are "profoundly moral works," ritualistic and symbolic in nature. Clifford Leech put the matter somewhat differently when he said that in *The Changeling* Middleton "has a sense of sin, though not of God" (*The John Fletcher Plays*, London, 1962), but felt that it is more difficult to undertand his "Weltanschauung" than that of many other Elizabethan dramatists. He ended by quoting Eliot, only a limited admirer of the play: "He has no point of view, is neither sentimental nor cynical; he is neither resigned, nor disillusioned, nor romantic; he has no message." Thus, once more, the same work of art often provokes its critics to opposite reactions.

A considerable amount of the criticism of the play has centered on two matters: the secondary plot and Alsemero's chemical tests for virginity and pregnancy. Few critics have been found to defend the latter, most of them calling the scene not only incredible but ridiculous. Ribner, however, found in it another of his dramatic symbols and suggested that "its very ludicrousness is a part of Middleton's design, to illustrate the futility of any probing into what only time can reveal," or "of human impotence in the face of divine will." To lend scientific credibility to his test, Alsemero says that he is quoting from *The Book of Experiment, Called Secrets in Nature*, by Antonius Mizaldus. Martin W. Sampson could not discover these particular tests in Mizaldus's *De Arcanis Naturae*, but found comparable ones in his *Centuriae IX. Memorabilium*.

The problem of the subplot exploiting the appeal of Bedlam, or in this case a private mental hospital, as a source of amusement to Elizabethans of course involves the collaboration of Middleton with Rowley, who is unanimously given credit for the comic scenes in the home of Dr. Alibius and for the opening and closing scenes of the play. A few critics with carefully attuned ears have felt themselves competent to assign other passages and even speeches to Rowley, on the basis of textual parallels, vocabulary, characteristic themes and images, and types of characters and situations. (For those interested in the subject, the following works are suggested: Pauline G. Wiggin, *An Inquiry into the Authorship of the Middleton-Rowley Plays*, Boston, 1897; Edward Engelberg, "A Middleton-Rowley Dispute," *NQ*, 1953, and "Tragic Blindness in *The Changeling* and *Women Beware Women*," *MLQ*, 1968; C. L. Barbour, "A Rare Use of 'Honour' as a Criterion of Middleton's Authorship," *ES*, 1957; Wilbur D. Dunkel, "Did Not Rowley Merely Revise Middleton?," *PMLA*, 1933; Dewar M. Robb, "The Canon of William Rowley's Plays," *MLR*, 1950; Schoenbaum; Stork; Barker; Bawcutt; and so forth.)

Until quite recently it was the custom to condemn this subplot, not only as an excrescence, but a tasteless one as well. Swinburne called it "very stupid, rather coarse and almost vulgar" in his introduction to Middleton in the old Mermaids (1887); E. H. C. Oliphant complained that it is "a pity that the silly underplot should have given its name to a tragedy that ranks among the very finest in the language" (*Shakespeare and His Fellow Dramatists*, New York, 1929); Eliot described it as "nauseous" (*The Use of Poetry and the Use of Criticism*, London, 1933); Ellis-Fermor thought it could well have been omitted; Barker said it "would be nice . . . if we could forget that the play has a comic story at all;" Schoenbaum called it the "play's worst blemish;" and Robert Ornstein shared this feeling (*The Moral Vision of Jacobean Tragedy*).

Recently, however, several critics have come to the defense of both Middleton and Rowley in their apparent joint decision to introduce a comical, even farcical, subplot, not only to appeal to the groundlings, but also to reinforce the main plot. (See William Empson, *Some Versions of Pastoral*, London, 1935; Muriel C. Bradbrook, *Themes and Conventions of Elizabethan Tragedy;* Karl L. Holzknecht, "The Dramatic Structure of *The Changeling*," *Renaissance Papers*, University of South Carolina Press, 1954;

George W. Williams, edition of the play for the Regents Renaissance Drama Series, University of Nebraska Press, 1966; Ribner; and so forth.) Ribner, for example, maintained not only that "the main plot and the sub-plot are united by a common theme" and that the two authors worked so closely together throughout that "the comic sub-plot . . . was subsumed into the thematic unity of the whole," but also that the subplot, in contrast with the main plot, "reveals the possibility of good, and this is one reason why Isabella and her lovers are so essential to the total play." But at the same time that Ribner argued that Isabella provides a conscious counterpart to Beatrice-Joanna and that the role of Antonio, sometimes in disguise as a fool but always wooing Isabella in his proper person, has a symbolic significance, along with the dividing of Alibius's house into fools and madmen, he also admitted that it would be futile to contend that these scenes are not "crude, farcical, generally in bad taste, and full of extraneous farcical horse play." Holzknecht, however, produced the most elaborate defense of the entire conception of the play by arguing that, in spite of the identification of Antonio in the dramatis personae as "the changeling," or the counterfeit fool, this word (not used anywhere in the play in its ordinary Elizabethan sense of a child secretly exchanged for another in its infancy) could also be applied, as suggested in the final speeches, in different senses to Beatrice-Joanna herself, to Alsemero, to Diaphanta, and to Franciscus, the counterfeit madman, so that the title might well have been in the plural. The story of Alsemero and Beatrice-Joanna is matched and paralleled by that of Jasperino and Diaphanta, and of Isabella and Alibius; and by bringing together and elaborating on the various mad transformations wrought by love, the collaborators created a play that is more structurally sound than most critics have supposed. Christopher Ricks also discussed "The Moral and Poetic Structure of *The Changeling*" (*Essays in Criticism*, 1960), finding that the play achieves form and meaning partly through its use of a particular group of words containing sexual innuendos. Robert S. Reed lent additional support to the verisimilitude of the madhouse scenes by contending that they were actually a burlesque reflection of the treatment of patients in Bethlehem Hospital in London and not a private asylum, and that Dr. Alibius (meaning "being in another place") and his lustful assistant Lollio were based on Dr. Hilkish Crooke and his steward, who, after a long period of maladministration, were finally tried in 1632 for fraud, misappropriation of funds, and neglect of duty. (See "A Factual Interpretation of *The Changeling's* Madhouse Scenes," *NQ*, 1950, and *Bedlam on the Jacobean Stage*, Harvard University Press, 1952.)

No immediate source has been found for the subplot of the play, but for the main plot the authors went to the fourth story of the first book of John Reynolds's *The Triumphs of God's Revenge against the Crying and Execrable Sin of Wilful and Premeditated Murther* (1621). Schoenbaum has made a detailed comparison with what he describes as Reynolds's lurid and preposterous story and the significant alterations made in it, notably in changing Deflores from "a gallant young gentleman, of the garrison of the castle," into a hideous, repulsive, lustful, but quick-witted villain. Although Reynolds denied that he had plagiarized or translated any of his thirty stories from French or Italian originals, modern scholars have pointed out various analogues, particularly that in a novel by Leonard Digges, *Gerardo, the Unfortunate Spaniard*, translated from the Spanish of G. de Cespedes y Meneses and entered in the Stationers' Register less than two months before *The Changeling* was licensed, on May 7, 1622. (For this whole background, see E. G. Matthews, "The Murdered Substitute Tale," *MLQ*, 1945; G. P. Baker, "A New Source of *The Changeling*," *Journal of Comparative Literature*, 1903; Karl Christ, *Quellenstudien zu den Dramen Thomas Middletons*, Leipzig, 1905; and Bertram Lloyd, "A Minor Source of *The Changeling*," *MLR*, 1924.)

Sir Henry Herbert, Master of the Revels, licensed the play to be acted by the Servants of the Queen of Bohemia, the Lady Elizabeth, at the Phoenix Theater. It was successful enough to be repeated at Whitehall on January 4, 1624 (Joseph Quincy Adams, *The Dramatic Records of Sir Henry Herbert*, Yale University Press, 1917).

The right to perform the play apparently resided in Christopher Beeston, the owner of the theater, who, after the disappearance of Lady Elizabeth's company during the outbreak of the plague in 1625, continued to give it with Queen Henrietta's company. When the play was first printed (not till 1653, as by "T. M. and W. R., gent."), its title page stated that it had been given both at the Phoenix and at the Salisbury Court.   In 1636 a new company, the King and Queen's Young Company, popularly known as "Beeston's Boys," kept it in its repertoire, as did William Beeston, who took over the company when his father died in 1638.   Several contemporary references in the 1640s and 1650s indicate the continued popularity of the play, especially because of the part of Antonio, the changeling.   Toward the end of the Commonwealth, *The Changeling* was one of several plays revived by John Rhodes at the Phoenix even before the Restoration of Charles II took place, and when Sir William D'avenant organized the Duke's Company in 1660 he continued to give performances of it, one of which was witnessed by Samuel Pepys.   Except for three productions of an inferior and unacknowledged adaptation by William Hayley in 1789, the play remained alive only in the library until an abridged version, without the subplot, was given by the British Broadcasting Company in 1950; a single performance was offered by the Pegasus Society at Wyndham's Theatre, London, in 1954; and two years later it was performed at Oxford by the Experimental Theatre Club.   (For this stage history, see G. E. Bentley, *The Jacobean and Caroline Stage*, supplemented by Bawcutt.)

After a reissue of the 1653 text in 1668, the play was not reprinted till 1815, in C. W. Dilke's *Old English Plays*.   Editions of the *Works* by the Rev. Alexander Dyce and A. H. Bullen appeared in 1840 and 1885 respectively.   Since then it has been reprinted in several anthologies and in individual modern editions in the Revels Plays (ed. Bawcutt, London, 1958), the New Mermaids (ed. Patricia Thomson, London, 1964), the Regents Renaissance Drama Series (ed. George W. Williams, University of Nebraska Press, 1966), and the Matthew Carey Library of English and American Literature (ed. Matthew W. Black, University of Pennsylvania Press, 1966).   In 1961 "A Bibliographical Study of Middleton and Rowley's *The Changeling*" was published in *The Library* by Robert G. Lawrence.   The present text is based on a photostat of the copy of the 1653 quarto in the Harvard College Library, but reference has also been made to the various other editions cited above.

# THE CHANGELING[1]

## BY

## THOMAS MIDDLETON AND WILLIAM ROWLEY

### DRAMATIS PERSONÆ

VERMANDERO, [governor of the castle of Alicant and] father to Beatrice.
TOMASO DE PIRACQUO, a noble lord.
ALONZO DE PIRACQUO, his brother, suitor to Beatrice.
ALSEMERO, a nobleman, afterwards married to Beatrice.
JASPERINO, his friend.
ALIBIUS, a jealous doctor.
LOLLIO, his man.
PEDRO, friend to Antonio.

ANTONIO, the changeling.
FRANCISCUS, the counterfeit madman.
DEFLORES, servant to Vermandero.
MADMEN.
SERVANTS.

BEATRICE [JOANNA], daughter to Vermandero.
DIAPHANTA, her waiting-woman.
ISABELLA, wife to Alibius.

THE SCENE: Alligant.[2]

[TIME: Contemporary.]

ACTUS PRIMUS. [SCENA PRIMA.

Outside a temple.]

Enter Alsemero.

[ALS.] 'Twas in the temple where I first beheld her,
And now again the same. What omen yet
Follows of that? None but imaginary.
Why should my hopes or fate be timorous?
The place is holy; so is my intent.
I love her beauties to the holy purpose;
And that, methinks, admits comparison
With man's first creation, the place blessed,
And is his right home back, if he achieve it.
The church hath first begun our interview,      10
And that's the place must join us into one;
So there's beginning and perfection too.

Enter Jasperino.

JAS. O sir, are you here? Come, the wind's fair with you;
Y' are like to have a swift and pleasant passage.
ALS. Sure, y' are deceived, friend; 'tis contrary,
In my best judgment.
JAS.                              What, for Malta?
If you could buy a gale amongst the witches,
They could not serve you such a lucky pennyworth      18
As comes a[3] God's name.
ALS.                              Even now I observed
The temple's vane to turn full in my face;
I know 'tis against me.
JAS.                              Against you?
Then you know not where you are.
ALS.                              Not well, indeed.
JAS. Are you not well, sir?
ALS.                              Yes, Jasperino,
Unless there be some hidden malady
Within me that I understand not.

[1] The title continues: "As It Was Acted with Great Applause at the Private House in Drury Lane, and Salisbury Court."   [2] Alicant, Spain.
[3] In.

415

Jas.                              And that
I begin to doubt,[1] sir. I never knew
Your inclinations to travels at a pause
With any cause to hinder it, till now.
Ashore you were wont to call your serv-
    ants up,
And help to trap [2] your horses for the
    speed;                                    30
At sea I have seen you weigh the anchor
    with 'em,
Hoist sails for fear to lose the foremost
    breath,
Be in continual prayers for fair winds—
And have you changed your orisons? [3]
Als.                              No, friend;
I keep the same church, same devotion.
Jas. Lover I'm sure y' are none; the stoic
    was [4]
Found in you long ago; your mother nor
Best friends, who have set snares of
    beauty, ay,
And choice ones too, could never trap
    you that way.
What might be the cause?
Als.                Lord, how violent   40
Thou art! I was but meditating of
Somewhat I heard within the temple.
Jas.                              Is this
Violence? 'Tis but idleness compared
With your haste yesterday.
Als.                    I'm all this while
A-going, man.

*Enter Servants.*

Jas. Backwards, I think, sir.  Look,
your servants.
1 Ser. The seamen call. Shall we board
your trunks?
Als. No, not today.                         50
Jas. 'Tis the critical day, it seems, and
the sign in Aquarius.[5]
2 Ser. We must not to sea today; this
smoke will bring forth fire.
Als. Keep all on shore; I do not know the
    end,
Which needs I must do, of an affair in
    hand
Ere I can go to sea.

1 Ser.                        Well, your pleasure.
2 Ser. Let him e'en take his leisure too;
we are safer on land.
                    *Exeunt Serv[ants].*

*Enter Beatrice Joanna,[6] Diaphanta, and
    Servants. [Alsemero kisses Beatrice.]*

Jas. [*Aside.*] How now! The laws  [60
of the Medes are changed sure.  Salute a
woman! He kisses too! Wonderful! Where
learnt he this? And does it perfectly too.
In my conscience,[7] he ne'er rehearsed it
before.  Nay, go on; this will be stranger
and better news at Valencia than if he had
ransomed half Greece from the Turk.
Bea. You are a scholar, sir?
Als.                      A weak one, lady.
Bea. Which of the sciences is this love you
    speak of?
Als. From your tongue I take it to be
    music.                                    70
Bea. You are skillful in 't; can sing at first
    sight.
Als. And I have showed you all my skill
    at once;
I want more words to express me further,
And must be forced to repetition.
I love you dearly.
Bea.                Be better advised, sir.
Our eyes are sentinels unto our judg-
    ments,
And should give certain judgment what
    they see;
But they are rash sometimes, and tell us
    wonders
Of common things, which, when our
    judgments find,
They can then check the eyes, and call
    them blind.                              80
Als. But I am further, lady; yesterday
Was mine eyes' employment, and hither
    now
They brought my judgment, where are
    both agreed.
Both houses[8] then consenting, 'tis agreed;
Only there wants the confirmation
By the hand royal. That's your part, lady.
Bea. O, there's one above me, sir.—
    [*Aside.*]  For five days past
To be recalled! Sure mine eyes were
    mistaken;

---

[1] Fear.          [2] Prepare.          [3] Prayers.
[4] In the original line ends with *stoic*. Other
instances of faulty line division later in the play
have been altered silently, and a few passages of
very rough verse have been printed as prose.
[5] *I.e.*, favorable for sailing.

[6] In the original *Joanna* appears after *Servants*.
[7] To my knowledge.
[8] Metaphorically, of Parliament.

This was the man was meant me. That
he should come
So near his time, and miss it!  90
JAS. We might have come by the carriers from Valencia, I see, and saved all our
sea-provision; we are at farthest sure. Methinks I should do something too; I meant
to be a venturer in this voyage. Yonder's
another vessel; I'll board her. If she be
lawful prize, down goes her topsail.
[*Goes to Diaphanta.*]

*Enter Deflores.*

DEF. Lady, your father—
BEA.                    Is in health, I hope.
DEF. Your eye shall instantly instruct you,
lady;
He's coming hitherward.
BEA.                    What needed then  100
Your duteous preface? I had rather
He had come unexpected; you must stall [1]
A good presence with unnecessary blab-
bing;
And how welcome for your part you are,
I'm sure you know.
DEF. [*Aside.*]            Will 't never mend,
this scorn,
One side nor other? Must I be enjoined
To follow still [2] whilst she flies from me?
Well,
Fates, do your worst, I'll please myself
with sight
Of her at all opportunities,
If but to spite her anger. I know she had
Rather see me dead than living; and yet
She knows no cause for 't but a peevish
will.                          112
ALS. You seemed displeaséd, lady, on the
sudden.
BEA. Your pardon, sir; 'tis my infirmity.
Nor can I other reason render you
Than his or hers, of [3] some particular thing
They must abandon as a deadly poison,
Which to a thousand other tastes were
wholesome;
Such to mine eyes is that same fellow
there,
The same that report speaks of the
basilisk. [4]                  120

ALS. This is a frequent frailty in our nature;
There's scarce a man amongst a thousand
sound
But hath his imperfection: one distastes
The scent of roses, which to infinites [5]
Most pleasing is and odoriferous;
One, oil, the enemy of poison;
Another, wine, the cheerer of the heart
And lively refresher of the countenance.
Indeed, this fault, if so it be, is general;
There's scarce a thing but is both loved
and loathed.                  130
Myself, I must confess, have the same
frailty.
BEA. And what may be your poison, sir?
I am bold with you.
ALS. And what might be your desire, per-
haps—a cherry?
BEA. I am no enemy to any creature
My memory has, but yon gentleman.
ALS. He does ill to tempt your sight, if he
knew it.
BEA. He cannot be ignorant of that, sir.
I have not spared to tell him so; and I
want
To help myself, since he's a gentleman
In good respect [6] with my father, and
follows him.                  140
ALS. He's out of his place then now.
[*They walk aside.*]
JAS. I am a mad wag, wench.
DIA. So methinks; but, for your comfort,
I can tell you we have a doctor in the city
that undertakes the cure of such.
JAS. Tush, I know what physic is best
for the state of mine own body.
DIA. 'Tis scarce a well-governed state, I
believe.
JAS. I could show thee such a  [150
thing with an ingredian [7] that we two would
compound together, and, if it did not tame
the maddest blood i' th' town for two hours
after, I'll ne'er profess physic again.
DIA. A little poppy, sir, were good to
cause you sleep.
JAS. Poppy? I'll give thee a pop i' th'
lips for that first, and begin there. Poppy
is one simple [8] indeed, and cuckoo [9] (what-
you-call 't) another. I'll discover no  [160
more now; another time I'll show thee all.
[*Exit.*]

[1] Forestall, anticipate.          [2] Always.
[3] Emended by Dyce. Original reads *or.*
[4] A fabulous creature whose look was supposed
to be fatal.

[5] Many people.        [7] Ingredience, mixture.
[6] Repute.            [8] Medicinal herb.
[9] The cuckoo-flower, with an obvious pun.

*Enter Vermandero and Servants.*

BEA. My father, sir.

VER.        O Joanna, I came to meet thee.
Your devotion's ended?

BEA.                        For this time, sir.—
[*Aside.*] I shall change my saint, I fear
me; I find
A giddy turning in me.—Sir, this while
I am beholding to this gentleman,
Who left his own way to keep me com-
pany,
And in discourse I find him much desir-
ous
To see your castle. He hath deserved it,
sir,
If ye please to grant it.

VER.        With all my heart, sir.    170
Yet there's an article between; I must
know
Your country. We use not to give survey
Of our chief strengths to strangers; our
citadels
Are placed conspicuous to outward view,
On promonts'[1] tops, but within our se-
crets.

ALS. A Valencian, sir.

VER.                        A Valencian?
That's native, sir. Of what name, I beseech you?

ALS. Alsemero, sir.

VER.                        Alsemero? Not the son
Of John de Alsemero?

ALS.                        The same, sir.

VER. My best love bids you welcome.

BEA.                        He was wont    [180
To call me so, and then he speaks a most
Unfeignéd truth.

VER.        O sir, I knew your father;
We two were in acquaintance long ago,
Before our chins were worth iulan down,[2]
And so continued till the stamp of time
Had coined us into silver. Well, he's
gone;
A good soldier went with him.

ALS. You went together in that, sir.

VER. No, by Saint Jacques, I came behind
him;
Yet I have done somewhat too. An un-
happy day    190
Swallowed him at last at Gibraltar,
In fight with those rebellious Hollanders.
Was it not so?

[1] Promontories'.

ALS.        Whose death I had revenged,
Or followed him in fate, had not the late
league[3]
Prevented me.

VER.        Ay, ay, 'twas time to breathe.—
O Joanna, I should ha' told thee news;
I saw Piracquo lately.

BEA. [*Aside.*]                        That's ill news.

VER. He's hot preparing for this day of
triumph;
Thou must be a bride within this sevennight.

ALS. [*Aside.*] Ha!                        200

BEA. Nay, good sir, be not so violent; with
speed
I cannot render satisfaction
Unto the dear companion of my soul,
Virginity, whom I thus long have lived
with,
And part with it so rude and suddenly.
Can such friends divide, never to meet
again,
Without a solemn farewell?

VER.        Tush, tush! There's a toy.[4]

ALS. [*Aside.*] I must now part, and never
meet again
With any joy on earth.—Sir, your pardon;
My affairs call on me.

VER.        How, sir? By no means.    210
Not changed so soon, I hope? You must
see my castle
And her best entertainment ere we part;
I shall think myself unkindly used else.
Come, come, let's on; I had good hope
your stay
Had been awhile with us in Alligant.
I might have bid you to my daughter's
wedding.

ALS. [*Aside.*] He means to feast me, and
poisons me beforehand.—
I should be dearly glad to be there, sir,
Did my occasions suit as I could wish.

BEA. I shall be sorry if you be not there
When it is done, sir; but not so suddenly.    221

VER. I tell you, sir, the gentleman's com-
plete,
A courtier and a gallant, enriched
With many fair and noble ornaments.
I would not change him for a son-in-law
For any he in Spain, the proudest he,
And we have great ones, that you know.

[2] The first growth of the beard.
[3] An armistice signed in 1609.        [4] Trifle.

ALS.                              He's much
Bound to you, sir.
VER.                    He shall be bound to me
As fast as this tie can hold him; I'll want
My will else.
BEA. [*Aside.*]    I shall want mine, if you
do it.                                          230
VER. But come. By the way I'll tell you
more of him.
ALS. [*Aside.*] How shall I dare to venture
in his castle,
When he discharges murderers[1] at the
gate?
But I must on, for back I cannot go.
BEA. [*Aside.*] Not this serpent[2] gone yet?
                              [*Drops her glove.*]
VER.          Look, girl, thy glove's fall'n.
Stay, stay. Deflores, help a little.
[*Exeunt Vermandero, Alsemero, and Serv-
ants.*]
DEF. [*Offering her her glove.*]    Here, lady.
BEA. Mischief on your officious forward-
ness!
Who bade you stoop? They touch my
hand no more.
There! For tother's[3] sake I part with
this.        [*Throws down the other glove.*]
Take um, and draw thine own skin off
with um!                                        240
*Exeunt* [*Beatrice, Diaphanta, and Attend-
ants*].
DEF. Here's a favor come with a mischief!
Now I know
She had rather wear my pelt tanned in a
pair
Of dancing pumps than I should thrust
my fingers
Into her sockets here. I know she hates me,
Yet cannot choose but love her.
No matter! If but to vex her, I'll haunt
her still;
Though I get nothing else, I'll have my
will.                                    *Exit.*

[SCENA SECUNDA.

*A room in the house of Alibius.*]

*Enter Alibius and Lollio.*

ALIB. Lollio, I must trust thee with a
secret,
But thou must keep it.
LOL. I was ever close to a secret, sir.

---

ALIB. The diligence that I have found in
thee,
The care and industry already past,
Assures me of thy good continuance.
Lollio, I have a wife.
LOL. Fie, sir, 'tis too late to keep her
secret; she's known to be married all the
town and country over.                          10
ALIB. Thou goest too fast, my Lollio.
That knowledge
I allow no man can be barred it;
But there is a knowledge which is
nearer,
Deeper, and sweeter, Lollio.
LOL. Well, sir, let us handle that be-
tween you and I.
ALIB. 'Tis that I go about, man. Lollio,
My wife is young.
LOL. So much the worse to be kept
secret, sir.                                    20
ALIB. Why, now thou meet'st the sub-
stance of the point;
I am old, Lollio.
LOL. No, sir, 'tis I am old Lollio.
ALIB. Yet why may not this concord and
sympathize?
Old trees and young plants often grow
together,
Well enough agreeing.
LOL. Ay, sir, but the old trees raise
themselves higher and broader than the
young plants.
ALIB. Shrewd application! There's the
fear, man;                                      30
I would wear my ring on my own finger;
Whilst it is borrowed, it is none of
mine,
But his that useth it.
LOL. You must keep it on still then; if
it but lie by, one or other will be thrusting
into 't.
ALIB. Thou conceiv'st me, Lollio. Here
thy watchful eye
Must have employment. I cannot al-
ways be at home.
LOL. I dare swear you cannot.
ALIB. I must look out.                          40
LOL. I know 't, you must look out; 'tis
every man's case.
ALIB. Here, I do say, must thy employ-
ment be—
To watch her treadings, and in my ab-
sence
Supply my place.

---

Lol. I'll do my best, sir; yet surely I cannot see who you should have cause to be jealous of.

Alib. Thy reason for that, Lollio? 'Tis a comfortable question.                    50

Lol. We have but two sorts of people in the house, and both under the whip—that's fools and madmen; the one has not wit enough to be knaves, and the other not knavery enough to be fools.

Alib. Ay, those are all my patients, Lollio.
I do profess the cure of either sort.
My trade, my living 'tis; I thrive by it.
But here's the care that mixes with my thrift:
The daily visitants, that come to see    60
My brainsick patients, I would not have
To see my wife.   Gallants I do observe
Of quick, enticing eyes, rich in habits,
Of stature and proportion very comely.
These are most shrewd temptations, Lollio.

Lol. They may be easily answered, sir. If they come to see the fools and madmen, you and I may serve the turn, and let my mistress alone.   She's of neither sort.

Alib. 'Tis a good ward; [1] indeed, come they to see                    70
Our madmen or our fools, let um see no more
Than what they come for.   By that consequent
They must not see her; I'm sure she's no fool.

Lol. And I'm sure she's no madman.

Alib. Hold that buckler fast.   Lollio, my trust
Is on thee, and I account it firm and strong.
What hour is 't, Lollio?

Lol.                    Towards belly hour, sir.

Alib. Dinner time?   Thou mean'st twelve a-clock?

Lol. Yes, sir, for every part has his hour: we wake at six and look about us—    [80 that's eye hour; at seven we should pray— that's knee hour; at eight walk—that's leg hour; at nine gather flowers and pluck a rose [2]—that's nose hour; at ten we

drink—that's mouth hour; at eleven lay about us for victuals—that's hand hour; at twelve go to dinner—that's belly hour.

Alib. Profoundly, Lollio!   It will be long
Ere all thy scholars learn this lesson, and
I did look to have a new one entered— stay,                    90
I think my expectation is come home.

*Enter Pedro, and Antonio like an idiot.*

Ped. Save you, sir.   My business speaks itself;
This sight takes off the labor of my tongue.

Alib. Ay, ay, sir, 'tis plain enough you mean him for my patient.

Ped. And, if your pains prove but commodious, to give but some little strength to his sick and weak part of nature in him, these are [*Gives him money.*] but patterns to show you of the whole pieces that will follow to you, beside the charge of diet, washing, and other necessaries, fully defrayed.

Alib. Believe it, sir, there shall no care be wanting.                    102

Lol. Sir, an officer in this place may deserve something.   The trouble will pass through my hands.

Ped. 'Tis fit something should come to your hands then, sir.        [*Gives him money.*]

Lol. Yes, sir, 'tis I must keep him sweet, [3] and read to him.   What is his name?

Ped. His name is Antonio; marry, we use but half to him, only Tony.        111

Lol. Tony, Tony, 'tis enough, and a very good name for a fool.—What's your name, Tony?

Ant. He, he, he!   Well, I thank you, cousin.   He, he, he!

Lol. Good boy, hold up your head.—He can laugh; I perceive by that he is no beast.

Ped. Well, sir,
If you can raise him but to any height,
Any degree of wit, might he attain,    121
As I might say, to creep but on all four
Towards the chair of wit, or walk on crutches,
'Twould add an honor to your worthy pains,
And a great family might pray for you,
To which he should be heir, had he discretion

---

[1] Guard, defense.        [2] *I.e.*, relieve ourselves.        [3] Clean.

To claim and guide his own.  Assure you, sir,
He is a gentleman.

Lol. Nay, there's nobody doubted that. At first sight I knew him for a gentleman; he looks no other yet.                    131

Ped. Let him have good attendance and sweet lodging.

Lol. As good as my mistress lies in, sir; and, as you allow us time and means, we can raise him to the higher degree of discretion.

Ped. Nay, there shall no cost want, sir.

Lol. He will hardly be stretched up to the wit of a magnifico.

Ped. O, no, that's not to be expected; far shorter will be enough.                 141

Lol. I'll warrant you [I'll] [1] make him fit to bear office in five weeks; I'll undertake to wind him up to the wit of constable.

Ped. If it be lower than that, it might serve turn.

Lol. No, fie; to level him with a headborough,[2] beadle, or watchman were but little better than he is.  Constable I'll [150 able him;[3] if he do come to be a justice afterwards, let him thank the keeper.  Or I'll go further with you.  Say I do bring him up to my own pitch; say I make him as wise as myself.

Ped. Why, there I would have it.

Lol. Well, go to; either I'll be as arrant a fool as he, or he shall be as wise as I, and then I think 'twill serve his turn.       159

Ped. Nay, I do like thy wit passing well.

Lol. Yes, you may; yet if I had not been a fool, I had had more wit than I have too.  Remember what state [4] you find me in.

Ped. I will, and so leave you.  Your best cares, I beseech you.    Ex[it] Ped[ro].

Alib. Take you none with you; leave um all with us.

Ant. O, my cousin's gone!  Cousin, cousin, O!                                        170

Lol. Peace, peace, Tony!  You must not cry, child; you must be whipped if you do.  Your cousin is here still; I am your cousin, Tony.

Ant. He, he!  Then I'll not cry, if thou beest my cousin.  He, he, he!

Lol. I were best try his wit a little, that I may know what form [5] to place him in.

Alib. Ay, do, Lollio, do.

Lol. I must ask him easy ques- [180 tions at first.—Tony, how many true [6] fingers has a tailor on his right hand?

Ant. As many as on his left, cousin.

Lol. Good.  And how many on both?

Ant. Two less than a deuce, cousin.

Lol. Very well answered.  I come to you again, cousin Tony.  How many fools goes to [7] a wise man?

Ant. Forty in a day sometimes, cousin.

Lol. Forty in a day?  How prove [190 you that?

Ant. All that fall out amongst themselves, and go to a lawyer to be made friends.

Lol. A parlous[8] fool!  He must sit in the fourth form at least, I perceive that.—I come again, Tony.  How many knaves make an honest man?

Ant. I know not that, cousin.

Lol. No, the question is too hard for you.  I'll tell you, cousin.  There's [200 three knaves may make an honest man—a serjeant, a jailor, and a beadle; the serjeant catches him, the jailor holds him, and the beadle lashes him; and, if he be not honest then, the hangman must cure him.

Ant. Ha, ha, ha!  That's fine sport, cousin.

Alib. This was too deep a question for the fool, Lollio.

Lol. Yes, this might have served [210 yourself, though I say 't.—Once more and you shall go play, Tony.

Ant. Ay, play at pushpin,[9] cousin. Ha, he!

Lol. So thou shalt.  Say how many fools are here.

Ant. Two, cousin; thou and I.

Lol. Nay, y' are too forward there, Tony.  Mark my question!  How many fools and knaves are here: a fool before a knave, a fool behind a knave, between [220 every two fools a knave—how many fools, how many knaves?

Ant. I never learnt so far, cousin.

Alib. Thou putt'st too hard questions to him, Lollio.

Lol. I'll make him understand it easily. —Cousin, stand there.

Ant. Ay, cousin.

---

[1] Supplied by Dyce.        [2] Petty constable.
[3] *I.e.*, qualify him for.        [4] Position.
[5] Class.        [6] Honest.        [7] Make.
[8] Clever.        [9] A child's game.

Lol. Master, stand you next the fool.

Alib. Well, Lollio. 230

Lol. Here's my place. Mark now, Tony, there a fool before a knave.

Ant. That's I, cousin.

Lol. Here's a fool behind a knave— that's I; and between us two fools there is a knave—that's my master; 'tis but we three, that's all.

Ant. We three, we three, cousin.

*Madmen within.*

1 [Mad.] (*Within.*) Put's head i' th' pillory; the bread's too little. 240

2 [Mad.] (*Within.*) Fly, fly, and he catches the swallow.

3 [Mad.] (*Within.*) Give her more onion, or the devil put the rope about her crag.[1]

Lol. You may hear what time of day it is; the chimes of Bedlam goes.

Alib. Peace, peace, or the wire [2] comes!

3 [Mad.] (*Within.*) Cat whore, cat [249 whore! Her parmasant, her parmasant! [3]

Alib. Peace, I say!—Their hour's come; they must be fed, Lollio.

Lol. There's no hope of recovery of that Welsh madman; was undone by a mouse that spoiled him a parmasant; lost his wits for 't.

Alib. Go to your charge, Lollio; I'll to mine.

Lol. Go you to your madmen's ward; let me alone with your fools. 260

Alib. And remember my last charge, Lollio. *Exit.*

Lol. Of which your patients do you think I am? Come, Tony, you must amongst your schoolfellows now. There's pretty scholars amongst um, I can tell you; there's some of 'em at *stultus, stulta, stultum.*[4]

Ant. I would see the madmen, cousin, if they would not bite me. 270

Lol. No, they shall not bite thee, Tony.

Ant. They bite when they are at dinner, do they not, coz?

Lol. They bite at dinner, indeed, Tony. Well, I hope to get credit by thee; I like thee the best of all the scholars that ever I brought up, and thou shalt prove a wise man, or I'll prove a fool myself. *Exeunt.*

---

[1] Neck.  [2] Whip.  [3] Parmesan cheese.
[4] The beginning of the Latin declension of *stupid.*

Actus Secundus. [Scena Prima.

*A room in the castle.*]

*Enter Beatrice and Jasperino severally.*

Bea. O, sir, I'm ready now for that fair service

Which makes the name of friend sit glorious on you!

Good angels and this conduct be your guide! [*Gives a paper.*]

Fitness of time and place is there set down, sir.

Jas. The joy I shall return rewards my service. *Exit.*

Bea. How wise is Alsemero in his friend!

It is a sign he makes his choice with judgment.

Then I appear in nothing more approved

Than making choice of him, for, 'tis a principle,

He that can choose 10

That bosom well who of his thoughts partakes,

Proves most discreet in every choice he makes.

Methinks I love now with the eyes of judgment,

And see the way to merit, clearly see it.

A true deserver like a diamond sparkles;

In darkness you may see him—that's in absence,

Which is the greatest darkness falls on love;

Yet is he best discerned then

With intellectual eyesight. What's Piracquo

My father spends his breath for? And his blessing 20

Is only mine as I regard his name,

Else it goes from me, and turns head against me,

Transformed into a curse. Some speedy way

Must be remembered. He's so forward too,

So urgent that way, scarce allows me breath

To speak to my new comforts.

*Enter Deflores.*

Def. [*Aside.*] Yonder's she;

Whatever ails me, now alate especially!

I can as well be hanged as refrain seeing her.

Some twenty times a day, nay, not so
  little,
Do I force errands, frame ways and ex-
  cuses,                30
To come into her sight; and I have small
  reason for 't,
And less encouragement, for she baits
  me still
Every time worse than other; does pro-
  fess herself
The cruelest enemy to my face in town;
At no hand can abide the sight of me,
As if danger or ill luck hung in my
  looks.
I must confess my face is bad enough,
But I know far worse has better fortune,
And not endured alone, but doted on;
And yet such pick-haired [1] faces, chins
  like witches',          40
Here and there five hairs, whispering
  in a corner
As if they grew in fear one of another,
Wrinkles like troughs, where swine-
  deformity swills
The tears of perjury, that lie there like
  wash
Fallen from the slimy and dishonest
  eye—
Yet such a one plucks sweets without
  restraint,
And has the grace of beauty to his sweet.
Though my hard fate has thrust me out
  to servitude,
I tumbled into th' world a gentleman.
She turns her blessèd eye upon me now,
And I'll endure all storms before I part
  with 't.           51
BEA. [*Aside*.] Again?
This ominous ill-faced fellow more dis-
  turbs me
Than all my other passions.
DEF. [*Aside*.]      Now 't begins again;
I'll stand this storm of hail, though the
  stones pelt me.
BEA. Thy business?   What's thy busi-
  ness?
DEF. [*Aside*.]        Soft and fair!
I cannot part so soon now.
BEA. [*Aside*.]     The villain's fixed.—
Thou standing toad-pool—
DEF. [*Aside*.]      The shower falls
  amain now.

BEA. Who sent thee?   What's thy errand?
  Leave my sight!
DEF. My lord your father charged me
  to deliver          60
A message to you.
BEA.        What, another since?
Do 't, and be hanged then; let me be rid
  of thee.
DEF. True service merits mercy.
BEA.         What's thy message?
DEF. Let beauty settle but in patience,
  You shall hear all.
BEA.     A dallying, trifling torment!
DEF. Signior Alonzo de Piracquo, lady,
  Sole brother to Tomaso de Piracquo—
BEA. Slave, when wilt make an end?
DEF.         Too soon I shall.
BEA. What all this while of him?
DEF.        The said Alonzo,
With the foresaid Tomaso—
BEA.         Yet again?  70
DEF. Is new alighted.
BEA.      Vengeance strike the news!
Thou thing most loathed, what cause
  was there in this
To bring thee to my sight?
DEF.       My lord your father
Charged me to seek you out.
BEA.      Is there no other
To send his errand by?
DEF.      It seems 'tis my luck
To be i' th' way still.
BEA.      Get thee from me!
DEF.          So.—
[*Aside*.] Why, am not I an ass to devise
  ways
Thus to be railed at?   I must see her still!
I shall have a mad qualm within this
  hour again,
I know 't; and, like a common Garden
  bull,[2]          80
I do but take breath to be lugged [3] again.
What this may bode I know not; I'll
  despair the less,
Because there's daily presidents [4] of
  bad faces
Beloved beyond all reason.   These foul
  chops
May come into favor one day mongst
  his fellows.
Wrangling has proved the mistress of
  good pastime.

---

[1] Thin-bearded.

[2] Bulls were baited at Paris Garden.
[3] Pulled, baited.        [4] Precedents.

As children cry themselves asleep, I
　ha' seen
Women have chid themselves abed to
　men.　　　　　　　*Exit Def[lores].*
BEA. I never see this fellow but I think
　Of some harm towards me; danger's
　in my mind still;　　　　　　　90
I scarce leave trembling of an hour after.
The next good mood I find my father in,
I'll get him quite discarded. O, I was
Lost in this small disturbance, and forgot
Affliction's fiercer torrent that now
　comes
To bear down all my comforts!

*Enter Vermandero, Alonzo, Tomaso.*

VER.　　　　　　Y' are both welcome,
But an especial one belongs to you, sir,
To whose most noble name our love
　presents
The addition [1] of a son, our son Alonzo.
ALON. The treasury of honor cannot bring
　forth　　　　　　　100
A title I should more rejoice in, sir.
VER. You have improved it well.—Daugh-
　ter, prepare;
The day will steal upon thee suddenly.
BEA. [*Aside.*] Howe'er, I will be sure to
　keep the night,[2]
If it should come so near me.
　　　[*Beatrice takes Vermandero aside.*]
TOM.　　　　　　Alonzo!
ALON.　　　　　　Brother?
TOM. In troth, I see small welcome in her
　eye.
ALON. Fie, you are too severe a censurer [3]
Of love in all points. There's no bring-
　ing on [4] you.
If lovers should mark everything a
　fault,　　　　　　　109
Affection would be like an ill-set book,
Whose faults might prove as big as half
　the volume.
BEA. That's all I do entreat.
VER.　　　　　　It is but reasonable;
I'll see what my son says to 't.—Son
　Alonzo,
Here's a motion made but to reprieve
A maidenhead three days longer; the
　request
Is not far out of reason, for indeed
The former time is pinching.

ALON.　　　　　　Though my joys
Be set back so much time as I could
　wish
They had been forward, yet, since she
　desires it,
The time is set as pleasing as before.　120
I find no gladness wanting.
VER.　　　　　　May I ever
Meet it in that point still! Y' are nobly
　welcome, sirs.
　　　*Exeunt Ver[mandero] and Bea[trice].*
TOM. So; did you mark the dullness of
　her parting now?
ALON. What dullness? Thou art so ex-
　ceptious [5] still!
TOM. Why, let it go then; I am but a fool
To mark your harms so heedfully.
ALON.　　　　　　Where's the oversight?
TOM. Come, your faith's cozened in her,
　strongly cozened.
Unsettle your affection with all speed
Wisdom can bring it to; your peace is
　ruined else.
Think what a torment 'tis to marry
　one　　　　　　　130
Whose heart is leaped into another's
　bosom.
If ever pleasure she receive from thee,
It comes not in thy name, or of thy gift.
She lies but with another in thine arms,
He the half-father unto all thy children
In the conception; if he get 'em not,
She helps to get 'em for him in his [6]
　passions, and how dangerous
And shameful her restraint may go in
　time to,
It is not to be thought on without suf-
　ferings.
ALON. You speak as if she loved some
　other, then.　　　　　　　140
TOM. Do you apprehend so slowly?
ALON.　　　　　　Nay, and that
Be your fear only, I am safe enough.
Preserve your friendship and your coun-
　sel, brother,
For times of more distress; I should de-
　part
An enemy, a dangerous, deadly one,
To any but thyself, that should but think
She knew the meaning of inconstancy,
Much less the use and practice; yet
　w' are friends.

---

[1] Title.　[2] *I.e.*, watch.　[3] Judge.　[4] Persuading.

[5] Captions.　　　　　　[6] *I.e.*, the husband's.

Pray, let no more be urged; I can endure
Much, till I meet an injury to her;   150
Then I am not myself.   Farewell, sweet
brother;
How much w' are bound to heaven to
depart lovingly.   *Exit.*
Tom. Why, here is love's tame madness;
thus a man
Quickly steals into his vexation.   *Exit.*

[Scena Secunda.

*Another room in the castle.*]

*Enter Diaphanta and Alsemero.*

Dia. The place is my charge; you have
kept your hour,
And the reward of a just meeting bless
you!
I hear my lady coming.   Complete
gentleman,
I dare not be too busy with my praises;
Th' are dangerous things to deal with.
                              *Exit.*
Als.                    This goes well;
These women are the ladies' cabinets,
Things of most precious trust are lock[ed]
into 'em.

*Enter Beatrice.*

Bea. I have within mine eye all my de-
sires.
Requests that holy prayers ascend
heaven for,
And brings 'em down to furnish our
defects,   10
Come not more sweet to our necessities
Than thou unto my wishes.
Als.                    W' are so like
In our expressions, lady, that, unless I
borrow
The same words, I shall never find their
equals.
Bea. How happy were this meeting, this
embrace,
If it were free from envy!   This poor
kiss
It has an enemy, a hateful one,
That wishes poison to 't.   How well were
I now,
If there were none such name known
as Piracquo,
Nor no such tie as the command of
parents!   20

I should be but too much blessed.
Als.                    One good service
Would strike off both your fears, and
I'll go near it too,
Since you are so distressed.   Remove
the cause,
The command ceases; so there's two
fears blown out
With one and the same blast.
Bea.          Pray, let me find [1] you, sir.
What might that service be, so strangely
happy?
Als. The honorablest piece 'bout man,
valor.
I'll send a challenge to Piracquo in-
stantly.
Bea. How?   Call you that extinguishing
of fear,
When 'tis the only way to keep it flam-
ing?   30
Are not you ventured in the action,
That's all my joys and comforts?
Pray, no more, sir.
Say you prevailed; you're danger's and
not mine then.
The law would claim you from me, or
obscurity
Be made the grave to bury you alive.
I'm glad these thoughts come forth;
O, keep not one
Of this condition, sir!   Here was a course
Found to bring sorrow on her way to
death;
The tears would ne'er 'a' dried, till dust
had choked 'em.
Blood guiltiness becomes a fouler vis-
age.—   40
[*Aside.*] And now I think on one; I was
to blame—
I ha' marred so good a market with my
scorn.
'T had been done questionless.   The
ugliest creature
Creation framed for some use!   Yet to
see
I could not mark so much where it should
be!
Als. Lady—
Bea. [*Aside.*]          Why, men of art make
much of poison,
Keep one to expel another.   Where was
my art?
Als. Lady, you hear not me.
[1] Understand.

BEA. I do especially, sir.
The present times are not so sure of our side
As those hereafter may be; we must use 'em then 50
As thrifty folks their wealth, sparingly now,
Till the time opens.
ALS. You teach wisdom, lady.
BEA. Within there, Diaphanta!

*Enter Diaphanta.*

DIA. Do you call, madam?
BEA. Perfect your service, and conduct this gentleman
The private way you brought him.
DIA. I shall, madam.
ALS. My love's as firm as love e'er built upon.
*Ex[eunt] Dia[phanta] and Als[emero].*

*Enter Deflores.*

DEF. [*Aside.*] I've watched this meeting, and do wonder much
What shall become of tother. I'm sure both
Cannot be served unless she transgress; happily [1] 59
Then I'll put in for one; for, if a woman
Fly from one point, from him she makes a husband,
She spreads and mounts then like arithmetic
(One, ten, a hundred, a thousand, ten thousand),
Proves in time sutler to an army royal.
Now do I look to be most richly railed at;
Yet I must see her.
BEA. [*Aside.*] Why, put case [2] I loathed him
As much as youth and beauty hates a sepulcher,
Must I needs show it? Cannot I keep that secret,
And serve my turn upon him? See, he's here.—
Deflores!
DEF. [*Aside.*] Ha, I shall run mad with joy! 70
She called me fairly by my name, Deflores,
And neither rogue nor rascal.

[1] Haply, perhaps.        [2] *I.e.*, suppose.

BEA. What ha' you done
To your face alate? Y'ave met with some good physician;
Y'ave pruned [3] yourself, methinks. You were not wont
To look so amorously. [4]
DEF. Not I.—[*Aside.*] 'Tis
The same physnomy, [5] to a hair and pimple,
Which she called scurvy scarce an hour ago.
How is this?
BEA. Come hither; nearer, man.
DEF. [*Aside.*] I'm up to the chin in heaven!
BEA. Turn, let me see.
Vaugh, 'tis but the heat of the liver, I perceive 't; 80
I thought it had been worse.
DEF. [*Aside.*] Her fingers touched me!
She smells all amber. [6]
BEA. I'll make a water for you shall cleanse this
Within a fortnight.
DEF. With your own hands, lady?
BEA. Yes, mine own, sir; in a work of cure
I'll trust no other.
DEF. [*Aside.*] 'Tis half an act of pleasure
To hear her talk thus to me.
BEA. When w' are used
To a hard face, 'tis not so unpleasing;
It mends still in opinion, hourly mends;
I see it by experience.
DEF. [*Aside.*] I was blessed 90
To light upon this minute; I'll make use on 't.
BEA. Hardness becomes the visage of a man well;
It argues service, resolution, manhood,
If cause were of employment.
DEF. 'Twould be soon seen
If e'er your ladyship had cause to use it;
I would but wish the honor of a service
So happy as that mounts to.
BEA. We shall try you.—
O, my Deflores!
DEF. [*Aside.*] How's that? She calls me hers
Already! "My Deflores!"—You were about
To sigh out somewhat, madam?

[3] Preened, trimmed.    [4] Like one to be loved.
[5] Physiognomy.        [6] Ambergris.

BEA.                     No, was I?   100
I forgot—O!—
DEF.               There 'tis again, the very
   fellow on 't.
BEA. You are too quick, sir.
DEF. There's no excuse for 't now; I
   heard it twice, madam;
That sigh would fain have utterance.
   Take pity on 't,
And lend it a free word.   'Las, how it
   labors
For liberty! I hear the murmur yet
Beat at your bosom.
BEA.                     Would creation—
DEF. Ay, well said, that's it.
BEA.                     Had formed me man!
DEF. Nay, that's not it.
BEA.           O, 'tis the soul of freedom!
I should not then be forced to marry
   one                                          110
I hate beyond all depths; I should have
   power
Then to oppose my loathings, nay, re-
   move 'em
Forever from my sight.
DEF. [Aside.]           O blessed occasion!—
Without change to your sex you have
   your wishes;
Claim so much man in me.
BEA.               In thee, Deflores?
There's small cause for that.
DEF.               Put it not from me;
It's a service that I kneel for to you.
                                        [Kneels.]
BEA. You are too violent to mean faith-
   fully.
There's horror in my service, blood and
   danger;
Can those be things to sue for?
DEF.               If you knew   120
How sweet it were to me to be employed
In any act of yours, you would say
   then
I failed, and used not reverence enough
When I receive the charge on 't.
BEA. [Aside.]           This is much,
Methinks; belike his wants are greedy;
   and,
To such, gold tastes like angel's food.
   Rise!
DEF. I'll have the work first.
BEA. [Aside.]           Possible his need
Is strong upon him.—There's to en-
   courage thee;               [Gives money.]

As thou art forward, and thy service
   dangerous,
Thy reward shall be precious.
DEF.           That I have thought on;   130
I have assured myself of that before-
   hand,
And know it will be precious; the thought
   ravishes!
BEA. Then take him to thy fury!
DEF.               I thirst for him.
BEA. Alonzo de Piracquo.
DEF. [Rising.]           His end's upon him;
He shall be seen no more.
BEA.               How lovely now
Dost thou appear to me!  Never was
   man
Dearlier rewarded.
DEF.                     I do think of that.
BEA. Be wondrous careful in the execu-
   tion.
DEF. Why, are not both our lives upon
   the cast?
BEA. Then I throw all my fears upon thy
   service.                                      140
DEF. They ne'er shall rise to hurt you.
BEA.               When the deed's done,
I'll furnish thee with all things for thy
   flight;
Thou mayst live bravely in another
   country.
DEF. Ay, ay;
We'll talk of that hereafter.
BEA. [Aside.]           I shall rid myself
Of two inveterate loathings at one
   time,
Piracquo, and his dog-face.        Exit.
DEF.               O my blood!
Methinks I feel her in mine arms already,
Her wanton fingers combing out this
   beard,
And, being pleased, praising this bad
   face.                                        150
Hunger and pleasure, they'll commend
   sometimes
Slovenly dishes, and feed heartily on
   'em—
Nay, which is stranger, refuse daintier
   for 'em.
Some women are odd feeders.—I'm too
   loud.
Here comes the man goes supperless
   to bed,
Yet shall not rise tomorrow to his din-
   ner.

*Enter Alonzo.*

ALON. Deflores.
DEF.                My kind, honorable lord?
ALON. I am glad I ha' met with thee.
DEF.                Sir?
ALON.                        Thou canst show me
The full strength of the castle?
DEF.                        That I can, sir.
ALON. I much desire it.
DEF.            And if the ways and straits 160
Of some of the passages be not too tedi-
ous for you,
I will assure you, worth your time and
sight, my lord.
ALON. Puh, that shall be no hindrance.
DEF.                I'm your servant, then.
'Tis now near dinner time; gainst [1]
your lordship's rising
I'll have the keys about me.
ALON.                Thanks, kind Deflores.
DEF. [*Aside.*] He's safely thrust upon me
beyond hopes.                *Exeunt.*

ACTUS TERTIUS. [SCENA PRIMA.

*The top of a narrow stairway in the castle.*]

*Enter Alonzo and Deflores.  (In the act
time [2] Deflores hides a naked rapier.)*

DEF. Yes, here are all the keys.  I was
afraid, my lord,
I'd wanted for the postern [3] —this
is it.
I've all, I've all, my lord.  This for the
sconce.[4]
ALON. 'Tis a most spacious and impreg-
nable fort.
DEF. You'll tell me more, my lord.  This
descent
Is somewhat narrow; we shall never
pass
Well with our weapons.  They'll but
trouble us.
ALON. Thou say[e]st true.
DEF.        Pray, let me help your lordship.
ALON. 'Tis done.  Thanks, kind Deflores.
DEF.                Here are hooks, my lord,
To hang such things on purpose.        10
                [*Hangs up the two swords.*]
ALON. Lead; I'll follow thee.
*Ex[eunt] at one door and enter at the other.*

[1] In anticipation of.
[2] *I.e.*, between the acts.
[3] Lacked the postern key.
[4] Isolated fortification.

[SCENA SECUNDA.

*A landing place on the stairway.*]

DEF. All this is nothing; you shall see
anon
A place you little dream on.
ALON.                I am glad
I have this leisure; all your master's house
Imagine I ha' taken a gondola.
DEF. All but myself, sir—[*Aside.*] which
makes up my safety.—
My lord, I'll place you at a casement here
Will show you the full strength of all the
castle.
Look, spend your eye awhile upon that
object.
ALON. Here's rich variety, Deflores.
DEF.                Yes, sir.
ALON. Goodly munition.
DEF.        Ay, there's ordnance, sir—   10
No bastard metal, will ring you a peal
like bells
At great men's funerals.  Keep your eye
straight, my lord.
Take special notice of that sconce before
you;
There you may dwell awhile.
        [*Takes the rapier which he has hidden.*]
ALON.                I am upon 't.
DEF. And so am I.                [*Stabs him.*]
ALON.                Deflores! O Deflores!
Whose malice hast thou put on?
DEF.                Do you question
A work of secrecy?  I must silence you.
                [*Stabs him.*]
ALON. O, O, O!
DEF.        I must silence you.—[*Stabs him.*]
So here's an undertaking well accom-
plished.
This vault serves to good use now.  Ha,
what's that                20
Threw sparkles in my eye?  O, 'tis a
diamond
He wears upon his finger.  It was well
found;
This will approve [5] the work.  What, so
fast on?
Not part in death?  I'll take a speedy
course then.
Finger and all shall off.  [*Cuts off the
finger.*]  So, now I'll clear
The passages from all suspect [6] or fear.
                *Exit with body.*

[5] Bear witness to.                [6] Suspicion.

[Scena Tertia.

*A room in the house of Alibius.*]

*Enter Isabella and Lollio.*

Isa. Why, sirrah! Whence have you commission
To fetter the doors against me? If you
Keep me in a cage, pray, whistle to me;
Let me be doing something.

Lol. You shall be doing, if it please you;
I'll whistle to you, if you'll pipe after.

Isa. Is it your master's pleasure, or your own,
To keep me in this pinfold?

Lol. 'Tis for my master's pleasure, lest, being taken in another man's [10 corn, you might be pounded[1] in another place.

Isa. 'Tis very well, and he'll prove very wise.

Lol. He says you have company enough in the house, if you please to be sociable, of all sorts of people.

Isa. Of all sorts? Why, here's none but fools and madmen.

Lol. Very well. And where will [20 you find any other, if you should go abroad? There's my master and I to boot, too.

Isa. Of either sort one, a madman and a fool.

Lol. I would ev'n participate of both then if I were as you. I know y' are half mad already; be half foolish too.

Isa. Y' are a brave, saucy rascal! Come on, sir;
Afford me then the pleasure of your bedlam.
You were commending once today to me    30
Your last-come lunatic—what a proper[2]
Body there was without brains to guide it,
And what a pitiful delight appeared
In that defect, as if your wisdom had found
A mirth in madness. Pray, sir, let me partake,
If there be such a pleasure.

Lol. If I do not show you the handsomest, discreetest madman, one that I may call the understanding madman, then say I am a fool.    40

Isa. Well, a match,[3] I will say so.

Lol. When you have a taste of the madman, you shall, if you please, see Fool's College, o' th' side. I seldom lock there; 'tis but shooting a bolt or two, and you are amongst 'em. [(*Ex*[*it*]. *Enter presently.*[4])—Come on, sir; let me see how handsomely you'll behave yourself now.

*Enter Loll*[*io*], *Franciscus.*

Fran. How sweetly she looks! O, but there's a wrinkle in her brow as deep as    [50 philosophy. Anacreon, drink to my mistress' health; I'll pledge it. Stay, stay, there's a spider in the cup! No, 'tis but a grapestone. Swallow it; fear nothing, poet; so, so, lift higher.

Isa. Alack, alack, 'tis too full of pity
To be laughed at! How fell he mad?
Canst thou tell?

Lol. For love, mistress. He was a pretty poet, too, and that set him forwards first. The Muses then forsook him;    [60 he ran mad for a chambermaid, yet she was but a dwarf neither.

Fran. Hail, bright Titania!
Why stand'st thou idle on these flow'ry banks?
Oberon is dancing with his Dryads;
I'll gather daisies, primrose, violets,
And bind them in a verse of poesy.

Lol. [*Showing him a whip.*] Not too near! You see your danger.    69

Fran. O, hold thy hand, great Diomede!
Thou feed'st thy horses well; they shall obey thee.
Get up! Bucephalus kneels.    [*Kneels.*]

Lol. You see how I awe my flock; a shepherd has not his dog at more obedience.

Isa. His conscience is unquiet; sure that was
The cause of this. A proper gentleman!

Fran. Come hither, Aesculapius; hide the poison.

Lol. [*Hiding the whip.*] Well, 'tis hid.    [79

Fran. Didst thou never hear of one Tiresias, a famous poet?

Lol. Yes, that kept tame wild geese.

Fran. That's he, I am the man.

Lol. No?

Fran. Yes; but make no words on 't. I was a man seven years ago.

---

[1] Impounded.    [2] Handsome.    [3] It is agreed.

[4] *I.e.*, after the following off-stage speech.

LOL. A stripling, I think, you might.

FRAN. Now I'm a woman, all feminine.

LOL. I would I might see that!

FRAN. Juno struck me blind.    90

LOL. I'll ne'er believe that; for a woman, they say, has an eye more than a man.

FRAN. I say she struck me blind.

LOL. And Luna made you mad; you have two trades to beg with.

FRAN. Luna is now big-bellied, and there's room

For both of us to ride with Hecate.

I'll drag thee up into her silver sphere,

And there we'll kick the Dog—and beat the bush—

That barks against the witches of the night.    100

The swift *lycanthropi* [1] that walks the round,

We'll tear their wolvish skins, and save the sheep.    [*Snatches at Lollio.*]

LOL. Is 't come to this? Nay, then, my poison comes forth again.    [*Shows the whip.*] Mad slave, indeed, abuse your keeper!

ISA. I prithee, hence with him, now he grows dangerous.

[*Let Franciscus*] *sing.*

FRAN. Sweet love, pity me;

Give me leave to lie with thee.

LOL. No, I'll see you wiser first. To your own kennel!    111

FRAN. No noise; she sleeps. Draw all the curtains round;

Let no soft sound molest the pretty soul

But love, and love creeps in at a mouse-hole.

LOL. I would you would get into your hole! (*Exit Fra[nciscus].*)—Now, mistress, I will bring you another sort; you shall be fooled another while.—Tony, come hither, Tony! Look who's yonder, Tony.

*Enter Antonio.*

ANT. Cousin, is it not my aunt? [2]    120

LOL. Yes, 'tis one of um, Tony.

ANT. He, he! How do you, uncle?

LOL. Fear him not, mistress; 'tis a gentle nidget; [3] you may play with him—as safely with him as with his bauble.

ISA. How long hast thou been a fool?

ANT. Ever since I came hither, cousin.

ISA. Cousin? I'm none of thy cousins, fool.    129

LOL. O, mistress, fools have always so much wit as to claim their kindred.

MADMAN. (*Within.*) Bounce, bounce! He falls, he falls!

ISA. Hark you, your scholars in the upper room are out of order.

LOL. Must I come amongst you there?—Keep you the fool, mistress; I'll go up and play left-handed Orlando amongst the madmen.    *Exit.*

ISA. Well, sir.    140

ANT. [*Revealing himself.*] 'Tis opportuneful now, sweet lady! Nay,

Cast no amazing [4] eye upon this change.

ISA. Ha!

ANT. This shape of folly shrouds your dearest love,

The truest servant to your powerful beauties,

Whose magic had this force thus to transform me.

ISA. You are a fine fool indeed!

ANT.    O, 'tis not strange!

Love has an intellect that runs through all

The scrutinous sciences, and, like

A cunning poet, catches a quantity  150

Of every knowledge, yet brings all home

Into one mystery, into one secret.

That he proceeds in.

ISA.    Y' are a parlous fool.

ANT. No danger in me; I bring naught but love

And his soft-wounding shafts to strike you with.

Try but one arrow; if it hurt you,

I'll stand you twenty back in recompense.    [*Kisses her.*]

ISA. A forward fool too!

ANT.    This was Love's teaching.

A thousand ways he [5] fashioned out my way,

And this I found the safest and the nearest,    160

To tread the galaxia to my star.

ISA. Profound withal! Certain, you dreamed of this;

Love never taught it waking.

---

[1] Lycanthropes, werewolves.

[2] Slang term for *procuress*.    [3] Idiot.

[4] Wondering.    [5] Original reads *she.*

ANT.                    Take no acquaintance
Of these outward follies.  There's within
A gentleman that loves you.
ISA.                    When I see him,
I'll speak with him; so, in the meantime, keep
Your habit; it becomes you well enough.
As you are a gentleman, I'll not discover you.
That's all the favor that you must expect.
When you are weary, you may leave the school,                                     170
For all this while you have but played the fool.

*Enter Lollio.*

ANT. And must again.—He, he!  I thank you, cousin;
I'll be your valentine tomorrow morning.
LOL. How do you like the fool, mistress?
ISA. Passing well, sir.
LOL. Is he not witty, pretty well, for a fool?
ISA. If he hold on as he begins, he is like to come to something.                          179
LOL. Ay, thank a good tutor.  You may put him to 't; he begins to answer pretty hard questions.—Tony, how many is five times six?
ANT. Five times six is six times five.
LOL. What arithmetician could have answered better?  How many is one hundred and seven?
ANT. One hundred and seven is seven hundred and one, cousin.
LOL. This is no wit to speak on!—Will you be rid of the fool now?             191
ISA. By no means; let him stay a little.
MADMAN. (*Within*.) Catch there, catch the last couple in hell! [1]
LOL. Again must I come amongst you?  Would my master were come home!  I am not able to govern both these wards together.                    *Exit.*
ANT. Why should a minute of love's hour be lost?                                       199
ISA. Fie, out again!  I had rather you kept
Your other posture; you become not your tongue
When you speak from [2] your clothes.

ANT.                    How can he freeze
Lives near so sweet a warmth?  Shall I alone
Walk through the orchard of the Hesperides,
And, cowardly, not dare to pull an apple?

*Enter Lol[lio] above.*

This with the red cheeks I must venter [3] for.                    [*Attempts to kiss her.*]
ISA. Take heed; there's giants keep 'em.
LOL. [*Aside*.]  How now, fool, are you good at that?  Have you read Lipsius? [4]
He's past *Ars Amandi*; [5]  I believe I  [210
must put harder questions to him, I perceive that.
ISA. You are bold without fear too.
ANT.                    What should I fear,
Having all joys about me?  Do you smile,
And love shall play the wanton on your lip,
Meet and retire, retire and meet again;
Look you but cheerfully, and in your eyes
I shall behold mine own deformity,
And dress myself up fairer.  I know this shape
Becomes me not, but in those bright mirrors                                          220
I shall array me handsomely.
LOL.                    Cuckoo, cuckoo!  *Exit.*
[*Cries of*] *Madmen above, some as birds,*
                              *others as beasts.*
ANT. What are these?
ISA.                    Of fear enough to part us;
Yet are they but our schools of lunatics,
That act their fantasies in any shapes,
Suiting their present thoughts: if sad, they cry;
If mirth be their conceit, [6] they laugh again;
Sometimes they imitate the beasts and birds,
Singing or howling, braying, barking—all
As their wild fancies prompt um.

*Enter Lollio.*

ANT.                    These are no fears.
ISA. But here's a large one, my man.
ANT. Ha, he!  That's fine sport, indeed, cousin.                                        232

[1] In the game of barleybreak the last couple left in the center were said to be in hell.
[2] Out of keeping with.

[3] Venture.                    [6] Thought.
[4] A humanist writer, with an obvious pun.
[5] Reference to Ovid's *Art of Love*.

Lol. I would my master were come home! 'Tis too much for one shepherd to govern two of these flocks; nor can I believe that one churchman can instruct two benefices at once. There will be some incurable mad of the one side, and very fools on the other.—Come, Tony.

Ant. Prithee, cousin, let me stay here still.                                              241

Lol. No, you must to your book now; you have played sufficiently.

Isa. Your fool has grown wondrous witty.

Lol. Well, I'll say nothing; but I do not think but he will put you down one of these days.          *Exeunt Lol[lio] and Ant[onio]*.

Isa. Here the restrainéd current might make breach,

Spite of the watchful bankers.[1] Would a woman stray,                          250

She need not gad abroad to seek her sin;

It would be brought home one ways or other.

The needle's point will to the fixéd north;

Such drawing artics [2] womens' beauties are.

### Enter Lollio.

Lol. How dost thou, sweet rogue?

Isa. How now?

Lol. Come, there are degrees; one fool may be better than another.

Isa. What's the matter?

Lol. Nay, if thou giv'st thy mind to fool's flesh, have at thee!               261

Isa. You bold slave, you!

Lol. I could follow now as t'other fool did.

"What should I fear,

Having all joys about me? Do you but smile,

And love shall play the wanton on your lip,

Meet and retire, retire and meet again;

Look you but cheerfully, and in your eyes

I shall behold my own deformity,      270

And dress myself up fairer. I know this shape

Becomes me not—"

And so as it follows. But is not this the more foolish way? Come, sweet rogue;

kiss me, my little Lacedaemonian. Let me feel how thy pulses beat. Thou hast a thing about thee would do a man pleasure; I'll lay my hand on 't.

Isa. Sirrah, no more! I see you have discovered

This love's knight errant, who hath made adventure                            280

For purchase of my love. Be silent, mute,

Mute as a statue, or his injunction

For me enjoying, shall be to cut thy throat;

I'll do it, though for no other purpose; and

Be sure he'll not refuse it.

Lol.                        My share, that's all;

I'll have my fool's part with you.

Isa.                        No more! Your master.

### Enter Alibius.

Alib. Sweet, how dost thou?

Isa.                        Your bounden servant, sir.

Alib. Fie, fie, sweetheart, no more of that.

Isa. You were best lock me up.

Alib. In my arms and bosom, my sweet Isabella,                             290

I'll lock thee up most nearly.—Lollio,

We have employment, we have task in hand.

At noble Vermandero's, our castle captain,

There is a nuptial to be solemnized—

Beatrice Joanna, his fair daughter, bride—

For which the gentleman hath bespoke our pains,

A mixture of our madmen and our fools,

To finish, as it were, and make the fag [3]

Of all the revels, the third night from the first;

Only an unexpected passage over,[4]      300

To make a frightful pleasure, that is all,

But not the all I aim at. Could we so act it,

To teach it in a wild, distracted measure,

Though out of form and figure, breaking time's head,

It were no matter—'twould be healed again

---

[1] Dike builders.   [2] *I.e.*, points of attraction.

[3] End.

[4] *I.e.*, of fools and **madmen across the stage.**

In one age or other, if not in this.
This, this, Lollio, there's a good reward
    begun,
And will beget a bounty, be it known.
LOL. This is easy, sir, I'll warrant you.
You have about you fools and madmen
that can dance very well; and, 'tis no    [311
wonder, your best dancers are not the wis-
est men; the reason is, with often jumping
they jolt their brains down into their feet,
that their wits lie more in their heels than
in their heads.
ALIB. Honest Lollio, thou giv'st me a good
    reason,
And a comfort in it.
ISA.                Y'ave a fine trade on 't.
    Madmen and fools are a staple com-
    modity.
ALIB. O wife, we must eat, wear clothes,
    and live.                              320
Just at the lawyer's haven we arrive—
By madmen and by fools we both do
    thrive.                        *Exeunt.*

### [SCENA QUARTA.

*A room in the castle.*]

*Enter Vermandero, Alsemero, Jasperino, and
                Beatrice.*

VER. Valencia speaks so nobly of you, sir,
I wish I had a daughter now for you.
ALS. The fellow of this creature were a
    partner
For a king's love.
VER.            I had her fellow once, sir,
But heaven has married her to joys
    eternal;
'Twere sin to wish her in this vale again.
Come, sir, your friend and you shall see
    the pleasures
Which my health chiefly joys in.
ALS. I hear the beauty of this seat largely.[1]
VER. It falls much short of that.
                *Exeunt. Manet[2] Beatrice.*
BEA.                So, here's one step    10
Into my father's favor; time will fix him.
I have got him now the liberty of the
    house.
So wisdom, by degrees, works out her
    freedom,
And if that eye be darkened that offends
    me—

[1] Widely.                    [2] Remains.

I wait but that eclipse—this gentleman
Shall soon shine glorious in my father's
    liking,
Through the refulgent virtue of my love.

*Enter Deflores.*

DEF. [*Aside.*] My thoughts are at a ban-
    quet; for the deed,
I feel no weight in 't; 'tis but light and
    cheap
For the sweet recompense that I set
    down for 't.                        20
BEA. Deflores!
DEF.        Lady!
BEA.                Thy looks promise cheerfully.
DEF. All things are answerable, time, cir-
    cumstance,
Your wishes, and my service.
BEA.                    Is it done, then?
DEF. Piracquo is no more.
BEA. My joys start at mine eyes; our
    sweet'st delights
Are evermore born weeping.
DEF.                I've a token for you.
BEA. For me?
DEF. But it was sent somewhat unwill-
    ingly;
I could not get the ring without the fin-
    ger.        [*Shows the finger and ring.*]
BEA. Bless me, what hast thou done?
DEF.                Why, is that more    30
Than killing the whole man? I cut his
    heartstrings;
A greedy hand thrust in a dish at court
In a mistake hath had as much as this.
BEA. 'Tis the first token my father made
    me send him.
DEF. And I made him send it back again
For his last token. I was loath to leave it,
And I'm sure dead men have no use of
    jewels;
He was as loath to part with 't, for it stuck
As if the flesh and it were both one sub-
    stance.
BEA. At the stag's fall, the keeper has his
    fees.                              40
'Tis soon applied; all dead men's fees are
    yours, sir.
I pray, bury the finger, but the stone
You may make use on shortly; the true
    value,
Take 't of my truth, is near three hundred
    ducats.

Def. 'Twill hardly buy a capcase [1] for
    one's conscience though,
To keep it from the worm, as fine as 'tis.
Well, being my fees, I'll take it;
Great men have taught me that, or else
    my merit
Would scorn the way on 't.
Bea.         It might justly, sir.
Why, thou mistak'st, Deflores; 'tis not
    given                       50
In state [2] of recompense.
Def.         No, I hope so, lady;
You should soon witness my contempt
    to 't then.
Bea. Prithee—thou look'st as if thou wert
    offended.
Def. That were strange, lady; 'tis not
    possible
My service should draw such a cause
    from you.
Offended? Could you think so? That
    were much
For one of my performance, and so warm
Yet in my service.
Bea. 'Twere misery in me to give you
    cause, sir.
Def. I know so much, it were so—
    misery                    60
In her most sharp condition.
Bea.           'Tis resolved then;
Look you, sir, here's three thousand
    golden florins;
I have not meanly thought upon thy
    merit.
Def. What! Salary? Now you move me.
Bea.             How, Deflores?
Def. Do you place me in the rank of ver-
    minous fellows,
To destroy things for wages? Offer
    gold?
The lifeblood of man? Is anything
Valued too precious for my recompense?
Bea. I understand thee not.
Def.        I could ha' hired   69
A journeyman in murder at this rate—
And mine own conscience might have
    [slept at ease] [3] —
And have had the work brought home.
Bea. [Aside.]       I'm in a labyrinth.
What will content him? I would fain be
    rid of him.
I'll double the sum, sir.

Def.             You take a course
To double my vexation; that's the good
    you do.
Bea. [Aside]. Bless me, I am now in worse
    plight than I was;
I know not what will please him.—For
    my fear's sake,
I prithee, make away with all speed
    possible;
And, if thou beest so modest not to name
The sum that will content thee, paper
    blushes not.              80
Send thy demand in writing; it shall
    follow thee.
But, prithee, take thy flight.
Def.        You must fly too, then.
Bea. I?
Def.     I'll not stir a foot else.
Bea.            What's your meaning?
Def. Why, are not you as guilty? In, I'm
    sure,
As deep as I? And we should stick to-
    gether.
Come, your fears counsel you but ill;
    my absence
Would draw suspect upon you instantly;
There were no rescue for you.
Bea. [Aside.]        He speaks home!
Def. Nor is it fit we two, engaged so
    jointly,
Should part and live asunder.
Bea.           How now, sir?   90
This shows not well.
Def.     What makes your lip so strange?
This must not be betwixt us.
Bea.          The man talks wildly!
Def. Come, kiss me with a zeal now.
Bea. [Aside.] Heaven, I doubt [4] him!
Def. I will not stand so long to beg 'em
    shortly.
Bea. Take heed, Deflores, of forgetfulness;
    'Twill soon betray us.
Def.         Take you heed first.
Faith, y' are grown much forgetful; y' are
    to blame in 't.
Bea. [Aside.] He's bold, and I am blamed
    for 't.
Def.     I have eased
You of your trouble; think on 't. I'm in
    pain,                  100
And must be eased of [5] you; 'tis a charity.
Justice invites your blood to understand
    me.

---

[1] Bandbox.                     [2] Place.
[3] Added by editor of 1816 edn.
[4] Fear.                            [5] By.

BEA. I dare not.
DEF.                Quickly!
BEA.                     O, I never shall!
  Speak it yet further off, that I may lose
  What has been spoken, and no sound
    remain on 't.
  I would not hear so much offense again
  For such another deed.
DEF.                     Soft, lady, soft!
  The last is not yet paid for. O, this act
  Has put me into spirit; I was as greedy
    on 't
  As the parched earth of moisture, when
    the clouds weep.                    110
  Did you not mark, I wrought myself
    into 't,
  Nay, sued and kneeled for 't? Why was
    all that pains took?
  You see I have thrown contempt upon
    your gold;
  Not that I want it,¹ for I do piteously.
  In order I will come unto 't, and make
    use on 't,
  But 'twas not held so precious to begin
    with,
  For I place wealth after the heels of
    pleasure;
  And, were not I resolved in my belief
  That thy virginity were perfect in thee,
  I should but take my recompense with
    grudging,                            120
  As if I had but half my hopes I agreed
    for.
BEA. Why, 'tis impossible thou canst be so
    wicked,
  Or shelter such a cunning cruelty,
  To make his death the murderer of my
    honor!
  Thy language is so bold and vicious
  I cannot see which way I can forgive it
  With any modesty.
DEF.        Push! ² You forget yourself.
  A woman dipped in blood, and talk of
    modesty!
BEA. O misery of sin! Would I'd been
    bound
  Perpetually unto my living hate      130
  In that Piracquo than to hear these
    words!
  Think but upon the distance that crea-
    tion
  Set twixt thy blood and mine, and keep
    thee there.

DEF. Look but into your conscience; read
    me there.
  'Tis a true book; you'll find me there
    your equal.
  Push! Fly not to your birth, but settle
    you
  In what the act has made you; y' are no
    more now.
  You must forget your parentage ³ to me;
  Y' are the deed's creature. By that name
  You lost your first condition, and I
    challenge you,                        140
  As peace and innocency has turned you
    out,
  And made you one with me.
BEA.            With thee, foul villain?
DEF. Yes, my fair murd'ress. Do you urge
    me,
  Though thou writ'st "maid," thou whore
    in thy affection?
  'Twas changed from thy first love, and
    that's a kind
  Of whoredom in thy heart; and he's
    changed now
  To bring thy second on, thy Alsemero,
  Whom, by all sweets that ever darkness
    tasted,
  If I enjoy thee not, thou ne'er enjoy'st!
  I'll blast the hopes and joys of mar-
    riage;                               150
  I'll confess all. My life I rate at nothing.
BEA. Deflores!
DEF.     I shall rest from all lovers' plagues
    then;
  I live in pain now; that shooting eye
  Will burn my heart to cinders.
BEA.                 O, sir, hear me!
DEF. She that in life and love refuses me,
  In death and shame my partner she shall
    be.
BEA. [Kneeling.] Stay, hear me once for
    all. I make thee master
  Of all the wealth I have in gold and
    jewels;
  Let me go poor unto my bed with honor,
  And I am rich in all things!
DEF.            Let this silence thee:  160
  The wealth of all Valencia shall not
    buy
  My pleasure from me.
  Can you weep Fate from its determined
    purpose?
  So soon may [you] ⁴ weep me.

_____
¹ I.e., want it not.               ² Pish!
³ Relationship.            ⁴ Added by Dyce.

BEA.                    Vengeance begins.
Murder, I see, is followed by more sins.
Was my creation in the womb so cursted
It must engender with a viper first?
DEF. [*Raising her.*] Come, rise and shroud
    your blushes in my bosom;
Silence is one of pleasure's best receipts.
Thy peace is wrought forever in this
    yielding.                              170
'Las! How the turtle[1] pants! Thou'lt
    love anon
What thou so fear'st and faint'st to
    venture on.                    *Exeunt.*

ACTUS QUARTUS.

[DUMB SHOW]

*Enter Gentlemen, Vermandero meeting them
with action of wonderment at the flight of
Piracquo. Enter Alsemero with Jasperino and Gallants; Vermandero points to
him, the Gentlemen seeming to applaud
the choice. Alsemero, Jasperino, and
Gentlemen; Beatrice the bride following
in great state, accompanied with Diaphanta, Isabella, and other Gentlewomen;
Deflores after All, smiling at the accident.[2] Alonzo's ghost appears to Deflores
in the midst of his smile, startles him,
showing him the hand whose finger he had
cut off. They pass over in great solemnity.*

[SCENA PRIMA.

*Alsemero's chamber in the castle.*]

*Enter Beatrice.*

BEA. This fellow has undone me endlessly;
Never was bride so fearfully distressed.
The more I think upon th' ensuing night,
And whom I am to cope with in em-
    braces,
One both ennobléd[3] in blood and mind,
So clear in understanding—that's my
    plague now—
Before whose judgment will my fault
    appear
Like malefactors' crimes before tri-
    bunals.
There is no hiding on 't, the more I dive
Into my own distress. How a wise
    man                                    10

---

[1] Turtledove.        [3] Original repeats *both* here.
[2] Event.

Stands for[4] a great calamity! There's
    no venturing
Into his bed, what course soe'er I light
    upon,
Without my shame, which may grow up
    to danger.
He cannot but in justice strangle me
As I lie by him, as a cheater use me.
'Tis a precious craft to play with a false
    die
Before a cunning gamester. Here's his
    closet,
The key left in 't, and he abroad i' th'
    park!
Sure 'twas forgot; I'll be so bold as look
    in 't.          [*Passes to the inner stage.*]
Bless me! A right physician's closet 'tis,
Set round with vials, every one her mark
    too.                                   21
Sure he does practice physic for his own
    use,
Which may be safely called your great
    man's wisdom.
What manuscript lies here? *The Book of
    Experiment,*
*Called Secrets in Nature.* So 'tis; 'tis so.
[*Reads.*] "How to know whether a woman
    be with child or no."
I hope I am not yet; if he should try
    though!
Let me see. [*Reads.*] "Folio forty-five"—
    here 'tis,
The leaf tucked down upon 't, the place
    suspicious.                           29
[*Reads.*] "If you would know whether a
woman be with child or not, give her two
spoonfuls of the white water in glass C——"
Where's that glass C? O yonder, I see 't
    now—
[*Reads.*] "and, if she be with child, she
sleeps full twelve hours after; if not, not."
None of that water comes into my belly;
I'll know you from a hundred. I could
    break you now,
Or turn you into milk, and so beguile
The master of the mystery; but I'll look
    to you.
Ha! That which is next is ten times
    worse:                               40
[*Reads.*] "How to know whether a
woman be a maid or not."
If that should be applied, what would
    become of me?

---

[4] Exposed to.

Belike he has a strong faith of my purity,
That never yet made proof; but this he calls
[*Reads.*] "A merry sleight, but true experiment; the author Antonius Mizaldus. Give the party you suspect the quantity of a spoonful of the water in the glass M, which, upon her that is a maid, makes [50 three several effects: 'twill make her incontinently [1] gape, then fall into a sudden sneezing, last into a violent laughing; else, dull, heavy, and lumpish."
Where had I been?
I fear it; yet 'tis seven hours to bedtime.

*Enter Diaphanta.*

DIA. Cud's,[2] madam, are you here?
BEA. [*Aside.*]      Seeing that wench now,
A trick comes in my mind; 'tis a nice piece
Gold cannot purchase.—I come hither, wench,
To look [3] my lord.
DIA.            Would I had such a cause  60
To look him too!—Why, he's i' th' park, madam.
BEA. There let him be.
DIA.            Ay, madam, let him compass
Whole parks and forests, as great rangers do;
At roosting-time a little lodge can hold 'em.
Earth-conquering Alexander, that thought the world
Too narrow for him, in the end had but his pit-hole.
BEA. I fear thou art not modest, Diaphanta.
DIA. Your thoughts are so unwilling to be known, madam.
'Tis ever the bride's fashion, towards bedtime,
To set light by her joys, as if she owed [4] 'em not.  70
BEA. Her joys? Her fears thou wouldst say.
DIA.      Fear of what?
BEA. Art thou a maid, and talk'st so to a maid?
You leave a blushing business behind;
Beshrew your heart for 't!
DIA.  Do you mean good sooth, madam?
BEA. Well, if I'd thought upon the fear at first,
Man should have been unknown.

DIA.                Is 't possible?
BEA. I will give a thousand ducats to that woman
Would try what my fear were, and tell me true
Tomorrow, when she gets from 't; as she likes,
I might perhaps be drawn to 't.
DIA.            Are you in earnest?  80
BEA. Do you get the woman, then challenge me,
And see if I'll fly from 't; but, I must tell you
This by the way, she must be a true maid.
Else there's no trial; my fears are not hers else.
DIA. Nay, she that I would put into your hands, madam,
Shall be a maid.
BEA.      You know I should be shamed else,
Because she lies for me.
DIA.            'Tis a strange humor!
But are you serious still? Would you resign
Your first night's pleasure, and give money too?
BEA. As willingly as live.—[*Aside.*] Alas, the gold  90
Is but a by-bet to wedge in the honor!
DIA. I do not know how the world goes abroad
For faith or honesty; there's both required in this.
Madam, what say you to me, and stray no further?
I've a good mind, in troth, to earn your money.
BEA. Y' are too quick, I fear, to be a maid.
DIA. How? Not a maid? Nay, then you urge me, madam;
Your honorable self is not a truer,
With all your fears upon you—
BEA. [*Aside.*]      Bad enough then.
DIA. Than I with all my lightsome joys about me.  100
BEA. I'm glad to hear 't. Then you dare put your honesty [5]
Upon an easy trial.
DIA.            Easy? Anything.
BEA. I'll come to you straight.
                    [*Goes to the closet.*]

[1] Immediately.   [2] God's, part of a mild oath.
[3] Look for.                    [4] Owned.

[5] Chastity.

DIA.        She will not search me, will she,
Like the forewoman of a female jury?
BEA. Glass M. Ay, this is it.  Look, Dia-
phanta;
You take no worse than I do.  [*Drinks.*]
DIA.                        And, in so doing,
I will not question what 'tis, but take it.
                                [*Drinks.*]
BEA. [*Aside.*]  Now if the experiment be
true, 'twill praise itself,
And give me noble ease.  Begins already.
                        [*Diaphanta gapes.*]
There's the first symptom; and what
haste it makes                        110
To fall into the second, there by this
time!        [*Diaphanta sneezes.*]
Most admirable secret!  On the contrary,
It stirs not me a whit, which most con-
cerns it.
DIA. Ha, ha, ha!
BEA. [*Aside.*]        Just in all things, and in
order
As if 'twere circumscribed; one accident [1]
Gives way unto another.
DIA. Ha, ha, ha!
BEA. How now, wench?
DIA.        Ha, ha, ha!  I'm so, so light
At heart—ha, ha, ha!—so pleasurable!
But one swig more, sweet madam.
BEA.                        Ay, tomorrow,  120
We shall have time to sit by 't.
DIA.                        Now I'm sad again.
BEA. [*Aside.*]  It lays [2] itself so gently
too!—Come, wench.
Most honest Diaphanta I dare call thee
now.
DIA. Pray, tell me, madam, what trick call
you this?
BEA. I'll tell thee all hereafter; we must
study
The carriage of this business.
DIA.                        I shall carry 't well,
Because I love the burthen.
BEA.                        About midnight
You must not fail to steal forth gently,
That I may use the place.
DIA.                        O, fear not, madam,
I shall be cool by that time.  The bride's
place,                        130
And with a thousand ducats!  I'm for a
justice now.
I bring a portion with me; I scorn small
fools.                        *Exeunt.*

[1] Effect, symptom.                        [2] Allays.

[SCENA SECUNDA.

*Another room in the castle.*]

*Enter Vermandero and Servant.*

VER. I tell thee, knave, mine honor is in
question,
A thing till now free from suspicion,
Nor ever was there cause.  Who of my
gentlemen
Are absent?  Tell me, and truly, how
many, and who?
SER. Antonio, sir, and Franciscus.
VER. When did they leave the castle?
SER. Some ten days since, sir, the one
intending to
Briamata, th' other for Valencia.
VER. The time accuses um.  A charge of
murder
Is brought within my castle gate, Pirac-
quo's murder.                        10
I dare not answer faithfully their ab-
sence.
A strict command of apprehension
Shall pursue um suddenly, and either
wipe
The stain off clear, or openly discover it.
Provide me wingéd warrants for the
purpose.                        *Exit Servant.*
See, I am set on again.

*Enter Tomaso.*

TOM. I claim a brother of you.
VER.                        Y' are too hot;
Seek him not here.
TOM.        Yes, 'mongst your dearest bloods,
If my peace find no fairer satisfaction.
This is the place must yield account for
him,                        20
For here I left him; and the hasty tie
Of this snatched marriage gives strong
testimony
Of his most certain ruin.
VER.                        Certain falsehood!
This is the place indeed.  His breach of
faith
Has too much marred both my abuséd
love,
The honorable love I reserved for him,
And mocked my daughter's joy.  The
prepared morning
Blushed at his infidelity; he left
Contempt and scorn to throw upon those
friends

Whose belief hurt 'em. O, 'twas most
  ignoble                         30
To take his flight so unexpectedly,
And throw such public wrongs on those
  that loved him!
Tom. Then this is all your answer?
Ver.                   'Tis too fair
For one of his alliance; and I warn you
That this place no more see you.   *Exit.*

*Enter Deflores.*

Tom.                 The best is
There is more ground to meet a man's
  revenge on.—
Honest Deflores?
Def.         That's my name indeed.
Saw you the bride? Good, sweet sir,
  which way took she?
Tom. I have blessed mine eyes from seeing
  such a false one.
Def. [*Aside.*] I'd fain get off; this man's
  not for my company.          40
I smell his brother's blood when I come
  near him.
Tom. Come hither, kind and true one; I
  remember
My brother loved thee well.
Def.         O, purely, dear sir!—
[*Aside.*] Methinks I am now again a-
  killing on him,
He brings it so fresh to me.
Tom.       Thou canst guess, sirrah—
One honest friend has an instinct of
  jealousy—
At some foul, guilty person.
Def. 'Las, sir, I am so charitable I think
  none
Worse than myself! You did not see the
  bride then?
Tom. I prithee, name her not. Is she not
  wicked?                   50
Def. No, no; a pretty, easy, round-
  packed sinner,
As your most ladies are, else you might
  think
I flattered her; but, sir, at no hand wicked,
Till th' are so old their chins and noses [1]
  meet,
And they salute witches. I'm called, I
  think, sir.—
[*Aside.*] His company ev'n o'erlays my
  conscience.              *Exit.*

[1] Emended by Dyce. Original reads *sins and vices.*

Tom. That Deflores has a wondrous honest
  heart!
He'll bring it out in time, I'm assured on 't.
O, here's the glorious master of the day's
  joy!
'T [2] will not be long till he and I do
  reckon.—Sir!              60

*Enter Alsemero.*

Als. You are most welcome.
Tom.       You may call that word back;
I do not think I am, nor wish to be.
Als. 'Tis strange you found the way to
  this house, then.
Tom. Would I'd ne'er known the cause!
  I'm none of those, sir,
That come to give you joy, and swill
  your wine.
'Tis a more precious liquor that must lay
The fiery thirst I bring.
Als.            Your words and you
Appear to me great strangers.
Tom.         Time and our swords
May make us more acquainted. This the
  business:
I should have a brother in your place; 70
How treachery and malice have disposed
  of him,
I'm bound to inquire of him which holds
  his right,
Which never could come fairly.
Als.            You must look
To answer for that word, sir.
Tom.             Fear you not,
I'll have it ready drawn at our next meet-
  ing.
Keep your day solemn. [3] Farewell, I dis-
  turb it not;
I'll bear the smart with patience for a
  time.                  *Exit.*
Als. 'Tis somewhat ominous this; a quar-
  rel entered
Upon this day. My innocence relieves me;

*Enter Jasperino.*

I should be wondrous sad else.—Jas-
  perino,                  80
I have news to tell thee, strange news.
Jasp.          I ha' some too,
I think as strange as yours. Would I
  might keep

[2] Emended by Dyce. Original reads *I.*
[3] *I.e.,* celebrate your wedding day.

Mine, so my faith and friendship might
be kept in 't!
Faith, sir, dispense a little with my zeal,
And let it cool in this.
Als. This puts me on,
And blames thee for thy slowness.
Jas. All may prove nothing,
Only a friendly fear that leaped from me,
sir.
Als. No question, it may prove nothing;
let's partake it though.
Jas. 'Twas Diaphanta's chance—for to
that wench
I pretend [1] honest love, and she deserves
it— 90
To leave me in a back part of the house,
A place we chose for private conference.
She was no sooner gone but instantly
I heard your bride's voice in the next
room to me,
And, lending more attention, found
Deflores
Louder than she.
Als. Deflores? Thou art out now.
Jas. You'll tell me more anon.
Als. Still I'll prevent [2] thee.
The very sight of him is poison to her.
Jas. That made me stagger too; but Dia-
phanta
At her return confirmed it.
Als. Diaphanta! 100
Jas. Then fell we both to listen, and words
passed
Like those that challenge interest in a
woman.
Als. Peace! Quench thy zeal; 'tis dan-
gerous to thy bosom.
Jas. Then truth is full of peril.
Als. Such truths are.
O, were she the sole glory of the earth,
Had eyes that could shoot fire into king's
breasts,
And touched,[3] she sleeps not here! Yet I
have time,
Though night be near, to be resolved [4]
hereof.
And, prithee, do not weigh me by my
passions.
Jas. I never weighed friend so.
Als. Done charitably! 110
That key will lead thee to a pretty secret,
[Gives key.]
By a Chaldean taught me, and I've
_____
[1] Profess. [2] Anticipate. [3] Tainted. [4] Satisfied.

My study upon some. Bring from my
closet
A glass inscribed there with the letter M,
And question not my purpose.
Jas. It shall be done, sir. Exit.
Als. How can this hang together? Not an
hour since
Her woman came pleading her lady's fears,
Delivered her for the most timorous virgin
That ever shrunk at man's name, and
so modest
She charged her weep out her request to
me 120
That she might come obscurely[5] to my
bosom.

*Enter Beatrice.*

Bea. [Aside.] All things go well; my wo-
man's preparing yonder
For her sweet voyage, which grieves me
to lose.
Necessity compels it. I lose all, else.
Als. [Aside.] Push! Modesty's shrine is
set in yonder forehead.
I cannot be too sure though.—My Jo-
anna!
Bea. Sir, I was bold to weep a message
to you;
Pardon my modest fears.
Als. [Aside.] The dove's not meeker;
She's abused, questionless.—O, are you
come, sir?

*Enter Jasperino [with vial].*

Bea. [Aside.] The glass, upon my life! I
see the letter. 130
Jas. [Giving vial.] Sir, this is M.
Als. 'T's it.
Bea. [Aside.] I am suspected.
Als. How fitly our bride comes to partake
with us!
Bea. What is 't, my lord?
Als. No hurt.
Bea. Sir, pardon me;
I seldom taste of any composition.
Als. But this, upon my warrant, you shall
venture on.
Bea. I fear 'twill make me ill.
Als. Heaven forbid that.
Bea. [Aside.] I'm put now to my cunning;
th' effects I know,
If I can now but feign 'em handsomely.
[Drinks.]
_____
[5] In the dark.

ALS. It has that secret virtue, it ne'er
    missed, sir,
Upon a virgin.
JAS.               Treble-qualitied?      140
              [*Beatrice gapes and sneezes.*]
ALS. By all that's virtuous it takes there—
    proceeds!
JAS. This is the strangest trick to know a
    maid by.
BEA. Ha, ha, ha!
You have given me joy of heart to drink,
    my lord.
ALS. No, thou hast given me such joy of
    heart
That never can be blasted.
BEA.             What's the matter, sir?
ALS. [*Aside.*] See now 'tis settled in a
    melancholy.
Keep both the time and method.—My
    Joanna,
Chaste as the breath of heaven, or
    morning's womb,
That brings the day forth! Thus my love
    encloses thee.        *Exeunt.*   150


[SCENA TERTIA.

*A room in the house of Alibius.*]

*Enter Isabella [with a letter,] and Lollio.*

ISA. O heaven! Is this the waning[1] moon?
Does love turn fool, run mad, and all at
    once?
Sirrah, here's a madman, akin to the fool
    too,
A lunatic lover.
LOL. No, no, not he I brought the letter
    from.
ISA. [*Giving him the letter.*] Compare his in-
    side with his out, and tell me.
LOL. The out's mad, I'm sure of that; I
had a taste on 't. [*Reads letter.*] "To the
bright Andromeda, chief chambermaid to
the Knight of the Sun, at the sign of  [10
Scorpio, in the middle region, sent by the
bellows-mender of Aeolus. Pay the post."
This is stark madness!
ISA. Now mark the inside. [*Takes the
letter and reads.*] "Sweet lady, having now
cast off this counterfeit cover of a madman,
I appear to your best judgment a true and
faithful lover of your beauty."
LOL. He is mad still.

[1] Emended by editor of 1816.  Original has
*waiting.*

ISA. "If any fault you find, chide  [20
those perfections in you which have made
me imperfect; 'tis the same sun that causeth
to grow and enforceth to wither—"
LOL. O rogue!
ISA. "Shapes and transshapes, destroys
and builds again. I come in winter to you,
dismantled of my proper ornaments; by
the sweet splendor of your cheerful smiles I
spring and live a lover."
LOL. Mad rascal still!               30
ISA. "Tread him not under foot, that
shall appear an honor to your bounties. I
remain—mad till I speak with you, from
whom I expect my cure,
    Yours all, or one beside himself,
                    FRANCISCUS."
LOL. You are like to have a fine time
on 't. My master and I may give over our
professions; I do not think but you can cure
fools and madmen faster than we, with
little pains too.                    40
ISA. Very likely.
LOL. One thing I must tell you,[2] mis-
tress: you perceive that I am privy to your
skill;[3] if I find you minister once, and set up
the trade, I put in for my thirds. I shall be
mad or fool else.
ISA. The first place is thine, believe it,
    Lollio,
If I do fall.
LOL.        I fall upon you.
ISA.                        So.
LOL. Well, I stand to my venture.
ISA. But thy counsel now. How  [50
shall I deal with 'em?
LOL. Why,[4] do you mean to deal with um?
ISA. Nay, the fair understanding[5]—how to
    use um.
LOL. Abuse[6] um! That's the way to
mad the fool, and make a fool of the mad-
man, and then you use um kindly.[7]
ISA. 'Tis easy; I'll practice. Do thou ob-
    serve it.
The key of thy wardrobe.
LOL. [*Giving key.*] There. Fit yourself
for um, and I'll fit um both for you.  [60
ISA. Take thou no further notice than the
    outside.               *Exit.*
LOL. Not an inch; I'll put you to the inside.

[2] Original reads *your*.        [3] Profession.
[4] Emended by Dyce.  Original reads *We*.
[5] *I.e.*, the proper meaning of my words.
[6] Deceive.        [7] According to their nature.

*Enter Alibius.*

ALIB. Lollio, art there? Will all be perfect,
    think'st thou?
    Tomorrow night, as if to close up the
    Solemnity, Vermandero expects us.

LOL. I mistrust the madmen most. The
fools will do well enough; I have taken pains
with them.

ALIB. Tush! They cannot miss. The more
    absurdity,
    The more commends it, so [1] no rough
    behaviors                   70
    Affright the ladies. They're nice [2] things,
    thou know'st.

LOL. You need not fear, sir; so long as
we are there with our commanding peesles [3]
they'll be as tame as the ladies themselves.

ALIB. I will see them once more rehearse
before they go.

LOL. I was about it, sir. Look you to
the madmen's morris, and let me alone with
the other. There is one or two that I mistrust their fooling. I'll instruct them, and [80
then they shall rehearse the whole measure.

ALIB. Do so; I'll see the music prepared.
    But, Lollio,
    By the way, how does my wife brook her
    restraint?
    Does she not grudge at it?

LOL. So, so. She takes some pleasure in
the house; she would abroad else. You must
allow her a little more length; she's kept
too short.

ALIB. She shall along to Vermandero's
    with us—                     89
    That will serve her for a month's liberty.

LOL. What's that on your face, sir?

ALIB. Where, Lollio? I see nothing.

LOL. Cry you mercy, [4] sir, 'tis your nose;
it showed like the trunk of a young elephant. [5]

ALIB. Away, rascal! I'll prepare the music,
    Lollio.              *Ex[it] Ali[bius].*

LOL. Do, sir, and I'll dance the whilst.—
Tony, where art thou, Tony?

*Enter Antonio.*

ANT. Here, cousin. Where art thou?

LOL. Come, Tony, the footmanship [100
I taught you.

---

[1] Provided that.          [2] Fastidious.
[3] Pizzles, whips.         [4] I beg your pardon.
[5] A variation on the jest about the cuckold's
horns.

---

ANT. I had rather ride, cousin.

LOL. Ay, a whip take you! But I'll keep
you out. Vault in. Look you, Tony! Fa, la,
la, la, la.                        *[Dances.]*

ANT. *[Dancing.]* Fa, la, la, la, la.

LOL. There, an honor. [6]

ANT. Is this an honor, coz?

LOL. Yes, and it please your worship. 109

ANT. Does honor bend in the hams, coz?

LOL. Marry, does it, as low as worship,
squireship, nay, yeomandry itself sometimes, from whence it first stiffened. There
rise, a caper.

ANT. Caper after an honor, coz?

LOL. Very proper, for honor is but a
caper, rise[s] as fast and high, has a knee or
two, and falls to th' ground again. You can
remember your figure, [7] Tony?       *Exit.*

ANT. Yes, cousin; when I see thy figure,
I can remember mine.              121

*Enter Isabella [, dressed as a madwoman].*

ISA. Hey, how she treads the air!
Shough, shough, tother way! He burns
his wings else. Here's wax enough below,
Icarus, more than will be canceled these
eighteen moons. He's down, he's down!
What a terrible fall he had!
    Stand up, thou son of Cretan Daedalus,
    And let us tread the lower labyrinth;
    I'll bring thee to the clue.         130

ANT. Prithee, coz, let me alone.

ISA.              Art thou not drowned?
    About thy head I saw a heap of clouds
    Wrapped like a Turkish turbant; on thy
    back
    A crook'd chameleon-colored rainbow
    hung
    Like a tiara down unto thy hams.
    Let me suck out those billows in thy
    belly;
    Hark, how they roar and rumble in the
    streets!
    Bless thee from the pirates!

ANT. Pox upon you, let me alone!

ISA. Why shouldst thou mount so high as
    Mercury,                     140
    Unless thou hadst reversion of [8] his place?
    Stay in the moon with me, Endymion,
    And we will rule these wild, rebellious
    waves,
    That would have drowned my love.

---

[6] Obeisance.    [7] Dance.    [8] Right to succeed to.

ANT. I'll kick thee, if again thou touch me,
Thou wild unshapen antic; I am no fool,
You bedlam!
ISA. But you are, as sure as I am, mad.
                    [*Reveals herself.*]
Have I put on this habit of a frantic,
With love as full of fury, to beguile  150
The nimble eye of watchful jealousy,
And am I thus rewarded?
ANT.                    Ha! Dearest beauty!
ISA. No, I have no beauty now,
Nor never had but what was in my gar-
    ments.
You a quick-sighted lover! Come not
    near me.
Keep your caparisons; y' are aptly clad.
I came a feigner, to return stark mad.
                                *Exit.*
ANT. Stay, or I shall change condition,
And become as you are.                159

### Enter Lollio.[1]

LOL. Why, Tony, whither now? Why, fool—
ANT. Whose fool, usher of idiots? You cox-
    comb!
I have fooled too much.
LOL. You were best be mad another while
    then.
ANT. So I am, stark mad; I have cause
    enough.
And I could throw the full effects on thee,
And beat thee like a fury.
LOL. Do not, do not; I shall not forbear
the gentleman under the fool, if you do.
Alas! I saw through your foxskin before
now! Come, I can give you comfort. [170
My mistress loves you; and there is as
arrant a madman i' th' house as you are a
fool, your rival, whom she loves not. If
after the masque we can rid her of him,
you earn her love, she says, and the fool
shall ride her.
ANT. May I believe thee?
LOL. Yes, or you may choose whether you
    will or no.
ANT. She's eased of him; I have a good
    quarrel on 't.
LOL. Well, keep your old station yet, and
    be quiet.                        180
ANT. Tell her *I* will deserve her love.
LOL. And you are like to have your desire.
                        [*Exit Antonio.*]

---

[1] This stage direction appears before Antonio's speech in the original.

### Enter Franciscus.

FRAN. [*Singing.*] "Down, down, down, a-
    down a-down—" and then with a
    horse trick [2]
To kick Latona's forehead, and break
    her bowstring.
LOL. [*Aside.*] This is tother counterfeit;
I'll put him out of his humor.—[*Reads Fran-
ciscus' letter.*] "Sweet lady, having now
cast this counterfeit cover of a madman,
I appear to your best judgment a  [189
true and faithful lover of your beauty."
This is pretty well for a madman.
FRAN. Ha! What's that?
LOL. "Chide those perfections in you
which [have] made me imperfect."
FRAN. I am discovered to the fool.
LOL. I hope to discover the fool in you
ere I have done with you. "Yours all, or one
beside himself, FRANCISCUS." This mad-
man will mend sure.
FRAN. What do you read, sirrah?    200
LOL. Your destiny, sir. You'll be hanged
for this trick, and another that I know.
FRAN. Art thou of counsel with thy
mistress?
LOL. Next her apron strings.
FRAN. Give me thy hand.
LOL. Stay, let me put yours in my pocket
first. [*Puts the letter away.*] Your hand
is true,[3] is it not? It will not pick? I  [209
partly fear it, because I think it does lie.
FRAN. Not in a syllable.
LOL. So if you love my mistress so well
as you have handled the matter here, you
are like to be cured of your madness.
FRAN. And none but she can cure it.
LOL. Well, I'll give you over then, and
she shall cast your water [4] next.
FRAN. Take for thy pains past.       218
                        [*Gives money.*]
LOL. I shall deserve more, sir, I hope.
My mistress loves you, but must have
some proof of your love to her.
FRAN. There I meet my wishes.
LOL. That will not serve; you must
meet her enemy and yours.
FRAN. He's dead already.
LOL. Will you tell me that, and I parted
but now with him?
FRAN. Show me the man.               228

---

[2] Caper.                    [3] Honest.
[4] *I.e.,* diagnose your disease.

Lol. Ay, that's a right course now. See him before you kill him, in any case; and yet it needs not go so far neither. 'Tis but a fool that haunts the house and my mistress in the shape of an idiot; bang but his fool's coat well-favoredly, and 'tis well.

Fran. Soundly, soundly!

Lol. Only reserve him till the masque be past; and, if you find him not now in the dance yourself, I'll show you. In, in! My master! [*Dances.*] [239

Fran. He handles him like a feather. Hey! [*Exit.*]

*Enter Alibius.*

Alib. Well said.[1] In a readiness, Lollio?

Lol. Yes, sir.

Alib. Away then, and guide them in, Lollio.

Entreat your mistress to see this sight.
Hark, is there not one incurable fool
That might be begged?[2] I have friends.

Lol. I have him for you, one that shall deserve it too.

Alib. Good boy, Lollio!

*The Madmen and Fools dance.*

'Tis perfect. Well, fit but once these strains, 250
We shall have coin and credit for our pains. *Exeunt.*

Actus Quintus. [Scena Prima.

*A corridor in the castle.*]

*Enter Beatrice. A clock strikes one.*

Bea. One struck, and yet she lies by 't!
O, my fears!
This strumpet serves her own ends, 'tis apparent now,
Devours the pleasure with a greedy appetite,
And never minds my honor or my peace,
Makes havoc of my right. But she pays dearly for 't;
No trusting of her life with such a secret
That cannot rule her blood to keep her promise.
Beside, I have some suspicion of her faith to me,
Because I was suspected of my lord, 9

And it must come from her. (*Strike two.*)[3]
Hark! By my horrors,
Another clock strikes two!

*Enter Deflores.*

Def. Pist! Where are you?

Bea. Deflores!

Def. Ay. Is she not come from him yet?

Bea. As I am a living soul, not!

Def. Sure the devil
Hath sowed his itch within her. Who'd trust a waiting-woman?

Bea. I must trust somebody.

Def. Push! They're termagants,
Especially when they fall upon their masters
And have their ladies' first fruits. Th' are mad whelps;
You cannot stave 'em off from game royal. Then
You are so harsh[4] and hardy, ask no counsel;
And I could have helped you to a apothecary's daughter 20
Would have fall'n off before eleven, and thank you too.

Bea. O me, not yet! This whore forgets herself.

Def. The rascal fares so well. Look, y' are undone;
The day-star, by this hand! See Phosphorus[5] plain yonder.

Bea. Advise me now to fall upon some ruin;
There is no counsel safe else.

Def. Peace! I ha 't now,
For we must force a rising; there's no remedy.

Bea. How? Take heed of that.

Def. Tush! Be you quiet, or else give over all. 29

Bea. Prithee, I ha' done then.

Def. This is my reach:[6] I'll set
Some part afire of Diaphanta's chamber.

Bea. How? Fire, sir? That may endanger the whole house.

Def. You talk of danger when your fame's on fire.

Bea. That's true; do what thou wilt now.

---

[1] Well done.
[2] Be appointed the fool's guardian to control and enjoy his estate.

[3] This stage direction in the original appears at the end of the speech. [4] Rough, rude.
[5] Original reads *Bosphorus*. [6] Trick.

DEF.                    Push! I aim
At a most rich success strikes all dead
   sure.
The chimney being afire, and some light
   parcels
Of the least danger in her chamber only,
If Diaphanta should be met by chance
   then
Far from her lodging, which is now sus-
   picious,
It would be thought her fears and af-
   frights then                             40
Drove her to seek for succor; if not seen
Or met at all, as that's the likeliest,
For her own shame she'll hasten towards
   her lodging.
I will be ready with a piece high-charged,
As 'twere to cleanse the chimney,
   there [1] 'tis proper now;
But she shall be the mark.

BEA.               I'm forced to love thee now,
Cause thou provid'st so carefully for
   my honor.

DEF. 'Slid, it concerns the safety of us
   both,
Our pleasure and continuance.

.BEA.                    One word now,
Prithee; how for the servants?

DEF.               I'll despatch them,   50
Some one way, some another in the
   hurry,
For buckets, hooks, ladders. Fear not you,
The deed shall find its time; and I've
   thought since
Upon a safe conveyance for the body
   too.
How this fire purifies wit! Watch you
   your minute.

BEA. Fear keeps my soul upon 't; I cannot stray from 't.

*Enter Alonzo's Ghost.*

DEF. Ha! What art thou that tak'st
   away the light
'Twixt that star and me? I dread thee
   not.—
'Twas but a mist of conscience; all's
   clear again.               [*Exit.*]

BEA. Who's that, Deflores? Bless me, it
   slides by!               [*Exit Ghost.*]  60
Some ill thing haunts the house; 't has
   left behind it

A shivering sweat upon me; I'm afraid
   now.
This night hath been so tedious!   O,
   this strumpet!
Had she a thousand lives, he should
   not leave her
Till he had destroyed the last.   List!
   O, my terrors!   *Struck three a-clock.*
Three struck by St. Sebastian's!

WITHIN.               Fire, fire, fire!

BEA. Already!   How rare is that man's
   speed!
How heartily he serves me!   His face
   loathes [2] one;
But, look upon his care, who would not
   love him?
The East is not more beauteous than
   his service.                             70

WITHIN. Fire, fire, fire!

*Enter Deflores; Servants pass over.   Ring
                              a bell.*

DEF. Away, despatch!   Hooks, buckets,
   ladders!   That's well said.
The fire bell rings; the chimney works.
   My charge!
The piece is ready.               *Exit.*

*Enter Diaphanta.*

BEA.               Here's a man worth loving!—
O, y' are a jewel!

DIA.               Pardon frailty, madam;
In troth, I was so well, I ev'n forgot myself.

BEA. Y' have made trim work!

DIA. What?

BEA.               Hie quickly to your chamber;
Your reward follows you.

DIA.                    I never made
So sweet a bargain.               *Exit.*

*Enter Alsemero.*

ALS.               O, my dear Joanna!  80
Alas, art thou risen too?   I was coming,
My absolute treasure!

BEA.                    When I missed you,
I could not choose but follow.

ALS.                    Th'art all sweetness
The fire is not so dangerous.

BEA.                    Think you so, sir?

ALS. I prithee, tremble not; believe me
   'tis not.

[1] Where.

[2] Repeis.

*Enter Vermandero, Jasperino.*

VER. O, bless my house and me!
ALS. 　　　　　　My lord your father.

*Enter Deflores with a piece.*

VER. Knave, whither goes that piece?
DEF. 　　　　　To scour the chimney. *Exit.*
VER. O, well said, well said!
　That fellow's good on all occasions. 89
BEA. A wondrous necessary man, my lord.
VER. He hath a ready wit; he's worth 'em
　all, sir.
　Dog [1] at a house of fire; I ha' seen him
　singed ere now.— *The piece goes off.*
　Ha, there he goes!
BEA. 　　　　　'Tis done!
ALS. 　　　　　Come, sweet, to bed now;
　Alas, thou wilt get cold.
BEA. 　　　　Alas, the fear keeps that out!
　My heart will find no quiet till I hear
　How Diaphanta, my poor woman, fares;
　It is her chamber, sir, her lodging cham-
　ber.
VER. How should the fire come there?
BEA. As good a soul as ever lady coun-
　tenanced, 　　　　　　　　　99
　But in her chamber negligent and heavy.
　She scaped a mine[2] twice.
VER. 　　　　　Twice?
BEA. 　　　　　Strangely twice, sir.
VER. Those sleepy sluts are dangerous in
　a house,
　And they be ne'er so good.

*Enter Deflores.*

DEF. 　　　　　O poor virginity,
　Thou hast paid dearly for 't!
VER. 　　　　　Bless us, what's that?
DEF. A thing you all knew once—Dia-
　phanta's burnt.
BEA. My woman! O, my woman!
DEF. 　　　　　Now the flames
　Are greedy of her; burnt, burnt, burnt
　to death, sir!
BEA. O, my presaging soul!
ALS. 　　　　　Not a tear more!
　I charge you by the last embrace I gave
　you 　　　　　　　　　　　109
　In bed before this raised us.
BEA. 　　　　　Now you tie me;
　Were it my sister, now she gets no more.

　[1] An adept. 　　　　　[2] Catastrophe.

*Enter Servant.*

VER. How now?
SER. 　　　All danger's past; you may now
　take
　Your rests, my lords; the fire is throughly
　quenched.
　Ah, poor gentlewoman, how soon was
　she stifled!
BEA. Deflores, what is left of her inter,
　And we as mourners all will follow her.
　I will entreat that honor to my servant
　Ev'n of my lord himself.
ALS. 　　　　　Command it, sweetness.
BEA. Which of you spied the fire first?
DEF. 　　　　　'Twas I, madam.
BEA. And took such pains in 't too? A
　double goodness! 　　　　　120
　'Twere well he were rewarded.
VER. 　　　　　He shall be.—
　Deflores, call upon me.
ALS. 　　　　　And upon me, sir.
　　　　　*Exeunt [All but Deflores].*
DEF. Rewarded? Precious! Here's a
　trick beyond me.
　I see in all bouts, both of sport and wit,
　Always a woman strives for the last
　hit. 　　　　　　　　　　*Exit.*

*[Scena Secunda.*

*A room in the castle].*

*Enter Tomaso.*

TOM. I cannot taste the benefits of life
　With the same relish I was wont to do.
　Man I grow weary of, and hold his
　fellowship
　A treacherous, bloody friendship, and,
　because
　I am ignorant in whom my wrath should
　settle,
　I must think all men villains, and the
　next
　I meet, whoe'er he be, the murderer
　Of my most worthy brother. Ha!
　What's he?

*Enter Deflores, passes over the stage.*

　O, the fellow that some call honest
　Deflores— 　　　　　　　9
　But methinks honesty was hard bestead
　To come there for a lodging; as if a
　queen

Should make her palace of a pesthouse.
I find a contrariety in nature
Betwixt that face and me.   The least
  occasion
Would give me game upon him; yet he's
  so foul
One would scarce touch [him] [1] with a
  sword he loved
And made account of—so most deadly
  venomous,
He would go near to poison any weapon
That should draw blood on him.   One
  must resolve
Never to use that sword again in fight   20
In way of honest manhood that strikes
  him.
Some river must devour 't; 'twere not fit
That any man should find it.   What,
  again?

*Enter Deflores.*

He walks a [2] purpose by, sure, to choke
  me up,
To infect my blood.
DEF.        My worthy, noble lord!
TOM.  Dost offer to come near and breathe
  upon me?        *[Strikes him.]*
DEF.  A blow!        *[Draws.]*
TOM.        Yea, are you so prepared?
I'll rather like a soldier die by th' sword
Than like a politician by thy poison.
        *[Draws.]*
DEF.  Hold, my lord, as you are honorable!
TOM.  All slaves that kill by poison are
  still cowards.        31
DEF.  *[Aside.]*  I cannot strike; I see his
  brother's wounds
Fresh-bleeding in his eye, as in a crys-
  tal.—
I will not question this; I know y' are
  noble.
I take my injury with thanks given, sir,
Like a wise lawyer, and as a favor
Will wear it for the worthy hand that
  gave it.—
*[Aside.]* Why this from him that yester-
  day appeared
So strangely loving to me?
O, but instinct is of a subtler strain!   40
Guilt must not walk so near his lodge
  again;
He came near me now.        *Exit.*

[1] Added by Dyce.        [2] On.

TOM.  All league with mankind I renounce
  forever,
Till I find this murderer; not so much
As common courtesy but I'll lock up;
For, in the state of ignorance I live in,
A brother may salute his brother's
  murderer,
And wish good speed to th' villain in a
  greeting.

*Enter Verman[dero], Ali[bius], and Isabella.*

VER.  Noble Piracquo!
TOM.        Pray, keep on your way, sir;
I've nothing to say to you.
VER.        Comforts bless you, sir.   50
TOM.  I have forsworn compliment, in troth
  I have, sir;
As you are merely man, I have not left
A good wish for you, nor any here.
VER.  Unless you be so far in love with
  grief,
You will not part from 't upon any
  terms.
We bring that news will make a welcome
  for us.
TOM.  What news can that be?
VER.        Throw no scornful smile
Upon the zeal I bring you; 'tis worth
  more, sir.
Two of the chiefest men I kept about me
I hide not from the law or your just
  vengeance.        60
TOM.  Ha!
VER.  To give your peace more ample
  satisfaction,
Thank these discoverers.
TOM.        If you bring that calm,
Name but the manner I shall ask for-
  giveness in
For that contemptuous smile upon you;
I'll perfect it with reverence that belongs
Unto a sacred altar.        *[Kneels.]*
VER.  *[Raising him.]*        Good sir, rise.
Why, now you overdo as much a this
  hand
As you fell short a tother.—Speak,
  Alibius.
ALIB.  'Twas my wife's fortune, as she is
  most lucky        70
At a discovery, to find out lately
Within our hospital of fools and madmen
Two counterfeits slipped into these
  disguises,

Their names Franciscus and Antonio.

VER. Both mine, sir, and I ask no favor
    for 'em.

ALIB. Now that which draws suspicion
    to their habits,
The time of their disguisings, agrees
    justly
With the day of the murder.

TOM.          O blessed revelation!

VER. Nay, more, nay, more, sir—I'll not
    spare mine own
In way of justice—they both feigned
    a journey        80
To Briamata, and so wrought out their
    leaves;
My love was so abused in 't.

TOM.          Time's too precious
To run in waste now; you have brought
    a peace
The riches of five kingdoms could not
    purchase.
Be my most happy conduct. I thirst for
    'em.
Like subtile lightning will I wind about
    'em,
And melt their marrow in 'em.   *Exeunt.*

[SCENA TERTIA.

*Alsemero's apartment in the castle.*]

*Enter Alsemero and Jasperino.*

JAS. Your confidence, I'm sure, is now of
    proof;
The prospect from the garden has
    showed
Enough for deep suspicion.

ALS.          The black mask
That so continually was worn upon 't
Condemns the face for ugly ere 't be seen,
Her despite to him, and so seeming
    bottomless.

JAS. Touch it home then; 'tis not a shallow
    probe
Can search this ulcer soundly; I fear
    you'll find it
Full of corruption. 'Tis fit I leave you.
She meets you opportunely from that
    walk;        10
She took the back door at his parting
    with her.    *Ex[it] Jas[perino].*

ALS. Did my fate wait for this unhappy
    stroke
At my first sight of woman?—She's here.

*Enter Beatrice.*

BEA. Alsemero!

ALS.          How do you?

BEA.              How do I?
Alas, how do you? You look not well.

ALS. You read me well enough; I am not
    well.

BEA. Not well, sir? Is 't in my power to
    better you?

ALS. Yes.

BEA. Nay, then y' are cured again.    19

ALS. Pray, resolve [1] me one question, lady.

BEA. If I can.

ALS. None can so sure: are you honest?

BEA. Ha, ha, ha! That's a broad question,
    my lord.

ALS. But that's not a modest answer, my
    lady.
Do you laugh? My doubts are strong
    upon me.

BEA. 'Tis innocence that smiles, and no
    rough brow
Can take away the dimple in her cheek.
Say I should strain a tear to fill the vault,
Which would you give the better faith to?

ALS. 'Twere but hypocrisy of a sadder
    color,        30
But the same stuff; neither your smiles
    nor tears
Shall move or flatter me from my belief:
You are a whore!

BEA.          What a horrid sound it hath!
It blasts a beauty to deformity;
Upon what face soever that breath falls,
It strikes it ugly. O, you have ruined
What you can ne'er repair again.

ALS. I'll all demolish, and seek out truth
    within you,
If there be any left. Let your sweet
    tongue
Prevent your heart's rifling; there I'll
    ransack    40
And tear out my suspicion.

BEA.          You may, sir;
'Tis an easy passage; yet, if you please,
Show me the ground whereon you lost
    your love.
My spotless virtue may but tread on that
Before I perish.

ALS.          Unanswerable.
A ground you cannot stand on. You fall
    down

[1] Answer.

Beneath all grace and goodness when
you set
Your ticklish heel on 't. There was a visor
O'er that cunning face, and that became
you;                                            49
Now Impudence in triumph rides upon 't.
How comes this tender reconcilement else
'Twixt you and your despite, your ran-
corous loathing,
Deflores? He that your eye was sore at
sight of,
He's now become your arm's supporter,
your
Lip's saint!

BEA.            Is there the cause?

ALS.                    Worse, your lust's devil,
Your adultery!

BEA.       Would any but yourself say that,
'Twould turn him to a villain!

ALS.                      'Twas witnessed
By the counsel of your bosom, Diaphanta.

BEA. Is your witness dead then?

ALS.                      'Tis to be feared
It was the wages of her knowledge; poor
soul,                                            60
She lived not long after the discovery.

BEA. Then hear a story of not much less
horror
Than this your false suspicion is beguiled
with;
To your bed's scandal I stand up innocence,
Which even the guilt of one black other
deed
Will stand for proof of; your love has
made me
A cruel murd'ress.

ALS.            Ha!

BEA.               A bloody one.
I have kissed poison for 't, stroked a
serpent,
That thing of hate, worthy in my esteem
Of no better employment; and him,
most worthy                                      70
To be so employed I caused to murder
That innocent Piracquo, having no
Better means than that worst to assure
Yourself to me.

ALS.       O, the place itself e'er since
Has crying been for vengeance, the
temple,
Where blood and beauty first unlaw-
fully

Fired their devotion and quenched the
right one!
'Twas in my fears at first; 'twill have it
now.
O, thou art all deformed!

BEA.               Forget not, sir,
It for your sake was done. Shall greater
dangers                                          80
Make the less welcome?

ALS.            O, thou shouldst have gone
A thousand leagues about to have
avoided
This dangerous bridge of blood! Here
we are lost.

BEA. Remember, I am true unto your bed.

ALS. The bed itself's a charnel, the sheets
shrouds
For murdered carcasses. It must ask pause
What I must do in this; meantime you
shall                                            87
Be my prisoner only. Enter my closet.
                              *Exit Beatrice.*
I'll be your keeper yet. O, in what part
Of this sad story shall I first begin?—Ha!
This same fellow has put me in.[1]—
Deflores!

*Enter Deflores.*

DEF. Noble Alsemero!

ALS.                    I can tell you
News, sir; my wife has her commended
to you.

DEF. That's news indeed, my lord; I
think she would
Commend me to the gallows if she could,
She ever loved me so well. I thank her.

ALS. What's this blood upon your band,[2]
Deflores?

DEF. Blood? No, sure; 'twas washed since.

ALS.                    Since when, man?

DEF. Since tother day I got a knock
In a sword-and-dagger school; I think
'tis out.                                        100

ALS. Yes, 'tis almost out, but 'tis per-
ceived though.
I had forgot my message. This it is—
What price goes murder?

DEF.            How, sir?

ALS.                    I ask you, sir.
My wife's behindhand with[3] you, she
tells me,

---

[1] Given me the cue.        [2] Collar.
[3] In arrears of payment to.

For a brave, bloody blow you gave for
her sake
Upon Piracquo.

DEF.          Upon? 'Twas quite through
him sure.
Has she confessed it?

ALS.          As sure as death to both of you;
And much more than that.

DEF.          It could not be much more.
'Twas but one thing, and that—she is a
whore.

ALS. I could not choose but follow. O cunning devils!                                        110
How should blind men know you from
fair-faced saints?

BEA. (*Within.*) He lies! The villain does
belie me!

DEF. Let me go to her, sir.

ALS.                    Nay, you shall to her.—
Peace, crying crocodile, your sounds are
heard.
Take your prey to you; get you into her,
sir.                              *Exit Def[lores]*.
I'll be your pander now; rehearse again
Your scene of lust, that you may be
perfect
When you shall come to act it to the
black audience,
Where howls and gnashings shall be
music to you.                              119
Clip [1] your adult'ress freely; 'tis the pilot
Will guide you to the *mare mortuum*,[2]
Where you shall sink to fadoms [3] bottom-
less.

*Enter Vermandero, Alibius, Isabella, To-
maso, Franciscus, and Antonio.*

VER. O Alsemero! I have a wonder for
you.

ALS. No, sir, 'tis I, I have a wonder for
you.

VER. I have suspicion near as proof itself
For Piracquo's murder.

ALS.                    Sir, I have proof
Beyond suspicion for Piracquo's murder.

VER. Beseech you, hear me; these two
have been disguised
E'er since the deed was done.

ALS.                    I have two other
That were more close disguised than
your two could be                              130
E'er since the deed was done.

VER. You'll hear me—these mine own
servants—

ALS. Hear me—those nearer than your
servants
That shall acquit them, and prove them
guiltless.

FRAN. That may be done with easy truth,
sir.

TOM. How is my cause bandied through
your delays!
'Tis urgent in blood and calls for haste.
Give me a brother alive or dead—
Alive, a wife with him; if dead, for
both                                        139
A recompense for murder and adultery.

BEA. (*Within.*) O, O, O!

ALS.                    Hark! 'Tis coming to you.

DEF. (*Within.*) Nay, I'll along for company.

BEA. (*Within.*)                    O, O!

VER. What horrid sounds are these?

ALS. Come forth, you twins of mischief!

*Enter Deflores, bringing in Beatrice
[wounded].*

DEF. Here we are. If you have any more
To say to us, speak quickly. I shall not
Give you the hearing else; I am so stout
yet,
And so, I think, that broken rib of man-
kind.

VER. An host of enemies entered my
citadel
Could not amaze like this! Joanna!
Beatrice Joanna!                              150

BEA. O, come not near me, sir; I shall
defile you!
I am that of your blood [4] was taken
from you
For your better health; look no more
upon 't,
But cast it to the ground regardlessly.
Let the common sewer [5] take it from
distinction.
Beneath the stars, upon yon meteor
                    [*Points to Deflores.*]
Ever hung [6] my fate 'mongst things cor-
ruptible;
I ne'er could pluck it from him; my
loathing

---

[1] Embrace.          [2] Dead sea.          [3] Fathoms.

[4] That part of your blood which.
[5] Original reads *shewer*.
[6] Emended by Dyce. Original has *hang*.

Was prophet to the rest, but ne'er
believed.
Mine honor fell with him, and now my
life.—                                                160
Alsemero, I am a stranger to your bed;
Your bed was cozened on the nuptial
night—
For which your false bride died.

ALS.                              Diaphanta!

DEF. Yes, and the while I coupled with
your mate
At barleybreak; now we are left in hell.

VER. We are all there; it circumscribes
[us] [1] here.

DEF. I loved this woman in spite of her
heart;
Her love I earned out of Piracquo's
murder.

TOM. Ha! My brother's murtherer?

DEF.        Yes, and her honor's prize  169
Was my reward. I thank life for nothing
But that pleasure; it was so sweet to me
That I have drunk up all, left none
behind
For any man to pledge me.

VER.                        Horrid villain!
Keep life in him for further tortures.

DEF.                                No!
I can prevent you; here's my penknife
still.
It is but one thread more [*Stabs him-
self.*]—and now 'tis cut.—
Make haste, Joanna, by that token to
thee,                                             177
Canst not forget, so lately put in mind;
I would not go to leave thee far behind.
                                          *Dies.*

BEA. Forgive me, Alsemero, all forgive!
'Tis time to die when 'tis a shame to live.
                                          *Dies.*

VER. O, my name is entered now in that
record
Where till this fatal hour 'twas never
read.

ALS. Let it be blotted out; let your heart
lose it,
And it can never look you in the face,
Nor tell a tale behind the back of life
To your dishonor. Justice hath so right
The guilty hit that innocence is quit
By proclamation, and may joy again.—
Sir, you are sensible of what truth hath
done;                                             190

[1] Added by Dyce.

'Tis the best comfort that your grief can
find.

TOM. Sir, I am satisfied; my injuries
Lie dead before me. I can exact no more,
Unless my soul were loose, and could
o'ertake
Those black fugitives that are fled from
thence,
To take a second vengeance; but there
are wraths
Deeper than mine, 'tis to be feared, about
'em.

ALS. What an opacous body had that
moon
That last changed on us! Here 's beauty
changed
To ugly whoredom; here servant-obe-
dience                                            200
To a master-sin, imperious murder;
I, a supposed husband, changed embraces
With wantonness—but that was paid
before.
Your change is come too, from an igno-
rant wrath
To knowing friendship.—Are there any
more on's?

ANT. Yes, sir, I was changed too from a
little ass as I was to a great fool as I am; and
had like to ha' been changed to the gallows,
but that you know my innocence [2] always
excuses me.                                       210

FRAN. I was changed from a little wit to
be stark mad,
Almost for the same purpose.

ISA. [*To Alibius.*]     Your change is still
Behind, but deserve best your transformation.
You are a jealous coxcomb, keep schools
of folly,
And teach your scholars how to break
your own head.

ALIB. I see all apparent, wife, and will
change now
Into a better husband, and never keep
Scholars that shall be wiser than myself.

ALS. [*To Vermandero.*] Sir, you have yet
a son's duty living.
Please you, accept it. Let that your
sorrow,                                           220
As it goes from your eye, go from your
heart.
Man and his sorrow at the grave must
part.

[2] Idiocy.

EPILOGUE

ALS. All we can do to comfort one an-
    other,
  To stay a brother's sorrow for a brother,
  To dry a child from the kind father's
    eyes,
  Is to no purpose—it rather multiplies.

Your only smiles have power to cause
    relive
The dead again, or in their rooms to give
Brother a new brother, father a child;
If these appear, all griefs are reconciled.
                  *Exeunt omnes.*

            FINIS.

# CYRIL TOURNEUR AND
# THE REVENGER'S TRAGEDY

The history of *The Revenger's Tragedy* presents one of the most remarkable and amusing stories in the annals of the English theater. The play was entered in the Stationers' Register on October 7, 1607, by a well-established publisher, George Eld, who put it into print in quarto form with the date 1607 on the title page. Under the old calendar this date would hold until March 25, when a new year would begin. After some sheets had been run off, the date was changed to 1608 and various corrections were made in the text, none of great importance. The title page also stated that the play "hath been sundry times acted by the King's Majesty's Servants." How many times "sundry" meant, no one knows, since no records or references exist to corroborate the claim. Inga-Stina Ekeblad, however, has demonstrated that the play was apparently written especially with the Globe theater in mind since a stage direction in V, iii, calls for the appearance of a "blazing star," or comet, in the heavens, and the Globe was the only Jacobean theater noted for this sort of firework ("A Note on *The Revenger's Tragedy*," *NQ*, 1955). As in the case of so many plays of the period, the title page carried no author's name.

After its one edition, the play then completely disappeared from public notice until 1656, when Edward Archer, in a list of Elizabethan and Stuart plays appended to his edition of *The Old Law* by Middleton, Massinger, and William Rowley, mentioned it as the work of "Tournour." Rogers and Ley did the same thing in their edition of Thomas Goffe's pastoral play, *The Careless Shepherdess*, in the same year. In 1661 and 1671 Francis Kirkman followed them and named "Cyril Tourneur" as the author in his lists of plays appended to *Tom Tyler and His Wife* and *Nicomede*. As usual in the Restoration and eighteenth century, compilers of bibliographical lists and biographical dictionaries trusted one another implicitly and copied their statements and ascriptions without any further investigation, as then did Gerard Langbaine in *Momus Triumphans* (1688) and *An Account of the English Dramatic Poets* (1691), Charles Gildon in *The Lives and Characters of the English Dramatic Poets* (1699), and Giles Jacob in *The Poetical Register* (1719), who called the author "Cyril Turner." Consequently, when the literary antiquarians got under way in the mid-eighteenth century and began to rediscover the older English drama, they meekly followed suit. This succession included Robert Dodsley in *A Select Collection of Old English Plays* (1744), continued by Isaac Reed (1780), John Payne Collier (1825–7), and W. C. Hazlitt (1874–6); Sir Walter Scott in *The Ancient British Drama* (1810); and J. Churton Collins in *The Plays and Poems of Cyril Tourneur* (1878). John Addington Symonds, too, in the original Mermaid Series edition of *The Best Plays of Webster and Tourneur* (1888), had no thought of challenging tradition. (For general discussions of these matters, see Allardyce Nicoll, *The Works of Cyril Tourneur*, London, [1930]; Samuel Schoenbaum, *Middleton's Tragedies;* and Peter B. Murray, *A Study of Cyril Tourneur*, University of Pennsylvania Press, 1964.)

So far, no one had had the iconoclasm or the originality to challenge Tourneur's authorship. But in 1891 this challenge was first made by the Rev. Frederick Gard Fleay, who had been known among his fellow students at Trinity College, Cambridge, as the "industrious flea," and who in 1874 had started a whole new trend in scholarly research by delivering a series of three papers "On Metrical Tests as Applied to Dramatic Poetry" before the newly born New Shakspere Society. Widely read, romantic, impressionistic, egotistic, always provocative, and with a tenacious memory, Fleay cut a considerable figure in the scholarly world for many years, most notably because he claimed to have an infallible ear and mind for the detection of all kinds of clues to the authorship of anonymous plays. Unfortunately, his fallibility, now generally recognized, was foreshadowed in 1891 by his sudden revelation that *The Revenger's Tragedy* was too good for Tourneur, and that its meter was "purely Websterian." (For a discussion of the whole problem of *Internal Evidence and Elizabethan Dramatic Authorship*, see Schoenbaum's skeptical book on the subject, published by the Northwestern University Press in 1966.) Though no one else ever developed an ear with the same kind of subtlety as Fleay's, Paul Wenzel later discovered similarly unconfirmed overtones of John Marston in the play (*Cyril Tourneurs Stellung in der Geschichte des Englischen Dramas*, Breslau, 1918). But it was the Australian scholar, E. H. C. Oliphant, who threw back the lid of the Pandora's box when he proposed Thomas Middleton as the previously unguessed author ("Problems of Authorship in Elizabethan Dramatic Literature," *MP*, 1911). Thus from 1911 right down to the present the battle has waged fiercely between the Tourneurian and the Middletonian forces, using the weapons of metrical tests, punctuation tests, vocabulary tests, spelling tests, reading tests, idea tests, imagery tests, stylistic tests, technical tests, typographical tests, *ad infinitum*, the Middletonians having to rely solely on internal evidence, since the little external evidence that exists is on the side of the Tourneurians. The line-up of champions behind Middleton has included Oliphant (with further articles), B. M. Wagner, Wilbur D. Dunkel, C. L. Barbour, F. L. Jones, Marco Mincoff, Richard H. Barker, George R. Price, and Samuel Schoenbaum, among others. In the traditional camp are found H. Dugdale Sykes, William Archer, T. S. Eliot, Una Ellis-Fermor, Inga-Stina Ekedal, Thomas Marc Parrott and Robert Hamilton Ball, Harold Jenkins, Henry Hitch Adams, and Irving Ribner, among others. The recent editors of *The Revenger's Tragedy* have generally refused to be converted by the Middletonians, and G. B. Harrison (Temple Dramatists, 1934), Richard C. Harrier (Jacobean Drama, 1963), R. A. Foakes (Revels Plays, 1966), and Brian Gibbons (New Mermaids, 1967) have all voted, with more or less hesitancy, for Tourneur. The position taken by Peter B. Murray, in the first full-length book on Tourneur, *A Study of Cyril Tourneur* (University of Pennsylvania Press, 1964), is perhaps typical of the present situation. Although in his preface Murray announces that "My study of *The Revenger's Tragedy* has turned up new and I think conclusive internal evidence that Thomas Middleton is the author," he devotes the longest chapter of his book on Tourneur to *The Revenger's Tragedy*, but heads it "The Anonymous *Revenger's Tragedy*." The ambiguity, if not the absurdity, of the situation is vividly illustrated by the fact that when Marco Mincoff and Una Ellis-Fermor made almost simultaneous studies of the imagery of the play to determine its authorship ("The Authorship of *The Revenger's Tragedy*," *Studia Historico-Philologica Serdicensia*, 1939, and "The Imagery of *The Revenger's Tragedy* and *The Atheist's Tragedy*," *MLR*, 1935, respectively), the former decided that the play must have been written by a townsman, Middleton, whereas the latter was quite sure that the author must have been a countryman, Tourneur.

Allardyce Nicoll himself, however, showed that he was capable of second thoughts, since in 1962 he contributed an article entitled "*The Revenger's Tragedy* and the Virtue of Anonymity" to *Essays on Shakespeare and Elizabethan Drama in Honor of Hardin Craig*. Beginning with the statement of Oliphant fifty years earlier that in his opinion *The Revenger's Tragedy* was the "greatest work of its period of that prolific writer *Anon*" and that "the establishment of the identity of the author" should be regarded "as one of the chief problems to be tackled by students of the Elizabethan drama," Nicoll ended his survey of the situation and his expression of his hope that "adequate attention will now be directed towards other significant aspects of the play" by quoting W. W. Greg's remark to him while compiling his monumental *Bibliography of the English Printed Drama to the Restoration* (London, 1939) that he was "trying to forget that these plays had authors at all." Nicoll agreed, and finished with his own opinion: "These thoughts therefore lead to the suggestion that . . . the establishment of the identity of the author of *The Revenger's Tragedy* is not today . . . one of the chief problems to be tackled . . . . *The Revenger's Tragedy* stands as an achievement in its own right." Just as Nicoll decided to forgo his earlier championship of Tourneur, so has Samuel Schoenbaum in his study of *Internal Evidence* abandoned the position he once took in what he now calls his "youthful" book on *Middleton's Tragedies:* "For this reason, in the 'Authors' column of my revised edition of Harbage's *Annals of English Drama*, the entry for *The Revenger's Tragedy* reads: Anonymous (Tourneur, C.? Middleton, T.?)."

Nevertheless, because of the prominence given the name of Cyril Tourneur as a result of this authorship controversy, because of his role as a minor playwright of the period, and also because of the probability of the survival of a fair number of Tourneurian proponents, a brief biographical sketch of the man is in place. Allardyce Nicoll in his de luxe edition of the *Works* is the chief authority, though he acknowledges his debt to the preliminary work of Gordon Goodwin (*Academy*, 1891) and Thomas Seccombe (*Dictionary of National Boigraphy*) in drawing attention to certain documents about Tourneur summarized in the *Calendar of State Papers.* Thus Seccombe suggested an apparent connection of Cyril Tourneur with a Captain Richard Tournour, who, like Cyril, was associated with the Cecils and with Sir Francis Vere. Captain Richard was for a time lieutenant-governor of the Dutch town of Brill, and probably died about 1598. Cyril, according to various letters and official documents, also had close connections with the Low Countries. The family of Captain Richard and his brother Edward came from the little town of Canons, Essex, but there is no evidence to connect Cyril with this place—or, in fact, with any other English place except London. Nicoll suggests vaguely that he was probably born between 1570 and 1580. Although the Richard-Edward family had associations with the Middle Temple, there is no evidence that Cyril ever went there for his education—or, in fact, anywhere else, except that his knowledge of Latin and Greek as shown in his authenticated works indicates that he must have attended one of the classical grammar schools.

The first firm fact known about him is that in 1598 he published a crabbed and obscure allegorical poem entitled *The Transformed Metamorphosis* and signed his dedication of it to Sir Christopher Heydon "Cyrill Turner." The name Cyril was, as Nicoll points out, a very rare one at this time. Nicoll also believes that at least part of the poem was written before 1598. Then, on October 16, 1609, the Stationers' Register recorded the listing of an elegy, soon printed as "A Funeral Poem upon the Death of the Most Worthy and True Soldier, Sir Francis Vere," and signed "Cyril Tourneur." References in the elegy suggest that Tourneur may have been with Vere in some minor capacity on the expedition of the Earl of Essex and Sir Francis Drake to Cadiz in 1596. Then, in the latter part of 1607, Tourneur's only extant signed play, *The Atheist's Tragedy, or The Honest Man's Revenge*, was registered and printed, "As in divers places it hath often been acted." Since no players' company was given, it has been speculated that it was performed by some minor group, perhaps on a provincial tour, whereas *The Revenger's Tragedy* had been given at the Globe. Not long afterward, on February 15, 1612, "Cyrill Tourneur" entered his play *The Nobleman* in the Stationers' Register, to be printed by Edward Blount. Although the Revels lists show that this play was performed at least twice by the King's Men at Court in 1612, the plans to publish it apparently never matured; nor did those of Humphrey Moseley in 1653. The manuscript seems to have survived until the middle of the eighteenth century, when it, along with fifty-five other rare play manuscripts, was destroyed by antiquarian John Warburton's unliterary cook, Betsy Baker, when they were "unluckily burned or put under pie bottoms" (W. W. Greg, "The Bakings of Betsy," *Library*, 1911). Only once more do the records show that Tourneur tried his hand at play writing. The *Henslowe Papers* (ed. W. W. Greg, London, 1907) contain a letter from the third-rate playwright, Robert Daborne, on June 5, 1613, telling his employer that, in completing an assignment, he had given Tourneur an act of *The Arraignment of London* to write. Apparently the collaboration on a dramatization of Dekker's *The Bellman of London* was not a success, since nothing more was heard of it. Tourneur also paid his further respects to his elegiac Muse by composing "A Grief on the Death of Prince Henry," printed in 1612, and a prose "Character of the Late Earl of Salisbury" in the same year, but not published till Nicoll found it. Salisbury was Robert Cecil, one of Tourneur's patrons. In 1931–2 there was a brief exchange between Bernard M. Wagner (*TLS*, April 23, 1931) and Samuel A. Tannenbaum (*MLN*, 1932) over the transcribing of the signatures on various copies of the "Character" which survive.

Thus ended Tourneur's proven literary activities, which presumably failed to support him satisfactorily, since in 1613 he returned to his service with the Cecils and spent much of his later life abroad. In 1613 he is recorded as carrying letters from London to Brussels, but in 1617 he must have made a misstep of some kind, since in September the Privy Council issued a warrant for his arrest, on unknown grounds. After a month in prison he was released on the bond of Sir Edward Cecil, nephew of Sir Robert. Toward the end of his life Tourneur held some sort of commission from the "States of Holland," since he had a pension of £60 a year from them as stated in a petition to the War Council by his widow. She also stated that her husband had been chosen to be secretary to that council by the Lord Viscount Wimbledon, when Wimbledon was made the general for a new action to attack the Spanish treasure fleet at Cadiz. Since Sir Edward Cecil was also made Lord Marshall for this action, Tourneur was appointed his secretary in addition to the other job. But just before the fleet sailed, the authorities decided that the salary of £400 a year would go much better to a court favorite named Glanvile. Thus Tourneur had only the less important secretaryship remaining when he sailed with the fleet on its fiasco of an expedition. He was one of the scores of diseased men who were dropped off at Kinsale, Ireland, as the fleet straggled home, and died there on February 28, 1626. The fate of his widow's petition for back pay on the canceled War Council secretaryship is unknown.

But Nicoll was unwilling to let his biography of Tourneur stop there, and so he devoted several pages to develop a suggestion that perhaps Cyril Tourneur and a certain Captain William Turner, who "first emerges from obscurity" in 1598 and becomes one of "the pawns in the vast system of Cecil's secret service," were the same man. The fact that no one seems to have accepted this supposition may perhaps be accounted for by James R. Sutherland's discovery of a very informative letter from James Bathurst to William Trumbull, dated from Nimuegen on August 14, 1616 (*TLS*, April 16, 1931): "The party whose letter I enclosed to you, and whose name you could not decipher, is one Mr. Cirrill Turner, that belongs to General Cecil and was in former times Secretary to Sir Francis Vere. He told me at his first coming to this town he had been in Brussels and received many courtesies from you. He is now gone to the army with his Colonel; otherwise he had written a second letter to you that you might have better known him." Obviously, then, Tourneur had some of the varied abilities of the earlier Renaissance man.

## THE REVENGER'S TRAGEDY

As the title immediately implies, *The Revenger's Tragedy*—whoever wrote it—is a sort of epitome of the Elizabethan tragedy of blood, lust, and revenge. As Moody E. Prior summarizes the incorporation of all the main elements of this genre in *The Language of Tragedy*, "All the features of this play can be duplicated in earlier revenge plays—the need for revenge against one beyond the law, the delay of the revenge, the passionate revulsion of the avenger against the open or concealed injustice and evil which he must combat, and his sardonic and melancholy reflections on his problem." Fredson T. Bowers, in his exhaustive study of *Elizabethan Revenge Tragedy/1587–1642* (Princeton University Press, 1940), places the play in the Kyd school, which he says had its "golden era" in the twenty years after 1587, and included Shakespeare's *Titus Andronicus* and *Hamlet*, its apex. Since in some of the plays in this "school of Kyd" the avenger had increasingly criminal elements, Bowers distinguishes the next phase of about a dozen years as "the reign of the villain," with Webster as its chief representative. (See also Clarence V. Boyer, *The Villain as Hero in Elizabethan Tragedy*.) Bowers makes it clear that there were really two antithetical attitudes toward private revenge: one, that of the professional moralists and preachers, who opposed it as contrary to Christian teaching and who believed that vengeance belonged properly only to God; the other, that of the general public, who not only tolerated it, but even sympathized with it when it was called for if base or extreme injuries had been inflicted or if the law did not provide a remedy. Percy Simpson devoted his Shakespeare lecture before the British Academy in 1936 to "The Theme of Revenge in Elizabethan Tragedy," and suggested that, by the time of *The Revenger's Tragedy*, the type had become a tradition of the English stage, no longer owing anything to Seneca as it had done with Kyd. Henry H. Adams ("Cyril Tourneur on Revenge," *JEGP*, 1949) and F. W. Wadsworth (*MLR*, 1955) took the attitude that the apparent glorification of private revenge in the play was not complete and that the strong disapproval of it in *The Atheist's Tragedy* was actually present in "seminal form" in the earliest play. It is also worth noting that the absence of any apostrophe in *Revengers* in the original title made it possible for Adams (*op. cit.*) and Irving Ribner (*Jacobean Tragedy/The Search for Moral Order*) to suggest that perhaps a plural possessive was intended or implied by the author in order to broaden out his theme, since the play presents nine cases in which the characters plan or have cause for private revenge, only one of which—that of Antonio for his ravished wife—suggests that the potential revenger "Trust in the Law above."

Because of the bringing together and concentration of so many of the elements of previous revenge tragedy, several critics of the play have refused to regard it as a serious tragedy and have suggested that it was intended as a burlesque, a parody, or a satire. Although Felix E. Schelling (*Elizabethan Drama/1558–1642*, Boston and New York, 1908) was so shocked by the play that he wrote that ". . . this species of drama, in the ingenuity of its horror, its straining of all the devices of tragedy, its pruriency in an attitude of assumed righteousness, and its bitterly cynical outlook on life, reaches the *ne plus ultra* of its kind," he failed to attain the depths of revulsion shown by William Archer, who had confessed (*The Old Drama and the New*): "I cannot, indeed, quite repress a suspicion that Tourneur wrote it with his tongue in his cheek, and would have been amazed and amused to think of Vendice [*sic*] being taken seriously by a whole school of critics after three centuries." Archer, the critic-colleague of Bernard Shaw, began by derisively quoting the hyperbolic opinion of the aesthetic poet-critic Swinburne, who had declared that Tourneur "recalls the passion and perfection, the fervour and the splendour and the harmony which we . . . recognize in the dialogue or the declamation of Aeschylus himself." In leading up to his suspicion that the play might have been intended as a sort of burlesque or parody, Archer used such phrases as "a hideous mind," "hideous themes," "hideous language," "sanguinary maniac," "a sort of crazy ingenuity in working up horrors," "a shambles," "such monstrous melodrama . . . , with its hideous sexuality and its lust for blood," "sheer barbarism," and "some pitiable psychopathic perversion." He could find no evidence of any ability to write poetry, or even verse, or of any truly "indignant morality under which he tries to dissemble his gloating appetite for horrors."

Murray, in accepting but redirecting Archer's comment on the author's intention, said that he "perhaps wrote truer than he meant" when he concluded from these grotesque farcical elements that the play is a "mere farrago of sanguinary absurdities," and berated modern criticism in taking seriously what its author might have intended as a burlesque of revenge melodrama.  Murray added that " . . . if the author had not been in part parodying the genre . . . he would have been breaking with the tradition he was attempting to epitomize," since such plays, like Shakespeare's *Hamlet* and Chettle's *The Tragedy of Hoffman, or A Revenge for a Father*, often contained scenes of burlesque and parody of their own type.  Murray also maintained that readers who approach the play as a dramatic satire, such as Alvin Kernan (*The Cankered Muse: Satire of the English Renaissance*, Yale University Press, 1959) and Inga-Stina Ekeblad ("On the Authorship of *The Revenger's Tragedy*," *ES*, 1960), "tend to detach Vindici's railing and moralizing from the play as a whole, leaving the way open for charges of cynicism and a horror of life on the part of the author himself."  Murray, however, regarded Marston as the playwright closest to *The Revenger's Tragedy* in point of view, as in *Antonio's Revenge* and, particularly, the "satiric revenge play," *The Malcontent*, "which it imitates very closely," but which shows what happens to a real malcontent as opposed to a reformed one.  John Peter, on the other hand, in his *Complaint and Satire in Early English Literature* (Oxford, 1956), believed that "Tourneur's" plays handled satire more competently than Marston's and compared them with Shakespeare's, coming to the conclusion that the "premeditated" and more flexible technique of *The Revenger's Tragedy* came much closer to the technique of the medieval morality play.  Peter also ("*The Revenger's Tragedy* Reconsidered," *Essays in Criticism*, 1956) took up arms against the group of critics like T. S. Eliot, Una Ellis-Fermor, and Henri Fluchère, who uphold Eliot's dictum in *Elizabethan Dramatists*: "The cynicism, the loathing and disgust of humanity . . . are immature in the respect that they exceed the object.  Their objective equivalents are characters practicing the grossest vices, characters which seem merely to be spectres projected from the poet's inner world of nightmare, some horror beyond words."  But T. W. Craik replied to Peter (*op. cit.*) that he had underestimated the moral difficulties to be found in the play.  And Peter Lisca attempted to shift the emphasis somewhat by asserting that "an intense and ubiquitous irony on two levels: action and language," is what marks the moral attitude of the play.

Many critics have felt that the play must be placed in the medieval morality tradition, which it perhaps brought to a close.  Murray, for instance, felt that through its fusion of the Italianate revenge tragedy with medieval and ritual forms, the play "dramatizes the conflict of Italian decadence with medieval values."  He found on the one hand the influence of the Italian *novelle* and their English translations and imitations and on the other of "the morality play, the sermon, the *memento mori*, and the Dance of Death."  (See also Schoenbaum, *Middleton's Tragedies*, and "*The Revenger's Tragedy*: Jacobean Dance of Death," *MLQ*, 1954; John Peter, "*The Revenger's Tragedy* Reconsidered;" Theodore Spencer, *Death and Elizabethan Tragedy*, Harvard University Press, 1936; and Leonard P. Kurtz, *The Dance of Death and the Macabre Spirit in European Literature*, New York, 1934.)  L. G. Salingar also developed the same point with many comparisons with late morality plays ("*The Revenger's Tragedy* and the Morality Tradition," *S*, 1938), and Robert Ornstein stressed it in *The Moral Vision of Jacobean Tragedy*.  Ribner carried the idea further in working out his pervasive general theme, the quest for moral order in Jacobean tragedy: "We cannot speak of *The Revenger's Tragedy* in terms of mere survival of an earlier morality play tradition; the play itself is one large dramatic symbol of which the morality play features are an appropriate part, and this total dramatic symbol is medieval both in its grotesqueness and in the view of life for which it provides the emotional equivalent."  Like almost every other commentator Ribner used the allegorical "humors" names to stress the artificiality of the whole production, which is at the opposite extreme from naturalism.

The appropriateness of the Italian words to the characters whom they name is more or less clarified by John Florio's *A World of Words* (1598). Lussorioso means luxurious in the common Elizabethan sense of lecherous, as well as riotous. Spurio obviously suggests a bastard. Ambitioso is ambitious, desirous of honor. Supervacuo, however, is not quite what might be expected—that is, super-empty—but rather superfluous, vain, or over-idle. Vindice (also spelled Vindici) is "a revenger of wrongs . . . and abuses, one that restoreth and setteth at liberty or out of danger." Piato is given various meanings: "a plea, a suit of law, a controversy, a process, a pleading;" "a dish . . . , a course served in at any feast;" "or, as an adjective, flat, plated, cowered down, or hidden." Nencio is a fool or idiot; Sordido a niggard, a dodger, a covetous wretch. Gratiana comes from *gratia*, or grace, and Castiza from *casta*, or chaste. And Dondolo, a gull, a fool, a thing to make sport, may have been suggested by Dandolo, a vulgar and bawdy servant in Marston's *The Fawn*. The remaining characters do not bear names which suggest obvious personifications of abstract qualities.

The structure of the play, likewise, has been both attacked and defended. Murray found the key to the play's "complex, unified structure" in the playwrights's consistent use of "moral and physical transformations" and "reversals." "Nearly every character in the play makes an attempt to transform something or someone." Vindice himself is a good example of this process, as he moves from his position as a just and honest avenger to his betrayal of chastity, his sadistic actions, and his final condemnation and execution. Alfred Harbage concluded that the play is a bad play, "less because of its intrigue, thickened to a point of coagulation, but because it has so little else to offer" ("Intrigue in Elizabethan Tragedy," *Essays on Shakespeare and Elizabethan Drama*). He also refused to accede to the general praise of the play's "widely acclaimed poetry," insisting that this appears only in a few bravura passages. Prior, although admitting that the play has many crudities, is full of exaggerations, and takes advantage of the lack of necessity to establish adequate motivations and probabilities because it was in the stream of a well-known dramatic tradition, praised its author as a "writer of real poetic gifts," and brought together the two elements of structure and style by asserting: "The almost geometrical trimness of the design, the lack of subtlety yet variety in the development, make possible the hard brilliance of the diction, the sharp oppositions and antitheses, the ironic contrasts and twists in the imagery." This imagery has to do largely with subjects such as disease, corruption, darkness, lust, luxury, and vice and virtue. The diction is carefully related to the "perverse and false values of a life of sin." But Prior concluded that, although the play gives opportunity for "fine and brilliant" things, it is nevertheless not quite a "fine and brilliant" play. Ribner also analyzed the play from the point of view of style and figurativeness, finding certain "leitmotifs," such as the skull as a *memento mori*, the use of the diamond or crystal as a symbol of "heaven and a harmonious cosmic order," the description of the human body as a building "subject to ruin and decay," the emphasis on time and change through allusions to haste, perpetual movement, and speeding minutes, and the employment of metaphors of fire. But Ribner concluded that all these things helped to shape the play "into a unified and consistent work of art," which preaches that "The only reality worth man's efforts is the heaven which always lies ahead and which may be attained by the kind of withdrawal from life, and cultivation of one's own piety, which is mirrored in Castiza and Antonio."

The search for the sources of the play has resulted in the general acceptance of the conclusion that the central situation is based on parts of the life of Alessandro di' Medici, Duke of Florence, who was assassinated by his nephew Lorenzino in January 1537. The playwright, however, did not go to any of the historical works of Renaissance Italians on the subject, but rather to Marguerite d'Angoulême, Queen of Navarre's, *Heptameron*, the twelfth novel of which became the fourteenth in William Painter's *The Palace of Pleasure* (1566–7). Another pertinent selection from the *Heptameron* was published in 1597. (See N. W. Bawcutt, *"The Revenger's Tragedy* and the Medici Family," *NQ*, 1957, which also sums up previous discussions of the same indebtedness by J. A. Symonds, Vernon Lee, and Samuel Schoenbaum; and Pierre Legouis, "Réflexions sur la Reserche de Sources à Propos de la *Tragedie du Vengeur*," *EA*, 1959.) To this main source J. K. Hunter added the suggestion that the episode in II, ii, was derived from the first book of Heliodorus's *Aethiopica*, probably through the translation by Thomas Underdowne in 1587. Finally, L. G. Salingar ("*The Revenger's Tragedy: Some Possible Sources*," *MLR*, 1965) proposed a long list of echoes and correspondences in passages in the play from the works of Giraldi, Bandello, Guicciardini, Harington, Fenton, and so forth. All these matters go to show that the author of *The Revenger's Tragedy*, whoever he was, was a man of fairly wide interests and reading, that helped to form his thoughts on virtue and sin, morality and corruption, earthly and heavenly vengeance and justice, Calvinism and predestination, repentance and salvation, which make the play much more than the sensational melodrama which it has seemed to be to many readers and critics. In 1966, at Stratford-on-Avon, it received its first performance since its initial production at the beginning of the seventeenth century.

The present text is based on Nicoll's reproduction of the British Museum's copy of the 1608 quarto, but R. A. Foakes's edition for the Revels Plays (London and Harvard 1966) and Brian Gibbons's for the New Mermaids (London, 1967) have also been consulted.

# THE REVENGER'S TRAGEDY[1]

## [DRAMATIS PERSONÆ

THE DUKE.

LUSSURIOSO, his son by a former marriage.

SPURIO, the Duke's bastard.

AMBITIOSO, the Duchess's eldest son by a former marriage.

SUPERVACUO, the Duchess's second son by a former marriage.

JUNIOR, her youngest son by a former marriage.

VINDICE, a revenger, sometimes disguised as PIATO ⎫ Sons of GRATIANA and brothers to
HIPPOLITO, also called CARLO ⎭ CASTIZA.

ANTONIO ⎫ Nobles.
PIERO ⎭

DONDOLO, Gentleman-usher to GRATIANA.

Nobles, Judges, Gentlemen, Officers, Keeper, Servants (two being called NENCIO and SORDIDO).

THE DUCHESS.

GRATIANA.

CASTIZA, her daughter.

SCENE: *A City in Italy.* TIME: *Sixteenth Century.*]

## ACT[US] I. SCE[NA] i.

[*A street outside the Duke's palace.*]

*Enter Vindice [with a skull in his hand]; [then] the Duke, Duchess, Lussurioso his son, Spurio the bastard, with a train, pass over the stage with torchlight.*

VIND. Duke, royal lecher! Go, grey-
    haired Adultery,
And thou his son, as impious steeped as
    he,
And thou his bastard, true-begot in evil,
And thou his duchess, that will do[2] with
    devil:
Four ex'lent characters!—O, that mar-
    rowless age
Would stuff the hollow bones with
    damned desires,

And, 'stead of heat, kindle infernal fires
Within the spendthrift veins of a dry
    duke,
A parched and juiceless luxur![3] O God!
    One
That has scarce blood enough to live
    upon,    10
And he to riot it like a son and heir?
O, the thought of that
Turns my abuséd heartstrings into fret.[4]
Thou sallow picture of my poisoned love,
My study's ornament, thou shell of
    Death,
Once the bright face of my betrothéd
    lady,
When life and beauty naturally filled out
These ragged imperfections,
When two heaven-pointed diamonds
    were set
In those unsightly[5] rings—then 'twas
    a face    20

---

[1] The title continues: As It Hath Been Sundry Times Acted by the King's Majesty's Servants." The absence of any apostrophe in "Revengers" makes it impossible to be sure whether the word should be a plural or a singular possessive.

[2] Deal, copulate.

[3] Lecher.

[4] Discord.

[5] Unseeing, ugly.

461

So far beyond the artificial shine
Of any woman's bought complexion
That the uprightest man—if such there
be,
That sin but seven times a day—broke
custom
And made up eight with looking after
her.
O, she was able to ha' made a usurer's
son
Melt all his patrimony in a kiss,
And, what his father fifty years told,[1]
To have consumed, and yet his suit been
cold:
But O, accursèd palace!               30
Thee, when thou wert apparelled in thy
flesh,
The old duke poisoned,
Because thy purer part would not
consent
Unto his palsy-lust; for old men lustful
Do show like young men angry—eager,
violent,
Outbid like their limited performances.
O, 'ware an old man hot and vicious!
"Age, as in gold, in lust is covetous."[2]
Vengeance, thou Murder's quitrent,[3] and
whereby
Thou show'st thyself tenant to
Tragedy               40
O, keep thy day, hour, minute, I beseech,
For those thou hast determined. Hum,
who e'er knew
Murder unpaid? Faith, give Revenge
her due;
Sh'as kept touch hitherto. Be merry,
merry,
Advance thee, O thou terror to fat folks,
To have their costly three-piled[4] flesh
worn off
As bare as this; for banquets, ease, and
laughter
Can make great men, as greatness goes
by clay;
But wise men, little, are more great than
they.

*Enter his[5] brother, Hippolito.*

HIP. Still sighing o'er Death's vizard?

VIND.               Brother, welcome! 50
What comfort bring'st thou? How go
things at court?
HIP. In silk and silver, brother; never
braver.[6]
VIND.                              Puh,
Thou play'st upon my meaning. Prithee,
say,
Has that bald madam, Opportunity,[7]
Yet thought upon's? Speak, are we
happy yet?
Thy wrongs and mine are for one scab-
bard fit.
HIP. It may prove happiness.
VIND.          What is't may prove?
Give me to taste.
HIP.     Give me your hearing then.
You know my place at court?
VIND.          Ay, the duke's chamber.
But 'tis a marvel thou'rt not turned out
yet!               60
HIP. Faith, I have been shoved at, but
'twas still my hap
To hold by the duchess' skirt—you guess
at that;
Whom such a coat keeps up can ne'er
fall flat.
But to the purpose:
Last evening, predecessor unto this,
The duke's son warily inquired for me,
Whose pleasure I attended. He began
By policy[8] to open and unhusk me
About the time and common rumor;
But I had so much wit to keep my
thoughts               70
Up in their built houses, yet afforded him
An idle satisfaction without danger.
But the whole aim and scope of his intent
Ended in this: conjuring me in private
To seek some strange-digested[9] fellow
forth
Of ill-contented nature, either disgraced
In former times, or by new grooms[10]
displaced
Since his stepmother's nuptials: such a
blood,[11]
A man that were for evil only good

---

[1] Counted, saved.
[2] As usual, quotation marks are used to call attention to sententious passages.
[3] Rent paid by a freehold tenant in lieu of otherwise required services.
[4] Thick, like velvet.     [5] Original reads *her.*
[6] Finer.
[7] Opportunity, or Occasion, was portrayed in emblems as being bald behind.
[8] Craftiness.
[9] Of peculiar temperament.
[10] Servants.
[11] Disorderly fellow.

To give you the true word, some base-
coined pander. 80
VIND. I reach[1] you, for I know his heat is
such,
Were there as many concubines as ladies,
He would not be contained; he must fly
out.
I wonder how ill-featured, vild[2]-propor-
tioned,
That one should be, if she were made for
woman,
Whom at the insurrection of his lust
He would refuse for once. Heart! I
think none.
Next to a skull, though more unsound
than one,
Each face he meets he strongly dotes
upon.
HIP. Brother, y'ave truly spoke him! 90
He knows not you, but I'll swear you
know him.
VIND. And therefore I'll put on[3] that knave
for once,
And be a right man then, a man a[4] th'
time,
For to be honest is not to be i' th' world.
Brother, I'll be that strange-composéd
fellow.
HIP. And I'll prefer[5] you, brother.
VIND. Go to, then!
The small'st advantage fattens wrongéd
men.
It may point out Occasion; if I meet her
I'll hold her by the fore-top fast enough,
Or like the French mole heave up hair
and all.[6] 100
I have a habit[7] that will fit it quaintly.[8]—
Here comes our mother.
HIP. And sister.
VIND. We must coin.[9]
Women are apt, you know, to take false
money;
But I dare stake my soul for these two
creatures—
Only excuse excepted—that they'll
swallow
Because their sex is easy in belief.

[1] Understand.
[2] Vile.
[3] Disguise myself as.
[4] Of.
[5] Recommend.
[6] The "French disease" was syphilis.
[7] Costume.
[8] Neatly.
[9] Counterfeit, pretend.

[*Enter Gratiana and Castiza.*]

MOTH[ER]. What news from court, son
Carlo?
HIP. Faith, mother,
'Tis whispered there the duchess' young-
est son
Has played a rape on Lord Antonio's
wife.
MOTH. On that religious lady! 110
CAST. Royal blood! Monster! He de-
serves to die,
If[10] Italy had no more hopes but he.
VIND. Sister, y'ave sentenced most direct,
and true.
The Law's a woman, and would she were
you.
Mother, I must take leave of you.
MOTH. Leave for what?
VIND. I intend speedy travel.
HIP. That he does, madam.
MOTH. Speedy, indeed!
VIND. For since my worthy father's
funeral,
My life's unnatural to me, e'en com-
pelled,[11]
As if I lived now when I should be
dead. 120
MOTH. Indeed, he was a worthy gentleman,
Had his estate been fellow to his mind.
VIND. The duke did much deject[12] him.
MOTH. Much?
VIND. Too much.
And through disgrace oft smothered in
his spirit
When it would mount. Surely I think he
died
Of discontent, the nobleman's consump-
tion.
MOTH. Most sure he did.
VIND. Did he? 'Lack,—you know all;
You were his midnight secretary.
MOTH. No,
He was too wise to trust me with his
thoughts.
VIND. [*Aside.*] I' faith then, father, thou
wast wise indeed; 130
"Wives are but made to go to bed and
feed."—
Come, mother, sister; you'll bring me
onward, brother?

[10] Even if.
[11] Forced.
[12] Degrade.

Hip. I will.
Vind. [*Aside.*]  I'll quickly turn into
     another.                    *Exeunt.*

[Scene ii.

*A hall of justice.*]

*Enter the old Duke, Lussurioso his son, the
Duchess, [Spurio] the bastard, the duchess'
two sons, Ambitioso and Supervacuo, the
third, her youngest, brought out with Officers
for the [trial for] rape; two Judges.*

Duke. Duchess, it is your youngest son.
     We're sorry
   His violent act has e'en drawn blood of
     honor
   And stained our honors,
   Thrown ink upon the forehead of our
     state,
   Which envious[1] spirits will dip their pens
     into
   After our death, and blot us in our tombs.
   For that which would seem treason in
     our lives
   Is laughter when we're dead.  Who dares
     now whisper
   That does not then speak out, and e'en
     proclaim
   With loud words and broad pens our
     closest[2] shame?                     10
[1] Judge. Your Grace hath spoke like to
     your silver years,
   Full of confirmed gravity; for what is it
     to have
   A flattering false insculption[3] on a tomb
   And in men's hearts reproach?  The
     'bowelled corpse
   May be cered[4] in, but, with free tongue
     I speak,
   "The faults of great men through their
     cerecloths break."
Duke. They do; we're sorry for't.  It is
     our fate
   To live in fear and die to live in hate.
   I leave him to your sentence; doom him,
     lords—
   The fact[5] is great—whilst I sit by and
     sigh.                              20
Duch. [*Kneels.*]  My gracious lord, I pray
     be merciful.

[1] Malicious.               [2] Most secret.
[3] Carved inscription.      [4] Sealed.
[5] Deed, crime.

Although his trespass far exceed his
     years,
   Think him to be your own, as I am yours.
   Call him not son-in-law.[6]  The law, I
     fear,
   Will fall too soon upon his name and him.
   Temper his fault with pity.
Luss.                    Good my lord,
   Then 'twill not taste so bitter and
     unpleasant
   Upon the judge's palate; for offences,
   Gilt o'er with mercy, show like fairest
     women,
   Good only for their beauties, which
     washed off,[7]                        30
   No sin is uglier.
Amb.              I beseech your grace,
   Be soft and mild; let not relentless Law
   Look with an iron forehead on our
     brother.
Spu. [*Aside.*]  He yields small comfort
     yet—hope he shall die;
   And if a bastard's wish might stand in
     force,
   Would all the court were turned into a
     corse.
Duch. [*Rises.*]  No pity yet?  Must I rise
     fruitless then—
   A wonder in a woman?  Are my knees
   Of such low metal that without respect—
1 Judge. Let the offender stand forth.  [40
   'Tis the duke's pleasure that impartial
     doom[8]
   Shall take first hold of his unclean
     attempt.[9]
   A rape!  Why, 'tis the very core of lust,
   Double adultery.
Jun.              So, sir!
2 Judge.              And, which was worse,
   Committed on the Lord Antonio's wife,
   That general-honest lady.[10]  Confess,
     my lord!
   What moved you to't?
Jun.          Why, flesh and blood, my lord.
   What should move men unto a woman
     else?
Luss. O, do not jest[11] thy doom!  Trust
     not an ax

[6] Stepson.
[7] In this and a few later passages the line division of the original has been regularized.
[8] Judgment.
[9] Assault.
[10] Invariably chaste.        [11] Jest about.

Or sword too far; the Law is a wise
serpent                                         50
And quickly can beguile thee of thy life.
Though marriage only has made thee
my brother,
I love thee so far; play not with thy
death.
JUN. I thank you, troth;[1] good admoni-
tions, faith,
If I'd the grace now to make use of them.
1 JUDGE. That lady's name has spread such
a fair wing
Over all Italy that if our tongues
Were sparing toward the fact, judgment
itself
Would be condemned and suffer in men's
thoughts.
JUN. Well then, 'tis done, and it would
please me well                              60
Were it to do again.   Sure, she's a
goddess,
For I'd no power to see her and to live;
It falls out true in this for I must die.
Her beauty was ordained to be my
scaffold;
And yet methinks I might be easier
'sessed.[2]
My fault being sport, let me but die in
jest.
1 JUDGE. This be the sentence—
DUCH. O, keep't upon your tongue; let it
not slip.
Death too soon steals out of a lawyer's
lip.
Be not so cruel-wise.
1 JUDGE.   Your Grace must pardon us, [70
'Tis but the justice of the law.
DUCH.                                    The law
Is grown more subtle than a woman
should be.
SPU. [Aside.] Now, now he dies!  Rid
'em away![3]
DUCH. [Aside.] O, what it is to have an
old cool duke
To be as slack in tongue as in performance.[4]
1 JUDGE. Confirmed, this be the doom
irrevocable.
DUCH. O!
1 JUDGE.          Tomorrow early—

DUCH.                    Pray be abed, my lord!
1 JUDGE. Your grace much wrongs your-
self.
AMB.                    No, 'tis that tongue.
Your too much right does do us too much
wrong.
1 JUDGE. Let that offender—
DUCH.               Live, and be in health.  80
1 JUDGE. Be on a scaffold—
DUKE.               Hold, hold, my lord.
SPU. [Aside.]                    Pox[5] on't,
What makes my dad speak now?
DUKE. We will defer the judgment till next
sitting.
In the meantime let him be kept close
prisoner.
Guard, bear him hence.
AMB. [Aside to Jun.] Brother, this makes
for thee.
Fear not, we'll have a trick to set thee
free.
JUN. [Aside.]  Brother, I will expect it
from you both,
And in that hope I rest.
SUPERV.               Farewell!  Be merry!
                    Exit [Jun.] with a guard.
SPU. [Aside.] Delayed!  Deferred!  Nay,
then, if judgment have
Cold blood, flattery and bribes will
kill it.                                        90
DUKE. About it then, my lords, with your
best powers.
More serious business calls upon our
hours.
                    Exe[unt]; manet Duchess.
DUCH. Was't ever known step-duchess was
so mild
And calm as I?  Some now would plot
his death
With easy doctors, those loose living men,
And make his withered grace fall to his
grave
And keep church better.[6]
Some second wife would do this, and
despatch
Her double loathéd lord at meat or[7] sleep.
Indeed, 'tis true an old man's twice a
child.                                          100
Mine cannot speak!  One of his single
words

[1] By my faith.          [2] Assessed, judged.
[3] Remove him.
[4] In bed.

[5] Original reads pax.
[6] Attend church better; that is, at his funeral.
[7] Original reads and.

Would quite have freed my youngest
    dearest son
From death or durance, and have made
    him walk
With a bold foot upon the thorny law,
Whose prickles should bow under him;
    but 't 'as not.
And therefore wedlock faith shall be
    forgot.
I'll kill him in his forehead; hate, there
    feed—
That wound is deepest though it never
    bleed;
And here comes he whom my heart
    points unto,
His bastard son, but my love's true-
    begot.    110
Many a wealthy letter have I sent him
Swelled up with jewels, and the timorous
    man
Is yet but coldly kind.

    [*Enter Spurio.*]

That jewel's mine that quivers in his ear,
Mocking his master's chillness and vain
    fear.—
H'as spied me now.
Spu.    Madam? Your Grace so private?
My duty on your hand.    [*Kisses it.*]
Duch. Upon my hand, sir! Troth, I think
    you'd fear
To kiss my hand too if my lip stood there.
Spu. Witness I would not, madam.
        [*Kisses her.*]
Duch.    'Tis a wonder,  120
For ceremony has made many fools.
It is as easy way unto a duchess
As to a hatted dame,[1] if her love answer,
But that, by timorous honors, pale
    respects,
Idle degrees of fear, men make their ways
Hard of themselves. What have you
    thought of me?
Spu. Madam, I ever think of you, in duty,
    Regard, and—
Duch.    Puh! Upon my love, I mean.
Spu. I would 'twere love, but 't 'as a fouler
    name
Than lust; you are my father's wife—
    your grace may guess now  130
What I could call it.

Duch.    Why, th'art his son but falsely,
'Tis a hard question whether he begot
    thee.
Spu. I' faith, 'tis true too; I'm an uncer-
    tain man
Of more uncertain woman. Maybe his
    groom
A'th' stable begot me—you know I know
    not.
He could ride a horse well—a shrewd
    suspicion, marry!
He was wondrous tall; he had his length,
    i' faith,
For peeping over half-shut holiday
    windows.
Men would desire him 'light.[2] When he
    was afoot
He made a goodly show under a pent-
    house,[3]  140
And when he rid[4] his hat would check
    the signs[5]
And clatter barbers' basins.[6]
Duch.    Nay, set you a horseback once
You'll ne'er 'light off.
Spu.    Indeed, I am a beggar.
Duch. That's more the sign thou art
    great—but to our love!
Let it stand firm both in thought and
    mind.
That the duke was thy father, as no
    doubt then
He bid fair for't, thy injury is the more;
For had he cut thee a right diamond,
Thou had'st been next set in the duke-
    dom's ring,
When his worn self like Age's easy
    slave  150
Had dropped out of the collet[7] into the
    grave.
What wrong can equal this? Canst thou
    be tame
And think upon't?
Spu.    No, mad and think upon't.
Duch. Who would not be revenged of such
    a father,
E'en the worst way? I would thank that
    sin

---

[1] Women of inferior position wore hats rather than headdresses.

[2] To alight.
[3] The projecting story of a building.
[4] Rode.
[5] Strike the shop signs.
[6] Hung in front of the shop.
[7] The setting for a jewel in a ring.

That could most injury him, and be in
    league with it.
O, what a grief 'tis that a man should live
But once i' the world, and then to live a
    bastard,
The curse a the womb, the thief of nature,
Begot against the seventh command-
    ment,               160
Half damned in the conception by the
    justice
Of that unbribéd, everlasting law.
SPU. O, I'd a hot-backed devil to my
    father.
DUCH. Would not this mad e'en patience,
    make blood rough?
Who but an eunuch would not sin, his
    bed
By one false minute disinherited?
SPU. Ay, there's the vengeance that my
    birth was wrapped in!
I'll be revenged for all! Now, hate,
    begin;
I'll call foul incest but a venial sin.
DUCH. Cold still? In vain then must a
    duchess woo?          170
SPU. Madam, I blush to say what I will do.
DUCH. [*Kisses him.*] Thence flew sweet
    comfort. Earnest[1] and farewell.
SPU. O, one incestuous kiss picks open hell!
DUCH. Faith, now, old duke, my vengeance
    shall reach high;
I'll arm thy brow with woman's heraldry.
                     *Exit.*
SPU. Duke, thou did'st do me wrong, and
    by thy act
Adultery is my nature;
Faith, if the truth were known, I was
    begot
After some gluttonous dinner—some
    stirring dish
Was my first father. When deep healths
    went round          180
And ladies' cheeks were painted red with
    wine,
Their tongues, as short and nimble as
    their heels,
Uttering words sweet and thick, and
    when they rise[2]
Were merrily disposed to fall again—
In such a whispering and withdrawing
    hour,

When base male bawds kept sentinel at
    stair-head,
Was I stol'n softly. O, damnation met
The sin of feasts, drunken adultery.
I feel it swell me; my revenge is just!
I was begot in impudent wine and
    lust.              190
Stepmother, I consent to thy desires;
I love thy mischief well but I hate thee
And those three cubs, thy sons, wishing
    confusion,
Death, and disgrace may be their
    epitaphs;
As for my brother, the duke's only son,
Whose birth is more beholding to report[3]
Than mine, and yet perhaps as falsely
    sown
—Women must not be trusted with their
    own—
I'll loose[4] my days upon him. Hate all I!
Duke, on thy brow I'll draw my bas-
    tardy;          200
For indeed a bastard by nature should
    make cuckolds
Because he is the son of a cuckold
    maker.          *Exit.*

### [SCENA iii.
*Near the palace.*]

*Enter Vindice and Hippolito, Vindice in dis-*
*guise to attend L[ord] Lussurioso,*
*the duke's son.*

VIND. What, brother, am I far enough
    from myself?
HIP. As if another man had been sent
    whole
Into the world and none wist[5] how he
    came.
VIND. It will confirm me bold—the child
    a th' court.
Let blushes dwell i' the country. Im-
    pudence,
Thou goddess of the palace, mistress of
    mistresses,
To whom the costly-perfumed people
    pray,
Strike thou my forehead into dauntless
    marble,
Mine eyes to steady sapphires; turn my
    visage,

---

[1] A deposit to seal a bargain.
[2] Riz (old form of *rose*).

[3] Beholden; indebted to fame.
[4] Spend.              [5] Knew.

And, if I must needs glow, let me blush
    inward                     10
That this immodest season may not spy
That scholar in my cheeks, fool bash-
    fulness,
That maid in the old time whose flush of
    grace
Would never suffer her to get good
    clothes.
Our maids are wiser and are less
    ashamed—
Save Grace the bawd, I seldom hear
    grace named!
HIP. Nay, brother, you reach out a th'
    verge[1] now—
'Sfoot,[2] the duke's son! Settle your
    looks.
VIND. Pray let me not be doubted.

          [Enter Lussurioso.]

HIP. My lord—
LUSS.       Hippolito?—[To Vindice.] Be
    absent, leave us.             20
        [Vindice withdraws to one side.]
HIP. My lord, after long search, wary
    inquiries,
And politic siftings, I made choice of
    yon fellow
Whom I guess rare for many deep
    employments.
This our age swims[3] within him; and if
    Time
Had so much hair I should take him for
    Time,
He is so near kin to this present minute.
LUSS.            'Tis enough.
We thank thee. Yet words are but great
    men's blanks;
Gold, though it be dumb, does utter the
    best thanks.     [Gives him money.]
HIP. Your plenteous honor! An ex'lent
    fellow, my lord.           30
LUSS. So, give us leave— [Exit Hippolito.]
[To Vindice.] Welcome, be not far off.
We must be better acquainted. Push,[4]
    be bold
With us. Thy hand—

VIND.       With all my heart, i' faith!
How dost, sweet musk-cat?[5] When
    shall we lie together?
LUSS. [Aside.] Wondrous knave!
Gather him into boldness. 'Sfoot, the
    slave's
Already as familiar as an ague
And shakes me at his pleasure.—Friend,
    I can
Forget myself in private, but elsewhere
I pray do you remember me.[6]     40
VIND. O, very well, sir. I conster[7] myself
    saucy!
LUSS. What has been—of what profession?
VIND. A bonesetter.
LUSS.         A bonesetter!
VIND.         A bawd, my lord,
One that sets bones together.
LUSS.         Notable bluntness!
Fit, fit for me, e'en trained up to my
    hand.—
Thou hast been scrivener to much
    knavery then?
VIND. Fool[8] to abundance, sir. I have
    been witness
To the surrenders of a thousand virgins
And not so little;
I have seen patrimonies washed
    apieces,             50
Fruit fields turned into bastards,
And in a world of acres
Not so much dust due to the heir 'twas
    left to
As would well gravel[9] a petition.
LUSS. [Aside.] Fine villain! Troth, I like
    him wonderously.
He's e'en shaped for my purpose.—Then
    thou know'st
In the world strange lust?
VIND.     O, Dutch lust! Fulsome lust!
Drunken procreation, which begets so
    many drunkards,
Some father dreads not, gone to bed in
    wine,
To slide from the mother and cling the
    daughter-in-law;       60
Some uncles are adulterous with their
    nieces,

[1] Beyond the limit.
[2] God's foot.
[3] The spirit of our age abounds.
[4] Pish!

[5] A perfumed fop or courtesan.
[6] I.e., remember my position.
[7] Construe, consider.
[8] Servant.
[9] Sand, blot.

Brothers with brothers' wives. O hour
  of incest!
Any kin now next to the rim[1] a th' sister
Is man's meat in these days, and in the
  morning,
When they are up and dressed and their
  mask on,
Who can perceive this, save that eternal
  eye
That sees through flesh and all? Well,
  if anything be damned,
It will be twelve-a-clock at night: that
  twelve
Will never 'scape.
It is the Judas of the hours, wherein  [70
Honest salvation is betrayed to sin.
Luss. In troth, it is too; but let this talk
  glide.
It is our blood to err, though hell gaped[2]
  loud.
Ladies know Lucifer fell, yet still are
  proud!
Now, sir, wert thou as secret as thou'rt
  subtle
And deeply fadomed[3] into all estates,[4]
I would embrace thee for a near employ-
  ment,
And thou should'st swell in money and
  be able
To make lame beggars crouch to thee.
Vind.               My lord,
Secret? I ne'er had that disease a th'
  mother,                80
I praise my father! Why are men made
  close
But to keep thoughts in best? I grant
  you this:
Tell but some woman a secret over night,
Your doctor may find it in the urinal i'
  th' morning;
But, my lord—
Luss.    So, thou'rt confirmed in me,
And thus I enter[5] thee.
                      [*Gives him money.*]
Vind.          This Indian devil[6]
Will quickly enter any man—but a
  usurer;
He prevents that by entering the devil
  first!

Luss. Attend me. I am past my depth in
  lust
And I must swim or drown. All my
  desires                90
Are leveled at a virgin not far from court,
To whom I have conveyed by messenger
Many waxed lines[7] full of my neatest
  spirit,
And jewels that were able to ravish her
Without the help of man, all which and
  more
She, foolish-chaste, sent back, the
  messengers
Receiving frowns for answers.
Vind.               Possible?
'Tis a rare phoenix whoe'er she be.
If your desires be such, she so repugnant,[8]
In troth, my lord I'd be revenged and
  marry her.             100
Luss. Push! The dowry of her blood and
  of her fortunes
Are both too mean—good enough to be
  bad withal.
I'm one of that number can defend
Marriage is good, yet rather keep a
  friend.[9]
Give me my bed by stealth—there's true
  delight;
What breeds a loathing in't but night by
  night?
Vind. A very fine religion!
Luss.            Therefore thus:
I'll trust thee in the business of my heart
Because I see thee well experienced
In this luxurious[10] day wherein we
  breathe.             110
Go thou and with a smooth, enchanting
  tongue
Bewitch her ears and cozen her of all
  grace;
Enter upon the portion of her soul,
Her honor, which she calls her chastity,
And bring it into expense,[11] for honesty[12]
Is like a stock of money laid to sleep
Which, ne'er so little broke, does never
  keep.
Vind. You have giv'n 't the tang, i' faith,
  my lord.

---

[1] Belly.        [6] *I.e.*, silver from the Indies.
[2] Yawned.
[3] Fathomed.
[4] All sorts of people.
[5] Admit.

[7] Sealed letters.
[8] Resistant.
[9] Mistress.
[10] Lecherous.
[11] Expanding.
[12] Chastity.

Make known the lady to me and my brain
Shall swell with strange invention.  I will move it          120
Till I expire with speaking and drop down
Without a word to save me; but I'll work—

Luss. We thank thee and will raise thee; receive her name.
It is the only daughter to Madam Gratiana,
The late widow.

Vind. [*Aside.*] O, my sister, my sister!

Luss. Why dost walk aside?

Vind. My lord, I was thinking how I might begin,
As thus—"O lady"—or twenty hundred devices.
Her very bodkin[1] will put a man in.

Luss. Ay, or the wagging of her hair.  [130

Vind. No, that shall put you in, my lord.

Luss. Shall't?  Why, content.  Dost know the daughter then?

Vind. O, ex'lent well by sight.

Luss.                    That was her brother
That did prefer thee to us.

Vind.               My lord, I think so.
I knew I had seen him somewhere.

Luss. And therefore, prithee let thy heart to him
Be as a virgin, close.

Vind.                    O, my good lord.

Luss. We may laugh at that simple age within him—

Vind. Ha! Ha! Ha!

Luss. Himself being made the subtle instrument          140
To wind up[2] a good fellow—

Vind.               That's I, my lord!

Luss. That's thou—
To entice and work his sister.

Vind.                    A pure novice!

Luss. 'Twas finely managed.

Vind. Gallantly carried!  A pretty, perfumed villain!

Luss. I've bethought me.
If she prove chaste still and immovable,
Venture upon the mother, and with gifts
As I will furnish thee, begin with her.

Vind. O, fie, fie, that's the wrong end, my lord.          150

'Tis mere[3] impossible that a mother by any gifts
Should become a bawd to her own daughter!

Luss. Nay, then I see thou'rt but a puny[4]
In the subtle mystery of a woman.
Why, 'tis held now no dainty dish.  The name[5]
Is so in league with age that nowadays
It does eclipse three quarters of a mother.

Vind. Does't so, my lord?
Let me alone then to eclipse the fourth.

Luss. Why, well said.  Come, I'll furnish thee.  But first          160
Swear to be true in all.

Vind.                    True?

Luss.                              Nay, but swear!

Vind. Swear?  I hope your honor little doubts my faith.

Luss. Yet, for my humor's sake, 'cause I love swearing—

Vind. 'Cause you love swearing, 'slud,[6] I will.

Luss. Why, enough.
Ere long, look to be made of better stuff.

Vind. That will do well indeed, my lord.

Luss.                    Attend me.[7]  [*Exit.*]

Vind. O,
Now let me burst; I've eaten noble poison!          170
We are made strange fellows, brother, innocent villains.
Wilt not be angry when thou hear'st on't, think'st thou?
I' faith, thou shalt.  Swear me to foul my sister!
Sword, I durst make a promise of him to thee:
Thou shalt dis-heir him.  It shall be thine honor.
And yet, now angry froth[8] is down in me,
It would not prove the meanest policy
In this disguise to try the faith of both;
Another might have had the selfsame office,
Some slave that would have wrought effectually,          180

---

[1] Hairpin.          [2] Engage.

[3] Completely.
[4] Beginner.
[5] *I.e.*, bawd.
[6] God's blood.
[7] Serve me.
[8] Frenzy.

Ay, and perhaps o'erwrought 'em; therefore, I,
Being thought traveled, will apply
myself
Unto the selfsame form, forget my
nature,
As if no part about me were kin to 'em,
So touch[1] 'em—though I durst almost for
good
Venture my lands in heaven upon their
good.                                    *Exit.*

[SCENA iv.
*A room in Antonio's house.*]

*Enter the discontented Lord Antonio (whose
wife the Duchess' youngest son ravished); he
discovering[2] the body of her, dead, to certain
lords and [to Piero and] Hippolito.*

ANT. Draw nearer, lords, and be sad
witnesses
Of a fair, comely building newly fall'n,
Being falsely undermínéd.  Violent rape
Has played a glorious act.  Behold, my
lords,
A sight that strikes man out of me.
PIERO. That virtuous lady!
ANT.                Precedent for wives!
HIP. The blush of[3] many women, whose
chaste presence
Would e'en call shame up to their cheeks
And make pale wanton sinners have
good colors.
ANT. Dead!                              10
Her honor first drunk poison; and her
life,
Being fellows in one house, did pledge[4]
her honor.
PIERO. O, grief of many!
ANT.        I marked not this before:
A prayerbook the pillow to her cheek.
This was her rich confection,[5] and
another
Placed in her right hand with a leaf
tucked up,
Pointing to these words:
*"Melius virtute mori, quam per dedecus
vivere."*[6]

---

[1] Test.                      [2] Revealing.
[3] The cause of blushing in.
[4] With the double meaning of *drink to* and
*redeem.*
[5] Preparation.
[6] "Better to die in virtue than to live in
shame."

True and effectual it is, indeed.
HIP. My lord, since you invite us to your
sorrows,                                20
Let's truly taste 'em, that with equal
comfort
As to ourselves we may relieve your
wrongs.
We have grief, too, that yet walks
without tongue:
*"Curae leves loquuntur, majores stupent."*[7]
ANT. You deal with truth, my lord.
Lend me but your attentions and I'll cut
Long grief into short words.  Last
reveling night,
When torchlight made an artificial noon
About the court, some courtiers in the
mask,
Putting on better faces than their
own,                                    30
Being full of fraud and flattery, amongst
whom
The duchess' youngest son—that moth
to honor—
Filled up a room, and, with long lust to
eat
Into my wearing, amongst all the ladies
Singled out that dear form, who ever
lived
As cold in lust as she is now in death—
Which that step-duchess' monster knew
too well—
And therefore in the height of all the
revels,
When music was heard loudest, courtiers
busiest,
And ladies great with laughter—O
vicious minute!                          40
Unfit, but for relation, to be spoke of—
Then with a face more impudent than
his vizard
He harried[8] her amidst a throng of
panders
That live upon damnation of both kinds
And fed the ravenous vulture of his lust.
O, death to think on't!  She, her honor
forced,
Deemed it a nobler dowry for her name
To die with poison than to live with
shame.
HIP. A wondrous lady of rare fire compact!

---

[7] "Light cares speak, greater are silent."
(From Seneca's *Hippolitus.*)
[8] Seized.

Sh'as made her name an empress by that
act.                                                        50
PIERO. My lord, what judgment follows
the offender?
ANT. Faith, none, my lord. It cools and
is deferred.
PIERO. Delay the doom for rape?
ANT. O, you must note who 'tis should
die—
The duchess' son. She'll look to be a
saver.[1]
"Judgment in this age is near kin to
favor."
HIP. [*Drawing his sword.*] Nay, then,
step forth, thou bribeless officer!
I bind you all in steel to bind you surely.
Here let your oaths meet, to be kept and
paid
Which else will stick like rust and shame
the blade.                                              60
Strengthen my vow that—if at the next
sitting
Judgment speak all in gold and spare
the blood
Of such a serpent—e'en before their
seats
To let his soul out, which long since was
found
Guilty in heaven.
ALL.        We swear it and will act it.
ANT. Kind gentlemen, I thank you in mine
ire.
HIP. 'Twere pity
The ruins of so fair a monument
Should not be dipped in the defacer's
blood.
PIERO. Her funeral shall be wealthy, for
her name                                                70
Merits a tomb of pearl. My lord
Antonio,
For this time wipe your lady from your
eyes;
No doubt our grief and yours may one
day court it[2]
When we are more familiar with revenge.
ANT. That is my comfort, gentlemen, and
I joy
In this one happiness above the rest,
Which will be called a miracle at last,
That, being an old man, I'd a wife so
chaste.                                        *Exeunt.*

---

[1] She'll take care to be his savior.
[2] Be shown at court.

ACTUS II. SCE[NA] i.
[*A room in Gratiana's house.*]

*Enter Castiza, the sister.*

CAST. How hardly shall that maiden be
beset
Whose only fortunes are her constant
thoughts,
That has no other child's-part[3] but her
honor
That keeps her low and empty in estate.
Maids and their honors are like poor
beginners:
Were not sin rich there would be fewer
sinners.
Why had not virtue a revenue? Well,
I know the cause: 'twould have
impoverished hell.

[*Enter Dondolo.*]

How now, Dondolo!
DON. Madonna, there is one, as they [10
say, a thing of flesh and blood—a man, I
take him by his beard, that would very
desirously mouth to mouth with you.
CAST. What's that?
DON. Show his teeth in your company.
CAST. I understand thee not.
DON. Why, speak with you, madonna.
CAST. Why, say so, madman, and cut off
a great deal of dirty way. Had it not
been better spoke, in ordinary words, that
one would speak with me?
DON. Ha, ha! That's as ordinary as
two shillings. I would strive a little to
show myself in my place.[4] A gentleman-
usher scorns to use the phrase and fancy
of a servingman.                                        20
CAST. Yours be your own,[5] sir; go direct
him hither.                    [*Exit Dondolo.*]
I hope some happy tidings from my
brother
That lately traveled, whom my soul
affects.[6]
Here he comes.

*Enter Vindice her brother, disguised.*

VIND. Lady, the best of wishes to your sex:
Fair skins and new gowns.

---

[3] Inheritance.
[4] Office.
[5] Original reads *one.*
[6] Loves.

CAST. O, they shall thank you, sir.
   Whence this?        [*He offers her a letter.*]
VIND.  O, from a dear and worthy friend,
   Mighty!
CAST.              From whom?
VIND.              The duke's son.
CAST.              Receive that!  30
        *A box a th' ear to her brother.*
I swore I'd put anger in my hand
And pass the virgin limits of myself
To him that next appeared in that base
   office,
To be his sin's attorney.  Bear to him
That figure of my hate upon thy cheek
Whilst 'tis yet hot, and I'll reward thee
   for't;
Tell him my honor shall have a rich name
When several harlots shall share his with
   shame.
Farewell; commend me to him in my
   hate!                    *Exit.*
VIND. It is the sweetest box that e'er my
   nose came nigh—                    40
The finest drawn-work cuff[1] that e'er was
   worn.
I'll love this blow forever, and this cheek
Shall still henceforward take the wall of[2]
   this.
O, I'm above my tongue![3]  Most con-
   stant sister,
In this thou hast right honorable shown.
Many are called by their honor that have
   none.
Thou art approved forever in my
   thoughts.
It is not in the power of words to taint
   thee,
And yet for the salvation of my oath,
As my resolve in that point, I will
   lay                    50
Hard siege unto my mother, though I
   know
A siren's tongue could not bewitch her so.
Mass! Fitly, here she comes.  Thanks,
   my disguise!—

[*Enter Gratiana.*]
Madam, good afternoon.
MOTH.        Y'are welcome, sir.
VIND. The next of Italy commends him to
   you,

[1] With a pun on an ornamental cuff.
[2] Take precedence of, be honored over.
[3] Powers of speech.

Our mighty expectation, the duke's son.
MOTH. I think myself much honored that
   he pleases
To rank me in his thoughts.
VIND.              So may you, lady!
One that is like to be our sudden duke—
The crown gapes for him every tide[4]—
   and then                    60
Commander o'er us all.  Do but think
   on him,
How blest were they now that could
   pleasure him,
E'en with anything almost.
MOTH.              Ay, save their honor.
VIND. Tut, one would let a little of that go
   too,
And ne'er be seen in't—ne'er be seen in't,
   mark you.
I'd wink and let it go—
MOTH.              Marry, but I would not.
VIND. Marry, but I would, I hope; I know
   you would too
If you'd that blood now which you gave
   your daughter.
To her indeed 'tis, this wheel[5] comes
   about;
That man that must be all this perhaps
   ere morning                    70
—For his white[6] father does but mold
   away—
Has long desired your daughter.
MOTH.              Desired?
VIND. Nay, but hear me.
He desires now that will command
   hereafter;
Therefore, be wise.  I speak as more a
   friend
To you than him.  Madam, I know y'are
   poor,
And, 'lack the day,
There are too many poor ladies already.
Why should you vex[7] the number?  'Tis
   despised.
Live wealthy, rightly understand the
   world,                    80
And chide away that foolish country girl
Keeps company with your daughter,
   Chastity.
MOTH. O fie, fie!  The riches of the world
   cannot hire

[4] Time, hour.
[5] Wheel of fortune.
[6] White-haired.
[7] Disturb, increase.

A mother to such a most unnatural task.
VIND. No, but a thousand angels[1] can.
　Men have no power; angels must work
　　you to it.
　The world descends into such baseborn
　　evils
　That forty angels can make four score
　　devils.
　There will be fools still, I perceive—still
　　fool[s].
　Would I be poor, dejected,[2] scorned of
　　greatness,                                90
　Swept from the palace, and see other
　　daughters
　Spring with the dew o'the court, having
　　mine own
　So much desired and loved by the duke's
　　son?
　No, I would raise my state upon her
　　breast
　And call her eyes my tenants; I would
　　count
　My yearly maintenance upon her cheeks,
　Take coach upon her lip, and all her parts
　Should keep men[3] after men, and I
　　would ride
　In pleasure upon pleasure.
　You took great pains for her, once when
　　it was;                                  100
　Let her requite it now, though it be but
　　some.
　You brought her forth; she may well
　　bring you home.
MOTH. O heavens! This overcomes me!
VIND. [Aside.] Not, I hope, already?
MOTH. [Aside.] It is too strong for me.
　　Men know, that know us,
　We are so weak their words can over-
　　throw us.
　He touched me nearly, made my virtues
　　bate,[4]
　When his tongue struck upon my poor
　　estate.
VIND. [Aside.] I e'en quake to proceed;
　　my spirit turns edge.[5]
　I fear me she's unmothered; yet I'll
　　venture,                                 110
　"That woman is all male whom none
　　can enter!"—

What think you now, lady? Speak, are
　you wiser?
What said advancement to you? Thus
　it said:
"The daughter's fall lifts up the mother's
　head."
Did it not, madam? But I'll swear it
　does
In many places. Tut, this age fears no
　man.
" 'Tis no shame to be bad, because 'tis
　common."
MOTH. Ay, that's the comfort on't.
VIND.　　　　　　The comfort on't!
　I keep the best for last. Can these per-
　　suade you
　To forget heaven—and—
　　　　　　　　　　[Gives her money.]
MOTH.　　　Ay, these are they—
VIND. O!                                    120
MOTH. —that enchant our sex. These are
　　the means
　That govern our affections. That wo-
　　man will
　Not be troubled with the mother[6] long
　That sees the comfortable shine of you.
　I blush to think what for your sakes I'll
　　do.
VIND. [Aside.] O suff'ring heaven, with
　　thy invisible finger
　E'en at this instant turn the precious side
　Of both mine eyeballs inward, not to see
　　myself!
MOTH. Look you, sir.
VIND.　　　　　　　Holla!
MOTH. [Giving him money.]　　　Let this
　　thank your pains.
VIND. O, you're a kind madam.[7]           130
MOTH. I'll see how I can move.
VIND.　　　　　　Your words will sting.
MOTH. If she be still chaste, I'll ne'er call
　her mine.
VIND. [Aside.]　　Spoke truer than you
　　meant it.
MOTH. Daughter Castiza!

　　　　　　[Enter Castiza.]

CAST.　　　　　Madam?
VIND.　　　　　O, she's yonder.
　Meet her.—[Aside.] Troops of celestial
　　soldiers guard her heart!

---

[1] Gold coins.
[2] Cast away.
[3] Servants.
[4] Abate, weaken.
[5] Becomes blunted.

[6] With a pun on the meaning of *hysteria*.
[7] With a pun on the meaning *bawd*. Original
reads *madman*.

Yon dam has devils enough to take her
part.

CAST. Madam, what makes[1] yon evil-officed
man

In presence of you?

MOTH.  Why?

CAST.  He lately brought
Immodest writing sent from the duke's
son

To tempt me to dishonorable act.  140

MOTH. Dishonorable act?  Good honor-
able fool,
That wouldst be honest 'cause thou
wouldst be so,
Producing no one reason but thy will;
And 't'as a good report, prettily com-
mended—
But pray by whom?  Mean people,
ignorant people!
The better sort I'm sure cannot abide it,
And by what rule should we square out
our lives
But by our betters' actions?  O, if thou
knew'st
What 'twere to lose it, thou would never
keep it.
But there's a cold curse laid upon all
maids;  150
Whilst others clip[2] the sun, they clasp
the shades!
Virginity is paradise locked up.
You cannot come by yourselves without
fee,
And 'twas decreed that man should keep
the key.
Deny advancement, treasure, the duke's
son!

CAST. I cry you mercy![3]  Lady, I mistook
you.
Pray, did you see my mother?  Which
way went you?
Pray God I have not lost her.

VIND. [Aside.]  Prettily put by.

MOTH. Are you as proud to me as coy to
him?
Do you not know me now?

CAST.  Why, are you she?  160
The world's so changed, one shape into
another,
It is a wise child now that knows her
mother.

VIND. [Aside.]  Most right, i' faith.

MOTH.  I owe your cheek my hand
For that presumption now, but I'll forget
it.
Come, you shall leave those childish
'haviors
And understand your time.  Fortunes
flow to you.
What, will you be a girl?
If all feared drowning that spy waves
ashore,
Gold would grow rich and all the mer-
chants poor.  170

CAST. It is a pretty saying of a wicked one,
But methinks now it does not show so well
Out of your mouth—better in his.

VIND. [Aside.]  Faith, bad enough in both,
Were I in earnest—as I'll seem no less.—
I wonder, lady, your own mother's words
Cannot be taken, nor stand in full force.
'Tis honesty you urge: what's honesty?
'Tis but heaven's beggar; and what
woman is
So foolish to keep honesty  180
And be not able to keep herself?  No,
Times are grown wiser and will keep less
charge.
A maid that has small portion now
intends
To break up house and live upon her
friends.
How blest are you!  You have happiness
alone.
Others must fall to thousands, you to one
Sufficient in himself to make your
forehead
Dazzle the world with jewels, and peti-
tionary people
Start at your presence.

MOTH.  O, if I were young,
I should be ravished!

CAST.  Ay, to lose your honor.  190

VIND. 'Slid, how can you lose your honor
To deal with my lord's grace?
He'll add more honor to it by his title;
Your mother will tell you how.

MOTH.  That I will.

VIND. O, think upon the pleasure of the
palace:
Secured ease and state; the stirring meats
Ready to move out of the dishes
That e'en now quicken[4] when· they're
eaten;

---

[1] Does.  [2] Hug.  [3] Beg your pardon.

[4] Make you feel lively, pregnant.

Banquets abroad by torchlight, musics, sports,

Bare-headed vassals that had ne'er the fortune                                    200

To keep on their own hats, but let horns wear 'em;[1]

Nine coaches waiting—hurry, hurry, hurry—

CAST. Ay, to the devil!

VIND. [*Aside*.] Ay, to the devil.—To th' duke, by my faith!

MOTH. Ay, to the duke. Daughter, you'd scorn to think

A th' devil and you were there once.

VIND. [*Aside*.] True, for most there are as proud as he

For his heart, i' faith.—

Who'd sit at home in a neglected room

Dealing her short-lived beauty to the pictures,                                  210

That are as useless as old men, when those

Poorer in face and fortune than herself

Walk with a hundred acres on their backs—

Fair meadows cut into green foreparts?[2]

O, it was the greatest blessing ever happened to women

When farmers' sons agreed, and met again,

To wash their hands and come up gentlemen!

The commonwealth has flourished ever since.

Lands that were mete[3] by the rod—that labor's spared—

Tailors ride down and measure 'em by the yard.[4]                            220

Fair trees, those comely foretops of the field,

Are cut to maintain head-tires.[5]  Much untold![6]

All thrives but Chastity; she lies a-cold.

Nay, shall I come nearer to you?  Mark but this:

Why are there so few honest women but

Because 'tis the poorer profession?

That's accounted best that's best followed;

Least in trade, least in fashion;

And that's not honesty, believe it; and do

But note the low and dejected price of it:                                        230

"Lose but a pearl, we search and cannot brook[7] it;

But that,[8] once gone, who is so mad to look[9] it?"

MOTH. Troth, he says true.

CAST.               False!  I defy you both!

I have endured you with an ear of fire;

Your tongues have struck hot irons on my face.

Mother, come from that poisonous woman there.

MOTH. Where?

CAST. Do you not see her?  She's too inward[10] then.

Slave, perish in thy office!  You heavens, please

Henceforth to make the mother a disease                                          240

Which first begins with me; yet I've outgone you.                    *Exit.*

VIND. [*Aside*.] O angels, clap your wings upon the skies

And give this virgin crystal plaudities![11]

MOTH. Peevish, coy, foolish!  But return this answer:

My lord shall be most welcome when his pleasure

Conducts him this way.  I will sway mine own.

Women with women can work best alone.                              *Exit.*

VIND. Indeed, I'll tell him so.—

O, more uncivil, more unnatural

Than those base-titled creatures that look downward,                            250

Why does not heaven turn black or with a frown

Undo the world?  Why does not earth start up

And strike the sins that tread upon 't?  O,

Were 't not for gold and women there would be no damnation.

Hell would look like a lord's great kitchen without fire in 't;

[1] Antlers used as hatracks, with, of course, a reference to cuckoldry.

[2] Parks; also ornamental stomachers.

[3] Measured.                                    [4] Yardstick.

[5] Headdresses.

[6] Much remains unsaid.

[7] Been the loss of.

[8] *I.e.*, chastity.                    [9] Look for.

[10] Intimate.                          [11] Applause.

But 'twas decreed before the world began
That they should be the hooks to catch
at man.                                        *Exit.*

[SCENA ii.
*The hall in the Duke's palace.*]

*Enter Lussurioso with Hippolito,*
*Vindice's brother.*

LUSS. I much applaud
  Thy judgment; thou art well-read in a
    fellow,
  And 'tis the deepest art to study man.
  I know this which I never learned in
    schools:
  The world's divided into knaves and
    fools.
HIP. [*Aside.*] "Knave" in your face, my
  lord—behind your back!
LUSS. And I much thank thee that thou
  hast preferred
  A fellow of discourse,[1] well mingléd,
  And whose brain time hath seasoned.
HIP.                                True, my lord,
  We shall find season once, I hope.—
  [*Aside.*] O villain,                    10
  To make such an unnatural slave of
  me!—But—

[*Enter Vindice, disguised.*]

LUSS. Mass, here he comes.
HIP. [*Aside.*]                And now shall I
  Have free leave to depart.
LUSS.                Your absence—leave us.
HIP. [*Aside.*] Are not my thoughts true?
  I must remove.
  But, brother, you may stay.
  Heart! We are both made bawds a new-
  found way!                            *Exit.*
LUSS. Now, we're an even number; a third
  man's
  Dangerous, especially her brother.
  Say, be free. Have I a pleasure toward?[2]
VIND.                        O my lord!
LUSS. Ravish me in thine answer. Art
  thou rare,[3]                          20
  Hast thou beguiled her of salvation
  And rubbed hell o'er with honey? Is
  she a woman?
VIND. In all but in desire.

[1] Reasoning power.
[2] At hand.
[3] Incomparable.

LUSS.                Then she's in nothing.
  I bate in courage[4] now.
VIND.                The word I brought
  Might well have made indifferent honest
    naught.[5]
  A right good woman in these days is
    changed
  Into white[6] money with less labor far.
  Many a maid has turned to Mahomet
  With easier working. I durst undertake,
  Upon the pawn and forfeit of my
    life,                                  30
  With half those words to flat[7] a Puritan's
    wife.
  But she is close and good.—[*Aside.*] Yet
    'tis a doubt
  By this time!—O, the mother, the
    mother!—
LUSS. I never thought their sex had been
  a wonder
  Until this minute. What fruit from the
    mother?
VIND. [*Aside.*] Now must I blister my
  soul, be forsworn,
  Or shame the woman that received me
    first.
  I will be true. Thou liv'st not to
    proclaim.[8]
  Spoke to a dying man shame has no
    shame.—
  My lord!
LUSS.        Who's that?
VIND.        Here's none but I, my lord.  40
LUSS. What would thy haste utter?
VIND.                Comfort.
LUSS.                                Welcome.
VIND. The maid being dull, having no mind
  to travel
  Into unknown lands, what did me straight
  But set spurs to the mother? Golden
    spurs
  Will put her to a false gallop in a trice.
LUSS. Is't possible that in this
  The mother should be damned before
    the daughter?
VIND. O, that's good manners, my lord;
  the mother for
  Her age must go foremost, you know.

[4] Desire.
[5] A reasonably chaste woman wicked.
[6] Silver.                    [7] Bring down.
[8] *I.e.*, Lussurioso will not live to publish
Gratiana's shame.

Luss. Thou'st spoke that true! But where
    comes in this comfort?          50
Vind. In a fine place, my lord. The un-
    natural mother
Did with her tongue so hard beset her
    honor
That the poor fool was struck to silent
    wonder;
Yet still the maid like an unlighted taper
Was cold and chaste, save that her
    mother's breath
Did blow fire on her cheeks. The girl
    departed;
But the good ancient madam, half mad,
    threw me
These promising words which I took
    deeply note of:
"My lord shall be most welcome"—
Luss.               Faith, I thank her!
Vind. "When his pleasure conducts him
    this way."                        60
Luss. That shall be soon, i' faith!
Vind.          "I will sway mine own;"—
Luss. She does the wiser; I commend her
    for 't.
Vind. "Women with women can work best
    alone."
    Luss. By this light,[1] and so they can.
Give 'em their due; men are not comparable
to 'em.
    Vind. No, that's true, for you shall have
one woman knit more in a hour than any
man can ravel again in seven and twenty
year.                                70
Luss. Now my desires are happy; I'll make
    'em freemen now.
Thou art a precious fellow. Faith, I
    love thee!
Be wise and make it thy revenue: beg,
    leg![2]
What office couldst thou be ambitious
    for?
Vind. Office, my lord? Marry, if I
might have my wish I would have one that
was never begged yet.
Luss. Nay, then thou canst have none.
    Vind. Yes, my lord, I could pick out
another office yet; nay, and keep a    80
horse and drab upon 't.
Luss. Prithee, good bluntness, tell me—
    Vind. Why, I would desire but this, my
lord: to have all the fees behind the arras,

and all the farthingales that fall plump
about twelve a clock at night upon the
rushes.
    Luss. Thou'rt a mad, apprehensive[3]
knave. Dost think to make any great
purchase[4] of that?                  90
Vind. O, 'tis an unknown thing, my
lord. I wonder 't 'as been missed so long!
Luss. Well, this night I'll visit her, and
    'tis till then
A year in my desires. Farewell, attend,
Trust me with thy preferment.    Exit.
Vind.               My loved lord.—
O, shall I kill him a th' wrong side now?
    No!
Sword, thou wast never a back-biter yet.
I'll pierce him to his face; he shall die
    looking upon me.
Thy veins are swelled with lust; this
    shall unfill 'em.
Great men were gods if beggars could
    not kill 'em.                    100
Forgive me, heaven, to call my mother
    wicked.
O, lessen not my days upon the earth!
I cannot honor her; by this I fear me
Her tongue has turned my sister into
    use.
I was a villain not to be forsworn
To this our lecherous hope, the duke's
    son;
For lawyers, merchants, some divines,
    and all
Count beneficial perjury a sin small.
It shall go hard yet but I'll guard her
    honor                           110
And keep the ports sure.

*Enter Hippol[ito].*

Hip. Brother, how goes the world? I
    would know news
Of you, but I have news to tell you.
Vind. What, in the name of knavery?
Hip.               Knavery, faith!
This vicious old duke's worthily abused;
The pen of his bastard writes him
    cuckold!
Vind. His bastard?
Hip.    Pray, believe it; he and the duchess
By night meet in their linen. They have
    been seen
By stair-foot panders.

---

[1] By God's daylight.    [2] Beg by bowing.    [3] Keen-witted.    [4] Profit.

VIND.                O sin foul and deep!
Great faults are winked at when the
    duke's asleep.                                    120
See, see, here comes the Spurio.
HIP.                    Monstrous luxur!
VIND. Unbraced.[1]  Two of his valiant
    bawds with him.
O, there's a wicked whisper; hell is in his
    ear.

[*Enter Spurio with two servants.*]

Stay, let's observe his passage.—
                                *[They retire.]*
SPUR.        O, but are you sure on't?
[1] SERV.  My lord, most sure on't, for 'twas
    spoke by one
That is most inward with the duke's
    son's lust:
That he intends within this hour to steal
Unto Hippolito's sister, whose chaste life
The mother has corrupted for his use.
SPUR. Sweet word!  Sweet occasion!
    Faith, then, brother,                             130
I'll disinherit you in as short time
As I was when I was begot in haste.
I'll damn you at your pleasure.  Precious
    deed!
After your lust, O, 'twill be fine to bleed!
Come, let our passing out be soft and
    wary.
                    *Exeunt* [*Spurio and two servants*].
VIND. Mark, there, there, that step!  Now
    to the duchess!
This their second meeting writes the
    duke cuckold
With new additions,[2] his horns newly
    revived.
Night, thou that look'st like funeral
    herald's fees[3]
Torn down betimes i' the morning, thou
    hang'st fitly                                      140
To grace those sins that have no grace
    at all.
Now 'tis full sea[4] abed over the world.
There's juggling of all sides.  Some that
    were maids
E'en at sunset are now perhaps i' th'
    toll-book;[5]

[1] With garments unfastened.
[2] Titles, honors.
[3] Feese, hangings of black cloth put up for a
funeral (Collins).
[4] High tide.
[5] Register of animals for sale at a fair.

This woman in immodest, thin apparel
Lets in her friend by water; here a
    dame,
Cunning, nails leather hinges to a door
To avoid proclamation.[6]
Now cuckolds are a-quoining,[7] apace,
    apace, apace, apace!
And careful sisters[8] spin that thread i' th'
    night                                             150
That does maintain them and their
    bawds i' th' day.
HIP. You flow well, brother.
VIND.            Puh!  I'm shallow yet,
Too sparing and too modest.  Shall I tell
    thee?
If every trick were told that's dealt by
    night,
There are few here that would not blush
    outright.
HIP. I am of that belief too.
VIND.                Who's this comes?

[*Enter Lussurioso.*]

The duke's son up so late!  Brother, fall
    back
And you shall learn some mischief.—

[*Hippolito retires.  Enter Lussurioso.*]

                        My good lord!
LUSS. Piato!  Why, the man I wished for!
    Come,
I do embrace this season for the
    fittest                                           160
To taste of that young lady.
VIND. [*Aside.*]                Heart and hell!
HIP. [*Aside.*] Damned villain!
VIND. [*Aside.*]  I ha' no way now to cross
    it, but to kill him.
LUSS. Come, only thou and I.
VIND.                My lord, my lord!
LUSS. Why dost thou start us?
VIND. I'd almost forgot—the bastard!
LUSS.                    What of him?
VIND. This night, this hour—this minute,
    now—
LUSS.        What?  What?
VIND. Shadows the duchess—
LUSS. Horrible word!
VIND.        And like strong poison eats
Into the duke your father's forehead.
LUSS.                            O!  170

[6] Public exposure as a whore.
[7] A-coining; being made.
[8] Disguised prostitutes.

VIND. He makes horn royal.

LUSS. 　　　　　　Most ignoble slave!

VIND. This is the fruit of two beds.

LUSS. 　　　　　　　　I am mad!

VIND. That passage he trod warily.

LUSS. 　　　　　　　　He did!

VIND. And hushed his villains every step he took.

LUSS. His villains! I'll confound them.

VIND. Take 'em finely, finely now.

LUSS. The duchess' chamber door shall not control me.

　　　　　　*Exeunt [Lussurioso and Vindice].*

HIP. Good, happy, swift! There's gunpowder i' th' court,
　Wildfire at midnight! In this heedless fury
　He may show violence to cross himself. 　　　　　　180
　I'll follow the event. 　　　　　*Exit.*

　　　　　　[SCENA iii.]

*[The Duchess's bedroom. The Duke and Duchess in bed.] Enter again [Lussurioso and Vindice, disguised].*

LUSS. 　　　　　Where is that villain?

VIND. Softly, my lord, and you may take 'em twisted.

LUSS. I care not how!

VIND. 　　　　　O, 'twill be glorious
　To kill 'em doubled, when they're heaped. Be soft, my lord!

LUSS. Away! My spleen is not so lazy—thus, and thus,
　I'll shake their eyelids ope and with my sword
　Shut 'em again for ever. Villain! Strumpet!

　　　　　　*[They pull the bed canopy apart.]*

DUKE. You upper guard, defend us!

DUCH. 　　　　　　Treason, treason!

DUKE. O, take me not in sleep! I have great sins.
　I must have days,
　Nay, months, dear son, with penitential heaves,[1] 　　　　　10
　To lift 'em out and not to die unclear;
　O, thou wilt kill me both in heaven and here.

LUSS. I am amazed to death.

DUKE. 　　　　　Nay villain, traitor,
　Worse than the foulest epithet, now I'll gripe thee

E'en with the nerves of wrath, and throw thy head
Amongst the lawyers.[2] Guard!

　　　*Enter [Guards,] Nobles, and Sons,
　[Ambitioso and Supervacuo, with Hippolito].*

1 NOB. How comes the quiet of your grace disturbed?

DUKE. This boy, that should be myself after me,
　Would be myself before me, and in heat 　　　　　20
　Of that ambition bloodily rushed in
　Intending to depose me in my bed.

2 NOB. Duty and natural loyalty forfend![3]

DUCH. He called his father villain and me strumpet,
　A word that I abhor to 'file my lips with.

AMB. That was not so well done, brother!

LUSS. 　　　　　　I am abused.
　I know there's no excuse can do me good.

VIND. [Aside to Hippolito.] 'Tis now good policy to be from sight;
　His vicious purpose to our sister's honor
　Is crossed beyond our thought. 　　　　30

HIP. [Aside.] You little dreamt his father slept here?

VIND. [Aside.] O, 'twas far beyond me.
　But since it fell so—without frightful word—
　Would he had killed him; 'twould have eased our swords.

　　　　　*Dissemble a flight [and steal away].*

DUKE. Be comforted, our duchess; he shall die.

LUSS. Where's this slave-pander now? Out of mine eye,
　Guilty of this abuse!

　　　　　*Enter Spurio with his villains.*

SPU. 　　　　　Y'are villains, fablers!
　You have knaves' chins and harlots' tongues, you lie,
　And I will damn you with one meal a day! 　　　　40

1 SERV. O, good my lord!

SPU. 　　'Sblood, you shall never sup.

2 SERV. O, I beseech you, sir!

SPU. 　　　　　To let my sword
　Catch cold so long and miss him!

---

[1] Sighs.

[2] Judges.

[3] Forbid, prevent.

1 SERV.                    Troth, my lord,
'Twas his intent to meet there.
SPU.            Heart, he's yonder!—
Ha? What news here?  Is the day out o'
the socket,
That it is noon at midnight, the court
up?
How comes the guard so saucy with his
elbows?
LUSS. [*Aside*.]  The bastard here?
Nay, then the truth of my intent shall
out.—
My lord and father, hear me.
DUKE.                Bear him hence.  50
LUSS. I can with loyalty excuse—
DUKE. Excuse?  To prison with the villain!
Death shall not long lag after him.
SPU. [*Aside*.]  Good, i' faith; then 'tis not
much amiss.
LUSS. Brothers, my best release lies on
your tongues.
I pray persuade for me.
AMB.                It is our duties.
Make yourself sure of us.
SUPERV.            We'll sweat in pleading.
LUSS. And I may live to thank you.
                *Exeunt [Lussurioso and guards]*.
AMB. [*Aside*.]            No, thy death
Shall thank me better.
SPU. [*Aside*.]      He's gone—I'll after him,
And know his trespass, seem to bear a
part                                      60
In all his ills—but with a Puritan[1] heart.
                                *Exit*.
AMB. Now, brother, let our hate and love
be woven
So subtlety together that in speaking
One word for his life, we may make three
for his death;
The craftiest pleader gets most gold for
breath.
SUPERV. Set on!  I'll not be far behind you,
brother.
DUKE. Is't possible a son should
Be disobedient as far as the sword?
It is the highest; he can go no farther.
AMB. My gracious lord, take pity.
DUKE.                Pity, boys?  70
AMB. Nay, we'd be loath to move your
grace too much.
We know the trespass is unpardonable,
Black, wicked, and unnatural.

[1] Hypocritical.

SUPERV. In a son, O, monstrous!
AMB.                Yet, my lord,
A duke's soft hand strokes the rough
head of law
And makes it lie smooth.
DUKE.      But my hand shall ne'er do't.
AMB. That as you please, my lord.
SUPERV.            We must needs confess,
Some father would have entered into hate
So deadly pointed that before his eyes
He would ha' seen the execution
sound[2]                                    80
Without corrupted favor.
AMB.                But, my lord,
Your grace may live the wonder of all
times
In pard'ning that offense which never yet
Had face to beg a pardon.
DUKE.            Honey, how's this?
AMB. Forgive him, good my lord; he's your
own son,
And—I must needs say—'twas the
vildlier[3] done.
SUPERV. He's the next heir; yet this true
reason gathers:
None can possess that dispossess their
fathers.
Be merciful!
DUKE. [*Aside*.]  Here's no stepmother's
wit:
I'll try 'em both upon their love and
hate.                                      90
AMB. Be merciful—although—
DUKE.            You have prevailed.
My wrath like flaming wax hath spent
itself,
I know 'twas but some peevish moon[4] in
him.
Go, let him be released.
SUPERV. [*Aside*.]  'Sfoot,  how  now,
brother?
AMB. Your Grace doth please to speak
beside your spleen;[5]
I would it were so happy.
DUKE.            Why, go release him.
SUPERV. O, my good lord, I know the
fault's too weighty
And full of general loathing, too in-
human,
Rather by all men's voices worthy death.

[2] Soundly performed.
[3] More vilely.
[4] Fit of lunacy.
[5] Without passion, impartially.

DUKE. 'Tis true too.  Here then, receive
    this signet;    [*Gives a seal ring.*]  [100
Doom shall pass.  Direct it to the judges.
He shall die ere many days.  Make haste.
AMB. All speed that may be.
    We could have wished his burden not so
    sore.
    We knew your grace did but delay
    before.
            *Exeunt* [*Ambitioso and Supervacuo*].
DUKE. Here's envy with a poor thin cover
    o'er it,
    Like scarlet hid in lawn, easily spied
    through;
    This their ambition by the mother's side
    Is dangerous and for safety must be
    purged.
    I will prevent their envies.[1]  Sure, it
    was                                        110
    But some mistaken fury in our son
    Which these aspiring boys would climb
    upon.
    He shall be released suddenly.[2]

            *Enter Nobles.*

1 NOB. Good morning to your grace.
DUKE.                    Welcome, my lords.
            [*The Nobles kneel.*]
2 NOB. Our knees shall take away the
    office of our feet for ever,
    Unless your grace bestow a father's eye
    Upon the clouded fortunes of your son,
    And in compassionate virtue grant him
    that
    Which makes e'en mean men happy:
    liberty.
DUKE. [*Aside.*]  How seriously their loves
    and honors woo                            120
    For that which I am about to pray them
    do,
    Which—Rise, my lords.  Your knees
    sign his release.
    We freely pardon him.
1 NOB. We owe your grace much thanks,
    and he much duty.    *Exeunt* [*Nobles*].
DUKE. It well becomes that judge to nod
    at crimes
    That does commit greater himself and
    lives.
    I may forgive a disobedient error
    That expect pardon for adultery,

And in my old days am a youth in lust.
Many a beauty have I turned to
    poison                                     130
In the denial,[3] covetous of all.
Age, hot, is like a monster to be seen:
My hairs are white and yet my sins are
    green.                            [*Exit.*]

            ACT[US] III. [SCENA i.
            *A room in the palace.*]

        *Enter Ambitioso and Supervacuo.*

SUPERV. Brother, let my opinion sway you
    once;
    I speak it for the best, to have him die
    Surest and soonest.  If the signet come
    Unto the judge's hands, why, then his
    doom
    Will be deferred till sittings and court-
    days,
    Juries and further.  Faiths are bought
    and sold;
    Oaths in these days are but the skin of
    gold.
AMB. In troth, 'tis true too.
SUPERV.        Then let's set by the judges
    And fall to the officers; 'tis but mistaking
    The duke our father's meaning, and
    where he named                             10
    "Ere many days," 'tis but forgetting
    that,
    And have him die i' th' morning.
AMB.                        Excellent!
    Then am I heir—duke in a minute!
SUPERV. [*Aside.*]                        Nay,
    And he were once puffed out, here is a pin
    Should quickly prick your bladder.
AMB.                        Blest[4] occasion!
    He being packed, we'll have some trick
    and wile
    To wind our younger brother out of
    prison
    That lies in for the rape; the lady's dead,
    And people's thoughts will soon be
    buriéd.
SUPERV. We may with safety do't and live
    and feed.                                  20
    The duchess' sons are too proud to bleed.
AMB. We are, i' faith, to say true.  Come,
    let's not linger.
    I'll to the officers.  Go you before
    And set an edge upon the executioner.

[1] Forestall their hatred.
[2] At once.

[3] When she denied me.
[4] Original reads *blast*.

SUPERV. Let me alone to grind him.   *Exit.*
AMB.                    Meet!¹  Farewell!
I am next now.  I rise just in that place
Where thou'rt cut off—upon thy neck,
   kind brother;
The falling of one head lifts up another.
                                   *Exit.*

[SCENA ii.
*Courtyard of a prison.*]

*Enter, with the Nobles, Lussurioso from
prison.*

LUSS. My lords, I am so much indebted to
   your loves
For this, O, this delivery.
1 NOB.                    But our duties,
My lord, unto the hopes that grow in
   you.
LUSS. If e'er I live to be myself, I'll thank
   you.
O  Liberty, thou sweet and heavenly
   dame!
But hell, for prison, is too mild a name!
                                   *Exeunt.*

*Enter Ambitioso and Supervacuo,
with Officers.*

AMB. Officers, here's the duke's signet,
   your firm warrant,
Brings the command of present death
   along with it
Unto our brother, the duke's son; we are
   sorry
That we are so unnaturally employed
In such an unkind office, fitter far
For enemies than brothers.
SU ERV.                    But you know
T.ie duke's command must be obeyed.
1 OFF. It must and shall, my lord.  This
   morning, then—
So suddenly?
AMB.                    Ay, alas, poor good soul,
He   must   breakfast   betimes;   the
   executioner                            10
Stands ready to put forth his cowardly
   valor.
2 OFF. Already?
SUPERV. Already, i' faith; O sir, destruc-
   tion hies,
And that² is least impudent, soonest dies.

¹ Fitting.
² He who.

1 OFF. Troth, you say true, my lord.  We
   take our leaves.
Our office shall be sound; we'll not delay
The third part of a minute.
AMB.                    Therein you show
Yourselves   good   men   and   upright
   officers.
Pray let him die as private as he may.
Do  him  that  favor,  for  the  gaping
   people                                 20
Will but trouble him at his prayers
And make him curse and swear and so
   die black.
Will you be so far kind?
1 OFF.              It shall be done, my lord.
AMB. Why, we do thank you; if we live to
   be,
You shall have a better office.
2 OFF.                    Your good lordship!
SUPERV. Commend us to the scaffold in
   our tears.
1 OFF. We'll weep and do your commenda-
   tions.                    *Exeunt [Officers].*
AMB. Fine fools in office!
SUPERV.              Things fall out so fit!
AMB. So happily!  Come, brother, ere next
   clock
His head will be made serve a bigger
   block.³              *Exeunt.*  [30

[SCENA iii.]

*Enter in prison junior brother.*

JUN. Keeper!
KEEP. [*Enters.*]  My lord?
JUN.    No news lately from our brothers?
Are they unmindful of us?
KEEP. My lord, a messenger came newly in
And brought this from 'em.
                    [*Gives him a letter.*]
JUN.              Nothing but paper comforts?
I looked for my delivery before this,
Had  they  been  worth  their  oaths.
Prithee, be from us.    [*Exit Keeper.*]
Now, what say you, forsooth?  Speak
   out, I pray:  [*He reads out the*] *letter.*
"Brother, be of good cheer."
'Slud, it begins like a whore with "good
   cheer"!
"Thou shalt not be long a prisoner."  10

³ With a pun on the meaning *hat block*.

Not five and thirty year like a bankrout,[1]
   I think so!
"We have thought upon a device to get
   thee out by a trick."
By a trick! Pox a' your trick and it be so
   long a-playing.
"And so rest comforted, be merry and
   expect it suddenly."
Be merry, hang merry, draw and quarter
   merry! I'll be mad!   [*Tears letter.*]
Is't not strange that a man should lie in
   a whole month for a woman? Well,
   we shall see how sudden our brothers
   will be in their promise. I must expect
   still a trick. I shall not be long a
   prisoner.

[*Enter Keeper.*]

        How now, what news?  20
KEEP. Bad news, my lord. I am discharged
   of you.
JUN. Slave, call'st thou that bad news? I
   thank you, brothers.
KEEP. My lord, 'twill prove so.  Here
   come the officers
Into whose hands I must commit you.
              [*Exit Keeper.*]
JUN. Ha, officers? What, why?

[*Enter Officers.*]

1 OFF. You must pardon us, my lord.
Our office must be sound; here is our
   warrant,
The signet from the duke. You must
   straight suffer.
JUN. Suffer? I'll suffer you to be gone;
   I'll suffer you
To come no more—what would you have
   me suffer?  30
2 OFF. My lord, those words were better
   changed to prayers.
The time's but brief with you; prepare
   to die.
JUN. Sure 'tis not so.
3 OFF.          It is too true, my lord.
JUN. I tell you 'tis not, for the duke my
   father
Deferred me till next sitting, and I look
E'en every minute, threescore times an
   hour,
For a release, a trick, wrought by my
   brothers.

1 Bankrupt.

1 OFF. A trick, my lord? If you expect
   such comfort,
Your hope's as fruitless as a barren
   woman.
Your brothers were the unhappy messengers  40
That brought this powerful token for
   your death.
JUN. My brothers! No, no!
2 OFF.          'Tis most true, my lord.
JUN. My brothers to bring a warrant for
   my death?
How strange this shows!
3 OFF.        There's no delaying time.
JUN. Desire 'em hither, call 'em up, my
   brothers—
They shall deny it to your faces!
1 OFF.              My lord,
They're far enough by this, at least at
   court,
And this most strict command they left
   behind 'em.
When grief swum in their eyes, they
   showed like brothers,
Brimful of heavy sorrow; but the
   duke  50
Must have his pleasure.
JUN.              His pleasure?
1 OFF. These were their last words which
   my memory bears:
"Commend us to the scaffold in our
   tears."
JUN. Pox dry their tears! What should I
   do with tears?
I hate 'em worse than any citizen's son
Can hate salt water.[2] Here came a letter
   now,
New-bleeding from their pens, scarce
   stinted yet.
Would I'd been torn in pieces when I
   tore it! [*Picks up some of the pieces.*]
Look, you officious whoresons,[3] words of
   comfort:
"Not long a prisoner."  60
1 OFF. It says true in that, sir, for you
   must suffer presently.
JUN. A villainous Duns[4] upon the letter!
   Knavish exposition!
Look you then here, sir: "We'll get thee
   out by a trick," says he.

2 *I.e.*, sea travel.
3 Rascals.
4 Referring to the subtle interpretations of
Duns Scotus.

2 Off. That may hold too, sir, for you
　　know
　A trick is commonly four cards, which
　　was meant
　By us four officers.
Jun.　　　　　Worse and worse dealing!
1 Off. The hour beckons us.
　The headsman waits. Lift up your eyes
　　to heaven.
Jun. I thank you, faith! Good, pretty,
　　wholesome counsel!
　I should look up to heaven as you
　　said　　　　　　　　　　　　　70
　Whilst he behind me cozens me of my
　　head!
　Ay, that's the trick.
3 Off.　　　You delay too long, my lord.
Jun. Stay, good authority's bastards.
　　Since I must
　Through brothers' perjury die, O, let me
　　venom
　Their souls with curses.
1 Off.　　　Come, 'tis no time to curse.
Jun. Must I bleed then without respect of
　　sign?[1] Well—
　My fault was sweet sport which the
　　world approves.
　I die for that which every woman
　　loves.　　　　　　　　　　*Exeunt.*

[SCENA iv.
*A lodge in the palace grounds.*]

*Enter Vindice [disguised], with Hippolito,
　　his brother.*

Vind. O, sweet, delectable, rare, happy,
　　ravishing!
Hip. Why, what's the matter, brother?
Vind.　　　　　　　　O, 'tis able
　To make a man spring up and knock his
　　forehead
　Against yon silver ceiling.
Hip.　　　　　　　Prithee, tell me
　Why may not I partake with you? You
　　vowed once
　To give me share to every tragic thought.
Vind. By th' Mass, I think I did too:
　Then I'll divide it to thee. The old duke,
　Thinking my outward shape and inward
　　heart
　Are cut out of one piece—for he that
　　prates his secrets,　　　　　　10

His heart stands a' th' outside—hires me
　　by price
To greet him with a lady
In some fit place veiled from the eyes o'
　　the court,
Some dark'ned, blushless angle that is
　　guilty
Of his forefathers' lusts, and great folks'
　　riots;
To which I easily, to maintain my shape,[2]
Consented, and did wish his impudent
　　grace
To meet her here in this unsunnéd lodge
Wherein 'tis night at noon, and here the
　　rather
Because unto the torturing of his
　　soul　　　　　　　　　　　20
The bastard and the duchess have
　　appointed
Their meeting too in this luxurious circle,
Which most afflicting sight will kill his
　　eyes
Before we kill the rest of him.
Hip. 'Twill, i' faith; most dreadfully
　　digested.[3]
　I see not how you could have missed me,
　　brother.
Vind. True; but the violence of my joy
　　forgot it.
Hip. Ay; but where's that lady now?
Vind.　　　　　　　O, at that word
　I'm lost again! You cannot find me yet.
　I'm in a throng of happy apprehen-
　　sions.　　　　　　　　　　30
　He's suited for a lady: I have took care
　For a delicious lip, a sparkling eye.
　You shall be witness, brother.
　Be ready; stand with your hat off. *Exit.*
Hip. Troth, I wonder what lady it should
　　be.
　Yet 'tis no wonder, now I think again,
　To have a lady stoop to a duke, that
　　stoops unto his men.
　'Tis common to be common[4] through the
　　world,
　And there's more private common
　　shadowing vices
　Than those who are known both by their
　　names and prices.　　　　　40
　'Tis part of my allegiance to stand bare
　To the duke's concubine—and here she
　　comes.

[1] Without regard to the proper sign of the
zodiac.

[2] Disguised.　　　　　　　[3] Arranged.
[4] A prostitute.

*Enter Vindice with the skull of his love
dressed up in tires.*[1]

VIND. Madam, his grace will not be absent
    long.
  "Secret?"  Ne'er doubt us, madam.
    'Twill be worth
Three velvet gowns to your ladyship.
    "Known?"
Few ladies respect that.  "Disgrace?"
    A poor thin shell!
'Tis the best grace you have to do it well.
I'll save your hand that labor; I'll
    unmask you.      [*Reveals the skull.*]

HIP. Why, brother, brother!

VIND. Art thou beguiled now?  Tut, a lady
    can      50
At such,[2] all hid, beguile a wiser man.
Have I not fitted the old surfeiter
With a quaint[3] piece of beauty?  Age and
    bare bone
Are e'er allied in action.  Here's an eye
Able to tempt a great man—to serve
    God;
A pretty hanging lip, that has forgot now
    to dissemble.
Methinks this mouth should make a
    swearer tremble,
A drunkard clasp his teeth, and not
    undo 'em,
To suffer wet damnation to run through
    'em.
Here's a cheek keeps her color.  Let the
    wind go whistle.      60
Spout, rain!  We fear thee not; be hot or
    cold,
All's one with us.  And is not he absurd
Whose fortunes are upon their faces set,
That fear no other God but wind and wet?

HIP. Brother, y'ave spoke that right.
Is this the form that, living, shone so
    bright?

VIND. The very same.
And now methinks I could e'en chide
    myself
For doting on her beauty, though her
    death
Shall be revenged after no common
    action.      70
Does the silkworm expend her yellow
    labors

For thee?  For thee does she undo
    herself?
Are lordships sold to maintain ladyships
For the poor benefit of a bewitching
    minute?
Why does yon fellow falsify highways[4]
And put his life between the judge's lips
To refine such a thing, keeps horse and
    men
To beat their valors[5] for her?
Surely we're all mad people and they,
Whom we think are, are not; we mistake
    those.      80
'Tis we are mad in sense; they but in
    clothes.

HIP. Faith, and in clothes too we—give us
    our due.

VIND. Does every proud and self-affecting
    dame
Camphor her face for this, and grieve
    her maker
In sinful baths of milk, when many an
    infant starves
For her superfluous outside—all for this?
Who now bids twenty pound a night,
    prepares
Music, perfumes, and sweetmeats?  All
    are hushed.
Thou may'st lie chaste now!  It were
    fine methinks
To have thee seen at revels, forgetful
    feasts,      90
And unclean brothels; sure, 'twould
    fright the sinner
And make him a good coward, put a
    reveler
Out of his antic[6] amble,
And cloy an epicure with empty dishes.
Here might a scornful and ambitious
    woman
Look through and through herself; see,
    ladies, with false forms
You deceive men but cannot deceive
    worms.
Now to my tragic business.  Look you,
    brother,
I have not fashioned this only for show
And useless property,[7] no—it shall bear a
    part      100
E'en in it[8] own revenge.  This very skull,

[1] Probably a wig, mask or veil, and headdress.
[2] Such a game as hide-and-seek.
[3] Dainty.

[4] Turn highwayman (?).
[5] Exhaust.      [6] Frolicsome.
[7] Stage property.
[8] A frequent neuter possessive.

Whose mistress the duke poisoned with
   this drug,
The mortal curse of the earth, shall be
   revenged
In the like strain[1] and kiss his lips to
   death.
As much as the dumb thing can, he shall
   feel.
What fails in poison we'll supply in steel.
HIP. Brother, I do applaud thy constant
   vengeance,
The quaintness of thy malice, above
   thought.
VIND. [*Poisoning the mouth of the skull.*]
   So, 'tis laid on! Now come and welcome,
   duke.
I have her for thee. I protest it,
   brother,                                    110
Methinks she makes almost as fair a sign
As some old gentlewoman in a periwig.
Hide thy face now for shame; thou
   hadst need have a mask now. [*Puts a
   mask on the skull.*]
'Tis vain when beauty flows, but when
   it fleets
This would become graves better than
   the streets.
HIP. You have my voice[2] in that. Hark,
   the duke's come.          [*Noises within.*]
VIND. Peace—let's observe what company
   he brings
And how he does absent 'em, for you
   know
He'll wish all private. Brother, fall you
   back a little
With the bony lady.
HIP.                    That I will. [*They retire.*]
VIND.                              So, so—   120
Now nine years' vengeance crowd into a
   minute.

[*Enter the Duke and Gentlemen.*]

DUKE. You shall have leave to leave us,
   with this charge:
Upon our lives, if we be missed by the
   duchess
Or any of the nobles, to give out
We're privately rid forth.
VIND. [*Aside.*]          O happiness!
DUKE. With some few honorable gentle-
   men, you may say.

¹ Manner.
² Agreement.

You may name those that are away from
   court.
GENT. Your will and pleasure shall be
   done, my lord.     [*Exeunt Gentlemen.*]
VIND. [*Aside.*] "Privately rid forth"!
He strives to make sure work on't.
   [*Advances.*]  Your good grace!     130
DUKE. Piato! Well done. Hast brought
   her? What lady is't?
VIND. Faith, my lord, a country lady, a
little bashful at first as most of them are,
but after the first kiss, my lord, the worst
is past with them. Your grace knows
now what you have to do. Sh'as somewhat
a grave look with her, but—
DUKE. I love that best. Conduct her.
VIND. [*Aside.*]              Have at all.
DUKE. In gravest looks the greatest faults
   seem less.
Give me that sin that's robed in holiness.
VIND. [*Aside.*]     Back with the torch.
   Brother, raise the perfumes.     140
DUKE. How sweet can a duke breathe?
   Age has no fault.
Pleasure should meet in a perfuméd mist.
Lady, sweetly encountered! I came from
   court.
I must be bold with you—[*Kisses the skull.*]
   O, what's this? O!
VIND. Royal villain! White[3] devil!
DUKE.                                    O!
VIND. Brother, place the torch here that
   his affrighted eyeballs
May start into those hollows. Duke,
   dost know
Yon dreadful vizard? View it well: 'tis
   the skull
Of Gloriana, whom thou poisonedst last.
DUKE. O, 't'as poisoned me!     150
VIND. Didst not know that till now?
DUKE.                    What are you two?
VIND. Villains all three! The very ragged
   bone
Has been sufficiently revenged.
DUKE. O Hippolito! Call treason! [*Falls.*]
HIP. Yes, my good lord. Treason, treason,
   treason!          *Stamping on him.*
DUKE. Then I'm betrayed.
VIND. Alas, poor lecher! In the hands of
   knaves
A slavish duke is baser than his slaves.
DUKE. My teeth are eaten out!

³ Deceptive, fair-appearing.

VIND.          Hadst any left?

HIP.                    I think but few.

VIND. Then those that did eat are eaten.

DUKE.                    O, my tongue! 160

VIND. Your tongue? 'Twill teach you to kiss closer,

Not like a slobbering[1] Dutchman. You have eyes still!

*[Throwing off his disguise.]*

Look, monster, what a lady hast thou made me—

My once betrothèd wife.

DUKE.    Is it thou, villain? Nay, then—

VIND. 'Tis I, 'tis Vindice, 'tis I!

HIP. And let this comfort thee. Our lord and father

Fell sick upon the infection of thy frowns

And died in sadness. Be that thy hope of life!

DUKE. O!

VIND. He had his tongue, yet grief made him die speechless.

Puh, 'tis but early yet. Now I'll begin          170

To stick thy soul with ulcers; I will make

Thy spirit grievous sore; it shall not rest

But, like some pestilent[2] man, toss in thy breast.

Mark me, duke,

Thou'rt a renownèd, high, and mighty cuckold!

DUKE. O!

VIND. Thy bastard, thy bastard, rides a-hunting in thy brow.

DUKE. Millions of deaths!

VIND.          Nay, to afflict thee more,

Here in this lodge they meet for damnèd clips.[3]

Those eyes shall see the incest of their lips.

DUKE. Is there a hell besides this, villains?

VIND.                    Villain? 180

Nay, heaven is just. Scorns are the hires[4] of scorns.

I ne'er knew yet adulterer without horns.

HIP. Once, ere they die, 'tis quitted.

*[Noises within.]*

VIND.                    Hark, the music!

Their banquet is prepared; they're coming—

DUKE. O, kill me not with that sight!

VIND. Thou shalt not lose that sight for all thy dukedom.

DUKE. Traitors! Murderers!

VIND. What, is not thy tongue eaten out yet?

Then we'll invent a silence. Brother, stifle the torch.

*[Hippolito extinguishes the torch.]*

DUKE. Treason! Murder!          190

VIND. Nay, faith, we'll have you hushed now with thy dagger.

Nail down his tongue, and mine shall keep possession

About his heart. If he but gasp he dies.

We dread not death to quittance[5] injuries. Brother,

If he but wink, not brooking[6] the foul object,

Let our two other hands tear up his lids

And make his eyes, like comets, shine through blood.

When the bad bleeds, then is the tragedy good.

HIP. Whist, brother! Music's at our ear; they come.

*Enter the Bastard meeting the Duchess.*

SPU. Had not that kiss a taste of sin, 'twere sweet.          200

DUCH. Why, there's no pleasure sweet but it is sinful.

SPU. True, such a bitter sweetness fate hath given;

Best side to us is the worst side to heaven.

DUCH. Push! Come, 'tis the old duke thy doubtful father.

The thought of him rubs heaven in thy way.[7]

But I protest, by yonder waxen fire,

Forget him or I'll poison him.

SPU. Madam, you urge a thought which ne'er had life.

So deadly do I loathe him for my birth

That, if he took me hasped[8] within his bed,          210

I would add murther to adultery

And with my sword give up his years to death.

---

[1] Original reads *flobbering*, which would mean *soiling*.

[2] Diseased.          [3] Embraces.

[4] Rewards.

[5] Requite.          [6] Being able to endure.

[7] Rubs out; puts an obstacle in thy way to happiness.

[8] Embraced.

Duch. Why, now thou'rt sociable. Let's in and feast.

    Loud'st music, sound! Pleasure is banquet's guest.

              *Exeunt [Spurio and Duchess].*

Duke. I cannot brook—          *[Dies.]*

Vind.      The brook is turned to blood.

Hip. Thanks to loud music.

Vind.        'Twas our friend, indeed.

    'Tis state in music for a duke to bleed.

    The dukedom wants a head, though yet unknown;

    As fast as they peep up let's cut 'em down.          *Exeunt.*

[Scena v.

*A room in the palace.*]

*Enter the duchess' two sons, Ambitioso and Supervacuo.*

Amb. Was not his execution rarely plotted? We are the duke's sons now.

Superv. Ay, you may thank my policy for that.

Amb. Your policy for what?

Superv. Why, was't not my invention, brother,

    To slip the judges, and, in lesser compass,

    Did not I draw the model of his death,

    Advising you to sudden officers

    And e'en extemporal[1] execution?

Amb. Heart, 'twas a thing I thought on too.            10

Superv. You thought on't too! 'Sfoot, slander not your thoughts

    With glorious untruth. I know 'twas from[2] you.

Amb. Sir, I say 'twas in my head.

[Superv.][3]      Ay, like your brains then

    Ne'er to come out as long as you lived.

Amb. You'd have the honor on't, forsooth, that your wit

    Led him to the scaffold.

Superv.        Since it is my due,

    I'll publish't—but I'll ha't, in spite of you.

Amb. Methinks y'are much too bold; you should a little

    Remember us, brother, next-to-be honest duke.[4]

Superv. *[Aside.]* Ay, it shall be as easy for you to be duke      20

[1] Immediate.          [2] Alien to.
[3] Original reads *Spu.*
[4] Remember that I am the next genuine duke.

    As to be honest, and that's never, i' faith.

Amb. Well, cold he is by this time, and because

    We're both ambitious, be it our amity,

    And let the glory be shared equally.

Superv. I am content to that.

Amb. This night our younger brother shall out of prison.

    I have a trick.

Superv.      A trick? Prithee, what is't?

Amb. We'll get him out by a wile.

Superv.        Prithee, what wile?

Amb. No, sir, you shall not know it till 't be done,

    For then you'd swear 'twere yours.

*[Enter an officer with a bleeding head in his hand.]*

Superv. How now, what's he?      30

Amb. One of the officers.

Superv.      Desired news!

Amb.        How now, my friend?

Off. My lords, under your pardon, I am allotted

    To that desertless office to present you

    With the yet bleeding head—

Superv. *[Aside.]*    Ha, ha! Excellent!

Amb. *[Aside.]* All's sure our own. Brother, canst weep, thinkst thou?

    'Twould grace our flattery much; think of some dame—

    'Twill teach thee to dissemble.

Superv. *[Aside.]* I have thought. Now for yourself.—

Amb. Our sorrows are so fluent.

    Our eyes o'erflow our tongues; words spoke in tears      40

    Are like the murmurs of the waters; the sound

    Is loudly heard but cannot be distinguished.

Superv. How died he, pray?

Off. O, full of rage and spleen.

Superv. He died most valiantly then. We're glad to hear it.

Off. We could not woo him once to pray.

Amb. He showed himself a gentleman in that.

    Give him his due.

Off.        But in the stead of prayer

    He drew forth oaths.

Superv.    Then did he pray, dear heart,

    Although you understood him not.

OFF.                          My lords,
  E'en at his last—with pardon be it
  spoke—                                        50
  He cursed you both.
SUPERV.   He cursed us? 'Las, good soul.
AMB. It was not in our powers, but the
  duke's pleasure.—
  [*Aside.*]   Finely dissembled both sides!
  Sweet fate!
  O happy opportunity!

*Enter Lussurioso.*

LUSS.          Now, my lords—
BOTH.                                          O!
LUSS. Why do you shun me, brothers?
  You may come nearer now.
  The savor of the prison has forsook me.
  I thank such kind lords as yourselves
  I'm free.
AMB. Alive!
SUPERV.          In health!
AMB.                          Released!
  We were both e'en amazed with joy to
  see it.
LUSS. I am much to thank you.          60
SUPERV. Faith, we spared no tongue unto
  my lord the duke.
AMB. I know your delivery, brother,
  Had not been half so sudden but for us.
SUPERV. O, how we pleaded!
LUSS.          Most deserving brothers,
  In my best studies I will think of it.
              *Exit Luss[urioso].*
AMB. O death and vengeance!
SUPERV.          Hell and torments!
AMB.                          Slave!
  Cam'st thou to delude us?
OFF.          Delude you, my lords?
SUPERV. Ay, villain!   Where's this head
  now?
OFF.                          Why, here, my lord!
  Just after his delivery you both came
  With warrant from the duke to behead
  your brother.                                  70
AMB. Ay, our brother, the duke's son.
OFF. The duke's son, my lord, had his
  release before you came.
AMB. Whose head's that, then?
OFF. His, whom you left command for—
  Your own brother's.
AMB.          Our brother's?   O, furies!
SUPERV.          Plagues!
AMB.          Confusions!
SUPERV.                          Darkness!

AMB.                          Devils!
SUPERV. Fell it out so accursedly?
AMB.                          So damnedly?
SUPERV.   Villain, I'll brain thee with it!
OFF.          O, my good lord!
SUPERV. The devil overtake thee!
AMB.                          O, fatal—
SUPERV. O, prodigious to our bloods!
AMB.                          Did we dissemble?
SUPERV. Did we make our tears women
  for thee?                                        80
AMB. Laugh and rejoice for thee?
SUPERV.          Bring warrant for thy death?
AMB. Mock off thy head?
SUPERV.                          You had a trick;
  You had a wile, forsooth!
  AMB. A murrain[1] meet 'em!   There's
none of these wiles that ever come to good.
I see now there is nothing sure in mortality
but mortality.   Well, no more words—
shalt be revenged, i' faith.   Come, throw
off clouds now, brother.   Think of ven-
geance and deeper settled hate.   Sirrah,
sit fast!   We'll pull down all.—[*Aside.*]
But thou shalt down at last.          *Exeunt.*

ACT[US] IV.  SCEN[A] i.
[*The grounds of the palace.*]

*Enter Lussurioso with Hippolito.*

LUSS. Hippolito!
HIP.          My lord!   Has your good lordship
  Aught to command me in?
LUSS.                          I prithee, leave us.
HIP. How's this?   Come, and leave us?
LUSS.                          Hippolito!
HIP. Your honor, I stand ready for any
  duteous employment.
LUSS. Heart, what mak'st thou here?
HIP. [*Aside.*] A pretty lordly humor!
  He bids me to be present; to depart;
  Something has stung his honor.
LUSS.          Be nearer; draw nearer.
  Y'are not so good, methinks; I'm angry
  with you.
HIP. With me, my lord?   I'm angry with
  myself for't.
LUSS. You did prefer a goodly fellow to
  me.                                              10
  'Twas wittily[2] elected, 'twas.   I thought
  H'ad been a villain, and he proves a
  knave—
  To me a knave.

---

[1] Plague.                              [2] Wisely.

Hip.    I chose him for the best, my lord.
'Tis much my sorrow if neglect in him
Breed discontent in you.
Luss.    Neglect? 'Twas will! Judge of it:
Firmly to tell of an incredible act
Not to be thought, less to be spoken of,
'Twixt my stepmother and the bastard—
O,
Incestuous sweets between 'em!
Hip.                        Fie, my lord!
Luss.    I, in kind loyalty to my father's
    forehead,                              20
Made this a desperate arm, and in that
    fury
Committed treason on the lawful bed
And with my sword e'en razed[1] my
    father's bosom,
For which I was within a stroke of death.
Hip.    Alack, I'm sorry! [Aside.] 'Sfoot,
    just upon the stroke,
Jars in[2] my brother; 'twill be villainous
    music!

*Enter Vindice [disguised].*

Vind.    My honored lord!
Luss.    Away! Prithee, forsake us! Here-
    after we'll not know thee.
Vind.    Not know me, my lord? Your lord-
    ship cannot choose.
Luss.    Begone, I say; thou art a false
    knave.                                 30
Vind.    Why, the easier to be known, my
    lord.
Luss.    Push! I shall prove too bitter with
    a word,
Make thee a perpetual prisoner,
And lay this ironage[3] upon thee.
Vind.  [Aside.]                    Mum,
For there's a doom would make a woman
    dumb.
Missing the bastard, next him, the wind's
    come about;
Now 'tis my brother's turn to stay, mine
    to go out.            *Exit Vin[dice].*
Luss.    H'as greatly moved me.
Hip.                Much to blame, i' faith.
Luss.    But I'll recover, to his ruin. 'Twas
    told me lately,
I know not whether falsely, that you'd a
    brother.                               40

Hip. Who, I?  Yes, my good lord, I have
    a brother.
Luss.    How chance the court ne'er saw
    him? Of what nature?
How does he apply his hours?
Hip.                Faith, to curse fates,
Who, as he thinks, ordained him to be
    poor;
Keeps at home full of want and discon-
    tent.
Luss.    There's hope in him, for discontent
    and want
Is the best clay to mold a villain of.
Hippolito, wish him repair to us.
If there be aught in him to please our
    blood
For thy sake we'll advance him, and
    build fair                            50
His meanest fortunes; for it is in us
To rear up towers from cottages.
Hip.    It is so, my lord; he will attend your
    honor.
But he's a man in whom much melan-
    choly dwells.
Luss.    Why, the better!  Bring him to
    court.
Hip.    With willingness and speed. [Aside.]
    Whom he cast off
E'en now, must now succeed.  Brother,
    disguise must off.
In thine own shape now I'll prefer thee
    to him.
How strangely does himself work to
    undo him!                    *Exit.*
Luss.    This fellow will come fitly; he shall
    kill                                  60
That other slave that did abuse my
    spleen
And made it swell to treason.  I have put
Much of my heart into him; he must die.
He that knows great men's secrets, and
    proves slight,[4]
That man ne'er lives to see his beard
    turn white.
Ay, he shall speed him.  I'll employ thee,
    brother.
Slaves are but nails to drive out one
    another.
He being of black condition, suitable
To want and ill-content, hope of pre-
    ferment
Will grind him to an edge.               70

---

[1] Scratched.
[2] Comes in discordantly.
[3] Either his sword or chains.

[4] Untrustworthy.

*The Nobles enter.*

1 [NOBLE]. Good days unto your honor.
LUSS. 　　　　　　My kind lords,
　I do return the like.
2 [NOBLE]. 　　Saw you my lord the duke?
LUSS. My lord and father? Is he from
　　court?
1 [NOBLE]. He's sure from court, but
　　where, which way his pleasure
　Took, we know not nor can we hear on't.

[*Enter other Nobles.*]

LUSS. Here come those should tell. Saw
　　you my lord and father?
3 [NOBLE]. Not since two hours before
　　noon, my lord,
　And then he privately rid forth.
LUSS. O, he's rode forth?
1 [NOBLE]. 　　'Twas wondrous privately.
2 [NOBLE]. There's none i' the court had
　　any knowledge on't. 　　　　　　80
LUSS. His grace is old and sudden; 'tis no
　　treason
　To say the duke my father has a humor
　Or such a toy[1] about him. What in us
　Would appear light, in him seems
　　virtuous.
3 [NOBLE]. 'Tis oracle, my lord. 　*Exeunt.*

[SCENA ii.
*A hall in the palace.*]

*Enter Vindice and Hippolito, Vind*[ice]
*out of his disguise.*

HIP. So, so, all's as it should be; y'are
　　yourself.
VIND. How that great villain puts me to
　　my shifts![2]
HIP. He that did lately in disguise reject
　　thee
　Shall, now thou art thyself, as much
　　respect thee.
VIND. 'Twill be the quainter fallacy. But,
　　brother,
　'Sfoot, what use will he put me to now,
　　think'st thou?
HIP. Nay, you must pardon me in that. I
　　know not.
　H'as some employment for you, but what
　　'tis

<hr>

[1] Whim.
[2] Tricks, disguises.

He and his secretary, the devil, knows
　best.
VIND. Well, I must suit my tongue to his
　　desires, 　　　　　　　　　　　10
　What color soe'er they be, hoping at last
　To pile up all my wishes on his breast.
HIP. Faith, brother, he himself shows the
　　way.
VIND. Now the duke is dead, the realm is
　　clad in clay;
　His death being not yet known, under
　　his name
　The people still are governed. Well,
　　thou his son
　Art not long-lived; thou shalt not 'joy
　　his death.
　To kill thee then I should most honor
　　thee,
　For 'twould stand firm in every man's
　　belief
　Thou'st a kind child, and only diedst
　　with grief. 　　　　　　　　　20
HIP. You fetch about[3] well; but let's talk
　　in present.
　How will you appear in fashion different,
　As well as in apparel, to make all things
　　possible?
　If you be but once tripped we fall for
　　ever.
　It is not the least[4] policy to be doubtful;
　You must change tongue—"familiar"
　　was your first.
VIND. Why, I'll bear me in some strain of
　　melancholy
　And string myself with heavy-sounding
　　wire
　Like such an instrument that speaks
　　merry things sadly.
HIP. Then 'tis as I meant; I gave you
　　out 　　　　　　　　　　　　30
　At first in discontent.
VIND. 　　　　I'll turn myself, and then—
HIP. 'Sfoot, here he comes! Hast thought
　　upon't?
VIND. Salute him; fear not me.

[*Enter Lussurioso.*]

LUSS. 　　　　　　Hippolito!
HIP. Your lordship.
LUSS. 　　　　　What's he yonder?
HIP. 'Tis Vindice, my discontented
　　brother,

<hr>

[3] Twist things. 　　　[4] Not in any way.

Whom, 'cording to your will, I'ave brought to court.

Luss. Is that thy brother? Beshrew me, a good presence;

I wonder h'as been from the court so long.—

Come nearer.

Hip. Brother: Lord Lussurioso, the duke's son.                                                    40

Luss. Be more near to us.  Welcome! Nearer yet!

[Vindice] snatches off his hat and makes legs to him.

Vind. How don you?  God you god den.[1]

Luss.                    We thank thee.—

[Aside.] How strangely such a coarse, homely salute

Shows in the palace, where we greet in fire—

Nimble and desperate tongues!  Should we name

God in a salutation, 'twould ne'er be stood on't.[2]  Heaven!—

Tell me, what has made thee so melancholy?

Vind. Why, going to law.

Luss. Why, will that make a man melancholy?

Vind. Yes, to look long upon ink  [50 and black buckram.  I went me to law in anno quadragesimo secundo,[3] and I waded out of it in anno sextagesimo tertio.[4]

Luss. What, three and twenty years in law?

Vind. I have known those that have been five and fifty, and all about pullin[5] and pigs.

Luss. May it be possible such men should breathe to vex the terms[6] so much?                                                [60

Vind. 'Tis food to some, my lord.  There are old men at the present that are so poisoned with the affectation of law words, having had many suits canvassed, that their common talk is nothing but Barbary[7] Latin; they cannot so much as pray, but in law, that their sins may be removed with a writ of error, and their souls fetched up to heaven with a sasarara.[8]

---

[Luss.][9] It seems most strange to me;  [70 Yet all the world meets round in the same bent.

Where the heart's set, there goes the tongue's consent.

How dost apply thy studies, fellow?

Vind. Study?  Why, to think how a great rich man lies a-dying, and a poor cobbler tolls the bell for him; how he cannot depart the world, and see the great chest stand before him; when he lies speechless, how he will point you readily to all the boxes, and, when he is past all  [80 memory, as the gossips guess, then thinks he of forfeitures and obligations.  Nay, when to all men's hearings he whurls and rottles[10] in the throat, he's busy threatening his poor tenants; and this would last me now some seven years thinking, or thereabouts!  But I have a conceit[11] a-coming in picture upon this.  I draw it myself, which, i' faith, la, I'll present to your honor; you shall not choose but like it, for your  [90 lordship shall give me nothing for it.

Luss. Nay, you mistake me then, For I am published[12] bountiful enough. Let's taste of your conceit.

Vind. In picture, my lord?

Luss.                    Ay, in picture.

Vind. Marry, this it is: A usuring father to be boiling in hell, and his son and heir with a whore dancing over him.

Hip. [Aside.] H'as pared him to the quick!

Luss. The conceit's pretty, i' faith—  [100 But, take't upon my life, 'twill ne'er be liked.

Vind. No?  Why, I'm sure the whore will be liked well enough!

Hip. [Aside.] Ay, if she were out a th' picture, he'd like her then himself.

Vind. And, as for the son and heir, he shall be an eyesore to no young revelers, for he shall be drawn in cloth-of-gold breeches.

Luss. And thou hast put my meaning in the pockets And canst not draw that out.  My thought was this:                                    [110 To see the picture of a usuring father Boiling in hell, our rich men would ne'er like it.

---

[1] Country dialect for: How do you do?  God give you good evening.

[2] Understood.        [3] The forty-second year.

[4] The sixty-third year.        [5] Poultry.

[6] Sessions of law courts.        [7] Barbarous.

[8] Corruption of certiorari, the name of a writ in law.

[9] Original reads Hip.

[10] Rumbles and rattles.

[11] Idea.        [12] Reported to be.

VIND. O, true, I cry you heart'ly
mercy. I know the reason: for some
of 'em had rather be damned indeed[1] than
damned in colors.[2]

LUSS. [*Aside.*] A parlous[3] melancholy!
　H'as wit enough
　To murder any man, and I'll give him
　　means.—
　I think thou art ill-moneyed?

VIND. 　　　　Money! Ho, ho!
　'T'as been my want so long 'tis now my
　　scoff;　　　　　　　　　　　120
　I've e'en forgot what color silver's of!

LUSS. [*Aside.*] It hits as I could wish.

VIND. 　　　　I get good clothes
　Of those that dread my humor; and for
　　table-room
　I feed on those that cannot be rid of me.

LUSS. [*Gives Vindice money.*] Somewhat to
　set thee up withal.

VIND. O, mine eyes!

LUSS. 　　　　How now, man?

VIND. 　　　　Almost struck blind!
　This bright, unusual shine to me seems
　　proud.[4]
　I dare not look till the sun be in a cloud.

LUSS. [*Aside.*] I think I shall affect[5] his
　melancholy.—[*Gives more money.*]
　How are they now?

VIND. 　The better for your asking.　130

LUSS. You shall be better yet if you but
　fasten
　Truly on my intent. Now y'are both
　　present,
　I will unbrace[6] such a close,[7] private
　　villain
　Unto your vengeful swords, the like ne'er
　　heard of,
　Who hath disgraced you much and in-
　　jured us.

HIP. Disgracéd us, my lord?

LUSS. 　　　　Ay, Hippolito.
　I kept it here[8] till now that both your
　　angers
　Might meet him at once.

VIND. 　　　　I'm covetous
　To know the villain.

LUSS. You know him—that slave pander,
　Piato, whom we threatened last　140
　With irons in perpetual prisonment.

VIND. [*Aside.*] All this is I!

HIP. 　　　　Is't he, my lord?

LUSS. I'll tell you—you first preferred[9]
　him to me.

VIND. Did you, brother?

HIP. 　　　　I did indeed.

LUSS. And the ungrateful villain
　To quit that kindness, strongly wrought
　　with me,
　Being as you see a likely man for pleasure,
　With jewels to corrupt your virgin sister.

HIP. O, villain!

VIND. 　He shall surely die that did it.

LUSS. I, far from thinking any virgin　[150
　harm,
　Especially knowing her to be as chaste
　As that part which scarce suffers to be
　　touched—
　The eye—would not endure him—

VIND. 　　　Would you not, my lord?
　'Twas wondrous honorably done.

LUSS. —But with some fine[10] frowns kept
　him out.

VIND. 　　　　Out, slave!

LUSS. What did me he, but in revenge of
　that
　Went of his own free will to make infirm
　Your sister's honor, whom I honor with
　　my soul
　For chaste respect; and, not prevailing
　　there
　—As 'twas but desperate folly to attempt
　it—　　　　　　　　　　　160
　In mere spleen, by the way, waylays your
　　mother,
　Whose honor being a coward, as it seems,
　Yielded by little force.

VIND. 　　　　Coward, indeed!

LUSS. He, proud of their advantage,[11] as he
　thought,
　Brought me these news for happy;
　　but I
　—Heaven forgive me for't—

VIND. 　　　What did your honor?

LUSS. —In rage pushed him from me,
　Trampled beneath his throat, spurned
　　him, and bruised.
　Indeed, I was too cruel, to say truth.

HIPP. Most nobly managed!

VIND. [*Aside.*] Has not heaven an
　　ear?　　　　　　　　　　　[170
　Is all the lightning wasted?

---

[1] In reality.　　　[2] In paint, in appearances.
[3] Perilous, shocking.
[4] Lordly.　　　[5] Like.　　　[6] Lay open.
[7] Secret.　　　[8] *I.e.*, in his mind.
[9] Recommended.
[10] Original reads *five.*
[11] The advantage won over them.

Luss. If I now were so impatient in a
 modest cause,
What should you be?
Vind.   Full mad! He shall not live
To see the moon change.
Luss.   He's about the palace.
Hippolito, entice him this way, that thy
 brother
May take full mark of him.
Hip. Heart! That shall not need, my lord.
I can direct him so far.
Luss.   Yet, for my hate's sake,
Go. Wind[1] him this way. I'll see him
 bleed myself.
Hip. [Aside.] What now, brother?
Vind. [Aside.] Nay, e'en what you
 will.          [180
Y'are put to't, brother?
Hip. [Aside.]  An impossible task,
 I'll swear,
To bring him hither that's already here.
        *Exit Hipp[olito].*
Luss. Thy name? I have forgot it.
Vind.   Vindice, my lord.
Luss. 'Tis a good name, that.
Vind.   Ay, a revenger.
Luss. It does betoken courage. Thou
 shouldst be valiant
And kill thine enemies.
Vind.  That's my hope, my lord.
Luss. This slave is one.
Vind.  I'll doom him.
Luss.   Then I'll praise thee.
Do thou observe[2] me best and I'll best
 raise thee.

    *Enter Hipp[olito].*

Vind. Indeed, I thank you.
Luss. Now, Hippolito, where's the slave-
 pander?         190
Hip. Your good lordship
Would have a loathesome sight of him,
 much offensive?
He's not in case[3] now to be seen, my
 lord.
The worst of all the deadly sins is in
 him:
That beggarly damnation, drunkenness.
Luss. Then he's a double slave.
Vind. [Aside.] 'Twas well conveyed,[4]
 upon a sudden wit.
Luss. What, are you both firmly resolved?
 I'll see him
Dead myself!

[1] Entice. [2] Gratify. [3] Condition. [4] Managed.

Vind.   Or else let not us live.
Luss. You may direct your brother to
 take note of him.     200
Hip. I shall.
Luss. Rise but in this and you shall never
 fall.
Vind. Your honor's vassals!
Luss. [Aside.]  This was wisely carried.
Deep policy in us makes fools of
 such.
Then must a slave die, when he knows
 too much.    *Exit Luss[urioso].*
Vind. O thou almighty patience, 'tis my
 wonder
That such a fellow, impudent and wicked,
Should not be cloven as he stood
Or with a secret wind burst open!
Is there no thunder left or is't  [210
 kept up
In stock for heavier vengeance? [*Thun-
der*.] There it goes!
Hip. Brother, we lose ourselves.
Vind.   But I have found it.
'Twill hold, 'tis sure; thanks, thanks to
 any spirit
That mingled it 'mongst my inventions.
Hip.      What is't?
Vind. 'Tis sound and good. Thou shalt
 partake it;
I'm hired to kill myself.
Hip.    True.
Vind.   Prithee, mark it;
And the old duke being dead, but not
 conveyed,[5]
For he's already missed too, and, you
 know,
Murder will peep out of the closest husk—
Hip. Most true!
Vind. What say you then to this [220
 device?
If we dressed up the body of the duke—
Hip. In that disguise of yours!
Vind.  Y'are quick; y'ave reached it.
Hip. I like it wonderously.
Vind. And, being in drink, as you have
 published him,
To lean him on his elbow as if sleep had
 caught him,
Which claims most interest in such
 sluggy[6] men.
Hip. Good yet; but here's a doubt.
We,[7] thought by th' duke's son to kill
 that pander,

[5] Put away, buried.    [6] Sluggish.
[7] Original reads *me*.

Shall, when he is known, be thought to
　kill the duke.
VIND. Neither, O thanks! It is sub-
　stantial;[1]　　　　　　　　　　230
For, that disguise being on him, which I
　wore,
It will be thought I, which he calls the
　pander,
Did kill the duke and fled away in
　his
Apparel, leaving him so disguised
To avoid swift pursuit.
HIP.　　　　　　　Firmer and firmer.
VIND. Nay, doubt not. 'Tis in grain,[2] I
　warrant
It hold color.
HIP.　　　　　　　Let's about it.
VIND. But, by the way too, now I think
　on't, brother,
Let's conjure that base devil out of our
　mother.　　　　　　　　Exeunt.

[SCENA iii.
A corridor in the palace.]

Enter the Duchess arm in arm with the
　Bastard. He seemeth[3] lasciviously to her.
　After them, enter Supervacuo running with
　a rapier. His brother stops him.

SPU. Madam, unlock yourself! Should it
　be seen,
Your arm would be suspected.
DUCH. Who is't that dares suspect or this
　or these?[4]
May not we deal our favors where we
　please?
SPU. I'm confident you may.
　　　　　Exeunt [Spurio and Duchess].
AMB. 'Sfoot, brother, hold!
SUPERV. Woul't let the bastard shame us?
AMB. Hold, hold, brother! There's fitter
　time than now.
SUPERV. Now, when I see it!
AMB.　　　　　'Tis too much seen already.
SUPERV. Seen and known.
The nobler she is, the baser is she
　grown.　　　　　　　　　　10
AMB. If she were bent lasciviously—the
　fault
Of mighty women that sleep soft—O
　death,

Must she needs choose such an unequal
　sinner
To make all worse?
SUPERV. A bastard! The duke's bastard!
　Shame heaped on shame!
AMB. O, our disgrace!
Most women have small waist the world
　throughout,
But their desires are thousand miles
　about.
SUPERV. Come, stay not here. Let's after
　and prevent,
Or else they'll sin faster than we'll
　repent.　　　　　　Exeunt. [20

[SCENA iv.
A room in Gratiana's house.]

Enter Vindice and Hippolito bringing out
their mother, one by one shoulder, and the
other by the other, with daggers in their hands.

VIND. O thou for whom no name is bad
　enough!
MOTH. What mean my sons? What, will
　you murder me?
VIND. Wicked, unnatural parent!
HIP.　　　　　　　Fiend of women!
MOTH. O! Are sons turned monsters?
　Help!
VIND.　　　　　　　　　　In vain.
MOTH. Are you so barbarous, to set iron
　nipples
Upon the breast that gave you suck?
VIND.　　　　　　　　That breast
Is turned to quarled[5] poison.
MOTH. Cut not your days for't! Am not
　I your mother?
VIND. Thou dost usurp that title now by
　fraud,
For in that shell of mother breeds a
　bawd.　　　　　　　　　　10
MOTH. A bawd! O name far loathsomer
　than hell!
HIP. It should be so, knew'st thou thy
　office[6] well.
MOTH. I hate it.
VIND. Ah, is't possible? Thou only?
　You powers on high,
That women should dissemble when
　they die!
MOTH. Dissemble?
VIND.　　　Did not the duke's son direct
A fellow of the world's condition hither

[1] Firm.　　　　　　　[2] Indelible.
[3] Behaves.
[4] I.e., her arm and her kisses.
[5] Curdled.　　　　　　[6] Duty.

That did corrupt all that was good in
  thee,
Made thee uncivilly forget thyself
And work our sister to his lust?
MOTH.                          Who, I?   20
  That had been monstrous! I defy that
    man
  For any such intent.  None lives so pure
  But shall be soiled with slander—
  Good son, believe it not.
VIND.                     O, I'm in doubt
  Whether I'm myself or no!
  Stay, let me look again upon this face.
  Who shall be saved when mothers have
    no grace?
HIP. 'Twould make one half despair.
VIND.                     I was the man.
  Defy me now! Let's see.  Do't modestly.
MOTH. O, hell unto my soul!            30
VIND. In that disguise, I, sent from the
    duke's son,
  Tried you and found you base metal
  As any villain might have done.
MOTH. O, no!  No tongue but yours could
  have bewitched me so.
VIND. O, nimble in damnation, quick in
    tune.
  There is no devil could strike fire so soon!
  I am confuted in a word.
MOTH. O sons, forgive me; to myself I'll
    prove more true.
  You that should honor me—I kneel to
    you.            [She kneels and weeps.]
VIND. A mother to give aim to her own
    daughter!                           40
HIP. True, brother.  How far beyond
    nature 'tis,
  Though many mothers do't!
                          [Draws his dagger.]
VIND. Nay, and you draw tears once, go
    you to bed;
  Wet will make iron blush and change
    to red.
  Brother, it rains.  'Twill spoil your
    dagger.  House it.
HIP. 'Tis done.
VIND. I' faith, 'tis a sweet shower; it does
    much good.
  The fruitful grounds and meadows of
    her soul
  Has been long dry.  Pour down, thou
    blessèd dew!
  Rise, mother; troth, this shower has
    made you higher.                    50

MOTH. O you heavens, take this infectious
    spot out of my soul!
  I'll rence[1] it in seven waters of mine eyes,
  Make my tears salt enough to taste of
    grace.
  To weep is to our sex naturally given,
  But to weep truly—that's a gift from
    heaven!
VIND. Nay, I'll kiss you now; kiss her,
    brother.
  Let's marry her to our souls, wherein's
    no lust,
  And honorably love her.
HIP.                          Let it be.
VIND. For honest women are so sild[2] and
    rare,
  'Tis good to cherish those poor few
    that are.                           60
  O you of easy wax,[3] do but imagine
  Now the disease has left you, how
    leprously
  That office would have clinged unto
    your forehead.
  All mothers that had any graceful hue
  Would have worn masks to hide their
    face at you.
  It would have grown to this, at your foul
    name
  Green-colored[4] maids would have turned
    red with shame.
HIP. And then our sister, full of hire and
    baseness—
VIND. There had been boiling lead again!
  The duke's son's great concubine.     70
  A drab of state, a cloth-a-silver slut,
  To have her train borne up and her soul
  Trail i' th' dirt—great!
HIP.               To be miserably great.
  Rich, to be eternally wretched.
VIND. O common madness!
  Ask but the thriving'st harlot in cold
    blood,
  She'd give the world to make her honor
    good.
  Perhaps you'll say, but only to th' duke's
    son
  In private—why, she first begins with
    one
  Who afterward to thousand proves a
    whore.                              80

[1] Rinse.
[2] Seld, seldom, infrequent.
[3] I.e., pliable.
[4] With the greensickness, chlorosis, anemia.

"Break ice in one place, it will crack in
    more."
MOTH. Most certainly applied!
HIP. O brother, you forget our business.
VIND. And well remembered. Joy's a
    subtle elf;
I think man's happiest when he forgets
    himself.
Farewell, once dried, now holy-watered
    mead;
Our hearts wear feathers that before
    wore lead.
MOTH. I'll give you this: that one I
    never knew[1]
Plead better for, and 'gainst, the devil
    than you.
VIND. You make me proud on't.        90
HIP. Commend us in all virtue to our
    sister.
VIND. Ay, for the love of heaven, to that
    true maid.
MOTH. With my best words.
VIND.        Why, that was motherly said.
        Exeunt [Vindice and Hippolito].
MOTH. I wonder now what fury did trans-
    port me.
I feel good thoughts begin to settle in me.
O, with what forehead[2] can I look on her
Whose honor I've so impiously beset?
And here she comes.

[Enter Castiza.]

CAST. Now, mother, you have wrought
    with me so strongly
That, what[3] for my advancement as to
    calm                                   100
The trouble of your tongue, I am content.
MOTH. Content, to what?
CAST.        To do as you have wished me,
To prostitute my breast to the duke's son
And put myself to common usury.
MOTH. I hope you will not so!
CAST.          Hope you I will not?
That's not the hope you look to be
    saved in.
MOTH. Truth, but it is.
CAST.        Do not deceive yourself.
I am, as you, e'en out of marble wrought.
What would you now? Are ye not
    pleased yet with me?

    ¹ That I never knew one.
    ² Dignity, self-respect.
    ³ As much.

You shall not wish me to be more
    lascivious                             110
Than I intend to be.
MOTH.               Strike not me cold!
CAST. How often have you charged me on
    your blessing
To be a curséd woman! When you knew
Your blessing had no force to make me
    lewd,
You laid your curse upon me. That did
    more.
The mother's curse is heavy; where that
    fights,
Sons set in storm and daughters lose
    their lights.
MOTH. Good child, dear maid, if there be
    any spark
Of heavenly intellectual fire within thee,
O, let my breath revive it to a flame. [120
Put not all out with woman's wilful
    follies.
I am recovered of that foul disease
That haunts too many mothers. Kind,
    forgive me!
Make me not sick in health. If then
My words prevailed when they were
    wickedness,
How much more now when they are just
    and good!
CAST. I wonder what you mean! Are not
    you she
For whose infect[4] persuasions I could
    scarce
Kneel out my prayers, and had much ado
In three hours' reading to untwist so
    much                                   130
Of the black serpent as you wound about
    me?
MOTH. 'Tis unfruitful, held tedious, to
    repeat what's past.
I'm now your present mother.
CAST.              Push! Now 'tis too late.
MOTH. Bethink again, thou know'st not
    what thou say'st.
CAST. No? Deny advancement, treasure,
    the duke's son?
MOTH. O see, I spoke those words, and
    now they poison me.
What will the deed do then?
Advancement? True; as high as shame
    can pitch.
For treasure? Who e'er knew a harlot
    rich
    ⁴ Infections.

Or could build by the purchase of her
　　sin　　　　　　　　　　　　　　140
An hospital to keep their bastards in?
The duke's son? O, when women are
　　young courtiers
They are sure to be old beggars.
To know the miseries most harlots taste
Thou'd'st wish thyself unborn when thou
　　art unchaste.

CAST. O mother, let me twine about your
　　neck
And kiss you till my soul melt on your
　　lips!
I did but this to try you.

MOTH.　　　　　　　　O, speak truth!

CAST. Indeed, I did not; for no tongue has
　　force
To alter me from honest.　　　　150
If maidens would, men's words could
　　have no power;
A virgin honor is a crystal tower
Which, being weak, is guarded with good
　　spirits;
Until she basely yields, no ill inherits.

MOTH. O happy child! Faith and thy
　　birth hath saved me.
'Mongst thousand daughters, happiest of
　　all others!
Be thou a glass[1] for maids, and I for
　　mothers.　　　　　　　　*Exeunt.*

[ACTUS V. SCENA i.[2]

*The Duke's lodge.*]

*Enter Vindice and Hippolito [with the duke's
　corpse lying on the couch].*

VIND. So, so, he leans well; take heed
you wake him not, brother.

HIP. I warrant you, my life for yours.

VIND. That's a good lay,[3] for I must
kill myself! Brother, that's I! That sits
for me; do you mark it? And I must stand
ready here to make away myself yonder.
I must sit to be killed, and stand to kill
myself. I could vary it not so little as
thrice over again; 't'as some eight　[10
returns, like Michaelmas Term.[4]

HIP. That's enow, a conscience.

_____
[1] Mirror, model.
[2] The original has no act or scene division
from here on.
[3] Bet.
[4] Return days, days fixed in law for the return
of writs. Michaelmas Term lasted eight weeks.

VIND. But, sirrah, does the duke's son
come single?　　　　　　　　　10

HIP. No, there's the hell on't! His
faith's too feeble to go alone. He brings
flesh-flies after him that will buzz against
supper time and hum for his coming out.

VIND. Ah, the fly-flop[5] of vengeance beat
'em to pieces! Here was the sweetest　[20
occasion, the fittest hour, to have made my
revenge familiar with him: show him the
body of the duke his father, and how
quaintly he died, like a politician, in
hugger-mugger;[6] made no man acquainted
with it; and in catastrophe[7] slain him over
his father's breast! And O, I'm mad to
lose such a sweet opportunity!

HIP. Nay, push! Prithee, be content!
There's no remedy present. May not　[30
hereafter times open in as fair faces as this?

VIND. They may, if they can paint so well.

HIP. Come now, to avoid all suspicion,
let's forsake this room and be going to
meet the duke's son.

VIND. Content. I'm for any weather.
Heart! Step close; here he comes!

*Enter Lussurioso.*

HIP. My honored lord!

LUSS. O me! You both present?　　[40

VIND. E'en newly, my lord, just as your
lordship entered now. About this place
we had notice given he should be, but in
some loathsome plight or other.

HIP. Came your honor private?

LUSS. Private enough for this. Only a few
　　Attend my coming out.

HIP. [*Aside.*]　　　　Death rot those few!

LUSS. Stay—yonder's the slave.

VIND. Mass, there's the slave, indeed,
　　my lord. [*Aside.*]
'Tis a good child; he calls his father
　　slave!　　　　　　　　　　　[50

LUSS. Ay, that's the villain, the damned
　　villain! Softly,
　　Tread easy.

VIND.　　　　　Puh! I warrant you, my lord,
　　We'll stifle in[8] our breaths.

LUSS.　　　　That will do well.
　—Base rogue, thou sleepest thy last!
　　[*Aside.*] 'Tis policy

_____
[5] Fly swatter.
[6] Like an intriguer, in secrecy.
[7] At the conclusion of the play.
[8] Hold.

To have him killed in's sleep, for, if he
 waked,
He would betray all to them.
VIND.     But, my lord—
LUSS. Ha? What say'st?
VIND. Shall we kill him now he's drunk?
LUSS.     Ay, best of all.
 VIND. Why, then he will ne'er live to be
sober.
 LUSS. No matter; let him reel to hell. [60
 VIND. But, being so full of liquor, I fear
he will put out all the fire.
 LUSS. Thou art a mad beast!
 VIND. [Aside.] And leave none to warm
your lordship's golls[1] withal.—For he that
dies drunk falls into hell fire like a bucket
a water: qush, qush!
 LUSS. Come, be ready! Nake[2] your
swords. Think of your wrongs. This
slave has injured you.     70
VIND. Troth, so he has, and he has paid
 well for't.
LUSS. Meet with him now.
VIND.   You'll bear us out, my lord?
LUSS. Puh, am I a lord for nothing, think
 you?
 Quickly now!
VIND.   Sa, sa, sa, thump! [He stabs
 the corpse.] There he lies!
LUSS. Nimbly done! [Approaches the
 corpse.] Ha! O villains, murderers,
 'Tis the old duke my father!
VIND. [Aside.]    That's a jest!
LUSS. What, stiff and cold already?
 O, pardon me to call you from your
  names.[3]
 'Tis none of your deed; that villain Piato,
 Whom you thought now to kill, has
  murdered him     80
 And left him thus disguised.
HIP.    And not unlikely.
VIND. O rascal! Was he not ashamed
 To put the duke into a greasy doublet?
LUSS. He has been cold and stiff—who
 knows how long?
VIND. [Aside.] Marry, that do I!
LUSS. No words, I pray, of anything
 intended!
VIND. O, my lord.
HIP. I would fain have your lordship think
 that we

Have small reason to prate.
LUSS. Faith, thou sayest true. I'll forth-
 with send to court     [90
 For all the nobles, Bastard, duchess, all—
 How here by miracle we found him dead
 And in his raiment that foul villain fled.
VIND. That will be the best way, my lord,
 to clear
 Us all; let's cast about to be clear.
LUSS. Ho! Nencio, Sordido, and the
 rest!

*Enter all [his servants].*

1 [SER.] My lord?
2 [SER.] My lord?
LUSS. Be witnesses of a strange spectacle.
 Choosing for private conference that sad
  room     100
 We found the duke my father 'gealed in
  blood.
1 [SER.]. My lord the duke! Run, hie thee,
 Nencio!
 Startle the court by signifying so much.
      [Exit Nencio.]
VIND. [Aside.] This much by wit a deep
 revenger can,[4]
 When murder's known, to be the clearest
  man.
 We're fordest[5] off, and with as bold an eye
 Survey his body as the standers-by.
LUSS. My royal father, too basely let blood
 By a malevolent slave!
HIPP. [Aside.]   Hark! He calls thee
 Slave again.
VIND. [Aside.]   H'as lost; he may!
LUSS.     O sight! 110
 Look hither; see, his lips are gnawn with
  poison!
VIND. How? His lips? By the Mass,
 they be!
LUSS. O villain! O rogue! O slave!
 O rascal!
HIP. [Aside.] O good deceit!—He quits
 him with like terms.

[Enter Nobles, preceding Ambitioso and
   Supervacuo.]

1 [NOBLE.] Where?
2 [NOBLE.] Which way?

---

[1] Hands.  [2] Unsheathe.  [3] Slander you.

[4] Knows how.
[5] Farthest.

AMB. Over what roof hangs this prodigious comet
In deadly fire?

Luss.  Behold, behold, my lords!
The duke my father's murdered by a vassal
That owes this habit,[1] and here left disguised.  120

[*Enter the Duchess and Spurio.*]

DUCH. My lord and husband!

2 [NOBLE].  Reverend majesty!

1 [NOBLE]. I have seen these clothes often attending on him.

VIND. [*Aside.*] That nobleman has been i'th' country, for he does not lie.

SUPERV. [*Aside.*] Learn of our mother— let's dissemble too!
I am glad he's vanished; so, I hope, are you?

AMB. [*Aside.*] Ay, you may take my word for't.

SPU. [*Aside.*]  Old dad dead?
I, one of his cast sins, will send the fates
Most hearty commendations by his own son.
I'll tug in the new stream till strength be done.

Luss. Where be those two that did affirm to us  130
My lord the duke was privately rid forth?

1 [GENT.]. O, pardon us, my lords. He gave that charge
Upon our lives, if he were missed at court,
To answer so. He rode not anywhere.
We left him private with that fellow, here.

VIND. [*Aside.*] Confirmed!

Luss.  O heavens! That false charge was his death.
Impudent beggars, durst you to our face
Maintain such a false answer? Bear him straight
To execution!

1 [GENT.].  My lord!

Luss.  Urge me no more.
In this, the excuse may be called half the murther.  140

<hr>

[1] Owns this clothing.

VIND. [*Aside.*] You've sentenced well.

Luss.  Away, see it be done!
[*Exit 1 Gentleman under guard.*]

VIND. [*Aside.*] Could you not stick?[2]
See what confession doth.
Who would not lie when men are hanged for truth?

HIP. [*Aside.*] Brother, how happy is our vengeance!

VIND. [*Aside.*]  Why, it hits
Past the apprehension of indifferent wits.[3]

Luss. My lord, let post horse be sent
Into all places to entrap the villain.

VIND. [*Aside.*] Post horse! Ha ha!

[1] NOBLE. My lord, we're something bold[4] to know our duty.
Your father's accidentally[5] departed;  [150
The titles that were due to him meet you.

Luss. Meet me? I'm not at leisure, my good lord;
I've many griefs to despatch out a th' way.—
[*Aside.*] Welcome, sweet titles!—Talk to me, my lords,
Of sepulchres and mighty emperors' bones;
That's thought for me.

VIND. [*Aside.*] So, one may see by this how foreign markets go:
Courtiers have feet o' the nines and tongues o' the twelves;[6]
They flatter dukes, and dukes flatter themselves.

2 [NOBLE]. My lord, it is your shine must comfort us.  160

Luss. Alas, I shine in tears like the sun in April.

1 [NOBLE]. You're now my lord's grace.

Luss. "My lord's grace"? I perceive you'll have it so.

2 [NOBLE]. 'Tis but your own.

Luss.  Then, heavens, give me grace to be so.

VIND. [*Aside.*] He prays well for himself!

1 [NOBLE].  Madam, all sorrows
Must run their circles into joys; no doubt but time

<hr>

[2] Stick to his original story.
[3] Ordinary intelligences.
[4] Rather eager.  [5] By chance.
[6] Tongues three sizes larger than their feet.

Will make the murderer bring forth
himself.

VIND. [*Aside.*]  He were an ass then, i'
faith!

1 [NOBLE].       In the mean season
Let us bethink the latest funeral honors
Due to the duke's cold body; and,  [170
withal,
Calling to memory our new happiness
Spread in his royal son—lords, gentle-
men,
Prepare for revels!

VIND. [*Aside.*]        Revels!

1 [NOBLE].        Time hath several falls.
Griefs lift up joys; feasts put down
funerals.

LUSS. Come then, my lords; my favors to
you all.
[*Aside.*] The duchess is suspected foully
bent;
I'll begin dukedom with her banishment.

*Exeunt Duke [Lussurioso], Nobles, and*
*Duchess.*

HIP. [*Aside.*] Revels!

VIND. [*Aside.*]         Ay, that's the word.
We are firm[1] yet.
Strike one strain more and then we crown
our wit.       *Exeu[nt] Bro[thers].*   180

SPU. [*Aside.*] Well, have[2] the fairest mark.
So said the duke when he begot me.
And, if I miss his heart or near about,
Then have at any—a bastard scorns to
be out.                       [*Exit.*]

SUPERV. Not'st thou that Spurio, brother?

AMB. Yes, I note him, to our shame.

SUPERV. He shall not live. His hair shall
not grow much longer. In this time of
revels tricks may be set afoot. Seest thou
yon new moon? It shall outlive [190
the new duke by much: this hand shall
dispossess him. Then we're mighty.
A masque is treason's license. That,
build upon.
'Tis murder's best face, when a vizard's
on!            *Exit Superv[acuo].*

AMB. Is't so? 'Tis very good!
And do you think to be duke then, kind
brother?
I'll see fair play. Drop one, and there
lies t'other.
                      *Exit Amb[itioso].*

*Enter Vindice and Hippolito, and Piero and*
*other Lords.*

VIND. My lords, be all of music! Strike
old griefs into other countries
That flow in too much milk and have
faint livers,
Not daring to stab home their discontents.
Let our hid flames break out as fire, as
lightning,
To blast this villainous dukedom vexed
with sin.
Wind up your souls to their full height
again.

PIERO. How?

1 [LORD].      Which way?

3 [LORD].  Any way! Our wrongs are such,
We cannot justly be revenged too much.

VIND. You shall have all enough. Revels
are toward,
And those few nobles that have long
suppressed you                       10
Are busied to the furnishing of a masque
And do affect[3] to make a pleasant tale
on't.
The masquing suits are fashioning. Now
comes in
That which must glad us all: we to take
pattern
Of all those suits, the color, trimming,
fashion,
E'en to an undistinguished hair almost.
Then, ent'ring first, observing the true
form,
Within a strain or two we shall find
leisure
To steal our swords out handsomely,
And, when they think their pleasure
sweet and good,                       20
In midst of all their joys they shall sigh
blood!

PIERO. Weightily, effectually!

3 [LORD].            Before the tother
Maskers come—

VIND.      We're gone, all done and past.

PIERO. But how for the duke's guard?

VIND.            Let that alone;
By one and one their strengths shall be
drunk down.

---

[1] Safe.          [2] Have at, aim at.       [3] Desire.

Hip. There are five hundred gentlemen in
   the action
   That will apply themselves and not
   stand idle.
Piero. O, let us hug your bosoms!
Vind.                    Come, my lords.
   Prepare for deeds; let other times have
   words.                              *Exeunt.*

[Scena iii.
*The banqueting hall of the palace.*]

*In a dumb show, the possessing*[1] *of the young
duke with all his Nobles; then sounding music.
A furnished table is brought forth. Then
enters [the Duke] and his Nobles to the banquet. A blazing-star*[2] *appeareth [later].*

[1] Noble. Many harmonious hours and
   choicest pleasures
   Fill up the royal numbers of your years!
Luss. My lords, we're pleased to thank
   you, though we know
   'Tis but your duty now to wish it so.
[1] Noble. That shine[3] makes us all happy.
3 Noble. [*Aside.*]          His grace frowns.
2 Noble. [*Aside.*]     Yet we must say he
   smiles.
1 Noble. [*Aside.*]          I think we must.
Luss. [*Aside.*]     That foul, incontinent
   duchess we have banished.
   The Bastard shall not live. After these
   revels,
   I'll begin strange ones; he and the
   stepsons
   Shall pay their lives for the first subsidies.                             10
   We must not frown so soon, else 't'ad
   been now.
1 Noble. My gracious lord, please you
   prepare for pleasure.
   The masque is not far off.
Luss.                    We are for pleasure.
                    [*The comet appears.*]
   Beshrew thee, what art thou? Madest
   me start!
   Thou hast committed treason! A
   blazing-star!
1 Noble. A blazing-star! O, where, my
   lord?
Luss.                    Spy out!
2 Noble. See, see, my lords! A wondrous
   dreadful one!

Luss. I am not pleased at that ill-knotted
   fire,
   That bushing,[4] flaring star. Am not I
   duke?
   It should not quake me now. Had it
   appeared                            20
   Before, it I might then have justly
   feared.
   But yet they say, whom art and learning
   weds,
   When stars wear locks they threaten
   great men's heads.
   Is it so? You are read,[5] my lords.
1 Noble.               May it please your grace,
   It shows great anger.
Luss.          That does not please our grace.
2 Noble. Yet here's the comfort, my lord:
   many times
   When it seems most, it threatens
   farthest off.
Luss. Faith, and I think so too.
1 Noble.               Beside, my lord,
   You're gracefully established with the
   loves
   Of all your subjects; and, for natural
   death,                              30
   I hope it will be threescore years
   a-coming.
Luss. True? No more but threescore
   years?
1 Noble. Fourscore, I hope, my lord.
2 Noble.               And fivescore I.
3 Noble. But 'tis my hope, my lord, you
   shall ne'er die.
Luss. Give me thy hand! These others I
   rebuke.
   He that hopes so, is fittest for a duke.
   Thou shalt sit next me. Take your
   places, lords.
   We're ready now for sports. Let 'em set
   on.
   [*To the comet.*] You thing! We shall
   forget you quite, anon.
3 Noble. I hear 'em coming, my lord.

*Enter the mask of revengers (the two Brothers
   and two Lords more).*

Luss.                    Ah, 'tis well!     40
   [*Aside.*] Brothers and Bastard, you
   dance next in hell!

---

[4] With a tail like a bush.
[5] Well-read, learned.

[1] Investiture.     [2] Comet.     [3] Smiling look.

*The revengers dance. At the end steal out their swords, and these four kill the four at the table, in their chairs. It thunders.*

VIND. Mark, thunder! Dost know thy cue, thou big-voiced crier?
    Duke's groans are thunder's watchwords.
HIP. So, my lords, you have enough.
VIND. Come, let's away—no ling'ring.
HIP.                Follow! Go!
    *Exeunt [all the masquers but Vindice].*
VIND. No power is angry when the lustful die.
    When thunder claps, heaven likes the tragedy.          *Exit.*
LUSS. O, O!

*Enter the other masque of intended murderers, stepsons, Bastard, and a fourth man coming in dancing. The duke recovers a little in voice and groans; calls "A guard! Treason!" At which they all start out of their measure and, turning towards the table, they find them all to be murdered.*

SPU. Whose groan was that?
LUSS.           Treason! A guard!
AMB. How now! All murdered!
SUPERV.               Murdered!    50
4 [LORD]. And those his nobles?
AMB. [*Aside.*]       Here's a labor saved!
    I thought to have sped him. 'Sblood, how came this?
[SUPERV.][1] Then I proclaim myself. Now I am duke.
AMB. Thou duke! Brother, thou liest!
             [*Stabs Supervacuo.*]
SPU.           Slave! So dost thou!
             [*Stabs Ambitioso.*]
4 [LORD]. Base villain, hast thou slain my lord and master?     [*Stabs Spurio.*]

*Enter the first men [Vindice, Hippolito, and two Lords].*

VIND. Pistols! Treason! Murder! Help, guard! My lord the duke!

[*Enter Antonio and the guard.*]

HIP. Lay hold upon this traitor![2]
          [*Guard seizes 4 Lord.*]
LUSS.               O!
VIND. Alas, the duke is murdered!
HIP.            And the nobles.

VIND. Surgeons, surgeons!—[*Aside.*] Heart, does he breathe so long?
ANT. A piteous tragedy, able to make    [60
    An old man's eyes bloodshot!
LUSS.                 O!
VIND. Look to my lord the duke. [*Aside.*]
    A vengeance throttle him!—
    Confess, thou murderous and unhallowed man,
    Didst thou kill all these?
4 [LORD].       None but the Bastard, I.
VIND. How came the duke slain then?
4 [LORD.]          We found him so.
LUSS. O, villain!
VIND.     Hark!
LUSS.     Those in the masque did murder us.
VIND. La you now,[3] sir!
    O, marble impudence! Will you confess now?
4 [LORD]. 'Sblood, 'tis all false!
ANT.     Away with that foul monster    70
    Dipped in a prince's blood.
4 [LORD].        Heart 'tis a lie.
ANT. Let him have bitter execution.
         [*Exit 4 Lord guarded.*]
VIND. [*Aside.*]    New marrow![4] No, I cannot be expressed.—
    How fares my lord the duke?
LUSS.             Farewell to all!
    He that climbs highest has the greatest fall.
    My tongue is out of office.
VIND.         Air, gentlemen, air!—
    [*Whispers.*] Now thou'lt not prate on't, 'twas Vindice murdered thee!
LUSS. O!
VIND. [*Whispers.*] Murdered thy father!
LUSS.             O!
VIND. [*Whispers.*]     And I am he!
    Tell nobody.—[*Lussurioso dies.*] So, so.
    The duke's departed.
ANT. It was a deadly hand that wounded him.            80
    The rest, ambitious who should rule and sway
    After his death, were so made all away.
VIND. My lord was unlikely.[5]
HIP.             Now the hope
    Of Italy lies in your reverend years.
VIND. Your hair will make the silver age again,

---

[1] Original reads *Spu.*
[2] Original reads *traitors.*
[3] Listen to that.
[4] Delicious food for his revenge.
[5] Unpromising, unfit.

When there was fewer, but more honest,
    men.
ANT. The burden's weighty and will press
    age down.
    May I so rule that heaven may keep the
    crown.
VIND. The rape of your good lady has been
    'quited
With death on death.
ANT.                Just is the law above.   90
    But of all things it puts me most to
    wonder
    How the old duke came murdered.
VIND.                    O, my lord!
ANT. It was the strangeliest carried.  I not
    heard of the like.
HIP. 'Twas all done for the best, my lord.
VIND. All for your grace's good.  We may
    be bold
    To speak it now.  'Twas somewhat witty
    carried,
    Though we say it.  'Twas we two mur-
    dered him!
ANT. You two?
VIND. None else, i' faith, my lord.  Nay,
    'twas well managed.
ANT. Lay hands upon those villains!
VIND.                How?  On us?  100
ANT. Bear 'em to speedy execution!
VIND. Heart!  Was't not for your good,
    my lord?
ANT. My good!  Away with 'em!  Such
    an old man as he!
    You that would murder him would
    murder me!
VIND. Is't come about?
HIP.        'Sfoot, brother, you begun.
VIND. May not we set as well as the duke's
    son?[1]
    Thou hast no conscience.  Are we not
    revenged?

[1] Pun on the setting of the sun.

Is there one enemy left alive amongst
    those?
'Tis time to die when we are ourselves
    our foes.
When murder[er]s shut deeds close this
    curse does seal 'em:                    110
If none disclose 'em, they themselves
    reveal 'em!
This murder might have slept in tongue-
    less brass
But for ourselves, and the world died an
    ass.
Now I remember, too, here was Piato
Brought forth a knavish sentence once:
"No doubt," said he, "but time
Will make the murderer bring forth
    himself."
'Tis well he died; he was a witch![2]
And now, my lord, since we are in
    forever,
This work was ours, which else might
    have been slipped;                      120
And, if we list,[3] we could have nobles
    clipped[4]
And go for less than beggars.  But we
    hate
To bleed so cowardly: we have enough—
I' faith, we're well—our mother turned,
    our sister true,
We die after a nest of dukes.  Adieu!
    *Exeunt [Vindice and Hippolito guarded].*
ANT. How subtly was that murder closed![5]
    Bear up
Those tragic bodies; 'tis a heavy season.
Pray heaven their blood may wash away
    all treason.        *Exit [with the rest].*

FINIS.

[2] A wizard, because he could foresee the future.
[3] Pleased.
[4] Punning reference to the chipping of gold
coins.
[5] Disclosed.

# FRANCIS BEAUMONT AND
# JOHN FLETCHER

When John Dryden, soon to become poet laureate of England, published his famous "An Essay of Dramatic Poesy" in 1668, he introduced into it a well-known digression concerning the merits and characteristics of the pre-Commonwealth poet-dramatists whom he considered to have contributed the most to the English theater. They were Shakespeare, Jonson, and Beaumont and Fletcher. Though, as Dryden put it, he admired Jonson, but loved Shakespeare, thus putting them first and second in his inventory, he at the same time had to admit that the plays of Beaumont and Fletcher "are now the most pleasant and frequent entertainments of the stage; two of theirs being acted through the year to one of Shakespeare's or Jonson's." And the reasons he gave for their popularity were that the gaiety in their comedies and the pathos in their more serious plays generally suited better "with all men's humors." Moreover, he believed that in them "the English language . . . arrived to its highest perfection," whereas "Shakespeare's language is . . . a little obsolete, and Ben Jonson's wit comes short of theirs." In addition, "they represented all the passions very lively, but above all, love."

And yet, when Eugene M. Waith published his *The Pattern of Tragi-Comedy in Beaumont and Fletcher* (Yale University Press, 1952), and Clifford Leech published his analysis of *The John Fletcher Plays* (London, 1962), Waith gave as the main reason for writing his book his desire to find a reason for the decline in the popular interest in these plays so great that "their plays are scarcely ever performed," and Leech stated that, although Fletcher received his tributes till the end of the seventeenth century, today he "remains a general target for disapproval" and is "nearly always thought of principally as the simple 'entertainer.'" This latter estimate was the general thesis of Lawrence B. Wallis's *Fletcher, Beaumont & Company/Entertainers to the Jacobean Gentry* (New York, 1947), though Leech resented his implication that "Fletcher, Beaumont & Company" (the "Company" represented chiefly by Philip Massinger) were never anything more than professional entertainers and "salesmen dramatists," and that their audiences consisted only of the "Jacobean gentry." But Leech agreed that Wallis was justified in naming Fletcher first, since he was certainly the leading and most prolific figure on the team, in spite of the fact that tradition established the two men as, in Swinburne's phrase, the Castor and Pollux of the Jacobean theater, and practically converted the pair into a single entity named Beaumont-and-Fletcher. Leech had gone so far as to announce that he would simply discuss the "John Fletcher Plays" without attempting to differentiate among their authors, though E. H. C. Oliphant, the first of the modern generation of Beaumont and Fletcher students, had worked for almost forty years on his *The Plays of Beaumont and Fletcher*, with its subtitle, *An Attempt to Determine Their Respective Shares and the Shares of Others* (Yale University Press, 1927). Samuel Schoenbaum, however, in his *Internal Evidence and Elizabethan Dramatic Authorship*, has not only discounted the reliability of this whole school of internal evidence research, but has called Oliphant's results "not a work of objective, disciplined scholarship, but of avowed impressionism." Nevertheless, Schoenbaum feels that Cyrus Hoy's *The Shares of Fletcher and His Collaborators in the Beaumont and*

*Fletcher Canon*, published serially in *Studies in Bibliography* (1956–62) and based on criteria of a linguistic nature, "is admirably lucid and well organized, and it displays throughout a refreshing sanity." Philip Edwards, in "The Art of John Fletcher: The Danger Not the Death" (*Jacobean Theatre, SAS*, 1960), also implied in his title that Fletcher was the main moving force, but his article is really a study of the combined collaborated work of Beaumont, Fletcher, and Massinger, and ends with a summary of the modern attitude toward the plays.

It is symptomatic of the new age of the Stuarts, as opposed to the old age of the Tudors, that in coming to two playwrights like Fletcher and Beaumont we are no longer dealing—as was so often the case previously—with out-at-elbows scholars, "popular" authors up from the ranks, bohemians, or self-educated hacks, but with gentlemen who had the entree into upper-class society and could mingle with the elite on equal terms. John Fletcher, the older and longer-lived of the two, was born, it is true, the son of a simple country rector, Richard Fletcher, in Rye, Sussex, and was baptized there on December 20, 1579. (The chief authority for the main facts about the lives of both dramatists remains C. M. Gayley's *Beaumont, the Dramatist/A Portrait with Some Account of His Circle, Elizabethan and Jacobean, and of His Association with John Fletcher*, New York, 1914. Alexander Dyce, in his edition of the *Works* in 1843–6, first discovered the baptismal date and various other details.) But the elder Fletcher was a rising ecclesiastic and became, first, prebendary of St. Paul's, then chaplain to Queen Elizabeth, next Dean of Peterborough, and finally, in succession, Bishop of Bristol, Worcester, and London. The important Spenserian poets, Giles and Phineas Fletcher, both clergymen, were John's first cousins, and his mother was also of good family. When the boy was seven, his father, as Dean of Peterborough, was chaplain at the execution of Mary, Queen of Scots, after having participated in her examination and indictment at Fotheringhay. Before he was twelve, young John was admitted as a pensioner to Bene't College, Cambridge (now Corpus Christi), of which his father had once been president. The fact that about two years later the boy was made one of the Bible-clerks, or readers, of the college would imply that he would take orders, like so many of the members of his family.

But Bishop Fletcher fell out of favor with his queen, partly because of his role in drawing up the rejected Lambeth Articles, with their Calvinistic leanings, and partly because of his second marriage, to the widow of Sir John Baker, a woman of somewhat dubious character. When he died suddenly in 1596, perhaps partly because of his suspension from office on account of this marriage and partly, as Swinburne suggested in his article on Beaumont and Fletcher in the *Encyclopedia Britannica*, because of "overmuch tobacco," he left eight children in such monetary distress that their uncle, Giles Fletcher, a diplomat, scholar, and poet, petitioned the Queen on their behalf. It is likely that these misfortunes caused young John to drop out of college, since there is no record of his graduation. What the young man did to earn a living for the next decade, until his emergence as a promising playwright, remains a blank, but Wallis speculates that he may have traveled on the Continent in the entourage of his uncle Giles, or even served him as a secretary. But Wallis also concludes from Fletcher's poem "Upon an Honest Man's Fortune" and his line "As sour fortune loves to use me," in his poem to Sir Robert Townsend, that he probably underwent a period of poverty before he decided to "declass" himself by turning professional playwright.

Francis Beaumont (generally called "Frank" by his family and friends) was born sometime between February 1584 and February 1585, probably on the family estate of Grace-Dieu in Charnwood Forest, Leicestershire. His father was a country squire and once a member of Parliament, Justice Francis Beaumont, who came from an ancient family of Anglo-Norman descent, as indicated by the surname. Both the father and the mother had aristocratic connections. Little is known of young Francis's childhood, except that one story has it that he had "already committed a tragedy or two in emulation of *Tamburlaine, Andronicus*, or *Jeronimo*" (as Swinburne put it) before he entered the fashionable Broadgates Hall (now Pembroke College), Oxford, on February 4, 1597, at the ripe age of twelve. His father, now a Judge of the Court of Common Pleas, died in the next year. On November 5, 1600, the boy was entered at the Inner Temple, without taking his degree at Oxford. But although his two older brothers stood sponsor for him and his father had also been an Inns of Court man, Francis Beaumont was obviously no more cut out to be a lawyer than John Fletcher was for a clergyman. He apparently spent more time writing poetry and going to the theater than he did studying law. Although the long erotic poem, *Salmacis and Hermaphroditus* (1602), on the model of Marlowe's *Hero and Leander*, has been attributed to him, his authorship is uncertain.

But there is no doubt he became acquainted with the celebrated Ben Jonson quite early, since he wrote commendatory verses "To My Dear Friend Mr. Ben Jonson" for *Volpone*, *Epicoene*, and *Catiline*. And Dryden has preserved the story that Jonson had such a high regard for the younger man's opinion that he "submitted all his writings to his censure and, 'tis thought, used his judgment in correcting, if not contriving, all his plots." If so, the influence was reciprocal, since both Beaumont and Fletcher apparently learned much about plot construction, characterization, satire, and even versification from their "master" (Mina Kerr, *The Influence of Ben Jonson on English Comedy, 1598–1642*, New York, 1912; also Wallis, and so forth). After all, they were all members of the Mermaid Tavern fellowship, of whose convivial and conversational meetings Beaumont later drew a vivid picture in a verse-letter to Jonson. Oliphant thinks that Beaumont himself began writing plays about 1604; Schelling guesses 1606 (*Elizabethan Drama*): At any rate, none of his plays amounted to anything until he met Fletcher, somewhere about this time. Before this meeting Fletcher too may have tried his hand at playwriting, but without producing anything that is traceable.

Although Oliphant believed that Fletcher could have started to write for the theater as early as 1602 or 1603, Wallis is very skeptical about such a date, and hypothesizes: "His whole output could be accounted for as belonging to the years between 1608 and 1625." The best claimant to priority, Wallis thinks, would perhaps be "the merry farce," *The Woman's Prize, or The Tamer Tamed*, which he would place before *The Faithful Shepherdess*. The first play to be published by either man was the anonymous *The Woman Hater*, which appeared in quarto in 1607 and was probably acted in the previous year. This play is now generally assigned to Beaumont, with perhaps some slight aid from Fletcher, in spite of the fact that when William D'avenant wrote his prologue to a revival of the play he assigned it unequivocally to Fletcher. These early plays, eventually identified as coming from one or the other of these playwrights, were given by the boys of the private theaters at Paul's and the Blackfriars.

When the two young men became acquainted, however, they immediately became close friends—so close, indeed, that tradition runs to the effect that they shared rooms on the Bankside and owned all things in common, including (according to one suspicious gossip) a mistress. From this time on they were very productive until about 1613, when Beaumont married Ursula Isley, a Kentish girl of good family and wealth, and at about the same time retired from London to his country estate. It was in this year too that his *Masque of the Gentlemen of Gray's Inn and the Inner Temple* was produced before King James. Fletcher and Beaumont during their years of partnership usually worked together, but sometimes produced some of their best work separately. Nevertheless, modern scholarship has reduced the number of their collaborated plays considerably, usually accepting only perhaps eight as probable, in spite of the fact that for many years after their deaths, despite the warning of the publishers, the public believed the implications of the title pages of the posthumous collected folios in 1647 (containing thirty-four plays and a masque) and 1679 (adding eighteen more plays), and accepted everything within their covers, including some manifestly spurious works, as the product of common labor.

Beaumont died in 1616; he was only thirty-one years old. Fletcher, however, not a man of independent income like his friend, continued to write plays of all types, though chiefly comedies and romances, till he died of the plague in 1625. Comedies of his last period, such as the very popular *The Wild Goose Chase* (about 1621), with its complicated plot based on the perennial skirmishes between male and female, which after five acts of intrigue bring them to the goal they have sought all along—each other's arms—predict the kind of comedy of manners which was to dominate the taste of the Restoration playgoer several decades later. Leech feels that, in spite of the fact that its hero is named Mirabel, the play is essentially more like Wycherley than Congreve. Though during his last years Fletcher was the leading figure in the London theatrical world, easily overshadowing Jonson in popularity, and collaborating with many authors, such as Massinger, Shakespeare, and William Rowley, and though he was loved and admired by almost everyone who knew and worked with him, modern criticism inclines to regard Beaumont, with his relatively few plays, as the greater dramatist.

## THE KNIGHT OF THE BURNING PESTLE

Although most readers today find *The Knight of the Burning Pestle* an amusingly good-humored and warm-hearted combination of fantasy and satirical comedy, its original audience obviously did not find it so, since Walter Burre, the publisher of the play, frankly admitted that this "unfortunate child" was so "utterly rejected" that it "was even ready to give up the ghost" except for the "cherishing" of it by Robert Keysar. Since Keysar was one of the managers of the Children of the Queen's Revels, who had been acting at the Blackfriars since 1600, it seems certain that this was the boys' company which first acted it. In the induction, the bluff citizen-grocer, in interrupting the regularly scheduled play, shows his knowledge of London theatrical history by reminding the actors, "This seven years there hath been plays at this house." This remark fitted the Blackfriars, where the Revels boys had been playing intermittently since the reorganization of the Chapel Children in 1600, rather than the Whitefriars, which the Children of the King's Revels did not occupy till 1608 (Chambers, *The Elizabethan Stage*). The play was not published, anonymously, until 1613, and the publisher, Burre, stated that he had "fostered it privately" in his bosom "these two years." Scholars today generally believe that it was a little longer before the reading public saw it and that it saw the stage not long after the mock-heroic *The Woman Hater*, perhaps in 1607 or 1608 (Baldwin Maxwell, *"The Knight of the Burning Pestle* and *Wily Beguiled,"* Studies in Beaumont, Fletcher, and Massinger, University of North Carolina Press, 1939; John Doebler, in his preface to the *Regents Renaissance Drama* edition of the play, University of Nebraska Press, 1967). A date of about 1610 had previously been argued by F. G. Fleay, *A Bibliographical Chronicle of the English Drama*, London, 1911; Herbert S. Murch, edition of the play in the *YSE*, New York, 1908; and Oliphant. Topical references in the play to other popular plays offer some slight difficulties in dating, however, since the earliest extant edition of *The Four Prentices of London* is 1615 and *The Travels of the Three English Brothers* is 1607. It is therefore necessary to posit an earlier edition of the *Four Prentices*, now lost, or at least an earlier production.

*The Knight of the Burning Pestle* must have had a greater success when it was revived "by Her Majesty's Servants at the Private House in Drury Lane" (that is, the Cockpit) in 1635, as stated on the title page of the quarto edition of that year where the two men are first named as the authors, since it was then performed at court early in the next year (*The Dramatic Records of Sir Henry Herbert*, ed. J. Q. Adams, Yale University Press, 1917). Various reasons have been offered for its initial failure. Alfred Harbage suggested that the aristocratic and fashionable Blackfriars audience perhaps expected a sharper satire on the middle class than it got (*Shakespeare and the Rival Traditions*,

New York, 1952, echoed by William W. Appleton, *Beaumont and Fletcher*, London, 1956); and Doebler wondered whether "the ironies were too finely spun for even a sophisticated audience." Wallis, on the other hand, emphasized the point that perhaps the grocer and his wife "were too uncomfortably like some of the burgesses seated in the audience." Leech also cited the presence of this couple and their apprentice Rafe as evidence of the attendance of this class of spectator, even though they were not quite at home there. But the play was well received in the Restoration, with the glamorous Nell Gwyn, the King's later mistress, acting in it, as shown by Arthur Colby Sprague in *Beaumont and Fletcher on the Restoration Stage* (Harvard University Press, 1926) and John Harold Wilson in *The Influence of Beaumont and Fletcher on Restoration Drama* (University of Chicago Press, 1928). In modern times there have been various academic revivals.

For a long time it was thought that Fletcher had at least a small part in the composition of the play, especially in the Jasper-Luce scenes, and the quartos in 1635 ascribe the play to "Francis Beaumont and John Fletcher, Gent." (Fleay, "On Metrical Tests as Applied to Dramatic Poetry," *New Shakespeare Society Transactions*, 1874; R. Boyle, "Beaumont, Fletcher, and Massinger," *Englische Studien*, 1881; and Oliphant). Wallis still clings to the speculation that the two friends "doubtless enjoyed discussing it during the time it was taking shape," even though the time of begetting and birth, as Burre admitted, covered only eight days. But the studies of Hoy and others now assign the play entirely to Beaumont. As for sources, modern scholars generally agree with Burre that those who think it "to be of the race of *Don Quixote*" are mistaken. Although Cervantes' satirical epic on the days of expiring chivalry was published in Spanish in 1605 and reprinted in Brussels in 1607, Thomas Shelton's English translation did not come out till 1612, its first translation into any language. There is no evidence that Beaumont knew any Spanish, though Edward M. Wilson, in "Did Fletcher Read Spanish?" (*PQ*, 1940), has proved that in some of his later plays Fletcher apparently was familiar with the original texts of novels by Cervantes and B. L. de Argensola. Murch has also shown that the common elements in the play and *Don Quixote* were quite conventional and can be paralleled in various places. For, in addition to poking fun at the taste and manners of the London tradesman, the play is a burlesque not only of such popular romantic dramas as *Mucedorus* and Heywood's *The Four Prentices of London* but also of such fictional romances, in both verse and prose, as Rafe's own favorite *Palmerin of England*. Though some critics, like Wallis, have felt that the rambling adventures of Rafe detract from the unity of the play, other recent studies, notably in German, take the opposite view (Robert Weimann, *Drama und Wirklichkeit in der Shakespearezeit*, Halle, 1958, and Inge Leimberg, "Das Spiel mit der Dramatischen Illusion in Beaumonts *The Knight of the Burning Pestle*," *Anglia*, 1963), and are supported by Doebler.

In addition to the editions of the play by Doebler and Murch, already cited, there is a long and minutely detailed French edition by M. T. Jones-Davies in the *Collection Bilingue des Classiques Étrangers* (Paris, 1957). The Fountainwell Drama Texts also offer an edition of the play by Andrew Gurr (1969). The present text is based on the 1613 quarto as reprinted by R. M. Alden in the Belles-Lettres Series (New York, 1912), but these readings have been checked by reference to those given by Murch in his critical edition, and by A. R. Waller in the Cambridge English Classics edition of the plays of Beaumont and Fletcher.

# THE KNIGHT OF THE BURNING PESTLE [1]

## BY

## FRANCIS BEAUMONT AND JOHN FLETCHER [2]

To His Many Ways Endeared Friend,
Master Robert Keysar [3]

Sir:

This unfortunate child, who in eight days, as lately I have learned, was begot and born, soon after was by his parents (perhaps because he was so unlike his brethren) exposed to the wide world, who, for want of judgment or not understanding the privy mark of irony about it (which showed it was no offspring of any vulgar brain), utterly rejected it, so that for want of acceptance it was even [10 ready to give up the ghost and was in danger to have been smothered in perpetual oblivion, if you out of your direct antipathy to ingratitude had not been moved both to relieve and cherish it, wherein I must needs commend both your judgment, understanding, and singular love to good wits. You afterwards sent it to me, yet being an infant and somewhat ragged. I have fostered it privately [20 in my bosom these two years, and now to show my love return it to you, clad in good, lasting clothes which scarce memory will wear out, and able to speak for itself, and withal, as it telleth me, desirous to try his fortune in the world, where, if yet it be welcome, father, foster-father, nurse, and child—all have their desired end. If it be slighted or traduced, it hopes his father will beget him a younger [30 brother who shall revenge his quarrel and challenge the world either of fond [4]

and merely literal interpretation or illiterate misprision. [5] Perhaps it will be thought to be of the race of *Don Quixote*. We both may confidently swear it is his elder above a year, and therefore may by virtue of his birthright challenge the wall of [6] him. I doubt not but they will meet in their adventures, and I hope [40 the breaking of one staff will make them friends; and perhaps they will combine themselves and travel through the world to seek their adventures. So I commit him to his good fortune, and myself to your love.

Your assured friend,
W. B. [7]

[To the Readers of This Comedy [8]

Gentlemen:

The world is so nice [9] in these our times that for apparel there is no fashion; for music (which is a rare art, though now slighted), no instrument; for diet, none but the French kickshews [10] that are delicate; and, for plays, no invention but that which now runneth an invective way, touching some particular person, or else it is contemned before it is thoroughly understood. This is all that I have to say: [10 that the author had no intent to wrong anyone in this comedy, but, as a merry passage, here and there interlaced it with delight, which he hopes will please all, and be hurtful to none.

---

[1] The title at the head of the text is *The Famous History of the Knight of the Burning Pestle*.

[2] The names of the authors do not appear until the second quarto (1635), but Fletcher's contribution is now doubted.

[3] A manager of the Children of the Queen's Revels.  [4] Foolish.

[5] Misapprehension.

[6] *I.e.*, take precedence of.

[7] Walter Burre, the publisher.

[8] The address "To the Readers," the prologue, and the dramatis personæ are all from the 1635 edn.

[9] Fastidious.

[10] Kickshaws.

## PROLOGUE [1]

Where the bee can suck no honey, she leaves her sting behind; and, where the bear cannot find origanum [2] to heal his grief, he blasteth all other leaves with his breath. We fear it is like to fare so with us—that, seeing you cannot draw from our labors sweet content, you leave behind you a sour mislike, and with open reproach blame our good meanings, because you cannot reap the wonted mirth. Our intent was at this time to move [11 inward delight, not outward lightness, and to breed (if it might be) soft smiling, not loud laughing, knowing it to the wise to be a great pleasure to hear counsel mixed with wit, as to the foolish to have sport mingled with rudeness. They were banished the theater of Athens, and from Rome hissed, that brought parasites on the stage with apish actions, or fools [20 with uncivil habits, or courtesans with immodest words. We have endeavored to be as far from unseemly speeches to make your ears glow as we hope you will be free from unkind reports or mistaking the author's intention (who never aimed at any one particular in this play) to make our cheeks blush. And thus I leave it, and thee to thine own censure, to like or dislike.—*Vale.*[3]]        30

## THE SPEAKERS' NAMES

THE PROLOGUE.
*Then* A CITIZEN.
THE CITIZEN'S WIFE, *and* RAFE,[4] *her man, sitting below amidst the spectators.*
[VENTUREWELL,] *a rich merchant.*
JASPER, *his apprentice.*
MASTER HUMPHREY, *a friend to the merchant.*
LUCE, *merchant's daughter.*
MISTRESS MERRYTHOUGHT, *Jasper's mother.*
MICHAEL, *a second son of Mistress Merrythought.*
OLD MASTER MERRYTHOUGHT.

[TIM,] *a squire.*
[GEORGE,] *a dwarf.*
A TAPSTER.
A BOY *that danceth and singeth.*
AN HOST.
A BARBER.
[THREE CAPTIVE] KNIGHTS.[5]
[CAPTIVE WOMAN.]
A CAPTAIN.
A SERGEANT.
SOLDIERS.
[BOYS.
POMPIONA, *daughter of the King of Moldavia.*

SCENE: *London, Moldavia, etc.*

TIME: *Indefinite.*

## INDUCTION

*Several Gentlemen sitting on stools on the stage; the Citizen, his Wife, and Rafe standing below among the audience.]*

*Enter Prologue.*

[PRO.] From all that's near the court, from all that's great,
Within the compass of the city[6] walls,
We now have brought our scene—

*Enter Citizen [, climbing onto the stage].*

CIT. Hold your peace, Goodman[7] Boy!
PRO. What do you mean, sir?
CIT. That you have no good meaning. This seven years there hath been plays at this house,[8] I have observed it, you have still girds[9] at citizens; and now you call your play *The London Merchant.* Down with your title,[10] boy! Down with [11 your title!
PRO. Are you a member of the noble city?
CIT. I am.

---

[1] This prologue is an almost exact reproduction of "The Prologue at the Blackfriars" prefixed to Lyly's *Sappho and Phao.*
[2] Marjoram.
[3] Farewell.
[4] Colloquial for *Ralph.*
[5] Early edns. read *Two Knights.*
[6] The business district of London, as opposed to Westminster, the court.

[7] Master.
[8] Probably Blackfriars, a private theater.
[9] Sneers.
[10] A sign hung or set on the stage to announce the name of the play.

PRO. And a freeman? [1]

CIT. Yea, and a grocer.

PRO. So, grocer, then, by your sweet favor, we intend no abuse to the city.

CIT. [2] No, sir! Yes, sir! If you were [20 not resolved to play the Jacks,[3] what need you study for new subjects, purposely to abuse your betters? Why could not you be contented, as well as others, with the legend of Whittington, or the life and death of Sir Thomas Gresham, with the building of the Royal Exchange, or the story of Queen Eleanor, with the rearing of London Bridge upon woolsacks? [4]     29

PRO. You seem to be an understanding man. What would you have us do, sir?

CIT. Why, present something notably in honor of the commons of the city.

PRO. Why, what do you say to the life and death of fat Drake, or the repairing of Fleet privies?

CIT. I do not like that; but I will have a citizen, and he shall be of my own trade.

PRO. O, you should have told us your mind a month since; our play is ready [40 to begin now.

CIT. 'Tis all one for that; I will have a grocer, and he shall do admirable [5] things.

PRO. What will you have him do?

CIT. Marry, I will have him—

WIFE. (*Below.*[6]) Husband, husband!

RAFE. (*Below.*[7]) Peace, mistress!

WIFE. Hold thy peace, Rafe; I know what I do, I warrant tee.[8] —Husband, [50 husband!

CIT. What sayst thou, cunny? [9]

WIFE. Let him kill a lion with a pestle, husband! Let him kill a lion with a pestle!

CIT. So he shall.—I'll have him kill a lion with a pestle.

WIFE. Husband! Shall I come up, husband?

CIT. Ay, cunny.—Rafe, help your mistress this way.—Pray, gentlemen, [60

_____
[1] In this case, a member of one of the great tradesmen's guilds.
[2] The original prints the remainder of this scene in extremely irregular verse.
[3] Act like low fellows.
[4] Allusions to actual plays of the period.
[5] Wonderful.
[6] Marginal note in the original reads *Wife below.*
[7] Marginal note in the original reads *Rafe below.*
[8] Thee.
[9] Cony, pet.

make her a little room.—I pray you, sir, lend me your hand to help up my wife. I thank you, sir.—So.

[*Wife is pulled onto the stage.*]

WIFE. By your leave, gentlemen all; I'm something troublesome. I'm a stranger here; I was ne'er at one of these plays, as they say, before; but I should have seen [10 Jane Shore once; and my husband hath promised me, any time this twelvemonth, to carry me to the Bold Beauchamps, [70 but in truth he did not. I pray you, bear with me.

CIT. Boy, let my wife and I have a couple stools and then begin; and let the grocer do rare things. [*Stools are brought.*]

PRO. But, sir, we have never a boy [11] to play him; everyone hath a part already.

WIFE. Husband, husband, for God's sake, let Rafe play him! Beshrew me, if I do not think he will go beyond them all. [80

CIT. Well remembered, wife.—Come up, Rafe.—I'll tell you, gentlemen; let them but lend him a suit of reparel [12] and necessaries, and, by Gad, if any of them all blow wind in the tail on him.[13] I'll be hanged.

[*Rafe leaps onto the stage.*]

WIFE. I pray you, youth, let him have a suit of reparel!—I'll be sworn, gentlemen, my husband tells you true. He will act you sometimes at our house that [90 all the neighbors cry out on him; he will fetch you up a couraging part so in the garret that we are all as feared, I warrant you, that we quake again. We'll fear [14] our children with him; if they be never so unruly, do but cry, "Rafe comes, Rafe comes!" to them, and they'll be as quiet as lambs.—Hold up thy head, Rafe; show the gentlemen what thou canst do. Speak a huffing [15] part; I warrant you, [100 the gentlemen will accept of it.

CIT. Do, Rafe, do.

RAFE. "By heaven, methinks, it were an easy leap

_____
[10] Was to have seen.
[11] The play was first performed by the Children of Her Majesty's Revels.
[12] Apparel.
[13] A vulgar expression for *find fault with him.*
[14] Frighten.
[15] Blustering.

To pluck bright honor from the pale-
faced moon,
Or dive into the bottom of the sea,
Where never fathom line touched any
ground,
And pluck up drownéd honor from the
lake of hell." [1]

CIT. How say you, gentlemen, is it not
as I told you?

WIFE. Nay, gentlemen, he hath [110
played before, my husband says, *Mucedorus,* before the wardens of our Company.

CIT. Ay, and he should have played
Jeronimo [2] with a shoemaker for a wager.

PRO. He shall have a suit of apparel,
if he will go in.

CIT. In, Rafe, in, Rafe, and set out the
grocery [3] in their kind,[4] if thou lov'st me.
[*Exit Rafe.*]

WIFE. I warrant, our Rafe will look
finely when he's dressed.        120

PRO. But what will you have it called?

CIT. *The Grocer's Honor.*

PRO. Methinks *The Knight of the Burning Pestle* were better.

WIFE. I'll be sworn, husband, that's
as good a name as can be.

CIT. Let it be so.—Begin, begin; my
wife and I will sit down.

PRO. I pray you, do.        129

CIT. What stately music have you?
You have shawms? [5]

PRO. Shawms? No.

CIT. No? I'm a thief if my mind did
not give [6] me so. Rafe plays a stately part,
and he must needs have shawms. I'll be
at the charge of them myself rather than
we'll be without them.

PRO. So you are like to be.

CIT. Why, and so I will be; there's
two shillings. [*Gives money.*] Let's [140
have the waits [7] of Southwark; they are
as rare fellows as any are in England;
and that will fetch them all o'er the water
with a vengeance, as if they were mad.

PRO. You shall have them. Will you
sit down then?

CIT. Ay.—Come, wife.

WIFE. Sit you merry all, gentlemen;

I'm bold to sit amongst you for my ease.
[*Citizen and Wife sit down.*]

PRO. From all that's near the court,
from all that's great,        150
Within the compass of the city walls,
We now have brought our scene. Fly
far from hence
All private taxes,[8] immodest phrases,
Whatever may but show like vicious!
For wicked mirth never true pleasure
brings,
But honest minds are pleased with hon-
est things.—

Thus much for that we do; but for
Rafe's part you must answer for yourself.

CIT. Take you no care for Rafe; he'll
discharge himself, I warrant you.        160
[*Exit Prologue.*]

WIFE. I' faith, gentlemen, I'll give my
word for Rafe.

ACTUS PRIMI SCENA PRIMA.[9]

[*A room in Venturewell's house.*]

*Enter Merchant [Venturewell] and Jasper,
his prentice.*

MERCH. Sirrah, I'll make you know you
are my prentice,
And whom my charitable love redeemed
Even from the fall of fortune; gave
thee heat
And growth, to be what now thou art;
new-cast [10] thee,
Adding the trust of all I have at home,
In foreign staples,[11] or upon the sea,
To thy direction; tied the good opinions
Both of myself and friends to thy en-
deavors.
So fair were thy beginnings. But with
these,
As I remember, you had never charge 10
To love your master's daughter, and
even then
When I had found a wealthy husband
for her.
I take it, sir, you had not. But, however,
I'll break the neck of that commission,
And make you know you are but a
merchant's factor.[12]

JASP. Sir, I do liberally confess I am yours,
Bound both by love and duty to your
service,

---

[1] A slightly inaccurate quotation from Shakespeare's *I Henry IV*, I, iii.
[2] The conventional allusion to *The Spanish
Tragedy.*        [5] Wind instruments.
[3] Grocers.        [6] Misgive.
[4] In their proper livery.        [7] Musicians.
[8] Criticisms of individuals.        [10] Remade.
[9] Scene one of act one.        [11] Markets.        [12] Agent.

In which my labor hath been all my
profit;
I have not lost in bargain, nor delighted
To wear your honest gains upon my
back;                                          20
Nor have I given a pension to my blood,[1]
Or lavishly in play consumed your stock;
These, and the miseries that do attend
them,
I dare with innocence proclaim are
strangers
To all my temperate actions.  For your
daughter,
If there be any love to my deservings
Borne by her virtuous self, I cannot
stop it;
Nor am I able to refrain [2] her wishes.
She's private to herself and best of
knowledge [3]
Whom she'll make so happy as to sigh
for;                                           30
Besides, I cannot think you mean to
match her
Unto a fellow of so lame a presence,
One that hath little left of nature in
him.
MERCH. 'Tis very well, sir; I can tell
your wisdom
How all this shall be cured.
JASP.               Your care becomes you.
MERCH. And thus it must be, sir: I here
discharge you
My house and service; take your liberty;
And, when I want a son, I'll send for
you.                                    *Exit.*
JASP. These be the fair rewards of them
that love!                                     39
O, you that live in freedom, never prove
The travail of a mind led by desire!

*Enter Luce.*

LUCE. Why, how now, friend?    Struck
with my father's thunder?
JASP. Struck, and struck dead, unless the
remedy
Be full of speed and virtue; I am now,
What I expected long, no more your
father's.
LUCE. But mine.
JASP.        But yours, and only yours, I am;

That's all I have to keep me from the
statute.[4]
You dare be constant still?
LUCE.                    O, fear me not!
In this I dare be better than a woman.
Nor shall his anger nor his offers move me,
Were they both equal to a prince's
power.                                        51
JASP. You know my rival?
LUCE.           Yes, and love him dearly,
Even as I love an ague or foul weather.
I prithee, Jasper, fear him not.
JASP.                        O, no!
I do not mean to do him so much kind-
ness.
But to our own desires: you know the plot
We both agreed on?
LUCE.              Yes, and will perform
My part exactly.
JASP.          I desire no more.
Farewell, and keep my heart; 'tis yours.
LUCE.                       I take it;
He must do miracles makes me forsake
it.                              *Exeunt.*  60

CIT. Fie upon 'em, little infidels! What
a matter's here now! Well, I'll be hanged
for a halfpenny, if there be not some
abomination knavery in this play. Well,
let 'em look to 't; Rafe must come, and if
there be any tricks a-brewing—
WIFE. Let 'em brew, and bake too,
husband, a [5] God's name; Rafe will find
all out, I warrant you, and [6] they were
older than they are.—                          70

*[Enter Boy.]*

I pray, my pretty youth, is Rafe ready?
BOY. He will be presently.
WIFE. Now, I pray you, make my commendations unto him, and withal carry
him this stick of licoras.[7] Tell him his
mistress sent it him, and bid him bite a
piece; 'twill open his pipes the better, say.
*[Exit Boy.]*

[SCENA SECUNDA.

*The same.]*

*Enter Merchant and Master Humphrey.*

MERCH. Come, sir, she's yours; upon my
faith, she's yours.

[1] A license to my passion.
[2] Restrain.
[3] *I.e.*, she is secret and knows best.
[4] Against masterless men.
[5] In.
[6] If.
[7] Licorice.

You have my hand. For other idle lets [1]
Between your hopes and her, thus with
    a wind
They are scattered and no more. My
    wanton prentice,
That like a bladder blew himself with
    love,
I have let out, and sent him to discover
New masters yet unknown.
HUM.                    I thank you, sir;
Indeed, I thank you, sir; and, ere I stir,
It shall be known, however you do deem,
I am of gentle blood and gentle seem.    10
MERCH. O, sir, I know it certain.
HUM.                    Sir, my friend,
Although, as writers say, all things have
    end,
And that we call a pudding hath his two,
O, let it not seem strange, I pray, to you,
If in this bloody simile I put
My love, more endless than frail things
    or gut!

WIFE. Husband, I prithee, sweet lamb,
tell me one thing, but tell me truly.—
Stay, youths, I beseech you, till I question
my husband.                    20
    CIT. What is it, mouse?
    WIFE. Sirrah, didst thou ever see a
prettier child? How it behaves itself, I
warrant ye, and speaks and looks and
perts [2] up the head!—I pray you, brother,
with your favor, were you never none of
M[aster] Monkester's [3] scholars?
    CIT. Chicken, I prithee heartily, con-
tain thyself; the childer [4] are pretty childer;
but, when Rafe comes, lamb—         30
    WIFE. Ay, when Rafe comes, conny!—
Well, my youth, you may proceed.

MERCH. Well, sir, you know my love, and
    rest, I hope,
Assured of my consent; get but my
    daughter's,
And wed her when you please. You must
    be bold,
And clap in close unto her; come, I know
You have language good enough to win
    a wench.

WIFE. A whoreson [5] tyrant! H'as been
an old stringer [6] in 's days, I warrant him.

HUM. I take your gentle offer, and withal
    Yield love again for love reciprocal.  [41
MERCH. What, Luce! Within there!

*Enter Luce.*

LUCE.                    Called you, sir?
MERCH.                    I did.
Give entertainment to this gentleman,
And see you be not froward.—To her,
    sir;
My presence will but be an eyesore to
    you.                    *Exit.*
HUM. Fair Mistress Luce, how do you do?
    Are you well?
Give me your hand, and then I pray
    you tell
How doth your little sister and your
    brother,
And whether you love me or any other.
LUCE. Sir, these are quickly answered.
HUM.                    So they are,    50
Where women are not cruel. But how
    far
Is it now distant from this place we are
    in,
Unto that blessed place, your father's
    warren?
LUCE. What makes you think of that, sir?
HUM.                    Even that face;
For, stealing rabbits whilom [7] in that
    place,
God Cupid, or the keeper, I know not
    whether,[8]
Unto my cost and charges brought you
    thither,
And there began—
LUCE.            Your game, sir.
HUM.                    Let no game,
Or anything that tendeth to the same,
Be evermore remembered, thou fair
    killer,                    60
For whom I sat me down, and brake my
    tiller.[9]

WIFE. There's a kind gentleman, I
warrant you; when will you do as much for
me, George?

---

[1] Obstacles.
[2] Cocks.
[3] Richard Mulcaster, until 1608 Headmaster
of St. Paul's School, encouraged the acting of
plays among his pupils.
[4] Children.

[5] Rascally.                    [8] Which.
[6] Libertine.                    [9] Crossbow.
[7] Formerly.

LUCE. Beshrew me, sir, I am sorry for
your losses,
But, as the proverb says, I cannot cry.
I would you had not seen me!

HUM.                    So would I,
Unless you had more maw [1] to do me
good.

LUCE. Why, cannot this strange passion
be withstood?                        69
Send for a constable, and raise the town.

HUM. O, no! My valiant love will batter
down
Millions of constables, and put to flight
Even that great watch of Midsummer
Day at night. [2]

LUCE. Beshrew me, sir, 'twere good I
yielded then;
Weak women cannot hope, where vai-
iant men
Have no resistance.

HUM.                    Yield, then; I am full
Of pity, though I say it, and can pull
Out of my pocket thus a pair of gloves.
Look, Lucy, look; the dog's tooth nor
the dove's
Are not so white as these; and sweet
they be,                              80
And whipped [3] about with silk, as you
may see.
If you desire the price, shoot [4] from your
eye
A beam to this place, and you shall espy
"F S," [5] which is to say, my sweetest
honey,
They cost me three and twopence, or
no money.

LUCE. Well, sir, I take them kindly, and
I thank you.
What would you more?

HUM.          Nothing.

LUCE.                    Why, then, farewell.

HUM. Nor so, nor so; for, lady, I must
tell,
Before we part, for what we met together.
God grant me time and patience and
fair weather!                        90

LUCE. Speak, and declare your mind in
terms so brief.

HUM. I shall.  Then, first and foremost,
for relief
I call to you, I, if that you can afford it;
I care not at what price, for, on my word,
it
Shall be repaid again, although it cost me
More than I'll speak of now, for love
hath tossed me
In furious blanket like a tennis ball,
And now I rise aloft, and now I fall.

LUCE. Alas, good gentleman, alas the
day!

HUM. I thank you heart[i]ly; and, as I
say,                                 100
Thus do I still continue without rest,
I' th' morning like a man, at night a
beast,
Roaring and bellowing mine own dis-
quiet,
That much I fear forsaking of my diet
Will bring me presently to that quan-
dary
I shall bid all adieu.

LUCE.                    Now, by S[t]. Mary,
That were great pity!

HUM.                    So it were, beshrew me;
Then, ease me, lusty [6] Luce, and pity
show me.

LUCE. Why, sir, you know my will is
nothing worth
Without my father's grant; get his
consent,                             110
And then you may with assurance try me.

HUM. The worshipful your sire will not
deny me;
For I have asked him, and he hath
replied,
"Sweet Master Humphrey, Luce shall
be thy bride."

LUCE. Sweet Master Humphrey, then
I am content.

HUM. And so am I, in truth.

LUCE.                    Yet take me with you; [7]
There is another clause must be annexed,
And this it is (I swore, and will perform
it):
No man shall ever joy [8] me as his wife
But he that stole me hence.  If you dare
venter, [9]                          120
I am yours (you need not fear; my
father loves you);
If not, farewell forever!

[1] Appetite, desire.
[2] The annual military muster of the guilds.
[3] Embroidered.
[4] From 1711 edn.  Original reads *sute*.
[5] Evidently the trade-mark or price mark.

[6] Jolly.                           [8] Enjoy.
[7] Understand me fully.             [9] Venture.

HUM.                    Stay, nymph, stay.
 I have a double gelding, colored bay,
 Sprung by his father from Barbarian [1]
    kind;
 Another for myself, though somewhat
    blind,
 Yet true as trusty tree.
LUCE.                    I am satisfied;
 And so I give my hand.  Our course
    must lie
 Through Waltham Forest, where I have
    a friend
 Will entertain us.  So, farewell, Sir Hum-
    phrey,
 And think upon your business.'
                              *Exit Luce.*
HUM.                    Though I die,  130
 I am resolved to venter life and limb
 For one so young, so fair, so kind, so
    trim.              *Exit Humphrey.*

WIFE.  By my faith and troth, George,
and as I am virtuous, it is e'en the kindest
young man that ever trod on shoe leather.
—Well, go thy ways; if thou hast her not,
'tis not thy fault, faith.

CIT.  I prithee, mouse, be patient; a [2]
shall have her, or I'll make some [of] [3] 'em
smoke [4] for 't.                        140

WIFE.  That's my good lamb, George.—
Fie, this stinking tobacco kills men! [5]
Would there were none in England!—Now,
I pray, gentlemen, what good does this
stinking tobacco do you?  Nothing, I war-
rant.  You make chimneys a [6] your faces!—
O, husband, husband, now, now!  There's
Rafe, there's Rafe.

### [SCENA TERTIA.]

*Enter Rafe, like a grocer in 's shop with
   two Prentices, [Tim and George,] reading* Palmerin of England.

CIT.  Peace, fool!  Let Rafe alone.—
Hark you, Rafe; do not strain yourself
too much at the first.—Peace!—Begin,
Rafe.

RAFE. [*Reading.*] [7]  "Then Palmerin and
Trineus, snatching their launces from

---

[1] *I.e.*, Barbary.
[2] He.
[3] From 1635 edn.
[7] The following passage is actually a con-
densed quotation from Munday's translation
of *Palmerin de Oliva*

[4] Suffer.
[5] Me(?).
[6] Of.

---

their dwarfs, and clasping their helmets,
galloped amain after the giant; and Palmerin, having gotten a sight of him, came
posting amain, saying, 'Stay, traitor-  [10
ous thief!  For thou mayst not so carry
away her that is worth the greatest lord
in the world;' and with these words gave
him a blow on the shoulder that he
stroke [8] him besides [9] his elephant.  And
Trineus, coming to the knight that had
Agricola behind him, set him soon besides
his horse, with his neck broken in the
fall, so that the princess, getting out of
the throng, between joy and grief,  [20
said, 'All happy knight, the mirror of all
such as follow arms, now may I be well
assured of the love thou bearest me.' "—
I wonder why the kings do not raise an
army of fourteen or fifteen hundred thousand men, as big as the army that the
Prince of Portigo brought against Rosicleer, and destroy these giants; they do
much hurt to wandering damsels that
go in quest of their knights.               30

WIFE.  Faith, husband, and Rafe says
true; for they say the King of Portugal
cannot sit at his meat but the giants and
the ettins [10] will come and snatch it from
him.

CIT.  Hold thy tongue!—On, Rafe!

RAFE.  And certainly those knights are
much to be commended, who, neglecting
their possessions, wander with a squire
and a dwarf through the deserts to  [40
relieve poor ladies.

WIFE.  Ay, by faith, are they, Rafe;
let 'em say what they will, they are indeed.  Our knights neglect their possessions well enough, but they do not the rest.

RAFE.  There are no such courteous
and fair well-spoken knights in this age;
they will call one "the son of a whore"
that Palmerin of England would have
called "fair sir"; and one that Rosi-  [50
cleer would have called "right beauteous
damsel" they will call "damned bitch."

WIFE.  I'll be sworn will they, Rafe;
they have called me so an hundred times
about a scurvy pipe of tobacco.

---

[8] Struck.
[9] Off.                    [10] Another word for *giants.*

RAFE. But what brave spirit could be content to sit in his shop, with a flappet [1] of wood and a blue apron before him, selling mithridatum and dragon's-water [2] to visited [3] houses, that might pursue [60 feats of arms, and, through his noble achievements, procure such a famous history to be written of his heroic prowess?

CIT. Well said, Rafe; some more of those words, Rafe!

WIFE. They go finely, by my troth.

RAFE. Why should not I then pursue this course, both for the credit of myself and our company? For, amongst all the worthy books of achievements, I do [70 not call to mind that I yet read of a grocer-errant. I will be the said knight.—Have you heard of any that hath wandered unfurnished of his squire and dwarf? My elder prentice Tim shall be my trusty squire, and little George my dwarf. Hence, my blue aporn! [4] Yet, in remembrance of my former trade, upon my shield shall be portrayed a burning pestle, and I will be called the Knight o' th' Burning Pestle.

WIFE. Nay, I dare swear thou wilt [81 not forget thy old trade; thou wert ever meek.

RAFE. Tim!

TIM. Anon.

RAFE. My beloved squire, and George my dwarf, I charge you that from henceforth you never call me by any other name but "the right courteous and valiant Knight of the Burning Pestle," and [90 that you never call any female by the name of a woman or wench, but "fair lady," if she have her desires; if not, "distressed damsel;" that you call all forests and heaths "deserts,' and all horses "palfreys."

WIFE This is very fine, faith.—Do the gentlemen like Rafe, think you, husband?

CIT. Ay, I warrant thee; the players would give all the shoes in their shop [100 for him.

RAFE. My beloved squire Tim, stand out. Admit this were a desert, and over it a knight-errant pricking, [5] and I should bid you inquire of his intents, what would you say?

TIM. Sir, my master sent me to know whither you are riding?

RAFE. No, thus: "Fair sir, the right courteous and valiant Knight of the [110 Burning Pestle commanded me to inquire upon what adventure you are bound, whether to relieve some distressed damsels, or otherwise."

CIT. Whoresome [6] blockhead, cannot remember!

WIFE. I' faith, and Rafe told him on 't before; all the gentlemen heard him.—Did he not, gentlemen? Did not Rafe tell him on 't?

GEORGE. Right courteous and valiant Knight of the Burning Pestle, here is a distressed damsel to have a halfpennyworth of pepper.

WIFE. That's a good boy! See, the little boy can hit it; by my troth, it's a fine child.

RAFE. Relieve her, with all courteous language. Now shut up shop; no more my prentice, but my trusty squire [130 and dwarf. I must bespeak my shield and arming [7] pestle. [Exeunt Tim and George.]

CIT. Go thy ways, Rafe! As I'm a true man, thou art the best on 'em all.

WIFE. Rafe, Rafe!

RAFE. What say you, mistress?

WIFE. I prithee, come again quickly, sweet Rafe.

RAFE. By-and-by. [8]                    Exit Rafe.

[SCENA QUARTA.

A room in Merrythought's house.]

Enter Jasper and his mother, Mistress
                              Merrythought.

MIST. MER. Give thee my blessing? No, I'll ne'er give thee my blessing; I'll

---

[1] Ledge, i.e., of the counter.
[2] Medicines used against the plague.
[3] I e., by the plague.                    [4] Apron.

[5] Spurring.                    [7] Heraldic
[6] Whoreson.                    [8] At once

see thee hanged first; it shall ne'er be said I gave thee my blessing. Th' art thy father's own son, of the right blood of the Merrythoughts. I may curse the time that e'er I knew thy father; he hath spent all his own and mine too; and, when I tell him of it, he laughs, and dances, and sings, and cries, "A merry heart lives [10 long-a." And thou art a wastethrift, and art run away from thy master that loved thee well, and art come to me; and I have laid up a little for my younger son Michael, and thou think'st to bezzle [1] that, but thou shalt never be able to do it.—Come hither, Michael! Come, Michael.

*Enter Michael.*

Down on thy knees; thou shalt have my blessing.                                          19
    MICH. [*Kneeling.*] I pray you, mother, pray to God to bless me.
    MIST. MER. God bless thee! [*Michael rises.*] But Jasper shall never have my blessing; he shall be hanged first; shall he not, Michael? How say'st thou?
    MICH. Yes, forsooth, mother, and grace of God.
    MIST. MER. That's a good boy!

    WIFE. Ay, faith, it's a fine-spoken child.

    JASP. Mother, though you forget a par-       ent's love,                          30
I must preserve the duty of a child.
I ran not from my master, nor return
To have your stock maintain my idle-       ness.

    WIFE. Ungracious child, I warrant him; hark, how he chops logic [2] with his mother!—Thou hadst best tell her she lies; do tell her she lies.
    CIT. If he were my son, I would hang him up by the heels, and flay him, and salt him, whoreson haltersack. [3]        40

    JASP. My coming only is to beg your       love,
Which I must ever, though I never gain       it;
And, howsoever you esteem of me,

---

There is no drop of blood hid in these       veins
But, I remember well, belongs to you
That brought me forth, and would be       glad for you
To rip them all again, and let it out.
    MIST. MER. Ay, faith, I had sorrow enough for thee, God knows; but I'll hamper thee well enough. Get thee [50 in, thou vagabond, get thee in, and learn of thy brother Michael.
        [*Exeunt Jasper and Michael.*]
    OLD MER. ([*Singing*] *within.*)

Nose, nose, jolly red nose,
And who gave thee this jolly red nose?

    MIST. MER. Hark, my husband! He's singing and hoiting, [4] and I'm fain to cark and care, and all little enough.—Husband! Charles! Charles Merrythought!

*Enter Old Merrythought.*

OLD MER. [*Singing.*]

Nutmegs and ginger, cinnamon and       cloves—
And they gave me this jolly red nose.  60

    MIST. MER. If you would consider your state, you would have little list [5] to sing, iwis. [6]
    OLD MER. It should never be con-sidered, while it were an estate, if I thought it would spoil my singing.
    MIST. MER. But how wilt thou do, Charles? Thou art an old man, and thou canst not work, and thou hast not forty shillings left, and thou eatest good [70 meat, and drinkest good drink, and laugh-est.
    OLD MER. And will do.
    MIST. MER. But how wilt thou come by it, Charles?
    OLD MER. How? Why, how have I done hitherto this forty years? I never came into my dining room but at eleven and six a-clock I found excellent meat and drink a th' table; my clothes were [80 never worn out but next morning a tailor brought me a new suit; and without ques-tion it will be so ever; use makes perfect-ness. If all should fail, it is but a little

---

straining myself extraordinary and laugh myself to death.

WIFE. It's a foolish old man this, is not he, George?

CIT. Yes, cunny.

WIFE. Give me a penny i' th' purse [90 while I live, George.

CIT. Ay, by Lady, cunny; hold thee there.[1]

MIST. MER. Well, Charles, you promised to provide for Jasper, and I have laid up for Michael. I pray you, pay Jasper his portion. He's come home, and he shall not consume Michael's stock; he says his master turned him away, but, I promise you truly, I think he ran away.      100

WIFE. No, indeed, Mistress Merrythought; though he be a notable gallows,[2] yet I'll assure you his master did turn him away, even in this place. 'Twas, i' faith, within this half hour, about his daughter; my husband was by.

CIT. Hang him, rogue! He served him well enough. Love his master's daughter! By my troth, cunny, if there were a thousand boys, thou wouldst spoil them [110 all with taking their parts. Let his mother alone with him.

WIFE. Ay, George; but yet truth is truth.

OLD MER. Where is Jasper? He's welcome, however. Call him in; he shall have his portion. Is he merry?

*Enter Jasper and Michael.*

MIST. MER. Ay, foul chive [3] him, he is too merry!—Jasper! Michael!

OLD MER. Welcome, Jasper! Though [120 thou runn'st away, welcome! God bless thee! 'Tis thy mother's mind thou shouldst receive thy portion. Thou hast been abroad, and I hope hast learned experience enough to govern it; thou art of sufficient years. Hold thy hand—one, two, three, four, five, six, seven, eight, nine, there's ten shillings for thee. [*Gives money.*] Thrust thyself into the world with that,

and take some settled course. If [130 fortune cross thee, thou hast a retiring place. Come home to me; I have twenty shillings left. Be a good husband,[4] that is, wear ordinary clothes, eat the best meat, and drink the best drink; be merry, and give to the poor; and, believe me, thou hast no end of thy goods.

JASP. Long may you live free from all thought of ill,
And long have cause to be thus merry still!
But, father—      140

OLD MER. No more words, Jasper; get thee gone. Thou hast my blessing; thy father's spirit upon thee! Farewell, Jasper! [*Sings.*]

But yet, or ere you part (O, cruel!),
Kiss me, kiss me, sweeting, mine own dear jewel!

So, now begone; no words.   *Exit Jasper.*

MIST. MER. So, Michael, now get thee gone too.

MICH. Yes, forsooth, mother; but I'll have my father's blessing first.      150

MIST. MER. No, Michael; 'tis no [5] matter for his blessing. Thou hast my blessing; begone. I'll fetch my money and jewels, and follow thee; I'll stay no longer with him, I warrant thee.—[*Exit Michael.*] Truly, Charles, I'll be gone too.

OLD MER. What, you will not?

MIST. MER. Yes, indeed will I.

OLD MER. [*Singing.*]

Heigh-ho, farewell, Nan!      159
I'll never trust wench more again, if I can.

MIST. MER. You shall not think, when all your own is gone, to spend that I have been scraping up for Michael.

OLD MER. Farewell, good wife; I expect it not. All I have to do in this world is to be merry, which I shall, if the ground be not taken from me; and, if it be, [*Sings.*]

When earth and seas from me are reft,
The skies aloft for me are left.      169
                    *Exeunt.*

*Boy danceth. Music.*

FINIS ACTUS PRIMI.

---

[1] Stand by your belief.
[2] Gallows bird.                    [3] Ill befall.

[4] Be economical.
[5] From 1635 edn. Original has *now.*

WIFE. I'll be sworn he's a merry old gentleman for all that. Hark, hark, husband, hark! Fiddles, fiddles! Now surely they go finely. They say 'tis present death for these fiddlers to tune their rebecks before the great Turk's grace, is 't not, George? But look, look! Here's a youth dances!—Now, good youth, do a turn a th' toe.—Sweetheart, i' faith, I'll have Rafe come and do some of his gambols.— He'll ride the wild mare,[1] gentle- [180 men, 'twould do your hearts good to see him.—I thank you, kind youth; pray, bid Rafe come.

CIT. Peace, cunny!—Sirrah, you scurvy boy, bid the players send Rafe; or, by God's——,[2] and they do not, I'll tear some of their periwigs beside their heads: this is all riffraff. [*Exit Boy.*]

ACTUS SECUNDI SCENA PRIMA.

[*A room in Venturewell's house.*]

*Enter Merchant and Humphrey.*

MERCH. And how, faith, how goes it now, son Humphrey?

HUM. Right worshipful, and my belovéd friend,
And father dear, this matter's at an end.

MERCH. 'Tis well; it should be so. I'm glad the girl
Is found so tractable.

HUM.                       Nay, she must whirl
From hence (and you must wink, for so, I say,
The story[3] tells) tomorrow before day.

WIFE. George, dost thou think in thy conscience now 'twill be a match? Tell me but what thou think'st, sweet [10 rogue. Thou seest the poor gentleman, dear heart, how it labors and throbs, I warrant you, to be at rest! I'll go move the father for 't.

CIT. No, no; I prithee, sit still, honeysuckle; thou'lt spoil all. If he deny him, I'll bring half a dozen good fellows myself, and in the shutting of an evening knock 't up, and there's an end.[4]

WIFE. I'll buss thee for that, i' [20 faith, boy. Well, George, well, you have been a wag in your days, I warrant you; but God forgive you, and I do with all my heart.

MERCH. How was it, son? You told me that tomorrow
Before daybreak you must convey her hence.

HUM. I must, I must; and thus it is agreed.
Your daughter rides upon a brown-bay steed,
I on a sorrel, which I bought of Brian, 29
The honest host of the red roaring Lion,
In Waltham situate. Then, if you may,
Consent in seemly sort, lest, by delay,
The Fatal Sisters come, and do the office,
And then you'll sing another song.

MERCH.                                Alas,
Why should you be thus full of grief to me,
That do as willing as yourself agree
To anything, so it be good and fair?
Then, steal her when you will, if such a pleasure
Content you both; I'll sleep and never see it,
To make your joys more full. But tell me why 40
You may not here perform your marriage?

WIFE. God's blessing a thy soul, old man! I' faith, thou art loath to part true hearts. I see a has her, George; and I'm as glad on 't!—Well, go thy ways, Humphrey; for a fair-spoken man, I believe thou hast not thy fellow within the walls of London; and I should say the suburbs too, I should not lie.—Why dost not rejoice with me, George? 50

CIT. If I could but see Rafe again, I were as merry as mine host, i' faith.

HUM. The cause you seem to ask, I thus declare—
Help me, O Muses nine! Your daughter sware
A foolish oath, and more it was the pity;
Yet none but myself within this city
Shall dare to say so, but a bold defiance
Shall meet him, were he of the noble science;[5]

---

[1] Perhaps the name of a dance step.
[2] To be filled in by the actor.
[3] *I.e.*, the plan of eloping.
[4] As in the closing of the shop shutters at night.
[5] *I.e.*, a fencer.

And yet she sware, and yet why did
   she swear?
Truly, I cannot tell, unless it were  60
For her own ease, for, sure, sometimes
   an oath,
Being sworn thereafter, is like cordial
   broth;
And thus it was she swore, never to
   marry
But such a one whose mighty arm could
   carry
(As meaning me, for I am such a one)
Her bodily away, through stick and
   stone,
Till both of us arrive, at her request,
Some ten miles off, in the wild Wal-
   tham Forest.
MERCH. If this be all, you shall not need
   to fear
Any denial in your love.  Proceed;  70
I'll neither follow, nor repent the deed.
HUM. Good night, twenty good nights,
   and twenty more,
And twenty more good nights—that
   makes threescore!     *Exeunt.*

[SCENA SECUNDA.

*Waltham Forest.*]

*Enter Mistress Merrythought and her son
Michael.*

MIST. MER. Come, Michael; art thou
not weary, boy?
MICH. No, forsooth, mother, not I.
MIST. MER. Where be we now, child?
MICH. Indeed, forsooth, mother, I cannot tell, unless we be at Mile End.  Is not
all the world Mile End, mother?
MIST. MER. No, Michael, not all the
world, boy; but I can assure thee, Michael,
Mile End is a goodly matter.  There  [10
has been a pitchfield,[1] my child, between
the naughty Spaniels and the Englishmen; and the Spaniels ran away, Michael,
and the Englishmen followed.  My neighbor Coxstone was there, boy, and killed
them all with a birding piece.
MICH. Mother, forsooth—
MIST. MER. What says my white[2] boy?
MICH. Shall not my father go with us
too?    20

MIST. MER. No, Michael, let thy father
go snick up;[3] he shall never come between
a pair of sheets with me again while he
lives.  Let him stay at home, and sing for
his supper, boy.  Come, child, sit down,
and I'll show my boy fine knacks, indeed.
[*They sit down; and she opens a casket.*]
Look here, Michael; here's a ring, and
here's a brooch, and here's a bracelet, and
here's two rings more, and here's money
and gold by th' eye,[4] my boy.    30
MICH. Shall I have all this, mother?
MIST. MER. Ay, Michael, thou shalt
have all, Michael.

CIT. How lik'st thou this, wench?
WIFE. I cannot tell; I would have Rafe,
George; I'll see no more else, indeed-law;[5]
and, I pray you, let the youths understand so much by word of mouth; for, I
tell you truly, I'm afraid a my boy.  Come,
come, George, let's be merry and  [40
wise; the child's a fatherless child; and
say they should put him into a strait pair
of gaskins,[6] 'twere worse than knotgrass;[7]
he would never grow after it.

*Enter Rafe, Squire, and Dwarf.*

CIT. Here's Rafe, here's Rafe!
WIFE. How do you do, Rafe?  You are
welcome, Rafe, as I may say.  It's a good
boy; hold up thy head, and be not afraid.
We are thy friends, Rafe; the gentlemen
will praise thee, Rafe, if thou play'st  [50
thy part with audacity.  Begin, Rafe, a
God's name!

RAFE. My trusty squire, unlace my
helm; give me my hat.  Where are we, or
what desert may this be?
DWARF. Mirror of knighthood, this
is, as I take it, the perilous Waltham
Down, in whose bottom stands the enchanted valley.
MIST. MER. O, Michael, we are be-  [60
trayed, we are betrayed!  Here be giants!
Fly, boy!  Fly, boy, fly!
*Exeunt Mother and Michael* [, *leaving the
casket*].

[1] Perhaps an allusion to a sham battle fought
on this drill ground by the trained bands.
[2] Dear.
[3] Go hang.
[4] In unlimited quantity.
[5] An exclamation of annoyance.
[6] Tight breeches.
[7] A concoction of this was supposed to retard
growth.

RAFE. Lace on my helm again. What noise is this?
A gentle lady, flying the embrace
Of some uncourteous knight! I will relieve her.
Go, squire, and say the knight that wears this pestle
In honor of all ladies swears revenge
Upon that recreant coward that pursues her.
Go, comfort her, and that same gentle squire
That bears her company.

SQUIRE.    I go, brave knight. [*Exit.*]  70

RAFE. My trusty dwarf and friend, reach me my shield,
And hold it while I swear. First, by my knighthood;
Then by the soul of Amadis de Gaul,
My famous ancestor; then by my sword
The beauteous Brionella girt about me;
By this bright burning pestle, of mine honor
The living trophy; and by all respect
Due to distresséd damsels, here I vow
Never to end the quest of this fair lady
And that forsaken squire till by my valor    80
I gain their liberty!

DWARF.    Heaven bless the knight
That thus relieves poor errant gentlewomen!    *Exit* [*with Rafe*].

WIFE. Ay, marry, Rafe, this has some savor in 't; I would see the proudest of them all offer to carry his books after him. But, George, I will not have him go away so soon; I shall be sick if he go away, that I shall. Call Rafe again, George, call Rafe again; I prithee, sweetheart, let him come fight before me, and let's ha' some [90 drums and some trumpets, and let him kill all that comes near him, and thou lov'st me, George!

CIT. Peace a little, bird; he shall kill them all, and they were twenty more on 'em than there are.

### Enter Jasper.

JASP. Now, Fortune, if thou beest not only ill,
Show me thy better face, and bring about

Thy desperate wheel, that I may climb at length,    99
And stand. This is our place of meeting,
If love have any constancy. O age
Where only wealthy men are counted happy!
How shall I please thee, how deserve thy smiles,
When I am only rich in misery?
My father's blessing and this little coin
Is my inheritance—a strong revenue!
From earth thou art, and to the earth I give thee.    [*Throws away the money.*]
There grow and multiply, whilst fresher air
Breeds me a fresher fortune.—(*Spies the casket.*)  How! Illusion?
What, hath the devil coined himself before me?    110
'Tis metal good; it rings well. I am waking,
And taking too, I hope. Now, God's dear blessing
Upon his heart that left it here!  'Tis mine;
These pearls, I take it, were not left for swine.    *Exit* [*with the casket*].

WIFE. I do not like that this unthrifty youth should embezzle away the money; the poor gentlewoman his mother will have a heavy heart for it, God knows.

CIT. And reason good, sweetheart.    119

WIFE. But let him go; I'll tell Rafe a tale in 's ear shall fetch him again with a wanion,[1] I warrant him, if he be above ground; and besides, George, here are a number of sufficient gentlemen can witness, and myself, and yourself, and the musicians, if we be called in question. But here comes Rafe, George; thou shalt hear him speak as [2] he were an emperal.[3]

### [SCENA TERTIA.

*Another part of the forest.*]

*Enter Rafe and Dwarf.*

RAFE. Comes not Sir Squire again?

DWARF.    Right courteous knight,
Your squire doth come, and with him comes the lady,

---

[1] Vengeance.
[2] From 1635 edn.; original reads *an*.
[3] Imperial, *i.e.*, emperor.

*Enter Mistress Merr[ythought] and Michael
and Squire.*

For and [1] the Squire of Damsels, as I
take it.

RAFE. Madam, if any service or devoir
Of a poor errant knight may right your
wrongs,
Command it; I am prest [2] to give you
succor,
For to that holy end I bear my armor.

MIST. MER. Alas, sir, I am a poor
gentlewoman, and I have lost my money
in this forest!                          10

RAFE. Desert, you would say, lady; and
not lost
Whilst I have sword and lance. Dry
up your tears,
Which ill befits the beauty of that face,
And tell the story, if I may request it,
Of your disastrous fortune.

MIST. MER. Out, alas! I left a thousand pound, a thousand pound, e'en all
the money I had laid up for this youth,
upon the sight of your mastership—you
looked so grim, and, as I may say it, [20
saving your presence, more like a giant
than a mortal man.

RAFE. I am as you are, lady; so are they
All mortal. But why weeps this gentle
squire?

MIST. MER. Has he not cause to weep,
do you think, when he hath lost his inheritance?

RAFE. Young hope of valor, weep not;
I am here
That will confound thy foe, and pay it
dear                                     29
Upon his coward head that dares deny
Distresséd squires and ladies equity.
I have but one horse, on which shall ride
This lady fair behind me, and, before,
This courteous squire. Fortune will
give us more
Upon our next adventure. Fairly speed
Beside us, squire and dwarf, to do us
need!                          *Exeunt.*

CIT. Did not I tell you, Nell, what
your man would do? By the faith of my
body, wench, for clean action and good
delivery they may all cast their caps [40
at him.[3]

WIFE. And so they may, i' faith, for,
I dare speak it boldly, the twelve companies of London cannot match him, timber for timber.[4] Well, George, and he be
not inveigled by some of these paltry players, I ha' much marvel. But, George, we
ha' done our parts, if the boy have any
grace to be thankful.

CIT. Yes, I warrant thee, duckling.  50

[SCENA QUARTA.

*Another part of the forest.*]

*Enter Humphrey and Luce.*

HUM. Good Mistress Luce, however I in
fault am
For your lame horse, you're welcome
unto Waltham;
But which way now to go, or what to
say,
I know not truly, till it be broad day.

LUCE. O, fear not, Master Humphrey;
I am guide
For this place good enough.

HUM.                    Then up and ride;
Or, if it please you, walk, for your repose;
Or sit, or, if you will, go pluck a rose [5]—
Either of which shall be indifferent
To your good friend and Humphrey,
whose consent                            10
Is so entangled ever to your will
As the poor harmless horse is to the mill.

LUCE. Faith, and you say the word, we'll
e'en sit down,
And take a nap.

HUM.            'Tis better in the town,
Where we may nap together, for, believe me,
To sleep without a snatch [6] would mickle
grieve me.

LUCE. You're merry, Master Humphrey.

HUM.                          So I am,
And have been ever merry from my dam.

LUCE. Your nurse had the less labor.

HUM.                        Faith, it may be,
Unless it were by chance I did beray [7]
me.                                      20

*Enter Jasper.*

JASP. Luce! Dear friend Luce!

LUCE.                    Here, Jasper.

---

[1] And also.
[2] Ready.          [3] Take off their hats to him.
[4] Man for man.              [6] Snack.
[5] A euphemism for *defecate.*    [7] Befoul.

JASP.                    You are mine.
HUM. If it be so, my friend, you use me
fine.
What do you think I am?
JASP.                    An arrant noddy.
HUM. A word of obloquy! Now, by God's
body,
I'll tell thy master, for I know thee well.
JASP. Nay, and you be so forward for to
tell,
Take that, and that! [*Beats him.*] And
tell him, sir, I gave it,
And say I paid you well.
HUM.                    O, sir, I have it,
And do confess the payment! Pray, be
quiet.
JASP. Go, get you to your nightcap
and the diet                    30
To cure your beaten bones.
LUCE.                    Alas, poor Humphrey!
Get thee some wholesome broth, with
sage and comfrey,[1]
A little oil of roses and a feather
To noint[2] thy back withal.
HUM.               When I came hether,[3]
Would I had gone to Paris with John
Dory![4]
LUCE. Farewell, my pretty nump;[5] I am
very sorry
I cannot bear thee company.
HUM.                    Farewell!
The devil's dam was ne'er so banged in
hell.     *Exeunt. Manet[6] Humphrey.*

WIFE. This young Jasper will prove me
anotherthings,[7] a my conscience, and    [40
he may be suffered. George, dost not see,
George, how a swaggers, and flies at the
very heads a folks, as he were a dragon?
Well, if I do not do his lesson[8] for wronging the poor gentleman, I am no true
woman. His friends that brought him
up might have been better occupied, iwis,
than ha' taught him these fegaries;[9] he's
e'en in the high way to the gallows, God
bless him!                    50
CIT. You're too bitter, cunny; the
young man may do well enough for all
this.

WIFE. Come hither, Master Humphrey;
has he hurt you? Now, beshrew his fingers
for 't! Here, sweetheart, here's some green
ginger for thee. Now, beshrew my heart,
but a has peppernel[10] in 's head as big as
a pullet's egg! Alas, sweet lamb, how thy
temples beat! Take the peace on him,[11]  [60
sweetheart, take the peace on him.

*Enter a Boy.*

CIT. No, no; you talk like a foolish
woman. I'll ha' Rafe fight with him, and
swinge him up well-favoredly.—Sirrah
Boy, come hither. Let Rafe come in and
fight with Jasper.
WIFE. Ay, and beat him well; he's an
unhappy[12] boy.
BOY. Sir, you must pardon us; the plot
of our play lies contrary, and 'twill    [70
hazard the spoiling of our play.
CIT. Plot me no plots! I'll ha' Rafe
come out; I'll make your house too hot
for you else.
BOY. Why, sir, he shall; but, if anything fall out of order, the gentlemen must
pardon us.
CIT. Go your ways, Goodman Boy!—
[*Exit Boy.*] I'll hold[13] him a penny he shall
have his bellyful of fighting now. Ho,   [80
here comes Rafe! No more![14]

*Enter Rafe, Mistress Merry[thought], Mi-
chael, Squire, and Dwarf.*

RAFE. What knight is that, squire? Ask
him if he keep
The passage, bound by love of lady fair,
Or else but prickant.[15]
HUM.               Sir, I am no knight,
But a poor gentleman, that this same
night
Had stolen from me, on yonder green,
My lovely wife, and suffered (to be seen
Yet extant on my shoulders) such a
greeting
That whilst I live I shall think of that
meeting.

WIFE. Ay, Rafe, he beat him un-    [90
mercifully, Rafe; and thou spar'st him,
Rafe, I would thou wert hanged.
CIT. No more, wife, no more.

[1] A herb used to cure wounds.     [3] Hither.
[2] Anoint.     [4] The subject of a popular song.
[5] Blockhead, or, perhaps, a nickname for Humphrey.
[6] Remains.     [8] Teach him.
[7] Otherwise.     [9] Vagaries, pranks.
[10] A lump.
[11] Have him bound to keep the peace.
[12] Mischievous.     [14] *I.e.*, Silence!
[13] Wager.     [15] Pricking, traveling.

RAFE. Where is the caitiff wretch hath done this deed?
Lady, your pardon, that I may proceed
Upon the quest of this injurious knight.—
And thou, fair squire, repute me not the worse
In leaving the great venture of the purse
And the rich casket, till some better leisure.

*Enter Jasper and Luce.*

HUM. Here comes the broker[1] hath purloined my treasure.                    100
RAFE. Go, squire, and tell him I am here,
An errant knight-at-arms, to crave delivery
Of that fair lady to her own knight's arms.
If he deny, bid him take choice of ground,
And so defy him.
SQUIRE.            From the knight that bears
The golden pestle, I defy thee, knight,
Unless thou make fair restitution
Of that bright lady.
JASP.   Tell the knight that sent thee
He is an ass; and I will keep the wench,
And knock his headpiece.
RAFE.   Knight, thou art but dead,   110
If thou recall not thy uncourteous terms.

WIFE. Break 's pate, Rafe; break 's pate, Rafe, soundly!

JASP. Come, knight; I am ready for you.
Now your pestle
                *(Snatches away his pestle.)*
Shall try what temper, sir, your mortar 's of.
"With that he stood upright in his stirrups,
And gave the Knight of the Calfskin such a knock      [Knocks Rafe down.]
That he forsook his horse and down he fell;
And then he leaped upon him, and, plucking off his helmet—"
HUM. Nay, and my noble knight be down so soon,   120
Though I can scarcely go,[2] I needs must run.   *Exeunt*[3] *Humphrey and Rafe.*

[1] With a pun on the meaning of *pander.*
[2] Walk.
[3] Original reads *Exit.*

WIFE. Run, Rafe; run, Rafe! Run for thy life, boy! Jasper comes, Jasper comes!

JASP. Come, Luce, we must have other arms for you;
Humphrey and golden pestle, both adieu!                    *Exeunt.*

WIFE. Sure the devil (God bless us!) is in this springald![4] Why, George, didst ever see such a firedrake?[5] I am afraid my boy's miscarried;[6] if he be, though he were Master Merrythought's son a thou-  [130 sand times, if there be any law in England, I'll make some of them smart for 't.
CIT. No, no; I have found out the matter, sweetheart. Jasper is enchanted; as sure as we are here, he is enchanted. He could no more have stood in Rafe's hands than I can stand in my lord mayor's. I'll have a ring to discover all enchantments, and Rafe shall beat him yet. Be no more vexed, for it shall be so.   140

[SCENA QUINTA.

*Before the Bell Inn at Waltham.]*

*Enter Rafe, Squire, Dwarf, Mistress Merrythought, and Michael.*

WIFE. O, husband, here's Rafe again!— Stay, Rafe, let me speak with thee. How dost thou, Rafe? Art thou not shrewdly[7] hurt?—The foul great lungis[8] laid unmercifully on thee; there's some sugar candy for thee. Proceed; thou shalt have another bout with him.
CIT. If Rafe had him at the fencing school, if he did not make a puppy of him, and drive him up and down the school,  [10 he should ne'er come in my shop more.

MIST. MER. Truly, Master Knight of the Burning Pestle, I am weary.
MICH. Indeed-law, mother, and I am very hungry.
RAFE. Take comfort, gentle dame, and you, fair squire;
For in this desert there must needs be placed
Many strong castles held by courteous knights;

[4] Young man.
[5] Fiery dragon.
[6] Ruined.
[7] Shrewdly, severely.
[8] Lout.

And, till I bring you safe to one of those,
I swear by this my order ne'er to leave
you.                                    20

WIFE. Well said, Rafe!—George, Rafe
was ever comfortable,[1] was he not?
CIT. Yes, duck.
WIFE. I shall ne'er forget him. When
we had lost our child (you know it was
strayed almost, alone, to Puddle Wharf,
and the criers were abroad for it, and there
it had drowned itself but for a sculler),
Rafe was the most comfortablest to me.
"Peace, mistress," says he, "let it go;    [30
I'll get you another as good." Did he not,
George, did he not say so?
CIT. Yes, indeed did he, mouse.

DWARF. I would we had a mess of
pottage and a pot of drink, squire, and
were going to bed!
SQUIRE. Why, we are at Waltham
town's end, and that's the Bell Inn.
DWARF. Take courage, valiant knight,
    damsel, and squire!
I have discovered, not a stonecast off,    40
An ancient castle, held by the old knight
Of the most holy Order of the Bell,
Who gives to all knights-errant enter-
    tain.[2]
There plenty is of food, and all pre-
    pared
By the white hands of his own lady
    dear.
He hath three squires that welcome
    all his guests:
The first, high[t] [3] Chamberlino, who
    will see
Our beds prepared, and bring us snowy
    sheets,
Where never footman stretched his
    buttered hams; [4]
The second, hight Ta[p]stero, who will
    see                                50
Our pots full filléd, and no froth therein;
The third, a gentle squire, Ostlero hight,
Who will our palfreys slick with wisps
    of straw,
And in the maunger [5] put them oats
    enough,

And never grease their teeth with candle
snuff.[6]

WIFE. That same dwarf's a pretty
boy, but the squire's a groutnole.[7]

RAFE. Knock at the gates, my squire,
    with stately lance.    [Squire knocks.]

*Enter Tapster.*

TAP. Who's there?—You're welcome,
gentlemen. Will you see a room?    60
DWARF. Right courteous and valiant
Knight of the Burning Pestle, this is the
Squire Tapstero.
RAFE. Fair Squire Tapstero, I a wander-
    ing knight,
Hight of the Burning Pestle, in the
    quest
Of this fair lady's casket and wrought
    purse,
Losing myself in this vast wilderness,
Am to this castle well by fortune
    brought,
Where, hearing of the goodly entertain
Your knight of holy Order of the Bell    70
Gives to all damsels and all errant
    knights,
I thought to knock, and now am bold
    to enter.
TAP. An 't please you see a chamber,
you are very welcome.            *Exeunt.*

WIFE. George, I would have something
done, and I cannot tell what it is.
CIT. What is it, Nell?
WIFE. Why, George, shall Rafe beat
nobody again? Prithee, sweetheart, let
him.                                80
CIT. So he shall, Nell; and, if I join with
him, we'll knock them all.

[SCENA SEXTA.

*A room in Venturewell's house.*]

*Enter Humphrey and Merchant.*

WIFE. O, George, here's Master Humphrey again now, that lost Mistress Luce,
and Mistress Lucy's father. Master Hum-

---

[1] Comforting.                    [3] Called.
[2] Entertainment.
[4] The calves of running footmen were greased
to prevent cramps.            [5] Manger.

[6] An ostler's trick to keep horses from eating
their feed.
[7] Blockhead.

phrey will do somebody's errant,[1] I'll warrant him.

HUM. Father, it's true in arms I ne'er shall clasp her,
For she is stol'n away by your man Jasper.

WIFE. I thought he would tell him.

MERCH. Unhappy that I am, to lose my child!                                              9
Now I begin to think on Jasper's words,
Who oft hath urged to me thy foolishness.
Why didst thou let her go? Thou lov'st her not,
That wouldst bring home thy life, and not bring her.

HUM. Father, forgive me.  Shall I tell you true?
Look on my shoulders; they are black and blue.
Whilst to and fro fair Luce and I were winding,
He came and basted me with a hedge binding.

MERCH. Get men and horses straight; we will be there
Within this hour.  You know the place again?

HUM. I know the place where he my loins did swaddle;                                    20
I'll get six horses, and to each a saddle.

MERCH. Meantime I'll go talk with Jasper's father.                    *Exeunt.*

WIFE. George, what wilt thou lay with me now, that Master Humphrey has not Mistress Luce yet?  Speak, George, what wilt thou lay with me?

CIT. No, Nell; I warrant thee Jasper is at Puckeridge with her by this.

WIFE. Nay, George, you must consider Mistress Lucy's feet are tender; and [30 besides 'tis dark; and, I promise you truly, I do not see how he should get out of Waltham Forest with her yet.

CIT. Nay, cunny, what wilt thou lay with me that Rafe has her not yet?

WIFE. I will not lay against Rafe, honey, because I have not spoken with him. But look, George; peace! Here comes the merry old gentleman again.

[SCENA SEPTIMA.

*A room in Merrythought's house.*]

*Enter Old Merrythought.*

OLD MER. [*Singing.*]

When it was grown to dark midnight,
    And all were fast asleep,
In came Margaret's grimely[2] ghost,
    And stood at William's feet.

I have money, and meat and drink beforehand, till tomorrow at noon; why should I be sad?  Methinks I have half a dozen jovial spirits within me!          [*Sings.*]

I am three merry men, and three merry men!

To what end should any man be sad  [10 in this world?  Give me a man that, when he goes to hanging, cries, "Troll[3] the black bowl to me!"—and a woman that will sing a catch in her travail!  I have seen a man come by my door with a serious face, in a black cloak, without a hatband, carrying his head as if he looked for pins in the street; I have looked out of my window half a year after, and have spied that man's head upon London Bridge.[4]  [20 'Tis vile.  Never trust a tailor that does not sing at his work; his mind is of nothing but filching.

WIFE. Mark this, George; 'tis worth noting: Godfrey my tailor, you know, never sings, and he had fourteen yards to make this gown; and, I'll be sworn, Mistress Pennistone the draper's wife had one made with twelve.                                          29

OLD MER. [*Singing.*]

'Tis mirth that fills the veins with blood,
More than wine, or sleep, or food.
Let each man keep his heart at ease;
No man dies of that disease.
He that would his body keep
From diseases, must not weep;
But whoever laughs and sings,
Never he his body brings
Into fevers, gouts, or rheums,

Or ling'ringly his lungs consumes,
Or meets with achës in the bone,        40
Or catarrhs or griping stone,
But contented lives for aye.
The more he laughs, the more he may.

WIFE. Look, George; how say'st thou
by this, George? Is 't not a fine old man?—
Now, God's blessing a thy sweet lips!—
When wilt thou be so merry, George?
Faith, thou art the frowning'st little thing,
when thou art angry, in a country.

*Enter Merchant.*

CIT. Peace, cony; thou shalt see    [50
him taken down too, I warrant thee. Here's
Luce's father come now.

OLD MER. [*Singing.*]

As you came from Walsingham,
    From that holy land,
There met you not with my true love
    By the way as you came?

MERCH. O, Master Merrythought, my
    daughter's gone!
This mirth becomes you not; my daugh-
    ter's gone!
OLD MER. [*Singing.*]

Why, an if she be, what care I?
    Or let her come, or go, or tarry.    60

MERCH. Mock not my misery; it is your
    son
(Whom I have made my own, when all
    forsook him)
Has stol'n my only joy, my child, away.
OLD MER. [*Singing.*]

He set her on a milk-white steed,
    And himself upon a gray;
He never turned his face again,
    But he bore her quite away.

MERCH. Unworthy of the kindness I have
    shown
To thee and thine! Too late I well per-
    ceive
Thou art consenting to my daughter's
    loss.        70
OLD MER. **Your daughter!** What a
stir 's here wi' your daughter? Let her go,
think no more on her, but sing loud. If

both my sons were on the gallows, I would
sing,

Down, down, down—they fall
Down, and arise they never shall.

MERCH. O, might I behold her once again,
    And she once more embrace her agéd
        sire!
OLD MER. Fie, how scurvily this goes! [80
"And she once more embrace her agéd
sire"? You'll make a dog on her, will
ye? She cares much for her agéd sire, I
warrant you.        [*Sings.*]

She cares not for her daddy,
    Nor she cares not for her mammy,
For she is, she is, she is, she is
    My Lord of Lowgave's lassy.

MERCH. For this thy scorn I will pursue
    That son of thine to death.        90
OLD MER. Do; and when you ha' killed
him,        [*Sings.*]

Give him flowers enow, palmer, give him
    flowers enow;
Give him red and white, and blue, green,
    and yellow.

MERCH. I'll fetch my daughter—
OLD MER. I'll hear no more a your
daughter; it spoils my mirth.
MERCH. I say, I'll fetch my daughter.
OLD MER. [*Singing.*]

Was never man for lady's sake—
    Down, down—        100
Tormented as I, poor Sir Guy—
    De derry down—
For Lucy's sake, that lady bright—
    Down, down—
As ever men beheld with eye—
    De derry down.

MERCH. I'll be revenged, by heaven!
        *Exeunt.*
*Music.*

FINIS ACTUS SECUNDI.

WIFE. How dost thou like this, George?
CIT. Why, this is well, cony; but, if
Rafe were hot once, thou shouldst see
more.        111
WIFE. The fiddlers go again, husband.

CIT. Ay, Nell; but this is scurvy music. I gave the whoreson gallows money, and I think he has not got me the waits of Southward. If I hear 'em [1] not anan,[2] I'll twinge him by the ears.—You musicians, play "Baloo"! [3]

WIFE. No, good George, let's ha' "Lachrymæ"!                    120

CIT. Why, this is it, cony.

WIFE. It's all the better, George. Now, sweet lamb, what story is that painted upon the cloth? The Confutation[4] of St. Paul?

CIT. No, lamb; that's [5] Rafe and Lucrece.

WIFE. Rafe and Lucrece? Which Rafe? Our Rafe?                    129

CIT. No, mouse; that was a Tartarian.[6]

WIFE. A Tartarian? Well, I would the fiddlers had done, that we might see our Rafe again!

ACTUS TERTIUS. SCENA PRIMA.

[*Waltham Forest.*]

*Enter Jasper and Luce.*

JASP. Come, my dear dear; though we
      have lost our way,
   We have not lost ourselves.   Are you
      not weary
   With this night's wand'ring, broken
      from your rest,
   And frighted with the terror that at-
      tends
   The darkness of this [7] wild unpeopled
      place?

LUCE. No, my best friend; I cannot either
      fear,
   Or entertain a weary thought, whilst
      you
   (The end of all my full desires) stand
      by me.
   Let them that lose their hopes, and live
      to languish                    9
   Amongst the number of forsaken lovers,
   Tell the long, weary steps, and number
      time,

[1] Original reads *him*.
[2] Anon, at once.
[3] A ballad tune.
[4] Her blunder for *Conversion*.
[5] From 1635 edn.   Original reads *that*.
[6] His blunder for *Tarquin*, who raped Lucrece.
*Tartarian* was also a cant term for *thief*.
[7] From 1635 edn.   Original has *these*.

Start at a shadow, and shrink up their
      blood,
   Whilst I, possessed with all content
      and quiet,
   Thus take my pretty love, and thus em-
      brace him.                    [*Embraces him.*]

JASP. You have caught me, Luce, so fast
      that, whilst I live,
   I shall become your faithful prisoner,
   And wear these chains forever.   Come,
      sit down,
   And rest your body, too-too delicate
   For these disturbances.   [*They sit down.*]
   So, will you sleep?
   Come, do not be more able [8] than you
      are;                    20
   I know you are not skillful in these
      watches,
   For women are no soliders.   Be not nice,[9]
   But take it;[10] sleep, I say.

LUCE.                    I cannot sleep;
   Indeed, I cannot, friend.

JASP.                    Why, then we'll sing,
   And try how that will work upon our
      senses.

LUCE. I'll sing, or say, or anything but
      sleep.

JASP. Come, little mermaid, rob me of
      my heart
   With that enchanting voice.

LUCE.                    You mock me, Jasper.

SONG

JASP. Tell me, dearest, what is love?
LUCE. 'Tis a lightning from above;                    30
      'Tis an arrow; 'tis a fire;
      'Tis a boy they call Desire;
         'Tis a smile
         Doth beguile
JASP. The poor hearts of men that prove.

   Tell me more, are women true?
LUCE. Some love change, and so do you.
JASP. Are they fair and never kind?
LUCE. Yes, when men turn with the wind.
JASP.    Are they froward?                    40
LUCE.       Ever toward,[11]
   Those that love, to love anew.

JASP. Dissemble it no more; I see the god
   Of heavy sleep lay on his heavy mace
   Upon your eyelids.
LUCE.       I am very heavy.   [*Sleeps.*]

[8] Capable of endurance.   [10] Acquiesce, agree.
[9] Foolish.       [11] Apt.

JASP. Sleep, sleep; and quiet rest crown
    thy sweet thoughts!
    Keep from her fair blood distempers,
      startings,
    Horrors, and fearful shapes! Let all her
      dreams
    Be joys and chaste delights, embraces,
      wishes,
    And such new pleasures as the ravished
      soul                     50
    Gives to the senses!—So; my charms
      have took.—
    Keep her, you powers divine, whilst I
      contemplate
    Upon the wealth and beauty of her mind!
    She is only fair and constant, only kind,
    And only to thee, Jasper. O, my joys!
    Whither will you transport me? Let
      not fullness
    Of my poor buried hopes come up to-
      gether
    And overcharge my spirits! I am weak.
    Some say (however ill) the sea and
      women
    Are governed by the moon; both ebb
      and flow,                60
    Both full of changes; yet to them that
      know,
    And truly judge, these but opinions are,
    And heresies, to bring on pleasing war
    Between our tempers, that without
      these were
    Both void of after-love and present
      fear,
    Which are the best of Cupid. O, thou
      child
    Bred from despair, I dare not enter-
      tain thee,
    Having a love without the faults of
      women,
    And greater in her perfect goods than
      men—
    Which to make good, and please my-
      self the stronger,       70
    Though certainly I am certain of her
      love,
    I'll try her, that the world and memory
    May sing to aftertimes her constancy.—
                  [*Draws his sword.*]
    Luce! Luce! Awake!
LUCE.       Why do you fright me, friend,
    With those distempered looks? What
      makes [1] your sword

[1] Does.

Drawn in your hand? Who hath of-
    fended you?
I prithee, Jasper, sleep; thou art wild
    with watching.
JASP. Come, make your way to heaven,
    and bid the world,
    With all the villainies that stick upon it,
    Farewell; you're for another life.
LUCE.              O, Jasper,  80
    How have my tender years committed
      evil,
    Especially against the man I love,
    Thus to be cropped untimely?
JASP.                Foolish girl,
    Canst thou imagine I could love his
      daughter
    That flung me from my fortune into
      nothing?
    Dischargéd me his service, shut the
      doors
    Upon my poverty, and scorned my
      prayers,
    Sending me, like a boat without a mast,
    To sink or swim? Come; by this hand
      you die.
    I must have life and blood to satisfy  90
    Your father's wrongs.

WIFE. Away, George, away! Raise
the watch at Ludgate, and bring a mittimus from the justice for this desperate
villain!—Now, I charge you, gentlemen,
see the king's peace kept!—O, my heart,
what a varlet's this to offer manslaughter
upon the harmless gentlewoman!
CIT. I warrant thee, sweetheart, we'll
have him hampered.             100

LUCE. O, Jasper, be not cruel!
    If thou wilt kill me, smile, and do it
      quickly,
    And let not many deaths appear before
      me.
    I am a woman, made of fear and love,
    A weak, weak woman; kill not with
      thy eyes;
    They shoot me through and through.
      Strike, I am ready;
    And, dying, still I love thee.

*Enter Merchant, Humphrey, and his Men.*
MERCH.               Whereabouts?
JASP. [*Aside.*] No more of this; now to
    myself again.

Hum. There, there he stands, with sword,
    like martial knight,
  Drawn in his hand; therefore beware
    the fight,            110
  You that be wise, for, were I good Sir
    Bevis,
  I would not stay his coming, by your
    leavës.
Merch. Sirrah, restore my daughter!
Jasp.                 Sirrah, no.
Merch. Upon him, then!
[*They set upon Jasper and take Luce from
him.*]

Wife. So; down with him, down with
him, down with him! Cut him i' th' leg,
boys, cut him i' th' leg!

Merch. Come your ways, minion; I'll
    provide a cage
  For you, you're grown so tame.—Horse
    her away.            119
Hum. Truly, I'm glad your forces have
    the day.    *Exeunt. Manet Jasper.*
Jasp. They are gone, and I am hurt; my
    love is lost,
  Never to get again. O, me unhappy!
  Bleed, bleed and die! I cannot. O, my
    folly,
  Thou hast betrayed me! Hope, where
    art thou fled?
  Tell me, if thou beest anywhere remain-
    ing.
  Shall I but see my love again? O, no!
  She will not deign to look upon her
    butcher,
  Nor is it fit she should; yet I must
    venter.
  O, Chance, or Fortune, or whate'er
    thou art
  That men adore for powerful, hear my
    cry,             130
  And let me loving live, or losing die!
                    *Exit.*

Wife. Is a gone, George?
Cit. Ay, cony.
Wife. Marry, and let him go, sweetheart. By the faith a my body, a has put
me into such a fright that I tremble (as
they say) as 'twere an aspine leaf. Look
a my little finger, George, how it shakes.
Now, i' truth, every member of my body
is the worse for 't.         140

Cit. Come, hug in mine arms, sweet
mouse; he shall not fright thee any
more. Alas, mine own dear heart, how it
quivers!

[Scena Secunda.

*Before the Bell Inn at Waltham.*]

*Enter Mistress Merrythought, Rafe, Michael,
Squire, Dwarf, Host, and a Tapster.*

Wife. O, Rafe! How dost thou, Rafe?
How hast thou slept tonight?[1] Has the
knight used thee well?
Cit. Peace, Nell; let Rafe alone.

Tap. Master, the reckoning is not paid.
Rafe. Right courteous knight, who, for
    the order's sake
  Which thou hast ta'en, hang'st out the
    holy Bell,
  As I this flaming pestle bear about,
  We render thanks to your puissant self,
  Your beauteous lady, and your gentle
    squires           10
  For thus refreshing of our wearied limbs,
  Stiffened with hard achievements in
    wild desert.
Tap. Sir, there is twelve shillings to pay.
Rafe. Thou merry Squire Tapstero,
    thanks to thee
  For comforting our souls with double
    jug;
  And, if advent'rous fortune prick thee
    forth,
  Thou jovial squire, to follow feats of
    arms,
  Take heed thou tender[2] every lady's
    cause,
  Every true knight, and every damsel
    fair;
  But spill the blood of treacherous Sara-
    cens,           20
  And false enchanters that with magic
    spells
  Have done to death full many a noble
    knight.
Host. Thou valiant Knight of the
Burning Pestle, give ear to me. There is
twelve shillings to pay, and, as I am a true
knight, I will not bate a penny.

Wife. George, I pray thee, tell me,
must Rafe pay twelve shillings now?

[1] Last night.         [2] Treat with care.

Cit. No, Nell, no; nothing but the old knight is merry with Rafe.    30

Wife. O, is 't nothing else? Rafe will be as merry as he.

Rafe. Sir Knight, this mirth of yours becomes you well;
But, to requite this liberal courtesy,
If any of your squires will follow arms,
He shall receive from my heroic hand
A knighthood, by the virtue of this pestle.

Host. Fair knight, I thank you for your noble offer;
Therefore, gentle knight,
Twelve shillings you must pay, or I must cap [1] you.    40

Wife. Look, George! Did not I tell thee as much? The Knight of the Bell is in earnest. Rafe shall not be beholding [2] to him; give him his money, George, and let him go snick up.

Cit. Cap Rafe? No.—Hold your hand, Sir Knight of the Bell; there's your money. [Gives money.] Have you anything to say to Rafe now? Cap Rafe?

Wife. I would you should know it,  [50 Rafe has friends that will not suffer him to be capped for ten times so much, and ten times to the end of that.—Now take thy course, Rafe.

Mist. Mer. Come, Michael; thou and I will go home to thy father. He hath enough left to keep us a day or two, and we'll set fellows abroad to cry [3] our purse and our casket. Shall we, Michael?

Mich. Ay, I pray, mother; in truth  [60 my feet are full of chilblains with traveling.

Wife. Faith, and those chilblains are a foul trouble. Mistress Merrythought, when your youth comes home, let him rub all the soles of his feet, and the heels, and his ankles, with a mouse skin; or, if none of your people can catch a mouse, when he goes to bed, let him roll his feet in the warm embers, and, I warrant you, he  [70 shall be well; and you may make him put his fingers between his toes, and smell to

them; it's very sovereign for his head, if he be costive.

Mist. Mer. Master Knight of the Burning Pestle, my son Michael and I bid you farewell. I thank your worship heartily for your kindness.

Rafe. Farewell, fair lady, and your tender squire.
If, pricking through these deserts, I do hear    80
Of any traitorous knight, who through his guile
Hath light [4] upon your casket and your purse,
I will despoil him of them, and restore them.

Mist. Mer. I thank your worship.
    *Exit with Michael.*

Rafe. Dwarf, bear my shield; squire, elevate my lance.
And now farewell, you Knight of holy Bell.

Cit. Ay, ay, Rafe, all is paid.

Rafe. But yet, before I go, speak, worthy knight,
If aught you do of sad [5] adventures know,
Where errant knight [6] may through his prowess win    90
Eternal fame, and free some gentle souls
From endless bonds of steel and ling'ring pain.

Host. Sirrah, go to Nick the barber, and bid him prepare himself, as I told you before, quickly.

Tap. I am gone, sir.    *Exit Tapster.*

Host. Sir Knight, this wilderness affordeth none
But the great venter, where full many a knight
Hath tried his prowess, and come off with shame,
And where I would not have you lose your life    100
Against no man, but furious fiend of hell.

Rafe. Speak on, Sir Knight; tell what he is and where,
For here I vow, upon my blazing badge,

[1] Arrest.    [2] Beholden.
[3] *I.e.*, have public criers announce the loss of.
[4] Lit.
[5] Important.    [6] Original reads *Knights*.

Never to blaze a day in quietness,
But bread and water will I only eat,
And the green herb and rock shall be
  my couch,
Till I have quelled [1] that man, or beast,
  or fiend
That works such damage to all errant
  knights.
HOST. Not far from hence, near to a
  craggy cliff,                              109
At the north end of this distresséd town,
There doth stand a lowly house,
Ruggedly builded, and in it a cave
In which an ugly giant now doth wone,[2]
Yclepéd Barbaroso;[3] in his hand
He shakes a naked lance of purest steel,
With sleeves turned up; and him be-
  fore he wears
A motley garment, to preserve his
  clothes
From blood of those knights which he
  massacres,
And ladies gent;[4] without his door doth
  hang
A copper basin on a prickant [5] spear,[6] 120
At which no sooner gentle knights can
  knock
But the shrill sound fierce Barbaroso
  hears,
And, rushing forth, brings in the errant
  knight
And sets him down in an enchanted
  chair;
Then with an engine,[7] which he hath
  prepared
With forty teeth, he claws his courtly
  crown,
Next makes him wink,[8] and underneath
  his chin
He plants a brazen piece of mighty
  bord,[9]
And knocks his bullets [10] round about
  his cheeks,
Whilst with his fingers and an instrument                                      130

With which he snaps his hair off he
  doth fill
The wretch's ears with a most hideous
  noise.
Thus every knight adventurer he doth
  trim,
And now no creature dares encounter
  him.
RAFE. In God's name, I will fight him.
  Kind sir,
Go but before me to this dismal cave,
Where this huge giant Barbaroso dwells,
And, by that virtue that [11] brave Rosi-
  cleer
That damnéd brood of ugly giants slew,
And Palmerin Frannarco overthrew, 140
I doubt not but to curb this traitor
  foul,
And to the devil send his guilty soul.
HOST. Brave-sprighted [12] knight, thus far
  I will perform
This your request: I'll bring you within
  sight
Of this most loathsome place inhabited
By a more loathsome man, but dare
  not stay,
For his main force soops [13] all he sees
  away.
RAFE. Saint George, set on before!
  March, squire and page!        *Exeunt.*

WIFE. George, dost think Rafe will
confound the giant?                        150
CIT. I hold my cap to a farthing he
does. Why, Nell, I saw him wrastle with
the great Dutchman, and hurl him.
WIFE. Faith, and that Dutchman was
a goodly man, if all things were answerable to his bigness. And yet they say there
was a Scotchman higher than he, and that
they two and a knight met, and saw one
another for nothing. But of all the sights
that ever were in London, since I was  [160
married, methinks the little child that was
so fair grown about the members was the
prettiest; that and the hermaphrodite.
CIT. Nay, by your leave, Nell, Ninivy [14]
was better.
WIFE. Ninivy! O, that was the story
of Jone and the wall,[15] was it not, George?
CIT. Yes, lamb.

---

[1] Killed.
[2] Dwell.
[3] Called Redbeard.
[4] Gentle, noble.
[5] With point upward.
[6] The basin and spear advertised the barber-surgeon.
[7] Instrument, *i.e.*, comb.
[8] *I.e.*, close his eyes to anoint them with per-fume.
[9] Circumference. The barber's basin, which was held up by the customer, had a semicircular opening to fit around his neck.
[10] Balls of soap.
[11] By which.  [12] Brave-spirited.  [13] Sweeps.
[14] A popular puppet show about Nineveh.
[15] *I.e.*, Jonah and the whale.

[SCENA TERTIA.

*Before Merrythought's house.*]

*Enter Mistress Merrythought.*

WIFE. Look, George, here comes Mistress Merrythought again! And I would have Rafe come and fight with the giant; I tell you true, I long to see 't.

CIT. Good Mistress Merrythought, be-gone, I pray you, for my sake; I pray you, forbear a little; you shall have audience presently. I have a little business.

WIFE. Mistress Merrythought, if it please you to refrain your passion a [10 little, till Rafe have despatched the giant out of the way, we shall think ourselves much bound to you. I thank you, good Mistress Merrythought.

*Exit Mist[ress] Merrythou[ght].*

*Enter a Boy.*

CIT. Boy, come hither. Send away Rafe and this whoreson giant quickly.

BOY. In good faith, sir, we cannot; you'll utterly spoil our play, and make it to be hissed; and it cost money; you will not suffer us to go on with our plot.— [20 I pray, gentlemen, rule him.

CIT. Let him come now and despatch this, and I'll trouble you no more.

BOY. Will you give me your hand of that?

WIFE. Give him thy hand, George, do; and I'll kiss him. I warrant thee, the youth means plainly.[1]

BOY. I'll send him to you presently.

WIFE. [*Kissing him.*] I thank you, [30 little youth.—(*Exit Boy.*) Faith, the child hath a sweet breath, George; but I think it be troubled with the worms. *Carduus Benedictus* [2] and mare's milk were the only thing in the world for 't.—O, Rafe's here, George!—God send thee good luck, Rafe!

[SCENA QUARTA.

*Before a barber's shop.*]

*Enter Rafe, Host, Squire, and Dwarf.*

HOST. Puissant knight, yonder his mansion is.

Lo, where the spear and copper basin are!

Behold that string, on which hangs many a tooth,

Drawn from the gentle jaw of wand'ring knights!

I dare not stay to sound;[3] he will appear.    *Exit Host.*

RAFE. O, faint not, heart! Susan, my lady dear,

The cobbler's maid in Milk Street, for whose sake

I take these arms, O, let the thought of thee

Carry thy knight through all adventerous deeds;

And, in the honor of thy beauteous self,    10

May I destroy this monster Barbaroso!—

Knock, squire, upon the basin till it break

With the shrill strokes, or till the giant speak. [*Squire knocks upon the basin.*]

*Enter Barber.*

WIFE. O, George, the giant, the giant!— Now, Rafe, for thy life!

BARBER. What fond unknowing wight is this that dares

So rudely knock at Barbaroso's cell,

Where no man comes but leaves his fleece behind?

RAFE. I, traitorous caitiff, who am sent by fate

To punish all the sad enormities    20

Thou hast committed against ladies gent

And errant knights. Traitor to God and men,

Prepare thyself! This is the dismal hour

Appointed for thee to give strict account

Of all thy beastly, treacherous villainies

BARBER. Foolhardy knight, full soon thou shalt aby [4]

This fond reproach; thy body will I bang;    *He takes down his pole.*

And, lo, upon that string thy teeth shall hang!

Prepare thyself, for dead soon shalt thou be.

RAFE. Saint George for me!    *They fight.*

BARBER.    Gargantua for me!    30

WIFE. To him, Rafe, to him! Hold up the giant; set out thy leg before, Rafe!

CIT. Falsify [1] a blow, Rafe, falsify a blow! The giant lies open on the left side.

WIFE. Bear 't off, bear 't off still! There, boy!—O, Rafe's almost down, Rafe's almost down!

RAFE. Susan, inspire me! Now have up again.

WIFE. Up, up, up, up, up! So, Rafe! Down with him, down with him, Rafe!

CIT. Fetch him o'er the hip, boy!   41
[*Rafe knocks the Barber down.*]

WIFE. There, boy! Kill, kill, kill, kill, kill, Rafe!

CIT. No, Rafe; get all out of him first.

RAFE. Presumptuous man, see to what desperate end
Thy treachery hath brought thee! The just gods,
Who never prosper those that do despise them,
For all the villainies which thou hast done
To knights and ladies, now have paid thee home
By my stiff arm, a knight adventurous.   50
But say, vile wretch, before I send thy soul
To sad Avernus, whither it must go,
What captives hold'st thou in thy sable cave?

BARBER. Go in, and free them all; thou hast the day.

RAFE. Go, squire and dwarf, search in this dreadful cave,
And free the wretched prisoners from their bonds.
*Exeunt [2] Squire and Dwarf.*

BARBER. I crave for mercy, as thou art a knight,
And scorn'st to spill the blood of those that beg.

RAFE. Thou showed'st no mercy, nor shalt thou have any;
Prepare thyself, for thou shalt surely die.   60

Enter Squire, leading One winking, with a basin under his chin.

SQUIRE. Behold, brave knight, here is one prisoner,
Whom this wild man hath uséd as you see.

WIFE. This is the first wise word I heard the squire speak.

RAFE. Speak what thou art, and how thou hast been used,
That I may give [him][3] condign punishment.

1 KNI. I am a knight that took my journey post
Northward from London; and in courteous wise
This giant trained me to his loathsome den   69
Under pretense of killing of the itch;
And all my body with a powder strewed,
That smarts and stings, and cut away my beard,
And my curled locks wherein were ribands tied,
And with a water washed my tender eyes
(Whilst up and down about me still he skipped),
Whose virtue is that, till my eyes be wiped
With a dry cloth, for this my foul disgrace
I shall not dare to look a dog i' th' face.

WIFE. Alas, poor knight!—Relieve him, Rafe; relieve poor knights, whilst you live.

RAFE. My trusty squire, convey him to the town,   81
Where he may find relief.—Adieu, fair knight.   *Exit [1] Knight.*

Enter Dwarf, leading One with a patch o'er his nose.

DWARF. Puissant knight, of the Burning Pestle hight,
See here another wretch, whom this foul beast

---

1 Counterfeit.
2 Original reads *Exit*.

3 From 1635 edn. Original reads *That that I may give.*

Hath scorched [1] and scored in this inhuman wise.

RAFE. Speak me thy name, and eke thy
place of birth,
And what hath been thy usage in this
cave.

2 KNI. I am a knight, Sir Pockhole is
my name,
And by my birth I am a Londoner,
Free by my copy,[2] but my ancestors    90
Were Frenchmen [3] all; and, riding hard
this way
Upon a trotting horse, my bones did
ache,
And I, faint knight, to ease my weary
limbs,
Light at this cave, when straight this
furious fiend
With sharpest instrument of purest
steel
Did cut the gristle of my nose away,
And in the place this velvet plaster
stands.
Relieve me, gentle knight, out of his
hands!

WIFE. Good Rafe, relieve Sir Pockhole, and send him away, for in truth his
breath stinks.    101

RAFE. Convey him straight after the
other knight.—
Sir Pockhole, fare you well.

2 KNI.        Kind sir, good night. *Exit.*
                                    *Cries within.*

MAN. Deliver us!
WOMAN. Deliver us!

WIFE. Hark, George, what a woeful
cry there is! I think some woman lies-in
there.

MAN. Deliver us!
WOMAN. Deliver us!    110
RAFE. What ghastly noise is this? Speak,
Barbaroso,
Or, by this blazing steel, thy head goes
off!

BARBER. Prisoners of mine, whom I in
diet keep.
Send lower down into the cave,

[1] Scotched, cut.
[2] Certificate of citizenship.
[3] In allusion to the "French disease," a common name for the pox or syphilis.

And in a tub that's heated smoking hot
There may they find them, and deliver
them.

RAFE. Run, squire and dwarf; deliver
them with speed.
                *Exeunt Squire and Dwarf.*

WIFE. But will not Rafe kill this giant?
Surely I am afeard, if he let him go, he
will do as much hurt as ever he did.    120

CIT. Not so, mouse, neither, if he could
convert him.

WIFE. Ay, George, if he could convert
him; but a giant is not so soon converted
as one of us ordinary people. There's a
pretty tale of a witch that had the devil's
mark about her (God bless us!), that had
a giant to her son, that was called Lob-lie-
by-the-fire; didst never hear it, George?

*Enter Squire, leading a Man, with a glass
of lotion in his hand, and the Dwarf,
leading a Woman, with diet bread [4] and
drink.*

CIT. Peace, Nell, here comes the prisoners.

DWARF. Here be these pinèd wretches,
manful knight,    131
That for these six weeks have not seen
a wight.

RAFE. Deliver what you are, and how
you came
To this sad cave, and what your usage
was.

MAN. I am an errant knight that followed
arms
With spear and shield; and in my tender
years
I stricken was with Cupid's fiery shaft,
And fell in love with this my lady dear,
And stole her from her friends in Turn-
bull Street,[5]
And bore her up and down from town
to town,    140
Where we did eat and drink, and music
hear,
Till at the length at this unhappy town
We did arrive, and, coming to this cave,
This beast us caught and put us in a
tub,
Where we this two months sweat, and
should have done

[4] Special bread prepared for invalids.
[5] A disreputable district.

Another month, if you had not relieved us.

WOMAN. This bread and water hath our diet been,
Together with a rib cut from a neck
Of burnéd mutton; hard hath been our fare.                                                    149
Release us from this ugly giant's snare!

MAN. This hath been all the food we have received;
But only twice a day, for novelty,
He gave a spoonful of this hearty broth
                              *Pulls out a syringe.*
To each of us, through this same slender quill.

RAFE. From this infernal monster you shall go,
That useth knights and gentle ladies so!—
Convey them hence.
                          *Exeunt Man and Woman.*

CIT. Cony, I can tell thee, the gentlemen like Rafe.

WIFE. Ay, George, I see it well [160
enough.—Gentlemen, I thank you all heartily for gracing my man Rafe; and, I promise you, you shall see him oft'ner.

BARBER. Mercy, great knight! I do recant my ill,
And henceforth never gentle blood will spill.

RAFE. I give thee mercy; but yet shalt thou swear
Upon my burning pestle, to perform
Thy promise uttered.

BARBER. I swear and kiss.
                          *[Kisses the pestle.]*

RAFE.            Depart then, and amend.—
                          *[Exit Barber.]*
Come, squire and dwarf; the sun grows towards his set,                                        170
And we have many more adventures yet.                          *Exeunt.*

CIT. Now Rafe is in this humor I know he would ha' beaten all the boys in the house, if they had been set on him.

WIFE. Ay, George, but it is well as it is. I warrant you, the gentlemen do consider what it is to overthrow a giant. But look, George; here comes Mistress Merrythought and her son Michael.—Now you

are welcome, Mistress Merrythought; [180 now Rafe has done, you may go on.

[SCENA QUINTA.

*Before Merrythought's house.*]

*Enter Mistress Merrythought and Michael.*

MIST. MER. Mick, my boy—

MICH. Ay, forsooth, mother.

MIST. MER. Be merry, Mick; we are at home now, where, I warrant you, you shall find the house flung out at the windows. [*Music within.*] Hark! Hey, dogs, hey! This is the old world,[1] i' faith, with my husband. If I get in among 'em, I'll play 'em such a lesson that they shall have little list to come scraping hither [10 again.—Why, Master Merrythought! Husband! Charles Merrythought!

OLD MER. (*Within.*)

If you will sing, and dance, and laugh,
    And hollo, and laugh again,
And then cry, "There, boys, there!" why, then,
    One, two, three, and four,
We shall be merry within this hour.

MIST. MER. Why, Charles, do you not know your own natural wife? I say, open the door, and turn me out those mangy [20 companions; 'tis more than time that they were fellow and fellowlike with you. You are a gentleman, Charles, and an old man, and father of two children; and I myself (though I say it) by my mother's side niece to a worshipful gentleman and a conductor;[2] ha[3] has been three times in his majesty's service at Chester, and is now the fourth time, God bless him and his charge, upon his journey.               30

OLD MER. [*Singing.*]

    Go from my window, love, go;
    Go from my window, my dear!
The wind and the rain will drive you back again;
    You cannot be lodgéd here.

Hark you, Mistress Merrythought, you that walk upon adventures, and forsake your husband, because he sings with never

---

[1] Way.
[2] Military leader.                          [3] He.

a penny in his purse, what shall I think myself the worse? Faith, no; I'll be merry.

You come not here; here's none but [40 lads of mettle, lives of a hundred years and upwards; care never drunk their bloods, nor want made 'em warble, "Heigh-ho, my heart is heavy."

MIST. MER. Why, Mr.[1] Merrythought, what am I that you should laugh me to scorn thus abruptly? Am I not your fellow-feeler, as we may say, in all our miseries? Your comforter in health and sickness? Have I not brought you [50 children? Are they not like you, Charles? Look upon thine own image, hard-hearted man! And yet for all this—

OLD MER. (*Within.*)

> Begone, begone, my juggy,[2] my puggy, [3]
> Begone, my love, my dear!
> The weather is warm, 'twill do thee no harm;
> Thou canst not be lodgéd here.—

Be merry, boys! Some light music, and more wine!

WIFE. He's not in earnest, I hope, [60 George, is he?

CIT. What if he be, sweetheart?

WIFE. Marry, if he be, George, I'll make bold to tell him he's an ingrant [4] old man to use his bedfellow so scurvily.

CIT. What! How does he use her, honey?

WIFE. Marry, come up, Sir Saucebox! I think you'll take his part, will you not? Lord, how hot you are grown! You [70 are a fine man, an you had a fine dog; [5] it becomes you sweetly!

CIT. Nay, prithee, Nell, chide not, for, as I am an honest man and a true Christian grocer, I do not like his doings.

WIFE. I cry you mercy, then, George! You know we are all frail and full of infirmities.—D'e hear, Mr. Merry-thought? May I crave a word with you?

OLD MER. (*Within.*) Strike up [80 lively, lads!

WIFE. I had not thought, in truth, Mr. Merrythought, that a man of your age and discretion (as I may say), being a gentleman, and therefore known by your gentle conditions,[6] could have used so little respect to the weakness of his wife, for your wife is your own flesh, the staff of your age, your yokefellow, with whose help you draw through the mire of [90 this transitory world; nay, she's your own rib! And again—

OLD MER. [*Singing.*]

> I come not hither for thee to teach;
> I have no pulpit for thee to preach;
> I would thou hadst kissed me under the breech,
> As thou art a lady gay.

WIFE. Marry, with a vengeance! I am heartily sorry for the poor gentle-woman, but, if I were thy wife, i' faith, graybeard, i' faith—    100

CIT. I prithee, sweet honeysuckle, be content.

WIFE. Give me such words, that am a gentlewoman born! Hang him, hoary rascal! Get me some drink, George; I am almost molten with fretting. Now, be-shrew his knave's heart for it!

[*Exit Citizen.*]

OLD MER. Play me a light lavalto.[7] Come, be frolic. Fill the good fellows wine.    110

MIST. MER. Why, Mr. Merrythought, are you disposed to make me wait here? You'll open, I hope; I'll fetch them that shall open else.

OLD MER. Good woman, if you will sing, I'll give you something; if not—

### SONG

> You are no love for me, Margret;
> I am no love for you.—

Come aloft,[8] boys, aloft!

MIST. MER. Now a churl's fart in [120 your teeth, sir!—Come, Mick, we'll not trouble him; a shall not ding us i' th' teeth

---

[1] Master.
[2] Diminutive of Joan.
[3] Term of endearment.
[4] Wife's confusion of *ignorant* and *ingrate*.
[5] A mark of gentility.

[6] Qualities.    [8] Be merry.
[7] Lavolta, a lively dance.

with his bread and his broth, that he shall not.  Come, boy; I'll provide for thee, I warrant thee.  We'll go to Master Venterwell's, the merchant; I'll get his letter to mine host of the Bell in Waltham; there I'll place thee with the tapster.  Will not that do well for thee, Mick?  And let me alone for that old cuckoldly knave [130 your father; I'll use him in his kind,[1] I warrant ye.                    [*Exeunt.*

*Enter Citizen with beer.*]

WIFE.  Come, George, where's the beer?
CIT.  Here, love.
WIFE.  This old fornicating fellow will not out of my mind yet.—Gentlemen, I'll begin to you all; and I desire more of your acquaintance with all my heart.—[*Drinks.*] Fill the gentlemen some beer, George.

FINIS ACTUS TERTII.

*Music.*

ACTUS QUARTUS.  SCENA PRIMA.

[*A street.*]
*Boy danceth.*

WIFE.  Look, George, the little boy 's come again; methinks he looks something like the Prince of Orange in his long stocking, if he had a little harness[2] about his neck.  George, I will have him dance "Fading."—"Fading" is a fine jig, I'll assure you, gentlemen.—Begin, brother.—Now a capers, sweetheart!—Now a turn a th' toe, and then tumble!  Cannot you tumble, youth?                                      10
BOY.  No, indeed, forsooth.
WIFE.  Nor eat fire?
BOY.  Neither.
WIFE.  Why, then, I thank you heartily; there's twopence to buy you points[3] withal.
                                        [*Exit Boy.*]

*Enter Jasper and Boy.*

JASP.  There, boy, deliver this.  [*Gives a letter.*]  But do it well.
Hast thou provided me four lusty fellows, Able to carry me?  And art thou perfect In all thy business?

BOY.          Sir, you need not fear;   19
I have my lesson here, and cannot miss it.
The men are ready for you and what else
Pertains to this employment.
JASP.          There, my boy.  [*Gives money.*]
Take it, but buy no land.
BOY.                Faith, sir, 'twere rare
To see so young a purchaser.  I fly,
And on my wings carry your destiny.
                                        [*Exit.*
JASP.  Go and be happy!—Now, my latest hope,
Forsake me not, but fling thy anchor out,
And let it hold!  Stand fixed, thou rolling stone,                                  28
Till I enjoy my dearest!  Hear me, all
You powers, that rule in men, celestial!
                                        [*Exit.*

WIFE.  Go thy ways; thou art as crooked a sprig as ever grew in London.  I warrant him, he'll come to some naughty end or other, for his looks say no less.  Besides, his father (you know, George) is none of the best; you heard him take me up like a flirt-gill,[4] and sing bawdy songs upon me; but, i' faith, if I live, George—
CIT.  Let me alone, sweetheart; I have a trick in my head shall lodge him in the [40 Arches[5] for one year, and make him sing *peccavi*[6] ere I leave him; and yet he shall never know who hurt him neither.
WIFE.  Do, my good George, do!
CIT.  What shall we have Rafe do now, boy?
BOY.  You shall have what you will, sir.
CIT.  Why, so, sir, go and fetch me him then, and let the Sophy of Persia come and christen him a child.[7]                       50
BOY.  Believe me, sir, that will not do so well; 'tis stale; it has been had before at the Red Bull.[8]
WIFE.  George, let Rafe travel over great hills, and let him be very weary, and come to the King of Cracovia's house, covered with velvet; and there let the king's daughter stand in her window, all in beaten gold, combing her golden locks

---

[1] According to his own nature.
[2] Armor.
[3] Laces for fastening clothes.
[4] Loose woman.   [5] A prison.   [6] I have sinned.
[7] *I. e.,* a member of his nation. (The passage alludes to *The Travels of the Three English Brothers,* a play by Day, Rowley, and Wilkins.)
[8] A rival theater.

with a comb of ivory; and let her spy [60
Rafe, and fall in love with him, and come
down to him, and carry him into her
father's house; and then let Rafe talk
with her.

CIT. Well said, Nell; it shall be so.—
Boy, let's ha't done quickly.

BOY. Sir, if you will imagine all this
to be done already, you shall hear them
talk together; but we cannot present a
house covered with black velvet, and [70
a lady in beaten gold.

CIT. Sir Boy, let's ha't as you can, then.

BOY. Besides, it will show ill-favoredly
to have a grocer's prentice to court a
king's daughter.

CIT. Will it so, sir? You are well read
in histories! [1] I pray you, what was Sir
Dagonet? Was not he prentice to a grocer
in London? Read the play of *The Four
Prentices of London*,[2] where they toss [80
their pikes so. I pray you, fetch him in, sir,
fetch him in.

BOY. It shall be done.—[*To audience.*]
It is not our fault, gentlemen.        *Exit.*

WIFE. Now we shall see fine doings, I
warrant tee, George. O, here they come;
how prettily the King of Cracovia's
daughter is dressed!

[SCENA SECUNDA.

*A hall in the palace of the King of Moldavia.*]

*Enter Rafe and the Lady, Squire, and Dwarf.*

CIT. Ay, Nell, it is the fashion of that
country, I warrant tee.

LADY. Welcome, Sir Knight, unto my
        father's court,
King of Moldavia, unto me, Pompiona,
His daughter dear! But, sure, you do
        not like
Your entertainment, that will stay with
        us
No longer but a night.

RAFE.                Damsel right fair,
I am on many sad adventures bound,
That call me forth into the wilderness;
Besides, my horse's back is something
        galled,                        10
Which will enforce me ride a sober pace.
But many thanks, fair lady, be to you

[1] Fiction.        [2] By Thomas Heywood.

For using errant knight with courtesy!

LADY. But say, brave knight, what is your
        name and birth?

RAFE. My name is Rafe; I am an
        Englishman,
As true as steel, a hearty Englishman,
And prentice to a grocer in the Strond [3]
By deed indent,[4] of which I have one
        part;
But, Fortune calling me to follow arms,
On me this holy order I did take        20
Of Burning Pestle, which in all men's
        eyes
I bear, confounding ladies' enemies.

LADY. Oft have I heard of your brave
        countrymen,
And fertile soil, and store of wholesome
        food;
My father oft will tell me of a drink
In England found, and nippitato [5] called,
Which driveth all the sorrow from your
        hearts.

RAFE. Lady, 'tis true; you need not lay
        your lips
To better nippitato than there is.

LADY. And of a wild fowl he will often
        speak,                        30
Which     poudered [6]-beef-and-mustard
        calléd is;
For there have been great wars twixt us
        and you.
But truly, Rafe, it was not long [7] of me.
Tell me then, Rafe, could you contented
        be
To wear lady's favor in your shield?

RAFE. I am a knight of religious order,
And will not wear a favor of a lady's
That trusts in Antichrist and false
        traditions.

CIT. Well said, Rafe! Convert her, if
thou canst.                        40

RAFE. Besides, I have a lady of my own
In merry England, for whose virtuous
        sake
I took these arms; and Susan is her name,
A cobbler's maid in Milk Street, whom I
        vow
Ne'er to forsake whilst life and pestle last.

LADY. Happy that cobbling dame, whoe'er
        she be,

[3] Strand.                        [6] Salted.
[4] Indenture.                     [7] Because.
[5] Strong liquor.

That for her own, dear Rafe, hath gotten thee!
Unhappy I, that ne'er shall see the day
To see thee more, that bear'st my heart
away!

RAFE. Lady, farewell; I needs must take
my leave.                                    50
LADY. Hard-hearted Rafe, that ladies dost
deceive!

CIT. Hark thee, Rafe; there's money
for thee. [*Gives money.*] Give something
in the King of Cracovia's house; be not
beholding to him.

RAFE. Lady, before I go, I must remember
Your father's officers, who, truth to tell,
Have been about me very diligent.
Hold up thy snowy hand, thou princely
maid!
There's twelvepence for your father's
chamberlain;                                 60
And another shilling for his cook,
For, by my troth, the goose was roasted
well;
And twelvepence for your father's
horse keeper,
For nointing my horse' back, and for
his butter [1]
There is another shilling; to the maid
That washed my boothose [2] there's an
English groat,
And twopence to the boy that wiped my
boots;
And last, fair lady, there is for yourself
Threepence to buy you pins at Bumbo
Fair.
LADY. Full many thanks; and I will keep
them safe                                    70
Till all the heads be off, for thy sake,
Rafe.
RAFE. Advance, my squire and dwarf! I
cannot stay.
LADY. Thou kill'st my heart in parting
thus away.                          *Exeunt.*

WIFE. I commend Rafe yet, that he
will not stoop to a Cracovian; there's
properer [3] women in London than any are
there, iwis. But here comes Master Humphrey and his love again now, George.
CIT. Ay, cony; peace.

[1] Used to rub the horse's back.
[2] Leggings.                    [3] Handsomer.

[SCENA TERTIA.

*A room in Venturewell's house.*]

*Enter Merchant, Humphrey, Luce, and a*
*Boy.*

MERCH. Go, get you up; [4] I will not be
entreated;
And, gossip [5] mine, I'll keep you sure
hereafter
From gadding out again with boys and
unthrifts.[6]
Come, they are women's tears; I know
your fashion.—
Go, sirrah, lock her in, and keep the key
Safe as you love your life.—
                    *Exeunt* [7] *Luce and Boy.*
Now, my son Humphrey,
You may both rest assuréd of my love
In this, and reap your own desire.
HUM. I see this love you speak of, through
your daughter,
Although the hole be little, and here-
after                                        10
Will yield the like in all I may or can,
Fitting a Christian and a gentleman.
MERCH. I do believe you, my good son,
and thank you,
For 'twere an impudence to think you
flattered.
HUM. It were, indeed; but shall I tell you
why?
I have been beaten twice about the
lie.
MERCH. Well, son, no more of compliment.
My daughter
Is yours again; appoint the time and
take her.
We'll have no stealing for it; I myself
And some few of our friends will see
you married.                                 20
HUM. I would you would, i' faith, for, be
it known,
I ever was afraid to lie alone.
MERCH. Some three days hence, then.
HUM.            Three days! Let me see;
'Tis somewhat of the most; [8] yet I
agree,
Because I mean against [9] the appointed
day
To visit all my friends in new array.

[4] Upstairs.              [7] Original reads *Exit.*
[5] Relative.              [8] Rather long.
[6] Prodigals.            [9] In preparation for

*Enter Servant.*

SER. Sir, there's a gentlewoman without would speak with your worship.

MERCH. What is she?

SER. Sir, I asked her not. 30

MERCH. Bid her come in. [*Exit Servant.*]

*Enter Mistress Merrythought and Michael.*

MIST. MER. Peace be to your worship! I come as a poor suitor to you, sir, in the behalf of this child.

MERCH. Are you not wife to Merry-thought?

MIST. MER. Yes, truly. Would I had ne'er seen his eyes! Ha has undone me and himself and his children; and there he lives at home, and sings and hoits [40 and revels among his drunken companions! But, I warrant you, where to get a penny to put bread in his mouth he knows not; and therefore, if it like your worship, I would entreat your letter to the honest host of the Bell in Waltham that I may place my child under the protection of his tapster, in some settled course of life.

MERCH. I'm glad the heavens have heard my prayers. Thy husband,

When I was ripe in sorrows, laughed at me; 50

Thy son, like an unthankful wretch, I having

Redeemed him from his fall, and made him mine,

To show his love again first stole my daughter,

Then wronged this gentleman, and, last of all,

Gave me that grief had almost brought me down

Unto my grave, had not a stronger hand

Relieved my sorrows. Go, and weep as I did,

And be unpitied, for I here profess

An everlasting hate to all thy name.

MIST. MER. Will you so, sir? How [60 say you by that? —Come, Mick; let him keep his wind to cool his porridge. We'll go to thy nurse's, Mick; she knits silk stockings, boy; and we'll knit too, boy, and be beholding to none of them all.

*Exeunt Michael and Mother.*

*Enter a Boy with a letter.*

BOY. Sir, I take it you are the master of this house.

MERCH. How then, boy?

BOY. Then to yourself, sir, comes this letter. 70

MERCH. From whom, my pretty boy?

BOY. From him that was your servant; but no more

Shall that name ever be, for he is dead.

Grief of your purchased [1] anger broke his heart.

I saw him die, and from his hand received

This paper, with a charge to bring it hither.

Read it, and satisfy yourself in all.

LETTER

MERCH. "Sir, that I have wronged your love I must confess, in which I have purchased to myself, besides mine [80 own undoing, the ill opinion of my friends. Let not your anger, good sir, outlive me, but suffer me to rest in peace with your forgiveness. Let my body (if a dying man may so much prevail with you) be brought to your daughter, that she may truly know my hot flames are now buried, and withal receive a testimony of the zeal I bore her virtue. Farewell forever, and be ever happy! JASPER."

God's hand is great in this. I do forgive him; 91

Yet I am glad he's quiet, where I hope

He will not bite again.—Boy, bring the body,

And let him have his will, if that be all.

BOY. 'Tis here without, sir.

MERCH.              So, sir; if you please,

You may conduct it in; I do not fear it.

HUM. I'll be your usher, boy, for, though I say it,

He owed me something once, and well did pay it.          *Exeunt.*

*Enter Luce, alone.*

LUCE. If there be any punishment inflicted

Upon the miserable more than yet I feel,          100

[1] Acquired.

Let it together seize me, and at once
Press down my soul! I cannot bear the pain
Of these delaying tortures.—Thou that art
The end of all, and the sweet rest of all,
Come, come, O Death! Bring me to thy peace,
And blot out all the memory I nourish
Both of my father and my cruel friend!—
O, wretched maid, still living to be wretched,
To be a say [1] to Fortune in her changes,
And grow to number times and woes together,                              110
How happy had I been, if, being born,
My grave had been my cradle!

*Enter Servant.*

SER.                            By your leave,
Young mistress, here's a boy hath brought a coffin.
What a would say, I know not; but your father
Charged me to give you notice. Here they come.    [*Exit.*]

*Enter Two bearing a coffin, Jasper in it.*

LUCE. For me I hope 'tis come, and 'tis most welcome.
BOY. Fair mistress, let me not add greater grief
To that great store you have already. Jasper
(That whilst he lived was yours, now dead
And here enclosed) commanded me to bring                          120
His body hither, and to crave a tear
From those fair eyes (though he deserved not pity)
To deck his funeral, for so he bid me
Tell her for whom he died.
LUCE.               He shall have many.—
Good friends, depart a little, whilst I take
My leave of this dead man that once I loved. *Exeunt Coffin Carrier and Boy.*
Hold yet a little, life, and then I give thee
To thy first heavenly being. O, my friend!
Hast thou deceived me thus, and got before me?

[1] Subject for experiment.

I shall not long be after. But, believe me,                          130
Thou wert too cruel, Jasper, gainst thyself,
In punishing the fault I could have pardoned,
With so untimely death. Thou didst not wrong me,
But ever wert most kind, most true, most loving,
And I the most unkind, most false, most cruel!
Didst thou but ask a tear? I'll give thee all,
Even all my eyes can pour down, all my sighs,
And all myself. Before thou goest from me
There are but sparing rites; but, if thy soul                          139
Be yet about this place, and can behold
And see what I prepare to deck thee with,
It shall go up, borne on the wings of peace,
And satisfied. First will I sing thy dirge,
Then kiss thy pale lips, and then die myself,
And fill one coffin and one grave together.

SONG

Come, you whose loves are dead,
    And, whiles I sing,
    Weep and wring
Every hand, and every head
Bind with cypress and sad yew;                          150
Ribands black and candles blue
For him that was of men most true!

Come with heavy mourning,[2]
    And on his grave
    Let him have
Sacrifice of sighs and groaning;
Let him have fair flowers enow,
White and purple, green and yellow,
For him that was of men most true!

Thou sable cloth, sad cover of my joys,
I lift thee up, and thus I meet with death.                          161
[*Removes the cloth, and Jasper rises out of the coffin.*]
JASP. And thus you meet the living!
LUCE.            Save me, heaven!

[2] Moaning(?).

JASP. Nay, do not fly me, fair; I am no
    spirit.
Look better on me; do you know me yet?
LUCE. O, thou dear shadow of my friend!
JASP.               Dear substance,
    I swear I am no shadow. Feel my hand;
    It is the same it was. I am your Jasper,
    Your Jasper that's yet living, and yet
      loving.
    Pardon my rash attempt, my foolish
      proof                       169
    I put in practice of your constancy,
    For sooner should my sword have drunk
      my blood,
    And set my soul at liberty than drawn
    The least drop from that body, for
      which boldness
    Doom me to anything; if death, I take it,
    And willingly.
LUCE.      This death I'll give you for it.
                     [*Kisses him.*]
    So, now I am satisfied you are no spirit,
    But my own truest, truest, truest friend.
    Why do you come thus to me?
JASP.           First, to see you;
    Then to convey you hence.
LUCE.             It cannot be;
    For I am locked up here, and watched
      at all hours,                180
    That 'tis impossible for me to scape.
JASP. Nothing more possible.    Within
    this coffin
    Do you convey yourself. Let me alone;
    I have the wits of twenty men about me;
    Only I crave the shelter of your closet [1]
    A little, and then fear me [2] not. Creep
      in,
    That they may presently convey you
      hence.
    Fear nothing, dearest love; I'll be your
      second.
[*Luce places herself in the coffin and Jasper
          puts the cloth over her.*]
    Lie close. So; all goes well yet.—Boy!

[*Enter Coffin Carrier and Boy.*]

BOY.                 At hand, sir.
JASP. Convey away the coffin, and be wary.
BOY. 'Tis done already.
[*Exeunt Coffin Carrier and Boy with the
                 coffin.*]
JASP.        Now must I go conjure.   191
                        *Exit.*

[1] Private room.       [2] *I.e.*, for me.

*Enter Merchant.*

MERCH. Boy, boy!

[*Enter Boy.*]

BOY. Your servant, sir.
MERCH. Do me this kindness, boy.
Hold, here's a crown. Before thou bury
the body of this fellow, carry it to his
old merry father, and salute him from me,
and bid him sing; he hath cause.
BOY. I will, sir.                199
MERCH. And then bring me word what
tune he is in, and have another crown; but
do it truly. I have fitted him a bargain now
will vex him.
BOY. God bless your worship's health,
sir!
MERCH. Farewell, boy.       *Exeunt.*

[SCENA QUARTA.

*Before Merrythought's house.*]

*Enter Master Merrythought.*

WIFE. Ah, old Merrythought, art thou
there again? Let's hear some of thy songs.
OLD MER. [*Singing.*]

    Who can sing a merrier note
    Than he that cannot change a groat?

Not a denier [3] left, and yet my heart leaps!
I do wonder yet, as old as I am, that any
man will follow a trade, or serve, that may
sing and laugh, and walk the streets. My
wife and both my sons are I know not
where; I have nothing left, nor know I   [10
how to come by meat to supper; yet am
I merry still, for I know I shall find it upon
the table at six a-clock; therefore, hang
thought!                   [*Sings.*]

    I would not be a serving-man
      To carry the cloak bag still,
    Nor would I be a falconer
      The greedy hawks to fill;
    But I would be in a good house,
      And have a good master too;    20
    But I would eat and drink of the best,
      And no work would I do.

This is it that keeps life and soul together—
mirth; this is the philosophers' stone that
they write so much on, that keeps a man
ever young.

[3] Penny.

*Enter a Boy.*

BOY. Sir, they say they know all your money is gone, and they will trust you for no more drink.

OLD MER. Will they not?    Let [30 am [1] choose! The best is, I have mirth at home, and need not send abroad for that. Let them keep their drink to themselves.

[*Sings.*]

For Jillian of Berry, she dwells on a hill,
And she hath good beer and ale to sell,
And of good fellows she thinks no ill;
    And thither will we go now, now, now,
        now,
    And thither will we go now.

And, when you have made a little stay,
You need not ask what is to pay,    40
But kiss your hostess, and go your way;
    And thither, etc.

*Enter another Boy.*

2 BOY. Sir, I can get no bread for supper.

OLD MER. Hang bread and supper! Let's preserve our mirth, and we shall never feel hunger, I'll warrant you. Let's have a catch. Boy, follow me; come, sing this catch.

    Ho, ho, nobody at home!    50
    Meat, nor drink, nor money ha' we none.
        Fill the pot, Eedy,
        Never more need I.

OLD MER. So, boys, enough.    Follow me.    Let's change our place, and we shall laugh afresh.    *Exeunt.*

WIFE. Let him go, George; a shall not have any countenance from us, nor a good word from any i' th' company, if I may strike stroke in 't.[2]    60

CIT. No more a sha' not, love. But, Nell, I will have Rafe do a very notable matter now, to the eternal honor and glory of all grocers.—Sirrah! You there, boy! Can none of you hear?

[*Enter Boy.*]

BOY. Sir, your pleasure?

CIT. Let Rafe come out on May Day in the morning, and speak upon a conduit, with all his scarfs about him, and his feathers, and his rings, and his knacks.    70

[1] 'Em.    [2] *I.e.,* have anything to do with it.

BOY. Why, sir, you do not think of our plot; what will become of that, then?

CIT. Why, sir, I care not what become on 't. I'll have him come out, or I'll fetch him out myself; I'll have something done in honor of the city. Besides, he hath been long enough upon adventures. Bring him out quickly; or, if I come in amongst you—

BOY. Well, sir, he shall come out, but if our play miscarry, sir, you are like [80 to pay for 't.    *Exit Boy.*

CIT. Bring him away then!

WIFE. This will be brave, i' faith! George, shall not he dance the morris too, for the credit of the Strand?

CIT. No, sweetheart, it will be too much for the boy. O, there he is, Nell! He's reasonable well in reparel; but he has not rings enough.

*Enter Rafe [dressed as the Lord of the May].*

RAFE. London, to thee I do present the
    merry month of May;    90
Let each true subject be content to
    hear me what I say.
For from the top of conduit head, as
    plainly may appear,
I will both tell my name to you, and
    wherefore I came here.
My name is Rafe, by due descent though
    not ignoble I,
Yet far inferior to the flock of gracious
    grocery;[3]
And by the common counsel of my fellows in the Strand,
With gilded staff and crosséd scarf, the
    May Lord here I stand.
Rejoice, O English hearts, rejoice! Rejoice, O lovers dear!
Rejoice, O city, town, and country!
    Rejoice, eke every shire!
For now the fragrant flowers do spring
    and sprout in seemly sort,    100
The little birds do sit and sing, the
    lambs do make fine sport;
And now the birchen tree doth bud,
    that makes the schoolboy cry;
The morris rings, while hobbyhorse doth
    foot it featously; [4]
The lords and ladies now abroad, for
    their disport and play,

[3] A parody of part of the Ghost's opening speech in *The Spanish Tragedy.*
[4] Neatly, expertly.

Do kiss sometimes upon the grass, and
   sometimes in the hay;
Now butter with a leaf of sage is good
   to purge the blood;
Fly Venus and phlebotomy, for they
   are neither good;
Now little fish on tender stone begin
   to cast their bellies,[1]
And sluggish snails, that erst were mute,[2]
   do creep out of their shellës;
The rumbling rivers now do warm, for
   little boys to paddle;        110
The sturdy steed now goes to grass,
   and up they hang his saddle;
The heavy hart, the bellowing buck,
   the rascal,[3] and the pricket[4]
Are now among the yeoman's peas,
   and leave the fearful thicket.
And be like them, O you, I say, of this
   same noble town,
And lift aloft your velvet heads, and,
   slipping off your gown,
With bells on legs, and napkins[5] clean
   unto your shoulders tied,
With scarfs and garters as you please,
   and "Hey for our town!" cried,
March out, and show your willing minds,
   by twenty and by twenty,
To Hogsdon or to Newington, where ale
   and cakes are plenty;
And let it ne'er be said for shame that
   we, the youths of London,     120
Lay thrumming of[6] our caps at home,
   and left our custom undone.
Up, then, I say, both young and old,
   both man and maid a-maying,
With drums and guns that bounce[7]
   aloud, and merry tabor playing!
Which to prolong, God save our king,
   and send his country peace,
And root out treason from the land!
   And so, my friends, I cease. [*Exit.*]

FINIS ACTUS QUARTI.


ACTUS QUINTUS. SCENA PRIMA.

[*A room in Venturewell's house.*]

*Enter Merchant, solus.*[8]

MERCH. I will have no great store of
company at the wedding—a couple of neighbors and their wives; and we will have a
capon in stewed broth, with marrow, and
a good piece of beef stuck with rosemary.

*Enter Jasper, his face mealed.*[9]

JASP. Forbear thy pains, fond man! It
   is too late.
MERCH. Heaven bless me! Jasper?
JASP.              Ay, I am his ghost,
   Whom thou hast injured for his con-
      stant love,
   Fond worldly wretch, who dost not
      understand
   In death that true hearts cannot parted
      be!                 10
   First, know thy daughter is quite borne
      away
   On wings of angels, through the liquid
      air,
   To far out of thy reach, and never more
   Shalt thou behold her face; but she
      and I
   Will in another world enjoy our loves,
   Where neither father's anger, poverty,
   Nor any cross that troubles earthly
      men
   Shall make us sever our united hearts.
   And never shalt thou sit or be alone
   In any place, but I will visit thee   20
   With ghastly looks, and put into thy
      mind
   The great offenses which thou didst to
      me.
   When thou art at thy table with thy
      friends,
   Merry in heart, and filled with swelling
      wine,
   I'll come in midst of all thy pride and
      mirth,
   Invisible to all men but thyself,
   And whisper such a sad tale in thine
      ear
   Shall make thee let the cup fall from
      thy hand,
   And stand as mute and pale as Death
      itself.
MERCH. Forgive me, Jasper! O, what
   might I do,              30
Tell me, to satisfy thy troubled ghost?
JASP. There is no means; too late thou
   think'st of this.
MERCH. But tell me what were best for
   me to do?

---

[1] Spawn.
[2] Mewed (?).
[3] A lean young deer.
[4] A yearling buck.
[5] Handkerchiefs.
[6] Setting tufts on.
[7] Boom, bang.
[8] Alone.
[9] Whitened with flour.

JASP. Repent thy deed, and satisfy my
    father,
And beat fond Humphrey out of thy
    doors.                    *Exit Jasper.*

*Enter Humphrey.*

WIFE. Look, George; his very ghost
would have folks beaten.

HUM. Father, my bride is gone, fair Mis-
    tress Luce;
    My soul's the fount of vengeance, mis-
    chief's sluice.
MERCH. Hence, fool, out of my sight;
    with thy fond passion             40
    Thou hast undone me.       [*Beats him.*]
HUM.                    Hold, my father dear,
    For Luce thy daughter's sake, that had
    no peer!
MERCH. Thy father, fool? There's some
    blows more; begone.—    [*Beats him.*]
    Jasper, I hope thy ghost be well appeased
    To see thy will performed. Now will
    I go
    To satisfy thy father for thy wrongs.
                            *Exit.*
HUM. What shall I do? I have been beaten
    twice,
    And Mistress Luce is gone. Help me,
    device!
    Since my true love is gone, I never more,
    Whilst I do live, upon the sky will pore,
    But in the dark will wear out my shoe
    soles                            51
    In passion in Saint Faith's Church under
    Paul's.[1]                    *Exit.*

WIFE. George, call Rafe hither; if you
love me, call Rafe hither. I have the
bravest [2] thing for him to do, George;
prithee, call him quickly.
CIT. Rafe! Why, Rafe, boy!

*Enter Rafe.*

RAFE. Here, sir.
CIT. Come hither, Rafe; come to thy
mistress, boy.                        60
WIFE. Rafe, I would have thee call
all the youths together in battle ray,[3] with
drums, and guns, and flags, and march
to Mile End in pompous fashion, and

there exhort your soldiers to be merry and
wise, and to keep their beards from burning, Rafe; and then skirmish, and let your
flags fly, and cry, "Kill, kill, kill!" My
husband shall lend you his jerkin, Rafe,
and there's a scarf; for the rest, the    [70
house shall furnish you, and we'll pay
for 't. Do it bravely, Rafe; and think before whom you perform, and what person
you represent.
RAFE. I warrant you, mistress; if I do
it not for the honor of the city and the
credit of my master, let me never hope for
freedom! [4]
WIFE. 'Tis well spoken, i' faith. Go
thy ways; thou art a spark indeed.    80
CIT. Rafe, Rafe, double your files
bravely, Rafe!
RAFE. I warrant you, sir.    *Exit Rafe.*
CIT. Let him look narrowly to his service; [5] I shall take him else. I was there myself a pikeman once, in the hottest of the
day, wench, had my feather shot sheer
away, the fringe of my pike burnt off with
powder, my pate broken with a scouring
stick,[6] and yet, I thank God, I am here.  90
                        *Drum within.*
WIFE. Hark, George, the drums!
CIT. Ran, tan, tan, tan; ran, tan! O,
wench, an thou hadst but seen little Ned
of Algate, Drum [7] Ned, how he made it
roar again, and laid on like a tyrant, and
then stroke softly till the ward [8] came up,
and then thundered again, and together
we go! "Sa, sa, sa, bounce!" quoth the
guns; "Courage, my hearts!" quoth the
captains; "Saint George!" quoth the   [100
pikemen; and withal, here they lay, and
there they lay. And yet for all this I am
here, wench.
WIFE. Be thankful for it, George, for
indeed 'tis wonderful.

[SCENA SECUNDA.

*A street in London.*]

*Enter Rafe and his Company with drums
and colors.*

RAFE. March fair, my hearts! Lieutenant, beat the rear up.—Ancient,[9] let
your colors fly; but have a great care of

[1] Near St. Paul's Cathedral.
[2] Finest.                    [3] Array.
[4] *I.e.,* full membership in his company.
[5] Equipment.
[6] Ramrod.                    [8] Guard.
[7] Drummer.                   [9] Standard bearer.

the butchers' hooks at Whitechapel; they have been the death of many a fair ancient.[1]—Open your files that I may take a view both of your persons and munition.—Sergeant, call a muster.

SERG. A stand![2]—William Hammerton, pewterer? 10

HAM. Here, captain.

RAFE. A corselet and a Spanish pike; 'tis well. Can you shake it with a terror?

HAM. I hope so, captain.

RAFE. Charge upon me. [*He charges on Rafe.*] 'Tis with the weakest; put more strength, William Hammerton, more strength. As you were, again!—Proceed, sergeant. 19

SERG. George Greengoose, poulterer?

GREEN. Here.

RAFE. Let me see your piece, Neighbor Greengoose. When was she shot in?

GREEN. And 't[3] like you, Master Captain, I made a shot even now, partly to scour her, and partly for audacity.

RAFE. It should seem so certainly, for her breath is yet inflamed; besides, there is a main[4] fault in the touchhole—it runs and stinketh; and I tell you, moreover, [30] and believe it, ten such touchholes would breed the pox in the army. Get you a feather,[5] neighbor, get you a feather, sweet oil, and paper, and your piece may do well enough yet. Where's your powder?

GREEN. Here.

RAFE. What, in a paper? As I am a soldier and a gentleman, it craves a martial court! You ought to die for 't. Where's your horn? Answer me to that. 40

GREEN. An 't like you, sir, I was oblivious.

RAFE. It likes me not you should be so; 'tis a shame for you, and a scandal to all our neighbors, being a man of worth and estimation, to leave your horn behind you; I am afraid 'twill breed example. But let me tell you no more on 't.—Stand, till I view you all. What's become o' th' nose of your flask? 50

1 SOLD. Indeed-law, captain, 'twas blown away with powder.

RAFE. Put on a new one at the city's charge.—Where's the stone of this piece?

2 SOLD. The drummer took it out to light tobacco.

RAFE. 'Tis a fault, my friend; put it in again.—You want a nose, and you a stone.—Sergeant, take a note on 't, for I mean to stop it in the pay.—Remove, [60] and march! [*They march.*] Soft and fair, gentlemen, soft and fair! Double your files! As you were! Faces about! Now, you with the sodden face, keep in there! Look to your match, sirrah; it will be in your fellow's flask anon! So; make a crescent now! Advance your pikes! Stand and give ear!—Gentlemen, countrymen, friends, and my fellow soldiers, I have brought you this day from the shops [70] of security and the counters of content to measure out in these furious fields honor by the ell and prowess by the pound. Let it not, O, let it not, I say, be told hereafter, the noble issue of this city fainted; but bear yourselves in this fair action like men, valiant men, and free men! Fear not the face of the enemy, nor the noise of the guns, for, believe me, brethren, the rude rumbling of a brewer's car is far [80] more terrible, of which you have a daily experience; neither let the stink of powder offend you, since a more valiant stink is nightly with you. To a resolved mind his home is everywhere. I speak not this to take away the hope of your return, for you shall see (I do not doubt it), and that very shortly, your loving wives again and your sweet children, whose care doth bear you company in baskets.[6] Remember, [90] then, whose cause you have in hand, and, like a sort[7] of true-born scavengers, scour me this famous realm of enemies. I have no more to say but this: stand to your tacklings,[8] lads, and show to the world you can as well brandish a sword as shake an apron. Saint George, and on, my hearts!

OMNES. St. George, St. George!

*Exeunt.*

WIFE. 'Twas well done, Rafe! I'll [100 send thee a cold capon afield and a bottle

---

1 Flag.
2 Halt!
3 If it. Emended by Dyce. Original reads *And*.
4 Serious.
5 A sharp blade placed in the musket rest.

6 Lunch baskets(?).
7 Company.    8 Tackle, equipment.

of March beer, and, it may be, come myself to see thee.

CIT. Nell, the boy has deceived me
much; I did not think it had been in him.
He has performed such a matter, wench,
that, if I live, next year I'll have him captain of the galley foist [1] or I'll want my will.

[SCENA TERTIA.

*A room in Merrythought's house.*]

*Enter Old Merrythought.*

OLD MER. Yet, I thank God, I break
not a wrinkle more than I had, not a stoop,
boys! Care, live with cats; I defy thee!
My heart is as sound as an oak; and, though
I want drink to wet my whistle, I can sing.
[*Sings.*]

Come no more there, boys, come no more
    there,
For we shall never whilst we live come any
    more there.

*Enter a Boy [and a Coffin Carrier] with a
                                    coffin.*

BOY. God save you, sir!
OLD MER. It's a brave boy. Canst
thou sing?                                    10
BOY. Yes, sir, I can sing; but 'tis not
so necessary at this time.
OLD MER. [*Singing.*]

Sing we, and chant it,
    Whilst love doth grant it.

BOY. Sir, sir, if you knew what I have
brought you, you would have little list
to sing.
OLD MER. [*Singing.*]

O, the Mimon[2] round,
Full long, long I have thee sought,
    And now I have thee found,          20
And what hast thou here brought?

BOY. A coffin, sir, and your dead son
Jasper in it.          [*Exit with Coffin Carrier.*]
OLD MER. Dead? Why, farewell he!
                                    [*Sings.*]

Thou wast a bonny boy, and I did love thee.

*Enter Jasper.*

JASP. Then, I pray you, sir, do so still.

[1] Barge used in the Lord Mayor's pageants.

OLD MER. Jasper's ghost?          [*Sings.*]

Thou art welcome from Stygian lake so
    soon;
Declare to me what wondrous things in
    Pluto's court are done.

JASP. By my troth, sir, I ne'er came [30
there; 'tis too hot for me, sir.
OLD MER. A merry ghost, a very merry
ghost!                                    [*Sings.*]

And where is your true love? O, where is
    yours?

JASP. Marry, look you, sir!
*Heaves up the coffin [, and Luce steps forth].*
OLD MER. Ah, ha! Art thou good at
that, i' faith?                              [*Sings.*]

With hey, trixy, terlery-whiskin,
    The world it runs on wheels;
When the young man's ——,          40
    Up goes the maiden's heels.

*Mistress Merrythought and Michael within.*

MIST. MER. What, Mr. Merrythought,
will you not let 's in? What do you think
shall become of us?
OLD MER. [*Singing.*]

What voice is that, that calleth at our door?

MIST. MER. You know me well enough;
I am sure I have not been such a stranger
to you.
OLD MER. [*Singing.*]

And some they whistled, and some they
    sung,
    "Hey, down, down!"                    50
And some did loudly say,
Ever as the Lord Barnet's horn blew,
    "Away, Musgrave, away!"

MIST. MER. You will not have us
starve here, will you, Mr. Merrythought?
JASP. Nay, good sir, be persuaded; she
is my mother. If her offenses have been
great against you, let your own love remember she is yours, and so forgive her.
LUCE. Good Mr. Merrythought, let [60
me entreat you; I will not be denied.
MIST. MER. Why, Mr. Merrythought,
will you be a vext[3] thing still?
OLD MER. Woman, I take you to my

[2] Minion(?).                    [3] Ill-tempered.

love again; but you shall sing before you enter; therefore despatch your song and so come in.

MIST. MER.   Well, you must have your will, when all's done.—Mick, what song canst thou sing, boy?                    70

MICH.   I can sing none, forsooth, but "A lady's daughter of Paris properly."

{ MIST. MER.
{ [MICH.]

SONG

It was a lady's daughter, etc.

[*Merrythought opens the door and Mistress Merrythought and Michael enter.*]

OLD MER.   Come, you're welcome home again.                    [*Sings.*]

If such danger be in playing,
   And jest must to earnest turn,
You shall gó no more a-maying—

MERCH. (*Within.*) Are you within, sir, Master Merrythought?                    80

JASP.   It is my master's voice!   Good sir, go hold him in talk, whilst we convey ourselves into some inward room.
                    [*Exit with Luce.*]

OLD MER.   What are you?   Are you merry?   You must be very merry, if you enter.

MERCH.   I am, sir.

OLD MER.   Sing, then.

MERCH.   Nay, good sir, open to me.

OLD MER.   Sing, I say, or, by the merry heart, you come not in!                    91

MERCH.   Well, sir, I'll sing.          [*Sings.*]

Fortune, my foe, etc.

[*Merrythought opens the door and Venture-well enters.*]

OLD MER.   You are welcome, sir; you are welcome.   You see your entertainment; pray you, be merry.

MERCH.   O, Mr. Merrythought, I'm come to ask you
Forgiveness for the wrongs I offered you
And your most virtuous son!   They're infinite;
Yet my contrition shall be more than they.                    100

I do confess my hardness broke his heart,
For which just heaven hath given me punishment
More than my age can carry.   His wand'ring spirit,
Not yet at rest, pursues me everywhere,
Crying, "I'll haunt thee for thy cruelty."
My daughter, she is gone, I know not how,
Taken invisible, and whether living
Or in grave, 'tis yet uncertain to me.
O, Master Merrythought, these are the weights
Will sink me to my grave!   Forgive me, sir.                    110

OLD MER.   Why, sir, I do forgive you; and be merry.
And, if the wag in 's lifetime played the knave,
Can you forgive him too?

MERCH.                    With all my heart, sir.

OLD MER.   Speak it again, and heartly.

MERCH.                    I do, sir.
Now, by my soul, I do.

OLD MER. [*Singing.*]

With that came out his paramour;
She was as white as the lily flower.
   Hey, troll, trolly, lolly!

*Enter Luce and Jasper.*

With that came out her own dear knight;
He was as true as ever did fight, etc. [120

Sir, if you will forgive him, clap their hands together; there's no more to be said[1] i' th' matter.

MERCH.   I do, I do.

CIT.   I do not like this!   Peace, boys! Hear me, one of you!   Everybody's part is come to an end but Rafe's, and he's left out.

BOY.   'Tis long[2] of yourself, sir; we have nothing to do with his part.                    130

CIT.   Rafe, come away!—Make on him, as you have done of the rest, boys; come.

WIFE.   Now, good husband, let him come out and die.

CIT.   He shall, Nell.—Rafe, come away quickly, and die, boy!

BOY.   'Twill be very unfit he should die

[1] From 1635 edn.   Original reads *sad.*
[2] Because.

sir, upon no occasion—and in a comedy too. 139

CIT. Take you no care of that, Sir Boy; is not his part at an end, think you, when he's dead?—Come away, Rafe!

*Enter Rafe, with a forked arrow through his head.*

RAFE.[1] When I was mortal, this my cos-
tive corpse
Did lap up figs and raisins in the Strand,
Where, sitting, I espied a lovely dame,
Whose master wrought with lingel [2]
and with awl,
And underground he vampied [3] many
a boot.
Straight did her love prick forth me,
tender sprig,
To follow feats of arms in warlike wise
Through Waltham Desert, where I did
perform 150
Many achievements, and did lay on
ground
Huge Barbaroso, that insulting giant,
And all his captives soon set at liberty.
Then honor pricked me from my native
soil
Into Moldavia, where I gained the love
Of Pompiona, his beloved daughter,
But yet proved constant to the black-
thumbed maid,
Susan, and scorned Pompiona's love;
Yet liberal I was, and gave her pins,
And money for her father's officers. 160
I then returned home, and thrust my-
self
In action, and by all men chosen was
Lord of the May, where I did flourish
it,
With scarfs and rings, and posy in my
hand.
After this action I preferred was,
And chosen city captain at Mile End,
With hat and feather, and with leading
staff,
And trained my men, and brought them
all off clear,
Save one man that berayed him with
the noise.

But all these things I Rafe did under-
take 170
Only for my beloved Susan's sake.
Then coming home, and sitting in my
shop
With apron blue, Death came into my
stall
To cheapen [4] *aqua vitæ;* but ere I
Could take the bottle down and fill a
taste,
Death caught a pound of pepper in his
hand,
And sprinkled all my face and body o'er,
And in an instant vanishéd away.

CIT. 'Tis a pretty fiction, i' faith.

RAFE. Then took I up my bow and shaft
in hand, 180
And walked into Moorfields to cool
myself;
But there grim cruel Death met me
again,
And shot this forkéd arrow through
my head.
And now I faint. Therefore be warned
by me,
My fellows every one, of forkéd heads!
Farewell, all you good boys in merry
London!
Ne'er shall we more upon Shrove Tues-
day meet,
And pluck down houses of iniquity.[5]—
My pain increaseth—I shall never more
Hold open, whilst another pumps both
legs, 190
Nor daub a satin gown with rotten eggs;
Set up a stake,[6] O, never more I shall!
I die! Fly, fly, my soul, to Grocers'
Hall!
O, O, O, etc.

WIFE. Well said, Rafe! Do your obeisance to the gentlemen, and go your ways.
Well said, Rafe! *Exit Rafe.*

OLD MER. Methinks all we, thus kindly
and unexpectedly reconciled, should not
depart without a song. 200

---

[1] Many parts of the following passage are a parody of the opening speech of Andrea's Ghost in *The Spanish Tragedy.*
[2] Waxed thread.
[3] Patched.

[4] Bargain for.
[5] An annual custom of the London apprentices.
[6] To which cocks were tied for targets to be thrown at.

MERCH. A good motion.

OLD MER. Strike up, then!

### SONG

Better music ne'er was known
Than a choir of hearts in one.
Let each other that hath been
Troubled with the gall or spleen
Learn of us to keep his brow
Smooth and plain, as ours are now.
Sing, though before the hour of dying;
He shall rise, and then be crying,    210
"Hey, ho, 'tis naught but mirth
That keeps the body from the earth!"

*Exeunt omnes.*

### EPILOGUS

CIT. Come, Nell, shall we go? The play's done.

WIFE. Nay, by my faith, George, I have more manners than so; I'll speak to these gentlemen first.—I thank you all, gentlemen, for your patience and countenance to Rafe, a poor fatherless child; and, if I might see you at my house,    [220 it should go hard but I would have a pottle [1] of wine and a pipe of tabacco for you, for, truly, I hope you do like the youth, but I would be glad to know the truth. I refer it to your own discretions, whether you will applaud him or no, for I will wink, and whilst [2] you shall do what you will. I thank you with all my heart. God give you good night!—Come, George.

*[Exeunt.]*

FINIS.

[1] A two-quart pot.    [2] In the meantime.

# JOHN FLETCHER

## THE FAITHFUL SHEPHERDESS

Just as it is now generally agreed that *The Knight of the Burning Pestle* was an independent work by Francis Beaumont, so it is agreed that *The Faithful Shepherdess* came from the single pen of John Fletcher. No serious questions have ever been raised about his complete authorship, since the first quarto (undated, but probably issued about 1609–10, a year or two after the production by the Children of the Queen's Revels) bears his name, as do the four other editions preceding the second folio, in which no distinction of authors was made. As Fletcher admitted in his address "To the Reader," the original audience, apparently not understanding his intention in his new kind of "pastoral tragicomedy," "began to be angry," and ruined the premier performance. Modern critics, however, have not been quite so unanimous in their reaction to the play and its theme, which, all of them agree, centers on the various types and degrees of love, chastity, and lust in a somewhat allegorical form. Homer Smith, in what F. E. Schelling in his *Elizabethan Drama* calls "an able, if somewhat conservative, monograph" ("Pastoral Influence in the English Drama," *PMLA*, 1897), grumbled that "few thoughtful men can accept the conclusions that Fletcher suggests, first, that constancy to a dead lover and a vow of virginity are supremely holy; secondly, that spiritual love between the sexes is necessarily destroyed by any taint of physical love, . . . and thirdly, that the deification of woman is in itself commendable." With this opinion Schelling found himself in essential agreement. Not long after Smith's article, W. W. Greg took a somewhat less emotional stand when he found in the play an "antagonism between Fletcher's own sympathies and the ideal he set before him" and discerned in this "the key to the enigma of his play" (*Pastoral Poetry and Pastoral Drama*, London, 1906). By 1936, however, Una Ellis-Fermor could write in her *Jacobean Drama* of the "enchantment," the "clear, remote radiance" of the play, despite the fact that "chastity, like the player-queen, doth protest too much," and thus gives the play "a pervading atmosphere of falseness and unreality." Leech, although admitting in 1962 that what happens "is for the most part frankly fantastic," stressed the play's uniqueness, both in its pastoral form and in its language and versification. In 1947, Wallis had already insisted that a Stuart audience would have been baffled by Ellis-Fermor's reservations, and lauded *The Faithful Shepherdess* as "the finest play in this kind, both as lyrical poetry and as theater, that was to be written in English." This would seem to be the majority attitude of critics today, although John Leon Lievsay has entered the minority opinion that there are very few English pastoral dramas, and that "aside from its pretty versification it is a confused and feeble play. So confused, in fact, that the reader is perfectly justified in asking who is the faithful shepherdess, Clorin or Amoret?" ("Italian *Favola Boscarecce* and Jacobean Stage Pastoralism," *Essays on Shakespeare and the Elizabethan Drama in Honor of Hardin Craig*).

Leech has concluded that *The Faithful Shepherdess* is characteristic of the work of Fletcher in its placing its chief emphasis on situation rather than on character, since Fletcher always strives to surprise his audience with some unusual circumstance or turn of plot, not always too plausible, but always striking and even sensational. At the same time, in this case we can see "an early demonstration of Fletcher's basic attitude toward the human spectacle: there is magic and nonsense enough, but both are presented with a certain wryness, a controlled humor; there is a shrewd interest in the possibilities of human behaviour, along with a reservation of judgement concerning the standards by which it should be judged." The situation in the play, Leech finds, involves what he calls the "day-night antinomy," according to which the beginning and the ending of the action take place in the clear light of day, but "the intervening night is a time of danger." The strangeness of the situation is also "heavily underlined" by making the god Pan the guardian of chastity, and leaving only the Sullen Shepherd, among the mortals, unreconciled to it at the end.

The investigation and discussion of Fletcher's models and predecessors have occupied many of his critics, although none of them has been able to emerge with any absolute sources. As in the case of Jonson's *The Sad Shepherd*, Guarini's *Il Pastor Fido* (itself modeled on Tasso's *Aminta*) and his *Il Compendia della Poesia Tragicomica* (1601) are at the root of it all. But in spite of the fact that Guarini was writing about a faithful shepherd and Fletcher about a faithful shepherdess, there is no similarity in the stories and little in the characters, except perhaps in the slight resemblance between Clorin and Corsica (see Lievsay). As Leech points out, however, "the world of Fletcher is far more complicated than the world of Guarini." Waith has concluded that Fletcher made a fairly close application of Guarini's principles of tragicomedy, as they are more or less echoed in Fletcher's own definition in his preface. Many other indirect influences on *The Faithful Shepherdess* from lyric and narrative poetry, prose fiction, and the drama have been suggested. These include, especially, Spenser, in both *The Shepherd's Calendar* and *The Fairy Queen* (particularly its third and fourth books illustrating the various aspects of love and lust); Michael Drayton's pastoral poems in *Idea, the Shepherd's Garland*; Sidney's *Arcadia;* and even certain plays such as Samuel Daniel's dull *The Queen's Arcadia*, which had been acted for Queen Anne at Christ Church College in 1605, and perhaps Shakespeare's *Pericles, Prince of Tyre*, and *A Midsummer Night's Dream* (see Wallis and Daniel M. McKeithan, *The Debt to Shakespeare in the Beaumont-and-Fletcher Plays, UTSE*, 1938). Quite properly, the influence of Fletcher's play was soon to show itself in Milton's *Comus*, in both theme and versification.

The dating of *The Faithful Shepherdess* about 1608 or a little later (Alfred Harbage, *Annals of the English Drama, 975 to 1700*, London, 1940) has allowed dramatic historians to regard it in some ways as a preparation for the famous series of more conventional—that is, nonpastoral—tragicomedies which were to come next from the combined pens of Fletcher and Beaumont (Frank H. Ristine, *English Tragicomedy/Its Origin and History*, Columbia University Press, 1910). Wallis has summed up these anticipatory elements as follows: a harmonious blending of a wide range of "passionate, threatening, idyllic, comic" effects; the evocation of an exotic atmosphere and world remote from actuality; a preoccupation with the aspects of love and lust; violent contrasts between characters and between juxtaposed situations; and "his anticipation, in some degree, of the lifting of emotional patterning to dominance in *Philaster*." And, of course, a potentially tragic situation must end happily for all the characters with whom the audience feels a sense of self-identification.

The present text follows the first quarto as given by Greg in the third volume of the Variorum Edition of the *Works* (London, 1908), but, since different copies of the quarto vary, in rare cases Waller's readings in the Cambridge English Classics have been adopted.

# THE FAITHFUL SHEPHERDESS

BY

## JOHN FLETCHER [1]

[*DRAMATIS PERSONÆ*

PERIGOT.
THENOT.
DAPHNIS.
ALEXIS.
SULLEN SHEPHERD.
OLD SHEPHERD.
PRIEST OF PAN.
GOD OF THE RIVER.

SATYR.
SHEPHERDS.

CLORIN.
AMORET.
AMARILLIS.
CLOE.
SHEPHERDESSES.

SCENE: *Thessaly.*

TIME: *Mythical.*]

### TO THE READER

If you be not reasonably assured of your knowledge in this kind of poem, lay down the book, or read this, which I would wish had been the prologue. It is a pastoral tragi-comedy, which the people, seeing when it was played, having ever had a singular gift in defining, concluded to be a play of country hired shepherds in gray cloaks, with curtailed dogs in strings, sometimes laughing together, and some- [10 times killing one another; and, missing Whitsun ales, cream, wassail, and morris dances, began to be angry. In their error I would not have you fall, lest you incur their censure.[2] Understand, therefore, a pastoral to be a representation of shepherds and shepherdesses with their actions and passions, which must be such as may agree with their natures, at least not exceeding former fictions and vul- [20 gar traditions; they are not to be adorned with any art but such improper[3] ones as nature is said to bestow, as singing and poetry, or such as experience may teach them, as the virtues of herbs and fountains, the ordinary course of the sun, moon, and stars, and suchlike. But you are ever to remember shepherds to be such as all the ancient poets, and modern of understanding, have received them; that [30 is, the owners of flocks, and not hirelings. A tragi-comedy is not so called in respect of mirth and killing, but in respect it wants deaths, which is enough to make it no tragedy, yet brings some near it, which is enough to make it no comedy, which must be a representation of familiar people, with such kind of trouble as no life be questioned,[4] so that a god is as lawful in this as in a tragedy, and mean people as in a [40 comedy. Thus much I hope will serve to justify my poem, and make you understand it; to teach you more for nothing, I do not know that I am in conscience bound.

JOHN FLETCHER.

[1] Commendatory verses by Nathan Field, Francis Beaumont, Ben Jonson, and George Chapman, and dedicatory verses to Sir Walter Aston, Sir William Skipwith, and Sir Robert Townshend follow here.

[2] *I.e.*, the criticism which they received.

[3] *I.e.*, common to all men.
[4] *I.e.*, be put in danger.

Actus Primi Scena Prima.[1]

[*A glade in a wood.*][2]

*Enter Clorin, a shepherdess, having buried
her love in an arbor.*

[Clorin.] Hail, holy earth, whose cold
    arms do embrace
The truest man that ever fed his flocks
By the fat plains of fruitful Thessaly!
Thus I salute thy grave; thus do I pay
My early vows and tribute of mine eyes
To thy still-lovéd ashes; thus I free
Myself from all ensuing heats and fires
Of love; all sports, delights, and games
That shepherds hold full dear, thus put
    I off.
Now no more shall these smooth brows
    be girt    10
With youthful coronals, and lead the
    dance;
No more the company of fresh fair
    maids
And wanton shepherds be to me de-
    lightful,
Nor the shrill, pleasing sound of merry
    pipes
Under some shady dell. when the cool
    wind
Plays on the leaves—all be far away,
Since thou art far away, by whose dear
    side
How often have I sat crowned with fresh
    flowers
For summer's queen, whilst every shep-
    herd's boy
Puts on his lusty green, with gaudy
    hook [3]    20
And hanging scrip of finest cordevan.[4]
But thou art gone, and these are gone
    with thee,
And all are dead but thy dear memory.
That shall outlive thee, and shall ever
    spring,
Whilst there are pipes, or jolly shep-
    herds sing.
And here will I, in honor of thy love,

Dwell by thy grave, forgetting all those
    joys
That former times made precious to
    mine eyes,
Only rememb'ring what my youth did
    gain
In the dark, hidden, virtuous [5] use of
    herbs.    30
That will I practice, and as freely give
All my endeavors, as I gained them free.
Of all green wounds I know the remedies
In men or cattle, be they stung with
    snakes,
Or charmed with powerful words of
    wicked art,
Or be they lovesick, or, through too
    much heat
Grown wild or lunatic, their eyes or ears
Thickened with misty film of dulling
    rheum;
These I can cure, such secret virtue lies
In herbs appliéd by a virgin's hand.    40
My meat shall be what these wild woods
    afford,
Berries and chestnuts, plantains, on
    whose cheeks
The sun sits smiling, and the lofty fruit
Pulled from the fair head of the
    straight-grown pine.
On these I'll feed with free content, and
    rest,
When night shall blind the world, by
    thy side blessed.

*Enter a Satyr* [*with a basket of fruit*].

Sat. Through[6] yon same bending plain,
That flings his arms down to the main,[7]
And through these thick woods have I
    run,
Whose bottom never kissed the sun    50
Since the lusty spring began;
All to please my master Pan,
Have I trotted without rest
To get him fruit, for at a feast
He entertains this coming night
His paramour, the Syrinx bright.—
But, behold, a fairer sight!
              *He stands amazed.*
By that heavenly form of thine,
Brightest fair, thou art divine,
Sprong[8] from great immortal race    60

---

[1] The first scene of the first act.
[2] The setting, which apparently remains unchanged throughout the play, consists of
Clorin's bower (or cottage) in the inner stage,
a wood on one side of the main stage, and a hill
with a well on the other.
[3] Crook.
[4] Pouch of Cordovan leather.

[5] Efficacious.       [7] Sea.       [8] Sprung.
[6] Perhaps pronounced *thorough*.

Of the gods; for in thy face
Shines more awful majesty
Than dull weak mortality
Dare with misty eyes behold,
And live.  Therefore on this mold
Lowly do I bend my knee
In worship of thy deity.
Deign it, goddess, from my hand
To receive whate'er this land
From her fertile womb doth send　　　70
Of her choice fruits, and but lend
Belief to that the satyr tells:
Fairer by the famous wells
To this present day ne'er grew,
Never better nor more true.
Here be grapes, whose lusty blood
Is the learnéd poets' good.
Sweeter yet did never crown
The head of Bacchus; nuts more brown
Than the squirrel's teeth that crack
　　them.　　　　　　　　　　　　80
Deign, O fairest fair, to take them!
For these black-eyed Dryope
Hath oftentimes commanded me
With my clasped knee to climb—
See how well the lusty time
Hath decked their rising cheeks in
　　red,
Such as on your lips is spread!
Here be berries for a queen—
Some be red, some be green;
These are of that luscious meat　　90
The great god Pan himself doth eat;
All these, and what the woods can yield,
The hanging mountain, or the field,
I freely offer, and ere long
Will bring you more, more sweet and
　　strong,
Till when, humbly leave I take,
Lest the great Pan do awake,
That sleeping lies in a deep glade
Under a broad beech's shade.
I must go, I must run　　　　　　　100
Swifter than the fiery sun.　　　*Exit.*
CLO.  And all my fears go with thee!
What greatness, or what private hidden
　　power,
Is there in me, to draw submission
From this rude man and beast?  Sure
　　I am mortal,
The daughter of a shepherd; he was
　　mortal,
And she that bore me mortal; prick my
　　hand,

And it will bleed; a fever shakes me, and
The selfsame wind that makes the young
　　lambs shrink
Makes me acold; my fear says I am
　　mortal.　　　　　　　　　　　110
Yet I have heard (my mother told it
　　me,
And now I do believe it), if I keep
My virgin-flower uncropped, pure, chaste,
　　and fair,
No goblin, wood god, fairy, elf, or fiend,
Satyr, or other power that haunts these
　　groves
Shall hurt my body, or by vain illusion
Draw me to wander after idle fires,
Or voices calling me in dead of night
To make me follow, and so toll me on
Through mires and standing pools.　120
Else why should this rough thing, who
　　never knew
Manners nor smooth humanity, whose
　　heats [1]
Are rougher than himself and more mis-
　　shapen,
Thus mildly kneel to me?  Sure there is
　　a power
In that great name of virgin that binds
　　fast
All rude, uncivil bloods, all appetites
That break their confines.  Then, strong
　　chastity,
Be thou my strongest guard, for here
　　I'll dwell
In opposition against fate and hell!
　　　　　　　　　　　　　　　*[Exit.]*

*Enter an Old Shepherd, with four couple of*
*　　Shepherds and Shepherdesses [, among*
*　　　whom are Perigot and Amoret].* [2]

OLD SHEP.  Now we have done this holy
　　festival　　　　　　　　　　130
In honor of our great god, and his rites
Performed, prepare yourselves for chaste
And uncorrupted fires, that, as the priest
With powerful hand shall sprinkle on
　　your brows
His pure and holy water, ye may be
From all hot flames of lust and loose
　　thoughts free.
Kneel, shepherds, kneel; here comes the
　　priest of Pan.　　　　*[They kneel.]*

[1] Passions.
[2] Added by Dyce.

*Enter Priest.*

PRIEST. [*Sprinkling them with water.*] Shep-
  herds, thus I purge away
Whatsoever this great day
Or the past hours gave not good        140
To corrupt your maiden blood.
From the high rebellious heat
Of the grapes, and strength of meat,
From the wanton quick desires
They do kindle by their fires
I do wash you with this water.
Be you pure and fair hereafter.
From your livers [1] and your veins
Thus I take away the stains;
All your thoughts be smooth and fair;        150
Be ye fresh and free as air.
Never more let lustful heat
Through your purgéd conduits [2] beat,
Or a plighted troth be broken,
Or a wanton verse be spoken
In a shepherdess's ear.
Go your ways; ye are all clear.
    *They rise and sing in praise of Pan.*

THE SONG

Sing his praises that doth keep
  Our flocks from harm,
Pan, the father of our sheep;        160
  And arm in arm
Tread we softly in a round,
Whilst the hollow neighboring ground
Fills the music with her sound.

Pan, O great god Pan, to thee
  Thus do we sing,
Thou that keep'st us chaste and free
  As the young spring!
Ever be thy honor spoke,
From that place the Morn is broke        170
To that place Day doth unyoke!

*Exeunt omnes but Perigot and Amoret.*
PERI. Stay, gentle Amoret, thou fair-
  browed maid;
Thy shepherd prays thee stay, that holds
  thee dear,
Equal with his soul's good.
AMO.          Speak; I give
Thee freedom, shepherd, and [3] thy
  tongue be still [4]
The same it ever was, as free from ill
As he whose conversation never knew
The court or city; be thou ever true!

[1] The supposed seat of desire.    [3] If.
[2] Veins.    [4] Always.

PERI. When I fall off from my affection,
  Or mingle my clean thoughts with foul
    desires,        180
First, let our great god cease to keep
  my flocks,
That, being left alone without a guard,
The wolf, or winter's rage, summer's
  great heat
And want of water, rots, or what to us
Of ill is yet unknown, fall speedily,
And in their general ruin let me go!
AMO. I pray thee, gentle shepherd, wish
  not so.
I do believe thee; 'tis as hard for me
To think thee false, and harder, than
  for thee
To hold me foul.
PERI.        O, you are fairer far        190
Than the chaste blushing morn, or that
  fair star
That guides the wand'ring seaman
  through the deep,
Straighter than the straightest pine
  upon the steep
Head of an aged mountain, and more
  white
Than the new milk we strip before day-
  light
From the full-freighted bags of our fair
  flocks;
Your hair more beauteous than those
  hanging locks
Of young Apollo!
AMO.        Shepherd, be not lost;
Y' are sailed too far already from the
  coast
Of our discourse.
PERI.      Did you not tell me once        200
I should not love alone, I should not
  lose
Those many passions, vows, and holy
  oaths
I've sent to heaven? Did you not give
  your hand,
Even that fair hand, in hostage? Do
  not, then,
Give back again those sweets to other
  men
You yourself vowed were mine.
AMO. Shepherd, so far as maiden's mod-
  esty
May give assurance, I am once more
  thine;
Once more I give my hand. Be ever free

From that great foe to faith, foul jeal-
   ousy!                                    210
PERI. I take it as my best good, and de-
   sire,
For stronger confirmation of our love,
To meet this happy night in that fair
   grove
Where all true shepherds have rewarded
   been
For their long service. Say, sweet, shall
   it hold?
AMO. Dear friend, you must not blame
   me if I make
A doubt of what the silent night may do,
Coupled with this day's heat, to move
   your blood.
Maids must be fearful. Sure you have
   not been
Washed white enough, for yet I see a
   stain                                    220
Stick in your liver; go and purge again.
PERI. O, do not wrong my honest, simple
   truth!
Myself and my affections are as pure
As those chaste flames that burn be-
   fore the shrine
Of the great Dian; only my intent
To draw you thither was to plight our
   troths,
With interchange of mutual chaste em-
   braces
And ceremonious tying of our souls.
For to that holy wood is consecrate
A virtuous well, about whose flowery
   banks                                    230
The nimble-footed fairies dance their
   rounds
By the pale moonshine, dipping often-
   times
Their stolen children, so to make them
   free
From dying flesh and dull mortality.
By this fair fount hath many a' shep-
   herd sworn,
And given away his freedom, many a
   troth
Been plight, which neither envy nor old
   time
Could ever break, with many a chaste
   kiss given
In hope of coming happiness. By this
Fresh fountain many a blushing maid 240
Hath crowned the head of her long-
   lovéd shepherd

With gaudy flowers, whilst he happy sung
Lays of his love and dear captivity.
There grows all herbs fit to cool looser
   flames
Our sensual parts provoke, chiding our
   bloods,
And quenching by their power those
   hidden sparks
That else would break out, and provoke
   our sense
To open fires; so virtuous is that place.
Then, gentle shepherdess, believe, and
   grant.
In troth, it fits not with that face to
   scant                                    250
Your faithful shepherd of those chaste
   desires
He ever aimed at, and—
AMO. Thou hast prevailed; farewell. This
   coming night
Shall crown thy chaste hopes with long-
   wished delight.
PERI. Our great god Pan reward thee for
   that good
Thou hast given thy poor shepherd!
   Fairest bud
Of maiden virtues, when I leave to be
The true admirer of thy chastity,
Let me deserve the hot polluted name
Of a wild woodman, or affect some dame
Whose often prostitution hath begot   261
More foul diseases than ever yet the hot
Sun bred through his burnings, whilst
   the Dog [1]
Pursues the raging Lion,[1] throwing fog
And deadly vapor from his angry breath,
Filling the lower world with plague and
   death!                  *Ex[it] Am[oret].*

*Enter [Amarillis,] another shepherdess that
                    is in love with Perigot.*

AMAR. Shepherd, may I desire to be be-
   lieved,
What I shall blushing tell?
PERI.                    Fair maid, you may.
AMAR. Then, softly thus: I love thee, Peri-
   got,
And would be gladder to be loved
   again                                    270
Than the cold earth is in his frozen arms
To clip [2] the wanton spring. Nay, do
   not start,

---

[1] Sign of the zodiac.                    [2] Embrace.

Nor wonder that I woo thee, thou that art
The prime of our young grooms, even the top
Of all our lusty shepherds. What dull eye,
That never was acquainted with desire,
Hath seen thee wrastle, run, or cast the stone
With nimble strength and fair delivery,
And hath not sparkled fire, and speedily
Sent secret heat to all the neighboring veins?          280
Who ever heard thee sing, that brought again
That freedom back was lent unto thy voice?
Then, do not blame me, shepherd, if I be
One to be numbered in this company,
Since none that ever saw thee yet were free.

PERI. Fair shepherdess, much pity I can lend
To your complaints; but sure I shall not love.
All that is mine, myself and my best hopes,
Are given already. Do not love him, then,
That cannot love again; on other men   290
Bestow those heats, more free, that may return
You fire for fire, and in one flame equal burn.

AMAR. Shall I rewarded be so slenderly
For my affection, most unkind of men?
If I were old, or had agreed with art
To give another nature to my cheeks,
Or were I common mistress to the love
Of every swain, or could I with such ease
Call back my love as many a wanton doth,
Thou mightst refuse me, shepherd, but to thee          300
I am only fixed and set. Let it not be
A sport, thou gentle shepherd, to abuse
The love of silly [1] maid.

PERI.                    Fair soul, you use
These words to little end; for, know, I may
Better call back that time was yesterday,

[1] Weak.

Or stay the coming night, than bring my love
Home to myself again, or recreant prove.
I will no longer hold you with delays.
This present night I have appointed been
To meet that chaste fair that enjoys my soul,          310
In yonder grove, there to make up our loves.
Be not deceived no longer; choose again.
These neighboring plains have many a comely swain,
Fresher and freer [2] far than I e'er was;
Bestow that love on them, and let me pass.
Farewell; be happy in a better choice!
                    Exit.

AMAR. Cruel, thou hast struck me deader with thy voice
Than if the angry heavens with their quick flames
Had shot me through. I must not leave [3] to love;
I cannot; no, I must enjoy thee, boy, 320
Though the great dangers twixt my hopes and that
Be infinite. There is a shepherd dwells
Down by the moor, whose life hath ever shown
More sullen discontent than Saturn's brow
When he sits frowning on the births of men—
One that doth wear himself away in loneness,
And never joys, unless it be in breaking
The holy plighted troths of mutual souls;
One that lusts after every several beauty,
But never yet was known to love or like,          330
Were the face fairer or more full of truth
Than Phœbe in her fullness, or the youth
Of smooth Lyæus, whose nigh-starvéd flocks
Are always scabby, and infect all sheep
They feed withal, whose lambs are ever last,
And die before their weaning, and whose dog
Looks, like his master, lean and full of scurf,

[2] More liberal.          [3] Cease.

Not caring for the pipe or whistle. This
   man may,
If he be well wrought, do a deed of won-
   der,                          339
Forcing me passage to my long desires.
And here he comes, as fitly to my pur-
   pose
As my quick thoughts could wish for.

*Enter Sullen [Shepherd].*

SULL. Fresh beauty, let me not be thought
   uncivil,
Thus to be partner of your loneness;
   'twas
My love (that ever-working passion)
   drew
Me to this place to seek some remedy
For my sick soul. Be not unkind and
   fair,
For such the mighty Cupid in his doom
Hath sworn to be avenged on. Then
   give room
To my consuming fires that so I may  350
Enjoy my long desires, and so allay
Those flames that else would burn my
   life away.
AMAR. Shepherd, were I but sure thy
   heart were sound
As thy words seem to be, means might
   be found
To cure thee of thy long pains; for to me
That heavy, youth-consuming misery
The lovesick soul endures never was
   pleasing.
I could be well content with the quick
   easing
Of thee and thy hot fires, might it
   procure
Thy faith and farther service to be
   sure.                          360
[SULL.] [1] Name but that work, danger, or
   what can
Be compassed by the wit or art of man,
And, if I fail in my performance, may
I never more kneel to the rising day!
AMAR. Then thus I try thee, shepherd.
   This same night
That now comes stealing on, a gentle pair
Have promised equal love, and do
   appoint
To make yon wood the place where
   hands and hearts

[1] From 1634 edn.

Are to be tied forever. Break their
   meeting
And their strong faith, and I am ever
   thine.                          370
SULL. Tell me their names, and, if I do
   not move,
By my great power, the center of their
   love
From his fixed being, let me never more
Warm me by those fair eyes I thus adore.
AMAR. Come; as we go, I'll tell thee what
   they are,
And give thee fit directions for thy work.
                                *Exeunt.*

*Enter Cloe.*

CLOE. How have I wronged the times or
   men, that thus
After this holy feast I pass unknown
And unsaluted? 'Twas not wont to be
Thus frozen with the younger com-
   pany                         380
Of jolly shepherds; 'twas not then held
   good
For lusty grooms [2] to mix their quicker
   blood
With that dull humor, most unfit to be
The friend of man, cold and dull chastity.
Sure I am held not fair, or am too old,
Or else not free enough, or from my
   fold
Drive not a flock sufficient great to
   gain
The greedy eyes of wealth-alluring
   swain.
Yet, if I may believe what others say,
My face has foil [3] enough; nor can they
   lay                          390
Justly too strict a coyness to my charge;
My flocks are many, and the downs as
   large
They feed upon. Then, let it ever be
Their coldness, not my virgin-modesty,
Makes me complain.

*Enter Thenot.*

THE.                Was ever man but I
Thus truly taken with uncertainty? [4]
Where shall that man be found that
   loves a mind

[2] Merry fellows.
[3] Beauty.
[4] Bewitched with "the desire of things incompatible" (Greg).

Made up in constancy, and dares not
   find
His love rewarded?  Here, let all men
   know,
A wretch that lives to love his mistress
   so.                           400
CLOE. Shepherd, I pray thee stay.  Where
   hast thou been?
Or whither go'st thou?  Here be woods as
   green
As any; air as fresh and sweet
As where smooth Zephyrus plays on
   the fleet
Face of the curléd streams, with flowers
   as many
As the young spring gives, and as choice
   as any;
Here be all new delights, cool streams
   and wells,
Arbors o'ergrown with woodbines, caves,
   and dells.
Choose where thou wilt, whilst I sit
   by and sing,
Or gather rushes, to make many a
   ring                            410
For thy long fingers; tell thee tales of
   love—
How the pale Phoebe, hunting in a
   grove,
First saw the boy Endymion, from whose
   eyes
She took eternal fire that never dies,
How she conveyed him softly in a sleep,
His temples bound with poppy, to the
   steep
Head of old Latmus, where she stoops
   each night,
Gilding the mountain with her brother's
   light,
To kiss her sweetest.
THE.            Far from me are these
Hot flashes, bred from wanton heat and
   ease;                        420
I have forgot what love and loving
   . meant;
Rhymes, songs, and merry rounds,[1] that
   oft are sent
To the soft ear of maid, are strange to
   me.
Only I live t' admire a chastity
That neither pleasing age,[2] smooth
   tongue, or gold
Could ever break upon, so sure a mold

Is that her mind was cast in.  'Tis to
   her
I only am reserved; she is my form I
   stir
By, breathe, and move; 'tis she, and
   only she,                  429
Can make me happy, or give misery.
CLOE. Good shepherd, may a stranger
   crave to know
To whom this dear observance [3] you do
   owe?
THE. You may, and by her virtue learn
   to square
And level out your life; for to be fair,
And nothing virtuous, only fits the eye
Of gaudy youth and swelling vanity.
Then, know, she's called the Virgin of
   the Grove,
She that hath long since buried her
   chaste love,
And now lives by his grave, for whose
   dear soul
She hath vowed herself into the holy
   roll                        440
Of strict virginity. 'Tis her I so ad-
   mire,
Not any looser blood or new desire.
                              [*Exit.*]
CLOE. Farewell, poor swain!  Thou art
   not for my bend; [4]
I must have quicker souls, whose
   words may tend
To some free action.  Give me him dare
   love
At first encounter, and as soon dare
   prove!

### THE SONG

Come, shepherds, come!
Come away without delay,
Whilst the gentle time doth stay.
  Green woods are dumb,         450
And will never tell to any
Those dear kisses and those many
Sweet embraces that are given—
Dainty pleasures that would even
Raise in coldest age a fire,
And give virgin-blood desire.
  Then, if ever,
  Now or never,
  Come and have it;
  Think not I               460
  Dare deny,
  If you crave it.

---

[1] Roundelays.              [2] Youth.        [3] Homage.         [4] Bent, purpose.

*Enter Daphnis.*

[CLOE. (*Aside.*)] Here comes another. Better be my speed,
Thou god of blood! But certain, if I read
Not false, this is that modest shepherd, he
That only dare salute, but ne'er could be
Brought to kiss any, hold discourse, or sing,
Whisper, or boldly ask that wishéd thing
We all are born for—one that makes loving faces,
And could be well content to covet graces,      470
Were they not got by boldness. In this thing
My hopes are frozen; and, but fate doth bring
Him hither, I would sooner choose
A man made out of snow, and freer use
An eunuch to my ends. But since he is here,
Thus I attempt him.—Thou, of men most dear,
Welcome to her that only for thy sake
Hath been content to live! Here, boldly take
My hand in pledge, this hand that never yet
Was given away to any, and but sit      480
Down on this rushy bank whilst I go pull
Fresh blossoms from the boughs, or quickly cull
The choicest delicates from yonder mead,
To make thee chains or chaplets, or to spread
Under our fainting bodies, when delight
Shall lock up all our senses. How the sight
Of those smooth rising cheeks renew the story
Of young Adonis, when in pride and glory
He lay infolded twixt the beating arms
Of willing Venus! Methinks stronger charms      490
Dwell in those speaking eyes, and on that brow
More sweetness than the painters can allow
To their best pieces. Not Narcissus, he
That wept himself away in memory
Of his own beauty, nor Silvanus' boy,
Nor the twice-ravished maid, for whom old Troy
Fell by the hand of Pyrrhus, may to thee
Be otherwise compared than some dead tree
To a young fruitful olive.

DAPH.                    I can love,   499
But I am loath to say so, lest I prove
Too soon unhappy.

CLOE.            Happy, thou wouldst say.
My dearest Daphnis, blush not. If the day
To thee and thy soft heats be enemy,
Then take the coming night.    Fair youth, 'tis free
To all the world. Shepherd, I'll meet thee, then,
When darkness hath shut up the eyes of men,
In yonder grove.    Speak, shall our meeting hold?
Indeed ye are too bashful; be more bold,
And tell me ay.

DAPH.                I am content to say so,
And would be glad to meet, might I but pray so      510
Much from your fairness, that you would be true.

CLOE. Shepherd, thou hast thy wish.

DAPH.                    Fresh maid, adieu.
Yet one word more. Since you have drawn me on
To come this night, fear not to meet alone
That man that will not offer to be ill,
Though your bright self would ask it, for his fill
Of this world's goodness. Do not fear him, then,
But keep your pointed [1] time.    Let other men
Set up their bloods to sale; mine shall be ever
Fair as the soul it carries, and unchaste never.    *Exit.*   520

CLOE. Yet am I poorer than I was before.
Is it not strange, among so many a score
Of lusty bloods, I should pick out these things

[1] Appointed.

Whose veins, like a dull river far from
  springs,
Is still the same, slow, heavy, and unfit
For stream or motion, though the strong
  winds hit
With their continual power upon his
  sides?
O, happy be your names that have been
  brides,
And tasted those rare sweets for which
  I pine!
And far more heavy be thy grief and
  tine,[1]                530
Thou lazy swain, that mayst relieve
  my needs,
Than his upon whose liver always feeds
A hungry vulture!

*Enter Alexis.*

ALEX.             Can such beauty be
Safe in his [2] own guard, and not draw
  the eye
Of him that passeth on, to greedy gaze
Or covetous desire, whilst in a maze
The better part contemplates, giving
  rein
And wishéd freedom to the laboring
  vein? [3]
Fairest and whitest, may I crave to
  know
The cause of your retirement, why ye
  go                  540
Thus all alone? Methinks the downs are
  sweeter,
And the young company of swains more
  meeter,
Than these forsaken and untrodden
  places.
Give not yourself to loneness, and those
  graces
Hide from the eyes of men, that were
  intended
To live amongst us swains.
CLOE.          Thou art befriended,
Shepherd; in all my life I have not seen
A man in whom greater contents hath
  been
Than thou thyself art. I could tell thee
  more,
Were there but any hope left to re-
  store               550
My freedom lost. O, lend me all thy red,

Thou shamefast [4] Morning, when from
  Tithon's bed
Thou risest ever maiden!
ALEX.               If for me,
Thou sweetest of all sweets, these flashes
  be,
Speak, and be satisfied. O, guide her
  tongue,
My better angel; force my name among
Her modest thoughts, that the first
  word may be—
CLOE. Alexis, when the sun shall kiss the
  sea,
Taking his rest by the white Thetis'
  side,
Meet me in the holy wood, where I'll
  abide             560
Thy coming, shepherd.
ALEX.          If I stay behind,
An everlasting dullness, and the wind,
That as he passeth by shuts up the
  stream
Of Rhine or Volga, whilst the sun's
  hot beam
Beats back again, seize me, and let me
  turn
To coldness more than ice! O, how I
  burn
And rise in youth and fire! I dare not
  stay.
CLOE. My name shall be your word.
ALEX.        Fly, fly, thou day! *Exit.*
CLOE. My grief is great, if both these
  boys should fail;
He that will use all winds must shift
  his sail.        *Exit.*  570

ACTUS SECUNDUS. SCENA PRIMA.

*[The same.]*

*Enter an Old Shepherd, with a bell ringing,*
    *and the Priest of Pan following.*

PRIEST. Shepherds all, and maidens fair,
Fold your flocks up, for the air
Gins [5] to thicken, and the sun
Already his great course hath run.
See the dewdrops, how they kiss
Every little flower that is,
Hanging on their velvet heads,
Like a rope of crystal beads.
See the heavy clouds low [6] falling,

---

[1] Teen, sorrow; loss.  [2] Its.  [3] *I.e.*, pulsing blood.
[4] Modest.
[5] Begins.
[6] From 1656 edn. Original reads *lowde.*

And bright Hesperus down calling 10
The dead Night from underground,
At whose rising mists unsound,[1]
Damps and vapors fly apace,
Hovering o'er the wanton face
Of these pastures, where they come,
Striking dead both bud and bloom.
Therefore, from such danger lock
Every one his lovéd flock;
And let your dogs lie loose without,
Lest the wolf come as a scout 20
From the mountain, and, ere day,
Bear a lamb or kid away;
Or the crafty thievish fox
Break upon your simple flocks.
To secure yourselves from these,
Be not too secure in ease.
Let one eye his watches keep,
Whilst the tother [2] eye doth sleep;
So you shall good shepherds prove,
And forever hold the love 30
Of our great god. Sweetest slumbers
And soft silence fall in numbers
On your eyelids! So, farewell.
Thus I end my evening's knell. *Exeunt.*

*Enter Clorin, the shepherdess, sorting of
　herbs, and telling the natures of them.*

CLO. Now let me know what my best
　　art hath done,
　Helped by the great power of the vir-
　　tuous moon
　In her full light. O, you sons of earth,
　You only brood, unto whose happy birth
　Virtue was given, holding more of nature
　Than man, her first-born and most
　　perfect creature, 40
　Let me adore you! You, that only can
　Help or kill nature, drawing out that
　　span
　Of life and breath even to the end of
　　time;
　You, that these hands did crop long
　　before prime
　Of day, give me your names, and, next,
　　your hidden power.
　This is the clote,[3] bearing a yellow
　　flower;
　And this, black horehound. Both are
　　very good

[1] Unwholesome.
[2] That other.
[3] The name is applied to both the burdock and
the yellow water lily.

For sheep or shepherd bitten by a wood [4]
Dog's venomed tooth. These rhamnus [5]
　branches are,
Which, stuck in entries or about the
　bar 50
That holds the door fast, kill all enchant-
　ments, charms
(Were they Medea's verses) that do
　harms
To men or cattle. These for frenzy be
A speedy and a sovereign remedy—
The bitter wormwood, sage, and mari-
　gold—
Such sympathy with man's good they do
　hold.
This tormentil, whose virtue is to part
All deadly killing poison from the heart.
And here, narcissus root, for swellings
　best;
Yellow lysimachus,[6] to give sweet rest 60
To the faint shepherd, killing, where it
　comes,
All busy gnats and every fly that hums.
For leprosy, darnel and celandine,
With calamint, whose virtues do refine
The blood of man, making it free and
　fair
As the first hour it breathed, or the best
　air.
Here, other two; but your rebellious use
Is not for me, whose goodness is abuse.
Therefore, foul standergrass,[7] from me
　and mine
I banish thee, with lustful turpentine— 70
You that entice the veins and stir the
　heat
To civil mutiny, scaling the seat
Our reason moves in, and deluding it
With dreams and wanton fancies till
　the fit
Of burning lust be quenched, by ap-
　petite
Robbing the soul of blessedness and
　light.
And thou, light varvin [8] too, thou must
　go after,
Provoking easy souls to mirth and
　laughter;
No more shall I dip thee in water now,

[4] Mad.
[5] A thorny shrub. Dyce's emendation for
*Ramuus.*
[6] Loosestrife.
[7] A variety of orchid.
[8] Vervain.

And sprinkle every post and every
bough                                    80
With thy well-pleasing juice, to make
the grooms
Swell with high mirth, as with joy all
the rooms.

*Enter Thenot.*[1]

THE. This is the cabin where the best of
all
Her sex that ever breathed, or ever
shall
Give heat or happiness to the shep-
herd's side,
Doth only to her worthy self abide.
Thou blessèd star, I thank thee for thy
light,
Thou by whose power the darkness of
sad night
Is banished from the earth, in whose
dull place
Thy chaster beams play on the heavy
face                                     90
Of all the world, making the blue sea
smile
To see how cunningly thou dost be-
guile
Thy brother of his brightness, giving
day
Again from chaos; whiter than that way
That leads to Jove's high court, and
chaster far
Than chastity itself, yon blessèd star
That nightly shines; thou, all the con-
stancy
That in all women was or e'er shall be,
From whose fair eyeballs flies that holy
fire
That poets[2] style the mother of de-
sire,                                    100
Infusing into every gentle breast
A soul of greater price, and far more
blessed
Than that quick power which gives a
difference
Twixt man and creatures of a lower
sense!
CLO. Shepherd, how cam'st thou hither
to this place?
No way is trodden; all the verdant grass

The spring shot up stands yet unbruisèd
here
Of any foot; only the dappled deer,
Far from the feared sound of crooked
horn,
Dwells in this fastness.
THE.            Chaster than the morn,   110
I have not wandered, or by strong
illusion
Into this virtuous place have made in-
trusion;
But hither am I come (believe me, fair)
To seek you out, of whose great good
the air
Is full, and strongly labors, whilst the
sound
Breaks against heaven, and drives into
a stound[3]
The amazèd shepherd, that such virtue
can
Be resident in lesser than a man.
CLO. If any art I have, or hidden skill,
May cure thee of disease or festered
ill                                      120
Whose grief or greenness to another's
eye
May seem unpossible of remedy,
I dare yet undertake it.
THE.                'Tis no pain
I suffer through disease, no beating vein
Conveys infection dangerous to the heart,
No part impostumed,[4] to be cured by art,
This body holds, and yet a feller[5] grief
Than ever skillful hand did give relief,
Dwells on my soul, and may be healed
by you,
Fair, beauteous virgin.
CLO.            Then, shepherd, let me sue   130
To know thy grief; that man yet never
knew
The way to health that durst not show
his sore.
THE. Then, fairest, know, I love you.
CLO.                Swain, no more!
Thou hast abused the strictness of this
place,
And offered sacrilegious foul disgrace
To the sweet rest of these interrèd
bones,
For fear of whose ascending, fly at
once,

---

[1] From 1629 edn. Original reads *Shepherd.*
The following speech heads also read *Shep.* in
the original.
[2] From 1629 edn. Original reads *ports.*

[3] Astonishment. From 1634 edn. Original has
*stround.*
[4] Abscessed.                    [5] Crueler.

Thou and thy idle passions, that the
    sight
Of death and speedy vengeance may
    not fright
Thy very soul with horror.
[The.] [1]                    Let me not, 140
Thou all perfection, merit such a blot
For my true, zealous faith.
Clo.                    Dar'st thou abide
To see this holy earth at once divide,
And give her body up? For sure it will,
If thou pursu'st with wanton flames
    to fill
This hallowed place; therefore repent
    and go,
Whilst I with praye[r]s appease his
    ghost below,
That else would tell thee what it were
    to be
A rival in that virtuous love that he
Embraces yet.
The.        'Tis not the white or red 150
Inhabits in your cheek that thus can
    wed
My mind to adoration; nor your eye,
Though it be full and fair; your fore-
    head high
And smooth as Pelops' shoulder; not
    the smile
Lies watching in those dimples to be-
    guile
The easy soul; your hands and fingers
    long,
With veins enameled richly, nor your
    tongue,
Though it spoke sweeter than Arion's
    harp;
Your hair woven into many a curious
    warp,
Able in endless error to infold [2]     160
The wand'ring soul; not the true, per-
    fect mold
Of all your body, which as pure doth
    show
In maiden whiteness as the Alpsian
    snow—
All these, were but your constancy
    away,
Would please me less than a black,
    stormy day
The wretched seaman toiling through
    the deep.

But, whilst this honored strictness you
    dare keep,
Though all the plagues that e'er be-
    gotten were
In the great womb of air were settled
    here,
In opposition, I would, like the tree, 170
Shake off those drops of weakness, and
    be free
Even in the arm of danger.
Clo.                    Wouldst thou have
Me raise again, fond [3] man, from silent
    grave
Those sparks that long ago were buried
    here
With my dead friend's cold ashes?
The.                    Dearest dear,
I dare not ask it, nor you must not
    grant;
Stand strongly to your vow, and do
    not faint.
Remember how he loved ye, and be
    still
The same opinion speaks ye. Let not
    will,[4]
And that great god of women, ap-
    petite,                    180
Set up your blood again; do not invite
Desire and fancy from their long exile,
To seat them once more in a pleasing
    smile.
Be, like a rock, made firmly up gainst
    all
The power of angry heaven or the
    strong fall
Of Neptune's battery. If ye yield, I
    die
To all affection; 'tis that loyalty
Ye tie unto this grave I so admire.
And yet there's something else I would
    desire,                    189
If you would hear me, but withal deny.
O, Pan, what an uncertain destiny
Hangs over all my hopes! I will retire,
For, if I longer stay, this double fire
Will lick my life up.
Clo.                Do; and let time wear out
What art and nature cannot bring about.
The. Farewell, thou soul of virtue, and be
    blessed
Forever, whilst I wretched rest
    Thus to myself! Yet grant me leave to
    dwell

[1] From 1629 edn.
[2] From 1634 edn. Original has *unfold*.

[3] Foolish.                    [4] Desire, lust.

In kenning [1] of this arbor; yon same dell,
O'ertopped with mourning cypress and
sad yew, 200
Shall be my cabin, where I'll early rue,
Before the sun hath kissed this dew
away,
The hard uncertain chance which faith
doth lay
Upon this head.
CLO. The gods give quick release
And happy cure unto thy hard disease! [2]
*Exeunt.*

*Enter Sullen Shepherd.*

SULL. I do not love this wench that I
should meet,
For never did my unconstant eye yet
greet
That beauty, were it sweeter or more fair
Than the new blossoms when the morn-
ing air
Blows gently on them, or the breaking
light 210
When many maiden blushes to our
sight
Shoot from his early face—were all
these set
In some neat form before me, 'twould
not get
The least love from me. Some desire it
might,
And present burning. All to me in sight
Are equal; be they fair or black or
brown,
Virgin or careless wanton, I can crown
My appetite with any; swear as oft,
And weep, as any; melt my words as
soft 219
Into a maiden's ears, and tell how long
My heart has been her servant, and
how strong
My passions are; call her unkind and
cruel;
Offer her all I have to gain the jewel
Maidens so highly praise; then loathe,
and fly.
This do I hold a blessèd destiny.

*Enter Amarillis.*

AMAR. Hail, shepherd! Pan bless both
thy flock and thee
For being mindful of thy word to me!

SULL. Welcome, fair shepherdess! Thy
loving swain
Gives thee the selfsame wishes back
again,
Who till this present hour ne'er knew
that eye 230
Could make me cross mine arms, or
daily die
With fresh consumings. Boldly tell
me, then,
How shall we part their faithful loves,
and when?
Shall I belie him to her? Shall I swear
His faith is false and he loves every-
where?
I'll say he mocked her the other day to
you,
Which will by your confirming show as
true,
For she [3] is of so pure an honesty,
To think, because she [3] will not, none
will lie.
Or else to him I'll slander Amoret, 240
And say she but seems chaste. I'll
swear she met
Me mongst the shady sycamores last
night,
And loosely offered up her flame and
sprite
Into my bosom, made a wanton bed
Of leaves and many flowers, where she
spread
Her willing body to be pressed by me.
There have I carved her name on many
a tree,
Together with mine own. To make this
show
More full of seeming—Hobinal, you
know,
Son to the aged shepherd of the glen, 250
Him I have sorted out of many men,
To say he found us at our private sport,
And roused us fore our time by his re-
sort.
This to confirm, I've promised to the
boy
Many a pretty knack and many a toy,
As gren [4] to catch him birds, with bow
and bolt
To shoot at nimble squirrels in the holt, [5]
A pair of painted buskins, and a lamb
Soft as his own locks or the down of
swan.

---

[1] View. [2] Dis-ease, discomfort.

[3] Early edns. read *he*. [4] Snare. [5] Wood.

This I have done to win ye, which doth
give                                        260
Me double pleasure.  Discord makes me
live.
AMAR.  Loved swain, I thank ye.  These
tricks might prevail
With other rustic shepherds, but will
fail
Even once to stir, much more to over-
throw,
His fixéd love from judgment, who doth
know
Your nature, my end, and his chosen's
merit.
Therefore some stronger way must force
his spirit,
Which I have found: give second,[1] and
my love
Is everlasting thine.
SULL.                          Try me, and prove.
AMAR.  These happy pair of lovers meet
straightway,                                270
Soon as they fold their flocks up with
the day,
In the thick grove bordering upon yon
hill,
In whose hard side nature hath carved a
well,
And, but that matchless spring which
poets know,
Was ne'er the like to this.  By it doth
grow
About the sides all herbs which witches
use,
All simples good for medicine or abuse,
All sweets that crown the happy nup-
tial day
With all their colors.  There the month
of May                                      279
Is ever dwelling; all is young and green:
There's not a grass on which was ever
seen
The falling autumn or cold winter's hand,
So full of heat and virtue is the land
About this fountain, which doth slowly
break,
Below yon mountain's foot, into a creek
That waters all the valley, giving fish
Of many sorts to fill the shepherd's
dish.
This holy well, my grandam that is
dead,
Right wise in charms, hath often to me
said,

Hath power to change the form of any
creature,                                   290
Being thrice dipped over the head, into
what feature
Or shape 'twould please the letter-down
to crave,
Who must pronounce this charm too,
which she gave        [Shows a scroll.]
Me on her deathbed, told me what, and
how,
I should apply unto the patients' brow
That would be changed, casting them
thrice asleep,
Before I trusted them into this deep.
All this she showed me, and did charge
me prove
This secret of her art, if crossed in
love.
I'll this attempt now, shepherd.    I
have here                                   300
All her prescriptions, and I will not
fear
To be myself dipped.  Come, my temples
bind
With these sad herbs, and, when I sleep
you find,
As you do speak your charm, thrice
down me let,
And bid the water raise me Amoret;
Which being done, leave me to my af-
fair,
And, ere the day shall quite itself out-
wear,
I will return unto my shepherd's arm.
Dip me again, and then repeat this
charm,
And pluck me up myself, whom freely
take,                                       310
And the hott'st fire of thine affection
slake.
SULL.  And, if I fit thee not, then fit not
me.
I long the truth of this well's power to
see.                              Exeun t.[2]

*Enter Daphnis.*

DAPH.  Here will I stay, for this the covert is
Where I appointed Cloe.  Do not miss,
Thou bright-eyed virgin; come, O, come,
my fair!

[1] Help.
[2] In the first quarto only here follows: "ACTUS
SECUNDUS. SCENA QUARTA"—the only attempt
in the play to divide acts into shorter scenes.

Be not abused [1] with fear, or let cold care
Of honor stay thee from thy shepherd's arm,
Who would as hard be won to offer harm
To thy chaste thoughts, as whiteness from the day, 320
Or yon great round [2] to move another way.
My language shall be honest, full of truth;
My flame, as smooth and spotless as my youth.
I will not entertain that wand'ring thought,
Whose easy current may at length be brought
To a loose vastness.

ALEX. (*Within.*) Cloe!
DAPH. 'Tis her voice,
And I must answer.—Cloe!—O, the choice
Of dear embraces, chaste and holy strains
Our hands shall give! I charge you, all my veins,
Through which the blood and spirit take their way, 330
Lock up your disobedient heats, and stay
Those mutinous desires that else would grow
To strong rebellion; do not wilder show
Than blushing modesty may entertain.

ALEX. (*Within.*) Cloe!
DAPH. There sounds that blesséd name again,
And I will meet it. Let me not mistake.

*Enter Alexis.*

This is some shepherd. Sure, I am awake.
What may this riddle mean? I will retire,
To give myself more knowledge.
[*Retires.*]
ALEX. O, my fire,
How thou consum'st me!—Cloe, answer me! 340
Alexis, strong Alexis, high and free,
Calls upon Cloe. See, mine arms are full
Of entertainment, ready for to pull
That golden fruit which too-too long hath hung

Tempting the greedy eye. Thou stayest too long;
I am impatient of these mad delays;
I must not leave unsought those many ways
That lead into this center, till I find
Quench for my burning lust. I come, unkind! *Exit Alexis.*
DAPH. [*Coming forward.*] Can my imagination work me so much ill 350
That I may credit this for truth and still
Believe mine eyes? Or shall I firmly hold
Her yet untainted, and these sights but bold
Illusion? Sure, such fancies oft have been
Sent to abuse true love, and yet are seen
Daring to blind the virtuous thought [3] with error.
But be they far from me with their fond terror!
I am resolved my Cloe yet is true.

CLOE. (*Within.*) Cloe!
[DAPH.] Hark! Cloe! Sure, this voice is new,
Whose shrillness, like the sounding of a bell, 360
Tells me it is a woman.—Cloe, tell
Thy blessed name again.

CLOE. (*Within.*) Here!
[DAPH.] O, what a grief is this, to be so near
And not encounter!

*Enter Cloe.*

CLOE. Shepherd, we are met;
Draw close into the covert, lest the wet,
Which falls like lazy mists upon the ground,
Soak through your startups. [4]
DAPH. Fairest, are you found?
How have we wandered, that the better part
Of this good night is perished? O, my heart!
How have I longed to meet ye, how to kiss 370
Those lily hands, how to receive the bliss
That charming tongue gives to the happy ear

---

[1] Cheated.  [2] *I.e.*, the moon.
[3] From 1634 edn. Original reads *though*.
[4] Rustic shoes.

Of him that drinks your language! But
   I fear
I am too much unmannered, far too
   rude,
And almost grown lascivious, to intrude
These hot behaviors, where regard of
   fame,
Honor, and modesty, a virtuous name,
And such discourse as one fair sister
   may
Without offense unto the brother say,
Should rather have been tendered. But,
   believe,                                          380
Here dwells a better temper. Do not
   grieve,
Then, ever-kindest, that my first salute
Seasons so much of fancy.[1] I am mute
Henceforth to all discourses but shall be
Suiting to your sweet thoughts and
   modesty.
Indeed, I will not ask a kiss of you,
No, not to wring your fingers, nor to sue
To those blessed pair of fixéd stars for
   smiles.
All a young lover's cunning, all his
   wiles,                                            389
And pretty wanton dyings shall to me
Be strangers; only to your chastity
I am devoted ever.
CLOE.                          Honest swain,
First let me thank you, then return
   again
As much of my love.—[Aside.]     No,
   thou art too cold,
Unhappy boy, not tempered to my
   mold;
Thy blood falls heavy downward. 'Tis
   not fear
To offend in boldness wins; they never
   wear
Deservéd favors that deny to take
When they are offered freely.    Do I
   wake,
To see a man of his youth, years, and
   feature,                                          400
And such a one as we call goodly crea-
   ture,
Thus backward?    What a world of
   precious art
Were merely[2] lost, to make him do his
   part!
But I will shake him off, that dares not
   hold.

[1] Amorousness.                    [2] Wholly.

Let men that hope to be beloved be
   bold.—
Daphnis, I do desire, since we are met
So happily, our lives and fortunes set
Upon one stake, to give assurance now,
By interchange of hands and holy vow,
Never to break again.    Walk you that
   way,                                              410
Whilst I in zealous meditation stray
A little this way.    When we both have
   ended
These rites and duties, by the woods be-
   friended
And secrecy of night, retire and find
An aged oak, whose hollowness may bind
Us both within his body.    Thither go.
It stands within yon bottom.
DAPH.               Be it so.    Ex[it] Daph[nis].
CLOE. And I will meet there never more
   with thee,
Thou idle shamefastness!
ALEX. [Within.]                    Cloe!
CLOE.                               'Tis he
That dare, I hope, be bolder.
ALEX. [Within.]                    Cloe!
CLOE.                              Now,   420
Great Pan, for Syrinx' sake, bid speed
   our plow!                         Exit Cloe.

ACTUS TERTIUS. SCENA PRIMA.

[The same.]

Enter the Sullen Shepherd, with Amarillis
                    in a sleep.

SULL. From thy forehead thus I take
These herbs, and charge thee not awake
Till in yonder holy well
Thrice, with powerful magic spell
Filled with many a baleful word,
Thou hast been dipped.    Thus, with my
   cord
Of blasted hemp, by moonlight twined,
I do thy sleepy body bind.
I turn thy head into the east,
And thy feet into the west,                    10
Thy left arm to the south put forth,
And thy right unto the north.
I take thy body from the ground,
In this deep and deadly sound,[3]
And into this holy spring
I let thee slide down by my string.—
          [Lowers her into the well.]
Take this maid, thou holy pit,

[3] Swound, swoon.

To thy bottom; nearer yet.
In thy water pure and sweet,
By thy leave I dip her feet.　　20
Thus I let her lower yet,
That her ankles may be wet.
Yet down lower, let her knee
In thy waters washéd be.
There stop.  Fly away,
Everything that loves the day!
Truth, that hath but one face,
Thus I charm thee from this place.
Snakes that cast your coats for new.
Chameleons that alter hue,　　30
Hares that yearly sexes change,
Proteus alt'ring oft and strange,
Hecate with shapës three,
Let this maiden changéd be,
With this holy water wet,
To the shape of Amoret!
Cynthia, work thou with my charm!—
Thus I draw thee, free from harm,
[*Draws her from the well, in the shape of Amoret.*]
Up out of this blesséd lake.
Rise both like her and awake!　　40
　　　　　　　　　　*She awaketh.*
AMAR.  Speak, shepherd, am I Amoret to
　　sight?
　　Or hast thou missed in any magic
　　rite,
　　For want of which any defect in me
　　May make our practices discovered be?
SULL.  By yonder moon, but that I here
　　do stand,
　　Whose breath hath thus re-formed thee,
　　and whose hand
　　Let thee down dry, and plucked thee up
　　thus wet,
　　I should myself take thee for Amoret!
　　Thou art in clothes, in feature, voice,
　　and hue
　　So like that sense cannot distinguish
　　you.　　50
AMAR.  Then this deceit, which cannot
　　crosséd be,
　　At once [1] shall lose her him, and gain
　　thee me.
　　Hither she needs must come, by promise
　　made;
　　And, sure, his nature never was so bad,
　　To bid a virgin meet him in the wood
　　When night and fear are up, but under-
　　stood

[1] Simultaneously.

'Twas his part to come first.  Being come,
　　I'll say
My constant love made me come first
　　and stay;
Then will I lead him further to the
　　grove.
But stay you here, and, if his own true
　　love　　60
Shall seek him here, set her in some wrong
　　path,
Which say her lover lately trodden hath.
I'll not be far from hence.  If need there
　　be,
Here is another charm [*Gives a scroll.*],
　　whose power will free
The dazzled sense, read by the moon-
　　beams clear,
And in my own true shape make me
　　appear.

*Enter Perigot.*

SULL.  Stand close; here's Perigot, whose
　　constant heart
Longs to behold her in whose shape thou
　　art.　　　　[*Retires with Amarillis.*]
PERI.  This is the place.—Fair Amoret!—
　　The hour
Is yet scarce come.  Here every sylvan
　　power　　70
Delights to be about yon sacred well,
Which they have blessed with many a
　　powerful spell;
For never traveler in dead of night,
Nor strayéd beasts have fall'n in; but,
　　when sight
Hath failed them, then their right way
　　they have found
By help of them, so holy is the ground.
But I will farther seek, lest Amoret
Should be first come, and so stray long
　　unmet.—
My Amoret, Amoret!　　　　　　*Exit.* [2]
AMAR.　　　　　　　　Perigot!
PERI.  [*Within.*] My love!
AMAR.　　　　　I come, my love!　*Exit.*
SULL.　　　　　Now she hath got　80
Her own desires, and I shall gainer be
Of my long-looked-for hopes as well as
　　she.
How bright the moon shines here, as if
　　she strove
To show her glory in this little grove

[2] Original reads *Ex. Amarillis. Perigot.*

*Enter Amoret.*

To some new-lovéd shepherd!—[*Aside.*]
    Yonder is
Another Amoret. Where differs this
From that? But that she Perigot hath
    met,
I should have ta'en this for the counter-
    feit.
Herbs, woods, and springs, the power
    that in you lies,
If mortal men could know your prop-
    erties!                                    90
AMO. Methinks it is not night; I have no
    fear,
Walking this wood, of lion or of bear,
Whose names at other times have made
    me quake,
When any shepherdess in her tale spake
Of some of them that underneath a wood
Have torn true lovers that together
    stood.
Methinks there are no goblins, and men's
    talk,
That in these woods the nimble fairies
    walk,
Are fables—such a strong heart I have
    got
Because I come to meet with Peri-
    got.—                                     100
My Perigot! Who's that? My Perigot?
SULL. Fair maid!
AMO.        Aye me, thou art not Perigot?
SULL. But I can tell ye news of Perigot.
An hour together under yonder tree
He sat with wreathéd arms, and called
    on thee
And said, "Why, Amoret, stayest thou
    so long?"
Then starting up, down yonder path he
    flung,
Lest thou hadst missed thy way. Were
    it daylight,
He could not yet have borne him out of
    sight.
AMO. Thanks, gentle shepherd; and be-
    shrew [1] my stay,                        110
That made me fearful I had lost my way.
As fast as my weak legs (that cannot be
Weary with seeking him) will carry me,
I'll follow; and, for this thy care of me,
Pray Pan thy love may ever follow thee!
                                         *Exit.*

[1] Curse.

SULL. How bright she was, how lovely
    did she show!
Was it not pity to deceive her so?
She plucked her garments up, and tripped
    away,
And with a virgin innocence did pray
For me that perjured [2] her.  Whilst
    she was here                             120
Methought the beams of light that did
    appear
Were shot from her; methought the
    moon gave none
But what it had from her.  She was
    alone
With me; if then her presence did so
    move,
Why did not I essay to win her love?
She would (not sure) [3] have yielded
    unto me.
Women love only opportunity,
And not the man; or, if she had denied,
Alone, I might have forced her to have
    tried
Who had been stronger.  O, vain fool,
    to let                                    130
Such blessed occasion pass! I'll follow yet.
My blood is up; I cannot now forbear.

*Enter Alex[is] and Cloe.*

I come, sweet Amoret!—[*Aside.*] Soft,
    who is here?
A pair of lovers? He shall yield her me;
Now lust is up, alike all women be.
                                    [*Retires.*]
ALEX. Where shall we rest? But for the
    love of me,
Cloe, I know, ere this would weary be.
CLOE. Alexis, let us rest here, if the place
Be private, and out of the common
    trace [4]                                 139
Of every shepherd; for, I understood,
This night a number are about the
    wood.
Then let us choose some place, where,
    out of sight,
We freely may enjoy our stol'n delight.
ALEX. Then boldly here, where we shall
    ne'er be found.
No shepherd's way lies here; 'tis hallowed
    ground.
No maid seeks here her strayéd cow
    or sheep.

[2] Swore falsely to.          [4] Track, path.
[3] *I.e.,* perhaps (?).

Fairies and fauns and satyrs do it keep.
Then, carelessly rest here, and clip and
kiss,
And let no fear make us our pleasures
miss.
CLOE. Then, lie by me; the sooner we
begin,                                         150
The longer ere the day descry our sin.
                                    [*They lie down.*]
SULL. [*Coming forward.*] Forbear to touch
my love; or, by yon flame,
The greatest power that shepherds
dare to name,
Here where thou sit'st, under this holy
tree,
Her to dishonor, thou shalt buried be!
ALEX. If Pan himself should come out
of the lawns,[1]
With all his troops of satyrs and of
fauns,
And bid me leave, I swear by her two
eyes
(A greater oath than thine), I would not
rise!
SULL. Then, from the cold earth never
thou shalt move,                               160
But lose at one stroke both thy life and
love.                          [*Wounds him.*]
CLOE. Hold, gentle shepherd!
SULL.                          Fairest shepherdess,
Come you with me; I do not love ye
less
Than that fond man that would have
kept you there
From me of more desert.
ALEX.                          O, yet forbear
To take her from me!  Give me leave to
die
By her!

*The Satyr enters; he [2] runs one way and
                                she another.*

SAT.        Now, whilst the moon doth rule
the sky,
And the stars, whose feeble light
Gives a pale shadow to the night,
Are up, great Pan commanded me         170
To walk this grove about, whilst he,
In a corner of the wood,
Where never mortal foot hath stood,
Keeps dancing, music, and a feast,
To entertain a lovely guest;
Where he gives her many a rose—

Sweeter than the breath that blows
The leaves—grapes, berries of the best.
I never saw so great a feast.            179
But to my charge.  Here must I stay,
To see what mortals lose their way,
And by a false fire, seeming bright,
Train them in and leave them right.
Then must I watch if any be
Forcing of a chastity.
If I find it, then in haste
Give my wreathéd horn a blast,
And the fairies all will run,
Wildly dancing by the moon,
And will pinch him to the bone           190
Till his lustful thoughts be gone.
ALEX. O, death!
SAT. Back again about this ground;
Sure, I hear a mortal sound.—
I bind thee by this powerful spell,
By the waters of this well,
By the glimmering moonbeams bright,
Speak again, thou mortal wight!
ALEX. O!
SAT.[3] Here the foolish mortal lies,     200
Sleeping on the ground.—Arise!—
The poor wight is almost dead;
On the ground his wounds have bled,
And his clothes fouled with his blood.
To my goddess in the wood
Will I lead him, whose hands pure
Will help this mortal wight to cure.
                          [*Exit, supporting Alexis.*]

*Enter Cloe again.*

CLOE. Since I beheld yon [4] shaggy man,
my breast
Doth pant; each bush, methinks, should
hide a beast.
Yet my desire keeps still above my
fear.                                          210
I would fain meet some shepherd, knew I
where,
For from one cause of fear I am most
free:
It is impossible to ravish me,
I am so willing.  Here upon this ground
I left my love, all bloody with his wound;
Yet, till that fearful shape made me
be gone,
Though he were hurt, I furnished was
of one;

[3] Original here repeats *Speak again, thou
mortal wight.*
[4] From 1634 edn.  Original has *you.*

But now both lost.—Alexis, speak or
move,
If thou hast any life; thou art yet my
love!—
He's dead, or else is with his little
might                                              220
Crept from the bank for fear of that ill
sprite.—
Then, where art thou that struck'st my
love? O, stay!
Bring me thyself in change, and then
I'll say
Thou hast some justice.  I will make
thee trim
With flowers and garlands that were
meant for him;
I'll clip thee round with both mine arms,
as fast
As I did mean he should have been em-
braced.
But thou art fled.—What hope is left
for me?
I'll run to Daphnis in the hollow tree,
Who I did mean to mock; though hope
be small                                          230
To make him bold, rather than none at
all,
I'll try him; his heart, and my behavior
too,
Perhaps may teach him what he ought
to do.                                        *Exit.*

*Enter the Sullen Shepherd.*

SULL. This was the place.  'Twas but my
feeble sight,
Mixed with the horror of my deed, and
night,
That shaped these fears, and made me
run away,
And lose my beauteous, hardly-gotten
prey.—
Speak, gentle shepherdess!  I am alone,
And tender love for love.—But she is gone
From me, that, having struck her lover
dead,                                              240
For silly fear left her alone and fled.
And see, the wounded body is removed
By her of whom it was so well beloved.

*Enter Perigot, and Amarillis in the shape of
Amoret.*

But all these fancies must be quite
forgot.

I must lie close; here comes young Peri-
got,
With subtle Amarillis in the shape
Of Amoret.    Pray, love, he may not
scape!                                 [*Retires.*]
AMAR. Beloved Perigot, show me some
place
Where I may rest my limbs weak with
the chase
Of thee, an hour before thou cam'st
at least.                                          250
PERI. Beshrew my tardy steps!    Here
shalt thou rest
Upon this holy bank.  No deadly snake
Upon this turf herself in folds doth make;
Here is no poison for the toad to feed.
Here boldly spread thy hands—no
venomed weed
Dares blister them; no slimy snail dare
creep
Over thy face when thou art fast asleep;
Here never durst the babbling cuckoo
spit; [1]
No slough [2] of falling star did ever hit
Upon this bank.  Let this thy cabin be;
This other, set with violets, for me.    261
                              [*They lie down.*]
AMAR. Thou dost not love me, Perigot.
PERI.                          Fair maid,
You only love to hear it often said;
You do not doubt.
AMAR.              Believe me, but I do.
PERI. What, shall we now begin again to
woo?
'Tis the best way to make your lover
last,
To play with him when you have caught
him fast.
AMAR. By Pan I swear, beloved Perigot,
And by yon moon, I think thou lov'st
me not.
PERI. By Pan I swear—and, if I falsely
swear,                                            270
Let him not guard my flocks.    Let
foxes tear
My earliest lambs, and wolves, whilst
I do sleep,
Fall on the rest—a rot among my sheep.
I love thee better than the careful ewe
The new-yeaned lamb that is of her own
hue.

[1] An allusion to cuckoo-spit, a frothy secre-
tion exuded by the larvæ of certain insects.
[2] Shell.

I dote upon thee more than that young lamb
Doth on the bag that feeds him from his dam!
Were there a sort [1] of wolves got in my fold,
And one ran after thee, both young and old
Should be devoured, and it should be my strife          280
To save thee whom I love above my life.

AMAR. How should I trust thee, when I see thee choose
Another bed, and dost my side refuse?

PERI. 'Twas only that the chaste thoughts might be shown
Twixt thee and me, although we were alone.

AMAR. Come, Perigot will show his power, that he
Can make his Amoret, though she weary be,
Rise nimbly from her couch and come to his.
Here, take thy Amoret; embrace and kiss.          [Comes to him.]

PERI. What means my love?

AMAR.          To do as lovers should,          290
That are to be enjoyed, not to be wooed.
There's ne'er a shepherdess in all the plain
Can kiss thee with more art; there's none can feign
More wanton tricks.

PERI.          Forbear, dear soul, to try
Whether my heart be pure; I'll rather die
Than nourish one thought to dishonor thee.

AMAR. Still think'st thou such a thing as chastity
Is amongst women? Perigot, there's none
That with her love is in a wood alone,
And would come home a maid; be not abused          300
With thy fond first belief; let time be used.          [Perigot rises.]
Why dost thou rise?

PERI.          My true heart thou hast slain!

AMAR. Faith, Perigot, I'll pluck thee down again.

_____
[1] Pack.

PERI. Let go, thou serpent, that into my breast
Hast with thy cunning dived!—Art not in jest?

AMAR. Sweet love, lie down.

PERI.          Since this I live to see,
Some bitter north wind blast my flocks and me!

AMAR. You swore you loved, yet will not do my will.

PERI. O, be as thou wert once, I'll love thee still!

AMAR. I am as still I was, and all my kind,          310
Though other shows we have, poor men to blind.

PERI. Then, here I end all love; and, lest my vain
Belief should ever draw me in again,
Before thy face, that hast my youth misled,
I end my life! My blood be on thy head!          [Offers to kill himself.]

AMAR. [Rising.] O, hold thy hands, thy Amoret doth cry!

PERI. Thou counsel'st well; first, Amoret shall die,
That is the cause of my eternal smart!
          He runs after her.

AMAR. O, hold!

PERI.          This steel shall pierce thy lustful heart!          [Exeunt.]

_The Sullen Shepherd steps out and uncharms her._

SULL. Up and down, everywhere,          320
I strew the herbs to purge the air.
Let your odor drive hence
All mists that dazzle sense.
Herbs and springs, whose hidden might
Alters shapes, and mocks the sight,
Thus I charge ye to undo
All before I brought ye to!
Let her fly, let her scape;
Give again her own shape!          [Retires.]

_Enter Amarillis [in her own shape] [2] [, followed by Perigot]._

AMAR. Forbear, thou gentle swain! Thou dost mistake;          330
She whom thou follow'dst fled into the brake,

_____
[2] From 1629 edn.

And, as I crossed thy way, I met thy
  wrath,
The only fear of which near slain me hath.
PERI. Pardon, fair shepherdess; my rage
  and night
Were both upon me, and beguiled my
  sight.
But far be it from me to spill the blood
Of harmless maids that wander in the
  wood!        *Ex[it Amarillis].*

*Enter Amoret.*

AMO. Many a weary step, in yonder path,
Poor hopeless Amoret twice trodden
  hath,          339
To seek her Perigot, yet cannot hear
His voice.—My Perigot! She loves thee
  dear
That calls.
PERI.         See yonder where she is!
How fair
She shows, and yet her breath infests
  the air!
AMO. My Perigot!
PERI.         Here.
AMO.            Happy!
PERI.            Hapless! First
It lights on thee; the next blow is the
  worst.         *[Wounds her.]*
AMO. Stay, Perigot! My love, thou art un-
  just.         *[Falls.]*
PERI. Death is the best reward that's
  due to lust.      *Exit Perigot.*
SULL. [*Aside.*] Now shall their love be
  crossed, for, being struck,
I'll throw her in the fount, lest being
  took
By some night-traveler, whose honest
  care         350
May help to cure her—
          *[Comes forward.]*
        Shepherdess, prepare
Yourself to die!
AMO.        No mercy I do crave.
Thou canst not give a worse blow than
  I have.
Tell him that gave me this, who loved
  him too,
He struck my soul, and not my body
  through;
Tell him, when I am dead, my soul
  shall be
At peace, if he but think he injured
  me.

SULL. In this fount be thy grave. Thou
  wert not meant
Sure for a woman, thou art so innocent.—
        *He flings her into the well.*
She cannot scape, for, underneath the
  ground,         360
In a long hollow the clear spring is bound,
Till on yon side, where the morn's sun
  doth look,
The struggling water breaks out in a
  brook.        *Exit.*

*The God of the River riseth with Amoret in*
*        his arms.*

GOD. What powerful charms my streams
  do bring
Back again unto their spring,
With such force that I their god,
Three times striking with my rod,
Could not keep them in their ranks?
My fishes shoot into the banks;
There's not one that stays and feeds;  370
All have hid them in the weeds.
Here's a mortal almost dead,
Fall'n into my riverhead,
Hallowed so with many a spell,
That till now none ever fell.
'Tis a female young and clear,
Cast in by some ravisher.
See, upon her breast a wound,
On which there is no plaster bound.
Yet, she's warm; her pulses beat;  380
'Tis a sign of life and heat.—
If thou be'st a virgin pure,
I can give a present cure.
Take a drop into thy wound,
From my watery lock[s], [1] more round
Than orient pearl, and far more pure
Than unchaste flesh may endure.—
See, she pants, and from her flesh
The warm blood gusheth out afresh.
She is an unpolluted maid;  390
I must have this bleeding stayed.
From my banks I pluck this flower
With holy hand, whose virtuous power
Is at once to heal and draw.
The blood returns. I never saw
A fairer mortal. Now doth break
Her deadly slumber.—Virgin, speak.
AMO. Who hath restored my sense, given
  me new breath,
And brought me back out of the arms of
  death?

[1] From 1629 edn.

GOD. I have healed thy wounds.
AMO.                              Ay me!    400
GOD. Fear not him that succored thee.
  I am this fountain's god; below,
  My waters to a river grow,
  And twixt two banks with osiers set,
  That only prosper in the wet,
  Through the meadows do they glide,
  Wheeling still on every side,
  Sometimes winding round about,
  To find the evenest channel out.
  And, if thou wilt go with me,        410
  Leaving mortal company,
  In the cool streams shalt thou lie,
  Free from harm as well as I.
  I will give thee for thy food
  No fish that useth [1] in the mud,
  But trout and pike, that love to swim
  Where tne gravel from the brim
  Through the pure streams may be seen;
  Orient pearl fit for a queen
  Will I give, thy love to win,          420
  And a shell to keep them in;
  Not a fish in all my brook
  That shall disobey thy look,
  But, when thou wilt, come sliding by,
  And from thy white hand take a fly;
  And, to make thee understand
  How I can my waves command,
  They shall bubble, whilst I sing,
  Sweeter than the silver string.

### THE SONG

  Do not fear to put thy feet          430
  Naked in the river sweet;
  Think not leech or newt or toad
  Will bite thy foot when thou hast trod;
  Nor let the water rising high,
  As thou wad'st in, make thee cry
  And sob; but ever live with me,
  And not a wave shall trouble thee.

AMO. Immortal power, that rul'st this
  holy flood,
  I know myself unworthy to be wooed
  By thee, a god, for ere this, but for
    thee,                             440
  I should have shown my weak mortality.
  Besides, by holy oath betwixt us twain,
  I am betrothed unto a shepherd swain,
  Whose comely face, I know, the gods
    above
  May make me leave to see, but not to
    love.

[1] Lives.

GOD. May he prove to thee as true!
  Fairest virgin, now adieu.
  I must make my waters fly,
  Lest they leave their channels dry,   449
  And beasts that come unto the spring
  Miss their morning's watering,
  Which I would not; for of late
  All the neighbor people sate
  On my banks, and from the fold
  Two white lambs of three weeks old
  Offered to my deity;
  For which this year they shall be free
  From raging floods that, as they pass,
  Leave their gravel in the grass;
  Nor shall their meads be overflown   460
  When their grass is newly mown.
AMO. For thy kindness to me shown,
  Never from thy banks be blown
  Any tree, with windy force,
  Cross [2] thy streams, to stop thy course;
  May no beast that comes to drink,
  With his horns cast down thy brink;
  May none that for thy fish do look,
  Cut thy banks to dam thy brook;
  Barefoot may no neighbor wade      470
  In thy cool streams, wife nor maid,
  When the spawns on stones do lie,
  To wash their hemp, and spoil the fry! [3]
GOD. Thanks, virgin. I must down again.
  Thy wound will put thee to no pain.
  Wonder not so soon 'tis gone;
  A holy hand was laid upon.         *Exit.*
AMO. And I, unhappy born to be,
  Must follow him that flies from me.
                *[Exit.]*

### [ACTUS QUARTUS. SCENA PRIMA [4]

#### *The same.]*

#### *Enter Perigot.*

PERI. She is untrue, unconstant, and
  unkind.
  She's gone, she's gone! Blow high, thou
    northwest wind,
  And raise the sea to mountains; let the
    trees
  That dare oppose thy raging fury leese [5]
  Their firm foundation, creep into the
    earth,

[2] Across.                    [3] Newly hatched fish.
[4] From 1629 edn. The act division in the original is indicated merely by *Finis actus terti[u]s.*
[5] Lose.

And shake the world as at the monstrous
   birth
Of some new prodigy, whilst I constant
   stand,
Holding this trusty boar spear in my
   hand,
And falling thus upon it.

*Enter to Perigot,*[1] *Amarillis running.*

AMAR. Stay thy dead-doing hand! Thou
   art too hot                                        10
Against thyself.  Believe me, comely
   swain,
If that thou diest, not all the showers of
   rain
The heavy clouds send down can wash
   away
That foul unmanly guilt the world will
   lay
Upon thee.  Yet thy love untainted
   stands.
Believe me, she is constant; not the
   sands
Can be so hardly numbered as she won.
I do not trifle, shepherd; by the moon
And all those lesser lights our eyes do
   view,
All that I told thee, Perigot, is true.     20
Then be a free man; put away despair
And will to die; smooth gently up that
   fair,
Dejected forehead; be as when those eyes
Took the first heat.
PERI.                          Alas, he double dies
That would believe, but cannot! 'Tis
   not well
Ye keep me thus from dying, here to
   dwell
With many worse companions.  But, O,
   death!
I am not yet enamored of this [2] breath
So much but I dare leave it; 'tis not pain
In forcing of a wound, nor after-gain     30
Of many days, can hold me from my
   will.
'Tis not myself, but Amoret, bids kill.
AMAR. Stay but a little, little—but one
   hour—
And, if I do not show thee, through the
   power
Of herbs and words I have, as dark as
   night,

Myself turned to thy Amoret, in sight,
Her very figure, and the robe she wears,
With tawny buskins, and the hook she
   bears
Of thine own carving, where your names
   are set,
Wrought underneath with many a
   curious fret,                                       40
The primrose-chaplet, tawdry-lace,[3] and
   ring,
Thou gav'st her for her singing, with
   each thing
Else that she wears about her, let me
   feel
The first fell stroke of that revenging
   steel!
PERI. I am contented, if there be a hope,
To give it entertainment for the scope
Of one poor hour.  Go; you shall find
   me next
Under yon shady beech, even thus per-
   plexed,
And thus believing.
AMAR.                          Bind, before I go,
Thy soul by Pan unto me, not to do     50
Harm or outrageous wrong upon thy
   life
Till my return.
PERI.                    By Pan, and by the strife
He had with Phœbus for the mastery,
When golden Midas judged their min-
   strelsy,
I will not!                                  *Exeunt.*

*Enter Satyr with Alexis, hurt.*

SAT. Softly gliding as I go,
With this burthen full of woe,
Through still silence of the night
Guided by the glowworm's light,
Hither am I come at last.                     60
Many a thicket have I passed;
Not a twig that durst deny me,
Not a bush that durst descry [4] me
To the little bird that sleeps
On the tender spray; nor creeps
That hardy worm with pointed tail,[5]
But if [6] I be under sail,
Flying faster than the wind,
Leaving all the clouds behind,
But doth hide her tender head            70
In some hollow tree, or bed

---

[1] Original reads *Perigot to enter.*
[2] From 1634 edn.  Original reads *his.*

[3] Lace bought at the fair of St. Audrey at Ely.
[4] Reveal.     [5] *I.e.,* a scorpion.     [6] Unless.

Of seeded nettles; not a hare
Can be started from his fare[1]
By my footing; nor a wish
Is more sudden, nor a fish
Can be found with greater ease
Cut the vast unbounded seas,
Leaving neither print nor sound,
Than I, when nimbly on the ground
I measure many a league an hour.            80
But, behold, the happy bower
That must ease me of my charge,
And by holy hand enlarge[2]
The soul of this sad man that yet
Lies fast bound in deadly fit.
Heaven and great Pan succor it!—
Hail, thou beauty of the bower,
Whiter than the paramour
Of my master! Let me crave            89
Thy virtuous help, to keep from grave
This poor mortal that here lies,
Waiting when the Destinies
Will undo his thread of life.
View the wound, by cruel knife
Trenched into him.

[*Enter Clorin.*]

CLO. What art thou call'st me from my
    holy rites,
    And with the fearéd name of death
        affrights
    My tender ears? Speak me thy name
        and will.
SAT. I am the satyr that did fill
    Your lap with early fruit, and will,            100
    When I hap to gather more,
    Bring ye better and more store.
    Yet I come not empty now:
    See, a blossom from the bough;
    But beshrew his heart that pulled it,
    And his perfect sight that culled it
    From the other springing blooms!
    For a sweeter youth the grooms
    Cannot show me, nor the downs,
    Nor the many neighboring towns.            110
    Low in yonder glade I found him;
    Softly in mine arms I bound him;
    Hither have I brought him sleeping
    In a trance, his wounds fresh weeping,
    In remembrance such youth may
    Spring and perish in a day.
CLO. Satyr, they wrong thee that do
    term thee rude;

Though thou be'st outward-rough and
    tawny-hued,
Thy manners are as gentle and as fair
As his who brags himself born only
    heir            120
To all humanity.—Let me see thy wound.
This herb will stay the current, being
    bound
Fast to the orifice, and this restrain
Ulcers and swellings, and such inward
    pain
As the cold air hath forced into the sore;
This to draw out such putrefying gore
As inward falls.
SAT.            Heaven grant it may do good!
CLO. Fairly wipe away the blood.
    Hold him gently, till I fling
    Water of a virtuous spring            130
    On his temples; turn him twice
    To the moonbeams; pinch him thrice,
    That the laboring soul may draw
    From his great eclipse.
SAT.            I saw
    His eyelids moving.
CLO.            Give him breath;
    All the danger of cold death
    Now is vanished! With this plaster
    And this unction do I master
    All the festered ill that may
    Give him grief another day.            140
SAT. See, he gathers up his sprite,
    And begins to hunt for light;
    Now a[3] gaps and breathes again.
    How the blood runs to the vein
    That erst was empty!
ALEX.            O my heart!
    My dearest, dearest Cloe! O, the smart
    Runs through my side! I feel some
        pointed thing
    Pass through my bowels, sharper than
        the sting
    Of scorpion.—
    Pan, preserve me!—What are you?            150
    Do not hurt me; I am true
    To my Cloe, though she fly,
    And leave me to this destiny.
    There she stands, and will not lend
    Her smooth white hand to help her
        friend.
    But I am much mistaken, for that face
    Bears more austerity and modest grace,
    More reproving and more awe,
    Than these eyes yet ever saw

---

[1] Path.            [2] Free.            [3] He.

In my Cloe. O, my pain                    160
Eagerly renews again!
Give me your help for his sake you love
    best.
CLO. Shepherd, thou canst not possible
    take rest,
Till thou hast laid aside all heats, desires,
Provoking thoughts that stir up lusty
    fires,
Commerce with wanton eyes, strong
    blood, and will
To execute. These must be purged until
The vein grow whiter; then repent, and
    pray
Great Pan to keep you from the like
    decay,
And I shall undertake your cure with
    ease;                    170
Till when, this virtuous plaster [1] will
    displease [2]
Your tender sides. Give me your hand,
    and rise!
Help him a little, satyr, for his thighs
Yet are feeble.
ALEX. [Rising.]      Sure, I have lost much
    blood.
SAT. 'Tis no matter; 'twas not good.
Mortal, you must leave your wooing;
Though there be a joy in doing,
Yet it brings much grief behind it.
They best feel it that do find it.
CLO. Come, bring him in; I will attend his
    sore.—                    180
When you are well, take heed you lust
    no more.                    [They retire.]
SAT. Shepherd, see what comes of kissing;
By my head, 'twere better missing.—
Brightest, if there be remaining
Any service, without feigning
I will do it. Were I set
To catch the nimble wind, or get
Shadows gliding on the green,
Or to steal from the great queen
Of fairies all her beauty,                    190
I would do it, so much duty
Do I owe those precious eyes.
CLO. I thank thee, honest satyr. If the
    cries
Of any other that be hurt or ill
Draw thee unto them, prithee, do thy
    will
To bring them hether.

[1] From 1629 edn. Original reads *Playsters.*
[2] Discomfort.

SAT. I will; and, when the weather
Serves to angle in the brook,
I will bring a silver hook,
With a line of finest silk,                    200
And a rod as white as milk,
To deceive the little fish.
So I take my leave, and wish
On this bower may ever dwell
Spring and summer!
CLO.                    Friend, farewell.
    *Exit [with Alexis and Satyr].*

*Enter Amoret, seeking her Love.*

AMO. This place is ominous; for here I lost
My love and almost life, and since have
    crossed
All these woods over; never a nook or
    dell,
Where any little bird or beast doth dwell,
But I have sought it; never a bending
    brow                    210
Of any hill, or glade the wind sings
    through,
Nor a green bank or shade where shep-
    herds use
To sit and riddle, sweetly pipe, or
    choose
Their valentines, but I have missed [3] to
    find
My love in. Perigot! O, too unkind,
Why hast thou fled me? Whither art
    thou gone?
How have I wronged thee? Was my
    love alone
To thee worthy this scorned recompense?
'Tis well;
I am content to feel it. But I tell
Thee, shepherd, and these lusty woods
    shall hear,                    220
Forsaken Amoret is yet as clear
Of any stranger fire as heaven is
From foul corruption, or the deep abyss
From light and happiness; and thou
    mayst know
All this for truth, and how that fatal
    blow
Thou gav'st me, never from desert of
    mine
Fell on my life, but from suspect [4] of
    thine,
Or fury more than madness. There-
    fore here,

[3] Failed.                    [4] Suspicion.

Since I have lost my life, my love, my
dear,
Upon this cursèd place, and on this
green                                    230
That first divorced us, shortly shall be
seen
A sight of so great pity that each eye
Shall daily spend his spring in memory
Of my untimely fall.

*Enter Amarillis.*

AMAR. [*Aside.*]        I am not blind,
Nor is it through the working of my
mind
That this shows Amoret. Forsake me, all
That dwell upon the soul, but what
men call
Wonder, or, more than wonder, miracle!
For, sure, so strange as this, the oracle
Never gave answer of; it passeth dreams,
Or madmen's fancy, when the many
streams                                  241
Of new imagination rise and fall.
'Tis but an hour since these ears heard
her call
For pity to young Perigot, whilst he,
Directed by his fury, bloodily
Lanched [1] up her breast, which bloodless
fell and cold;
And, if belief may credit what was told,
After all this, the melancholy swain
Took her into his arms, being almost
slain,
And to the bottom of the holy well    250
Flung her, forever with the waves to
dwell.
'Tis she, the very same, 'tis Amoret,
And living yet! The great powers will
not let
Their virtuous love be crossed.—Maid,
wipe away
Those heavy drops of sorrow, and allay
The storm that yet goes high, which,
not depressed,
Breaks heart and life and all before it
rest.
Thy Perigot—
AMO.        Where, which is Perigot?
AMAR. Sits there below, lamenting much,
God wot,
Thee and thy fortune. Go and comfort
him:                                     260

[1] Lanced.

And thou shalt find him underneath a
brim
Of sailing [2] pines that edge yon mountain in.
AMO. I go, I run. Heaven grant me I may
win
His soul again!        [*Exit Amoret.*] [3]

*Enter Sullen.*

SULL.        Stay, Amarillis, stay!
You are too fleet; 'tis two hours yet to
day.
I have performed my promise; let us sit
And warm our bloods together, till the
fit
Come lively on us.
AMAR.        Friend, you are too keen;
The morning riseth, and we shall be seen.
Forbear a little.
SULL.        I can stay no longer.  270
AMAR. Hold, shepherd, hold! Learn not
to be a wronger
Of your word. Was not your promise
laid,
To break their loves first?
SULL.        I have done it, maid.
AMAR. No; they are yet unbroken, met
again,
And are as hard to part yet as the stain
Is from the finest lawn.
SULL.        I say they are
Now at this present parted, and so far
That they shall never meet.
AMAR.        Swain, 'tis not so;
For do but to yon hanging mountain go,
And there believe your eyes.
SULL.        You do but hold  280
Off with delays and trifles.—Farewell,
cold
And frozen bashfulness, unfit for men!—
Thus I salute thee, virgin!
        [*Attempts to seize her.*]
AMAR.        And thus, then,
I bid you follow; catch me if you can!
        *Exit.*
SULL. And, if I stay behind, I am no
man!        [*Exit, running after her.*]

*Enter Perigot.*

PERI. Night, do not steal away; I woo
thee yet
To hold a hard hand o'er the rusty bit

[2] "*I.e.*, of which masts are made" (Greg).
[3] From 1629 edn.

That guides thy lazy team.  Go back
    again,
Boötes, thou that driv'st thy frozen
    wain
Round as a ring, and bring a second
    night                         290
To hide my sorrows from the coming
    light;
Let not the eyes of men stare on my
    face
And read my falling; give me some black
    place,
Where never sunbeam shot his whole-
    some light,
That I may sit and pour out my sad
    sprite
Like running water, never to be known
After the forcéd fall and sound is gone.

*Enter Amoret, looking of* [1] *Perigot.*

Amo. This is the bottom.[2]—Speak, if
    thou be here,
My Perigot! Thy Amoret, thy dear,
Calls on thy lovéd name.
Peri.          What [art] [3] thou dare   300
    Tread these forbidden paths, where
    death and care
Dwell on the face of darkness?
Amo.               'Tis thy friend,
Thy Amoret, come hither to give end
To these consumings.  Look up, gentle
    boy;
I have forgot those pains and dear
    annoy
I suffered for thy sake, and am content
To be thy love again.  Why hast thou
    rent
Those curléd locks where I have often
    hung
Ribands and damask-roses, and have
    flung
Waters distilled, to make thee fresh
    and gay,                   310
Sweeter than nosegays on a bridal day?
Why dost thou cross thine arms, and
    hang thy face
Down to thy bosom, letting fall apace
From those two little heavens, upon the
    ground,
Showers of more price, more orient, and
    more round
Than those that hang upon the moon's
    pale brow?

[1] For.       [2] Dale.      [3] From 1629 edn.

Cease these complainings, shepherd; I
    am now
The same I ever was, as kind and free,
And can forgive before you ask of me;
Indeed, I can and will.
Peri.             So spoke my fair!  320
    O, you great working powers of earth
    and air,
Water and forming fire, why have you
    lent
Your hidden virtues of so ill intent?
Even such a face, so fair, so bright of
    hue,
Had Amoret; such words, so smooth
    and new,
Came flowing from her tongue; such
    was her eye,
And such the pointed sparkle that did
    fly
Forth like a bleeding shaft.  All is the
    same,
The robe and buskins, painted hook,
    and frame
Of all her body.  O me, Amoret!   330
Amo. Shepherd, what means this riddle?
    Who hath set
So strong a difference twixt myself and
    me
That I am grown another? Look, and see
The ring thou gav'st me, and about my
    wrist
That curious bracelet thou thyself didst
    twist
From those fair tresses.  Know'st thou
    Amoret?
Hath not some newer love forced thee
    forget
Thy ancient faith?
Peri.         Still nearer to my love!
    These be the very words she oft did
    prove
Upon my temper; so she still would
    take                      340
Wonder into her face, and silent make
Signs with her head and hand, as who
    would say,
"Shepherd, remember this another day."
Amo. Am I not Amoret?  Where was I
    lost?
Can there be heaven and time and men,
    [and] [4] most
Of these unconstant?    Faith, where
    art thou fled?

[4] From 1629 edn.

Are all the vows and protestations
    dead,
The hands held up, the wishes and the
    heart?
Is there not one remaining, not a part
Of all these to be found? Why, then, I
    see                                          350
Men never knew that virtue, constancy.
PERI. Men ever were most blessed, till
    cross fate
Brought love and women forth, unfor-
    tunate
To all that ever tasted of their smiles;
Whose actions are all double, full of
    wiles,
Like to the subtle hare, that fore the
    hounds
Makes many turnings, leaps, and many
    rounds,
This way and that way, to deceive the
    scent
Of her pursuers.
AMO.              'Tis but to prevent
Their speedy coming on, that seek her
    fall—                                        360
The hands of cruel men, more bestial,
And of a nature more refusing good
Than beasts themselves, or fishes of the
    flood.
[PERI.] [1] Thou art all these, and more than
    nature meant
When she created all: frowns, joys,
    content;
Extreme fire for an hour, and presently
Colder than sleepy poison, or the sea
Upon whose face sits a continual frost;
Your actions ever driven to the most,
Then down again as low, that none can
    find                                         370
The rise or falling of a woman's mind.
AMO. Can there be any age or days or time
Or tongues of men guilty so great a crime
As wronging simple maid? O, Perigot,
Thou that wast yesterday without a
    blot,
Thou that wast every good and every-
    thing
That men call blessèd, thou that wast the
    spring
From whence our looser grooms drew all
    their best,
Thou that wast always just and al-
    ways blessed

[1] From 1629 edn.

In faith and promise, thou that hadst
    the name                                     380
Of virtuous given thee, and made good
    the same
Ev'n from thy cradle, thou that wast
    that all
That men delighted in! O, what a fall
Is this, to have been so, and now to be
The only best in wrong and infamy!
And I to live to know this! And by me,
That loved thee dearer than mine eyes, or
    that
Which we esteem our honor, virgin
    state!
Dearer than swallows love the early
    morn,
Or dogs of chase the sound of merry
    horn;                                        390
Dearer than thou canst love thy new
    love, if thou hast
Another, and far dearer than the last;
Dearer than thou canst love thyself,
    though all
The self-love were within thee that did
    fall
With that coy swain that now is made
    a flower,
For whose dear sake Echo weeps many a
    shower!
And am I thus rewarded for my flame?
Loved worthily to get a wanton's name?
Come, thou forsaken willow, wind my
    head,
And noise it to the world, my love is
    dead!                                        400
I am forsaken, I am cast away,
And left for every lazy groom to say
I was unconstant, light, and sooner lost
Than the quick clouds we see, or the
    chill frost
When the hot sun beats on it! Tell me
    yet,
Canst thou not love again thy Amoret?
PERI. Thou art not worthy of that blessed
    name;
I must not know thee. Fling thy wanton
    flame
Upon some lighter blood that may be
    hot                                          409
With words and feignèd passions; Perigot
Was ever yet unstained, and shall not
    now
Stoop to the meltings of a borrowed
    brow.

Amo. Then hear me, heaven, to whom
    I call for right,
And you, fair twinkling stars, that crown
    the night;
And hear me, woods, and silence of this
    place,
And ye, sad hours, that move a sullen
    pace;
Hear me, ye shadows, that delight to
    dwell
In horrid darkness, and ye powers of
    hell,
Whilst I breathe out my last! I am that
    maid,                                      419
That yet-untainted Amoret, that played
The careless prodigal, and gave away
My soul to this young man that now
    dares say
I am a stranger, not the same, more
    wild;
And thus with much belief I was be-
    guiled.
I am that maid that have delayed,
    denied,
And almost scorned the loves of all
    that tried
To win me but this swain, and yet
    confess
I have been wooed by many with no
    less
Soul of affection, and have often had
Rings, belts, and cracknels[1] sent me from
    the lad                                    430
That feeds his flocks down westward;
    lambs and doves
By young Alexis; Daphnis sent me
    gloves—
All which I gave to thee. Nor these
    nor they
That sent them did I smile on, or e'er
    lay
Up to my after-memory. But why
Do I resolve to grieve, and not to die?
Happy had been the stroke thou gav'st,
    if home,
By this time had I found a quiet room,
Where every slave is free, and every
    breast,
That living bred new care, now lies at
    rest;                                      440
And thither will poor Amoret.
Peri.                              Thou must.
    Was ever any man so loath to trust
    His eyes as I? Or was there ever yet

Any so like as this to Amoret?
For whose dear sake I promise, if there
    be
A living soul within thee, thus to free
Thy body from it.    *He hurts her again.*
Amo. [*Falling.*]    So, this work hath end.
    Farewell, and live; be constant to thy
        friend
    That loves thee next.

*Enter Satyr; Perigot runs off.*

Sat. See, the day begins to break,       450
    And the light shoots[2] like a streak
    Of subtle fire; the wind blows cold,
    Whilst the morning doth unfold;
    Now the birds begin to rouse,
    And the squirrel from the boughs
    Leaps to get him nuts and fruit.
    The early lark, that erst was mute,
    Carols to the rising day
    Many a note and many a lay;
    Therefore here I end my watch,       460
    Lest the wand'ring swain should catch
    Harm, or lose himself.
Amo.                              Ah me!
Sat. Speak again, whate'er thou be.
    I am ready; speak, I say!
    By the dawning of the day,
    By the power of night and Pan,
    I enforce thee, speak again!
Amo. O, I am most unhappy!
Sat. Yet more blood!
    Sure, these wanton swains are wood.   470
    Can there be a hand or heart
    Dare commit so vild[3] a part
    As this murder? By the moon,
    That hid herself when this was done,
    Never was a sweeter face;
    I will bear her to the place
    Where my goddess keeps,[4] and crave
    Her to give her life or grave.    *Exeunt.*

*Enter Clorin.*

Clo. Here whilst one patient takes his
    rest secure,                             479
    I steal abroad to do another cure.—
    Pardon, thou buried body of my love,
    That from thy side I dare so soon
        remove;
    I will not prove unconstant, nor will leave
    Thee for an hour alone. When I deceive

---

[1] Biscuits.
[2] From 1634 edn.  Original reads *shutts.*
[3] Vile.                              [4] Dwells.

My first-made vow, the wildest of the
    wood
Tear me, and o'er thy grave let out my
    blood!
I go by wit to cure a lover's pain,
Which no herb can; being done, I'll
    come again.                    *Exit.*

*Enter Thenot.*

THE. Poor shepherd, in this shade for-
    ever lie
And, seeing thy fair Clorin's cabin,
    die!            [*Lies down.*]    490
O, hapless love, which being answered,
    ends!
And, as a little infant cries and bends
His tender brows, when, rolling of his
    eye,
He hath espied something that glisters
    nigh,
Which he would have, yet, give it him,
    away
He throws it straight, and cries afresh
    to play
With something else—such my affection,
    set
On that which I should loathe, if I could
    get.

*Enter Clorin.*

CLO. [*Aside.*]  See, where he lies!  Did
    ever man but he
Love any woman for her constancy   500
To her dead lover, which she needs
    must end
Before she can allow him for her friend,
And he himself must needs the cause
    destroy
For which he loves, before he can en-
    joy?
Poor shepherd, heaven grant I at once
    may free
Thee from thy pain, and keep my loy-
    alty!—
Shepherd, look up.
THE.            Thy brightness doth amaze;
So Phœbus may at noon bid mortals
    gaze.
Thy glorious constancy appears so bright,
I dare not meet the beams with my
    weak sight.                    510
CLO. Why dost thou pine away thyself
    for me?

THE. Why dost thou keep such spotless
    constancy?
CLO. Thou holy shepherd, see what for
    thy sake
Clorin, thy Clorin, now dare undertake.
                    *He starts up.*
THE. Stay there, thou constant Clorin!
    If there be
Yet any part of woman left in thee,
To make thee light, think yet before
    thou speak.
CLO. See, what a holy vow for thee I
    break—
I, that already have my fame far spread
For being constant to my lover dead.
THE. Think yet, dear Clorin, of your love,
    how true,                    521
If you had died, he would have been to
    you.
CLO. Yet, all I'll lose for thee—
THE.            Think but how blessed
A constant woman is above the rest!
CLO. And offer up myself, here on this
    ground,
To be disposed by thee.
THE.            Why dost thou wound
His heart with malice against women
    more,
That hated all the sex but thee before?
How much more pleasant had it been to
    me
To die than [to] [1] behold this change in
    thee!                    530
Yet, yet return; let not the woman sway!
CLO. Insult not on [2] her now, nor use de-
    lay,
Who for thy sake hath ventured all her
    fame. [3]
THE. Thou hast not ventured, but bought
    certain shame.
Your sex's curse, foul falsehood, must
    and shall,
I see, once in your lives light on you all.
I hate thee now.  Yet turn!
CLO.            Be just to me;
Shall I at once lose both my fame and
    thee?
THE. Thou hadst no fame; that which
    thou didst like good
Was but thy appetite that swayed thy
    blood                    540
For that time to the best, for as a blast

[1] From 1634 edn.            [3] Reputation.
[2] Do not behave insolently toward.

That through a house comes, usually
doth cast
Things out of order, yet by chance may
come
And blow some one thing to his proper
room,
So did thy appetite, and not thy zeal,
Sway thee by chance to do some one
thing well.
Yet turn!
CLO.        Thou dost but try me, if I would
Forsake thy dear embraces for my old
Love's, though he were alive; but do not
fear.
THE. I do contemn thee now, and dare
come near,                          550
And gaze upon thee; for methinks that
grace,
Austerity, which sate upon that face,
Is gone, and thou like others.  False
maid, see,
This is the gain of foul inconstancy!
                              *Exit.*
CLO. 'Tis done.—Great Pan, I give thee
thanks for it!—
What art could not have healed is cured
by wit.

*Enter Thenot again.*

THE. Will ye be constant yet?  Will ye
remove
Into the cabin to your buried love?
CLO. No, let me die, but by thy side re-
main.
THE. There's none shall know that thou
didst ever stain                    560
Thy worthy strictness, but shalt honored
be,
And I will lie again under this tree,
And pine and die for thee with more
delight
Than I have sorrow now to know thee
light.
CLO. Let me have thee, and I'll be where
thou wilt.
THE. Thou art of women's race, and full
of guilt.
Farewell all hope of that sex!  Whilst I
thought
There was one good, I feared to find
one naught;
But, since their minds I all alike espy,
Henceforth I'll choose, as others, by
mine eye.                [*Exit.*] 570

CLO. Blessed be ye powers that gave such
quick redress,
And for my labors sent so good success!
I rather choose, though I a woman be,
He should speak ill of all than die for
me.                         [*Exit.*] [1]

ACTUS QUINTUS.  SCENA PRIMA.

[*The same.*]

*Enter Priest and Old Shepherd.*

PRIEST. Shepherds, rise, and shake off
sleep!
See, the blushing morn doth peep
Through the windows, whilst the sun
To the mountain tops is run,
Gilding all the vales below
With his rising flames, which grow
Greater by his climbing still.
Up, ye lazy grooms, and fill
Bag and bottle for the field!          9
Clasp your cloaks fast, lest they yield
To the bitter northeast wind.
Call the maidens up, and find
Who lay longest, that she may
Go without a friend all day;
Then reward your dogs, and pray
Pan to keep you from decay.
So unfold, and then away!—
What, not a shepherd stirring?  Sure,
the grooms
Have found their beds too easy, or the
rooms
Filled with such new delight and heat
that they                          20
Have both forgot their hungry sheep and
day.
Knock, that they may remember what
a shame
Sloth and neglect lays on a shepherd's
name.
OLD SHEP. It is to little purpose.  Not a
swain
This night hath known his lodging here,
or lain
Within these cotes.  The woods, or
some near town
That is a neighbor to the bordering down,
Hath drawn them thither 'bout some
lusty sport,
Or spicéd wassail bowl, to which resort
All the young men and maids of many
a cote,                          30

[1] Original edn. here adds *Finis actus quartus.*

Whilst the trim minstrel strikes his
    merry note.
PRIEST. God pardon sin!—Show me the
    way that leads
To any of their haunts.
OLD SHEP.            This to the meads,
    And that down to the woods.
PRIEST.           Then, this for me.
Come, shepherd, let me crave your
    company.               *Exeunt.*

*Enter Clorin in her cabin, Alexis with her.*[1]

CLO. Now your thoughts are almost pure,
    And your wound begins to cure.
    Strive to banish all that's vain,
    Lest it should break out again.
ALEX. Eternal thanks to thee, thou holy
    maid!                    40
    I find my former wand'ring thoughts
      well stayed
    Through thy wise precepts; and my
      outward pain
    By thy choice herbs is almost gone again.
    Thy sex's vice and virtue are revealed
    At once; for what one hurt another
      healed.
CLO. May thy grief more appease!
    Relapses are the worst disease.
    Take heed how you in thought offend;
    So mind and body both will mend.

*Enter Satyr with Amoret.*

AMO. Be'st thou the wildest creature of
    the wood,                 50
    That bear'st me thus away, drowned in
      my blood,
    And dying, know I cannot injured be;
    I am a maid; let that name fight for me.
SAT. Fairest virgin, do not fear
    Me, that doth thy body bear,
    Not to hurt, but healed to be;
    Men are ruder far than we.—
    See, fair goddess, in the wood
    They have let out yet more blood.
    Some savage man hath struck her
      breast,                  60
    So soft and white, that no wild beast
    Durst 'a' touched, asleep or wake—
    So sweet that adder, newt, or snake
    Would have lain, from arm to arm,
    On her bosom to be warm

[1] Early edns. here erroneously add *and Amarillis.*

All a night, and, being hot,
Gone away and stung her not.
Quickly clap herbs to her breast.
A man, sure, is a kind of beast.    69
CLO. With spotless hand on spotless breast
    I put these herbs, to give thee rest—
    Which, till it heal thee, there will bide,
    If both be pure; if not, off slide.—
    See, it falls off from the wound!
    Shepherdess, thou art not sound,
    Full of lust.
SAT.          Who would have thought it?
    So fair a face!
CLO.          Why, that hath brought it.
AMO. For aught I know or think, these
    words my last,
    Yet Pan so help me as my thoughts are
      chaste!
CLO. And so may Pan bless this my
    cure,                    80
    As all my thoughts are just and pure!
    Some uncleanness nigh doth lurk,
    That will not let my medicines work.—
    Satyr, search if thou canst find it.
SAT. Here away methinks I wind [2] it.
    Stronger yet!—O, here they be;
    Here, here, in a hollow tree
    Two fond mortals have I found.
CLO. Bring them out; they are unsound.

*Enter Cloe and Daphnis.*

SAT. By the fingers thus I wring ye;    90
    To my goddess thus I bring ye;
    Strife is vain; come gently in.—
    I scented them; they're full of sin.
CLO. Hold, satyr; take this glass,
    Sprinkle over all the place,
    Purge the air from lustful breath,
    To save this shepherdess from death,
    And stand you still whilst I do dress
    Her wound, for fear the pain increase.
SAT. From this glass I throw a drop    100
    Of crystal water on the top
    Of every grass, on flowers a pair.—
    Send a fume, and keep the air
    Pure and wholesome, sweet and blessed,
    Till this virgin's wound be dressed.
CLO. Satyr, help to bring her in.
SAT. By Pan, I think she hath no sin,
    [*Carries Amoret into the bower.*]
    She is so light.—Lie on these leaves.
    Sleep, that mortal sense deceives,

[2] *I.e.*, catch wind of.

Crown thine eyes and ease thy pain; 110
Mayst thou soon be well again!
CLO. Satyr, bring the shepherd near;
Try him, if his mind be clear.
SAT. Shepherd, come.
DAPH.  My thoughts are pure.
SAT. The better trial to endure.
CLO. In this flame his finger thrust,
Which will burn him if he lust;
But if not, away will turn,
As loath unspotted flesh to burn.
[*Satyr holds Daphnis' finger to the flame.*]
See, it gives back; let him go.  120
SAT.[1] Farewell, mortal; keep thee so.—
  [*Exit Daphnis.*]
Stay, fair nymph; fly not so fast;
We must try if you be chaste.—
Here's a hand that quakes for fear;
Sure, she will not prove so clear.
CLO. Hold her finger to the flame;
That will yield her praise or shame.
SAT. To her doom she dares not stand,
  [*Holds Cloe's finger to the flame.*]
But plucks away her tender hand,
And the taper darting sends  130
His hot beams at her fingers' ends.—
O, thou art foul within, and hast
A mind, if nothing else, unchaste!
ALEX. Is not that Cloe? 'Tis my love,
'tis she!
Cloe, fair Cloe!
CLOE.  My Alexis!
ALEX.  He.
CLOE. Let me embrace thee.
CLO.  Take her hence,
Lest her sight disturb his sense.
ALEX. Take not her; take my life first!
CLO. See, his wound again is burst!
Keep her near, here in the wood,  140
Till I have stopped these streams of
blood.  [*Exeunt Cloe and Satyr.*]
Soon again he ease shall find,
If I can but still his mind.
This curtain thus I do display,
To keep the piercing air away.
  [*Draws the traverse across the bower.*]

*Enter Old Shepherd and Priest.*

PRIEST. Sure, they are lost forever; 'tis
in vain
To find them out with trouble and
much pain

[1] In the original, this speech head has dropped
so that it precedes the next line.

That have a ripe desire and forward will
To fly the company of all but ill.
What shall be counseled now?  Shall
we retire,  150
Or constant follow still that first desire
We had to find them?
OLD SHEP.  Stay a little while,
For, if the morning's mist do not be-
guile
My sight with shadows, sure I see a
swain;
One of this jolly troop's come back
again.

*Enter Thenot.*

PRIEST. Dost thou not blush, young
shepherd, to be known
Thus without care leaving thy flocks
alone,
And following what desire and present
blood
Shapes out before thy burning sense
for good,
Having forgot what tongue hereafter
may  160
Tell to the world thy falling off, and say
Thou art regardless both of good and
shame,
Spurning at virtue and a virtuous name?
And like a glorious,[2] desperate man that
buys
A poison of much price, by which he
dies,
Dost thou lay out for lust, whose only
gain
Is foul disease, with present age and
pain,
And then a grave? These be the fruits
that grow
In such hot veins, that only beat to know
Where they may take most ease, and
grow ambitious  170
Through their own wanton fire and
pride delicious.
THE. Right holy sir, I have not known this
night
What the smooth face of mirth was, or
the sight
Of any looseness; music, joy, and ease
Have been to me as bitter drugs to
please
A stomach lost with weakness, not a
game

[2] Boastful.

That I am skilled at throughly; nor a
dame,
Went her tongue smoother than the
feet of time,
Her beauty ever-living like the rhyme
Our blesséd Tityrus[1] did sing of yore;
No, were she more enticing than the
store                                        181
Of fruitful summer, when the loaden
tree
Bids the faint traveler be bold and
free,
'Twere but to me like thunder gainst
the bay,
Whose lightning may inclose, but never
stay
Upon his charméd branches; such am I
Against the catching flames of woman's
eye.
PRIEST. Then, wherefore hast thou wan-
dered?
THE.          'Twas a vow
That drew me out last night, which I
have now
Strictly performed, and homewards go
to give                                       190
Fresh pasture to my sheep, that they
may live.
PRIEST. 'Tis good to hear ye, shepherd,
if the heart
In this well-sounding music bear his
part.
Where have you left the rest?
[THE.] [2]                    I have not seen,
Since yesternight we met upon this
green
To fold our flocks up, any of that train;
Yet have I walked these woods round,
and have lain
All this long night under an agéd tree;
Yet neither wand'ring shepherd did I
see,                                          199
Or shepherdess; or drew into mine ear
The sound of living thing, unless it were
The nightingale, among the thick-leaved
spring,
That sits alone in sorrow, and doth sing
Whole nights away in mourning; or the
owl,
Or our great enemy,[3] that still doth
howl
Against the moon's cold beams.

PRIEST.                    Go, and beware
Of after-falling.
THE.               Father, 'tis my care.
                              *Exit Thenot.*

          *Enter Daphnis.*

OLD SHEP. Here comes another straggler.
Sure I see
A shame in this young shepherd.—
Daphnis?
DAPH.          He.
PRIEST. Where hast left the rest, that
should have been                              210
Long before this grazing upon the green
Their yet-imprisoned flocks?
DAPH.               Thou holy man,
Give me a little breathing, till I can
Be able to unfold what I have seen—
Such horror, that the like hath never
been
Known to the ear of shepherd. O, my
heart
Labors a double motion to impart
So heavy tidings!   You all know the
bower
Where the chaste Clorin lives, by whose
great power
Sick men and cattle have been often
cured.                                        220
There lovely Amoret, that was assured [4]
To lusty Perigot, bleeds out her life,
Forced by some iron hand and fatal
knife;
And, by her, young Alexis.

*Enter Amarillis, running from her Sullen
                              Shepherd.*

AMAR.                    If there be
Ever a neighbor brook or hollow tree,
Receive my body, close me up from lust
That follows at my heels! Be ever just,
Thou god of shepherds, Pan, for her
dear sake
That loves the rivers' brinks, and still
doth shake
In cold remembrance of thy quick pur-
suit.                                         230
Let me be made a reed, and, ever mute,
Nod to the waters' fall, whilst every
blast
Sings through my slender leaves that I
was chaste!

[1] Either Virgil or Chaucer.  [3] *I.e.*, the wolf.
[2] From 1629 edn.
[4] Affianced.

PRIEST. This is a night of wonder.—
Amarill,
Be comforted; the holy gods are still
Revengers of these wrongs.
AMAR.                    Thou blessèd man,
Honored upon these plains, and loved
of Pan,
Hear me, and save from endless infamy
My yet unblasted flower, virginity!
By all the garlands that have crowned
that head,                              240
By thy chaste office, and the marriage
bed
That still is blessed by thee, by all the
rites
Due to our god, and by those virgin
lights
That burn before his altar, let me not
Fall from my former state, to gain the
blot
That never shall be purged! I am not
now
That wanton Amarillis; here I vow
To heaven and thee, grave father, if I
may
Scape this unhappy night, to know the
day
A virgin, never after to endure       250
The tongues or company of men un-
pure!
I hear him come; save me!
PRIEST.                    Retire awhile
Behind this bush, till we have known
that vile
Abuser of young maidens.  [They retire.]

*Enter Sullen.*

SULL.                    Stay thy pace,
Most lovèd Amarillis; let the chase
Grow calm and milder; fly me not so
fast;
I fear the pointed brambles have unlaced
Thy golden buskins. Turn again, and see
Thy shepherd follow, that is strong and
free,                                    259
Able to give thee all content and ease.
I am not bashful, virgin; I can please
At first encounter, hug thee in mine
arm,
And give thee many kisses, soft and warm
As those the sun prints on the [1] smiling
cheek

[1] From 1634 edn. Original has *thy.*

Of plums or mellow peaches; I am sleek
And smooth as Neptune when stern
Æolus
Locks up his surly winds, and nimbly
thus
Can show my active youth. Why dost
thou fly?
Remember, Amarillis, it was I        269
That killed Alexis for thy sake, and set
An everlasting hate twixt Amoret
And her belovèd Perigot; 'twas I
That drowned her in the well, where she
must lie
Till time shall leave to be. Then, turn
again,
Turn with thy open arms, and clip the
swain
That hath performed all this; turn, turn,
I say;
I must not be deluded.
PRIEST. [*Coming forward.*]      Monster,
stay!
Thou that art like a canker to the state
Thou liv'st and breath'st in, eating with
debate [2]
Through every honest bosom, forcing
still                                    280
The veins of any men may serve thy
will;
Thou that hast offered with a sinful hand
To seize upon this virgin that doth stand
Yet trembling here!
SULL.               Good holiness, declare
What had the danger been, if being bare
I had embraced her; tell me, by your
art,
What coming wonders would that sight
impart?
PRIEST. Lust and branded soul.
SULL.                    Yet, tell me more;
Hath not our mother Nature, for her
store
And great increase, said it is good and
just,                                    290
And willed that every living creature
must
Beget his like?
PRIEST.          Ye are better read than I,
I must confess, in blood and lechery.—
Now to the bower, and bring this beast
along,
Where he may suffer penance for his
wrong.                          [*Exeunt.*]

[2] Discord.

*Enter Perigot, with his hand bloody.*

PERI. Here will I wash it in the morning's
    dew,
Which she on every little grass doth
    strew
In silver drops against the sun's appear.[1]
'Tis holy water, and will make me
    clear.—
My hand will not be cleansed.—My
    wrongéd love,     300
If thy chaste spirit in the air yet move,
Look mildly down on him that yet doth
    stand
All full of guilt, thy blood upon his hand.
And, though I struck thee undeservedly,
Let my revenge on her that injured thee
Make less a fault which I intended not,
And let these dewdrops wash away my
    spot!—
It will not cleanse. O, to what sacred
    flood
Shall I resort to wash away this blood?
Amidst these trees the holy Clorin
    dwells     310
In a low cabin of cut boughs, and heals
All wounds; to her I will myself ad-
    dress,
And my rash faults repentantly confess;
Perhaps she'll find a means by art or
    prayer,
To make my hand, with chaste blood
    stained, fair.
That done, not far hence, underneath
    some tree
I'll have a little cabin built, since she
Whom I adored is dead; there will I give
Myself to strickness,[2] and, like Clorin,
    live.     *Exit.*

*The curtain is drawn; Clorin appears sitting
in the cabin, Amoret sitting on the one
side of her, Alexis and Cloe on the other,
the Satyr standing by.*

CLO. Shepherd, once more your blood is
    stayed;     320
Take example by this maid,
Who is healed ere you be pure,
So hard it is lewd lust to cure.
Take heed, then, how you turn your eye
On these other lustfully.—
And, shepherdess, take heed lest you
Move his willing eye thereto;

Let no wring nor pinch nor smile
Of yours his weaker sense beguile.—
Is your love yet true and chaste,     330
And forever so to last?
ALEX. I have forgot all vain desires,
All looser thoughts, ill-tempered fires.
True love I find a pleasant fume,
Whose moderate heat can ne'er con-
    sume.
CLOE. And I a new fire feel in me,
Whose chaste flame [3] is not quenched to
    be.
CLO. Join your hands with modest touch,
And forever keep you such.

*Enter Perigot.*

PERI. [*Aside.*] Yon is her cabin; thus far
    off I'll stand,     340
And call her forth; for my unhallowed
    hand
I dare not bring so near yon sacred
    place.—
Clorin, come forth, and do a timely
    grace
To a poor swain.
CLO.     What art thou that dost call?
Clorin is ready to do good to all.
Come near.
PERI.     I dare not.
CLO.     Satyr, see
Who it is that calls on me.
SAT. There, at hand,[4] some swain doth
    stand,
Stretching out a bloody hand.
PERI. Come, Clorin, bring thy holy waters
    clear,     350
To wash my hand.
CLO.     What wonders have been here
Tonight! Stretch forth thy hand, young
    swain;
Wash and rub it, whilst I rain
Holy water.
PERI.     Still you pour,
But my hand will never scour.
CLO. Satyr, bring him to the bower.
We will try the sovereign power
Of other waters.
SAT.     Mortal, sure,
'Tis the blood of maiden pure
That stains thee so.

[1] Appearance.     [2] Strictness.

[3] From 1656 edn. Original reads *base end.*
[4] From 1634 edn. Original reads *there's a
hand.*

*The Satyr leadeth him to the bower, where*
*he spieth Amoret, and kneeleth down;*
*she knoweth him.*

PERI.　　　　　Whate'er thou be,　360
Beest thou her sprite, or some divinity
That in her shape thinks good to walk
this grove,
Pardon poor Perigot!

AMO.　　　　　I am thy love,
Thy Amoret, forevermore thy love;
Strike[1] once more on my naked breast,
I'll prove
As constant still. O, canst thou love me
yet,
How soon could I my former griefs forget!

PERI. So overgreat with joy that you live,
now
I am, that no desire of knowing how
Doth seize me. Hast thou still power to
forgive?　370

AMO. Whilst thou hast power to love, or I
to live.
More welcome now than hadst thou
never gone
Astray from me!

PERI.　　　And, when thou lov'st alone,
And not I, death or some ling'ring pain
That's worse, light on me!

CLO.　　　　Now your stain
Perhaps will cleanse thee[2] once again.
See, the blood that erst[3] did stay,
With the water drops away.
All the powers again are pleased,
And with this new knot are appeased.　380
Join your hands, and rise together;
Pan be blessed that brought you hither!

*Enter Priest and Old Shepherd.*

Go back again, whate'er thou art; unless
Smooth maiden thoughts possess thee,
do not press
This hallowed ground.—Go, satyr, take
his hand,
And give him present trial.

SAT.　　　　　Mortal, stand,
Till by fire I have made known
Whether thou be such a one
That mayst freely tread this place.
Hold thy hand up.—[*Holds the Priest's*
*hand to the flame.*] Never was　390
More untainted flesh than this.—
Fairest, he is full of bliss.

CLO. Then boldly speak; why dost thou
seek this place?

PRIEST. First, honored virgin, to behold
thy face,
Where all good dwells that is; next, for
to try
The truth of late report was given to
me—
Those shepherds that have met with
foul mischance
Through much neglect and more ill
governance,
Whether the wounds they have may yet
endure
The open air, or stay a longer cure;　400
And lastly, what the doom may be shall
light
Upon those guilty wretches, through
whose spite
All this confusion fell;[4] for to this place,
Thou holy maiden, have I brought the
race
Of these offenders, who have freely told
Both why and by what means they gave
this bold
Attempt upon their lives.

CLO.　　　　Fume all the ground,
And sprinkle holy water, for unsound
And foul infection gins to fill the air;
It gathers yet more strongly; [take a
pair][5]　410
Of censers filled with frankincense and
myrrh,
Together with cold camphire;[6] quickly
stir
Thee, gentle satyr, for the place begins
To sweat and labor with the abhorréd
sins
Of those offenders. Let them not come
nigh,
For full of itching flame and leprosy
Their very souls are, that the ground
goes back,
And shrinks to feel the sullen weight of
black
And so unheard-of venom.—Hie thee
fast,
Thou holy man, and banish from the
chaste　420
These manlike monsters; let them never
more

---

[4] From 1629 edn. Original reads *full*.
[5] From 1629 edn.
[6] Camphor, supposedly an antaphrodisiac.

[1] From 1634 edn. Original reads *stick*.
[2] *I.e.*, be cleansed for thee.　　[3] Formerly.

Be known upon these downs, but, long
    before
The next sun's rising, put them from
    the sight
And memory of every honest wight.
Be quick in expedition, lest the sores
Of these weak patients break into new
    gores.          *Ex[it] Priest.*
PERI.  My dear, dear Amoret, how happy
    are
Those blesséd pairs, in whom a little jar
Hath bred an everlasting love, too
    strong          429
For time or steel or envy to do wrong!
How do you feel your hurts?  Alas, poor
    heart,
How much I was abused!  Give me the
    smart,
For it is justly mine.
AMO.          I do believe.
It is enough, dear friend; leave off to
    grieve,
And let us once more, in despite of ill,
Give hands and hearts again.
PERI.          With better will
Than e'er I went to find in hottest day
Cool crystal of the fountain, to allay
My eager thirst.  May this band never
    break!
Hear us, O heaven!
AMO.          Be constant.
PERI.          Else Pan wreak     440
With double vengeance my disloyalty!
Let me not dare to know the company
Of men, or any more behold those eyes!
AMO.  Thus, shepherd, with a kiss all envy [1]
    dies.

*Enter Priest.*

PRIEST.  Bright maid, I have performed
    your will.  The swain
In whom such heat and black rebellions
    reign
Hath undergone your sentence [and dis-
    grace]; [2]
Only the maid I have reserved,[3] whose
    face
Shows much amendment; many a tear
    doth fall
In sorrow of her fault.  Great fair,
    recall          450
Your heavy doom, in hope of better
    days,

[1] Ill will.  [2] From 1629 edn.  [3] Preserved.

Which I dare promise; once again up-
    raise
Her heavy spirit, that near drownéd
    lies
In self-consuming care that never dies.
CLO.  I am content to pardon; call her in.—
The air grows cool again, and doth be-
    gin
To purge itself.  How bright the day
    doth show
After this stormy cloud!—Go, satyr, go,
And with this taper boldly try her hand.
If she be pure and good, and firmly
    stand          460
To be so still, we have performed a work
Worthy the gods themselves.
        *Satyr brings Amarillis in.*
SAT.  Come forward, maiden; do not lurk,
Nor hide your face with grief and shame.
Now or never get a name
That may raise thee, and recure [4]
All thy life that was impure.
Hold your hand unto the flame.
If thou beest a perfect dame,
Or hast truly vowed to mend,          470
This pale fire will be thy friend.—
        [*Holds her hand to the flame.*]
See, the taper hurts her not!
Go thy ways; let never spot
Henceforth seize upon thy blood.
Thank the gods, and still be good.
CLO.  Young shepherdess, now ye are
    brought again
To virgin state, be so, and so remain
To thy last day, unless the faithful love
Of some good shepherd force thee to
    remove;
Then labor to be true to him, and
    live          480
As such a one that ever strives to give
A blessed memory to aftertime;
Be famous for your good, not for your
    crime.—
Now, holy man, I offer up again
These patients, full of health and free
    from pain.
Keep them from after-ills; be ever near
Unto their actions; teach them how to
    clear
The tedious way they pass through from
    suspect;
Keep them from wrong in others, or neg-
    lect

[4] Recover, cure.

Of duty in themselves; correct the
blood                                              490
With thrifty bits [1] and labor; let the
flood
Or the next neighboring spring give
remedy
To greedy thirst and travail, not the
tree
That hangs with wanton clusters; let
not wine,
Unless in sacrifice or rites divine,
Be ever known of shepherds; have a care,
Thou man of holy life! Now do not spare
Their faults through much remissness,
nor forget
To cherish him whose many pains and
sweat
Hath giv'n increase and added to the
downs.                                             500
Sort all your shepherds from the lazy
clowns
That feed their heifers in the budded
brooms. [2]
Teach the young maidens strictness,
that the grooms
May ever fear to tempt their blowing
youth.
Banish all compliment, but single truth,
From every tongue and every shepherd's
heart;
Let them use persuading, but no art.
Thus, holy priest, I wish to thee and
these
All the best goods and comforts that
may please.
ALL. And all those blessings heaven did
ever give,                                         510
We pray upon this bower may ever live.
PRIEST. Kneel, every shepherd, whilst with
powerful hand
I bless your after-labors, and the land
You feed your flocks upon. Great Pan
defend you
From misfortune, and amend you;
Keep you from those dangers still
That are followed by your will;
Give ye means to know at length
All your riches, all your strength,
Cannot keep your foot from falling  520
To lewd lust, that still is calling
At your cottage, till his power
Bring again that golden hour
Of peace and rest to every soul;

May his care of you control
All diseases, sores, or pain
That in aftertime may reign
Either in your flocks or you;
Give ye all affections new,
New desires, and tempers new,      530
That ye may be ever true!
Now rise, and go; and, as ye pass away,
Sing to the God of Sheep that happy lay
That honest Dorus [3] taught ye—Dorus, he
That was the soul and god of melody.
*They all sing [and strew flowers on the ground].*

### THE SONG

All ye woods and trees and bowers,
All ye virtues and ye powers
That inhabit in the lakes,
In the pleasant springs or brakes,
    Move your feet                          540
        To our sound,
    Whilst we greet
        All this ground
With his honor and his name
That defends our flocks from blame. [4]

He is great, and he is just;
He is ever good, and must
Thus be honored. Daffadillies,
Roses, pinks, and lovéd lilies,
    Let us fling,                            550
    Whilst we sing,
    Ever holy,
    Ever holy,
Ever honored, ever young!
Thus great Pan is ever sung!

*Exeunt [all except Clorin and Satyr].*

SAT. Thou divinest, fairest, brightest,
Thou most powerful maid and whitest,
Thou most virtuous and most blesséd,
Eyes of stars, and golden-tresséd
Like Apollo, tell me, sweetest,        560
What new service now is meetest
For the satyr? Shall I stray
In the middle air, and stay
The sailing rack, or nimbly take
Hold by the moon, and gently make
Suit to the pale queen of the night
For a beam to give thee light?
Shall I dive into the sea,
And bring thee coral, making way
Through the rising waves that fall     570

[1] Scanty fare.  [2] Bushes.

[3] Probably a reference to Spenser and *The
Shepherd's Calendar.*
[4] Harm.

In snowy fleeces?  Dearest, shall
I catch thee wanton fauns, or flies
Whose woven wings the summer dyes
Of many colors, get thee fruit,
Or steal from heaven old Orpheus' lute?
All these I'll venter [1] for, and more,
To do her service all these woods adore.

CLO. No other service, satyr, but thy
    watch
About these thicks,[2] lest harmless people
    catch
Mischief or sad mischance.        580

SAT. Holy virgin, I will dance
Round about these woods as quick
As the breaking light, and prick [3]
Down the lawns and down the vales
Faster than the windmill-sails.
So I take my leave, and pray
All the comforts of the day,
Such as Phœbus' heat doth send
On the earth, may still befriend
Thee and this arbor!

CLO.                    And to thee    590
All thy master's love be free!    *Exeunt.*

[1] Venture.        [2] Thickets.        [3] Spur, speed.

FINIS.  THE PASTORAL OF THE FAITHFUL SHEPHERDESS.

# FRANCIS BEAUMONT AND
# JOHN FLETCHER

## PHILASTER

After *The Knight of the Burning Pestle* and *The Faithful Shepherdess* failed with their original Jacobean audiences, Wallis theorizes that their authors went to work to contrive a new type of play combining "a variety of content and theatre craft" that adjusted to the taste of a "playgoing public unappreciative of their best." However this may be, in *Philaster, or Love Lies a-Bleeding*, the play which most critics believe is their first in double harness, Beaumont & Fletcher turned out an immediate hit. They established a type which was to have a far-reaching effect on the English drama for many decades—the romantic tragicomedy. It was produced at the Globe by "His Majesty's Servants" not later than 1610, and then given at the Blackfriars, their new winter home. At the Restoration it was allotted to Killigrew in the division of the older classics between him and D'avenant, and was produced at the Theatre Royal, with Charles II present at least twice (see playlists in Allardyce Nicoll, *A History of Restoration Drama, 1660–1700*, Cambridge University Press, 1923, 1928). It was not among the several Beaumont and Fletcher plays, most of them comedies, revived at the playhouses in the first half of the eighteenth century (Nicoll, *A History of Early Eighteenth Century Drama, 1700–1750*, Cambridge University Press, 1925). But in 1763 George Colman the Elder, noting that there had been a change in public taste, adapted it and offered it with some success to audiences at the Drury Lane in London and at Bath, after shortening it and clearing it "of ribaldry and obscenity" (Nicoll, *A History of Late Eighteenth Century Drama, 1750–1800*, Cambridge University Press, 1927; and Wallis). There were occasional London performances into the nineteenth century, but apparently none in the twentieth, in spite of Archer's praise of it in 1923 as "unquestionably one of the more charming, one of the least offensive, of the Jacobean romances. There is something really attractive in the characters both of Arethusa and Bellario, and the writing is often beautiful." But Archer at the same time admitted that the effects of the play were often "gained by a flagrant defiance both of material probability and psychological plausibility" and focused his criticism on the motivation of Euphrasia-Bellario and Philaster himself.

Although no one questions the joint authorship of the play, speculations have been raised as to the individual contributions of each man to the elements and proportions of the play as a whole. The highly speculative Wallis, after emphasizing the unusually close relationship of the pair in comparison with other Elizabethan cases of collaboration, would like to give Fletcher more responsibility for the construction than generally believed, though at the same time he stresses "the indications that the critically minded Beaumont, as the stronger personality in this Damon and Pythias partnership, was the chief polisher and reviser." Indeed, recalling the fact that among the fourteen performances of plays given by the King's Men at court during the season 1612–13, this play is once listed as *Philaster* and once as *Love Lies a-Bleeding*, Wallis goes so far as to suggest that Fletcher, perhaps aided by Nathan Field or someone else, wrote a first version under the title of its final subtitle, and that Beaumont then reworked it and polished it under its final main title. Beaumont, says Wallis, always had the more critical mind, Fletcher the more creative. Oliphant, indeed, believed the play to be mostly by Beaumont.

Thus *Philaster* has given scholars an excellent opportunity to apply their tests of authorship to its various parts. These tests, after eliminating the negligible external evidence, depend upon the following internal elements: versification, especially Fletcher's free approximation of conversational prose effects by the use of weak (i.e., double, triple, or even quadruple) endings for his lines, with a general avoidance of rhyme (*The Faithful Shepherdess* is an obvious exception, because of its nature), and a favoring of the end-stop; diction and recurring rhetorical devices, such as repetition of words, constructions, and ideas; and mental attitude, shown in the use of certain types of material, such as Fletcher's greater fondness for questionable moral situations and furtive innuendo, and Beaumont's more truly philosophical and speculative outlook.

No direct source for the story of *Philaster* has been discovered, though resemblances to parts of Sidney's *Arcadia* and Montemayor's *Diana* have been noted. James E. Savage, however, in "Beaumont and Fletcher's *Philaster* and Sidney's *Arcadia*" (*ELH*, 1947), has argued that *Arcadia*, rather than *Diana*, was the main source and that the materials were transmitted through Fletcher's *Cupid's Revenge*. But various other influences or resemblances have also been suggested. Wallis goes so far as to intimate that Marston and Webster's *The Malcontent* "in some ways . . . definitely foreshadows *Philaster*," these ways apparently being that both combine a "comical satirical" treatment of material with a tragicomic plot and construction. He also suggests Shakespeare's *Pericles, Prince of Tyre*, as a forerunner, and both he and Leech agree that *Hamlet*, with its basic situation of a wronged son trying to gain his rightful throne from a usurper, may have offered a new treatment to the younger men.

These suggestions of a relationship with Shakespeare, however remote, immediately bring up the once hotly argued question of the direction of the influence of *Philaster* and *Cymbeline* on the establishment of the tragicomic genre. At the beginning of this century Ashley H. Thorndike published *The Influence of Beaumont and Fletcher on Shakspere* (Worcester, Mass., 1901), and temporarily persuaded many people that in *Cymbeline*, *The Winter's Tale*, and *The Tempest*, Shakespeare had been inspired by the successful examples of Fletcher and Beaumont plays like *Philaster*, *A King and No King*, and *Bonduca*. More recent scholars, however, have decided that if there was any relationship between these two groups of plays it probably proceeded from the fact that *Pericles* preceded both and that they both descended from it. Wallis, however, not wishing to take any credit away from either the younger men or the older one, suggests that during the simultaneous writing of *Cymbeline* and *Philaster* there may have been a parallel cross-fertilization, since all three men were composing for the King's Company and may well have talked over their plans together, and even discussed them while listening to preliminary readings by the casts. In any case, there is some evidence that, after Beaumont's retirement from the theater, an actual collaboration between Shakespeare and Fletcher took place, and that Fletcher worked with the veteran playwright in *Henry VIII* (perhaps doing the greater share), as well as in *The Two Noble Kinsmen* and the lost *Cardenio* (Leech; Kenneth Muir, *Shakespeare as Collaborator*, London, 1960). Massinger and Field also collaborated with Fletcher after the death of Shakespeare, while Fletcher was dominating the later Jacobean stage.

The setting of *Philaster* was Fletcher and Beaumont's favorite one of a court, with all its intrigues of love and politics; thus the play discloses a great deal about its authors' views on both subjects. Though they have often been accused of salaciousness and of having a positive preoccupation with sex, as shown in the behavior of Prince Pharamond of Spain and Megra in this play, Wallis maintains that if proper allowance is made for the freedom of language and situation permitted by the age (also seen in the plays of Shakespeare, Jonson, Middleton, Chapman, and the rest), "Fletcher can be seen to have handled sex themes with a cold, swift, surface brittleness that compares not unfavorably with similar situations in modern sophisticated comedies." Leech maintains that "he shows, I believe, a genuine interest in the moral twistings of the human situation, the quirks of destiny, and this leads him again and again to the scene that is sexually charged."

As for the court settings, which were very rarely placed in England, Leech found that they usually had a rather paradoxical effect: on the one hand they created an atmosphere "of an impossible and fantastic remoteness" while on the other they clearly related themselves to the kind of court that at least some of the audience were familiar with. Although Wallis felt that there was nothing in either the backgrounds or educations of Fletcher and Beaumont to make them susceptible to the divine right propaganda of James I and that their social consciousness was that of a ruling class which "looked forward to leadership in the affairs of the land rather than to servile compliance with dictatorship or tyranny" (that is, their position was between that of democracy and absolute monarchy), Mary A. M. Adkins, in her article "The Citizens in *Philaster,* Their Function and Their Significance" (*SP*, 1946), pointed out that this play was an exception to the general run of Jacobean plays, because the citizens in it are the dominating political force. Leech observed that, although the seating of the prince was accomplished by action, he himself did not take an active part in the revolt. Adkins suggested that since the leading passages on the subject in the play are generally assigned to Beaumont, it is possible that he was inclining toward more democratic ideas, whereas Fletcher remained an uncompromising royalist. On the other hand, Wallis felt that Fletcher, in joining with Massinger in 1619 to write *The Tragedy of Sir John Olden Barnavelt* (not published until 1883), showed great courage in daring to write on this independent and liberal Dutchman. Leech also regarded the astonishing fight in IV, iii, in which the "Country Fellow" easily defeats Philaster, as an anti-aristocratic sign and as evidence that "a common citizen's patience may reach a point of exhaustion against great lords." In fact, the whole court in the play is made to look very unattractive. Baldwin Maxwell, in "The Attitude toward the Duello in the Beaumont and Fletcher Plays" (*Studies in Beaumont, Fletcher, and Massinger*), contended that even if the playwrights of the King's Men had to take their stand against dueling after 1615–16 because of James's attempt to stop the practice, this fact came out of necessity and not because they were servile royalists. The most thorough examination of the political implications to be found in *Philaster*, however, has been made by Peter Davison ("The Serious Concerns of *Philaster*," *ELH*, 1963), who discovered some striking parallels between passages in the play and in the *Works* of James, dealing with the nature of kings, the precise character of the contract between God and a king, and the rights of subjects to question their king and demand reasons for his conduct. But Davison concluded only that *Philaster* was thus an excellent mirror of contemporary political thought, not that the authors were attempting to reflect the ideas of James. The somewhat different endings in the quartos of 1620 and 1622, he felt, showed the awareness of the dramatists that some reconciliation must be effected between King and Parliament, and that the ending of *Philaster* reflected the "balance of all the elements" demanded by the urge for order in Elizabethan society.

Finally, the literary style of the authors, especially of Fletcher, has engaged the attention of the critics. Thorndike said of him: "Every line helps to give the effect of unpremeditated speech," but he also noted that, paradoxically, there was "an extraordinary cultivation of parenthesis," which is more noticeable as an obstacle to a reader than to an audience. Waith attributed some of this rather intricate rhetorical structure to the Renaissance cult of oratory and the stress on the art of declamation which was part of every boy's education. Waith also noted that there is "comparatively little imagery" in Fletcher's language, but that his "verbal texture"—that is, the mere sound of the words arranged in more or less formal patterns—is what chiefly pleases.

Similarly, John Danby (*Poets on Fortune's Hill*, London, 1952) stressed the importance of relating the language of the Beaumont and Fletcher plays to the individual dramatic situation and to the total effect.

The basis of the present text is the 1622 quarto ("second impression, corrected and amended") as reproduced by A. H. Thorndike in the Belles-Lettres Series (New York, 1906), but these readings have been checked with those of the same quarto as given in the Variorum edition by P. A. Daniel and in the Cambridge edition by Waller.

# PHILASTER,
# OR
# LOVE LIES A-BLEEDING [1]

## BY

## FRANCIS BEAUMONT AND JOHN FLETCHER

*[The scene being in Sicily.*
*The persons represented in the play are these, viz.:*

THE KING.
PHILASTER, *heir to the crown.*
PHARAMOND, *Prince of Spain.*
DION, *a lord.*
CLEREMONT } *noble gentlemen,*
THRASILINE } *his associates.*
ARETHUSA, *the king's daughter.*
GALATEA, *a wise, modest lady attending the*
*princess.*
MEGRA, *a lascivious lady.*

AN OLD WANTON LADY, *or crone.*
ANOTHER LADY *attending the princess.*
EUPHRASIA, *daughter of Dion, but disguised*
*like a page and called Bellario.*
AN OLD CAPTAIN.
FIVE CITIZENS.
A COUNTRY FELLOW.
TWO WOODMEN.
THE KING'S GUARD AND TRAIN.] [2]

[TIME: *Indefinite.*]

## ACTUS I. SCENA i.

*[The presence chamber in the palace.]*

*Enter Dion, Cleremont, and Thrasiline.* [3]

CLE. Here's nor lords nor ladies.

DI. Credit me, gentlemen, I wonder at it. They received strict charge from the king to attend here; besides, it was boldly published that no officer should forbid any gentleman that desired to attend and hear.

CLE. Can you guess the cause?

DI. Sir, it is plain—about the Spanish prince that's come to marry our king- [10 dom's heir and be our sovereign.

THRA. Many that will seem to know much say she looks not on him like a maid in love.

DI. Faith, sir, the multitude, that seldom know anything but their own opinions, speak that they would have; but the prince, before his own approach, received so many confident messages from the state that I think she's resolved to be ruled. 20

CLE. Sir, it is thought with her he shall enjoy both these kingdoms of Sicily and Calabria.

DI. Sir, it is without controversy so meant. But 'twill be a troublesome labor for him to enjoy both these kingdoms with safety, the right heir to one of them living, and living so virtuously—especially, the people admiring the bravery of his mind and lamenting his injuries. 30

CLE. Who? Philaster?

DI. Yes; whose father, we all know, was by our late King of Calabria unrighteously deposed from his fruitful Sicily. Myself drew some blood in those wars, which I would give my hand to be washed from.

CLE. Sir, my ignorance in state policy will not let me know why, Philaster being

[1] The title-page continues: "As It Hath Been Divers Times Acted at the Globe and Black-friars by His Majesty's Servants."
[2] From 1630 edn.
[3] So all other quartos. 1622 edn. reads *Trasiline.*

heir to one of these kingdoms, the king should suffer him to walk abroad with [40 such free liberty.

DI. Sir, it seems your nature is more constant than to inquire after state news. But the king, of late, made a hazard of both the kingdoms, of Sicily and his own, with offering but to imprison Philaster, at which the city was in arms, not to be charmed down by any state order or proclamation, till they saw Philaster ride through the streets pleased and without a guard, [50 at which they threw their hats and their arms from them, some to make bonfires, some to drink, all for his deliverance— which wise men say is the cause the king labors to bring in the power of a foreign nation to awe his own with.

*Enter Galatea, Megra, and a Lady.*[1]

THRA. See, the ladies! What's the first?

DI. A wise and modest gentlewoman that attends the princess.

CLE. The second? 60

DI. She is one that may stand still discreetly enough and ill-favoredly dance her measure, simper when she is courted by her friend, and slight her husband.

CLE. The last?

DI. Faith, I think she is one whom the state keeps for the agents of our confederate princes; she'll cog[2] and lie with a whole army, before the league shall break. Her name is common through the kingdom, [70 and the trophies of her dishonor advanced beyond Hercules' Pillars. She loves to try the several constitutions of men's bodies, and, indeed, has destroyed the worth of her own body by making experiment upon it for the good of the commonwealth.

CLE. She's a profitable member.

LA. Peace, if you love me! You shall see these gentlemen stand their ground and not court us. 80

GAL. What if they should?

MEG. What if they should!

LA. [*To Galatea.*] Nay, let her alone.— What if they should? Why, if they should,

---

[1] The order of the last two characters has been transposed and the speech heads *La.* and *Meg.* reversed by all other modern editors in the dialogue preceding the entrance of the King. But the *Lady* is probably the "old wanton lady, or crone."

[2] Cheat.

I say they were never abroad. What foreigner would do so? It writes them directly untraveled.

GAL. Why, what if they be?

MEG. What if they be!

LA. [*To Galatea.*] Good madam, let [90 her go on.—What if they be? Why, if they be, I will justify, they cannot maintain discourse with a judicious lady, nor make a leg[3] nor say, "Excuse me."

GAL. Ha, ha, ha!

LA. Do you laugh, madam?

DI. Your desires upon you, ladies!

LA. Then you must sit beside us.

DI. I shall sit near you then, lady.

LA. Near me, perhaps; but there's a lady endures no stranger; and to me [101 you appear a very strange fellow.

MEG. Methinks he's not so strange; he would[4] quickly to be acquainted.

THRA. Peace, the king!

*Enter King, Pharamond, Arethusa, and Train.*

KING. To give a stronger testimony of love
Than sickly promises (which commonly
In princes find both birth and burial
In one breath), we have drawn you, worthy sir,
To make your fair endearments to our daughter, 110
And worthy services known to our subjects,
Now loved and wondered at; next, our intent
To plant you deeply our immediate heir
Both to our blood and kingdoms. For this lady
(The best part of your life, as you confirm me,
And I believe), though her few years and sex
Yet teach her nothing but her fears and blushes,
Desires without desire, discourse and knowledge
Only of what herself is to herself,
Make her feel moderate health; and, when she sleeps, 120
In making no ill day, knows no ill dreams.
Think not, dear sir, these undivided parts

---

[3] Bow.  [4] Wishes.

That must mold up a virgin, are put on
To show her so, as borrowed ornaments
To talk of her perfect love to you, or add
An artificial shadow to her nature.
No, sir; I boldly dare proclaim her yet
No woman. But woo her still, and think
    her modesty
A sweeter mistress than the offered lan-
    guage
Of any dame, were she a queen, whose
    eye                                          130
Speaks common loves and comforts to
    her servants.[1]
Last, noble son (for so I now must call
    you),
What I have done thus public is not only
To add comfort in particular
To you or me, but all, and to confirm
The nobles and the gentry of these king-
    doms
By oath to your succession, which shall
    be
Within this month at most.
THRA. [*Aside*.] This will be hardly done.
CLE. [*Aside*.] It must be ill done, if it be
    done.                                        140
DI. [*Aside*.!] When 'tis at best, 'twill be but
    half done, whilst [2]
So brave a gentleman is wronged and
    flung off.
THRA. [*Aside*.] I fear.
CLE. [*Aside*.] Who does not?
DI. [*Aside*.] I fear not for myself, and
    yet I fear too.
Well, we shall see, we shall see. No more.
PHA. Kissing your white hand, mistress, I
    take leave
To thank your royal father, and thus far
To be my own free trumpet. Under-
    stand,
Great king, and these your subjects, mine
    that must be                                 150
(For so deserving you have spoke me,
    sir,
And so deserving I dare speak myself),
To what a person, of what eminence,
Ripe expectation, of what faculties,
Manners, and virtues, you would wed
    your kingdoms;
You in me have your wishes. O, this
    country!

By more than all the gods, I hold **it**
    happy—
Happy in their dear memories that have
    been
Kings great and good; happy in yours
    that is;                                     159
And from you (as a chronicle to keep
Your noble name from eating age) do I
Open [3] myself most happy.    Gentle-
    men,
Believe me in a word, a prince's word,
There shall be nothing to make up a
    kingdom
Mighty and flourishing, defensèd, feared,
Equal to be commanded and obeyed,
But through the travails of my life I ll
    find it,
And tie it to this country.    By all the
    gods,
My reign shall be so easy to the subject
That every man shall be his prince him-
    self,                                        170
And his own law—yet I his prince and
    law.
And, dearest lady, to your dearest self
(Dear in the choice of him whose name
    and luster
Must make you more and mightier) let
    me say
You are the blessed'st living, for, sweet
    princess,
You shall enjoy a man of men to be
Your servant; you shall make him yours,
    for whom
Great queens must die,
THRA. [*Aside*.] [4] Miraculous!
CLE. [*Aside*.] This speech calls him    [180
Spaniard, being nothing but a large inven-
tory of his own commendations.

*Ent[er] Philaster.*

DI. [*Aside*.] I wonder what's his price,
for certainly he'll sell himself, he has so
praised his shape.—But here comes one
more worthy those large speeches than the
large speaker of them. Let me be swallowed
quick, if I can find, in all the anatomy of
yon man's virtues, one sinew sound enough
to promise for him he shall be con-    [190
stable. By this sun, he'll ne'er make king

---

[1] Lovers.
[2] Here and in a few other passages the line
division has been regularized.

[3] Reveal, declare.
[4] In several speeches, such as the following, although prose is used, it may be scanned as
rough iambics.

unless it be of trifles, in my poor judgment.

PHI. [*Kneeling*.] Right noble sir, as low as my obedience,

And with a heart as loyal as my knee,

I beg your favor.

KING. Rise; you have it, sir.
[*Philaster rises*.]

DI. Mark but the king, how pale he looks! He fears!

O, this same whoreson [1] conscience, how it jades us!

KING. Speak your intent, sir.

PHI. Shall I speak um freely? Be still my royal sovereign.

KING. As a subject, 200
We give you freedom.

DI. [*Aside*.] Now it heats.

PHI. Then thus I turn
My language to you, prince—you, foreign man!

Ne'er stare nor put on wonder, for you must

Endure me, and you shall. This earth you tread upon

(A dowry, as you hope, with this fair princess),

By my dead father (O, I had a father,

Whose memory I bow to!) was not left [2]

To your inheritance, and I up and living—

Having myself about me and my sword,

The souls of all my name and memories,

These arms and some few friends beside the gods—  211

To part so calmly with it, and sit still

And say, "I might have been." I tell thee, Pharamond,

When thou art king, look I be dead and rotten,

And my name ashes, as I; for, hear me, Pharamond,

This very ground thou goest on, this fat earth

My father's friends made fertile with their faiths,

Before that day of shame shall gape and swallow

Thee and thy nation, like a hungry grave,

Into her hidden bowels. Prince, it shall.

By the just gods, it shall!

PHA. He's mad; beyond cure, mad.  221

DI. [*Aside*.] Here's a fellow has some fire in 's veins;

The outlandish [3] prince looks like a tooth-drawer.

PHI. Sir Prince of Poppingjays,[4] I'll make it well appear

To you I am not mad.

KING. You displease us;
You are too bold.

PHI. No, sir, I am too tame,
Too much a turtle,[5] a thing born without passion,

A faint shadow that every drunken cloud
Sails over, and makes nothing.

KING. I do not fancy this.
Call our physicians; sure, he's somewhat tainted.[6]  230

THRA. [*Aside*.] I do not think 'twill prove so.

DI. [*Aside*.] H'as given him a general purge already, for all the right he has; and now he means to let him blood. Be constant, gentlemen; by heaven, I'll run his hazard,[7] although I run my name out of the kingdom!

CLE. [*Aside*.] Peace, we are all one soul.

PHA. What you have seen in me to stir offense  239

I cannot find, unless it be this lady,

Offered into mine arms with the succession,

Which I must keep (though it hath pleased your fury

To mutiny within you) without disputing

Your genealogies, or taking knowledge

Whose branch you are. The king will leave it me,

And I dare make it mine. You have your answer.

PHI. If thou wert sole inheritor to him

That made the world his,[8] and couldst see no sun

Shine upon anything but thine; were Pharamond

As truly valiant as I feel him cold,  250

And ringed amongst the choicest of his friends

(Such as would blush to talk such serious follies,

---

[1] Rascally.
* The order of this and the preceding line is reversed in the original.

[3] Foreign.
[4] Popinjays.
[5] Turtledove.
[6] Mentally unbalanced.
[7] *I.e.*, I'll run a risk for him.
[8] *I.e.*, Alexander the Great.

Or back such belied [1] commendations),
And from this presence, spite of [all] [2]
    these bugs, [3]
You should hear further from me.
KING. Sir, you wrong the prince;
    I gave you not this freedom to brave our
    best friends.
    You deserve our frown. Go to; be better
    tempered.
PHI. It must be, sir, when I am nobler
    used.
GAL. [Aside.] Ladies,                    260
    This would have been a pattern of suc-
    cession,
    Had he ne'er met this mischief. By my
    life,
    He is the worthiest the true name of
    man
    This day within my knowledge.
MEG. [Aside.] I cannot tell what you may
    call your knowledge;
    But the other is the man set in my eye.
    O, 'tis a prince of wax! [4]
GAL. [Aside.]              A dog it is. [5]
KING. Philaster, tell me
    The injuries you aim at in your riddles.
PHI. If you had my eyes, sir, and suffer-
    ance, [6]                              270
    My griefs upon you, and my broken
    fortunes,
    My wants great, and now-nothing hopes
    and fears,
    My wrongs would make ill riddles to be
    laughed at.
    Dare you be still my king, and right me
    [not]? [7]
KING. Give me your wrongs in private.
PHI.                        Take them,
    And ease me of a load would bow strong
    Atlas.              They whisper.
CLE. [Aside.] He dares not stand the
    shock.
DI. [Aside.] I cannot blame him; there's
    danger in 't. Every man in this age [280
    has not a soul of crystal for all men to read
    their actions through; men's hearts and faces
    are so far asunder that they hold no intelli-
    gence. Do but view yon stranger well, and
    you shall see a fever through all his bravery, [8]

and feel him shake like a true tenant. [9] If he
give not back his crown again upon the report of an elder gun, [10] I have no augury.
KING. Go to;
    Be more yourself, as you respect our
    favor;                                290
    You'll stir us else. Sir, I must have you
    know
    That y' are and shall be, at our pleasure,
    what fashion we
    Will put upon you. Smooth your brow,
    or by the gods—
PHI. I am dead, sir; y' are my fate. It was
    not I
    Said I was wronged. I carry all about
    me
    My weak stars lead me to, all my weak
    fortunes.
    Who dares in all this presence speak (that
    is
    But man [11] of flesh, and may be mortal),
    tell me
    I do not most entirely love this prince,
    And honor his full virtues!
KING.            Sure, he's possessed!  300
PHI. Yes, with my father's spirit.    It's
    here, O king,
    A dangerous spirit!  Now he tells me,
    king,
    I was a king's heir, bids me be a king,
    And whispers to me these are all my
    subjects.
    'Tis strange he will not let me sleep, but
    dives
    Into my fancy, and there gives me shapes
    That kneel and do me service, cry me
    king.
    But I'll suppress him; he's a factious
    spirit,
    And will undo me.—[To Pharamond.]
    Noble sir, your hand;
    I am your servant.
KING.       Away!  I do not like this.  310
    I'll make you tamer, or I'll dispossess you
    Both of life and spirit. For this time
    I pardon your wild speech, without so
    much
    As your imprisonment.
Exeunt K[ing], Pha[ramond], Are[thusa, and
                                    Train].

---

[1] Lying.
[2] Supplied from other quartos.
[3] Bugbears.
[4] I.e., perfect like a wax model.
[5] "A dog of wax" was a cant phrase indicating contempt.
[6] Suffering.   [7] From 1628 edn.   [8] Insolence.

[9] I.e., "one who has only temporary possession" (Dyce).
[10] Popgun.
[11] From 1620 edn. Original reads men.

DI. I thank you, sir; you dare not for the people.

GAL. Ladies, what think you now of this brave fellow?

MEG. A pretty talking fellow, hot at hand. But eye yon stranger; is he not a fine complete gentleman? O, these strangers, I do affect[1] them strangely! [320 They do the rarest home-things, and please the fullest! As I live, I could love all the nation over and over for his sake.

GAL. Gods comfort your poor headpiece, lady! 'Tis a weak one, and had need of a nightcap.                    *Exeunt*[2] *Ladies*.

DI. [*Aside*.] See, how his fancy labors! Has he not spoke
Home and bravely? What a dangerous train
Did he give fire to! How he shook the king,
Made his soul melt within him, and his blood                                    330
Run into whey! It stood upon his brow
Like a cold, winter dew.

PHI.                    Gentlemen,
You have no suit to me? I am no minion.[3]
You stand, methinks, like men that would be courtiers,
If you[4] could well be flattered at a price
Not to undo your children. Y' are all honest.
Go, get you home again, and make your country
A virtuous court, to which your great ones may,
In their diseasèd age, retire and live recluse.

CLE. How do you, worthy sir?

PHI.                    Well, very well;   340
And so well that, if the king please, I find
I may live many years.

DI.                    The king must please,
Whilst we know what you are and who you are,
Your wrongs and injuries. Shrink not, worthy sir,
But add your father to you, in whose name
We'll waken all the gods, and conjure up
The rods of vengeance, the abusèd people,
Who, like to raging torrents, shall swell high,

And so begirt the dens of these male dragons
That, through the strongest safety, they shall beg                                    350
For mercy at your sword's point.

PHI.                    Friends, no more;
Our ears may be corrupted. 'Tis an age
We dare not trust our wills to. Do you love me?

THRA. Do we love heaven and honor?

PHI. My Lord Dion, you had
A virtuous gentlewoman called you father;
Is she yet alive?

DI.                    Most honored sir, she is,
And, for the penance but of an idle dream,
Has undertook a tedious pilgrimage.

*Enter a Lady.*

PHI. Is it to me, or any of these gentlemen, you come?                                    360

LA. To you, brave lord; the princess would entreat
Your present company.

PHI. The princess send for me! Y' are mistaken.

LA. If you be called Philaster, 'tis to you.

PHI. Kiss her fair hand, and say I will attend her.                    [*Exit Lady*.]

DI. Do you know what you do?

PHI. Yes; go to see a woman.

CLE. But do you weigh the danger you are in?

PHI. Danger in a sweet face?
By Jupiter, I must not fear a woman!   370

THRA. But are you sure it was the princess sent?
It may be some foul train[5] to catch your life.

PHI. I do not think it, gentlemen; she's noble.
Her eye may shoot me dead, or those true red
And white friends in her face may steal my soul out;
There's all the danger in 't. But, be what may,
Her single[6] name hath armèd me.

                    *Exit Phil[aster]*.

DI.                    Go on.
And be as truly happy as thou'rt fearless!—

---

[1] Admire.
[2] Original reads *Exit*.
[3] Servile favorite.
[4] Mason suggests *I*.
[5] Trick, plot.
[6] Mere.

Come, gentlemen, let's make our friends acquainted,
Lest the king prove false.                    380

*Exeunt* [1] *Gentlemen.*

[Scena ii.

*Arethusa's chambers in the palace.*]

*Enter Arethusa and a Lady.*

Are. Comes he not?
La.                    Madam?
Are.                    Will Philaster come?
La.  Dear madam, you were wont
To credit me at first.
Are.  But didst thou tell me so?
I am forgetful, and my woman's strength
Is so o'ercharged with dangers like to grow
About my marriage that these under-things
Dare not abide in such a troubled sea.
How looked he when he told thee he would come?
La.  Why, well.                    10
Are.  And not a little fearful?
La.  Fear, madam?  Sure, he knows not what it is.
Are.  You all are of his faction; the whole court
Is bold in praise of him, whilst I
May live neglected, and do noble things,
As fools in strife throw gold into the sea,
Drowned in the doing.  But I know he fears.
La.  Fear, madam!  Methought, his looks hid more
Of love than fear.
Are.        Of love?  To whom?  To you?
Did you deliver those plain words I sent,
With such a winning gesture and quick look                    21
That you have caught him?
La.                    Madam, I mean to you.
Are.  Of love to me!  Alas, thy ignorance
Lets thee not see the crosses of our births!
Nature, that loves not to be questionéd
Why she did this or that, but has her ends,
And knows she does well, never gave the world
Two things so opposite, so contrary,
As he and I am.  If a bowl of blood

[1] Original reads *Exit.*

Drawn from this arm of mine would poison thee,                    30
A draught of his would cure thee.  Of love to me!
La.  Madam, I think I hear him.
Are.        Bring him in.—[*Exit Lady.*]
You gods, that would not have your dooms withstood,
Whose holy wisdoms at this time it is
To make the passions of a feeble maid
The way unto your justice, I obey.

*Enter Phil[aster with Lady].*

La.  Here is my Lord Philaster.
Are.                    O, it is well.
Withdraw yourself.                    [*Exit Lady.*]
Phi.        Madam, your messenger
Made me believe you wished to speak with me.
Are.  'Tis true, Philaster; but the words are such                    40
I have to say and do so ill beseem
The mouth of woman that I wish them said,
And yet am loath to speak them.  Have you known
That I have aught detracted from your worth?
Have I in person wronged you, or have set
My baser instruments to throw disgrace
Upon your virtues?
Phi.                    Never, madam, you.
Are.  Why, then, should you, in such a public place,
Injure a princess, and a scandal lay    49
Upon my fortunes, famed to be so great,
Calling a great part of my dowry in question?
Phi.  Madam, this truth which I shall speak will be
Foolish; but, for your fair and virtuous self,
I could afford myself to have no right
To anything you wished.
Are.                    Philaster, know
I must enjoy these kingdoms.
Phi.                    Madam, both?
Are.  Both, or I die; by heaven, I die, Philaster,
If I not calmly may enjoy them both.
Phi.  I would do much to save that noble life,
Yet would be loath to have posterity    60

Find in our stories that Philaster gave
His right unto a scepter and a crown
To save a lady's longing.
ARE.                              Nay, then, hear:
I must and will have them, and more—
PHI.                              What more?
ARE. Or lose that little life the gods pre-
    pared
To trouble this poor piece of earth withal.
PHI. Madam, what more?
ARE.                    Turn then away thy face.
PHI. No.
ARE. Do.
PHI. I can endure it.  Turn away my
    face?                                        70
I never yet saw enemy that looked
So dreadfully but that I thought myself
As great a basilisk [1] as he, or spake
So horrible but that I thought my tongue
Bore thunder underneath, as much as his,
Nor beast that I could turn from.  Shall
    I then
Begin to fear sweet sounds?  A lady's
    voice,
Whom I do love?  Say you would have
    my life.
Why, I will give it you, for it is of me
A thing so loathed, and unto you that
    ask                                          80
Of so poor use, that I shall make no price.
If you entreat, I will unmovedly hear.
ARE. Yet, for my sake, a little bend thy
    looks.
PHI. I do.
ARE.       Then know I must have them
    and thee.
PHI. And me?
ARE.            Thy love—without which all
    the land
Discovered yet will serve me for no use
But to be buried in.
PHI.                    Is 't possible?
ARE. With it, it were too little to bestow
    On thee.  Now, though thy breath do
        strike me dead
    (Which, know, it may), I have unripped
        my breast.                              90
PHI. Madam, you are too full of noble
    thoughts
To lay a train for this contemnéd life,
Which you may have for asking.  To sus-
    pect

Were base, where I deserve no ill.  Love
    you!
By all my hopes, I do, above my life!
But how this passion should proceed
    from you
So violently, would amaze a man
That would be jealous.[2]
ARE. Another soul into my body shot
Could not have filled me with more
    strength and spirit                          100
Than this thy breath.  But spend not
    hasty time
In seeking how I came thus.  'Tis the gods,
The gods, that make me so; and, sure,
    our love
Will be the nobler and the better blessed,
In that the secret justice of the gods
Is mingled with it.  Let us leave, and kiss,
Lest some unwelcome guest should fall
    betwixt us,
And we should part without it.
PHI.                              'Twill be ill
I should abide here long.
ARE.                    'Tis true; and worse
You should come often.  How shall we
    devise                                        110
To hold intelligence,[3] that our true loves,
On any new occasion, may agree
What path is best to tread?
PHI.                        I have a boy,
Sent by the gods, I hope, to this intent,
Not yet seen in the court.  Hunting the
    buck,
I found him sitting by a fountain's side,
Of which he borrowed some to quench his
    thirst,
And paid the nymph again as much in
    tears.
A garland lay him by, made by himself
Of many several flowers bred in the bay,[4]
Stuck in that mystic order that the rare-
    ness                                          121
Delighted me; but ever when he turned
His tender eyes upon um, he would weep,
As if he meant to make um grow again.
Seeing such pretty, helpless innocence
Dwell in his face, I asked him all his
    story.
He told me that his parents gentle died,
Leaving him to the mercy of the fields,

[1] A fabulous creature whose breath and look
were fatal.

[2] Suspicious.
[3] Communication.
[4] "An indentation, recess in a range of hills,
etc." (N.E.D.)

Which gave him roots; and of the crystal
  springs,
Which did not stop their courses; and the
  sun,                                                  130
Which still, he thanked him, yielded him
  his light.
Then took he up his garland, and did
  show
What every flower, as country people
  hold,
Did signify, and how all, ordered thus,
Expressed his grief, and, to my thoughts,
  did read
The prettiest lecture of his country art
That could be wished, so that methought
  I could
Have studied it.   I gladly entertained
Him, who was glad to follow, and have
  got
The trustiest, loving'st, and the gentlest
  boy                                                  140
That ever master kept.   Him will I send
To wait on you, and bear our hidden love.
ARE. 'Tis well; no more.

### Enter Lady.

LA. Madam, the prince is come to do
  his service.
ARE. What will you do, Philaster, with
  yourself?
PHI. Why, that which all the gods have
  appointed out for me.
ARE. Dear, hide thyself!—
  Bring in the prince.          [Exit Lady.]
PHI.                Hide me from Pharamond!
  When thunder speaks, which is the voice
  of God,
  Though I do reverence, yet I hide me
  not;                                                  150
  And shall a stranger prince have leave to
  brag
  Unto a foreign nation that he made
  Philaster hide himself?
ARE.                He cannot know it.
PHI. Though it should sleep forever to the
  world,
  It is a simple sin to hide myself,
  Which will forever on my conscience lie.
ARE. Then, good Philaster, give him scope
  and way
  In what he says, for he is apt to speak
  What you are loath to hear.   For my
  sake, do.
PHI. I will.                                             160

### Enter Pharamond [with Lady].

PHA. My princely mistress, as true lovers
  ought,                              [Exit Lady.]
  I come to kiss these fair hands, and to
  show,
  In outward ceremonies, the dear love
  Writ in my heart.
PHI. If I shall have an answer no directlier,
  I am gone.
PHA.          To what would he have answer?
ARE. To his claim unto the kingdom.
PHA. Sirrah, I forbare [1] you before the
  king—
PHI. Good sir, do so still; I would not talk
  with you.
PHA. But now the time is fitter.   Do but
  offer                                                170
  To make mention of right to any king-
  dom,
  Though it be scarce habitable—
PHI.                          Good sir, let me go.
PHA. And, by the gods—
PHI.          Peace, Pharamond!   If thou—
ARE. Leave us, Philaster.
PHI. I have done.
PHA. You are gone!   By heaven, I'll fetch
  you back.
PHI. You shall not need.
PHA.                What now?
PHI.                          Know, Pharamond,
  I loathe to brawl with such a blast as
  thou,
  Who art naught but a valiant voice, but,
  if
  Thou shalt provoke me further, men shall
  say                                                  180
  Thou wert—and not lament it.
PHA.                          Do you slight
  My greatness so, and in the chamber of
  the princess?
PHI. It is a place to which I must confess
  I owe a reverence; but, were 't the
  church,
  Ay, at the altar, there's no place so safe,
  Where thou dar'st injure me, but I dare
  kill thee.
  And for your greatness, know, sir, I can
  grasp
  You and your greatness thus, thus into
  nothing.
  Give not a word, not a word back!   Fare-
  well.                                            Exit.

[1] Forbore.

PHA. 'Tis an odd fellow, madam; we must
    stop                                     190
His mouth with some office when we are
    married.
ARE. You were best make him your con-
    troller.
PHA. I think he would discharge it well.
    But, madam,
I hope our hearts are knit; but yet so slow
The ceremonies of state are that 'twill be
    long
Before our hands be so.  If then you
    please,
Being agreed in heart, let us not wait
For dreaming form, but take a little
    stolen
Delights, and so prevent [1] our joys to
    come.
ARE. If you dare speak such thoughts, 200
I must withdraw in honor.
                        *Exit Are[thusa].*
PHA. The constitution of my body will
never hold out till the wedding; I must seek
elsewhere.            *Exit Ph[aramond].*

### ACTUS II. SCENA i.

*[A hall in the palace.]*

*Enter Philaster and Bellario.*

PHI. And thou shalt find her honorable,
    boy,
Full of regard unto thy tender youth,
For thine own modesty, and, for my sake,
Apter to give than thou wilt be to ask,
Ay, or deserve.
BEL.             Sir, you did take me up
When I was nothing, and only yet am
    something
By being yours.  You trusted me un-
    known,
And that which you were apt to conster [2]
A simple innocence in me, perhaps
Might have been craft, the cunning of a
    boy                                       10
Hardened in lies and theft, yet ventured
    you
To part my miseries and me, for which
I never can expect to serve a lady
That bears more honor in her breast than
    you.
PHI. But, boy, it will prefer [3] thee.  Thou
    art young,

[1] Anticipate.               [3] Advance.
[2] Construe, interpret.

And bearest a childish, overflowing love
To them that clap thy cheeks and speak
    thee fair yet;
But, when thy judgment comes to rule
    those passions,
Thou wilt remember best those careful
    friends
That placed thee in the noblest way of
    life.                                     20
She is a princess I prefer thee to.
BEL. In that small time that I have seen
    the world,
I never knew a man hasty to part
With a servant he thought trusty.  I
    remember
My father would prefer the boys he kept
To greater men than he, but did it not
Till they were grown too saucy for him-
    self.
PHI. Why, gentle boy, I find no fault at all
In thy behavior.
BEL.              Sir, if I have made  29
A fault of ignorance, instruct my youth;
I shall be willing, if not apt, to learn.
Age and experience will adorn my mind
With larger knowledge; and, if I have
    done
A willful fault, think me not past all hope
For once.   What master holds so strict a
    hand
Over his boy that he will part with him
Without one warning?  Let me be cor-
    rected
To break my stubbornness, if it be so,
Rather than turn me off; and I shall
    mend.
PHI. Thy love doth plead so prettily to
    stay                                      40
That, trust me, I could weep to part
    with thee.
Alas, I do not turn thee off!  Thou
    knowest
It is my business that doth call thee hence;
And, when thou art with her, thou
    dwellest with me.
Think so, and 'tis so; and, when time is
    full,
That thou hast well discharged this
    heavy trust,
Laid on so weak a one, I will again
With joy receive thee.  As I live, I will!
Nay, weep not, gentle boy.  'Tis more
    than time
Thou didst attend the princess.

BEL.                    I am gone.  50
  But, since I am to part with you, my
    lord,
  And none knows whether I shall live to
    do
  More service for you, take this little
    prayer:
  Heaven bless your loves, your fights, all
    your designs!
  May sick men, if they have your wish, be
    well,
  And heaven hate those you curse, though
    I be one!                    *Exit.*
PHI.  The love of boys unto their lords is
    strange.
  I have read wonders of it; yet this boy
  For my sake (if a man may judge by
    looks
  And speech) would outdo story.  I may
    see                    60
  A day to pay him for his loyalty.
                *Exit Phi[laster].*

*Enter Pharamond.*

PHA.  Why should these ladies stay so
long?  They must come this way.  I know
the queen employs um not, for the reverend
mother [1] sent me word they would all be
for the garden.  If they should all prove
honest [2] now, I were in a fair taking.[3]  I
was never so long without sport in my life,
and, in my conscience, 'tis not my fault.
O, for our country ladies! [4]—Here's one  [70
bolted; I'll hound at her.—[Madam!] [5]

*Enter Galatea.*

GAL.  Your grace!
PHA.  Shall I not be a trouble?
GAL.  Not to me, sir.
PHA.  Nay, nay, you are too quick.  By
this sweet hand—
GAL.  You'll be forsworn, sir; 'tis but
an old glove.  If you will talk at distance,
I am for you; but, good prince, be not
bawdy, nor do not brag; these two I  [80
bar; and then, I think, I shall have
sense enough to answer all the weighty
apothegms your royal blood shall manage.

PHA.  Dear lady, can you love?
GAL.  "Dear," prince?  How dear?  I
ne'er cost you a coach yet, nor put you to
the dear repentance of a banquet.  Here's
no scarlet, sir, to blush the sin out it was
given for.  This wire [6] mine own hair  [90
covers; and this face has been so far from
being dear to any that it ne'er cost penny
painting; and, for the rest of my poor
wardrobe, such as you see, it leaves no
hand [7] behind it to make the jealous mercer's
wife curse our good doings.
PHA.  You mistake me, lady.
GAL.  Lord, I do so; would you or I
could help it!
PHA.  Do ladies of this country use  [100
to give no more respect to men of my
full being?
GAL.  Full being!  I understand you not,
unless your grace means growing to fatness;
and then your only remedy (upon my
knowledge, prince) is, in a morning, a cup
of neat white wine brewed with carduus,[8]
then fast till supper—about eight you may
eat; use exercise, and keep a sparrow
hawk; you can shoot in a tiller;[9] but,  [110
of all, your grace must fly phlebotomy,[10]
fresh pork, conger, and clarified whey; they
are all dullers of the vital spirits.
PHA.  Lady, you talk of nothing all this
while.
GAL.  'Tis very true, sir; I talk of you.
PHA.  [*Aside.*]  This is a crafty wench; I
like her wit well; 'twill be rare to stir up a
leaden appetite.  She's a Danaë, and must
be courted in a shower of gold.—  [120
[*Shows her money.*]  Madam, look here; all
these, and more than—
GAL.  What have you there, my lord?
Gold?  Now, as I live, 'tis fair gold!  You
would have silver for it, to play with the
pages.  You could not have taken me in a
worse time; but, if you have present use,
my lord, I'll send my man with silver and
keep your gold for you.
PHA.  Lady, lady!                    130
GAL.  She's coming, sir, behind, will take
white money.[11]—[*Aside.*]  Yet for all this
I'll match ye.  [*Takes gold.*]
    *Exit* GAL[ATEA] *behind the hangings.*

---

1 *I.e.*, the lady in charge of the maids of honor.
2 Chaste.
3 Dilemma.
4 *I.e.*, ladies of our country (Spain).
5 From 1620 edn.

6 Used as a frame for the headdress.
7 Record of indebtedness.        10 Bloodletting.
8 A panacea made from a kind of thistle.
9 With a crossbow.                    11 *I.e.*, silver.

PHA. If there be but two such more in this kingdom, and near the court, we may even hang up our harps. Ten such camphire[1] constitutions as this will call the golden age again in question, and teach the old way for every ill-faced husband to get his own children; and what a mis-  [140 chief that will breed, let all consider!—

*Enter Megra.*

Here's another; if she be of the same last, the devil shall pluck her on.—Many fair mornings, lady!

MEG. As many mornings bring as many days,
Fair, sweet, and hopeful to your grace!

PHA. [*Aside.*] She gives good words yet; sure this wench is free.—
If your more serious business do not call you,
Let me hold quarter[2] with you; we'll talk
An hour out quickly.

MEG.        What would your grace talk of?

PHA. Of some such pretty subject as yourself.                        151
I'll go no further than your eye, or lip;
There's theme enough for one man for an age.

MEG. Sir, they stand right, and my lips are yet even,
Smooth, young enough, ripe enough, and red enough,
Or my glass wrongs me.

PHA. O, they are two twinned cherries dyed in blushes,
Which those fair suns above with their bright beams
Reflect upon and ripen. Sweetest beauty,
Bow down those branches, that the long-ing taste                        160
Of the faint looker-on may meet those blessings,
And taste and live.                [*They kiss.*][3]

MEG. [*Aside.*]                O, delicate, sweet prince!
She that hath snow enough about her heart
To take the wanton spring of ten such lines off,
May be a nun without probation.—Sir,

[1] Camphor was formerly considered to possess the property of coldness.
[2] Friendly intercourse.
[3] From 1620 edn.

You have in such neat poetry gathered a kiss
That, if I had but five lines of that number,
Such pretty, begging blanks,[4] I should commend
Your forehead or your cheeks, and kiss you too.

PHA. Do it in prose; you cannot miss it, madam.                        170

MEG. I shall, I shall.

PHA.        By my life, but you shall not;
I'll prompt you first. [*Kisses her.*] Can you do it now?

MEG. Methinks 'tis easy, now I ha' done 't before;
But yet I should stick at it. [*Kisses him.*]

PHA.                Stick till tomorrow;
I'll ne'er part you, sweetest. But we lose time.
Can you love me?

MEG. Love you, my lord? How would you have me love you?

PHA. I'll teach you in a short sentence, cause I will not load your memory. This is all: love me, and lie with me.                        180

MEG. Was it "lie with you" that you said? 'Tis impossible.

PHA. Not to a willing mind, that will endeavor. If I do not teach you to do it as easily in one night as you'll go to bed, I'll lose my royal blood for 't.

MEG. Why, prince, you have a lady of your own that yet wants teaching.

PHA. I'll sooner teach a mare the old measures[5] than teach her anything  [190 belonging to the function. She's afraid to lie with herself if she have but any masculine imaginations about her. I know, when we are married, I must ravish her.

MEG. By mine honor, that's a foul fault, indeed; but time and your good help will wear it out, sir.

PHA. And for any other I see, excepting your dear self, dearest lady, I had rather be Sir Tim the schoolmaster, and  [200 leap a dairymaid, madam.

MEG. Has your grace seen the court star, Galatea?

PHA. Out upon her! She's as cold of her favor as an apoplex;[6] she sailed by but now.

MEG. And how do you hold her wit, sir?

[4] Blank verses.
[5] Stately dances.
[6] Apoplexy.

PHA. I hold her wit? The strength of all the guard cannot hold it, if they were tied to it; she would blow um out of the kingdom. They talk of Jupiter; he's but [210 a squib-cracker to her. Look well about you, and you may find a tongue-bolt.[1] But speak, sweet lady, shall I be freely welcome?

MEG. Whither?

PHA. To your bed. If you mistrust my faith, you do me the unnoblest wrong.

MEG. I dare not, prince, I dare not.

PHA. Make your own conditions, my purse shall seal um, and what you [220 dare imagine you can want, I'll furnish you withal. Give two hours to your thoughts every morning about it. Come, I know you are bashful. Speak in my ear; will you be mine? Keep this. [*Gives a ring*.] And, with it, me. Soon I will visit you.

MEG. My lord, my chamber's most unsafe; but, when 'tis night, I'll find some means to slip into your lodging; till [230 when—

PHA. Till when, this and my heart go with thee!    *Exeunt*.

*Enter Galatea from behind the hangings.*

GAL. O, thou pernicious petticoat prince, are these your virtues? Well, if I do not lay a train to blow your sport up, I am no woman; and, Lady Towsabel,[2] I'll fit you for 't.    *Exit Gal[atea]*.

[SCENA ii.

*Arethusa's chambers in the palace.*]

*Enter Arethusa and a Lady.*

ARE. Where's the boy?

LA. Within, madam.

ARE. Gave you him gold to buy him clothes?

LA. I did.

ARE. And has he done 't?

LA. Yes, madam.

ARE. 'Tis a pretty, sad-talking [3] boy, is it not? Asked you his name?

LA. No, madam.    10

[1] With an allusion to Jupiter's thunderbolt.
[2] A contemptuous form of Dowsabell, a sweetheart.
[3] Serious-talking.

*Enter Galatea.*

ARE. O, you are welcome. What good news?

GAL. As good as anyone can tell your grace, That says she has done that you would have wished.

ARE. Hast thou discovered?

GAL. I have strained a point of modesty for you.

ARE. I prithee, how?

GAL. In listening after bawdry. I see, let a lady live never so modestly, she shall be sure to find a lawful time to hearken after bawdry. Your prince, brave Phara- [20 mond, was so hot on 't!

ARE. With whom?

GAL. Why, with the lady I suspected. I can tell the time and place.

ARE. O, when, and where?

GAL. Tonight, his lodging.

ARE. Run thyself into the presence;[4] mingle there again
With other ladies; leave the rest to me.—
    [*Exit Galatea*.]
If destiny (to whom we dare not say,
Why thou didst this) have not decreed it so,    30
In lasting leaves (whose smallest characters
Were never altered), yet this match shall break.—
Where's the boy?

LA. Here, madam.

*Enter Bellario.*

ARE. Sir, you are sad to change your service, is 't not so?

BEL. Madam, I have not changed; I wait on you,
To do him service.

ARE.    Thou disclaim'st [5] in me.
Tell me thy name.

BEL. Bellario.

ARE. Thou canst sing and play?    40

BEL. If grief will give me leave, madam, I can.

ARE. Alas, what kind of grief can thy years know?
Hadst thou a curst [6] master when thou went'st to school?
Thou art not capable of other grief;
Thy brows and cheeks are smooth as waters be

[4] Presence chamber.    [6] Ill-tempered.
[5] Renouncest all share.

When no breath troubles them. Believe me, boy,
Care seeks out wrinkled brows and hol- low eyes,
And builds himself caves, to abide in them.
Come, sir, tell me truly, doth your lord love me?

BEL. Love, madam? I know not what it is. 50

ARE. Canst thou know grief, and never yet knew'st love?
Thou art deceived, boy. Does he speak of me
As if he wished me well?

BEL. If it be love
To forget all respect of his own friends
With thinking of your face; if it be love
To sit cross-armed and think away the day,
Mingled with starts, crying your name as loud
And hastily as men i' the streets do fire;
If it be love to weep himself away
When he but hears of any lady dead 60
Or killed, because it might have been your chance;
If, when he goes to rest (which will not be),
Twixt every prayer he says, to name you once,
As others drop a bead, be to be in love,
Then, madam, I dare swear he loves you.

ARE. O, y' are a cunning boy, and taught to lie
For your lord's credit! But thou knowest a lie
That bears this sound is welcomer to me
Than any truth that says he loves me not.
Lead the way, boy.—[To Lady.] Do you attend me too.— 70
'Tis thy lord's business hastes me thus. Away! Exeunt.

[SCENA iii.

Before Pharamond's lodging in the palace yard.]

Enter Dion, Cleremont, Thrasiline, Megra, Galatea.

DI. Come, ladies, shall we talk a round? As men

Do walk a mile, women should talk an hour
After supper; 'tis their exercise.

GAL. 'Tis late.

MEG. 'Tis all
My eyes will do to lead me to my bed.

GAL. I fear they are so heavy they'll scarce find
The way to your own lodging with um tonight.

*Enter Pharamond.*

THRA. The prince!

PHA. Not abed, ladies? Y' are good sit- ters-up. 10
What think you of a pleasant dream, to last
Till morning?

MEG. I should choose, my lord, a pleasing wake before it.

*Enter Arethusa and Bellario.*

ARE. 'Tis well, my lord; y' are courting of these ladies.—
Is 't not late, gentlemen?

CLE. Yes, madam.

ARE. Wait you there. *Exit Arethusa.*

MEG. [*Aside.*] She's jealous, as I live.—
Look you, my lord,
The princess has a Hylas, an Adonis.

PHA. His form is angel-like. 20

MEG. Why, this is he must, when you are wed,
Sit by your pillow, like young Apollo, with
His hand and voice binding your thoughts in sleep;
The princess does provide him for you and for herself.

PHA. I find no music in these boys.

MEG. Nor I.
They can do little, and that small they do,
They have not wit to hide.

DI. Serves he the princess?

THRA. Yes.

DI. 'Tis a sweet boy; how brave [1] she keeps him!

PHA. Ladies all, good rest; I mean to kill a buck

_____
[1] Richly dressed.

Tomorrow morning ere y'ave done your
   dreams.                30
MEG. All happiness attend your grace!—
   [*Exit Pharamond.*] Gentlemen, good
   rest.—
   Come, shall we to bed?
GAL.           Yes.—All, good night.
           *Exit Gal[atea with] Meg[ra].*
DI. May your dreams be true to you!—
   What shall we do, gallants? 'Tis late.
   The king
   Is up still; see, he comes, a guard
   along
   With him.

*Enter King, Arethusa, and Guard.*

KING.     Look your intelligence be true.
ARE. Upon my life, it is; and I do hope
   Your highness will not tie me to a
   man
   That in the heat of wooing throws me
   off,
   And takes another.        40
DI. What should this mean?
KING. If it be true,
   That lady had been better have em-
   braced
   Cureless diseases. Get you to your rest.
        *Ex[eunt] Are[thusa], Bell[ario].*
   You shall be righted.—Gentlemen, draw
   near;
   We shall employ you. Is young Phara-
   mond
   Come to his lodging?
DI.          I saw him enter there.
KING. Haste, some of you, and cunningly
   discover
   If Megra be in her lodging. [*Exit Dion.*]
CLE. Sir,             50
   She parted hence but now, with other
   ladies.
KING. If she be there, we shall not need to
   make
   A vain discovery of our suspicion.—
   [*Aside.*] You gods, I see that who un-
   righteously
   Holds wealth or state from others shall
   be cursed
   In that which meaner men are blessed
   withal;
   Ages to come shall know no male of
   him
   Left to inherit, and his name shall be

Blotted from earth; if he have any child
It shall be crossly matched; the gods
   themselves           60
Shall sow wild strife betwixt her lord and
   her.
Yet, if it be your wills, forgive the sin
I have committed; let it not fall
Upon this understanding child of mine!
She has not broke your laws. But how
   can I
Look to be heard of gods that must be
   just,
Praying upon the ground I hold by
   wrong?

*Enter Dion.*

DI. Sir, I have asked, and her women
swear she is within; but they, I think, are
bawds. I told um I must speak with  [70
her; they laughed, and said their lady lay
speechless. I said my business was important; they said their lady was about it.
I grew hot, and cried my business was a
matter that concerned life and death; they
answered, so was sleeping, at which their
lady was. I urged again, she had scarce
time to be so since last I saw her. They
smiled again, and seemed to instruct me
that sleeping was nothing but lying  [80
down and winking.[1] Answers more direct
I could not get; in short, sir, I think she is
not there.
KING. 'Tis then no time to dally.—You o'
   th' guard,
   Wait at the back door of the prince's
   lodging,
   And see that none pass thence, upon your
   lives.—         [*Exeunt Guards.*]
   Knock, gentlemen; knock loud; louder
   yet.             [*They knock.*]
   What, has their pleasure taken off their
   hearing?—
   I'll break your meditations.—Knock
   again!—
   Not yet? I do not think he sleeps, having
   this               90
   Larum [2] by him.—Once more.—Pharamond! Prince!

*Pharamond above.*

PHA. What saucy groom knocks at this
   dead of night?

[1] Closing the eyes.          [2] Alarum.

Where be our waiters? [1] By my vexéd
    soul,
He meets his death that meets me, for
    this boldness.
KING. Prince, you wrong your thoughts;
    we are your friends.
Come down.
PHA.          The king?
KING.          The same, sir. Come down;
We have cause of present counsel with
    you.
PHA. If your grace please
To use me, I'll attend you to your
    chamber.

*Pha[ramond] below.*

KING. No, 'tis too late, prince; I'll make
    bold with yours.          100
PHA. I have some private reasons to my-
    self
Makes me unmannerly, and say you
    cannot.—
Nay, press not forward, gentlemen; he
    must come
Through my life that comes here.
KING. Sir, be resolved [2] I must and will
    come.—Enter!
PHA. I will not be dishonored.
He that enters, enters upon his
    death.
Sir, 'tis a sign you make no stranger of
    me,
To bring these renegadoes to my cham-
    ber
At these unseasoned hours.
KING.          Why do you   110
Chafe yourself so? You are not wronged
    nor shall be;
Only I'll search your lodging, for some
    cause
To ourself known.—Enter, I say.
PHA.          I say, no.

*Meg[ra] above.*

MEG. Let um enter, prince, let um en-
    ter;
I am up and ready. [3] I know their
    business;
'Tis the poor breaking of a lady's
    honor
They hunt so hotly after; let um enjoy
    it.—

You have your business, gentlemen. I
    lay here.
O, my lord the king, this is not noble in
    you
To make public the weakness of a
    woman!          120
KING. Come down.
MEG. I dare, my lord. Your whootings [4]
    and your clamors,
Your private whispers and your broad
    fleerings,
Can no more vex my soul than this base
    carriage. [5]
But I have vengeance yet in store for
    some
Shall, in the most contempt you can
    have of me,
Be joy and nourishment.
KING.          Will you come down?
MEG. Yes, to laugh at your worst; but I
    shall wring you,
If my skill fail me not.          [*Exit above.*]
KING. Sir, I must dearly chide you for
    this looseness;          130
You have wronged a worthy lady; but
    no more.—
Conduct him to my lodging and to bed.
    [*Exeunt Pharamond and Attendants.*]
CLE. Get him another wench, and you
bring him to bed indeed.
DI. 'Tis strange a man cannot ride a
    stag [6]
Or two, to breathe himself, without a
    warrant.
If this gear [7] hold, that lodgings be
    searched thus,
Pray God we may lie with our own wives
    in safety,
That they be not by some trick of state
    mistaken!

*Enter [Attendants] with Megra.*

KING. Now, lady of honor, where's your
    honor now?          140
No man can fit your palate but the
    prince.
Thou most ill-shrouded rottenness, thou
    piece
Made by a painter and a pothe-
    cary,

[1] Attendants.   [2] Convinced.   [3] Dressed.
[4] Hootings.   [5] Behavior.   [6] A romping girl.   [7] Matter.

Thou troubled sea of lust, thou wilderness
Inhabited by wild thoughts, thou swoln
cloud
Of infection, thou ripe mine of all dis-
eases,
Thou all-sin, all-hell, and, last, all-devils,
tell me,
Had you none to pull on with your
courtesies
But he that must be mine, and wrong my
daughter?
By all the gods, all these, and all the
pages,                                            150
And all the court shall hoot thee through
the court,
Fling  rotten  oranges,  make  ribald
rhymes,
And sear thy name with candles upon
walls!
Do you laugh, Lady Venus?
Meg. Faith, sir, you must pardon me;
I cannot choose but laugh to see you
merry.
If you do this, O king, nay, if you dare
do it,
By all those gods you swore by, and as
many
More of my own, I will have fellows, and
such
Fellows  in  it  as  shall  make  noble
mirth!                                            160
The princess, your dear daughter, shall
stand by me
On walls, and sung in ballads, any-
thing.
Urge me no more; I know her and her
haunts,
Her lays,[1] leaps, and outlays, and will
discover all,
Nay, will dishonor her. I know the
boy
She keeps, a handsome boy, about
eighteen,
Know what she does with him, where,
and when.
Come, sir, you put me to a woman's madness,
The glory of a fury; and, if I do
not                                               169
Do it to the height—
King.       What boy is this she raves
at?

[1] Hiding places.

Meg. Alas, good-minded prince, you know
not these things?
I am loath to reveal um. Keep this
fault
As you would keep your health from the
hot air
Of the corrupted people, or, by heaven,
I will not fall alone. What I have
known
Shall be as public as a print; all
tongues
Shall speak it as they do the language
they
Are born in, as free and commonly; I'll
set it,
Like a prodigious star,[2] for all to gaze
at,
And so high and glowing that other king-
doms far and foreign                              180
Shall read it there, nay, travel with it,
till they find
No tongue to make it more, nor no more
people;
And then behold the fall of your fair
princess!
King. Has she a boy?
Cle. So please your grace, I have seen a
boy wait
On her, a fair boy.
King.            Go, get you to your quarter,
For this time I'll study to forget you.
Meg. Do you study to forget me, and I'll
study
To forget you.
              Ex[eunt] K[ing], Meg[ra], Guard.
Cle. Why, here's a male spirit fit   [190
for Hercules. If ever there be Nine Worthies of women, this wench shall ride astride
and be their captain.
Di. Sure, she has a garrison of devils in
her tongue, she uttered such balls of wildfire. She has so nettled[3] the king that all
the doctors in the country will scarce cure
him. That boy was a strange-found-out antidote to cure her infection; that boy, that
princess' boy; that brave, chaste, vir-   [200
tuous lady's boy! And a fair boy, a well-
spoken boy, all these considered, can make
nothing else—but there I leave you, gentlemen.
Thra. Nay, we'll go wander with you.
                                          Exeunt.

[2] Portentous comet.
[3] From 1620 edn. Original reads metled.

Actus III. Scena i.

*[The court of the palace.]*

*Enter Cle[remont], Di[on], Thra[siline].*

Cle. Nay, doubtless, 'tis true.

Di. Ay; and 'tis the gods
That raised this punishment to scourge
    the king
With his own issue. Is it not a shame
For us that should write noble [1] in the
    land,
For us that should be freemen, to behold
A man that is the bravery of his age,
Philaster, pressed down from his royal
    right
By this regardless [2] king, and only look
And see the scepter ready to be cast     10
Into the hands of that lascivious lady
That lives in lust with a smooth boy, now
    to be
Married to yon strange prince, who, but
    that people
Please to let him be a prince, is born a
    slave
In that which should be his most noble
    part,
His mind?

Thra.            That man that would not stir
    with you
To aid Philaster, let the gods forget
That such a creature walks upon the
    earth!

Cle. Philaster is too backward in 't him-
    self.                                       19
The gentry do await it, and the people
Against their nature are all bent for
    him,
And like a field of standing corn, that's
    moved
With a stiff gale, their heads bow all one
    way.

Di. The only cause that draws Philaster
    back
From this attempt is the fair princess'
    love,
Which he admires, and we can now con-
    fute.

Thra. Perhaps he'll not believe it.

Di. Why, gentlemen, 'tis without question
    so.

Cle. Ay, 'tis past speech she lives dis-
    honestly.

---

[1] *I.e.*, rank as nobles.          [2] Neglectful.

But how shall we, if he be curious,[3]
    work                                       30
Upon his faith?

Thra. We all are satisfied within our-
    selves.

Di. Since it is true, and tends to his own
    good,
I'll make this new report to be my knowl-
    edge;
I'll say I know it; nay, I'll swear I saw it.

Cle. It will be best.

Thra.            'Twill move him.

*Enter Philas[ter].*

Di.                     Here he comes.
Good morrow to your honor; we have
    spent
Some time in seeking you.

Phi.                     My worthy friends,
You that can keep your memories to
    know
Your friend in miseries, and cannot
    frown                                       40
On men disgraced for virtue, a good day
Attend you all! What service may I do
Worthy your acceptation?

Di.                     My good lord,
We come to urge that virtue, which we
    know
Lives in your breast, forth.  Rise, and
    make a head; [4]
The nobles and the people are all dulled
With this usurping king, and not a man
That ever heard the word, or knew such a
    thing
As virtue, but will second your attempts.

Phi. How honorable is this love in you   50
To me that have deserved none!  Know,
    my friends
(You that were born to shame your poor
    Philaster
With too much courtesy), I could afford
To melt myself in thanks; but my designs
Are not yet ripe.  Suffice it that ere long
I shall employ your loves; but yet the
    time
Is short of what I would.

Di. The time is fuller, sir, than you expect;
That which hereafter will not, perhaps,
    be reached
By violence, may now be caught.  As for
    the king,                                  60

---

[3] Scrupulous, skeptical.     [4] Raise an army.

You know the people have long hated
   him;
But now the princess, whom they
   loved—
PHI. Why, what of her?
DI.                    Is loathed as much as he.
PHI. By what strange means?
DI.                    She's known a whore.
PHI.                    Thou liest!
DI. My lord—
PHI. Thou liest,
                  *Offers to draw and is held.*
And thou shalt feel it! I had thought
   thy mind
Had been of honor. Thus to rob a lady
Of her good name is an infectious sin
Not to be pardoned. Be it false as
   hell,                                    70
'Twill never be redeemed, if it be sown
Amongst the people, fruitful to increase
All evil they shall hear. Let me alone
That I may cut off falsehood whilst it
   springs!
Set hills on hills betwixt me and the man
That utters this, and I will scale them all,
And from the utmost top fall on his neck,
Like thunder from a cloud.
DI.                    This is most strange;
Sure, he does love her.
PHI.              I do love fair truth.   79
She is my mistress, and who injures her
Draws vengeance from me. Sirs, let go
   my arms.
THRA. Nay, good my lord, be patient.
CLE. Sir, remember this is your honored
   friend
That comes to do his service, and will
   show you
Why he uttered this.
PHI.              I ask your pardon, sir;
My zeal to truth made me unmannerly.
Should I have heard dishonor spoke of
   you,
Behind your back, untruly, I had been
As much distempered and enraged as
   now.
DI. But this, my lord, is truth.
PHI.                    O, say not so!   90
Good **sir**, forbear to say so. 'Tis then
   **truth**
**That** womankind is false. Urge it no
   **more**;
**It is** impossible. Why should you think
**The** princess light?

DI.              Why, she was taken at it.
PHI. 'Tis false! By heaven, 'tis false! It
   cannot be!
Can it? Speak, gentlemen; for God's
   love, speak!
Is 't possible? Can women all be damned?
DI. Why, no, my lord.
PHI.                    Why, then, it cannot be.
DI. And she was taken with her boy.
PHI.                    What boy?
DI. A page, a boy that serves her.
PHI.                    O, good gods!   100
A little boy?
DI.              Ay; know you him, my lord?
PHI. [*Aside.*] Hell and sin know him!—
Sir, you are deceived;
I'll reason it a little coldly with you.
If she were lustful, would she take a
   boy,
That knows not yet desire? She would
   have one
Should meet her thoughts and know the
   sin he acts,
Which is the great delight of wickedness.
You are abused,[1] and so is she, and I.
DI. How you, my lord?
PHI.              Why, all the world's abused
In an unjust report.
DI.              O, noble sir, your virtues   110
Cannot look into the subtle thoughts of
   woman!
In short, my lord, I took them, I myself.
PHI. Now, all the devils, thou didst! Fly
   from my rage!
Would thou hadst ta'en devils engend'-
   ring plagues,
When thou didst take them! Hide thee
   from mine eyes!
Would thou hadst ta'en thunder on thy
   breast
When thou didst take them, or been
   strucken dumb
Forever, that this foul deed might have
   slept
In silence!
THRA. [*Aside.*]        Have you known him
   so ill-tempered?
CLE. [*Aside.*] Never before.
PHI.              The winds that are let loose   120
From the four several corners of the
   earth,
And spread themselves all over sea and
   land,

[1] Deceived.

Kiss not a chaste one. What friend bears a sword
To run me through?

DI.　　　　　　　　Why, my lord, are you
So moved at this?

PHI.　　　　　　When any fall from virtue,
I am distracted; I have an interest in 't.

DI. But, good my lord, recall yourself, and think
What's best to be done.

PHI.　　　　　　I thank you; I will do it.
Please you to leave me; I'll consider of it.
Tomorrow I will find your lodging
　　forth,　　　　　　　　　　　　　130
And give you answer.

DI.　　　　　　　All the gods direct you
The readiest way!

THRA. [*Aside.*]　　　He was extreme impatient.

CLE. [*Aside.*]　It was his virtue and his noble mind.

*Exit Di[on, with] Cle[remont], Thra[siline].*

PHI. I had forgot to ask him where he took them;
I'll follow him. O, that I had a sea
Within my breast to quench the fire I feel!
More circumstances will but fan this fire.
It more afflicts me now, to know by whom
This deed is done, than simply that 'tis
　　done,　　　　　　　　　　　　　139
And he that tells me this is honorable,
As far from lies as she is far from truth,
O, that like beasts we could not grieve ourselves
With that we see not! Bulls and rams will fight
To keep their females, standing in their sight;
But take um from them, and you take at once
Their spleens away, and they will fall again
Unto their pastures, growing fresh and fat,
And taste the waters of the springs as sweet
As 'twas before, finding no start in sleep.
But miserable man—

*Enter Bellario.*

[*Aside.*]　　　　　See, see, you gods,　150
He walks still; and the face you let him wear

When he was innocent is still the same,
Not blasted! Is this justice? Do you mean
To entrap mortality, that you allow
Treason so smooth a brow? I cannot now
Think he is guilty.

BEL.　　　　　　Health to you, my lord!
The princess doth commend her love, her life,
And this, unto you.　　[*Gives a letter.*]

PHI.　　　　　　　O, Bellario,
Now I perceive she loves me; she does show it
In loving thee, my boy; she has made thee brave.　　　　　　　　　　　　160

BEL. My lord, she has attired me past my wish,
Past my desert, more fit for her attendant,
Though far unfit for me who do attend.

PHI. Thou art grown courtly, boy.—
[*Aside.*] O, let all women
That love black deeds, learn to dissemble here,
Here, by this paper! She does write to me
As if her heart were mines of adamant
To all the world besides; but, unto me,
A maiden snow that melted with my looks.—
Tell me, my boy, how doth the princess use thee?　　　　　　　　　　　170
For I shall guess her love to me by that.

BEL. Scarce like her servant, but as if I were
Something allied to her, or had preserved
Her life three times by my fidelity;
As mothers fond do use their only sons,
As I'd use one that's left unto my trust,
For whom my life should pay if he met harm,
So she does use me.

PHI.　　　　　Why, this is wondrous well.
But what kind language does she feed thee with?

BEL. Why, she does tell me she will trust my youth　　　　　　　　　　　180
With all her loving secrets, and does call me
Her pretty servant; bids me weep no more
For leaving you; she'll see my services
Regarded; and such words of that soft strain

That I am nearer weeping when she ends
Than ere she spake.

PHI.                    This is much better still.

BEL. Are you not ill, my lord?

PHI.                         Ill? No, Bellario.

BEL. Methinks your words
Fall not from off your tongue so evenly,
Nor is there in your looks that quietness
That I was wont to see.

PHI.            Thou art deceived, boy.   191
And she strokes thy head?

BEL. Yes.

PHI. And she does clap thy cheeks?

BEL.                    She does, my lord.

PHI. And she does kiss thee, boy? Ha!

BEL.                    How, my lord?

PHI. She kisses thee?

BEL.            Never, my lord, by heaven.

PHI. That's strange; I know she does.

BEL.                    No, by my life.

PHI. Why, then she does not love me.
Come, she does.
I bade her do it; I charged her, by all
charms
Of love between us, by the hope of
peace          200
We should enjoy, to yield thee all de-
lights
Naked as to her bed; I took her oath
Thou shouldst enjoy her. Tell me, gentle
boy,
Is she not parallelless? Is not her breath
Sweet as Arabian winds when fruits are
ripe?
Are not her breasts two liquid ivory
balls?
Is she not all a lasting mine of joy?

BEL. Ay, now I see why my disturbéd
thoughts
Were so perplexed. When first I went to
her,          209
My heart held augury. You are abused;
Some villain has abused you. I do
see
Whereto you tend. Fall rocks upon his
head
That put this to you! 'Tis some subtile
train
To bring that noble frame of yours to
naught.

PHI. Thou think'st I will be angry with
thee. Come,
Thou shalt know all my drift. I hate her
more

Than I love happiness, and placed thee
there
To pry with narrow eyes into her deeds.
Hast thou discovered? Is she fall'n to
lust,
As I would wish her? Speak some comfort to me.          220

BEL. My lord, you did mistake the boy
you sent.
Had she the lust of sparrows or of goats,
Had she a sin that way, hid from the
world,
Beyond the name of lust, I would not aid
Her base desires; but what I came to
know
As servant to her, I would not reveal
To make my life last ages.

PHI. [Aside.]                    O, my heart!
This is a salve worse than the main
disease.—
Tell me thy thoughts, for I will know the
least
That dwells within thee, or will rip thy
heart          230
To know it. I will see thy thoughts as
plain
As I do now thy face.

BEL.                    Why, so you do.
She is (for aught I know), by all the
gods,
As chaste as ice! But, were she foul as
hell,
And I did know it thus, the breath of
kings,
The points of swords, tortures, nor bulls
of brass [1]
Should draw it from me.

PHI.                    Then 'tis no time
To dally with thee; I will take thy life,
For I do hate thee. I could curse thee
now.

BEL. If you do hate, you could not curse
me worse;          240
The gods have not a punishment in store
Greater for me than is your hate.

PHI.                              Fie, fie,
So young and so dissembling! Tell me
when
And where thou didst enjoy her, or let
plagues
Fall on me, if I destroy thee not!
                         [Draws his sword.]

[1] An instrument of torture causing death by
roasting.

Bel. By heaven, I never did; and, when I
    lie
To save my life, may I live long and
    loathed!
Hew me asunder, and, whilst I can think,
I'll love those pieces you have cut away
Better than those that grow, and kiss
    those limbs                                    250
Because you made um so.
Phi.                        Fear'st thou not death?
Can boys contemn that?
Bel.                        O, what boy is he
Can be content to live to be a man,
That sees the best of men thus passion-
    ate,
Thus without reason?
Phi.                        O, but thou dost not know
What 'tis to die.
Bel.                        Yes, I do know, my lord.
'Tis less than to be born, a lasting sleep,
A quiet resting from all jealousy,
A thing we all pursue. I know, besides,
It is but giving over of a game            260
That must be lost.
Phi.            But there are pains, false boy,
For perjured souls. Think but on those,
    and then
Thy heart will melt, and thou wilt utter
    all.
Bel. May they fall all upon me whilst I
    live,
If I be perjured, or have ever thought
Of that you charge me with! If I be false,
Send me to suffer in those punishments
You speak of; kill me!
Phi. [Aside.]                        O, what should I do?
Why, who can but believe him? He
    does swear
So earnestly that, if it were not true,      270
The gods would not endure him.—Rise,
    Bellario;
Thy protestations are so deep, and thou
Dost look so truly when thou utter'st
    them
That, though I know um false as were
    my hopes,
I cannot urge thee further. But thou wert
To blame to injure me, for I must love
Thy honest looks, and take no revenge
    upon
Thy tender youth. A love from me to
    thee
Is firm, whate'er thou doest; it troubles
    me

That I have called the blood out of thy
    cheeks,                                    280
That did so well become thee. But, good
    boy,
Let me not see thee more; something is
    done
That will distract me, that will make me
    mad,
If I behold thee. If thou tender'st [1] me,
Let me not see thee.
Bel.                        I will fly as far
As there is morning, ere I give distaste
To that most honored mind.      But,
    through these tears
Shed at my hopeless parting, I can see
A world of treason practiced upon you,
And her, and me.  Farewell forevermore!
If you shall hear that sorrow struck me
    dead,                                    291
And after find me loyal, let there be
A tear shed from you in my memory,
And I shall rest at peace.
                              Exit Bell[ario].
Phi.                        Blessing be with thee,
Whatever thou deserv'st!    O, where
    shall I
Go bathe this body? Nature too unkind,
That made no medicine for a troubled
    mind!                        Ex[it] Phi[laster].

[Scena ii.

Arethusa's chambers in the palace.]

Enter Arethusa.

Are. I marvel my boy comes not back
    again;
But that I know my love will question
    him
Over and over—how I slept, waked,
    talked,
How I remembered him when his dear
    name
Was last spoke, and how, when I sighed,
    wept, sung,
And ten thousand such—I should be
    angry at his stay.

Enter King.

King. What, at your meditations? Who
    attends you?
Are. None but my single self. I need no
    guard;
I do no wrong, nor fear none.

[1] Regardest.

KING. Tell me, have you not a boy?

ARE.                          Yes, sir.  10

KING. What kind of boy?

ARE.                A page, a waiting-boy.

KING. A handsome boy?

ARE.                I think he be not ugly;
    Well qualified and dutiful I know him;
    I took him not for beauty.

KING. He speaks and sings and plays?

ARE.                          Yes, sir.

KING. About eighteen?

ARE.                I never asked his age.

KING. Is he full of service?

ARE. By your pardon, why do you ask?

KING. Put him away.

ARE.    Sir?

KING.                Put him away, I say.
    H'as done you that good service shames
        me to speak of.                20

ARE. Good sir, let me understand you.

KING.                If you fear me,
    Show it in duty; put away that boy.

ARE. Let me have reason for it, sir, and
        then
    Your will is my command.

KING. Do not you blush to ask it?  Cast
        him off,
    Or I shall do the same to you.  Y' are one
    Shame with me, and so near unto my-
        self
    That, by my life, I dare not tell myself
    What you, myself, have done.

ARE. What I have done, my lord?    30

KING. 'Tis a new language, that all love
        to learn;
    The common people speak it well al-
        ready;
    They need no grammar.  Understand
        me well;
    There be foul whispers stirring.  Cast
        him off,
    And suddenly.  Do it!  Farewell.

                          *Exit King.*

ARE. Where may a maiden live securely
        free,
    Keeping her honor fair?  Not with the
        living.
    They feed upon opinions, errors, dreams,
    And make um truths; they draw a
        nourishment                39
    Out of defamings, grow upon disgraces,
    And, when they see a virtue fortified
    Strongly above the battery of their
        tongues,

O, how they cast [1] to sink it, and, de-
    feated
(Soul-sick with poison), strike the mon-
    uments
Where noble names lie sleeping, till
    they sweat,
And the cold marble melt.

*Enter Philaster.*

PHI. Peace to your fairest thoughts, dear-
    est mistress!

ARE. O, my dearest servant, I have a war
    within me!

PHI. He must be more than man that
    makes these crystals
    Run into rivers.  Sweetest fair, the
        cause?                50
    And, as I am your slave, tied to your
        goodness,
    Your creature, made again from what
        I was
    And newly-spirited, I'll right your honor.

ARE. O, my best love, that boy!

PHI.                          What boy?

ARE. The pretty boy you gave me—

PHI.                          What of him?

ARE. Must be no more mine.

PHI.    Why?

ARE.                They are jealous of him.

PHI. Jealous!  Who?

ARE.                The king.

PHI. [*Aside.*]                O, my misfortune!
    Then 'tis no idle jealousy.—Let him go.

ARE. O, cruel!
    Are you hard-hearted too?  Who shall
        now tell you                60
    How much I loved you?  Who shall
        swear it to you,
    And weep the tears I send?  Who shall
        now bring you
    Letters, rings, bracelets?  Lose his health
        in service?
    Wake tedious nights in stories of your
        praise?
    Who shall sing your crying elegies,
    And strike a sad soul into senseless
        pictures,
    And make them mourn?  Who shall
        take up his lute,
    And touch it till he crown a silent sleep
    Upon my eyelids, making me dream,
        and cry,
    "O, my dear, dear Philaster!"

[1] Plan.

PHI. [*Aside.*]                     O, my heart!  70
Would he had broken thee, that made
thee know
This lady was not loyal!—Mistress,
Forget the boy; I'll get thee a far better.
ARE. O, never, never such a boy again
As my Bellario!
PHI.             'Tis but your fond affection.
ARE. With thee, my boy, farewell forever
All secrecy in servants! Farewell, faith,
And all desire to do well for itself!
Let all that shall succeed thee for thy
wrongs
Sell and betray chaste love!            80
PHI. And all this passion for a boy?
ARE. He was your boy, and you put him
to me,
And the loss of such must have a mourn-
ing for.
PHI. O, thou forgetful woman!
ARE.                     How, my lord?
PHI. False Arethusa!
Hast thou a medicine to restore my wits,
When I have lost um? If not, leave to
talk
And do thus.
ARE.       Do what, sir? Would you sleep?
PHI. Forever, Arethusa. O, you gods,
Give me a worthy patience! Have I
stood,                                        90
Naked, alone, the shock of many for-
tunes?
Have I seen mischiefs numberless and
mighty
Grow like a sea upon me? Have I taken
Danger as stern as death into my
bosom,
And laughed upon it, made it but a
mirth,
And flung it by? Do I live now like him,
Under this tyrant king, that languish-
ing
Hears his sad bell and sees his mourners?
Do I
Bear all this bravely, and must sink
at length
Under a woman's falsehood? O, that
boy,                                          100
That curséd boy! None but a villain
boy
To ease your lust?
ARE.             Nay, then, I am betrayed.
I feel the plot cast for my overthrow.
O, I am wretched!

PHI. Now you may take that little right
I have
To this poor kingdom. Give it to your
joy,
For I have no joy in it. Some far place,
Where never womankind durst set her
foot
For [1] bursting with her poisons, must
I seek,
And live to curse you.                     110
There dig a cave, and preach to birds
and beasts
What woman is, and help to save them
from you:
How heaven is in your eyes, but in
your hearts
More hell than hell has; how your
tongues, like scorpions,
Both heal and poison; how your thoughts
are woven
With thousand changes in one subtle
web,
And worn so by you: how that foolish
man,
That reads the story of a woman's face
And dies believing it, is lost forever;
How all the good you have is but a
shadow,                                       120
I' th' morning with you, and at night
behind you,
Past and forgotten; how your vows are
frosts,
Fast for a night, and with the next sun
gone;
How you are, being taken all together,
A mere confusion, and so dead a chaos
That love cannot distinguish. These
sad texts,
Till my last hour, I am bound to utter
of you.
So, farewell all my woe, all my delight!
                              *Exit Phi[laster].*
ARE. Be merciful, ye gods, and strike me
dead!
What way have I deserved this? Make
my breast                                     130
Transparent as pure crystal, that the
world,
Jealous of me, may see the foulest
thought
My heart holds. Where shall a woman
turn her eyes
To find out constancy?

[1] For fear of.

*Enter Bell[ario].*

Save me, how black
And guiltily, methinks, that boy looks
now!—
O, thou dissembler, that, before thou
spak'st,
Wert in thy cradle false, sent to make
lies
And betray innocents!  Thy lord and
thou
May glory in the ashes of a maid
Fooled by her passion; but the con-
quest is                                        140
Nothing so great as wicked.  Fly away!
Let my command force thee to that
which shame
Would do without it.  If thou under-
stood'st
The loathéd office thou hast undergone,
Why, thou wouldst hide thee under heaps
of hills,
Lest men should dig and find thee.
BEL.                          O, what god,
Angry with men, hath sent this strange
disease
Into the noblest minds?  Madam, this
grief
You add unto me is no more than drops
To seas, for which they are not seen to
swell.                                          150
My lord hath struck his anger through
my heart,
And let out all the hope of future joys.
You need not bid me fly; I came to part,
To take my latest leave.  Farewell for-
ever!
I durst not run away in honesty
From such a lady, like a boy that stole
Or made some grievous fault.  The power
of gods
Assist you in your sufferings!  Hasty
time
Reveal the truth to your abuséd lord
And mine, that he may know your worth,
whilst I                                        160
Go seek out some forgotten place to
die!                          *Exit Bell[ario].*
ARE. Peace guide thee!  Th'ast over-
thrown me once;
Yet, if I had another Troy to lose,
Thou, or another villain with thy looks,
Might talk me out of it, and send me
naked,

My hair disheveled, through the fiery
streets.

*Enter a Lady.*

LA. Madam, the king would hunt, and
calls for you
With earnestness.
ARE.                    I am in tune to hunt!
Diana, if thou canst rage with a maid
As with a man,[1] let me discover thee    170
Bathing, and turn me to a fearful hind,
That I may die pursued by cruel hounds,
And have my story written in my
wounds!                          *Exeunt.*

ACTUS IV.  SCENA i.

[*Outside the palace.*]

*Enter King, Pharamond, Arethusa, Gala-*
*tea, Megra, Dion, Cleremont, Thrasi-*
*line, and Attendants.*

KING. What, are the hounds before and
all the woodmen?
Our horses ready and our bows bent?
DI.                                        All, sir.
KING. [*To Pharamond.*] Y' are cloudy,
sir.  Come, we have forgotten
Your venial trespass; let not that sit
heavy
Upon your spirit; here's none dare utter it.
DI. [*Aside.*] He looks like an old surfeited stallion after his leaping, dull as a
dormouse.  See how he sinks!  The wench
has shot him between wind and water,
and, I hope, sprung a leak.               10
THRA. [*Aside.*] He needs no teaching;
he strikes sure enough.  His greatest fault
is, he hunts too much in the purlieus; would
he would leave off poaching!
DI. [*Aside.*] And, for his horn, h'as left
it at the lodge where he lay late.  O, he's
a precious limehound![2]  Turn him loose
upon the pursue[3] of a lady, and, if he lose
her, hang him up i' th' slip.[4]  When my
fox bitch, Beauty, grows proud,[5] I'll  [20
borrow him.
KING. Is your boy turned away?

[1] *I.e.,* Actaeon.
[2] A hunting dog led by a lime, or leash.
[3] Pursuit.
[4] Noose by which hounds are held.
[5] Sexually excited.

ARE. You did command, sir, and I obeyed you.

KING. 'Tis well done. Hark ye further. [*All except Cleremont, Dion, and Thrasiline retire. The King and Arethusa talk apart.*]

CLE. Is 't possible this fellow should repent? Methinks that were not noble in him; and yet he looks like a mortified member, as if he had a sick man's salve [1] in 's mouth. If a worse man had done [30 this fault now, some physical justice [2] or other would presently (without the help of an almanac [3]) have opened the obstructions of his liver, and let him blood with a dog whip.

DI. See, see how modestly yon lady looks, as if she came from churching with her neighbors! Why, what a devil can a man see in her face but that she's honest?

THRA. Faith, no great matter to [40 speak of—a foolish twinkling with the eye, that spoils her coat; [4] but he must be a cunning herald that finds it.

DI. See how they muster [5] one another! O, there's a rank regiment where the devil carries the colors, and his dam drum major! Now the world and the flesh come behind with the carriage. [6]

CLE. Sure this lady has a good turn done her against her will; before, she [50 was common talk; now none dare say cantharides [7] can stir her. Her face looks like a warrant, willing and commanding all tongues, as they will answer it, to be tied up and bolted when this lady means to let herself loose. As I live, she has got her a goodly protection and a gracious, and may use her body discreetly for her health' sake, once a week, excepting Lent and dog days. O, if they were to be [60 got for money, what a large sum would come out of the city for these licenses!

KING. To horse, to horse! We lose the morning, gentlemen. *Exeunt.*

[SCENA ii.

*A forest.*]

*Enter two Woodmen.*

1 WOOD. What, have you lodged [8] the deer?

2 WOOD. Yes, they are ready for the bow.

1 WOOD. Who shoots?

2 WOOD. The princess.

1 WOOD. No, she'll hunt.

2 WOOD. She'll take a stand, I say.

1 WOOD. Who else?

2 WOOD. Why, the young stranger [10 prince.

1 WOOD. He shall shoot in a stone-bow [9] for me. [10] I never loved his beyond-sea-ship since he forsook the say, for paying ten shillings. [11] Hew as there at the fall of a deer, and would needs (out of his mightiness) give ten groats for the dowcets; [12] marry, the steward would have the velvethead, [13] into the bargain, to turf [14] his hat withal. I think he should love venery; [20 he is an old Sir Tristram; [15] for, if you be remembered, he forsook the stag once to strike a rascal milking [16] in a meadow, and her he killed in the eye. Who shoots else?

2 WOOD. The Lady Galatea.

1 WOOD. That's a good wench, and [17] she would not chide us for tumbling of her women in the brakes. She's liberal, and, by the gods, they say she's honest, and whether that be a fault, I have nothing [30 to do. There's all?

2 WOOD. No, one more—Megra.

1 WOOD. That's a firker, [18] i' faith, boy. There's a wench will ride her haunches as hard after a kennel of hounds as a hunting saddle, and, when she comes home, get um clapped, [19] and all is well again. I have known her lose herself three times in one afternoon (if the woods have been answerable [20]), and it has been work enough [40 for one man to find her, and he has sweat

---

[1] An allusion to such religious pamphlets as Thomas Becon's *The Sick Man's Salve* (1561) and William Perkins' *Salve for a Sick Man* (1595).

[2] *I.e.*, a justice acting as a physician.

[3] Almanacs gave directions for bloodletting.

[4] "The allusion is to mullets, or stars, introduced into coats of arms to distinguish the younger branches of a family, which of course denote inferiority" (Mason).

[5] Set off.    [6] Baggage.    [7] A provocative.

[8] Entrapped.

[9] With a crossbow for shooting stones.

[10] For all I care.

[11] Refused the assay, or slitting of the deer, to avoid paying the customary keeper's fee.

[12] Doucets, testicles.

[13] The down-covered horns of a young deer.

[14] Re-cover.        [17] If.    [18] A lively one.

[15] An expert huntsman.        [19] Rubbed.

[16] A lean doe feeding.        [20] Suitable.

for it.  She rides well and she pays well.
Hark!  Let's go.                    *Exeunt.*

*Enter Philaster.*

PHI.  O, that I had been nourished in these
        woods
    With milk of goats and acorns, and not
        known
    The right of crowns nor the dissembling
        trains
    Of women's looks, but digged myself a
        cave
    Where I, my fire, my cattle, and my
        bed
    Might have been shut together in one
        shed,
    And then had taken me some mountain
        girl,                                  50
    Beaten with winds, chaste as the hard-
        ened rocks
    Whereon she dwells, that might have
        strewed my bed
    With leaves and reeds, and with the skins
        of beasts,
    Our neighbors, and have borne at her big
        breasts
    My large, coarse issue!  This had been a
        life
    Free from vexation.

*Enter Bellario.*

BEL.  [*To himself.*]        O, wicked men!
    An innocent may walk safe among
        beasts;
    Nothing assaults me here.  See, my
        grieved lord
    Sits as his soul were searching out a way
    To leave his body!—Pardon me, that
        must                                   60
    Break thy last commandment, for I
        must speak.
    You that are grieved can pity; hear,
        my lord!
PHI.  Is there a creature yet so miserable
    That I can pity?
BEL.                    O, my noble lord,
    View my strange fortune, and bestow
        on me,
    According to your bounty (if my service
    Can merit nothing), so much as may
        serve
    To keep that little piece I hold of life
    From cold and hunger!

PHI.                        Is it thou?  Begone!
    Go, sell those misbeseeming clothes thou
        wear'st,                              70
    And feed thyself with them.
BEL.  Alas, my lord, I can get nothing for
        them!
    The silly country people think 'tis trea-
        son
    To touch such gay things.
PHI.                    Now, by the gods, this is
    Unkindly done, to vex me with thy
        sight.
    Th' art fall'n again to thy dissembling
        trade.
    How shouldst thou think to cozen me
        again?
    Remains there yet a plague untried for
        me?
    Even so thou wep[t]'st, and look[ed]'st,
        and spok'st when first                79
    I took thee up.  Curse on the time!  If thy
    Commanding tears can work on any
        other,
    Use thy art;  I'll not betray it.  Which
        way
    Wilt thou take, that I may shun thee,
    For thine eyes are poison to mine, and I
    Am loath to grow in rage?  This way, or
        that way?
BEL.  Any will serve; but I will choose to
        have
    That path in chase that leads unto my
        grave.
    *Exit Phi[laster, with] Bel[lario], severally.*

*Enter Dion and the Woodmen.*

DI.  This is the strangest sudden chance!
    —You, woodmen!
1 WOOD.  My lord Dion?
DI.  Saw you a lady come this way    [90
on a sable horse studded with stars of
white?
2 WOOD.  Was she not young and tall?
DI.  Yes.  Rode she to the wood or to the
    plain?
2 WOOD.  Faith, my lord, we saw none.
                        *Exeunt* [1] *Woodmen.*
DI.  Pox of your questions then!—

*Enter Cleremont.*

                        What, is she found?
CLE.  Nor will be, I think.

[1] Original reads *Exit.*

DI. Let him seek his daughter himself. She cannot stray about a little necessary natural business, but the whole court [100 must be in arms. When she has done, we shall have peace.

CLE. There's already a thousand fatherless tales amongst us. Some say her horse ran away with her; some, a wolf pursued her; others, 'twas a plot to kill her, and that armed men were seen in the wood; but questionless she rode away willingly.

*Enter King and Thrasiline.*

KING. Where is she?
CLE.                    Sir, I cannot tell.
KING.                              How's that? Answer me so again!
CLE.                    Sir, shall I lie?    110
KING. Yes, lie and damn, rather than tell me that.
    I say again, where is she? Mutter not!—
    Sir, speak you; where is she?
DI.                    Sir, I do not know.
KING. Speak that again so boldly, and, by heaven,
    It is thy last!—You, fellows, answer me;
    Where is she? Mark me, all; I am your king.
    I wish to see my daughter; show her me.
    I do command you all, as you are subjects,
    To show her me! What! Am I not your king?
    If ay, then am I not to be obeyed?    120
DI. Yes, if you command things possible and honest.
KING. Things possible and honest! Hear me, thou,
    Thou traitor, that dar'st confine thy king to things
    Possible and honest! Show her me,
    Or, let me perish, if I cover not
    All Sicily with blood!
DI.                    Faith, I cannot,
    Unless you tell me where she is.
KING. You have betrayed me; y' have let me lose
    The jewel of my life. Go, bring her me,    129
    And set her here before me. 'Tis the king
    Will have it so, whose breath can still the winds,
    Uncloud the sun, charm down the swelling sea,

And stop the floods of heaven. Speak, can it not?
DI. No.
KING.    No? Cannot the breath of kings do this?
DI. No; nor smell sweet itself, if once the lungs
    Be but corrupted.
KING.                    Is it so? Take heed!
DI. Sir, take you heed how you dare the powers
    That must be just.
KING.            Alas! What are we kings?
    Why do you gods place us above the rest,
    To be served, flattered, and adored, till we    140
    Believe we hold within our hands your thunder?
    And, when we come to try the power we have,
    There's not a leaf shakes at our threat'-nings.
    I have sinned, 'tis true, and here stand to be punished;
    Yet would not thus be punished. Let me choose
    My way, and lay it on!
DI. [*Aside.*] He articles [1] with the gods. Would somebody would draw bonds for the performance of covenants betwixt them!    150

*Enter Pha[ramond], Galatea, and Megra.*

KING. What, is she found?
PHA.    No; we have ta'en her horse;
    He galloped empty by. There's some treason.
    You, Galatea, rode with her into the wood.
    Why left you her?
GAL. She did command me.
KING. Command! You should not.
GAL. 'Twould ill become my fortunes and my birth
    To disobey the daughter of my king.
KING. Y' are all cunning to obey us for our hurt;
    But I will have her.
PHA.            If I have her not,    160
    By this hand, there shall be no more Sicily.

_____
[1] Bargains.

Dɪ. [*Aside.*]  What, will he carry it to
Spain in 's pocket?

Pʜᴀ. I will not leave one man alive but
the king,
A cook, and a tailor.

Dɪ. [*Aside.*]  Yes; you may do well to
spare your lady-bedfellow; and her you may
keep for a spawner.

Kɪɴɢ. [*Aside.*]  I see the injuries I have
done must be revenged.

Dɪ. Sir, this is not the way to find her
out.

Kɪɴɢ. Run all; disperse yourselves. The
man that finds her,                              170
Or (if she be killed) the traitor, I'll make
him great.

Dɪ. I know some would give five thousand
pounds to find her.

Pʜᴀ. Come, let us seek.

Kɪɴɢ. Each man a several way; here I myself.

Dɪ. Come, gentlemen, we here.

Cʟᴇ. Lady, you must go search too.

Mᴇɢ. I had rather be searched myself.

                              *Exeunt* [1] *omnes.*

[Sᴄᴇɴᴀ iii.

*Another part of the forest.*]

*Enter Arethusa.*

Aʀᴇ. Where am I now?   Feet, find me out
a way,
Without the counsel of my troubled head.
I'll follow you boldly about these woods,
O'er mountains, through brambles, pits,
and floods.
Heaven, I hope, will ease me.   I am sick.
                    [*She sits down.*] [2]

*Enter Bellario.*

Bᴇʟ. [*Aside.*]  Yonder's my lady.   God
knows I want nothing,
Because I do not wish to live; yet I
Will try her charity.—O, hear, you that
have plenty!
From that flowing store drop some on
dry ground.—See,                              9
The lively red is gone to guard her heart!
I fear she faints.—Madam, look up!—
She breathes not.—
Open once more those rosy twins, and
send

[1] Original reads *Exit.*    [2] From 1620 edn.

Unto my lord your latest farewell!—O,
she stirs.—
How is it, madam?   Speak comfort.

Aʀᴇ. 'Tis not gently done,
To put me in a miserable life,
And hold me there.   I prithee, let me
go.
I shall do best without thee; I am well.

*Enter Philaster.*

Pʜɪ. [*Aside.*]  I am to blame to be so
much in rage.
I'll tell her coolly when and where I
heard                                          20
This killing truth.   I will be temperate
In speaking, and as just in hearing.—
O, monstrous!   Tempt me not, you gods!
Good gods,
Tempt not a frail man!   What's he that
has a heart
But he must ease it here!

Bᴇʟ. My lord, help, help!   The princess!

Aʀᴇ. I am well; forbear.

Pʜɪ. [*Aside.*]  Let me love lightning; let me
be embraced
And kissed by scorpions, or adore the
eyes                                           29
Of basilisks, rather than trust the tongues
Of hell-bred woman!   Some good god
look down,
And shrink these veins up!   Stick me
here a stone,
Lasting to ages in the memory
Of this damned act!—Hear me, you
wicked ones!
You have put hills of fire into this
breast,
Not to be quenched with tears, for which
may guilt
Sit on your bosoms!   At your meals and
beds
Despair await you!   What, before my
face?
Poison of asps between your lips!   Dis-
eases
Be your best issues!   Nature make a
curse,                                         40
And throw it on you!

Aʀᴇ.                    Dear Philaster, leave
To be enraged, and hear me.

Pʜɪ.                    I have done;
Forgive my passion.   Not the calméd
sea,
When Aeolus locks up his windy brood,

Is less disturbed than I. I'll make you
   know 't.
Dear Arethusa, do but take this sword,
   [*Offers his drawn sword.*] [1]
And search how temperate a heart I
   have;
Then you and this your boy may live and
   reign
In lust without control.—Wilt thou,
   Bellario?
I prithee, kill me; thou art poor, and
   mayst                                          50
Nourish ambitious thoughts; when I am
   dead,
This way were freer. Am I raging now?
If I were mad, I should desire to live.
Sirs,[2] feel my pulse, whether you have
   known
A man in a more equal tune to die.
BEL. Alas, my lord, your pulse keeps mad-
   man's time!
So does your tongue.
PHI.               You will not kill me, then?
ARE. Kill you?
BEL.               Not for the world.
PHI.               I blame not thee,
   Bellario; thou has done but that which
      gods
   Would have transformed themselves to
      do. Begone;                                60
   Leave me without reply. This is the
      last
   Of all our meeting.—(*Exit Bell[ario].*)
   Kill me with this sword.
   Be wise, or worse will follow; we are two
   Earth cannot bear at once. Resolve to
      do,
   Or suffer.
ARE. If my fortune be so good to let me
   fall
Upon [3] thy hand, I shall have peace in
   death.
Yet tell me this: will there be no slan-
   ders,
No jealousy in the other world, no ill
   there?
PHI. No.                                        70
ARE. Show me then the way.
PHI. Then guide my feeble hand,
   You that have power to do it, for I must
   Perform a piece of justice!—If your
      youth

Have any way offended heaven, let
   prayers
Short and effectual reconcile you to it.
ARE. I am prepared.

*Enter a Country Fellow.*

COUN. [*Aside.*] I'll see the king, if he be
in the forest; I have hunted him these two
hours. If I should come home and not [80
see him, my sisters would laugh at me. I
can see nothing but people better horsed
than myself, that outride me; I can hear
nothing but shouting. These kings had
need of good brains; this whooping is able
to put a mean man out of his wits.—
There's a courtier with his sword drawn;
by this hand, upon a woman, I think!
PHI. Are you at peace?
ARE.               With heaven and earth. 89
PHI. May they divide thy soul and body!
                                    [*Wounds her.*]
COUN. Hold, dastard! Strike a woman!
Th' art a craven. I warrant thee, thou
wouldst be loath to play half a dozen venies
at wasters [4] with a good fellow for a
broken head.
PHI. Leave us, good friend.
ARE. What ill-bred man art thou, to in-
   trude thyself
Upon our private sports, our recreations?
COUN. God 'uds [5] me, I understand you
not; but I know the rogue has hurt you.
PHI. Pursue thy own affairs. It will be ill
   To multiply blood upon my head, which
      thou                                       102
   Wilt force me to.
COUN. I know not your rhetoric; but I
can lay it on, if you touch the woman.
                                    *They fight.*
PHI. Slave, take what thou deservest!
ARE.               Heavens guard my lord!
COUN. O, do you breathe?
PHI. I hear the tread of people. I am hurt.
   The gods take part against me. Could
      this boor
   Have held me thus else? I must shift
      for life,                                  110
   Though I do loathe it. I would find a
      course
   To lose it rather by my will than force.
                                    *Exit Philaster.*
COUN. I cannot follow the rogue. I
pray thee, wench, come and kiss me now.

*Enter Phara[mond], Dion, Cle[remont], Thra-*
*si[line], and Woodmen.*

PHA. What art thou?

COUN. Almost killed I am for a foolish woman; a knave has hurt her.

PHA. The princess, gentlemen!—Where's the wound, madam?  Is it dangerous?

ARE. He has not hurt me.                    120

COUN. By God, she lies; h'as hurt her in the breast; look else.

PHA. O sacred spring of innocent blood!

DI. 'Tis above wonder!  Who should dare this?

ARE. I felt it not.

PHA. Speak, villain, who has hurt the princess?

COUN. Is it the princess?

DI. Ay.                                     130

COUN. Then I have seen something yet.

PHA. But who has hurt her?

COUN. I told you, a rogue; I ne'er saw him before, I.

PHA. Madam, who did it?

ARE.                    Some dishonest wretch;
Alas, I know him not, and do forgive him!

COUN. He's hurt too; he cannot go far;
I made my father's old fox [1] fly about his ears.

PHA. How will you have me kill    [140
him?

ARE. Not at all; 'tis some distracted fellow.

PHA. By this hand, I'll leave ne'er a piece of him bigger than a nut, and bring him all to you in my hat.

ARE. Nay, good sir,
If you do take him, bring him quick [2] to me,
And I will study for a punishment
Great as his fault.                         149

PHA. I will.

ARE.           But swear.

PHA.                By all my love, I will.—
Woodmen, conduct the princess to the king,
And bear that wounded fellow to dress-
ing.—
Come, gentlemen, we'll follow the chase close.

*Exeunt [3] Are[thusa], Pha[ramond], Di[on],*
*Cle[remont], Thra[siline], and 1 Wood-*
*man.*

COUN. I pray you, friend, let me see the king.

2 WOOD. That you shall, and receive thanks.

COUN. If I get clear with this, I'll go to see no more gay sights.        *Exeunt.[4]*

[SCENA iv.

*Another part of the forest.]*

*Enter Bellario.*

BEL. A heaviness near death sits on my brow,
And I must sleep.  Bear me, thou gentle bank,
Forever, if thou wilt.  You sweet ones all,                    [*Lies down.*]
Let me unworthy press you; I could wish
I rather were a corse [5] strewed o'er with you
Than quick above you.  Dullness shuts mine eyes,
And I am giddy.  O, that I could take
So sound a sleep that I might never wake!                      [*Sleeps.*]

*Enter Philaster.*

PHI. I have done ill; my conscience calls me false
To strike at her that would not strike at me.                           10
When I did fight, methought I heard her pray
The gods to guard me.  She may be abused,
And I a loathéd villain; if she be,
She will conceal who hurt her.  He has wounds
And cannot follow; neither knows he me.
Who's this?  Bellario sleeping?  If thou beest
Guilty, there is no justice that thy sleep                    *Cry within.*
Should be so sound, and mine, whom thou hast wronged,
So broken.  Hark! I am pursued.  You gods,
I'll take this offered means of my escape.                              20
They have no mark to know me but my wounds,

---

[1] Broad sword.          [3] Original reads *Exit.*
[2] Alive.

[4] In original, stage direction appears at end of preceding speech.        [5] Corpse.

If she be true; if false, let mischief light
On all the world at once! Sword, print
    my wounds
Upon this sleeping boy! I ha' none, I
    think,
Are mortal, nor would I lay greater on
    thee.                    *Wounds him.*
BEL. O, death, I hope, is come! Blessed
    be that hand!
It meant me well. Again, for pity's sake!
PHI. I have caught myself;
                    *Phi[laster] falls.*
The loss of blood hath stayed my flight.
    Here, here
Is he that stroke [1] thee. Take thy full
    revenge;                                    30
Use me, as I did mean thee, worse than
    death;
I'll teach thee to revenge. This luckless
    hand
Wounded the princess; tell my followers [2]
Thou didst receive these hurts in staying
    me,
And I will second thee. Get a reward.
BEL. Fly, fly, my lord, and save yourself!
PHI.                              How's this?
Wouldst thou I should be safe?
BEL.                              Else were it vain
For me to live. These little wounds I
    have
Ha' not bled much. Reach me that noble
    hand;
I'll help to cover you.
PHI.                    Art thou true to me? 40
BEL. Or let me perish loathed! Come,
    my good lord,
Creep in among those bushes. Who does
    know
But that the gods may save your much-
    loved breath?
PHI. Then I shall die for grief, if not for
    this,
That I have wounded thee. What wilt
    thou do?
BEL. Shift for myself well. Peace! I hear
    um come. [*Philaster conceals himself.*]
[VOICES.] (*Within.*) Follow, follow, follow!
    That way they went.
BEL. With my own wounds I'll bloody
    my own sword.
I need not counterfeit to fall; heaven
    knows
That I can stand no longer. [*Falls.*] 50

[1] Struck.                    [2] Pursuers.

*Enter Pharamond, Dion, Cleremont, Thrasi-*
                                        *line.*

PHA. To this place we have tracked him
    by his blood.
CLE. Yonder, my lord, creeps one away.
DI. Stay, sir! What are you?
BEL. A wretched creature, wounded in
    these woods
By beasts. Relieve me, if your names
    be men,
Or I shall perish.
DI.                    This is he, my lord,
Upon my soul, that hurt her. 'Tis the
    boy,
That wicked boy that served her.
PHA.                    O, thou damned
In thy creation! What cause couldst
    thou shape
To hurt the princess?
BEL.              Then I am betrayed. 60
DI. Betrayed! No, apprehended.
BEL.                    I confess
(Urge it no more) that, big with evil
    thoughts,
I set upon her, and did make my aim
Her death. For charity, let fall at once
The punishment you mean, and do not
    load
This weary flesh with tortures.
PHA.                    I will know
Who hired thee to this deed.
BEL.                    Mine own revenge.
PHA. Revenge! For what?
BEL.                    It pleased her to receive
Me as her page and, when my fortunes
    ebbed,
That men strid [3] o'er them careless, she
    did shower                                70
Her welcome graces on me, and did swell
My fortunes till they overflowed their
    banks,
Threat'ning the men that crossed um,
    when, as swift
As storms arise at sea, she turned her
    eyes
To burning suns upon me, and did dry
The streams she had bestowed, leaving
    me worse
And more contemned than other little
    brooks,
Because I had been great. In short, I
    knew

[3] Strode.

I could not live, and therefore did desire
To die revenged.

PHA.        If tortures can be found  80
Long as thy natural life, resolve to feel
The utmost rigor.

*Philaster creeps out of a bush.*

CLE.        Help to lead him hence.

PHI. Turn back, you ravishers of innocence!
Know ye the price of that you bear away
So rudely?

PHA.    Who's that?

DI.        'Tis the Lord Philaster.

PHI. 'Tis not the treasure of all kings in one,
The wealth of Tagus, nor the rocks of pearl
That pave the court of Neptune, can weigh down
That virtue. It was I that hurt the princess.
Place me, some god, upon a pyramis [1]  90
Higher than hills of earth, and lend a voice
Loud as your thunder to me, that from thence
I may discourse to all the underworld
The worth that dwells in him!

PHA.        How's this?

BEL.        My lord, some man
Weary of life, that would be glad to die.

PHI. Leave these untimely courtesies, Bellario.

BEL. Alas, he's mad! Come, will you lead me on?

PHI. By all the oaths that men ought most to keep,
And gods do punish most when men do break,
He touched her not.—Take heed, Bellario,  100
How thou dost drown the virtues thou hast shown
With perjury.—By all that's good, 'twas I!
You know she stood betwixt me and my right.

PHA. Thy own tongue be thy judge!

CLE.        It was Philaster.

DI. Is 't not a brave boy?
Well, sirs, I fear me we were all deceived.

PHI. Have I no friend here?

[1] Pyramid.

DI.        Yes.

PHI.        Then show it. Some
Good body lend a hand to draw us nearer.
Would you have tears shed for you when you die?
Then lay me gently on his neck, that there  110
I may weep floods and breathe forth my spirit.
'Tis not the wealth of Plutus, nor the gold  [*Embraces Bellario.*]
Locked in the heart of earth, can buy away
This armful from me; this had been a ransom
To have redeemed the great Augustus Cæsar,
Had he been taken. You hard-hearted men,
More stony than these mountains, can you see
Such clear, pure blood drop, and not cut your flesh
To stop his life, to bind whose bitter wounds
Queens ought to tear their hair, and with their tears  120
Bathe um?—Forgive me, thou that art the wealth
Of poor Philaster!

*Enter King, Arethusa, and a Guard.*

KING.        Is the villain ta'en?

PHA. Sir, here be two confess the deed; but say [2]
It was Philaster—

PHI.        Question it no more;
It was.

KING.    The fellow that did fight with him
Will tell us that.

ARE.        Ay me! I know he will.

KING. Did not you know him?

ARE.        Sir, if it was he,
He was disguised.

PHI.        I was so.—O, my stars,
That I should live still!

KING.        Thou ambitious fool,
Thou that hast laid a train for thy own life!—  130
Now[3] I do mean to do, I'll leave to talk.[4]
Bear him to prison.

[2] Suppose.    [3] Now that.    [4] Stop talking.

ARE. Sir, they did plot together to take hence
This harmless life; should it pass unrevenged,
I should, to earth go weeping. Grant me, then,
By all the love a father bears his child,
Their custodies, and that I may appoint
Their tortures and their deaths.

DI. Death? Soft; our law will not reach that for this fault.

KING. 'Tis granted; take um to you with a guard.—    140
Come, princely Pharamond, this business past,
We may with more security go on
To your intended match.

CLE. [*Aside.*] I pray that this action lose not Philaster the hearts of the people.

DI. [*Aside.*] Fear it not; their overwise heads will think it but a trick.

*Exeunt omnes.*[1]

Actus V. Scena i.

[*Outside the palace.*]

*Enter Dion, Cleremont, Thrasiline.*

THRA. Has the king sent for him to death?

DI. Yes; but the king must know 'tis not in his power to war with heaven.

CLE. We linger time; the king sent for Philaster and the headsman an hour ago.

THRA. Are all his wounds well?

DI. All. They were but scratches, but the loss of blood made him faint.

CLE. We dally, gentlemen.    10

THRA. Away!

DI. We'll scuffle hard before he perish.

*Exeunt.*

[Scena ii.

*A room in a prison.*]

*Enter Philaster, Arethusa, Bellario.*

ARE. Nay, faith, Philaster, grieve not; we are well.

BEL. Nay, good my lord, forbear; we're wondrous well.

PHI. O, Arethusa, O, Bellario,
Leave to be kind!

I shall be shut[2] from heaven, as now from earth,
If you continue so. I am a man
False to a pair of the most trusty ones
That ever earth bore; can it bear us all?
Forgive, and leave me. But the king hath sent
To call me to my death. O, show it me,    10
And then forget me! And for thee, my boy,
I shall deliver words will mollify
The hearts of beasts to spare thy innocence.

BEL. Alas, my lord, my life is not a thing
Worthy your noble thoughts! 'Tis not a life;
'Tis but a piece of childhood thrown away.
Should I outlive you, I should then outlive
Virtue and honor; and, when that day comes,
If ever I shall close these eyes but once,
May I live spotted for my perjury,    20
And waste my[3] limbs to nothing!

ARE. And I (the woeful'st maid that ever was,
Forced with my hands to bring my lord to death)
Do by the honor of a virgin swear
To tell no hours beyond it![4]

PHI.        Make me not hated so.

ARE. Come from this prison all joyful to our deaths!

PHI. People will tear me, when they find you true
To such a wretch as I; I shall die loathed.
Enjoy your kingdoms peaceably, whilst I    29
Forever sleep forgotten with my faults.
Every just servant, every maid in love,
Will have a piece of me, if you be true.

ARE. My dear lord, say not so.

BEL.        A piece of you?
He was not born of women that can cut
It and look on.

PHI. Take me in tears betwixt you, for my heart
Will break with shame and sorrow.

---

[1] In the original *Finis actus quarti* is inserted here.

[2] From 1620 edn. Original reads *shot*.

[3] From 1630 edn. Original reads *by*.

[4] *I.e.,* to die.

ARE.                          Why, 'tis well.
BEL. Lament no more.
PHI.               What would you have done
    If you had wronged me basely, and had
      found
    Your [1] life no price compared to mine?[1]
    For love, sirs,                              40
    Deal with me truly.
BEL.               'Twas mistaken, sir.
PHI. Why, if it were?
BEL.         Then, sir, we would have asked
    Your pardon.
PHI.           And have hope to enjoy it?
ARE. Enjoy it? Ay.
PHI.             Would you indeed? Be plain.
BEL. We would, my lord.
PHI.                     Forgive me, then.
ARE.                                    So, so.
BEL. 'Tis as it should be now.
PHI.               Lead to my death. *Exeunt.*

[SCENA iii.

*A state room in the palace.*]

*Enter King, Dion, Cleremont, Thrasiline.*

KING. Gentlemen, who saw the prince?
CLE. So please you, sir, he's gone to see
      the city
    And the new platform,[2] with some gentle-
      men
    Attending on him.
KING.               Is the princess ready
    To bring her prisoner out?
THRA.             She waits your grace.
KING. Tell her we stay.
                    [*Exit Thrasiline.*][3]
DI. [*Aside.*]      King, you may be de-
      ceived yet.
    The head you aim at cost more setting
      on
    Than to be lost so lightly. If it must off,
    Like a wild overflow, that soops[4] be-
      fore him
    A golden stack, and with it shakes down
      bridges,                                   10
    Cracks the strong hearts of pines, whose
      cable-roots
    Held out a thousand storms, a thousand
      thunders,
    And, so made mightier, takes whole
      villages

[1] Mason's emendation for *my . . . yours* of
all early edns.        [2] For mounting guns.
[3] From 1620 edn.        [4] Sweeps.

Upon his back, and in that heat of pride
Charges strong towns, towers, castles,
    palaces,
And lays them desolate, so shall thy
    head,
Thy noble head, bury the lives of thou-
    sands,
That must bleed with thee like a sacri-
    fice,
In thy red ruins.

*Enter Philaster, Arethusa, Bellario in a
    robe and garland [, and Thrasiline].*

KING.       How now? What masque is this?
BEL. Right royal sir, I should         20
    Sing you an epithalamion of these lovers,
    But having lost my best airs with my
      fortunes,
    And wanting a celestial harp to strike
    This blessed union on, thus in glad story
    I give you all. These two fair cedar
      branches,
    The noblest of the mountain where they
      grew,
    Straightest and tallest, under whose
      still shades
    The worthier beasts have made their
      lairs, and slept
    Free from [the fervor of][5] the Sirian
      star
    And the fell thunderstroke, free from
      the clouds                                 30
    When they were big with humor,[6] and
      delivered
    In thousand spouts their issues to the
      earth
    (O, there was none but silent quiet
      there),
    Till never-pleaséd Fortune shot up
      shrubs,
    Base underbrambles, to divorce these
      branches;
    And for a while they did so, and did reign
    Over the mountain, and choke up his
      beauty
    With brakes, rude thorns, and thistles,
      till the sun
    Scorched them even to the roots and
      dried them there.                          39
    And now a gentle gale hath blown again,
    That made these branches meet and
      twine together,
    Never to be divided. The god that sings

[5] From 1620 edn.        [6] Moisture.

His holy numbers [1] over marriage beds
Hath knit their noble hearts; and here
    they stand,
Your children, mighty king; and I have
    done.

KING. How, how?

ARE.       Sir, if you love it in plain truth
(For now there is no masquing in 't),
    this gentleman,
The prisoner that you gave me, is be-
    come
My keeper, and through all the bitter
    throes
Your jealousies and his ill fate have
    wrought him,                                50
Thus nobly hath he struggled, and at
    length
Arrived here my dear husband.

KING.              Your dear husband!—
Call in the Captain of the Citadel—
There you shall keep your wedding.
    I'll provide
A masque shall make your Hymen turn
    his saffron
Into a sullen coat, and sing sad requiems
To your departing souls.
Blood shall put out your torches; and,
    instead
Of gaudy flowers about your wanton
    necks,
An ax shall hang, like a prodigious
    meteor,                                    60
Ready to crop your loves' sweets. Hear,
    you gods!
From this time do I shake all title off
Of father to this woman, this base
    woman;
And what there is of vengeance in a
    lion
Chased among dogs or robbed of his
    dear young,
The same, enforced more terrible, more
    mighty,
Expect from me!

ARE. Sir, by that little life I have left to
    swear by,
There's nothing that can stir me from
    myself.
What I have done, I have done without
    repentance,                              70
For death can be no bugbear unto me,
So long as Pharamond is not my heads-
    man.

[1] Verses.

DI. [Aside.] Sweet peace upon thy soul,
    thou worthy maid,
Whene'er thou diest! For this time I'll
    excuse thee,
Or be thy prologue. [2]

PHI.              Sir, let me speak next,
And let my dying words be better with
    you
Than my dull, living actions. If you aim
At the dear life of this sweet innocent,
Y' are a tyrant and a savage monster.
Your memory shall be as foul behind
    you,                                       80
As you are living; all your better deeds
Shall be in water writ, but this in marble;
No chronicle shall speak you, though
    your own,
But for the shame of men. No monu-
    ment,
Though high and big as Pelion, shall be
    able
To cover this base murther, make it
    rich
With brass, with purest gold, and shin-
    ing jasper,
Like the pyramidës; lay on epitaphs
Such as make great men gods; my little
    marble,
That only clothes my ashes, not my
    faults,                                    90
Shall far outshine it. And for after-
    issues [3]
Think not so madly of the heavenly
    wisdoms
That they will give you more for your
    mad rage
To cut off, unless it be some snake, or
    something
Like yourself, that in his birth shall
    strangle you.
Remember my father, king! There was
    a fault,
But I forgive it. Let that sin persuade
    you
To love this lady; if you have a soul,
Think, save her, and be savéd. For my-
    self,                                      99
I have so long expected [4] this glad hour,
So languished under you, and daily
    withered,
That, by the gods, it is a joy to die;
I find a recreation in 't.

[2] I.e., precede thee in death.       [4] Awaited.
[3] Future offspring.

*Enter a Messenger.*

MESS. Where's the king?

KING.    Here.

MESS.            Get you to your strength,
And rescue the Prince Pharamond from
    danger.
He's taken prisoner by the citizens,
Fearing [1] the Lord Philaster.

DI. [*Aside.*]        O, brave followers!
Mutiny, my fine, dear countrymen,
    mutiny!
Now, my brave, valiant foremen, show
    your weapons
In honor of your mistresses!        110

*Enter another Messenger.*

[2] MESS. Arm, arm, arm, arm!

KING. A thousand devils take um!

DI. [*Aside.*] A thousand blessings on um!

[2] MESS. Arm, O king! The city is in
    mutiny,
Led by an old gray ruffian, who comes
    on
In rescue of the Lord Philaster.

KING. Away to the citadel!—

*Exit with Are[thusa], Phi[laster], Bellario.*
                    I'll see them safe,
And then cope with these burghers. Let
    the guard
And all the gentlemen give strong at-
    tendance.

*Exit King; manent [2] Dion, Cleremont,
                    Thrasiline.*

CLE. The city up! This was above our
    wishes.        120

DI. Ay, and the marriage too. By my
life, this noble lady has deceived us all.
A plague upon myself, a thousand plagues,
for having such unworthy thoughts of her
dear honor! O, I could beat myself! Or
do you beat me, and I'll beat you, for we
had all one thought.

CLE. No, no, 'twill but lose time.

DI. You say true. Are your swords
sharp?—Well, my dear countrymen [130
What-ye-lacks,[3] if you continue, and fall
not back upon the first broken shin, I'll
have ye chronicled and chronicled, and
cut and chronicled, and all-to [4] bepraised
and sung in sonnets, and bathed [5] in new,

brave ballads, that all tongues shall troll
you *in sæcula sæculorum,*[6] my kind can-
carriers.

THRA. What if a toy [7] take um i' th'
heels now, and they run all away, [140
and cry, "The devil take the hind-
most"?

DI. Then the same devil take the foremost too, and souse him for his breakfast!
If they all prove cowards, my curses fly
among them and be speeding! May they
have murrains [8] reign to keep the gentlemen at home unbound in easy frieze!
May the moths branch [9] their velvets, and
their silks only be worn before sore [150
eyes! May their false lights undo um, and
discover presses,[10] holes, stains, and old-
ness in their stuffs, and make them shop-
rid! May they keep whores and horses,
and break,[11] and live mewed up with necks
of beef and turnips! May they have many
children, and none like the father! May
they know no language but that gibber-
ish they prattle to their parcels,[12] unless
it be the goatish [13] Latin they write in [160
their bonds—and may they write that false,
and lose their debts!

*Enter the King.*

KING. Now the vengeance of all the
gods confound them! How they swarm
together! What a hum they raise!—Devils
choke your wild throats!—If a man had
need to use their valors, he must pay a
brokage for it, and then bring um on, and
they will fight like sheep. 'Tis Philaster,
none but Philaster, must allay this [170
heat. They will not hear me speak, but
fling dirt at me and call me tyrant. O, run,
dear friend, and bring the Lord Philaster!
Speak him fair; call him prince; do him
all the courtesy you can; commend me to
him. O, my wits, my wits!

                    *Exit Cleremont.*

DI. [*Aside.*]   O, my brave countrymen!
As I live, I will not buy a pin out of your
walls [14] for this. Nay, you shall cozen me,
and I'll thank you, and send you [180
brawn and bacon, and soil [15] you every long

---

[1] Fearing for.        [4] Completely.
[2] Remain.            [5] Heath suggests *bawled.*
[3] Shopkeepers, who used this cry.

[6] Forever and ever.        [11] "Go broke."
[7] Trifle, whim.            [12] Conveyances.
[8] Plagues.                 [13] Foul.
[9] Eat patterns on.         [14] Outside of your shops.
[10] Creases.                [15] Fatten.

vacation a brace of foremen,[1] that at Michaelmas shall come up fat and kicking.

KING. What they will do with this poor prince, the gods know, and I fear.

DI. [*Aside.*] Why, sir, they'll flay him, and make church buckets[2] on 's skin, to quench rebellion; then clap a rivet in 's sconce, and hang him up for [a][3] sign.

*Enter Cleremont with Philaster.*

KING. O, worthy sir, forgive me! Do not make                                              190
Your miseries and my faults meet together,
To bring a greater danger. Be yourself,
Still sound amongst diseases. I have wronged you;
And, though I find it last, and beaten to it,
Let first your goodness know it. Calm the people,
And be what you were born to. Take your love,
And with her my repentance, all my wishes,
And all my prayers. By the gods, my heart speaks this;
And, if the least fall from me not performed,
May I be strook with thunder!
PHI.                    Mighty sir,      200
I will not do your greatness so much wrong,
As not to make your word truth. Free the princess
And the poor boy, and let me stand the shock
Of this mad sea-breach, which I'll either turn,
Or perish with it.
KING.          Let your own word free them.
PHI. Then thus I take my leave, kissing your hand,
And hanging on your royal word. Be kingly,
And be not moved, sir. I shall bring your peace
Or never bring myself back.
KING. All the gods go with thee.
                              *Exeunt omnes.*

*Enter an old Captain and Citizens with Pharamond.*

CAP. Come, my brave myrmidons, let's fall on. Let your[4] caps swarm, my boys, and your nimble tongues forget your mother-gibberish of "what do you lack?" And set your mouths up,[5] children, till your palates fall frighted half a fathom past the cure of bay salt and gross pepper, and then cry, "Philaster, brave Philaster!" Let Philaster be deeper in request, my dingdongs,[6] my pairs of dear indentures, [10 kings of clubs,[7] than your cold water chamblets[8] or your paintings spitted with copper.[9] Let not your hasty [10] silks, or your branched cloth of bodkin, [11] or your tissues, dearly beloved of spiced cake and custards, your Robin Hoods, Scarlets, and Johns, tie your affections in darkness to your shops. No, dainty duckers, [12] up with your three-piled spirits, your wrought valors; [13] and let your uncut cholers [14] make the king [20 feel the measure of your mightiness. Philaster! Cry, my rose-nobles,[15] cry!

ALL. Philaster! Philaster!

CAP. How do you like this, my lord prince? These are mad boys, I tell you; these are things that will not strike their topsails to a foist,[16] and let a man of war, an argosy, hull and cry "cockles." [17]

PHA. Why, you rude slave, do you know what you do?

CAP. My pretty prince of puppets, we do know,                                            30
And give your greatness warning that you talk
No more such bug's [18] words, or that soldered crown

[4] From 1620 edn. Original reads *our*.
[5] 1620 edn. has *ope*.
[6] Hearties.
[7] *I.e.*, apprentices, who were bound by indentures and preferred the club as a weapon.
[8] Camlets, a kind of watered cloth.
[9] Painted cloths interwoven with copper.
[10] Shoddy.
[11] Embroidered cloth of gold and silk.
[12] *I.e.*, those who bow before their customers.
[13] With a pun on *velours*.
[14] With a pun on *collars*.
[15] Name of a coin.
[16] A small pleasure boat.
[17] Lie idle and be meanly engaged.
[18] Bugbear's; *i.e.*, swaggering.

Shall be scratched with a musket.  Dear
   Prince Pippin,
Down with your noble blood, or, as I
   live,
I'll have you coddled.—Let him loose,
   my spirits;
Make us a round ring with your bills,[1] my
   Hectors,
And let me see what this trim man
   dares do.
Now, sir, have at you!  Here I lie,
And with this swashing blow (do you
   see, sweet prince?)
I could hulk [2] your grace, and hang you
   up cross-legged,                              40
Like a hare at a poulter's,[3] and do this
   with this wiper.[4]

PHA.  You will not see me murdered,
   wicked villains?

1 CIT.  Yes, indeed, will we, sir; we have
   not seen one for a great while.

CAP.  He would have weapons, would he?
Give him a broadside, my brave boys,
with your pikes; branch me his skin in
flowers like a satin, and between every
flower a mortal cut.—Your royalty shall
ravel!—Jag him, gentlemen; I'll have him
cut to the kell,[5] then down the seams. [50
O, for a whip to make him galloon-laces! [6]
I'll have a coachwhip.

PHA.  O, spare me, gentlemen!

CAP.  Hold, hold; the man begins to fear
and know himself.  He shall for this time
only be seeled up,[7] with a feather through
his nose, that he may only see heaven, and
think whither he's going.  Nay, my beyond-
sea sir, we will proclaim you.  You would
be king!  Thou tender heir apparent  [60
to a church ale,[8] thou slight prince of
single sarcenet,[9] thou royal ringtail,[10] fit to
fly at nothing but poor men's poultry, and
have every boy beat thee from that too
with his bread and butter!

PHA.  Gods keep me from these hell-
hounds!

1 CIT.  Shall 's geld him, captain?

---

[1] A pike-like weapon.
[2] Disembowel.
[3] Poulterer's.
[4] Ramrod.
[5] Caul.
[6] Tape used for trimming or binding.
[7] As a hawk's eyelids were temporarily sewed together.
[8] I.e., a bastard child conceived at a church festivity.
[9] Thin silk.
[10] A sort of hawk, the "hen harrier."

CAP.  No, you shall spare his dowcets, my
   dear donsels; [11]
As you respect the ladies, let them
   flourish.                                     70
The curses of a longing woman kills
As speedy as a plague, boys.

1 CIT.  I'll have a leg, that's certain.

2 CIT.  I'll have an arm.

3 CIT.  I'll have his nose, and at mine
own charge build a college and clap 't upon
the gate.[12]

4 CIT.  I'll have his little gut to string a
kit [13] with; for certainly a royal gut will
sound like silver.                              80

PHA.  Would they were in thy belly, and
I past my pain once!

5 CIT.  Good captain, let me have his
liver to feed ferrets.

CAP.  Who will have parcels else?  Speak.

PHA.  Good gods, consider me!  I shall
be tortured.

1 CIT.  Captain, I'll give you the trimming of your two-hand sword, and let me
have his skin to make false scabbards.       90

2 CIT.  He had no horns, sir, had he?

CAP.  No, sir, he's a pollard.[14]  What
wouldst thou do with horns?

2 CIT.  O, if he had had, I would have
made rare hafts and whistles of um; but
his shin bones, if they be sound, shall
serve me.

*Enter Philaster.*

ALL.  Long live Philaster, the brave
   Prince Philaster!

PHI.  I thank you, gentlemen.  But why are
   these
Rude weapons brought abroad, to teach
   your hands                                   100
Uncivil trades?

CAP.                    My royal Rosicleer,
We are thy myrmidons, thy guard, thy
   roarers;
And, when thy noble body is in durance,
Thus do we clap our musty murrions [15]
   on,
And trace [16] the streets in terror.  Is it
   peace,
Thou Mars of men?  Is the king sociable,
And bids thee live?  Art thou above thy
   foemen,

---

[11] Young dons, young fellows.
[12] In allusion to Brasenose College, Oxford.
[13] Cittern, guitar.
[14] Unhorned animal.
[15] Helmets.
[16] Walk.

And free as Phœbus? Speak. If not, this stand [1]
Of royal blood shall be abroach, atilt,
And run even to the lees of honor.      110
PHI. Hold, and be satisfied. I am myself,
Free as my thoughts are; by the gods, I am!
CAP. Art thou the dainty darling of the king?
Art thou the Hylas to our Hercules?
Do the lords bow, and the regarded scarlets [2]
Kiss their gummed golls,[3] and cry, "We are your servants"?
Is the court navigable and the presence stuck
With flags of friendship? If not, we are thy castle,
And this man sleeps.
PHI. I am what I do desire to be, your friend;      120
I am what I was born to be, your prince.
PHA. Sir, there is some humanity in you;
You have a noble soul. Forget my name,
And know my misery; set me safe aboard
From these wild cannibals, and, as I live,
I'll quit this land forever.   There is nothing—
Perpetual prisonment, cold, hunger, sickness
Of all sorts, of all dangers, and altogether
The worst company of the worst men, madness, age,      129
To be as many creatures as a woman,
And do as all they do, nay, to despair—
But I would rather make it a new nature,
And live with all these, than endure one hour
Amongst these wild dogs.
PHI. I do pity you.—Friends, discharge your fears;
Deliver me the prince. I'll warrant you
I shall be old enough to find my safety.
3 CIT. Good sir, take heed he does not hurt you;
He's a fierce man, I can tell you, sir.
CAP. Prince, by your leave, I'll have a surcingle,[4]      140

And make [5] you like a hawk. (*He strives.*)[6]
PHI. Away, away, there is no danger in him!
Alas, he had rather sleep to shake his fit off!
Look you, friends, how gently he leads! Upon my word,
He's tame enough; he need[s] no further watching.
Good my friends, go to your houses,
And by me have your pardons and my love;
And know there shall be nothing in my power
You may deserve, but you shall have your wishes.
To give you more thanks were to flatter you.      150
Continue still your love; and for an earnest
Drink this.      [*Gives money.*]
ALL. Long mayst thou live, brave prince, brave prince, brave prince!
      *Exeunt* [7] *Phi*[*laster*] *and Pharamond.*
CAP. Go thy ways, thou art the king of courtesy!—
Fall off again, my sweet youths. Come,
And every man trace to his house again,
And hang his pewter up; then to the tavern,
And bring your wives in muffs. We will have music;
And the red grape shall make us dance and rise, boys.      *Exeunt.*

[SCENA v.

*An apartment in the palace.*]

*Enter King, Arethusa, Galatea, Megra,
Cleremont, Dion, Thrasiline, Bellario, and
Attendants.*

KING. Is it appeased?
DI. Sir, all is quiet as this dead of night,
As peaceable as sleep. My Lord Philaster
Brings on the prince himself.
KING.                    Kind gentlemen,
I will not break the least word I have given
In promise to him.  I have heaped a world
Of grief upon his head, which yet I hope
To wash away.

---

[1] Cask, *i.e.*, Pharamond.   [3] Perfumed hands.
[2] Courtiers clad in scarlet.   [4] Band.
[5] Train.      [7] Original reads *Exit.*
[6] *I.e.*, Pharamond tries to get away.

*Enter Philaster and Pharamond.*

CLE.                    My lord is come.

KING.                                My son!
Blessed be the time that I have leave to
    call
Such virtue mine!   Now thou art in
    mine arms,                                    10
Methinks I have a salve unto my breast
For all the stings that dwell there.
    Streams of grief
That I have wrought thee, and as much
    of joy
That I repent it, issue from mine eyes;
Let them appease thee.  Take thy right.
    Take her
(She is thy right too), and forget to urge
My vexéd soul with that I did before.

PHI.  Sir, it is blotted from my memory,
Past and forgotten.—For you, Prince of
    Spain,
Whom I have thus redeemed, you have
    full leave                                    20
To make an honorable voyage home.
And, if you would go furnished to your
    realm
With fair provision, I do see a lady,
Methinks, would gladly bear you com-
    pany.
How like you this piece?

MEG.                    Sir, he likes it well,
For he hath tried it, and hath found it
    worth
His princely liking.  We were ta'en
    abed;
I know your meaning.  I am not the first
That nature taught to seek a fellow
    forth.
Can shame remain perpetually in me,   30
And not in others?   Or have princes
    salves
To cure ill names, that meaner people
    want?

PHI.  What mean you?

MEG.            You must get another ship,
To bear the princess and her boy to-
    gether.

DI.  How now!

MEG.  Others took me, and I took her and
    him
At that all women may be ta'en some-
    time.
Ship us all four, my lord; we can endure
Weather and wind alike.

KING.  Clear thou thyself, or know not me
    for father.                                   40

ARE.  This earth, how false it is!   What
    means is left for me
To clear myself?  It lies in your belief.
My lords, believe me; and let all things
    else
Struggle together to dishonor me.

BEL.  O, stop your ears, great king, that I
    may speak
As freedom would!  Then I will call this
    lady
As base as are her actions.  Hear me, sir;
Believe your heated blood when it
    rebels
Against your reason, sooner than this
    lady.

MEG.  By this good light, he bears it
    handsomely.                                   50

PHI.  This lady?  I will sooner trust the
    wind
With feathers, or the troubled sea with
    pearl,
Than her with anything.  Believe her
    not.
Why, think you, if I did believe her
    words,
I would outlive 'em?  Honor cannot take
Revenge on you.  Then what were to be
    known
But death?

KING.        Forget her, sir, since all is knit
Between us.  But I must request of you
One favor, and will sadly be denied.

PHI.  Command, whate'er it be.

KING.                    Swear to be true   60
To what you promise.

PHI.                    By the powers above,
Let it not be the death of her or him,
And it is granted!

KING.                    Bear away that boy
To torture; I will have her cleared or
    buried.

PHI.  O, let me call my word back, worthy
    sir!
Ask something else; bury my life and
    right
In one poor grave; but do not take away
My life and fame at once.

KING.  Away with him!  It stands irrevo-
    cable.

PHI.  Turn all your eyes on me.   Here
    stands a man,                                 70
The falsest and the basest of this world.

Set swords against this breast, some
    honest man,
For I have lived till I am pitiéd!
My former deeds were hateful; but this
    last
Is pitiful, for I unwillingly
Have given the dear preserver of my
    life
Unto his torture. Is it in the power
Of flesh and blood to carry this, and live?
                  *Offers to kill himself.*

ARE. Dear sir, be patient yet! O, stay
    that hand!

KING. Sirs, strip that boy.

DI.         Come, sir; your tender flesh  80
Will try [1] your constancy.

BEL.            O, kill me, gentlemen!

DI. No.—Help, sirs!

BEL.          Will you torture me?

KING.               Haste there.
Why stay you?

BEL.    Then I shall not break my vow,
You know, just gods, though I discover
    all.

KING. How's that? Will he confess?

DI.               Sir, so he says.

KING. Speak then.

BEL.        Great king, if you command
This lord to talk with me alone, my
    tongue
Urged by my heart, shall utter all the
    thoughts
My youth hath known; and stranger
    things than these
You hear not often.

KING.      Walk aside with him.  90
        [*Dion and Bellario walk apart.*]

DI. Why speak'st thou not?

BEL.      Know you this face, my lord?

DI. No.

BEL.    Have you not seen it, nor the like?

DI. Yes, I have seen the like, but readily
I know not where.

BEL.       I have been often told
In court of one Euphrasia, a lady,
And daughter to you, betwixt whom
    and me
They that would flatter my bad face
    would swear
There was such strange resemblance
    that we two
Could not be known asunder, dressed
    alike.

[1] From 1620 edn. Original reads *tire*.

DI. By heaven, and so there is!

BEL.         For her fair sake,  100
Who now doth spend the springtime of
    her life
In holy pilgrimage, move to the king
That I may scape this torture.

DI.             But thou speak'st
As like Euphrasia as thou dost look.
How came it to thy knowledge that she
    lives
In pilgrimage?

BEL.        I know it not, my lord;
But I have heard it, and do scarce
    believe it.

DI. O, my shame! Is't possible? Draw
    near
That I may gaze upon thee. Art thou
    she,
Or else her murderer? [2] Where wert
    thou born?            110

BEL. In Syracusa.

DI.            What's thy name?

BEL.                 Euphrasia.

DI. O, 'tis just, 'tis she!
Now I do know thee. O, that thou hadst
    died,
And I had never seen thee nor my
    shame!
How shall I own thee? Shall this tongue
    of mine
E'er call thee daughter more?

BEL. Would I had died indeed! I wish it
    too;
And so [I] [3] must have done by vow, ere
    published
What I have told, but that there was no
    means
To hide it longer. Yet I joy in this,  [120
The princess is all clear.—

KING.           What, have you done?

DI. All's discovered.

PHI.         Why then hold you me?
All is discovered! Pray you, let me go.
              *He offers to stab himself.*

KING. Stay him!

ARE.       What is discovered?

DI.              Why, my shame.
It is a woman; let her speak the rest.

PHI. How? That again!

DI. It is a woman.

[2] Some barbarous peoples believed that the murderer assumed the shape of the person he murdered.

[3] From 1620 edn.

PHI. Blessed be you powers that favor innocence!

KING. Lay hold upon that lady.

[*Megra is seized.*]

PHI. It is a woman, sir!—Hark, gentlemen,   130

It is a woman!—Arethusa, take
My soul into thy breast, that would be gone
With joy. It is a woman! Thou art fair,
And virtuous still to ages, in despite
Of malice.

KING. Speak you, where lies his shame?

BEL.                    I am his daughter.

PHI. The gods are just.

DI. I dare accuse none; but, before you two,
The virtue of our age, I bend my knee
For mercy.                    [*Kneels.*]

PHI. [*Raising him.*]    Take it freely, for I know,   140
Though what thou didst were undiscreetly done,
'Twas meant well.

ARE. And, for me,
I have a power to pardon sins, as oft
As any man has power to wrong me.

CLE. Noble and worthy!

PHI.                    But, Bellario
(For I must call thee still so), tell me why
Thou didst conceal thy sex. It was a fault,
A fault, Bellario, though thy other deeds
Of truth outweighed it. All these jealousies   150
Had flown to nothing if thou hadst discovered
What now we know.

BEL.          My father oft would speak
Your worth and virtue; and, as I did grow
More and more apprehensive,[1] I did thirst
To see the man so raised. But yet all this
Was but a maiden longing, to be lost
As soon as found, till, sitting in my window,
Printing my thoughts in lawn,[2] I saw a god,
I thought (but it was you), enter our gates.

[1] Quick to understand.   [2] *I.e.*, embroidering.

My blood flew out and back again, as fast   160
As I had puffed it forth and sucked it in
Like breath. Then was I called away in haste
To entertain you. Never was a man,
Heaved from a sheepcote to a scepter, raised
So high in thoughts as I. You left a kiss
Upon these lips then, which I mean to keep
From you forever. I did hear you talk,
Far above singing. After you were gone,
I grew acquainted with my heart, and searched   169
What stirred it so. Alas, I found it love,
Yet far from lust, for, could I but have lived
In presence of you, I had had my end.
For this I did delude my noble father
With a feigned pilgrimage, and dressed myself
In habit of a boy; and, for I knew
My birth no match for you, I was past hope
Of having you; and, understanding well
That when I made discovery of my sex
I could not stay with you, I made a vow,
By all the most religious things a maid
Could call together, never to be known,
Whilst there was hope to hide me from men's eyes,   182
For other than I seemed, that I might ever
Abide with you. Then sat I by the fount,
Where first you took me up.

KING.                    Search out a match
Within our kingdom, where and when thou wilt,
And I will pay thy dowry; and thyself
Wilt well deserve him.

BEL.                    Never, sir, will I
Marry; it is a thing within my vow.
But, if I may have leave to serve the princess,   190
To see the virtues of her lord and her,
I shall have hope to live.

ARE.                    I, Philaster,
Cannot be jealous, though you had a lady
Dressed like a page to serve you; nor will I
Suspect her living here.—Come, live with me;

Live free as I do. She that loves my
   lord,
Cursed be the wife that hates her!

PHI. I grieve such virtue should be laid in
   earth
Without an heir.—Hear me, my royal
   father.
Wrong not the freedom of our souls so
   much,                 200
To think to take revenge of that base
   woman;
Her malice cannot hurt us. Set her free
As she was born, saving from shame and
   sin.

KING. Set her at liberty.—But leave the
   court;
This is no place for such.—You, Pharamond,
Shall have free passage, and a conduct
   home
Worthy so great a prince. When you
   come there,

Remember 'twas your faults that lost
   you her,
And not my purposed will.

PHA.                I do confess,
Renownéd sir.               210

KING. Last, join your hands in one. En-
   joy, Philaster,
This kingdom, which is yours, and,
   after me,
Whatever I call mine. My blessing on
   you!
All happy hours be at your marriage
   joys,
That you may grow yourselves over all
   lands,
And live [1] to see your plenteous branches
   spring
Wherever there is sun! Let princes learn
By this to rule the passions of their blood;
For what heaven wills can never be
   withstood.           *Exeunt omnes.*

[1] From 1620 edn. Original reads *like.*

FINIS.

# FRANCIS BEAUMONT AND
# JOHN FLETCHER

## THE MAID'S TRAGEDY

*The Maid's Tragedy*, written not later than 1611 and acted by the King's Men at the Blackfriars, was the first tragedy to be attempted by the collaborators. Oliphant gives Beaumont credit for the major part of it, but later critics like Leech make Fletcher chiefly responsible for shaping its pattern and direction. Although it immediately became popular with audiences and actors, and remained so for over two centuries, most twentieth-century critics have pretended to look down on it, and, like Leech, have cited it as one reason why they would rank the authors as "third-rate" dramatists, not really fitted to write tragedy at all. Some have declared that the abilities of the authors should have been confined to comedy and tragicomedy, and Wallis has applied to the play the phrase "twin-form" of tragicomedy, that is, a play incorporating all the features of the "middle mood" except its happy ending, which in this case seems almost to have been prepared for up to the very last scene. In fact, by 1685 the poet Edmund Waller had twice attempted to turn it into a tragicomedy, without hitting the public taste. In 1677 the critic Thomas Rymer, in his notorious *The Tragedies of the Last Age, Considered and Examined by the Practice of the Ancients and by the Common Sense of All Ages*, had attacked the play violently for lack of unity, unnaturalness, improbability of plot, and inconsistency of characters. In 1923 William Archer, the Thomas Rymer of modern criticism of the Elizabethan drama, went even further. After quoting St. Loe Strachey's dictum in editing the play for the old Mermaid series that "Judged as plays, *The Maid's Tragedy* and *Philaster* stand above all else that is not Shakespeare's which can be brought for comparison in our dramatic literature," he demolished the older critic by ending his own drastic analysis of the plot and characters thus: "I say nothing of the brutal grossness of the play; but I do say that if a modern dramatist wrote a play so full of psychological improbabilities and enigmas, he would certainly not find the critics assign him a place only a little lower than Shakespeare." But Wallis, although admitting the faults of the play, took a more sensibly moderate position when he declared: "*The Maid's Tragedy* is fundamentally an independent play, and a play of more merit than is customarily recognized."

After all, it is scarcely plausible that a play with such a stage history as that of *The Maid's Tragedy* could be as devoid of merit as many recent critics have called it. After it was first printed anonymously in 1619, issued in a revised edition in 1622, and given a third edition in 1630, using the authors' names for the first time, it continuously underwent many other editions in every century to the present. The great Richard Burbage played the role of Melantius in the first production. The play was given before the King and Queen in 1636, and continued to be acted until the closing of the theaters by law in 1642. At the Restoration it was immediately revived by Killigrew, with Michael Mohun, Charles Hart, and Anne Marshall in the leads, and by 1668 Sam Pepys had seen it at least five times, first calling it "too sad and melancholy," but later admitting that it was "a good play." Dryden praised its "labyrinth of design" in 1668. But for a time it was forbidden by King Charles, perhaps because he saw too close an analogy between the amorous exploits of the play's King and his own liaisons, or perhaps because he disapproved of some of its political comments.

In the eighteenth century it was revived by the great but aging Thomas Betterton, with Mrs. Barry and Mrs. Bracegirdle; in fact, Melantius was the role Betterton was playing at the time of his death in 1710. The Drury Lane gave the play in the 1728–29 season, and Lewis Theobald mentioned a performance about 1742. The Norwich provincial company kept it in its repertoire between 1721 and 1750. In the nineteenth century, the leading actor-manager, William Macready, and the well-meaning playwright, James Sheridan Knowles, collaborated on a slight revision, *The Bridal*, in 1837, and Macready acted in it with some success. In 1833 Thomas Babington Macaulay had reported in his essay on Beaumont that *The Maid's Tragedy* "still occasionally appears on the stage." (For later revivals of various Beaumont and Fletcher plays by groups like the Elizabethan Stage Society and the Phoenix Society, see Anna Irene Miller, *The Independent Theater in Europe, 1887 to the Present*, New York, 1931.)

The essence of the modern criticism of *The Maid's Tragedy* is perhaps offered by Irving Ribner in his *Jacobean Tragedy: The Search for Moral Order:* that although Beaumont and Fletcher present certain political, social, and ethical problems in the play, not only is their treatment shallow but their vision is limited. They never wrote "truly moral tragedy," suggests Ribner, "because of their very attachment to a past social ideal which may never have fully existed except in men's minds, and because the ethical paradoxes they examine are related only to artificial—and ultimately unimportant—patterns of social conduct, and never to the larger problem of the relationship of good to evil in the world." As T. S. Eliot put it, there is no evidence of "a struggle for harmony in the soul of the poet." For this reason, although *The Maid's Tragedy* "rings its many changes on the themes of honour, love and friendship" —values dear to the Elizabethan world of great country estates—Ribner excludes the play from a full examination in his study because it does not fit into the pattern of his book. But he accepts J. F. Danby's analysis of the main characters as symbolic representations of the nostalgia for Elizabethan values of the elegant aristocratic life which could no longer survive in the seventeenth century: Aspatia as a symbol of these rejected values, Amintor as a debased shadow of the conception of honor shown only in outward appearance, and Melantius as a symbol of the true code of honor and integrity. Leech has made the same charge in somewhat different words, saying that the play is "out of tune with our common conception of tragic writing" partly because the situation in which Amintor and Melantius debate "whether or not it is right to kill a guilty king, whether as a king he has a privilege not accorded to other men," is not a situation which finds itself immediately echoed in common experience, but even more because of "its lack of concern with the cosmic." Leech adds that although Fletcher shows an interest in religious belief (though not much in the supernatural, except in casual references to fate or the gods), "he is interested in it because he is interested in the way the human mind behaves," but "His characters are not pitted against the universe and its darkness: they exist only within a web of human intrigue."

From the purely theatrical point of view, however, opinion is almost unanimous that *The Maid's Tragedy* is highly effective, from the expository building up of the situation in which the romantic and brave but weak Amintor (the most interesting and complex character in the play) finds that the fascinating woman he has married is already the secret mistress of the King, through the victorious return of her brother Melantius from battle and his joining with Amintor in their determination to get revenge, and finally to the rather too sudden repentance and reformation of the formerly ambitious and lustful sister Evadne and her murder of her lover. Especially powerful scenes, as Leech sees them, are those in which the tigress Evadne stabs the King in his bed, her taunting revelation of her relationship with the King to the stunned but acquiescent Amintor, and, for relief, the comic deception of the King by Melantius against the persistent accusations of Calianax. Fletcher's successful use of "patterned repetition of behaviour" is illustrated in the scene where Amintor and Melantius alternately draw their swords on one another—a quarrel scene for which Wallis has special praise. The introduction of the masque in the first act, although it is longer than most scenes of this kind in the Elizabethan and Jacobean drama, lends an element of spectacular appeal and helps to create Fletcher's favorite court setting. The element of violence throughout, of course, continues to have a strong audience appeal. The male disguise of the pathetic, lovelorn Aspatia and her suicidal death by the sword of her lover, the resistant but ignorant Amintor, who then kills himself, have a lurid, masochistic aspect which was certainly capable of communicating an emotional thrill. And the final scene of catharsis, in which the new king, Lysippus, declares his attitude toward the duties and responsibilities of kingship, reveals a compromise between Fletcher's usual partisanship toward the doctrine of the divine right of kings and self-restraint under the eye of God.

No source has been discovered for the plot of the play, though many students have noticed that Aspatia has several resemblances to Sidney's deserted Parthenia in the *Arcadia*, and that Calianax offers a rather new version of the old braggart soldier type.

As for the language of the tragedy, as Moody E. Prior sees it in his book, *The Language of Tragedy*, in spite of the fact that so many of the features of the characteristic Elizabethan dramatic style can be found in the Beaumont and Fletcher plays and that older critics often ranked the pair next to Shakespeare, their writing actually differed radically in many respects from that of the best of their contemporaries. The most conspicuous difference is that Beaumont and Fletcher's use of verse is not so much organic as it is "a superficial means for securing poetic effects." At the same time, certain "metrical eccentricities," such as weak syllables at the ends of lines, double and triple endings, and so on, produce a quality of abruptness which makes their verse seem unlike verse. The effect of this characteristic is both to "open a back door to verisimilitude" and also to allow the introduction of poetic effects where desirable. The diction in the plays is less metaphorical than in most of the contemporary plays, but it is lucid and energetic. Only relatively rarely do the authors use figurative language or hyperbole. Their rhythms give the speeches effective balance and accent as well as conversational ease. As a consequence, the characters are usually reduced to the "merest outline," though the intrigue is "brilliantly manipulated." Prior concludes that *The Maid's Tragedy* is a "striking performance" of its kind, but that it is not "in the strictest sense poetically conceived tragedy" because its poetry is only "an adjunct of the brilliant moment, a final refinement of the emphasis."

The present text follows Thorndike's reprint of the 1622 quarto in the Belles-Lettres Series (New York, 1906), checked by the readings of the same quarto given in the Variorum Edition by Daniel and in the Cambridge edition by Waller. The play has been edited for the Fountainwell Drama Texts by Andrew Gurr (1969).

# THE MAID'S TRAGEDY[1]

## BY

## FRANCIS BEAUMONT AND JOHN FLETCHER[2]

### SPEAKERS

KING.
LYSIPPUS, *brother to the king.*
AMINTOR [, *a noble gentleman*].[3]
EVADNE, *wife to Amintor.*
MELANTIUS ⎫
DIPHILUS ⎭ *brothers to Evadne.*
ASPATIA, *troth-plight wife to Amintor.*
CALIANAX, *an old humorous* [4] *lord, and father to Aspatia.*
CLEON ⎫
STRATO ⎭ *gentlemen.*
DIAGORAS, *a servant.*

[LORDS, GENTLEMEN, SERVANTS, *etc.*]
ANTIPHILA ⎫ *waiting gentlewomen to As-*
OLYMPIAS ⎭ *patia.*
DULA, *a lady* [, *attendant on Evadne*].
[LADIES.]

NIGHT ⎫
CYNTHIA ⎪
NEPTUNE ⎪
ÆOLUS ⎬ *masquers.*
[SEA GODS] ⎪
[WINDS] ⎭

[SCENE: *Rhodes.*

TIME: *Indefinite.*]

ACTUS I. SCEN[A] i.

[*An apartment in the palace.*]

*Enter Cleon, Strato, Lysippus, Diphilus.*

CLE. The rest are making ready, sir.

LYS.[5] So let them; there's time enough.

DIPH. You are the brother to the king, my lord; we'll take your word.

LYS. Strato, thou hast some skill in poetry; what think'st [thou] [6] of the [7] masque? Will it be well?

STRA. As well as masques can be.

LYS. As masques can be?

STRA. Yes; they must commend [10 their king, and speak in praise of the assembly, bless the bride and bridegroom in person of some god; they're tied to rules of flattery.

CLE. See, good my lord, who is returned!

*Enter Melantius.*

LYS. Noble Melantius, the land by me welcomes thy virtues home to Rhodes— thou that with blood abroad buyest our peace! The breath of kings is like the breath of gods; my brother wished [20 thee here, and thou art here. He will be too kind, and weary thee with often welcomes; but the time doth give thee a welcome above his or all the world's.

MEL. My lord, my thanks; but these scratched limbs of mine have spoke my love and truth unto my friends more than my tongue e'er could. My mind's the same it [8]

Ever was to you. Where I find worth,
I love the keeper till he let it go, 31
And then I follow it.

DIPH. Hail, worthy brother!
He that rejoices not at your return
In safety is mine enemy forever.

MEL. I thank thee, Diphilus. But thou art faulty:

---

[1] The title continues: "As It Hath Been Divers Times Acted at the Blackfriars by the King's Majesty's Servants."

[2] The authors' names do not appear until the third quarto (1630).

[3] From 1630 edn. [4] Temperamental.

[5] From 1619 edn. Original reads *Stra.*

[6] From 1619 edn.

[7] Suggested by Seward. Early edns. read *a.*

[8] Although the preceding passage is printed as prose in all the early edns., it may be scanned in rough iambics.

653

I sent for thee to exercise thine arms
With me at Patria; thou cam'st not,
　　Diphilus;
'Twas ill.
DIPH.　　　My noble brother, my excuse
Is my king's strict command, which
　　you, my lord,
Can witness with me.
LYS.　　　　　　'Tis true, Melantius; 40
He might not come till the solemnity
Of this great match were past.
DIPH.　　　　　　　Have you heard of it?
MEL. Yes, I have given cause to those
　　that
Envy my deeds abroad to call me game-
　　some.
I have no other business here at Rhodes.
LYS. We have a masque tonight, and you
　　must tread
A soldier's measure.
MEL. These soft and silken wars are not
　　for me;
The music must be shrill and all con-
　　fused
That stirs my blood; and then I dance
　　with arms.　　　　　　　　　50
But is Amintor wed?
DIPH. This day.
MEL. All joys upon him, for he is my
　　friend.
Wonder not that I call a man so young
　　my friend.
His worth is great; valiant he is and
　　temperate,
And one that never thinks his life his
　　own,
If his friend need it.　When he was a
　　boy,
As oft as I returned (as, without boast,
I brought home conquest), he would
　　gaze upon me
And view me round to find in what one
　　limb　　　　　　　　　　　60
The virtue lay to do these things he
　　heard;
Then would he wish to see my sword,
　　and feel
The quickness of the edge, and in his
　　hand
Weigh it.　He oft would make me smile
　　at this.
His youth did promise much, and his
　　ripe years
Will see it all performed.—

*Enter Aspatia, passing by.*

　　　　　　　　　　Hail, maid and wife!
Thou fair Aspatia, may the holy knot
That thou hast tied today last till the
　　hand
Of age undo 't!　Mayst thou bring a
　　race　　　　　　　　　　　69
Unto Amintor that may fill the world
Successively with soldiers!
ASP.　　　　　　　My hard fortunes
Deserve not scorn, for I was never
　　proud
When they were good.　　*Exit Aspatia.*
MEL.　　　　　How's this?
LYS.　　　　　　　You are mistaken,[1]
For she is not married.
MEL.　　　　　You said Amintor was.
DIPH. 'Tis true; but—
MEL.　　　　　Pardon me; I did receive
Letters at Patria from my Amintor,
That he should marry her.
DIPH.　　　　　　　And so it stood
In all opinion long; but your arrival
Made me imagine you had heard the
　　change.
MEL. Who hath he taken then?
LYS.　　　　　　A lady, sir,　80
That bears the light about her, and
　　strikes dead
With flashes of her eye—the fair Evadne,
Your virtuous sister.
MEL.　　　Peace of heart betwixt them!
But this is strange.
LYS.　　　　　The king, my brother, did it
To honor you; and these solemnities
Are at his charge.
MEL. 'Tis royal, like himself.　But I am
　　sad
My speech bears so unfortunate a sound
To beautiful Aspatia.　There is rage
Hid in her father's breast.　Calianax　90
Bent long against me, and he should
　　not think,
If I could call it back, that I would take
So base revenges as to scorn the state
Of his neglected daughter.　Holds he still
His greatness with the king?
LYS.　　　　　　Yes.　But this lady
Walks discontented, with her wat'ry eyes
Bent on the earth.　The unfrequented
　　woods

[1] Here and in a few other passages the line
division has been regularized.

Are her delight; and, when she sees a
bank
Stuck full of flowers, she with a sigh will
tell                                            99
Her servants what a pretty place it were
To bury lovers in, and make her maids
Pluck 'em, and strow her over like a
corse.[1]
She carries with her an infectious grief
That strikes all her beholders; she will
sing
The mournful'st things that ever ear
hath heard,
And sigh, and sing again; and, when the
rest
Of our young ladies, in their wanton[2]
blood,
Tell mirthful tales in course,[3] that fill
the room
With laughter, she will with so sad a
look                                            109
Bring forth a story of the silent death
Of some forsaken virgin, which her grief
Will put in such a phrase that, ere she
end,
She'll send them weeping one by one
away.
MEL. She has a brother under my com-
mand,
Like her—a face as womanish as hers,
But with a spirit that hath much out-
grown
The number of his years.

*Enter Amintor.*

CLE.                My lord the bridegroom!
MEL. I might run fiercely, not more hast-
ily,
Upon my foe. I love thee well, Amintor.
My mouth is much too narrow for my
heart;                                          120
I joy to look upon those eyes of thine.
Thou art my friend, but my disordered
speech
Cuts off my love.
AMIN.            Thou art Melantius;
All love is spoke in that. A sacrifice,
To thank the gods Melantius is returned
In safety! Victory sits on his sword,
As she was wont. May she build there
and dwell,
And may thy armor be, as it hath been,

Only thy valor and thine innocence!
What endless treasures would our ene-
mies give                                       130
That I might hold thee still thus!
MEL.                            I am poor
In words; but credit me, young man,
thy mother
Could no more but weep for joy to see
thee
After long absence. All the wounds I
have
Fetched not so much away, nor all the
cries
Of widowéd mothers. But this is peace,
And that was war.
AMIN.              Pardon, thou holy god
Of marriage bed, and frown not I am
forced,
In answer of such noble tears as those,
To weep upon my wedding day!       140
MEL. I fear thou art grown too fickle,
for I hear
A lady mourns for thee, men say, to
death,
Forsaken of thee, on what terms[4] I
know not.
AMIN. She had my promise; but the king
forbade it,
And made me make this worthy change,
thy sister,
Accompanied with graces about her,
With whom I long to lose my lusty
youth
And grow old in her arms.
MEL.                        Be prosperous!

*Enter Messenger.*

MESS.[5] My lord, the masquers rage for
you.
LYS. We are gone. Cleon, Strato, Diphi-
lus!                                            150
AMIN. We'll all attend you.—
[*Exeunt All but Amintor and Melantius.*]
                          We shall trouble you
With our solemnities.
MEL.                    Not so, Amintor;
But, if you laugh at my rude carriage
In peace, I'll do as much for you in war,
When you come thither. Yet I have a
mistress
To bring to your delights; rough though
I am,

---

[1] Corpse.        [2] Lively.        [3] Turn.

[4] Under what circumstances.
[5] Original reads *Serv.*

I have a mistress, and she has a heart,
She says; but, trust me, it is stone, no
    better.
There is no place that I can challenge.
But you stand still, and here my way
    lies.        *Exit* [*with Amintor*].   160

[SCENA ii.

*A hall in the palace, with Spectators in a
                                    balcony.*]

*Enter Calianax with Diagoras.*

CAL. Diagoras, look to the doors better,
for shame! You let in all the world, and
anon the king will rail at me. Why, very
well said.[1] By Jove, the king will have the
show i' th' court!

DIAG. Why do you swear so, my lord?
You know he'll have it here.

CAL. By this light, if he be wise, he
will not.

DIAG. And, if he will not be wise, [10
you are forsworn.

CAL. One may swear[2] his heart out
with swearing, and get thanks on no side.
I'll be gone, look to 't who will.

DIAG. My lord, I shall never keep
them out. Pray, stay; your looks will
terrify them.

CAL. My looks terrify them, you cox-
combly ass, you! I'll be judge[d] by all
the company whether thou hast not a  [20
worse face than I.

DIAG. I mean, because they know you
and your office.

CAL. Office! I would I could put it
off! I am sure I sweat quite through my
office. I might have made room at my
daughter's wedding—they ha' near killed
her among them; and now I must do service for him that hath forsaken her. Serve[3]
that will!        *Exit Calianax.*   30

DIAG. He's so humorous since his daughter was forsaken! (*Knock within.*) Hark,
hark! There, there! So, so! Codes, codes![4]
What now?

MEL. (*Within.*) Open the door!

DIAG. Who's there?

MEL. Melantius.

DIAG. I hope your lordship brings no
troop with you, for, if you do, I must
return them.        [*Opens the door.*]   40

---

[1] Done.        [3] Let him serve.
[2] Folio reads *wear.*        [4] Corruption of *God's* (?).

*Enter Melantius and a Lady.*

MEL. None but this lady, sir.

DIAG. The ladies are all placed above,
save those that come in the king's troop;
the best of Rhodes sit there, and there's
room.

MEL. I thank you, sir.—When I have
seen you placed, madam, I must attend
the king; but, the masque done, I'll wait
on you again.
        [*Exit Melantius, Lady, other door.*][5]

DIAG. Stand back there!—Room for [50
my Lord Melantius!—Pray, bear back
—this is no place for such youths and
their trulls—let the doors shut again.—
Ay!—Do your heads itch? I'll scratch
them for you. [*Shuts door.*] So, now
thrust and hang.—[*Knocking within.*]
Again! Who is 't now?—I cannot blame
my Lord Calianax for going away. Would
he were here! He would run raging among
them, and break a dozen wiser heads [60
than his own in the twinkling of an eye.
—What's the news now?

[VOICE.] (*Within.*)   I pray you, can
you help me to the speech of the master
cook?

DIAG. If I open the door, I'll cook some
of your calves' heads. Peace, rogues!—
[*Knocking within.*] Again! Who is 't?

MEL. (*Within.*) Melantius.

*Enter Calianax to Melantius.*

CAL. Let him not in.                     70

DIAG. O, my lord, a[6] must.—

[*Opens door. Enter Melantius.*]

Make room there for my lord.—Is your
lady placed?

MEL. Yes, sir.
    I thank you.—My Lord Calianax, well
        met.
    Your causeless hate to me I hope is
        buried.

CAL. Yes, I do service for your sister here,
    That brings my own poor child to time-
        less[7] death.
    She loves your friend Amintor, such
        another
    False-hearted lord as you.

---

[5] From 1619 edn. Thus, Diagoras is guarding
two doors, one to the gallery, and one to the
outside.        [6] He.        [7] Untimely.

MEL.                    You do me wrong,   80
A most unmanly one, and I am slow
In taking vengeance; but be well advised.
CAL. It may be so.—Who placed the lady
there
So near the presence of the king?
MEL.                                    I did.
CAL. My lord, she must not sit there.
MEL.                                    Why?
CAL. The place is kept for women of more
worth.
MEL. More worth than she?     It mis-
becomes your age
And place to be thus womanish. Forbear!
What you have spoke, I am content to
think
The palsy shook your tongue to.
CAL.               Why, 'tis well,   90
If I stand here to place men's wenches.
MEL.                                    I
Shall forget this place, thy age, my
safety,
And, through all, cut that poor sickly
week
Thou hast to live away from thee.
CAL. Nay, I know you can fight for your
whore.
MEL. Bate [1] the king, and, be he flesh and
blood,
A lies that says it!     Thy mother at
fifteen
Was black and sinful to her.
DIAG.                    Good my lord—
MEL. Some god pluck threescore years
from that fond [2] man,
That I may kill him and not stain mine
honor!                                  100
It is the curse of soldiers that in peace
They shall be braved by such ignoble
men
As, if the land were troubled, would
with tears
And knees beg succor from 'em. Would
that blood,
That sea of blood, that I have lost in
fight,
Were running in thy veins, that it might
make thee
Apt to say less, or able to maintain,
Shouldst thou say more!   This Rhodes,
I see, is naught
But a place privileged to do men wrong.
CAL. Ay, you may say your pleasure.

*Enter Amintor.*

AMIN.                What vild [3] injury   110
Has stirred my worthy friend, who is
as slow
To fight with words as he is quick of
hand?
MEL. That heap of age, which I should
reverence
If it were temperate—but testy years
Are most contemptible.
AMIN.                Good sir, forbear.
CAL. There is just such another as your-
self.
AMIN. He will wrong you, or me, or any
man,
And talk as if he had no life to
lose,
Since this our match. The king is coming
in;
I would not for more wealth than I
enjoy                                    120
He should perceive you raging.  He did
hear
You were at difference now, which has-
tened him.        *Hautboys play within.*
CAL. Make room there!

*Enter King, Evadne, Aspatia, Lords, and*
*Ladies.*

KING. Melantius, thou art welcome, and
my love
Is with thee still; but this is not a
place
To brabble [4] in.—Calianax, join hands.
CAL. He shall not have mine hand.
KING.                    This is no time
To force you to 't.   I do love you
both.
Calianax, you look well to your office;
And you, Melantius, are welcome
home.—                                  130
Begin the masque.
MEL. Sister, I joy to see you and your
choice;
You looked with my eyes when you
took that man.
Be happy in him!     *Recorders [play].*
EVAD.                O, my dearest brother,
Your presence is more joyful than this
day
Can be unto me.

---

[1] Except.          [2] Foolish.          [3] Vile.          [4] Quarrel.

THE MASQUE

*Night rises in mists.*

NIGHT. Our reign is come, for in the raging
    sea
    The sun is drowned, and with him fell
      the Day.
    Bright Cynthia, hear my voice! I am
      the Night,
    For whom thou bear'st about thy bor-
      rowed light.           140
    Appear! No longer thy pale visage
      shroud,
    But strike thy silver horns quite through
      a cloud,
    And send a beam upon my swarthy
      face,
    By which I may discover all the place
    And persons, and how many longing
      eyes
    Are come to wait on our solemnities.

*Enter Cynthia.*

How dull and black am I! I could not
    find
    This beauty[1] without thee, I am so
      blind;
    Methinks they show like to those east-
      ern streaks
    That warn us hence before the morning
      breaks.           150
    Back, my pale servant, for these eyes
      know how
    To shoot far more and quicker rays
      than thou.
CYNTH. Great queen, they be a troop for
    whom alone
    One of my clearest moons I have put on—
    A troop that looks as if thyself and I
    Had plucked our reins in and our whips
      laid by,
    To gaze upon these mortals that appear
    Brighter than we.
NIGHT.           Then let us keep 'em here,
    And never more our chariots drive
      away,
    But hold our places and outshine the
      Day.           160
CYNTH. Great queen of shadows, you are
    pleased to speak
    Of more than may be done. We may not
      break

[1] Referring to the ladies of the court.

The gods' decrees, but, when our time
    is come,
    Must drive away, and give the Day our
      room.
    Yet, whilst our reign lasts, let us stretch
      our power
    To give our servants one contented
      hour,
    With such unwonted solemn grace and
      state
    As may forever after force them hate
    Our brother's glorious beams, and wish
      the Night
    Crowned with a thousand stars and our
      cold light,           170
    For almost all the world their service
      bend
    To Phœbus, and in vain my light I
      lend,
    Gazed on unto my setting from my rise
    Almost of none but of unquiet eyes.
NIGHT. Then shine at full, fair queen,
    and by thy power
    Produce a birth—to crown this happy
      hour—
    Of nymphs and shepherds; let their
      songs discover,
    Easy and sweet, who is a happy lover;
    Or, if thou woot,[2] then call thine own
      Endymion           179
    From the sweet flow'ry bed he lies upon,
    On Latmus' top, thy pale beams drawn
      away,
    And of this long night let him make
      this day.
CYNTH. Thou dream'st, dark queen; that
    fair boy was not mine,
    Nor went I down to kiss him. Ease and
      wine
    Have bred these bold tales. Poets,
      when they rage,
    Turn gods to men, and make an hour
      an age.
    But I will give a greater state and
      glory,
    And raise to time a noble memory
    Of what these lovers are.—Rise, rise, I
      say,
    Thou power of deeps, thy surges laid
      away,           196
    Neptune, great king of waters, and by
      me
    Be proud to be commanded!

[2] Wilt.

*Neptune rises.*

NEP.                              Cynthia, see
Thy word hath fetched me hither; let
    me know
Why I ascend.
CYNTH.              Doth this majestic show
Give thee no knowledge yet?
NEP.                            Yes, now I see
Something intended, Cynthia, worthy
    thee.
Go on; I'll be a helper.
CYNTH.                        Hie thee, then,
And charge the Wind fly from his rocky
    den;
Let loose thy subjects; only Boreas,  199
Too foul for our intentions as he was,
Still keep him fast chained.  We must
    have none here
But vernal blasts and gentle winds
    appear,
Such as blow flowers, and through the
    glad boughs sing
Many soft welcomes to the lusty spring.
These are our music.  Next, thy wat'ry
    race
Bring on in couples (we are pleased to
    grace
This noble night), each in their richest
    things
Your own deeps or the broken vessel
    brings.
Be prodigal, and I shall be as kind  209
And shine at full upon you.
NEP.                            O, the wind-
Commanding Æolus!

*Enter Æolus out of a rock.*

ÆOL.                          Great Neptune!
NEP.                                    He.
ÆOL.  What is thy will?
NEP.            We do command thee free
Favonius and thy milder winds, to wait
Upon our Cynthia; but tie Boreas
    strait.
He's too rebellious.
ÆOL.                    I shall do it.  [*Exit.*]
NEP.                                    Do.
[ÆOL. (*Within*.)]  Great master of the flood
    and all below,
Thy full command has taken.—O, the
    Main!
Neptune!
NEP.        Here.

[*Enter Æolus with Favonius and other
                                    Winds.*]

ÆOL.            Boreas has broke his chain,
And, struggling with the rest, has got
    away.
NEP. Let him alone; I'll take him up at
    sea.                                    220
He will not long be thence.  Go once
    again,
And call out of the bottoms of the main
Blue Proteus and the rest; charge them
    put on
Their greatest pearls, and the most
    sparkling stone
The beaten rock breeds, till this night
    is done
By me a solemn honor to the Moon.
Fly, like a full sail.
ÆOL.                    I am gone.  [*Exit.*]
CYNTH.                        Dark Night,
Strike a full silence, do a thorough
    right
To this great chorus, that our music
    may
Touch high as heaven, and make the
    east break day                            230
At midnight.                          *Music.*

[FIRST] SONG

[*During the song enter Proteus and other Sea
                                    Deities.*]
Cynthia, to thy power and thee
        We obey.
Joy to this great company!
        And no day
Come to steal this night away,
    Till the rites of love are ended,
And the lusty bridegroom say,
    "Welcome, light, of all befriended!"

Pace out, you wat'ry powers below;   240
        Let your feet,
Like the galleys when they row,
        Even beat.
Let your unknown measures, set
    To the still winds, tell to all
That gods are come, immortal, great,
    To honor this great nuptial.
                            *The measure.*

SECOND SONG

Hold back thy hours, dark Night, till we
    have done;
    The Day will come too soon.

Young maids will curse thee, if thou
   steal'st away,      250
And leav'st their blushes open to the day.
    Stay, stay, and hide
    The blushes of the bride.

Stay, gentle Night, and with thy darkness
   cover
    The kisses of her lover.
Stay, and confound her tears and her shrill
   cryings,
Her weak denials, vows, and often-dyings.
    Stay, and hide all.
    But help not, though she call.

NEP. Great queen of us and heaven, hear
   what I bring      260
To make this hour a full one.
              *Another measure.*[1]
CYNTH.          Speak, sea's king.
NEP. Thy tunes my Amphitrite joys to
   have,
When they will dance upon the rising
   wave,
And court me as the sails. My Tritons,
   play
Music to lead a storm! I'll lead the way.
              *Measure.*

[THIRD] SONG

To bed, to bed! Come, Hymen, lead the
   bride,
And lay her by her husband's side.
    Bring in the virgins every one,
    That grieve to lie alone,
That they may kiss while they may say, "A
   maid;"      270
Tomorrow 'twill be other [2] kissed and said.
    Hesperus, be long a-shining,
    Whilst these lovers are a-twining.

ÆOL. [*Within.*] Ho, Neptune!
NEP.          Æolus!

[*Enter Æolus.*]

ÆOL.         The sea goes high;
Boreas hath raised a storm. Go and
   apply
Thy trident; else, I prophesy, ere day
Many a tall ship will be cast away.
Descend with all the gods and all their
   power,
To strike a calm.

[1] Fleay's emendation for *if not her measure.*
[2] Otherwise.

CYNTH. A thanks to everyone and to
   gratulate      280
So great a service, done at my desire,
Ye shall have many floods, fuller and
   higher
Than you have wishéd for; no ebb shall
   dare
To let the Day see where your dwelling[s]
   are.
Now back unto your government in
   haste,
Lest your proud charge should swell
   above the waste,
And win upon the island.
NEP.             We obey.
*Neptune descends and the Sea Gods.* [*Exeunt*
             *Favonius and other Winds.*]
CYNTH. Hold up thy head, dead Night;
   see'st thou not Day?
The east begins to lighten. I must down,
And give my brother place.
NIGHT.        O, I could frown
To see the Day, the Day that flings his
   light      291
Upon my kingdoms and contemns old
   Night!
Let him go on and flame! I hope to see
Another wildfire in his axletree,
And all fall drenched. But I forget.—
   Speak, queen.
The Day grows on; I must no more be
   seen.
CYNTH. Heave up thy drowsy head again
   and see
A greater light, a greater majesty,
Between our set [3] and us! Whip up thy
   team.
The Day breaks here, and yon same
   flashing stream [4]      300
Shot from the south. Say, which way
   wilt thou go?
NIGHT. I'll vanish into mists.
CYNTH.         I into Day. *Exeunt.*

FINIS MASQUE

KING. Take lights there!—Ladies, get the
   bride to bed.—
We will not see you laid. Good night,
   Amintor.
We'll ease you of that tedious cere-
   mony.

[3] Seward's emendation for *sect.*
[4] The "effulgence of the court" (Thorndike).

Were it my case, I should think time
    run slow.
If thou beest noble, youth, get me a boy
That may defend my kingdoms from my
    foes.
AMIN. All happiness to you!
KING.                Good night, Melantius.
                        *Exeunt.*

ACTUS II. [SCENA i.

*Anteroom to Evadne's bedchamber.]*

*Enter Evadne, Aspatia, Dula, and other*
                                    *Ladies.*

DUL. Madam, shall we undress you for
    this fight?
The wars are nak'd that you must make
    tonight.
EVAD. You are very merry, Dula.
DUL.                    I should be
Far merrier, madam, if it were with me
As it is with you.
[EVAD.            How's that?
DUL.                    That I might go
To bed with him wi' th' credit that you
    do.]¹
EVAD. Why, how now, wench?
DUL.            Come, ladies, will you help?
EVAD. I am soon undone.
DUL.                    And as soon done;
Good store of clothes will trouble you at
    both.
EVAD. Art thou drunk, Dula?
DUL.        Why, here's none but we. 10
EVAD. Thou think'st belike² there is no
    modesty
When we are alone.
DUL.                    Ay, by my troth,
You hit my thoughts aright.
EVAD. You prick me, lady.
DUL.                'Tis against my will.
Anon you must endure more and lie still;
You're best to practice.
EVAD.            Sure, this wench is mad.
DUL. No, faith, this is a trick that I have
    had
Since I was fourteen.
EVAD.        'Tis high time to leave it.
DUL. Nay, now I'll keep it till the trick
    leave me.                        19
A dozen wanton words put in your head
Will make you livelier in your husband's
    bed.

¹ From 1619 edn.        ² Perhaps.

EVAD. Nay, faith, then take it.³
DUL.            Take it, madam! Where?
We all, I hope, will take it that are here.
EVAD. Nay, then I'll give you o'er.
DUL.                    So will I make
The ablest man in Rhodes, or his heart,
    ache.
EVAD. Wilt take my place tonight?
DUL.                I'll hold your cards
Against any two I know.
EVAD.            What wilt thou do?
DUL. Madam, we'll do 't, and make 'em
    leave play too.
EVAD. Aspatia, take her part.
DUL.                    I will refuse it.
She will pluck down a side;⁴ she does not
    use it.                        30
EVAD. Do, I prithee.⁵
DUL.            You will find the play
Quickly, because your head lies well
    that way.
EVAD. I thank thee, Dula. Would thou
    couldst instill
Some of thy mirth into Aspatia!
Nothing but sad thoughts in her breast
    do dwell;
Methinks, a mean betwixt you would
    do well.
DUL. She is in love; hang me, if I were so,
But I could run⁶ my country. I love too
To do those things that people in love
    do.
ASP. It were a timeless smile should prove
    my cheek.⁷                    40
It were a fitter hour for me to laugh,
When at the altar the religious priest
Were pacifying the offended powers
With sacrifice than now. This should
    have been
My night; and all your hands have been
    employed
In giving me a spotless offering
To young Amintor's bed, as we are now
For you. Pardon, Evadne. Would my
    worth
Were great as yours, or that the king,
    or he,
Or both, thought so! Perhaps he found
    me worthless,                    50
But till he did so, in these ears of mine,

³ *I.e.,* the trick.
⁴ Cause the loss of the game.
⁵ From 1619 edn. Original reads *Why, do.*
⁶ Ride at a hot pace.        ⁷ Audacity.

These credulous ears, he poured the sweetest words
That art or love could frame. If he were false,
Pardon it, heaven! And, if I did want
Virtue, you safely may forgive that too,
For I have lost none that I had from you.

EVAD. Nay, leave this sad talk, madam.

ASP. Would I could!
Then I should leave the cause.

EVAD. See, if you have not spoiled all Dula's mirth!

ASP. Thou think'st thy heart hard; but, if thou beest caught,           60
Remember me; thou shalt perceive a fire
Shot suddenly into thee.

DUL. That's not so good;
Let 'em shoot anything but fire, I fear 'em not.

ASP. Well, wench, thou mayst be taken.

EVAD. Ladies, good night; I'll do the rest myself.

DUL. Nay, let your lord do some.

ASP. [Singing.]

Lay a garland on my hearse
    Of the dismal yew—

EVAD. That's one of your sad songs, madam.

ASP. Believe me, 'tis a very pretty one. 70

EVAD. How is it, madam?

### SONG

ASP. Lay a garland on my hearse
    Of the dismal yew;
Maidens, willow branches bear;
    Say I diéd true.

My love was false, but I was firm
    From my hour of birth.
Upon my buried body lay
    Lightly gentle earth!

EVAD. Fie on 't, madam! The words   [80
are so strange, they are able to make one
dream of hobgoblins.—"I could never
have the power"—sing that, Dula.

DUL. [Singing.]

I could never have the power
    To love one above an hour,
But my heart would prompt mine eye
    On some other man to fly.

Venus, fix mine eyes fast,
Or, if not, give me all that I shall see at last!           89

EVAD. So, leave me now.

DUL. Nay, we must see you laid.

ASP. Madam, good night. May all the marriage joys
That longing maids imagine in their beds
Prove so unto you! May no discontent
Grow twixt your love and you! But, if there do,
Inquire of me, and I will guide your moan,
Teach you an artificial [1] way to grieve,
To keep your sorrow waking. Love your lord
No worse than I; but, if you love so well,
Alas, you may displease him! So did I.
This is the last time you shall look on me.—           100
Ladies, farewell. As soon as I am dead,
Come all and watch one night about my hearse;
Bring each a mournful story and a tear,
To offer at it when I go to earth;
With flattering ivy clasp my coffin round;
Write on my brow my fortune; let my bier
Be borne by virgins that shall sing by course
The truth of maids and perjuries of men.

EVAD. Alas, I pity thee. Exit Evadne.

OMNES. Madam, good night.

1 LADY. Come, we'll let in the bridegroom.

DUL. Where's my lord?           110

1 LADY. Here, take this light.

### Enter Amintor.

DUL. You'll find her in the dark.

1 LADY. Your lady's scarce abed yet; you must help her.

ASP. Go, and be happy in your lady's love.
May all the wrongs that you have done to me
Be utterly forgotten in my death!
I'll trouble you no more; yet I will take

[1] Artful.

A parting kiss, and will not be denied.
                              [*Kisses Amintor.*]
You'll come, my lord, and see the vir-
   gins weep
When I am laid in earth, though you
   yourself
Can know no pity. Thus I wind my-
   self                                    120
Into this willow garland, and am prouder
That I was once your love, though now
   refused,
Than to have had another true to me.
So with [my] [1] prayers I leave you, and
   must try
Some yet unpracticed way to grieve and
   die.                        *Exit Aspatia.*
DUL. Come, ladies, will you go?
OMNES.               Good night, my lord.
AMIN. Much happiness unto you all!
                     *Exeunt* [*Dula and*] *Ladies.*
I did that lady wrong. Methinks, I feel
Her grief shoot suddenly through all
   my veins;
Mine eyes run. This is strange at such
   a time.                                130
It was the king first moved me to 't; but
   he
Has not my will in keeping. Why do I
Perplex myself thus? Something whis-
   pers me,
"Go not to bed." My guilt is not so
   great
As mine own conscience, too sensible, [2]
Would make me think; I only brake a
   promise,
And 'twas the king that forced me.
   Timorous flesh,
Why shak'st thou so? Away, my idle
   fears!

*Enter Evadne.*

Yonder she is, the luster of whose eye
Can blot away the sad remembrance 140
Of all these things.--O, my Evadne,
   spare
That tender body; let it not take cold!
The vapors of the night will not fall
   here.
To bed, my love; Hymen will punish us
For being slack performers of his rites.
Cam'st thou to call me?
EVAD.               No.

AMIN.               Come, come, my love,
And let us lose ourselves to one another.
Why art thou up so long?
EVAD.               I am not well.
AMIN. To bed then; let me wind thee in
   these arms
Till I have banished sickness.
EVAD.               Good my lord,   150
I cannot sleep.
AMIN.               Evadne, we'll watch;
I mean no sleeping.
EVAD.               I'll not go to bed.
AMIN. I prithee, do.
EVAD.               I will not for the world.
AMIN. Why, my dear love?
EVAD.        Why? I have sworn I will not.
AMIN. Sworn!
EVAD.        Ay.
AMIN.               How? Sworn, Evadne?
EVAD. Yes, sworn, Amintor—and will
   swear again,
If you will wish to hear me.
AMIN. To whom have you sworn this?
EVAD. If I should name him, the matter
   were not great.
AMIN. Come, this is but the coyness of
   a bride.                                160
EVAD. The coyness of a bride?
AMIN.               How prettily
That frown becomes thee!
EVAD.               Do you like it so?
AMIN. Thou canst not dress thy face in
   such a look
But I shall like it.
EVAD.        What look likes [3] you best?
AMIN. Why do you ask?
EVAD. That I may show you one less
   pleasing to you.
AMIN. How's that?
EVAD. That I may show you one less
   pleasing to you.
AMIN. I prithee, put thy jests in milder
   looks;
It shows as thou wert angry.
EVAD.               So perhaps   170
I am indeed.
AMIN.        Why, who has done thee wrong?
Name me the man, and by thyself I
   swear,
Thy yet unconquered self, I will revenge
   thee!
EVAD. Now I shall try thy truth. If thou
   dost love me,

---

[1] From 1630 edn.        [2] Sensitive.        [3] Pleases.

Thou weigh'st not anything compared
    with me.
Life, honor, joys eternal, all delights
This world can yield, or hopeful people
    feign,
Or in the life to come, are light as air
To a true lover when his lady frowns,
And bids him, "Do this." Wilt thou
    kill this man?    180
Swear, my Amintor, and I'll kiss the sin
Off from thy lips.

AMIN.    I wo' not swear, sweet love,
Till I do know the cause.

EVAD.    I would thou wouldst.
Why, it is thou that wrong'st me. I
    hate thee.
Thou shouldst have killed thyself.

AMIN. If I should know that, I should
    quickly kill
The man you hated.

EVAD.    Know it, then, and do 't.

AMIN. O, no! What look soe'er thou
    shalt put on
To try my faith, I shall not think thee
    false;
I cannot find one blemish in thy face, 190
Where falsehood should abide. Leave,
    and to bed.
If you have sworn to any of the virgins
That were your old companions, to
    preserve
Your maidenhead a night, it may be done
Without this means.

EVAD.    A maidenhead, Amintor,
At my years?

AMIN.    Sure she raves. This cannot be
Thy natural temper. Shall I call thy
    maids?
Either thy healthful sleep hath left
    thee long,
Or else some fever rages in thy blood.

EVAD. Neither, Amintor. Think you I
    am mad,    200
Because I speak the truth?

AMIN.    [Is this the truth?] [1]
Will you not lie with me tonight?

EVAD.    Tonight?
You talk as if [you thought] [1] I would
    hereafter.

AMIN. Hereafter? Yes, I do.

EVAD.    You are deceived.
Put off amazement, and with patience
    mark

[1] From 1619 edn.

What I shall utter, for the oracle
Knows nothing truer. 'Tis not for a
    night
Or two that I forbear thy bed, but ever.

AMIN. I dream. Awake, Amintor!

EVAD.    You hear right;  209
I sooner will find out the beds of snakes,
And with my youthful blood warm their
    cold flesh,
Letting them curl themselves about
    my limbs,
Than sleep one night with thee. This is
    not feigned,
Nor sounds it like the coyness of a bride.

AMIN. Is flesh so earthly to endure all
    this?
Are these the joys of marriage? Hymen,
    keep
This story, that will make succeeding
    youth
Neglect thy ceremonies, from all ears;
Let it not rise up for thy shame and
    mine
To after ages; we will scorn thy laws, 229
If thou no better bless them. Touch the
    heart
Of her that thou hast sent me, or the
    world
Shall know; there's not an altar that
    will smoke
In praise of thee; we will adopt us sons;
Then virtue shall inherit, and not blood.
If we do lust, we'll take the next we
    meet,
Serving ourselves as other creatures do,
And never take note of the female more,
Nor of her issue.—I do rage in vain;
She can but jest.—O, pardon me, my
    love!    230
So dear the thoughts are that I hold of
    thee,
That I must break forth. Satisfy my
    fear;
It is a pain, beyond the hand of death,
To be in doubt. Confirm it with an oath,
If this be true.

EVAD.    Do you invent the form;
Let there be in it all the binding words
Devils and conjurers can put together,
And I will take it. I have sworn be-
    fore,
And here by all things holy do again,
Never to be acquainted with thy bed!
Is your doubt over now?    241

AMIN. I know too much; would I had
   doubted still!
Was ever such a marriage night as this!
You powers above, if you did ever mean
Man should be used thus, you have
   thought a way
How he may bear himself, and save
   his honor.
Instruct me in it, for to my dull eyes
There is no mean, no moderate course
   to run;
I must live scorned, or be a murderer.
Is there a third? Why is this night so
   calm?                                    250
Why does not heaven speak in thunder
   to us,
And drown her voice?
EVAD.            This rage will do no good.
AMIN. Evadne, hear me. Thou has ta'en
   an oath,
But such a rash one that to keep it
   were
Worse than to swear it. Call it back to
   thee;
Such vows as those never ascend to
   the heaven;
A tear or two will wash it quite away.
Have mercy on my youth, my hopeful
   youth,
If thou be pitiful, for, without boast,
This land was proud of me. What lady
   was there                               260
That men called fair and virtuous in
   this isle,
That would have shunned my love? It
   is in thee
To make me hold this worth. O, we
   vain men,
That trust all our reputation
To rest upon the weak and yielding
   hand
Of feeble woman! But thou art not
   stone;
Thy flesh is soft, and in thine eyes doth
   dwell
The spirit of love; thy heart cannot be
   hard.
Come, lead me from the bottom of de-
   spair
To all the joys thou hast, I know thou
   wilt,                                   270
And make me careful lest the sudden
   change
O'ercome my spirits.

EVAD.        When I call back this oath,
The pains of hell environ me!
AMIN. I sleep, and am too temperate.
   Come to bed!
Or by those hairs, which, if thou hast
   a soul
Like to thy locks, were threads for kings
   to wear
About their arms——
EVAD.            Why, so perhaps they are.
AMIN. I'll drag thee to my bed, and make
   thy tongue
Undo this wicked oath, or on thy flesh
I'll print a thousand wounds to let out
   life!                                   280
EVAD. I fear thee not; do what thou
   dar'st to me!
Every ill-sounding word or threat'ning
   look
Thou show'st to me will be revenged at
   full.
AMIN. It will not, sure, Evadne.
EVAD. Do not you hazard that.
AMIN.            Ha' ye your champions?
EVAD. Alas, Amintor, think'st thou I
   forbear
To sleep with thee because I have put
   on
A maiden's strictness? Look upon
   these cheeks,
And thou shalt find the hot and rising
   blood                                   289
Unapt for such a vow. No; in this heart
There dwells as much desire and as
   much will
To put that wished act in practice as
   ever yet
Was known to woman; and they have
   been shown
Both. But it was the folly of thy youth
To think this beauty, to what land[1]
   soe'er
It shall be called, shall stoop to any
   second.
I do enjoy the best, and in that height
Have sworn to stand or die. You guess
   the man.
AMIN. No; let me know the man that
   wrongs me so,
That I may cut his body into motes,  300
And scatter it before the northern wind.
EVAD. You dare not strike him.

[1] Bullen suggests *hand*, to fit the figure of
falconry in the passage.

AMIN.                Do not wrong me so.
Yes, if his body were a poisonous plant
That it were death to touch, I have a
    soul
Will throw me on him.
EVAD.                Why, 'tis the king.
AMIN.                The king!
EVAD. What will you do now?
AMIN.                'Tis not the king!
EVAD. What did he make this match for,
    dull Amintor?
AMIN. O, thou hast named a word that
    wipes away
All thoughts revengeful! In that sacred
    name,
"The king," there lies a terror. What
    frail man                310
Dares lift his hand against it? Let the
    gods
Speak to him when they please; till
    when, let us
Suffer and wait.
EVAD. Why should you fill yourself so
    full of heat,
And haste so to my bed? I am no virgin.
AMIN. What devil put it in thy fancy,
    then,
To marry me?
EVAD.                Alas, I must have one
To father children, and to bear the name
Of husband to me, that my sin may be
More honorable!
AMIN.        What a strange thing am I! 320
EVAD. A miserable one; one that myself
Am sorry for.
AMIN.                Why, show it then in this:
If thou hast pity, though thy love be
    none,
Kill me; and all true lovers, that shall
    live
In after ages crossed in their desires,
Shall bless thy memory, and call thee
    good,
Because such mercy in thy heart was
    found,
To rid a ling'ring wretch.
EVAD.                I must have one
To fill thy room again, if thou wert
    dead;
Else, by this night, I would! I pity
    thee.                330
AMIN. These strange and sudden injuries
    have fall'n
So thick upon me that I lose all sense

Of what they are. Methinks, I am not
    wronged;
Nor is it aught, if from the censuring
    world
I can but hide it. Reputation,
Thou art a word, no more!—But thou
    hast shown
An impudence so high that to the world
I fear thou wilt betray or shame thy-
    self.
EVAD. To cover shame, I took thee;
    never fear
That I would blaze [1] myself.
AMIN.                Nor let the king  340
Know I conceive he wrongs me; then
    mine honor
Will thrust me into action; that my flesh
Could bear with patience.  And it is
    some ease
To me in these extremes that I know
    this
Before I touched thee; else, had all the
    sins
Of mankind stood betwixt me and the
    king,
I had gone through 'em to his heart and
    thine.
I have lost one desire; 'tis not his crown
Shall buy me to thy bed, now I resolve [2]
He has dishonored thee.  Give me thy
    hand.                350
Be careful of thy credit, and sin close; [3]
'Tis all I wish.  Upon thy chamber floor
I'll rest tonight, that morning visitors
May think we did as married people
    use.
And, prithee, smile upon me when they
    come,
And seem to toy, as if thou hadst been
    pleased
With what we did.
EVAD.                Fear not; I will do this.
AMIN. Come, let us practice; and, as wan-
    tonly
As ever loving bride and bridegroom met,
Let's laugh and enter here.
EVAD.                I am content.  360
AMIN. Down all the swellings of my
    troubled heart!
When we walk thus entwined, let all
    eyes see
If ever lovers better did agree.
                *Exit* [*with Evadne*].

[1] Proclaim.    [2] Am convinced.    [3] Privately.

[SCENA ii.

*A room in the house of Calianax.*]

*Enter Aspatia, Antiphila, and Olympias.*

ASP. Away, you are not sad! Force it no
    further.
Good gods, how well you look! Such a
    full color
Young bashful brides put on; sure, you
    are new married!
ANT. Yes, madam, to your grief.
ASP.                     Alas, poor wenches!
Go learn to love first; learn to lose your-
    selves;
Learn to be flattered, and believe and
    bless
The double tongue that did it; make a
    faith
Out of the miracles of ancient lovers,
Such as speak truth and died in 't; and,
    like me,
Believe all faithful, and be miserable.    10
Did you ne'er love yet, wenches? Speak,
    Olympias;[1]
Thou hast an easy temper, fit for stamp.[2]
OLYM. Never.
ASP.            Nor you, Antiphila?
ANT.                            Nor I.
ASP. Then, my good girls, be more than
    women, wise;
At least be more than I was; and be sure
You credit anything the light gives life
    to,
Before a man.  Rather believe the sea
Weeps for the ruined merchant, when he
    roars;
Rather, the wind courts but the preg-
    nant sails,
When the strong cordage cracks; rather,
    the sun                                20
Comes but to kiss the fruit in wealthy
    autumn,
When all falls blasted.  If you needs
    must love
(Forced by ill fate), take to your maiden
    bosoms
Two dead-cold aspics,[3] and of them make
    lovers.
They cannot flatter nor forswear; one
    kiss
Makes a long peace for all.  But man—

---

[1] This line follows l. 8 in original.  Emended
by Theobald.    [2] Impression.    [3] Asps.

O, that beast man!  Come, let's be sad,
    my girls;
That down-cast of thine eye, Olympias,
Shows a fine sorrow.—Mark, Antiphila;
Just such another was the nymph
    Oenone's,                            30
When Paris brought home Helen.—
    Now, a tear;
And then thou art a piece expressing
    fully
The Carthage queen, when from a cold
    sea rock,
Full with her sorrow, she tied fast her
    eyes
To the fair Trojan ships, and, having
    lost them,
Just as thine does, down stole a tear.—
    Antiphila,
What would this wench do, if she were
    Aspatia?
Here she would stand, till some more
    pitying god
Turned her to marble!—  'Tis enough,
    my wench!
Show me the piece of needlework you
    wrought.                            40
ANT. Of Ariadne, madam?
ASP. [*Examining the needlework.*]    Yes,
    that piece.—
This should be Theseus; h'as a cozening
    face.—
You meant him for a man?
ANT.                        He was so, madam.
ASP. Why, then, 'tis well enough.—Never
    look back;
You have a full wind and a false heart,
    Theseus.—
Does not the story say his keel was
    split,
Or his masts spent, or some kind rock
    or other
Met with his vessel?
ANT.                    Not as I remember.
ASP. It should ha' been so.  Could the
    gods know this,
And not, of all their number, raise a
    storm?                              50
But they are all as ill.  This false smile
Was well expressed; just such another
    caught me.—
[*To Theseus.*] You shall not go so.—
Antiphila, in this place work a quick-
    sand,
And over it a shallow, smiling water,

And his ship plowing it, and then a
Fear.

Do that Fear to the life, wench.

ANT.                    'Twill wrong the story.

ASP. 'Twill make the story, wronged by
wanton poets,

Live long and be believed. But where's
the lady?

ANT. There, madam.                    60

ASP. Fie, you have missed it here, Antiphila;

You are much mistaken, wench.

These colors are not dull and pale
enough

To show a soul so full of misery

As this sad lady's was. Do it by me,

Do it again by me, the lost Aspatia;

And you shall find all true but the wild
island.

I stand upon the sea-breach now, and
think

Mine arms thus, and mine hair blown
with the wind,

Wild as that desert; and let all about
me                    70

Tell that I am forsaken. Do my face

(If thou hadst ever feeling of a sorrow)

Thus, thus, Antiphila: strive to make
me look

Like Sorrow's monument; and the trees
about me,

Let them be dry and leafless; let the
rocks

Groan with continual surges; and, behind me,

Make all a desolation. Look, look,
wenches,

A miserable life [1] of this poor picture!

OLYM. Dear madam!

ASP.    I have done. Sit down; and let us

Upon that point fix all our eyes, that
point there.                    80

Make a dull silence, till you feel a sudden
sadness

Give us new souls.

*Enter Calianax.*

CAL. The king may do this, and he may
not do it.

My child is wronged, disgraced.—Well,
how now, huswives? [2]

What, at your ease? Is this a time to
sit still?

Up, you young lazy whores, up, or I'll
swenge [3] you!

OLYM. Nay, good my lord—

CAL. You'll lie down shortly. Get you in,
and work!

What, are you grown so resty [4] you want
heats?

We shall have some of the court boys do
that office.                    90

ANT. My lord, we do no more than we
are charged.

It is the lady's pleasure we be thus

In grief; she is forsaken.

CAL.                    There's a rogue too,

A young dissembling slave!—Well, get
you in.—

I'll have a bout with that boy. 'Tis high
time

Now to be valiant; I confess my youth

Was never prone that way. What, made
an ass?

A court stale? [5] Well, I will be valiant,

And beat some dozen of these whelps; I
will!

And there's another of 'em, a trim,
cheating soldier;                    100

I'll maul that rascal; has outbraved me
twice;

But now, I thank the gods, I am valiant.—

Go, get you in.—I'll take a course with
all.                    *Exeunt om[nes].*

## ACTUS III. [SCENA i.

*Anteroom to Evadne's bedchamber.*]

*Enter Cleon, Strato, and Diphilus.*

CLE. Your sister is not up yet.

DIPH. O, brides must take their morning's rest; the night is troublesome.

STRA. But not tedious.

DIPH. What odds, he has not my
sister's maidenhead tonight?

STRA. No; it's odds against any bridegroom living, he ne'er gets it while he
lives.

DIPH. Y' are merry with my sister; [10
you'll please to allow me the same freedom
with your mother.

---

[1] Living representation.          [2] Hussies.

[3] Swinge, beat.          [5] Laughingstock.
[4] Restive, sluggish.

STRA. She's at your service.

DIPH. Then she's merry enough of herself; she needs no tickling.—Knock at the door.

STRA. We shall interrupt them.

DIPH. No matter; they have the year before them.—[*Strato knocks.*] Good morrow, sister. Spare yourself today; the [20 night will come again.

*Enter Amintor.*

AMIN. Who's there? My brother! I'm no readier yet. Your sister is but now up.

DIPH. You look as you had lost your eyes tonight; I think you ha' not slept.

AMIN. I' faith, I have not.

DIPH.        You have done better, then.

AMIN. We ventured for a boy; when he is twelve,

A shall command against the foes of Rhodes.

Shall we be merry?                          29

STRA. You cannot; you want sleep.

AMIN.        'Tis true.—(*Aside.*) But she,

As if she had drunk Lethe, or had made

Even with heaven, did fetch so still a sleep,

So sweet and sound——

DIPH.                        What's that?

AMIN.                        Your sister frets

This morning, and does turn her eyes upon me,

As people on their headsman. She does chafe,

And kiss, and chafe again, and clap my cheeks.

She's in another world.

DIPH. Then I had lost; I was about to lay

You had not got her maidenhead tonight.[1]

AMIN. [*Aside.*] Ha! He does not mock me? —Y'ad lost indeed;                    40

I do not use to bungle.

CLE.                    You do deserve her.

AMIN. (*Aside.*) I laid my lips to hers, and that wild breath,

That was so rude and rough to me last night,

Was sweet as April. I'll be guilty too,

If these be the effects.

[1] Last night.

*Enter Melantius.*

MEL. Good day, Amintor, for to me the name

Of brother is too distant; we are friends,

And that is nearer.

AMIN.                    Dear Melantius!

Let me behold thee. Is it possible?

MEL. What sudden gaze is this?

AMIN.            'Tis wondrous strange!  50

MEL. Why does thine eye desire so strict a view

Of that it knows so well? There's nothing here

That is not thine.

AMIN.            I wonder much, Melantius,

To see those noble looks that make me think

How virtuous thou art; and, on the sudden,

'Tis strange to me thou shouldst have worth and honor,

Or not be base, and false, and treacherous,

And every ill. But——

MEL.                    Stay, stay, my friend;

I fear this sound will not become our loves.

No more embrace me.

AMIN.                O, mistake me not!  60

I know thee to be full of all those deeds

That we frail men call good; but by the course

Of nature thou shouldst be as quickly changed

As are the winds, dissembling as the sea,

That now wears brows as smooth as virgins' be,

Tempting the merchant to invade his face,

And in an hour calls his billows up,

And shoots 'em at the sun, destroying all

A carries on him.—(*Aside.*) O, how near am I

To utter my sick thoughts!                70

MEL. But why, my friend, should I be so by nature?

AMIN. I have wed thy sister, who hath virtuous thoughts

Enough for one whole family; and it is strange

That you should feel no want.

MEL. Believe me, this is compliment too cunning for me.

DIPH. What should I be then by the course
of nature,
They having both robbed me of so much
virtue?
STRA. O, call the bride, my Lord Amin-
tor, that we may see her blush, and turn
her eyes down. It is the prettiest sport!
AMIN. Evadne!
EVAD. (*Within.*)      My lord?
AMIN.        Come forth, my love;  81
Your brothers do attend to wish you joy.
EVAD. I am not ready yet.
AMIN.            Enough, enough.
EVAD. They'll mock me.
AMIN.        Faith, thou shalt come in.

*Enter Evadne.*

MEL. Good morrow, sister. He that under-
stands
Whom you have wed, need not to wish
you joy.
You have enough; take heed you be not
proud.
DIPH. O, sister, what have you done?
EVAD. I done! Why, what have I done?
STRA. My Lord Amintor swears you are
no maid now.        90
EVAD. Push!
STRA. I' faith, he does.
EVAD.    I knew I should be mocked.
DIPH. With a truth.
EVAD.        If 'twere to do again,
In faith I would not marry.
AMIN. (*Aside.*)      Nor I, by heaven!
DIPH. Sister, Dula swears she heard you
cry two rooms off.
EVAD. Fie, how you talk!
DIPH. Let's see you walk.
EVAD.        By my troth, y' are spoiled.
MEL.            Amintor!
AMIN. Ha!
MEL.    Thou art sad.
AMIN.        Who, I? I thank you for that.
Shall Diphilus, thou, and I sing a catch?
MEL. How!        100
AMIN. Prithee, let's.
MEL. Nay, that's too much the other way.
AMIN. I am so lightened with my hap-
piness!—
How dost thou, love? Kiss me.
EVAD. I cannot love you; you tell tales of
me.
AMIN. Nothing but what becomes us.—
Gentlemen,

Would you had all such wives, and all
the world,
That I might be no wonder! Y' are all
sad.
What, do you envy me? I walk, me-
thinks,        109
On water, and ne'er sink, I am so light.
MEL. 'Tis well you are so.
AMIN.        Well! How can I be other,
When she looks thus?—Is there no
music there?
Let's dance.
MEL.    Why, this is strange, Amintor!
AMIN. I do not know myself; yet I could
wish
My joy were less.
DIPH. I'll marry too, if it will make one
thus.
EVAD. (*Aside.*) Amintor, hark.
AMIN. [*Aside.*] What says my love?—I
must obey.
EVAD. [*Aside.*] You do it scurvily; 'twill
be perceived.        119
CLE. My lord, the king is here.

*Enter King and Lysip[pus].*

AMIN.            Where?
STRA.            And his brother.
KING. Good morrow, all!—
Amintor, joy on joy fall thick upon
thee!—
And, madam, you are altered since I
saw you;
I must salute you; you are now an-
other's.
How liked you your night's rest?
EVAD.            Ill, sir.
AMIN.            Indeed,
She took but little.
LYS.        You'll let her take more,
And thank her too, shortly.
KING. Amintor, wert thou truly honest [1] till
Thou wert married?
AMIN.    Yes, sir.
KING.        Tell me, then, how shows
The sport unto thee?
AMIN.        Why, well.
KING.            What did you do?  130
AMIN. No more, nor less, than other
couples use;
You know what 'tis; it has but a coarse
name.

[1] Chaste.

KING. But, prithee, I should think, by her
black eye,
And her red cheek, she should be quick
and stirring
In this same business; ha?
AMIN.                    I cannot tell;
I ne'er tried other, sir, but I perceive
She is as quick [1] as you deliveréd.
KING. Well, you'll trust me then, Amintor,
to choose
A wife for you again?
AMIN.                    No, never, sir.
KING. Why, like you this so ill?
AMIN.                    So well I like her.  140
For this I bow my knee in thanks to
you,
And unto heaven will pay my grateful
tribute
Hourly, and do hope we shall draw out
A long contented life together here,
And die both, full of gray hairs, in one
day,
For which the thanks is yours. But, if
the powers
That rule us please to call her first
away,
Without pride spoke, this world holds
not a wife
Worthy to take her room.
KING. [Aside.]           I do not like this.—
All forbear the room but you, Amin-
tor,                                      150
And your lady.
[Exeunt All but the King, Amintor, and
Evadne.]
                    I have some speech with you,
That may concern your after living well.
AMIN. [Aside.] A will not tell me that he
lies with her?
If he do, something heavenly stay my
heart,
For I shall be apt to thrust this arm of
mine
To acts unlawful!
KING.               You will suffer me
To talk with her, Amintor, and not have
A jealous pang?
AMIN.           Sir, I dare trust my wife
With whom she dares to talk, and not be
jealous.                         [Retires.]
KING. How do you like Amintor?
EVAD.                    As I did, sir.  160
KING. How's that?

[1] I.e., quickened with child.

EVAD. As one that, to fulfill your will and
pleasure,
I have given leave to call me wife and
love.
KING. I see there is no lasting faith in sin;
They that break word with heaven will
break again
With all the world, and so dost thou
with me.
EVAD. How, sir?
KING.           This subtle woman's ignorance
Will not excuse you; thou hast taken
oaths,
So great that, methought, they did mis-
become
A woman's mouth, that thou wouldst
ne'er enjoy                          170
A man but me.
EVAD.               I never did swear so;
You do me wrong.
KING.               Day and night have heard it.
EVAD. I swore indeed that I would never
love
A man of lower place; but, if your for-
tune
Should throw you from this height, I
bade you trust
I would forsake you, and would bend to
him
That won your throne. I love with my
ambition,
Not with my eyes. But, if I ever yet
Touched any other, leprosy light here
Upon my face, which for your royalty
I would not stain!                    181
KING. Why, thou dissemblest, and it is
in me
To punish thee.
EVAD.           Why, it is in me, then,
Not to love you, which will more afflict
Your body than your punishment can
mine.
KING. But thou hast let Amintor lie with
thee.
EVAD. I ha' not.
KING.     Impudence! He says himself so.
EVAD. A lies.
KING.       A does not.
EVAD.               By this light, he does,
Strangely and basely, and I'll prove it
so!
I did not only shun him for a night,  190
But told him I would never close with
him.

KING. Speak lower; 'tis false.

EVAD.                    I am no man
To answer with a blow; or, if I were,
You are the king. But urge [me] [1] not;
'tis most true.

KING. Do not I know the uncontrolléd
    thoughts
That youth brings with him, when his
    blood is high
With expectation and desire of that
He long hath waited for? Is not his
    spirit,
Though he be temperate, of a valiant
    strain
As this our age hath known? What could
    he do,                                    200
If such a sudden speech had met his
    blood,
But ruin thee forever, if he had not killed
    thee?
He could not bear it thus; he is as we,
Or any other wrongèd man.

EVAD.                    It is dissembling.

KING. Take him!    Farewell; henceforth
    I am thy foe,
And what disgraces I can blot thee with
    look for.

EVAD. Stay, sir!—Amintor!—You shall
    hear.—Amintor!

AMIN. [Coming forward.] What, my love?

EVAD. Amintor, thou hast an ingenious [2]
    look,
And shouldst be virtuous; it amazeth
    me                                        210
That thou canst make such base, mali-
    cious lies!

AMIN. What, my dear wife?

EVAD.        Dear wife! I do despise thee.
Why, nothing can be baser than to sow
Dissension amongst lovers.

AMIN.                    Lovers! Who?

EVAD. The king and me—

AMIN.                    O, God!

EVAD. Who should live long, and love
    without distaste,
Were it not for such pickthanks [3] as
    thyself.
Did you lie with me? Swear now, and be
    punished
In hell for this!

AMIN. [Aside.] The faithless sin I made
To fair Aspatia is not yet revenged;      220
It follows me.—I will not lose a word

To this wild [4] woman; but to you, my
    king,
The anguish of my soul thrusts out this
    truth:
Y' are a tyrant!—and not so much to
    wrong
An honest man thus, as to take a pride
In talking with him of it.

EVAD.                    Now, sir, see
How loud this fellow lied!

AMIN. You that can know to wrong, should
    know how men
Must right themselves—what punish-
    ment is due
From me to him that shall abuse my
    bed.                                       230
It is not death; nor can that satisfy,
Unless I send your lives [5] through all
    the land,
To show how nobly I have freed my-
    self.

KING. Draw not thy sword; thou knowest
    I cannot fear
A subject's hand. But thou shalt feel
    the weight
Of this, if thou dost rage.

AMIN.                    The weight of that!
If you have any worth, for heaven's
    sake, think
I fear not swords; for, as you are mere
    man,
I dare as easily kill you for this deed   239
As you dare think to do it. But there is
Divinity about you that strikes dead
My rising passions; as you are my king,
I fall before you, and present my sword
To cut mine own flesh, if it be your will.
Alas, I am nothing but a multitude
Of walking [6] griefs! Yet, should I mur-
    der you,
I might before the world take the ex-
    cuse
Of madness; for, compare [7] my injuries,
And they will well appear too sad a
    weight                                    249
For reason to endure. But fall I [8] first
Amongst my sorrows, ere my treacher-
    ous hand
Touch holy things! But why (I know
    not what

_____
[1] From 1630 edn.  [2] Ingenuous.  [3] Talebearers.
[4] Dyce suggests vild, i.e., vile.
[5] Life histories.
[6] So all edns. except original, which reads
waking.
[7] Examine.        [8] I.e., may I fall.

I have to say), why did you choose out me

To make thus wretched?   There were thousands, fools

Easy to work on, and of state [1] enough, Within the island.

EVAD.                    I would not have a fool;
It were no credit for me.

AMIN.                    Worse and worse!
Thou, that dar'st talk unto thy husband thus,

Profess thyself a whore, and, more than so,

Resolve to be so still!—It is my fate    260
To bear and bow beneath a thousand griefs,

To keep that little credit with the world!—

But there were wise ones too; you might have ta'en

Another.

KING.          No; for I believe thee honest,
As thou wert valiant.

AMIN.                    All the happiness [2]
Bestowed upon me turns into disgrace.

Gods, take your honesty again, for I

Am loaden with it!—Good my lord the king,

Be private in it.

KING.          Thou mayst live, Amintor,
Free as thy king, if thou wilt wink at this,                                    270

And be a means that we may meet in secret.

AMIN. A bawd! Hold, hold, my breast! A bitter curse

Seize me, if I forget not all respects

That are religious, on another word [3]

Sounded like that, and through a sea of sins

Will wade to my revenge, though I should call

Pains here and after life upon my soul!

KING. Well, I am resolute [4] you lay not with her;

And so I leave you.          Exit King.

EVAD.          You must needs be prating;
And see what follows!

AMIN.                    Prithee, vex me not.  280
Leave me; I am afraid some sudden start

Will pull a murther on me.

[1] Estate, position.                    [4] Convinced.
[2] Good fortune.
[3] I.e., a repetition of bawd (?).

EVAD.                    I am gone;
I love my life well.          Exit Evadne.

AMIN.                    I hate mine as much.
This 'tis to break a troth!  I should be glad,

If all this tide of grief would make me mad.                    Exit.

[SCENA ii.

A room in the palace.]

Enter Melantius.

MEL. I'll know the cause of all Amintor's griefs,

Or friendship shall be idle. [5]

Enter Calianax.

CAL.                    O, Melantius,
My daughter will die!

MEL.                    Trust me, I am sorry;
Would thou hadst ta'en her room!

CAL.                    Thou art a slave,
A cutthroat slave, a bloody, treacherous slave!

MEL. Take heed, old man; thou wilt be heard to rave,

And lose thine offices.

CAL.                    I am valiant grown
At all these years, and thou art but a slave!

MEL. Leave!  Some company will come, and I respect

Thy years, not thee, so much that I could wish                    10

To laugh at thee alone.

CAL.                    I'll spoil your mirth.
I mean to fight with thee.  There lie, my cloak!

This was my father's sword, and he durst fight.

Are you prepared?

MEL.                    Why wilt thou dote thyself
Out of thy life?  Hence, get thee to bed,

Have careful looking-to, and eat warm things,

And trouble not me; my head is full of thoughts

More weighty than thy life or death can be.

CAL. You have a name in war, where you stand safe

Amongst a multitude; but I will try    20

[5] Vain.

What you dare do unto a weak old man
In single fight. You'll give ground, I fear.
Come, draw!

MEL.   I will not draw, unless thou pull'st
thy death
Upon thee with a stroke. There's no
one blow
That thou canst give hath strength
enough to kill me.
Tempt me not so far, then; the power
of earth
Shall not redeem thee.

CAL. [Aside.]          I must let him alone;
He's stout and able; and, to say the
truth,
However I may set a face and talk,   30
I am not valiant. When I was a youth,
I kept my credit with a testy trick
I had amongst cowards, but durst never
fight.

MEL.   I will not promise to preserve your
life,
If you do stay.

CAL. [Aside.]          I would give half my land
That I durst fight with that proud man
a little.
If I had men to hold him, I would beat
him
Till he ask me mercy.

MEL.                    Sir, will you be gone?

CAL. [Aside.] I dare not stay; but I will
go home, and beat my servants all   [40
over for this.               Exit Calianax.

MEL. This old fellow haunts me.
But the distracted carriage of mine
Amintor
Takes deeply on me.[1] I will find the
cause;
I fear his conscience cries he wronged
Aspatia.

*Enter Amintor.*

AMIN. [Aside.] Men's eyes are not so
subtle to perceive
My inward misery; I bear my grief
Hid from the world. How art thou
wretched then?
For aught I know, all husbands are
like me;
And every one I talk with of his wife   50
Is but a well dissembler of his woes,
As I am. Would I knew it! For the
rareness

Afflicts me now.

MEL. Amintor, we have not enjoyed
our friendship of late, for we were wont
to charge [2] our souls in talk.

AMIN. Melantius, I can tell thee a
good jest of Strato and a lady the last day.

MEL. How was 't?

AMIN. Why, such an odd one!   60

MEL. I have longed to speak with you,
not of an idle jest, that's forced, but of
matter you are bound to utter to me.

AMIN. What is that, my friend?

MEL. I have observed your words fall
from your tongue
Wildly, and all your carriage
Like one that strove to show his merry
mood,
When he were ill disposed. You were
not wont
To put such scorn into your speech, or
wear
Upon your face ridiculous jollity.   70
Some sadness sits here, which your
cunning would
Cover o'er with smiles, and 'twill not
be.
What is it?

AMIN.          A sadness here! What cause
Can fate provide for me to make me so?
Am I not loved through all this isle?
The king
Rains greatness on me. Have I not
received
A lady to my bed, that in her eye
Keeps mounting fire, and on her tender
cheeks
Inevitable [3] color, in her heart   79
A prison for all virtue? Are not you,
Which is above all joys, my constant
friend?
What sadness can I have? No; I am
light,
And feel the courses of my blood more
warm
And stirring than they were. Faith,
marry too,
And you will feel so unexpressed [4] a joy
In chaste embraces that you will indeed
Appear another.

MEL.          You may shape, Amintor,
Causes to cozen the whole world withal,
And yourself too; but 'tis not like a
friend

[1] Affects me deeply.

[2] Weigh down.   [3] Irresistible.   [4] Inexpressible.

To hide your soul from me. 'Tis not
    your nature                                            90
To be thus idle. I have seen you stand
As you were blasted midst of all your
    mirth,
Call thrice aloud, and then start, feign-
    ing joy
So coldly!—World, what do I here? A
    friend
Is nothing.  Heaven, I would ha' told
    that man
My secret sins! I'll search [1] an unknown
    land,
And there plant friendship; all is with-
    ered here.
Come with a compliment! I would have
    fought,
Or told my friend a lied, ere soothed [2]
    him so.—
Out of my bosom!                                       100
AMIN. But there is nothing.
MEL.               Worse and worse! Farewell!
From this time have acquaintance, but
    no friend.
AMIN. Melantius, stay; you shall know
    what that is.
MEL. See how you played with friendship!
    Be advised
How you give cause unto yourself to say
You ha' lost a friend.
AMIN.               Forgive what I ha' done,
For I am so o'ergone with injuries
Unheard of, that I lose consideration
Of what I ought to do. O, O!
MEL.                     Do not weep.
What is 't? May I once but know the
    man                                                       110
Hath turned my friend thus!
AMIN.               I had spoke at first
But that—
MEL.       But what?
AMIN.               I held it most unfit
For you to know. Faith, do not know
    it yet.
MEL. Thou seest my love, that will keep
    company
With thee in tears; hide nothing, then,
    from me,
For, when I know the cause of thy dis-
    temper,
With mine old armor I'll adorn myself,
My resolution, and cut through thy
    foes,

Unto thy quiet, till I place thy heart
As peaceable as spotless innocence.   120
What is it?
AMIN.               Why, 'tis this—it is too big
To get out—let my tears make way
    awhile.
MEL. Punish me strangely, heaven, if he
    escape
Of life or fame, that brought this youth
    to this!
AMIN. Your sister—
MEL.               Well said.
AMIN.                     You'll wish 't unknown,
When you have heard it.
MEL.               No.
AMIN.                          —is much to blame,
And to the king has given her honor
    up,
And lives in whoredom with him.
MEL.                          How's this?
Thou art run mad with injury indeed;
Thou couldst not utter this else. Speak
    again,                                                    130
For I forgive it freely; tell thy griefs.
AMIN. She's wanton; I am loath to say
    "a whore,"
Though it be true.
MEL. Speak yet again, before mine anger
    grow
Up beyond throwing down. What are
    thy griefs?
AMIN. By all our friendship, these.
MEL.                          What, am I tame?
After mine actions, shall the name of
    friend
Blot all our family, and strike the brand
Of whore upon my sister, unrevenged?
My shaking flesh, be thou a witness for
    me,                                                        140
With what unwillingness I go to scourge
This railer, whom my folly hath called
    friend?
I will not take thee basely; thy sword
                          [Draws his sword.]
Hangs near thy hand; draw it, that I
    may whip
Thy rashness to repentance. Draw thy
    sword!
AMIN. Not on thee, did thine anger go as
    high
As the wild surges. Thou shouldst do
    me ease
Here and eternally, if thy noble hand
Would cut me from my sorrows.

MEL.                              This is base
And fearful.[1]  They that use to utter
    lies                                    150
Provide not blows but words to qualify [2]
The men they wronged.  Thou hast a
    guilty cause.
AMIN. Thou pleasest me; for so much
    more like this
Will raise my anger up above my griefs
(Which is a passion easier to be borne)
And I shall then be happy.
MEL.                        Take, then, more
To raise thine anger: 'tis mere coward-
    ice
Makes thee not draw; and I will leave
    thee dead,
However.  But, if thou art so much
    pressed
With guilt and fear as not to dare to
    fight,                                  160
I'll make thy memory loathed, and fix
    a scandal
Upon thy name forever.
AMIN. [Drawing his sword.]        Then I
    draw,
As justly as our magistrates their
    swords
To cut offenders off.  I knew before
'Twould grate your ears; but it was
    base in you
To urge a weighty secret from your
    friend,
And then rage at it.  I shall be at ease,
If I be killed; and, if you fall by me,
I shall not long outlive you.
MEL.                        Stay awhile.—  169
The name of friend is more than family,
Or all the world besides; I was a fool.
Thou searching human nature, that
    didst wake
To do me wrong, thou art inquisitive,
And thrusts me upon questions that
    will take
My sleep away!  Would I had died, ere
    known
This sad dishonor!—Pardon me, my
    friend!            [Sheathes his sword.]
If thou wilt strike, here is a faithful
    heart;
Pierce it, for I will never heave my
    hand
To thine.  Behold the power thou hast
    in me!

I do believe my sister is a whore,     180
A leprous one.  Put up thy sword, young
    man.
AMIN. How should I bear it, then, she
    being so?
I fear, my friend, that you will lose me
    shortly;           [Sheathes his sword.]
And I shall do a foul act on myself,
Through these disgraces.
MEL.                        Better half the land
Were buried quick [3] together.  No,
    Amintor;
Thou shalt have ease.  O, this adulter-
    ous king
That drew her to 't!  Where got he the
    spirit
To wrong me so?
AMIN.                What is it, then, to me,
If it be wrong to you?
MEL.                Why, not so much.     190
The credit of our house is thrown away.
But from his iron den I'll waken Death,
And hurl him on this king.  My honesty
Shall steel my sword; and on my horrid
    point
I'll wear my cause, that shall amaze
    the eyes
Of this proud man, and be too glittering
For him to look on.
AMIN. I have quite undone my fame.[4]
MEL. Dry up thy watery eyes,     199
And cast a manly look upon my face,
For nothing is so wild as I, thy friend,
Till I have freed thee.  Still this swell-
    ing breast.
I go thus from thee, and will never
    cease
My vengeance till I find my heart at
    peace.
AMIN. It must not be so.  Stay.  Mine
    eyes would tell
How loath I am to this; but, love and
    tears,
Leave me awhile, for I have hazarded
All that this world calls happy!—Thou
    hast wrought
A secret from me, under name of friend,
Which art could ne'er have found, nor
    torture wrung                          210
From out my bosom.  Give it me again,
For I will find it, wheresoe'er it lies,
Hid in the mortal'st part.  Invent a way
To give it back.

[1] Cowardly.        [2] Mollify.        [3] Alive.        [4] Reputation.

MEL. Why would you have it back?
I will to death pursue him with revenge.

AMIN. Therefore I call it back from thee,
for I know
Thy blood so high that thou wilt stir
in this,
And shame me to posterity. Take to
thy weapon! [*Draws his sword.*]

MEL. Hear thy friend, that bears more
years than thou.

AMIN. I will not hear. But draw, or I—

MEL. Amintor! 220

AMIN. Draw, then; for I am full as reso-
lute
As fame and honor can enforce me be.
I cannot linger. Draw!

MEL. [*Drawing his sword.*] I do. But is
not
My share of credit equal with thine,
If I do stir?

AMIN. No; for it will be called
Honor in thee to spill thy sister's blood,
If she her birth abuse; and on the king
A brave revenge; but on me, that have
walked
With patience in it, it will fix the name
Of fearful cuckold. O, that word! Be
quick. 230

MEL. Then, join with me.

AMIN. I dare not do a sin,
Or else I would. Be speedy.

MEL. Then, dare not fight with me, for
that's a sin.—
[*Aside.*] His grief distracts him.—Call
thy thoughts again,
And to thyself pronounce the name of
friend,
And see what that will work. I will not
fight.

AMIN. You must.

MEL. [*Sheathing his sword.*] I will be
killed first. Though my passions
Offered the like to you, 'tis not this earth
Shall buy my reason to it. Think awhile,
For you are (I must weep when I speak
that) 240
Almost besides yourself.

AMIN. [*Sheathing his sword.*] O, my soft
temper!
So many sweet words from thy sister's
mouth
I am afraid would make me take her to
Embrace, and pardon her. I am mad
indeed,
And know not what I do. Yet have a
care
Of me in what thou doest.

MEL. Why, thinks my friend
I will forget his honor, or, to save
The bravery of our house, will lose his
fame,
And fear to touch the throne of majesty?

AMIN. A curse will follow that; but rather
live 250
And suffer with me.

MEL. I will do what worth
Shall bid me, and no more.

AMIN. Faith, I am sick,
And desperately I hope; yet, leaning
thus,
I feel a kind of ease.

MEL. Come, take again
Your mirth about you.

AMIN. I shall never do 't.

MEL. I warrant you. Look up; we'll
walk together.
Put thine arm here; all shall be well
again.

AMIN. Thy love (O, wretched!), ay, thy
love, Melantius.
Why, I have nothing else.

MEL. Be merry, then. *Exeunt.*

*Enter Melantius again.*

MEL. This worthy young man may do
violence 260
Upon himself; but I have cherished
him
To my best power, and sent him smiling from me,
To counterfeit again. Sword, hold thine
edge;
My heart will never fail me.—

*Enter Diphilus.*[1]

Diphilus!
Thou com'st as [2] sent.

DIPH. Yonder has been such laughing.

MEL. Betwixt whom?

DIPH. Why, our sister and the king.
I thought their spleens would break;
they laughed us all
Out of the room.

MEL. They must weep, Diphilus.

DIPH. Must they?

[1] In original, direction appears a line later
[2] As if.

Mel.                              They must.
Thou art my brother; and, if I did be-
    lieve                                        270
Thou hadst a base thought, I would rip
    it out,
Lie where it durst.
Diph.              You should not; I would first
Mangle myself and find it.
Mel.                          That was spoke
According to our strain.  Come, join
    thy hands to mine,
And swear a firmness to what project I
Shall lay before thee.
Diph.              You do wrong us both.
People hereafter shall not say there
    passed
A bond, more than our loves, to tie our
    lives
And deaths together.                      279
Mel.  It is as nobly said as I would wish.
Anon [1] I'll tell you wonders: we are
    wronged.
Diph.  But I will tell you now, we'll right
    ourselves.
Mel.  Stay not; prepare the armor in my
    house;
And what friends you can draw unto
    our side,
Not knowing of the cause, make ready
    too.
Haste, Diph[ilus]; the time requires it,
    haste!—                  *Exit Diphilus.*
I hope my cause is just; I know my blood
Tells me it is; and I will credit it.
To take revenge, and lose myself withal,
Were idle, and to scape impossible   290
Without I had the fort, which (misery!)
Remaining in the hands of my old en-
    emy,
Calianax—but I must have it.  See

*Enter Calianax.*

Where he comes shaking by me!—Good
    my lord,
Forget your spleen to me.  I never
    wronged you,
But would have peace with every man.
Cal.                              'Tis well.
If I durst fight, your tongue would lie
    at quiet.
Mel.  Y' are touchy without all cause.
Cal.                          Do, mock me.

Mel.  By mine honor, I speak truth.
Cal.              Honor?  Where is 't?
Mel.  See, what starts you make        300
Into your hatred, to my love
And freedom to you.  I come with resolu-
    tion
To obtain a suit of you.
Cal.                          A suit of me!
'Tis very like it should be granted, sir.
Mel.  Nay, go not hence.
'Tis this: you have the keeping of the
    fort,
And I would wish you, by the love you
    ought
To bear unto me, to deliver it
Into my hands.
Cal.              I am in hope thou art mad,
To talk to me thus.
Mel.              But there is a reason  310
To move you to it: I would kill the king
That wronged you and your daughter.
Cal.                              Out, traitor!
Mel.  Nay, but stay; I cannot scape, the
    deed once done,
Without I have this fort.
Cal.              And should I help thee?
Now thy treacherous mind betrays it-
    self.
Mel.  Come, delay me not.
Give me a sudden answer, or already
Thy last is spoke!  Refuse not offered
    love                                        318
When it comes clad in secrets.
Cal.  [*Aside.*]              If I say
I will not, he will kill me; I do see 't
Writ in his looks; and should I say I will,
He'll run and tell the king.—I do not
    shun
Your friendship, dear Melantius; but
    this cause
Is weighty.  Give me but an hour to
    think.
Mel.  Take it.—[*Aside.*] I know this goes
    unto the king;
But I am armed.        *Exit Melantius.*
Cal.              Methinks I feel myself
But twenty now again.  This fighting
    fool                                        327
Wants policy;[2] I shall revenge my girl,
And make her red[3] again.  I pray my legs
Will last that pace that I will carry them;
I shall want breath before I find the
    king.                              *Exit.*

ACTUS IV. [SCENA i.

*Evadne's apartment.*]

*Enter Melantius, Evadne, and Ladies.*[1]

MEL. Save you!

EVAD.                Save you, sweet brother.

MEL. In my blunt eye, methinks, you look [2] Evadne.

EVAD. Come, you would make me blush.

MEL.                I would, Evadne;
I shall displease my ends else.

EVAD.                You shall, if you
Commend [3] me; I am bashful.  Come, sir, how do
I look?

MEL.    I would not have your women hear me
Break into commendations of you; 'tis not
Seemly.

EVAD. [*To Ladies.*]        Go wait me in the gallery.—
Now speak.

MEL.            I'll lock the door first.
                        *Exeunt Ladies.*

EVAD.                        Why?

MEL. I will not have your gilded things, that dance        10
In visitation with their Milan skins,[4]
Choke up my business.

EVAD.        You are strangely disposed, sir.

MEL. Good madam, not to make you merry.

EVAD. No; if you praise me, 'twill make me sad.

MEL. Such a sad commendations I have for you.

EVAD. Brother,
The court hath made you witty, and learn to riddle.

MEL. I praise the court for 't; has it learned you nothing?

EVAD. Me?

MEL.        Ay, Evadne; thou art young and handsome,
A lady of a sweet complexion,        20
And such a flowing carriage that it cannot
Choose but inflame a kingdom.

EVAD.                Gentle brother!

MEL. 'Tis yet in thy repentance, foolish woman,
To make me gentle.

EVAD.                How is this?

MEL.                'Tis base;
And I could blush, at these years, through all
My honored scars, to come to such a parley.

EVAD. I understand you not.

MEL.                You dare not, fool!
They that commit thy faults fly the remembrance.

EVAD. My faults, sir!  I would have you know I care not
If they were written here, here in my forehead.        30

MEL. Thy body is too little for the story,
The lusts of which would fill another woman,[5]
Though she had twins within her.

EVAD.                This is saucy.
Look you intrude no more!  There's your way.

MEL. Thou art my way, and I will tread upon thee
Till I find truth out.

EVAD.    What truth is that you look for?

MEL. Thy long-lost honor.  Would the gods had set me
Rather to grapple with the plague, or stand [6]
One of their loudest bolts!  Come, tell me quickly,        39
Do it without enforcement, and take heed
You swell me not above my temper.

EVAD.                How, sir?
Where got you this report?

MEL.                Where there was people,
In every place.

EVAD.        They and the seconds of it
Are base people.  Believe them not; they lied.

MEL. Do not play with mine anger; do not, wretch!        [*Seizes her.*]
I come to know that desperate fool that drew thee
From thy fair life.  Be wise, and lay him open.

EVAD. Unhand me, and learn manners!  Such another
Forgetfulness forfeits your life.

---

[1] Original has *a Lady.*        [4] Gloves.
[2] *I.e.*, look like.
[3] Theobald's emendation for *Command.*

[5] The account of whose lusts would cover the body of another woman.        [6] Withstand.

MEL. Quench me this mighty humor, and
    then tell me                              50
Whose whore you are; for you are one,
    I know it.
Let all mine honors perish but I'll find
    him,
Though he lie locked up in thy blood!
    Be sudden;
There is no facing it;[1] and be not flattered.
The burnt air, when the Dog reigns, is
    not fouler
Than thy contagious name, till thy re-
    pentance
(If the gods grant thee any) purge thy
    sickness.
EVAD. Begone!    You are my brother;
    that's your safety.
MEL. I'll be a wolf first. 'Tis, to be thy
    brother,
An infamy below the sin of coward.  60
I am as far from being part of thee
As thou art from thy virtue.  Seek a
    kindred
Mongst sensual beasts, and make a goat
    thy brother;
A goat is cooler.  Will you tell me yet?
EVAD. If you stay here and rail thus, I
    shall tell you
I'll ha' you whipped!  Get you to your
    command,
And there preach to your sentinels, and
    tell them
What a brave man you are.  I shall laugh
    at you.
MEL. Y' are grown a glorious[2] whore!
    Where be your fighters?
What mortal fool durst raise thee to
    this daring,                              70
And I alive!  By my just sword, h'ad safer
Bestride a billow when the angry North
Plows up the sea, or made heaven's fire
    his food!
Work me no higher.  Will you discover
    yet?
EVAD. The fellow's mad.  Sleep, and speak
    sense.
MEL. Force my swoln heart no further;
    I would save thee.
Your great maintainers are not here—
    they dare not.
Would they were all, and armed!    I
    would speak loud;

Here's one should thunder to 'em!  Will
    you tell me?
Thou hast no hope to scape.  He that
    dares most,                              80
And damns away his soul to do thee serv-
    ice,
Will sooner snatch meat from a hungry
    lion
Than come to rescue thee.  Thou hast
    death about thee—
Has undone thine honor, poisoned thy
    virtue,
And, of a lovely rose, left thee a canker.[3]
EVAD. Let me consider.
MEL.              Do, whose child thou wert,
Whose honor thou hast murdered, whose
    grave opened,
And so pulled on[4] the gods that in their
    justice
They must restore him flesh again and
    life,
And raise his dry bones to revenge this
    scandal.                                 90
EVAD. The gods are not of my mind; they
    had better
Let 'em lie sweet still in the earth; they'll
    stink here.
MEL. Do you raise mirth out of my easi-
    ness?
Forsake me, then, all weaknesses of
    nature
That make men women!  [Draws his
    sword.]  Speak, you whore, speak truth,
Or, by the dear soul of thy sleeping
    father,
This sword shall be thy lover!  Tell,
    or I'll kill thee;
And, when thou hast told all, thou wilt
    deserve it.
EVAD. You will not murther me?         99
MEL. No; 'tis a justice, and a noble one,
To put the light out of such base of-
    fenders.
EVAD. Help!
MEL. By thy foul self, no human help
    shall help thee,
If thou criest!  When I have killed thee,
    as I
Have vowed to do, if thou confess not,
    naked
As thou hast left thine honor will I
    leave thee,

---

[1] I.e., there is nothing to be gained by maintaining a false appearance.        [2] Boasting.

[3] Dog-rose; also a disease of plants.
[4] Provoked.

That on thy branded flesh the world
  may read
Thy black shame and my justice. Wilt
  thou bend yet?
EVAD. Yes.
MEL. Up, and begin your story.    110
EVAD. O, I am miserable!
MEL. 'Tis true, thou art.  Speak truth
  still.
EVAD. I have offended; noble sir, forgive
  me!
MEL. With what secure [1] slave?
EVAD.        Do not ask me, sir;
  Mine own remembrance is a misery
  Too mighty for me.
MEL.        Do not fall back again;
  My sword's unsheathéd yet.
EVAD.        What shall I do?
MEL. Be true, and make your fault less.
EVAD.        I dare not tell.
MEL. Tell, or I'll be this day a-killing thee.
EVAD. Will you forgive me, then?    120
MEL. Stay; I must ask mine honor first.
  I have too much foolish nature in me.
  Speak.
EVAD. Is there none else here?
MEL. None but a fearful conscience;
  that's too many.
  Who is 't?
EVAD.    O, hear me gently!  It was
  the king.
MEL. No more!  My worthy father's and
  my services
  Are liberally rewarded!  King, I thank
  thee!
  For all my dangers and my wounds thou
  hast paid me
  In my own metal: these are soldiers'
  thanks!—
  How long have you lived thus, Evadne?
EVAD.      Too long.  130
MEL. Too late you find it.  Can you be
  sorry?
EVAD. Would I were half as blameless!
MEL. Evadne, thou wilt to thy trade
  again.
EVAD. First to my grave.
MEL.        Would gods thou
  hadst been so blessed!
  Dost thou not hate this king now?
  Prithee, hate him.
  Couldst thou not curse him?  I com-
  mand thee, curse him;

[1] Overconfident.

Curse till the gods hear, and deliver
  him
To thy just wishes.  Yet I fear, Evadne,
You had rather play your game out.
EVAD.        No; I feel
  Too many sad confusions here, to let
  in  140
Any loose flame hereafter.
MEL. Dost thou not feel, amongst all
  those, one brave anger
  That breaks out nobly, and directs
  thine arm
  To kill this base king?
EVAD.    All the gods forbid it!
MEL. No, all the gods require it;
  They are dishonored in him.
EVAD.        'Tis too fearful.
MEL. Y' are valiant in his bed, and bold
  enough
  To be a stale whore, and have your
  madam's name
  Discourse for grooms and pages, and
  hereafter,
  When his cool majesty hath laid you
  by,  150
  To be at pension with some needy sir
  For meat and coarser clothes; thus far
  you know
  No fear.  Come, you shall kill him.
EVAD.        Good sir!
MEL. An 'twere to kiss him dead, thou'dst
  smother him.
  Be wise, and kill him.  Canst thou live,
  and know
  What noble minds shall make thee,
  see thyself
  Found out with every finger, made the
  shame
  Of all successions, and in this great
  ruin
  Thy brother and thy noble husband
  broken?
  Thou shalt not live thus.  Kneel, and
  swear to help me,  160
  When I shall call thee to it; or, by
  all
  Holy in heaven and earth, thou shalt
  not live
  To breathe a full hour longer; not a
  thought!
  Come, 'tis a righteous oath.  Give me
  thy hand[s],
  And, both to heaven held up, swear, by
  that wealth

This lustful thief stole from thee, when
  I say it,
To let his foul soul out.

EVAD.                Here I swear it;
And, all you spirits of abusèd ladies,
  Help me in this performance!

MEL. Enough. This must be known to
  none                      170
But you and I, Evadne—not to your
  lord,
Though he be wise and noble, and a
  fellow
Dares step as far into a worthy action
As the most daring, ay, as far as justice.
Ask me not why. Farewell!
                     *Exit Mel[antius].*

EVAD. Would I could say so to my black
  disgrace!
O, where have I been all this time?
  How friended,
That I should lose myself thus desper-
  ately,
And none for pity show me how I
  wandered?               179
There is not in the compass of the light
A more unhappy creature; sure, I am
  monstrous,
For I have done those follies, those mad
  mischiefs,
Would dare [1] a woman. O, my loaden
  soul,
Be not so cruel to me; choke not up
The way to my repentance!—

*Enter Amintor.*

                     O, my lord!

AMIN. How now?

EVAD.   My much abusèd lord! [*Kneels.*]

AMIN.             This cannot be!

EVAD. I do not kneel to live; I dare not
  hope it.
The wrongs I did are greater. Look
  upon me,
Though I appear with all my faults.

AMIN.            Stand up!   189
This is no new way to beget more sorrow!
Heaven knows I have too many. Do
  not mock me;
Though I am tame, and bred up with
  my wrongs,
Which are my foster-brothers, I may
  leap,

Like a hand-wolf,[2] into my natural
  wildness,
And do an outrage. Prithee, do not
  mock me.

EVAD. My whole life is so leprous, it
  infects
All my repentance. I would buy your
  pardon,
Though at the highest set,[3] even with
  my life,
That slight contrition—that's [4] no sacrifice
For what I have committed.

AMIN.         Sure, I dazzle;   200
There cannot be a faith in that foul
  woman,
That knows no god more mighty than
  her mischiefs.
Thou dost still worse, still number on
  thy faults,
To press my poor heart thus. Can I
  believe
There's any seed of virtue in that woman
Left to shoot up, that dares go on in
  sin
Known, and so known as thine is? O,
  Evadne!
Would there were any safety [5] in thy
  sex
That I might put a thousand sorrows
  off,
And credit thy repentance! But I must
  not.                     210
Thou hast brought me to that dull
  calamity,
To that strange misbelief of all the world
And all things that are in it, that I
  fear
I shall fall like a tree, and find my grave,
Only rememb'ring that I grieve.

EVAD.              My lord,
Give me your griefs. You are an inno-
  cent,
A soul as white as heaven. Let not my
  sins
Perish [6] your noble youth. I do not fall
  here
To shadow by dissembling with my
  tears                  219
(As all say women can) or to make less

[1] Frighten.

[2] Hand-raised, tamed wolf.
[3] Stake.
[4] From 1630 edn. Original reads *that.*
[5] Trustworthiness.         [6] Destroy.

What my hot will hath done, which
heaven and you
Knows to be tougher than the hand of
time
Can cut from man's remembrance. No,
I do not.
I do appear the same, the same Evadne,
Dressed in the shames I lived in, the
same monster.
But these are names of honor to what
I am;
I do present myself the foulest creature,
Most poisonous, dangerous, and de-
spised of men,
Lerna e'er bred or Nilus. I am hell,
Till you, my dear lord, shoot your light
into me,                            230
The beams of your forgiveness; I am
soul-sick,
And wither with the fear of one con-
demned,
Till I have got your pardon.

AMIN.                        Rise, Evadne!
Those heavenly powers that put this
good into thee
Grant a continuance of it! I forgive thee.
Make thyself worthy of it, and take
heed,
Take heed, Evadne, this be serious.
Mock not the powers above, that can
and dare
Give thee a great example of their jus-
tice
To all ensuing eyes, if thou play'st  240
With thy repentance, the best sacrifice.

EVAD. I have done nothing good to win
belief,
My life hath been so faithless. All the
creatures,
Made for heaven's honors, have their
ends, and good ones,
All but the cozening crocodiles, false
women.
They reign here like those plagues, those
killing sores,
Men pray against; and, when they die,
like tales
Ill told and unbelieved, they pass away,
And go to dust forgotten. But, my
lord,
Those short days I shall number to my
rest                              250
(As many must not see me), shall—
though too late.

Though in my evening—yet perceive
a will
(Since I can do no good, because a
woman)
Reach constantly at something that is
near it.
I will redeem one minute of my age,
Or, like another Niobe, I'll weep
Till I am water.

AMIN.                I am now dissolved.
My frozen soul melts. May each sin
thou hast,
Find a new mercy! Rise; I am at
peace.
Hadst thou been thus, thus excellently
good                              260
Before that devil-king tempted thy
frailty,
Sure thou hadst made a star. Give me
thy hand;
From this time I will know thee; and,
as far
As honor gives me leave, be thy Amintor.
When we meet next. I will salute thee
fairly,
And pray the gods to give thee happy
days.
My charity shall go along with thee,
Though my embraces must be far from
thee.
I should ha' killed thee, but this sweet
repentance
Locks up my vengeance, for which thus
I kiss thee—                      270
The last kiss we must take—and would
to heaven
The holy priest that gave our hands to-
gether
Had given us equal virtues! Go,
Evadne;
The gods thus part our bodies. Have a
care
My honor falls no farther. I am well,
then.

EVAD. All the dear joys here, and above
hereafter,
Crown thy fair soul! Thus I take leave,
my lord;
And never shall you see the foul
Evadne
Till she have tried all honored means
that may
Set her in rest and wash her stains
away.                *Exeunt.* 280

[SCENA ii.

*A hall in the palace.*]

*Banquet. Enter King, Calianax. Hautboys play within.*

KING. I cannot tell how I should credit this
From you, that are his enemy.
CAL.                    I am sure
He said it to me; and I'll justify it
What way he dares oppose—but with my sword.
KING. But did he break,[1] without all cir-cumstance,[2]
To you, his foe, that he would have the fort
To kill me, and then scape?
CAL.                    If he deny it,
I'll make him blush.
KING.                    It sounds incredibly.
CAL. Ay, so does everything I say of late.
KING. Not so, Calianax.
CAL.                    Yes, I should sit  10
Mute, whilst a rogue with strong arms cuts your throat.
KING. Well, I will try him; and, if this be true,
I'll pawn my life I'll find it; if 't be false,
And that you clothe your hate in such a lie,
You shall hereafter dote in your own house,
Not in the court.
CAL.                    Why, if it be a lie,
Mine ears are false, for I'll be sworn I heard it.
Old men are good for nothing; you were best
Put me to death for hearing, and free him
For meaning it. You would 'a' trusted me  20
Once, but the time is altered.
KING.                    And will still,
Where I may do with justice to the world.
You have no witness.
CAL.                    Yes, myself.
KING.                    No more,
I mean, there were that heard it.
CAL.                    How? No more?
Would you have more? Why, am not I enough
To hang a thousand rogues?

KING                    But so you may
Hang honest men too, if you please.
CAL.                    I may!
'Tis like I will do so; there are a hun-dred
Will swear it for a need too, if I say it.
KING. Such witnesses we need not.
CAL.                    And 'tis hard  30
If my word cannot hang a boisterous knave.
KING. Enough.—Where's Strato?
STRA. Sir?

*Enter Strat[o].*

KING. Why, where's all the company? Call Amintor in;
Evadne.    Where's my brother, and Melant:us?
Bid him come too; and Diphilus. Call all
That are without there.—(*Exit Strat[o].*)
If he should desire
The combat of you, 'tis not in the power
Of all our laws to hinder it, unless
We mean to quit 'em.
CAL.                    Why, if you do think  40
'Tis fit an old man and a councilor
To fight for what he says, then you may grant it.

*Enter Amint[or], Evad[ne], Melant[ius], Diph[ilus], Lysip[pus], Cle[on], Stra[to], Diag[oras].*

KING. Come, sirs!—Amintor, thou art yet a bridegroom,
And I will use thee so; thou shalt sit down.—
Evadne, sit; and you, Amintor, too;
This banquet is for you, sir.—Who has brought
A merry tale about him, to raise laughter
Amongst our wine? Why, Strato, where art thou?
Thou wilt chop out with them[3] un-seasonably,
When I desire 'em not.  50
STRA. 'Tis my ill luck, sir, so to spend them, then.
KING. Reach me a bowl of wine.—Melantius, thou
Art sad.
MEL.[4]    I should be, sir, the merriest here,

[3] *I.e.,* blurt out tales.
[4] From 1619 edn. Original reads *Amint.*

[1] Impart.        [2] Without any ceremony.

But I ha' ne'er a story of mine own
Worth telling at this time.
KING.                    Give me the wine.—
Melantius, I am now considering
How easy 'twere for any man we trust
To poison one of us in such a bowl.
MEL. I think it were not hard, sir, for a
  knave.
CAL. [*Aside.*] Such as you are.        60
KING. I' faith, 'twere easy. It becomes
  us well
To get plain-dealing men about our-
  selves,
Such as you all are here.—Amintor, to
  thee,
And to thy fair Evadne.        [*Drinks.*]
MEL. (*Aside.*)        Have you thought
Of this, Calianax?
CAL. [*Aside.*]        Yes, marry, have I.
MEL. [*Aside.*] And what's your resolu-
  tion?
CAL. [*Aside.*]        Ye shall have it—
[*To himself.*] Soundly, I warrant you.
KING. Reach to Amintor, Strato.
AMIN.                    Here, my love.
    [*Drinks and hands the cup to Evadne.*]
This wine will do thee wrong, for it will
  set
Blushes upon thy cheeks; and, till thou
  dost                                70
A fault, 'twere pity.
KING.                Yet I wonder much
Of [1] the strange desperation of these
  men
That dare attempt such acts here in our
  state.
He could not scape that did it.
MEL.                Were he known,
Unpossible.
KING.        It would be known, Melantius.
MEL. It ought to be. If he got then away,
He must wear all our lives upon his
  sword.
He need not fly the island; he must
  leave
No one alive.
KING.        No; I should think no man
Could kill me, and scape clear, but that
  old man.                            80
CAL. But I! Heaven bless me! I! Should
  I, my liege?
KING. I do not think thou wouldst; but
  yet thou mightst,

[1] At.

For thou hast in thy hands the means
  to scape,
By keeping of the fort.—He has, Melan-
  tius,
And he has kept it well.
MEL.                From cobwebs, sir,
'Tis clean swept; I can find no other
  art
In keeping of it now.    'Twas ne'er be-
  sieged
Since he commanded.
CAL.                I shall be sure
Of your good word; but I have kept it
  safe
From such as you.
MEL.        Keep your ill temper in.  90
I speak no malice; had my brother kept
  it,
I should ha' said as much.
KING.                You are not merry.
Brother, drink wine. Sit you all still!—
(*Aside.*) Calianax,
I cannot trust thus. I have thrown out
  words
That would have fetched warm blood
  upon the cheeks
Of guilty men, and he is never moved;
He knows no such thing.
CAL.                Impudence may scape,
When feeble virtue is accused.
KING.                    A must,
If he were guilty, feel an alteration
At this our whisper, whilst we point
  at him.                            100
You see he does not.
CAL.        Let him hang himself.
What care I what he does? This he did
  say.
KING. Melan[tius], you can easily con-
  ceive
What I have meant, for men that are
  in fault
Can subtly apprehend when others aim
At what they do amiss; but I forgive
Freely before this man. Heaven do so
  too!
I will not touch thee, so much as with
  shame
Of telling it. Let it be so no more.
CAL. Why, this is very fine!
MEL.                I cannot tell   110
What 'tis you mean; but I am apt[2]
  enough
Rudely to thrust into ignorant fault.

[2] Likely.

But let me know it. Happily [1] 'tis naught
But misconstruction; and, where I am clear,
I will not take forgiveness of the gods,
Much less of you.

KING.　　　　　Nay, if you stand so stiff,
I shall call back my mercy.

MEL.　　　　　I want smoothness
To thank a man for pardoning of a crime
I never knew.

KING. Not to instruct your knowledge,
　　but to show you　　　　　　120
My ears are everywhere; you meant to kill me,
And get the fort to scape.

MEL.　　　　　Pardon me, sir;
My bluntness will be pardoned. You preserve
A race of idle people here about you,
Eaters and talkers, to defame the worth
Of those that do things worthy. The man that uttered this
Had perished without food, be 't who it will,
But for this arm, that fenced him from the foe;
And, if I thought you gave a faith to this,
The plainness of my nature would speak more.　　　　　　130
Give me a pardon (for you ought to do 't)
To kill him that spake this.

CAL. [Aside.]　　　　　Ay, that will be
The end of all; then I am fairly paid
For all my care and service.

MEL.　　　　　That old man,
Who calls me enemy, and of whom I
(Though I will never match my hate so low)
Have no good thought, would yet, I think, excuse me,
And swear he thought me wronged in this.

CAL.　　　　　Who, I?
Thou shameless fellow, didst thou not speak to me
Of it thyself?

MEL.　　　O, then it came from him! 140

CAL. From me! Who should it come from but from me?

MEL. Nay, I believe your malice is enough;

[1] Haply.

But I ha' lost my anger.—Sir, I hope
You are well satisfied.

KING.　　　　　Lysip[pus], cheer
Amintor and his lady.—There's no sound
Comes from you; I will come and do 't myself.

AMIN. [Aside.] You have done already, sir, for me, I thank you.

KING. Melantius, I do credit this from him,
How slight soe'er you make 't.

MEL.　　　'Tis strange you should.

CAL. 'Tis strange a should believe an old man's word　　　　　　150
That never lied in 's life!

MEL.　　　　　I talk not to thee.—
Shall the wild words of this distempered man,
Frantic with age and sorrow, make a breach
Betwixt your majesty and me? 'Twas wrong
To hearken to him; but to credit him,
As much at least as I have power to bear—
But pardon me—whilst I speak only truth,
I may commend myself—I have bestowed
My careless blood with you, and should be loath
To think an action that would make me lose　　　　　　160
That and my thanks too. When I was a boy,
I thrust myself into my country's cause,
And did a deed that plucked five years from time,
And styled me man then. And for you, my king,
Your subjects all have fed by virtue of
My arm. This sword of mine hath plowed the ground,
And reaped the fruit in peace;
And you yourself have lived at home in ease.
So terrible I grew that, without swords,
My name hath fetched you conquest; and my heart　　　　　　170
And limbs are still the same; my will as great
To do you service. Let me not be paid
With such a strange distrust.

KING.                    Melant[ius],
I held it great injustice to believe
Thine enemy, and did not; if I did,
I do not; let that satisfy.—What, struck
With sadness,[1] all?  More wine!
CAL.                    A few fine words
Have overthrown my truth.  Ah, thou'rt
  a villain!
MEL. (*Aside.*) Why, thou wert better
  let me have the fort.
Dotard, I will disgrace thee thus for-
  ever.                                    180
There shall no credit lie upon thy words.
Think better, and deliver it.
CAL.                    My liege,
He's at me now again to do it.—Speak!
Deny it, if thou canst.—Examine him
Whilst he is hot, for, if he cool again,
He will forswear it.
KING.                    This is lunacy,
I hope, Melantius.
MEL.          He hath lost himself
Much, since his daughter missed the
  happiness
My sister gained; and, though he call
  me foe,
I pity him.
CAL.        A pity!  A pox upon you!  190
MEL. Mark his disordered words; and
  at the masque
Diagoras knows he raged and railed
  at me,
And called a lady "whore," so innocent
She understood him not.  But it be-
  comes
Both you and me too to forgive dis-
  traction.[2]
Pardon him, as I do.
CAL.          I'll not speak for thee,
For[3] all thy cunning.—If you will be
  safe,
Chop off his head, for there was never
  known
So impudent a rascal.
KING.          Some that love him
Get him to bed.  Why, pity should not
  let                                     200
Age make itself contemptible; we must
  be
All old.  Have him away.
MEL. [*Aside.*]          Calianax,
The king believes you.  Come, you shall
  go home,

And rest; you ha' done well.  You'll
  give it up,
When I have used you thus a month,
  I hope.
CAL. Now, now, 'tis plain, sir; he does
  move me still.
He says he knows I'll give him up the
  fort,
When he has used me thus a month.  I
  am mad,
Am I not, still?
OMNES. Ha, ha, ha!                        210
CAL. I shall be mad indeed, if you do
  thus.
Why should you trust a sturdy fellow
  there
(That has no virtue in him; all's in his
  sword)
Before me?  Do but take his weapons
  from him,
And he's an ass; and I am a very fool,
Both with him and without him, as you
  use me.
OMNES. Ha, ha, ha!
KING. 'Tis well, Cal[ianax]; but, if you
  use
This once again, I shall entreat some
  other
To see your offices be well discharged.—
Be merry, gentlemen.—It grows some-
  what late.—                            221
Amintor, thou wouldst be abed again.
AMIN. Yes, sir.
KING.          And you, Evadne.—Let me take
Thee in my arms, Melantius, and be-
  lieve
Thou art, as thou deservest to be, my
  friend
Still and forever.—Good Cal[ianax],
Sleep soundly; it will bring thee to
  thyself.
*Exeunt omnes.  Manent[4] Mel[antius] and*
                    *Cal[ianax].*
CAL. Sleep soundly!  I sleep soundly now,
  I hope;
I could not be thus else.—How dar'st
  thou stay
Alone with me, knowing how thou hast
  used me?                                230
MEL. You cannot blast me with your
  tongue, and that's
The strongest part you have about you.
CAL.                                      I

[1] Seriousness.    [2] Madness.    [3] In spite of.
[4] Remain.

Do look for some great punishment for
this,
For I begin to forget all my hate,
And take 't unkindly that mine enemy
Should use me so extraordinarily scur-
vily.
MEL. I shall melt too, if you begin to take
Unkindnesses; I never meant you hurt.
CAL. Thou'lt anger me again. Thou
wretched rogue,
"Meant me no hurt"! Disgrace me with
the king!                                       240
Lose all my offices! This is no hurt,
Is it? I prithee, what dost thou call
hurt?
MEL. To poison men, because they love
me not;
To call the credit of men's wives in ques-
tion;
To murder children betwixt me and
land—
This I call hurt.
CAL.          All this thou think'st is sport;
For mine is worse. But use thy will
with me;
For betwixt grief and anger I could cry.
MEL. Be wise, then, and be safe; thou
mayst revenge—
CAL. Ay, o' th' king! I would revenge of
thee.                                          250
MEL. That you must plot yourself.
CAL.                    I'm a fine plotter.
MEL. The short is, I will hold thee with
the king
In this perplexity, till peevishness
And thy disgrace have laid thee in thy
grave.
But, if thou wilt deliver up the fort,
I'll take thy trembling body in my arms,
And bear thee over dangers. Thou
shalt hold
Thy wonted state.
CAL.             If I should tell the king,
Canst thou deny 't again?
MEL.                    Try, and believe.
CAL. Nay, then, thou canst bring any-
thing about.                                   260
Thou shalt have the fort.
MEL. Why, well.
Here let our hate be buried; and this
hand
Shall right us both. Give me thy agéd
breast
To compass.

CAL.          Nay, I do not love thee yet;
I cannot well endure to look on thee;
And, if I thought it were a courtesy,
Thou shouldst not have it. But I am
disgraced;
My offices are to be ta'en away;
And, if I did but hold this fort a day,
I do believe the king would take it from
me,                                            271
And give it thee, things are so strangely
carried.
Ne'er thank me for 't; but yet the king
shall know
There was some such thing in 't I told
him of,
And that I was an honest man.
MEL.                              He'll buy
That knowledge very dearly.—

*Enter Diphilus.*

                              Diph[ilus],
What news with thee?
DIPH.                    This were a night indeed
To do it in; the king hath sent for her.
MEL. She shall perform it then.—Go,
Diph[ilus],
And take from this good man, my
worthy friend,                                 280
The fort; he'll give it thee.
DIPH.                    Ha' you got that?
CAL. Art thou of the same breed? Canst
thou deny
This to the king too?
DIPH.                    With a confidence
As great as his.
CAL. Faith, like enough.
MEL. Away, and use him kindly.
CAL.                    Touch not me;
I hate the whole strain. If thou follow
me
A great way off, I'll give thee up the
fort—
And hang yourselves!
MEL.          Begone.
DIPH.                    He's finely wrought.[1]
          *Exeunt Cal[ianax], Diph[ilus].*
MEL. This is a night, spite of astrono-
mers,[2]                                       290
To do the deed in. I will wash the stain
That rests upon our house off with his
blood.

---

[1] Wrought up, excited.
[2] Astrologers.

*Enter Amintor.*

AMIN. Melantius, now assist me. If thou
    beest
    That which thou say'st, assist me. I
    have lost
    All my distempers, and have found a
    rage
    So pleasing! Help me.
MEL. [*Aside.*]      Who can see him thus,
    And not swear vengeance?—What's
    the matter, friend?
AMIN. Out with thy sword; and, hand in
    hand with me,
    Rush to the chamber of this hated king,
    And sink him with the weight of all his
    sins                      300
    To hell forever.
MEL.        'Twere a rash attempt,
    Not to be done with safety. Let your
    reason
    Plot your revenge, and not your passion.
AMIN. If thou refusest me in these ex-
    tremes,
    Thou art no friend. He sent for her to
    me;
    By heaven, to me, myself! And, I must
    tell ye,
    I love her as a stranger; there is worth
    In that vild woman, worthy things,
    Melantius;
    And she repents. I'll do 't myself alone,
    Though I be slain. Farewell.
MEL. [*Aside.*]      He'll overthrow  310
    My whole design with madness.—
    Amintor,
    Think what thou doest. I dare as much
    as valor,
    But 'tis the king, the king, the king,
    Amintor,
    With whom thou fightest!—(*Aside.*) I
    know he's honest,[1]
    And this will work with him.
AMIN.           I cannot tell
    What thou hast said; but thou hast
    charmed my sword
    Out of my hand, and left me shaking
    here,
    Defenseless.
MEL.         I will take it up for thee.
AMIN. What a wild beast is uncollected[2]
    man!

[1] Loyal.
[2] Not self-controlled.

The thing that we call honor bears us all
Headlong unto sin, and yet itself is
    nothing.                     321
MEL. Alas, how variable are thy thoughts!
AMIN. Just like my fortunes. I was run
    to [3] that
    I purposed to have chid thee for. Some
    plot
    I did distrust thou hadst against the
    king,
    By that old fellow's carriage. But take
    heed;
    There's not the least limb growing to
    a king
    But carries thunder in 't.
MEL.             I have none
    Against him.
AMIN.        Why, come, then; and still
    remember
    We may not think revenge.
MEL.      I will remember. *Exeunt.*  330

ACTUS V. [SCENA i.

*An anteroom opening upon the king's bed-
    chamber curtained off on the inner
                     stage.]*

*Enter Evadne and a Gentleman [of the bed-
                  chamber].*

EVAD. Sir, is the king abed?
GENT.           Madam, an hour ago.
EVAD. Give me the key, then, and let
    none be near;
    'Tis the king's pleasure.
GENT. I understand you, madam; would
    'twere mine!
    I must not wish good rest unto your
    ladyship.
EVAD. You talk, you talk.
GENT. 'Tis all I dare do, madam; but
    the king
    Will wake, and then—
EVAD. Saving your imagination, pray,
    good night, sir.
GENT. A good night be it, then, and a
    long one, madam.               10
    I am gone.                    *Exit.*
EVAD. The night grows horrible, and all
    about me
    Like my black purpose. O, the con-
    science              *King abed.*
    Of a lost virgin, whither wilt thou pull
    me?

[3] *I.e.*, just on the point of doing.

To what things dismal as the depth of
hell
Wilt thou provoke me?  Let no woman
dare
From this hour be disloyal, if her heart
be flesh,
If she have blood, and can fear.  'Tis a
daring
Above that desperate fool's that left
his peace,
And went to sea to fight; 'tis so many
sins,                                          20
An age cannot prevent [1] 'em, and so
great
The gods want mercy for.  Yét I must
through 'em.
I have begun a slaughter on my honor,
And I must end it there.—A sleeps.
Good heavens!
Why give you peace to this untemperate
beast,
That hath so long transgressed you?
I must kill him,
And I will do 't bravely; the mere joy
Tells me, I merit in it.  Yet I must not
Thus tamely do it as he sleeps—that
were
To rock him to another world.   My
vengeance                                      30
Shall take him waking, and then lay be-
fore him
The number of his wrongs and punish-
ments.
I'll shape his sins like Furies, till I
waken
His evil angel, his sick conscience,
And then I'll strike him dead.—King,
by your leave!—
        *Ties his arms to the bed.*
I dare not trust your strength; your
grace and I
Must grapple upon even terms no more.
So, if he rail me not from my resolu-
tion,
I shall be strong enough.—My lord the
king!
My lord!—A sleeps, as if he meant to
wake                                           40
No more.—My lord!—Is he not dead
already?—
Sir!  My lord!
KING.  Who's that?
EVAD.  O, you sleep soundly, sir!

[1] Recount (?).  1619 edn. has *repent.*

KING.                    My dear Evadne,
I have been dreaming of thee; come to
bed.
EVAD.  I am come at length, sir; but how
welcome?
KING.  What pretty new device is this,
Evadne?
What, do you tie me to you?  By my love,
This is a quaint one.  Come, my dear,
and kiss me.
I'll be thy Mars; to bed, my Queen of
Love.                                          50
Let us be caught together, that the
gods
May see and envy our embraces.
EVAD.                    Stay, sir, stay;
You are too hot, and I have brought
you physic
To temper your high veins.
KING.  Prithee, to bed then; let me take
it warm.
There thou shalt know the state of my
body better.
EVAD.  I know you have a surfeited, foul
body,
And you must bleed.  [*Draws a knife.*]
KING.  Bleed!
EVAD.  Ay, you shall bleed.  Lie still; and,
if the devil,                                  60
Your lust, will give you leave, repent.
This steel
Comes to redeem the honor that you
stole,
King, my fair name, which nothing but
thy death
Can answer to the world.
KING.                    How's this, Evadne?
EVAD.  I am not she; nor bear I in this
breast
So much cold spirit to be called a woman.
I am a tiger; I am anything
That knows not pity.  Stir not!  If thou
dost,
I'll take thee unprepared, thy fears
upon thee,
That make thy sins look double, and
so send thee                                   70
(By my revenge, I will!) to look [2] those
torments
Prepared for such black souls.
KING.  Thou dost not mean this; 'tis im-
possible.
Thou art too sweet and gentle.
[2] Behold.

EVAD.                    No, I am not;
I am as foul as thou art, and can number
As many such hells here.  I was once
    fair;
Once I was lovely, not a blowing rose
More chastely sweet, till thou, thou,
    thou, foul canker
(Stir not!), didst poison me.  I was a
    world of virtue,
Till your cursed court and you (hell
    bless you for 't!)                    80
With your temptations on temptations
Made me give up mine honor, for which,
    king,
I am come to kill thee.
KING.                    No!
EVAD.                    I am.
KING.                    Thou art not!
I prithee, speak not these things.  Thou
    art gentle,
And wert not meant thus rugged.
EVAD.                    Peace, and hear me.
Stir nothing but your tongue, and that
    for mercy
To those above us, by whose lights I vow,
Those blessed fires [1] that shot to see
    our sin,
If thy hot soul had substance with thy
    blood,
I would kill that too; which, being past
    my steel,                    90
My tongue shall reach.  Thou art a
    shameless villain,
A thing out of the overcharge of nature,
Sent like a thick cloud to disperse a
    plague
Upon weak, catching [2] women—such
    a tyrant
That for his lust would sell away his
    subjects,
Ay, all his heaven hereafter!
KING.                    Hear, Evadne,
Thou soul of sweetness, hear!  I am thy
    king.
EVAD. Thou art my shame!  Lie still;
    there's none about you,
Within your cries; all promises of safety
Are but deluding dreams.  Thus, thus,
    thou foul man,                    100
Thus I begin my vengeance! *Stabs him.*
KING.                    Hold, Evadne!
I do command thee hold.
EVAD.                    I do not mean, sir,

To part so fairly with you; we must
    change
More of these love tricks yet.
KING.                    What bloody villain
Provoked thee to this murther?
EVAD.                    Thou, thou monster!
KING. O!
EVAD. Thou kept'st me brave [3] at court,
    and whored me, king;
Then married me to a young, noble
    gentleman,
And whored me still.
KING.                    Evadne, pity me!
EVAD. Hell take me, then!  This for my
    lord, Amintor!                    110
This for my noble brother!  And this
    stroke
For the most wronged of women!
                    *Kills him.*
KING.                    O, I die!
EVAD. Die all our faults together!  I for-
    give thee.                    *Exit.* [4]

*Enter Two of the bedchamber.*

    1. Come, now she's gone, let's enter;
the king expects it, and will be angry.
    2. 'Tis a fine wench; we'll have a snap
at her one of these nights, as she goes from
him.
    1. Content.  How quickly he had done
with her!  I see kings can do no more  [120
that way than other mortal people.
    2. How fast [5] he is!  I cannot hear him
    breathe.
    1. Either the tapers give a feeble light,
Or he looks very pale.
    2.                    And so he does.
Pray heaven he be well; let's look.—
    Alas!
He's stiff, wounded, and dead!  Treason,
    treason!
    1. Run forth and call! *Exit* [2] *Gent[leman].*
    2. Treason, treason!
    1.                    This will be laid on us.
Who can believe a woman could do this?

*Enter Cleon and Lysippus.*

CLE. How now!  Where's the traitor?
    1. Fled, fled away; but there her woeful
    act                    131
Lies still.

[1] Shooting stars.          [2] Easily infected.
[3] Well-dressed.            [5] Fast asleep.
[4] Original reads *Exeunt.*

CLE. Her act! A woman!

LYS.                    Where's the body?

1.                              There.

LYS. Farewell, thou worthy man! There
    were two bonds
  That tied our loves, a brother and a
    king,
  The least of which might fetch a flood
    of tears;
  But such the misery of greatness is,
  They have no time to mourn.  Then,
    pardon me!
  Sirs, which way went she?

*Enter Strato.*

STRA.                    Never follow her,
  For she, alas, was but the instrument.
  News is now brought in that Melantius
  Has got the fort, and stands upon the
    wall,                              142
  And with a loud voice calls those few
    that pass
  At this dead time of night, delivering
  The innocence of this act.

LYS.                        Gentlemen,
  I am your king.

STRA.            We do acknowledge it.

LYS. I would I were not!  Follow, all;
    for this
  Must have a sudden stop.        *Exeunt.*

[SCENA ii.

*Before the fort.*]

*Enter Melant[ius], Diph[ilus], Cal[ianax] on
                              the walls.*

MEL. If the dull people can believe I am
    armed
  (Be constant, Diph[ilus]), now we have
    time
  Either to bring our banished honors
    home,
  Or create new ones in our ends.

DIPH.                       I fear not;
  My spirit lies not that way.—Courage,
    Calianax!

CAL. Would I had any!  You should
    quickly know it.

MEL. Speak to the people; thou art elo-
    quent.

CAL. 'Tis a fine eloquence to come to the
    gallows.
  You were born to be my end: the devil
    take you!

Now must I hang for company?  'Tis
    strange                            10
  I should be old, and neither wise nor
    valiant.

*Enter Lysip[pus], Diag[oras], Cleon, Strat[o],
                              Guard.*

LYS. See where he stands, as boldly con-
    fident
  As if he had his full command about
    him.

STRA. He looks as if he had the better
    cause, sir;
  Under your gracious pardon, let me
    speak it!
  Though he be mighty-spirited, and for-
    ward
  To all great things, to all things of that
    danger
  Worse men shake at the telling of, yet
    certainly
  I do believe him noble, and this action
  Rather pulled on than sought.    His
    mind was ever                      20
  As worthy as his hand.

LYS.              'Tis my fear, too.
  Heaven forgive all!—Summon him,
    Lord Cleon.

CLE. Ho, from the walls there!

MEL.            Worthy Cleon, welcome.
  We could 'a' wished you here, lord;
    you are honest.

CAL. (*Aside.*) Well, thou art as flatter-
    ing a knave, though
  I dare not tell thee so—

LYS.              Melantius!

MEL.                        Sir?

LYS. I am sorry that we meet thus; our
    old love
  Never required such distance.    Pray
    heaven,
  You have not left yourself, and sought
    this safety
  More out of fear than honor!  You have
    lost                              30
  A noble master, which your faith, Me-
    lantius,
  Some think might have preserved; yet
    you know best.

CAL. [*Aside.*] When time was,[1] I was mad;
    some that dares fight
  I hope will pay this rascal.

[1] Once upon a time.

MEL. Royal young man, those tears look
　　lovely on thee;
Had they been shed for a deserving one,
They had been lasting monuments. Thy
　　brother,
Whilst he was good, I called him king,
　　and served him
With that strong faith, that most un-
　　wearied valor,
Pulled people from the farthest sun to
　　seek him,　　　　　　　　　　40
And buy his friendship. I was then his
　　soldier.
But, since his hot pride drew him to
　　disgrace me,
And brand my noble actions with his
　　lust
(That never-cured dishonor of my sister,
Base stain of whore, and, which is worse,
　　the joy
To make it still so), like myself, thus I
Have flung him off with my allegiance,
And stand here, mine own justice, to
　　revenge
What I have suffered in him, and this
　　old man
Wronged almost to lunacy.
CAL.　　　　　　　　　　Who, I?　50
　　You would draw me in. I have had no
　　wrong;
I do disclaim ye all.
MEL.　　　　　　　The short is this:
'Tis no ambition to lift up myself
Urgeth me thus; I do desire again
To be a subject, so I may be free.
If not, I know my strength, and will
　　unbuild
This goodly town. Be speedy, and be
　　wise,
In a reply.
STRA.　　　　　Be sudden, sir, to tie
All up again. What's done is past re-
　　call,
And past you to revenge; and there are
　　thousands　　　　　　　　　　60
That wait for such a troubled hour as
　　this.
Throw him the blank.
LYS.　　　　　　Melantius, write in that
Thy choice; my seal is at it.
　　　　　　[Throws a paper to Melantius.]
MEL. It was our honors drew us to this act,
Not gain; and we will only work our
　　pardons.

CAL. Put my name in too.
DIPH.　　　　　You disclaimed us all
But now, Calianax.
CAL.　　　　　　That's all one.
I'll not be hanged hereafter by a trick;
I'll have it in.
MEL.　　　　You shall, you shall.—
Come to the back gate, and we'll call
　　you king,　　　　　　　　　　70
And give you up the fort.
LYS.　　　　Away, away!　*Exeunt omnes.*

[SCENA iii.

*An anteroom to Amintor's apartment.*]

*Enter Aspatia in man's apparel [and with
　　her face disguised with counterfeit scars].*

ASP. This is my fatal hour.　Heaven
　　may forgive
My rash attempt, that causelessly hath
　　laid
Griefs on me that will never let me rest,
And put a woman's heart into my
　　breast.
It is more honor for you that I die,
For she that can endure the misery
That I have on me, and be patient
　　too,
May live and laugh at all that you can
　　do.—

*Enter Servant.*

God save you, sir!
SER.　　　　And you, sir!　What's your
　　business?
ASP. With you, sir, now; to do me the
　　fair office　　　　　　　　　　10
To help me to your lord.
SER.　　　　What, would you serve him?
ASP. I'll do him any service; but, to haste,
For my affairs are earnest, I desire
To speak with him.
SER. Sir, because you are in such haste,
　　I would
Be loath to delay you longer. You can
　　not.
ASP. It shall become you, though, to tell
　　your lord.
SER. Sir, he will speak with nobody.
ASP.　　　　　　This is most strange.
Art thou gold-proof? There's for thee;
　　help me to him.　　　[*Gives money.*]
SER. Pray be not angry, sir; I'll do my
　　best.　　　　　　　　*Exit.*　20

Asp. How stubbornly this fellow answered me!
There is a vild, dishonest trick in man,
More than in women. All the men I meet
Appear thus to me, are harsh and rude,
And have a subtilty in everything,
Which love could never know; but we fond women
Harbor the easiest and the smoothest thoughts,
And think all shall go so. It is unjust
That men and women should be matched together.

*Enter Amintor and his Man.*

Amin. Where is he?
Ser. There, my lord.
Amin. What would you, sir? 30
Asp. Please it your lordship to command your man
Out of the room, I shall deliver things
Worthy your hearing.
Amin. Leave us. [*Exit Servant.*]
Asp. (*Aside.*) O, that that shape
Should bury falsehood in it!
Amin. Now your will, sir.
Asp. When you know me, my lord, you needs must guess
My business; and I am not hard to know;
For, till the chance of war marked this smooth face
With these few blemishes, people would call me
My sister's picture, and her mine. In short, 39
I am the brother to the wronged Aspatia.
Amin. The wronged Aspatia! Would thou wert so too
Unto the wronged Amintor! Let me kiss
That hand of thine, in honor that I bear
Unto the wronged Aspatia. Here I stand
That did it. Would he could not! Gentle youth,
Leave me, for there is something in thy looks
That calls my sins in a most hideous form
Into my mind; and I have grief enough
Without thy help.

Asp. I would I could with credit!
Since I was twelve years old, I had not seen 50
My sister till this hour I now arrived;
She sent for me to see her marriage—
A woeful one! But they that are above
Have ends in everything. She used few words,
But yet enough to make me understand
The baseness of the injuries you did her.
That little training I have had is war;
I may behave myself rudely in peace;
I would not, though. I shall not need to tell you
I am but young, and would be loath to lose 60
Honor, that is not easily gained again.
Fairly I mean to deal; the age is strict
For [1] single combats; and we shall be stopped,
If it be published. If you like your sword,
Use it; if mine appear a better to you,
Change; for the ground is this, and this the time,
To end our difference. [*Draws.*]
Amin. Charitable youth,
If thou beest such, think not I will maintain
So strange a wrong; and, for thy sister's sake,
Know that I could not think that desperate thing 70
I durst not do; yet, to enjoy this world,
I would not see her, for, beholding thee,
I am I know not what. If I have aught
That may content thee, take it, and be-gone,
For death is not so terrible as thou;
Thine eyes shoot guilt into me.
Asp. Thus, she swore
Thou wouldst behave thyself, and give me words
That would fetch tears into my eyes; and so
Thou dost indeed. But yet she bade me watch
Lest I were cozened; and be sure to fight 80
Ere I returned.
Amin. That must not be with me.
For her I'll die directly; but against her
Will never hazard it.

[1] Against.

Asp.                    You must be urged.
    I do not deal uncivilly with those
    That dare to fight; but such a one as you
    Must be used thus.        *She strikes him.*
Amin.        I prithee, youth, take heed.
    Thy sister is a thing to me so much
    Above mine honor that I can endure
    All this—Good gods! A blow I can en-
        dure!
    But stay not, lest thou draw a timeless
        death                                    90
    Upon thyself.
Asp.            Thou art some prating fellow,
    One that hath studied out a trick to
        talk,
    And move soft-hearted people; to be
        kicked—            *She kicks him.*
    Thus to be kicked!—(*Aside.*)    Why
        should he be so slow
    In giving me my death?
Amin.                        A man can bear
    No more, and keep his flesh. Forgive
        me, then!
    I would endure yet, if I could.    Now
        show                        [*Draws.*]
    The spirit thou pretendest, and under-
        stand
    Thou hast no hour to live.
            *They fight [; Aspatia is wounded].*
                    What dost thou mean?
    Thou canst not fight. The blows thou
        mak'st at me                            100
    Are quite besides;[1] and those I offer
        at thee,
    Thou spread'st thine arms, and tak'st
        upon thy breast,
    Alas, defenseless!
Asp.            I have got enough,
    And my desire. There is no place so fit
    For me to die as here.        [*Falls.*]

*Enter Evadne, her hands bloody, with a*
                            *knife.*

Evad. Amintor, I am loaden with events,
    That fly to make thee happy; I have
        joys
    That in a moment can call back thy
        wrongs,
    And settle thee in thy free state again.
    It is Evadne still that follows thee,    110
    But not her mischiefs.
Amin. Thou canst not fool me to believe
        again;

[1] To one side.

But thou hast looks and things so full
    of news
    That I am stayed.
Evad. Noble Amintor, put off thy amaze,
    Let thine eyes loose, and speak. Am I
        not fair?
    Looks not Evadne beauteous with these
        rites now?
    Were those hours half so lovely in thine
        eyes
    When our hands met before the holy
        man?
    I was too foul within to look fair then; 120
    Since I knew ill, I was not free till now.
Amin. There is presage of some impor-
        tant thing
    About thee, which it seems thy tongue
        hath lost.
    Thy hands are bloody, and thou hast
        a knife.
Evad. In this consists thy happiness and
        mine.
    Joy to Amintor, for the king is dead!
Amin. Those have most power to hurt us
        that we love;
    We lay our sleeping lives within their
        arms.
    Why, thou hast raised up mischief to
        his height,
    And found one to outname[2] thy other
        faults;                                130
    Thou hast no intermission of thy sins,
    But all thy life is a continued ill.
    Black is thy color now, disease thy na-
        ture.
    "Joy to Amintor!" Thou hast touched
        a life,
    The very name of which had power to
        chain
    Up all my rage, and calm my wildest
        wrongs.
Evad. 'Tis done; and, since I could not
        find a way
    To meet thy love so clear as through
        his life,
    I cannot now repent it.
Amin. Couldst thou procure the gods to
        speak to me,                            140
    To bid me love this woman and forgive,
    I think I should fall out with them. Be-
        hold,
    Here lies a youth whose wounds bleed
        in my breast,

[2] Surpass.

Sent by a violent fate to fetch his death
From my slow hand! And, to augment
   my woe,
You now are present, stained with a
   king's blood
Violently shed. This keeps night here,
And throws an unknown wilderness [1]
   about me.

ASP. O, O, O!

AMIN. No more; pursue me not.

EVAD.                    Forgive me then, 150
And take me to thy bed; we may not
   part.                    [Kneels.]

AMIN. Forbear, be wise, and let my rage
go this way.

EVAD. 'Tis you that I would stay, not it.

AMIN.                    Take heed;
It will return with me.

EVAD.                    If it must be,
I shall not fear to meet it. Take me
home.

AMIN. Thou monster of cruelty, forbear!

EVAD. For heaven's sake, look more calm!
   Thine eyes are sharper
Than thou canst make thy sword.

AMIN.                    Away, away!
Thy knees are more to me than violence.
I am worse than sick to see knees fol-
   low me                    160
For that I must not grant. For God's
sake, stand.

EVAD. Receive me, then.

AMIN.          I dare not stay thy language.
In midst of all my anger and my grief,
Thou dost awake something that trou-
   bles me,
And says I loved thee once. I dare not
   stay;
There is no end of woman's reasoning.
                 *Leaves her.*

EVAD. [*Rising.*] Amintor, thou shalt love
me now again.
Go; I am calm. Farewell, and peace
   forever!
Evadne, whom thou hat'st, will die
   for thee.          *Kills herself.* 169

AMIN. I have a little human nature yet,
That's left for thee, that bids me stay
   thy hand.                    *Returns.*

EVAD. Thy hand was welcome, but it
came too late.
O, I am lost! The heavy sleep makes
   haste.                    *She dies.*

[1] Wildness.

ASP. O, O, O!

AMIN. This earth of mine doth tremble,
   and I feel
A stark affrighted motion in my blood.
My soul grows weary of her house, and I
All over am a trouble to myself.
There is some hidden power in these
   dead things                    179
That calls my flesh into 'em; I am cold.
Be resolute and bear 'em company.
There's something yet, which I am loath
   to leave.
There's man enough in me to meet the
   fears
That death can bring; and yet would it
   were done!
I can find nothing in the whole dis-
   course
Of death I durst not meet the boldest
   way;
Yet still, betwixt the reason and the act,
The wrong I to Aspatia did stands up;
I have not such another fault to answer.
Though she may justly arm herself
   with scorn                    190
And hate of me, my soul will part less
   troubled,
When I have paid to her in tears my
   sorrow.
I will not leave this act unsatisfied,
If all that's left in me can answer it.

ASP. Was it a dream? There stands Amintor still,
Or I dream still.

AMIN. How dost thou? Speak; receive
   my love and help.
Thy blood climbs up to his old place
   again;
There's hope of thy recovery.

ASP. Did you not name Aspatia?

AMIN.                    I did. 200

ASP. And talked of tears and sorrow unto
   her?

AMIN. 'Tis true; and, till these happy
   signs in thee
Stayéd my course, 'twas thither I was
   going.

ASP. Thou art there already, and these
   wounds are hers.
Those threats I brought with me sought
   not revenge,
But came to fetch this blessing from thy
   hand.
I am Aspatia yet.

AMIN. Dare my soul ever look abroad again?

ASP. I shall sure live, Amintor; I am well.
A kind of healthful joy wanders within
    me.     210

AMIN. The world wants lines to excuse
    thy loss;
Come, let me bear thee to some place
    of help.

ASP. Amintor, thou must stay; I must
    rest here;
My strength begins to disobey my will.
How dost thou, my blessed soul? I would
    fain live
Now, if I could. Wouldst thou have
    loved me, then?

AMIN. Alas,
All that I am 's not worth a hair from
    thee!

ASP. Give me thy hand; mine hands grope
    up and down,
And cannot find thee; I am wondrous
    sick.     220
Have I thy hand, Amintor?

AMIN. Thou greatest blessing of the world,
    thou hast.

ASP. I do believe thee better than my
    sense.
O, I must go! Farewell!     *Dies.*

AMIN. She sounds.[1]—Aspatia!—Help! For
    God's sake, water,
Such as may chain life ever to this
    frame!—
Aspatia, speak!—What, no help? Yet I
    fool![2]
I'll chafe her temples. Yet there noth-
    ing stirs.
Some hidden power tell her Amintor
    calls,
And let her answer me!—Aspatia,
    speak!—     230
I have heard, if there be any life, but
    bow
The body thus, and it will show itself.
O, she is gone! I will not leave her yet.
Since out of justice we must challenge
    nothing,
I'll call it mercy, if you'll pity me,
You heavenly powers, and lend for some
    few years
The blessèd soul to this fair seat again!
No comfort comes; the gods deny me
    too.

    Swounds, swoons.     [2] Act foolishly.

I'll bow the body once again.—Aspa-
    tia!—
The soul is fled forever, and I wrong     240
Myself, so long to lose her company.
Must I talk now? Here's to be with
    thee, love!     *Kills himself.*

*Enter Servant.*

SER. This is a great grace to my lord,
to have the new king come to him. I must
tell him he is entering.—O, God!—Help,
help!

*Enter Lysip[pus], Melant[ius], Cal[ianax],*
*Cleon, Diph[ilus], Strato.*

LYS. Where's Amintor?

STRA. O, there, there!

LYS. How strange is this!

CAL.     What should we do here?

MEL. These deaths are such acquainted
    things with me     250
That yet my heart dissolves not. May
    I stand
Stiff here forever! Eyes, call up your
    tears!
This is Amintor. Heart, he was my
    friend.
Melt! Now it flows.—Amintor, give a
    word
To call me to thee.

AMIN. O!

MEL. Melantius calls his friend Amintor.
    O!
Thy arms are kinder to me than thy
    tongue!
Speak, speak!

AMIN. What?     260

MEL. That little word was worth all the
    sounds
That ever I shall hear again.

DIPH.     O, brother,
Here lies your sister slain! You lose
    yourself
In sorrow there.

MEL.     Why, Diphilus, it is
A thing to laugh at, in respect of this.
Here was my sister, father, brother,
    son—
All that I had.—Speak once again;
    what youth
Lies slain there by thee?

AMIN.     'Tis Aspatia.

My last is said. Let me give up my soul
Into thy bosom.            [*Dies.*]    270
CAL. What's that? What's that? Aspatia!
MEL.                    I never did
    Repent the greatness of my heart till
        now;
    It will not burst at need.
    CAL. My daughter dead here too! And
you have all fine new tricks to grieve; but
I ne'er knew any but direct crying.
MEL. I am a prattler; but no more.
                    [*Offers to stab himself.*]
DIPH.                    Hold, brother!
LYS. Stop him.
DIPH. Fie, how unmanly was this offer
    in you!
    Does this become our strain?    280
    CAL. I know not what the matter
is, but I am grown very kind, and am
friends with you. You have given me that
among you will kill me quickly; but I'll
go home, and live as long as I can. [*Exit.*]

MEL. His spirit is but poor that can be
    kept
    From death for want of weapons.
    Is not my hands a weapon sharp enough
    To stop my breath? Or, if you tie down
        those,
    I vow, Amintor, I will never eat,    290
    Or drink, or sleep, or have to do with
        that
    That may preserve life! This I swear
        to keep.
LYS. Look to him, though, and bear those
    bodies in.
    May this a fair example be to me
    To rule with temper; [1] for, on lustful
        kings,
    Unlooked-for, sudden deaths from God
        are sent,
    But cursed is he that is their instrument.
                        [*Exeunt.*]
                    FINIS.
[1] Temperance, self-restraint.

# PHILIP MASSINGER

Just as Fletcher dominated the field of English playwriting from Beaumont's retirement till his own death in 1625, Philip Massinger, who had been Fletcher's quondam collaborator, dominated it from 1625 till his own death in 1640, though few modern critics, with the exception of William Archer, would place him in the same rank as his predecessors. Archer, however, after having praised Thomas Middleton as "a real dramatist, who, in another environment, would have been capable of working up to higher standards," went on: "And if this is true of Middleton, far more is it true of Philip Massinger." After adding that "Massinger's fate has been curious and significant," Archer continued judiciously, "As a matter of fact, Massinger was, in a sane and sober way, one of the best writers of the period." In other words, in accordance with Archer's thesis in *The Old Drama and the New*, Massinger was one of the very few playwrights of the time who did not allow the poetic element in his plays to master the dramatic element: "But when we come to specifically dramatic gifts . . . we find him head and shoulders above the average of his fellows. Shakespeare apart, of course, his only rivals are Beaumont and Fletcher; and in my judgment he not only had a cleaner, saner mind than they, but more real ingenuity and a truer sense of dramatic effect." After then comparing Massinger's conception of the drama with that of Lope de Vega and Calderon, Dumas *père* and Victor Hugo, Archer extended his encomium by finding that for once he could agree with Swinburne, who in his *Contemporaries of Shakespeare* had stated: "In his own day Massinger would seem to have received, if not such honours as lovers of English dramatic poetry might think due to him in such days as ours, yet undoubtedly very much more recognition than was accorded to poets of far purer and more potent inspiration." Admitting that as a poet Massinger could not be classed with Shakespeare, Webster, Tourneur, or Ford (arranged in descending order), Swinburne asserted that "it is no less certain that the best of them cannot be ranked as an artist, I do not say equal, but comparable, to Massinger." And Swinburne quoted Coleridge's opinion that Massinger is "always entertaining" and that "his plays have the interest of novels," to support his own view that this was "but one of the excellent qualities which make the long eclipse of his fame so inexplicable."

Strangely enough, Massinger's most recent and most thorough biographer, T. A. Dunn, stops rather short of these praises in his *Philip Massinger/The Man and the Playwright* (Edinburgh and London, 1957), where early in his preface he declares: "He is not, it must be admitted, a great, or even always a very good, dramatist. Nevertheless, his plays are of considerable interest as samples of the romantic tragicomedies that held the stage after the death of Shakespeare." Warning his readers that he would go only incidentally into the "tangled undergrowth of collaboration that surrounds the Beaumont-Fletcher *corpus*," and would concentrate on the plays which are definitely Massinger's, Dunn explained why his own thorough study of Massinger's dedications, prologues, epilogues, and so forth, in addition to new research in the records of Wiltshire and Gloucestershire, had enabled him to produce the first full-length biography in English, and that Thomas Davies's "Some Account of the Life and Writings of Philip Massinger" in 1789 was outdated, J. Phelan's research article, "The Life of Philip Massinger" (*Anglia*, 1879–80) was speculative and unreliable,

Alfred H. Cruickshank's *Philip Massinger* (Oxford, 1920) was inadequate, and Maurice Chelli's *Le Drame de Massinger* (Lyons, 1923) was "youthful." The condition of Massinger criticism is further illustrated by the fact that when the *Times Literary Supplement* published a feature article on the tercentenary of Massinger's death ("Philip Massinger, 1583–1640," *TLS*, March 16, 1940), in which the anonymous author suggested that a modern film producer would find first-class material for scenarios in Massinger's plays, Clifford Leech felt called upon to protest various points in the article and to maintain that only Massinger in the Caroline age had inherited the masculine outlook of Jonson and Chapman (*TLS*, March 23, 1940).

In spite of Dunn's disclaimer of interest in the problem of Massinger's collaboration with other dramatists, several modern scholars have attempted to attack this problem from new angles. Frederic L. Jones has made "An Experiment with Massinger's Verse" (*PMLA*, 1932), dealing statistically with Massinger's use of the words *of* and *to* as parts of split phrases at the ends of lines; W. J. Lawrence has studied his use of full stops and commas in stage directions ("Massinger's Punctuation," *Criterion*, 1932), and Cyrus Hoy has written on "Verbal Formulae in the Plays of Philip Massinger" (*SP*, 1959).

As established by Dunn, the records of the parish church of St. Thomas's, Salisbury, register the baptism of "Philip Messanger, the son of Arthur," on November 24, 1583. Since the register adds, "Mr. Messenger's wiffe churched the xvi of December, her crisom xii d.," Dunn concluded from this ceremony and payment that the child was probably born in Salisbury, and not at Wilton, the nearby estate of the Earl of Pembroke, his father's employer and patron. Though the name of Massinger (usually spelled "Messager" or "Messenger") appears often in the Gloucester and Gloucestershire records, Dunn decided that Arthur's branch of the family had been established in Wiltshire, and especially in Salisbury, for a long time, and had been quite prominent in the town, particularly in the legal profession, for which both the boy's father and his uncle, Walter, had been prepared at Oxford. Though nothing is known about his mother, his father graduated from St. Alban's Hall, Oxford, in 1571, was elected a Fellow at Merton in 1572, and proceeded M.A. in 1577. Arthur Massinger, however, must have had something of the adventurer in his nature, since Mark Eccles discovered a document (*TLS*, July 13, 1931) which showed that after Sir Humphrey Gilbert's first attempt to sail to the New World in 1578 and some of his company had refused to put to sea with him again, one of the "asured friends" who continued with him and Sir Walter Raleigh was an "Arthure Messinger, gent." Dunn is confident that, although there were apparently at least two other Arthur Messingers living in England at this time, Philip's father is the only one for whom clear connections with the courtly circle which planned such ventures can be found.

Of Philip's childhood, nothing is known. Dunn discounts the speculation of Francis Cunningham in his edition of the *Plays* in 1871 that the boy may have become a page in the service of the Countess of Pembroke, as Massinger lamented in his dedication of *The Bondman* (1624) (to Philip, Earl of Montgomery, the younger son of his father's patron and a man of his own age) that he "could never arrive at the happiness to be made known to your lordship." But the boy was probably educated at the Salisbury grammar school, and very likely saw Pembroke's troupe of players act at Wilton, where his father had become house-steward and agent to Henry Herbert, second Earl of Pembroke, and, on the Earl's death, retained this position with his son, the third Earl, who, with his brother, was to have the first folio of Shakespeare dedicated to him. Arthur Massinger was also a member of Parliament for Weymouth in 1588–9 and 1592–3, and for Shaftesbury in 1601, seats undoubtedly controlled by the Earl. Thus Philip's family was a good, respectable one of the professional class, in between that of the court and that of the tradesman. Certainly Philip regarded himself as a "gentleman" and often signed himself so. Since the Pembrokes spent much of their time in London as well as at Wilton, Arthur Massinger undoubtedly made frequent business trips there, and probably sometimes took his family with him. At any rate, by 1603 he had established a permanent residence there.

By this time young Philip was a student at St. Alban's Hall, his father's old college at Oxford. He matriculated there on May 14, 1602, as "Sarisburiensis generosi filius" —that is, "of Salisbury, son of a gentleman." Although Anthony à Wood later wrote in his *Athenae Oxonienses* (1691–2) that Massinger spent more time on poetry and romances than he did on logic and philosophy, Gerard Langbaine simultaneously stated in his *An Account of the English Dramatic Poets* that Massinger "closely pursued his studies in Alban Hall, for 3 or 4 years space." Whether Massinger was a good or a bad student at Oxford, he never took his degree. Wood, stating that the boy stayed in college for about four years, while he was financed by Pembroke, implied that he had to leave because Pembroke withdrew his support when he decided that the other was devoting too much attention to literature. But Dunn, rejecting Wood's speculation as unlikely because of the interest of all the Herberts in the arts, believed that Massinger must have been financed by his father. While at Oxford, the boy—to judge from his later writing—gleaned a sufficient knowledge of classical mythology and Greek and Roman history to allude to them with fair facility, though Dunn suggests that he could also have got this knowledge from general works in English such as Golding's *Metamorphoses*, North's *Plutarch*, or Lodge's *Seneca*. His apparent ability to read both French and Spanish with some ease came from outside his college courses, since modern languages were not yet taught at the universities. Although William Gifford in his edition of the *Plays* in 1813 used the rumored conversion of Massinger to Roman Catholicism while at college as a reason for the boy's leaving prematurely, the playwright's religious affiliations are only speculative, though there are some hints in his later writings that he may have become a convert at some time in his life.

In other words, there is no contemporary documentary evidence on Massinger's life from the time of his matriculation at Oxford until 1613, when he and two other young playwrights, Robert Daborne and Nathan Field, wrote a tripartite letter from some unspecified debtors' prison asking Philip Henslowe (whom they deferentially called "Mr. Hinchlow") to advance them money on the next play they were working on (W. W. Greg, *Henslowe Papers*). Whether or not Henslowe bailed them out at this time, two years later Daborne and Massinger gave him their bond for £3, presumably to pay off more debts. There is no good reason to suppose, as J. Meissner did in "Die Englischen Komoedianten żur Zeit Shakespeares in Oesterreich" (*Beiträge zur Geschichte der Deutschen Litteratur*, Vienna, 1884), that Massinger was one of the company of English actors who toured Germany under John Greene, since in his works he shows no knowledge of German or the German character. And although he alludes many times to soldiering and often, as in *The Maid of Honor*, shows a close knowledge of military techniques and practices (a profession which he usually defends and praises), there is only this sort of unreliable internal evidence to support the theory that he spent some of these "lost years" in the army.

Thus, in spite of his aristocratic connections, Massinger got his first start in the drama as so many of his colleagues did—in the play factory of the leading business man in the Elizabethan theater. Philip Edwards has speculated at some length on why a moralistic gentleman like Massinger should have turned to the popular stage, and describes him as "one of the reluctant artists of his age; a gentleman in reduced circumstances who became a playwright as gentlewomen later became governesses" ("Massinger the Censor," *Essays on Shakespeare and Elizabethan Drama*). Many of the plays—independent works, collaborations, and revisions—were published either separately or in the 1647 Beaumont and Fletcher folio, but the only ones credited to him on their title pages during his lifetime were *The Virgin Martyr*, with Dekker (published 1622), and *The Fatal Dowry*, with his and Field's initials (published 1632). Dunn summarizes his total output as having consisted of twelve extant plays in which he collaborated, eleven which he probably simply revised, and fifteen which he wrote alone, besides at least fifteen, now lost, which are named in Herbert's Office Book or in the list of plays whose manuscripts John Warburton said were burned by his cook Betsy in the eighteenth century (W. W. Greg, "The Bakings of Betsy," *Library*, 1911). Thus in a period of some thirty years of industrious labor Massinger produced at least fifty-three plays, a figure placing him next to Thomas Heywood in output.

After thus serving his practical apprenticeship in playmaking, Massinger set out to acquire as many patrons as possible, most of them of minor prominence but of some wealth, as his dedications—often in a very humble and sycophantic vein—to some ten persons show. Several of these men, however, became his personal friends, though only one—the much younger Sir Aston Cokayne—remains known to literary historians today. But his main relations of this sort were with the Herbert family whom his father served. Dunn thinks that Lord Lovell's remark in III, i, of *A New Way to Pay Old Debts* about a "fitting difference between my footboy/And a gentleman by want compelled to serve me" was intended by Massinger as a description of himself. From the political point of view, some of the passages in Massinger's uncollaborated works like *The Bondman* and *The Maid of Honor*, produced in 1623 and 1626 by the King's Men, obliquely reflected the views held by the Herberts on King James and his favorite Duke of Buckingham. The Herberts were in the party of opposition, especially William, the third Earl of Pembroke. (Perhaps the most thorough discussion of Massinger's political views and his conception of monarchy is in Benjamin T. Spencer's "Philip Massinger," *Seventeenth Century Studies by Members of the Graduate School, University of Cincinnati*, Princeton University Press, 1933.) But Dunn, recalling Massinger's rhymed begging letter to the Earl in the late 1610s, concludes that this earl was of very little assistance, whereas he found William's brother Philip, Earl of Montgomery and later fourth Earl of Pembroke, much more approachable. In fact, John Aubrey, in his *Brief Lives, Chiefly of Contemporaries*, in the late Restoration, stated that Pembroke had paid Massinger a pension of £30 a year, and that this pension continued to be paid to his widow. No other reference to Massinger's marriage exists. The only suggestion that he had any children is found in a news item in *The London Magazine* for August 4, 1762, recording the death of "Miss Henrietta Massinger, a descendant of Massinger, the dramatic poet."

Massinger's later biography therefore consists almost entirely of his plays. For a period of two or three years between 1623 and 1626 he left the King's Men and went over to the Queen's Men under Beeston at the Cockpit, but he soon returned to the Blackfriars and the Globe. His output fell off slightly during his last years, and in the two years before he produced *The Guardian* in 1633 he had two serious failures, as the prologue frankly admitted. Apparently the usually quiet and modest Massinger had been accused of "arrogance" and "self-love" by another playwright, whom Dunn suspects of having been the aging Ben Jonson. Although Jonson never mentioned Massinger anywhere by name, this was the time at which Ben was at his most quarrelsome and pugnacious as a result of the failure of his *The New Inn* and his running fight with Inigo Jones. It had been suggested long before by Davies that Massinger had fallen afoul of Jonson well before 1630, but Dunn thinks this would have been unlikely for a newcomer like Massinger. Dunn's only explanation for this quarrel is that perhaps, "with Fletcher dead and Shirley hardly yet in the full flood of his production, for a brief period he allowed himself to feel, quite justifiably, cock of the theatrical walk." If so, however, this proud mood did not last, since soon afterward, although only in his early fifties, Massinger referred to himself in the epilogue to *The Bashful Lover* (acted 1636; printed 1655) as "a strange old fellow" and in the epilogue to *The Guardian* (acted 1633; printed 1655) complained that "he grows old."

According to Aubrey, Massinger died "about the 66th yeare of his age: went to bed well, and dyed suddenly—but not of the plague." The records of the church of St. Saviour (now Southwark Cathedral) show that he was buried on March 18, 1640.

The somewhat peculiar entry reads: "Philip Massenger, Strang, in ye church. G— £2.0.0," but why he was regarded as a "Stranger," or outsider, in a Bankside parish is unexplained. Perhaps it was because he was, after all, a Roman Catholic. Another unusual circumstance of his burial is indicated in the title of an elegiac poem written by his good friend, Sir Aston Cokayne: "an Epitaph on Mr. John Fletcher and Mr. Philip Massinger, Who Lie Buried Both in One Grave in St. Mary Overy's Church in Southwark." Aubrey, telling of his own examination of the register of St. Saviour's ("vulgo St. Mary's Overy's," as he puts it—that is, colloquially known under the latter name), was apparently wrongly informed "at the place where he dyed, which was at the Bankes side, near the then playhouse," that Massinger was buried in the churchyard near the Bullhead Tavern instead of in the church itself, as shown in the record. Cokayne's poem, however, together with other remarks by him, shows how the tradition of the community of relationship between Massinger and Fletcher was physically as well as symbolically preserved. Cokayne's efforts to maintain his friend's reputation continued till his death in 1684, but there are few other references to him in the late seventeenth century. In the eighteenth century several adaptations of Massinger's plays led to a brief revival, aided by the editions of Thomas Coxeter in 1759 and 1761 and J. Monck Mason in 1779. The twice reprinted edition by William Gifford (1805, 1813, 1850), together with Cunningham's revision of it in 1870, kept public interest alive in the nineteenth century. Twentieth-century opinion has already been discussed.

## A NEW WAY TO PAY OLD DEBTS

Although Massinger wrote only two unaided comedies of social satire, *A New Way to Pay Old Debts* and *The City Madam* (acted 1626; printed 1658), it is hard to understand why he did not write more. The tragicomedy *The Roman Actor* (acted 1626; printed 1629) was his own favorite, but it has been *A New Way* which has survived on the living stage down to our own time, largely because its villain, Sir Giles Overreach, offered such a tempting role to successive generations of great actors. In fact, the remarkable stage history of this character drew Robert H. Ball to write a whole book about it, *The Amazing Career of Sir Giles Overreach* (Princeton University Press, 1939), in which he traced the history of the role (and therefore of the play) from its first impersonation by Richard Perkins of the Queen's Company to the present. Strangely enough, as A. H. Cruickshank pointed out in his old spelling edition of the play (Oxford, 1926), it was not reprinted in the seventeenth century after the 1633 quarto and not revived during the Restoration or the early eighteenth century. But in 1781 it started a remarkable new life on both sides of the Atlantic. Miss St. Clare Byrne, in her introduction to her edition of the play (Falcon Educational Books, 1950), suggests that the reason for this revival was that "as a high-class melodrama" it had "distinct affinities with the sentimental drama of the eighteenth century" and thus anticipated the "natural taste of the predominantly middle-class audiences of the early nineteenth century theatre." It has often been revived by modern academic groups, and was given a professional production by Donald Wolfit, who, however, confessed to Dunn that "it was not a success with the public."

This robust comedy was probably written and performed in 1625, although a few scholars (e.g., A. K. McIlwraith, "On the Date of *A New Way to Pay Old Debts*," *MLR*, 1933) have argued for 1621 or 1622 on the basis of some of its historical references and certain of its metrical and literary characteristics. T. W. Craik, however, in the preface to his edition of the play in the New Mermaids series (London, 1964), has found no strong reason in content, style, or Massinger's circumstances as a dramatist to prefer the earlier date, and has accepted Furnace's allusion (I, ii) to the siege of Breda (lifted on July 1, 1625) as sufficient evidence for the later. Actually, a state of war, as described through Lord Lovell's campaign in the Low Countries, existed until peace was declared with France in 1629 and Spain in 1630.

Several influences were apparently at work on Massinger when he wrote the play. Most obvious and most usually emphasized was the presence of Middleton's successful *A Trick to Catch the Old One*, now perhaps twenty years old. Actually, however, a comparison of the two plays shows that Massinger could have taken little more than a bare outline of the central situation from the other play, since the whole cast of characters and the moral atmosphere are utterly different. As Cruickshank points out, even Wellborn, though labeled "a prodigal" in the dramatis personae, is a far remove from the adventurer Witgood because of Wellborn's model moral speech that first recommends him to Lady Allworth and his final redemption of his past reputation by accepting a military command under Lord Lovell. The working out of the plot situation is also entirely different, and Dunn, in illustrating Massinger's skill in plotting, even diagrams its "six-strand" plot. Dunn also calls attention to the similarity of Massinger's characterization at times to the old morality play technique, with Overreach as "anti-Christ, the principle of evil personified," Marall, his henchman, as "Accessory Wickedness, a minor devil," and Justice Greedy, his hanger-on, as "the deadly sin of Gluttony." Perhaps this type of characterization might be applied to other characters also, such as Wellborn, as the reforming prodigal, and Lady Allworth, as the spirit of beneficence. Nor is it possible to overlook the influence of Ben Jonson in the presence of humors names like Greedy, Furnace, Watchall, and of course Overreach himself.

For many years much has also been made of the possible indebtedness of Massinger to the notorious Sir Giles Mompesson and his accomplice, Sir Francis Mitchell, in creating Sir Giles Overreach and his creature Greedy. Cruickshank and Craik, however, have devoted considerable space to showing that such resemblances, after all, were superficial, consisting of the use of the common name, Giles, and the partnership of both men with a sort of justice of the peace. Mompesson had also been closely connected with Wiltshire, Massinger's original county. Moreover, Mompesson had been brought to justice because of his abuse of his monopoly on tavern-licenses, chiefly by charging exorbitant fees and taking bribes, but little of this characterization is left in Overreach except his power over Tapwell—a rather minor element in the plot. Nor does Greedy seem to have any real resemblance to Mitchell, who was scarcely a farcical Plautine figure like Greedy. Cruickshank believes that the object of Massinger's attack on Overreach was not his abuse of his monopoly but his viciousness in usury, extortion, and rural oppression, which of course Mompesson may have practised before he came under public scrutiny, but which was not the primary factor in his trial and sentence.

As for Massinger's literary style in the play, Cruickshank labels it a "middle type" of blank verse, perhaps influenced by Jonson and Fletcher, at times little better than "versified prose," but therefore capable of a "natural and flexible delivery." John L. Lyons, in an article on "Massinger's Imagery" (*Renaissance Papers*, Rice University Press, 1955), showed how Massinger used a specialized imagery directly and metaphorically related to the narrative or plot of each play to form a parallel comment on its theme. Thus in *A New Way* the recurrent imagery is that of war, weapons, and power, whereas in *The City Madam* it is that of clothes, and so on.

The present text is based on a copy of the 1633 edition in the Newberry Library in Chicago, compared with Cruickshank's text and that of Brander Matthews in volume three of Gayley's *Representative English Comedies*. The recent editions of Bryne and Craik have also been consulted.

# A NEW WAY TO PAY OLD DEBTS[1]

## BY

## PHILIP MASSINGER

### DRAMATIS PERSONÆ

LOVELL, *an English lord.*
SIR GILES OVERREACH, *a cruel extortioner.*
[FRANK] WELLBORN, *a prodigal.*
[TOM] ALLWORTH, *a young gentleman, page to Lord Lovell.*
GREEDY, *a hungry justice of peace.*
MARALL, *a term driver;[2] a creature of Sir Giles Overreach.*
ORDER [, *a steward*] ⎫
AMBLE [, *an usher*] ⎪ *servants to the Lady*
FURNACE [, *a cook*] ⎬ *Allworth.*
WATCHALL [, *a porter*] ⎭

WILLDO, *a parson.*
TAPWELL, *an alehouse keeper.*
THREE CREDITORS [, SERVANTS, *etc.*]

THE LADY ALLWORTH, *a rich widow.*
MARGARET, *Overreach his daughter.*
WAITING-WOMAN.
CHAMBERMAID.
FROTH, *Tapwell's wife.*

[SCENE: *The country near Nottingham.*

TIME: *Contemporary.*]

ACTUS PRIMUS. SCENA PRIMA.

[*Before Tapwell's house.*]

*Wellborn, Tapwell, Froth.*

WELL. No booze? Nor no tobacco?
TAP.                Not a suck, sir,
Nor the remainder of a single can
Left by a drunken porter, all night
    palled[3] too.
FROTH. Not the dropping of the tap for
    your morning's draught, sir.
'Tis verity, I assure you.
WELL.            Verity, you brach![4]
The devil turned precisian?[5]   Rogue,
    what am I?

TAP. Troth, durst I trust you with a look-
    ing-glass
To let you see your trim shape, you
    would quit[6] me
And take the name yourself.
WELL.             How, dog?
TAP.                 Even so, sir.
And I must tell you, if you but ad-
    vance                      10
Your Plimworth cloak[7] you shall be soon
    instructed
There dwells, and within call, if it please
    your worship,
A potent monarch called the constable,
That does command a citadel called the
    stocks,
Whose guards are certain files of rusty
    billmen[8]
Such as with great dexterity will hale
Your tattered, lousy—
WELL.       Rascal! Slave!
FROTH.                No rage, sir.

---

[1] The title continues: "A Comedy. As It Hath Been Often Acted at the Phœnix in Drury Lane by the Queen's Majesty's Servants." On the following pages appear the dedication to the Earl of Carnarvon and two commendatory poems by Sir Henry Moody and Sir Thomas Jay.
[2] One who moves from court to court during sessions.
[3] Paled, become flat.
[4] Bitch.           [5] Puritan.
[6] Acquit.
[7] Plymouth cloak; *i.e.*, a cudgel.
[8] Watchmen armed with pikes.

TAP. At his own peril. Do not put yourself
In too much heat, there being no water
  near
  To quench your thirst; and sure, for
    other liquor,                                    20
  As mighty ale or beer, they are things, I
    take it,
  You must no more remember—not in a
    dream, sir.
WELL. Why, thou unthankful villain,
  dar'st thou talk thus?
  Is not thy house, and all thou hast, my
    gift?
TAP. I find it not in chalk; and Timothy
  Tapwell
Does keep no other register.
WELL.                                    Am not I he
  Whose riots fed and clothed thee? Wert
    thou not
  Born on my father's land, and proud to
    be
  A drudge in his house?
TAP.          What I was, sir, it skills [1] not;
  What you are, is apparent. Now, for a
    farewell,                                    30
  Since you talk of father, in my hope it
    will torment you,
  I'll briefly tell your story. Your dead
    father,
  My quondam master, was a man of wor-
    ship,
  Old Sir John Wellborn, justice of peace
    and quorum, [2]
  And stood fair to be *custos rotulorum;* [3]
  Bare the whole sway of the shire, kept a
    great house,
  Relieved the poor, and so forth; but, he
    dying,
  And the twelve hundred a year coming
    to you,
  Late Master Francis, but now forlorn
    Wellborn—
WELL. Slave, stop, or I shall lose my-
  self!
FROTH.                          Very hardly;    40
  You cannot out of your way.
TAP.                          But to my story.
  You were then a lord of acres, the prime
    gallant,
  And I your underbutler. Note the change
    now.

[1] Matters.
[2] One of the most eminent justices.
[3] Custodian of the records.

You had a merry time of 't—hawks and
  hounds,
With choice of running horses; mistresses
Of all sorts and all sizes, yet so hot
As their embraces made your lordships [4]
  melt,
Which your uncle, Sir Giles Overreach,
  observing,
Resolving not to lose a drop of 'em
On foolish mortgages, statutes, and
  bonds,                                    50
For a while supplied your looseness, and
  then left you.
WELL. Some curate hath penned this in-
  vective, mongrel,
  And you have studied it.
TAP.                          I have not done yet.
  Your land gone, and your credit not
    worth a token, [5]
  You grew the common borrower; no man
    scaped
  Your paper pellets, [6] from the gentle-
    man
  To the beggars on highways, that sold
    you switches
  In your gallantry.
WELL.          I shall switch your brains out!
TAP. Where poor Tim Tapwell, with a
  little stock,
  Some forty pounds or so, bought a small
    cottage,                                    60
  Humbled myself to marriage with my
    Froth here,
  Gave entertainment—
WELL.                          Yes, to whores and canters, [7]
  Clubbers by night.
TAP.          True, but they brought in profit,
  And had a gift to pay for what they
    called for,
  And stuck [8] not like your mastership.
    The poor income
  I gleaned from them hath made me in my
    parish
  Thought worthy to be scavenger, and in
    time
  May rise to be overseer of the poor,
  Which if I do, on your petition, Wellborn,
  I may allow you thirteenpence a quarter,
  And you shall thank my worship.

[4] Estates.
[5] A counter used as a substitute for money.
[6] *I.e.,* I.O.U's.
[7] Users of thieves' cant.
[8] *I. e.,* delayed payment.

WELL.                Thus, you dogbolt,[1]  71
And thus—        *Beats and kicks him.*
TAP. [*To Froth.*]        Cry out for help!
WELL.                Stir, and thou diest.
Your potent prince, the constable, shall
    not save you.
Hear me, ungrateful hellhound! Did
    not I
Make purses for you? Then you licked
    my boots,
And thought your holy day [2] cloak too
    coarse to clean 'em.
'Twas I that, when I heard thee swear if
    ever
Thou couldst arrive at forty pounds thou
    wouldst
Live like an emperor, 'twas I that
    gave it
In ready gold. Deny this, wretch!
TAP.                I must, sir,  80
For, from the tavern to the taphouse, all,
On forfeiture of their licenses, stand
    bound
Never to remember who their best guests
    were,
If they grew poor like you.
WELL.        They are well rewarded
That beggar themselves to make such
    cuckolds rich.
Thou viper, thankless viper! Impudent
    bawd!
But, since you are grown forgetful, I will
    help
Your memory, and tread thee into mor-
    tar,
Not leave one bone unbroken.
                [*Beats him again.*]
TAP.                O!
FROTH.                Ask mercy.

*Enter Allworth.*

WELL. 'Twill not be granted.
ALL.        Hold—for my sake, hold!  90
Deny me, Frank? They are not worth
    your anger.
WELL. For once thou hast redeemed them
    from this scepter. [*Shows*] *his cudgel.*
But let 'em vanish, creeping on their
    knees,
And, if they grumble, I revoke my par-
    don.

[1] A worthless arrow, *i.e.*, a contemptible
fellow.        [2] Holiday.

FROTH. This comes of your prating, hus-
    band; you presumed
On your ambling wit, and must use your
    glib tongue,
Though you are beaten lame for 't.
TAP.                Patience, Froth;
There's law to cure our bruises.
        *They go off on their hands and knees.*
WELL.        Sent to your mother?
ALL. My lady, Frank, my patroness, my
    all!
She's such a mourner for my father's
    death,                100
And, in her love to him, so favors me
That I cannot pay too much observance
    to her.
There are few such stepdames.
WELL.                'Tis a noble widow,
And keeps her reputation pure and clear
From the least taint of infamy; her life,
With the splendor of her actions, leaves
    no tongue
To envy or detraction. Prithee, tell me,
Has she no suitors?
ALL.        Even the best of the shire, Frank,
My lord excepted, such as sue and send,
And send and sue again, but to no pur-
    pose.                110
Their frequent visits have not gained her
    presence.
Yet she's so far from sullenness and
    pride
That I dare undertake you shall meet
    from her
A liberal entertainment. I can give you
A catalogue of her suitors' names.
WELL.                Forbear it,
While I give you good counsel. I am
    bound to it;
Thy father was my friend, and that
    affection
I bore to him, in right descends to
    thee.
Thou art a handsome and a hopeful
    youth,
Nor will I have the least affront stick on
    thee,                120
If I with any danger can prevent it.
ALL. I thank your noble care; but, pray
    you, in what
Do I run the hazard?
WELL.                Art thou not in love?
Put it not off with wonder.
ALL.                In love, at my years?

WELL. You think you walk in clouds, but
    are trans[pa]rent.
I have heard all, and the choice that you
    have made,
And with my finger can point out the
    north star
By which the loadstone of your folly's
    guided.
And, to confirm this true, what think
    you of                   129
Fair Margaret, the only child and heir
Of cormorant Overreach? Does it blush
    and start,
To hear her only named? Blush at your
    want
Of wit and reason.
ALL.            You are too bitter, sir.
WELL. Wounds of this nature are not to be
    cured
With balms, but corrosives. I must be
    plain:
Art thou scarce manumised [1] from the
    porter's lodge [2]
And yet sworn servant to the pantofle,[3]
And dar'st thou dream of marriage? I
    fear
'Twill be concluded for impossible
That there is now, nor e'er shall be here-
    after,                   140
A handsome page or player's boy of
    fourteen
But either loves a wench, or drabs love
    him—
Court-waiters [4] not exempted.
ALL.               This is madness.
Howe'er you have discovered my in-
    tents,
You know my aims are lawful; and, if
    ever
The queen of flowers, the glory of the
    spring,
The sweetest comfort to our smell, the
    rose,
Sprang from an envious brier, I may
    infer
There's such disparity in their condi-
    tions
Between the goddess of my soul, the
    daughter,                150
And the base churl of her father.

[1] Manumitted, freed.
[2] Where servants were punished.
[3] Slipper; *i.e.*, he is still a page.
[4] Pages at court.

WELL.             Grant this true,
As I believe it, canst thou ever hope
To enjoy a quiet bed with her whose
    father
Ruined thy state?
ALL.            And yours too.
WELL.              I confess it.
True, I must tell you as a friend, and
    freely,
That, where impossibilities are apparent,
'Tis indiscretion to nourish hopes.
Canst thou imagine (let not self-love
    blind thee)
That Sir Giles Overreach, that, to make
    her great
In swelling titles, without touch of con-
    science                160
Will cut his neighbor's throat, and I hope
    his own too,
Will e'er consent to make her thine?
    Give o'er,
And think of some course suitable to thy
    rank,
And prosper in it.
ALL.         You have well advised me.
But in the meantime you that are so
    studious
Of my affairs wholly neglect your own.
Remember yourself, and in what plight
    you are.
WELL. No matter, no matter.
ALL.         Yes, 'tis much material.[5]
You know my fortune and my means;
    yet something
I can spare from myself to help your
    wants.
WELL.     How's this?        170
ALL. Nay, be not angry; there's eight
    pieces
To put you in better fashion.
WELL.          Money from thee?
From a boy? A stipendary? [6] One that
    lives
At the devotion of a stepmother
And the uncertain favor of a lord?
I'll eat my arms first. Howsoe'er blind
    Fortune
Hath spent the utmost of her malice on
    me—
Though I am vomited out of an alehouse,
And, thus accoutered,[7] know not where
    to eat,

[5] Very important.        [7] Fitted out.
[6] Stipendiary.

Or drink, or sleep, but underneath this
   canopy [1]—  180
Although I thank thee, I despise thy
   offer,
And, as I in my madness broke my state
Without th' assistance of another's brain,
In my right wits I'll piece it; at the worst,
Die thus and be forgotten.
ALL.  A strange humor!  *Exeunt.*

ACTUS PRIMI SCENA SECUNDA.[2]

[*A room in Lady Allworth's house.*]

*Order, Amble, Furnace, Watchall.*

ORD.  Set all things right, or, as my name is
   Order,
And by this staff of office that commands
   you,
This chain and double ruff, symbols of
   power,
Whoever misses in his function,
For one whole week makes forfeiture of
   his breakfast
And privilege in the wine cellar.
AMB.  You are merry,
   Good Master Steward.
FURN.  Let him; I'll be angry.
AMB.  Why, fellow Furnace, 'tis not twelve
   a-clock yet,
Nor dinner taking up; then, 'tis allowed,
Cooks by their places may be choleric.
FURN.  You think you have spoke wisely,
   Goodman Amble,  11
My lady's go-before! [3]
ORD.  Nay, nay, no wrangling.
FURN.  Twit me with the authority of the
   kitchen?
At all hours and all places, I'll be angry;
And, thus provoked, when I am at my
   prayers,
I will be angry.
AMB.  There was no hurt meant.
FURN.  I am friends with thee; and yet I
   will be angry.
ORD.  With whom?
FURN.  No matter whom—yet, now I
   think on 't,
I am angry with my lady.
WATCH.  Heaven forbid, man!
ORD.  What cause has she given thee?

FURN.  Cause enough, Master
   Steward.  20
I was entertained [4] by her to please her
   palate,
And, till she forswore eating, I performed
   it.
Now, since our master, noble Allworth,
   died,
Though I crack my brains to find out
   tempting sauces,
And raise fortifications in the pastry [5]
Such as might serve for models in the
   Low Countries,
Which, if they had been practised at
   Breda,
Spinola might have thrown his cap at it, [6]
   and ne'er took it—
AMB.  But you had wanted matter there to
   work on.
FURN.  Matter?  With six eggs and a
   strike [7] of rye meal  30
I had kept the town till doomsday, per-
   haps longer.
ORD.  But what's this to your pet [8] against
   my lady?
FURN.  What's this?  Marry, this: when I
   am three parts roasted
And the fourth part parboiled to prepare
   her viands,
She keeps her chamber, dines with a
   panada [9]
Or water gruel my sweat never thought
   on.
ORD.  But your art is seen in the dining
   room.
FURN.  By whom?
By such as pretend love to her, but come
To feed upon her.  Yet, of all the harpies
That do devour her, I am out of charity
With none so much as the thin-gutted
   squire  41
That's stolen into commission.
ORD.  Justice Greedy?
FURN.  The same, the same.  Meat's cast
   away upon him;
It never thrives.  He holds this para-
   dox:
Who eats not well, can ne'er do justice
   well.

[1] *I.e.*, the sky.
[2] The second scene of the first act.
[3] *I.e.*, usher.
[4] Employed.  [5] Room where pastry is made.
[6] Given it up as a bad job.
[7] A measure varying from one-half to four
bushels.  [8] Peevishness.
[9] A boiled bread pudding.

His stomach's as insatiate as the grave,
Or strumpets' ravenous appetites.

WATCH.                    One knocks.

*Allworth knocks, and enters.*

ORD. Our late young master!
AMB.                    Welcome, sir.
FURN.                    Your hand.
    If you have a stomach, a cold bakemeat's
        ready.
ORD. His father's picture in little.
FURN.        We are all your servants.   50
AMB. In you he lives.
ALL.                    At once, my thanks to
        all;
    This is yet some comfort.  Is my lady
        stirring?

*Enter the Lady Allworth, Waiting-Woman,*
                        *Chambermaid.*

ORD. Her presence answer for us.
LADY.                    Sort those silks well.
    I'll take the air alone.
*Exeunt Waiting-Woman and Chambermaid.*
FURN.                    You air and air;
    But will you never taste but spoonmeat [1]
        more?
    To what use serve I?
LADY.                    Prithee, be not angry;
    I shall, ere long.  I' the meantime, there
        is gold
    To buy thee aprons and a summer
        suit.
FURN. I am appeased, and Furnace now
        grows cook.
LADY. And, as I gave directions, if this
        morning                    60
    I am visited by any, entertain 'em
    As heretofore; but say, in my excuse,
    I am indisposed.
ORD.        I shall, madam.
LADY.                    Do, and leave me.—
    Nay, stay you, Allworth.
*Exeunt Order, Amble, Furnace, Watchall.*
ALL.                    I shall gladly grow here,
    To wait on your commands.
LADY.                    So soon turned courtier!
ALL. Style not that courtship, madam,
        which is duty
    Purchased on your part.
LADY.                    Well, you shall o'ercome;
    I'll not contend in words.  How is it with
    Your noble master?

[1] Liquid diet.

ALL.                    Ever like himself,
    No scruple lessened in the full weight of
        honor.                    70
    He did command me, pardon my pre-
        sumption,
    As his unworthy deputy to kiss
    Your ladyship's fair hands.
LADY.                    I am honored in
    His favor to me.  Does he hold his pur-
        pose
    For the Low Countries?
ALL.                    Constantly, good madam;
    But he will in person first present his
        service.
LADY. And how approve you of his course?
    You are yet,
    Like virgin parchment, capable of any
    Inscription, vicious or honorable.
    I will not force your will, but leave you
        free                    80
    To your own election.
ALL.                    Any form you please
    I will put on; but, might I make my
        choice,
    With humble emulation I would follow
    The path my lord marks to me.
LADY.                    'Tis well answered,
    And I commend your spirit.  You had a
        father—
    Blessed be his memory!—that some few
        hours
    Before the will of heaven took him from
        me,
    Who did commend you, by the dearest
        ties
    Of perfect love between us, to my charge;
    And therefore what I speak you are
        bound to hear                    90
    With such respect as if he lived in me.
    He was my husband, and, howe'er you
        are not
    Son of my womb, you may be of my love,
    Provided you deserve it.
ALL.                    I have found you,
    Most honored madam, the best mother to
        me,
    And, with my utmost strengths of care
        and service,
    Will labor that you never may repent
    Your bounties showered upon me.
LADY.                    I much hope it.
    These were your father's words: "If e'er
        my son                    99
    Follow the war, tell him it is a school

Where all the principles tending to
honor
Are taught, if truly followed.  But for
such
As repair thither as a place in which
They do presume they may with license
practice
Their lusts and riots, they shall never
merit
The noble name of soldiers.  To dare
boldly
In a fair cause, and for the country's
safety
To run upon the cannon's mouth un-
daunted;
To obey their leaders, and shun muti-
nies;                                        109
To bear with patience the winter's
cold
And summer's scorching heat, and not to
faint,
When plenty of provision fails, with
hunger—
Are the essential parts make up a sol-
dier,
Not swearing, dice, or drinking."
ALL.                    There's no syllable
You speak but is to me an oracle,
Which but to doubt were impious.
LADY.                    To conclude:
Beware ill company, for often men
Are like to those with whom they do con-
verse;
And from one man I warned you, and
that's Wellborn,
Not cause he's poor—that rather claims
your pity—                              120
But that he's in his manners so de-
bauched,
And hath to vicious courses sold him-
self.
'Tis true, your father loved him while he
was
Worthy the loving; but, if he had lived
To have seen him as he is, he had cast
him off,
As you must do.
ALL.               I shall obey in all things.
LADY.  You follow me to my chamber; you
shall have gold
To furnish you like my son, and still
supplied
As I hear from you.
ALL.        I am still your creature.  *Exeunt.*

ACTUS PRIMI SCENA TERTIA.

[*A hall in the same.*]

*Overreach, Greedy, Order, Amble, Furnace,
Watchall, Marall.*

GREEDY.  Not to be seen?
OVER.        Still cloistered up?  Her rea-
son,
I hope, assures her, though she make
herself
Close prisoner ever for her husband's
loss,
'Twill not recover him.
ORD.                    Sir, it is her will,
Which we that are her servants ought
to serve it
And not dispute.  Howe'er, you are
nobly welcome;
And, if you please to stay, that you may
think so,
There came not six days since from
Hull a pipe
Of rich Canary, which shall spend itself
For my lady's honor.
GREEDY.            Is it of the right race?  10
ORD.  Yes, Master Greedy.
AMB.  [*Aside.*]      How his mouth runs
o'er!
FURN.  [*Aside.*]  I'll make it run, and run.—
Save your good worship!
GREEDY.  Honest Master Cook, thy hand
again!  How I love thee!
Are the good dishes still in being?  Speak,
boy.
FURN.  If you have a mind to feed, there
is a chine
Of beef, well seasoned.
GREEDY.            Good!
FURN.               A pheasant, larded.
GREEDY.  That I might now give thanks
for 't!
FURN.        Other kuckshaws.[1]
Besides, there came last night from the
forest of Sherwood
The fattest stag I ever cooked.
GREEDY.                    A stag, man?
FURN.  A stag, sir—part of it prepared for
dinner,                                    20
And baked in puff paste.
GREEDY.            Puff paste too, Sir Giles!
A ponderous chine of beef!  A pheasant
larded!

[1] Kickshaws.

And red deer too, Sir Giles, and baked
in puff paste!
All business set aside, let us give thanks
here.
FURN. How the lean skeleton's raped! [1]
OVER.                You know we cannot.
MAR. Your worships are to sit on a com-
mission,
And, if you fail to come, you lose the
cause.
GREEDY. Cause me no causes. I'll prove
't, for such a dinner
We may put off a commission: you shall
find it
*Henrici decimo quarto* [2] —
OVER.            Fie, Master Greedy!   30
Will you lose me a thousand pounds
for a dinner?
No more, for shame! We must forget
the belly
When we think of profit.
GREEDY.       Well, you shall o'errule me.
I could ev'n cry now.—Do you hear,
Master Cook?
Send but a corner of that immortal
pasty,
And I in thankfulness will by your boy
Send you—a brace of threepences.
FURN.        Will you be so prodigal?

*Enter Wellborn.*

OVER. Remember me to your lady.—
Who have we here?
WELL. You know me.
OVER.        I did once, but now I will not;
Thou art no blood•of mine. Avaunt,
thou beggar!                          40
If ever thou presume to own me more,
I'll have thee caged and whipped.
GREEDY.        I'll grant the warrant.
Think of Pie Corner, Furnace!
*Exeunt Overreach, Greedy, Marall.*
WATCH.        Will you out, sir?
I wonder how you durst creep in.
ORD.                This is rudeness
And saucy impudence.
AMB.                Cannot you stay
To be served, among your fellows, from
the basket, [3]
But you must press into the hall?

[1] Rapt, transported.
[2] In a law enacted in the fourteenth year of
Henry's reign.
[3] Of scraps.

FURN.                Prithee, vanish
Into some outhouse, though it be the
pigsty;
My scullion shall come to thee.

*Enter Allworth.*

WELL.                This is rare.
O, here's Tom Allworth.—Tom!
ALL.        We must be strangers;   50
Nor would I have you seen here for a
million.                *Exit Allworth.*
WELL. Better and better. He contemns
me too!

*Enter [Waiting-] Woman and Chambermaid.*

WOMAN. Foh, what a smell's here! What
thing's this?
CHAM.        A creature
Made out of the privy; let us hence,
for love's sake,
Or I shall sown. [4]
WOMAN.        I begin to feel faint already.
*Exeunt [Waiting-] Woman and Chamber-
maid.*
WATCH. Will you know your way?
AMB.        Or shall we teach it you
By the head and shoulders?
WELL.                No; I will not stir.
Do you mark, I will not. Let me see
the wretch
That dares attempt to force me. Why,
you slaves,                          59
Created only to make legs [5] and cringe,
To carry in a dish and shift a trencher,
That have not souls only to hope a
blessing
Beyond blackjacks [6] or flagons—you that
were born
Only to consume meat and drink, and
batten
Upon reversions! [7]—Who advances? Who
Shows me the way?
ORD.                My lady!

*Enter Lady, [Waiting-] Woman, Chamber-
maid.*

CHAM.                Here's the monster.
WOMAN. Sweet madam, keep your glove
to your nose.

[4] Sound, swoon.        [6] Leather jugs.
[5] Bows.                [7] Fatten on left-overs.

CHAM.                    Or let me
Fetch some perfumes may be predomi-
    nant;
You wrong yourself else.
WELL.               Madam, my designs
Bear me to you.
LADY.  To me?
WELL.       And, though I have met with          70
But ragged entertainment from your
    grooms here,
I hope from you to receive that noble
    usage
As may become the true friend of your
    husband,
And then I shall forget these.
LADY.                    I am amazed
To see and hear this rudeness.  Dar'st
    thou think,
Though sworn, that it can ever find belief
That I, who to the best men of this
    country
Denied my presence since my husband's
    death,
Can fall so low as to change words with
    thee?                                          79
Thou son of infamy, forbear my house,
And know and keep the distance that's
    between us,
Or, though it be against my gentler
    temper,
I shall take order you no more shall be
An eyesore to me.
WELL.            Scorn me not, good lady;
But, as in form you are angelical,
Imitate the heavenly natures and vouch-
    safe
At the least awhile to hear me.  You will
    grant
The blood that runs in this arm is as
    noble
As that which fills your veins; those
    costly jewels,
And those rich clothes you wear, your
    men's observance                              90
And women's flattery are in you no
    virtues,
Nor these rags, with my poverty, in
    me vices.
You have a fair fame, and, I know, de-
    serve it;
Yet, lady, I must say, in nothing more
Than in the pious sorrow you have
    shown
For your late noble husband.

ORD. [Aside.]               How she starts!
FURN. [Aside.]  And hardly can keep finger
    from the eye
To hear him named.
LADY.       Have you aught else to say?
WELL. That husband, madam, was once
    in his fortune
Almost as low as I; want, debts, and
    quarrels                                     100
Lay heavy on him.  Let it not be thought
A boast in me, though I say I relieved
    him.
'Twas I that gave him fashion; mine
    the sword
That did on all occasions second his;
I brought him on and off with honor,
    lady;
And, when in all men's judgments he
    was sunk
And in his own hopes not to be bunged[1]
    up,
I stepped unto him, took him by the
    hand,
And set him upright.
FURN. [Aside.]        Are not we base rogues,
That could forget this?
WELL.       I confess, you made him       110
Master of your estate; nor could your
    friends,
Though he brought no wealth with him,
    blame you for 't,
For he had a shape, and to that shape
    a mind,
Made up of all parts either great or
    noble—
So winning a behavior not to be
Resisted, madam.
LADY.               'Tis most true, he had.
WELL. For his sake, then, in that I was
    his friend,
Do not contemn me.
LADY.       For what's past, excuse me;
I will redeem it.—Order, give the gentle-
    man
A hundred pounds.
WELL.       No, madam, on no terms.      120
I will nor beg nor borrow sixpence of
    you,
But be supplied elsewhere, or want
    thus ever.
Only one suit I make, which you deny
    not                        Whispers to her.
To strangers; and 'tis this.

_____
[1] Craik suggests *buoyed*.

LADY.                    Fie! Nothing else?

WELL. Nothing, unless you please to charge your servants

To throw away a little respect upon me.

LADY. What you demand is yours.

WELL.                    I thank you, lady.

Now what can be wrought out of such a suit

Is yet in supposition. I have said all;

When you please, you may retire.—[*Exit Lady.*] Nay, all's forgotten;    130

And for a lucky omen to my project

Shake hands and end all quarrels in the cellar.

ORD. Agreed, agreed.

FURN.            Still merry Master Wellborn!

*Exeunt.*

ACTUS SECUNDI SCENA PRIMA.

[*A room in Overreach's house.*]

*Overreach, Marall.*

OVER. He's gone, I warrant thee; this commission crushed him.

MAR. Your worship have the way on 't,[1] and ne'er miss

To squeeze these unthrifts[2] into air; and yet

The chapfallen justice did his part, returning

For your advantage the certificate,

Against his conscience and his knowledge too

(With your good favor), to the utter ruin

Of the poor farmer.

OVER.            'Twas for these good ends

I made him a justice; he that bribes his belly

Is certain to command his soul.

MAR.                    I wonder,    10

Still with your license, why your worship, having

The power to put this thin-gut in commission,

You are not in 't yourself?

OVER.                Thou art a fool.

In being out of office I am out of danger;

Where,[3] if I were a justice, besides the trouble,

I might or [4] out of willfulness or error

Run myself finely into a *præmunire*,[5]

And so become a prey to the informer.

No, I'll have none of 't. 'Tis enough I keep

Greedy at my devotion;[6] so he serve    20

My purposes, let him hang or damn, I care not.

Friendship is but a word.

MAR.                You are all wisdom.

OVER. I would be worldly wise; for the other wisdom,

That does prescribe as a well-governed life,

And to do right to others as ourselves,

I value not an atom.

MAR.                What course take you,

With your good patience, to hedge in the manor

Of your neighbor, Master Frugal, as 'tis said

He will nor sell nor borrow nor exchange?

And his land, lying in the midst of your many lordships,    30

Is a foul blemish.

OVER.        I have thought on 't, Marall,

And it shall take. I must have all men sellers,

And I the only purchaser.

MAR.                'Tis most fit, sir.

OVER. I'll therefore buy some cottage near his manor,

Which done, I'll make my men break ope his fences,

Ride o'er his standing corn, and in the night

Set fire on his barns, or break his cattle's legs.

These trespasses draw on suits, and suits, expenses,

Which I can spare, but will soon beggar him.

When I have harried him thus two or three year,    40

Though he sue *in forma pauperis*,[7] in spite

Of all his thrift and care he'll grow behindhand.

MAR. The best I ever heard! I could adore you.

OVER. Then, with the favor of my man of law,

---

[1] Emended by Gifford. Original reads *out.*
[2] Spendthrifts.
[3] Whereas.                    [4] Either.

[5] A legal writ; here a scrape or predicament.
[6] *I. e.*, interests.
[7] In the status of a pauper.

I will pretend some title. Want will force him
To put it to arbitrament; then, if he sell
For half the value, he shall have ready money,
And I possess his land.

MAR. 'Tis above wonder!
Wellborn was apt [1] to sell, and needed not
These fine arts, sir, to hook him in.

OVER. Well thought on. 50
This varlet, Marall, lives too long to upbraid me
With my close cheat [2] put upon him. Will nor cold
Nor hunger kill him?

MAR. I know not what to think on 't.
I have used all means, and the last night I caused
His host, the tapster, to turn him out of doors,
And have been since with all your friends and tenants
And on the forfeit of your favor charged them, [3]
Though a crust of moldy bread would keep him from starving,
Yet they should not relieve him. This is done, sir.

OVER. That was something, Marall; but thou must go further, 60
And suddenly, Marall.

MAR. Where and when you please, sir.

OVER. I would have thee seek him out and, if thou canst,
Persuade him that 'tis better steal than beg;
Then, if I prove he has but robbed a henroost,
Not all the world shall save him from the gallows.
Do anything to work him to despair,
And 'tis thy masterpiece.

MAR. I will do my best, sir.

OVER. I am now on my main work with the Lord Lovell,
The gallant-minded, popular Lord Lovell,
The minion [4] of the people's love. I hear 70
He's come into the country, and my aims are

To insinuate myself into his knowledge,
And then invite him to my house.

MAR. I have you;
This points at my young mistress.

OVER. She must part with
That humble title, and write "honorable,"
"Right honorable," Marall, my "right honorable" daughter,
If all I have, or e'er shall get, will do it.
I will have her well attended; there are ladies
Of errant knights decayed and brought so low
That for cast [5] clothes and meat will gladly serve her. 80
And 'tis my glory, though I come from the city,
To have their issue whom I have undone,
To kneel to mine as bondslaves.

MAR. 'Tis fit state, sir.

OVER. And therefore I'll not have a chambermaid
That ties her shoes, or any meaner office,
But such whose fathers were right worshipful.
'Tis a rich man's pride, there having ever been
More than a feud, a strange antipathy,
Between us and true gentry.

*Enter Wellborn.*

MAR. See who's here, sir.

OVER. Hence, monster! Prodigy!

WELL. Sir, your wife's nephew; 90
She and my father tumbled in one belly.

OVER. Avoid my sight! Thy breath's infectious, rogue!
I shun thee as a leprosy or the plague.—
Come hither, Marall.—[*Aside.*] This is the time to work him.

MAR. I warrant you, sir.

*Exit Over[reach].*

WELL. By this light, I think he's mad.

MAR. Mad? Had you took compassion on yourself,
You long since had been mad.

WELL. You have took a course,
Between you and my venerable uncle,·
To make me so

[1] Prepared, willing.     [2] Secret trick.
[3] Matthews' reading; original reads *him*.
[4] Favorite.     [5] Cast-off.

MAR.            The more pale-spirited you,
That would not be instructed. I swear
    deeply—                                    100
WELL. By what?
MAR.                       By my religion.
WELL. [*Aside.*]                Thy religion!
    The devil's creed!—But what would
    you have done?
MAR. Had there been but one tree in all
    the shire,
Nor any hope to compass a penny
    halter,
Before, like you, I had outlived my
    fortunes,
A withe had served my turn to hang
    myself.
I am zealous in your cause; pray you,
    hang yourself,
And presently,[1] as you love your credit.
WELL.                     I thank you.
MAR. Will you stay till you die in a ditch,
    or lice devour you?
Or, if you dare not do the feat your-
    self,                                       110
But that you'll put the state to charge
    and trouble,
Is there no purse to be cut, house to be
    broken,
Or market women with eggs, that you
    may murther,
And so despatch the business?
WELL.                    Here's variety,
I must confess; but I'll accept of
    none
Of all your gentle offers, I assure you.
MAR. Why, have you hope ever to eat
    again,
Or drink, or be the master of three
    farthings?
If you like not hanging, drown your-
    self! Take some course
For your reputation.
WELL.    'Twill not do, dear tempter,   120
With all the rhetoric the fiend hath
    taught you.
I am as far as thou art from despair;
Nay, I have confidence, which is more
    than hope,
To live, and suddenly, better than ever.
MAR. Ha, ha! These castles you build
    in the air
Will not persuade me or to give or lend
A token to you.

[1] At once.

WELL.            I'll be more kind to thee.
Come, thou shalt dine with me.
MAR.                     With you?
WELL.               Nay, more, dine gratis.
MAR. Under what hedge, I pray you?
    Or at whose cost?
Are they padders[2] or Abram-men[3]
    that are your consorts?              130
WELL. Thou art incredulous; but thou
    shalt dine
Not alone at her house, but with a
    gallant lady—
With me and with a lady.
MAR.               Lady? What lady?
With the Lady of the Lake,[4] or Queen
    of Fairies?
For I know it must be an enchanted
    dinner.
WELL. With the Lady Allworth, knave.
MAR.                Nay, now there's hope
Thy brain is cracked.
WELL.        Mark there, with what respect
I am entertained.
MAR.        With choice, no doubt, of dog
    whips.
Why, dost thou ever hope to pass her
    porter?
WELL. 'Tis not far off; go with me. Trust
    thine own eyes.                       140
MAR. Troth, in my hope, or my assurance
    rather,
To see thee curvet and mount like a dog
    in a blanket,
If ever thou presume to pass her thresh-
    old,
I will endure thy company.
WELL.            Come along then. *Exeunt.*

ACTUS SECUNDI SCENA SECUNDA.

[*A room in Lady Allworth's house.*]

*Allworth, Waiting-Woman, Chambermaid,
    Order, Amble, Furnace, Watchall.*

WOMAN. Could you not command your
    leisure one hour longer?
CHAM. Or half an hour?
ALL.    I have told you what my haste is.
Besides, being now another's, not mine
    own,
Howe'er I much desire to enjoy you
    longer,

[2] Footpads.
[3] Beggars who feigned insanity.
[4] In the *Morte d'Arthur.*

My duty suffers, if, to please myself,
I should neglect my lord.
WOMAN.          Pray you, do me the favor
To put these few quince cakes into your
pocket;
They are of mine own preserving.
CHAM.          And this marmulade;[1]
'Tis comfortable for your stomach.
WOMAN.          And, at parting,
Excuse me if I beg a farewell from you.  10
CHAM. You are still before me. I move the
same suit, sir.
          [Allworth] kisses 'em severally.
FURN. How greedy these chamberers are
of a beardless chin!
I think the tits[2] will ravish him.
ALL.          My service
To both.
WOMAN.          Ours waits on you.
CHAM.          And shall do ever.
ORD. You are my lady's charge; be there-
fore careful
That you sustain your parts.
WOMAN.     We can bear, I warrant you.
Exeunt [Waiting-] Woman and Chambermaid.
FURN. Here, drink it off. The ingredients
are cordial,
And this the true elixir; it hath boiled
Since midnight for you.  'Tis the quin-
tessence
Of five cocks of the game, ten dozen of
sparrows,          20
Knuckles of veal, potato roots and mar-
row,
Currall[3] and ambergris. Were you two
years elder,
And I had a wife or gamesome mistress,
I durst trust you with neither. You need
not bait[4]
After this, I warrant you, though your
journey's long;
You may ride on the strength of this till
tomorrow morning.
ALL. Your courtesies overwhelm me.  I
much grieve
To part from such true friends, and yet
find comfort—          28
My attendance on my honorable lord,
Whose resolution holds to visit my lady,
Will speedily bring me back.
Knocking at the gate; Marall and Wellborn
within. [Exit Watchall.]

MAR.          Dar'st thou venture further?
WELL. Yes, yes, and knock again.
ORD.          'Tis he; disperse!
AMB. Perform it bravely.
FURN.     I know my cue; ne'er doubt me.
They go off several ways [, Allworth re-
maining.

Enter Watchall with Wellborn and Marall.]

WATCH. Beast that I was, to make you
stay! Most welcome;
You were long since expected.
WELL.          Say so much
To my friend, I pray you.
WATCH.     For your sake, I will, sir.
MAR. [Aside.] For his sake!
WELL. [Aside.]     Mum; this is nothing.
MAR.          More than ever
I would have believed, though I had
found it in my primer.[5]
ALL. When I have given you reasons for
my late harshness,
You'll pardon and excuse me, for, be-
lieve me,          40
Though now I part abruptly, in my
service
I will deserve it.
MAR. [Aside.]     Service! With a ven-
geance!
WELL. I am satisfied. Farewell, Tom.
ALL.          All joy stay with you!
          Exit Allw[orth].

Enter Amble.

AMB. You are happily encountered; I yet
never
Presented one so welcome as I know
You will be to my lady.
MAR. [Aside.]     This is some vision,
Or, sure, these men are mad, to worship
a dunghill;
It cannot be a truth.
WELL.          Be still a pagan,
An unbelieving infidel; be so, miscreant,
And meditate on blankets and on dog
whips!          50

Enter Furnace.

FURN. I am glad you are come; until I
know your pleasure
I knew not how to serve up my lady's
dinner.

[1] Marmalade.
[2] Chits.
[3] Coral, lobster ovaries.
[4] Eat.
[5] "The original primers were books of prayers for children" (Cruickshank).

MAR. [*Aside*.] His pleasure! Is it pos-
sible?
WELL.                    What's thy will?
FURN. Marry, sir, I have some grouse, and
turkey chicken,
Some rails and quails, and my lady willed
me ask you
What kind of sauces best affect your
palate
That I may use my utmost skill to
please it.
MAR. [*Aside*.] The devil's entered this
cook. Sauce for his palate,
That, on my knowledge, for almost this
twelvemonth
Durst wish but cheese parings, and
brown bread on Sundays.          60
WELL. That way I like 'em best.
FURN.                    It shall be done, sir.
                              *Exit Furnace.*
WELL. What think you of "the hedge we
shall dine under"?
Shall we feed gratis?
MAR. [*Aside*.] I know not what to
think.
Pray you, make me not mad.

*Enter Order.*

ORD.          This place becomes you not;
Pray you, walk, sir, to the dining room.
WELL.                    I am well here,
Till her ladyship quits her chamber.
MAR. [*Aside*.]          Well here, say you?
'Tis a rare change! But yesterday you
thought
Yourself well in a barn, wrapped up in
peas-straw.

*Enter [Waiting-] Woman and Chambermaid.*

WOMAN. O, sir, you are wished for.
CHAM.          My lady dreamt, sir, of you.
WOMAN. And the first command she gave,
after she rose,          70
Was, her devotions done, to give her
notice
When you approached here.
CHAM.          Which is done, on my virtue.
MAR. [*Aside*.] I shall be converted; I begin
to grow
Into a new belief, which saints nor
angels
Could have won me to have faith in.
WOMAN.                    Sir, my lady!

*Enter Lady [Allworth].*

LADY. I come to meet you, and languished
till I saw you.
This first kiss is for form; I allow a sec-
ond
To such a friend.          [*Kisses Wellborn.*]
MAR. [*Aside*.]          To such a friend!
Heaven bless me!
WELL. I am wholly yours; yet, madam,
if you please
To grace this gentleman with a sa-
lute—                    80
MAR. [*Aside*.] Salute me at his bidding!
WELL.                    I shall receive it
As a most high favor.
LADY.          Sir, you may command me.
[*Advances to kiss Marall, who draws back.*]
WELL. Run backward from a lady? And
such a lady?
MAR. To kiss her foot is to poor me a
favor
I am unworthy of—
                    *Offers to kiss her foot.*
LADY.                    Nay, pray you, rise,
And, since you are so humble, I'll exalt
you.
You shall dine with me today at mine
own table.
MAR. Your ladyship's table? I am not
good enough
To sit at your steward's board.
LADY.                    You are too modest;
I will not be denied.

*Enter Furnace.*

FURN.          Will you still be babbling  90
Till your meat freeze on the table? The
old trick still;
My art ne'er thought on!
LADY.     Your arm, Master Wellborn.—
[*To Marall.*] Nay, keep us company.
MAR.          I was never so graced.
*Exeunt Wellborn, Lady [Allworth], Amble,
     Marall, [Waiting-] Woman [, and
                    Chambermaid].*
ORD. So we have played our parts, and are
come off well;
But, if I know the mystery, why my
lady
Consented to it, or why Master Well-
born
Desired it, may I perish!

FURN.                    Would I had
The roasting of his heart that cheated
   him,
And forces the poor gentleman to these
   shifts!
By fire (for cooks are Persians, and
   swear by it),                    100
Of all the griping and extorting tyrants
I ever heard or read of, I ne'er met
A match to Sir Giles Overreach.
WATCH.            What will you take
To tell him so, fellow Furnace?
FURN.                    Just as much
As my throat is worth, for that would be
   the price on 't.
To have a usurer that starves himself
And wears a cloak of one-and-twenty
   years
On a suit of fourteen groats, bought of
   the hangman,
To grow rich, and then purchase,[1] is too
   common;
But this Sir Giles feeds high, keeps many
   servants,                    110
Who must at his command do any out-
   rage.
Rich in his habit, vast in his expenses,
Yet he to admiration[2] still increases
In wealth and lordships.
ORD.    He frights men out of their estates,
And breaks through all law nets, made
   to curb ill men,
As they were cobwebs.  No man dares
   reprove him.
Such a spirit to dare and power to do
   were never
Lodged so unluckily.

*Enter Amble.*

AMB.                Ha, ha!  I shall burst.
ORD.  Contain thyself, man.
FURN.                Or make us partakers
Of your sudden mirth.
AMB.        Ha, ha!  My lady has got  120
Such a guest at her table—this term
   driver, Marall,
This snip of an attorney!
FURN.            What of him, man?
AMB.  The knave thinks still he's at the
   cook's shop in Ram Alley,[3]

Where the clerks[4] divide, and the elder
   is to choose;[5]
And feeds so slovenly!
FURN.                    Is this all?
AMB.                    My lady
Drank to him for fashion' sake, or to
   please Master Wellborn.
As I live, he rises, and takes up a dish
In which there were some remnants of a
   boiled capon,
And pledges her in white broth!
FURN.                Nay, 'tis like  129
The rest of his tribe.
AMB.        And, when I brought him wine,
He leaves his stool and after a leg or two
Most humbly thanks my worship.
ORD.                Rose already!
AMB.  I shall be chid.

*Enter Lady [Allworth], Wellborn, Marall.*

FURN. [*Aside.*]        My lady frowns.
LADY.                You wait well!
Let me have no more of this; I observed
   your jeering.
Sirrah, I'll have you know, whom I
   think worthy
To sit at my table, be he ne'er so mean,
When I am present, is not your com-
   panion.[6]
ORD. [*Aside.*] Nay, she'll preserve what's
   due to her.
FURN. [*Aside.*]        This refreshing
Follows your flux of laughter.
LADY. [*To Wellborn.*]        You are master
Of your own will.  I know so much of
   manners                    140
As not to inquire your purposes; in a
   word,
To me you are ever welcome, as to a
   house
That is your own.
WELL. [*Aside to Marall.*]        Mark that.
MAR. [*Aside.*]        With reverence, sir,
And it like[7] your worship.
WELL.            Trouble yourself no farther,
Dear madam; my heart's full of zeal and
   service,
However in my language I am sparing.—
Come, Master Marall.
MAR.            I attend your worship.
        *Exeunt Wellb[orn], Mar[all].*

---

[1] Acquire real estate by any other means than
inheritance.
[2] In a wonderful fashion.
[3] A street in London famous for its restaurants.
[4] Lawyers.
[5] Have first choice of his portion.
[6] *I.e.*, kind.                    [7] If it please.

LADY. I see in your looks you are sorry,
and you know me
An easy mistress. Be merry; I have for-
got all.—
Order and Furnace, come with me; I
must give you                         150
Further directions.
ORD.          What you please.
FURN.          We are ready. [*Exeunt.*]

ACTUS SECUNDI SCENA TERTIA.

[*The country near Lady Allworth's house.*]

*Wellborn, Marall.*

WELL. I think I am in a good way.
MAR.               Good sir, the best way,
The certain best way.
WELL.               There are casualties
That men are subject to.
MAR.               You are above 'em;
And, as you are already worshipful,
I hope ere long you will increase in wor-
ship,
And be right worshipful.
WELL.               Prithee, do not flout me.
What I shall be, I shall be. Is 't for your
ease
You keep your hat off?
MAR.          Ease, and it like your worship?
I hope Jack Marall shall not live so long,
To prove himself such an unmannerly
beast,                              10
Though it hail hazelnuts, as to be covered
When your worship's present.
WELL. (*Aside.*)     Is not this a true rogue
That, out of mere hope of a future
coz'nage,[1]
Can turn thus suddenly?     'Tis rank
already.
MAR. I know your worship's wise, and
needs no counsel;
Yet, if in my desire to do you service
I humbly offer my advice (but still
Under correction), I hope I shall not
Incur your high displeasure.
WELL.               No; speak freely.
MAR. Then, in my judgment, sir, my
simple judgment                    20
(Still with your worship's favor), I could
wish you
A better habit, for this cannot be
But much distasteful to the noble lady

[1] With a pun on *cousinage*, intimacy.

(I say no more) that loves you, for, this
morning
To me (and I am but a swine to her),
Before th' assurance of her wealth
perfumed you,
You savored not of amber.[2]
WELL.               I do now then?
[*Marall*] *kisses the end of his* [*Wellborn's*]
                                *cudgel.*
MAR. This your batoon [3] hath got a touch
of it.
Yet, if you please, for change I have
twenty pounds here
Which out of my true love I presently   30
Lay down at your worship's feet; 'twill
serve to buy you
A riding suit.
WELL.          But where's the horse?
MAR.                    My gelding
Is at your service; nay, you shall ride me
Before your worship shall be put to the
trouble
To walk afoot. Alas, when you are lord
Of this lady's manor, as I know you will
be,
You may with the lease of glebe land,
called Knave's Acre,
A place I would manure,[4] requite your
vassal.
WELL. I thank thy love, but must make no
use of it.
What's twenty pounds?
MAR.          'Tis all that I can make, sir.   40
WELL. Dost thou think, though I want
clothes, I could not have 'em
For one word to my lady?
MAR.                    As I know not that!
WELL. Come, I'll tell thee a secret, and so
leave thee.
I'll not give her the advantage, though
she be
A gallant-minded lady, after we are
married
(There being no woman but is sometimes
froward),
To hit me in the teeth, and say she was
forced
To buy my wedding clothes, and took
me on
With a plain riding suit and an ambling
nag.

[2] Ambergris.
[3] Baton, stick.
[4] Maneuver, operate, possess.

No, I'll be furnished something like
   myself,                      50
And so farewell. For thy suit touching
   Knave's Acre,
When it is mine, 'tis thine.
MAR.         I thank your worship.—
                     *Exit Wellb[orn].*
How [I][1] was cozened in the calcula-
   tion
Of this man's fortune! My master
   cozened too,
Whose pupil I am in the art of undoing
   men,
For that is our profession! Well, well,
   Master Wellborn,
You are of a sweet nature and fit again
   to be cheated,
Which, if the Fates please, when you are
   possessed
Of the land and lady, you, sans question,
   shall be.
I'll presently think of the means.
                 *Walk by, musing.*[2]

*Enter Overreach.*

OVER. [*To a Servant within.*]     Sirrah,
   take my horse.                60
I'll walk to get me an appetite; 'tis but a
   mile,
And exercise will keep me from being
   pursy.
Ha! Marall! Is he conjuring? Perhaps
The knave has wrought the prodigal to
   do
Some outrage on himself, and now he
   feels
Compunction in his conscience for 't.
   No matter,
So it be done.—Marall!
MAR.         Sir.
OVER.            How succeed we
In our plot on Wellborn?
MAR.             Never better, sir.
OVER. Has he hanged or drowned himself?
MAR.            No, sir, he lives—
Lives once more to be made a prey to
   you,                    70
A greater prey than ever.
OVER.          Art thou in thy wits?
If thou art, reveal this miracle, and
   briefly.

[1] Added by Cruickshank.
[2] Matthews' reading; original reads *masing.*

MAR. A lady, sir, is fall'n in love with him.
OVER. With him? What lady?
MAR.          The rich Lady Allworth.
OVER. Thou dolt! How dar'st thou speak
   this?
MAR.         I speak truth;
And I do so but once a year, unless
It be to you, sir. We dined with her
   ladyship,
I thank his worship.
OVER.          His worship!
MAR.              As I live, sir,
I dined with him at the great lady's
   table,
Simple as I stand here, and saw when she
   kissed him,              80
And would at his request have kissed
   me too;
But I was not so audacious as some
   youths are,
And dare do anything, be it ne'er so
   absurd,
And sad after performance.
OVER.           Why, thou rascal,
To tell me these impossibilities!
Dine at her table? And kiss him? Or
   thee?
Impudent varlet, have not I myself,
To whom great countesses' doors have
   oft flew open,
Ten times attempted, since her hus-
   band's death,
In vain to see her, though I came—a
   suitor?               90
And yet your good solicitorship and
   rogue Wellborn
Were brought into her presence, feasted
   with her!
But that I know thee a dog that cannot
   blush,
This most incredible lie would call up
   one
On thy buttermilk cheeks.
MAR.       Shall I not trust my eyes, sir,
Or taste? I feel her good cheer in my
   belly.
OVER. You shall feel me, if you give not
   over, sirrah.
Recover your brains again, and be no
   more gulled
With a beggar's plot, assisted by the
   aids
Of serving-men and chambermaids, for
   beyond these            100

Thou never saw'st a woman, or I'll quit [1]
you
From my employments.

MAR.                    Will you credit this yet?
On my confidence of their marriage, I
offered Wellborn—
(*Aside.*) I would give a crown now I
durst say "his worship"—
My nag and twenty pounds.

OVER.                    Did you so, idiot? [2]
                              *Strikes him down.*
Was this the way to work him to despair,
Or rather to cross me?

MAR.          Will your worship kill me?

OVER. No, no; but drive the lying spirit
out of you.

MAR. He's gone.

OVER.                    I have done then. Now,
forgetting
Your late imaginary feast and lady,    110
Know my Lord Lovell dines with me
tomorrow.
Be careful naught be wanting to receive
him;
And bid my daughter's women trim her
up;
Though they paint her, so she catch the
lord I'll thank 'em.
There's a piece for my late blows.
                              [*Gives money.*]

MAR. (*Aside.*)          I must yet suffer.
But there may be a time—

OVER.          Do you grumble?

MAR.                    No, sir. [*Exeunt.*]

ACTUS TERTII SCENA PRIMA.

[*The country near Overreach's house.*]

*Lovell, Allworth, Servants.*

LOV. Walk the horses down the hill. Something in private
I must impart to Allworth. *Exeunt servi.* [3]

ALL.                    O, my lord,
What sacrifice of reverence, duty, watch-
ing,
Although I could put off the use of sleep,
And ever wait on your commands [to]
serve 'em,
What dangers, though ne'er so horrid
shapes,

Nay, death itself, though I should run
to meet it,
Can I, and with a thankful willingness,
suffer!
But still the retribution will fall short
Of your bounties showered upon me.

LOV.                    Loving youth,    10
Till what I purpose be put into act,
Do not o'erprize it.    Since you have
trusted me
With your soul's nearest, nay, her
dearest secret,
Rest confident 'tis in a cabinet locked
Treachery shall never open.    I have
found you
(For so much to your face I must profess,
Howe'er you guard [4] your modesty with a
blush for 't)
More zealous in your love and service
to me
Than I have been in my rewards.

ALL.                    Still great ones,
Above my merit.

LOV.    Such your gratitude calls 'em;    20
Nor am I of that harsh and rugged tem-
per
As some great men are taxed with, who
imagine
They part from the respect due to their
honors
If they use not all such as follow 'em,
Without distinction of their births, like
slaves.
I am not so conditioned; I can make
A fitting difference between my footboy
And a gentleman by want compelled to
serve me.

ALL. 'Tis thankfully acknowledged. You
have been                              29
More like a father to me than a master.
Pray you, pardon the comparison.

LOV.                    I allow it;
And, to give you assurance I am pleased
in 't,
My carriage and demeanor to your mis-
tress,
Fair Margaret, shall truly witness for me
I can command my passions.

ALL.                    'Tis a conquest
Few lords can boast of when they are
tempted.—O!

LOV. Why do you sigh?    Can you be
doubtful of me?

---

[1] Release, discharge.
[2] Emended by Coxeter. Original reads *I doe.*
Cf. V, i, 215.
[3] Servants.
[4] Adorn.

By that fair name I in the wars have
    purchased
And all my actions hitherto untainted,
I will not be more true to mine own
    honor                 40
Than to my Allworth!
ALL.      As you are the brave Lord Lovell,
    Your bare word only given is an assur-
    ance
Of more validity and weight to me
Than all the oaths bound up with im-
    precations,
Which, when they would deceive, most
    courtiers practice;
Yet, being a man (for, sure, to style you
    more
Would relish of gross flattery), I am
    forced
Against my confidence of your worth and
    virtues
To doubt, nay, more, to fear.
LOV.          So young, and jealous?
ALL. Were you to encounter with a single
    foe,                 50
The victory were certain; but to stand
The charge of two such potent enemies,
At once assaulting you, as wealth and
    beauty,
And those too seconded with power, is
    odds
Too great for Hercules.
LOV.      Speak your doubts and fears,
    Since you will nourish 'em, in plainer
    language
That I may understand 'em.
ALL.             What's your will,
    Though I lend arms against myself
    (provided
They may advantage [1] you), must be
    obeyed.
My much-loved lord, were Margaret
    only fair,              60
The cannon of her more than earthly
    form,
Though mounted high, commanding all
    beneath it,
And rammed with bullets of her sparkling
    eyes,
Of all the bulwarks that defend your
    senses
Could batter none [2] but that which
    guards your sight.

But, when the well-tuned accents of her
    tongue
Make music to you, and with numerous [3]
    sounds
Assault your hearing (such as if Ulysses
Now lived again, howe'er he stood the
    Sirens,
Could not resist), the combat must grow
    doubtful          70
Between your reason and rebellious
    passions.
Add this too: when you feel her touch,
    and breath
Like a soft western wind when it glides
    o'er
Arabia, creating gums and spices,
And, in the van, the nectar of her lips,
Which you must taste, bring the battalia [4]
    on,
Well armed, and strongly lined [5] with her
    discourse
And knowing manners, to give enter-
    tainment—
Hippolytus himself would leave Diana
To follow such a Venus.
LOV.        Love hath made you  80
    Poetical, Allworth.
ALL.              Grant all these beat off
    (Which, if it be in man to do, you'll do it),
Mammon, in Sir Giles Overreach, steps
    in
With heaps of ill-got gold, and so much
    land,
To make her more remarkable, as would
    tire
A falcon's wings in one day to fly over.
O my good lord! These powerful aids,
    which would
Make a misshapen negro beautiful
(Yet are but ornaments to give her
    luster,          89
That in herself is all perfection), must
Prevail for her. I here release your
    trust;
'Tis happiness enough for me to serve
    you
And sometimes with chaste eyes to look
    upon her.
LOV. Why, shall I swear?
ALL.          O, by no means, my lord;
    And wrong not so your judgment to the
    world

---

[1] Help.
[2] Emended by Gifford. Original reads *more*.
[3] Rhythmical.
[4] Army.  [5] Strengthened. Original reads *liv'd*.

As from your fond indulgence to a boy,
Your page, your servant, to refuse a
     blessing
Divers great men are rivals for.
Lov.                              Suspend
Your judgment till the trial. How far is it
To Overreach' house?
ALL.          At the most, some half hour's
     riding;                                    100
You'll soon be there.
Lov.               And you the sooner freed
From your jealous fears.
ALL.               O, that I durst but hope it!
                                   *Exeunt.*

ACTUS TERTII SCENA SECUNDA.

[*A room in Overreach's house.*]

*Overreach, Greedy, Marall.*

OVER. Spare for no cost; let my dressers
     crack with the weight
Of curious viands.
GREEDY.               *Store indeed's no sore,*[1] sir.
OVER. That proverb fits your stomach,
     Master Greedy.
And let no plate be seen but what's pure
     gold,
Or such whose workmanship exceeds the
     matter
That it is made of; let my choicest linen
Perfume the room, and, when we wash,
     the water,
With precious powders mixed, so please
     my lord
That he may with envy wish to bathe so
     ever.
MAR. 'Twill be very chargeable.[2]
OVER.               Avaunt, you drudge!     10
Now all my labored ends are at the
     stake,
Is 't a time to think of thrift? Call in my
     daughter.—               [*Exit Marall.*]
And, Master Justice, since you love
     choice dishes,
And plenty of 'em—
GREEDY.               As I do, indeed, sir,
Almost as much as to give thanks for 'em.
OVER. I do confer that providence, with
     my power
Of absolute command to have abun-
     dance,
To your best care.

Store indeed—

GREEDY.               I'll punctually discharge it
And give the best directions. Now am I
In mine own conceit[3] a monarch—at
     the least,                                20
Archpresident of the boiled, the roast,
     the baked,
For which I will eat often and give
     thanks
When my belly's braced up like a drum—
     and that's pure justice.
OVER. I[t] must be so. Should the foolish
     girl prove modest,          *Exit Greedy.*
She may spoil all. She had it not from
     me,
But from her mother; I was ever forward,
As she must be, and therefore I'll pre-
     pare her.

[*Enter*] *Margaret.*

Alone—and let your women wait without.
MARG. Your pleasure, sir?
OVER.               Ha, this is a neat dressing!
These orient pearls and diamonds well
     placed too!                              30
The gown affects[4] me not; it should have
     been
Embroidered o'er and o'er with flowers
     of gold;
But these rich jewels and quaint fashion
     help it.
And how below, since oft the wanton
     eye,
The face observed, descends unto the
     foot,
Which, being well proportioned, as
     yours is,
Invites as much as perfect white and red,
Though without art?     How like you
     your new woman,
The Lady Downfall'n?
MARG.               Well, for a companion;
Not as a servant.
OVER.               Is she humble, Meg, 40
And careful too, her ladyship forgotten?
MARG. I pity her fortune.
OVER.               Pity her? Trample on her!
I took her up in an old tamine[5] gown
(Even starved for want of twopenny
     chops) to serve thee;
And, if I understand she but repines
To do thee any duty, though ne'er so
     servile,

---

[1] Harm. Sententious sayings are frequently
indicated by italics.          [2] Costly.

[3] Thought, opinion.
[4] Pleases.          [5] Thin woolen stuff.

I'll pack her to her knight, where I have
  lodged him,
Into the Counter [1] and there let 'em
  howl together.
MARG. You know your own ways; but, for
  me, I blush
When I command her that was once
  attended                      50
With persons not inferior to myself
In birth.
OVER.        In birth? Why, art thou not
  my daughter,
The blessed child of my industry and
  wealth?
Why, foolish girl, was 't not to make thee
  great
That I have ran, and still pursue, those
  ways
That hale down curses on me, which I
  mind not?
Part with these humble thoughts, and
  apt [2] thyself
To the noble state I labor to advance
  thee,
Or, by my hopes to see thee honorable,
I will adopt a stranger to my heir,      60
And throw thee from my care. Do not
  provoke me.
MARG. I will not, sir; mold me which way
  you please.

*Enter Greedy.*

OVER. How! Interrupted?
GREEDY.        'Tis matter of importance.
  The cook, sir, is self-willed, and will not
    learn
  From my experience. There's a fawn
    brought in, sir,
  And, for my life, I cannot make him
    roast it
  With a Norfolk dumpling in the belly of
    it;
  And, sir, we wise men know, without the
    dumpling
  'Tis not worth threepence.
OVER.    Would it were whole in thy belly,
  To stuff it out! Cook it any way; prithee,
    leave me.                        70
GREEDY. Without order for the dumpling?
OVER.               Let it be dumpled
  Which way thou wilt, or tell him I will
    scald him
  In his own caldron.

GREEDY.            I had lost my stomach
  Had I lost my Mistress Dumpling I'll
  give thanks for.
OVER. But to our business, Meg. You
  have heard who dines here?
                         *Exit Greedy.*
MARG. I have, sir.
OVER.             'Tis an honorable man;
  A lord, Meg, and commands a regiment
  Of soldiers, and, what's rare, is one
    himself,
  A bold and understanding one; and to be
  A lord and a good leader, in one volume,
  Is granted unto few but such as rise [3]
    up                               81
  The kingdom's glory.

*Enter Greedy.*

GREEDY.           I'll resign my office,
  If I be not better obeyed.
OVER.        'Slight, art thou frantic?
GREEDY. Frantic?    'Twould make me
  a frantic [4] and stark mad,
  Were I not a justice of peace and coram [5]
    too,
  Which this rebellious cook cares not a
    straw for.
  There are a dozen of woodcocks—
OVER.            Make thyself
  Thirteen, the baker's dozen.
GREEDY.          I am contented,
  So they may be dressed to my mind. He
    has found out
  A new device for sauce, and will not dish
    'em                              90
  With toasts and butter. My father was a
    tailor,
  And my name, though a justice, Greedy
    Woodcock;
  And, ere I'll see my linage [6] so abused,
  I'll give up my commission.
OVER. [*To Cook within.*] Cook! Rogue,
  obey him!
  I have given the word; pray you, now
  remove yourself
  To a collar of brawn,[7] and trouble me no
  farther.
GREEDY. I will, and meditate what to eat
  at dinner.               *Exit Greedy.*

---

[3] Raise.
[4] *I.e.*, an insane person.
[5] Obsolete corruption of *quorum*.
[6] Lineage.            [7] Neck of a boar.

[1] One of the London prisons.      [2] Fit.

OVER. And, as I said, Meg, when this gull
    disturbed us,
This honorable lord, this colonel,[1]
I would have thy husband.
MARG.    There's too much disparity   100
Between his quality and mine to hope it.
OVER. I more than hope 't, and doubt not
    to effect it.
Be thou no enemy to thyself; my wealth
Shall weigh his titles down, and make
    you equals.
Now for the means to assure him thine,
    observe me:
Remember he's a courtier and a soldier,
And not to be trifled with; and, therefore,
    when
He comes to woo you, see you do not
    coy it.[2]
This mincing modesty hath spoiled many
    a match   109
By a first refusal, in vain after hoped
    for.
MARG. You'll have me, sir, preserve the
    distance that
Confines a virgin?
OVER.    Virgin me no virgins!
I must have you lose that name, or you
    lose me.
I will have you private—start not—I
    say, private.
If thou art my true daughter, not a
    bastard,
Thou wilt venture alone with one man,
    though he came
Like Jupiter to Semele, and come off,
    too;
And therefore, when he kisses you, kiss
    close.
MARG. I have heard this is the strumpet's
    fashion, sir,
Which I must never learn.
OVER.    Learn anything,   120
And from any creature that may make
    thee great—
From the devil himself.
MARG. [Aside.]    This is but devilish
    doctrine!
OVER. Or, if his blood grow hot, suppose
    he offer
Beyond this, do not you stay till it
    cool,
But meet his ardor; if a couch be near,
Sit down on 't, and invite him.

[1] Trisyllabic here.    [2] Behave coyly.

MARG.    In your house,
Your own house, sir? For heaven's sake,
    what are you then?
Or what shall I be, sir?
OVER.    Stand not on form;
Words are no substances.
MARG.    Though you could dispense
With your own honor, cast aside re-
    ligion,   130
The hopes of heaven or fear of hell,
    excuse me.
In worldly policy this is not the way
To make me his wife; his whore, I grant
    it may do.
My maiden honor so soon yielded up,
Nay, prostituted, cannot but assure him
I, that am light to him, will not hold
    weight
When he is tempted by others; so, in
    judgment,
When to his lust I have given up my
    honor,
He must and will forsake me.
OVER.    How? Forsake thee?
Do I wear a sword for fashion? Or is this
    arm   140
Shrunk up or withered? Does there live a
    man
Of that large list I have encountered
    with
Can truly say I e'er gave inch of
    ground
Not purchased with his blood that did
    oppose me?
Forsake thee when the thing is done?
    He dares not.
Give me but proof he has enjoyed thy
    person,
Though all his captains, echoes to his
    will,
Stood armed by his side to justify the
    wrong,
And he himself in the head of his bold
    troop,   149
Spite of his lordship and his colonel-
    ship,
Or the judge's favor, I will make him
    render
A bloody and a strict accompt,[3] and
    force him,
By marrying thee, to cure thy wounded
    honor!
I have said it.

[3] Account.

*Enter Marall.*

MAR.        Sir, the man of honor's come,
Newly alighted.
OVER.                    In, without reply.
And do as I command, or thou art lost.
                              *Exit Marg[aret].*
Is the loud music I gave order for
Ready to receive him?
MAR.                    'Tis, sir.
OVER.                         Let 'em sound
A  princely  welcome.—[*Exit  Marall.*]
Roughness, awhile leave me,
For fawning now, a stranger to my
    nature,                              160
Must make way for me.

*Loud music.   Enter Lovell, Greed[y], All-
             w[orth], Mar[all].*
LOV.              Sir, you meet your trouble.
OVER. What you are pleased to style so is
    an honor
Above my worth and fortunes.
ALL. [*Aside.*]           Strange, so humble.
OVER. A justice of peace, my lord.
                    *Presents Greedy to him.*
LOV.                    Your hand, good sir.
GREEDY. [*Aside.*] This is a lord, and some
    think this a favor;
But I had rather have my hand in my
    dumpling.
OVER. Room for my lord.
LOV.              I miss, sir, your fair daughter
To crown my welcome.
OVER.              May it please my lord
To taste a glass of Greek wine first, and
    suddenly
She shall attend my lord.
LOV.              You'll be obeyed, sir.   170
             *Exeunt omnes præter* [1] *Over[reach].*
OVER. 'Tis to my wish. As soon as come,
    ask for her!—
Why, Meg! Meg Overreach!—

             [*Enter Margaret.*]

                    How! Tears in your eyes!
Ha!  Dry 'em quickly, or I'll dig 'em
    out.
Is this a time to whimper?  Meet that
    greatness
That flies into thy bosom; think what 'tis
For me to say, "My honorable daugh-
    ter,"

[1] All except.

And thou, when I stand bare, to say,
    "Put on," [2]
Or, "Father, you forget yourself." No
    more.
But  be  instructed,  or  expect—He
    comes.—

*Enter  Lovell,  Greedy,  Allworth,  Marall.*
                              *They salute.*
A black-browed girl, my lord.
LOV. [*Kissing her.*]              As I live,
    a rare one.                              180
ALL. [*Aside.*] He's took already.  I am
    lost.
OVER. [*Aside.*]         That kiss
Came twanging off; I like it.—Quit the
    room.—                    *The Rest off.*
A little bashful, my good lord, but you,
I hope, will teach her boldness.
LOV.                    I am happy
In such a scholar, but—
OVER.              I am past learning,
And therefore leave you to yourselves.—
(*To his Daughter.*)  Remember!
                              *Exit Overreach.*
LOV. You see, fair lady, your father is
    solicitous
To have you change the barren name of
    virgin
Into a hopeful wife
MARG.              His [3] haste, my lord,
Holds no power o'er my will.
LOV.                    But o'er your duty.  190
MARG. Which, forced too much, may
    break.
LOV.              Bend rather, sweetest.
Think of your years.
MARG.        Too few to match with yours—
And choicest fruits, too soon plucked,
    rot and wither.
LOV.  Do you think I am old?
MARG.              I am sure I am too young.
LOV.  I can advance you.
MARG.                    To a hill of sorrow,
Where every hour I may expect to fall,
But never hope firm footing.  You are
    noble,
I of a low descent, however rich;
And  tissues [4]  matched  with  scarlet [5]
    suit but ill.

[2] *I.e.*, put on your hat.
[3] Emended by Gifford. Original reads *he.*
[4] Silk clothes.
[5] A scarlet gown, worn as a mark of dignity.

O, my good lord, I could say more, but
 that            200
I dare not trust these walls.

Lov.    Pray you, trust my ear then.

*Enter Over[reach behind], list'ning.*

Over. Close at it! Whispering! This is
 excellent!
And, by their postures, a consent on
 both parts.

*Enter Greed[y behind].*

Greedy. Sir Giles, Sir Giles!

Over.     The great fiend stop
 that clapper!

Greedy. It must ring out, sir, when my
 belly rings noon.
The baked-meats are run out, the roast
 turned powder.

Over. I shall powder you.

Greedy.  Beat me to dust, I care not;
In such a cause as this, I'll die a martyr.

Over. Marry, and shall, you barathrum
 of the shambles!¹   *Strikes him.*

Greedy. How! Strike a justice of peace?
 'Tis petty treason,     210
*Edwardi quinto.*² But that you are my
 friend,
I could commit you without bail or
 mainprize.³

Over. Leave your bawling, sir, or I shall
 commit you
Where you shall not dine today. Disturb my lord
When he is in discourse?

Greedy.    Is 't a time to talk
When we should be munching?

Lov.    Ha! I heard some noise.

Over. Mum, villain; vanish! Shall we
 break a bargain
Almost made up?  *Thrust Greedy off.*

Lov.    Lady, I understand you,
And rest most happy in your choice,
 believe it;
I'll be a careful pilot to direct  220
Your yet uncertain bark to a port of
 safety.

Marg. So shall your honor save two lives,
 and bind us
Your slaves forever.

¹ Gulf of the butcher shops; glutton.
² According to a law enacted in the fifth year
of Edward's reign.
³ An undertaking of suretyship.

Lov.    I am in the act rewarded,
Since it is good; howe'er, you must put
 on
An amorous carriage towards me to
 delude
Your subtle father.

Marg.    I am prone to that.

Lov. Now break we off our conference.—
 Sir Giles!
Where is Sir Giles?

*Enter Overreach and the Rest.*

Over.    My noble lord! And how
Does your lordship find her?

Lov.    Apt, Sir Giles, and coming;
And I like her the better.

Over.    So do I too.  230

Lov. Yet, should we take forts at the first
 assault,
'Twere poor in the defendant; I must
 confirm her
With a love letter or two, which I must
 have
Delivered by my page, and you give way
 to 't.

Over. With all my soul—a towardly gen-
 tleman!—
Your hand, good Master Allworth.
 Know my house
Is ever open to you.

All. (*Aside.*)   'Twas shut till now.

Over. Well done, well done, my honorable
 daughter!
Th' art so already. Know this gentle
 youth,
And cherish him, my honorable daughter.    240

Marg. I shall, with my best care.
   *Noise within, as of a coach.*

Over.    A coach!

Greedy.    More stops
Before we go to dinner! O my guts!

*Enter Lady [Allworth] and Wellborn.*

Lady.    If I find welcome,
You share in it; if not, I'll back again,
Now I know your ends, for I come armed
 for all
Can be objected.

Lov.   How! The Lady Allworth!

Over. And thus attended!

*Lovell salutes the Lady; the Lady salutes*
         *Margaret.*

MAR.                          No, I am a dolt!
The spirit of lies had entered me!
OVER.                        Peace, patch! [1]
'Tis more than wonder! An astonish-
    ment
That does possess me wholly!
LOV.                          Noble lady,
This is a favor, to prevent [2] my visit,   250
The service of my life can never equal.
LADY. My lord, I laid wait for you, and
    much hoped
You would have made my poor house
    your first inn;
And therefore, doubting that you might
    forget me
Or too long dwell here, having such
    ample cause
In this unequaled beauty for your stay,
And fearing to trust any but myself
With the relation of my service to
    you,
I borrowed so much from my long re-
    straint
And took the air in person to invite
    you.                                    260
LOV. Your bounties are so great they rob
    me, madam,
Of words to give you thanks.
LADY.        Good Sir Giles Overreach!—
                            *Salutes him.*
How doest thou, Marall? Liked you my
    meat so ill
You'll dine no more with me?
GREEDY.          I will, when you please,
And it like your ladyship.
LADY.            When you please, Master
    Greedy;
If meat can do it, you shall be satisfied.—
And now, my lord, pray take into your
    knowledge
This gentleman; howe'er his outside's
    coarse,            *Presents Wellborn.*
His inward linings are as fine and fair
As any man's. Wonder not I speak at
    large.[3]                              270
And howsoe'er his humor carries him
To be thus accoutered, or what taint
    soever
For his wild life hath stuck upon his
    fame,[4]
He may ere long with boldness rank
    himself

With some that have contemned him.—
Sir Giles Overreach,
If I am welcome, bid him so.
OVER.                        My nephew!
He has been too long a stranger. Faith,
    you have;
Pray, let it be mended.
            *Lovell conferring with Wellborn.*
MAR.        Why, sir, what do you mean?
This is "rogue Wellborn, monster,
    prodigy,
That should hang or drown himself;"
    no man of worship,                    280
Much less your nephew.
OVER.        Well, sirrah, we shall reckon
For this hereafter.
MAR. [*Aside.*]        I'll not lose my jeer,
Though I be beaten dead for 't.
WELL.            Let my silence plead
In my excuse, my lord, till better leisure
Offer itself to hear a full relation
Of my poor fortunes.
LOV.        I would hear, and help 'em.
OVER. Your dinner waits you.
LOV.            Pray you, lead; we follow.
LADY. Nay, you are my guest.—Come,
    dear Master Wellborn.
                    *Exeunt. Manet* [5] *Greedy.*
GREEDY. "Dear Master Wellborn!" so
    she said. Heaven! Heaven!
If my belly would give me leave, I could
    ruminate                              290
All day on this. I have granted twenty
    warrants
To have him committed, from all prisons
    in the shire,
To Nottingham jail. And now "Dear
    Master Wellborn"!
And "My good nephew"!—but I play
    the fool
To stand here prating, and forget my
    dinner.—

                    *Enter Marall.*

Are they set, Marall?
MAR.    Long since. Pray you, a word, sir.
GREEDY. No wording now.
MAR.            In troth, I must. My master,
Knowing you are his good friend, makes
    bold with you
And does entreat you, more guests being
    come in                               299
Than he expected, especially his nephew,

_____
[1] Fool.                    [3] Freely.
[2] Anticipate.              [4] Reputation.
                             [5] Remains.

The table being full too, you would
excuse him
And sup with him on the cold meat.
GREEDY.                    How! No dinner
After all my care?
MAR.                    'Tis but a penance for
A meal; besides, you broke your fast.
GREEDY.                          That was
But a bit to stay my stomach. A man
in commission
Give place to a tatterdemalion!
MAR.                    No bug [1] words, sir;
Should his worship hear you—
GREEDY.               Lose my dumpling too,
And buttered toasts, and woodcocks?
MAR.                    Come, have patience.
If you will dispense a little with your
worship,
And sit with the waiting-women, you
have dumpling,                          310
Woodcock, and buttered toasts too.
GREEDY.                    This revives me;
I will gorge there sufficiently.
MAR.          This is the way, sir. *Exeunt.*

ACTUS TERTII SCENA TERTIA.

[*The same.*]

*Overreach, as from dinner.*

OVER. She's caught! O women! She
neglects my lord,
And all her compliments applied to
Wellborn!
The garments of her widowhood laid
by,
She now appears as glorious as the
spring.
Her eyes fixed on him, in the wine she
drinks,
He being her pledge, she sends him
burning kisses,
And sits on thorns till she be private
with him.
She leaves my meat to feed upon his
looks,
And, if in our discourse he be but named,
From her a deep sigh follows. But why
grieve I                          10
At this? It makes for me; if she prove
his,
All that is hers is mine, as I will work
him.

[1] Pompous, conceited.

*Enter Marall.*

MAR. Sir, the whole board is troubled at
your rising.
OVER. No matter, I'll excuse it. Prithee,
Marall,
Watch an occasion to invite my nephew
To speak with me in private.
MAR.                    Who? "The rogue
The lady scorned to look on"?
OVER.                    You are a wag.

*Enter Lady [Allworth] and Wellborn.*

MAR. See, sir, she's come, and cannot
be without him.
LADY. With your favor, sir, after a plen-
teous dinner,                          19
I shall make bold to walk a turn or two
In your rare garden.
OVER.                    There's an arbor too,
If your ladyship please to use it.
LADY.               Come, Master Wellborn.
*Exeunt Lady [Allworth] and Wellborn.*
OVER. Grosser and grosser! Now I be-
lieve the poet
Feigned not, but was historical, when
he wrote
Pasiphaë was enamored of a bull.
This lady's lust's more monstrous.—
My good lord,

*Enter Lord Lovell, Margaret, and the Rest.*

Excuse my manners.
LOV.               There needs none, Sir Giles—
I may ere long say father, when it
pleases
My dearest mistress to give warrant
to it.
OVER. She shall seal to it, my lord, and
make me happy.                          30

*Enter Wellb[orn] and the Lad[y].*

MARG. My lady is returned.
LADY.                    Provide my coach;
I'll instantly away. My thanks, Sir
Giles,
For my entertainment.
OVER.                    'Tis your nobleness
To think it such.
LADY.          I must do you a further wrong
In taking away your honorable guest.
LOV. I wait on you, madam; farewell,
good Sir Giles.

LADY. Good Mistress Margaret!—Nay, come, Master Wellborn,
  I must not leave you behind; in sooth, I must not.
OVER. Rob me not, madam, of all joys at once;
  Let my nephew stay behind. He shall have my coach,     40
  And, after some small conference between us,
  Soon overtake your ladyship.
LADY.           Stay not long, sir.
LOV. This parting kiss! [Kisses Margaret.]
  You shall every day hear from me
  By my faithful page.
ALL.        'Tis a service I am proud of.
Exeunt Lovell, Lady [Allworth], Allworth, Margaret, Marall.
OVER. Daughter, to your chamber.—
  You may wonder, nephew,
  After so long an enmity between us,
  I should desire your friendship.
WELL.          So I do, sir;
  'Tis strange to me.
OVER.       But I'll make it no wonder;
  And, what is more, unfold my nature to you.
  We worldly men, when we see friends and kinsmen     50
  Past hopes sunk in their fortunes, lend no hand
  To lift 'em up, but rather set our feet
  Upon their heads to press 'em to the bottom,
  As, I must yield, with you I practiced it.
  But, now I see you in a way to rise,
  I can and will assist you. This rich lady
  (And I am glad of 't) is enamored of you;
  'Tis too apparent, nephew.
WELL.         No such thing—
  Compassion rather, sir.
OVER.        Well, in a word,
  Because your stay is short, I'll have you seen     60
  No more in this base shape; nor shall she say
  She married you like a beggar, or in debt.
WELL. (Aside.) He'll run into the noose and save my labor.
OVER. You have a trunk of rich clothes not far hence

In pawn; I will redeem 'em. And, that no clamor
  May taint your credit for your petty debts,
  You shall have a thousand pounds to cut 'em off,
  And go a free man to the wealthy lady.
WELL. This done, sir, out of love, and no ends else—
OVER. As it is, nephew.
WELL.      Binds me still your servant.   70
OVER. No compliments; you are stayed for. Ere y'ave supped,
  You shall hear from me.—My coach, knaves, for my nephew!—
  Tomorrow I will visit you.
WELL.           Here's an uncle
  In a man's extremes! [1] How much they do belie you,
  That say you are hard-hearted!
OVER.           My deeds, nephew,
  Shall speak my love; what men report I weigh not.     Exeunt.

FINIS ACTUS TERTII.

ACTUS QUARTI SCENA PRIMA.

[A room in Lady Allworth's house.]

Lovell, Allworth.

LOV. 'Tis well; give me my cloak; I now discharge you
  From further service. Mind your own affairs;
  I hope they will prove successful.
ALL.          What is blessed
  With your good wish, my lord, cannot but prosper.
  Let aftertimes report, and to your honor,
  How much I stand engaged,[2] for I want language
  To speak my debt. Yet, if a tear or two
  Of joy for your much goodness can supply
  My tongue's defects, I could—
LOV.          Nay, do not melt;
  This ceremonial thanks to me 's superfluous.     10
OVER. (Within.) Is my lord stirring?
LOV. 'Tis he! O, here's your letter. Let him in.

_____
[1] Extremities.                [2] Indebted.

*Enter Over[reach], Greed[y], Mar[all].*

OVER. A good day to my lord!

Lov.                    You are an early riser,
Sir Giles.

OVER.        And reason, to attend your
lordship.

Lov. And you too, Master Greedy, up
so soon?

GREEDY. In troth, my lord, after the sun
is up,
I cannot sleep, for I have a foolish stom-
ach
That croaks for breakfast. With your
lordship's favor,
I have a serious question to demand  19
Of my worthy friend Sir Giles.

Lov.            Pray you, use your pleasure.

GREEDY. How far, Sir Giles, and, pray
you, answer me
Upon your credit, hold you it to be
From your manor house to this of my
Lady Allsworth's?

OVER. Why, some four mile.

GREEDY.        How! Four mile? Good Sir
Giles,
Upon your reputation think better,
For, if you do abate but one half-quarter
Of five, you do yourself the greatest
wrong
That can be in the world; for four miles'
riding
Could not have raised so huge an appe-
tite                                              29
As I feel gnawing on me.

MAR.                    Whether you ride
Or go afoot, you are that way still pro-
vided,
And it please your worship.

OVER.        How now, sirrah? Prating
Before my lord! No difference? Go to
my nephew,
See all his debts discharged, and help
his worship
To fit on his rich suit.

MAR. [*Aside.*]            I may fit you too.
Tossed like a dog still!    *Exit Marall.*

Lov.            I have writ this morning
A few lines to my mistress, your fair
daughter.

OVER. 'Twill fire her, for she's wholly
yours already.—
Sweet Master Allworth, take my ring.
'Twill carry you

To her presence, I dare warrant you;
and there plead                          40
For my good lord, if you shall find occasion.
That done, pray ride to Nottingham;
get a license,
Still by this token. I'll have it despatched,
And suddenly, my lord, that I may
say
My "honorable," nay, "right honorable"
daughter.

GREEDY. Take my advice, young gentleman; get your breakfast.
'Tis unwholesome to ride fasting. I'll
eat with you
And eat to purpose.

OVER.            Some Fury's in that gut!
Hungry again! Did you not devour this
morning
A shield of brawn,[1] and a barrel of Colchester oysters?                          50

GREEDY. Why, that was, sir, only to
scour my stomach,
A kind of a preparative. Come, gentleman,
I will not have you feed like the hangman of Vlushing [2]
Alone, while I am here.

Lov.                    Haste your return.

ALL. I will not fail, my lord.

GREEDY.                    Nor I, to line
My Christmas coffer.[3]
                    *Exeunt Greedy and Allworth.*

OVER.        To my wish, we are private.
I come not to make offer with my daugh-
ter
A certain portion—that were poor and
trivial.
In one word, I pronounce all that is
mine,                                        59
In lands or leases, ready coin or goods,
With her, my lord, comes to you; nor
shall you have
One motive to induce you to believe
I live too long, since every year I'll
add
Something unto the heap, which shall
be yours too.

Lov. You are a right kind father.

[1] "The thick skin on the flanks of a boar; a
piece of this was filled up with meat and cooked
till soft" (Cruickshank).
[2] Flushing.        [3] *I.e.*, his stomach.

Over.                    You shall have reason
To think me such.  How do you like
    this seat?
It is well wooded, and well watered, the
    acres
Fertile and rich.  Would it not serve
    for change,
To entertain your friends in a summer
    progress?[1]                             69
What thinks my noble lord?
Lov.                     'Tis a wholesome air,
And well-built pile; and she that's mis-
    tress of it
Worthy the large revenue.
Over.                    She the mistress?
It may be so for a time, but, let my lord
Say only that he likes it, and would
    have it,
I say, ere long 'tis his.
Lov.                          Impossible.
Over.  You do conclude too fast, not know-
    ing me,
Nor the engines[2] that I work by.  'Tis
    not alone
The Lady Allworth's lands, for those
    once Wellborn's
(As by her dotage on him I know they will
    be)
Shall soon be mine; but point out any
    man's                                   80
In all the shire, and say they lie con-
    venient
And useful for your lordship, and once
    more
I say aloud, they are yours.
Lov.                    I dare not own
What's by unjust and cruel means ex-
    torted;
My fame and credit are more dear to
    me
Than so to expose 'em to be censured by
The public voice.
Over.        You run, my lord, no hazard.
Your reputation shall stand as fair
In all good men's opinions as now;
Nor can my actions, though condemned
    for ill,                                90
Cast any foul aspersion upon yours,
For, though I do contemn report my-
    self
As a mere sound, I still will be so tender
Of what concerns you, in all points of
    honor,

That the immaculate whiteness of your
    fame
Nor your unquestioned integrity
Shall e'er be sullied with one taint or
    spot
That may take from your innocence and
    candor.[3]
All my ambition is to have my daugh-
    ter
Right honorable, which my lord can
    make her.                              100
And, might I live to dance upon my
    knee
A young Lord Lovell, borne by her unto
    you,
I write *nil ultra*[4] to my proudest hopes.
As for possessions and annual rents,
Equivalent to maintain you in the port[5]
Your noble birth and present state re-
    quires,
I do remove that burthen from your
    shoulders
And take it on mine own, for, though
    I ruin
The country to supply your riotous
    waste,
The scourge of prodigals, want, shall
    never find you.                        110
Lov. Are you not frighted with the im-
    precations
And curses of whole families, made
    wretched
By your sinister practices?
Over.                     Yes, as rocks are,
When foamy billows split themselves
    against
Their flinty ribs, or as the moon is moved
When wolves, with hunger pined, howl
    at her brightness.
I am of a solid temper and like these
Steer on a constant course.  With mine
    own sword,
If called into the field, I can make that
    right
Which fearful enemies murmured at as
    wrong.                                 120
Now, for these other piddling com-
    plaints
Breathed out in bitterness, as when they
    call me
Extortioner, tyrant, cormorant, or in-
    truder

[1] Journey.                    [2] Devices.
[3] Immaculateness.
[4] Nothing beyond.        [5] Style of living.

On my poor neighbor's right, or grand
   incloser
Of what was common, to my private
   use,
Nay, when my ears [1] are pierced with
   widows' cries,
And undone orphants [2] wash with tears
   my threshold,
I only think what 'tis to have my daugh-
   ter
Right honorable; and 'tis a powerful
   charm                                      129
Makes me insensible of remorse or pity
Or the least sting of conscience.
Lov.                            I admire [3]
The toughness of your nature.
Over.                        'Tis for you,
   My lord, and for my daughter, I am
      marble;
Nay, more, if you will have my char-
   acter
In little, I enjoy more true delight
In my arrival to my wealth these dark
And crooked ways than you shall e'er
   take pleasure
In spending what my industry hath
   compassed.
My haste commands me hence.  In one
   word, therefore,                          139
Is it a match?
Lov.       I hope that is past doubt now.
Over. Then rest secure; not the hate of
   all mankind here,
Nor fear of what can fall on me here-
   after
Shall make me study aught but your
   advancement
One story higher.  An earl, if gold can
   do it!
Dispute not my religion nor my faith.
Though I am borne thus headlong by
   my will,
You may make choice of what belief
   you please;
To me they are equal.  So, my lord,
   good  morrow.                        Exit.
Lov. He's gone—I wonder how the earth
   can bear
Such a portent!  I, that have lived a
   soldier,                                  150
And stood the enemy's violent charge
   undaunted,

To hear this blasphemous beast am
   bathed all over
In a cold sweat.  Yet, like a mountain,
   he,
Confirmed in atheistical [4] assertions,
Is no more shaken than Olympus is
When angry Boreas loads his double
   head
With sudden drifts of snow.

*Enter Amble, Lady [Allworth], [Waiting-]*
*Woman.*

Lady.                        Save you, my lord!
   Disturb I not your privacy?
Lov.                        No, good madam,
   For your own sake I am glad you came
      no sooner,
Since this bold, bad man, Sir Giles
   Overreach,                               160
Made such a plain discovery [5] of himself,
And read this morning such a devilish
   matins
That I should think it a sin next to his
But to repeat it.
Lady.              I ne'er pressed, my lord,
   On others' privacies; yet, against my
      will,
Walking, for health' sake, in the gallery
Adjoining to your lodgings, I was made
(So vehement and loud he was) partaker
Of his tempting offers.
Lov.               Please you to command
   Your servants hence, and I shall gladly
      hear                                   170
Your wiser counsel.
Lady.              'Tis, my lord, a woman's,
   But true and hearty.—[*To Amble.*] Wait
      in the next room,
But be within call; yet not so near to
   force me
To whisper my intents.
Amb.                We are taught better
   By you, good madam.
Woman.        And well know our distance.
Lady. Do so, and talk not; 'twill become
   your breeding.—
        *Exeunt Amble and [Waiting-] Woman.*
   Now, my good lord, if I may use my
      freedom,
As to an honored friend—
Lov.                You lessen else
   Your favor to me.

---

[1] Original read *cares.*
[2] Orphans.                    [3] Wonder at.
[4] Godless.                    [5] Revelation.

LADY.          I dare then say thus:  179
As you are noble (howe'er common men
Make sordid wealth the object and sole
end
Of their industrious aims), 'twill not
agree
With those of eminent blood, who are
engaged
More to prefer [1] their honors than to
increase
The state left to 'em by their ances-
tors,
To study large additions to their for-
tunes
And quite neglect their births—though
I must grant
Riches, well got, to be a useful servant,
But a bad master.
LOV.          Madam, 'tis confessed.  189
But what infer you from it?
LADY.                    This, my lord:
That as all wrongs, though thrust into
one scale,
Slide of themselves off when right fills
the other
And cannot bide the trial, so all wealth,
I mean if ill-acquired, cemented to
honor
By virtuous ways achieved and bravely
purchased,
Is but as rubbage [2] poured into a river
(Howe'er intended to make good the
bank),
Rendering the water, that was pure be-
fore,
Polluted and unwholesome. I allow
The heir of Sir Giles Overreach,
Margaret,                    200
A maid well qualified and the richest
match
Our north part can make boast of; yet
she cannot,
With all that she brings with her, fill [3]
their mouths,
That never will forget who was her
father,
Or that my husband Allworth's lands
and Wellborn's
(How wrung from both needs now no
repetition)
Were real motive that more worked
your lordship

To join your families than her form and
virtues.
You may conceive the rest.
LOV.                    I do, sweet madam,
And long since have considered it.  I
know,                    210
The sum of all that makes a just man
happy
Consists in the well choosing of his wife;
And there, well to discharge it, does
require
Equality of years, of birth, of fortune,
For beauty, being poor and not cried
up
By birth or wealth, can truly mix with
neither.
And wealth, where there's such differ-
ence in years
And fair descent, must make the yoke
uneasy.
But I come nearer.
LADY.                    Pray you, do, my lord.
LOV. Were Overreach' states thrice cen-
tupled, his daughter                    220
Millions of degrees much fairer than
she is,
Howe'er I might urge presidents [4] to
excuse me,
I would not so adulterate my blood
By marrying Margaret, and so leave my
issue
Made up of several pieces, one part
scarlet
And the other London blue.[5] In my own
tomb
I will inter my name first.
LADY. (*Aside*.)     I am glad to hear this.—
Why then, my lord, pretend you mar-
riage to her?
Dissimulation but ties false knots
On that straight line by which you
hitherto                    230
Have measured all your actions.
LOV.                    I make answer,
And aptly, with a question. Wherefore
have you
That, since your husband's death, have
lived a strict
And chaste nun's life, on the sudden
given yourself
To visits and entertainments? Think
you, madam,

[1] Promote.
[2] Rubbish.                    [3] *I.e.*, stop.

[4] Precedents.
[5] Cloth symbolical of the servant class.

'Tis not grown public conference? Or
  the favors
Which you too prodigally have thrown
  on Wellborn,
Being too reserved before, incur not
  censure?
LADY. I am innocent here; and, on my
  life, I swear             239
  My ends are good.
LOV.          On my soul, so are mine
To Margaret; but leave both to the
  event. [1]
And, since this friendly privacy does serve
But as an offered means unto ourselves
To search each other farther, you having
  shown
Your care of me, I my respect to you,
Deny me not, but still in chaste words,
  madam,
An afternoon's discourse.
LADY.     So I shall hear you. [*Exeunt.*]

ACTUS QUARTI SCENA SECUNDA.

[*Before Tapwell's house.*]

*Tapwell, Froth.*

TAP. Undone, undone! This was your
  counsel, Froth.
FROTH. Mine! I defy thee. Did not Mas-
  ter Marall
  (He has marred all, I am sure) strictly
    command us,
On pain of Sir Giles Overreach' dis-
  pleasure,
To turn the gentleman out of doors?
TAP.               'Tis true;
But now he's his uncle's darling, and has
  got
Master Justice Greedy, since he filled
  his belly,
At his commandment, to do anything.
  Woe, woe to us!
FROTH.     He may prove merciful.  9
TAP. Troth, we do not deserve it at his
  hands.
Though he knew all the passages [2] of our
  house,
As the receiving of stolen goods, and
  bawdry,
When he was rogue Wellborn no man
  would believe him,
And then his information could not hurt
  us;

But now he is "right worshipful" again,
Who dares but doubt [3] his testimony?
  Methinks,
I see thee, Froth, already in a cart,
For a close [4] bawd, thine eyes ev'n pelted
  out
With dirt and rotten eggs, and my hand
  hissing             19
If I scape the halter, with the letter R [5]
Printed upon it.
FROTH.     Would that were the worst!
That were but nine days' wonder. As
  for credit,
We have none to lose, but we shall lose
  the money
He owes us, and his custom—there's the
  hell on 't.
TAP. He has summoned all his creditors
  by the drum,
And they swarm about him like so many
  soldiers
On the pay day, and has found out such
  a new way
To pay his old debts as 'tis very likely
He shall be chronicled for it!
FROTH.           He deserves it
More than ten pageants. But are you
  sure his worship         30
Comes this way, to my lady's?
  *A cry within: "Brave Master Wellborn!"*
TAP.           Yes. I hear him.
FROTH. Be ready with your petition and
  present it
To his good grace.

*Enter Wellb[orn] in a rich habit, [Marall,]*
  *Greed[y], Ord[er], Furn[ace], three Credi-*
  *tors; Tapw[ell], kneeling, delivers his*
                    *bill of debt.*

WELL.     How's this? Petitioned, too?
But note what miracles the payment of
A little trash, and a rich suit of clothes,
Can work upon these rascals! I shall be,
I think, Prince Wellborn.
MAR.     When your worship's married,
You may be—I know what I hope to
  see you.
WELL. Then look thou for advancement.
MAR.             To be known
Your worship's bailiff is the mark I shoot
  at.               40

[1] Outcome.           [2] Occurrences.

[3] Fear.
[4] Secret.        [5] Standing for "Rogue."

WELL. And thou shalt hit it.

MAR.          Pray you, sir, despatch
These needy followers, and for my ad-
   mittance,[1]
Provided you'll defend me from Sir Giles,
*This interim, Tapwell and Froth flattering*
               *and bribing Justice Greedy.*
Whose service I am weary of, I'll say
   something
You shall give thanks for.

WELL.          Fear me not [2] Sir Giles.

GREEDY. Who? Tapwell? I remember
   thy wife brought me
Last New Year's tide a couple of fat
   turkeys.

TAP. And shall do every Christmas, let
   your worship
But stand my friend now.

GREEDY.     How? With Master Wellborn?
I can do anything with him on such
   terms.—                     50
[*To Wellborn.*] See you this honest cou-
   ple? They are good souls
As ever drew cut faucet. Have they
   not
A pair of honest faces?

WELL.          I o'erheard you,
And the bribe he promised. You are
   cozened in 'em,
For of all the scum that grew rich by my
   riots
This, for a most unthankful knave, and
   this,
For a base bawd and whore, have worst
   deserved me,[3]
And therefore speak not for 'em. By
   your place
You are rather to do me justice. Lend me
   your ear.—
[*Aside.*] Forget his turkeys, and call in
   his license,                 60
And at the next fair I'll give you a yoke
   of oxen
Worth all his poultry.

GREEDY.       I am changed on the sudden
In my opinion!—Come near; nearer,
   rascal.
And, now I view him better, did you e'er
   see
One look so like an archknave? His very
   countenance,

Should an understanding judge but look
   upon him,
Would hang him, though he were innocent.

TAP.   ⎫
FROTH. ⎬                Worshipful sir!

GREEDY. No, though the great Turk came,
   instead of turkeys,
To beg any favor, I am inexorable.
Thou hast an ill name; besides thy musty
   ale,                           70
That hath destroyed many of the king's
   liege people,
Thou never hadst in thy house, to stay
   men's stomachs,
A piece of Suffolk cheese or gammon of
   bacon,
Or any esculent, as the learned call it,
For their emolument, but sheer drink
   only,
For which gross fault I here do damn thy
   license,
Forbidding thee ever to tap or draw;
For instantly I will in mine own person
Command the constable to pull down
   thy sign,
And do it before I eat.

FROTH.          No mercy?

GREEDY.             Vanish!   80
If I show any, may my promised oxen
   gore me!

TAP. Unthankful knaves are ever so rewarded.
           *Exeunt Greedy, Tapwell, Froth.*

WELL. Speak, what are you?

1 CRED.         A decayed vintner, sir,
That might have thrived, but that your
   worship broke me
With trusting you with muscadine and
   eggs,
And five-pound suppers, with your after-
   drinkings,
When you lodged upon the Bankside.

WELL.          [I] [4] remember.

1 CRED. I have not been hasty, nor e'er
   laid to arrest you;
And therefore, sir—

WELL.      Thou art an honest fellow. 89
I'll set thee up again; see his bill paid.—
What are you?

2 CRED.        A tailor once, but now
   mere botcher.[5]
I gave you credit for a suit of clothes,

---

[1] *I.e.*, admittance to his service.
[2] *I.e.*, fear not.
[3] Have deserved worst in respect to me.
[4] Supplied by Gifford.         [5] Mender.

Which was all my stock, but, you failing
  in payment,
I was removed from the shopboard,[1] and
  confined
Under a stall.[2]
WELL.        See him paid—and botch
  no more.
2 CRED. I ask no interest, sir.
WELL.        Such tailors need not;
If their bills are paid in one-and-twenty
  year,
They are seldom losers.—[*To 3 Creditor*.]
  O, I know thy face;
Thou wert my surgeon. You must tell
  no tales;
Those days are done. I will pay you in
  private.                100
ORD. A royal gentleman!
FURN.        Royal as an emperor!
He'll prove a brave master; my good
  lady knew
To choose a man.
WELL.    See all men else discharged;
And, since *old debts are cleared by a new
  way*,
A little bounty will not misbecome me.
There's something, honest cook, for thy
  good breakfasts.—
[*To Order*.] And this, for your respect.
  Take 't; 'tis good gold,
And I able to spare it.
ORD.        You are too munificent.
FURN. He was ever so.
WELL.        Pray you, on before.
3 CRED.        Heaven bless you!
MAR. At four a-clock the rest know where
  to meet me.             110
  *Exeunt Ord*[er], *Furn*[ace], *Credit*[ors].
WELL. Now, Master Marall, what's the
  weighty secret
You promised to impart?
MAR.        Sir, time nor place
Allow me to relate each circumstance.
This only, in a word: I know Sir Giles
Will come upon you for security
For his thousand pounds, which you
  must not consent to.
As he grows in heat, as I am sure he
  will,
Be you but rough, and say he's in your
  debt
Ten times the sum, upon sale of your
  land.

[1] A tailor's workbench.      [2] Bench.

I had a hand in 't (I speak it to my
  shame)            120
When you were defeated [3] of it.
WELL.        That's forgiven.
MAR. I shall deserve 't then. Urge him to
  produce
The deed in which you passed it over to
  him,
Which I know he'll have about him, to
  deliver
To the Lord Lovell with many other
  writings
And present monies. I'll instruct you
  further,
As I wait on your worship. If I play not
  my price [4]
To your full content and your uncle's
  much vexation,
Hang up Jack Marall.
WELL.        I rely upon thee. *Exeunt.*


ACTUS QUARTI SCENA ULTIMA.[5]

[*A room in Overreach's house.*]

*Allworth, Margaret.*

ALL. Whether to yield the first praise to
  my lord's
Unequaled temperance or your constant
  sweetness
That I yet live, my weak hands fastened
  on
Hope's anchor, spite of all storms of
  despair,
I yet rest doubtful.
MARG.        Give it to Lord Lovell,
For what in him was bounty, in me's
  duty.
I make but payment of a debt to which
My vows, in that high office[6] registered,
Are faithful witnesses.
ALL.        'Tis true, my dearest;
Yet, when I call to mind how many fair
  ones           10
Make willful shipwrack of their faiths,
  and oaths
To God and man, to fill the arms of great-
  ness,
And you rise up [no] [7] less than a glorious
  star,

[3] Defrauded.
[4] Prize (in a game); *i.e.*, part.
[5] The last scene of the fourth act.
[6] *I.e.*, heaven.      [7] Added by Dodsley.

To the amazement of the world, that hold
   out
Against the stern authority of a father,
And spurn at honor when it comes to
   court you,
I am so tender of your good that, faintly,[1]
With your wrong I can wish myself that
   right
You yet are pleased to do me.

MARG.                              Yet and ever.
To me what's title, when content is want-
   ing?                                                20
Or wealth, raked up together with much
   care
And to be kept with more, when the
   heart pines
In being dispossessed of what it longs for
Beyond the Indian[2] mines?  Or the
   smooth brow
Of a pleased sire, that slaves me to his
   will,
And, so his ravenous humor may be
   feasted
By my obedience, and he see me great,
Leaves to my soul nor faculties nor power
To make her own election?

ALL.                              But the dangers
That follow the repulse—

MARG.          To me they are nothing.  30
Let Allworth love, I cannot be unhappy.
Suppose the worst, that in his rage he
   kill me.
A tear or two, by you dropped on my
   hearse
In sorrow for my fate, will call back life
So far as but to say that I die yours;
I then shall rest in peace.  Or should he
   prove
So cruel, as one death would not suffice
His thirst of vengeance, but with ling'ring
   torments
In mind and body I must waste to air,
In poverty joined with banishment, so
   you share                                       40
In my afflictions, which I dare not wish
   you,
So high I prize you, I could undergo 'em
With such a patience as should look
   down
With scorn on his worst malice.

ALL.                              Heaven avert
Such trials of your true affection to me!
Nor will it unto you, that are all mercy,

[1] Half-heartedly.          [2] Of the Indies.

Show so much rigor.  But, since we must
   run
Such desperate hazards, let us do our best
To steer between 'em.

MARG.          Your lord's ours, and sure;
And, though but a young actor, second
   me                                              50
In doing to the life what he has plotted,

*Enter Overreach [behind].*

The end may yet prove happy.  Now, my
   Allworth—                    [*Sees her father.*]

ALL. [*Aside.*]  To your letter, and put on a
   seeming anger.

MARG.  I'll pay my lord all debts due to his
   title;
And when, with terms not taking from
   his honor,
He does solicit me, I shall gladly hear
   him.
But in this peremptory, nay, command-
   ing way,
To appoint a meeting and, without my
   knowledge,
A priest to tie the knot can ne'er be
   undone
Till death unloose it, is a confidence[3]    60
In his lordship will deceive him.

ALL.                              I hope better,
Good lady.

MARG.          Hope, sir, what you please.
   For me
I must take a safe and secure course; I
   have
A father, and without his full consent,
Though all lords of the land kneeled for
   my favor,
I can grant nothing.

OVER. [*Coming forward.*]     I like this obe-
   dience.—
But whatsoever my lord writes must and
   shall be
Accepted and embraced.  Sweet Master
   Allworth,
You show yourself a true and faithful
   servant
To your good lord; he has a jewel of
   you.                                             70
How?  Frowning, Meg?  Are these looks
   to receive
A messenger from my lord?  What's this?
   Give me it.

[3] Presumption.

MARG. A piece of arrogant paper, like th'
   inscriptions. *Overreach read[s] the letter.*
OVER. "Fair mistress, from your servant
   learn, all joys
   That we can hope for, if deferred, prove
   toys;
   Therefore this instant, and in private,
   meet
   A husband, that will gladly at your
   feet
   Lay down his honors, tend'ring them to
   you
   With all content, the church being paid
   her due."—                               79
   Is this the arrogant piece of paper? Fool,
   Will you still be one? In the name of
   madness what
   Could his good honor write more to
   content you?
   Is there aught else to be wished, after
   these two,
   That are already offered: marriage first,
   And lawful pleasure after? What would
   you more?
MARG. Why, sir, I would be married like
   your daughter,
   Not hurried away i' th' night I know not
   whither,
   Without all ceremony—no friends invited
   To honor the solemnity.
ALL.                An 't please your honor,
   For so before tomorrow I must style
   you,                                      90
   My lord desire[s] this privacy, in respect
   His honorable kinsmen are far off,
   And his desires to have it done brook
   not
   So long delay as to expect [1] their com-
   ing;
   And yet he stands resolved, with all due
   pomp,
   As running at the ring, plays, masques,
   and tilting,
   To have his marriage at court celebrated,
   When he has brought your honor up to
   London.
OVER. He tells you true; 'tis the fashion,
   on my knowledge.
   Yet the good lord, to please your peevish-
   ness,                                     100
   Must put it off, forsooth, and lose a night,
   In which perhaps he might get two boys
   on thee.

[1] Wait on.

Tempt me no farther; if you do, this
   goad [2]              [*Points to his sword.*]
Shall prick you to him.
MARG.                    I could be contented,
   Were you but by to do a father's part
   And give me in the church.
OVER.                    So my lord have you,
   What do I care who gives you? Since
   my lord
   Does purpose to be private, I'll not cross
   him.
   I know not, Master Allworth, how my
   lord
   May be provided, and therefore there's a
   purse                                     110
   Of gold—'twill serve this night's expense;
   tomorrow
   I'll furnish him with any sums. In the
   meantime,
   Use my ring to my chaplain; he is
   beneficed
   At my manor of Gotam,[3] and called
   Parson Willdo.
   'Tis no matter for a license; I'll bear him
   out in 't.
MARG. With your favor, sir, what warrant
   is your ring?
   He may suppose I got that twenty ways,
   Without your knowledge; and then to be
   refused
   Were such a stain upon me! If you
   pleased, sir,
   Your presence would do better.
OVER.                    Still perverse?  120
   I say again, I will not cross my lord;
   Yet I'll prevent you too.—Paper and
   ink there!
ALL. I can furnish you.
OVER.    I thank you; I can write then.
                       *Writes on his book.*
ALL. You may, if you please, put out the
   name of my lord,
   In respect he comes disguised, and only
   write,
   "Marry her to this gentleman."
OVER.    Well advised.—(*Margaret kneels.*)
   'Tis done; away!—My blessing, girl?
   Thou hast it.
   Nay, no reply; begone.—Good Master
   Allworth,
   This shall be the best night's work you
   ever made.

[2] Emended by Gifford.   Original reads *good*.
[3] Gotham.                          [4] Forestall.

ALL. I hope so, sir.                          130
*Exeunt Allworth and Margaret.*
OVER. Farewell!—Now all's cocksure.
Methinks I hear already knights and
    ladies
Say, "Sir Giles Overreach, how is it with
Your honorable daughter?    Has her
    honor
Slept well tonight?" or, "Will her honor
    please
To accept this monkey?    Dog?    Or
    paraquit?" [1]
(This is state in ladies) "Or my eldest son
To be her page, and wait upon her
    trencher?"
My ends, my ends are compassed!    Then
    for Wellborn
And the lands.    Were he once married to
    the widow,                          140
I have him here.    I can scarce contain
    myself,
I am so full of joy, nay, joy all over. *Exit.*

THE END OF THE FOURTH ACT

ACTUS QUINTI SCENA PRIMA.[2]

[*A room in Lady Allworth's house.*]

*Lovell, Lady* [*Allworth*], *Amble.*

LADY. By this you know how strong the
    motives were
That did, my lord, induce me to dispense
A little with my gravity to advance,
In personating some few favors to him,
The plots and projects of the downtrod
    Wellborn.
Nor shall I e'er repent, although I suffer
In some few men's opinions for 't, the
    action,
For he that ventured all for my dear
    husband
Might justly claim an obligation from
    me
To pay him such a courtesy, which
    had I                                10
Coyly or overcuriously[3] denied,
It might have argued me of little love
To the deceased.
LOV.               What you intended, madam,
For the poor gentleman hath found good
    success,
For, as I understand, his debts are paid,

And he once more furnished for fair em-
    ployment.
But all the arts that I have used to raise
The fortunes of your joy and mine, young
    Allworth,
Stand yet in supposition, though I hope
    well,
For the young lovers are in wit more
    pregnant                            20
Than their years can promise; and for
    their desires,
On my knowledge, they are equal.
LADY.                    —As my wishes
Are with yours, my lord.    Yet give me
    leave to fear
The building, though well grounded.    To
    deceive
Sir Giles, that's both a lion and a fox
In his proceedings, were a work beyond
The strongest undertakers—not the trial
Of two weak innocents.
LOV.               Despair not, madam.
*Hard things are compassed oft by easy
    means;*
And judgment, being a gift derived from
    heaven,                            30
Though sometimes lodged i' th' hearts of
    worldly men,
That ne'er consider from whom they re-
    ceive it,
Forsakes such as abuse the giver of it—
Which is the reason that the politic
And cunning statesman, that believes he
    fathoms
The counsels of all kingdoms on the
    earth,
Is by simplicity oft overreach[ed].[4]
LADY. May he be so!    Yet in his name to
    express it
Is a good omen.
LOV.               May it to myself      39
Prove so, good lady, in my suit to you!
What think you of the motion?[5]
LADY.               Troth, my lord,
My own unworthiness may answer for
    me,
For had you, when that I was in my
    prime
(My virgin flower uncropped), presented
    me
With this great favor, looking on my
    lowness
Not in a glass of self-love, but of truth,

[1] Parakeet.
[2] Original reads *Quinta*.        [3] Overcarefully.
[4] Added by Coxeter.               [5] Proposal.

I could not but have thought it as a blessing
Far, far beyond my merit.

Lov. You are too modest,
And undervalue that which is above
My title, or whatever I call mine. 50
I grant, were I a Spaniard, to marry
A widow might disparage me; but, being
A true-born Englishman, I cannot find
How it can taint my honor. Nay, what's more,
That which you think a blemish is to me
The fairest luster. You already, madam,
Have given sure proofs how dearly you can cherish
A husband that deserves you, which confirms me
That, if I am not wanting in my care
To do you service, you'll be still the same 60
That you were to your Allworth. In a word,
Our years, our states, our births are not unequal,
You being descended nobly, and allied so;
If then you may be won to make me happy,
But join your lips to mine, and that shall be
A solemn contract.

Lady. I were blind to my own good
Should I refuse it. [*Kisses him.*] Yet, my lord, receive me
As such a one, the study of whose whole life
Shall know no other object but to please you.

Lov. If I return not with all tenderness 70
Equal respect to you, may I die wretched!

Lady. There needs no protestation, my lord,
To her that cannot doubt.—

*Enter Wellborn [handsomely appareled].*[1]

You are welcome, sir.
Now you look like yourself.

Well. And will continue
Such in my free acknowledgment that I am

[1] In the original the stage direction follows Lady Allworth's speech.

Your creature, madam, and will never hold
My life mine own, when you please to command it.

Lov. It is a thankfulness that well becomes you.
You could not make choice of a better shape
To dress your mind in.

Lady. For me, I am happy 80
That my endeavors prospered. Saw you of late
Sir Giles, your uncle?

Well. I heard of him, madam,
By his minister, Marall; he's grown into strange passions
About his daughter. This last night he looked for
Your lordship at his house, but, missing you,
And she not yet appearing, his wisehead [2]
Is much perplexed and troubled.

Lov. It may be,
Sweetheart, my project took.

*Enter Over[reach], with distracted looks, driving in Marall before him [with a box].*

Lady. I strongly hope.

Over. Ha! Find her, booby, thou huge lump of nothing;
I'll bore thine eyes out else.

Well. [*Aside.*] May it please your lordship, 90
For some ends of mine own but to withdraw
A little out of sight, though not of hearing,
You may perhaps have sport.

Lov. You shall direct me. *Steps aside.*

Over. I shall *sol fa*[3] you, rogue!

Mar. Sir, for what cause
Do you use me thus?

Over. Cause, slave? Why, I am angry,
And thou a subject only fit for beating,
And so to cool my choler. Look to the writing;
Let but the seal be broke upon the box
That has slept in my cabinet these three years,
I'll rack thy soul for 't.

Mar. (*Aside.*) I may yet cry quittance, 100
Though now I suffer, and dare not resist.

[2] *I.e.*, his "wisehood," "wisdomship."
[3] Play a tune on, beat.

Over. Lady, by your leave, did you see my
    daughter, lady?
And the lord her husband?  Are they in
    your house?
If they are, discover, that I may bid 'em
    joy;
And, as an entrance to her place of honor,
See your ladyship on her left hand, and
    make curtseys
When she nods on you, which you must
    receive
As a special favor.
Lady.                When I know, Sir Giles,
Her state requires such ceremony, I shall
    pay it;                                    109
But in the meantime, as I am myself,
I give you to understand I neither
    know
Nor care where her honor is.
Over.                When you once see her
Supported and led by the lord her hus-
    band,
You'll be taught better.—Nephew!
Well.                                        Sir.
Over.                                    No more?
Well. 'Tis all I owe you.
Over.                Have your redeemed rags
Made you thus insolent?
Well. (*In scorn.*)        Insolent to you?
Why, what are you, sir, unless in your
    years,
At the best, more than myself?
Over. [*Aside.*]        His fortune swells him.
'Tis rank [1] he's married.
Lady.                        This is excellent!
Over. Sir, in calm language, though I sel-
    dom use it,                                120
I am familiar with the cause that makes
    you
Bear up thus bravely.  There's a certain
    buzz
Of a stol'n marriage—do you hear?—of a
    stol'n marriage,
In which, 'tis said, there's somebody
    hath been cozened.
I name no parties.
Well.        Well, sir, and what follows?
Over. Marry, this, since you are peremp-
    tory: remember,
Upon mere hope of your great match, I
    lent you
A thousand pounds.  Put me in good
    security,

[1] Gross, plain.

And suddenly, by [2] mortgage or by stat-
    ute,
Of some of your new possessions, or I'll
    have you                                   130
Dragged in your lavender [3] robes to the
    jail.  You know me,
And therefore do not trifle.
Well.                        Can you be
So cruel to your nephew, now he's in
The way to rise?  Was this the courtesy
You did me "in pure love, and no ends
    else"?
Over. End me no ends!  Engage the whole
    estate,
And force your spouse to sign it, you
    shall have
Three or four thousand more, to roar and
    swagger
And revel in bawdy taverns.
Well.                    And beg after—   139
Mean you not so?
Over.        My thoughts are mine, and free.
Shall I have security?
Well.                No, indeed, you shall not,
Nor bond, nor bill, nor bare acknowledg-
    ment;
Your great looks fright not me.
Over.                        But my deeds shall.
Outbraved?
            *They both draw.  The Servants enter.*
Lady.        Help, murther!  Murther!
Well.                        Let him come on,
With all his wrongs and injuries about
    him,
Armed with his cutthroat practices to
    guard him;
The right that I bring with me will de-
    fend me,
And punish his extortion.
Over.                    That I had thee
But single in the field!
Lady.                You may; but make not
My house your quarreling scene.
Over.            Were 't in a church, 150
By heaven and hell, I'll do 't!
Mar. [*Aside to Wellborn.*]        Now put
    him to
The showing of the deed.
Well.                    This rage is vain, sir.
For fighting, fear not, you shall have your
    hands full
Upon the least incitement; and whereas

[2] Emended by Coxeter.  Original reads *my.*
[3] Laid in lavender; *i.e.,* pawned.

You charge me with a debt of a thousand
    pounds,
If there be law (howe'er you have no
    conscience),
Either restore my land or I'll recover
A debt that's truly due to me from you,
In value ten times more than what you
    challenge.[1]
OVER. I in thy debt! O impudence! Did
    I not purchase           160
The land left by thy father, that rich
    land
That had continuéd in Wellborn's name
Twenty descents, which, like a riotous
    fool,
Thou didst make sale of? Is not here
    inclosed
The deed that does confirm it mine?
MAR. [*Aside.*]           Now, now!
WELL. I do acknowledge none; I ne'er
    passed o'er
Any such land. I grant for a year or two
You had it in trust, which if you do
    discharge,
Surrend'ring the possession, you shall
    ease
Yourself and me of chargeable suits in
    law,           170
Which, if you prove not honest, as I
    doubt it,
Must of necessity follow.
LADY.           In my judgment
He does advise you well.
OVER.         Good! Good! Conspire
With your new husband, lady; second
    him
In his dishonest practices; but, when
This manor is extended [2] to my use,
You'll speak in an humbler key, and sue
    for favor.
LADY. Never; do not hope it.
WELL.         Let despair first seize me.
OVER. Yet, to shut up thy mouth, and
    make thee give
Thyself the lie, the loud lie, I draw
    out           180
The precious evidence; if thou canst for-
    swear
Thy hand and seal, and make a forfeit of
    *Opens the box [and shows the document]*.
Thy ears to the pillory—see, here's that
    will make
My interest clear.—Ha!

[1] Claim.         [2] Seized for debt.

LADY.         A fair skin of parchment.
WELL. Indented,[3] I confess, and labels
    too;
But neither wax nor words. How! Thun-
    derstrook?[4]
Not a syllable to insult with? My wise
    uncle,
Is this your precious evidence? Is this
    that makes
Your interest clear?
OVER.     I am o'erwhelmed with wonder!
What prodigy is this? What subtle
    devil           190
Hath razed out the inscription, the wax
Turned into dust? The rest of my deeds
    whole
As when they were delivered, and this
    only
Made nothing! Do you deal with
    witches, rascal?
There is a statute for you, which will
    bring
Your neck in a hempen circle; yes, there
    is.
And now 'tis better thought, for, cheater,
    know
This juggling shall not save you.
WELL.           To save thee
Would beggar the stock of mercy.
OVER.           Marall!
MAR.                Sir.
OVER. (*Flattering him.*) Though the wit-
    nesses are dead, your testimony— 200
Help with an oath or two; and for thy
    master,
Thy liberal master, my good honest
    servant,
I know you will swear anything to dash
This cunning sleight. Besides, I know
    thou art
A public notary, and such stand in law
For a dozen witnesses. The deed, being
    drawn too
By thee, my careful Marall, and deliv-
    ered
When thou wert present, will make good
    my title.
Wilt thou not swear this?
MAR.           I? No, I assure you.
I have a conscience not seared up like
    yours;           210
I know no deeds.
OVER.           Wilt thou betray me?

[3] Cut on a zigzag line.     [4] Thunderstruck.

MAR.　　　　　　　　　　　Keep him
From using of his hands, I'll use my
　tongue
To his no little torment.
OVER.　　　　　　　Mine own varlet
Rebel against me?
MAR.　　　　　Yes, and uncase [1] you too.
The "idiot," the "patch," the "slave,"
　the "booby,"
The property fit only to be beaten
For your morning exercise, your "foot-
　ball," or
"Th' unprofitable lump of flesh," your
　"drudge,"
Can now anatomize [2] you, and lay open
All your black plots, and level with the
　earth　　　　　　　　　　　　220
Your hill of pride, and, with these
　gabions [3] guarded,
Unload my great artillery and shake,
Nay, pulverize the walls you think de-
　fend you.
LADY.　How he foams at the mouth with
　rage!
WELL.　　　To him again.
OVER.　O, that I had thee in my gripe; I
　would tear thee
Joint after joint!
MAR.　　　　　　I know you are a tearer,
But I'll have first your fangs pared off,
　and then
Come nearer to you, when I have dis-
　covered, [4]
And made it good before the judge, what
　ways　　　　　　　　　　　　229
And devilish practices you used to cozen
With an army of whole families, who yet
　live,
And, but [5] enrolled for soldiers, were able
To take in [6] Dunkirk.
WELL.　　　　　All will come out.
LADY.　　　　　　　The better.
OVER.　But that I will live, rogue, to torture
　thee,
And make thee wish, and kneel in vain,
　to die,
These swords that keep thee from me
　should fix here,
Although they made my body but one
　wound,

But I would reach thee.
LOV. (*Aside.*)　　Heaven's hand is in this;
One bandog [7] worry the other!
OVER.　　　　　　　I play the fool,
And make my anger but ridiculous;　240
There will be a time and place, there will
　be, cowards,
When you shall feel what I dare do.
WELL.　　　　　　　　I think so.
You dare do any ill, yet want true valor
To be honest and repent.
OVER.　　　They are words I know not,
Nor e'er will learn.　Patience, the beg-
　gar's virtue,

*Enter Greedy and Parson Willdo.*

Shall find no harbor here.—After these
　storms
At length a calm appears.　Welcome,
　most welcome!
There's comfort in thy looks.　Is the deed
　done?
Is my daughter married?　Say but so, my
　chaplain,　　　　　　　　　　249
And I am tame.
WILLDO.　　Married? Yes, I assure you.
OVER.　Then vanish, all sad thoughts!
　There's more gold for thee.
My doubts and fears are in the titles
　drowned
Of my "right honorable," my "right
　honorable" daughter.
GREEDY.　Here will I be feasting!　At least
　for a month
I am provided.　Empty guts, croak no
　more.
You shall be stuffed like bagpipes, not
　with wind,
But bearing [8] dishes.
OVER.　　　　　　Instantly be here?
　　　　　　　　*Whisp'ring to Willdo.*
To my wish!　To my wish!　Now you that
　plot against me,
And hoped to trip my heels up, that
　contemned me,　　　　*Loud music.*
Think on 't and tremble.—They come!
I hear the music.　　　　　　　260
A lane there for my lord!
WELL.　　　　　This sudden heat
May yet be cooled, sir.
OVER.　　　Make way there for my lord!

---

[1] Flay.　　　　　　　　　　[2] Dissect.
[3] Cylinders filled with earth and used for
fortification.　　　　　　　　[5] If only.
[4] Revealed.　　　　　　　[6] Capture.
[7] A ferocious dog kept chained.
[8] Substantial.

*Enter Allworth and Margaret.*

MARG. Sir, first your pardon, then your blessing, with
Your full allowance of the choice I have made,
As ever you could make use of your reason.    *Kneeling.*
Grow not in passion, since you may as well
Call back the day that's past, as untie the knot
Which is too strongly fastened.  Not to dwell
Too long on words, this's my husband.
OVER.    How!
ALL. So I assure you; all the rites of marriage,    270
With every circumstance, are past. Alas, sir,
Although I am no lord, but a lord's page,
Your daughter and my loved wife mourns not for it;
And, for "right honorable" son-in-law, you may say,
Your "dutiful" daughter.
OVER.    Devil! Are they married?
WILLDO. Do a father's part, and say, "Heaven give 'em joy!"
OVER. Confusion and ruin!  Speak, and speak quickly,
Or thou art dead.
WILLDO.    They are married.
OVER.    Thou hadst better
Have made a contract with the king of fiends
Than these.  My brain turns!
WILLDO.    Why this rage to me?    280
Is not this your letter, sir, and these the words?
"Marry her to this gentleman."
OVER.    It cannot—
Nor will I e'er believe it—'sdeath, I will not!—
That I, that in all passages I touched
At worldly profit have not left a print
Where I have trod for the most curious search
To trace my footsteps, should be gulled by children,
Baffled and fooled, and all my hopes and labors
Defeated and made void.

WELL.    As it appears,
You are so, my grave uncle.
OVER.    Village nurses    290
Revenge their wrongs with curses; I'll not waste
A syllable, but thus I take the life
Which, wretched, I gave to thee.
    *Offers to kill Margaret.*
LOV. [*Rushing forward.*]    Hold, for your own sake!
Though charity to your daughter hath quite left you,
Will you do an act, though in your hopes lost here,
Can leave no hope for peace or rest hereafter?
Consider; at the best you are but a man,
And cannot so create your aims but that
They may be crossed.
OVER.    Lord, thus I spit at thee    299
And at thy counsel, and again desire thee,
And as thou art a soldier, if thy valor
Dares show itself where multitude and example
Lead not the way, let's quit the house, and change
Six words in private.
LOV.    I am ready.
LADY.    Stay, sir.
Contest with one distracted?
WELL.    You'll grow like him,
Should you answer his vain challenge.
OVER.    Are you pale? [1]
Borrow his help; though Hercules call it odds,
I'll stand against both, as I am hemmed in thus.
Since, like Libyan lion in the toil,
My fury cannot reach the coward hunters,    310
And only spends itself, I'll quit the place.
Alone I can do nothing; but I have servants
And friends to second me; and, if I make not
This house a heap of ashes (by my wrongs,
What I have spoke I will make good!) or leave [2]
One throat uncut—if it be possible,
Hell add to my afflictions!
    *Exit Overreach.*

[1] Afraid.
[2] Emended by Gifford.  Original reads *leav'd*.

MAR.                    Is 't not brave sport?

GREEDY.  Brave sport?  I am sure it has
    ta'en away my stomach;
I do not like the sauce.

ALL.                    Nay, weep not, dearest,
    Though it express your pity; what's
      decreed                                     320
Above, we cannot alter.

LADY.                    His threats move me
    No scruple, madam.

MAR.                    Was it not a rare trick,
    And it please your worship, to make the
      deed nothing?
I can do twenty neater, if you please
To purchase and grow rich, for I will be
Such a solicitor and steward for you
As never worshipful had.

WELL.                    I do believe thee.
    But first discover the quaint [1] means you
      used
To raze out the conveyance?

MAR.                    They are mysteries
    Not to be spoke in public: certain min-
      erals                                     330
Incorporated in the ink and wax.
Besides, he gave me nothing, but still
    fed me
With hopes and blows; and that was the
    inducement
To this conumbrum.[2]  If it please your
    worship
To call to memory, this mad beast once
    caused me
To urge you or to drown or hang your-
    self;
I'll do the like to him, if you command
    me.

WELL.  You are a rascal!  He that dares be
    false
To a master, though unjust, will ne'er be
    true                                          339
To any other.  Look not for reward
Or favor from me; I will shun thy sight
As I would do a basilisk's.  Thank my
    pity
If thou keep thy ears; howe'er, I will take
    order
Your practice shall be silenced.

GREEDY.                    I'll commit him,
    If you'll have me, sir.

WELL.          That were to little purpose;
    His conscience be his prison.  Not a word,
But instantly begone!

ORD.                    Take this kick with you.

AMB.  And this.

FURN.          If that I had my cleaver here,
    I would divide your knave's head.

MAR.                    This is the haven   349
    False servants still arrive at.

                            *Exit Mar[all].*

                *Enter Over[reach].*

LADY.                    Come again!

LOV.  Fear not, I am your guard.

WELL.                    His looks are ghastly.

WILLDO.  Some little time I have spent,
    under your favors,
In physical [3] studies, and, if my judg-
    ment err not,
He's mad beyond recovery.  But observe
    him,
And look to yourselves.

OVER.          Why, is not the whole world
    Included in myself?  To what use then
Are friends and servants?  Say there were
    a squadron
Of pikes, lined through with shot, [4] when
    I am mounted
Upon my injuries, shall I fear to charge
    'em?
No; I'll through the battalia, and, that
    routed,                                        360
      *Flourishing his sword sheathed.*[5]
I'll fall to execution.  Ha!  I am feeble;
Some undone widow sits upon mine arm,
And takes away the use of 't; and my
    sword,
Glued to my scabbard with wronged
    orphans' tears,
Will not be drawn.  Ha!  What are these?
    Sure, hangmen
That come to bind my hands, and then
    to drag me
Before the judgment seat.  Now they are
    new shapes,
And do appear like Furies, with steel
    whips
To scourge my ulcerous soul.  Shall I
    then fall
Ingloriously, and yield?  No; spite of
    Fate,                                          370
I will be forced to hell like to myself.

[3] Medical.
[4] Interspersed with musketeers.
[5] Emended by Gifford.  Original reads *unsheathed.*

[1] Ingenious.                    [2] Conundrum.

Though you were legions of accursèd
  spirits,
Thus would I fly among you.
           *[Runs forward and falls.]*
WELL.[1]         There's no help;
  Disarm him first, then bind him.
GREEDY.        Take a *mittimus*,[2]
  And carry him to Bedlam.
LOV.          How he foams!
WELL.  And bites the earth!
WILLDO.   Carry him to some dark room;
  There try what art can do for his recov-
  ery.
MARG.  O my dear father!
         *They force Overreach off.*
ALL.      You must be patient, mistress.
LOV.  Here is a president to teach wicked
  men
  That when they leave religion, and turn
    atheists,                380
  Their own abilities leave 'em.  Pray you,
    take comfort;
  I will endeavor you shall be his guardians
  In his distractions.  And for your land,
    Master Wellborn,
  Be it good or ill in law, I'll be an umpire
  Between you and this, th' undoubted
    heir
  Of Sir Giles Overreach.  For me, here's
    the anchor
  That I must fix on.
ALL.         What you shall determine,
  My lord, I will allow of.[3]

---

[1] This speech head is placed before the preceding line in the original.
[2] A writ of committal.
[3] Agree to.

WELL.            'Tis the language
  That I speak too; but there is something
    else
  Beside the repossession of my land   390
  And payment of my debts, that I must
    practice.
  I had a reputation, but 'twas lost
  In my loose course, and, till I redeem it
  Some noble way, I am but half made up.
  It is a time of action; if your lordship
  Will please to confer a company upon me
  In your command, I doubt not in my
    service
  To my king and country but I shall do
    something
  That may make me right again.
LOV.           Your suit is granted
  And you loved for the motion.
WELL.  *[To the audience.]*      Nothing
  wants then                 400
  But your allowance—

## THE EPILOGUE

But your allowance, and in that our all
Is comprehended, it being known nor we
Nor he that wrote the comedy can be
  free
Without your manumission, which if you
Grant willingly, as a fair favor due
To the poet's and our labors (as you may,
For we despair not, gentlemen, of the
  play),
We jointly shall profess your grace hath
  might                    409
To teach us action, and him how to write.
                     *[Exeunt.]*
       FINIS.

# PHILIP MASSINGER

## THE MAID OF HONOR

*The Maid of Honor* is one of the best and most representative of Massinger's tragi-comedies.  Although the title page of the first edition in 1632 assigns it to the Queen's Men at the Phoenix (or Cockpit), it apparently does not appear in the Office Book of Sir Henry Herbert, unless it was disguised under some other title.  Dunn believes that the attempts to identify it with *The Honor of Women,* licensed in 1628, have not been convincing.  Although the play was performed in 1632, almost simultaneously with its first printing, critical opinion of today based on various allusions in the play assigns its first production to 1625 or 1626.  Whereas it seems to have remained alive on the stage in pre-Commonwealth times, it was barely remembered in the Restoration and early eighteenth century.  It impressed George Lillo sufficiently, however, for him to introduce several echoes of it into his *Fatal Curiosity* in 1731.  In 1785 the great actor John Philip Kemble paid tribute to it by making an adaptation and acting in it as Adorni in support of his sister, the dazzling Mrs. Sarah Siddons, as Camiola.  But their great names and reputation were not enough to draw the public to it in any numbers.  Nevertheless, in 1831 another member of this illustrious theatrical dynasty, Frances Anne Kemble, better known on both sides of the Atlantic as Fanny Kemble, was similarly impressed by the play when she read it and offered it in her own revival, saying that the role of Camiola was the only one which she had ever selected for herself.  Her production had somewhat more popular success than her uncle's and aunt's had had, but it failed to establish the play in the living theater.  (For its general stage history, see Dunn and Eva A. W. Bryne's critical edition, London, 1927.)

The first scholar to discuss the source of Massinger's plot was Emil Koeppel, in his monograph, "Quellenstudien zu den Dramen George Chapmans, Philip Massingers, und John Fords," *Quellen und Forschungen zur Sprach-und-Kultur-Geschichte der Germanischen Völker* (Strassburg, 1897).  Koeppel's article was developed and expanded by Karl Raebel in his *Massingers Drama "The Maid of Honour" in Seinem Verhältnis zu Painters "Palace of Pleasure"* (Halle, 1911).  Massinger, like so many of his predecessors in the English drama, went back to that warehouse of ideas published in 1566–7, William Painter's *The Palace of Pleasure.*  Here he found Painter's version of Giovanni Boccaccio's tale of "Camiola and Rolande," which he reoriented to shift its main theme from liberality to love and honor.  (Bryne gives a detailed summary and comparison of the different versions of the story.)

Honor was always one of Massinger's favorite themes.  Edwards, in his "Massinger the Censor," gives perhaps the best brief description of this aspect of the play, though Dunn, Bryne, and others also deal with it.  These discussions all concern themselves with analyses of the leading characters from this point of view: Bertoldo's "essential shallowness" and disregard of his vows as a Knight of Malta when faced with various female temptations; Camiola's high principles, undermined somewhat in the estimation of the modern reader by her treatment of Bertoldo, Adorni, and the silly Sylli; and Adorni's unshaken integrity and nobility.  In view of Massinger's constant introduction of new turns in his plot to illustrate the various aspects of his theme, many critics have used the term "drama of surprise" in addition to "tragicomedy" to classify the play and show its skillfully built basic construction, even though it is not always completely plausible.

The treatment of honor is closely related to Massinger's conception of religion, and is also dealt with chiefly in *The Renegado* (acted 1624; printed 1630) and *The Virgin Martyr* (licensed 1620; printed 1622). In this connection Massinger's alleged conversion to Roman Catholicism reappears. But Dunn concludes that "an examination of the plays, however, reveals no particularly individual religious ideas nor indeed anything religiously eccentric," and, while stressing Massinger's fundamental piety, seriousness, and orthodoxy, uses the phrase "undenominationally religious." Whatever his exact religious affiliation, he was essentially tolerant, and, in fact, displayed a sort of Christian Stoicism in his attitude. In the case of *The Maid of Honor* Dunn even suggests that perhaps "a great deal of the religious element is part and parcel of, is indeed demanded by, the exigencies of the drama of surprise." It is really, he thinks, the conflict between reason and passion in Camiola which gives the play its title. Bryne felt once more the morality influence in the struggle between good and evil and in names like Astutio, Fulgentio, and Adorni.

Politically, *The Maid of Honor* reëmphasizes the audacity of so many of the playwrights of the age in criticizing and giving advice to the government and even to the rulers themselves. Practically all the critics of the play, from T. Monck Mason in his edition of Massinger's works in 1779, the historian S. R. Gardiner, in his article on "The Political Element in Massinger" (*Contemporary Review*, 1876), to the modern editors, have called attention to the importance of this element in Massinger's writing. Bryne comments on the similarities between the situations in England and in Sicily, the scene of the play, and remarks on the fact that both are islands somewhat cut off from the mainland. Although she detected the presence of certain reflections of the early years of the Thirty Years' War in the conflict between Urbin and Siena, she warned against its overemphasis. But, like Dunn and others, she stressed the bold way in which Massinger mirrored the characters and relations of the extravagant and somewhat unreliable James and his favorite, the Duke of Buckingham, through Roberto, King of Sicily, and his "minion," the beautiful, elegant, arrogant, and dissolute Fulgentio, who, like Buckingham, has risen from a relative obscurity of birth to a position of great power in the state. Although Massinger seems to be covertly warning the present king, Charles I, to take heed from his father's example, he also portrays Roberto as a tolerant, well-meaning ruler, believing in his own impartiality in the administration of justice and the affairs of his kingdom, internal and external. Dunn ascribed the error of Roberto in the play as rising "from an isolated interference of a prince with a subject's liberty of choice as regards marriage, in which sphere the law gave him no authority." Nevertheless, Dunn believed that Massinger remained essentially loyal to Charles and would have fought for him in the coming civil wars as the "divinely-appointed ruler," in spite of his disapproval of some of the royal actions. Chelli thought he detected a foreshadowing of the modern feministic movement in many of Massinger's women, especially in Camiola, with her high-mindedness, independence of thought and action, and representation of an equality of the sexes. Dunn, however, convinced that many of Massinger's highly praised "good women" were "too much taken up with their own virtue" without always acting in accordance to their own pronouncements, suggested that Chelli (who wrote early in the twentieth century when the movement for women's rights was at its height) probably overemphasized the importance of this element in Massinger's plays.

In his chapter on Massinger's "Stagecraft" Dunn commented on the frequent artificiality of many of the playwright's soliloquies and asides, illustrating with a case from IV, iv, of *The Maid of Honor*. Bryne called attention to Massinger's habit of self-repetition in plots, characters, motives, language, and so on, and saw a strong resemblance between *The Maid of Honor* and *The Knight of Malta* (about 1619), in which Massinger assisted Fletcher. In commenting on the "realistically conversational" impression created by his blank verse, in spite of some of his "long, involved parentheses in the classical manner," and his lack of much real poetry, Bryne concluded that among "the less extravagant emotions of a play like *The Maid of Honor*" Massinger was most "at home."

In addition to the critical edition of the play by Bryne, a translation into French prose by Maurice Chelli, with textual and marginal notes and an "avant-propos," along with an introduction by A. Kozul, was published in 1933, in which the English and the French texts appear on opposite pages. The present text is based on Bryne's edition, compared with that in a copy of the 1632 quarto in the Newberry Library. Bryne's readings themselves are drawn from a collation of nine copies of the quarto, corrections apparently having been made by the printers as the sheets went through the press.

# THE MAID OF HONOR [1]

## BY

## PHILIP MASSINGER

### THE ACTORS' NAMES

ROBERTO, *King of Sicily.*
FERDINAND, *Duke of Urbin.*
BERTOLDO, *the king's natural brother, a Knight of Malta.*
GONZAGA, *a Knight of Malta, general to the Duchess of Siena.*
ASTUTIO, *a counselor of state.*
FULGENTIO, *the minion*[2] *of Roberto.*
ADORNI, *a follower of Camiola's father.*
AMBASSADOR *from the Duke of Urbin.*
SIGNIOR SYLLI, *a foolish self-lover.*
ANTHONIO ⎫
GASPARO ⎬ *two rich heirs, city bred.*
PIERIO, *a colonel to Gonzaga.*
RODERIGO ⎫
JACOMO ⎬ *captains to Gonzaga.*

DRUSO ⎫
LIVIO ⎬ *captains to Duke Ferdinand.*
PAULO, *a priest, Camiola's confessor.*
[BISHOP.]
[PAGE.]
SCOUT.
SOLDIERS.
SERVANTS.
JAILOR.
DWARF.
MUTES.

AURELIA, *Duchess of Siena.*
CAMIOLA, *the Maid of Honor.*
CLARINDA, *her woman.*[3]

[SCENE: *Sicily and the Sienese.*

TIME: *Fourteenth century.*]

ACT I. SCENE i.

[*The council chamber in the palace at Palermo.*]

*Astutio, Adorni.*

ADOR. Good day to your lordship.
AST.                              Thanks, Adorni.
ADOR. May I presume to ask if the ambassador
  Employed by Ferdinand, the Duke of Urbin,
  Hath audience this morning?

*Enter Fulgent[io].*

AST.                              'Tis uncertain;
  For, though a counselor of state, I am not
  Of the cabinet council. But there's one,
    if he please,
  That may resolve[4] you.
ADOR.              I will move[5] him.—Sir![6]
FUL. If you have a suit, show water;[7] I am
  blind else.
ADOR. A suit, yet of a nature not to prove
  The quarry[8] that you hawk for. If your
    words                                    10

---

[1] The title continues: "As It Hath Been Often Presented with Good Allowance at the Phœnix in Drury Lane by the Queen's Majesty's Servants." After the half-title follows the phrase, "A Tragi-Comedy."    [2] Favorite.
[3] Here follow a dedication to Sir Francis Foljambe and Sir Thomas Bland and a commendatory poem by Aston Cokayne.

[4] Satisfy, inform.          [5] Appeal to.
[6] As frequently the original reads *Sr.*, a form which may sometimes be an abbreviation for *Signior.*
[7] Give me an eye wash (*i.e.*, a bribe) to clear my sight.
[8] "A hunting phrase, meaning to try out a special prey on the hawk which is being trained to capture that particular kind of game" (Bryne).

Are not like Indian wares, and every
  scruple
To be weighed and rated, one poor syl-
  lable
Vouchsafed in answer of a fair demand
Cannot deserve a fee.

FUL.          It seems you are ignorant.
I neither speak nor hold my peace for
  nothing—
And yet for once I care not if I answer
One single question gratis.

ADOR.         I much thank you.
Hath the ambassador audience, sir, today?

FUL. Yes.

ADOR.     At what hour?

FUL.          I promised not so much.
A syllable you begged; my charity gave
  it.                            20
Move me no further.    *Exit Fulgentio.*

AST.          This you wonder at?
With me, 'tis usual.

ADOR.      Pray you, sir, what is he?

AST. A gentleman, yet no lord. He hath
  some drops
Of the king's blood running in his veins,
  derived
Some ten degrees off. His revenue lies
In a narrow compass, the king's ear, and
  yields him
Every hour a fruitful harvest. Men may
  talk
Of three crops in a year in the Fortunate
  Islands,
Or profit made by wool; but, while there
  are suitors,
His sheep shearing, nay, shaving to the
  quick,                          30
Is in every quarter of the moon, and
  constant.
In the time of trussing a point,[1] he can
  undo
Or make a man. His play or recrea-
  tion
Is to raise this up, or pull down that, and,
  though
He never yet took orders, makes more
  bishops
In Sicily than the pope himself.

*Enier Bertoldo, Gasparo, Anthonio, a*
*                         Servant.*

ADOR.             Most strange!

[1] Tying the laces of the hose.

AST. The presence fills. He in the Malta
  habit
Is the natural brother of the king—a by-
  blow.[2]

ADOR. I understand you.

GASP.          Morrow to my uncle

ANT. And my late guardian.—But at
  length I have                     40
The reins in my own hands.

AST.         Pray you, use 'em well,
Or you'll too late repent it.

BERT.         With this jewel,
Presented to Camiola, prepare
This night a visit for me.—(*Exit Servant.*)
  I shall have
Your company, gallants, I perceive, if
  that
The king will hear of war.

ANT.          Sir, I have horses
Of the best breed in Naples, fitter far
To break a rank than crack a lance,[3] and
  are
In their career of such incredible swift-
  ness
They outstrip swallows.

BERT.       And such may be useful   50
To run away with, should we be defeated.
You are well provided, signior.

ANT.             Sir, excuse me.
All of their race by instinct know a
  coward
And scorn the burthen. They come on
  like lightning,
Foundered in a retreat.

BERT.        By no means back 'em,
Unless you know your courage sym-
  pathize
With the daring of your horse.

ANT.         My lord, this is bitter.

GASP. I will raise me a company of foot,
And, when at push of pike I am to enter
A breach, to show my valor I have
  bought me                      60
An armor cannon-proof.

BERT.         You will not leap then
O'er an outwork in your shirt?

GASP.         I do not like
Activity that way.

BERT.        You had rather stand
A mark to try their muskets on?

GASP.           If I do
No good, I'll do no hurt.

BERT.        'Tis in you, signior,

[2] Illegitimate child.   [3] *I.e.*, in a tournament.

A Christian resolution, and becomes you!
But I will not discourage you.
Ant.                              You are, sir,
A Knight of Malta, and, as I have heard,
Have served against the Turk.
Bert.                    'Tis true.
Ant.                          Pray you, show us
The difference between the city valor  70
And service in the field.
Bert.                       'Tis somewhat more
Than roaring [1] in a tavern or a brothel,
Or to steal a constable from a sleeping
    watch,
Then burn their halberds, or, safe
    guarded by
Your tenants' sons, to carry away a
    Maypole
From a neighbor village.  You will not
    find there
Your masters of dependencies [2] to take up
A drunken brawl or to get you the names
Of valiant chevaliers, fellows that will be,
For a cloak with thrice-dyed velvet, and
    a cast [3] suit,                          80
Kicked down the stairs.  A knave with
    half a britch [4] there
And no shirt (being a thing superfluous
And worn out of his memory), if you bear
    not
Yourselves both in and upright,[5] with a
    provant [6] sword
Will slash your scarlets and your plush a
    new way,
Or, with the hilts, thunder about your
    ears
Such music as will make your worships
    dance
To the doleful tune of "Lachryma." [7]
Gasp.                        I must tell you
In private, as you are my princely friend,
I do not like such fiddlers.
Bert.             No?  They are useful  90
For your imitation.  I remember you
When you came first to the court and
    talked of nothing

But your rents and your entradas,[8] ever
    chiming
The golden bells in your pockets; you be-
    lieved
The taking of the wall [9] as a tribute due
    to
Your gaudy clothes, and could not walk
    at midnight
Without a causeless quarrel, as if men
Of coarser outsides were in duty bound
To suffer your affronts; but, when you
    had been
Cudgeled well twice or thrice, and from
    the doctrine [10]                         100
Made profitable uses, you concluded
The sovereign means to teach irregular [11]
    heirs
Civility, with conformity of manners,
Were two or three sound beatings.
Ant.                             I confess
They did much good upon me.
Gasp.                         And on me [12] —
The principles that they read were sound.
Bert.                          You'll find
The like instructions in the camp.
Ast.                               The king!

*A flourish.  Enter Roberto, Fulgentio, Am-
    bassador, Attendants.*

Rob. [*Ascending the throne.*]  We sit pre-
    pared to hear.
Amb.                    Your majesty
Hath been long since familiar, I doubt
    not,
With the desperate fortunes of my lord;
    and pity                              110
Of the much that your confederate hath
    suffered,
You being his last refuge, may persuade
    you
Not alone to compassionate, but to lend
Your royal aids to stay him in his fall
To certain ruin.  He too late is conscious
That his ambition to encroach upon
His neighbor's territories with the danger
    of
His liberty, nay, his life, hath brought in
    question

[1] Roistering.
[2] Bravoes who managed duels between inexperienced contestants.
[3] Cast-off.
[4] Breech, a pair of breeches.
[5] *I.e.,* erectly, like a soldier.
[6] Provided by the quartermaster; *i.e.,* of
inferior quality.
[7] Generally "Lachrymæ," meaning "Tears,"
a popular song by Dowland.

[8] Income.
[9] In passing a person, walking nearest the wall,
where the street was cleanest.
[10] Lesson.        [11] Unruly.
[12] Here and in a few other passages the line
division has been regularized.

His own inheritance; but youth and heat
Of blood, in your interpretation, may
Both plead and mediate for him. I must
    grant it                 121
An error in him, being denied the favors
Of the fair Princess of Siena (though
He sought her in a noble way) t' endeavor
To force affection by surprisal of
Her principal seat, Siena.

ROB.              Which now proves
The seat of his captivity, not triumph.
Heaven is still just.

AMB.          And yet that justice is
To be with mercy tempered, which
    heaven's deputies
Stand bound to minister. The injured
    duchess,                130
By reason taught, as nature, could not,
    with
The reparation of her wrongs, but aim at
A brave revenge; and my lord feels too
    late
That innocence will find friends. The
    great Gonzaga,
The honor of his Order (I must praise
Virtue, though in an enemy), he whose
    fights
And conquests hold one number, rallying
    up
Her scattered troops, before we could get
    time
To victual or to man the conquered city,
Sat down before it, and, presuming
    that                140
'Tis not to be relieved, admits no parley,
Our flags of truce hung out in vain; nor
    will he
Lend an ear to composition,[1] but exacts,
With the rendering up the town, the
    goods and lives
Of all within the walls and of all sexes
To be at his discretion.

ROB.             Since injustice
In your duke meets this correction, can
    you press us,
With any seeming argument of reason,
In foolish pity to decline [2] his dangers,
To draw 'em on ourself? Shall we not
    be                150
Warned by his harms? The league pro-
    claimed between us
Bound neither of us farther than to aid
Each other, if by foreign force invaded;

---

[1] Making of terms.         [2] Turn aside.

And so far in my honor I was tied.
But, since without our counsel or allow-
    ance
He hath took arms, with his good leave
    he must
Excuse us if we steer not on a rock
We see and may avoid. Let other mon-
    archs
Contend to be made glorious by proud
    war
And with the blood of their poor subjects
    purchase           160
Increase of empire and augment their
    cares
In keeping that which was by wrongs
    extorted,
Gilding unjust invasions with the trim
Of glorious conquests; we, that would be
    known
The father of our people, in our study
And vigilance for their safety must not
    change
Their plowshares into swords, or force
    them from
The secure shade of their own vines to be
Scorched with the flames of war, or for
    our sport
Expose their lives to ruin.

AMB.          Will you then   170
In his extremity forsake your friend?

ROB. No; but preserve ourself.

BERT.         Cannot the beams
Of honor thaw your icy fears?

ROB.              Who's that?

BERT. A kind of brother, sir, howe'er your
    subject;
Your father's son, and one who blushes
    that
You are not heir to his brave spirit and
    vigor,
As to his kingdom.

ROB.            How's this?

BERT.            Sir, to be
His living chronicle and to speak his
    praise
Cannot deserve your anger.

ROB.          Where's your warrant
For this presumption?

BERT.     Here, sir, in my heart.   180
Let sycophants, that feed upon your
    favors,
Style coldness in you caution, and prefer
Your ease before your honor, and con-
    clude

To eat and sleep supinely is the end
Of human blessings. I must tell you, sir,
Virtue, if not in action, is a vice,
And, when we move not forward, we go
    b&#807;ckward.
Nor is this peace, the nurse of drones and
    cowards,
Our health, but a disease.
GASP.             Well urged, my lord.
ANT. Perfit [1] what is so well begun.
AMB.              And bind   190
My lord your servant.
ROB.      Hair-brained fool! What reason
Canst thou infer [2] to make this good?
BERT.            A thousand,
Not to be contradicted. But consider
Where your command lies. 'Tis not, sir,
    in France,
Spain, Germany, Portugal, but in Sicily,
An island, sir. Here are no mines of gold
Or silver to enrich you; no worm spins
Silk in her womb to make distinction
Between you and a peasant in your
    habits;
No fish lives near our shores, whose blood
    can dye                   200
Scarlet or purple; all that we possess,
With beasts we have in common. Nature
    did
Design us to be warriors, and to break
    through
Our ring, the sea, by which we are en-
    vironed;
And we by force must fetch in what is
    wanting
Or precious to us. Add to this, we are
A populous nation, and increase so fast
That, if we by our providence are not
    sent
Abroad in colonies, or fall by the sword,
Not Sicily, though now it were more
    fruitful                210
Than when 'twas styled the "granary of
    great Rome,"
Can yield our numerous fry bread. We
    must starve,
Or eat up one another.
ADOR [*Aside.*]        The king hears
With much attention.
AST. [*Aside.*] And seems moved with what
Bertoldo hath delivered.
BERT.       May you live long, sir,
The king of peace, so you deny not us

The glory of the war; let not our nerves
Shrink up with sloth, nor for want of em-
    ployment
Make younger brothers thieves. 'Tis
    their swords, sir,
Must sow and reap their harvest. If
    examples            220
May move you more than arguments,
    look on England,
The empress of the European isles,
And unto whom alone ours yields prece-
    dence.
When did she flourish so as when she was
The mistress of the ocean? Her navies,
Putting a girdle round about the world
When the Iberian [3] quaked, her worthies
    named; [4]
And the fair flower-de-luce [5] grew pale,
    set by
The red rose and the white! Let not our
    armor
Hung up, or our unrigged armada, make
    us                      230
Ridiculous to the late poor snakes our
    neighbors,
Warmed in our bosoms, and to whom
    again
We may be terrible, while we spend our
    hours
Without variety, confined to drink,
Dice, cards, or whores. Rouse us, sir,
    from the sleep
Of idleness, and redeem our mortgaged
    honors.
Your birth, and justly, claims my father's
    kingdom;
But his heroic mind descends to me.
I will confirm so much.
ADOR.          In his looks he seems
To break ope Janus' temple.
AST.         How these younglings   240
Take fire from him!
ADOR.        It works an alteration
Upon the king.
ANT.        I can forbear no longer.
War, war, my sovereign!
FUL.           The king appears
Resolved, and does prepare to speak.
ROB.               Think not
Our counsel's built upon so weak a base

---

[1] Perfect.               [2] Bring forward,

[3] Spaniard, in reference to the Spanish
Armada.
[4] *I.e.,* England's navy made her great men.
[5] *I.e.,* France.

As to be overturned or shaken with
Tempestuous winds of words. As I, my
   lord,
Before resolved you, I will not engage
My person in this quarrel, neither press
My subjects to maintain it; yet, to
   show      250
My rule is gentle and that I have feeling
Of your master's sufferings, since these
   gallants, weary
Of the happiness of peace, desire to taste
The bitter sweets of war, we do con-
   sent
That, as adventure[r]s and volunteers,
No way compelled by us, they may make
   trial
Of their boasted valors.

BERT.            We desire no more.
ROB. 'Tis well; and, but my grant in this,
   expect not
Assistance from me.     Govern as you
   please
The province you make choice of, for I
   vow,      260
By all things sacred, if that thou mis-
   carry
In this rash undertaking, I will hear it
No otherwise than as a sad disaster
Fallen on a stranger, nor will I esteem
That man my subject who in thy ex-
   tremes
In purse or person aids thee. Take your
   fortune.
You know me; I have said it. So, my
   lord,
You have my absolute answer.

AMB.            My prince pays
In me his duty.
ROB.           Follow me, Fulgentio,
And you, Astutio.

*Exeunt Roberto, Fulgentio, Astutio, Attend-*
                          *ants.*

GASP.      What a frown he threw    270
At his departure on you!
BERT.            Let him keep
His smiles for his state catamite;[1] I care
   not.
ANT. Shall we aboard tonight?
AMB.           Your speed, my lord,
Doubles the benefit.
BERT.          I have a business
Requires despatch; some two hours hence
I'll meet you.            *Exeunt.*

[1] Male prostitute.

## ACT I. SCENE ii.

[*A room in Camiola's house at Palermo.*]

*Signior Sylli, walking fantastically before,*
    *followed by Camiola and Clarinda.*

CAM. Nay, signior, this is too much cere-
   mony
In my own house.
SYL.           What's gracious abroad
Must be in private practiced.
CLAR.         For your mirth' sake
Let him alone; he has been all this morn-
   ing
In practice with a peruged [2] gentleman
   usher,
To teach him his true amble and his
   postures

*Sylli walking by and practicing his postures.*
   When he walks before a lady.
SYL.          You may, madam,
Perhaps, believe that I in this use art
To make you dote upon me by exposing
My more than most rare features to
   your view.      10
But I, as I have ever done, deal simply,
A mark of sweet simplicity ever noted
I' the family of the Syllis. Therefore,
   lady,
Look not with too much contemplation
   on me;
If you do, you are i' the suds.[3]
CAM.          You are no barber?
SYL. Fie, no! Not I. But my good parts
   have drawn
More loving hearts out of fair ladies'
   bellies
Than the whole trade have done teeth.[4]
CAM.           Is 't possible?
SYL. Yes, and they live too, marry, much
   condoling [5]
The scorn of their Narcissus, as they
   call me,      20
Because I love myself—
CAM.           Without a rival.
What philters or love powders do you
   use
To force affection? I see nothing in
Your person but I dare look on, yet
   keep
My own poor heart still.

[2] Peruked, bewigged.
[3] *I.e.*, in a pickle.
[4] The barber was also surgeon and dentist.
[5] Lamenting.

SYL. You are warned—be armed;
And do not lose the hope of such a husband
In being too soon enamored.

CLAR. Hold in your head,
Or you must have a martingale.

SYL. I have sworn
Never to take a wife but such a one
(O, may your ladyship prove so strong!) as can 30
Hold out a month against me.

CAM. Never fear it;
Though your best taking part, your wealth, were trebled,
I would not woo you. But, since in your pity
You please to give me caution, tell me what
Temptations I must fly from.

SYL. The first is
That you never hear me sing, for I am a Syri.[1]
If you observe, when I warble, the dogs howl
As ravished with my ditties, and you will
Run mad to hear me.

CAM. I will stop my ears,
And keep my little wits.

SYL. Next, when I dance, 40
And come aloft thus [Capers.], cast not a sheep's eye
Upon the quivering of my calf.

CAM. Proceed, sir.

SYL. But on no terms (for 'tis a main point) dream not
Of the strength of my back, though it will bear a burthen
With any porter.

CAM. I mean not to ride you.

SYL. [2] Nor I your little ladyship, till you have
Performed the covenants. Be not taken with
My pretty spider-fingers, nor my eyes
That twinkle [3] on both sides.

CAM. [Aside.] Was there ever such
A piece of motley [4] heard of!—(One

knocks.) Who's that?—You may spare
The catalogue of my dangers.
Exit Clarinda.

SYL. No, good madam; 51
I have not told you half.

CAM. Enough, good signior;
If I eat more of such sweetmeats, I shall surfeit.—

Enter Clarinda.

Who is 't?

CLAR. The brother of the king.

SYL. Nay, start not.
The brother of the king! Is he no more?
Were it the king himself, I'll give him leave
To speak his mind to you, for I am not jealous;
And, to assure your ladyship of so much,
I'll usher him in—[Aside.] and, that done, hide myself. Exit Syl[li].

CAM. Camiola, if ever, now be constant. 60
This is indeed a suitor whose sweet presence,
Courtship,[5] and loving language would have staggered
The chaste Penelope; and, to increase
The wonder, did not modesty forbid it,
I should ask that from him he sues to me for.
And yet my reason, like a tyran,[6] tells me
I must nor give nor take it.

Enter Sylli and Bertoldo.

SYL. I must tell you
You lose your labor. 'Tis enough to prove it,
Signior Sylli came before you; and you know
First come, first served; yet you shall have my countenance 70
To parley with her, and I'll take special care
That none shall interrupt you.

BERT. You are courteous.

SYL. Come, wench, wilt thou hear wisdom?

CLAR. Yes, from you, sir.
Steps aside [with Sylli].

[1] A double pun on Siren and Sirius, the Dog Star (Bryne).
[2] Original has Cam.
[3] Wink.
[4] I.e., fool.
[5] Courtliness.
[6] Tyrant.

BERT. (*Kisseth her.*) If forcing this sweet favor from your lips,
Fair madam, argue me of too much boldness,
When you are pleased to understand I take
A parting kiss, if not excuse, at least
'Twill qualify, the offense.

CAM.                                    A parting kiss, sir?
What nation, envious of the happiness
Which Sicily enjoys in your sweet presence,                                             80
Can buy you from her, or what climate yield
Pleasures transcending those which you enjoy here,
Being both beloved and honored, the North Star
And guider of all hearts, and, to sum up
Your full accompt [1] of happiness in a word,
The brother of the king?

BERT.                                    Do you alone
And with an unexampled cruelty
Enforce my absence and deprive me of
Those blessings which you with a polished phrase
Seem to insinuate that I do possess,   90
And yet tax me as being guilty of
My willful exile? What are titles to me,
Or popular suffrage,[2] or my nearness to
The king in blood, or fruitful Sicily
Though it confessed no sovereign but myself,
When you, that are the essence of my being,
The anchor of my hopes, the real substance
Of my felicity, in your disdain
Turn all to fading and deceiving shadows?

CAM. You tax me without cause.

BERT.                    You must confess it.   100
But, answer love with love, and seal the contract
In the uniting of our souls, how gladly
(Though now I were in action, and assured,
Following my fortune, that plumed Victory
Would make her glorious stand upon my tent)
Would I put off my armor in my heat

Of conquest and like Anthony pursue
My Cleopatra! Will you yet look on me
With an eye of favor?

CAM.                    Truth bear witness for me
That in the judgment of my soul you are                                             110
A man so absolute and circular[3]
In all those wished-for rarities that may take
A virgin captive that, though at this instant
All sceptered monarchs of our western world
Were rivals with you, and Camiola worthy
Of such a competition, you alone
Should wear the garland.

BERT.                    If so, what diverts
Your favor from me?

CAM.                    No mulct[4] in yourself,
Or in your person, mind, or fortune.

BERT.                                    What then?

CAM.   The consciousness of mine own wants. Alas, sir,                              120
We are not parallels, but, like lines divided,
Can ne'er meet in one center. Your birth, sir,
Without addition,[5] were an ample dowry
For one of fairer fortunes, and this shape,
Were you ignoble, far above all value;
To this, so clear a mind, so furnished with
Harmonious faculties molded from heaven,
That, though you were Thersites in your features,
Of no descent, and Irus in your fortunes,
Ulysses-like, you would force all eyes and ears                                       130
To love, but seen, and, when heard, wonder at
Your matchless story. But all these bound up
Together in one volume! Give me leave
With admiration to look upon 'em,
But not presume in my own flattering hopes
I may or can enjoy 'em.

BERT.                                    How you ruin
What you would seem to build up! I know no

---

[1] Account.          [2] Favor.

[3] Perfect, complete.   [4] Defect.   [5] Title, rank.

Disparity between us; you are an heir
Sprung from a noble family, fair, rich,
    young,
And every way my equal.
CAM.                        Sir, excuse me;  140
    One ærie with proportion ne'er dis-
        closes [1]
    The eagle and the wren.  Tissue [2] and
        frieze
    In the same garment, monstrous!  But
        suppose
    That what's in you excessive were di-
        minished,
    And my desert supplied; the strongest
        bar,
    Religion, stops our entrance.  You are, sir,
    A Knight of Malta, by your Order
        bound
    To a single life; you cannot marry me,
    And I assure myself you are too noble
    To seek me, though my frailty should
        consent,                          150
    In a base path.
BERT.                    A dispensation, lady,
    Will easily absolve me.
CAM.                        O, take heed, sir!
    When what is vowed to heaven is dis-
        pensed with,
    To serve our ends on earth, a curse must
        follow,
    And not a blessing.
BERT.                    Is there no hope left me?
CAM.  Nor to myself, but is a neighbor to
    Impossibility.  True love should walk
    On equal feet; in us it does not, sir.
    But rest assured, excepting this, I shall
        be
    Devoted to your service.
BERT.                    And this is your  160
    Determinate sentence?
CAM.                        Not to be revoked.
BERT.  Farewell then, fairest cruel!  All
        thoughts in me
    Of women perish.  Let the glorious light
    Of noble war extinguish Love's dim
        taper,
    That only lends me light to see my folly.
    Honor, be thou my ever-living mistress,
    And fond affection, as thy bondslave,
        serve thee!            Exit Ber[toldo].
CAM.  How soon my sun is set, he being
        absent,

Never to rise again!  What a fierce
    battle
Is fought between my passions!—Me-
    thinks                                170
We should have kissed at parting.
SYL.  [Aside.]              I perceive
He has his answer; now must I step in
To comfort her.—[Comes forward.] You
    have found, I hope, sweet lady,
Some difference between a youth of my
    pitch [3]
And this bugbear [4] Bertoldo.  Men are
    men;
The king's brother is no more.  Good
    parts will do it,
When titles fail.  Despair not; I may be
In time entreated.
CAM.              Be so now—to leave me.—
Lights for my chamber.  O my heart!
            Exeunt Camiola and Clarinda.
SYL.                              She now,
I know, is going to bed to ruminate
Which way to glut herself upon my
    person.                                181
But for my oath' sake I will keep her
    hungry,
And, to grow full myself, I'll straight—
to supper.                        Exit.

### THE END OF THE FIRST ACT.


### ACT II. SCENE i.

[*The council chamber in the palace at Pal-
        ermo.*]

*Roberto, Fulgentio, Astutio.*

ROB.  Embarked tonight, do you say?
FUL.                    I saw him aboard, sir.
ROB.  And without taking of his leave?
AST.                              'Twas strange!
ROB.  Are we grown so contemptible?
FUL.                                'Tis far
From me, sir, to add fuel to your anger,
That, in your ill opinion of him, burns
Too hot already; else I should affirm
It was a gross neglect.
ROB.                    A willful scorn
Of duty and allegiance; you give it
Too fair a name.  But we shall think on 't.
    Can you

_____
[1] One nest of natural dimensions never hatches.
[2] Rich cloth.

[3] The height to which falcons were trained to
fly.
[4] Hobgoblin.

Guess what the numbers were that followed him                                        10
In his desperate action?

FUL.[1]                    More than you think, sir.
All ill-affected spirits in Palermo,
Or [2] to your government or person, with
The turbulent swordmen, such whose
poverty forced 'em
To wish a change, are gone along with
him—
Creatures devoted to his undertakings,
In right or wrong—and to express their
zeal
And readiness to serve him, ere they
went,
Profanely took the sacrament on their
knees
To live and die with him.

ROB.                    O most impious!  20
Their loyalty to us forgot?

FUL.                              I fear so.

AST. Unthankful as they are!

FUL.                    Yet this deserves not
One troubled thought in you, sir; with
your pardon,
I hold that their remove from hence
makes more
For your security than danger.

ROB.                              True;
And, as I'll fashion it, they shall feel it
too.
Astutio, you shall presently be des-
patched
With letters, writ and signed with our
own hand,
To the Duchess of Siena, in excuse
Of these forces sent against her. If you
spare                                       30
An oath to give it credit, that we never
Consented to it, swearing for the king,
Though false, it is no perjury.

AST.                              I know it.
They are not fit to be state agents, sir,
That witnout scruple of their conscience
cannot
Be prodigal in such trifles.

FUL.                    Right, Astutio.

ROB. You must, beside, from us take some
instructions
To be imparted, as you judge 'em use-
ful,
To the general, Gonzaga. Instantly
Prepare you for your journey.

[1] Original reads *Roberto*.                    [2] Either.

AST.                    With the wings  40
Of loyalty and duty.        *Exit Astutio.*

FUL.                    I am bold
To put your majesty in mind—

ROB.                    Of my promise
And aids to further you in your amorous
project
To the fair and rich Camiola. There's
my ring;
Whatever you shall say that I entreat,
Or can command by power, I will make
good.

FUL. Ever your majesty's creature.

ROB.                    Venus prove
Propitious to you!        *Exit Robert[o].*

FUL.                    All sorts to [3] my wishes.
Bertoldo was my hindrance; he removed,
I now will court her in the conquerous [4]
style:                                        50
"Come, see, and overcome."[5]—Boy!

*Enter Page.*

PAGE.                    Sir, your pleasure?

FUL. Haste to Camiola; bid her prepare
An entertainment suitable to a fortune
She could not hope for. Tell her I vouch-
safe
To honor her with a visit.

PAGE.                    'Tis a favor
Will make her proud.

FUL.        I know it.

PAGE.                    I am gone, sir. *Exit Page.*

FUL. Entreaties fit not me; a man in
grace
May challenge awe and privilege by
his place.        *Exit Fulgentio.*

ACT II. SCENE ii.

[*A room in Camiola's house.*]

*Sylli, Adorni, Clarinda.*

ADOR. So melancholy, say you?

CLAR.                    Never given
To such retirement.

ADOR.                    Can you guess the cause?

CLAR. If it hath not its birth and being
from
The brave Bertoldo's absence, I confess
It is past my apprehension.

SYL.                    You are wide,[6]

[3] Consorts with, fits.                    [4] Conquering.
[5] Cæsar's famous phrase.
[6] Wide of the mark.

The whole field wide. I, in my under-
standing,
Pity your ignorance; yet, if you will
Swear to conceal it, I will let you know
Where her shoe wrings her.
CLAR.            I vow, signior,
By my virginity.
SYL.          A perilous oath  10
In a waiting-woman of fifteen, and is,
indeed,
A kind of nothing.
ADOR.       I'll take one of something,
If you please to minister it.
SYL.         Nay, you shall not swear.
I had rather take your word, for, should
you vow,
"Damn me, I'll do this!"—you are sure
to break.
ADOR. I thank you, signior; but resolve
us.
SYL.      Know, then,
Here walks the cause: she dares not
look upon me;
My beauties are so terrible and enchant-
ing
She cannot endure my sight.
ADOR.          There I believe you.
SYL. But the time will come, be com-
forted, when I will     20
Put off this visor of unkindness to her,
And show an amorous and yielding
face.
And, until then, though Hercules him-
self
Desire to see her, he had better eat
His club than pass her threshold, for
I'll be
Her Cerberus to guard her.
ADOR.          A good dog!

*Enter Page.*

CLAR. Worth twenty porters.
PAGE.       Keep you open house here?
No groom to attend a gentleman? O,
I spy one.
SYL. He means not me, I am sure.
PAGE.         You, Sirrah Sheepshead,
With a face cut on a catstick,[1] do you
hear?           30
You, yeoman fewterer,[2] conduct me to

[1] Stick used in the game of cat, here referring
to a pair of thin legs.
[2] A menial attendant of dogs.

The lady of the mansion, or my poniard
Shall disembogue thy soul.
SYL.       O, terrible! "Disembogue"!
I talk of Hercules, and here is one
Bound up in *decimo sexto.*[3]
PAGE.           Answer, wretch!
SYL. Pray you, little gentleman, be not
so furious.
The lady keeps her chamber.
PAGE.        And we present?
Sent in an embassy to her? But here is
Her gentlewoman. Sirrah, hold my
cloak,
While I take a leap at her lips. Do it,
and neatly,     40
Or, having first tripped up thy heels,
I'll make
Thy back my footstool.
              *Page kisses Clar[inda].*
SYL.        Tamburlaine in little!
Am I turned Turk? What an office am
I put to!
CLAR. My lady, gentle youth, is indis-
posed.
PAGE. Though she were dead and buried,
only tell her
The great man in the court, the brave
Fulgentio,
Descends to visit her, and it will raise
her
Out of the grave for joy.

*Enter Fulgen[tio].*

SYL.        Here comes another!
The devil, I fear, in his holiday clothes.
PAGE.           So soon!
My part is at an end then.—Cover my
shoulders;     50
When I grow great, thou shalt serve
me.
FUL. [*To Sylli.*]      Are you, sirrah,
An implement of the house?
SYL.        Sure, he will make
A joins-stool[4] of me!
FUL. [*To Adorni.*]      Or, if you belong
To the lady of the place, command her
hither.
ADOR. I do not wear her livery, yet ac-
knowledge
A duty to her, and as little bound
To serve your peremptory will as she
is

[3] A very small book; hence a diminutive person.
[4] Joint stool.

To obey your summons. 'Twill become you, sir,
To wait her leisure; then, her pleasure known,
You may present your duty.

FUL.            Duty? Slave,   60
I'll teach you manners.

ADOR.     I am past learning. Make not
A tumult in the house.

FUL.           Shall I be braved thus?
                       *They draw.*

SYL. O, I am dead! And now I soun. [1]
                 *Falls on his face.*

CLAR.             Help! Murther!

PAGE. Recover, sirrah; the lady's here.

*Enter Cam[iola].*

SYL.                Nay, then
I am alive again, and I'll be valiant.
                       *[Rises.]*

CAM. What insolence is this?   Adorni, hold,
Hold, I command you!

FUL.          Saucy groom!

CAM.             Not so, sir;
However in his life he had dependence
Upon my father, he is a gentleman
As well born as yourself. Put on your hat.   70

FUL. In my presence, without leave?

SYL.         He has mine, madam.

CAM. And I must tell you, sir, and in plain language,
Howe'er your glittering outside promise gentry, [2]
The rudeness of your carriage and behavior
Speaks you a coarser thing.

SYL.         She means a clown, sir—
I am her interpreter for want of a better.

CAM. I am a queen in mine own house, nor must you
Expect an empire here.

SYL.          Sure, I must love her
Before the day, the pretty soul's so valiant.

CAM. What are you, and what would you with me?

FUL.          Proud one,   80
When you know what I am, and what I came for,

And may on your submission proceed to, [3]
You in your reason must repent the coarseness
Of my entertainment.

CAM.    Why, fine man? What are you?

FUL. A kinsman of the king's.

CAM.           I cry you mercy, [4]
For his sake, not your own. But grant you are so,
'Tis not impossible but a king may have
A fool to his kinsman—no way meaning you, sir.

FUL. You have heard of Fulgen[tio]?

CAM.             Long since, sir—
A suit-broker in court. He has the worst   90
Report among good men I ever heard of,
For bribery and extortion. In their prayers
Widows and orphans curse him for a canker
And caterpillar in the state. I hope, sir,
You are not the man, much less employed by him
As a smock-agent [5] to me.

FUL.           I reply not
As you deserve, being assured you know me—
Pretending ignorance of my person only
To give me a taste of your wit. 'Tis well and courtly;
I like a sharp wit well.

SYL.         I cannot endure it,   100
Nor any of the Syllis.

FUL.         More I know too.
This harsh induction [6] must serve as a foil
To the well-tuned observance [7] and respect
You will hereafter pay me, being made
Familiar with my credit with the king,
And that (contain your joy) I deign to love you.

CAM. Love me? I am not raped [8] with it.

[3] So all editors except Bryne who reads *so,* stating "the *s* in *so* not clear.' However, the Newberry copy plainly reads *fo.*
[4] I beg forgiveness.
[5] Pander.        [7] Deference.
[6] Introduction.    [8] Rapt, transported.

[1] Sound, swoon.   [2] Gentility, good breeding.

FUL.                    Hear 't again:
I love you honestly.  Now you admire [1]
me.
CAM. I do indeed, it being a word so sel-
dom
Heard from a courtier's mouth.  But,
pray you, deal plainly,          110
Since you find me simple.  What might
be the motives
Inducing you to leave the freedom of
A bachelor's life, on your soft neck to
wear
The stubborn yoke of marriage?  And,
of all
The beauties in Palermo, to choose me,
Poor me?  That is the main point you
must treat of.
FUL. Why, I will tell you.  Of a little
thing
You are a pretty peat,[2] indifferently [3]
fair too,
And, like a new-rigged ship, both tight
and yare,[4]
Well trussed to bear.  Virgins of giant
size                              120
Are sluggards at the sport, but for my
pleasure
Give me a neat, well-timbered gamester
like you;
Such need no spurs—the quickness of
your eye
Assures an active spirit.
CAM.                 You are pleasant, sir;
Yet I presume that there was one thing
in me,
Unmentioned yet, that took you more
than all
Those parts you have remembered.
FUL.              What?
CAM.                    My wealth, sir.
FUL. You are i' the right; without that,
beauty is
A flower worn in the morning, at night
trod on.
But, beauty, youth, and fortune meet-
ing in you,                       130
I will vouchsafe to marry you.
CAM.                 You speak well;
And in return excuse me, sir, if I
Deliver reasons why upon no terms
I'll marry you.  I fable not.

[1] Wonder at.
[2] A term of endearment.
[3] Tolerably.          [4] Trim and lively.

SYL. [Aside.]              I am glad
To hear this; I began to have an ague.
FUL. Come, your wise reasons.
CAM. Such as they are, pray you, take
them:
First, I am doubtful whether you are
a man,
Since, for your shape, trimmed up in a
lady's dressing,
You might pass for a woman; now I
love                              140
To deal on certainties.  And, for the
fairness
Of your complexion, which you think
will take me,
The color, I must tell you, in a man
Is weak and faint, and never will hold
out
If put to labor—give me the lovely
brown,
A thick-curled hair of the same dye,
broad shoulders,
A brawny arm full of veins, a leg with-
out
An artificial calf.  I suspect yours—
But let that pass.
SYL. [Aside.]        She means me all this
while,
For I have every one of those good
parts.                            150
O Sylli!  Fortunate Sylli!
CAM.                  You are moved, sir.
FUL. Fie!  No; go on.
CAM.              Then, as you are a courtier,
A graced one too, I fear you have been
too forward.
And so much for your person.  Rich
you are,
Devilish rich, as 'tis reported, and sure
have
The aids of Satan's little fiends to get it;
And what is got upon his back must be
Spent, you know where—the proverb's
stale.  One word more,
And I have done.
FUL.     I'll ease you of the trouble,  159
Coy and disdainful!
CAM.       Save me, or else he'll beat me!
FUL. No, your own folly shall; and, since
you put me
To my last charm, look upon this and
tremble.       Shows the king's ring.
CAM. At the sight of a fair ring?  The
king's, I take it.

I have seen him wear the like. If he
hath sent it
As a favor to me—

FUL.                    Yes, 'tis very likely,
His dying mother's gift, prized at [1] his
crown!
By this he does command you to be
mine;
By his gift you are so. You may yet
redeem all.

CAM. You are in a wrong account still.
Though the king may
Dispose of my life and goods, my mind's
mine own,                                    170
And shall be never yours. The king—
heaven bless him!—
Is good and gracious, and, being in himself
Abstemious from base and goatish loose-
ness,
Will not compel, against their wills,
chaste maidens
To dance in his minions' circles. I be-
lieve,
Forgetting it when he washed his hands,
you stole it
With an intent to awe me. But you are
cozened;
I am still myself, and will be.

FUL.                    A proud haggard,[2]
And not to be reclaimed! Which of
your grooms,
Your coachman, fool, or footman, min-
isters                                        180
Night-physic to you?

CAM.            You are foul-mouthed.

FUL.                    Much fairer
Than thy black soul; and so I will proclaim thee.

CAM. Were I a man, thou durst not speak
this.

FUL.       Heaven
So prosper me, as I resolve to do it
To all men, and in every place. Scorned
by
A tit of tenpence![3]
        *Exeunt* [4] *Fulgentio and his Page.*

SYL.            Now I begin to be valiant.
Nay, I will draw my sword. O, for a
brother! [5]

---

[1] *I.e.*, at the value of.   [2] Wild female hawk.
[3] A girl not worth tenpence.
[4] Original reads *Exit.*
[5] *I.e.*, a sworn brother. Some copies of the
original read *butcher, i.e.*, bravo.

---

Do a friend's part; pray you, carry him
the length of 't.
I give him three years and a day to
match my Toledo,
And then we'll fight like dragons.

ADOR.        Pray, have patience.        190

CAM. I may live to have vengeance. My
Bertoldo
Would not have heard this.

ADOR.            Madam—

CAM.                    Pray you, spare
Your language.—[*To Sylli.*] Prithee, fool
and make me merry.

SYL. That is my office ever.

ADOR.                    I must do,
Not talk; this glorious[6] gallant shall hear
from me.                                *Exeunt.*

### ACT II. SCENE iii.

*[Before the walls of Siena.]*

*The chambers[7] discharged; a flourish as
to an assault. Gonzaga, Pierio, Roderigo, Jacomo, Soldiers.*

GONZ.   Is the breach made assaultable?

PIER.                    Yes, and the moat
Filled up; the cannoneer hath done his
parts.
We may enter six abreast.

ROD.                There's not a man
Dares show himself upon the wall.

JAC.                        Defeat not
The soldiers' hoped-for spoil.

PIER.                    If you, sir,
Delay the assault, and the city be given
up
To your discretion, you in honor cannot
Use the extremity of war—but, in
Compassion to 'em, you to us prove
cruel.

JAC. And an enemy to yourself.

ROD.                A hindrance to   10
The brave revenge you have vowed.

GONZ.                Temper your heat
And lose not by too sudden rashness
that
Which, be but patient, will be offered
to you.
Security[8] ushers ruin; proud contempt
Of an enemy three parts vanquished,
with desire

---

[6] Bragging.
[7] Small cannon used for theatrical purposes.
[8] Want of caution.

And greediness of spoil, have often wrested
A certain victory from the conqueror's gripe.
Discretion is the tutor of the war,
Valor the pupil; and, when we command
With lenity, and your direction's followed        20
With cheerfulness, a prosperous end must crown
Our works well undertaken.

ROD.                    Ours are finished—

PIER. If we make use of fortune.

GONZ.                    Her false smiles
Deprive you of your judgments. The condition
Of our affairs exacts a double care,
And, like bifronted Janus, we must look
Backward as forward. Though a flattering calm
Bids us urge on, a sudden tempest raised,
Not feared, much less expected, in our rear
May foully fall upon us, and distract [1] us        30
To our confusion.—

*Enter Scout.*

Our scout! What brings
Thy ghastly looks and sudden speed?

SCOUT.                    Th' assurance
Of a new enemy.

GONZ.        This I foresaw and feared.
What are they, know'st thou?

SCOUT.        They are by their colors
Sicilians, bravely mounted, and the brightness
Of their rich armors doubly gilded with
Reflection of the sun.

GONZ.                    From Sicily?
The king in league! No war proclaimed!
'Tis foul;
But this must be prevented, not disputed.
Ha, how is this? Your estridge [2] plumes, that but        40
E'en now like quills of porcupines seemed to threaten
The stars, drop at the rumor of a shower,
And like to captive colors sweep the earth!
Bear up; but, in great dangers, greater minds

Are never proud. Shall a few loose troops, untrained
But in a customary ostentation,
Presented as a sacrifice to your valors,
Cause a dejection in you?

PIER.                    No dejection.

ROD. However startled, where you lead we'll follow.

GONZ. 'Tis bravely said. We will not stay their charge,        50
But meet 'em man to man, and horse to horse.
Pierio, in our absence hold our place,
And with our footmen [3] and those sickly troops
Prevent a sally. I in mine own person,
With part of the cavallerie,[4] will bid
These hunters welcome to a bloody breakfast.—
But I lose time.

PIER.        I'll to my charge. *Exit Pierio.*

GONZ.                    And we
To ours. I'll bring you on.

JAC.                    If we come off,
It is not amiss; if not, my state is settled.        *Exeunt. Alarm.*

## ACT II. SCENE iv.

[*The citadel of Siena.*]

*Ferdinand, Druso, Livio, above.*[5]

FER. No aids from Sicily? Hath hope forsook us,
And that vain comfort to affliction, pity,
By our vowed friend denied us? We can nor live
Nor die with honor. Like beasts in a toil,
We wait the leisure of the bloody hunter,
Who is not so far reconciled unto us,
As in one death to give a period
To our calamities; but in delaying
The fate we cannot fly from, starved with wants,        9
We die this night to live again tomorrow
And suffer greater torments.

DRU.                    There is not
Three days' provision for every soldier,
At an ounce of bread a day, left in the city.

LIV. To die the beggar's death, with hunger made

[1] Draw apart, scatter.        [2] Ostrich.

[3] Foot soldiers.
[4] Cavalry.        [5] *I.e.*, on the walls.

Anatomies [1] while we live, cannot but crack
Our heartstrings with vexation.

FER.                    Would they would break,
Break altogether!  How willingly, like Cato,
Could I tear out my bowels rather than
Look on the conqueror's insulting face,
But that religion and the horrid dream
To be suffered in the other world denies it!                                    21

*Enter Soldier.*

What news with thee?

SOLD.               From the turret of the fort,
By the rising clouds of dust, through which, like lightning,
The splendor of bright arms sometimes brake through,
I did descry some forces making towards us;
And from the camp, as emulous of their glory,
The general (for I know him by his horse),
And bravely seconded, encountered 'em.
Their greetings were too rough for friends, their swords
And not their tongues exchanging courtesies.                                   30
By this the main battalias are joined,
And, if you please to be spectators of
The horrid issue, I will bring you where
As in a theater you may see their fates
In purple gore presented.

FER.                              Heaven, if yet
Thou art appeased for my wrong done to Aurelia,
Take pity of my miseries!—Lead the way, friend.                    [*Exeunt.*]

ACT II. SCENE v.

[*A plain near the walls.*]

*A long charge; after, a flourish for victory.*
*Gonzaga; Jacomo; Roderigo, wounded.*
*Bertoldo, Gasparo, Anthonio prisoners.*
                    [*Officers and Soldiers.*]

GONZ. We have 'em yet, though they cost us dear.  This was
Charged home, and bravely followed. (*To Jacomo and Roderigo.*)  Be to yourselves

True mirrors to each other's worth; and, looking
With noble emulation on his [2] wounds,
The glorious livery of triumphant war,
Imagine these with equal grace appear
Upon yourself.[3]  The bloody sweat you have suffered
In this laborious, nay, toilsome harvest,
Yields a rich crop of conquest; and the spoil,
Most precious balsam to a soldier's hurts,                                    10
Will ease and cure 'em.  Let me look upon
The prisoners' faces.—(*To Gasparo and Anthon[io].*)  O, how much transformed
From what they were!  O Mars!  Were these toys fashioned
To undergo the burthen of thy service?
The weight of their defensive armor bruised
Their weak, effeminate limbs, and would have forced 'em
In a hot day without a blow to yield.

ANT. This insultation [4] shows not manly in you.

GONZ. To men I had forborne it; you are women,
Or, at the best, loose carpet knights.[5]
What fury                                    20
Seduced you to exchange your ease in court
For labor in the field?  Perhaps you thought
To charge through dust and blood an arméd foe
Was but like graceful running at the ring [6]
For a wanton mistress' glove, and the encounter
A soft impression on her lips.  But you
Are gaudy butterflies, and I wrong myself
In parling [7] with you.

GASP.                    *Væ victis!* [8]  Now we prove it.

ROD. But here's one fashioned in another mold,

---

[1] Skeletons.
[2] *I.e.*, Roderigo's.          [3] *I.e.*, Jacomo.
[4] Scornful exultation.
[5] Knights who have been created in court, not on the battlefield.
[6] One of the favorite sports at a tournament.
[7] Parleying, speaking.
[8] Woe to the vanquished!

And made of tougher metal.

GONZ.                    True; I owe him  30
For this wound bravely given.

BERT.                    O, that mountains
Were heaped upon me that I might ex-
    pire,
A wretch no more remembered!

GONZ.                    Look up, sir.
To be o'ercome deserves no shame.  If
    you
Had fallen ingloriously, or could accuse
Your want of courage in resistance,
    'twere
To be lamented; but, since you per-
    formed
As much as could be hoped for from a
    man,
Fortune his enemy, you wrong your-
    self
In this direction.[1]  I am honored in  40
My victory o'er you; but to have these
My prisoners is, in my true judgment,
    rather
Captivity than a triumph.  You shall
    find
Fair quarter from me, and your many
    wounds,
Which I hope are not mortal, with such
    care
Looked to and cured, as if your nearest
    friend
Attended on you.

BERT.          When you know me better,
You will make void this promise.  Can
    you call me
Into your memory?          [Shows his face.]

GONZ.          The brave Bertoldo!
A brother of our order!  By Saint John,
Our holy patron, I am more amazed,  51
Nay, thunderstrook [2] with thy apostasy
And precipice [3] from the most solemn
    vows
Made unto heaven, when this, the
    glorious badge
Of our Redeemer, was conferred upon
    thee
By the great master, than if I had seen
A reprobate Jew, an atheist, Turk, or
    Tartar
Baptized in our religion!

BERT.                    This I looked for,
And am resolved to suffer.

GONZ.                    Fellow soldiers,
Behold this man, and, taught by his
    example,  60
Know that 'tis safer far to play with
    lightning
Than trifle in things sacred.  In my
    rage          Weeps.
I shed these at the funeral of his virtue,
Faith, and religion.  Why, I will tell
    you
He was a gentleman so trained up and
    fashioned
For noble uses, and his youth did prom-
    ise
Such certainties, more than hopes, of
    great achievements,
As—if the Christian world had stood
    opposed
Against the Ottoman race to try the
    fortune
Of one encounter—this Bertoldo had
    been,  70
For his knowledge to direct, and match-
    less courage
To execute, without a rival by
The votes of good men chosen general,
As the prime soldier and most deserv-
    ing
Of all that wear the cross, which now
    in justice
I thus tear from him.

BERT.          Let me die with it
Upon my breast.

GONZ.          No; by this thou wert sworn
On all occasions as a knight to guard
Weak ladies from oppression, and never
To draw thy sword against 'em, where-
    as thou,  80
In hope of gain or glory, when a prin-
    cess,
And such a princess as Aurelia is,
Was dispossessed by violence of what
    was
Her true inheritance, against thine oath
Hast to thy uttermost labored to up-
    hold
Her falling enemy.  But thou shalt pay
A heavy forfeiture, and learn too late
Valor employed in an ill quarrel turns
To cowardice, and Virtue then puts on
Foul Vice's visor.  This is that which
    cancels  90
All friendship's bands between us.—
    Bear 'em off;

---

[1] Gifford reads dejection.
[2] Thunderstruck.          [3] Headlong fall.

I will hear no reply. And let the ransom
Of these, for they are yours, be highly
    rated.
In this I do but right, and let it be
Styled justice and not willful cruelty.
                                *Exeunt.*

THE END OF THE SECOND ACT.


ACT III. SCENE i.

[*Before the walls of Siena.*]

*Gonzaga, Astutio, Roderigo, Jacomo.*

GONZ. What I have done, sir, by the law
    of arms
I can and will make good.
AST.                    I have no commission
To expostulate [1] the act. These letters
    speak
The king my master's love to you, and
    his
Vowed service to the duchess, on whose
    person
1 am to give attendance.
GONZ.                    At this instant
She's at Pienza. You may spare the
    trouble
Of riding thither; I have advertised her
Of our success, and on what humble
    terms                                    9
Siena stands. Though presently [2] I can
Possess it, I defer it, that she may
Enter her own, and, as she please, dispose
    of
The prisoners and the spoil.
AST.                    I thank you, sir.
I' the meantime, if I may have your
    license,
I have a nephew, and one once my ward,
For whose liberties and ransoms I would
    gladly
Make composition.
GONZ.            They are, as I take it,
Called Gasparo and Anthonio.
AST.                    The same, sir.
GONZ. For them, you must treat with
    these [*Indicating Roderigo and Jacomo*];
    but, for Bertoldo,
He is mine own. If the king will ransom
    him,                                    20
He pays down fifty thousand crowns;
    if not,
He lives and dies my slave.

[1] Discuss, examine.        [2] Immediately.

AST.                    Pray you, a word.—
[*Aside to Gonzaga.*] The king will rather
    thank you to detain him
Than give one crown to free him.
GONZ. [*Aside.*]            At his pleasure.—
I'll send the prisoners under guard; my
    business
Calls me another way.        *Exit Gonzaga.*
AST.                    My service waits you.—
Now, gentlemen, do not deal like mer-
    chants with me,
But noble captains; you know, in great
    minds,
*Posse et nolle nobile.* [3]
ROD.                    Pray you, speak
Our language.
JAC.        I find not in my commission    30
An officer's bound to speak or under-
    stand
More than his mother tongue.
ROD.                    If he speaks that
After midnight, 'tis remarkable.
AST.                    In plain terms, then,
Anthonio is your prisoner; Gasparo,
    yours.
JAC. You are i' the right.
AST.                At what sum do you rate
Their several ransoms?
ROD.                    I must make my market
As the commodity cost me.
AST.                    As it cost you?
You did not buy your captainship?
    Your desert,
I hope, advanced you.
ROD.                    How? It well appears
You are no soldier. Desert in these
    days?                                    40
Desert may make a sergeant to a colo-
    nel,
And it may hinder him from rising
    higher;
But, if it ever get a company,
A company, pray you, mark me, with-
    out money
Or private service done for the general's
    mistress,
With a commendatory epistle from
    her,
I will turn lanceprisado. [4]
JAC.                    Pray you, observe, sir:
I served two prenticeships, just fourteen
    year,

[3] It is noble to have the power and to refuse.
[4] Lance-corporal.

Trailing the puissant pike, and half so
    long
Had the right-hand file; and I fought
    well, 'twas said, too.        50
But I might have served, and fought,
    and served till doomsday,
And never have carried a flag but for the
    legacy
A buxom widow of threescore bequeathed
    me;
And that too, my back knows, I labor[ed]
    hard for,
But was better paid.
Ast.        You are merry with yourselves.
But this is from the purpose.
Rod.            To the point then.
Prisoners are not ta'en every day; and,
    when
We have 'em, we must make the best
    use of 'em.
Our pay is little to the part we should
    bear,
And that so long a-coming that 'tis
    spent        60
Before we have it, and hardly wipes off
    scores
At the tavern and the ordinary.
Jac.           You may add, too,
Our sport took up [1] on trust.
Rod.        Peace, thou smock vermin!
Discover commanders' secrets!—In a
    word, sir,
We have required,[2] and find our prison-
    ers rich.
Two thousand crowns apiece our com-
    panies cost us,
And so much each of us will have, and
    that
In present pay.
Jac.          It is too little; yet,
Since you have said the word, I am con-
    tent,
But will not go a gazet [3] less.
Ast.          Since you are not   70
To be brought lower, there is no evad-
    ing;
I'll be your paymaster.
Rod.         We desire no better.
Ast. But not a word of what's agreed be-
    tween us,
Till I have schooled my gallants.
Jac.          I am dumb, sir.

[1] Obtained.
[2] Inquired, investigated.    [3] A small coin.

*Enter a Guard; Bertoldo, Anthonio, Gasparo,*
*in irons.*

Bert. And where removed now? Hath the
    tyrant found out
Worse usage for us?
Ant.            Worse it cannot be.
My grewhound [4] has fresh straw and
    scraps in his kennel;
But we have neither.
Gasp.          Did I ever think
To wear such garters [5] on silk stockings,
    or
That my too curious [6] appetite, that
    turned        80
At the sight of godwits, [7] pheasant,
    partridge, quails,
Larks, woodcocks, calvered [8] salmon, as
    coarse diet,
Would leap at a moldy crust?
Ant.           And go without it,
So oft as I do? O, how have I jeered
The city entertainment! A huge shoulder
Of glorious, fat ram-mutton, seconded
With a pair of tame cats [9] or conies, [10] a
    crab [11] tart,
With a worthy loin of veal, and valiant
    capon,
Mortified [12] to grow tender—these I
    scorned,
From their plentiful horn of abundance,
    though invited.        90
But now I could carry my own stool to a
    tripe,
And call their chitterlings charity, and
    bless the founder.
Bert. O, that I were no farther sensible
Of my miseries than you are! You, like
    beasts,
Feel only stings of hunger, and complain
    not
But when you are empty; but your
    narrow souls,
If you have any, cannot comprehend
How insupportable the torments are
Which a free and noble soul, made cap-
    tive, suffers.
Most miserable men! And what am I,
    then,        100

[4] Greyhound.
[5] *I.e.*, shackles.
[6] Finical.
[7] Snipes.
[8] Sliced alive and perhaps pickled.
[9] Hares.
[10] Rabbits.
[11] Crab apple.
[12] Castrated.

That envy you? Fetters, though made of
    gold,
Express base thralldom; and all delicates
Prepared by Median cooks for epicures,
When not our own, are bitter; quilts
    filled high
With gossamer and roses cannot yield
The body soft repose, the mind kept
    waking
With anguish and affliction.
AST.                        My good lord—
BERT. This is no time nor place for
    flattery, sir.
    Pray you, style me as I am, a wretch for-
        saken
    Of the world, as myself.
AST.                    I would it were   110
    In me to help you.
BERT. Ay, if that you want power, sir,
    Lip-comfort cannot cure me. Pray you,
        leave me
    To mine own private thoughts. *Walks by.*[1]
AST.                    My valiant nephew!
    And my more than warlike ward! I am
        glad to see you
    After your glorious conquests. Are these
        chains
    Rewards [2] for your good service? If they
        are,
    You should wear 'em on your necks,
        since they are massy,
    Like aldermen [3] of the war.
ANT.                    You jeer us too!
GASP. Good uncle, name not, as you are a
    man of honor,
    That fatal word of war; the very sound [4]
        of 't                        120
    Is more dreadful than a cannon.
ANT.                    But redeem us
    From this captivity, and I'll vow here-
        after
    Never to wear a sword, or cut my
        meat
    With a knife that has an edge or point;
        I'll starve first.
GASP. I will cry "broom" or "cat's
    meat" [5] in Palermo,
    Turn porter, carry burthens—anything
    Rather than live a soldier.

[1] Stage direction follows next line in original.
[2] Original reads *rewardee.*
[3] London aldermen still wear heavy gold
chains.
[4] The Newberry copy reads *summon.*
[5] Common cries of public vendors.

AST.                    This should have
    Been thought upon before. At what
        price, think you,
    Your two wise heads are rated?
ANT.                    A calf's head is
    More worth than mine; I am sure it had
        more brains in't,                130
    Or I had never come here.
ROD.                    And I will eat it
    With bacon, if I have not speedy ran-
        som.
ANT. And a little garlic too, for your own
    sake, sir;
    'Twill boil in your stomach else.
GASP.                    Beware of mine,
    Or the horns [6] may choke you; I am
        married, sir.
ANT. You shall have my row of houses
    near the palace.
GASP. And my villa; all—
ANT.                    All that we have.[7]
AST. Well, have more wit hereafter; for
    this time,
    You are ransomed.
JAC.                    Off with their irons.
ROD.                    Do, do.
    If you are ours again, you know your
        price.                        140
ANT. Pray you, despatch [8] us. I shall ne'er
    believe
    I am a free man, till I set my foot
    In Sicily again, and drink Palermo,
    And in Palermo too.
AST.                    The wind sits fair;
    You shall aboard tonight. With the
        rising sun
    You may touch upon the coast. But
        take your leaves
    Of the late general first.
GASP.                    I will be brief.
ANT. And I. My lord, heaven keep you!
GASP.                    Yours, to use
    In the way of peace; but as your soldiers,
        never.
ANT. A pox of [9] war! No more of war.
*Exeunt Roderig[o], Jaco[mo], Anthonio,*
                        *Gasparo.*
BERT.                    Have you  150
    Authority to loose their bonds, yet leave

[6] The time-worn allusion to the sign of
cuckoldry.
[7] In the original here follows the unnecessary
stage direction, *To Astutio.*
[8] Hasten.                    [9] A plague on.

The brother of your king, whose worth
   disdains
Comparison with such as these, in irons?
If ransom may redeem them, I have
   lands,
A patrimony of mine own, assigned me
By my deceaséd sire, to satisfy
Whate'er can be demanded for my
   freedom.
Ast. I wish you had, sir; but the king,
   who yields
No reason for his will, in his displeasure
Hath seized on all you had; nor will
   Gonzaga,                                        160
Whose prisoner now you are, accept of
   less
Than fifty thousand crowns.
Bert.                              I find it now
   That misery ne'er comes alone. But,
   grant
The king is yet inexorable, time
May work him to a feeling of my suffer-
   ings.
I have friends that swore their lives and
   fortunes were
At my devotion—and among the rest
Yourself, my lord, when, forfeited to the
   law
For a foul murther, and in cold blood
   done,
I made your life my gift, and reconciled
   you                                            170
To this incenséd king and got your par-
   don.
Beware ingratitude. I know you are rich,
And may pay down the sum.
Ast.                              I might, my lord;
   But pardon me.
Bert.              And will Astutio prove then
(To please a passionate man—the king's
   no more)
False to his maker and his reason,
   which
Commands more than I ask? O summer
   friendship,
Whose flattering leaves, that shadowed
   us in our
Prosperity, with the least gust drop off
In th' autumn of adversity! How      180
   like
A prison is to a grave! When dead, we
   are
With solemn pomp brought thither, and
   our heirs.

Masking their joy in false, dissembled
   tears,
Weep o'er the hearse; but earth no
   sooner covers
The earth brought thither, but they turn
   away
With inward smiles, the dead no more
   remembered.
So, entered in a prison—
Ast.                              My occasions
Command me hence, my lord.
Bert.                    Pray you, leave me, do;
And tell the cruel king that I will wear
These fetters till my flesh and they are
   one                                            190
Incorporated substance. In myself,
As in a glass, I'll look on human frailty,
And curse the height of royal blood,
   since I,
In being born near to Jove, am near his
   thunder.
Cedars once shaken with a storm, their
   own                              *Exit Astutio.*
Weight grubs their roots out.—Lead me
   where you please;
I am his, not fortune's, martyr, and will
   die
The great example of his cruelty.
                   *Exit cum suis.*[1]

### Act III. Scene ii.

*[A grove near the palace near Palermo.]*

*Adorni.*

Ador. He undergoes my challenge and
   contemns it,
And threatens me with the late edict
   made
Gainst duelists—the [2] altar cowards fly to.
But I, that am engaged, and nourish in
   me
A higher aim than fair Camiola dreams
   of,
Must not sit down thus. In the court I
   dare not
Attempt him; and in public he's so
   guarded
With a herd of parasites, clients, fools,
   and suitors
That a musket cannot reach him. My
   designs

[1] With his attendants.
[2] Suggested by Davies. Original reads *then.*

Admit of no delay.  This is her birth-
day,                                            10
Which, with a fit and due solemnity,
Camiola celebrates; and on it all such
As love or serve her usually present
A tributary duty.  I'll have something
To give, if my intelligence prove true,
Shall find acceptance.  I am told, near
this grove
Fulgentio every morning makes his
markets [1]
With his petitioners; I may present him
With a sharp petition!—Ha, 'tis he!
My fate
Be ever blessed for 't!          [*Retires.*]

*Enter* [2] *Fulgen[tio and Page].*

FUL.          Command such as wait me    20
Not to presume, at the least for half an
hour,
To press on my retirements.
PAGE.                    I will say, sir,
You are at your prayers.
FUL.          That will not find belief;
Courtiers have something else to do.
Begone, sir.—                    [*Exit Page.*]
Challenged!  'Tis well!  And by a groom!
Still better!
Was this shape made to fight?  I have a
tongue yet,
Howe'er no sword, to kill him; and what
way
This morning I'll resolve of.
                              *Exit Fulgentio.*
ADOR.                    I shall cross
Your resolution, or suffer for you.
                              *Exit Adorni.*

ACT III. SCENE iii.

[*A room in Camiola's house.*]

*Camiola, divers Servants with presents,*
*Sylli, Clarinda.*

SYL.  What are all these?
CLAR.          Servants with several presents,
And rich ones too.
1 SERV.          With her best wishes, madam,
Of many such days to you, the Lady
Petula
Presents you with this fan.
2 SERV.                    This diamond
From your aunt Honoria.

[1] Dealings.          [2] Original reads *Exit.*

3 SERV.                    This piece of plate
From your uncle, old Vincentio, with
your arms
Graven upon it.
CAM.          Good friends they are too—
Munificent in their love and favor to
me.—
[*To Clarinda.*] Out of my cabinet return
such jewels                                        9
As this directs you.—[*Gives Servants*
*money.*] For your pains; and yours;
Nor must you be forgotten.    Honor
me
With the drinking of a health.
1 SERV.                    Gold, on my life!
2 SERV.  She scorns to give base silver.
3 SERV.                    Would she had been
Born every month in the year!
1 SERV.                    Month?  Every day.
2 SERV.  Show such another maid.
3 [SERV.]          All happiness wait you!
SYLLI.  I'll see your will done.
              *Exeunt Sylli, Clarinda, Servants.*

*Enter Adorni, wounded.*

CAM.                    How, Adorni wounded?
ADOR.  A scratch got in your service, else
not worth
Your observation.  I bring not, madam,
In honor of your birthday, antique plate
Or pearl for which the savage Indian
dives                                            20
Into the bottom of the sea, nor diamonds
Hewn from steep rocks with danger.
Such as give
To those that have what they themselves
want, aim at
A glad return with profit.  Yet despise
not
My offering at the altar of your favor,
Nor let the lowness of the giver lessen
The height of what's presented, since it is
A precious jewel, almost forfeited,
And dimmed with clouds of infamy,
redeemed
And in its natural splendor, with addi-
tion,                                            30
Restored to the true owner.
CAM.                    How is this?
ADOR.  Not to hold you in suspense, I
bring you, madam,
Your wounded reputation cured, the
sting

Of virulent malice, festering your fair
　name,
Plucked out and trod on. That proud
　man, that was
Denied the honor of your bed, yet durst
With his untrue reports strumpet your
　fame,
Compelled by me, hath given himself the
　lie,
And in his own blood wrote it. [*Gives her
　a paper.*] You may read
"Fulgentio" subscribed.
CAM.　　　　　　　　I am amazed!　40
ADOR. It does deserve it, madam. Com-
　mon service
Is fit for hinds, and the reward propor-
　tioned
To their conditions. Therefore, look not
　on me
As a follower of your father's fortunes, or
One that subsists on yours. You frown!
　My service
Merits not this aspect.
CAM.　　　　　　　　Which of my favors,
I might say bounties, hath begot and
　nourished
This more than rude presumption?
　Since you had
An itch to try your desperate valor,
　wherefore
Went you not to the war? Couldst thou
　suppose　　　　　　　　　　　　50
My innocence could ever fall so low
As to have need of thy rash sword to
　guard it
Against malicious slander? O, how much
Those ladies are deceived and cheated
　when
The clearness and integrity of their
　actions
Do not defend themselves, and stand
　secure
On their own bases! Such as in a color [1]
Of seeming service give protection to 'em,
Betray their own strengths. Malice
　scorned puts out　　　　　　　　　59
Itself, but argued gives a kind of credit
To a false accusation. In this, this your
Most memorable service, you believed
You did me right; but you have wronged
　me more
In your defense of my undoubted honor
Than false Fulgentio could.

ADOR.　　　　　　　I am sorry what was
So well intended is so ill received;
Yet, under your correction, you wished

*Ente[r] Clarinda.*

Bertoldo had been present.
CAM.　　　　　　　　　　True, I did.
But he and you, sir, are not parallels,
Nor must you think yourself so.
ADOR.　　　　　　　　　I am what　70
You'll please to have me.
CAM.　　　　　　　　　If Bertoldo had
Punished Fulgentio's insolence, it had
　shown
His love to her whom in his judgment he
Vouchsafed to make his wife—a height,
　I hope,
Which you dare not aspire to. The same
　actions
Suit not all men alike. But I perceive
Repentance in your looks. For this time,
　leave me;
I may forgive, perhaps forget, your
　folly.
Conceal yourself till this storm be blown
　over.
You will be sought for, yet, for my
　estate [2]　　　　　　　　　　　80
Can hinder it, shall not suffer in my
　service.　　　*Gives him her hand to kiss.*
ADOR. [*Aside.*] This is something yet,
　though I missed the mark I shot at.
　　　　　　　　　　　　　*Exit Adorni.*
CAM. This gentleman is of a noble temper,
And I too harsh, perhaps, in my reproof.
Was I not, Clarinda?
CLAR.　　　　　　I am not to censure [3]
Your actions, madam; but there are a
　thousand
Ladies, and of good fame, in such a cause
Would be proud of such a servant.
CAM.　　　　　　　　　　It may be.

*Enter a Servant.*

Let me offend in this kind.—Why,
　uncalled for?
SERV. The signiors, madam, Gasparo and
　Anthonio,　　　　　　　　　　　90
Selected friends of the renowned Ber-
　toldo,
Put ashore this morning.
CAM.　　　　　　　　　　Without him?

---

[1] Pretense.　　　[2] Rank, position.　　　[3] Judge.

SERV. I think so.

CAM.        Never think more then.

SERV.        They have been at court,
Kissed the king's hand, and, their first
    duties done
To him, appear ambitious [1] to tender
To you their second service.

CAM.    Wait 'em hither. *Exit* [2] *Servant.*
Fear, do not rack me! Reason, now if
    ever,
Haste with thy aids and tell me such a
    wonder
As my Bertoldo is, with such care
    fashioned,
Must not, nay, cannot, in heaven's
    providence                    100

*Enter Anthonio, Gasparo, Serv[ant].*

So soon miscarry!—Pray you, forbear;
    ere you
Take the privilege, as strangers, to
    salute me—
Excuse my manners—make me first
    understand
How it is with Bertoldo.

GASP. [3]        The relation
Will not, I fear, deserve your thanks.

ANT.        I wish
Some other should inform you.

CAM.        Is he dead?
You see, though with some fear, I dare
    inquire it.

GASP. Dead! Would that were the worst;
    a debt were paid then
Kings in their birth owe nature.

CAM.        Is there aught
More terrible than death?

ANT.        Yes, to a spirit    110
Like his: cruel imprisonment, and that
Without the hope of freedom.

CAM.        You abuse me.
The royal king cannot, in love to virtue,
Though all springs of affection were dried
    up,
But pay his ransom.

GASP.        When you know what 'tis,
You will think otherwise. No less will do
    it
Than fifty thousand crowns.

CAM.        A pretty sum,
The price weighed with the purchase!
    Fifty thousand?
To the king 'tis nothing. He that can
    spare more
To his minion for a masque cannot but
    ransom                    120
Such a brother at a million. You wrong
The king's magnificence.

ANT.        In your opinion;
But 'tis most certain. He does not alone
In himself refuse to pay it, but forbids
All other men.

CAM.        Are you sure of this?

GASP.        You may read
The edict to that purpose, published by
    him;
That will resolve you.

CAM.        Possible! Pray you, stand off.
If I do not mutter treason to myself,
My heart will break. Yet I will not curse
    him;
He is my king. The news you have de-
    livered                    130
Makes me weary of your company; we'll
    salute
When we meet next. I'll bring you to the
    door.
Nay, pray you, no more compliments.

GASP.        One thing more,
And that's substantial: let your Adorni
Look to himself.

ANT.        The king is much incensed
Against him for Fulgentio.

CAM.        As I am,
For your slowness to depart.

BOTH.        Farewell, sweet lady.
        *Exeunt Gaspa[ro], Antho[nio].*

CAM. O more than impious times, when
    not alone
Subordinate ministers of justice are
Corrupted and seduced, but kings them-
    selves,                    140
The greater wheels by which the lesser
    move,
Are broken or disjointed! Could it be,
    else,
A king, to soothe his politic ends, should
    so far
Forsake his honor as at once to break
Th' adamant chains of nature and
    religion
To bind up atheism [4] as a defense

---

[1] Emended by Gifford. Original reads *am-bitions.*

[2] Original reads *Exeunt.*

[3] Original reads *Ber.*

[4] Godlessness, dishonor.

To his dark counsels? Will it ever be
That to deserve too much is dangerous,
And virtue, when too eminent, a crime?
Must she serve fortune still, or, when
   stripped of                                    150
Her gay and glorious favors, lose the
   beauties
Of her own natural shape? O my Ber-
   toldo,
Thou only sun in honor's sphere, how
   soon
Art thou eclipsed and darkened—not the
   nearness
Of blood prevailing on the king, nor
   all
The benefits to the general good dis-
   pensed,
Gaining a retribution! But that
To owe a courtesy to a simple virgin
Would take from the deserving, I find in
   me
Some sparks of fire, which, fanned with
   honor's breath,                               160
Might rise into a flame and in men
   darken
Their usurped splendor. Ha! My aim is
   high,
And, for the honor of my sex, to fall so
Can never prove inglorious. 'Tis re-
   solved.—
Call in Adorni.
CLAR.          I am happy in
Such employment, madam.
                 *Exit Clarin[da].*
CAM.              He's a man,
I know, that at a reverend distance
   loves me;
And such are ever faithful. What a sea
Of melting ice I walk on! What strange
   censures
Am I to undergo! But good intents   170
Deride all future rumors.

     *Enter [1] Clarin[da] and Adorn[i].*

ADOR.             I obey
Your summons, madam.
CAM.       Leave the place, Clarinda;
One woman, in a secret of such weight,
Wise men may think too much.—
              *[Exit Clarinda.]*
              Nearer, Adorni.
I warrant it with a smile.
[1] Original reads *Exit.*

ADOR.          I cannot ask
Safer protection. What's your will?
CAM.             To doubt
Your ready desire to serve me, or prepare
   you
With the repetition of former merits,
Would, in my diffidence, wrong you. But
   I will,
And without circumstance, in the trust
   that I                                        180
Impose upon you, free you from sus-
   picion.
ADOR. I foster none of you.
CAM.         I know you do not.
You are, Adorni, by the love you owe
   me—
ADOR. The surest conjuration.
CAM.       Take me with you [2] —
Love born of duty. But advance no
   further.
You are, sir, as I said, to do me service,
To undertake a task in which your faith,
Judgment, discretion—in a word, your
   all
That's good—must be engaged; nor
   must you study,                               189
In the execution, but what may make
For the ends I aim at.
ADOR.        They admit no rivals.
CAM. You answer well. You have heard
   of Bertoldo's
Captivity, and the king's neglect, the
   greatness
Of his ransom—fifty thousand crowns,
   Adorni,
Two parts of my estate?
ADOR. *[Aside.]*    To what tends this?
CAM. Yet I so love the gentleman, for to
   you
I will confess my weaknesses, that I
   purpose
Now, when he is forsaken by the king
And his own hopes, to ransom him and
   receive him
Into my bosom as my lawful hus-
   band—                                          200
    *Adorni starts and seems troubled.*
Why change you color?
ADOR.        'Tis in wonder of
Your virtue, madam.
CAM.      You must therefore to
Siena for me, and pay to Gonzaga
This ransom for his liberty; you shall
[2] I.e., don't go too fast.

Have bills of exchange along with you.
Let him swear
A solemn contract to me; for you must
be
My principal witness, if he should—but
why
Do I entertain these jealousies? [1] You
will do this?

ADOR. Faithfully, madam—(*Aside*.) but
not live long after.

CAM. One thing I had forgot: besides his
freedom          210
He may want accommodations; furnish
him
According to his birth. And from Cami-
ola
Deliver this kiss, printed on your lips,
*Kisses him.*
Sealed on his hand. You shall not see my
blushes.
I'll instantly despatch you.
*Exit Camiola.*

ADOR.          I am half
Hanged out of the way already.—Was
there ever
Poor lover so employed against himself
To make way for his rival? I must do it.
Nay, more, I will. If loyalty can find
Recompense beyond hope or imagina-
tion,          220
Let it fall on me in the other world
As a reward, for in this I dare not hope
it.          *Exit.*

THE END OF THE THIRD ACT.

ACT IV. SCENE i.

[*Before the walls of Siena.*]

*Gonzaga, Pierio, Roderigo, Jacomo.*

GONZ. You have seized upon the citadel,
and disarmed
All that could make resistance?

PIER.          Hunger had
Done that before we came, nor was the
soldier
Compelled to seek for prey; the famished
wretches,
In hope of mercy, as a sacrifice offered
All that was worth the taking.

GONZ.          You proclaimed,
On pain of death, no violence should be
offered
To any woman?

[1] Suspicions.

ROD.          But it needed not,
For famine had so humbled 'em, and took
off
The care of their sex's honor that there
was not          10
So coy a beauty in the town but would
For half a moldy biscuit sell herself
To a poor bezonian,[2] and without shriek-
ing.

GONZ. Where is the duke of Urbin?

JAC.          Under guard,
As you directed.

GONZ.          See the soldiers set
In rank and file, and, as the duchess
passes,
Bid 'em vail [3] their ensigns; and charge
'em on their lives
Not to cry "whores"!

JAC.          The devil cannot fright 'em
From their military license. Though
they know
They are her subjects, and will part with
being          20
To do her service, yet, since she is a
woman,
They will touch at her britch [4] with their
tongues; and that is all
That they can hope for.

*A shout, and a general cry within,"Whores,*
*whores!"*

GONZ.          O, the devil! They are at it!
Hell stop their bawling throats. Again!
Make up,
And cudgel them into jelly.

ROD.          To no purpose;
Though their mothers [5] were there, they
would have the same name for 'em.
*Exeunt.*

ACT IV. SCENE ii.

[*Another part of the camp.*]

*Roderigo, Jacomo, Pierio, Gonzaga, Aurelia,*
*under a canopy. Astutio presents her*
*with letters. Loud music. She reads the*
*letters.*

GONZ. I do beseech your highness not to
ascribe
To the want of discipline the barbarous
rudeness
Of the soldier in his profanation of
Your sacred name and virtues.

[2] Recruit, beggar.          [3] Lower.          [4] Breech.
[5] Emended by Gifford. Original reads *mouthes*.

AUR.                              No, lord general;
I've heard my father say oft 'twas a
custom
Usual in the camp, nor are they to be
· punished
For words, that have in fact ¹ deserved
so well.
Let the one excuse the other.
ALL.                              Excellent, princess!
AUR. But, for ² these aids from Sicily sent
against us
To blast our spring of conquest in the
bud,                                                    10
I cannot find, my lord ambassador,
How we should entertain 't but as a
wrong,
With purpose to detain us from our own,
Howe'er the king endeavors in his letters
To mitigate the affront.
AST.                              Your grace hereafter
May hear from me such strong assur-
ances
Of his unlimited desires to serve you
As will, I hope, drown in forgetfulness
The memory of what's past.
AUR.                              We shall take time
To search the depth of 't further, and
proceed                                                 20
As our council shall direct us.
GONZ.                              We present you
With the keys of the city; all lets ³ are
removed.
Your way is smooth and easy; at your
feet
Your proudest enemy falls.
AUR.                              We thank your valors.
A victory without blood is twice achieved,
And the disposure of it, to us tendered,
The greatest honor.  Worthy captains,
thanks!
My love extends itself to all.
GONZ.                              Make way there!
*A Guard made.  Aurelia passes thorough 'em.*
*Loud music.  Exeunt.*

ACT IV.  SCENE iii.

·[*A room in the prison at Siena.*]

*Bertoldo, with a small book, in fetters.*
*Jailor.*⁴

BERT.  'Tis here determined (great exam-
ples, armed
With arguments, produced to make it
good)
That neither tyrants nor the wrested
laws,
The people's frantic rage, sad exile, want,
Nor that which I endure, captivity,
Can do a wise man any injury.
Thus Seneca, when he wrote it, thought.
But then
Felicity courted him.  His wealth exceed-
ing
A private man's, happy in the embraces
Of his chaste wife Paulina, his house full
Of children, clients, servants, flattering
friends,                                                11
Soothing his lip-positions,⁵ and created
Prince of the senate, by the general voice,
As his pupils' new ⁶ suffrage ⁷—then no
doubt
He held and did believe this.  But no
sooner
The prince's frowns and jealousies had
thrown him
Out of security's lap, and a centurion
Had offered him what choice of death he
pleased,
But told him die he must, when straight
the armor
Of his so boasted fortitude fell off,      20
                              *Throws away the book.*
Complaining of his frailty.  Can it then
Be censured womanish weakness in me,
if,
Thus clogged with irons, and the period
To close up all calamities ⁸ denied me,
Which was presented Seneca, I wish
I ne'er had being, at least never knew
What happiness was, or argue with
heaven's justice,
Tearing my locks, and in defiance throw-
ing
Dust in the air, or, falling on the ground,
thus
With my nails and teeth to dig a grave,
or rend                                                30
The bowels of the earth, my stepmother,
And not a natural parent, or thus prac-
tice

---

¹ Deed, achievement.
² As for.
³ Hindrances.
⁴ Probably on guard on the outer stage.

⁵ Utterances.
⁶ Emended by Bryne.  Original reads *pupil
news.*
⁷ Choice by vote.          ⁸ *I.e.,* death.

To die, and, as I were insensible,
Believe I had no motion? *Lies on his face.*

*Enter Gonzaga, Adorn[i], Jailor.*

GONZ. There he is.
I'll not inquire by whom his ransom's
paid—
I am satisfied that I have it—nor allege
One reason to excuse his cruel usage,
As you may interpret it. Let it suffice
It was my will to have it so. He is yours
now;
Dispose of him as you please.
*Exit Gonzaga.*
ADOR. Howe'er I hate him, 40
As one preferred before me, being a man
He does deserve my pity. Sir, he sleeps.
Or is he dead? Would he were a saint in
heaven
('Tis all the hurt I wish him), but was not
Born to such happiness. (*Kneels by him.*)
—No, he breathes—come near,
And, if 't be possible without his feeling,
Take off his irons. (*His irons taken off.*)
So; now leave us private. *Exit Jailor.*
He does begin to stir; and, as trans-
ported
With a joyful dream, how he stares and
feels his legs,
As yet uncertain whether it can be 50
True or fantastical!
BERT. [*Rising.*] Ministers of mercy,
Mock not calamity. Ha, 'tis no vision!
Or, if it be, the happiest that ever
Appeared to sinful flesh! Who's here?
His face
Speaks him Adorni—but some glorious
angel,
Concealing its divinity in his shape,
Hath done this miracle, it being not an
act
For wolvish man. Resolve me, if thou
look'st for
Bent knees in adoration?
ADOR. O, forbear, sir!
I am Adorni, and the instrument 60
Of your deliverance; but the benefit
You owe another.
BERT. If he has a name,
As soon as spoken, 'tis writ on my heart
I am his bondman.
ADOR. To the shame of men,
This great act is a woman's.

BERT. The whole sex
For her sake must be deified. How I
wander
In my imagination, yet cannot
Guess who this phœnix should be!
ADOR. 'Tis Camiola.
BERT. Pray you, speak 't again; there's
music in her name.
Once more, I pray you, sir.
ADOR. Camiola, 70
The Maid of Honor.
BERT. Cursed atheist [1] that I was,
Only to doubt it could be any other,
Since she alone, in the abstract of her-
self,
That small but ravishing substance, com-
prehends
Whatever is, [2] or can be wished, in the
Idea [3] of a woman! O, what service
Or sacrifice of duty can I pay her,
If not to live and die her charity's slave?
Which is resolved already!
ADOR. She expects not 79
Such a dominion o'er you. Yet, ere I
Deliver her demands, give me your hand.
On this, as she enjoined me, with my
lips
I print her love and service, by me sent
you.
BERT. I am o'erwhelmed with wonder!
ADOR. You must now,
Which is the sum of all that she desires,
By a solemn contract bind yourself,
when she
Requires it, as a debt due for your free-
dom,
To marry her.
BERT. This does engage me further.
A payment! An increase of obligation.
To marry her!—'Twas my *nil ultra* [4]
ever— 90
The end of my ambition! O, that now
The holy man, she present, were pre-
pared
To join our hands, but with that speed
my heart
Wishes mine eyes might see her!
ADOR. You must swear this.
BERT. Swear it? Collect all oaths and im-
precations,
Whose least breach is damnation, and
those

[1] Skeptic.
[2] Original reads *it*.
[3] Ideal pattern.
[4] Nothing beyond.

Ministered to me in a form more dread-
ful;
Set heaven and hell before me, I will take
'em.
False to Camiola? Never.—Shall I now
Begin my vows to you?

ADOR.       I am no churchman;  100
Such a one must file it on record. You
are free;
And, that you may appear like to yourself,
For so she wished, there's [1] gold, with
which you may
Redeem your trunks and servants, and
whatever
Of late you lost. I have found out the
captain
Whose spoil they were; his name is Roderigo.

BERT.  I know him.

ADOR.       I have done my parts.

BERT.          So much, sir,
As I am ever yours for 't. Now, me-
thinks,
I walk in air! Divine Camiola—
But words cannot express thee. I'll build
to thee       110
An altar in my soul, on which I'll offer
A still-increasing sacrifice of duty.
                 *Exit Ber[toldo].*

ADOR.  What will become of me now is
apparent.
Whether a poniard or a halter be
The nearest way to hell (for I must
thither
After I have killed myself) is somewhat
doubtful.
This Roman resolution of self-murther
Will not hold water at the high tribunal
When it comes to be argued; my good
genius       119
Prompts me to this consideration. He
That kills himself to avoid misery fears
it,
And, at the best, shows but a bastard
valor.
This life's a fort committed to my trust,
Which I must not yield up till it be
forced.
Nor will I. He's not valiant that dares
die,
But he that boldly bears calamity. *Exit.*

ACT IV. SCENE iv.

*[The council chamber in the palace at Siena.]*

*A flourish. Pierio, Roderigo, Jacomo, Gon-
   zaga, Aurelia, Ferdinand, Astutio,
                      Attendants.*

AUR.  A seat here for the duke! It is our
glory
To overcome with courtesies, not rigor.
The lordly Roman, who held it the
height
Of human happiness to have kings and
queens
To wait by his triumphant chariot
wheels,
In his insulting pride, deprived himself
Of drawing near the nature of the gods,
Best known for such, in being merciful.
Yet give me leave, but still with gentle
language
And with the freedom of a friend, to
tell you       10
To seek by force what courtship could
not win
Was harsh [2] and never taught in Love's
mild school.
Wise poets feign that Venus' coach is
drawn
By doves and sparrows, not by bears and
tigers.
I spare the application.

FER.              In my fortune,
Heaven's justice hath confirmed it; yet,
great lady,
Since my offense grew from excess of love,
And [3] not to be resisted, having paid too
With the loss of liberty the forfeiture
Of my presumption, in your clemency  20
It may find pardon.

AUR.       You shall have just cause
To say it hath. The charge of the long
siege
Defrayed, and the loss my subjects have
sustained
Made good, since so far I must deal with
caution,
You have your liberty.

FER.          I could not hope for
Gentler conditions.

AUR.          My Lord Gonzaga,

[2] Emended by Gifford. Original reads *not
harsh.*
   [3] *I.e.,* and a love, etc.

Since my coming to Siena, I have heard
   much
Of your prisoner, brave Bertoldo.
Gonz.                                    Such an one,
   Madam, I had.
Ast.                And have still, sir, I hope.
Gonz. Your hopes deceive you. He is ran-
   somed, madam.                                    30
Ast. By whom, I pray you, sir?
Gonz.                    You had best inquire
Of your intelligencer. I am no informer.
Ast. [*Aside.*] I like not this.
Aur.                    He is, as 'tis reported,
   A goodly gentleman, and of noble parts—
   A brother of your order.
Gonz.                    He was, madam,
   Till he against his oath wronged you, a
     princess,
   Which his religion bound him from.
Aur.                                    Great minds
   For trial of their valors oft maintain
   Quarrels that are unjust, yet without
     malice;
   And such a fair construction I make of
     him.                                    40
   I would see that brave enemy.
Gonz.                                    My duty
   Commands me to seek for him.
Aur.                                    Pray you, do,
   And bring him to our presence.
                     *Exit Gonzaga.*
Ast. [*Aside.*]                I must blast
   His entertainment.—May it please your
     excellency,
   He is a man debauched, and, for his riots,
   Cast off by the king my master; and that,
    I hope, is
   A crime sufficient.
Fer.                    To you, his subjects,
   That like as your king likes.

     *Enter Gonzaga, Bertoldo, richly habited;*
                    *Adorni.*

Aur.                                    But not to us;
   We must weigh with our own scale.—
   [*Aside.*] This is he, sure.
   How soon mine eye had found him!
     What a port                                    50
   He bears! How well his bravery [1] be-
     comes him!
   A prisoner, nay, a princely suitor, rather!
   But I am too sudden.

[1] Fine clothes.

Gonz.                    Madam, 'twas his suit,
   Unsent for, to present his service to you
   Ere his departure.
Aur. [*Aside.*]                With what majesty
   He bears himself!
Ast.        The devil, I think, supplies him.
   Ransomed, and thus rich too!
     *Bertoldo,[2] kneeling, kisses her hand.*
Aur.                                    You ill deserve
   The favor of our hand—(We are not well;
   Give us more air.)
                 *She descends suddenly.*
Gonz.                    What sudden qualm is this?
Aur.—That lifted yours against me.
Bert. [*Kissing her hand.*]                Thus
   once more                                    60
   I sue for pardon.
Aur. (*Aside.*)        Sure his lips are poisoned
   And through these veins force passage to
     my heart,
   Which is already seized upon.
Bert.                    I wait, madam,
   To know what your commands are; my
     designs
   Exact me in another place.
Aur.                                    Before
   You have our license to depart? If man-
     ners,
   Civility of manners, cannot teach you
   T' attend our leisure, I must tell you, sir,
   That you are still our prisoner—[*To
     Gonzaga.*] nor had you
   Commission to free him.
Gonz.                    How's this, madam?  70
Aur. You were my substitute and wanted
   power
   Without my warrant to dispose of him.
   I will pay back his ransom ten times over
   Rather than quit my interest.
Bert.                                    This is
   Against the law of arms.
Aur. (*Aside.*)                But not of love.—
   Why, hath your entertainment, sir, been
     such,
   In your restraint, that with the wings of
     fear
   You would fly from it?
Bert.                    I know no man, madam,
   Enamored of his fetters, or delighting
   In cold or hunger, or that would in
     reason                                    80
   Prefer straw in a dungeon before
   A down bed in a palace.

[2] Original reads *Ferdinand.*

Aur.　　　　　How!—[*To Gonzaga.*] Come nearer.
Was his usage such?

Gonz.　　　　　Yes; and it had been worse
Had I foreseen this.

Aur.　　　　　O thou misshaped monster!
In thee it is confirmed that such as have
No share in nature's bounties know no pity
To such as have 'em. Look on him with my eyes,
And answer, then, whether this were a man
Whose cheeks of lovely fullness should be made　　　89
A prey to meager famine? Or these eyes,
Whose every glance store Cupid's emptied quiver,
To be dimmed with tedious watching? Or these lips,
These ruddy lips, of whose fresh color cherries
And roses were but copies, should grow pale
For want of nectar? Or these legs, that bear
A burthen of more worth than is supported
By Atlas' wearied shoulders, should be cramped
With the weight of iron? O, I could dwell ever
On this description!

Bert.　　　　　Is this in derision
Or pity of me?

Aur.　　　　　In your charity　　　100
Believe me innocent. Now you are my prisoner,
You shall have fairer quarter. You will shame
The place where you have been, should you now leave it
Before you are recovered. I'll conduct you
To more convenient lodgings, and it shall be
My care to cherish you. Repine who dare;
It is our will. You'll follow me?

Bert.　　　　　To the center,
Such a Sybilla guiding me.

*Exeunt Aurelia, Bertoldo [, and Attendants].*

Gonz.　　　　　Who speaks first?

Fer.　　　　　We stand as we had seen Medusa's head.　　　*All amazed.*

Pier.　　I know not what to think, I am so amazed.　　　110

Rod. Amazed! I am thunderstrook.

Jac.　　　　　We are enchanted,
And this is some illusion.

Ador. [*Aside.*]　　　　　Heaven forbid!
In dark despair it shows a beam of hope.
Contain thy joy, Adorni.

Ast.　　　　　Such a princess,
And of so long-experienced reservedness,
Break forth, and on the sudden, into flashes
Of more than doubted [1] looseness!

*[Enter Aurelia and Bertoldo.]*

Gonz. [*Aside.*]　　　　　They come again,
Smiling, as I live, his arm circling her waist!
I shall run mad. Some fury hath possessed her.
If I speak, I may be blasted. Ha! I'll mumble　　　120
A prayer or two, and cross myself, and then,
Though the devil fart fire, have at him.

Aur.　　　　　Let not, sir,
The violence of my passions nourish in you
An ill opinion; or, grant my carriage
Out of the road and garb of private women,
'Tis still done with decorum. As I am
A princess, what I do is above censure,
And to be imitated.

Bert.　　　　　Gracious madam,　128
Vouchsafe a little pause, for I am so rapt
Beyond myself that, till I have collected
My scattered faculties, I cannot tender
My resolution.

Aur.　　　　　Consider of it.
I will not be long from you.
　　　　　　*Bertoldo walking by, musing.*

Gonz. [*Aside.*]　　　　　Pray I cannot!
This curséd object strangles my devotion.
I must speak, or I burst.—Pray you, fair lady,
If you can, in courtesy direct me to
The chaste Aurelia.

Aur.　　Are you blind? Who are we?

Gonz. Another kind of thing. Her blood was governed

[1] Suspected.

By her discretion, and not ruled her
  reason.
The reverence and majesty of Juno    140
Shined in her looks, and, coming to the
  camp,
Appeared a second Pallas. I can see
No such divinities in you. If I
Without offense may speak my thoughts,
  you are,
As it were, a wanton Helen.

AUR.                        Good! Ere long
You shall know me better.

GONZ.              Why, if you are Aurelia,
How shall I dispose of the soldier?

AST.                        May it please you
To hasten my despatch?

AUR.                        Prefer your suits
Unto Bertoldo; we will give him hearing,
And you'll find him your best advocate.
                    *Exit Aurelia.*

AST.              This is rare!    150

GONZ. What are we come to?

ROD.              Grown up in a moment
A favorite!

FERD.              He does take state[1] already.

BERT. [*Aside.*] No, no, it cannot be. Yet
  but[1] Camiola
There is no step between me and a crown.
Then my ingratitude—a sin in which
All sins are comprehended! Aid me,
  virtue,
Or I am lost.

GONZ.              May it please your excellence—
Second me, sir.

BERT. [*Aside.*]    Then my so horrid
  oaths,
And hell-deep imprecations made against
  it!

AST. The king, your brother, will thank
  you for th' advancement    160
Of his affairs.

BERT. [*Aside.*]    And yet who can hold
  out
Against such batteries as her power and
  greatness
Raise up against my weak defenses!

GONZ.                        Sir,

*Enter Aurelia.*

Do you dream, waking?—'Slight,[2] she's
  here again;

---

[1] The chain of state.        [2] Except for.
[3] By God's light, a mild oath.

BERT. Walks she on woolen feet!

AUR.                        You dwell too long
In your deliberation, and come
With a cripple's pace to that which you
  should fly to.

BERT. It is confessed. Yet why should I,
  to win
From you that hazard all to my poor
  nothing,
By false play send you off a loser from
  me?    170
I am already too-too much engaged
To the king my brother's anger; and who
  knows
But that his doubts and politic fears,
  should you
Make me his equal, may draw war
  upon
Your territories? Were that breach made
  up,
I should with joy embrace what now I
  fear
To touch but with due reverence.

AUR.                        That hinderance
Is easily removed. I owe the king
For a royal visit, which I straight will
  pay him;
And, having first reconciled you to his
  favor,    180
A dispensation shall meet with us.

BERT. I am wholly yours.

AUR.                        On this book seal it.

GONZ. [*Aside.*] What, hand and lip too!
  Then the bargain's sure.—
You have no employment for me?

AUR.                        Yes, Gonzaga;
Provide a royal ship.

GONZ.                        A ship? Saint John,
Whither are we bound now?

AUR.              You shall know hereafter.
My lord, your pardon for my too much
  trenching
Upon your patience.

ADOR. (*Whispers to Bertoldo.*)    Camiola!

AUR. How do you?

BERT.              Indisposed; but I attend you.
             *Exeunt [All but Adorni].*

ADOR. The heavy curse that waits on perjury    190
And foul ingratitude pursue thee ever!
Yet why from me this? In this breach of
  faith
My loyalty finds reward! What poisons
  him

Proves mithridate [1] to me. I have per-
    formed
All she commanded, punctually, and now
In the clear mirror of my truth she may
Behold his falsehood. O, that I had
    wings
To bear me to Palermo! This, once
    known,
Must change her love into a just disdain,
And work her to compassion of my
    pain.                    *Exit.*  200

### Act IV. Scene v.

[*A room in Camiola's house.*]

*Sylli, Camiola, Clarinda, at several doors.*

Syl. Undone! Undone! Poor I, that
    whilom [2] was
The top and ridge of my house, am on
    the sudden
Turned to the pitifullest animal
Of the lignage [3] of the Syllis!
Cam.                    What's the matter?
Syl. The king—break, girdle, break!
Cam.                    Why, what of him?
Syl. Hearing how far you doted on my
    person,
Growing envious of my happiness, and
    knowing
His brother nor his favorite, Fulgentio,
Could get a sheep's eye from you, I being
    present,
Is come himself a suitor, with the awl   10
Of his authority to bore my nose,
And take you from me—O, O, O!
Cam.                    Do not roar so.
    The king?
Syl.    The king! Yet loving Sylli is not
So sorry for his own as your misfortune;
If the king should carry you, or you bear
    him,
What a loser should you be! He can but
    make you
A queen, and what a simple thing is that
To the being my lawful spouse. The
    world can never
Afford you such a husband.
Cam.                    I believe you.
But how are you sure the king is so
    inclined?                    20
Did not you dream this?

Syl.                    With these eyes I saw him
Dismiss his train and lighting from his
    coach,
Whispering Fulgentio in the ear.
Cam.                    If so,
I guess the business.
Syl.                    It can be no other
But to give me the bob,[4] that being a
    matter
Of main importance. Yonder they are; I
    dare not
Be seen, I am so desperate. If you forsake
    me,

*Enter [5] Rob[erto], Ful[gentio].*

Send me word that I may provide a
    willow garland
To wear when I drown myself. O Sylli,
    O Sylli!                    *Exit, crying.*
Ful. It will be worth your pains, sir, to
    observe                    30
The constancy and bravery of her spirit.
Though great men tremble at your
    frowns, I dare
Hazard my head your majesty, set off [6]
With terror, cannot fright her.
Rob.                    May she answer
My expectation!
Ful.                    There she is.
Cam.                    My knees thus
Bent to the earth, while my vows are
    sent upward
For the safety of my sovereign, pay the
    duty
Due for so great an honor, in this favor
Done to your humblest handmaid.
Rob.                    You mistake me;   39
I come not, lady, that you may report
The king, to do you honor, made your
    house
(He being there) his court, but to correct
Your stubborn disobedience. A pardon
For that, could you obtain it, were well
    purchased
With this humility.
Cam.                    A pardon, sir?
Till I am conscious of an offense,
I will not wrong my innocence to beg one.
What is my crime, sir?
Rob.                    Look on him I favor,
By you scorned and neglected.
Cam.                    Is that all, sir?

---

[1] Antidote against poisons.
[2] Formerly.                    [3] Lineage.

[4] *I.e.*, to cheat me.
[5] Original reads *Exit.*                    [6] Invested.

Rob. No, minion, though that were too
　　much. How can you　　　　　　50
　　Answer the setting on your desperate
　　bravo
　　To murther him?

Cam.　　　　　With your leave, I must not
　　kneel, sir,
　　While I reply to this, but thus rise up
　　In my defense and tell you as a man
　　(Since, when you are unjust, the deity
　　Which you may challenge as a king parts
　　from you)
　　'Twas never read in Holy Writ, or moral,
　　That subjects on their loyalty were
　　obliged
　　To love their sovereign's vices. Your
　　grace, sir,
　　To such an undeserver is no virtue.　60

Ful. What think you now, sir?

Cam.　　　　　Say you should love wine,
　　You being the king, and, cause[1] I am
　　your subject,
　　Must I be ever drunk? Tyrants, not
　　kings,
　　By violence from humble vassals force
　　The liberty of their souls. I could not
　　love him;
　　And to compel affection, as I take it,
　　Is not found in your prerogative.

Rob. (Aside.)　　　　　Excellent virgin!
　　How I admire her confidence!

Cam.　　　　　He complains
　　Of wrong done him; but be no more a
　　king
　　Unless you do me right. Burn your
　　decrees,　　　　　　　　　　70
　　And of your laws and statutes make a
　　fire
　　To thaw the frozen numbness of delin-
　　quents,
　　If he escape unpunished. Do your edicts
　　Call it death in any man that breaks into
　　Another's house to rob him, though of
　　trifles?
　　And shall Fulgentio, your Fulgentio, live,
　　Who hath committed more than sacri-
　　lege
　　In the pollution of my clear fame
　　By his malicious slanders?

Rob.　　　　　Have you done this?
　　Answer truly, on your life.

Ful.　　　　　In the heat of blood　80
　　Some such thing I reported.

[1] Because.

Rob.　　　　　Out of my sight!
　　For I vow, if by true penitence thou win
　　not
　　This injured virgin to sue out thy pardon,
　　Thy grave is digged already.

Ful. [Aside.]　　　　　By my own folly
　　I have made a fair hand of 't.
　　　　　　　　　　　　Exit Fulgentio.

Rob.　　　　　You shall know, lady,
　　While I wear a crown, justice shall use
　　her sword
　　To cut offenders off, though nearest to us.

Cam. Ay, now you show whose deputy
　　you are.
　　If now I bath[2] your feet with tears, it
　　cannot
　　Be censured superstition.

Rob.　　　　　You must rise;　90
　　Rise in our favor and protection ever.
　　　　　　　　　　　　Kisses her.

Cam. Happy are subjects, when the prince
　　is still
　　Guided by justice, not his passionate
　　will.　　　　　　　　　　Exeunt.

Then End of the Fourth Act.

## Act V. Scene i.

### [The same.]

### Camiola, Sylli.

Cam. You see how tender I am of the quiet
　　And peace of your affection, and what
　　great ones
　　I put off in your favor.

Syl.　　　　　You do wisely,
　　Exceeding wisely; and, when I have said
　　I thank you for 't, be happy.

Cam.　　　　　And good reason,
　　In having such a blessing.

Syl.　　　　　When you have it;
　　But the bait is not yet ready. Stay the
　　time,
　　While I triumph by myself. King, by
　　your leave,
　　I have wiped your royal nose[3] without a
　　napkin.[4]
　　You may cry, "Willow, willow!"[5] for
　　your brother;　　　　　　10
　　I'll only say, "Go by!"[6] for my fine
　　favorite,

[2] Bathe.　　　　　[4] Handkerchief.
[3] I.e., cheated you.　　[5] A cry of sorrow.
[6] Wait a little. The well-known catch phrase
from The Spanish Tragedy.

He may graze where he please; his lips
may water
Like a puppy's o'er a fermenty [1] pot,
while Sylli
Out of his two-leaved cherry-stone dish, [2]
drinks nectar!
I cannot hold out any longer; heaven forgive me!
'Tis not the first oath I have broke; I
must take
A little for a preparative.

*Offers to kiss and embrace her.*

CAM.                           By no means.
If you forswear yourself, we shall not
prosper.
I'll rather lose my longing.

SYL.                          Pretty soul!
How careful it is of me! Let me buss
yet                                             20
Thy little dainty foot for 't. That, I'm
sure, is
Out of my oath.

CAM.                    Why, if thou canst dis-
pense with 't
So far, I'll not be scrupulous; such a favor
My amorous shoemaker steals.

SYL.                        O most rare leather!

*Kisses her shoe often.*

I do begin at the lowest, but in time
I may grow higher.

CAM.        Fie, you dwell too long there!
Rise, prithee, rise.

*Enter Clarinda, hastily.*

SYL.                    O, I am up already.

CAM. How I abuse my hours!—What news
with thee now?

CLAR. Off with that gown; 'tis mine, mine
by your promise.
Signior Adorni is returned! Now upon
entrance! [3]                                    30
Off with it, off with it, madam!

CAM.                       Be not so hasty.
When I go to bed, 'tis thine.

SYL.               You have my grant, [4] too.
But, do you hear, lady, though I give
way to this,
You must hereafter ask my leave be-
fore
You part with things of moment.

---

[1] Frumenty, hulled wheat boiled in milk.
[2] *I.e.*, Camiola's lips.
[3] Now ready to enter.            [4] Consent.

CAM.                                Very good;
When I'm yours, I will be governed.

SYL.                          Sweet obedience!

*Enter Adorni.*

CAM. You are well returned.

ADOR.               I wish that the success
Of my service had deserved it.

CAM.                          Lives Bertoldo?

ADOR. Yes, and returned with safety.

CAM.                            'Tis not then
In the power of fate to add to or take
from                                            40
My perfit happiness; and yet he should
Have made me his first visit.

ADOR.                    So I think too;
But he—

SYL.      Durst not appear, I being present;
That's his excuse, I warrant you.

CAM.                    Speak, where is he?
With whom? Who hath deserved more
from him, or
Can be of equal merit? I in this
Do not except the king.

ADOR.                     He's at the palace
With the Duchess of Siena. One coach
brought 'em hither,
Without a third. He's very gracious with
her;
You may conceive the rest.

CAM.                My jealous fears     50
Make me to apprehend.

ADOR.                Pray you, dismiss
Signior Wisdom, and I'll make relation
to you
Of the particulars.

CAM.               Servant, [5] I would have you
To haste unto the court.

SYL.                    I will outrun
A footman for your pleasure.

CAM.                     There observe
The duchess' train and entertainment.

SYL.                          Fear not;
I will discover all that is of weight,
To the liveries of her pages and her foot-
men.
This is fit employment for me.

*Exit Sylli.*

CAM.                     Gracious with
The duchess! Sure, you said so?

ADOR.               I will use   60
All possible brevity to inform you,
madam,

---

[5] This word also meant *lover.*

Of what was trusted to me, and discharged
With faith and loyal duty.

CAM.                    I believe it.
You ransomed him, and supplied his
wants—imagine
That is already spoken. And what vows
Of service he made to me is apparent;
His joy of me, and wonder too, per-
spicuous.
Does not your story end so?

ADOR.                    Would the end
Had answered [1] the beginning! In a
word,                                        69
Ingratitude and perjury at the height
Cannot express him.

CAM.               Take heed.

ADOR.                    Truth is armed,
And can defend itself. It must out,
madam.
I saw (the presence [2] full) the amorous
duchess
Kiss and embrace him; on his part ac-
cepted
With equal ardor; and their willing hands
No sooner joined, but a remove [3] was
published,
And put in execution.

CAM.                    The proofs are
Too pregnant. O Bertoldo!

ADOR.                    He's not worth
Your sorrow, madam.

CAM.          Tell me, when you saw this,
Did not you grieve, as I do now to hear
it?                                          80

ADOR. His precipice from goodness raising
mine,
And serving as a foil to set my faith off,
I had little reason.

CAM.                    In this you confess
The devilish malice of your disposition.
As you were a man, you stood bound to
lament it,
And not, in flattery of your false hopes,
To glory in it. When good men pursue
The path marked out by virtue, the
blessed saints
With joy look on it, and seraphic angels
Clap their celestial wings in heavenly
plaudits                                     90
To see [4] a scene of grace so well presented,

The fiends and men made up of envy
mourning,
Whereas now, on the contrary, as far
As their divinity can partake of passion,
With me they weep, beholding a fair
temple,
Built in Bertoldo's loyalty, turned to
ashes
By the flames of his inconstancy, the
damned
Rejoicing in the object.—'Tis not well
In you, Adorni.

ADOR. [Aside.]      What a temper dwells
In this rare virgin!—Can you pity him
That hath shown none to you?

CAM.                    I must not be   101
Cruel by his example. You, perhaps,
Expect now I should seek recovery
Of what I have lost, by tears, and with
bent knees
Beg his compassion. No; my towering
virtue,
From the assurance of my merit, scorns
To stoop so low. I'll take a nobler
course
And, confident in the justice of my cause,
The king his brother and new mistress,
judges,
Ravish him from her arms. You have
the contract                                110
In which he swore to marry me?

ADOR.                    'Tis here, madam.

CAM. He shall be then against his will
my husband;
And, when I have him, I'll so use him!
Doubt not
But that, your honesty being unques-
tioned,
This writing, with your testimony, clears
all.

ADOR. [Aside.] And buries me in the dark
mists of error.

CAM. I'll presently to court; pray you, give
order
For my caroche. [5]

ADOR. [Aside.]      A cart for me were
fitter,
To hurry me to the gallows.

                              Exit Ador[ni].

CAM.                    O false men!
Inconstant! Perjured! My good angel
help me                                     120
In these my extremities!

[1] Corresponded to.      [2] Presence chamber.
[3] Removal, withdrawal from the room.
[4] Gifford's reading. Original reads be.
[5] Carriage.

*Enter Sylli.*

Syl.  If you ever will see brave sight,
   Lose it not now.  Bertoldo and the
      duchess
   Are presently to be married.  There's
      such pomp
   And preparation.
Cam.               If I marry, 'tis
   This day or never.
Syl.               Why, with all my heart;
   Though I break this, I'll keep the next
      oath I make,
   And then it is quit.
Cam.               Follow me to my cabinet.[1]
   You know my confessor, Father Paulo?
Syl.                       Yes.  Shall he
   Do the feat for us?
Cam.               I will give in writing
   Directions to him, and attire myself    130
   Like a virgin bride; and something I will
      do
   That shall deserve men's praise—and
      wonder too.
Syl.  And I, to make all know I am not
      shallow,
   Will have my points of cochineal and
      yellow.                    *Exeunt.*

### Act V. Scene ii.

[*The presence chamber in the palace at
      Palermo.*]

*Loud music.  Astutio, Gonzaga, Roderigo,
   Jacomo, Pierio, Roberto, Bertoldo, Aurelia, [ Ferdinand,] Bishop, with Attend-
      ants.*

Rob.  Had our division been greater,
      madam,
   Your clemency, the wrong being done to
      you,
   In pardon of it, like the rod of concord,
   Must make a perfect union.—Once more
   With a brotherly affection we receive you
   Into our favor.  Let it be your study
   Hereafter to deserve this blessing, far
   Beyond your merit.
Bert.               As the princess' grace
   To me is without limit, my endeavors
   With all obsequiousness to serve her
      pleasures                    10
   Shall know no bounds; nor will I, being
      made

Her husband, e'er forget the duty that
   I owe her as a servant.
Aur.               I expect not
   But fair equality, since I well know,
   If that superiority be due,
   'Tis not to me.  When you are made my
      consort,
   All the prerogatives of my high birth
      canceled,
   I'll practice the obedience of a wife,
   And freely pay it.  Queens themselves,
      if they
   Make choice of their inferiors, only aim-
      ing                    20
   To feed their sensual appetites, and to
      reign
   Over their husbands, in some kind com-
      mit
   Authorized whoredom; nor will I be
      guilty
   In my intent of such a crime.
Gonz.                       This done,
   As it is promised, madam, may well
      stand for
   A president[2] to great women; but, when
      once
   The griping hunger of desire is cloyed,
   And the poor fool advanced, brought on
      his knees,
   Most of your eagle breed, I'll not say all,
   Ever excepting you, challenge[3] again    30
   What in hot blood they parted from.
Aur.                       You are ever
   An enemy of our sex; but you, I hope,
      sir,
   Have better thoughts.
Bert.               I dare not entertain
   An ill one of your goodness.
Rob.                       To my power
   I will enable[4] him, to prevent all danger
   Envy can raise against your choice.  One
      word more
   Touching the articles.

*Enter Fulgen[tio], Cam[iola], Syl[li], Ador[ni].*

Ful.                       In you alone
   Lie all my hopes; you can or kill or save
      me.
   But pity in you will become you better
   (Though I confess in justice 'tis denied
      me)                    40
   Than too much rigor.

[1] Private room.
[2] Precedent.
[3] Lay claim to, demand.
[4] Elevate.

CAM.                    I will make your peace
As far as it lies in me, but must first
Labor to right myself.
AUR. [*To Roberto.*]          Or add or alter
What you think fit. In him I have my all;
Heaven make me thankful for him!
ROB.                    On to the temple!
CAM. [*Kneeling.*] Stay, royal sir; and, as
you are a king,
Erect[1] one here, in doing justice to
An injured maid.
AUR.                    How's this?
BERT. [*Aside.*]          O, I am blasted!
ROB. I have given some proof, sweet lady,
of my promptness
To do you right; you need not, therefore,
doubt me.                              50
And rest assured that, this great work
despatched,
You shall have audience and satisfaction
To all you can demand.
CAM.                    To do me justice
Exacts your present care, and can admit
Of no delay. If, ere my cause be heard,
In favor of your brother you go on, sir,
Your scepter cannot right me. He's the
man,
The guilty man, whom I accuse; and you
Stand bound in duty, as you are supreme,
To be impartial. Since you are a judge,
As a delinquent look on him, and not   61
As on a brother. Justice painted blind
Infers her ministers are obliged to hear
The cause, and, truth the judge, deter-
mine of it,
And, not swayed or by favor or affection,
By a false gloss or wrested comment, alter
The true intent and letter of the law.
ROB. Nor will I, madam.
AUR. [*To Bertoldo.*]          You seem trou-
bled, sir.
GONZ. His color changes, too.
CAM.                    The alteration
Grows from his guilt. The goodness of
my cause                              70
Begets such confidence in me that I bring
No hired tongue to plead for me, that
with gay,
Rhetorical flourishes may palliate
That which, stripped naked, will appear
deformed.
I stand here mine own advocate; and my
truth,
Delivered in the plainest language, will

Make good itself; nor will I, if the king
Give suffrage to it, but admit of you,
My greatest enemy, and this stranger
prince,
To sit assistants with him.
AUR.               I ne'er wronged you.  80
CAM. In your knowledge of the injury, I
believe it;
Nor will you, in your justice, when you
are
Acquainted with my interest in this man
Which I lay claim to.
ROB.               Let us take our seats.
What is your title to him?
CAM. [*Rising and giving a paper to the
King.*]     By this contract,
Sealed solemnly before a reverend man,
I challenge him for my husband.
SYL. [*Aside.*]               Ha! Was I
Sent for the friar for this? O Sylli!
Sylli!—
Some cordial, or I faint.
ROB.               This writing is
Authentical.
AUR.     But, done in heat of blood,  90
Charmed by her flatteries as no doubt he
was,
To be dispensed with.
FER.               Add this, if you please:
The distance and disparity between
Their births and fortunes.
CAM.     What can Innocence hope for,
When such as sit her judges are cor-
rupted!
Disparity of birth or fortune, urge you?
Or Siren charms? Or, at his best, in me
Wants[2] to deserve him? Call some few
days back
And, as he was, consider him, and you
Must grant him my inferior. Imagine
You saw him now in fetters, with his
honor,                              101
His liberty lost, with her black wings
Despair
Circling his miseries, and this[3] Gonzaga
Trampling on his afflictions; the great
sum
Proposed for his redemption; the king
Forbidding payment of it; this near kins-
man,[4]

[1] Raise.
[2] Deficiencies.
[3] Emended by all editors. Original has *his*.
[4] The reading of the Princeton copy. Other
copies examined by Bryne read *kinsmen.*

With his protesting followers and friends,
Falling off from him; by the whole world
    forsaken;
Dead to all hope, and buried in the grave
Of his calamities; and then weigh duly
What she deserved, whose merits now
    are doubted,              111
That as his better angel in her bounties
Appeared unto him, his great ransom
    paid,
His wants, and with a prodigal hand,
    supplied—
Whether then, being my manumised [1]
    slave,
He owed not himself to me?
AUR.                  Is this true?
ROB. In his silence 'tis acknowledged.
GONZ.              If you want
A witness to this purpose, I'll depose it.
CAM. If I have dwelt too long on my
    deservings
To this unthankful man, pray you,
    pardon me;            120
The cause required it. And, though now
    I add
A little in my painting to the life
His barbarous ingratitude, to deter
Others from imitation, let it meet with
A fair interpretation. This serpent,
Frozen to numbness, was no sooner
    warmed
In the bosom of my pity and compassion,
But in return he ruined his preserver,
The prints the irons had made in his
    flesh               129
Still ulcerous; but all that I had done,
My benefits, in sand or water writ-
    ten,
As they had never been, no more re-
    membered!
And on what ground but his ambitious
    hopes
To gain this duchess' favor?
AUR.             Yes; the object—
Look on it better, lady—may excuse
The charge of [2] his affection.
CAM.               The object!
In what? Forgive me, modesty, if I say
You look upon your form in the false
    glass
Of flattery and self-love, and that de-
    ceives you.

[1] Manumitted, freed.
[2] Accusation against.

That you were a duchess, as I take it, was
    not               140
Charactered on your face; and, that not
    seen,
For other feature,[3] make all these that are
Experienced in women judges of 'em,
And, if they are not parasites, they must
    grant,[4]
For beauty without art, though you
    storm at it,
I may take the right-hand file.
GONZ.           Well said, i' faith!
I see fair women on no terms will yield
Priority in beauty.
CAM.            Down, proud heart!
Why do I rise up in defense of that
Which, in my cherishing of it, hath un-
    done me?            150
No, madam, I recant—you are all
    beauty,
Goodness, and virtue, and poor I not
    worthy
As a foil to set you off. Enjoy your con-
    quest,
But do not tyrannize. Yet, as I am,
In my lowness, from your height you may
    look on me
And in your suffrage to me make him know
That, though to all men else I did appear
The shame and scorn of women, he
    stands bound
To hold me as her masterpiece.
ROB. [To Bertoldo.]       By my life,
You have shown yourself of such an
    abject temper,       160
So poor and low-conditioned, as I grieve
    for
Your nearness to me.
FER.           I am changed in my
Opinion of you, lady, and profess
The virtues of your mind an ample fortune
For an absolute monarch.
GONZ. [To Bertoldo.]       Since you
    are resolved
To damn yourself, in your forsaking of
Your noble order for a woman, do it
For this. You may search through the
    world, and meet not
With such another phœnix.
AUR.            On the sudden
I feel all fires of love quenched in the
    water            170

[3] I.e., as far as other features are concerned.
[4] Supply that.

Of compassion.—Make your peace; you have
My free consent; for here I do disclaim
All interest in you, and, to further your
Desires, fair maid, composed of worth and honor,
The dispensation procured by me,
Freeing Bertoldo from his vow, makes way
To your embraces.

BERT.             O, how have I strayed,
And willfully, out of the noble tract [1]
Marked me by virtue! Till now, I was never
Truly a prisoner. To excuse my late    180
Captivity, I might allege the malice
Of fortune, you, that conquered me, confessing
Courage in my defense was no way wanting.
But now I have surrendered up my strengths
Into the power of vice, and on my forehead
Branded with mine own hand in capital letters,
DISLOYAL and INGRATEFUL. Though barred from
Human society, and hissed into
Some desert ne'er yet haunted with the curses    189
Of men and women, sitting as a judge
Upon my guilty self, I must confess
It justly falls upon me, and one tear,
Shed in compassion of my sufferings, more
Than I can hope for.

CAM.             This compunction
For the wrong that you have done me, though you should
Fix here, and your true sorrow move no further,
Will, in respect I loved once, make these eyes
Two springs of sorrow for you.

BERT.             In your pity
My cruelty shows more monstrous; yet I am not,
Though most ingrateful, grown to such a height    200
Of impudence as in my wishes only
To ask your pardon. If, as now I fall
Prostrate before your feet, you will vouchsafe          [He kneels.]

[1] Track, course.

To act your own revenge, treading upon me
As a viper eating through the bowels of
Your benefits, to whom with liberty
I owe my being, 'twill take from the burthen·
That now is insupportable.

CAM. [Raising him.]         Pray you, rise.
As I wish peace and quiet to my soul,
I do forgive you heartily. Yet, excuse me,    210
Though I deny myself a blessing that,
By the favor of the duchess, seconded
With your submission, is offered to me,
Let not the reason I allege for 't grieve you:
You have been false once. I have done. And if,
When I am married, as this day I will be,
As a perfit sign of your atonement [2] with me,
You wish me joy, I will receive it for
Full satisfaction of all obligations
In which you stand bound to me.

BERT.             I will do it,    220
And, what's more, in despite of sorrow, live
To see myself undone, beyond all hope
To be made up again.

SYL. [Aside.]           My blood begins
To come to my heart again.

CAM.             Pray you, Signior Syl,
Call in the holy friar. He's prepared
For finishing the work.

SYL.             I knew I was
The man. Heaven make me thankful!

ROB.             Who is this?

AST. His father was the banker of Palermo,
And this the heir of his great wealth; his wisdom
Was not hereditary.

SYL.     Though you know me not,    230
Your majesty owes me a round sum; I have
A seal or two to witness. Yet, if you please
To wear my colors and dance at my wedding,
I'll never sue you.

ROB.          And I'll grant your suit.

SYL. Gracious madonna, noble general,
Brave captains, and my quondam rivals, wear 'em,

[2] Reconciliation.

Since I am confident you dare not harbor
A thought but that way current.[1] *Exit.*
AUR.                For my part
    I cannot guess the issue.

     *Enter Syl[li] with [Father Paulo].*

SYL.               Do your duty;
    And with all speed you can you may des-
      patch us.                     240
PAUL. Thus, as a principal ornament to
    the church,
    I seize her.
ALL.        How!
ROB.           So young, and so religious!
PAUL. She has forsook the world.
SYL.               And Sylli too!
    I shall run mad.
ROB.             Hence with the fool!—
    (*Syl[li] thrust off.*) Proceed, sir.
PAUL. Look on this Maid of Honor, now
    Truly honored in her vow
    She pays to heaven. Vain delight
    By day or pleasure of the night
    She no more thinks of. This fair hair
    (Favors for great kings to wear)     250
    Muw [2] now be shorn; her rich array
    Changed into a homely gray.
    The dainties with which she was fed
    And her proud flesh pamperéd
    Must not be tasted; from the spring,
    For wine, cold water we will bring,
    And with fasting mortify
    The feasts of sensuality.
    Her jewels, beads; and she must look
    Not in a glass, but holy book,     260
    To teach her the ne'er-erring way
    To immortality. O, may
    She, as she purposes to be
    A child new-born to piety,
    Persever [3] in it, and good men,
    With saints and angels, say, Amen!
CAM. This is the marriage, this the port to
    which
    My vows must steer me! Fill my spread-
     ing sails
    With the pure wind of your devotions
     for me
    That I may touch the secure haven,
     where                     270
    Eternal happiness keeps her residence,
    Temptations to frailty never entering!
    I am dead to the world, and thus dispose

Of what I leave behind me; and, dividing
My state into three parts, I thus be-
    queath it:
The first to the fair nunnery, to which
I dedicate the last and better part
Of my frail life; a second portion
To pious uses; and the third to thee,    279
Adorni, for thy true and faithful service.
And, ere I take my last [4] farewell, with
    hope
To find a grant, my suit to you is that
You would for my sake pardon this
    young man,
And to his merits love him, and no
    further.
ROB. I thus confirm it.
               *Gives his hand to Fulgen[tio].*
CAM. (*To Bertoldo.*) And, as e'er you hope,
    Like me, to be made happy, I conjure
     you
    To reassume your order, and, in fighting
    Bravely against the enemies of our faith,
    Redeem your mortgaged honor.
GONZ.[5]             I restore this.
            *[Gives him] the white cross.*
    Once more brothers in arms.
BERT.          I'll live and die so.    290
CAM. To you my pious wishes! And, to
    end
    All differences, great sir, I beseech you
    To be an arbitrator, and compound
    The quarrel long continuing between
    The duke and duchess.
ROB.            I'll take it into
    My special care.
CAM.     I am then at rest. Now, father,
    Conduct me where you please.
            *Exeunt Paulo and Camiola.*
ROB.            She well deserves
    Her name, the Maid of Honor! May
     she stand
    To all posterity a fair example      299
    For noble maids to imitate, since to live
    In wealth and pleasure is common, but to
     part with
    Such poisoned baits is rare, there being
     nothing
    Upon this stage of life to be commended,
    Though well begun, till it be fully ended.
                      *Exeunt.*

### THE END.

---

[1] Tending in that direction.
[2] May.                  [3] Persevere.

[4] Emended by all editors. Original reads
*mytake lust.*        [5] Original reads *Rob.*

# JOHN FORD

John Ford might almost be described as a startling discovery of the nineteenth and twentieth centuries. Clifford Leech, in *John Ford and the Drama of His Time* (London, 1957), wrote that, apart from the second issue of the little known *The Sun's Darling/A Moral Masque* in 1657, not one of Ford's plays was reprinted in the seventeenth century, nor were they often even referred to. And G. E. Bentley, in commenting on *'Tis Pity She's a Whore*, the Ford tragedy that is perhaps his most talked-about play today, though not necessarily his best, remarked that there is no evidence that this or any other of his plays attracted much attention in the seventeenth century itself, and added, ". . . until very recent years the story is one of almost uniform neglect" (*The Jacobean and Caroline Stage*). Actually, the resuscitation of Ford took place in the early nineteenth century, after his name and plays had almost totally disappeared in the eighteenth, but the twentieth-century revival of interest has far exceeded that of the nineteenth and has opened a new perspective on his writings.

Yet it was Gerard Langbaine who in 1691 really anticipated and focused the modern controversy in *An Account of the English Dramatic Poets*, when he asserted of *'Tis Pity She's a Whore*: "All that I can say is, that it equals any of our author's plays; and were to be commended did not the author paint the incestuous love of Giovanni and his sister Annabella in too beautiful colors." Nevertheless, Langbaine did not suggest that Ford was attempting to effect a revolution in the code of sexual morality or of social ethics as one school of modern critics has done. M. Joan Sargeaunt, in her comprehensive study, *John Ford* (Oxford, 1935), remarked that "It is unfortunate, though perhaps inevitable, that questions of morality seem to have become inextricably bound up with questions of art in the criticism of Ford's plays;" but she attempted to correct the imbalance of much modern criticism when she added that perhaps this school "has been inclined to read into Ford's plays a more consciously modern outlook, in this sense, than is really there." George F. Sensabaugh, however, in *The Tragic Muse of John Ford* (Stanford University Press, 1944), while admitting the presence of many elements in Ford's work which would justify those critics who have called him "the high priest of decadence," preferred to treat him as "a prophet of the modern world," and contended that Ford's plays "stand closer, both in nature and function, to the tragedies of Henrik Ibsen and Eugene O'Neill than to those of Shakespeare and Webster."

The two camps were actually formed in the early nineteenth century when the two critics, the romantic and impressionistic Charles Lamb and the almost equally subjective William Hazlitt, reacted in quite opposite ways to the plays. Lamb, in *Specimens of English Dramatic Poets Contemporary with Shakespeare* (1808), placed Ford in "the first order of poets," and argued that, although sometimes his moral views seem somewhat confused, at his best his deep and objective analysis of human behavior revealed a higher rather than a lower morality, since Ford emphasized the exalting power of love and the nobility of the endurance of suffering in adverse times. The opposite party, on the other hand, adopted the views expressed by Hazlitt in *Lectures on the Dramatic Literature in the Age of Elizabeth* (1821) to the effect that Ford was in conscious revolt against the established moral order and showed this by his decadent delight in melodramatic plots and licentious scenes.

Practically all the writers on Ford in the twentieth century devote considerable space to surveying the disciples of these two leaders, along with their individual attitudes and prejudices (that is, Sargeaunt; Leech; Irving Ribner, *Jacobean Tragedy/The Search for Moral Order;* Robert Ornstein, *The Moral Vision of Jacobean Tragedy;* Mark Stavig, *John Ford and the Traditional Moral Order,* University of Wisconsin Press, 1968). Lamb's partisans were as enthusiastic as their master, though perhaps not so numerous as Hazlitt's. Lamb's eulogy encouraged the first attempt to bring out a collected edition of Ford—H. Weber's miserably edited *The Dramatic Works of John Ford* (Edinburgh, 1811), which was attacked by the free-swinging Francis Jeffrey in *The Edinburgh Review,* and inspired a more moderate article, probably by John Herman Merivale, in *The Monthly Review.* Weber's edition was followed by a somewhat improved one by William Gifford in 1827, the text of which was reprinted in 1839 with an introduction by Hartley Coleridge. Alexander Dyce's re-editing of Gifford in 1869 was followed by A. H. Bullen's reissue of Dyce in 1895. These editions, with their prefaces, which were textual as well as critical, proved that the public interest in Ford had been aroused. Havelock Ellis's edition of five plays in the Mermaid series in 1888 took the attitude toward Ford that would have been expected from a leader in the movement for more liberal sexual freedom, and Algernon Charles Swinburne wrote both an essay and a poem in the same vein. Abroad, the French critic Hippolyte Taine and the Belgian dramatist Maurice Maeterlinck wrote appreciatively about Ford.

But the academics on both sides of the ocean were generally hostile, and the Americans were much more upset than the English. George Saintsbury, of the University of Edinburgh, successfully resisted the poet's appeal, but in the United States the professors in the early years of the century, like Felix E. Schelling, of the University of Pennsylvania, in *The Elizabethan Drama,* Ashley H. Thorndike, of Columbia University, in *Tragedy* (Boston and New York, 1910), and William Allan Neilson, of Harvard, in *The Cambridge History of English Literature* (Cambridge University Press, 1910), although recognizing Ford's genius, qualified their estimates by speaking, respectively, of his "quality of a strange, unnatural originality like a gorgeous and scented but poisonous exotic of the jungle," of "the stifling hothouse in which they [the seeds of fatal passions] luxuriate," and of "an assault at once so insidious and so daring upon the foundations of accepted morality." Although T. S. Eliot realized that *'Tis Pity* was not an apology for incest (see *Elizabethan Dramatists*), he was still sufficiently blind to Ford's real significance so that Clifford Bax, a great admirer of most of Ford's plays, felt enforced to write a reply to Eliot's original anonymous article in the *Times Literary Supplement* (May 5 and 12, 1932).

It was Professor Stuart Pratt Sherman, of the University of Illinois, who became the chief modern spokesman for the Hazlitt school when he made the first real attempt to arrive at what Stavig calls "a systematic statement of Ford's ethical thought," and accepted Hazlitt's belief that "the plays deal with daring subject matter in an unnatural way." Sherman interpreted them as expressions of their author's sympathy with his sinful heroes and heroines without recognizing the evidence in the entire body of Ford's work, both dramatic and non-dramatic, that he was by no means an enemy of traditional morality. (Sherman's ideas were first stated in his article, "Ford's Contribution to the Decadence of the Drama," *John Fordes Dramatische Werke,* in W. Bang's *Materialen zur Kunde des Alteren Englischen Dramas,* Louvain, 1908, and repeated in his introduction to the Belles Lettres Series edition of *'Tis Pity She's a Whore and The Broken Heart,* Boston and London, 1915.) Sherman treated all three of Ford's tragedies as a kind of problem play, justifying illicit love and, as Sargeaunt puts it, "using the stage as a pulpit from which to preach his gospel." Most of the more recent Ford scholars have refused to make such a conscious rebel out of him, but Stavig agrees that Sherman's "analysis of Ford's Platonic bias and of his sympathy for the victims of passion is still widely influential in a modified form." These more recent scholars follow generally in the path of Sargeaunt, treating Ford as a sensitive and perceptive analyst of the psychological problems of his characters, both normal and abnormal, and as a dramatist who was at the same time somewhat restricted by the necessity of writing for an audience that craved sensation and excitement. These writers would include Muriel C. Bradbrook (*Themes and Conventions of Elizabethan Tragedy*), Una M. Ellis-Fermor (*Jacobean Drama/An Interpretation*), H. J. Oliver (*The Problem of John Ford*, Melbourne University Press, 1955), and Clifford Leech. A study that looks at Ford as a modern before his time, with a habit of mind resembling that of Henry James or the existentialists more than that of the dramatists or ethical thinkers of his own age, is that of R. J. Kaufmann ("Ford's Tragic Perspective," *Texas Studies in Language and Literature*, 1960).

The writer who precipitated such controversy with the meager output of eight plays, a masque, two or three poems (not all clearly his), and two or three short prose works (also not all clearly his) was baptized in the little Devonshire village of Ilsington, on the edge of Dartmoor, on April 17, 1586. (The chief authorities on the biography of Ford are Sargeaunt and Robert Davril, *Le Drame·de John Ford*, Paris, 1954.) His parents, Thomas and Elizabeth Ford, had two daughters and he was the second of four boys. The Fords came from the oldest branch of an old Devonshire family, established at Chagford at least as early as the end of the fifteenth century. Sargeaunt points out that John's great grandfather had a grant of arms made to him and his descendants in 1524. Thomas Ford owned considerable property in Ilsington and other neighboring villages, and in 1588 was assessed £12 on these properties, the second largest amount for the nine parishes named on the list. The boy's mother came from an even more distinguished line. She was Elizabeth Popham, second daughter of Edward Popham of Huntworthy in Somerset, and niece of the famous Sir John Popham, Lord Chief Justice during the last years of the reign of Elizabeth and the early years of the reign of James. The Fords also had connections with many others of the landed gentry of the county. Their manor house remained standing till about 1870.

But nothing is known of John's childhood and rearing, though Sargeaunt assumes from his later use of west-country provincialisms in his plays that he grew up in Ilsington. She also expresses surprise that he made practically no attempt to introduce into his plays anything of "the beauties of nature or of outdoor life" which he would have experienced in this charming countryside, but preferred indoor scenes in the rooms of state and the bedchambers of palaces and castles. *The Broken Heart* has some of its scenes laid in a garden, but it seems as formal, shut-in, and "airless" as the house to which it belongs and in which the jealous Bassanes keeps his beautiful young wife confined. It is not even certain that Ford ever returned to this early home after he started to grow up, though he did own some property in two nearby villages, quaintly named Ipplepen and Torbryan. Nor is it even clear where he started his college education, though on March 26, 1601, a "John Ford Devon. gent." matriculated at Exeter College, Oxford, at the age of sixteen—a figure which would not quite fit with the birth date at Ilsington. There were other John Fords in Devonshire, one of whom was the later dramatist's own cousin. However, the authorities at Exeter College seem to have had no doubt of the identification since they have officially laid claim to him by installing in the college hall a stained glass memorial window in his name, along with similar windows to other illustrious alumni.

In any case, if John entered Exeter he did not stay long, since the first certain record there is of him after his baptism shows his admission to the Middle Temple on November 16, 1602. The names of Ford and Popham appear frequently in the Middle Temple records, both before and after this time. Somewhere in the course of his education Ford obtained a knowledge of Plato, Aristotle, and the principal Latin classics, along with a command of some Italian and perhaps some Spanish. He was of course familiar with the well-known works of English literature, including the drama, but although in the preface to *The Lover's Melancholy* he calls himself a "scholar" there is little evidence that he ever went very deeply into any of his studies.

While living and studying among the lawyers, however, young John Ford found ways of distinguishing himself which were not exactly in the line of academic duty. By the Hilary term of 1606 he had run up his buttery (or pantry) bill so far without payment that he was expelled, and was not readmitted till June 10, 1608, on condition that he not only pay his back bill plus a fine of forty shillings, but also acknowledge "his fault with penitency" and give new sureties for future good conduct. Such financial transgressions were not uncommon among students then, but the long gap between the offense and its rectification remains unaccounted for. Ford apparently stayed on his good behavior for many years, since he continued to reside in his chambers in the Middle Temple even though there is no record of his passing his bar examinations. Sargeaunt and others have therefore speculated that he probably supported himself with some sort of legal work, in spite of the fact that he was not a barrister. But even after he was thirty he remained in conflict with the academic authorities, since on May 30, 1617, his name stood tenth on a list of forty delinquents (arranged in order of seniority) who had joined in "a conspiracy of and among dyvers gentlemen of the fellowship to break the auncient custom of wearing cappes" in the Temple church and in the dining hall. Seemingly these rebels had attempted to show their independence of thought and defiance of the faculty by wearing hats instead of the traditional caps. Presumably Ford along with the others submitted so that his chambers would not be "seized forfeyted and disposed of to the use of the house."

There is evidence that between these two dates in the Middle Temple records, John Ford had committed other acts which alienated him from his family, although Sargeaunt refuses to do more than state the bare facts. When his father died at Ilsington in April 1610 and his will, dated May 9, 1609, was proved, it was discovered that he had left his three shares of the manor to his wife during her lifetime and then to his oldest son Henry. To the two youngest sons, Thomas and Edward, he provided that each should be paid an annuity of £10 to be increased to £20 on their mother's death. But to his second son, John, he bequeathed only a lump sum of £10. Sargeaunt refused to speculate on the reasons for this apparent discrimination, but it at least raises some suspicions as to John Ford's behavior toward his family. This domestic situation was further complicated by the terms of his brother Henry's will, which he made only two days before his death on September 19, 1616. This will provided for an annuity of £20 to be paid to "Iohn Ford gent." "for the terme of his lief," to be met out of the revenues of Henry's valuable parsonage at Ipplepen, which had come into the hands of the Ford family on the dissolution of the College of St. Mary Ottery in the time of Henry VIII. But in exchange for this annuity the will stipulated that John "surrender the estate he hath in two tenements called Glandfeilds groundes Bilver parke and willow meade lying in Iplepen and Torbryan to the vse of my children." How these two "tenements" or houses came into John's hands is unknown, but the whole affair looks as if Henry might have been trying to equalize the income of his three younger brothers and that John preferred a regular income to what he might receive through his two "tenements." In any case, his private income did not provide him with any affluence.

Perhaps the fact that he had rather haltingly begun his literary career about the time of his temporary expulsion from law school for not paying his bills may have had some bearing on all these dealings, but if so it could not at first have added much to his revenue. Sargeaunt and Stavig divide Ford's literary career into three main parts: his non-dramatic writing (1606–20); his dramatic writing in collaboration (about 1620 to about 1625); and his independent dramatic writing (about 1625 to about 1639). The first of these periods is inconsequential except that it may throw some light on what Stavig calls "Ford's Early Ethical Thought" and bases on three main works: a long religious poem, *Christ's Bloody Sweat, or The Son of God in His Agony;* and two prose pamphlets, *The Golden Mean* and *The Line of Life* (1620). But the first two of these have only been attributed to him by recent scholars on internal evidence. Ford had tried his prentice hand, however, in two signed publications in 1606: *Fame's Memorial,* an elegiac poem on the death of the Earl of Devonshire, his home county, praising the earl for his military conquests in Ireland and for his fame as a lover and as the eventual husband of Penelope Rich, or "Stella" (whom Ford incidentally vindicated in her guilty connection with the earl while still married to Rich); and a prose pamphlet, *Honor Triumphant*, all about love, beauty, and valor, and apparently written as part of the entertainment of the King of Denmark on his visit to England. Since Ford dedicated his poem to the Countess of Devonshire and his pamphlet to the Countess of Pembroke and Montgomery, he seems to have been cultivating the right people.

Then for seven years nothing apparently emanated from his pen until in 1613 *Christ's Bloody Sweat* was published, with a dedication to the Earl of Pembroke, signed "I. F." In this dedication the author confessed that he had recently undergone a conversion from his "doubts of folly, youth, and opinion" and asserted that sinners could be saved only "by partaking in that Agony." In the same year came the anonymously published pamphlet *The Golden Mean*, which extolled "the nobleness of perfect virtue in extremes" of the Earl of Northumberland, imprisoned in the Tower since 1605 for complicity in the Gunpowder Plot. On November 25, 1615, the Stationers' Register recorded the entry of a work to be entitled *Sir Thomas Overbury's Ghost, Containing the History of His Life and Untimely Death by John Ford, Gent.* Although no copy is known to be extant, the mere title shows, as Sargeaunt puts it, "his extreme sympathy with such characters as the Earl and Countess of Devonshire, the Earl of Essex, Sir Walter Raleigh, and Sir Thomas Overbury, the victims of flattery and envy," that is, for such suffering characters as were to appear later in his plays. Finally, in 1620, Ford published under his name his moral and didactic prose pamphlet, *A Line of Life*, dedicated to Viscount Dorchester, but admitting that the author was "an unknown stranger to his noble patron." None of these early non-dramatic works would seem to have anything but the most remote connection with the plays that were soon to come from Ford's pen. Stavig sums them up by asserting: "We may conclude from these early works that Ford was a traditional and quite orthodox Christian who was deeply influenced by classical ethics. Ford believed that man, through reason, resolution, and perseverance, could steer between the extremes of passion and achieve the golden mean of a well-ordered life." Ford's overall approach to life was that of "a Christian neo-Stoic."

The only suggestion that Ford may have written at all for the stage before 1621 comes from the fact that the publisher Humphrey Moseley, on September 9, 1653, entered in the Stationers' Register his intention to publish four plays by John Ford, and on June 29, 1660, made a similar entry concerning three comedies. But if Moseley ever printed any of these, no copies are extant. John Warburton listed the titles of four of these among the manuscripts which his cook Betsy used for her baking, but doubts have been cast on his credibility by recent criticism (Greg, "The Bakings of Betsy"). In "Elizabethan-Restoration Palimpsest" (*MLR*, 1940), Alfred Harbage, in claiming that several supposedly original Restoration plays were really adaptations of "lost" Elizabethan ones, suggested that Sir Robert Howard's *The Great Favorite, or The Duke of Lerma* (1668) had originally been written by Ford, and Sensabaugh has endorsed this ascription ("Another Play by Ford," *MLQ*, 1940). Leech, in a four-page appendix, has discussed Ford's "Lost Plays (Including Some of Doubtful Authorship)."

However this may be, during the period 1621–25 the evidence is pretty clear that Ford wrote at least five plays in collaboration with Thomas Dekker, William Rowley, and John Webster. His verifiable career as a dramatist began with *The Witch of Edmonton*, written and produced in 1621 in collaboration with Rowley and Dekker, the latter of whom had been recently released from prison and was industriously turning out plays for any company that would buy them. *The Witch of Edmonton* was acted at court by the Prince's Men, "with singular applause," and fixed Ford's attention on the theater as the basis for his future literary career. In 1624 he and Dekker turned out no less than four plays, only one of which is extant—*The Sun's Darling*, though others were licensed and produced.

This spurt of collaborative activity not only seems to have exhausted Ford temporarily, but when he returned to the stage in 1628 with *The Lover's Melancholy* he decided to go it alone from then on.  This play, reflecting Ford's involvement in the Platonic love cult which was sweeping Queen Henrietta Maria's court, was acted at both the Blackfriars and the Globe by the King's Men, and when published in 1629 it was dedicated to Nathaniel Finch, to the author's similarly named cousin John Ford, and to "All the Rest of the Noble Society of Gray's Inn."  Sargeaunt speculates that since Finch was the lawyer who signed Dekker's deposition in the *Keep the Widow Waking* case he may have been the person who had brought the young and the old playwrights together for their collaborations.  Scholars have been unable to decide on an acceptable chronology for most of the remainder of Ford's plays, which included tragedy, tragicomedy, comedy, and history, but the most important of them were the tragedies, *The Broken Heart, Love's Sacrifice,* and *'Tis Pity She's a Whore*, all published in 1633, and *The Chronicle History of Perkin Warbeck*, published in 1634.  Ford's dedication of *'Tis Pity* to the Earl of Peterborough as "These First Fruits of My Leisure" confuses the picture, since *The Lover's Melancholy* was entered in the Stationers' Register on November 24, 1628.  (Bentley makes the most thorough survey of these problems in *The Jacobean and Caroline Stage*.)

Ford's life during the 1620s and 1630s is known only through the publication of his plays, their dedications, and the dedications and occasional poems of others written to him.  He collaborated with Dekker, Rowley, Webster, and perhaps Middleton, and was acquainted with Shirley, Massinger, and Brome, to judge from various commendatory verses.  He dedicated four of the seven plays published with his name during his lifetime to well-known noble patrons of literature, but was apparently personally acquainted only with Peterborough.  Sargeaunt asks the question of what became of Ford after the production of his tragicomedy, *The Lady's Trial*, in the early summer of 1638 and its subsequent publication in 1639, and has tried to answer it by referring to an article by Bertram Lloyd (*RES*, 1925) on a little hymeneal poem, "A Contract of Love and Truth," in an unprinted *Poetical Miscellany* sometime before 1645.  It is signed "J. Ford" and according to Lloyd may well have been written by the "lawyer dramatist for one of his clients."

It has generally been assumed on purely negative evidence that Ford died shortly after the publication of *The Lady's Trial*.  However, in 1873 *Notes and Queries* printed a letter from a correspondent saying that she owned a volume with an inscription, "John Ford Middle Temple 15 Jully 1641."  It is possible, though, that this volume belonged to the John Forde of Chewford, Somerset, who entered the Middle Temple in 1616.  Long before this, Gifford stated without indicating his source that "Faint traditions in the neighborhood of his birthplace" suggest that Ford, "having from his legal pursuits acquired a sufficient fortune, retired home to pass the remainder of his days among the youthful connections whom time had yet spared him."  Sargeaunt finds some support for the notion that Ford actually did not die before the civil wars, but retired to Devonshire during their waging, from the presence of a commendatory poem signed "Jo: Ford" prefixed to a little volume entitled *Dia Poemata* published by an Edmund Elys in 1655.  Elys's father was rector in a little village a few miles from Ilsington, East Allington.  Since young Elys had taken his B.A. at Balliol, Oxford, on October 16, 1655, Sargeaunt suggests that it would be quite possible that he had visited his father during the vacation period, and that Ford, knowing the family, had generously written a verse for the book.  But even if the dramatist were alive in Devonshire in 1655, Sargeaunt is rather sure that he did not die in Ilsington, since the burials of his younger brothers and his sister Jane are recorded in that parish, but his name does not appear.

John Ford, in spite of some of his youthful escapades, was apparently never a very conspicuous man.  A possible sidelight on his appearance and impression is to be found in an amusing burlesque "Elegy on Randolph's Finger" by William Hemminge, written probably about 1632.  In it, in more or less conventional manner, both the living and the dead poets escort the severed finger to the banks of the Styx, and Ford is pictured in the following couplet:

> Deep in a dump Jack Ford alone was got
> With folded arms and melancholy hat.

Sargeaunt speculates on whether this description should be applied literally to Ford's physical appearance and lonely character or whether it is only a symbolic reference to *The Lover's Melancholy*.  However, she also calls attention to Sherman's allusion to the frontispiece of Robert Burton's *The Anatomy of Melancholy* (1621), which depicts "a tall, elegantly attired young gentleman standing with folded hands and wide hat pulled down over his eyes."  Perhaps Ford, who, like most of his contemporaries, was much struck by Burton's book, had in his early middle age assumed the characteristics and guise of the melancholy man.  Richard Crashaw's epigram, published in *The Delights of the Muses* in 1648, may also have some bearing on the subject:

> Thou cheat'st us, Ford, mak'st one seem two by art:
> What is *Love's Sacrifice* but *The Broken Heart?*

## THE WITCH OF EDMONTON

*The Witch of Edmonton*, one of the best of the popular witch plays of the era, was acted by the Prince's Servants at Whitehall on December 29, 1621, and, as the title page of the first edition in 1658 stated, "Often at the Cockpit in Drury Lane," and always "with Singular Applause."  On April 19, 1621, a poor old woman named Elizabeth Sawyer had been executed at Edmonton for witchcraft, and on April 27 Henry Good-cole's *The Wonderful Discovery of Elizabeth Sawyer, a Witch, Late of Edmonton* was entered in the Stationers' Register and soon printed.  The popular curiosity about this event attracted the "Divers Well-Esteemed Poets, William Rowley, Thomas Dekker, John Ford, etc." to turn this "Known True Story" (as it was described on the title page) into the subject of their play.  No sources for the main plot have ever been discovered, nor have the identities of the writers behind the mysterious "etc." ever been detected, since scholars have felt satisfied with their ability to assign definite parts of the play to the playwrights designated, though they have not always agreed on which parts to give to which authors.  In general, however, as Stavig sums up the results of the critics' analysis, Dekker is given credit for most of the witch scenes and for the character of Susan, who belongs to the Patient Griselda type which was a favorite of his in other plays.  The low comedy scenes involving Cuddy Banks and his friends have been assigned to Rowley, and Ford has been made responsible for the Frank-Winnifride plot.  Sargeaunt and Oliver, following H. Dugdale Sykes (*NQ*, 1926), have made their more specific assignments of individual scenes and parts of scenes, according to their own tastes, and Leech has agreed with Sargeaunt that in some places Dekker and Ford may have worked intimately together on the same scene.  No one, however, has been able to suggest a good reason why Ford was given his particular part of the action, since it is utterly unlike anything he had written before.  But Sargeaunt conjectures that the veteran playwright Dekker may have drawn it from the lives of the kind of people he was accustomed to write about, and then turned it over to the neophyte Ford to develop under his supervision.  Bentley thinks that the play was probably revived about 1635–6 by the Queen's Men.  It then disappeared from the stage until the Phoenix Society resurrected it in London in 1921, and the Old Vic did the same in 1926, with a notable cast, including Edith Evans as Mother Sawyer, Beatrix Lehmann as Winnifride, and Marius Goring as Frank.  In an article on "The Significance of *The Witch of Edmonton*" (*Criterion*, 1937), Edward Sackville-West attacked the opinion of one reviewer that the play "was merely something quaint—a period piece—a minor hotchpotch," and maintained that its central problem, that of Good vs. Evil, is as real today as it ever was.

The publisher of the 1658 edition of the play described it as a tragicomedy, using the term in a rather different sense from Fletcher's. Stavig called it a "domestic tragedy, combined with some elements of topical comedy"—"exciting theater" in its mixture of elements, but little more. Henry H. Adams, however, in his *English Domestic or Homiletic Tragedy, 1575–1642* (Columbia University Press, 1943), placed it squarely at the end of the line of domestic murder plays, best represented in the sixteenth century by the anonymous *A Yorkshire Tragedy, Arden of Feversham*, and Heywood's *A Woman Killed with Kindness*. Sargeaunt thought that Ford's part of the play had been quite well constructed, but that—perhaps because the play as a whole had been pretty hastily thrown together to take advantage of the popular interest in the affair—little attempt had been made to weld it and the witch plot closely together. Stavig—on the other hand, felt that the plots themselves "are interconnected thematically so that each segment of the play contributes to an overall structure and meaning. The authors are constantly shaping the play to suggest a generalized commentary on the human situation."

The characters impressed Sargeaunt as being carefully drawn, especially Winnifride, Susan, and her father Carter. She felt that Winnifride would have had to be Ford's creation because of her "courage, combined with a certain tenderness and strength of feeling" characteristic of all his women. The theme of the father-daughter relationship illustrated in the Carters was also of peculiar interest to Ford as shown in his later plays such as *'Tis Pity, The Broken Heart*, and *Perkin Warbeck*. The related theme of enforced marriage also continued to attract him. But Stavig felt that the characters were largely two-dimensional. Granting that Frank Thorney was the most fully developed of these characters and that "Modern readers are apt to see the shrewd study of Frank's vacillations as indications of a sensitive psychologist at work," Stavig concluded that Ford actually only gave him "so much surface vitality that we can be fooled into taking him primarily as a psychological study instead of seeing his more important functional role in the development of the play's themes." Stavig then proceeded to examine the other characters as stereotypes, used largely as moral symbols and developed according to symbolic techniques "directed toward clarifying the subtleties of moral responsibility." The question of repentance and redemption bulked large with Ford, as critics have realized. Leech commented on the presence of "a strain of religious speculation" characteristic of Ford, and found that at the end "the Christian element in Ford's feeling is stronger than the sense of tragedy. Frank is to know repentance and the prospect of salvation is with him at his execution." Adams also emphasized that the play was based on popular religious beliefs, but found that the playwrights carefully avoided the question of whether Mother Sawyer herself could hope for redemption and grace, even though she was drawn with some sympathy, because "The feeling pervades the play that the onus should rest on the shoulders of the people who drove her to make a contract with the Devil." Nevertheless, although she too repents at the end, "her sin is so much greater than that of murder that it would have been dangerous for anyone except a churchman or a practiced theologian to hazard a guess as to her chance of salvation."

The role of the devil-dog is of course an important factor in the situation. Adams compared his relationship to Mother Sawyer with that of Mephistopheles to Faustus or of the Vice to the protagonists in the moralities, but neither he nor anyone else seems to have theorized as to how the part was actually performed on the stage. Stavig used the role as "an instructive illustration of the ways in which symbolism, realism, psychology, and morality are often linked in seventeenth century plays," since the devil has no power over human beings unless they voluntarily or subconsciously seek his aid, as do both Mother Sawyer and Frank Thorney. R. H. West, as part of his examination of *The Invisible World: A Study of Pneumatology in Elizabethan Drama* (University of Georgia Press, 1946), has discussed "the homelier English variety" of witchcraft in *The Witch of Edmonton* as distinguished from "the darker continental variety" in other plays.  Of course, as in *Doctor Faustus*, this element can be used for contrasting scenes of farce and horseplay along with the ominous scenes of super-natural menace and tragedy.

In the matter of style, Adams points out that the main plot involving the hero-villain Frank is about four-fifths in verse, whereas the witch plot (and also the Banks plot, father and son), being concerned with lower class persons, is largely in prose. Oliver expresses surprise that so many critics have charged Ford with an inability to write great single lines of poetry and even goes so far as to attack "the persistence of that other heresy, . . . that Ford owed little to Shakespeare."

The present text is based on photostats of the 1658 quarto in the Harvard College Library; some use has also been made of the Gifford-Dyce edition of Ford's works.

# THE WITCH OF EDMONTON[1]

## BY

## JOHN FORD, WILLIAM ROWLEY, AND THOMAS DEKKER

### ACTORS' NAMES

SIR ARTHUR CLARINGTON.
OLD THORNEY, *a gentleman.*
OLD CARTER, *a rich yeoman.*
OLD BANKS, *a countryman.*
W. MAGO [2]
W. HAMLUC [2] } *two countrymen.*
THREE OTHER COUNTRYMEN.
WARBECK
SOMERTON } *suitors to Carter's daughters.*
FRANK, *Thorney's son.*
YOUNG CUDDY BANKS, *the clown.*
FOUR MORRIS DANCERS.[3]
OLD RATCLIFFE.
SAWGUT, *an old fiddler.*
POLDAVIS, *a barber's boy.*[4]

JUSTICE.
CONSTABLE.
OFFICERS.
SERVING-MEN.
DOG, *a familiar.*[5]
A SPIRIT.

### WOMEN

MOTHER SAWYER, *the witch.*
ANN, *Ratcliffe's wife.*
SUSAN
KATHERINE } *Carter's daughters.*
WINNIFRIDE, *Sir Arthur's maid.*
[JANE, *Carter's maid.*

SCENE: *Edmonton and its vicinity; London.*

TIME: *Early seventeenth century.*]

*The whole argument is this distich.*

Forced marriage, murder; murder, blood
    requires.
Reproach, revenge; revenge, hell's help
    desires.

### PROLOGUE

The town of Edmonton hath lent the stage
A devil [6] and a witch, both in an age.
To make comparisons it were uncivil
Between so even a pair, a witch and devil;

But, as the year doth with his plenty bring
As well a latter as a former spring,
So has this witch enjoyed the first, and
    reason
Presumes she may partake the other season.
In acts deserving name, the proverb says,
"Once good, and ever." Why not so in
    plays?     10
Why not in this, since, gentlemen, we
    flatter
No expectation? Here is mirth and matter.
                 MR. BIRD.[7]

### ACT[US] I. SCEN[A] i.

[*A room in Sir Arthur's House at Edmonton.*]

*Enter Frank Thorney; Winnifride, with child.*[8]

FRANK. Come, wench. Why, here's a
    business soon despatched.
  Thy heart I know is now at ease; thou
    need'st not

---

[1] The title continues: "A Known True Story, Composed into a Tragi-Comedy by Divers Well-Esteemed Poets, William Rowley, Thomas Dekker, John Ford, etc. Acted by the Prince's Servants, Often at the Cockpit in Drury Lane, Once at Court, with Singular Applause."
[2] Probably the names of actual actors. W. Mago, however, is not referred to by name in the play itself.
[3] Who appear first as the above-mentioned countrymen.
[4] Merely referred to in the play.
[5] *I.e.*, a familiar spirit.
[6] An allusion to *The Merry Devil of Edmonton*, printed anonymously in 1608.
[7] Master Theophilus Bird.   [8] *I.e.*, pregnant.

Fear what the tattling gossips in their cups

Can speak against thy fame. Thy child shall know

Who to call dad now.

WIN. You have discharged [1]
The true part of an honest man; I cannot
Request a fuller satisfaction
Than you have freely granted. Yet methinks
'Tis an hard case, being lawful man and wife,
We should not live together.

FRANK. Had I failed 10
In promise of my truth[2] to thee, we must
Have then been ever sundered; now the longest
Of our forbearing either's company
Is only but to gain a little time
For our continuing thrift, that so hereafter
The heir that shall be born may not have cause
To curse his hour of birth, which made him feel
The misery of beggary and want—
Two devils that are occasions to enforce
A shameful end. My plots aim but to keep 20
My father's love.

WIN. And that will be as difficult
To be preserved, when he shall understand
How you are married, as it will be now,
Should you confess it to him.

FRANK. Fathers are
Won by degrees, not bluntly, as our masters
Or wrongéd friends are; and besides I'll use
Such dutiful and ready means that ere
He can have notice of what's past, th' inheritance
To which I am born heir shall be assured.
That done, why, let him know it; if he like it not, 30
Yet he shall have no power in him left
To cross the thriving of it.

WIN. You who had
The conquest of my maiden love may easily

Conquer the fears of my distrust. And whither
Must I be hurried?

FRANK. Prithee, do not use
A word so much unsuitable to the constant
Affections of thy husband. Thou shalt live
Near Waltham Abbey with thy uncle Selman.
I have acquainted him with all at large.[3]
He'll use thee kindly; thou shalt want no pleasures 40
Nor any other fit supplies whatever
Thou canst in heart desire.

WIN. All these are nothing
Without your company.

FRANK. Which thou shalt have
Once every month at least.

WIN. Once every month!
Is this to have an husband?

FRANK. Perhaps oft'ner;
That's as occasion serves.

WIN. Ay, ay; in case
No other beauty tempt your eye, whom you
Like better, I may chance to be remembered,
And see you now and then. Faith, I did hope
You'ld not have used me so; 'tis but my fortune. 50
And yet, if not for my sake, have some pity
Upon the child I go with, that's your own.
And, less[4] you'll be a cruel-hearted father,
You cannot but remember that.
Heaven knows how—

FRANK. To quit which fear at once,
As by the ceremony late performed
I plighted thee a faith as free from challenge
As any double thought, once more, in hearing
Of heaven and thee, I vow that never henceforth
Disgrace, reproof, lawless affections, threats, 60
Or what can be suggested gainst our marriage,
Shall cause me falsify that bridal oath
That binds me thine. And, Winnifride, whenever

---

[1] Here and in a few later passages the line division has been regularized. Some passages printed in the original as prose have been divided into verse. [2] Troth, promise.

[3] At length, fully. [4] Unless.

The wanton heat of youth, by subtle
    baits
Of beauty, or what woman's art can
    practice,[1]
Draw me from only loving thee, let
    heaven
Inflict upon my life some fearful ruin!
I hope thou dost believe me.
WIN.                          Swear no more;
    I am confirmed, and will resolve to do
What you think most behooveful for us.
FRANK.                    Thus, then: 70
    Make thyself ready; at the furthest house
Upon the green without the town your
    uncle
Expects you. For a little time, farewell!
WIN.                              Sweet,
    We shall meet again as soon as thou
    canst possibly?
FRANK. We shall. One kiss!—Away!
                        [*Exit Winnifride.*]


*Ent[er] Sir Art[hur] Clarington.*

SIR ART.              Frank Thorney!
FRANK.                          Here, sir.
SIR ART. Alone? Then must I tell thee in
    plain terms
Thou hast wronged thy master's house
    basely and lewdly.
FRANK. Your house, sir?
SIR ART.        Yes, sir. If the nimble devil
    That wantoned in your blood rebelled
    against                              79
All rules of honest duty, you might, sir,
Have found out some more fitting place
    than here
To have built a stews in. All the country
    whispers
How shamefully thou hast undone a
    maid,
Approved for modest life, for civil car-
    riage,
Till thy prevailing perjuries enticed her
To forfeit shame. Will you be honest yet,
Make her amends and marry her?
FRANK.                          So, sir,
    I might bring both myself and her to
    beggary;
And that would be a shame worse than
    the other.
SIR ART. You should have thought on this
    before, and then                    90

Your reason would have overswayed the
    passion
Of your unruly lust. But, that you may
Be left without excuse, to salve the
    infamy
Of my disgracéd house, and cause [2] you
    are
A gentleman, and both of you my serv-
    ants,
I'll make the maid a portion.
FRANK.              So you promised me
Before, in case I married her. I know
Sir Arthur Clarington deserves the credit
Report hath lent him, and presume you
    are
A debtor to your promise. But upon  100
What certainty shall I resolve? Excuse me
For being somewhat rude.
SIR ART.              'Tis but reason.
    Well, Frank, what think'st thou of two
    hundred pounds
And a continual friend?
FRANK.            Though my poor fortunes
    Might happily [3] prefer me to a choice
Of a far greater portion, yet, to right
A wrongéd maid and to preserve your
    favor,
I am content to accept your proffer.
SIR ART.                    Art thou?
FRANK. Sir, we shall every day have need
    to employ
The use of what you please to give.
SIR ART.        Thou shalt have 't.  110
FRANK. Then I claim your promise. We
    are man and wife.
SIR ART. Already?
FRANK.              And more than so; I have
    promised her
Free entertainment in her uncle's house
Near Waltham Abbey, where she may
    securely
Sojourn, till time and my endeavors work
My father's love and liking.
SIR ART.              Honest Frank!
FRANK. I hope, sir, you will think I can-
    not keep her
Without a daily charge.
SIR ART.              As for the money,
    'Tis all thine own! And, though I can-
    not make thee
A present payment, yet thou shalt be
    sure                              120
I will not fail thee.

[1] Scheme.

[2] Because.        [3] Haply, perhaps.

FRANK.            But our occasions—

SIR ART.            Nay, nay,
Talk not of your occasions.  Trust my
bounty;
It shall not sleep.  Hast married her,
i' faith, Frank?
'Tis well, 'tis passing well!  Then, Winni-
fride,
Once more thou art an honest [1] woman.
Frank,
Thou hast a jewel.  Love her; she'll
deserve it.
And when to Waltham?

FRANK.            She is making ready;
Her uncle stays for her.

SIR ART.            Most provident speed.
Frank, I will be [thy] [2] friend, and such a
friend!
Thou'lt bring her thither?

FRANK.            Sir, I cannot; newly    130
My father sent me word I should come
to him.

SIR ART. Marry, and do; I know thou
hast a wit
To handle him.

FRANK.            I have a suit t' ye.

SIR ART.            What is 't?
Anything, Frank; command it.

FRANK.            That you'll please
By letters to assure my father that
I am not married.

SIR ART.            How!

FRANK.            Someone or other
Hath certainly informed him that I
purposed
To marry Winnifride, on which he
threatened
To disinherit me.  To prevent it,
Lowly I crave your letters, which he,
seeing,                                              140
Will credit; and I hope, ere I return,
On such conditions as I'll frame, his lands
Shall be assured.

SIR ART.            But what is there [3] to quit [4]
My knowledge of the marriage?

FRANK.            Why, you were not
A witness to it.

SIR ART.            I conceive; and then—
His land confirmed, thou wilt acquaint
him throughly
With all that's past.

---

[1] Chaste.        [2] Added in Gifford-Dyce edn.
[3] Emended by Gifford.  Original reads *that*.
[4] *I.e.*, rid myself of.

---

FRANK.            I mean no less.

SIR ART.            Provided
I never was made privy to it.

FRANK.            Alas, sir,
Am I a talker?

SIR ART.            Draw thyself the letter;
I'll put my hand to it.  I commend thy
policy;                                              150
Th' art witty, witty Frank; nay, nay,
'tis fit.
Despatch it.

FRANK.        I shall write effectually.  *Exit.*

SIR ART. Go thy way, cuckoo.  Have I
caught the young man?
One trouble, then, is freed.  He that will
feast
At other's cost must be a bold-faced
guest.

*Enter Win[nifride] in a riding suit.*

WIN. I have heard the news; all now is
safe;
The worst is past.

SIR ART.            Thy lip, wench!  [*Kisses her.*]
I must bid
Farewell, for fashion's sake; but I will
visit thee
Suddenly, girl.  This was cleanly carried;
Ha!  Was 't not, Win?

WIN.            Then were my happiness,    160
That I in heart repent I did not bring him
The dower of a virginity.  Sir, forgive me;
I have been much to blame.  Had not
my lewdness [5]
Given way to your immoderate waste of
virtue,
You had not with such eagerness pur-
sued
The error of your goodness.

SIR ART.            Dear, dear Win,
I hug this art of thine; it shows how
cleanly
Thou canst beguile, in case occasion
serve
To practice; it becomes thee.  Now we
share
Free scope enough, without control or
fear,                                                170
To interchange our pleasures; we will
surfeit
In our embraces, wench.  Come, tell me,
when
Wilt thou appoint a meeting?

---

[5] Suggested by Dyce.  Original reads *laundress.*

WIN.                          What to do?

SIR ART.  Good, good, to con the lesson of
    our loves,
Our secret game.

WIN.               O, blush to speak it further!
As y' are a noble gentleman, forget
A sin so monstrous; 'tis not gently done
To open a cured wound.  I know you
    speak
For trial; troth, you need not.

SIR ART.                          I for trial?
Not I, by this good sunshine!

WIN.                     Can you name  180
    That syllable of good, and yet not
    tremble
To think to what a foul and black in-
    tent
You use it for an oath?  Let me resolve [1]
    you:
If you appear in any visitation
That brings not with it pity for the
    wrongs
Done to abuséd Thorney, my kind hus-
    band;
If you infect mine ear with any breath
That is not throughly perfuméd with
    sighs        •
For former deeds of lust, may I be
    cursed                          189
Even in my prayers, when I vouchsafe
To see or hear you!  I will change my
    life
From a loose whore to a repentant wife.

SIR ART.  Wilt thou turn monster now?
    Art not ashamed
After so many months to be honest at
    last?
Away, away!  Fie on 't!

WIN.                     My resolution
    Is built upon a rock.  This very day
Young Thorney vowed, with oaths not
    to be doubted,
That never any change of love should
    cancel
The bonds in which we are to either
    bound
Of lasting truth—and shall I, then, for
    my part                          200
Unfile the sacred oath set on record
In heaven's book?  Sir Arthur, do not
    study
To add to your lascivious lust the sin
Of sacrilege, for, if you but endeavor

[1] Inform.

By any unchaste word to tempt my
    constancy,
You strive as much as in you lies to ruin
A temple hallowed to the purity
Of holy marriage.  I have said enough;
You may believe me.

SIR ART.               Get you to your nunnery;
There freeze in your old cloister!  This
    is fine!                          210

WIN.  Good angels guide me!  Sir, you'll
    give me leave
To weep and pray for your conversion?

SIR ART.                          Yes.
Away to Waltham!  Pox on your honesty!
Had you no other trick to fool me?  Well,
You may want money yet.

WIN.               None that I'll send for
To you, for hire of a damnation.
When I am gone, think on my just com-
    plaint.
I was your devil; O, be you my saint!
                  *Exit Win[nifride].*

SIR ART.  Go, go thy ways, as changeable a
    baggage
As ever cozened knight.  I'm glad I'm
    rid of her.                          220
Honest?  Marry, hang her!  Thorney is
    my debtor;
I thought to have paid him too; but fools
have fortune.          *Exit S[ir] A[rthur].*

SCEN[A] ii.

[*A room in Carter's house at Edmonton.*]

*Enter Old Thorney and Old Carter.*

O. THOR.  You offer, Mr. Carter, like a
gentleman; I cannot find fault with it, 'tis
so fair.

O. CART.  No gentleman I, Mr. Thorney.
Spare the mastership; call me by my name,
John Carter.  "Master" is a title my father,
nor his before him, were acquainted with—
honest Hertfordshire yeomen.  Such an one
am I; my word and my deed shall be proved
one at all times.  I mean to give you  [10
no security for the marriage money.

O. THOR.  How?  No security?  Although
it need not so long as you live, yet who is
he has surety of his life one hour?  "Men,"
the proverb says, "are mortal;" else, for
my part, I distrust you not, were the sum
double.

O. CART.  Double, treble, more or less,

I tell you, Mr. Thorney, I'll give no security.
Bonds and bills are but terriers to  [20
catch fools, and keep lazy knaves busy; my
security shall be present payment. And we
here about Edmonton hold present payment as sure as an alderman's bond in
London, Mr. Thorney.

O. THOR. I cry you mercy,[1] sir; I understood you not.

O. CART. I like young Frank well; so
does my Susan too. The girl has a fancy
to him, which makes me ready in my  [30
purse. There be other suitors within, that
make much noise to little purpose. If Frank
love Sue, Sue shall have none but Frank.
'Tis a mannerly girl, Mr. Thorney, though
but an homely man's daughter. There
have worse faces looked out of black bags,
man.

O. THOR. You speak your mind freely
and honestly. I marvel my son comes not;
I am sure he will be here some time  [40
today.

O. CART. Today or tomorrow, when he
comes he shall be welcome to bread, beer,
and beef, yeoman's fare; we have no kickshaws: full dishes, whole bellyfulls. Should
I diet three days at one of the slender city suppers, you might send me to
Barber-Surgeons' Hall [2] the fourth day,
to hang up for an anatomy.[3] Here come
they that—How now, girls? Every day  [50
playday with you?

*Enter Warbeck with Susan, Somerton with*
*Katherine.*

Valentine's day too, all by couples? Thus
will young folks do when we are laid in our
graves, Mr. Thorney; here's all the care they
take. And how do you find the wenches,
gentlemen? Have they any mind to a loose
gown and a strait shoe? Win 'em and wear
'em. They shall choose for themselves by
my consent.

WARB. You speak like a kind father.—
[*The young people stand aside in pairs.*]
Sue, thou hearest                          60
The liberty that's granted thee; what
   sayest thou?
Wilt thou be mine?

[1] I beg your pardon.
[2] Many barbers performed duties now given
to surgeons.
[3] Skeleton.

Sus.              Your what, sir? I dare swear
Never your wife.

WARB.              Canst thou be so unkind,
Considering how dearly I affect [4] thee,
Nay, dote on thy perfections?

Sus.              You are studied,
Too scholarlike in words; I understand
   not.
I am too coarse for such a gallant's love
As you are.

WARB.              By the honor of gentility—

Sus. Good sir, no swearing; yea and nay
   with us                                69
Prevails above all oaths you can invent.

WARB. By this white hand of thine—

Sus.              Take a false oath?
Fie, fie! Flatter the wise; fools not regard
   it—
And one of these am I.

WARB.              Dost thou despise me?

O. CART. Let 'em talk on, Mr. Thorney;
I know Sue's mind. The fly may buzz about
the candle; he shall but singe his wings
when all's done. Frank, Frank is he has
her heart.

SOM. But shall I live in hope, Kate?     79

KAT. Better so than be a desperate man.

SOM. Perhaps thou think'st it is thy por-
   tion
I level at. Wert thou as poor in fortunes
As thou art rich in goodness, I would
   rather
Be suitor for the dower of thy virtues
Than twice thy father's whole estate;
   and, prithee,
Be thou resolved [5] so.

KAT.              Mr. Somerton,
It is an easy labor to deceive
A maid that will believe men's subtile
   promises;
Yet I conceive of you as worthily
As I presume you do deserve.

SOM.              Which is    90
As worthily in loving thee sincerely
As thou art worthy to be so beloved.

KAT. I shall find time to try you.

SOM.              Do, Kate, do;
And, when I fail, may all my joys forsake
   me!

O. CART. Warbeck and Sue are at it still.
I laugh to myself, Mr. Thorney, to see how
earnestly he beats the bush, while the bird
is flown into another's bosom. A very un-

[4] Love.                          [5] Convinced.

thrift, Mr. Thorney; one of the country roaring lads. We have such as well as the [100 city, and as arrant rakehells as they are, though not so nimble at their prizes of wit. Sue knows the rascal to an hair's breadth, and will fit him accordingly.

O. THOR. What is the other gentleman?

O. CART. One Somerton—the honester man of the two by five pounds in every stone weight; a civil fellow. He has a fine, convenient estate of land in West Ham, by Essex. M[aster] Ranges, that dwells [110 by Enfield, sent him hither. He likes Kate well; I may tell you I think she likes him as well. If they agree, I'll not hinder the match for my part. But that Warbeck is such another—I use him kindly for Mr. Somerton's sake, for he came hither first as a companion of his. Honest men, Mr. Thorney, may fall into knaves' company now and then.

WARB. Three hundred a year jointure, Sue.

SUS.                    Where lies it?   120
By sea or by land? I think by sea.

WARB. Do I look like a captain?

SUS.                    Not a whit, sir.
Should all that use the seas be reckoned captains,
There's not a ship should have a scullion in her
To keep her clean.

WARB.               Do you scorn me, Mrs.[1] Susan?
Am I a subject to be jeered at?

SUS.                              Neither
Am I a property for you to use
As stale[2] to your fond,[3] wanton, loose discourse.
Pray, sir, be civil.

WARB.               Wilt be angry, wasp?

O. CART. God-a-mercy, Sue! She'll [130 firk[4] him, on my life, if he fumble with her.

### Enter Frank.

Mr. Francis Thorney, you are welcome indeed; your father expected your coming. How does the right worshipful knight, Sir Arthur Clarington, your master?

FRANK. In health this morning.—Sir, my duty.

O. THOR.        Now
You come as I could wish.

WARB. [Aside.]        Frank Thorney, ha!

SUS. You must excuse me.

FRANK.               Virtuous Mrs. Susan!
Kind Mrs. Katherine! (Salutes[5] them.)—
Gentlemen, to both                139
Good time o' th' day.

SOM.               The like to you.

WARB. [Aside to Somerton.]        'Tis he.
A word, friend. On my life, this is the man
Stands fair in crossing Susan's love to me.

SOM. [Aside to Warbeck.] I think no less;
be wise, and take no notice on 't.
He that can win her, best deserves her.

WARB. [Aside to Somerton.]        Marry
A serving-man? Mew!

SOM. [Aside to Warbeck.]        Prithee,
friend, no more.

O. CART. Gentlemen all, there's within a slight dinner ready, if you please to taste of it. Mr. Thorney, Mr. Francis, Mr. Somerton!—Why, girls! What, huswives! Will you spend all your fore- [150 noon in tittle-tattles? Away! It's well, i' faith.—Will you go in, gentlemen?

O. THOR. We'll follow presently; my son and I
Have a few words of business.

O. CART.               At your pleasure.
                    Ex[eunt] the Rest.

O. THOR. I think you guess the reason, Frank, for which
I sent for you.

FRANK.               Yes, sir.

O. THOR.               I need not tell you
With what a labyrinth of dangers daily
The best part of my whole estate's encumbered;
Nor have I any clew to wind it out   159
But what occasion proffers me, wherein
If you should falter, I shall have the shame,
And you the loss. On these two points rely
Our happiness or ruin. If you marry
With wealthy Carter's daughter, there's a portion
Will free my land, all which I will instate,[6]
Upon the marriage, to you; otherwise
I must be of necessity enforced
To make a present sale of all; and yet,
For aught I know, live in as poor distress,

---

[1] Mistress.   [2] Dupe.   [3] Foolish.   [4] Chastise.        [5] Kisses.        [6] Assign.

Or worse, than now I do. You hear the
sum?                                            170
I told you thus before. Have you con-
sidered on 't?
FRANK. I have, sir; and however I could
wish
To enjoy the benefit of single freedom—
For that I find no disposition in me
To undergo the burthen of that care
That marriage brings with it—yet, to
secure
And settle the continuance of your credit,
I humbly yield to be directed by you
In all commands.
O. THOR.                    You have already used
Such thriving protestations to the maid
That she is wholly yours. And—speak
the truth—                                       181
You love her, do you not?
FRANK.                       'Twere pity, sir,
I should deceive her.
O. THOR.            Better y' had been unborn.
But is your love so steady that you
mean—
Nay, more, desire—to make her your
wife?
FRANK.        Else, sir,
It were a wrong not to be righted.
O. THOR.                                True,
It were. And you will marry her?
FRANK.                    Heaven prosper it,
I do intend it.
O. THOR.               O, thou art a villain!
A devil like a man! Wherein have I    189
Offended all the powers so much, to be
Father to such a graceless, godless son?
FRANK. To me, sir, this? O, my cleft heart!
O. THOR.                            To thee,
Son of my curse. Speak truth and blush,
thou monster!
Hast thou not married Winnifride, a maid
Was fellow servant with thee?
FRANK. [Aside.]           Some swift spirit
Has blown this news abroad; I must out-
face it.
O. THOR. D' you study for excuse? Why,
all the country
Is full on 't.
FRANK.        With your license, 'tis not
charitable,
I am sure it is not fatherly, so much
To be o'erswayed with credulous con-
ceit ¹                                            200

¹ Thought, belief.

Of mere ² impossibilities; but fathers
Are privileged to think and talk at
pleasure.
O. THOR. Why, canst thou yet deny thou
hast no wife?
FRANK. What do you take me for? An
atheist?
One that nor hopes the blessedness of
life
Hereafter, neither fears the vengeance
due
To such as make the marriage bed an
inn,
Which travelers day and night,
After a toilsome lodging, leave at pleas-
ure?
Am I become so insensible of losing   210
The glory of creation's work, my soul?
O, I have lived too long!
O. THOR.               Thou hast, dissembler.
Darest thou persever ³ yet, and pull
down wrath
As hot as flames of hell to strike thee
quick
Into the grave of horror? I believe thee
not;
Get from my sight!
FRANK.                    Sir, though mine
innocence
Needs not a stronger witness than the
clearness
Of an unperished conscience, yet for that⁴
I was informed how mainly you had been
Possessed of this untruth, to quit all
scruple,                                          220
Please you peruse this letter; 'tis to you.
O. THOR. From whom?
FRANK.                       Sir Arthur Clar-
ington, my master.
O. THOR. [After reading.] Well, sir.
FRANK. [Aside.]            On every side
I am distracted,
Am waded deeper into mischief
Than virtue can avoid. But on I must.
Fate leads me; I will follow.—There you
read
What may confirm you.
O. THOR.                       Yes, and wonder
at it.
Forgive me, Frank; credulity abused me.
My tears express my joy, and I am
sorry
I injured innocence.

² Absolute.        ³ Persevere.        ⁴ Because.

FRANK.                    Alas, I knew  230
Your rage and grief proceeded from your
love
To me; so I conceived it.
O. THOR.                    My good son,
I'll bear with many faults in thee here-
after;
Bear thou with mine.
FRANK.                    The peace is soon
concluded.

*Enter Old Carter [and Susan].*

O. CART.  Why, Mr. Thorney, d' ye mean
to talk out your dinner?  The company
attends your coming.  What must it be,
Mr. Frank, or son Frank?  I am plain Dun-
stable.[1]
O. THOR.  Son, brother, if your daughter
like to have it so.  .            240
FRANK.  I dare be confident she's not al-
tered
From what I left her at our parting last.
Are you, fair maid?
SUS.                    You took too sure
possession
Of an engagéd heart.
FRANK.            Which now I challenge.
O. CART.  Marry, and much good may
it do thee, son.  Take her to thee.  Get me a
brace of boys at a burthen, Frank; the nurs-
ing shall not stand thee in a penny-worth
of milk.  Reach her home and spare not!
When's the day?            250
O. THOR.  Tomorrow, if you please.  To use
ceremony
Of charge and custom were to little
purpose;
Their loves are married fast enough
already.
O. CART.  A good motion.  We'll e'en have
an household dinner, and let the fiddlers go
scrape.  Let the bride and bridegroom dance
at night together; no matter for the guests.
Tomorrow, Sue, tomorrow.—Shall 's to
dinner now?
O. THOR.  We are on all sides pleased, I
hope.            260
SUS.  Pray heaven I may deserve the bless-
ing sent me.
Now my heart is settled.
FRANK.                    So is mine.
O. CART.  Your marriage money shall be

[1] Proverbial for outspoken and honest.

received before your wedding shoes can
be pulled on.  Blessing on you both!
FRANK.  [*Aside.*]  No man can hide his
shame from heaven that views him;
In vain he flees whose destiny pursues
him.                    *Exeunt omnes.*

ACT[US] II.  SCEN[A] i.

[*A field near Edmonton.*]

*Enter Elizabeth Sawyer gathering sticks.*

SAWY.  And why on me?  Why should the
envious world
Throw all their scandalous malice upon
me?
Cause I am poor, deformed, and igno-
rant,
And like a bow buckled and bent to-
gether
By some more strong in mischiefs than
myself,
Must I for that be made a common
sink
For all the filth and rubbish of men's
tongues
To fall and run into?  Some call me
witch,
And, being ignorant of myself, they go
About to teach me how to be one, urg-
ing            10
That my bad tongue—by their bad
usage made so—
Forspeaks[2] their cattle, doth bewitch
their corn,
Themselves, their servants, and their
babes at nurse.
This they enforce upon me, and in part

*Enter O[ld] Banks.*

Make me to credit it.  And here comes
one
Of my chief adversaries.
O. BANK.  Out, out upon thee, witch!
SAWY.            Dost call me witch?
O. BANK.  I do, witch, I do; and worse
I would, knew I a name more hateful.
What makest[3] thou upon my ground?  [20
SAWY.  Gather a few rotten sticks to
warm me.
O. BANK.  Down with them when I bid
thee, quickly; I'll make thy bones rattle in
thy skin else.

[2] Bewitches.            [3] Doest.

SAWY. You won't, churl, cutthroat, miser! There they be. [*Throws them down.*] Would they stuck cross thy throat, thy bowels, thy maw, thy midriff!

O. BANK. Say'st thou me so? Hag, [30 out of my ground!            [*Beats her.*]

SAWY. Dost strike me, slave, curmudgeon? Now, thy bones aches, thy joints cramps, and convulsions stretch and crack thy sinews!

O. BANK. Cursing, thou hag!  Take that and that!    [*Beats her and*] *exit.*

SAWY. Strike, do, and withered may
    that hand and arm
Whose blows have lamed me drop from
    the rotten trunk.
Abuse me!  Beat me!  Call me hag and
    witch!                             40
What is the name, where and by what
    art learned,
What spells, what charms, or invocations,
May the thing called Familiar be purchased?

*Enter Young Banks and three or four more*
                    [*Countrymen*].

Y. BANK. A new head for the tabor, and silver tipping for the pipe; remember that, and forget not five leash of new bells.

1 [COUNT.] Double bells! Crooked Lane[1] ye shall have 'em straight in.  Crooked Lane! Double bells all, if it be possible.

Y. BANK. Double bells?  Double [50 coxcombs! Trebles, buy me trebles, all trebles, for our purpose is to be in the altitudes.

2 [COUNT.] All trebles? Not a mean?[2]

Y. BANK. Not one.  The morris is so cast we'll have neither mean nor bass in our company, fellow Rowland.

3 [COUNT.] What?  Nor a counter?[3]

Y. BANK. By no means, no hunting counter;[4] leave that to Enfield[5] Chase [60 men.  All trebles, all in the altitudes.  Now for the disposing of parts in the morris, little or no labor will serve.

2 [COUNT.] If you that be minded to follow your leader know me—an ancient

honor belonging to our house—for a fore-horse [i' th'][6] team and fore-gallant[7] in a morris, my father's stable is not unfurnished.

3 [COUNT.] So much for the fore- [70 horse; but how for a good hobbyhorse?[8]

Y. BANK. For a hobbyhorse?  Let me see an almanac.  Midsummer moon, let me see ye.  "When the moon's in the full, then's wit in the wane."  No more.  Use your best skill; your morris will suffer an eclipse.

1 [COUNT.] An eclipse?

Y. BANK. A strange one.

2 [COUNT.] Strange?                    80

Y. BANK. Yes, and most sudden.  Remember the fore-gallant, and forget the hobbyhorse!  The whole body of your morris will be darkened.—There be of us—but 'tis no matter.  Forget the hobbyhorse!

1 [COUNT.] Cuddy Banks, have you forgot since he paced[9] it from Enfield Chase to Edmonton?  Cuddy, honest Cuddy, cast thy stuff.[10]              90

Y. BANK. Suffer may ye all!  It shall be known, I can take mine ease as well as another man.  Seek your hobbyhorse where you can get him.

1 [COUNT.] Cuddy, honest Cuddy, we confess, and are sorry for our neglect.

2 [COUNT.] The old horse shall have a new bridle.

3 [COUNT.] The caparisons new painted.

4 [COUNT.] The tail repaired.  The [100 snaffle and the bosses new saffroned o'er.[11]

1 [COUNT.] Kind—

2 [COUNT.] Honest—

3 [COUNT.] Loving, ingenious—

4 [COUNT.] Affable Cuddy.

Y. BANK. To show I am not flint, but affable, as you say, very well stuffed, a kind of warm dough or puffpaste, I relent, I connive, most affable Jack.  Let the hobbyhorse provide a strong back, [110 he shall not want a belly when I am in 'em—but [*Sees Sawyer.*]—'uds me,[12] Mother Sawyer!

---

[1] A shopping district in London.

[2] Tenor.        [3] Countertenor.

[4] Following the trail in the wrong direction.

[5] The original spelling, *Envile*, indicates the pronunciation.

[6] Added in Gifford-Dyce edn.

[7] Leader of the dancers.

[8] A performer in a morris.        [9] Danced.

[10] *I.e.*, play the part as the hobbyhorse.

[11] The original gives this sentence to the first countryman.

[12] God's me; a mild oath.

1 [COUNT.] The old witch of Edmonton!
If our mirth be not crossed—
2 [COUNT.] Bless us, Cuddy, and let her
curse her tother [1] eye out.—What dost
now?
Y. BANK. "Ungirt, unblessed," says
the proverb; but my girdle shall [120
serve [2] a riding knot; [3] and a fig for all the
witches in Christendom!—What wouldst
thou?
1 [COUNT.] The devil cannot abide to
be crossed.
2 [COUNT.] And scorns to come at any
man's whistle.
3 [COUNT.] Away—
4 [COUNT.] With the witch!
OMN[ES]. Away with the witch [130
of Edmonton! *Ex[eunt] in strange posture.*
SAWY. Still vexed? Still tortured? That
curmudgeon Banks
Is ground of all my scandal; I am
shunned
And hated like a sickness, made a scorn
To all degrees and sexes. I have heard
old beldams
Talk of familiars in the shape of mice,
Rats, ferrets, weasels, and I wot not
what,
That have appeared, and sucked, some
say, their blood;
But by what means they came ac-
quainted with them
I'm now ignorant. Would some power,
good or bad,                     140
Instruct me which way I might be re-
venged
Upon this churl, I'd go out of myself,
And give this fury leave to dwell within
This ruined cottage ready to fall with
age,
Abjure all goodness, be at hate with
prayer,
And study curses, imprecations,
Blasphemous speeches, oaths, detested
oaths,
Or anything that's ill, so I might work
Revenge upon this miser, this black
cur,
That barks and bites, and sucks the
very blood                        150
Of me and of my credit. 'Tis all one

To be a witch as to be counted one.
Vengeance, shame, ruin light upon that
canker!

*Enter Dog.*

DOG. Ho! Have I found thee cursing?
Now thou art
Mine own.
SAWY.          Thine? What art thou?
DOG.               He thou hast so often
Importuned to appear to thee, the devil.
SAWY. Bless me! The devil?
DOG. Come, do not fear; I love thee much
too well
To hurt or fright thee; if I seem terrible,
It is to such as hate me. I have
found                             160
Thy love unfeigned, have seen and
pitiéd
Thy open wrongs, and come, out of my
love,
To give thee just revenge against thy foes.
SAWY. May I believe thee?
DOG.          To confirm 't, command me
Do any mischief unto man or beast,
And I'll effect it, on condition
That, uncompelled, thou make a deed
of gift
Of soul and body to me.
SAWY.                    Out, alas!
My soul and body?
DOG.               And that instantly,
And seal it with thy blood. If thou
deniest,                          170
I'll tear thy body in a thousand pieces.
SAWY. I know not where to seek relief.
But shall I,
After such covenants sealed, see full
revenge
On all that wrong me?
DOG.               Ha, ha! Silly woman!
The devil is no liar to such as he loves.
Didst ever know or hear the devil a liar
To such as he affects?
SAWY. Then [4] I am thine; at least so
much of me
As I can call mine own.
DOG.                    Equivocations?
Art mine or no? Speak, or I'll tear—
SAWY.                    All thine. 180
DOG. Seal 't with thy blood.
*Sucks her arm. Thunder and lightning.*
See! Now I dare call thee mine!

[1] Other.        [2] *I.e.*, serve as.
[3] Running knot, slip knot, used for hanging.
Original reads *knit.*
[4] Emended by Dyce. Original reads *when.*

For proof, command me; instantly I'll
run
To any mischief; goodness can I none.
SAWY. And I desire as little. There's an
old churl,
One Banks—
DOG.       That wronged thee: he lamed
thee, called thee witch.
SAWY. The same; first upon him I'ld be
revenged.
DOG. Thou shalt; do but name how.
SAWY.                Go, touch his life.
DOG. I cannot.
SAWY. Hast thou not vowed?   Go, kill
the slave!
DOG.            I wonnot.
SAWY. I'll cancel, then, my gift.
DOG.            Ha, ha!
SAWY.                Dost laugh?  190
Why wilt not kill him?
DOG.                Fool, because I cannot.
Though we have power, know it is cir-
cumscribed
And tied in limits.  Though he be cursed
to thee,
Yet of himself he is loving to the world,
And charitable to the poor.  Now men
That, as he, love goodness, though in
smallest measure,
Live without compass of our reach.  His
cattle
And corn I'll kill and mildew; but his
life—
Until I take him, as I late found thee,
Cursing and swearing—I have no power
to touch.               200
SAWY. Work on his corn and cattle, then.
DOG.            I shall.
The witch of Edmonton shall see his
fall,
If she at least put credit in my power,
And in mine only, make orisons to me,
And none but me.
SAWY.        Say how and in what manner.
DOG. I'll tell thee.  When thou wishest
ill,
Corn, man, or beast wouldst spoil or
kill,
Turn thy back against the sun,
And mumble this short orison:
"If thou to death or shame pursue
'em,               210
Sanctibicetur nomen tuum."[1]

[1] Hallowed be thy name.

SAWY. "If thou to death or shame pur-
sue 'em,
Sanctibicetur nomen tuum."
DOG. Perfect!  Farewell.  Our first-made
promises
We'll put in execution against Banks.
                Exit.
SAWY. Contaminetur nomen tuum.[2]  I'm
an expert scholar,
Speak Latin, or I know not well what
language,
As well as the best of 'em.  But who
comes here?

Enter Y[oung] Ba[nks].

The son of my worst foe. "To death pur-
sue 'em,
Ei sanctibicetur nomen tuum."      220
Y. BANK. [Aside.] What's that she mum-
bles?   The devil's paternoster?   Would
it were else!—Mother Sawyer, good mor-
row.
SAWY. Ill morrow to thee, and all the
world that flout
A poor old woman! "To death pursue
'em,
And sanctibicetur nomen tuum."
Y. BANK.  Nay, good Gammer[3] Sawyer,
whate'er it pleases
My father to call you, I know you are—
SAWY.                A witch.
Y. BANK. A witch?  Would you were else,
i' faith!
SAWY.        Your father      230
Knows I am by this.[4]
Y. BANK.        I would he did.
SAWY. And so in time may you.
Y. BANK. I would I might else!  But,
witch or no witch, you are a motherly
woman, and, though my father be a kind
of God-bless-us, as they say, I have an
earnest suit to you; and, if you'll be so
kind to ka me one good turn, I'll be so
courteous as to kob you another.[5]
SAWY. What's that? To spurn, beat me,
and call me witch,      240
As your kind father doth?
Y. BANK.  My father?  I am ashamed
to own him.  If he has hurt the head of thy
credit, there's money to buy thee a plaster.
[Gives money.]  And a small courtesy I
would require at thy hands.

[2] Cursed be thy name.   [4] I.e., by this time.
[3] Old woman.   [5] Serve me, and I'll serve you.

SAWY. You seem a good young man, and—
    [*Aside.*] I must dissemble,
The better to accomplish my revenge.—
But—for this silver, what wouldst have
    me do?
Bewitch thee?                                    250
Y. BANK. No, by no means; I am be-
witched already. I would have thee so
good as to unwitch me, or witch another
with me for company.
SAWY. I understand thee not; be plain,
    my son.
Y. BANK. As a pikestaff, mother. You
know Kate Carter?
SAWY. The wealthy yeoman's daughter?
    What of her?
Y. BANK. That same party has be-
witched me.                                      260
SAWY. Bewitched thee?
Y. BANK. Bewitched me, *hisce auribus.*[1]
I saw a little devil fly out of her eye like
a burbolt,[2] which sticks at this hour up
to the feathers in my heart. Now, my request is, to send one of thy what-d'ye-
call-'ems either to pluck that out, or stick
another as fast in hers. Do, and here's
my hand; I am thine for three lives.
SAWY. [*Aside.*] We shall have sport.—
    Thou art in love with her?              270
Y. BANK. Up to the very hilts, mother.
SAWY. And thou'ldst have me make her
love thee too?
Y. BANK. [*Aside.*] I think she'll prove
a witch in earnest.—Yes, I could find in
my heart to strike her three-quarters deep
in love with me too.
SAWY. But dost thou think that I can
    do 't, and I alone?
Y. BANK. Truly, Mother Witch, I do
verily believe so; and, when I see it done,
I shall be half persuaded so too.       280
SAWY. It's enough. What art can do be
    sure of.
Turn to the west, and, whatsoe'er thou
    hearest
Or seest, stand silent, and be not afraid.

*She stamps. Enter the Dog. He fawns and
                    leaps upon her.*

Y. BANK. Afraid, Mother  Witch?—
[*Aside.*] Turn my face to the west? I

said I should always have a backfriend[3]
of her; and now it's out. And[4] her little
devil should be hungry, come sneaking behind me, like a cowardly catchpole,[5] and
clap his talents[6] on my haunches!—   [290
'Tis woundy[7] cold, sure.—[*Aside.*] I dud-
der[8] and shake like an aspen leaf, every
joint of me.
SAWY. "To scandal and disgrace pursue
    'em,
    *Et sanctibicetur nomen tuum." Exit Dog.*
    How now, my son, how is 't?
Y. BANK. Scarce in a clean life, Mother
Witch. But did your goblin and you spout
Latin together?
SAWY. A kind of charm I work by. Didst
    thou hear me?                              300
Y. BANK. I heard I know not the devil
what mumble in a scurvy bass tone, like
a drum that had taken cold in the head
the last muster. Very comfortable words;
what were they? And who taught them
you?
SAWY. A great learned man.
Y. BANK. Learned man? Learned devil,
it was as soon! But what? What comfortable news about the party?         310
SAWY. Who? Kate Carter? I'll tell
thee. Thou know'st the stile at the west
end of thy father's peasfield. Be there
tomorrow night after sunset, and the first
live thing thou seest be sure to follow, and
that shall bring thee to thy love.
Y. BANK. In the peasfield? Has she
a mind to codlings[9] already? The first
living thing I meet, you say, shall bring
me to her?                                       320
SAWY. To a sight of her, I mean. She
will seem wantonly coy, and flee thee;
but follow her close and boldly. Do but
embrace her in thy arms once, and she is
thine own.
Y. BANK. At the stile at the west end
of my father's peasland, the first live thing
I see, follow and embrace her, and she
shall be thine. Nay, and I come to embracing once, she shall be mine; I'll   [330
go near to make at eaglet[10] else.   *Exit.*

---

[1] By these ears.
[2] Blunt-headed arrow.

[3] This word meant both *supporter* and *secret
enemy.*
[4] If.
[5] Sheriff's officer.
[6] Talons.
[7] Extremely.
[8] Dodder, shiver.
[9] Green peas, with a pun on *cuddlings.*
[10] Probably a term from some game of the
period.

ŠAWY. A ball well bandied! Now the set's half won.

The father's wrong I'll wreak upon the son.                                     *Exit.*

### Scen[a] ii.

*[Old Carter's house.]*

*Enter Carter, Warbeck, Somerton.*

[O.] CART. How now, gentlemen! Cloudy? I know, Mr. Warbeck, you are in a fog about my daughter's marriage.

WARB. And can you blame me, sir?

[O.] CART. Nor you me justly. Wedding and hanging are tied up both in a proverb; and destiny is the juggler that unties the knot. My hope is you are reserved to a richer fortune than my poor daughter.

WARB. However, your promise—          10

[O.] CART. Is a kind of debt, I confess it.

WARB. Which honest men should pay.

[O.] CART. Yet some gentlemen break in that point now and then, by your leave, sir.

SOM. I confess thou hast had a little wrong in the wench; but patience is the only salve to cure it. Since Thorney has won the wench, he has most reason to wear her.          20

WARB. Love in this kind admits no reason to wear her.

[O.] CART. Then Love's a fool, and what wise man will take exception?

SOM. Come, frolic Ned, were every man master of his own fortune, Fate might pick straws, and Destiny go a-woolgathering.

WARB. You hold yours in a string, though. 'Tis well; but, if there be any [30 equity, look thou to meet the like usage ere long.

SOM. In my love to her sister Katherine? Indeed, they are a pair of arrows drawn out of one quiver, and should fly at an even length, if she do run after her sister.

WARB. Look for the same mercy at my hands as I have received at thine.

SOM. She'll keep a surer compass; I have too strong a confidence to mistrust her.          40

WARB. And that confidence is a wind that has blown many a married man ashore at Cuckold's Haven, I can tell you; I wish yours more prosperous though.

[O.] CART. Whate'er you wish, I'll master my promise to him.

WARB. Yes, as you did to me.

[O.] CART. No more of that, if you love me. But for the more assurance, the next offered occasion shall consummate the [50 marriage; and that once sealed—

*Enter Young Thorney and Susan [, and stand aside].*

SOM. Leave the manage of the rest to my care. But see, the bridegroom and bride comes—the new pair of Sheffield knives, fitted both to one sheath.

WARB. The sheath might have been better fitted, if somebody had their due. But—

[O.] CART. No harsh language, if thou lovest me. Frank Thorney has done—          [60

WARB. No more than I, or thou, or any man, things so standing, would have attempted.

SOM. Good morrow, Mr. Bridegroom.

WARB. Come, give thee joy. Mayst thou live long and happy in thy fair choice!

Y. THOR. I thank ye, gentlemen. Kind Mr. Warbeck, I find you loving.

WARB. Thorney, that creature (much good do thee with her!)—

Virtue and beauty hold fair mixture in her;          70

She's rich, no doubt, in both. Yet were she fairer,

Thou art right worthy of her. Love her, Thorney.

'Tis nobleness in thee; in her but duty.

The match is fair and equal; the success I leave to censure.[1] Farewell, Mrs. Bride!

Till now elected, thy old scorn deride.

                                     *Exit.*

SOM. Good Mr. Thorney—

[O.] CART. Nay, you shall not part till you see the barrels run atilt, gentlemen.

                    *Exit [with Somerton].*

SUS. Why change you your face, [80 sweetheart?

Y. THOR. Who, I? For nothing.

SUS. Dear, say not so; a spirit of your constancy cannot endure this change for nothing. I have observed strange variations in you.

Y. THOR. In me?

[1] Judgment.

Sus. In you, sir. Awake, you seem to dream, and in your sleep you utter sudden and distracted accents, like one at en-  [90 mity with peace. Dear loving husband, if I
  May dare to challenge any interest in you,
  Give me the reason fully; you may trust
  My breast as safely as your own.
Y. Thor.                          With what?
  You half amaze me; prithee—
Sus.                    Come, you shall not,
  Indeed you shall not, shut me from partaking
  The least dislike that grieves you; I am all yours.
Y. Thor. And I all thine.
Sus.                You are not, if you keep
  The least grief from me. But I find the cause;
  It grew from me.
Y. Thor.        From you?
Sus.                From some distaste  100
  In me or my behavior; you are not kind
  In the concealment. 'Las, sir, I am young,
  Silly, and plain; more, strange to those contents
  A wife should offer. Say but in what I fail,
  I'll study satisfaction.
Y. Thor.                    Come, in nothing.
Sus. I know I do; knew I as well in what,
  You should not long be sullen. Prithee, love,
  If I have been immodest or too bold,
  Speak 't in a frown; if peevishly too nice,
  Show 't in a smile. Thy liking is the glass
  By which I'll habit my behavior.      111
Y. Thor. Wherefore dost weep now?
Sus.                You, sweet, have the power
  To make me passionate as an April day—
  Now smile, then weep; now pale, then crimson red.
  You are the powerful moon of my blood's sea,
  To make it ebb or flow into my face,
  As your looks change.
Y. Thor.     Change thy conceit,[1] I prithee.
  Thou art all perfection: Diana herself
  Swells in thy thoughts and moderates thy beauty.                         119

[1] Figure of speech.

Within thy left eye amorous Cupid sits,
Feathering love shafts, whose golden heads he dipped
In thy chaste breast; in the other lies
Blushing Adonis scarfed in modesties;
And, still as wanton Cupid blows love fires,
Adonis quenches out unchaste desires;
And from these two I briefly do imply
A perfect emblem of thy modesty.
Then, prithee, dear, maintain no more dispute,
For, where thou speak'st, it's fit all tongues be mute.
Sus. Come, come, those golden strings of flattery                              130
  Shall not tie up my speech, sir; I must know
  The ground of your disturbance.
Y. Thor.                Then look here,
  For here, here is the fen in which this hydra
  Of discontent grows rank.
Sus.                Heaven shield it! Where?
Y. Thor. In mine own bosom; here the cause has root.
  The poisoned leeches twist about my heart,
  And will, I hope, confound me.
Sus.                You speak riddles.
Y. Thor. Take 't plainly, then. 'Twas told me by a woman
  Known and approved in palmistry,
  I should have two wives.
Sus.        Two wives? Sir, I take it   140
  Exceeding likely; but let not conceit
  Hurt you. You are afraid to bury me?
Y. Thor. No, no, my Winnifride.
Sus. How say you? Winnifride? You forget me.
Y. Thor. No, I forget myself, Susan.
Sus.                          In what?
Y. Thor. Talking of wives, I pretend Winnifride,
  A maid that at my mother's waited on me
  Before thyself.
Sus.            I hope, sir, she may live
  To take my place. But why should all this move you?
Y. Thor. [Aside.] The poor girl! She has 't before thee,                      150
  And that's the fiend torments me.
Sus.                    Yet why should this

Raise mutiny within you? Such presages
Prove often false. Or say it should be
true?
Y. Thor. That I should have another wife?
Sus.                          Yes, many;
If they be good, the better.
Y. Thor.                     Never any
Equal to thee in goodness.
Sus. Sir, I could wish I were much better
for you,
Yet, if I knew your fate
Ordained you for another, I could wish—
So well I love you and your hopeful
pleasure—                              160
Me in my grave, and my poor virtues
added
To my successor.
Y. Thor.          Prithee, prithee, talk not
Of death or graves; thou art so rare a
goodness
As Death would rather put itself to
death
Than murther thee. But we, as all
things else,
Are mutable and changing.
Sus.                      Yet you still move
In your first sphere of discontent. Sweet,
chase
Those clouds of sorrow, and shine clearly
on me.
Y. Thor. At my return I will.
Sus.                      Return? Ah me!
Will you, then, leave me?
Y. Thor.          For a time I must.   170
But how? As birds their young, or
loving bees
Their hives, to fetch home richer dain-
ties.
Sus.          Leave me?
Now has my fear met its effect. You
shall not;
Cost it my life, you shall not.
Y. Thor.          Why? Your reason?
Sus. Like to the lapwing have you all
this while
With your false love deluded me, pre-
tending
Counterfeit senses for your discontent;
And now at last it is by chance stole
from you.
Y. Thor. What? What by chance?
Sus.          Your preappointed meeting
Of single combat with young Warbeck.
Y. Thor.                      Ha!   180

Sus. Even so. Dissemble not; 'tis too
apparent.
Then in his look I read it. Deny it not;
I see 't apparent. Cost it my undoing,
And unto that my life, I will not leave
you.
Y. Thor. Not until when?
Sus.          Till he and you be friends.
Was this your cunning? And then flam
me off
With an old witch, two wives, and
Winnifride?
Y 'are not so kind, indeed, as I imagined.
Y. Thor. [Aside.] And you more fond [1]
by far than I expected.   189
It is a virtue that attends thy kind.—
But of our business within. And, by
this kiss,
I'll anger thee no more; troth, chuck,
I will not.
Sus. You shall have no just cause.
Y. Thor.          Dear Sue, I shall not.
                                   Exeunt.

Act[us] III. Scen[a] i.

[The village green in Edmonton.]

Enter Cuddy Banks and Morris Dancers.

1 [Dan.] Nay, Cuddy, prithee, do not
leave us now; if we part all this night, we
shall not meet before day.

2 [2] [Dan.] I prithee, Banks, let's keep
together now.

Clow.[3] If you were wise, a word would
serve; but, as you are, I must be forced to
tell you again, I have a little private business, an hour's work. It may prove but an
half hour's, as luck may serve: and [10
then I take horse, and along with you.
Have we e'er a witch in the morris?

1 [Dan.] No, no; no woman's part but
Maid Marian and the hobbyhorse.

Clow. I'll have a witch; I love a witch.

1 [Dan.] Faith, witches themselves are
so common nowadays that the counterfeit
will not be regarded. They say we have
three or four in Edmonton besides Mother
Sawyer.   20

2 [Dan.] I would she would dance her
part with us.

[1] With a pun on the meaning *foolish*.
[2] Original reads *1*.
[3] *I.e.. Clown*, previously *Young Banks*.

3 [Dan.] So would not I, for, if she comes, the devil and all comes along with her.

Clow. Well, I'll have a witch; I have loved a witch ever since I played at cherry pit.[1] Leave me, and get my horse dressed. Give him oats; but water him not till I come. Whither do we foot it first?  30

2 [Dan.] To Sir Arthur Clarington's first; then whither thou wilt.

Clow. Well, I am content. But we must up to Carter's, the rich yeoman; I must be seen on hobbyhorse there.

1 [Dan.] O, I smell him now! I'll lay my ears Banks is in love, and that's the reason he would walk melancholy by himself.

Clow. Ha! Who was that said I [40 was in love?

1 [Dan.] Not I.

2 [Dan.] Nor I.

Clow. Go to, no more of that. When I understand what you speak, I know what you say; believe that.

1 [Dan.] Well, 'twas I; I'll not deny it. I meant no hurt in 't. I have seen you walk up to Carter's of Chessum. Banks, were not you there last Shrovetide?  50

Clow. Yes, I was ten days together there the last Shrovetide.

2 [Dan.] How could that be, when there are but seven days in the week?

Clow. Prithee, peace! I reckon *stila nova*[2] as a traveler; thou understandest as a freshwater farmer that never sawest a week beyond sea. Ask any soldier that ever received his pay but in the Low Countries, and he'll tell thee there are eight days [60 in the week there hard by. How dost thou think they rise in High Germany, Italy, and those remoter places?

3 [Dan.] Ay, but simply there are but seven days in the week yet.

Clow. No, simply as thou understandest. Prithee, look but in the lover's almanac. When he has been but three days absent, "O," says he, "I have not seen my love these seven years." There's a long [70 cut! When he comes to her again and embraces her, "O," says he, "now methinks I am in heaven." And that's a pretty step! He that can get up to heaven in ten days

need not repent his journey; you may ride a hundred days in a caroche,[3] and be further off than when you set forth. But, I pray you, good morris mates, now leave me. I will be with you by midnight.

1 [Dan.] Well, since he will be [80 alone, we'll back again and trouble him no more.

Omn[es]. But remember, Banks.

Clow. The hobbyhorse shall be remembered. But hark you; get Poldavis, the barber's boy, for the witch, because he can show his art better than another.—

*Exeunt [All but Clown].*

Well, now to my walk. I am near the place where I should meet—I know not what. Say I meet a thief, I must follow him, [90 if to the gallows; say I meet a horse, or hare, or hound, still I must follow. Some slow-paced beast, I hope. Yet love is full of lightness in the heaviest lovers. Ha! My guide is come.

*[Enter the Dog.]*

A water dog! I am thy first man, sculler; I go with thee; ply no other but myself. Away with the boat! Land me but at Katherine's Dock, my sweet Katherine's Dock, and I'll be a fare to thee. [100 That way? Nay, which way thou wilt; thou know'st the way better than I. Fine, gentle cur it is, and well brought up, I warrant him. We go a-ducking, spaniel; thou shalt fetch me the ducks, pretty, kind rascal.

*Enter Spirit in shape of Katherine, vizarded,*
*and takes it[4] off.*

Spir. [*Aside.*] Thus throw I off mine own
    essential horror,
And take the shape of a sweet, lovely
    maid
Whom this fool dotes on. We can meet
    his folly,  109
But from his virtues must be runaways.
We'll sport with him; but, when we
    reckoning call,
We know where to receive; th' witch
    pays for all.  *Dog barks.*

Clow. Ay? Is that the watchword? She's come. Well, if ever we be married,

---

[1] A children's game.

[2] According to the new style of dating.

[3] Coach.

[4] *I.e.*, his vizard, or natural appearance.

it shall be at Barking Church, in memory of thee. Now come behind, kind cur.

And have I met thee, sweet Kate?
I will teach thee to walk so late.

O, see, we meet in meter. [*The Spirit moves away.*] What! Dost thou trip from [120 me? O, that I were upon my hobbyhorse; I 'would mount after thee so nimble! "Stay, nymph; stay, nymph," singed Apollo.

" Tarry and kiss me. Sweet nymph, stay!
Tarry and kiss me, sweet."

We will to Chessum Street, and then to the house stands in the highway.—Nay, by your leave, I must embrace you.
*Ex*[*eunt*] *Spir*[*it*] *and Banks.*
[*Within.*] O, help, help! I am drowned, I am drowned!    *Enter wet.* [130
Dog. Ha, ha, ha, ha!
Clow. This was an ill night to go a-wooing in. I find it now in Pond's almanac. Thinking to land at Katherine's Dock, I was almost at Gravesend. I'll never go to a wench in the dog days again; yet 'tis cool enough.—Had you never a paw in this dog-trick? A mangie [1] take that black hide of yours! I'll throw you in at Limehouse in some tanner's pit or other.    140
Dog. Ha, ha, ha, ha!
Clow. How now! Who's that laughs at me? Hist to him!—(*Dog barks.*) Peace, peace! Thou didst but thy kind [2] neither; 'twas my own fault.
Dog. Take heed how thou trustest the devil another time.
Clow. How now! Who's that speaks? I hope you have not your reading tongue about you.    150
Dog. Yes, I can speak.
Clow. The devil you can! You have read Æsop's fables, then; I have played one of your parts then—the dog that catched at the shadow in the water. Pray you, let me catechize you a little. What might one call your name, dog?
Dog. My dame calls me Tom.
Clow. 'Tis well, and she may call me Ass; so there's an whole one betwixt [160 us, Tom-Ass. She said I should follow you, indeed. Well, Tom, give me thy fist; we

are friends. You shall be mine ingle. [3] I love you, but, I pray you, let's have no more of these ducking devices.
Dog. Not, if you love me. Dogs love where they are beloved; cherish me, and I'll do anything for thee.
Clow. Well, you shall have jowls and livers; I have butchers to my friends [170 that shall bestow 'em. And I will keep crusts and bones for you, if you'll be a kind dog, Tom.
Dog. Anything; I'll help thee to thy love.
Clow. Wilt thou? That promise shall cost me a brown loaf, though I steal it out of my father's cupboard. You'll eat stolen goods, Tom, will you not?
Dog. O, best of all; the sweetest [180 bits those.
Clow. You shall not starve, ningle [4] Tom; believe that. If you love fish, I'll help you to maids [5] and soles; I'm acquainted with a fishmonger.
Dog. Maids and soles? O, sweet bits! Banqueting stuff those.
Clow. One thing I would request you, ningle, as you have played the knavish cur with me a little, that you would [190 mingle amongst our morris dancers in the morning. You can dance?
Dog. Yes, yes, anything; I'll be there, but unseen to any but thyself. Get thee gone before; fear not my presence. I have work tonight; I serve more masters, more dames, than one.
Clow. He can serve Mammon and the devil too.
Dog. It shall concern thee and thy love's purchase.    200
There's a gallant rival loves the maid, And likely is to have her. Mark what a mischief,
Before the morris ends, shall light on him!
Clow. O, sweet ningle, thy neuf [6] once again; friends must part for a time. Farewell, with this remembrance; shalt have bread too when we meet again. If ever there were an honest devil, 'twill be the devil of Edmonton, I see. Farewell, Tom; I prithee, dog[7] me as soon as thou canst. [210
*Ex*[*it*] *Banks.*

---

[1] Mange.    [2] *I.e.*, according to thy nature.

[3] Crony.    [4] *I.e.*, mine ingle.
[5] Female skates.    [6] Fist.    [7] Follow.

Dog. I'll not miss thee, and be merry
with thee.
Those that are joys denied must take
delight
In sins and mischiefs; 'tis the devil's
right.  *Ex[it] Dog.*

[Scena ii.

*The neighborhood of Edmonton.*]

*Enter Young Thorney, Winnifride as a boy.*

Frank. Prithee, no more! Those tears
give nourishment
To weeds and briers in me, which shortly
will
O'ergrow and top my head; my shame
will sit
And cover all that can be seen of me.
Win. I have not shown this cheek in
company.
Pardon me now. Thus singled with
yourself,
It calls a thousand sorrows round about,
Some going before, and some on either
side,
But infinite behind, all chained together.
Your second adulterous marriage leads;
That's the sad eclipse—th' effects must
follow,                                    11
As plagues of shame, spite, scorn, and
obloquy.
Y. Thor. Why, hast thou not left one
hour's patience
To add to all the rest? One hour bears us
Beyond the reach of all these enemies.
Are we not now set forward in the flight,
Provided with the dowry of my sin
To keep us in some other nation?
While we together are, we are at home
In any place.
Win.          'Tis foul, ill-gotten coin,  20
Far worse than usury or extortion.
Y. Thor. Let my father, then, make the
restitution,
Who forced me take the bribe. It is his
gift
And patrimony to me; so I receive it.
He would not bless, nor look a father on
me,
Until I satisfied his angry will.
When I was sold, I sold myself again—
Some knaves have done 't in lands, and I
in body—

For money, and I have the hire. But,
sweet, no more;                            29
'Tis hazard of discovery, our discourse;
And then prevention takes off all our
hopes.
For only but to take her leave of me
My wife is coming.
Win.          Who coming? Your wife?
Y. Thor. No, no; thou art here. The
woman—I knew
Not how to call her now; but after this
day
She shall be quite forgot and have no
name
In my remembrance. See, see! She's
come.

*Enter Susan.*

Go lead
The horses to the hill's top; there I'll
meet thee.
Sus. Nay, with your favor let him stay a
little;
I would part with him too, because he
is                                         40
Your sole companion; and I'll begin with
him,
Reserving you the last.
Y. Thor.          Ay, with all my heart.
Sus. You may hear, if it please you, sir.
Y. Thor.          No, 'tis not fit.
Some rudiments, I conceive, they must
be,
To overlook my slippery footings. And
so—
Sus. No, indeed, sir.
Y. Thor.          Tush, I know it must be so,
And 'tis necessary. On! But be brief.
                              [*Walks forward.*]
Win. What charge soe'er you lay upon
me, mistress,
I shall support it faithfully—being hon-
est—
To my best strength.
Sus.          Believe 't shall be no other.  50
I know you were commended to my hus-
band
By a noble knight.
Win.          O, gods! O, mine eyes!
Sus. How now! What ail'st thou, lad?
Win. Something hit mine eye—it makes it
water still—
Even as you said "commended to my
husband."

Some dor [1] I think it was. I was, for-
sooth,
Commended to him by Sir Arthur Clar-
ington.
Sus. Whose servant once my Thorney was
himself.
That title, methinks, should make you
almost fellows,
Or at the least much more than a ser-
vant;                                        60
And I am sure he will respect you so.
Your love to him, then, needs no spur
from me,
And what for my sake you will ever do,
'Tis fit it should be bought with some-
thing more
Than fair entreats. Look, here's a jewel
for thee,
A pretty, wanton label for thine ear;
And I would have it hang there, still to
whisper
These words to thee, "Thou hast my
jewel with thee."
It is but earnest of a larger bounty,
When thou return'st with praises of thy
service,                                     70
Which I am confident thou wilt deserve.
Why, thou art many now besides thyself:
Thou mayst be servant, friend, and wife
to him;
A good wife is, then, all. A friend can
play
The wife and servant's part, and shift
enough;
No less the servant can the friend and
wife.
'Tis all but sweet society, good counsel,
Interchanged loves, yes, and counsel-
keeping.
Y. Thor. Not done yet?
Sus. Even now, sir.                          80
Win. Mistress, believe my vow; your
severe eye,
Were it present to command, your boun-
teous hand,
Were it then by to buy or bribe my
service,
Shall not make me more dear or near
unto him
Than I shall voluntary. I'll be all your
charge,
Servant, friend, wife to him.
Sus.                            Wilt thou?

<hr>

[1] Beetle.

Now blessings go with thee for 't! Cour-
tesies
Shall meet thee coming home.
Win.                    Pray you, say plainly,
Mistress, are you jealous of him? If you
be,
I'll look to him that way too.
Sus.                        Say'st thou so?  90
I would thou hadst a woman's bosom
now;
We have weak thoughts within us. Alas,
There's nothing so strong in us as sus-
picion;
But I dare not, nay, I will not think
So hardly of my Thorney.
Win.                    Believe it, mistress,
I'll be no pander to him; and, if I find
Any loose, lubric[2] scapes[3] in him, I'll
watch him,
And at my return protest I'll show you
all.
He shall hardly offend without my
knowledge.                                   99
Sus. Thine own diligence is that I press,
And not the curious eye over his faults.
Farewell. If I should never see thee more,
Take it forever.
Y. Thor. (Gives his sword.) Prithee, take
that along with thee, and haste thee
To the hill's top; I'll be there instantly.
                          Ex[it] Win[nifride].
Sus. No haste, I prithee; slowly as thou
canst.
Pray, let him obey me now; 'tis happily
His last service to me. My power is
e'en
A-going out of sight.
Y. Thor.              Why would you delay?
We have no other business now but to
part.                                        110
Sus. And will not that, sweetheart, ask a
long time?
Methinks it is the hardest piece of work
That e'er I took in hand.
Y. Thor.                    Fie, fie! Why, look,
I'll make it plain and easy to you—
farewell!                          Kisses.
Sus. Ah, 'las, I am not half perfect in it
yet;
I must have it read over an hundred
times.
Pray you, take some pains; I confess my
dullness.

<hr>

[2] Lubricous, lascivious.    [3] Misdemeanors.

Y. Thor. [*Aside.*] What a thorn this rose
　　grows on! Parting were sweet;
　But what a trouble 'twill be to obtain
　　it!—
　Come, again and again, farewell!—
　　(*Kisses.*) Yet wilt return?          120
　All questions of my journey, my stay,
　　employment,
　And revisitation, fully I have answered
　　all.
　There's nothing now behind but—
　　nothing.
Sus.　　　　　And
　That "nothing" is more hard than any-
　　thing,
　Than all the everythings. This request—
Y. Thor.　　　　　　What is it?
Sus. That I may bring you through one
　　pasture more
　Up to yon knot of trees; amongst those
　　shadows
　I'll vanish from you—they shall teach
　　me how.
Y. Thor. Why, 'tis granted; come, walk,
　　then.
Sus.　　　Nay, not too fast.
　They say slow things have best perfec-
　　tion;          130
　The gentle shower wets to fertility,
　The churlish storm may mischief with
　　his bounty;
　The baser beasts take strength even from
　　the womb,
　But the lord lion's whelp is feeble long.
　　　　　　　　　　　　　*Exeunt.*

[Scena iii.

*A field with a small grove.*]

*Enter Dog.*[1]

Dog. Now for an early mischief and a
　　sudden!
　The mind's about it now; one touch from
　　me
　Soon sets the body forward.

*Enter Young Thorney, Susan.*

Y. Thor. Your request is out; yet will you
　　leave me?
Sus. What? So churlishly? You'll make
　　me stay forever
　Rather than part with such a sound from
　　you.

[1] The Dog is, of course, invisible to all but the
audience.

Y. Thor. Why, you almost anger me.
　　Pray you, begone.
　You have no company, and 'tis very
　　early;
　Some hurt may betide you homewards.
Sus.　　　　　Tush! I fear none;
　To leave you is the greatest hurt I can
　　suffer.          10
　Besides, I expect your father and mine
　　own
　To meet me back, or overtake me with
　　you.
　They began to stir when I came after you.
　I know they'll not be long.
Y. Thor. [*Aside.*] So! I shall have more
　　trouble. (*Dog rubs him.*) Thank you
　　for that.
　Then I'll ease all at once. 'Tis done
　　now—
　What I ne'er thought on.—You shall not
　　go back.
Sus. Why, shall I go along with thee?
　　Sweet music!
Y. Thor. No, to a better place.
Sus.　　　　　Any place I;
　I'm there at home where thou pleasest to
　　have me.          20
Y. Thor. At home? I'll leave you in your
　　last lodging;
　I must kill you.
Sus.　　　O, fine! You'ld fright me from
　　you.
Y. Thor. You see I had no purpose; I'm
　　unarmed;
　'Tis this minute's decree, and it must be.
　Look, this will serve your turn.
　　　　　　　　　　　　[*Draws a knife.*]
Sus.　　　　　I'll not turn from it,
　If you be ear[ne]st, sir; yet you may tell
　　me
　Wherefore you'll kill me.
Y. Thor.　　　Because you are a whore.
Sus. There's one deep wound already. A
　　whore!
　'Twas ever further from me than the
　　thought
　Of this black hour. A whore?
Y. Thor.　　　Yes, I'll prove it,          30
　And you shall confess it. You are my
　　whore—
　No wife of mine; the word admits no
　　second.
　I was before wedded to another, have her
　　still.

I do not lay the sin unto your charge;
'Tis all mine own. Your marriage was
  my theft,
For I espoused your dowry, and I have
  it.
I did not purpose to have added mur-
  ther;
The devil did not prompt me. Till this
  minute
You might have safe returned; now you
  cannot.
You have dogged your own death.
                         *Stabs her.*

Sus.             And I deserve it;   40
I'm glad my fate was so intelligent.[1]
'Twas some good spirit's motion. Die?
  O, 'twas time!
How many years might I have slept in
  sin,
Sin of my most hatred, too, adultery?
Y. THOR. Nay, sure, 'twas likely that the
  most was past,
For I meant never to return to you
After this parting.
Sus.       Why, then, I thank you more.
You have done lovingly, leaving yourself,
That you would thus bestow me on
  another.
Thou art my husband, Death, and I em-
  brace thee                     50
With all the love I have. Forget the stain
Of my unwitting sin; and then I come
A crystal virgin to thee. My soul's purity
Shall with bold wings ascend the doors
  of Mercy,
For Innocence is ever her companion.
Y. THOR. Not yet mortal? I would not
  linger you,
Or leave you a tongue to blab.
                       *[Stabs her again.]*
Sus. Now heaven reward you ne'er the
  worse for me!
I did not think that Death had been so
  sweet,
Nor I so apt to love him. I could ne'er
  die better,                     60
Had I stayed forty years for preparation,
For I'm in charity with all the world.
Let me for once be thine example,
  heaven;
Do to this man as I him free forgive,
And may he better die and better live.
                       *Moritur.*[2]

[1] Communicative.          [2] She dies.

Y. THOR. 'Tis done; and I am in! Once
  past our height,
We scorn the deep'st abyss. This follows
  now,
To hele [3] her wounds by dressing of the
  weapon.
Arms, thighs, hands, any place; we musт
  not fail                 *Wounds himself.*
Light scratches, giving such deep ones.
  The best I can                 70
To bind myself to this tree. Now's the
  storm,
Which if blown o'er, many fair days may
  follow.                   *Dog ties him.*
So, so, I'm fast; I did not think I could
Have done so well behind me. How
  prosperous
And effectual mischief sometimes isſ
  Help! Help!
Murther, murther, murther!

*Enter Carter and Old Thorney.*

[O.] CART. Ha! Whom tolls the bell for?
Y. THOR.          O, O!
O. THOR.              Ah me!
The cause appears too soon. My child,
  my son!
[O.] CART. Susan, girl, child! Not speak
  to thy father? Ha!
Y. THOR. O, lend me some assistance to
  o'ertake                     80
This hapless woman.
O. THOR.      Let's o'ertake the murtherers.
Speak whilst thou canst; anon may be too
  late.
I fear thou hast death's mark upon thee
  too.
Y. THOR. I know them both; yet such an
  oath is passed
As pulls damnation up if it be broke.
I dare not name 'em. Think what forced
  men do.
O. THOR. Keep oath with murtherers?
  That were a conscience
To hold the devil iɪ.
Y. THOR.      Nay, sir, I can describe 'em,
Shall show them as familiar as their
  names.                     89
The taller of the two at this time wears
His satin doublet white, but crimson-
  lined,
Hose of black satin, cloak of scarlet—

[3] *I.e.,* conceal the source of.

O. Thor.                 Warbeck,
  Warbeck, Warbeck!—Do you list to this,
    sir?

[O.] Cart. Yes, yes, I listen you; here's
  nothing to be heard.

Y. Thor. Th' other's cloak branched [1] velvet, black, velvet-lined his suit.

O. Thor. I have 'em already. Somerton,
  Somerton!
  Binal [2] revenge all this. Come, sir, the
    first work
  Is to pursue the murtherers, when we
    have
  Removed these mangled bodies hence.

[O.] Cart. Sir, take that carcass there,
  and give me this.            100
  I'll not own her now; she's none of mine.
  Bob [3] me off with a dumb show? No, I'll
    have life.
  This is my son too, and, while there's life
    in him,
  'Tis half mine; take you half that silence
    for 't.—
  When I speak, I look to be spoken to.
  Forgetful slut!

O. Thor.          Alas, what grief may do
  now!—
  Look, sir, I'll take this load of sorrow
    with me.

[O.] Cart. Ay, do, and I'll have this.—[Exit
  Old Thorney, carrying Susan.] How do
  you, sir?

Y. Thor. O, very ill, sir.

[O.] Cart. Yes, I think so; but 'tis well
  you can speak yet.            110
  There's no music but in sound; sound it
    must be.
  I have not wept these twenty years be-
    fore,
  And that I guess was ere that girl was
    born;
  Yet now methinks, if I but knew the way,
  My heart's so full I could weep night and
    day.                  *Exeunt.*

[Scena iv.
*Before Sir Arthur Clarington's house.*]

*Enter Sir Arthur Clarington, Warbeck,*
                 *Somerton.*

Sir Art. Come, gentlemen, we must all
  help to grace
The nimble-footed youth of Edmonton,

That are so kind
To call us up today with an high morris.

Warb. I could wish it for the best it
were the worst now. Absurdity's in my
opinion ever the best dancer in a morris.

Som. I could rather sleep than see 'em.

Sir Art. Not well, sir?

Som. Faith, not ever thus leaden;   [10
yet I know no cause for 't.

Warb. Now am I beyond mine own
condition highly disposed to mirth.

Sir Art. Well, you may have yet a morris
  to help both:
To strike you in a dump, and make him
  merry.

*Enter Fiddler and Morris, all but Banks.*

Fiddl. Come, will you set yourselves
in morris ray? [4] The fore-bell, second bell,
tenor, and great bell; Maid Marian for the
same bell. But where's the weathercock
now? The hobbyhorse?          20

1 [Dan.] Is not Banks come yet? What
a spite 'tis!

Sir Art. When set you forward, gentlemen?

1 [Dan.] We stay but for the hobbyhorse, sir; all our footmen are ready.

Som. 'Tis marvel your horse should be
behind your foot.

2 [Dan.] Yes, sir, he goes further about;
we can come in at the wicket, but the   [30
broad gate must be opened for him.

*Enter Banks, Hobbyhorse, and Dog.*

Sir Art. O, we stayed for you, sir.

Clow. Only my horse wanted a shoe,
sir; but we shall make you amends ere we
part.

Sir Art. Ay? Well said. Make 'em drink
  ere they begin.

*Ent[er] Serv[ants] with beer.*

Clow. A bowl, I prithee, and a little for
my horse; he'll mount the better. Nay,
give me. I must drink to him; he'll not
pledge else.—[Drinks.] Here, hobby.   [40
(*Holds him the bowl.*) I pray you. No? Not
drink?—You see, gentlemen, we can but
bring our horse to the water; he may
choose whether he'll drink or no.

---

[1] Embroidered with a figured pattern.
[2] Twofold.                        [3] Deceive.
[4] Array.

Som. A good moral made plain by history.

1 [Dan.] Strike up, Father Sawgut, strike up.

Fiddl. E'en when you will, children. Now in the name of the best foot for- [50 ward!—[*The fiddle makes no sound.*] How now! Not a word in thy guts? I think, children, my instrument has caught cold on the sudden.

Clow. [*Aside.*] My ningle's knavery; black Tom's doing.

Omn[es]. Why, what mean you, Father Sawgut?

Clow. Why, what would you have him do? You hear his fiddle is speechless.    60

Fiddl. I'll lay mine ear to my instrument that my poor fiddle is bewitched. I played "The Flowers in May" e'en now, as sweet as a violet; now 'twill not go against the hair. You see I can make no more music than a beetle of a cow turd.

Clow. Let me see, Father Sawgut. [*Takes the fiddle.*] Say once you had a brave hobbyhorse that you were beholding [1] to. I'll play and dance too.—Ningle, [70 away with it.

*Dog plays the morris, which ended, enter a Constable and Officers.*

Omn[es]. Ay, marry, sir!

Con. Away with jollity! 'Tis too sad an hour.—

Sir Arthur Clarington, your own assistance,

In the king's name, I charge, for apprehension

Of these two murderers, Warbeck and Somerton.

Sir Art. Ha! Flat murtherers?

Som. Ha, ha, ha! This has awakened my melancholy.

Warb. And struck my mirth down [80 flat.—Murtherers?

Con. The accusation is flat against you, gentlemen.—

Sir, you may be satisfied with this.— [*Shows warrant.*]

I hope you'll quietly obey my power; 'Twill make your cause the fairer.

Ambo.[2] O, with all our hearts, sir.

[1] Beholden.
[2] *I.e.*, both Somerton and Warbeck.

Clow. There's my rival taken up for hangman's meat. Tom told me he was about a piece of villainy.—Mates and morris men, you see here's no longer [90 piping, no longer dancing; this news of murder has slain the morris. You that go the footway, fare ye well; I am for a gallop. —Come, ningle.

*Exe[unt Banks and Dog].*

Fiddl. (*Strikes his fiddle.*) Ay? Nay, and my fiddle be come to himself again, I care not. I think the devil has been abroad amongst us today; I'll keep thee out of thy fit now, if I can.

*Exe[unt Fiddler and Morris].*

Sir Art. These things are full of horror, full of pity.    100

But, if this time be constant to the proof, The guilt of both these gentlemen I dare take

Upon mine own danger; yet, howsoever, sir,

Your power must be obeyed.

Warb.    O, most willingly, sir. 'Tis a most sweet affliction; I could not meet

A joy in the best shape with better will. Come, fear not, sir; nor judge nor evidence

Can bind him o'er who's freed by conscience.

Som. Mine stands so upright to the middle zone    109

It takes no shadow to 't; it goes alone.

*Exeunt.*

Act[us] IV. Scen[a] i.

[*The village green in Edmonton.*]

*Enter Old Banks and two or three Countrymen.*

O. Bank. My horse this morning runs most piteously of the glanders, whose nose yesternight was as clean as any man's here now coming from the barber's; and this, I'll take my death upon 't, is long [3] of this jadish witch, Mother Sawyer.

1 [Count.] I took my wife and a servingman in our town of Edmonton, thrashing in my barn together such corn as country wenches carry to market, and, examin- [10 ing my polecat [4] why she did so, she swore

[3] Because.    [4] Harlot.

in her conscience she was bewitched. And what witch have we about us but Mother Sawyer?

2 [COUNT.] Rid the town of her, else all our wives will do nothing else but dance about other country Maypoles.

3 [COUNT.] Our cattle fall, our wives fall, our daughters fall, and maidservants fall; and we ourselves shall not be able to [20 stand, if this beast be suffered to graze amongst us.

*Enter W. Hamluc with thatch and a link.*[1]

HAML. Burn the witch, the witch, the witch, the witch!

OMN[ES]. What hast got there?

HAML. A handful of thatch plucked off a hovel of hers; and they say, when 'tis burning, if she be a witch, she'll come running in.

O. BANK. Fire it, fire it! I'll stand [30 between thee and home for any danger.

*As that burns enter the Witch.*

SAWY. Diseases, plagues, the curse of an old woman follow and fall upon you!

OMN[ES]. Are you come, you old trot?

O. BANK. You hot whore, must we fetch you with fire in your tail?

1 [COUNT.] This thatch is as good as a jury to prove she is a witch.

OMN[ES]. Out, witch! Beat her, kick her, set fire on her! 40

SAWY. Shall I be murthered by a bed of serpents? Help, help!

*Enter Sir Arthur Clarington and a Justice.*

OMN[ES]. Hang her, beat her, kill her!

JUST. How now? Forbear this violence!

SAWY. A crew of villains, a knot of bloody hangmen, set to torment me, I know not why.

JUST. Alas, neighbor Banks, are you a ringleader in mischief? Fie, to abuse an aged woman! 50

O. BANK. Woman? A she-hellcat, a witch! To prove her one, we no sooner set fire on the thatch of her house, but in she came running as if the devil had sent her in a barrel of gunpowder, which trick as surely proves her a witch as the pox in a snuffling nose is a sign a man is a whoremaster.

[1] Torch.

JUST. Come, come. Firing her thatch? Ridiculous!

Take heed, sirs, what you do; unless your proofs

Come better armed, instead of turning her 60

Into a witch, you'll prove yourselves stark fools.

OMN[ES]. Fools?

JUST. Arrant fools.

O. BANK. Pray, Mr. Justice What-do-you-call-'em, hear me but in one thing: this grumbling devil owes me I know no good will ever since I fell out with her.

SAWY. And breakedst my back with beating me.

O. BANK. I'll break it worse. 70

SAWY. Wilt thou?

JUST. You must not threaten her; 'tis against law. Go on.

O. BANK. So, sir, ever since, having a dun cow tied up in my backside,[2] let me go thither, or but cast mine eye at her, and, if I should be hanged, I cannot choose, though it be ten times in an hour, but run to the cow, and, taking up her tail, kiss—saving your worship's reverence—my cow [80 behind, that the whole town of Edmonton has been ready to bepiss themselves with laughing me to scorn.

JUST. And this is long of her?

O. BANK. Who the devil else? For is any man such an ass to be such a baby, if he were not bewitched?

SIR ART. Nay, if she be a witch, and the harms she does end in such sports, she may scape burning. 90

JUST. Go, go! Pray, vex her not; she is a subject,

And you must not be judges of the law To strike her as you please.

OMN[ES]. No, no, we'll find cudgel enough to strike her.

O. BANK. Ay; no lips to kiss but my cow's—!

*Exeunt [Old Banks and Countrymen].*

SAWY. Rots and foul maladies eat up thee and thine!

JUST. Here's none now, Mother Sawyer, but this gentleman,

Myself, and you. Let us to some mild questions; 100

Have you mild answers. Tell us honestly

[2] Back yard.

And with a free confession—we'll do
    our best
To wean you from it—are you a witch,
    or no?
SAWY. I am none!
JUST.                    Be not so furious.
SAWY.                         I am none!
    None but base curs so bark at me. I'm
    none.
    Or would I were!  If every poor old
    woman
    Be trod on thus by slaves, reviled,
    kicked, beaten,
    As I am daily, she to be revenged
    Had need turn witch.
SIR ART.          And you to be revenged
    Have sold your soul to th' devil.
SAWY.          Keep thine own from him.
JUST. You are too saucy and too bitter.
SAWY.                    Saucy?  111
    By what commission can he send my soul
    On the devil's errand more than I can
    his?
    Is he a landlord of my soul, to thrust it,
    When he list, out of door?
JUST.          Know whom you speak to.
SAWY. A man; perhaps no man.  Men in
    gay clothes,
    Whose backs are laden with titles and
    honors,
    Are within far more crooked than I am,
    And, if I be a witch, more witchlike.
SIR ART. Y' are a base hellhound.—  120
    And now, sir, let me tell you, far and near
    She's bruited for[1] a woman that maintains
    A spirit that sucks her.
SAWY.                    I defy thee.
SIR ART.                         Go, go.
    I can, if need be, bring an hundred voices,
    E'en here in Edmonton, that shall loud
    proclaim
    Thee for a secret and pernicious witch.
SAWY. Ha, ha!
JUST.     Do you laugh?  Why laugh you?
SAWY.                    At my name,
    The brave name this knight gives me—
    witch.
JUST. Is the name of witch so pleasing to
    thine ear?
SIR ART. Pray, sir, give way, and let her
    tongue gallop on.          130
SAWY. A witch!  Who is not?
    Hold not that universal name in scorn,
    then.

What are your painted things in princes'
    courts,
Upon whose eyelids lust sits, blowing
    fires
To burn men's souls in sensual hot de-
    sires,
Upon whose naked paps a lecher's
    thought
Acts sin in fouler shapes than can be
    wrought?
JUST. But those work not as you do.
SAWY.                    No, but far worse.
    These by enchantments can whole lord-
    ships[2] change
    To trunks of rich attire, turn plows and
    teams          140
    To Flanders mares and coaches, and huge
    trains
    Of servitors to a French butterfly.
    Have you not city witches who can turn
    Their husbands' wares, whole standing
    shops of wares,
    To sumptuous tables, gardens of stol'n
    sin,
    In one year wasting what scarce twenty
    win?
    Are not these witches?
JUST.               Yes, yes: but the law
    Casts not an eye on these.
SAWY.               Why then on me,
    Or any lean old beldam?  Reverence once
    Had wont to wait on age; now an old
    woman,          150
    Ill-favored grown with years, if she be
    poor,
    Must be called bawd or witch.  Such so
    abused
    Are the coarse witches; tother are the
    fine,
    Spun for the devil's own wearing.
SIR ART.                    And so is thine.
SAWY. She on whose tongue a whirlwind
    sits to blow
    A man out of himself, from his soft
    pillow
    To lean his head on rocks and fighting
    waves,
    Is not that scold a witch?  The man of
    law
    Whose honeyed hopes the credulous
    client draws—
    As bees by tinkling basins—to swarm to
    him          160

    [1] Reported as.                    [2] Estates.

From his own hive to work the wax in
his—
He is no witch, not he!
SIR ART.              But these men-witches
Are not in trading with hell's merchan-
dise,
Like such as you are, that for a word, a
look,
Denial of a coal of fire, kill men,
Children, and cattle.
SAWY.              Tell them, sir, that do so.
Am I accused for such an one?
SIR ART.              Yes; 'twill be sworn.
SAWY.    Dare any swear I ever tempted
maiden
With golden hooks flung at her chastity
To come and lose her honor; and, being
lost,                                          170
To pay not a denier[1] for 't? Some slaves
have done it.
Men-witches can, without the fangs of
law
Drawing once one drop of blood, put
counterfeit pieces
Away for true gold.
SIR ART              By one thing she speaks
I know now she's a witch, and dare no
longer
Hold conference with the fury.
JUST.              Let's, then, away.—
Old woman, mend thy life; get home and
pray. *Exeunt [Sir Arthur and Justice].*
SAWY.  For his confusion!—

*Enter Dog.*

My dear Tom-boy, welcome!
I'm torn in pieces by a pack of curs
Clapped all upon me, and for want of
thee.                                          180
Comfort me; thou shalt have the teat
anon.
DOG.  Bow, wow! I'll have it now.
SAWY.              I am dried up
With cursing and with madness, and
have yet
No blood to moisten these sweet lips of
thine.
Stand on thy hind legs up—kiss me, my
Tommy,
And rub away some wrinkles on my
brow
By making my old ribs to shrug for joy

Of thy fine tricks. What has thou done?
Let's tickle.
Hast thou struck the horse lame as I bid
thee?
DOG.        Yes;
And nipped the sucking child.
SAWY.              Ho, ho, my dainty,   190
My little pearl! No lady loves her hound,
Monkey, or parrakeet, as I do thee.
DOG. The maid has been churning butter
nine hours, but it shall not come.
SAWY. Let 'em eat cheese and choke.
DOG.              I had rare sport
Among the clowns i' th' morris.
SAWY.              I could dance
Out of my skin to hear thee. But, my
curl-pate,
That jade, that foul-tongued whore, Nan
Ratcliffe,
Who, for a little soap licked by my sow,
Struck and almost had lamed it, did not
I charge thee                                  200
To pinch that quean[2] to th' heart?
DOG.              Bow, wow, wow! Look
here else.

*Enter Ann Ratcliffe mad.*

RATC.  See, see, see! The man i' th'
moon has built a new windmill; and what
running there's from all quarters of the
city to learn the art of grinding!
SAWY.  Ho, ho, ho! I thank thee, my
sweet mongrel.
RATC.  Hoyda! A pox of the devil's false
hopper! All the golden meal runs into the
rich knaves' purses, and the poor  [210
have nothing but bran. Hey derry down!—
Are not you Mother Sawyer?
SAWY. No, I am a lawyer.
RATC.  Art thou? I prithee, let me
scratch thy face, for thy pen has flayed off
a great many men's skins. You'll have
brave doings in the vacation, for knaves
and fools are at variance in every village.
I'll sue Mother Sawyer, and her own sow
shall give in evidence against her.    220
SAWY.  *[To Dog.]* Touch her.
RATC.  O, my ribs are made of a paned
hose,[3] and they break! There's a Lan-
cashire hornpipe in my throat; hark, how
it tickles it, with doodle, doodle, doodle,
doodle! Welcome, serjeants![4] Welcome,

[1] Penny.        [2] Hussy.        [3] Striped in strips.        [4] Sheriff's officers.

devil!—Hands, hands! Hold hands, and dance around, around, around.  [*Dances.*]

*Enter Old Banks, his son the Clown, Old Ratcliffe, Country Fellows.*

O. RATC.  She's here; alas, my poor wife is here!                                            230

O. BANK.  Catch her fast, and have her into some close chamber, do, for she's, as many wives are, stark mad.

CLOW.  The witch! Mother Sawyer, the witch, the devil!

O. RATC.  O, my dear wife! Help, sirs!
                              *Car[ry] her* ¹ *off.* ²

O. BANK.  You see your work, Mother Bumby.³

SAWY.  My work? Should she and all you here run mad, is the work mine? [240

CLOW.  No, on my conscience, she would not hurt a devil of two years old.—

*Enter Old Ratcliffe and the Rest.*

How now? What's become of her?

O. RATC.  Nothing; she's become nothing but the miserable trunk of a wretched woman. We were in her hands as reeds in a mighty tempest. Spite of our strengths, away she brake; and nothing in her mouth being heard but "the devil, the witch, the witch, the devil!" she beat out her [250 own brains, and so died.

CLOW.  It's any man's case, be he never so wise, to die when his brains go a-wool-gathering.

O. BANK.  Masters, be ruled by me; let's all to a justice.—Hag, thou hast done this, and thou shalt answer it.

SAWY.  Banks, I defy thee.

O. BANK.  Get a warrant first to examine her; then ship her to Newgate. Here's [260 enough, if all her other villainies were pardoned, to burn her for a witch.— You have a spirit, they say, comes to you in the likeness of a dog; we shall see your cur at one time or other. If we do, unless it be the devil himself, he shall go howling to the goal ⁴ in one chain, and thou in another.

SAWY.  Be hanged thou in a third, and do thy worst!

CLOW.  How, father? You send the [270

poor dumb thing howling to th' goal? He that makes him howl makes me roar.

O. BANK.  Why, foolish boy, dost thou know him?

CLOW.  No matter if I do or not. He's bailable, I am sure, by law. But, if the dog's word will not be taken, mine shall.

O. BANK.  Thou bail for a dog?

CLOW.  Yes, or a bitch either, being my friend. I'll lie by the heels myself [280 before puppison ⁵ shall; his dog days are not come yet, I hope.

O. BANK.  What manner of dog is it? Didst ever see him?

CLOW.  See him? Yes, and given him a bone to gnaw twenty times. The dog is no court foisting ⁶ hound that fills his belly full by base wagging his tail; neither is it a citizen's water spaniel, enticing his master to go a-ducking twice or thrice a week, [290 whilst his wife makes ducks and drakes at home. This is no Paris Garden ban-dog ⁷ neither, that keeps a bow-wow-wowing to have butchers bring their curs thither; and, when all comes to all, they run away like sheep. Neither is this the Black Dog of Newgate.⁸

O. BANK.  No, Goodman Son-fool, but the dog of hellgate.

CLOW.  I say, Goodman Father- [300 fool, it's a lie.

OMN[ES].  He's bewitched.

CLOW.  A gross lie, as big as myself. The devil in St. Dunstan's will as soon drink with this poor cur as with any Temple Bar laundress that washes and wrings lawyers.

DOG.  Bow, wow, wow, wow!

OMN[ES].  O, the dog's here, the dog's here.                                            309

O. BANK.  It was the voice of a dog.

CLOW.  The voice of a dog? If that voice were a dog's, what voice had my mother? So am I a dog. Bow, wow, wow! It was I that barked so, father, to make coxcombs of these clowns.

O. BANK.  However, we'll be coxcombed no longer. Away, therefore, to th' justice for a warrant; and then, Gammer Gurton, have at your needle of witchcraft!⁹

¹ *I.e.*, Ann Ratcliffe.
² This stage direction follows the preceding line in the original.
³ A reference to Lyly's *Mother Bombic.*
⁴ Gaol, jail.

⁵ Probably equivalent to *his puppyship.*
⁶ Cheating; also stinking.
⁷ Fierce dog used for bear baiting.
⁸ A probable allusion to a lost play of a similar title.    ⁹ A reference to *Gammer Gurton's Needle.*

SAWY. And prick thine own eyes out. Go,
peevish fools!  320
*Exe[unt Old Banks, Ratcliffe, and Coun-
trymen].*

CLOW. Ningle, you had liked to have
spoiled all with your bow-ings. I was glad
to put 'em off with one of my dogtricks
on a sudden; I am bewitched, little Cost-
me-naught, to love thee.—A pox!—That
morris makes me spit in thy mouth. I
dare not stay. Farewell, ningle; you
whoreson [1] dog's nose!—Farewell, witch!
*Exit.*

DOG. Bow, wow, wow, wow!

SAWY. Mind him not; he's not [330
worth thy worrying. Run at a fairer
game, that foul-mouthed knight, scurvy Sir
Arthur. Fly at him, my Tommy, and pluck
out 's throat.

DOG. No, there['s] a dog already biting 's
conscience.

SAWY. That's a sure bloodhound. Come,
let's home and play;
Our black work ended, we'll make holiday.  *Exeunt.*

### SCEN[A] ii.

*[A bedroom in Carter's house.]*

*Enter Katherine. A bed thrust forth; on it
Frank in a slumber.*

KAT. Brother, brother! So sound asleep?
That's well.

FRANK. *[Waking.]* No, not I, sister; he
that's wounded here
As I am—all my other hurts are bitings
Of a poor flea—but he that here once
bleeds
Is maimed incurably.

KAT.  My good sweet brother—
For now my sister must grow up in you—
Though her loss strikes you through,
and that I feel
The blow as deep, I pray thee, be not
cruel
To kill me too, by seeing you cast away
In your own helpless sorrow. Good love,
sit up;  10
And, if you can give physic to yourself,
I shall be well.

FRANK.  I'll do my best.

KAT.  I thank you.
What do you look about for?

[1] Rascally.

FRANK.  Nothing, nothing;
But I was thinking, sister—

KAT.  Dear heart, what?

FRANK. Who but a fool would thus be
bound to a bed,
Having this room to walk in?

KAT.  Why do you talk so?
Would you were fast asleep!

FRANK.  No, no; I'm not idle.[2]
But here's my meaning: being robbed as
I am,
Why should my soul, which married was
to hers,
Live in divorce, and not fly after her?  20
Why should not I walk hand in hand
with Death,
To find my love out?

KAT.  That were well indeed,
Your time being come; when Death is
sent to call you,
No doubt you shall meet her.

FRANK.  Why should not I
Go without calling?

KAT.  Yes, brother, so you might,
Were there no place to go when y' are
gone
But only this.

FRANK.  Troth, sister, thou say'st true,
For, when a man has been an hundred
years
Hard traveling o'er the tottering bridge
of age,  29
He's not the thousand part upon his way.
All life is but a wand'ring to find home;
When we are gone, we are there. Happy
were man,
Could here his voyage end; he should
not, then,
Answer how well or ill he steered his soul
By heaven's or by hell's compass; how
he put in—
Losing blessed goodness' shore—at such
a sin;
Nor how life's dear provision he has
spent;
Nor how far he in 's navigation went
Beyond commission. This were a fine
reign,
To do ill and not hear of it again;  40
Yet then were man more wretched than
a beast;
For, sister, our dead pay [3] is sure the
best.

[2] Light-headed.  [3] Retribution.

KAT. 'Tis so, the best or worst; and I wish
        heaven
    To pay—and so I know it will—that
        traitor,
    That devil Somerton, who stood in mine
        eye
    Once as an angel, home to his deservings.
    What villain but himself, once loving me,
    With Warbeck's soul would pawn his
        own to hell
    To be revenged on my poor sister?
FRANK.                              Slaves!
    A pair of merciless slaves! Speak no
        more of them.                        50
KAT. I think this talking hurts you.
FRANK. Does me no good, I'm sure;
    I pay for 't everywhere.
KAT.                    I have done, then.
    Eat, if you cannot sleep; you have these
        two days
    Not tasted any food.—[Calls.] Jane, is it
        ready?
FRANK. What's ready? What's ready?
KAT. I have made ready a roasted chicken
    for you.

[Enter Jane with chicken.]

    Sweet, wilt thou eat?
FRANK. A pretty stomach on a sudden,
        yes.
    There's one in the house can play upon
        a lute.                              60
    Good girl, let's hear him too.
KAT.               You shall, dear brother.
                                    [Exit Jane.]
    Would I were a musician; you should
        hear                     Lute plays.
    How I would feast your ear! Stay, mend
        your pillow,
    And raise you higher.
FRANK.              I am up too high,
    Am I not, sister, now?
KAT.                    No, no; 'tis well.
    Fall to, fall to.—A knife! Here's never
        a knife.
    Brother, I'll look out yours.
                        [Picks up his coat.]

Enter Dog, shrugging as it were for joy, and
                                    dances.

FRANK.                    Sister, O sister,
    I am ill upon a sudden, and can eat
        nothing.

KAT. In very deed you shall. The want of
        food
    Makes you so faint. Ha! [Sees the bloody
        knife.] Here's none in your pocket;  70
    I'll go fetch a knife.                Exit.
FRANK.                    Will you? 'Tis well;
    All's well.

She gone, he searches first one, then the other,
    pocket. Knife found. Dog runs off.
    He lies on one side. The Spirit of
    Susan, his second wife, comes to the
    bed's side. He stares at it, and, turning
    to the other side, it's there too. In the
    meantime, Winnifride as a page comes
    in, stands at his bed's feet sadly. He,
    frighted, sits upright. The Spirit van-
                                    ishes.

FRANK.                    What art thou?
WIN.                    A lost creature.
FRANK. So am I too.—Win? Ah, my
    she-page!
WIN. For your sake I put on
    A shape that's false; yet do I wear a
        heart
    True to you as your own.
FRANK.              Would mine and thine
    Were fellows in one house! Kneel by me
        here.
    On this side now? How dar'st thou come
        to mock me
    On both sides of my bed?
WIN.                    When?
FRANK.                    But just now.
    Outface me, stare upon me with strange
        postures,                            80
    Turn my soul wild by a face in which
        were drawn
    A thousand ghosts leaped newly from
        their graves
    To pluck me into a winding sheet!
WIN.                    Believe it,
    I came no nearer to you than yon place
    At your bed's feet, and of the house had
        leave,
    Calling myself your horse boy, in to
        come
    And visit my sick master.
FRANK.              Then 'twas my fancy—
    Some windmill in my brains for want of
        sleep.
WIN. Would I might never sleep, so you
    could rest!

But you have plucked a thunder on your
head,                                            90
Whose noise cannot cease suddenly.
Why should you
Dance at the wedding of a second
wife,
When scarce the music which you heard
at mine
Had ta'en a farewell of you? O, this was
ill!
And they who thus can give both hands
away
In th' end shall want their best limbs.

FRANK.                          Winnifride—
The chamber door fast?

WIN.                              Yes.

FRANK.                    Sit thee, then, down,
And, when th'ast heard me speak, melt
into tears.
Yet I, to save those eyes of thine from
weeping,
Being to write a story of us two,       100
Instead of ink dipped my sad pen in
blood.
When of thee I took leave, I went abroad
Only for pillage, as a freebooter,
What gold soe'er I got to make it
thine.
To please a father, I have heaven dis-
pleased;
Striving to cast two wedding rings in
one,
Through my bad workmanship I now
have none.
I have lost her and thee.

WIN.                    I know she's dead;
But you have me still.

FRANK.                    Nay, her this hand
Murdered; and so I lose thee too.

WIN.                              O me!    110

FRANK. Be quiet, for thou my evidence
art,
Jury, and judge. Sit quiet, and I'll tell all.

*As they whisper, enter at one end o' th' stage
Old Carter and Katherine, Dog at th'
other, pawing softly at Frank.*

KAT. I have run madding up and down to
find you,
Being laden with the heaviest news that
ever
Poor daughter carried.

[O.] CART.        Why? Is the boy dead?

KAT.                              Dead, sir!
O father, we are cozened. You are told
The murtherer sings in prison, and he
laughs here.
This villain killed my sister. See else,
see,
A bloody knife in 's pocket!

[O.] CART.              Bless me, patience!

FRANK. [*Seeing them.*] The knife, the knife,
the knife!                                       120

KAT. What knife?              *Exit Dog.*

FRANK.              To cut my chicken up,
my chicken!—
Be you my carver, father.

[O.] CART.                    That I will.

KAT. [*Aside.*] How the devil steels our
brows after doing ill!

FRANK. My stomach and my sight are
taken from me;
All is not well within me.

[O.] CART. I believe thee, boy—I that
have seen so many moons clap their horns
on other men's foreheads to strike them
sick, yet mine to scape and be well; I that
never cast away a fee upon urinals,   [130
but am as sound as an honest man's conscience when he's dying, I should cry out
as thou dost, "All is not well within me,"
felt I but the bag of thy imposthumes.[1] Ah,
poor villain! Ah, my wounded rascal! All
my grief is, I have now small hope of thee.
thee.

FRANK. Do the surgeons say my wounds
are dangerous then?

[O.] CART. Yes, yes, and there's no   [140
way with thee but one.

FRANK. Would he were here to open
them!

[O.] CART. I'll go to fetch him; I'll make
an holiday to see thee as I wish.
                              *Exit to fetch Officers.*

FRANK. A wondrous kind old man!

WIN. [*Aside to Frank.*] Your sin's the
blacker so to abuse his goodness.—Master,
how do you?

FRANK. Pretty well now, boy; I   [150
have such odd qualms come cross my
stomach. I'll fall to; boy, cut me.

WIN. [*Aside.*] You have cut me, I'm
sure.—A leg or wing, sir?

FRANK. No, no, no! A wing?—[*Aside.*]
Would I had wings but to soar up you
tower! But here's a clog that hinders me.—
What's that?

---

[1] Abscesses.

*Father with her in a coffin.*

[O.] Cart. That? What? O, now I see her; 'tis a young wench, my daughter, [160 sirrah, sick to the death; and, hearing thee to be an excellent rascal for letting blood, she looks out at a casement, and cries, "Help, help! Stay that man! Him I must have or none."

Frank. For pity's sake, remove her! See, she stares

With one broad open eye still in my face!

[O.] Cart. Thou puttest both hers out, like a villain as thou art; yet, see, she is willing to lend thee one again to [170 find out the murtherer, and that's thyself.

Frank. Old man, thou liest!

[O.] Cart.          So shalt thou— i' th' goal.

Run for officers!

Kat.         O, thou merciless slave! She was—though yet above ground—in her grave

To me; but thou hast torn it up again.

Mine eyes, too much drowned, now must feel more rain.

[O.] Cart. Fetch officers.

*Exit Katherine.*

Frank. For whom?

[O.] Cart. For thee, sirrah, sirrah! Some knives have foolish posies [1] upon [180 them, but thine has a villainous one. [*Takes knife from Frank's pocket.*] Look! O, it is enameled with the heart blood of thy hated wife, my beloved daughter! What say'st thou to this evidence? Is 't not sharp? Does 't not strike home? Thou canst not answer honestly and without a trembling heart to this one point, this terrible, bloody point.

Win. I beseech you, sir, strike [190 him no more; you see he's dead already.

[O.] Cart. O, sir, you held his horses; you are as arrant a rogue as he. Up go you too.

Frank. As y' are a man, throw not upon that woman

Your loads of tyranny, for she's innocent.

[O.] Cart. How? How? A woman? Is 't grown to a fashion for women in all countries to wear the breeches?

Win. I am not as my disguise [200

[1] Inscriptions.

speaks me, sir, his page, but his first, only wife, his lawful wife.

[O.] Cart. How? How? More fire i' th' bedstraw!

Win. The wrongs which singly fell on your daughter

On me are multiplied; she lost a life,

But I an husband and myself must lose

If you call him to a bar for what he has done.

[O.] Cart. He has done it, then?

Win. Yes, 'tis confessed to me.

Frank.       Dost thou betray me? 210

Win. O, pardon me, dear heart! I am mad to lose thee,

And know not what I speak; but, if thou didst,

I must arraign this father for two sins, Adultery and murther.

*Enter Katherine.*

Kat.          Sir, they are come.

[O.] Cart. Arraign me for what thou wilt, all Middlesex knows me better for an honest man than the middle of a market place knows thee for an honest woman.— Rise, sirrah, and don your tacklings; rig yourself for the gallows, or I'll carry [220 thee thither on my back. Your trull shall to th' goal go with you. There be as fine Newgate birds as she, that can draw him in. Pox on 's wounds!

Frank. I have served thee, and my wages now are paid;

Yet my worst punishment shall, I hope, be stayed.          *Exeunt.*

Act[us] V. Scen[a] i.

[*Mother Sawyer's hut.*]

*Enter Mother Sawyer alone.*

Sawy. Still wronged by every slave, and not a dog

Bark in his dame's defense? I am called witch,

Yet am myself bewitched from doing harm.

Have I given up myself to thy black lust

Thus to be scorned? Not see me in three days?

I'm lost without my Tomalin. Prithee, come;

Revenge to me is sweeter far than life.
Thou art my raven, on whose coal-
    black wings
Revenge comes flying to me. O, my
    best love!
I am on fire, even in the midst of ice,  10
Raking my blood up, till my shrunk
    knees feel
Thy curled head leaning on them. Come,
    then, my darling;
If in the air thou hover'st, fall upon me
In some dark cloud; and, as I oft have
    seen
Dragons and serpents in the elements,
Appear thou now so to me. Art thou i'
    th' sea?
Muster up all the monsters from the
    deep,
And be the ugliest of them, so that my
    bulch [1]
Show but his swarth cheek to me, let
    earth cleave
And break from hell, I care not! Could
    I run                              20
Like a swift powder mine beneath the
    world,
Up would I blow it, all to find out thee,
Though I lay ruined in it.   Not yet
    come!
I must, then, fall to my old prayer:
*Sanctibicetur nomen tuum.*

Not yet come!   Worrying of wolves,
biting of mad dogs, the manges, and the—

*Enter Dog [, now white].*

Dog. How now! Whom art thou cursing?
Sawy. Thee! Ha! No, 'tis my black cur
    I am cursing
For not attending on me.
Dog.                 I am that cur.  30
Sawy. Thou liest.  Hence!  Come not
    nigh me.
Dog.            Baw, waw!
Sawy. Why dost thou thus appear to me
    in white,
As if thou wert the ghost of my dear
    love?
Dog. I am dogged—list[2] not to tell
thee; yet, to torment thee, my whiteness
puts thee in mind of thy winding sheet.[3]
    Sawy. Am I near death?

[1] Bull calf, a term of endearment.
[2] I desire.        [3] Original reads *sweet.*

Dog. Yes, if the dog of hell be near
thee; when the devil comes to thee as a
lamb, have at thy throat!            40
    Sawy. Off, cur!
Dog. He has the back of a sheep, but
the belly of an otter; devours by sea and
land. Why am I in white? Didst thou not
pray to me?
    Sawy. Yes,   thou   dissembling  hell-
hound! Why now in white more than at
other times?
Dog. Be blasted with the news! Whiteness is day's footboy, a forerunner  [50
to light, which shows thy old riveled[4]
face.  Villains are stripped naked; the
witch must be beaten out of her cockpit.
Sawy. Must she?  She shall not; thou
    art a lying spirit.
Why to mine eyes art thou a flag of
    truce?
I am at peace with none; 'tis the black
    color,
Or none, which I fight under. I do not like
Thy puritan paleness; glowing furnaces
Are far more hot than they which flame
    outright.
If thou my old dog art, go and bite
    such                              60
As I shall set thee on.
Dog. I will not.
Sawy. I'll sell myself to twenty thou-
    sand fiends
To have thee torn in pieces, then.
Dog. Thou canst not; thou art so ripe
to fall into hell, that no more of my kennel
will so much as bark at him that hangs
thee.
    Sawy. I shall run mad.
Dog. Do so; thy time is come to  [70
curse, and rave, and die. The glass of thy
sins is full, and it must run out at gallows.
Sawy. It cannot, ugly cur.  I'll confess
    nothing;
And, not confessing, who dare come
    and swear
I have bewitched them? I'll not confess
    one mouthful.
Dog. Choose, and be hanged or burned.
Sawy. Spite of the devil and thee, I'll
    muzzle up
My tongue from telling tales.
Dog. Spite of thee and the devil, thou'lt
    be condemned.

[4] Shriveled.

Sawy. Yes, when?

Dog.          And, ere the executioner    80
Catch thee full in 's claws, thou'lt confess all.

Sawy. Out, dog!

Dog.     Out, witch! Thy trial is at hand.
Our prey being had, the devil does
laughing stand. *The Dog stands aloof.*

*Enter Old Banks, Ratcliffe, and Countrymen.*

O. Bank. She's here; attach her.—
Witch, you must go with us.
                    [*They seize her.*]

Sawy. Whither? To hell?

O. Bank. No, no, no, old crone; your
mittimus shall be made thither, but your
own jailors shall receive you.—Away with
her!                                    90

Sawy. My Tommy! My sweet Tom-boy!
O, thou dog!
Dost thou now fly to thy kennel and for-
sake me?
Plagues and consumptions—
                    *Exeunt [All but Dog].*

Dog. Ha, ha, ha, ha!
Let not the world witches or devils
condemn;
They follow us, and then we follow them.

*[Enter] Young Banks to the Dog.*

Clow. I would fain meet with mine
ingle once more. He has had a claw
amongst um. My rival that loved my
wench is like to be hanged like an    [100
innocent.[1]    A kind cur where he takes,
but, where he takes not, a dogged rascal. I
know the villain loves me. No!—(*[Dog]
barks.*) Art thou there? [*Sees Dog.*]—That's
Tom's voice, but 'tis not he; this is a dog
of another hair, this. Bark, and not speak
to me? Not Tom, then; there's as much
difference betwixt Tom and this as betwixt
white and black.

Dog. Hast thou forgot me?          110

Clow. That's Tom again.—Prithee,
ningle, speak. Is thy name Tom?

Dog. Whilst I served my old Dame
Sawyer, 'twas; I'm gone from her now.

Clow.[2] Gone? Away with the witch,
then, too! She'll never thrive if thou
leav'st her; she knows no more how to
kill a cow, or a horse, or a sow, without
thee, than she does to kill a goose.

[1] Fool, idiot.          [2] Original reads *Dog.*

Dog. No, she has done killing now, [120
but must be killed for what she has done;
she's shortly to be hanged.

Clow. Is she? In my conscience, if
she be, 'tis thou hast brought her to the
gallows, Tom.

Dog. Right. I served her to that purpose; 'twas part of my wages.

Clow. This was no honest servant's
part, by your leave, Tom. This remember,
I pray you, between you and I; I    [130
entertained you ever as a dog, not as a
devil.

Dog. True; and so I used thee doggedly,
not devilishly;
I have deluded thee for sport to laugh
at.
The wench thou seek'st after thou never
spakest with,
But a spirit in her form, habit, and
likeness.
Ha, ha!

Clow. I do not, then, wonder at the
change of your garments, if you can enter
into shapes of women too.          140

Dog. Any shape, to blind such silly
eyes as thine; but chiefly those coarse
creatures, dog, or cat, hare, ferret, frog,
toad.

Clow. Louse or flea?

Dog. Any poor vermin.

Clow. It seems you devils have poor,
thin souls, that you can bestow yourselves
in such small bodies. But, pray you, Tom,
one question at parting—I think I    [150
shall never see you more—where do you
borrow those bodies that are none of your
own? The garment-shape you may hire
at broker's.

Dog. Why wouldst thou know that?
Fool, it avails thee not.

Clow. Only for my mind's sake, Tom,
and to tell some of my friends.

Dog. I'll thus much tell thee: thou never
art so distant                          159
From an evil spirit but that thy oaths,
Curses, and blasphemies pull him to
thine elbow.
Thou never tell'st a lie but that a devil
Is within hearing it; thy evil purposes
Are ever haunted; but, when they come
to act—
As thy tongue slandering, bearing false
witness,

Thy hand stabbing, stealing, cozening,
　　cheating—
He's then within thee.　Thou play'st;
　　he bets upon thy part.
Although thou lose, yet he will gain by
　　thee.
Clow. Ay? Then he comes in the shape
　　of a rook.
Dog. The old cadaver of some self-
　　strangled wretch　　　　　　　170
We sometimes borrow, and appear
　　human;
The carcass of some disease-slain strum-
　　pet
We varnish fresh, and wear as her first
　　beauty.
Didst never hear?　If not, it has been
　　done.
An hot, luxurious lecher in his twines,
When he has thought to clip his dal-
　　liance,
There has provided been for his em-
　　brace
A fine, hot, flaming devil in her place.
　　Clow. Yes, I am partly a witness to
this, but I never could embrace her. [180
I thank thee for that, Tom.　Well, again I
thank thee, Tom, for all this counsel;
without a fee too!　There's few lawyers of
thy mind now.　Certainly, Tom, I begin to
pity thee.
　　Dog. Pity me?　For what?
　　Clow. Were it not possible for thee to
become an honest dog yet?　'Tis a base
life that you lead, Tom, to serve witches,
to kill innocent children, to kill [190
harmless cattle, to stroy corn and fruit,
etc.　'Twere better yet to be a butcher and
kill for yourself.
　　Dog. Why, these are all my delights,
my pleasures, fool.
　　Clow. Or, Tom, if you could give your
mind to ducking—I know you can swim,
fetch, and carry—some shopkeeper in
London would take great delight in you,
and be a tender master over you.　Or [200
if you have a mind to the game either at
bull or bear, I think I could prefer you
to Moll Cutpurse.
　　Dog. Ha, ha!　I should kill all the game
—bulls, bears, dogs, and all; not a cub to
be left.
　　Clow. You could do, Tom; but you
must play fair; you should be staved off

else.　Or, if your stomach did better like to
serve in some nobleman's, knight's, [210
or gentleman's kitchen, if you could brook[1]
the wheel and turn the spit (your labor
could not be much) when they have roast
meat (that's but once or twice in the week
at most), here you might lick your own
toes very well.　Or, if you could translate
yourself into a lady's arming puppy, there
you might lick sweet lips, and do many
pretty offices.　But to creep under an old
witch's coats, and suck like a great [220
puppy!　Fie upon 't!　I have heard beastly
things of you, Tom.
　　Dog. Ha, ha!
　　The worse thou heard'st of me, the bet-
　　　ter 'tis.
　　Shall I serve thee, fool, at the selfsame
　　　rate?
　　Clow. No, I'll see thee hanged; thou
shalt be damned first!　I know thy qualities
too well; I'll give no suck to such whelps.
Therefore henceforth I defy thee.　Out,
and avaunt!　　　　　　　　230
　　Dog. Nor will I serve for such a silly
　　　soul.
　　I am for greatness now, corrupted great-
　　　ness;
　　There I'll shug[2] in, and get a noble
　　　countenance;
　　Serve some Briarean footcloth-strider,[3]
　　That has an hundred hands to catch at
　　　bribes,
　　But not a finger's nail of charity.
　　Such, like the dragon's tail, shall pull
　　　down hundreds
　　To drop and sink with him.　I'll stretch
　　　myself,
　　And draw this bulk small as a silver
　　　wire,　　　　　　　　239
　　Enter at the least pore tobacco fume
　　Can make a breach for.　Hence, silly
　　　fool!
　　I scorn to prey on such an atom soul.
　　Clow. Come out, come out, you cur!
I will beat thee out of the bounds of
Edmonton, and tomorrow we go in pro-
cession, and after thou shalt never come
in again.　If thou goest to London, I'll
make thee go about by Tyburn, stealing
in by Thieving Lane.　If thou canst rub
thy shoulder against a lawyer's gown, [250

---

[1] Use, operate.　　　　　　[2] Crawl, sneak.
[3] A rider on a horse decked out for show.

as thou passest by Westminster Hall, do; if not, to the stairs amongst the bandogs; take water,[1] and the devil go with thee!

*Exeunt Y[oung] Banks, Dog barking.*

[SCENA ii.

*Near Tyburn.*]

*Enter Justice, Sir Arthur, [Somerton,] Warbeck, Carter, Kate.*

JUST. Sir Arthur, though the bench hath mildly censured your errors, yet you have indeed been the instrument that wrought all their misfortunes; I would wish you paid down your fine speedily and willingly.

SIR ART. I'll need no urging to it.

[O.] CART. If you should, 'twere a shame to you, for, if I should speak my conscience, you are worthier to be [10 hanged of the two, all things considered; and now make what you can of it. But I am glad these gentlemen are freed.

WARB. We knew our innocence.

SOM.                    And therefore feared it not.

KAT. But I am glad that I have you safe.

*Noise within.*

JUST. How now! What noise is that?

[O.] CART. Young Frank is going the wrong way. Alas, poor youth! Now I begin to pity him.                    [*Exeunt.*]

[SCENA iii.

*Another place near Tyburn.*]

*Enter Y[oung] Thorney and Halberts. Enter, as to see the execution, O[ld] Carter, O[ld] Thorney, Katherine, Winnifride weeping.*

O. THOR. Here let our sorrows wait him; to press nearer
The place of his sad death, some apprehensions
May tempt our grief too much, at height already.—
Daughter, be comforted.

WIN.                    Comfort and I
Are too far separated to be joined,
But in eternity. I share too much
Of him that's going thither.

[O.] CART. Poor woman, 'twas not thy fault; I grieve to see
Thee weep for him that hath my pity too.

WIN. My fault was lust; my punishment was shame.                    10
Yet I am happy that my soul is free
Both from consent, foreknowledge, and intent
Of any murther but of mine own honor,
Restored again by a fair satisfaction,
And since not to be wounded.

O. THOR.                    Daughter, grieve not
For what necessity forceth; rather resolve
To conquer it with patience.—Alas, she faints!

WIN. My griefs are strong upon me; my weakness scarce
Can bear them.

[VOICES.] (*within.*) Away with her! Hang her, witch!

*Enter Sawyer to execution; Officers with halberts; Country People.*

[O.] CART. The witch, that instru- [20 ment of mischief! Did not she witch the devil into my son-in-law, when he killed my poor daughter?—Do you hear, Mother Sawyer?

SAWY. What would you have? Cannot a poor old woman
Have your leave to die without vexation?

[O.] CART. Did not you bewitch Frank to kill his wife? He could never have done 't without the devil.

SAWY. Who doubts it? But is every devil mine?                    30
Would I had one now whom I might command
To tear you all in pieces! Tom would have done 't
Before he left me.

[O.] CART. Thou didst bewitch Ann Ratcliffe to kill herself.

SAWY. Churl, thou liest; I never did her hurt.
Would you were all as near your ends as I am,
That gave evidence against me for it!

[1] COUNT. I'll be sworn, Mr. Carter, she bewitched Gammer Washbowl's sow to cast her pigs a day before she would have [40 farried.[2] Yet they were sent up to London and sold for as good Westminster dog pigs[3]

_____

[1] *I.e.*, over the river.                    [3] Male pigs.
[2] Farrowed.

at Bartholomew Fair as ever great-bellied
alewife longed for.

SAWY. These dogs will mad me; I was
    well resolved
    To die in my repentance. Though 'tis
    true
I would live longer if I might, yet since
I cannot, pray, torment me not; my
    conscience
Is settled as it shall be. All take heed
How they believe the devil; at last he'll
    cheat you.                                    50
[O.] CART. Th'adst best confess all truly.
SAWY.                          Yet again?
    Have I scarce breath enough to say my
    prayers,
    And would you force me to spend that
    in bawling?
Bear witness, I repent all former evil;
There is no damnéd conjuror like the
    devil.
OMN[ES]. Away with her, away!
                            [She is led away.]


*Enter Frank to execution, Officers, Justice,*
        *Sir Arthur, Warbeck, Somerton.*


O. THOR. Here's the sad object which I
    yet must meet
With hope of comfort, if a repentant end
Make him more happy than misfortune
    would
Suffer him here to be.
FRANK.          Good sirs, turn from me.   60
    You will revive affliction almost killed
    With my continual sorrow.
O. THOR.                    O, Frank, Frank!
    Would I had sunk in mine own wants,
    or died
    But one bare minute ere thy fault was
    acted!
FRANK. To look upon your sorrows
    executes me
    Before my execution.
WIN.                    Let me pray you, sir—
FRANK. Thou much-wronged woman, I
    must sigh for thee,
    As he that's only loath to leave the
    world
For that he leaves thee in it unprovided,
Unfriended; and for me to beg a pity
From any man to thee when I am gone
Is more than I can hope; nor, to say
    truth,                                        72

Have I deserved it. But there is a pay-
    ment
Belongs to goodness from the great
    exchequer
Above; it will not fail thee, Winnifride.
Be that thy comfort.
O. THOR.              Let it be thine too,
    Untimely-lost young man.
FRANK.                    He is not lost
    Who bears his peace within him. Had I
    spun
    My web of life out at full length, and
    dreamed
Away my many years in lusts, in sur-
    feits,                                        80
Murthers of reputations, gallant sins
Commended or approved, then, though
    I had
Died easily, as great and rich men do,
Upon my own bed, not compelled by
    justice,
You might have mourned for me indeed;
    my miseries
Had been as everlasting as remediless.
But now the law hath not arraigned,
    condemned
With greater rigor my unhappy fact [1]
Than I myself have every little sin
My memory can reckon from my child-
    hood.                                         90
A court hath been kept here, where I
    am found
Guilty; the difference is, my impartial
    judge
Is much more gracious than my faults
Are monstrous to be named; yet they
    are monstrous.
O. THOR. Here's comfort in this penitence.
WIN.                          It speaks
    How truly you are reconciled, and
    quickens
My dying comfort, that was near expiring
With my last breath. Now this re-
    pentance makes thee
As white as innocence; and my first sin
    with thee,
Since which I knew none like it, by my
    sorrow                                        100
Is clearly canceled. Might our souls
    together
Climb to the height of their eternity,
And there enjoy what earth denied us,
    happiness!

[1] Deed.

But, since I must survive, and be the monument
Of thy loved memory, I will preserve it
With a religious care, and pay thy ashes
A widow's duty, calling that end best
Which, though it stain the name, makes the soul blessed.

FRANK. Give me thy hand, poor woman; do not weep.
Farewell! Thou dost forgive me?

WIN. 'Tis my part 110
To use that language.

FRANK. O, that my example
Might teach the world hereafter what a curse
Hangs on their heads who rather choose to marry
A goodly portion than a dower of virtues!—
Are you there, gentlemen? There is not one
Amongst you whom I have not wronged.—[To Carter.] You most—
[I] ¹ robbed you of a daughter; but she is
In heaven, and I must suffer for it willingly.

[O.] CART. Ay, ay, she's in heaven, and I am glad to see thee so well prepared [120 to follow her. I forgive thee with all my heart; if thou hadst not had ill counsel, thou wouldst not have done as thou didst—the more shame for them.

SOM. Spare your excuse to me; I do conceive
What you would speak. I would you could as easily
Make satisfaction to the law as to my wrongs.
I am sorry for you.

WARB. And so am I,
And heartily forgive you.

KAT. I will pray for you
For her sake, who I am sure did love you dearly. 130

SIR ART. Let us part friendly too; I am ashamed
Of my part in thy wrongs.

FRANK. You are all merciful,
And send me to my grave in peace. Sir Arthur,

Heavens send you a new heart!—[To Old Thorney.] Lastly, to you, sir;
And, though I have deserved not to be called
Your son, yet give me leave upon my knees
To beg a blessing. [Kneels.]

O. THOR. Take it; let me wet
Thy cheeks with the last tears my griefs have left me.
O, Frank, Frank, Frank!

FRANK. Let me beseech you, gentlemen,
To comfort my old father, keep him with ye; 140
Love this distressèd widow, and, as often
As you remember what a graceless man
I was, remember likewise that these are
Both free, both worthy of a better fate
Than such a son or husband as I have been.
All help me with your prayers.—On, on; 'tis just
That law should purge the guilt of blood and lust. Exit [with Officers].

[O.] CART. Go thy ways. I did not think to have shed one tear for thee, but thou hast made me water my plants spite [150 of my heart.—M[aster] Thorney, cheer up, man; whilst I can stand by you, you shall not want help to keep you from falling. We have lost our children, both on 's,² the wrong way, but we cannot help it; better or worse, 'tis now as 'tis.

O. THOR. I thank you, sir; you are more kind than I
Have cause to hope or look for.

[O.] CART. Mr. Somerton, is Kate yours or no? 160

SOM. We are agreed.

KAT. And, but my faith is passed, I should fear to be married, husbands are so cruelly unkind. Excuse me that I am thus troubled.

SOM. Thou shalt have no cause.

JUST.³ Take comfort, Mistress Winnifride.
—Sir Arthur,

¹ The spreading of the type in the original shows that this word has obviously fallen out.

² Of us.
³ The content of the following speech indicates that it should be assigned to the Justice rather than to Old Carter, as in the original.

For his abuse to you and to your husband,
Is by the bench enjoined to pay you
down　　　　　　　　　　　　169
A thousand marks.

SIR ART.　　　Which I will soon discharge.

WIN. Sir, 'tis too great a sum to be employed
Upon my funeral.

[O.] CART. Come, come! If luck had
served, Sir Arthur, and every man had his
due, somebody might have tottered ere
this, without paying fines, like it as you
list.—Come to me, Winnifride; shalt be welcome.—Make much of her, Kate, I charge
you. I do not think but she's a good wench,
and hath had wrong as well as we. [180
So let's every man home to Edmonton with
heavy hearts, yet as merry as we can, though
not as we would.

JUST. Join, friends, in sorrow; make of
all the best.
Harms past may be lamented, not
redressed.　　　　　　　　　*Exeunt.*

### EPILOGUE

*Win[nifride].*

I am a widow still, and must not sort [1]
A second choice without a good report,
Which though some widows find, and
few deserve,
Yet I dare not presume, but will not
swerve
From modest hopes. All noble tongues
are free;　　　　　　　　　　　190
The gentle may speak one kind word for
me.

　　　　　　　　　　　　　PHEN. [2]

FINIS.

[1] Select.　　　[2] This author is unidentified.

# JOHN FORD

By universal agreement Ford's forte lay in tragedy, which he practised in all its major types. He was perhaps least successful in the domestic genre, like *The Witch of Edmonton*, which was after all a collaborated play and was not really typical of his true interests. The critics' choice of his best play has always lain among *The Broken Heart*, *'Tis Pity She's a Whore*, and *Perkin Warbeck*. The last, however, falls into the specialized category of the historical tragedy, leaving the decision involving the purely romantic tragedy between *The Broken Heart* and *'Tis Pity*, even though Adams has pointed out that Ford, in specifically stating that Giovanni and Annabella, the brother and sister lovers in *'Tis Pity*, were the children of a well-to-do citizen, and thus not of the aristocracy, has introduced a slightly alien note into what would otherwise have been a purely romantic tragedy. Oliver thought that *The Broken Heart* "falls short of *'Tis Pity*, and seems to be a less mature play." William Archer estimated that *The Broken Heart* enjoys a reputation "only second" to that of *The Duchess of Malfi*, but although he felt that "Ford's spirit was, indeed, more subtle than that of Webster," he nevertheless applied his usual test of plausibility and found the play wanting. Leech felt that, although *'Tis Pity* might well be Ford's best play, it is not his most characteristic, as are *The Broken Heart* and *Perkin Warbeck*. Prior, somewhat similarly, concluded that "*The Broken Heart* is perhaps the most satisfactory of his tragedies for detailed study." Stavig described it as "a tragedy that is at once his most ambitious and his most complex," and Sargeaunt wrote: "*The Broken Heart* stands alone among Ford's own plays as among those of his contemporaries. It cannot well be compared to any other dramatic poem . . . . Its beauties are not of a kind that appeal to popular imagination, but there will always be some who will afford it a high place among the great tragedies of our literature." In fact, as Prior saw it, "The notoriety of *'Tis Pity She's a Whore*, with its story of incest between brother and sister, has tended to place all of Ford's work in a distorted focus, particularly in discussions of 'decadence' in the drama." One might indeed suggest that, if it were not for the sensationalism of its somewhat misleading title, *'Tis Pity* would not have supplanted *The Broken Heart* in the general interest today. After all, the sinning and suffering Annabella is by no means a whore in the professional sense that Dekker's Bellafront was, even though the latter did eventually turn "honest." Nor did the final scene in which the twisted and tortured Giovanni rushes onto the stage bearing on the point of his dagger the heart of his sister, whom he has murdered, have less appeal to the jaded and sensation-seeking Jacobean audience than it does to readers and spectators inured to violence today. These are some of the reasons, positive and negative, that have motivated the present editors to select *The Broken Heart* rather than *'Tis Pity* to represent Ford as a writer of romantic tragedy.

*The Broken Heart* was entered in the Stationers' Register on March 28, 1633, and published by Hugh Beeston in the same year. This quarto was the only contemporary edition of the play. According to the title page it was acted by "the King's Majesty's Servants at the Private House in the Blackfriars," but the date of the acting is uncertain, W. J. Lawrence, noticing the reference to the popular miscellany, *The Garden of Goodwill*, in IV, ii, argued a date between 1631 and 1633 (*TLS*, July 12, 1923), but it was discovered later that the title had appeared in the Register as early as 1593, and that an edition may also have appeared in 1604 (F. O. Mann, *The Works of Thomas Deloney*, Oxford, 1912). However, as Brian Morris says (introduction to the New Mermaids edition of the play, London, 1965): "Nevertheless, the 1631 edition might well have aroused interest and its evidence should not be completely discounted." On the other hand, Bentley concluded that "*The Broken Heart* must have been close in date to *Beauty in a Trance* and *The Lover's Melancholy*, or about 1627–31." Morris, after collating the texts of the copies of the quarto in the British Museum and the Bodleian Library, concluded that in spite of the bad printing, the literal errors, the wrong assignment of some speeches, and the garbled state of some passages, the careful and detailed stage directions suggest that the copy used by the printer was the author's own manuscript. There is no indication that the play was performed after its first run until the end of the nineteenth century. Although it and *The Lover's Melancholy* were named on a supplementary list of plays assigned to D'avenant on August 20, 1668 (Nicoll, *Restoration Drama*), he apparently did not stage either of them. On June 11, 1898, however, William Poel produced *The Broken Heart* as part of his series of seventeenth-century revivals at St. George's Hall, London, but he abridged much of the material and entirely omitted the scene of the suicide of Orgilus. In November 1904 the Mermaid Society gave its version of the play at the Royalty Theatre (Robert Speaight, *William Poel and the Elizabethan Revival*, London, 1954; and Sargeaunt).

As in the case of most of Ford's plays, his independence of mind is shown not only in his single authorship but also in the lack of any single source for the main action of the story. Several subsidiary, but general, sources, however, have been suggested. Sherman was the first to venture the idea that Sir Philip Sidney may have been in the background not only in the reflection of the general influence of the *Arcadia* and its atmosphere but also in the possible parallel between certain events in the play and the relationship among Sidney, Mountjoy, and Penelope Rich ("Stella and *The Broken Heart*," *PMLA*, 1909). Most critics have agreed that the still pervasive magnetism of the *Arcadia* continued to show itself in the play, and Morris has narrowed this similarity to the story of Argalus and Parthenia, which he says "shares several details with the story of Orgilus and Penthea, and celebrates the same qualities of heroic calm in a tragic situation." Oliver has recalled that Ford had already showed his interest in Lady Rich in his *Fame's Memorial*. Sargeaunt, however, is rather dubious about the parallel with the Sidney-Rich-Mountjoy affair, and suggests that if any of the play is founded on fact, as the prologue hints, it is more probable that Ford "knew of some true story of tragic love nearer to his own plot."

The attempts to relate part of the main action of the play to actual events and character have grown from four lines in the prologue:

> What may be here thought a fiction, when Time's youth
> Wanted some riper years, was known a truth,
> In which, if words have clothed the subject right,
> You may partake a pity with delight.

Looking at these lines, Giovanni M. Carsaniga, while admitting that the oracle in the play "is contrived with the same ingenious and clever antithesis" as that in the *Arcadia* and that in both the play and the novel, the characters, through their very names, are presented from a moralistic point of view, suggested that Ford might rather have had in mind in these lines the scene of the murder of Ithocles by Orgilus, with its device of the trap-chair ("The 'Truth' in John Ford's *The Broken Heart*," *Comparative Literature*, 1958). On March 17, 1551, a similar murder was performed in Antwerp by a Lucchese merchant on one of his fellow citizens. Such wide publicity resulted throughout Europe that Matteo Bandello preserved the story in Part IV of his *Novelle*. Dyce had already mentioned Bandello as a possible source for the episode without realizing that it was based on truth and not fiction, and therefore relevant to the prologue. Without knowing of the actual event, Sargeaunt also recalled Gifford's statement that such a chair had been described by the second century Greek traveler and geographer Pausanias in *Attica* and that Barnabe Barnes had used a similar device in *The Devil's Charter* in 1607. In any case, Ford must be denied any originality in his use of such an "engine." Davril followed this plot thread to its conclusion in the final scene where the crowned corpse of Ithocles, brought before the temple altar, is married by the Princess Calantha before she dies of a broken heart ("John Ford and La Corda's *Inés de Castro*," *MLN*, 1951; also discussed in his biography of Ford). Davril detected a somewhat similar scene in this Spanish play by Mejia de la Corda, but, although there is some similarity in the stage directions of the two tragedies, there is no way of telling whether Ford knew this play—or even knew Spanish.

The general influence of English dramatists other than Barnes has also been claimed by certain critics. Stavig has maintained that when Ford wrote tragedies he turned to "the Italianate tragedy of intrigue," as previously practised by Kyd, Marlowe, Shakespeare, Chapman, Tourneur, Webster, Fletcher, Middleton, and others, and specifically cited *Bussy d'Ambiois*, *The White Devil*, *The Duchess of Malfi*, *The Changeling*, and *Women, Beware Women* as being in the background of *The Broken Heart*, *'Tis Pity*, and *Love's Sacrifice*. Morris also felt Ford's debt to Webster in some passages, particularly from *The White Devil*, and detected some echoes from Shakespeare, especially in the mad scene. Davril, too, after citing the linking of the names of Ford and Shakespeare by earlier writers like Thomas May, Charles Macklin, and Charles Lamb, asserted that the influence of Shakespeare is manifest in almost all of Ford's independent plays, not only in many transformed phrases, but in the resemblance of the madness of Calantha to that of Ophelia and Cordelia ("Shakespeare and Ford," *SJ*, 1958).

Perhaps the most discussed of all the influences on Ford's romantic tragedies and tragicomedies were those of the two contemporary schools of Platonic love and Burtonian melancholy. Stavig, in his chapter on "Ford and the Drama of His Time," has summarized these. Pointing out that Ford seems to have had no close personal associations with the court, he concluded that the playwright nevertheless could not escape the influence of Queen Henrietta Maria's Platonic love cult, which differed from the brand of Platonism reverenced in Elizabeth's day in that in the latter there was more stress on marriage whereas in the former the emphasis was placed on rational, spiritual, non-physical love. Two modern writers on the influence of this cult on Ford have disagreed in their conclusions, though both have based them on the same plays. George F. Sensabaugh, in *The Tragic Muse of John Ford*, after examining all the plays and masques on this subject presented at court during the Caroline period, concluded that they all reveal libertine tendencies and justify Ford's reputation as the "decadent high priest" of Caroline drama, drawing characters defying convention and arguing in favor of adultery and even incest—characters struggling in a world of physical forces crossing swords with the laws of society. This, Stavig thought, is a different and lower form of tragic suffering from that in the Greeks and Shakespeare, where man's free will is not fettered and moral values are not confused. Alfred Harbage, on the other hand, in his book on *The Cavalier Drama*, regarded most of these court plays as essentially innocent and moral, and saw little connection between them and Ford. Stavig concluded that Harbage was right about the innocence of the themes of the plays, but that Sensabaugh was right in arguing that the cult did influence Ford, though at the same time he misunderstood the nature of the influence in failing to give proper stress to the element of satire in the court dramatists' treatment of Platonic love. In the court itself there was a considerable difference between theory and practice. Ford succeeded in taking advantage of the popularity of the Platonic cult and the Burtonian vogue at the same time, under the bias of his own particular outlook on life. Sensabaugh considered both these influences corrupting.

Much has been written in recent years, especially by Americans, on Burton's *The Anatomy of Melancholy* as a forerunner of modern psychoanalysis and even psychiatry (e.g., Bergen Evans, *The Psychiatry of Robert Burton*, Columbia University Press, 1944). So far as Ford is concerned, the most complete studies have been those of Sensabaugh, Davril, and especially S. Blaine Ewing, *Burtonian Melancholy in the Plays of John Ford* (Princeton University Press, 1940), supplemented by articles by Mary Cochnower and Lawrence Babb. Stavig, while admitting his indebtedness to their work, qualifies his acceptance of the influence of Burton on Ford by reminding his readers that, since Burton was "writing a compendium of the learning of his day," Ford's direct debt might well have been far less than many have supposed. As did most of the medical and psychological theorists of the time, Burton believed that the emotions and passions of the mind and spirit were closely associated with the humors, or physical elements of the body, and that a disturbance in the balance of the latter resulted in excesses which found release in the passions; that is, in what was essentially a disease. As Stavig summarized the Burtonian theory, ". . . the rational soul must control the sensitive soul." Moreover, since in the seventeenth century "medical science was still the handmaiden of Christian ethics," it was vital that prayer accompany treatment. Since love has always been one of the major passions affecting human character and life, Burton believed that when it is controlled by reason it is noble, but if not so controlled it is ignoble. He thus went back eventually to Plato and to the Renaissance theory of Marsilio Ficino and others that there are two Venuses and two kinds of love. Though Burton discussed the various kinds of worthy love, he was mostly preoccupied with love as a disease, "commonly described as heroical love, or love-melancholy." Unfortunately, but also naturally, men often—undeliberately—confused the "honorable intentions of divine or Platonic love with their lustful desires for fleshly woman." Stavig concluded, before examining both Ford's tragicomedies and his tragedies from this point of view, that Ford's debt to Burton's ideas on love-melancholy was great, but that his plays nevertheless did not conform to a mere application of the other's ideas to imagined situations. He seems to suggest that "even the most villainous behavior can be understood if we seek out the causes." Ribner, too, would reject the view of the ultra-Burtonian school that Ford's characters are primarily clinical case-studies, and that Ford is simply a scientific determinist, who "removes human activity from the realm of ethical choice, and anticipating the exponents of modern thought, looks at life with amoral eyes." Though both Eliot (*Elizabethan Dramatists*) and Bradbrook (*Themes and Conventions of Elizabethan Tragedy*) accused Ford of writing without any real ethical or moral purpose, Ribner suggested that "Ford struggled as fully as his predecessors had struggled with the problem of man's position in the universe . . . . What sets Ford apart from his contemporaries is not a disregard for moral issues, but an inability to lead his audience to a full resolution of the moral problems which he poses." Ribner attributes this inconclusiveness of his "tragedies of paradox" to the fact that they were the "products of a skeptical age which can no longer accept without question the doctrine of a human law reflecting the will of God in a perfectly reasonable and harmonious universe."

From the standpoint of Ford's use of the passion of love in *The Broken Heart*, Morris points out that there are three contrasting pairs of lovers, one acting as a norm and a foil to the other two, whose passion is outside that norm. As many critics have remarked (e.g., Ewing, Morris, Oliver), Bassanes is a living illustration of the symptoms of the type of Burtonian melancholy which springs particularly from the knowledge of one's own sterility and sometimes brings a man close to insanity. Oliver has found Bassanes scarcely credible in his jealousy, in fact even comically absurd, when he bursts in on Penthea and her brother Ithocles and accuses them of "bestial incest." But then he defends Ford in his skillful use of this device to accomplish Bassanes' self-reform which turns him into a believable and even likable figure at the end—a man whose new-found dignity and stoicism justify Calantha in appointing him Sparta's marshal. Other critics, like Sargeaunt, have felt that Bassanes' character is still too unstable to deserve such trust. There has also been some criticism of the consistency of the motivation of some of the other characters, such as Calantha herself, particularly in the remarkable scene (so fulsomely praised by Lamb) in which she stoically, without interrupting her dance, successively hears the whispered announcements of the deaths of her father the king, of Penthea, and of Ithocles.

To Ford, presumably, this almost inhuman control of the emotions was part of building the Spartan setting and atmosphere. Sargeaunt has called attention to Ford's departure in this play from his usual custom of choosing an Italianate background for his plays because of the English concept of Renaissance Italy. Here, however, the tone is entirely different because, although the motivating passions are as great, "they lie concealed for the time in a depth whose surface is calm." Sherman observed that, although the Sparta of this play is modeled on the Sparta of the *Arcadia*, it is really only used as a disguise to hide the real significance of the plot. Morris has voiced the opinion that this Sparta is not only that of the *Arcadia* but of Plutarch's life of Lycurgus as well. But to Sargeaunt the Ford of *The Broken Heart* is "indeed the Ford of Swinburne's sonnet, hewing from hard marble the figures of Orgilus, Ithocles, and Calantha," who are all Spartan in the popular sense of the word. Even the handling of the deaths is Spartan and classical, in contrast to those of *'Tis Pity*—perishing by self-starvation, murder accepted in cold blood, suicide by calm vein-slitting, quiet death by a broken heart. (No critic, however, seems to have questioned the old myth that a human heart can actually break and cause death for this reason alone.) Tecnicus, the artist-philosopher, heightens the Spartan atmosphere with his instructions to the disguised Orgilus. Stavig remarks that in attempting to account for the "coldness and restraint" and the "grave and chill dignity" of the play scholars have called attention to Ford's introduction of spectacle, music, dance, and ritual. But "no one has sufficiently stressed that these devices are like the symbolic techniques of the masques and the emblem books." Nevertheless, although the play may seem at first glance to be one in which the characters, at least in their own eyes if not in those of the other characters, are "helplessly and heroically" struggling against an uncontrollable fate, their tragedies are at least partially due to their acceptance of the Spartan ideal which calls for an unyielding submission to that fate. At the same time, Sparta itself, as Tecnicus describes it to Orgilus, is in a state of moral chaos which Orgilus attempts to purge and thus provide the basis for a better future society, though actually his motives for all his actions may not be so high-minded as he pretends.

In view of what has already been said or implied about Ford's plots, it may come as a surprise to hear that, as R. J. Kaufmann states it, "The strange silences which attend the movements of Ford's heroes have been remarked by the critics. They are silent because their personal reasons are sufficient; the world's claims are thus not opposed and equal, but negligible and incommensurate ("Ford's Tragic Perspective," *Elizabethan Drama: Modern Essays in Criticism*, New York and Oxford, 1961). Ribner, in *Jacobean Tragedy*, has similarly called attention to the unity of tone in *The Broken Heart*, described by Ellis-Fermor as "a quality of stillness" (*Jacobean Drama*). As these two see it, in spite of the fact that the play is filled with violence, suffering, and death, we do not feel "the turbulence of passion." Nevertheless, to Ribner, this very quality is the play's weakness as tragedy, since it induces a "sense of detachment" so that it is difficult to feel the "vitality and the significance of the moral issues the play poses." Leech, too, saw in Ford's three most characteristic tragedies, *Love's Sacrifice*, *The Broken Heart*, and *Perkin Warbeck*, a comparative indifference to event, a "cultivation of the static scene," which contrasts so strongly with the impression given by *'Tis Pity*. Morris and others have commented on the structure of the play from this point of view. Morris remarked on the slight amount of real action, in which "characters come and go, usually in ceremonial groups and processions, and dialogues frequently reach the very edge of silence before the pressure is released." This kind of austere, almost episodic, dramaturgy builds up to the three great spectacular scenes at the end: the death of Ithocles, the dance scene, and the temple scene before the altar.

Although Sargeaunt found Ford's conduct of plot "entirely satisfactory" only in *The Broken Heart* and *Perkin Warbeck*, the former being "perhaps the greatest of Ford's achievements," Leech thought he had detected some "clumsinesses" in the action, and referred to Emil Koeppel's speculation that Ford had originally intended a love affair between Ithocles and Euphrania, Orgilus's sister, but had forgotten it as his play developed (*Quellenstudien zu den Dramen George Chapmans, Philip Massingers, und John Fords*). Strangely and contradictorily enough, it was the Belgian poet-dramatist Maurice Maeterlinck who in his preface to his French adaptation of *'Tis Pity* under the title of *Annabella* had first introduced this idea of "les silences" and "les intervalles qu'il y a entre les scènes" as a special trait of Ford's plays. This observation, however, might be expected from a playwright who was noted for his own theory that the best drama is one of silences and stasis.

A point constantly reiterated by Stavig and his school is that in spite of the sensational events in Ford's plays he was not primarily a commercial exploiter of sensationalism and that, although he seems to sympathize with his convention-breaking characters, he does so without excusing them. In fact, by showing the disasters which follow when the social codes are broken, even if they are in a corrupt society, he clearly does not question the moral order. This attitude Stavig epitomizes in the phrase "concord in discord." Prior agrees that in *The Broken Heart* Ford was as much preoccupied with its moral problems, "with reference both to the social forms and laws which conflict in the claims of love, and to the demands of personal honor which the characters, caught in various dilemmas, must try to satisfy," as he was with his sympathetic probing of psychological distortions. This question of honor becomes one of the themes of the play, and its different and often conflicting concepts afford some of its major clashes, as in the situation in which, as Ribner puts it, honor becomes dishonor and dishonor honor when Orgilus feels he must kill his admired friend, but at the same time forfeits his honor in the manner of the killing. Such are often the paradoxes of the revenge tragedy. The main reason for the introduction of Tecnicus into the story is to provide "an ideal of honor against which the actions of the other characters may be measured."

A weighty aspect of this problem of honor has to do with Ford's conception of the relationship between love and marriage, and the conditions of a true marriage. Actually, as Peter Ure decided in his article on "Marriage and the Domestic Drama in Heywood and Ford" (*ES*, 1957), Ford's attitude toward marriage in *The Broken Heart* was the orthodox one. Sargeaunt emphatically disagreed with Sherman's opinion that it was "a mere subservience to conventionality" that made Penthea hold out against the pleadings of Orgilus. Although her brother has forced her to marry Bassanes against her will, and without love on her part, she is still convinced that her personal morality will not permit her to be unfaithful to her detested husband. George H. Blayney, in "Convention, Plot, and Structure in *The Broken Heart*" (*MP*, 1958), made the same point and reinforced it with a discussion of the importance of the betrothal ceremony as a virtual equivalent of marriage in the seventeenth century. The conflict of these two conventions is responsible for the main plot of the play, and makes the problem of the "enforced marriage" a dominant theme.

*The Broken Heart* is also exceptional among English tragedies in ways other than those already reviewed. As Oliver noted, ". . . the play has been called, not altogether unaptly, 'a revenge play without a villain,'" or, as Ribner put it, "There is no active force of evil in *The Broken Heart*." The characters are all of "exemplary virtue" in their various ways, but they are caught in the inescapable consequences of a past action growing from "commitments to social codes which at last seem arbitrary and without meaning." Nor does the play have a real protagonist since, as Eliot remarked, ". . . the plot is somewhat overloaded and distracted by the affairs of unfortunate personages, all of whom have an equal claim on our attention." Morris, dissenting from Eliot's criticisms of the plot, agreed with him on the lack of a central figure, and added that, even as "a 'de casibus' tragedy, about the fall of a noble man," its tragic pattern is blurred; since "the major characters are neither great nor little, there is no fall from great happiness to great despair, because no great happiness has ever existed in the play." It is also lacking in any humor, a deficiency which to Leech's mind is an asset, since Ford's humor in other tragedies and tragicomedies was of a pretty farcical and crude type. Similarly, as Stavig saw, the satirical element, so strong in *'Tis Pity* and *Love's Sacrifice*, is almost entirely absent; thus Ford was able to concentrate more on the understanding of suffering and less on the exposure of weakness. In spite of these missing elements, and because of the prevailing unity of tone throughout, few readers today would agree with Charles C. McDonald, who, in "The Design of John Ford's *The Broken Heart*" (*SP*, 1962), concluded that the play "clearly has not the strength or vigour of the early Stuart tragedies; it is fragile, more uneven, and more pathetic than tragic in its effects . . . ."

Whether Ford's language and verse are as harmonious with the Spartan atmosphere he wished to create has been questioned by some critics. Although Anderson, in his article, "The Heart of the Banquet: Imagery in Ford's *'Tis Pity She's a Whore* and *The Broken Heart*" (*Studies in English Literature, 1500–1900*, 1962), spoke of Ford's masterful handling of imagery, Morris felt that the immediate impression in reading his plays is the remarkable absence of figures of speech, unlike the virtuosity of so much Jacobean writing. Contrariwise, Prior, although remarking on the thinness and crudeness of much of Ford's diction, compared him with the preceding poetic dramatists in his having "the same interest in the figurative use of language, and the same desire to employ verse and the language of poetry not merely as a convenient or ornate instrument of dialogue but as an essential part of a serious dramatic art." Sargeaunt, perhaps, saw the closest harmony between Ford's style and his matter, and credited him with perfecting "a unique mode of expression in dramatic blank verse." She found the chief characteristics to be "an extreme simplicity of diction with a free use of colloquialism, and a carefully regulated, and, indeed, . . . an almost rigid form of blank verse," and maintained that, although he did not entirely forgo the use of metaphor, "when his language is most truly characteristic it goes straight to the heart of the matter and reveals the truth in her naked perfection." Thus Sargeaunt seems to feel that Ford has forged a truly Spartan language to go with his Spartan material and setting. She also felt that he did not use "looseness of metrical structure" to give the effect of real speech and commented on his sparing employment of extrametrical style at the ends of lines and also on his sparing use of couplets. (In citing the article by F. E. Pierce, "The Collaboration of Dekker and Ford," *Anglia*, 1912, she stated that she believed that Pierce's statistical percentages in many of these matters were far too high.) Anderson, on the other hand, while admitting that Ford has "moments of profound simplicity," maintained that they are usually set in the context of "an elaborate and courtly language," in which "the core of the meaning is overlaid with a complicated yet loosely articulated syntax which gives . . . an aureate grandeur of utterance." Even though this "periphrastic manner" implies a civilized social code, the question might well be raised as to whether a more laconic style might not be more appropriate to Spartans. Leech, in fact, while praising Ford for creating "an imaginable world consistently peopled," whose inhabitants speak in "fittingly noble accents," wondered whether Ford was not "expressing a wish for a proud and yet affectionate courtliness which he cannot fully credit." Stavig, while commenting on the "simplicity and economy" of Ford's language, which nevertheless makes for an atmosphere of formality and elevation, and which he relates to Ford's philosophy, also described it as "concord in discord."

Ford's desire to set his characters in abstract frames, as in the descriptive phrases in the dramatis personae, also contributes to the disciplined, regulated, or, as Leech put it, almost emblematic atmosphere of the play. Though at first the reader might find this device a little irksome, Leech agreed with Davril that it lent a more immutable quality to each character. But both Leech and Morris had to admit that some of Ford's

labels seem arbitrary and almost without point.   Morris traced the name Amyclas
to the early settlement of the same name close to the city of Sparta and also to the
name of the Laconian, or Lacedemonian, king in the *Arcadia*, the probable direct source.
Amelas, Morris discovered, really means "neglectful," not "trusty."   He was unable
to trace the word Groneas at all, but pointed out that the name Hemophil in the 1633
quarto was usually printed as Lemophil, which would mean "lover of the wine-vat"
rather than the "glutton" of the dramatis personae.

The present text is based on Henry de Vocht's reprint of the 1633 quarto in the
Royal Library of The Hague, but reference has also been made to the Gifford-Dyce
edition of Ford's works.   Brian Morris's edition in the New Mermaids series in 1965
has also been useful.

# THE BROKEN HEART[1]

## BY

### JOHN FORD[2]

THE SCENE: *Sparta.*

[THE TIME: *About the eighth century, B.C.*]

## THE SPEAKERS' NAMES FITTED TO THEIR QUALITIES

AMYCLAS, *common* [3] *to the kings of Laconia.*
ITHOCLES, *Honor of Loveliness: a favorite.*
ORGILUS, *Angry: son to Crotolon.*
BASSANES, *Vexation: a jealous nobleman.*
ARMOSTES, *an Appeaser: a councilor of state.*
CROTOLON, *Noise: another councilor.*
PROPHILUS, *Dear: friend to Ithocles.*
NEARCHUS, *Young Prince: Prince of Argos.*
TECNICUS, *Artist: a philosopher.*
HEMOPHIL, *Glutton* ⎫
GRONEAS, *Tavern Haunter* ⎬ *two courtiers.*
AMELUS, *Trusty: friend to Nearchus.*
PHULAS, *Watchful: servant to Bassanes.*

CALANTHA, *Flower of Beauty: the king' daughter.*
PENTHEA, *Complaint: sister to Ithocles* [*and wife to Bassanes*].
EUPHRANEA, *Joy: a maid of honor* [*and daughter to Crotolon*].
CHRISTALLA, *Crystal* ⎫
PHILEMA, *a Kiss* ⎬ *maids of honor.*
GRAUSIS,[4] *Old Beldam: overseer of Penthea.*

### PERSONS INCLUDED

THRASUS, *Fierceness: Father of Ithocles.*
APLOTES, *Simplicity: Orgilus so disguised.*
[COURTIERS, OFFICERS, ATTENDANTS, ETC.]

## THE PROLOGUE

Our scene is Sparta. He whose best of art
Hath drawn this piece calls it *The Broken Heart.*
The title lends no expectation here
Of apish laughter, or of some lame jeer
At place or persons; no pretended clause [5]
Of jests, fit for a brothel, courts applause
From vulgar admiration; such low songs,
Tuned to unchaste ears, suit not modest tongues.
The Virgin Sisters[6] then deserved fresh bays
When Innocence and Sweetness crowned their lays;                          10
Then vices gasped for breath, whose whole commerce
Was whipped to exile by unblushing verse.
This law we keep in our presentment now,
Not to take freedom more than we allow;[7]
What may be here thought a fiction, when Time's youth
Wanted some riper years, was known a truth,
In which, if words have clothed the subject right,
You may partake a pity with delight.

[1] The title continues: "A Tragedy. Acted by the King's Majesty's Servants at the Private House in the Blackfriars. *Fide Honor.*"
[2] The author's name does not appear on the title-page, but is affixed to the adulatory dedication (here omitted) to William, Lord Craven, Baron of Hampsted Marshall. The Latin motto is also an anagram of Ford's name, used elsewhere instead of his signature.
[3] *I.e.*, a name common.
[4] Throughout the text of the original, almost invariably misprinted *Gransis.*
[5] Close; *i.e.*, implication through a double meaning.
[6] The Muses.
[7] Sanction.

Actus Primus. Scena Prima.

[*A room in Crotolon's house.*]

*Enter Crotolon and Orgilus.*

Crot. Dally not further; I will know the reason
That speeds thee to this journey.
Org.                    Reason? Good sir,
I can yield many.
Crot.           Give me one, a good one;
Such I expect, and ere we part must have.
Athens? Pray, why to Athens? You intend not
To kick against the world, turn cynic, stoic,
Or read the logic lecture, or become
An Areopagite,[1] and judge in causes
Touching the commonwealth? For, as I take it,
The budding of your chin cannot prognosticate                     10
So grave an honor.
Org.               All this I acknowledge.
Crot. You do! Then, son, if books and love of knowledge
Inflame you to this travel, here in Sparta
You may as freely study.
Org.                'Tis not that, sir.
Crot. Not that, sir! As a father, I command thee
To acquaint me with the truth.
Org.                Thus I obey 'e.
After so many quarrels as dissension,
Fury, and rage had broached in blood, and sometimes
With death to such confederates as sided
With now-dead Thrasus and yourself, my lord,                     20
Our present king, Amyclas, reconciled
Your eager swords and sealed a gentle peace.
Friends you professed yourselves, which to confirm,
A resolution for a lasting league
Betwixt your families was entertained,
By joining in a Hymenean bond
Me and the fair Penthea, only daughter
To Thrasus.
Crot.    What of this?
Org.        Much, much, dear sir.  28
A freedom of converse, an interchange
Of holy and chaste love, so fixed our souls

In a firm growth of [2] union, that no time
Can eat into the pledge; we had enjoyed
The sweets our vows expected, had not cruelty
Prevented all those triumphs [3] we prepared for,
By Thrasus his untimely death.
Crot.                    Most certain.
Org. From this time sprouted up that poisonous stalk
Of aconite, whose ripened fruit hath ravished
All health, all comfort of a happy life,
For Ithocles, her brother, proud of youth,
And prouder in his power, nourished closely                     40
The memory of former discontents,
To glory in revenge. By cunning partly,
Partly by threats, a [4] woos at once and forces
His virtuous sister to admit a marriage
With Bassanes, a nobleman, in honor
And riches, I confess, beyond my fortunes.
Crot. All this is no sound reason to importune
My leave for thy departure.
Org.                Now it follows.
Beauteous Penthea, wedded to this torture                     49
By an insulting brother, being secretly
Compelled to yield her virgin freedom up
To him who never can usurp her heart,
Before contracted mine, is now so yoked
To a most barbarous thralldom, misery,
Affliction, that he savors not humanity,
Whose sorrow melts not into more than pity
In hearing but her name.
Crot.               As how, pray?
Org.                    Bassanes,
The man that calls her wife, considers truly
What heaven of perfections he is lord of
By thinking fair Penthea his; this thought                     60
Begets a kind of monster-love, which love
Is nurse unto a fear so strong and servile
As brands all dotage with a jealousy.
All eyes who gaze upon that shrine of beauty,

---

[1] A member of the highest Athenian court of justice.
[2] Some copies of the original insert *holy* here.
[3] Celebrations.                     [4] He.

He doth resolve,[1] do homage to the miracle;
Someone, he is assured, may now or then,
If opportunity but sort,[2] prevail.
So much, out of a self-unworthiness,
His fears transport him—not that he finds cause  69
In her obedience, but his own distrust.

CROT. You spin out your discourse.

ORG.  My griefs are violent;
For, knowing how the maid was heretofore
Courted by me, his jealousies grow wild
That I should steal again into her favors,
And undermine her virtues, which the gods
Know I nor dare nor dream of. Hence, from hence
I undertake a voluntary exile—
First, by my absence to take off the cares
Of jealous Bassanes; but chiefly, sir,
To free Penthea from a hell on earth; 80
Lastly, to lose the memory of something
Her presence makes to live in me afresh.

CROT. Enough, my Orgilus, enough. To Athens
I give a full consent.—Alas, good lady!—
We shall hear from thee often?

ORG.  Often.

CROT.  See,
Thy sister comes to give a farewell.

*Enter Euphranea.*

EUPH.  Brother!

ORG. Euphranea, thus upon thy cheeks I print
A brother's kiss, more careful of thine honor,
Thy health, and thy well-doing than my life.  89
Before we part, in presence of our father,
I must prefer a suit to 'e.

EUPH.  You may style it,
My brother, a command.

ORG.  That you will promise
To pass never to any man, however [3]
Worthy, your faith, till, with our father's leave,
I give a free consent.

<hr/>

[1] Conclude.
[2] Occur.
[3] Here and in a few other passages the line division has been regularized.

CROT.  An easy motion! [4]
I'll promise for her, Orgilus.

ORG.  Your pardon.
Euphranea's oath must yield me satisfaction.

EUPH. By Vesta's sacred fires I swear.

CROT.  And I
By great Apollo's beams join in the vow,
Not without thy allowance to bestow her
On any living.

ORG.  Dear Euphranea, 101
Mistake me not; far, far 'tis from my thought,
As far from any wish of mine, to hinder
Preferment to an honorable bed
Or fitting fortune. Thou art young and handsome,
And 'twere injustice—more, a tyranny—
Not to advance thy merit. Trust me, sister,
It shall be my first care to see thee matched
As may become thy choice and our contents.
I have your oath.

EUPH.  You have. But mean you, brother, 110
To leave us, as you say?

CROT.  Ay, ay, Euphranea;
He has just grounds direct him. I will prove
A father and a brother to thee.

EUPH.  Heaven
Does look into the secrets of all hearts.
Gods, you have mercy with 'e, else—

CROT.  Doubt nothing
Thy brother will return in safety to us.

ORG. Souls sunk in sorrows never are without 'em;
They change fresh airs, but bear their griefs about 'em.  *Exeunt omnes.*

## Scene ii.

[*A room in the palace.*]

*Flourish. Enter Amyclas the king, Armostes, Prophilus, and Attendants.*

AMY. The Spartan gods are gracious; our humility
Shall bend before their altars, and perfume
Their temples with abundant sacrifice.

<hr/>

[4] Proposal.

See, lords, Amyclas, your old king, is
ent'ring
Into his youth again! I shall shake off
This silver badge of age, and change this
snow
For hairs as gay as are Apollo's locks;
Our heart leaps in new vigor.
ARM. May old time
Run back to double your long life, great
sir!
AMY. It will, it must, Armostes; thy bold
nephew, 10
Death-braving Ithocles, brings to our
gates
Triumphs and peace upon his conquering
sword.
Laconia is a monarchy at length,
Hath in this latter war trod under
foot
Messene's pride; Messene bows her neck
To Lacedemon's royalty. O, 'twas
A glorious victory, and doth deserve
More than a chronicle—a temple, lords,
A temple to the name of Ithocles!—
Where didst thou leave him, Prophilus?
PRO. At Pephon, 20
Most gracious sovereign; twenty of the
noblest
Of the Messenians there attend your
pleasure
For such conditions as you shall propose
In settling peace and liberty of life.
AMY. When comes your friend, the gen-
eral?
PRO. He promised
To follow with all speed convenient.

*Enter Crotolon, Calantha, Christalla, Philema
[with a garland], and Euphranea.*

AMY. Our daughter!—Dear Calantha, the
happy news,
The conquest of Messene, hath already
Enriched thy knowledge.
CAL. With the circumstance
And manner of the fight, related faith-
fully 30
By Prophilus himself.—But, pray, sir,
tell me
How doth the youthful general demean[1]
His actions in these fortunes?
PRO. Excellent princess,
Your own fair eyes may soon report a
truth

Unto your judgment, with what modera-
tion,
Calmness of nature, measure, bounds,
and limits
Of thankfulness and joy, a doth digest
Such amplitude of his success as would
In others, molded of a spirit less clear,
Advance 'em to comparison with heaven.
But Ithocles—
CAL. Your friend—
PRO. He is so, madam, 41
In which the period[2] of my fate consists;
He, in this firmament of honor, stands
Like a star fixed, not moved with any
thunder
Of popular applause or sudden lightning
Of self-opinion; he hath served his coun-
try,
And thinks 'twas but his duty.
CROT. You describe
A miracle of man.
AMY. Such, Crotolon,
On forfeit of a king's word, thou wilt find
him.—
Hark, warning of his coming! All attend
him. *Flourish.* 50

*Enter Ithocles, Hemophil, and Groneas, the
rest of the Lords ushering him in.*

AMY. Return into these arms, thy home,
thy sanctuary,
Delight of Sparta, treasure of my bosom,
Mine own, own Ithocles!
ITH. Your humblest subject.
ARM. Proud of the blood I claim an in-
terest in,
As brother to thy mother, I embrace
thee,
Right noble nephew.
ITH. Sir, your love's too partial.
CROT. Our country speaks by me, who by
thy valor,
Wisdom, and service shares in this great
action,
Returning thee, in part[3] of thy due merits,
A general welcome.
ITH. You exceed in bounty. 60
CAL. Christalla, Philema, the chaplet.—
[*Takes the chaplet from them.*] Ith-
ocles,
Upon the wings of Fame the singular
And chosen fortune of an high attempt

---

[1] Conduct.  [2] Summation.  [3] On behalf.

Is borne so past the view of common
    sight
That I myself with mine own hands have
    wrought,
To crown thy temples, this provincial
    garland.[1]
Accept, wear, and enjoy it as our gift
Deserved, not purchased.

ITH.                        Y' are a royal maid.

AMY. She is in all our daughter.

ITH.                            Let me blush,
Acknowledging how poorly I have
    served,                                    70
What nothings I have done, compared
    with th' honors
Heaped on the issue of a willing mind;
In that lay mine ability, that only.
For who is he so sluggish from his birth,
So little worthy of a name or country,
That owes not out of gratitude for life
A debt of service, in what kind soever
Safety or counsel of the commonwealth
Requires, for payment?

CAL.            A speaks truth.

ITH.                        Whom heaven
Is pleased to style victorious, there, to
    such,                                       80
Applause runs madding, like the drunken
    priests
In Bacchus' sacrifices, without reason,
Voicing the leader-on a demigod,
Whenas, indeed, each common soldier's
    blood
Drops down as current coin in that hard
    purchase
As his whose much more delicate condi-
    tion
Hath sucked the milk of ease. Judgment
    commands,
But resolution executes. I use not,
Before this royal presence, these fit
    slights
As in contempt of such as can direct;  90
My speech hath other end—not to at-
    tribute
All praise to one man's fortune, which is
    strengthéd
By many hands. For instance, here is
    Prophilus,
A gentleman—I cannot flatter truth—
Of much desert; and, though in other
    rank,

Both Hemophil and Groneas were not
    missing
To wish their country's peace; for, in a
    word,
All there did strive their best, and 'twas
    our duty.

AMY. Courtiers turn soldiers?—We vouch-
    safe our hand.
    [Hemophil and Groneas kiss his hand.]
Observe [2] your great example.

HEM.                    With all diligence. 100

GRO. Obsequiously and hourly.

AMY.                        Some repose
After these toils are needful. We must
    think on
Conditions for the conquered; they ex-
    pect [3] 'em.
On!—Come, my Ithocles.

EUPH.                    Sir, with your favor,
I need not a supporter.

PRO.                    Fate instructs me.

Exeunt. Manent [4] Hemophil, Groneas, Chris-
    talla, et Philema.    Hemophil stays
    Christalla; Groneas, Philema.

CHRIS. With me?

PHIL.            Indeed, I dare not stay.

HEM.                        Sweet lady,
Soldiers are blunt—your lip.

CHRIS.                    Fie, this is rudeness;
You went not hence such creatures.

GRO.                        Spirit of valor
Is of a mounting nature.

PHIL.                    It appears so.—  109
Pray, in earnest, how many men apiece
Have you two been the death of?

GRO.                    Faith, not many;
We were composed of mercy.

HEM.                        For our daring,
You heard the general's approbation
Before the king.

CHRIS.        You "wished your country's
    peace;"
That showed your charity. Where are
    your spoils,
Such as the soldier fights for?

PHIL.                    They are coming.

CHRIS. By the next carrier, are they not?

GRO.                    Sweet Philema,
When I was in the thickest of mine
    enemies,
Slashing off one man's head, another's
    nose,
Another's arms and legs—

---

[1] I.e., one "conferred on those who . . . had
added a *Province* to the empire" (Gifford).

[2] Do homage to.    [3] Await.    [4] Remain.

PHIL.            And all together [1]—    120

GRO. Then would I with a sigh remember
    thee,
    And cry, "Dear Philema, 'tis for thy sake
    I do these deeds of wonder!"—Dost not
    love me
    With all thy heart now?

PHIL.            Now as heretofore.
    I have not put my love to use; [2] the
    principal
    Will hardly yield an interest.

GRO.            By Mars,
    I'll marry thee!

PHIL.        By Vulcan, y' are forsworn,
    Except my mind do alter strangely.

GRO.            One word.

CHRIS. You lie beyond all modesty. For-
    bear me!    129

HEM. I'll make thee mistress of a city; 'tis
    Mine own by conquest.

CHRIS.            By petition; sue for 't
    In forma pauperis. [3] City? Kennel! [4] Gal-
    lants,
    Off with your feathers; [5] put on aprons,
    gallants.
    Learn to reel, [6] thrum, [7] or trim a lady's
    dog,
    And be good, quiet souls of peace, hob-
    goblins!

HEM. Christalla!

CHRIS.        Practice to drill hogs, in hope
    To share in the acorns. Soldiers? Corn-
    cutters,
    But not so valiant; they ofttimes draw
    blood,
    Which you durst never do. When you
    have practiced    139
    More wit or more civility, we'll rank 'e
    I' th' list of men; till then, brave things-
    at-arms,
    Dare not to speak to us—most potent
    Groneas!—

PHIL. And Hemophil the hardy!—at your
    services.

GRO. They scorn us as they did before we
    went.

HEM. Hang 'em! Let us scorn them, and
    be revenged.
        Exeunt Chri[stalla] et Philema.

[1] Gifford-Dyce reading. Original reads altogether.
[2] I.e., lent it out for profit.
[3] In the status of a pauper.    [4] Doghouse.
[5] Gifford-Dyce reading. Original reads fathers.
[6] Wind yarn.        [7] Make tufts.

GRO. Shall we?

HEM. We will; and, when we slight them
    thus,
    Instead of following them, they'll follow
    us;
    It is a woman's nature.

GRO.        'Tis a scurvy one. Exeunt omnes.

### SCENE iii.

[The palace gardens adjoining a grove.]

Enter Tecnicus, a philosopher, and Orgilus
            disguised like a scholar of his.

TEC. Tempt not the stars, young man;
    thou canst not play
    With the severity of fate. This change
    Of habit and disguise in outward view
    Hides not the secrets of thy soul within
    thee
    From their quick-piercing eyes, which
    dive at all times
    Down to thy thoughts; in thy aspect I
    note
    A consequence of danger.

ORG.            Give me leave,
    Grave Tecnicus, without foredooming
    destiny,
    Under thy roof to ease my silent griefs,
    By applying to my hidden wounds the
    balm    10
    Of thy oraculous lectures. If my fortune
    Run such a crooked byway as to wrest
    My steps to ruin, yet thy learnéd pre-
    cepts
    Shall call me back and set my footings
    straight.
    I will not court the world.

TEC.            Ah, Orgilus,
    Neglects in young men of delights and
    life
    Run often to extremities; they care not
    For harms to others who contemn their
    own.

ORG. But I, most learnéd artist, am not so
    much
    At odds with nature that I grutch [8]
    the thrift    20
    Of any true deserver; nor doth malice [9]
    Of present hopes so check them with
    despair
    As that I yield to thought of more
    affliction

[8] Grudge.        [9] Misfortune.

Than what is incident to frailty; where-
fore
Impute not this retiréd course of living
Some little time to any other cause
Than what I justly render—the infor-
mation
Of an unsettled mind; as the effect
Must clearly witness.

TEC.                    Spirit of truth inspire thee!
On these conditions I conceal thy
change,                                                    30
And willingly admit thee for an audi-
tor.—
I'll to my study.

ORG.                    I to contemplations
In these delightful walks.—

                                        [*Exit Tecnicus.*]
                    Thus metamorphized [1]
I may without suspicion hearken after
Penthea's usage and Euphranea's faith.
Love, thou art full of mystery!   The
deities
Themselves are not secure [2] in search-
ing out
The secrets of those flames, which,
hidden, waste
A breast made tributary to the laws
Of beauty; physic yet hath never
found                                                        40
A remedy to cure a lover's wound.—
Ha!  Who are those that cross yon
private walk
Into the shadowing grove in amorous
foldings?

*Prophilus passeth over, supporting Euphra-
nea, and whispering.*

My sister—O, my sister?  'Tis Euphra-
nea
With Prophilus!   Supported too!   I
would
It were an apparition!  Prophilus
Is Ithocles his friend.   It strangely
puzzles me.
Again?  Help me, my book; this scholar's
habit
Must stand my privilege; [3] my mind is
busy,
Mine eyes and ears are open.

                                        *Walk by, reading.*

[1] Metamorphosed.
[2] Certain.
[3] *I.e.*, must become my right to walk here.

*Enter again Prophilus and Euphranea.*

PRO.                                        Do not waste   50
The span of this stol'n time, lent by the
gods
For precious use, in niceness. [4]   Bright
Euphranea,
Should I repeat old vows, or study new
For purchase of belief to my desires—

ORG. [*Aside.*] Desires?

PRO.                    My service, my integrity—

ORG. [*Aside.*] That's better.

PRO.                    I should but repeat a lesson
Oft conned without a prompter but
thine eyes.
My love is honorable.

ORG. [*Aside.*]                    So was mine
To my Penthea—chastely honorable.

PRO. Nor wants there more addition to
my wish                                                    60
Of happiness than having thee a wife—
Already sure of Ithocles, a friend
Firm and unalterable.

ORG. [*Aside.*]                    But a brother
More cruel than the grave.

EUPH.                    What can you look for,
In answer to your noble protestations,
From an unskillful maid, but language
suited
To a divided mind?

ORG. [*Aside.*]                    Hold out, Euphranea!

EUPH. Know, Prophilus, I never under-
valued,
From the first time you mentioned
worthy love,
Your merit, means, or person; it had
been                                                          70
A fault of judgment in me, and a dull-
ness
In my affections, not to weigh and thank
My better stars that offered me the
grace
Of so much blissfulness.  For, to speak
truth,
The law of my desires kept equal pace
With yours, nor have I left that resolu-
tion;
But only, in a word, whatever choice
Lives nearest in my heart must first
procure
Consent both from my father and my
brother,
Ere he can own me his.

[4] Coyness.

ORG. [*Aside*.] She is forsworn else. 80

PRO. Leave me that task.

EUPH. My brother, ere he parted
To Athens, had my oath.

ORG. [*Aside*.] Yes, yes, a had, sure.

PRO. I doubt not, with the means the
court supplies,
But to prevail at pleasure.

ORG. [*Aside*.] Very likely!

PRO. Meantime, best, dearest, I may
build my hopes
On the foundation of thy constant
suff'rance
In any opposition.

EUPH. Death shall sooner
Divorce life and the joys I have in living
Than my chaste vows from truth.

PRO. On thy fair hand
I seal the like.

ORG. [*Aside*.] There is no faith in
woman. 90
Passion, O, be contained! My very
heartstrings
Are on the tenters.[1]

EUPH. Sir, we are overheard.
Cupid protect us! 'Twas a stirring, sir,
Of someone near.

PRO. Your fears are needless, lady;
None have access into these private
pleasures
Except some near in court, or bosom
student
From Tecnicus his oratory,[2] granted
By special favor lately from the king
Unto the grave philosopher.

EUPH. Methinks
I hear one talking to himself—I see
him. 100

PRO. 'Tis a poor scholar, as I told you,
lady.

ORG. [*Aside*.] I am discovered.—[*As if
studying aloud*.] Say it: is it possible,
With a smooth tongue, a leering countenance,
Flattery, or force of reason—I come t'e,[3]
sir—
To turn or to appease the raging sea?
Answer to that.—Your art? What art
to catch
And hold fast in a net the sun's small
atoms?

No, no; they'll out, they'll out; ye may
as easily
Outrun a cloud driven by a northern
blast
As fiddle-faddle so! Peace, or speak
sense. 110

EUPH. Call you this thing a scholar? 'Las,
he's lunatic.

PRO. Observe him, sweet; 'tis but his recreation.

ORG. But will you hear a little! You are
so tetchy.
You keep no rule in argument. Philoso-
phy
Works not upon impossibilities,
But natural conclusions.—Mew!—Ab-
surd!
The metaphysics are but speculations
Of the celestial bodies, or such accidents
As, not mixed perfectly, in the air en-
gendered
Appear to us unnatural; that's all. 120
Prove it; yet, with a reverence to your
gravity,
I'll balk illiterate sauciness, submitting
My sole opinion to the touch of writers.

PRO. Now let us fall in with him.
[*They come forward*.]

ORG. Ha, ha, ha!
These apish boys, when they but taste
the grammates [4]
And principles of theory, imagine
They can oppose their teachers. Con-
fidence
Leads many into errors.

PRO. By your leave, sir.

EUPH. Are you a scholar, friend?

ORG. I am, gay creature,
With pardon of your deities, a mush-
room 130
On whom the dew of heaven drops now
and then;
The sun shines on me too, I thank his
beams!
Sometime I feel their warmth; and eat
and sleep.

PRO. Does Tecnicus read [5] to thee?

ORG. Yes, forsooth.
He is my master surely; yonder door
Opens upon his study.

PRO. Happy creatures!
Such people toil not, sweet, in heats of
state,

[1] Tenterhooks.
[2] Lecture hall.
[3] He addresses an imaginary opponent.
[4] Rudiments.
[5] Lecture.

Nor sink in thaws of greatness; their affections
Keep order with the limits of their modesty; [1]
Their love is love of virtue.—What's thy name?                                         140
ORG. Aplotes, sumptuous master, a poor wretch.
EUPH. Dost thou want anything?
ORG.                    Books, Venus, books.
PRO. Lady, a new conceit [2] comes in my thought,
And most available for both our comforts.
EUPH. My lord—
PRO.        Whiles I endeavor to deserve
Your father's blessing to our loves, this scholar
May daily at some certain hours attend [3]
What notice I can write of my success,
Here in this grove, and give it to your hands;
The like from you to me. So can we never,                                              150
Barred of our mutual speech, want sure intelligence,
And thus our hearts may talk when our tongues cannot.
EUPH. Occasion is most favorable; use it.
PRO. Aplotes, wilt thou wait us twice a day,
At nine i' the morning and at four at night,
Here in this bower, to convey such letters
As each shall send to other? Do it willingly,
Safely, and secretly, and I will furnish
Thy study, or what else thou canst desire.
ORG. Jove, make me thankful, thankful, I beseech thee,                                160
Propitious Jove! I will prove sure and trusty.
You will not fail me books?
PRO.               Nor aught besides
Thy heart can wish. This lady's name's Euphranea,
Mine Prophilus.
ORG.        I have a pretty memory;
It must prove my best friend. I will not miss
One minute of the hours appointed.
PRO.                              Write

The books thou wouldst have bought thee in a note,
Or take thyself some money.
ORG.                    No, no money;
Money to scholars is a spirit invisible;
We dare not finger it. Or [4] books or nothing.                                        170
PRO. Books of what sort thou wilt. Do not forget
Our names.
ORG.            I warrant 'e, I warrant 'e.
PRO. Smile, Hymen, on the growth of our desires;
We'll feed thy torches with eternal fires!
                    *Exeunt. Manet Org[ilus].*
ORG. Put out thy torches, Hymen, or their light
Shall meet a darkness of eternal night!
Inspire me, Mercury, with swift deceits.
Ingenious Fate has leapt into mine arms,
Beyond the compass of my brain. Mortality
Creeps on the dung of earth, and cannot reach                                          180
The riddles which are purposed by the gods.
Great arts best write themselves in their own stories;
They die too basely who outlive their glories.                            *Exit.*

ACTUS SECUNDUS. SCENA PRIMA.

[*A room in Bassanes' house.*]

*Enter Bassanes and Phulas.*

BASS. I'll have that window next the street dammed up;
It gives too full a prospect to temptation,
And courts a gazer's glances. There's a lust
Committed by the eye, that sweats and travails,
Plots, wakes, contrives, till the deformed bear whelp,
Adultery, be licked into the act,
The very act. That light shall be dammed up;
D'e hear, sir?
PHU.        I do hear, my lord; a mason
Shall be provided suddenly.[5]

---

[1] Moderation.        [2] Idea.        [3] Await.        [4] Either.        [5] At once.

BASS.                              Some rogue, 9
  Some rogue of your confederacy, factor [1]
  For slaves and strumpets, to convey
    close [2] packets
  From this spruce springal [3] and the
    tother [4] youngster,
  That gaudy earwrig, [5] or my lord your
    patron,
  Whose pensioner you are! I'll tear thy
    throat out,
  Son of a cat, ill-looking hound's head,
    rip up
  Thy ulcerous maw, if I but scent a paper,
  A scroll but half as big as what can
    cover
  A wart upon thy nose, a spot, a pimple,
  Directed to my lady; it may prove
  A mystical preparative to lewdness.    20
PHU. Care shall be had. I will turn every
    thread
  About me to an eye.—[*Aside.*] Here's a
    sweet life!
BASS. The city housewives, cunning in the
    traffic
  Of chamber merchandise, set all at
    price
  By wholesale; yet they wipe their
    mouths and simper,
  Cull, [6] kiss, and cry "sweetheart," and
    stroke the head
  Which they have branched; [7] and all is
    well again!
  Dull clods of dirt, who dare not feel the
    rubs [8]
  Stuck on the foreheads.
PHU.                          'Tis a villainous world;
  One cannot hold his own in 't.
BASS.                          Dames at court,    30
  Who flaunt in riots, run another bias; [9]
  Their pleasure heaves the patient ass that
    suffers
  Up on the stilts of office, titles, in-
    comes;
  Promotion justifies the shame, and sues
    for 't.
  Poor Honor, thou art stabbed, and
    bleed'st to death
  By such unlawful hire! The country
    mistress

Is yet more wary, and in blushes hides
Whatever trespass draws her troth to
  guilt.
But all are false. On this truth I am
  bold:
No woman but can fall, and doth, or
  would.—                                40
Now for the newest news about the
  city;
What blab the voices, sirrah?
PHU.                              O, my lord,
  The rarest, quaintest, strangest, tickling
    news
  That ever—
BASS.    Heyday! Up and ride me, rascal!
  What is 't?
PHU.    Forsooth, they say, the king has
    mewed [10]
  All his gray beard, instead of which is
    budded
  Another of a pure carnation color,
  Speckled with green and russet.
BASS.                              Ignorant block!
PHU. Yes, truly; and 'tis talked about the
    streets
  That, since Lord Ithocles came home,
    the lions                              50
  Never left roaring, at which noise the
    bears
  Have danced their very hearts out.
BASS.                              Dance out thine too.
PHU. Besides, Lord Orgilus is fled to
    Athens
  Upon a fiery dragon, and 'tis thought
  A never can return.
BASS.                              Grant it, Apollo!
PHU. Moreover, please your lordship,
    'tis reported
  For certain that whoever is found jealous
  Without apparent proof that 's wife is
    wanton
  Shall be divorced; but this is but she-
    news—
  I had it from a midwife. I have more
    yet.                                  60
BASS. Antic, no more! Idiots and stupid
    fools
  Grate my calamities. Why to be fair
  Should yield presumption of a faulty
    soul? [11]
  Look to the doors.

---

[1] Agent.                        [3] Youth.
[2] Secret.                       [4] That other.
[5] Earwig, secret confidant.
[6] Coll, "neck," embrace.
[7] A conventional allusion to cuckoldry.
[8] Knobs, horns.                 [9] Direction.

[10] Moulted.
[11] *I.e.*, why should beauty arouse suspicion of a
faulty soul?

Phu. [*Aside*.]        The horn of plenty crest
    him!                                   *Exit Phul*[*as*].
Bass. Swarms of confusion huddle in my
    thoughts
In rare distemper.—Beauty? O, it is
An unmatched blessing or a horrid curse.

*Enter Penthea and Grausis, an old lady.*

[*Aside*.] She comes, she comes! So shoots
    the morning forth,
Spangled with pearls of transparent
    dew.
The way to poverty is to be rich,        70
As I in her am wealthy; but for her,
In all contents a bankrupt.—Loved
    Penthea!
How fares my heart's best joy?
Grau.                          In sooth, not well.
    She is so oversad.
Bass.               Leave chattering, magpie.—
Thy brother is returned, sweet, safe and
    honored
With a triumphant victory; thou shalt
    visit him.
We will to court, where, if it be thy
    pleasure,
Thou shalt appear in such a ravishing
    luster
Of jewels above value that the dames
Who brave it there, in rage to be out-
    shined,                                80
Shall hide them in their closets, and un-
    seen
Fret in their tears, whiles every won-
    d'ring eye
Shall crave none other brightness but thy
    presence.
Choose thine own recreations; be a
    queen
Of what delights thou fanciest best, what
    company,
What place, what times; do anything, do
    all things
Youth can command, so thou wilt chase
    these clouds
From the pure firmament of thy fair
    looks.
Grau. Now 'tis well said, my lord.—What,
    lady! Laugh;
Be merry! Time is precious.
Bass. [*Aside*.]         Furies whip thee!  90
Pen. Alas, my lord, this language to your
    handmaid

Sounds as would music to the deaf; I need
No braveries [1] nor cost of art to draw
The whiteness of my name into offense,
Let such, if any such there are, who covet
A curiosity of admiration,
By laying out their plenty to full view,
Appear in gaudy outsides; my attires
Shall suit the inward fashion of my
    mind,
From which, if your opinion, nobly
    placed,                              100
Change not the livery your words be-
    stow,
My fortunes with my hopes are at the
    highest.
Bass. This house, methinks, stands some-
    what too much inward; [2]
It is too melancholy. We'll remove
Nearer the court. Or what thinks my
    Penthea
Of the delightful island we command?
Rule me as thou canst wish.
Pen.                          I am no mistress.
Whither you please, I must attend; all
    ways
Are alike pleasant to me.
Grau.                          Island? Prison!
A prison is as gaysome; we'll no is-
    lands.                              110
Marry, out upon 'em! Whom shall we
    see there?
Seagulls, and porpoises, and water rats,
And crabs, and mews, [3] and dogfish—
    goodly gear
For a young lady's dealing—or an old
    one's!
On no terms islands; I'll be stewed first.
Bass. [*Aside*.]                       Grausis,
You are a juggling bawd.—This sadness,
    sweetest,
Becomes not youthful blood.—[*Aside*.]
    I'll have you pounded. [4]—
For my sake put on a more cheerful
    mirth;
Thou'lt mar thy cheeks, and make me old
    in griefs.—
[*Aside*.] Damnable bitch fox!
Grau.               I am thick of hearing  120
Still, [5] when the wind blows southerly.—
    What think 'e,
If your fresh lady breed young bones, my
    lord?

---

[1] Fineries.     [2] Secret, secluded.     [3] Gulls.
[4] Impounded.                              [5] Always.

Would not a chopping[1] boy d'e good at heart?
But, as you said—

BASS. [*Aside.*]    I'll spit thee on a stake, Or chop thee into collops!

GRAU.                    Pray, speak louder.
Sure, sure the wind blows south still.

PEN.                    Thou prat'st madly.

BASS. 'Tis very hot; I sweat extremely.— Now?

*Enter Phulas.*

PHU.  A herd of lords, sir.

BASS.                    Ha?

PHU.                    A flock of ladies.

BASS.  Where?

PHU.        Shoalds[2] of horses.

BASS.                    Peasant, how?

PHU.  .                    Caroches[3]
In drifts; th' one enter, th' other stand without, sir.                    130
And now I vanish.        *Exit Phulas.*

*Enter Prophilus, Hemophil, Groneas, Chris-
talla, and Philema.*

PRO.                    Noble Bassanes!

BASS.  Most welcome, Prophilus; ladies, gentlemen,
To all my heart is open; you all honor me—
[*Aside.*] A tympany[4] swells in my head al- ready—
Honor me bountifully.—[*Aside.*] How they flutter,
Wagtails and jays together!

PRO.                    From your brother
By virtue of your love to him, I require
Your instant presence, fairest.

PEN.                    He is well, sir?

PRO.  The gods preserve him ever! Yet, dear beauty,
I find some alteration in him lately,    140
Since his return to Sparta.—My good lord,
I pray, use no delay.

BASS.        We had not needed
An invitation, if his sister's health
Had not fallen into question.—Haste, Penthea,
Slack not a minute.—Lead the way, good Prophilus;
I'll follow step by step.

¹ Strapping.                    ³ Coaches.
² Shoals.                    ⁴ Distension.

PRO.                    Your arm, fair madam.
*Exeunt omnes sed[5] Bass[anes] et Grau[sis].*

BASS.  One word with your old bawdship: th' hadst been better
Railed at the sins thou worshipp'st than have thwarted
My will.  I'll use thee cursedly.

GRAU.                    You dote;    149
You are beside yourself.  A politician
In jealousy?  No, y' are too gross, too vulgar.
Pish, teach not me my trade; I know my cue.
My crossing you sinks me into her trust,
By which I shall know all; my trade's a sure one.

BASS.  Forgive me, Grausis; 'twas consid- eration
I relished[6] not; but have a care now.

GRAU.                    Fear not,
I am no new-come-to 't.

BASS.        Thy life's upon it,
And so is mine.  My agonies are infinite.
                    *Exeunt omnes.*

SCENE ii.

[*Ithocles' apartment in the palace.*]

*Enter Ithocles, alone.*

ITH.  Ambition?  'Tis of vipers' breed; it gnaws
A passage through the womb that gave it motion.
Ambition, like a seelèd[7] dove, mounts upward,
Higher and higher still, to perch on clouds,
But tumbles headlong down with heavier ruin.
So squibs and crackers fly into the air;
Then, only breaking with a noise, they vanish
In stench and smoke.  Morality,[8] applied
To timely practice, keeps the soul in tune,
At whose sweet music all our actions dance.                    10
But this is form of books and school- tradition;[9]
It physics not the sickness of a mind

⁵ But.                    ⁸ Moralization.
⁶ Understood.                ⁹ *I.e.*, pedantry.
⁷ With eyelids sewed together.

Broken with griefs.  Strong fevers are
   not eased
With counsel, but with best receipts
   and means—
Means, speedy means and certain; that's
   the cure.

*Enter Armostes and Crotolon.*

ARM. You stick, Lord Crotolon, upon a
   point
Too nice and too unnecessary; Prophilus
Is every way desertful.  I am confident
Your wisdom is too ripe to need instruc-
   tion
From your son's tutelage.
CROT.          Yet not so ripe,  20
My Lord Armostes, that it dares to dote
Upon the painted [1] meat of smooth
   persuasion,
Which tempts me to a breach of faith.
ITH.               Not yet
Resolved, my lord?  Why, if your son's
   consent
Be so available,[2] we'll write to Athens
For his repair [3] to Sparta.  The king's
   hand
Will join with our desires; he has been
   moved to 't.
ARM. Yes, and the king himself impor-
   tuned Crotolon
For a despatch.
CROT.     Kings may command; their wills
Are laws not to be questioned.
ITH.           By this marriage  30
You knit an union so devout, so hearty,
Between your loves to me and mine to
   yours,
As if mine own blood had an interest in
   it;
For Prophilus is mine, and I am his.
CROT. My lord, my lord!—
ITH.      What, good sir?  Speak your
   thought.
CROT. Had this sincerity been real once,
My Orgilus had not been now unwived,
Nor your lost sister buried in a bridebed.
Your uncle here, Armostes, knows this
   truth,
For, had your father Thrasus lived—
   but peace  40
Dwell in his grave!  I have done.
ARM.        Y' are bold and bitter.

ITH. [*Aside.*] A presses home the injury;
   it smarts.—
No reprehensions, uncle; I deserve 'em.
Yet, gentle sir, consider what the heat
Of an unsteady youth, a giddy brain,
Green indiscretion, flattery of greatness,
Rawness of judgment, willfulness in
   folly,
Thoughts vagrant as the wind and as
   uncertain,
Might lead a boy in years to; 'twas a
   fault,
A capital fault, for then I could not
   dive  50
Into the secrets of commanding love,
Since when, experience, by the ex-
   tremities [4] (in others),
Hath forced me to collect.[5]  And, trust
   me, Crotolon,
I will redeem those wrongs with any
   service
Your satisfaction can require for current.
ARM. Thy acknowledgment is satisfac-
   tion.
What would you more?
CROT.      I'm conquered; if Euphranea
Herself admit the motion, let it be so;
I doubt not my son's liking.
ITH.            Use my fortunes,
Life, power, sword, and heart—all are
   your own.  60

*Enter Bassanes, Prophilus, Calantha, Pen-*
*   thea, Euphranea, Christalla, Philema,*
*                  and Grausis.*

ARM. The princess, with your sister.
CAL.             I present 'e
A stranger here in court, my lord, for,
   did not
Desire of seeing you draw her abroad,
We had not been made happy in her
   company.
ITH. You are a gracious princess.—Sister,
   wedlock
Holds too severe a passion in your na-
   ture,
Which can engross all duty to your hus-
   band,
Without attendance on so dear a mis-
   tress.—
[*To Bassanes.*]  'Tis not my brother's
   pleasure, I presume,
T' immure her in a chamber.

---

[1] Counterfeit.    [2] Serviceable.    [3] Return.

[4] Extremes.               [5] Understand.

BASS.                    'Tis her will; 70
    She governs her own hours.    Noble
        Ithocles,
    We thank the gods for your success and
        welfare.
    Our lady has of late been indisposed,
    Else we had waited on you with the first.
ITH.  How does Penthea now?
PEN.               You best know, brother,
    From whom my health and comforts
        are derived.
BASS. [Aside.]  I like the answer well; 'tis
        sad ¹ and modest.
    There may be tricks yet, tricks.—Have
        an eye, Grausis!
CAL.  Now, Crotolon, the suit we joined in
        must not
    Fall by too long demur.²
CROT.               'Tis granted, princess, 80
        For my part.
ARM.               With condition that his son
    Favor the contract.
CAL.               Such delay is easy.—
    The joys of marriage make thee, Pro-
        philus,
    A proud deserver of Euphranea's love,
    And her of thy desert!
PRO.                  Most sweetly gracious!
BASS.  The joys of marriage are the heaven
        on earth,
    Life's paradise, great princess, the soul's
        quiet,
    Sinews of concord, earthly immortality,
    Eternity of pleasures—no restoratives
    Like to a constant woman!—[Aside.]
    But where is she?              90
    'Twould puzzle all the gods but to create
    Such a new monster.—I can speak by
        proof,
    For I rest in Elysium; 'tis my happiness.
CROT.  Euphranea, how are you resolved—
        speak freely—
    In your affections to this gentleman?
EUPH.  Nor more nor less than as his love
        assures me,
    Which—if your liking with my brother's
        warrants—
    I cannot but approve in all points
        worthy.
CROT. So, so!—[To Prophilus.]  I know
    your answer.
ITH.                  'T had been pity 99
    To sunder hearts so equally concented.³

¹ Serious.        ² Delay.        ³ Harmonized.

*Enter Hemophil.*

HEM.  The king, Lord Ithocles, commands
    your presence—
    And, fairest princess, yours.
CAL.               We will attend him.

*Enter Groneas.*

GRO.  Where are the lords?  All must unto
    the king
    Without delay; the Prince of Argos—
CAL.               Well, sir?
GRO.  Is coming to the court, sweet lady.
CAL.               How!
    The Prince of Argos?
GRO.               'Twas my fortune, madam,
    T' enjoy the honor of these happy tid-
        ings.
ITH.  Penthea!—
PEN.          Brother?
ITH.               Let me an hour hence
    Meet you alone within the palace grove;
    I have some secret with you.—Prithee,
        friend,              110
    Conduct her thither, and have special
        care
    The walks be cleared of any to disturb us.
PRO.  I shall.
BASS. [Aside.]        How's that?
ITH.               Alone, pray be alone.—
    I am your creature, princess.—On, my
        lords!        *Exeunt [All but] Bassanes.*
BASS.  Alone, alone?    What means that
        word "alone"?
    Why might not I be there?—Hum!—
    He's her brother.
    Brothers and sisters are but flesh and
        blood,
    And this same whoreson ⁴ court ease is
        temptation
    To a rebellion in the veins; besides,
    His fine friend Prophilus must be her
        guardian.              120
    Why may not he despatch a business
        nimbly
    Before the other come?—Or—pand'ring,
        pand'ring
    For one another—be 't to sister, mother,
    Wife, cousin, anything—'mongst youths
        of mettle
    Is in request; it is so—stubborn fate!
    But, if I be a cuckold, and can know it,
    I will be fell,⁵ and fell.

⁴ Rascally.                    ⁵ Ruthless.

*Enter Groneas.*

GRO.        My lord, y' are called for.

BASS. Most heartily I thank ye. Where's
my wife, pray?

GRO. Retired amongst the ladies.

BASS.        Still I thank 'e.
There's an old waiter [1] with her; saw you
her too?        130

GRO. She sits i' th' presence lobby fast
asleep, sir.

BASS. Asleep? Sleep, sir?

GRO.        Is your lordship troubled?
You will not to the king?

BASS.        Your humblest vassal.

GRO. Your servant, my good lord.

BASS.        I wait your footsteps.
*Exeunt.*

SCENE THE THIRD.

[*The palace gardens adjoining a grove.*]

[*Enter*] *Prophilus, Penthea.*

PRO. In this walk, lady, will your brother
find you;
And, with your favor, give me leave a
little
To work a preparation. In his fashion
I have observed of late some kind of
slackness
To such alacrity as nature [once] [2]
And custom took delight in, sadness
grows
Upon his recreations, which he hoards
In such a willing [3] silence that to question
The grounds will argue [little][2] skill in
friendship,
And less good manners.

PEN.        Sir, I'm not inquisitive   10
Of secrecies without an invitation.

PRO. With pardon, lady, not a syllable
Of mine implies so rude a sense; the
drift—

*Enter Orgilus* [, *disguised as before*].

[*To Orgilus.*] Do thy best
To make this lady merry for an hour.
*Exit.*

ORG. Your will shall be a law, sir.

PEN.        Prithee, leave me;

[1] Attendant, watcher.
[2] Supplied by Gifford-Dyce.
[3] Resolute.

I have some private thoughts I would
account with;
Use thou thine own.

ORG.        Speak on, fair nymph; our souls
Can dance as well to music of the spheres
As any's who have feasted with the
gods.        20

PEN. Your school terms [4] are too troublesome.

ORG.        What heaven
Refines mortality from dross of earth
But such as uncompounded [5] beauty
hallows
With glorified perfection?

PEN.        Set thy wits
In a less wild proportion.

ORG.        Time can never
On the white table of unguilty faith
Write counterfeit dishonor; turn those
eyes,
The arrows of pure love, upon that fire,
Which once rose to a flame, perfumed
with vows
As sweetly scented as the incense smok-
ing        30
The holiest artars,[6] virgin tears (like
On Vesta's odors), sprinkled dews to
feed 'em[7]
And to increase their fervor.

PEN.        Be not frantic!

ORG. All pleasures are but mere imagina-
tion,
Feeding the hungry appetite with steam
And sight of banquet, whilst the body
pines,
Not relishing the real taste of food;
Such is the leanness of a heart divided
From intercourse of troth-contracted
loves;
No horror should deface that precious
figure        40
Sealed with the lively stamp of equal
souls.

PEN. Away! Some Fury hath bewitched
thy tongue.
The breath of ignorance, that flies from
thence,
Ripens a knowledge in me of afflictions

[4] *I.e.*, rhetorical language.
[5] Unadorned, simple.        [6] Attars, perfumes.
[7] This incoherency may be intentional, but
Gifford emends as follows:
"On Vesta's altars . . .
. . . the holiest odors, virgins' tears,
. . . sprinkled, like dews, to feed them."

Above all suff'rance.—Thing of talk,
begone!
Begone, without reply!

ORG.          Be just, Penthea,
In thy commands; when thou send'st
forth a doom
Of banishment, know first on whom it
lights.
Thus I take off the shroud, in which my
cares
Are folded up from view of common
eyes.      [*Discloses himself.*]    50
What is thy sentence next?

PEN.       Rash man! Thou layest
A blemish on mine honor, with the
hazard
Of thy too desperate life; yet I profess,
By all the laws of ceremonious wedlock,
I have not given admittance to one
thought
Of female change since cruelty enforced
Divorce betwixt my body and my heart.
Why would you fall from goodness thus?

ORG.          O, rather
Examine me, how I could live to say
I have been much, much wronged. 'Tis
for thy sake    60
I put on this imposture; dear Penthea,
If thy soft bosom be not turned to
marble,
Thou't [1] pity our calamities; my interest
Confirms me thou art mine still.

PEN.       Lend your hand;
With both of mine I clasp it thus, thus
kiss it
Thus kneel before ye.

ORG.      You instruct my duty.

PEN. We may stand up.—Have you aught
else to urge
Of new demand? As for the old, forget it;
'Tis buried in an everlasting silence,
And shall be, shall be ever. What more
would ye?    70

ORG. I would possess my wife; the equity
Of very reason bids me.

PEN.        Is that all?

ORG. Why, 'tis the all of me, myself.

PEN.       Remove
Your steps some distance from me.—At
this space
A few words I dare change; but first
put on
Your borrowed shape.

ORG.      You are obeyed; 'tis done.
     [*He resumes his disguise.*]

PEN. How, Orgilus, by promise I was thine
The heavens do witness; they can wit-
ness too
A rape done on my truth; [2] how I do
love thee    79
Yet, Orgilus, and yet, must best appear
In tendering [3] thy freedom, for I find
The constant preservation of thy merit,
By thy not daring to attempt my fame [4]
With injury of any loose conceit,
Which might give deeper wounds to
discontents.
Continue this fair race; [5] then, though I
cannot
Add to thy comfort, yet I shall more
often
Remember from what fortune I am
fallen,
And pity mine own ruin.—Live, live
happy,
Happy in thy next choice, that thou
mayst people    90
This barren age with virtues in thy issue!
And O, when thou art married, think on
me
With mercy, not contempt! I hope thy
wife,
Hearing my story, will not scorn my
fall.—
Now let us part.

ORG.      Part! Yet advise thee better:
Penthea is the wife to Orgilus,
And ever shall be.

PEN.       Never shall nor will.

ORG. How!

PEN.       Hear me; in a word I'll tell
thee why.
The virgin dowry which my birth be-
stowed    99
Is ravished by another; my true love
Abhors to think that Orgilus deserved
No better favors than a second bed.

ORG. I must not take this reason.

PEN.       To confirm it
Should I outlive my bondage, let me
meet
Another worse than this and less desired,
If, of all men alive, thou shouldst but
touch
My lip or hand again?

[2] Troth.             [4] Reputation, honor.
[3] Having a care of.      [5] Course.

[1] Thou wilt.

ORG.                          Penthea, now
  I tell 'e, you grow wanton in my suffer-
    ance;
  Come, sweet, th' art mine.
PEN.                    Uncivil sir, forbear,   109
  Or I can turn affection into vengeance!
  Your reputation, if you value any,
  Lies bleeding at my feet.   Unworthy
    man,
  If ever henceforth thou appear in lan-
    guage,
  Message, or letter to betray my frailty,
  I'll call thy former protestations lust,
  And curse my stars for forfeit of my
    judgment.
  Go thou, fit only for disguise and
    walks,[1]
  To hide thy shame.   This once I spare
    thy life.
  I laugh at mine own confidence; my
    sorrows
  By thee are made inferior to my for-
    tunes.                                   120
  If ever thou didst harbor worthy love,
  Dare not to answer.   My good genius
    guide me
  That I may never see thee more!—Go
    from me!
ORG. I'll tear my veil of politic French[2]
    off,
  And stand up like a man resolved to
    do;
  Action, not words, shall show[3] me.—O
    Penthea!                    *Exit Orgilus.*
PEN. A sighed my name, sure, as he
    parted from me;
  I fear I was too rough.   Alas, poor
    gentleman,
  A looked not like the ruins of his
    youth,                                   129
  But like the ruins of those ruins.  Honor,
  How much we fight with weakness to
    preserve thee!            [*Walks aside.*]

### Enter Bassanes and Grausis.

BASS. Fie on thee!  Damn thee, rotten
    maggot, damn thee!
  Sleep?  Sleep at court?  And now?  Aches,[4]
    convulsions,

Imposthumes,[5] rhemes,[6] gouts, palsies
  clog thy bones
  A dozen years more yet!
GRAU.                    Now y' are in hu-
    mors.
BASS.  She's by herself; there's hope of
    that.  She's sad too;
  She's in strong contemplation; yes, and
    fixed.
  The signs are wholesome.
GRAU.                    Very wholesome, truly.
BASS.  Hold your chops,[7] nightmare!—
    Lady, come; your brother
  Is carried to his closet;[8] you must
    thither.                                  140
PEN. Not well, my lord?
BASS.                    A sudden fit; 'twill off!
  Some surfeit or disorder.—How dost,
    dearest?
PEN. Your news is none o' the best.

### Enter Prophilus.

PRO.                    The chief of men,
  The excellentest Ithocles, desires
  Your presence, madam.
BASS.                    We are hasting to him.
PEN. In vain we labor in this course of
    life
  To piece our journey out at length, or
    crave
  Respite of breath; our home is in the
    grave.
BASS.  Perfect philosophy!
[PEN.][9]
                 Then let us care
  To live so, that our reckonings may fall
    even                                     150
  When w' are to make account.
PRO.                    He cannot fear
  Who builds on noble grounds; sickness
    or pain
  Is the deserver's exercise;[10] and such
  Your virtuous brother to the world is
    known.
  Speak comfort to him, lady; be all
    gentle.
  Stars fall but in the grossness of our
    sight;
  A good man dying, th' earth doth lose a
    light.                    *Exeunt omnes.*

---

[1] *I.e.*, for secret meeting.
[2] A characteristic Elizabethan anachronism.
[3] Reveal.
[4] Pronounced *aitches.*

[5] Abscesses.
[6] Rheums.
[9] Emended by Gifford-Dyce. Original assigns
this speech to Bassanes.

[7] Jaws.
[8] Chamber.
[10] Discipline.

ACTUS TERTIUS. SCENA PRIMA.

*[The study of Tecnicus.]*

*Enter Tecnicus, and Orgilus in his own shape.*

TEC. Be well advised; let not a resolution
Of giddy rashness choke the breath of
　reason.
ORG. It shall not, most sage master.
TEC. 　　　　　　　　　I am jealous,[1]
For, if the borrowed shape so late put on
Inferred a consequence, we must con-
　clude
Some violent design of sudden nature
Hath shook that shadow off, to fly upon
A new-hatched execution.[2] Orgilus,
Take heed thou hast not, under our
　integrity,
Shrouded unlawful plots; our mortal
　eyes　　　　　　　　　　　　　10
Pierce not the secrets of your hearts;
　the gods
Are only privy to them.
ORG. 　　　　　　　　Learned Tecnicus,
Such doubts are causeless; and, to clear
　the truth
From misconceit,[3] the present state com-
　mands me.
The Prince of Argos comes himself in
　person
In quest of great Calantha for his bride,
Our kingdom's heir; besides, mine only
　sister,
Euphranea, is disposed to Prophilus;
Lastly, the king is sending letters for me
To Athens, for my quick repair to
　court.　　　　　　　　　　　　20
Please to accept these reasons.
TEC. 　　　　　　　Just ones, Orgilus,
Not to be contradicted; yet beware
Of an unsure foundation; no fair colors[4]
Can fortify a building faintly jointed.
I have observed a growth in thy aspect
Of dangerous extent, sudden, and—
　look to 't—
I might add, certain—
ORG. 　　　　　　My aspect? Could art
Run through mine inmost thoughts, it
　should not sift
An inclination there more than what
　suited
With justice of mine honor.

TEC. 　　　　　　　　I believe it. 30
But know then, Orgilus, what honor is.
Honor consists not in a bare opinion
By doing any act that feeds content,
Brave in appearance, cause we think it
　brave;
Such honor comes by accident, not
　nature,
Proceeding from the vices of our passion,
Which makes our reason drunk. But real
　honor
Is the reward of virtue, and acquired
By justice or by valor which for bases
Hath justice to uphold it. He then
　fails　　　　　　　　　　　　40
In honor, who for lucer [or][5] revenge
Commits thefts, murthers, treasons, and
　adulteries,
With suchlike, by intrenching on just
　laws,
Whose sovereignty is best preserved by
　justice.
Thus, as you see how honor must be
　grounded
On knowledge, not opinion—for opinion
Relies on probability and accident,
But knowledge on necessity and truth—
I leave thee to the fit consideration
Of what becomes the grace of real
　honor,　　　　　　　　　　　50
Wishing success to all thy virtuous mean-
　ings.
ORG. The gods increase thy wisdom, rev-
　erend oracle,
And in thy precepts make me ever
　thrifty! 　　　　　*Exit Org[ilus].*
TEC. I thank thy wish.—Much mystery
　of fate
Lies hid in that man's fortunes; curiosity
May lead his actions into rare attempts.
But let the gods be moderators still,
No human power can prevent their
　will.—

*Enter Armostes [with a casket].*

From whence come 'e?
ARM. 　　　　From King Amyclas—pardon
My interruption of your studies. Here,
In this sealed box, he sends a treasure
　dear　　　　　　　　　　　　61
To him as his crown. A prays your grav-
　ity,

[1] Suspicious.　[2] Achievement, enterprise.
[3] Misconception.　[4] Reasons, excuses.

[5] Emended by Gifford. Original has *of.*

You would examine, ponder, sift, and
    bolt
The pith and circumstance of every tittle
The scroll within contains.
TEC.                    What is 't, Armostes?
ARM.  It is the health of Sparta, the king's
    life,
Sinews and safety of the common-
    wealth—
The sum of what the oracle delivered
When last he visited the prophetic
    temple
At Delphos.  What his reasons are, for
    which,                                              70
After so long a silence, he requires
Your counsel now, grave man, his
    majesty
Will soon himself acquaint you with.
TEC.  [Taking the casket.]              Apollo
Inspire my intellect!—The Prince of
    Argos
Is entertained?
ARM.              He is, and has demanded
Our princess for his wife, which I con-
    ceive
One special cause the king importunes
    you
For resolution [1] of the oracle.
TEC.  My duty to the king, good peace to
    Sparta,
And fair day to Armostes!
ARM.      Like to Tecnicus!    Exeunt.  80

[SCENE ii.

Ithocles' apartment in the palace.]

Soft music.

A SONG

Can you paint a thought, or number
Every fancy in a slumber?
Can you count soft minutes roving
From a dial's point by moving?
Can you grasp a sigh, or, lastly,
Rob a virgin's honor chastely?
    No, O, no!  Yet you may
Sooner do both that and this,
This and that, and never miss,
    Than by any praise display         10
Beauty's beauty—such a glory,
As beyond all fate, all story,
        All arms, all arts,
        All loves, all hearts,
    Greater than those or they,
    Do, shall, and must obey.

[1] Interpretation.

During which time enters Prophilus, Bas-
    sanes, Penthea, Grausis, passing over
    the stage; Bassanes and Grausis enter
    again softly, stealing to several stands,[2]
                                    and listen.

BASS.  All silent, calm, secure.—Grausis,
    no creaking?
No noise?  Dost hear nothing?
GRAU.                        Not a mouse,
    Or whisper of the wind.
BASS.                    The floor is matted;
The bedposts sure are steel or marble.—
    Soldiers                                          20
Should not affect, methinks, strains so
    effeminate;
Sounds of such delicacy are but fawn-
    ings
Upon the sloth of luxury; [3] they heighten
Cinders of covert lust up to a flame.
GRAU.  What do you mean, my lord?
    Speak low; that gabbling
Of yours will but undo us.
BASS.                    Chamber combats
    Are felt, not heard.
PRO.  [Within.]        A wakes.
BASS.                        What's that?
ITH.  [Within.]              Who's there?
Sister?—All quit the room else.
BASS.                        'Tis consented!

Enter Prophilus.

PRO.  Lord Bassanes, your brother would
    be private;
We must forbear; his sleep hath newly
    left him.                                          30
Please 'e withdraw.
BASS.              By any means; 'tis fit.
PRO.  Pray, gentlewoman, walk too.
GRAU.        Yes, I will, sir.  Exeunt omnes.

Ithocles discovered [4] in a chair, and Penthea.
ITH.  Sit nearer, sister, to me; nearer yet.
We had one father, in one womb took
    life,
Were brought up twins together, yet
    have lived
At distance, like two strangers.  I could
    wish
That the first pillow whereon I was
    cradled
Had proved to me a grave.

[2] Different positions.                        [3] Lust.
[4] By the drawing of the curtain from the inner
stage.

PEN.                    You had been happy;
Then had you never known that sin
    of life
Which blots all following glories with
    a vengeance,                          40
For forfeiting the last will of the dead,
From whom you had your being.
ITH.                        Sad Penthea,
Thou canst not be too cruel; my rash
  . spleen
Hath with a violent hand plucked from
    thy bosom
A lover-blessed heart, to grind it into dust
For which mine's now a-breaking.
PEN.                    Not yét, heaven,
I do beseech thee! First let some wild
    fires
Scorch, not consume it! May the heat
    be cherished
With desires infinite, but hopes impos-
    sible!
ITH. Wronged soul, thy prayers are heard.
PEN.              Here, lo, I breathe,   50
A miserable creature, led to ruin
By an unnatural brother!
ITH.                        I consume
In languishing affections [1] for that tres-
    pass,
Yet cannot die.
PEN.          The handmaid to the wages
Of country toil drinks the untroubled [2]
    streams
With leaping kids and with the bleating
    lambs,
And so allays her thirst secure,[3] whiles I
Quench my hot sighs with fleetings [4] of
    my tears.
ITH. The laborer doth eat his coarsest
    bread,
Earned with his sweat, and lies him
    down to sleep,                        60
Whiles [5] every bit I touch turns in di-
    gestion
To gall as bitter as Penthea's curse.
Put me to any penance for my tyranny,
And I will call thee merciful.
PEN.                    Pray, kill me;
Rid me from living with a jealous hus-
    band.

[1] Emotions.
[2] The last two words are misplaced at the head of the line in the original.
[3] Unmolested.
[4] Flowings, streams.
[5] Gifford-Dyce reading. Original reads *Which.*

Then we will join in friendship, be again
Brother and sister.—Kill me, pray; nay,
    will 'e?
ITH. How does thy lord esteem thee?
PEN.                    Such an one
As only you have made me: a faith-
    breaker,
A spotted whore. Forgive me. I am
    one                                    70
In art,[6] not in desires, the gods must wit-
    ness.
ITH. Thou dost belie thy friend.
PEN.              I do not, Ithocles;
For she that's wife to Orgilus, and lives
In known adultery with Bassanes,
Is at the best a whore. Wilt kill me now?
The ashes of our parents will assume
Some dreadful figure, and appear to
    charge
Thy bloody guilt, that hast betrayed
    their name                            78
To infamy in this reproachful match.
ITH. After my victories abroad, at home
I meet despair; ingratitude of nature
Hath made my actions monstrous.
    Thou shalt stand
A deity, my sister, and be worshipped
For thy resolvéd martyrdom; wronged
    maids
And married wives shall to thy hallowed
    shrine
Offer their orisons, and sacrifice
Pure turtles,[7] crowned with myrtle, if
    thy pity
Unto a yielding brother's pressure lend
One finger but to ease it.
PEN.                        O, no more!
ITH. Death waits to waft me to the
    Stygian banks,                        90
And free me from this chaos of my
    bondage;
And, till thou wilt forgive, I must en-
    dure.
PEN. Who is the saint you serve?
ITH.                    Friendship, or [nearness] [8]
Of birth to any but my sister, durst not
Have moved that question; as a secret,
    sister,
I dare not murmur to myself—
PEN.                        Let me,
By your new protestations I conjure 'e,
Partake her name.

[6] Act, practice (?).          [8] Supplied by Gifford.
[7] Turtledoves.

ITH.                Her name?—'Tis—'tis—
    I dare not.
PEN. All your respects [1] are forged.
ITH.                    They are not.—Peace!
    Calantha is—the princess—the king's
        daughter—                        100
    Sole heir of Sparta.—Me most miser-
        able,
    Do I now love thee?  For my injuries,
    Revenge thyself with bravery, and gos-
        sip
    My treasons to the king's ears; do.
        Calantha
    Knows it not yet, nor Prophilus, my
        nearest.
PEN. Suppose you were contracted to her,
        would it not
    Split even your very soul to see her
        father
    Snatch her out of your arms against
        her will,
    And force her on the Prince of Argos?
ITH.                        Trouble not
    The fountains of mine eyes with thine
        own story;                        110
    I sweat in blood for 't.
PEN.                    We are reconciled.
    Alas, sir, being children, but two
        branches
    Of one stock, 'tis not fit we should divide.
    Have comfort; you may find it.
ITH.                        Yes, in thee;
    Only in thee, Penthea mine.
PEN.                        If sorrows
    Have not too much dulled my infected
        brain,
    I'll cheer invention for an active strain.[2]
ITH. Mad man!  Why have I wronged a
    maid so excellent?

*Enter Bassanes with a poniard; Prophilus,
    Groneas, Hemophil, and Grausis.*

BASS. I can forbear no longer; more, I
    will not.
    Keep off your hands, or fall upon my
        point.                            120
    Patience is tired, for, like a slow-paced
        ass,
    Ye ride my easy nature, and proclaim
    My sloth to vengeance a reproach and
        property.[3]

ITH. The meaning of this rudeness?
PRO.                        He's distracted.
PEN. O, my grieved lord!—
GRAU.            Sweet lady, come not near
        him;
    He holds his perilous weapon in his
        hand
    To prick a cares not whom nor where—
        see, see, see!
BASS. My birth is noble.  Though the
        popular blast
    Of vanity, as giddy as thy youth,
    Hath reared thy name up to bestride
        a cloud,                          130
    Or progress in the chariot of the sun,
    I am no clod of trade, to lackey pride,
    Nor, like your slave of expectation,[4]
        wait [5]
    The bawdy hinges of your doors, or
        whistle
    For mystical conveyance to your bed
        sports.
GRO. Fine humors!  They become him.
HEM.                    How a stares,
    Struts, puffs, and sweats!  Most ad-
        mirable [6] lunacy!
ITH. But that I may conceive the spirit
    of wine
    Has took possession of your soberer
        custom,
    I'd say you were unmannerly.
PEN.                Dear brother!—    140
BASS. Unmannerly!—Mew,    kitling! [7]—
        Smooth Formality
    Is usher to the rankness of the blood,
    But Impudence bears up the train.  In-
        deed, sir,
    Your fiery mettle, or your springal [8]
        blaze
    Of huge renown, is no sufficient royalty [9]
    To print upon my forehead the scorn,
        "cuckold."
ITH. His jealousy has robbed him of his
        wits;
    A talks a knows not what.
BASS.                Yes, and a knows
    To whom a talks—to one that franks [10]
        his lust
    In swine-security of bestial incest.    150
ITH. Ha, devil!

[1] Supply *for me.*
[2] *I.e.*, I will try to contrive some plan.
[3] Characteristic condition.

[4] Attendance.        [8] Youthful.
[5] Attend.            [9] Right.
[6] Wonderful.         [10] Fattens.
[7] Kitten.

BASS.          I will hallo [1] 't, though I blush more
To name the filthiness than thou to act it.

ITH. Monster!

PRO.          Sir, by our friendship—

PEN.          By our bloods—
Will you quite both undo us, brother?

GRAU.          Out on him!
These are his megrims,[2] firks,[3] and melancholies.

HEM. Well said, old touchhole!

GRO.          Kick him out at doors!

PEN. With favor, let me speak.—My lord, what slackness
In my obedience hath deserved this rage?
Except humility and silent duty
Have drawn on your unquiet, my simplicity          160
Ne'er studied your vexation.

BASS.          Light of beauty,
Deal not ungently with a desperate wound!
No breach of reason dares make war with her
Whose looks are sovereignty, whose breath is balm.
O, that I could preserve thee in fruition
As in devotion!

PEN.          Sir, may every evil
Locked in Pandora's box shower, in your presence,
On my unhappy head, if, since you made me
A partner in your bed, I have been faulty
In one unseemly thought against your honor!          170

ITH. Purge not his griefs, Penthea.

BASS.          Yes, say on,
Excellent creature!—[To Ithocles.] Good, be not a hinderance
To peace and praise of virtue.—O, my senses
Are charmed with sounds celestial!—On, dear, on;
I never gave you one ill word; say, did I?
Indeed, I did not.

PEN.          Nor, by Juno's forehead,
Was I e'er guilty of a wanton error.

BASS. A goddess! Let me kneel.

[1] Proclaim.     [2] Headaches, fancies.     [3] Freaks.

GRAU.          Alas, kind animal!

ITH. No; but for penance—

BASS.          Noble sir, what is it?
With gladness I embrace it; yet, pray, let not          180
My rashness teach you to be too unmerciful.

ITH. When you shall show good proof that manly wisdom,
Not overswayed by passion or opinion,
Knows how to lead judgment, then this lady,
Your wife, my sister, shall return in safety
Home, to be guided by you; but, till first
I can out of clear evidence approve it,
She shall be my care.

BASS.          Rip my bosom up,
I'll stand the execution with a constancy;
This torture is unsufferable.

ITH.          Well, sir,          190
I dare not trust her to your fury.

BASS.          But
Penthea says not so.

PEN.          She needs no tongue
To plead excuse who never purposed wrong.

HEM. [To Grausis.] Virgin of reverence and antiquity,
Stay you behind.

GRO. [To Grausis.]          The court wants not your diligence.

*Exeunt omnes sed Bass[anes] et Graus[is].*

GRAU. What will you do, my lord? My lady's gone;
I am denied to follow.

BASS.          I may see her,
Or speak to her once more?

GRAU.          And feel her too, man;
Be of good cheer, she's your own flesh and bone.

BASS. Diseases desperate must find cures alike.          200
She swore she has been true.

GRAU.          True, on my modesty.

BASS. Let him want truth who credits not her vows!
Much wrong I did her, but her brother infinite;
Rumor will voice me the contempt of manhood,

Should I run on thus. Some way I must try
To outdo art, and cry [1] a jealousy.

*Exeunt omnes.*

[SCENE iii.

*A room in the palace.*]

*Flourish. Enter Amyclas, Nearchus, leading Calantha, Armostes, Crotolon, Euphranea, Christalla, Philema, and Amelus.*

AMY. Cousin of Argos, what the heavens have pleased
In their unchanging counsels to conclude
For both our kingdoms' weal, we must submit to;
Nor can we be unthankful to their bounties,
Who, when we were even creeping to our graves,
Sent us a daughter, in whose birth our hope
Continues of succession. As you are
In title next, being grandchild to our aunt,
So we in heart desire you may sit nearest
Calantha's love, since we have ever vowed          10
Not to enforce affection by our will,
But by her own choice to confirm it gladly.
NEAR. You speak the nature of a right just father.
I come not hither roughly to demand
My cousin's thralldom, but to free mine own.
Report of great Calantha's beauty, virtue,
Sweetness, and singular perfections, courted
All ears to credit what I find was published
By constant truth, from which, if any service
Of my desert can purchase fair construction,          20
This lady must command it.
CAL.                              Princely sir,
So well you know how to profess observance [2]

That you instruct your hearers to become
Practitioners in duty, of which number
I'll study to be chief.
NEAR.                    Chief, glorious virgin,
In my devotions, as in all men's wonder.
AMY. Excellent cousin, we deny no liberty;
Use thine own opportunities.—Armostes,
We must consult with the philosophers;
The business is of weight.
ARM.                    Sir, at your pleasure.    30
AMY. You told me, Crotolon, your son's returned
From Athens? Wherefore comes a not to court
As we commanded?
CROT.                    He shall soon attend
Your royal will, great sir.
AMY.                              The marriage
Between young Prophilus and Euphranea
Tastes of too much delay.
CROT.                    My lord—
AMY.                              Some pleasures
At celebration of it would give life
To th' entertainment of the prince our kinsman;
Our court wears gravity more than we relish.
ARM. Yet the heavens smile on all your high attempts          40
Without a cloud.
CROT.                    So may the gods protect us.
CAL. A prince a subject?
NEAR.                    Yes, to beauty's scepter;
As all hearts kneel, so mine.
CAL.                    You are too courtly.

*To them, Ithocles, Orgilus, Prophilus.*

ITH. Your safe return to Sparta is most welcome;
I joy to meet you here, and, as occasion
Shall grant us privacy, will yield you reasons
Why I should covet to deserve the title
Of your respected friend; for, without compliment,
Believe it, Orgilus, 'tis my ambition.
ORG. Your lordship may command me your poor servant.          50
ITH. [*Aside.*] So amorously close? So soon? My heart!

[1] Decry, disprove.          [2] Courtship.

PRO. What sudden change is next?

ITH.                              Life to the
    king,
To whom I here present this noble
    gentleman,
New come from Athens.    Royal sir,
    vouchsafe
Your gracious hand in favor of his
    merit.

CROT. [*Aside.*] My son preferred by Itho-
    cles!

AMY.          Our bounties
Shall open to thee, Orgilus; for in-
    stance—
Hark in thine ear—if, out of those in-
    ventions
Which flow in Athens, thou hast there
    engrossed [1]
Some rarity of wit, to grace the nup-
    tials                                        60
Of thy fair sister, and renown our court
In th' eyes of this young prince, we
    shall be debtor
To thy conceit; think on 't.

ORG.          Your highness honors me.

NEAR. My tongue and heart are twins.

CAL.                    A noble birth,
Becoming such a father.—Worthy Or-
    gilus,
You are a guest most wished for.

ORG.                    May my duty
Still rise in your opinion, sacred prin-
    cess!

ITH. Euphranea's brother, sir; a gentle-
    man
Well worthy of your knowledge.

NEAR.               We embrace him,
Proud of so dear acquaintance.

AMY.               All prepare    70
For revels and disport; the joys of Hy-
    men,
Like Phœbus in his luster, puts to
    flight
All mists of dullness.   Crown the hours
    with gladness.
No sounds but music, no discourse but
    mirth!

CAL. Thine arm, I prithee, Ithocles.—
    Nay, good
My lord, keep on your way; I am pro-
    vided.

NEAR. I dare not disobey.

ITH.          Most heavenly lady!    *Exeunt.*

[1] Acquired, learned.

[SCENE iv

*A room in Crotolon's house.*]

*Enter Crotolon, Orgilus.*

CROT. The king hath spoke his mind.

ORG.                    His will he hath;
But, were it lawful to hold plea against
The power of greatness, not the reason,
    haply
Such undershrubs as subjects sometimes
    might
Borrow of nature justice, to inform
That license [2] sovereignty holds without
    check
Over a meek obedience.

CROT.               How resolve you
Touching your sister's marriage?   Pro-
    philus
Is a deserving and a hopeful youth.    9

ORG. I envy not his merit, but applaud it;
Could wish [3] him thrift [4] in all his best
    desires,
And with a willingness inleague our blood
With his, for purchase of full growth in
    friendship.
He never touched on any wrong that
    maliced [5]
The honor of our house nor stirred our
    peace;
Yet, with your favor, let me not forget
Under whose wing he gathers warmth
    and comfort,
Whose creature he is bound, made, and
    must live so.

CROT. Son, son, I find in thee a harsh con-
    dition; [6]
No courtesy can win it; 'tis too ran-
    corous.                                    20

ORG. Good sir, be not severe in your con-
    struction.
I am no stranger to such easy calms
As sit in tender bosoms.   Lordly Ithocles
Hath graced my entertainment in abun-
    dance,
Too humbly hath descended from that
    height
Of arrogance and spleen which wrought
    the rape
On grieved Penthea's purity; his scorn
Of my untoward fortunes is reclaimed

[2] To control that authority.
[3] Suggested by Gifford-Dyce.   Original reads
*with.*
[4] Success.
[5] Sought to injure.
[6] Disposition.

Unto a courtship, almost to a fawning.
I'll kiss his foot, since you will have it
   so.                            30
CROT. Since I will have it so? Friend, I
   will have it so,
Without our ruin by your politic plots,
Or wolf of hatred snarling in your breast.
You have a spirit, sir, have ye? A fa-
   miliar
That posts i' th' air for your intelligence?
Some such hobgoblin hurried you from
   Athens,
For yet you come unsent for.
ORG.                  If unwelcome,
I might have found a grave there.
CROT.          Sure, your business
Was soon despatched, or your mind al-
   tered quickly.
ORG. 'Twas care, sir, of my health cut
   short my journey;              40
For there a general infection
Threatens a desolation.
CROT.             And I fear
Thou hast brought back a worse infection
   with thee—
Infection of thy mind, which, as thou
   say'st,
Threatens the desolation of our family.
ORG. Forbid it, our dear genius![1] I will
   rather
Be made a sacrifice on Thrasus' monu-
   ment,
Or kneel to Ithocles, his son, in dust,
Than woo a father's curse. My sister's
   marriage
With Prophilus is from my heart con-
   firmed.                        50
May I live hated, may I die despised,
If I omit to further it in all
That can concern me!
CROT.        I have been too rough.
My duty to my king made me so earnest.
Excuse it, Orgilus.
ORG.             Dear sir!—

*Enter to them, Prophilus, Euphranea, Itho-*
        *cles, Groneas, Hemophil.*

CROT.            Here comes
Euphranea with Prophilus and Ithocles.
ORG. Most honored! Ever famous!
ITH.            Your true friend;
On earth not any truer.—With smooth [2]
   eyes

[1] Tutelary spirit.               [2] Kindly.

Look on this worthy couple; your consent
Can only make them one.
ORG.          They have it.—Sister,    60
Thou pawn'dst to me an oath, of which
   engagement
I never will release thee, if thou aim'st
At any other choice than this.
EUPH.             Dear brother
At him, or none.
CROT.       To which my blessing's added.
ORG. Which, till a greater ceremony per-
   fect—
Euphranea, lend thy hand. Here, take
   her, Prophilus;
Live long a happy man and wife; and
   further,
That these in presence may conclude an
   omen,
Thus for a bridal song I close my wishes:

Comforts lasting; loves increasing,    70
Like soft hours never ceasing;
Plenty's pleasure; peace complying,
Without jars, or tongues envying;
Hearts by holy union wedded
More than theirs by custom bedded;
Fruitful issues; life so gracéd,
Not by age to be defacéd,
Budding, as the year ensu'th,
Every spring another youth—
All what thought can add beside    80
Crown this bridegroom and this bride!

PRO. You have sealed joy close to my
   soul.—Euphranea,
Now I may call thee mine.
ITH.            I but exchange
One good friend for another.
ORG.           If these gallants
Will please to grace a poor invention
By joining with me in some slight device,
I'll venture on a strain my younger days
Have studied for delight.
HEM.       With thankful willingness
I offer my attendance.
GRO.           No endeavor
Of mine shall fail to show itself.
ITH.          We will    90
All join to wait on thy directions, Orgilus.
ORG. O, my good lord, your favors flow
   towards
A too unworthy worm—but as you
   please;
I am what you will shape me.
ITH.            A fast friend.

CROT. I thank thee, son, for this acknowledgment;
It is a sight of gladness.
ORG. But my duty. *Exeunt omnes.*

*Calantha's apartment in the palace.]*

*Enter Calantha, Penthea, Christalla, Philema.*

CAL. Whoe'er would speak with us, deny his entrance;
Be careful of our charge.
CHRIS. We shall, madam.
CAL. Except the king himself, give none admittance;
Not any.
PHIL. Madam, it shall be our care.

*Exeunt [All but] Calantha, Penthea.*

CAL. Being alone, Penthea, you have granted
The opportunity you sought, and might
At all times have commanded.
PEN. 'Tis a benefit
Which I shall owe your goodness even in death for.
My glass [1] of life, sweet princess, hath few minutes
Remaining to run down; the sands are spent, 10
For by an inward messenger I feel
The summons of departure short and certain.
CAL. You feed too much your melancholy.
PEN. Glories
Of human greatness are but pleasing dreams
And shadows soon decaying; on the stage
Of my mortality my youth hath acted
Some scenes of vanity, drawn out at length
By varied pleasures, sweetened in the mixture,
But tragical in issue; beauty, pomp,
With every sensuality our giddiness 20
Doth frame an idol, are unconstant friends,
When any troubled passion makes assault
On the unguarded castle of the mind.
CAL. Contemn not your condition for the proof

[1] Hourglass.

Of bare opinion only.[2] To what end
Reach all these moral texts?
PEN. To place before 'e
A perfect mirror, wherein you may see
How weary I am of a ling'ring life,
Who count the best a misery.
CAL. Indeed
You have no little cause; yet none so great 30
As to distrust a remedy.
PEN. That remedy
Must be a winding sheet, a fold of lead,
And some untrod-on corner in the earth.—
Not to detain your expectation, princess,
I have an humble suit.
CAL. Speak; I enjoy it.
PEN. Vouchsafe, then, to be my executrix,
And take that trouble on 'e to dispose
Such legacies as I bequeath, impartially.
I have not much to give—the pains are easy;
Heaven will reward your piety, and thank it 40
When I am dead. For sure I must not live;
I hope I cannot.
CAL. Now, beshrew thy sadness;
Thou turn'st me too much woman.
[*Weeps.*]
PEN. [*Aside.*] Her fair eyes
Melt into passion. Then I have assurance
Encouraging my boldness.—In this paper
My will was charactered, which you, with pardon,
Shall now know from mine own mouth.
CAL. Talk on, prithee;
It is a pretty earnest.[3]
PEN. I have left me
But three poor jewels to bequeath. The first is
My youth, for, though I am much old in griefs, 50
In years I am a child.
CAL. To whom that?
PEN. To virgin wives, such as abuse not wedlock
By freedom of desires, but covet chiefly
The pledges of chaste beds for ties of love,
Rather than ranging of their blood; and next

[2] On account of your experience from mere public opinion.
[3] A small advance payment, a foretaste.

To married maids, such as prefer the
  number
Of honorable issue in their virtues
Before the flattery of delights by mar-
  riage.
May those be ever young!

CAL.              A second jewel
You mean to part with?

PEN.         'Tis my fame, I trust  60
  By scandal yet untouched; this I be-
    queath
To Memory, and Time's old daughter,
  Truth.
If ever my unhappy name find mention
When I am fall'n to dust, may it deserve
Beseeming charity without dishonor!

CAL. How handsomely thou play'st with
  harmless sport
Of mere imagination! Speak the last.
I strangely like thy will.

PEN.         This jewel, madam,
Is dearly precious to me; you must use
The best of your discretion to employ  70
This gift as I intend it.

CAL.           Do not doubt me.

PEN. 'Tis long agone since first I lost my
  heart;
Long I have lived without it, else for cer-
  tain
I should have given that too; but instead
Of it, to great Calantha, Sparta's heir,
By service bound and by affection vowed,
I do bequeath, in holiest rites of love,
Mine only brother, Ithocles.

CAL.          What said'st thou?

PEN. Impute not, heaven-blessed lady, to
  ambition                   79
A faith as humbly perfect as the prayers
Of a devoted suppliant can endow it.
Look on him, princess, with an eye of
  pity.
How like the ghost of what he late ap-
  peared
A moves before you!

CAL.        Shall I answer here,
Or lend my ear too grossly?

PEN.        First his heart
Shall fall in cinders, scorched by your
  disdain,
Ere he will dare, poor man, to ope an eye
On these divine looks, but with low-bent
  thoughts
Accusing such presumption, as, for
  words,

A dares not utter any but of service.   90
Yet this lost creature loves 'e. Be a
  princess
In sweetness as in blood; give him his
  doom,
Or raise him up to comfort.

CAL.         What new change
Appears in my behavior, that thou dar'st
Tempt my displeasure?

PEN.     I must leave the world
To revel [in] [1] Elysium, and 'tis just
To wish my brother some advantage
  here;
Yet, by my best hopes, Ithocles is ig-
  norant
Of this pursuit. But, if you please to kill
  him,
Lend him one angry look or one harsh
  word,                   100
And you shall soon conclude how strong
  a power
Your absolute authority holds over
His life and end.

CAL.       You have forgot, Penthea,
How still I have a father.

PEN.         But remember
I am a sister, though to me this brother
Hath been, you know, unkind, O, most
  unkind!

CAL. Christalla, Philema, where are 'e?—
  Lady,
Your check [2] lies in my silence.

*Enter Christalla and Philema.*

BOTH.             Madam, here.

CAL. I think 'e sleep, 'e drones! Wait on
  Penthea
Unto her lodging.—[*Aside.*] Ithocles?
  Wronged lady!             110

PEN. My reckonings are made even;
  death or fate
Can now nor strike too soon, nor force
  too late.          *Exeunt.*

ACTUS QUARTUS. SCENA PRIMA.

[*Ithocles' apartment in the palace.*]

*Enter Ithocles and Armostes.*

ITH. Forbear your inquisition; curiosity
Is of too subtle and too searching nature,
In fears of love too quick, too slow of
  credit.

[1] Supplied by Gifford-Dyce.     [2] Censure.

I am not what you doubt [1] me.

ARM.          Nephew, be, then,
As I would wish.—[*Aside.*] All is not
right.—Good heaven
Confirm your resolutions for dependence
On worthy ends, which may advance
your quiet!

ITH. I did the noble Orgilus much injury,
But grieved Penthea more; I now repent
it.
Now, uncle, now; this "now" is now too
late.        10
So provident [2] is folly in sad issue
That after-wit, like bankrupts' debts,
stand tallied [3]
Without all possibilities of payment.
Sure, he's an honest, very honest gentle-
man;
A man of single [4] meaning.

ARM.          I believe it;
Yet, nephew, 'tis the tongue informs our
ears;
Our eyes can never pierce into the
thoughts,
For they are lodged too inward. But I
question
No truth in Orgilus.—The princess, sir.

ITH. The princess? Ha!

ARM.    With her the Prince of Argos. 20

*Enter Nearchus, leading Calantha; Amelus,*
*Christalla, Philema.*

NEAR. Great fair one, grace my hopes
with any instance
Of livery,[5] from the allowance of your
favor;
This little spark—
     [*Tries to take a ring from her finger.*]

CAL.       A toy!

NEAR.       Love feasts on toys,
For Cupid is a child. Vouchsafe this
bounty;
It cannot be [de][6]nied.

CAL.       You shall not value,
Sweet cousin, at a price, what I count
cheap,
So cheap that let him take it who dares
stoop for 't,
And give it at next meeting to a mistress;

[1] Suspect.
[2] Productive.
[5] Badge of service.
[6] Supplied by Gifford-Dyce.
[3] Reckoned up.
[4] Sincere.

She'll thank him for 't, perhaps.
       *Casts it to Ithocles.*

AME.       The ring, sir, is 29
The princess's; I could have took it up.

ITH. Learn manners, prithee.—To the
blessed owner,
Upon my knees—

NEAR.       Y' are saucy.

CAL.          This is pretty!
I am, belike, "a mistress." Wondrous
pretty!
Let the man keep his fortune, since he
found it;
He's worthy on 't.—On, cousin!

ITH. [*To Amelus.*]    Follow, spaniel;
I'll force 'e to a fawning else.

AME.       You dare not.
    *Exeunt. Manent Itho[cles] et Armost[es].*

ARM. My lord, you were too forward.

ITH.       Look 'e, uncle,
Some such there are whose liberal con-
tents
Swarm without care in every sort of
plenty,
Who after full repasts can lay them
down        40
To sleep; and they sleep, uncle—in which
silence
Their very dreams present 'em choice of
pleasures,
Pleasures—observe me, uncle—of rare
object;
Here heaps of gold, there increments of
honors,
Now change of garments, then the votes
of people,
Anon varieties of beauties, courting,
In flatteries of the night, exchange of
dalliance.
Yet these are still but dreams. Give me
felicity
Of which my senses waking are par-
takers,
A real, visible, material happiness;    50
And then, too, when I stagger in ex-
pectance
Of the least comfort that can cherish
life—
I saw it, sir, I saw it, for it came
From her own hand.

ARM.       The princess threw it t'e.

ITH. True; and she said—well I remember
what.
Her cousin prince would beg it.

ARM.                          Yes, and parted
    In anger at your taking on 't.
ITH.                                    Penthea,
    O, thou hast pleaded with a powerful
        language!
    I want a fee to gratify thy merit;
    But I will do—
ARM.                    What is 't you say?
ITH.                                In anger, 60
    In anger let him part, for could his
        breath,
    Like whirlwinds, toss such servile slaves
        as lick
    The dust his footsteps print into a vapor,
    It durst not stir a hair of mine, it should
        not;
    I'd rend it up by th' roots first.  To be
        anything
    Calantha smiles on is to be a blessing
    More sacred than a petty prince of Argos
    Can wish to equal, or in worth or title.
ARM.  Contain yourself, my lord.  Ixion,
        aiming                            69
    To embrace Juno, bosomed but a cloud,
    And begat Centaurs; 'tis an useful
        moral.
    Ambition hatched in clouds of mere opin-
        ion
    Proves but in birth a prodigy.
ITH.                            I thank 'e;
    Yet, with your license, I should seem un-
        charitable
    To gentler fate, if, relishing the dainties
    Of a soul's settled peace, I were so feeble
    Not to digest it.
ARM.                  He deserves small trust
    Who is not privy counselor to himself.


*Enter Nearchus, Orgilus, and Amelus.*

NEAR.  Brave me?
ORG.                    Your excellence mistakes
        his temper,
    For Ithocles in fashion of his mind      80
    Is beautiful, soft, gentle, the clear mirror
    Of absolute perfection.
AME.                        Was 't your modesty
    Termed any of the prince his servants
        "spaniel"?
    Your nurse, sure, taught you other lan-
        guage.
ITH.            Language!
NEAR.  A gallant man-at-arms is here, a
        doctor

In feats of chivalry, blunt and rough-
    spoken,
Vouchsafing not the fustian of civility,
Which [less] [1] rash spirits style good man-
    ners!
ITH.        Manners!
ORG.  No more, illustrious sir; 'tis match-
    less Ithocles.
NEAR.  You might have understood who I
    am.
ITH.        Yes,                            90
    I did; else—but the presence [2] calmed
        th' affront—
    Y' are cousin to the princess.
NEAR.                        To the king, too;
    A certain instrument that lent support-
        ance
    To your colossic greatness—to that king
        too,
    You might have added.
ITH.                        There is more divinity
    In beauty than in majesty.
ARM.                            O, fie, fie!
NEAR.  This odd youth's pride turns heretic
    in loyalty.
    Sirrah, low mushrooms never rival ce-
        dars!        *Exeunt Nearchus et Amelus.*
ITH.  Come back!—What pitiful dull thing
    am I
    So to be tamely scolded at!    Come
        back!—                          100
    Let him come back, and echo once
        again
    That scornful sound of "mushroom"!
        Painted colts—
    Like heralds' coats gilt o'er with crowns
        and scepters—
    May bait a muzzled lion.
ARM.                        Cousin, cousin,
    Thy tongue is not thy friend.
ORG.                        In point of honor
    Discretion knows no bounds.  Amelus
        told me
    'Twas all about a little ring.
ITH.                            A ring
    The princess threw away, and I took up.
    Admit she threw 't to me, what arm of
        brass
    Can snatch it hence?  No; could a grind
        the hoop                        110
    To powder, a might sooner reach my
        heart

_____
[1] Supplied by Gifford.
[2] *I.e.*, of the princess.

Than steal and wear one dust [1] on 't. Orgilus,
I am extremely wronged.

ORG.                              A lady's favor
Is not to be so slighted.

ITH.                        Slighted!

ARM.                              Quiet
These vain, unruly passions, which will render ye
Into a madness.

ORG.              Griefs will have their vent.

*Enter Tecnicus [with a scroll].*

ARM. Welcome; thou com'st in season, reverend man,
To pour the balsam of a suppling [2] patience
Into the festering wound of ill-spent fury.

ORG. [*Aside.*] What makes he here?

TEC.      The hurts are yet but [3] mortal,
Which shortly will prove deadly.    To the king,                              121
Armostes, see in safety thou deliver
This sealed-up counsel; bid him with a constancy
Peruse the secrets of the gods.—O Sparta,
O Lacedemon!  Double-named, but one
In fate!  When kingdoms reel—mark well my saw—[4]
Their heads must needs be giddy.    Tell the king
That henceforth he no more must inquire after
My agéd head; Apollo wills it so.
I am for Delphos.

ARM.        Not without some conference
With our great master.

TEC.        Never more to see him;    131
A greater prince commands me.—Ithocles,
*When youth is ripe, and age from time doth part,*
*The lifeless trunk shall wed the broken heart.*

ITH. What's this, if understood?

TEC.                        List, Orgilus;
Remember what I told thee long before;
These tears shall be my witness.

[1] One particle.
[2] Healing. Suggested by Gifford-Dyce; original reads *supplying.*
[3] Gifford-Dyce suggests *not* but retains original.
[4] Proverb.

ARM.                        'Las, good man!

TEC. *Let craft with courtesy awhile confer;*
*Revenge proves its own executioner.*

ORG. Dark sentences are for Apollo's priests;                              140
I am not Œdipus.

TEC.                        My hour is come.
Cheer up the king; farewell to all.—O Sparta,
O Lacedemon!              *Exit Tecn[icus].*

ARM.              If prophetic fire
Have warmed this old man's bosom, we might construe
His words to fatal sense.

ITH.                        Leave to the powers
Above us the effects of their decrees;
My burthen lies within me.    Servile fears
Prevent no great effects.—Divine Calantha!

ARM. The gods be still propitious!
                    *Exeunt.  Manet Org[ilus].*

ORG.                        Something oddly
The bookman prated, yet a talked it weeping:                              150
" *Let craft with courtesy awhile confer;*
*Revenge proves its own executioner.*"
Con it again.—For what?  It shall not puzzle me;
'Tis dotage of a withered brain.—Penthea
Forbade me not her presence; I may see her,
And gaze my fill.  Why, see her, then, I may,
When, if I faint to speak—I must be silent.              *Exit Org[ilus].*

[SCENE ii.

*A room in Bassanes' house.*]

*Enter Bassanes, Grausis, and Phulas.*

BASS. Pray, use your recreations; all the service
I will expect is quietness amongst 'e;
Take liberty at home, abroad, at all times,
And in your charities appease the gods,
Whom I, with my distractions, have offended.

GRAU. Fair blessings on thy heart!

PHU. [*Aside.*]        Here's a rare change!

My lord, to cure the itch, is surely
    gelded;
The cuckold in conceit [1] hath cast his
    horns.
Bass. Betake 'e to your several occasions;
And, wherein I have heretofore been
    faulty,    10
Let your constructions mildly pass it
    over.
Henceforth I'll study reformation; more
I have not for employment.
Grau.                O sweet man!
Thou art the very "Honeycomb of
    Honesty."
Phu. The "Garland of Goodwill." [2] —Old
    lady, hold up
Thy reverend snout, and trot behind me
    softly,
As it becomes a moil [3] of ancient carriage.
          *Exeunt. Manet Bass[anes].*
Bass. Beasts, only capable of sense, enjoy
The benefit of food and ease with thank-
    fulness;
Such silly creatures, with a grudging,
    kick not    20
Against the portion nature hath be-
    stowed;
But men, endowed with reason and the
    use
Of reason, to distinguish from the chaff
Of abject scarcity the quintessence,
Soul, and elixir of the earth's abundance,
The treasures of the sea, the air, nay,
    heaven,
Repining at these glories of creation,
Are verier beasts than beasts; and of
    those beasts
The worst am I—I, who was made a
    monarch
Of what a heart could wish for—a chaste
    wife—    30
Endeavored what in me lay to pull down
That temple built for adoration only,
And level 't in the dust of causeless
    scandal.
But, to redeem a sacrilege so impious,
Humility shall pour, before the deities
I have incensed, a largeness [4] of more pa-
    tience
Than their displeaséd altars can require.

No tempests of commotion shall disquiet
The calms of my composure.

*Enter Orgilus.*

Org.              I have found thee,
Thou patron of more horrors than the
    bulk    40
Of manhood, hooped about with ribs of
    iron,
Can cram within thy breast. Penthea,
    Bassanes,
Cursed by thy jealousies—more, by thy
    dotage—
Is left a prey to words. [5]
Bass.              Exercise
Your trials for addition to my penance;
I am resolved.
Org.          Play not with misery
Past cure; some angry minister of fate
    hath
Deposed the empress of her soul, her
    reason,
From its most proper throne; but, what's
    the miracle
More new, I, I have seen it, and yet
    live!    50
Bass. You may delude my senses, not my
    judgment;
'Tis anchored into a firm resolution;
Dalliance of mirth or wit can ne'er unfix
    it.
Practice [6] yet further.
Org.      May thy death of love to her
Damn all thy comforts to a lasting fast
From every joy of life! Thou barren
    rock,
By thee we have been split in ken [7] of
    harbor.

*Enter Ithocles, Penthea, her hair about her*
    *ears, [Armostes,] Philema, Christalla.*

Ith. Sister, look up; your Ithocles, your
    brother,
Speaks t'e; why do you weep? Dear,
    turn not from me.—
Here is a killing sight; lo, Bassanes,    60
A lamentable object!
Org.            Man, dost see 't?
Sports are more gamesome; am I yet in
    merriment?
Why dost not laugh?

---

[1] Imagination.
[2] A popular miscellany of the time.
[3] Mule.
[4] Bounty, liberality.
[5] *I.e.*, scandal.    [6] Carry on.    [7] Sight.

BASS.                    Divine and best of ladies,
Please to forget my outrage; mercy ever
Cannot but lodge under a roof [1] so ex-
cellent.
I have cast off that cruelty of frenzy
Which once appeared impostors, and then
    juggled
To cheat my sleeps of rest.
ORG.                    Was I in earnest?
PEN.  Sure, if we were all Sirens, we should
    sing pitifully.
And 'twere a comely music, when in
    parts                                        70
One sung another's knell.  The turtle
    sighs
When he hath lost his mate; and yet
    some say
A must be dead first.  'Tis a fine deceit
To pass away in a dream; indeed, I've
    slept
With mine eyes open a great while.  No
    falsehood
Equals a broken faith; there's not a hair
Sticks on my head but, like a leaden
    plummet,
It sinks me to the grave.  I must creep
    thither;
The journey is not long.
ITH.                    But thou, Penthea,
Hast many years, I hope, to number
    yet,                                        80
Ere thou canst travel that way.
BASS.                    Let the sun [2] first
Be wrapped up in an everlasting dark-
    ness,
Before the light of nature, chiefly formed
For the whole world's delight, feel an
    eclipse
So universal!
ORG.                    Wisdom, look 'e, begins
To rave!—Art thou mad too, antiquity?
PEN.  Since I was first a wife, I might have
    been
Mother to many pretty, prattling babes;
They would have smiled when I smiled,
    and for certain
I should have cried when they cried.—
    Truly, brother,                              90
My father would have picked me out a
    husband,

And then my little ones had been no
    bastards;
But 'tis too late for me to marry now—
I am past childbearing; 'tis not my fault.
BASS.  Fall on me, if there be a burning
    Ætna,
And bury me in flames!  Sweats hot as
    sulphur
Boil through my pores!  Affliction hath
    in store
No torture like to this.
ORG.                    Behold a patience!
Lay by thy whining, gray dissimulation;
Do something worth a chronicle.  Show
    justice                                     100
Upon the author of this mischief; dig out
The jealousies that hatched this thrall-
    dom first
With thine own poniard.  Every antic
    rapture [3]
Can roar as thine does.
ITH.                    Orgilus, forbear.
BASS.  Disturb him not; it is a talking
    motion [4]
Provided for my torment.  What a fool
    am I
To bawdy passion!  Ere I'll speak a word,
I will look on and burst.
PEN.  [To Orgilus.]                    I loved you once.
ORG.  Thou didst, wronged creature, in de-
    spite of malice;
For it I love thee ever.
PEN.                    Spare your hand; 110
Believe me, I'll not hurt it.
ORG.                    Pain my heart too.
[PEN.] [5]  Complain not though I wring it
    hard.  I'll kiss it;
O, 'tis a fine soft palm!—Hark, in thine
    ear;
Like whom do I look, prithee?—Nay, no
    whispering.
Goodness!  We had been happy; too
    much happiness
Will make folk proud, they say—but that
    is he—                    Points at Ithocles.
And yet he paid for 't home.  Alas, his
    heart
Is crept into the cabinet of the princess;
We shall have points [6] and bride laces. [7]
    Remember,

---

[1] Emended by Gifford-Dyce; original reads
*root.*
[2] Emended by Gifford-Dyce; original reads
*swan.*

[3] Actor's passion.                    [4] Puppet.
[5] This speech is assigned to Orgilus in the
original.
[6] Tagged laces.    [7] *I.e.*, as wedding souvenirs.

When we last gathered roses in the gar-
den,                                    120
I found my wits, but truly you lost yours.
That's he, and still 'tis he.
ITH.                    Poor soul, how idly [1]
Her fancies guide her tongue!
BASS. [Aside.]          Keep in, vexation,
And break not into clamor.
ORG. [Aside.]          She has tutored me;
Some powerful inspiration checks my
laziness.[2]—
Now let me kiss your hand, grieved
beauty.
PEN.                    Kiss it.—
Alack, alack, his lips be wondrous cold.
Dear soul, h'as lost his color; have 'e
seen
A straying heart? All crannies! Every
drop
Of blood is turn[é]d to an amethyst,   130
Which married bachelors hang in their
ears.
ORG. Peace usher her into Elysium!—
If this be madness, madness is an oracle.
                        Exit Org[ilus].
ITH. Christalla, Philema, when slept my
sister,
Her ravings are so wild?
CHRIS.                  Sir, not these ten days.
PHIL. We watch by her continually; be-
sides,
We cannot any way pray her to eat.
BASS. O, misery of miseries!
PEN.                    Take comfort;
You may live well, and die a good old
man.
By yea and nay, an oath not to be
broken,                                 140
If you had joined our hands once in the
temple—
'Twas since my father died, for had he
lived
He would have done 't—I must have
called you father.
O, my wracked honor, ruined by those
tyrants,
A cruel brother and a desperate dotage!
There is no peace left for a ravished
wife
Widowed by lawless marriage; to all
memory
Penthea's, poor Penthea's, name is
strumpeted.

But, since her blood was seasoned by
the forfeit
Of noble shame with mixtures of pollu-
tion,                                   150
Her blood—'tis just—be henceforth
never heightened
With taste of sustenance! Starve; let
that fullness
Whose plurisy [3] hath fevered faith and
modesty—
Forgive me; O, I faint!
        [Falls into the arms of her Attendants.]
ARM.                    Be not so willful,
Sweet niece, to work thine own destruc-
tion.
ITH.          Nature
Will call her daughter monster!—What!
Not eat?
Refuse the only ordinary means
Which are ordained for life? Be not, my
sister,
A murth'ress to thyself.—Hear'st thou
this, Bassanes?
BASS. Foh! I am busy, for I have not
thoughts                                160
Enow to think; all shall be well anon.
'Tis tumbling in my head; there is a
mastery
In art to fatten and keep smooth the
outside;
Yes, and to comfort up the vital spirits
Without the help of food, fumes or per-
fumes,
Perfumes or fumes. Let her alone; I'll
search out
The trick on 't.
PEN.          Lead me gently; heavens reward
ye.
Griefs are sure friends; they leave with-
out control
Nor cure nor comforts for a leprous soul.
        Exeunt the Maids supporting Penthea.
BASS. I grant 'e, and will put in practice
instantly                               170
What you shall still admire.[4] 'Tis won-
derful;
'Tis super-singular, not to be matched;
Yet, when I've done 't, I've done 't.—Ye
shall all thank me.     Exit Bassanes.
ARM. The sight is full of terror.
ITH.                    On my soul
Lies such an infinite clog of massy dull-
ness

[1] Madly.          [2] Procrastination.          [3] Superabundance.          [4] Wonder at.

As that I have not sense enough to feel
it.—
See, uncle, th' augury [1] thing returns
again;
Shall 's welcome him with thunder? We
are haunted,
And must use exorcism to conjure down
This spirit of malevolence.
Arm.                        Mildly, nephew.   180

*Enter Nearchus and Amelus.*

Near. I come not, sir, to chide your late
disorder,
Admitting that th' inurement to a rough-
ness
In soldiers of your years and fortunes,
chiefly,
So lately prosperous, hath not yet shook
off
The custom of the war in hours of leisure;
Nor shall you need excuse, since y' are to
render
Account to that fair excellence, the
princess,
Who in her private gallery expects it
From your own mouth alone.  I am a
messenger
But to her pleasure.
Ith.               Excellent Nearchus,  190
Be prince still of my services, and con-
quer
Without the combat of dispute; I hon-
or 'e.
Near.  The king is on a sudden indisposed;
Physicians are called for.  'Twere fit,
Armostes,
You should be near him.
Arm.               Sir, I kiss your hands.
      *Exeunt. Manent Nearchus et Amelus.*
Near.  Amelus,  I  perceive  Calantha's
bosom
Is warmed with other fires than such as
can
Take strength from any fuel of the love
I might address to her.  Young Ithocles,
Or ever I mistake, is lord ascendant  200
Of her devotions—one, to speak him
truly,
In every disposition nobly fashioned.
Ame.  But can your highness brook to be
so rivaled,
Considering th' inequality of the persons?

[1] Foreboding.      [2] An astrological figure.

Near.  I can, Amelus, for affections in-
jured
By tyranny or rigor of compulsion,
Like tempest-threatened trees unfirmly
rooted,
Ne'er spring to timely growth.  Observe,
for instance,
Life-spent Penthea and unhappy Orgilus.
Ame.  How does your grace determine?
Near.               To be jealous  210
In public of what privately I'll further;
And, though they shall not know, yet
they shall find it.       *Exeunt omnes.*

[Scene iii.

*An apartment in the palace.*]

*Enter Hemophil and Groneas leading Amy-
clas, and placing him in a chair; followed
by Armostes [with a box], Crotolon, and
Prophilus.*

Amy.  Our daughter is not near?
Arm.               She is retired, sir,
Into her gallery.
Amy.        Where's the prince our cousin?
Pro.  New walked into the grove, my lord.
Amy.               All leave us
Except Armostes, and you, Crotolon;
We would be private.
Pro.        Health unto your majesty!
      *Exeunt Prophilus, Hemophil, et Groneas.*
Amy. What! Tecnicus is gone?
Arm.               He is to Delphos,
And to your royal hands presents this
box.
Amy. Unseal it, good Armostes; therein
lies
The secrets of the oracle.  Out with it.
      [*Armostes removes the scroll.*]
Apollo live our patron!  Read, Ar-
mostes.                        10
Arm.  "*The plot in which the vine takes root
Begins to dry from head to foot;
The stock soon withering, want of sap
Doth cause to quail*[3] *the budding grape;
But from the neighboring elm a dew
Shall drop, and feed the plot anew.*"
Amy.        That is the oracle.  What exposi-
tion
Makes the philosopher?
Arm.               This brief one only.
"*The plot is Sparta; the dried vine the king;*

[3] Quell, die.

*The quailing grape his daughter; but the*
*    thing*                                        20
*Of most importance, not to be revealed,*
*Is a near prince, the elm—the rest con-*
*    cealed.*

TECNICUS."

AMY. Enough; although the opening [1] of
    this riddle
Be but itself a riddle, yet we construe
How near our laboring age draws to a
    rest.
But must Calantha quail too? That
    young grape
Untimely budded! I could mourn for her;
Her tenderness hath yet deserved no rigor
So to be crossed by fate.

ARM.                    You misapply, sir.   29
With favor let me speak it—what Apollo
Hath clouded in hid sense. I here con-
    jecture
Her marriage with some neighb'ring
    prince, the dew
Of which befriending elm shall ever
    strengthen
Your subjects with a sovereignty of
    power.

CROT. Besides, most gracious lord, the
    pith of oracles
Is to be then digested when th' events
Expound their truth, not brought as soon
    to light
As uttered. Truth is child of Time; and
    herein
I find no scruple, rather cause of comfort,
With unity of kingdoms.

AMY.                    May it prove so,   40
For weal of this dear nation!—Where is
    Ithocles?—
Armostes, Crotolon, when this withered
    vine
Of my frail carcass, on the funeral pile
Is fired into its ashes, let that young man
Be hedged about still with your cares and
    loves.
Much owe I to his worth, much to his
    service.—
Let such as wait come in now.

ARM.                    All attend here!

*Enter Ithocles, Calantha, Prophilus, Orgilus,*
*    Euphranea, Hemophil, and Groneas.*

CAL. Dear sir! King! Father!
ITH.                    O my royal master!

¹ *I.e.*, interpretation.

AMY. Cleave not my heart, sweet twins of
    my life's solace,
With your forejudging fears; there is no
    physic                                        50
So cunningly restorative to cherish
The fall of age, or call back youth and
    vigor,
As your consents in duty. I will shake off
This languishing disease of time, to
    quicken
Fresh pleasures in these drooping hours
    of sadness.
Is fair Euphranea married yet to Pro-
    philus?

CROT. This morning, gracious lord.
ORG.                    This very morning,
Which, with your highness' leave, you
    may observe too.
Our sister looks, methinks, mirthful and
    sprightly,
As if her chaster fancy could already   60
Expound the riddle of her gain in losing
A trifle maids know only that they know
    not.
Pish! Prithee, blush not; 'tis but honest
    change
Of fashion in the garment, loose for
    strait,
And so the modest maid is made a wife.
Shrewd business—is 't not, sister?

EUPH.                    You are pleasant.
AMY. We thank thee, Orgilus; this mirth
    becomes thee.
But wherefore sits the court in such a
    silence?
A wedding without revels is not seemly.

CAL. Your late indisposition, sir, forbade
    it.                                            70
AMY. Be it thy charge, Calantha, to set
    forward
The bridal sports, to which I will be
    present;
If not, at least consenting.—Mine own
    Ithocles,
I have done little for thee yet.

ITH.                    Y' have built me
To the full height I stand in.

CAL. [*Aside.*]                    Now or never!—
May I propose a suit?

AMY.                    Demand, and have it.
CAL. Pray, sir, give me this young man,
    and no further
Account him yours than he deserves in
    all things

To be thought worthy mine; I will
esteem him
According to his merit.

AMY.      Still th' art my daughter, 80
Still grow'st upon my heart.—[*To
Ithocles.*] Give me thine hand.—
Calantha, take thine own. In noble
actions
Thou'lt find him firm and absolute.—I
would not
Have parted with thee, Ithocles, to any
But to a mistress who is all what I am.

ITH. A change, great king, most wished
for, cause the same![1]

CAL. [*Aside to Ithocles.*] Th' art mine. Have
I now kept my word?

ITH. [*Aside to Calantha.*]      Divinely.

ORG. Rich fortunes guard, the[2] favor of a
princess
Rock thee, brave man, in ever-crownéd
plenty!
Y' are minion of the time; be thankful for
it.—      90
[*Aside.*] Ho! Here's a swinge[3] in destiny.
Apparent,
The youth is up on tiptoe, yet may stum-
ble.

AMY. On to your recreations.—Now convey me
Unto my bedchamber. None on his forehead
Wear a distempered look.

OMNES.      The gods preserve 'e!

CAL. [*Aside to Ithocles.*]      Sweet, be not
from my sight.

ITH. [*Aside to Calantha.*]      My whole
felicity!

*Exeunt, carrying out of the King; Orgilus*
*stays Ithocles.*

ORG. Shall I be bold, my lord?

ITH.      Thou canst not, Orgilus.
Call me thine own, for Prophilus must
henceforth
Be all thy sister's. Friendship, though it
cease not      99
In marriage, yet is oft at less command
Than when a single freedom can dispose
it.

ORG. Most right, my most good lord, my
most great lord,
My gracious, princely lord, I might add,
royal.

ITH. Royal! A subject royal?

ORG.      Why not, pray, sir?
The sovereignty of kingdoms in their
nonage
Stooped to desert, not birth; there's as
much merit
In clearness of affection[4] as in puddle
Of generations.[5] You have conquered
love
Even in the loveliest; if I greatly err not,
The son of Venus hath bequeathed his
quiver      110
To Ithocles his manage,[6] by whose
arrows
Calantha's breast is opened.

ITH.      Can 't be possible?

ORG. I was myself a piece of suitor once,
And forward in preferment too—so for-
ward
That, speaking truth, I may without
offense, sir,
Presume to whisper that my hopes and
—hark 'e—
My certainty of marriage stood assured
With as firm footing—by your leave—as
any's
Now at this very instant—but—

ITH.      'Tis granted;
And, for a league of privacy between
us,      120
Read o'er my bosom and partake a
secret:
The princess is contracted mine.

ORG.      Still, why not?
I now applaud her wisdom; when your
kingdom
Stands seated in your will, secure and
settled,
I dare pronounce you will be a just mon-
arch;
Greece must admire and tremble.

ITH.      Then the sweetness
Of so imparadised a comfort, Orgilus!
It is to banquet with the gods.

ORG.      The glory
Of numerous children, potency of nobles,
Bent knees, hearts paved to tread on!

ITH.      With a friendship 130
So dear, so fast as thine.

ORG.      I am unfitting
For office; but for service—

---

[1] Because they are the same.      [3] Sway.
[2] Emended by Gifford-Dyce; original reads *to*
[4] Nobility of mental tendencies.
[5] Birth.
[6] To Ithocles' management.

ITH.                              We'll distinguish
Our fortunes merely in the title; partners
In all respects else but the bed.
ORG.                                    The bed?
Forfend[1] it, Jove's own jealousy, till
    lastly
We slip down in the common earth to-
    gether,
And there our beds are equal, save some
    monument
To show this was the king, and this the
    subject.—
List, what sad sounds are these?—Ex-
    tremely sad ones!
ITH. Sure, from Penthea's lodgings.
ORG.                    Hark! A voice too.  140

*Soft, sad music.*

A SONG

O, no more, no more, too late
    Sighs are spent; the burning tapers
Of a life as chaste as fate,
    Pure as are unwritten papers,
Are burnt out. No heat, no light
Now remains; 'tis ever night.

Love is dead; let lovers' eyes,
    Locked in endless dreams,
    Th' extremes of all extremes,
Ope no more, for now Love dies,        150
    Now Love dies, implying
Love's martyrs must be ever, ever dying.

ITH. O, my misgiving heart!
ORG.                    A horrid stillness
Succeeds this deathful air; let's know the
    reason.
Tread softly; there is mystery in mourn-
    ing.                                *Exeunt.*

[SCENE iv.

*Penthea's apartment in the palace.*]

*Enter Christalla and Philema, bringing in*
    *Penthea in a chair, veiled; two other*
    *Servants placing two chairs, one on the*
    *one side, and the other with an engine[2]*
    *on the other. The Maids sit down at her*
    *feet, mourning. The Servants go out;*
    *meet them Ithocles and Orgilus.*

SERV. [*Aside to Orgilus.*] 'Tis done; that on
    her right hand.

    [1] Forbid.        [2] Mechanical contrivance.

ORG.                        Good; begone!
                            [*Exeunt Servants.*]
ITH. Soft peace enrich this room!
ORG.                        How fares the lady?
PHIL. Dead!
CHRIS.        Dead!
PHIL.        Starved!
CHRIS.        Starved!
ITH.                        Me miserable!
ORG.                                Tell us
How parted she from life.
PHIL.                    She called for music,
And begged some gentle voice to tune a
    farewell
To life and griefs. Christalla touched the
    lute;
I wept the funeral song.
CHRIS.                Which scarce was ended
But her last breath sealed up these hollow
    sounds,
"O, cruel Ithocles and injured Orgilus!"
So down she drew her veil, so died.
ITH.                        So died!  10
ORG. Up! You are messengers of death; go
    from us;
Here's woe enough to court without a
    prompter!
Away; and—hark ye—till you see us
    next,
No syllable that she is dead.—Away;
        *Exeunt Phil[ema] et Chri[stalla].*
Keep a smooth brow.—My lord—
ITH.                        Mine only sister!
Another is not left me.
ORG.                        Take that chair;
I'll seat me here in this. Between us sits
The object of our sorrows; some few
    tears
We'll part among us; I perhaps can mix
One lamentable story to prepare 'em.—
There, there; sit there, my lord.
ITH.                    Yes, as you please.  21
*Ithocles sits down, and is catched in the*
                                *engine.*
What means this treachery?
ORG.                    Caught! You are caught,
Young master; 'tis thy throne of corona-
    tion,
Thou fool of greatness! See, I take this
    veil off;
Survey a beauty withered by the flames
Of an insulting Phaëton, her brother.
ITH. Thou mean'st to kill me basely.
ORG.                        I foreknew

The last act of her life, and trained [1] thee
    hither
To sacrifice a tyrant to a turtle.
You dreamt of kingdoms, did 'e? How to
    bosom                                         30
The delicacies of a youngling princess,
How with this nod to grace that subtle
    courtier,
How with that frown to make this noble
    tremble,
And so forth, whiles Penthea's groans and
    tortures,
Her agonies, her miseries, afflictions
Ne'er touched upon your thought? As
    for my injuries,
Alas, they were beneath your royal
    pity;
But yet they lived, thou proud man, to
    confound thee.
Behold thy fate, this steel!
                            [*Draws a dagger.*]
ITH.                    Strike home! A courage
    As keen as thy revenge shall give it wel-
    come.                                          40
But, prithee, faint not; if the wound
    close up,
Tent [2] it with double force, and search it
    deeply.
Thou look'st that I should whine and beg
    compassion,
As loath to leave the vainness of my
    glories.
A statelier resolution arms my confidence,
To cozen thee of honor; neither could I
With equal trial of unequal fortune
By hazard of a duel; 'twere a bravery
Too mighty for a slave intending mur-
    ther.
On to the execution, and inherit          50
A conflict with thy horrors!
ORG.                              By Apollo,
    Thou talk'st a goodly language! For
    requital
I will report thee to thy mistress richly,
And take this peace along: some few
    short minutes
Determined,[3] my resolves shall quickly
    follow
Thy wrathful ghost; then, if we tug for
    mastery,
Penthea's sacred eyes shall lend new
    courage.

---
[1] Lured.        [3] Brought to a termination.
[2] Probe.

Give me thy hand; be healthful in thy
    parting
From lost mortality! Thus, thus I free it!
                              *Kills him.*
ITH. Yet, yet, I scorn to shrink.
ORG.                    Keep up thy spirit.  60
    I will be gentle even in blood; to linger [4]
Pain, which I strive to cure, were to be
    cruel.                    [*Stabs him again.*]
ITH. Nimble in vengeance, I forgive thee.
    Follow
Safety, with best success.   O, may it
    prosper!—
Penthea, by thy side thy brother
    bleeds—
The earnest of his wrongs to thy forced
    faith.
Thoughts of ambition, or delicious ban-
    quet,
With beauty, youth, and love, together
    perish
In my last breath, which on the sacred
    altar
Of a long-looked-for peace—now—moves
    —to heaven.              *Moritur.*[5] 70
ORG. Farewell, fair spring of manhood.
    Henceforth welcome
Best expectation of a noble suff'rance.
I'll lock the bodies safe, till what must
    follow
Shall be approved.—Sweet twins, shine
    stars forever!—
In vain they build their hopes whose life
    is shame;
No monument lasts but a happy name.
                            *Exit Orgilus.*


ACTUS QUINTUS.  SCENA PRIMA.

[*A room in Bassanes' house.*]

*Enter Bassanes, alone.*

BASS. Athens!—To Athens I have sent,
    the nursery
Of Greece for learning and the fount of
    knowledge,
For here in Sparta there's not left
    amongst us
One wise man to direct; we're all turned
    madcaps.
'Tis said Apollo is the god of herbs;
Then certainly he knows the virtue of
    'em.

---
[4] Prolong.                    [5] He dies.

To Delphos I have sent too.  If there
    can be
A help for nature, we are sure yet.

*Enter Orgilus.*

ORG.                              Honor
Attend thy counsels ever!
BASS.                     I beseech thee
With all my heart, let me go from thee
    quietly;                                  10
I will not aught to do with thee of all
    men.
The doubles [1] of a hare—or, in a morning,
Salutes from a splay-footed witch—to
    drop
Three drops of blood at th' nose just
    and no more—
Croaking of ravens, or the screech of
    owls—
Are not so boding mischief as thy cross-
    ing
My private meditations.  Shun me,
    prithee;
And, if I cannot love thee heartily,
I'll love thee as well as I can.
ORG.                    Noble Bassanes,
Mistake me not.
BASS.        Phew!    Then we shall be
    troubled.                                  20
Thou wert ordained my plague—heaven
    make me thankful,
And give me patience too, heaven, I
    beseech thee.
ORG.  Accept a league of amity, for hence-
    forth
I vow by my best genius, in a syllable,
Never to speak vexation.  I will study
Service and friendship, with a zealous
    sorrow
For my past incivility towards 'e.
BASS.  Heyday, good words, good words!  I
    must believe 'em,
And be a coxcomb for my labor.
ORG.                              Use not
So hard a language; your misdoubt is
    causeless.                                 30
For instance, if you promise to put on
A constancy of patience, such a patience
As chronicle or history ne'er mentioned,
As follows not example, but shall stand
A wonder and a theme for imitation,

[1] Doublings.  Reading of Gifford-Dyce; original
reads *doublers*.

The first, the index [2] pointing to a second,
I will acquaint 'e with an unmatched
    secret,
Whose knowledge to your griefs shall
    set a period.
BASS.  Thou canst not, Orgilus; 'tis in the
    power                                      39
Of the gods only; yet, for satisfaction,
Because I note an earnest in thine
    utterance,
Unforced and naturally free, be resolute [3]
The virgin bays shall not withstand the
    lightning
With a more careless [4] danger than my
    constancy
The full of thy relation.  Could it move
Distraction in a senseless marble statue,
It should find me a rock.  I do expect
    now
Some truth of unheard moment.
ORG.                    To your patience
You must add privacy, as strong in
    silence
As mysteries locked up in Jove's own
    bosom.                                     50
BASS.  A skull hid in the earth a treble age
Shall sooner prate.
ORG.              Lastly, to such direction
As the severity of a glorious action
Deserves to lead your wisdom and your
    judgment,
You ought to yield obedience.
BASS.                    With assurance
Of will and thankfulness.
ORG.                With manly courage
Please then to follow me.
BASS.                Where'er, I fear not.
                    *Exeunt omnes.*

SCENE ii.

*[A room of state in the palace.]*

*Loud music.  Enter Groneas and Hemophil,
    leading Euphranea; Christalla and
    Philema, leading Prophilus; Nearchus
    supporting Calantha; Crotolon and
    Amelus.  Cease loud music; All make a
                                    stand.*

CAL.  We miss our servant Ithocles and
    Orgilus;
On whom attend they?
CROT.        My son, gracious princess,

[2] Finger.
[3] Certain.
[4] *I.e.*, heedlessness of.

Whispered some new device, to which these revels
Should be but usher, wherein 1 conceive
Lord Ithocles and he himself are actors.

CAL. A fair excuse for absence. As for Bassanes,
Delights to him are troublesome. Armostes
Is with the king?

CROT. He is.

CAL. On to the dance!—
Dear cousin, hand you the bride; the bridegroom must be
Intrusted to my courtship. Be not jealous,                          10
Euphranea; I shall scarcely prove a temptress.—
Fall to our dance.                                *Music.*

*Nearchus dance with Euphranea, Prophilus with Calantha, Christalla with Hemophil, Philema with Groneas. Dance the first change,[1] during which enter Armostes.*

ARM. (*In Calantha's ear.*)          The king your father's dead.

CAL. To the other change.

ARM. Is 't possible?          *Dance again.*

*Enter Bassanes.*

BASS. [*In Calantha's ear.*]          O, madam! Penthea, poor Penthea's starved.

CAL.          Beshrew thee!—
Lead to the next.

BASS.          Amazement dulls my senses.
                                     *Dance again.*

*Enter Orgilus.*

ORG. [*In Calantha's ear.*] Brave Ithocles is murthered, murthered cruelly.

CAL. How dull this music sounds! Strike up more sprightly;
Our footings are not active like our heart,
Which treads the nimbler measure.

ORG.          I am thunderstrook.
                          *Last change. Cease music.*

CAL. So! Let us breathe awhile.—Hath not this motion                          20
Raised fresher color on your cheeks?

NEAR.                          Sweet princess,
A perfect purity of blood enamels
The beauty of your white.

CAL.          We all look cheerfully;
And, cousin, 'tis, methinks, a rare presumption
In any who prefers our lawful pleasures
Before their own sour censure, to interrupt
The custom of this ceremony bluntly.

NEAR. None dares, lady.

CAL. Yes, yes; some hollow voice delivered to me
How that the king was dead.

ARM.          The king is dead.          30
That fatal news was mine; for in mine arms
He breathed his last, and with his crown bequeathed 'e
Your mother's wedding ring, which here I tender.

CROT. Most strange!

CAL.          Peace crown his ashes! We are queen, then.

NEAR. Long live Calantha! Sparta's sovereign queen!

OMNES. Long live the queen!

CAL.          What whispered Bassanes?

BASS. That my Penthea, miserable soul, Was starved to death.

CAL.          She's happy; she hath finished
A long and painful progress.[2]—A third murmur
Pierced mine unwilling ears.

ORG.                          That Ithocles          40
Was murthered—rather butchered—had not bravery
Of an undaunted spirit, conquering terror,
Proclaimed his last act triumph over ruin.

ARM. How? Murthered!

CAL.          By whose hand?

ORG.          By mine; this weapon
Was instrument to my revenge. The reasons
Are just, and known; quit him of these, and then
Never lived gentleman of greater merit,
Hope, or abiliment[3] to steer a kingdom.

CROT. Fie, Orgilus!

EUPH.          Fie, brother!

CAL.          You have done it?

---

[1] Figure of the dance.

[2] Journey.          [3] Mental equipment.

BASS. How it was done let him report, the forfeit                             50
Of whose allegiance to our laws doth covet
Rigor of justice; but that done it is,
Mine eyes have been an evidence of credit
Too sure to be convinced.[1] Armostes, rent[2] not
Thine arteries with hearing the bare circumstances
Of these calamities. Thou 'st lost a nephew,
A niece, and I a wife. Continue man still;[3]
Make me the pattern of digesting[4] evils,
Who can outlive my mighty ones, not shrinking                             59
At such a pressure as would sink a soul
Into what 's most of death, the worst of horrors.
But I have sealed a covenant with sadness,
And entered into bonds without condition,
To stand these tempests calmly. Mark me, nobles,
I do not shed a tear, not for Penthea! Excellent misery!

CAL.                              We begin our reign
With a first act of justice: thy confession,
Unhappy Orgilus, dooms thee a sentence;
But yet thy father's or thy sister's presence
Shall be excused.—Give, Crotolon, a blessing                             70
To thy lost son; Euphranea, take a farewell;
And both be gone.

CROT. [To Orgilus.]                              Confirm thee, noble sorrow,
In worthy resolution!

EUPH.                              Could my tears speak, My griefs were slight.

ORG.        All goodness dwell amongst ye!
Enjoy my sister, Prophilus; my vengeance
Aimed never at thy prejudice.

CAL.                              Now withdraw.
*Exeunt Crotolon, Prophilus, et Euphranea.*

[1] Confuted.        [3] Continue still to be a man.
[2] Rend.            [4] Stomaching, enduring.

Bloody relater of thy stains in blood,
For that thou hast reported him, whose fortunes
And life by thee are both at once snatched from him,
With honorable mention, make thy choice                             80
Of what death likes thee best; there's all our bounty.—
But, to excuse delays, let me, dear cousin,
Entreat you and these lords see execution
Instant before 'e part.

NEAR.                              Your will commands us.

ORG. One suit, just queen, my last: vouchsafe your clemency
That by no common hand I be divided
From this my humble frailty.

CAL.                              To their wisdoms
Who are to be spectators of thine end
I make the reference. Those that are dead
Are dead; had they not now died, of necessity                             90
They must have paid the debt they owed to nature
One time or other.—Use despatch, my lords;
We'll suddenly prepare our coronation.
*Exeunt Calantha, Philema, Christalla.*

ARM. 'Tis strange these tragedies should never touch on
Her female pity.

BASS.                              She has a masculine spirit;
And wherefore should I pule, and, like a girl,
Put finger in the eye? Let's be all toughness,
Without distinction betwixt sex and sex.

NEAR. Now, Orgilus, thy choice?

ORG.                              To bleed to death.

ARM. The executioner?

ORG.                              Myself, no surgeon;   100
I am well skilled in letting blood. Bind fast
This arm, that so the pipes may from their conduits
Convey a full stream; here's a skillful instrument.        [Shows his dagger.]
Only I am a beggar to some charity
To speed me in this execution
By lending th' other prick to th' tother arm,
When this is bubbling life out.

BASS.                    I am for 'e;
It most concerns my art, my care, my
    credit.—
Quick, fillet both his [1] arms.
ORG.                    Gramercy, friendship!
Such courtesies are real which flow
    cheerfully                    110
Without an expec[ta]tion of requital.
Reach me a staff in this hand.
                    [*They give him a staff.*]
                    If a proneness
Or custom in my nature from my
    cradle
Had been inclined to fierce and eager
    bloodshed,
A coward guilt, hid in a coward quaking,
Would have betrayed fame to ignoble
    flight
And vagabond pursuit of dreadful safety;
But look upon my steadiness, and scorn
    not
The sickness of my fortune, which,
    since Bassanes
Was husband to Penthea, had lain
    bedrid.                    120
We trifle time in words. Thus I show
    cunning
In opening of a vein too full, too lively.
                    [*Opens the vein.*]
ARM. Desperate courage!
ORG.                    Honorable infamy!
HEM. I tremble at the sight.
GRO.                    Would I were loose!
BASS. It sparkles like a lusty wine new
    broached;
The vessel must be sound from which it
    issues.
Grasp hard this other stick; I'll be as
    nimble—
But, prithee, look not pale. Have at
    'e! Stretch out
Thine arm with vigor and unshook
    virtue.        [*Opens the other vein.*]
Good! O, I envy not a rival, fitted    130
To conquer in extremities. This pastime
Appears majestical; some high-tuned
    poem
Hereafter shall deliver to posterity
The writer's glory and his subject's
    triumph.
How is 't, man? Droop not yet.
ORG.                    I feel no palsies.

On a pair-royal [2] do I wait in death:
My sovereign, as his liegeman; on my
    mistress,
As a devoted servant; and on Ithocles,
As if no brave, yet no unworthy enemy.
Nor did I use an engine to entrap    140
His life out of a slavish fear to combat
Youth, strength, or cunning, [3] but for
    that I durst not
Engage [4] the goodness of a cause on for-
    tune,
By which his name might have outfaced
    my vengeance.
O Tecnicus, inspired with Phœbus' fire!
I call to mind thy augury; 'twas per-
    fect:
"*Revenge proves its own executioner.*"
When feeble man is bending to his
    mother,
The dust a was first framed on, thus he
    totters.
BASS. Life's fountain is dried up.
ORG.            So falls the standards    150
Of my prerogative in being a creature!
A mist hangs o'er mine eyes; the sun's
    bright splendor
Is clouded in an everlasting shadow.
Welcome, thou ice, that sitt'st about my
    heart;
No heat can ever thaw thee.    *Dies.*
NEAR.            Speech hath left him.
BASS. A has shook hands with time; his
    funeral urn
Shall be my charge. Remove the blood-
    less body.
The coronation must require attendance;
That past, my few days can be but one
    mourning.            *Exeunt.*

[SCENE iii.

*A temple.*]

*An altar covered with white; two lights of
virgin wax, during which music of
recorders. Enter Four bearing Ithocles
on a hearse, or in a chair, in a rich
robe, and a crown on his head; place
him on one side of the altar. After
him enter Calantha in a white robe
and crowned; Euphranea, Philema,
Christalla, in white; Nearchus, Armostes
Crotolon, Prophilus, Amelus, Bassanes*

---

[1] Emended by Gifford-Dyce; original reads
*tnis.*

[2] In cards, three of the same denomination.
[3] Skill.                    [4] Stake.

*Hemophil, and Groneas.  Calantha
goes and kneels before the altar;  the
Rest stand off, the women kneeling behind.  Cease recorders during her devotions.  Soft music.  Calantha and the
Rest rise, doing obeisance to the altar.*

CAL. Our orisons are heard; the gods are
    merciful.—
  Now tell me, you whose loyalties pays
    tribute
  To us your lawful sovereign, how un-
    skillful
  Your duties or obedience is to render
  Subjection to the scepter of a virgin,
  Who have been ever fortunate in princes
  Of masculine and stirring composi-
    tion.
  A woman has enough to govern wisely
  Her own demeanors, passions, and di-
    visions.[1]
  A nation warlike and inured to prac-
    tice                                        10
  Of policy and labor cannot brook
  A feminate authority; we therefore
  Command your counsel how you may
    advise us
  In choosing of a husband whose abili-
    ties
  Can better guide this kingdom.
NEAR.                              Royal lady,
  Your law is in your will.
ARM.                    We have seen tokens
  Of constancy too lately to mistrust it.
CROT. Yet, if your highness settle on a
    choice
  By your own judgment both allowed and
    liked of,
  Sparta may grow in power, and pro-
    ceed                                        20
  To an increasing height.
CAL.                    Hold you the same
    mind?
BASS. Alas, great mistress, reason is so
    clouded
  With the thick darkness of my infinite
    woes
  That I forecast nor dangers, hopes, or
    safety.
  Give me some corner of the world to wear
    out
  The remnant of the minutes I must
    number,

[1] Uncertainties.

  Where I may hear no sounds but sad
    complaints
  Of virgins who have lost contracted
    partners;
  Of husbands howling that their wives
    were ravished
  By some untimely fate; of friends
    divided                                     30
  By churlish opposition; or of fathers
  Weeping upon their children's slaugh-
    tered carcasses;
  Or daughters groaning o'er their fathers'
    hearses;
  And I can dwell there, and with these
    keep consort [2]
  As musical as theirs.  What can you
    look for
  From an old, foolish, peevish, doting man
  But craziness of age?
CAL. Cousin of Argos!
NEAR.                    Madam?
CAL.                              Were I presently
  To choose you for my lord, I'll open
    freely
  What articles I would propose to treat
    on                                          40
  Before our marriage.
NEAR.                    Name them, virtuous lady.
CAL. I would presume you would retain
    the royalty
  Of Sparta in her own bounds; then in
    Argos
  Armostes might be viceroy; in Messene
  Might Crotolon bear sway; and Bas-
    sanes—
BASS. I, queen? Alas, what I?
CAL.                    Be Sparta's mar-
    shal.
  The multitudes of high employments
    could not
  But set a peace to private griefs. These
    gentlemen,
  Groneas and Hemophil, with worthy
    pensions,
  Should wait upon your person in your
    chamber.                                     50
  I would bestow Christalla on Amelus;
  She'll prove a constant wife.  And
    Philema
  Should into Vesta's temple.
BASS.                    This is a testament!
  It sounds not like conditions on a
    marriage.

[2] Harmony.

NEAR. All this should be performed.

CAL. Lastly, for Prophilus,
He should be, cousin, solemnly invested
In all those honors, titles, and prefer-
ments
Which his dear friend and my neglected
husband
Too short a time enjoyed.

PRO. I am unworthy
To live in your remembrance.

EUPH. Excellent lady! 60

NEAR. Madam, what means that word,
"neglected husband"?

CAL. Forgive me.—Now I turn to thee,
thou shadow
Of my contracted lord! Bear witness
all,
I put my mother's [1] wedding ring upon
His finger; 'twas my father's last be-
quest.

[Places a ring on the finger of Ithocles.]
Thus I new-marry him whose wife I
am;
Death shall not separate us. O my
lords,
I but deceived your eyes with antic
gesture,[2]
When one news straight came huddling
on another
Of death, and death, and death! Still
I danced forward; 70
But it strook home, and here, and in an
instant.
Be[3] such mere women, who with shrieks
and outcries
Can vow a present end to all their sor-
rows,
Yet live to vow new pleasures, and out-
live them.
They are the silent griefs which cut the
heartstrings;
Let me die smiling.

NEAR. 'Tis a truth too ominous.

CAL. One kiss on these cold lips, my last!—
[Kisses Ithocles.] Crack, crack!—
Argos now's Sparta's king.—Command
the voices
Which wait at th' altar now to sing the
song
I fitted for my end.

NEAR. Sirs, the song! 80

---

[1] Original reads *mother*, perhaps a survival of
an old genitive.
[2] Actor's demeanor. [3] *I.e.*, there be.

---

A SONG

ALL. Glories, pleasures, pomps, delights,
and ease
Can but please
[Th']⁴ outward senses when the mind
Is⁵ untroubled or by peace refined.

1 [VOICE.] Crowns may flourish and decay;
Beauties shine, but fade away.

2 [VOICE.] Youth may revel, yet it must
Lie down in a bed of dust.

3 [VOICE.] Earthly honors flow and waste;
Time alone doth change and
last. 90

ALL. Sorrows mingled with contents pre-
pare
Rest for care;
Love only reigns in death, though art
Can find no comfort for a broken
heart.

[Calantha dies.]

ARM. Look to the queen!

BASS. Her heart is broke, indeed.
O, royal maid, would thou hadst missed
this part;
Yet 'twas a brave one. I must weep
to see
Her smile in death.

ARM. Wise Tecnicus! Thus said he:
"When youth is ripe, and age from time
doth part,
The lifeless trunk shall wed the broken
heart." 100
'Tis here fulfilled.

NEAR. I am your king.

OMNES. Long live
Nearchus, King of Sparta!

NEAR. Her last will
Shall never be digressed from; wait in
order
Upon these faithful lovers, as becomes
us.—
The counsels of the gods are never known
Till men can call th' effects of them
their own. [Exeunt.]

FINIS.

THE EPILOGUE

WHERE noble judgments and clear eyes
are fixed
To grace endeavor, there sits Truth,
not mixed

---

⁴ A space here indicates that something has
dropped out.
⁵ Original reads *Is not*.

With ignorance; those censures [1] may
  command
Belief which talk not till they under-
  stand.
Let some say, "This was flat;" some,
  "Here the scene
Fell from its height;" another, that
  the mean [2]
Was "ill observed" in such a growing
  passion
As it transcended either state or fash-
  ion.

[1] Opinions.    [2] Means, method.

Some few may cry, "'Twas pretty well,"
  or so,
"But—" and there shrug in silence;
  yet we know      10
Our writer's aim was in the whole
  addressed
Well to deserve of *all*, but please the
  *best*,
Which granted, by th' allowance of this
  strain,
The *Broken Heart* may be pieced up
  again.

FINIS.

# JOHN FORD

## PERKIN WARBECK

In 1932 T. S. Eliot somewhat startled the critics with one of his iconoclastic judgments on the earlier masterpieces of English literature by announcing in an anonymous leading article in the *Times Literary Supplement* that *Perkin Warbeck* was "unquestionably Ford's highest achievement" and "one of the very best historical plays outside of Shakespeare in the whole Elizabethan and Jacobean drama," ranking above both *'Tis Pity* and *The Broken Heart*. Although some readers with realistic or semi-realistic tastes will undoubtedly agree with Eliot, Ribner's estimate in his study of the English historical play is perhaps more representative of general opinion when he judges it only on its rank among other members of its particular type: "What is significant about *Perkin Warbeck* is that in it we find a major dramatist attempting to revive a dead dramatic genre, going to the finest extant species of that genre for his models, and, with the examples of Marlowe and Shakespeare before him, creating a history play which may rank with the finest of the earlier age." A distinctly minor view, however, was placed on record by Clifford Bax, generally an admirer of Ford, who wrote a letter to the *Times Literary Supplement* in reply to its anonymous feature article ("Patmore and Ford," May 12, 1932) which called *Perkin Warbeck* the dullest of all Ford's plays. This verdict was somewhat precariously backed up by Bax, who said that in his copy of the 1811 edition of Ford's works, once owned by the Victorian poet and critic Coventry Patmore, there were fewer appreciative marginal comments than for any other of Ford's plays.

Anderson, in his edition of the play for the Regents Renaissance Drama series (University of Nebraska Press, 1965), has brought together the ascertainable facts about its history. It was entered in the Stationers' Register on February 24, 1634, for the publisher Hugh Beeston, "under the hands of Sir Henry Herbert and Master Aspley, warden (observing the caution of the license) a tragedy called *Perkin Warbeck* by John Fford." The play was printed in the same year. The title page, however, described it as a "chronicle history," not a "tragedy," and added the statement that it had been "Acted (Sometimes) by the Queen's Majesty's Servants at the Phoenix in Drury Lane." The word "Sometimes," combined with the phrase "observing the caution of the license," made Bentley conjecture that there might have been some unknown relationship between the wording of the two statements, possibly involving a suppression of performance because of the political overtones of the play. This was the only printing of *Perkin Warbeck* in the seventeenth century, but in 1714 a duodecimo edition was issued, containing a thirteen-page preface on the history of the Warbeck affair. In the Bodleian Library at Oxford there is a copy of the play, based on the 1634 quarto, with numerous alterations and with initials before the names of the dramatis personae, apparently indicating the actors who were to take the roles. According to Davril the hand is late seventeenth century, and he therefore suggested that this version was prepared "vers l'epoque de l'affaire Monmouth." Bentley placed the hand as late seventeenth century or early eighteenth century, but wondered whether this version had anything to do with the first and only recorded acting revival of the play at the Goodman's Fields theater in 1745. Anderson has tried to prove that this abridged and revised version was actually prepared for this production ("The Date and Handwriting of a Manuscript Copy of Ford's *Perkin Warbeck*," NQ, 1963).

The play then dropped from public attention till Henry Weber reprinted it in his edition of the dramatic works in 1811, followed by Gifford's edition of the *Works* in 1827; Hartley Coleridge's inclusion of it in *The Dramatic Works of Massinger and Ford* in 1840; Dyce's additions to Gifford in 1869; Havelock Ellis's Mermaid edition of the play in 1888; and Mildred C. Struble's *A Critical Edition of Ford's Perkin Warbeck* (Seattle, 1926). One comparatively modern author paid Ford the compliment of imitation. In 1892 John Aizlewood published *Warbeck/A Historical Play in Two Parts Partly Founded on the Perkin Warbeck of Ford.* Leech, however, in commenting on this piece, decided that its length alone, with a dramatic prologue and two five-act parts, would make performance "almost unthinkable." In this view all potential producers have agreed. Bentley has speculated on the possibility that the play may have been acted some years before its publication, and has taken 1622 as the earliest limiting date, because of the publication of one of Ford's principal sources in that year. Harbage, in the process of giving his evidence for the possibility that the new characteristics in the writing and materials of the play may be accounted for by the assumption that Ford had an unrecognized collaborator in the person of Thomas Dekker, suggests 1625 as a reasonable date, just after the time of the known collaboration between the two men ("The Mystery of *Perkin Warbeck*," *Studies in English Renaissance Drama, in Honor of Karl J. Holzknecht*, New York University Press, 1959).

The main source of the subject matter of the play would obviously be the chronicles of English history. Sargeaunt declared her belief that the germ of the whole situation and of Ford's interpretation of Warbeck's character could be found concentrated in a single sentence from Francis Bacon's *A History of the Reign of King Henry the Seventh* (1622): ". . . it was generally believed (as well amongst great persons as amongst the vulgar) that he was indeed Duke Richard. Nay, himself, with long and continual counterfeiting, and with oft telling a lie, was turned by habit almost into the thing he seemed to be, and from a liar to a believer." Earlier writers like LeGay Brereton ("The Sources of *Perkin Warbeck*," *Anglia*, 1911) thought that Ford had also drawn from the chronicles of Edward Hall and Raphael Holinshed, but in 1926 Mildred Struble showed that he had actually pilfered from Thomas Gainsford's *The True and Wonderful History of Perkin Warbeck* (1618), which had itself used both Hall and Holinshed. Her discovery was first announced in "The Indebtedness of Ford to Gainsford" (*Anglia*, 1924), and was reproduced in her edition of the play in 1926. Koeppel, in his source studies of Chapman, Massinger, and Ford, had already referred to Gainsford, but without working out the details of the relationship. Many passages in the play are simply versifications of Gainsford and other works. Ford's reference in his dedication to a "late . . . and an honorable pen" is very likely an allusion to Bacon. Anderson concluded that Ford borrowed from him and Gainsford almost equally, with Bacon's contribution found mostly in Acts II and V and Gainsford's mostly in III and IV, with an almost equal contribution from both in Act I. Only six of the eighteen scenes show no use of any of the sources. Ribner thought that Ford might also have consulted the chronicles of John Stow and John Speed, but if so their influence was negligible. In 1955 John O'Connor further suggested that Ford had gone to Book VII of William Warner's long and serialized historical poem in "fourteeners," *Albion's England* (1586 ff.), for his unique characterization of the beautiful, loyal, and dutiful Lady Katherine Gordon and his creation of Lord Daliell—important elements in the play for which Ford himself had previously been given credit ("William Warner and Ford's *Perkin Warbeck*," *NQ*, 1955). The bluff and honest father, the Earl of Huntley, would seem to be mostly Ford's own creation. O'Connor also found a passage in Gainsford's *A History of the Earl of Tyrone* (1619) which suggested that Gainsford had seen a play, now lost, on the subject of Warbeck and that Ford may have known this play and been influenced by it ("A Lost Play of Perkin Warbeck," *MLN*, 1955). Although Ribner and others have found Ford's play to be full of echoes of Shakespeare's powerful historical plays, Sargeaunt has discounted these borrowings, and has instead offered the suggestion that "Ford's greatest debt to Shakespeare may be in his appreciation of the fact that a person whose mental powers have been deranged by a great sorrow and severe emotional strain can excite intense dramatic sympathy."

In using these sources, Ford has shown great skill in constructing a tightly knit plot through omission, addition, and alteration. He has followed Bacon more closely than Gainsford in portraying the character of Henry VII, but, as Anderson points out, has treated him even more favorably than Bacon by "often changing the sequence of historical events to enhance Henry's foresight." Ford's chief case of addition occurred in the last act, where he felt it dramatically necessary to bring Henry and Warbeck face to face, in spite of the fact that Bacon stated clearly that, although Warbeck was brought to the English court, and Henry "(to satisfy his curiosity) saw him sometimes out of a window or in a passage," the two never confronted one another. Ford also added the final dialogue between Warbeck and Simnel, the submissive and repentant pretender, to bring the tragic situation and its meaning to a focus. Moreover, he carefully suppressed the escape of Warbeck from the Tower with the true Earl of Warwick in 1499, their apprehension, and the hanging of the earl. Unlike the play, on this occasion Warbeck was put in the stocks, and was made to repeat his previous public confession that he was an impostor and had to review his whole life from his birth in Flanders, his nomadic adventures throughout Europe and Ireland, to his exploitation by Margaret, sister of Edward IV, in her support of the Yorkist cause. Similarly, although in the play Katherine swears that she will never remarry and is given pensions and land grants by Henry, she actually married three more times before her death in 1537. Sargeaunt has remarked, however, that this play is exceptional among Ford's works in that it is the only one in which he has made the love interest secondary.

But the most significant departure from the picture in the chronicles has been discussed by Lawrence Babb in his article, "Abnormal Psychology in John Ford's *Perkin Warbeck*" (*MLN*, 1936), which depicts Warbeck as a Burtonian "melancholic with delusions of grandeur" who has come to believe in his own pretensions to greatness, whereas the chronicles had usually drawn him as "an impudent impostor who is under no illusions regarding his own base origin." Since Ford very wisely never appeals to the audience for the sympathy merely given to the sick and always makes Warbeck talk with absolute self-assurance, not like a man deranged, Davril has refused to accept Babb's diagnosis of Perkin as an afflicted man. Stavig, on the other hand, has noted that the only scene in which Ford raises the question of Warbeck's sanity is that in which he confronts the king, and has thus prolonged the suspense. Since the author never actually suggests that Warbeck's claim may be valid, the only question is whether he is hypocritical or demented, with the final scenes leaving no doubt that the latter alternative is correct. Sympathy for him is also maintained by the loving loyalty of his wife.

Despite these changes in characterization and motivation that Ford found it desirable to make for dramatic reasons, he clearly and positively ranged himself on the side of Ben Jonson in his theory of treating history truthfully and not simply as a stimulus to the imagination of the writer of fiction. He made his commitment clear in the lines from his prologue in which he asserted without equivocation:

> He shows a history couched in a play—
> A history of noble mention, known
> Famous and true; most noble 'cause our own . . . .

Thus Ford not only made his appeal to English patriotism, but he also declared that he felt his presentation of a well-known episode in English history was a true and not a fabricated one. "Truth and state," he said, were his objectives, by "state" apparently meaning "stateliness" or "dignity," since he had just said that he had rejected "Unnecessary mirth forced, to endear a multitude." He regarded himself as a historian as well as a poet and playwright. Oliver, however, felt that Ford "is not really concerned at all with the fortunes of England, with its traditions, its politics, and its countryside; of these he treats solely because of their effects on the somewhat fantastic character, as he conceived it, that chance has called on to play a leading part for a short time in the historical scene."

Most critics, however, have adopted Struble's theory that Ford, because of his interest in political thought, intended to contrast the Tudor doctrine of responsible and limited sovereignty with the Stuart position of divine right and infallibility. Oliver even hazarded the untenable guess that Ford's "main interest in the play could have been as a problem of technique." Ribner, however, saw as one of Ford's main purposes "to offer a political point of view which the excesses of King Charles I were causing many thinking men to embrace," and to read the play partly as "a plea against the doctrine of the divine right of kings which Charles I was so flagrantly abusing . . . and an argument that responsibility both to God and to subjects must be a cardinal element of kingship." Like Struble, Ribner felt that Henry's statement of his position was essentially an affirmation of the principle of the social contract. He also pointed out that since both English Henry VII and Scotch James IV were ancestors of Charles I, the play contained an implicit plea that Charles follow the example of his Tudor rather than his Stuart forebear in always seeking the advice of his council instead of acting unilaterally in following his own will, as James did in at first embracing the cause of the pretender, Warbeck. On the other hand, Anderson, in "Kingship in Ford's *Perkin Warbeck*" (*ELH*, 1960), decided that on the whole, but not invariably, the play should not be interpreted as reflecting contemporary events or as criticizing the government of Charles. Nor should it be read as an attack on the doctrine of the divine right of kings, since on several occasions Henry himself supports it; nevertheless, it does stress the *de facto* basis of sovereignty practised by Henry, as opposed to the *de jure* basis as offered by Warbeck and temporarily accepted by James. In other words, Henry holds his position by his skill and cleverness in maintaining his military power, somewhat in the school of Bacon and Machiavelli, whereas both Warbeck and James reveal their weakness and inadequacy as leaders. Warbeck's motley crew of supporters—"the abject scum of mankind," as Frion himself calls them—is in itself a proof of his inability to judge other human beings and obtain the support of anyone who is both intelligent and disinterested. Political skill rather than a claim to hereditary right wins the day. In his prose pamphlet, *The Line of Life*, in 1620, Ford had already described the able ruler as a statesman and a promoter of international peace, and had used James I of England as an example. Still, as Oliver points out, there is no real villain in the play, except perhaps Frion or Stanley, the turncoat, who are only minor villains. Although, as Anderson sees it, Warbeck is the play's dramatic protagonist, Henry is its political protagonist, and the whole play is, by implication, a study in the requirements and ideals of kingship. Ribner, in *Jacobean Tragedy*, takes the same attitude and states that Henry has been set up as a model ruler in contrast to the imperfections of James and Warbeck.

Ribner also remarks on the paradoxical nature of the whole play—the most realistic of all Ford's plays in its setting and characters, yet one which raises the profound question of the true nature of reality. Since Warbeck, the central character, "goes to the gallows convinced of his own truth, the audience is left in a state of doubt and ambivalence." Since it "cannot really choose between the values of Perkin and King Henry," it "is unable finally to distinguish appearance from reality." (This was of course the same problem that Pirandello was to examine so thoroughly, notably in plays like *Henry IV*.) Thus "*Perkin Warbeck* more than anything else is a play about the impossibility of belief." It is "the tragedy of man's inability to find certainty, to understand reality, or to grasp his own position in the universe." Ultimately, Ribner finds, the play is "a perfect expression of the Caroline skepticism for which Ford stands." It is "the product of a search for moral order which can only resolve itself in paradox."

Ford, in spite of his admiration for the Elizabethans and his desire to imitate them, could never attain the kind of certainty which most, if not all, of his Elizabethan predecessors had attained.

Critics have generally praised Ford for his language and poetic style in *Perkin Warbeck*, and Leech goes so far as to assert: "As a model of style, if for no other reason, he has an enduring value." He was a poet not only in his conceptions but in his words, although these avoided the "older fashioned rhetoric" and the use of "the compressed or violent image" of his predecessors. With a quieter, more natural tone of speaking, in keeping with the tastes of the new audience, he still cultivated "a simple fluency and melody of language," with imagery drawn in particular from common life. However, he resisted the tendency of his age to break down the established structure of blank verse, and composed regular lines, with relatively few feminine endings or run-on constructions. Oliver, too, emphasized Ford's "quite exceptional" gift of clarity and simplicity, preserving this atmosphere without moving halfway toward prose, as Massinger and Shirley were doing, and maintaining this feeling "even—or particularly —in moments of greatest emotional stress." It is true, however, that sometimes an everyday, matter-of-fact effect springs from Ford's versification of passages from his prose sources. Oliver also commented on Ford's surprising avoidance of the soliloquy, not one of which is given to Warbeck in spite of the potential usefulness of this conventional device to a psychological dramatist. Ford preferred more dramatic methods than those of self-exposition. Stavig noted that the imagery throughout the play associated Warbeck with witchcraft and the devil and King Henry with heaven and the forces of good.

The present text is based on Henry de Vocht's reprint of the 1634 quarto, but reference has been made to the Gifford-Dyce edition of Ford's works, to the critical edition by Mildred C. Struble, and to the edition by Donald K. Anderson, Jr.

# THE CHRONICLE HISTORY OF PERKIN WARBECK[1]

## BY

### JOHN FORD

THE SCENE: *The continent of Great Britain.*

[THE TIME: *1499 and the years preceding.*]

## THE PERSONS PRESENTED

HENRY THE SEVENTH.
[LORD] DAWBNEY.[2]
SIR WILLIAM STANLEY.
[EARL OF] OXFORD.
[EARL OF] SURREY.
[FOX,] *Bishop of Durham.*
URSWICK, *chaplain to King Henry.*
SIR ROBERT CLIFFORD.
LAMBERT SIMNEL.
HIALAS,[3] *a Spanish agent.*
CONSTABLE, OFFICERS, [POST,][4] SERVING-MEN *and* SOLDIERS.

JAMES THE FOURTH, *King of Scotland.*
EARL OF HUNTLEY.

EARL OF CRAWFORD.
LORD DALIELL.
MARCHMOUNT, *a herald.*

PERKIN WARBECK.
[STEPHEN] FRION, *his secretary.*
[JOHN A WATER,] *Mayor of Cork.*
HERON, *a mercer.*
SKETON, *a tailor.*
ASTLEY, *a scrivener.*

### WOMEN

LADY KATHERINE GORDON, *wife to Perkin.*
COUNTESS OF CRAWFORD.
JANE DOUGLAS, *Lady Kath[erine's] maid*

## PROLOGUE

Studies have of this nature been of late
So out of fashion, so unfollowed, that
It is become more justice[6] to revive
The antic[7] follies of the times than strive
To countenance wise industry.   No want
Of art doth render wit or[8] lame or scant
Or slothful in the purchase of fresh bays,

But want of truth in them who give the
   praise
To their self-love, presuming to outdo
The writer, or—for need—the actors too. 10
But such this author's silence best befits,
Who bids them be in love with their own
   wits.
From him to clearer judgments we can
   say
He shows a history couched in a play—
A history of noble mention, known
Famous and true; most noble, cause[9] our
   own;
Not forged from Italy, from France, from
   Spain,
But chronicled at home; as rich in strain
Of brave attempts as ever fertile rage[10]
In action could beget to grace the stage. 20

---

[1] The title continues· "A Strange Truth. Acted (Sometimes) by the Queen's Majesty's Servants at the Phœnix in Drury Lane. *Fide Honor.*"   The Latin motto is an anagram of Ford's name used elsewhere instead of his signature.
[2] *I.e.*, Giles, Baron Daubeney.
[3] *I.e.*, Don Pedro Ayala.        [4] Messenger.
[5] Here follow the dedicatory epistle to William Cavendish, Earl of Newcastle, signed by John Ford, and five commendatory poems.
[6] Judiciousness, wisdom.        [8] Either.
[7] Either antique, ancient; or grotesque.
[9] Because.        [10] Poetic inspiration.

905

We cannot limit scenes, for the whole land
Itself appeared too narrow to withstand
Competitors for kingdoms; nor is here
Unnecessary mirth forced, to endear
A multitude. On these two rests the fate
Of worthy expectation—truth and state.

ACTUS PRIMUS. SCENA PRIMA.

[*The presence chamber at Westminster.*]

*Enter King Henry, Durham, Oxford, Sur-*
*rey, Sir William Stanley, Lord Cham-*
*berlain, Lord Dawbney; the King*
*supported to his throne by Stanley and*
*Durham. A Guard.*

KING. Still [1] to be haunted, still to be
    pursued,
Still to be frighted with false appari-
    tions
Of pageant majesty and new-coined
    greatness,
As if we were a mockery king in state,
Only ordained to lavish sweat and blood
In scorn and laughter to the ghosts of
    York, [2]
Is all below our merits; yet, my lords,
My friends and counselors, yet we sit
    fast
In our own royal birthright. The rent
    face
And bleeding wounds of England's
    slaughtered people        10
Have been by us as by the best physi-
    cian
At last both throughly cured and set in
    safety;
And yet for all this glorious work of
    peace
Ourself is scarce secure.
DUR.            The rage of malice
    Conjures fresh spirits with the spells of
    York.
For ninety years ten English kings and
    princes,
Threescore great dukes and earls, a
    thousand lords
And valiant knights, two hundred fifty
    thousand
Of English subjects have in civil wars
Been sacrificed to an uncivil thirst    20

Of discord and ambition.    This hot
    vengeance
Of the just powers above to utter ruin
And desolation had reigned on, but that
Mercy did gently sheathe the sword
    of justice
In lending to this blood-shrunk common-
    wealth
A new soul, new birth, in your sacred
    person.
DAW. Edward the Fourth, after a doubt-
    ful fortune,
Yielded to nature, leaving to his sons,
Edward and Richard, the inheritance
Of a most bloody purchase. [3]    These
    young princes,        30
Richard the tyrant, [4] their unnatural
    uncle,
Forced to a violent grave, so just is
    heaven.
Him hath your majesty by your own
    arm,
Divinely strengthened, pulled from his
    boar's sty [5]
And struck the black usurper to a car-
    cass.
Nor doth the house of York decay in
    honors,
Though Lancaster doth repossess his
    right,
For Edward's daughter is King Henry's
    queen,
A blesséd union, and a lasting blessing
For this poor panting island, if some
    shreds,        40
Some useless remnant of the house of
    York,
Grudge not at this content.
OX.            Margaret of Burgundy [6]
Blows fresh coals of division.
SUR.            Painted fires,
Without or heat to [7] scorch or light to
    cherish.
DAW. York's headless trunk, her father;
    Edward's fate,
Her brother king; the smothering of her
    nephews
By tyrant Gloucester, [8] brother to her
    nature;

---

[1] Always.
[2] *I.e.*, Simnel and Warbeck, pretenders to the throne, who were supported by the Yorkist faction, with its emblem, the White Rose.
[3] Acquisition.    [4] *I.e.*, Richard III.
[5] A reference to the arms of Richard III.
[6] Sister of Edward IV and widow of Charles the Bold.
[7] Emended by Gifford-Dyce. Original reads *to heat or.*    [8] *I.e.*, Richard III.

Nor Gloucester's own confusion (all decrees

Sacred in heaven) can move this woman-monster,

But that she still from the unbottomed mine                                    50

Of devilish policies doth vent the ore

Of troubles and sedition.

Ox.                                        In her age—

Great sir, observe the wonder—she grows fruitful,

Who in her strength of youth was always barren,

Nor are her births as other mothers' are,

At nine or ten months' end—she has been with child

Eight or seven years at least; whose twins [1] being born—

A prodigy in nature—even the youngest

Is fifteen years of age at his first entrance

As soon as known i' th' world, tall striplings, strong                          60

And able to give battle unto kings,

Idols of Yorkish malice.

Daw. [2]                              And but idols!

A steely hammer crushes 'em to pieces.

King. Lambert, the eldest, lords, is in our service,

Preferred by an officious care of duty

From the scullery to a falc'ner—strange example!—

Which shows the difference between noble natures

And the baseborn.  But for the upstart duke,

The new revived York, Edward's second son,

Murdered long since i' th' Tower, he lives again                                 70

And vows to be your king.

Stan.                          The throne is filled, sir.

King. True, Stanley; and the lawful heir sits on it.

A guard of angels and the holy prayers

Of loyal subjects are a sure defense

Against all force and counsel of intrusion.

But now, my lords, put case [3] some of our nobles,

Our great ones, should give countenance and courage

To trim Duke Perkin.  You will all confess

Our bounties have unthriftily been scattered

Amongst unthankful men.

Daw.                              Unthankful beasts,  80

Dogs, villains, traitors!

King.                          Dawbney, let the guilty

Keep silence; I accuse none, though I know

Foreign attempts against a state and kingdom

Are seldom without some great friends at home.

Stan. Sir, if no other abler reasons else

Of duty or allegiance could divert

A headstrong resolution, yet the dangers

So lately passed by men of blood and fortunes

In Lambert Simnel's party must command

More than a fear, a terror, to conspiracy.                                       90

The highborn Lincoln, son to De la Pole,

The Earl of Kildare, [the] [4] Lord Geraldine,

Francis, Lord Lovell, and the German baron

Bold Martin Swart, with Broughton and the rest—

Most spectacles of ruin, some of mercy—

Are presidents [5] sufficient to forewarn

The present times, or any that live in them,

What folly, nay, what madness, 'twere to lift

A finger up in all defense but yours,

Which can be but impostorous in a title.                                        100

King. Stanley, we know thou lov'st us, and thy heart

Is figured on thy tongue; nor think we less

Of any's here.—How closely we have hunted

This cub, since he unlodged, from hole to hole,

Your knowledge is our chronicle.  First Ireland,

The common stage of novelty, presented

---

[1] These youths were not actually her sons, but were impostors put forward by her as Edward's not-dead sons.

[2] Gifford-Dyce's emendation for *Ox.*

[3] Suppose.

[4] Supplied by Gifford-Dyce.   [5] Precedents.

This gewgaw to oppose us; there the Geraldines
And Butlers once again stood in support
Of this colossic statue.    Charles of France                                          109
Thence called him into his protection,
Dissembled him the lawful heir of England;
Yet this was all but French dissimulation,
Aiming at peace with us, which being granted
On honorable terms on our part, suddenly
This smoke of straw was packed from France again
T' infect some grosser air.  And now we learn—
Mauger[1] the malice of the bastard Nevill,
Sir Taylor, and a hundred English rebels—
They're all retired to Flanders, to the dam
That nursed this eager whelp, Margaret of Burgundy.                                     120
But we will hunt him there too; we will hunt him,
Hunt him to death, even in the beldam's closet,[2]
Though the archduke were his buckler.
Sur.  She has styled him "the fair white rose of England."
Daw.  Jolly gentleman, more fit to be a swabber
To the Flemish after a drunken surfeit.

*Enter Urswick.*

Ur.  Gracious sovereign, please you peruse this paper.        [*The King reads.*]
Dur.  The king's countenance gathers a sprightly blood.
Daw.  Good news, believe it.
King.                     Urswick, thine ear.
Th'ast lodged[3] him?
Ur.                     Strongly safe, sir.    130
King.  Enough.  Is Barley come too?
Ur.                     No, my lord.
King.  No matter—phew, he's but a running weed,
At pleasure to be plucked up by the roots!

But more of this anon.—I have bethought me.
My lords, for reasons which you shall partake,
It is our pleasure to remove our court
From Westminster to th' Tower.  We will lodge
This very night there; give, Lord Chamberlain,
A present order for it.
Stan.  [*Aside.*]    The Tower!—I shall, sir.
King.  Come, my true, best, fast friends.
These clouds will vanish;                    140
The sun will shine at full; the heavens are clearing.    *Exeunt.  Flourish.*

[Scena Secunda.

*A room in Huntley's house at Edinburgh.*]

*Enter Huntley and Daliell.*

Hunt.  You trifle time, sir.
Dal.                     O, my noble lord,
You conster[4] my griefs to so hard a sense
That where the text is argument[5] of pity,
Matter of earnest love, your gloss corrupts it
With too much ill-placed mirth.
Hunt.                     Much mirth, Lord Daliell?
Not so, I vow.  Observe me, sprightly gallant.
I know thou art a noble lad, a handsome,
Descended from an honorable ancestry,
Forward and active, dost resolve to wrestle
And ruffle in the world by noble actions                                    10
For a brave mention to posterity.
I scorn not thy affection to my daughter,
Not I, by good St. Andrew; but this bugbear,
This whoresome[6] tale of honor—honor, Daliell!—
So hourly chats and tattles in mine ear
The piece of royalty that is stitched up
In my Kate's blood[7] that 'tis as dangerous
For thee, young lord, to perch so near an eaglet
As foolish for my gravity to admit it.
I have spoke all at once.

DAL. Sir, with this truth 20
You mix such wormwood that you leave
no hope
For my disordered palate e'er to relish
A wholesome taste again. Alas, I know,
sir,
What an unequal distance lies between
Great Huntley's daughter's birth and
Daliell's fortunes.
She's the king's kinswoman, placed near
the crown,
A princess of the blood, and I a subject.
HUNT. Right; but a noble subject—put in
that too.
DAL. I could add more, and in the rightest
line 29
Derive my pedigree from Adam Mure,
A Scottish knight, whose daughter was
the mother
To him who first begot the race of
Jameses
That sway the scepter to this very day.
But kindreds are not ours when once the
date
Of many years have swallowed up the
memory
Of their originals; so pasture fields
Neighboring too near the ocean are
sooped [1] up
And known no more; for, stood I in my
first
And native [2] greatness, if my princely
mistress
Voutsafed [3] me not her servant,[4] 'twere
as good 40
I were reduced to clownery,[5] to nothing,
As to a throne of wonder.
HUNT. [*Aside.*] Now, by Saint Andrew,
A spark of mettle! [6] A [7] has a brave fire
in him.
I would a had my daughter, so I knew 't
not.
But must not be so, must not.—Well,
young lord,
This will not do yet. If the girl be head-
strong
And will not hearken to good counsel,
steal her
And run away with her; dance galliards,[8]
do,

And frisk about the world to learn the
languages.
'Twill be a thriving trade; you may set up
by 't. 50
DAL. With pardon, noble Gordon, this dis-
dain
Suits not your daughter's virtue or my
constancy.
HUNT. You are angry.—[*Aside.*] Would a
would beat me; I deserve it.—
Daliell, thy hand; w' are friends. Follow
thy courtship.
Take thine own time and speak; if thou
prevail'st
With passion more than I can with my
counsel,
She's thine. Nay, she is thine; 'tis a fair
match,
Free and allowed. I'll only use my
tongue,
Without a father's power; use thou thine.
Self do, self have. No more words; win
and wear her. 60
DAL. You bless me; I am now too poor
in thanks
To pay the debt I owe you.
HUNT. Nay, th' art poor [9]
Enough.—[*Aside.*] I love his spirit in-
finitely.—
Look ye, she comes. To her now, to her,
to her!

*Enter Katherine and Jane.*

KATH. The king commands your presence,
sir.
HUNT. The gallant—
This—this—this lord—this servant,
Kate, of yours—
Desires to be your master.
KATH. I acknowledge him
A worthy friend of mine.
DAL. Your humblest creature.
HUNT. [*Aside.*] So, so, the game's afoot!
I'm in cold hunting;
The hare and hounds are parties.[10]
DAL. Princely lady, 70
How most unworthy I am to employ
My services in honor of your virtues,
How hopeless my desires are to enjoy

---

[1] Supped.  [5] Base birth.
[2] Inherited.  [6] A high-spirited young man.
[3] Vouchsafed.  [7] He.
[4] Suitor.  [8] Lively dances.

[9] Here, as in many other passages throughout
the play, lines which have obviously been
wrongly divided by the printer have been silently
regularized.
[10] Confederates.

Your fair opinion, and much more your
   love,
Are only matter of despair, unless
Your goodness give large warrant to my
   boldness,
My feeble-winged ambition.
HUNT. [*Aside.*]        This is scurvy.[1]
KATH. My lord, I interrupt you not.
HUNT. [*Aside.*]         Indeed!
   Now, on my life, she'll court him.—Nay,
   nay, on, sir.
DAL. Oft have I tuned the lesson of my
   sorrows             80
To sweeten discord and enrich your pity;
But all in vain. Here had my comforts
   sunk,
And never risen again to tell a story
Of the despairing lover, had not now,
Even now, the earl your father—
HUNT. [*Aside.*]      A means me, sure.
DAL. After some fit disputes of your con-
   dition,
Your highness and my lowness, given a
   license
Which did not more embolden than en-
   courage
My faulting [2] tongue.
HUNT.       How, how? How's that?
   Embolden?
Encourage? I encourage ye? D'e [3] hear,
   sir?             90
A subtle trick, a quaint one! Will you
   hear, man?
What did I say to you? Come, come, to
   th' point.
KATE. It shall not need, my lord.
HUNT.        Then hear me, Kate.—
Keep you on that hand of her, I on
   this.—
Thou stand'st between a father and a
   suitor,
Both striving for an interest in thy heart.
He courts thee for affection, I for duty;
He as a servant pleads; but, by the
   privilege
Of nature though I might command, my
   care          99
Shall only counsel what it shall not force.
Thou canst but make one choice; the
   ties of marriage
Are tenures not at will, but during life.
Consider whose thou art, and who—a
   princess,

A princess of the royal blood of Scotland,
In the full spring of youth and fresh in
   beauty.
The king that sits upon the throne is
   young,
And yet unmarried, forward in attempts
On any least occasion to endanger
His person; wherefore, Kate, as I am
   confident
Thou dar'st not wrong thy birth and
   education        110
By yielding to a common servile rage
Of female wantonness, so I am confident
Thou wilt proportion all thy thoughts to
   side [4]
Thy equals, if not equal thy superiors.
My Lord of Daliell, young in years, is
   old
In honors, but nor eminent in titles
Or in estate that may support or add to
The expectation of thy fortunes. Settle
Thy will and reason by a strength of
   judgment,
For, in a word, I give thee freedom; take
   it.           120
If equal fates have not ordained to pitch
Thy hopes above my height, let not thy
   passion
Lead thee to shrink mine honor in ob-
   livion.
Thou art thine own; I have done.
DAL.        O, y' are all oracle,
The living stock and root of truth and
   wisdom!
KATH. My worthiest lord and father, the
   indulgence
Of your sweet composition [5] thus com-
   mands
The lowest of obedience. You have
   granted
A liberty so large that I want skill   129
To choose without direction of example,
From which I daily learn by how much
   more
You take off from the roughness of a
   father,
By so much more I am engaged to tender
The duty of a daughter. For respects
Of birth, degrees of title, and advance-
   ment,
I nor admire nor slight them; all my
   studies
Shall ever aim at this perfection only—

---

[1] Wretched.     [2] Failing.     [3] Do ye.     [4] Match.     [5] Nature.

To live and die so, that you may not blush
In any course of mine to own me yours.

HUNT. Kate, Kate, thou grow'st upon my heart like peace,                    140
Creating every other hour a jubilee.

KATE. To you, my Lord of Daliell, I address
Some few remaining words. The general fame,
That speaks your merit even in vulgar tongues,
Proclaims it clear; but in the best, a president.[1]

HUNT. Good wench, good girl, i' faith!

KATH.                    For my part, trust me,
I value mine own worth at higher rate
Cause you are pleased to prize it. If the stream
Of your protested service—as you term it—
Run in a constancy more than a compliment,                    150
It shall be my delight that worthy love
Leads you to worthy actions, and these guide ye
Richly to wed an honorable name.[2]
So every virtuous praise in after ages
Shall be your heir, and I in your brave mention
Be chronicled the mother of that issue,
That glorious issue.

HUNT. [Aside.] O, that I were young again!
She'd make me court proud danger, and suck spirit
From reputation.

KATH.                    To the present motion[3]
Here's all that I dare answer: when a ripeness                    160
Of more experience, and some use of time,
Resolves to treat the freedom of my youth
Upon exchange of troths, I shall desire
No surer credit of a match with virtue
Than such as lives in you. Meantime my hopes are
Preserved secure in having you a friend.

DAL. You are a blessed lady, and instruct
Ambition not to soar a farther flight
Than in the perfumed air of your soft voice.—

My noble Lord of Huntley, you have lent                    170
A full extent of bounty to this parley,
And for it shall command your humblest servant.

HUNT. Enough. We are still friends, and will continue
A hearty love.—O, Kate, thou art mine own!—
No more. My Lord of Crawford!

*Enter Crawford.*

CRAW.                    From the king
I come, my Lord of Huntley, who in council
Requires your present aid.

HUNT.                    Some weighty business!

CRAW. A secretary from a Duke of York,
The second son to the late English Edward,
Concealed I know not where these fourteen years,                    180
Craves audience from our master; and 'tis said
The duke himself is following to the court.

HUNT. Duke upon duke! 'Tis well, 'tis well; here's bustling
For majesty. My lord, I will along with ye.

CRAW. My service, noble lady!

KATH.                    Please ye walk, sir?

DAL. [Aside.] "Times have their changes; sorrow makes men wise;
The sun itself must set as well as rise."[4]
Then, why not I?—Fair madam, I wait on ye.                    *Exeunt omnes.*

[SCENA TERTIA.

*A room in the Tower of London.*]

*Enter Durham, Sir Robert Clifford, and Urswick. Lights.*

DUR. You find, Sir Robert Clifford, how securely
King Henry, our great master, doth commit
His person to your loyalty; you taste
His bounty and his mercy even in this,
That at a time of night so late, a place
So private as his closet, he is pleased

---

[1] Model, pattern.
[2] Reputation, career.                    [3] Proposal.
[4] Quotation marks were often used to call attention to sententious passages.

To admit you to his favor.  Do not falter
In your discovery; [1] but, as you covet
A liberal grace and pardon for your
follies,
So labor to deserve it by laying open  10
All plots, all persons that contrive against
it.
URS.  Remember not the witchcraft or the
magic,
The charms and incantations, which the
sorceress
Of Burgundy hath cast upon your rea-
son.
Sir Robert, be your own friend now; dis-
charge
Your conscience freely.  All of such as
love you
Stand sureties for your honesty and
truth.
Take heed you do not dally with the
king;
He is wise as he is gentle.
CLIF.                       I am miserable,
If Henry be not merciful.
URS.                    The king comes.  20

*Enter King Henry.*

KING.  Clifford!
CLIF.  [*Kneeling.*]        Let my weak knees
rot on the earth,
If I appear as leap'rous [2] in my treach-
eries
Before your royal eyes, as to mine own
I seem a monster by my breach of truth.
KING.  Clifford, stand up; for instance [3] of
thy safety,
I offer thee my hand.
CLIF.                      A sovereign balm
For my bruised soul, I kiss it with a
greediness.                    [*Rises.*]
Sir, you are a just master, but I—
KING.                            Tell me,
Is every circumstance thou hast set down
With thine own hand within this paper
true?                                    30
Is it a sure intelligence of all
The progress of our enemies' intents
Without corruption?
CLIF.                  True, as I wish heaven,
Or my infected honor white again.
KING.  We know all, Clifford, fully, since
this meteor,

This airy apparition, first discradled [4]
From Tournay into Portugal, and thence
Advanced his fiery blaze for adoration
To th' superstitious Irish; since the
beard                                    39
Of this wild comet, conjured into France,
Sparkled in antic flames in Charles his
court,
But shrunk again from thence, and, hid
in darkness,
Stole out of [5] Flanders, flourishing the
rags
Of painted power on the shore of Kent
Whence he was beaten back with shame
and scorn,
Contempt, and slaughter of some naked
outlaws.
But tell me what new course now shapes
Duke Perkin?
CLIF.  For Ireland, mighty Henry; so in-
structed
By Stephen Frion, sometimes [6] secretary
In the French tongue unto your sacred
excellence,                              50
But Perkin's tutor now.
KING.                       A subtle villain,
That Frion, Frion.  You, my Lord of Dur-
ham,
Knew well the man.
DUR.        French both in heart and actions.
KING.  Some Irish heads work in this mine
of treason;
Speak [7] 'em.
CLIF.        Not any of the best; your fortune
Hath dulled their spleens.  Never had
counterfeit
Such a confuséd rabble of lost bank-
routs [8]
For counselors: first Heron, a broken
mercer;
Then John a Water, sometimes Major [9] of
Cork;
Sketon, a tailor; and a scrivener      60
Called Astley.  And whate'er these list [10]
to treat of,
Perkin must hearken to; but Frion, cun-
ning
Above these dull capacities, still prompts
him

---

[4] Left its cradle, emerged.
[5] Suggested by Struble.  Original reads *into*.
[6] Sometime, formerly.
[7] Reveal.                          [9] **Mayor.**
[8] Bankrupts.                       [10] **Please.**

To fly to Scotland to young James the
   Fourth,
And sue for aid to him. This is the latest
Of all their resolutions.

KING.                          Still more Frion!
Pestilent adder, he will hiss out poison
As dang'rous as infectious.  We must
   match 'em.
Clifford, thou hast spoke home; we give
   thee life.
But, Clifford, there are people of our
   own                                                        70
Remain behind untold; who are they,
   Clifford?
Name those, and we are friends, and will
   to rest.
'Tis thy last task.

CLIF.                    O, sir, here I must break
A most unlawful oath to keep a just one.

KING. Well, well, be brief, be brief.

CLIF.                         The first in rank
Shall be John Ratcliffe, Lord Fitzwater,
   then
Sir Simon Mountford and Sir Thomas
   Thwaites,
With William Dawbney, Cressoner, Ast-
   wood,
Worsley the Dean of Paul's, two other
   friars,                                                     79
And Robert Ratcliffe.

KING.           Churchmen are turned devils.
These are the principal?

CLIFF.                     One more remains
Unnamed, whom I could willingly forget.

KING. Ha, Clifford! One more?

CLIF.             Great sir, do not hear him;
For, when Sir William Stanley, your lord
   chamberlain,
Shall come into the list, as he is chief,
I shall lose credit with ye; yet this lord
Last named is first against you.

KING.                        Urswick, the light!
View well my face, sirs; is there blood
   left in it?

DUR. You alter strangely, sir.

KING.                        Alter, Lord Bishop?
Why, Clifford stabbed me, or I dreamed
   a stabbed me.—                                             90
Sirrah, it is a custom with the guilty
To think they set their own stains off by
   laying
Aspersions on some nobler than them-
   selves.
Lies wait on treasons, as I find it here.

Thy life again is forfeit; I recall
My word of mercy, for I know thou
   dar'st
Repeat the name no more.

CLIF.                I dare, and once more,
Upon my knowledge, name Sir William
   Stanley
Both in his counsel and his purse the
   chief                                                       99
Assistant to the feign[é]d Duke of York.

DUR. Most strange!

URS.                        Most wicked!

KING.                     Yet again, once more.

CLIF. Sir William Stanley is your secret
   enemy,
And, if time fit, will openly profess it.

KING. Sir William Stanley!  Who?  Sir
   William Stanley?
My chamberlain, my counselor, the love,
The pleasure of my court, my bosom
   friend,
The charge and the controlment of my
   person,
The keys and secrets of my treasury,
The all of all I am!  I am unhappy.   109
Misery of confidence—let me turn traitor
To mine own person, yield my scepter up
To Edward's sister and her bastard duke!

DUR. You lose your constant temper.

KING.                     Sir William Stanley!
O, do not blame me; he, 'twas only he,
Who, having rescued me in Bosworth
   Field
From Richard's bloody sword, snatched
   from his head
The kingly crown, and placed it first on
   mine.
He never failed me.  What have I de-
   served
To lose this good man's heart, or he his
   own?

URS. The night doth waste.  This passion
   ill becomes ye;                                            120
Provide against your danger.

KING.                            Let it be so.
Urswick, command straight Stanley to
   his chamber;
'Tis well we are i' th' Tower; set a guard
   on him.
Clifford, to bed; you must lodge here to-
   night.
We'll talk with you tomorrow.  My sad
   soul
Divines strange troubles.

DAW. [*Within.*] Ho! The king, the king!
I must have entrance.
KING.    Dawbney's voice! Admit him.
What new combustions huddle next, to keep
Our eyes from rest?—The news?

*Enter Dawbney.*

DAW.    Ten thousand Cornish,
Grudging to pay your subsidies, have gathered    130
A head.[1] Led by a blacksmith and a lawyer,
They make for London, and to them is joined
Lord Audley. As they march, their number daily
Increases; they are—
KING.    Rascals!—Talk no more;
Such are not worthy of my thoughts to-night.
And, if I cannot sleep, I'll wake.—To bed.
When counsels fail, and there's in man no trust,
Even then an arm from heaven fights for the just.    *Exeunt.*

FINIS ACTUS PRIMI.

ACTUS SECUNDUS. SCENA PRIMA.

[*The presence chamber in the palace at Edinburgh.*]

*Enter above, Countess of Crawford, Katherine, Jane, with other Ladies.*

COUN. Come, ladies, here's a solemn preparation
For entertainment of this English prince;
The king intends grace more than ordinary.
'Twere pity now if a should prove a counterfeit.
KATH. Bless the young man, our nation would be laughed at
For honest [2] souls through Christendom. My father
Hath a weak stomach to the business, madam,
But that the king must not be crossed.
COUN.    A brings
A goodly troop, they say, of gallants with him,

But very modest people, for they strive not    10
To fame [3] their names too much; their godfathers
May be beholding [4] to them, but their fathers
Scarce owe them thanks. They are disguiséd princes,
Brought up, it seems, to honest trades. No matter,
They will break forth in season.
JANE.    Or break out; [5]
For most of 'em are broken, by report.—
The king!
KATH.    Let us observe 'em and be silent.
    *Flourish.*

*Enter [below] King James, Huntley, Crawford, and Daliell [, with other Noblemen].*

K. JA. The right of kings, my lords, extends not only
To the safe conservation of their own,
But also to the aid of such allies    20
As change of time and state hath oftentimes
Hurled down from careful crowns to undergo
An exercise of sufferance in both fortunes.
So English Richard, surnamed Cœur-de-Lion,
So Robert Bruce, our royal ancestor,
Forced by the trial of the wrongs they felt,
Both sought and found supplies from foreign kings
To repossess their own. Then grudge not,[6] lords,
A much distresséd prince. King Charles of France
And Maximilian of Bohemia both    30
Have ratified his credit by their letters.
Shall we then be distrustful? No, compassion
Is one rich jewel that shines in our crown,
And we will have it shine there.
HUNT.    Do your will, sir.
K. JA. The young duke is at hand. Daliell, from us
First greet him, and conduct him on; then Crawford

[1] Armed force.    [2] Trusting, simple.
[3] Boast.    [5] I.e., rebel.
[4] Beholden.    [6] Do not begrudge aid to.

Shall meet him next; and Huntley, last of all,
Present him to our arms. Sound sprightly music,
Whilst majesty encounters majesty.

*Hautboys.*

*Daliell goes out, brings in Perkin at the door, where Crawford entertains him, and from Crawford, Huntley salutes him and presents him to the King. They embrace; Perkin in state retires some few paces back, during which ceremony the noblemen slightly salute Frion, Heron, a mercer, Sketon, a tailor, Astley, a scrivener, with John a Water,[1] all Perkin's followers. Salutations ended, cease music.*

WAR. Most high, most mighty king! That now there stands     40
Before your eyes, in presence of your peers,
A subject of the rarest kind of pity
That hath in any age touched noble hearts,
The vulgar [2] story of a prince's ruin
Hath made it too apparent. Europe knows,
And all the western world, what persecution
Hath raged in malice against us, sole heir
To the great throne of old Plantagenets.
How from our nursery we have been hurried
Unto the sanctuary, from the sanctuary     50
Forced to the prison, from the prison haled
By cruel hands to the tormentor's fury
Is registered already in the volume
Of all men's tongues, whose true relation draws
Compassion, melted into weeping eyes
And bleeding souls. But our misfortunes since
Have ranged a larger progress through strange lands,
Protected in our innocence by heaven.
Edward the Fift, our brother, in his tragedy
Quenched their hot thirst of blood, whose hire to murther     60

Paid them their wages of despair and horror.
The softness of my childhood smiled upon
The roughness of their task, and robbed them farther
Of hearts to dare, or hands to execute.
Great king, they spared my life, the butchers spared it,
Returned the tyrant, my unnatural uncle,
A truth [3] of my despatch. I was conveyed
With secrecy and speed to Tournay, fostered
By obscure means, taught to unlearn myself.     69
But, as I grew in years, I grew in sense
Of fear and of disdain—fear of the tyrant
Whose power swayed the throne then, when disdain
Of living so unknown, in such a servile
And abject lowness, prompted me to thoughts
Of recollecting who I was. I shook off
My bondage, and made haste to let my aunt
Of Burgundy acknowledge me her kinsman,
Heir to the crown of England, snatched by Henry
From Richard's head—a thing scarce known i' th' world.
K. JA. My lord, it stands not with your counsel now     80
To fly upon invectives. If you can
Make this apparent what you have discoursed
In every circumstance, we will not study
An answer, but are ready in your cause.
WAR. You are a wise and just king, by the powers
Above reserved beyond all other aids
To plant me in mine own inheritance,
To marry these two kingdoms in a love
Never to be divorced while time is time.
As for the manner, first of my escape,     90
Of my conveyance next, of my life since,
The means and persons who were instruments,

---

[1] Original reads *Watring.*       [2] Common.       [3] Pledge.

Great sir, 'tis fit I overpass in silence,
Reserving the relation to the secrecy
Of your own princely ear, since it con-
    cerns
Some great ones living yet, and others
    dead,
Whose issue might be questioned. For
    your bounty,
Royal magnificence to him that seeks it,
We vow hereafter to demean ourself
As if we were your own and natural
    brother,                                       100
Omitting no occasion in our person
To express a gratitude beyond example.
K. Ja. He must be more than subject
    who can utter
The language of a king, and such is
    thine.
Take this for answer: be whate'er thou
    art,
Thou never shalt repent that thou hast
    put
Thy cause and person into my protection.
Cousin of York, thus once more we em-
    brace thee.
Welcome to James of Scotland! For thy
    safety,
Know such as love thee not shall never
    wrong thee.                                    110
Come, we will taste awhile our court de-
    lights,
Dream hence afflictions past, and then
    proceed
To high attempts of honor. On, lead on!
Both thou and thine are ours, and we will
    guard ye.
Lead on! *Exeunt. Manent* [1] *Ladies above.*
Coun.        I have not seen a gentleman
Of a more brave aspect or goodlier car-
    riage;
His fortunes move not him.—Madam,
    y' are passionate.[2]
Kath. Beshrew me,[3] but his words have
    touched me home,
As if his cause concerned me. I should
    pity him                                       119
If a should prove another than he seems.

### Enter Crawford.

Craw. Ladies, the king commands your
    presence instantly
For entertainment of the duke.

Kath.                          The duke
Must then be entertained, the king
    obeyed;
It is our duty.
Coun.                We will all wait on him.
                                        *Exeunt.*

### [Scena Secunda.

*A room in the Tower of London.*]

*Flourish.        Enter King Henry [and his
    Train]; Oxford, Durham, Surrey.*

King. Have ye condemned my chamber-
    lain?
Dur.          His treasons
Condemned him, sir, which were as
    clear and manifest
As foul and dangerous. Besides, the guilt
Of his conspiracy pressed him so nearly [4]
That it drew from him free confession
Without an importunity.
King.                    O, lord bishop,
This argued shame and sorrow for his
    folly,
And must not stand in evidence against
Our mercy and the softness of our na-
    ture.
The rigor and extremity of law         10
Is sometimes too-too bitter, but we
    carry
A chancery [5] of pity in our bosom.
I hope we may reprieve him from the sen-
    tence
Of death; I hope we may.
Dur.                You may, you may,
And so persuade your subjects that the
    title
Of York is better, nay, more just and
    lawful,
Than yours of Lancaster! So Stanley
    holds—
Which if it be not treason in the highest,
Then we are traitors all, perjured and
    false,
Who have took oath to Henry and the
    justice                                        20
Of Henry's title: Oxford, Surrey, Dawb-
    ney,
With all your other peers of state and
    church,

---

[1] Remain.                         [3] A mild oath.
[2] Compassionate, moved.
[4] Closely.
[5] A chancellorship, whose holder could lighten
sentences.

Forsworn, and Stanley true alone to
   heaven
And England's lawful heir!
Ox.                       By Vere's old honors,
   I'll cut his throat dares speak it.
Sur.                          'Tis a quarrel
   To engage a soul in.
King.                       What a coil [1] is here
   To keep my gratitude sincere and per-
      fect!
   Stanley was once my friend, and came
      in time
   To save my life; yet, to say truth, my
      lords,
   The man stayed long enough t' endan-
      ger it.                                    30
   But I could see no more into his heart
   Than what his outward actions did
      present,
   And for 'em have rewarded 'em so fully
   As that there wanted nothing in our
      gift
   To gratify his merit, as I thought,
   Unless I should divide my crown with
      him,
   And give him half—though now I well
      perceive
   'Twould scarce have served his turn
      without the whole.
   But I am charitable, lords; let justice
   Proceed in execution, whiles I mourn   40
   The loss of one whom I esteemed a
      friend.
Dur. Sir, he is coming this way.
King.                       If a speak to me,
   I could deny him nothing; to prevent it,
   I must withdraw. Pray, lords, commend
      my favors
   To his last peace, which I with him will
      pray for.
   That done, it doth concern us to consult
   Of other following troubles.
        *Exeunt [King Henry with his Train].*
Ox.                          I am glad
   He's gone. Upon my life, he would have
      pardoned
   The traitor, had a seen him.
Sur.                          'Tis a king
   Composed of gentleness.
Dur.                    Rare and unheard of!   50
   But every man is nearest to [2] himself;
   And that the king observes. 'Tis fit a
      should.
------
[1] Tumult.   [2] Closest to most concerned for.

*Enter Stanley, Executioner, Urswick, and*
                                      *Dawbney.*

Stan. May I not speak with Clifford ere
   I shake
   This piece of frailty off?
Daw.                    You shall; he's sent for.
Stan. I must not see the king?
Dur.                    From him, Sir William,
   These lords and I am sent; he bade us
      say
   That he commends his mercy to your
      thoughts,
   Wishing the laws of England could
      remit
   The forfeit of your life as willingly
   As he would in the sweetness of his
      nature                                    60
   Forget your trespass. But howe'er your
      body
   Fall into dust, he vows, the king him-
      self
   Doth vow to keep a requiem for your
      soul,
   As for a friend close treasured in his
      bosom.
Ox. Without remembrance of your errors
      past,
   I come to take my leave, and wish you
      heaven.
Sur. And I. Good angels guard ye!
Stan.                       O, the king,
   Next to my soul, shall be the nearest
      subject
   Of my last prayers. My grave Lord of
      Durham,
   My Lords of Oxford, Surrey, Dawbney,
      all,                                      70
   Accept from a poor dying man a fare-
      well.
   I was as you are, once—great, and stood
      hopeful
   Of many flourishing years; but fate and
      time
   Have wheeled about to turn me into
      nothing.

*Enter Clifford.*

Daw. Sir Robert Clifford comes—the
      man, Sir William,
   You so desire to speak with.
Dur.                    Mark their meeting.
Clif. Sir William Stanley, I am glad your
      conscience

Before your end hath emptied every
  burthen
Which charged it, as that [1] you can
  clearly witness
How far I have proceeded in a duty   80
That both concerned my truth and the
  state's safety.
STAN. Mercy, how dear is life to such as
  hug it!
Come hither; by this token think on me!
*Makes a cross on Clifford's face with his
                   finger.*
CLIF. This token? What? I am abused!
STAN.              You are not.
I wet upon your cheeks a holy sign,
The cross, the Christian's badge, the
  traitor's infamy.
Wear, Clifford, to thy grave this painted
  emblem;
Water shall never wash it off; all eyes
That gaze upon thy face shall read there
  written   89
A state-informer's character, more ugly
Stamped on a noble name than on a
  base.
The heavens forgive thee! Pray, my
  lords, no change [2]
Of words; this man and I have used too
  many.
CLIF. Shall I be disgraced
Without reply?
DUR.       Give losers leave to talk;
  His loss is irrecoverable.
STAN.             Once more,
To all a long farewell! The best of great-
  ness
Preserve the king! My next suit is, my
  lords,
To be remembered to my noble brother,
Derby, my much-grieved brother. O,
  persuade him   100
That I shall stand no blemish to his
  house
In chronicles writ in another age.
My heart doth bleed for him and for his
  sighs.
Tell him, he must not think the style [3]
  of Derby,
Nor being husband to King Henry's
  mother,
The league with peers, the smiles of for-
  tune, can
Secure his peace above the state of man.

[1] So that.    [2] Exchange.    [3] Title.

I take my leave, to travel to my dust.
"Subjects deserve their deaths whose
  kings are just."—
[*To Urswick.*] Come, confessor.—[*To
  Executioner.*] On with thy ax, friend,
  on!   110
*Exeunt [Urswick, Stanley, and Executioner].*
CLIF. Was I called hither by a traitor's
  breath
To be upbraided? Lords, the king shall
  know it.

*Enter King Henry with a white staff.* [4]

KING. The king doth know it, sir; the
  king hath heard
What he or you could say. We have
  given credit
To every point of Clifford's information,
The only evidence gainst Stanley's
  head.
A dies for 't; are you pleased?
CLIF.             I pleased, my lord!
KING. No echoes. For your service we
  dismiss
Your more attendance on the court.
  Take ease,
And live at home; but, as you love your
  life,   120
Stir not from London without leave
  from us.
We'll think on your reward. Away!
CLIF.         I go, sir.   *Exit Clifford.*
KING. Die all our griefs with Stanley!
  Take this staff
Of office, Dawbney; henceforth be our
  chamberlain.
DAW. I am your humblest servant.
KING.           We are followed
By enemies at home, that will not cease
To seek their own confusion. 'Tis most
  true
The Cornish under Audley are marched
  on
As far as Winchester. But let them
  come;
Our forces are in readiness; we'll catch
  'em   130
In their own toils.
DAW.       Your army, being mustered,
Consists in all, of horse and foot, at least
In number six-and-twenty thousand—
  men

[4] Emblematic of the Lord Chamberlain's office.

Daring and able, resolute to fight,
And loyal in their truths.
KING.                We know it, Dawbney.
For them we order thus:   Oxford in
    chief,
Assisted by bold Essex and the Earl
Of Suffolk, shall lead on the first bat-
    talia.[1] —
Be that your charge.
Ox.            I humbly thank your majesty.
KING. The next division we assign to
    Dawbney.                                    140
These must be men of action, for on
    those
The fortune of our fortunes must rely.
The last and main ourself commands in
    person,
As ready to restore the fight at all
    times
As to consummate an assuréd victory.
DAW.  The king is still oraculous.[2]
KING.                    But, Surrey,
We have employment of more toil for
    thee,
For our intelligence comes swiftly to
    us
That James of Scotland late hath enter-
    tained
Perkin the counterfeit with more than
    common                                        150
Grace and respect, nay, courts him with
    rare favors.
The Scot is young and forward; we must
    look for
A sudden storm to England from the
    north,
Which to withstand, Durham shall post
    to Norham
To fortify the castle and secure
The frontiers against an invasion
    there.
Surrey shall follow soon, with such an
    army
As may relieve the bishop and en-
    counter
On all occasions the death-daring
    Scots.
You know your charges all; 'tis now a
    time                                          160
To execute, not talk.  Heaven is our
    guard still.
War must breed peace; such is the fate
    of kings.                          *Exeunt.*

[1] Division.                    [2] Oracular, wise.

*A room in the palace at Edinburgh.*]

*Enter Crawford and Daliell.*

CRAW.  'Tis more than strange; my reason
    cannot answer
Such argument of fine imposture,
    couched
In witchcraft of persuasion, that it fash-
    ions
Impossibilities, as if appearance
Could cozen truth itself.  This dukeling
    mushroom
Hath doubtless charmed the king.
DAL.                    A courts the ladies
As if his strength of language chained
    attention
By power of prerogative.
CRAW.                It madded
My very soul to hear our master's mo-
    tion.                                          9
What surety both of amity and honor
Must of necessity ensue upon
A match betwixt some noble of our nation
And this brave prince, forsooth!
DAL.                    'Twill prove too fatal;
Wise Huntley fears the threat'ning.
    Bless the lady
From such a ruin.
CRAW.            How the council privy
Of this young Phaëton do screw their
    faces
Into a gravity their trades, good people,
Were never guilty of!  The meanest of
    'em
Dreams of at least an office in the state.
DAL. Sure, not the hangman's; 'tis be-
    spoke already                                20
For service to their rogueships.—Silence!

*Enter King James and Huntley.*

K. JA.                        Do not
Argue against our will; we have de-
    scended
Somewhat—as we may term it—too
    familiarly
From justice of our birthright to examine
The force of your allegiance—sir, we
    have—
But find it short of duty.
HUNT.                Break my heart,
Do, do, king! Have my services, my
    loyalty—

Heaven knows untainted ever—drawn upon me
Contempt now in mine age, when I but wanted [1]    29
A minute of a peace not to be troubled,
My last, my long one?  Let me be a dotard,
A bedlam,[2] a poor sot,[3] or what you please
To have me, so you will not stain your blood,
Your own blood, royal sir, though mixed with mine,
By marriage of this girl to a straggler!
Take, take my head, sir; whilst my tongue can wag,
It cannot name him other.

K. JA.                    Kings are counterfeits
In your repute, grave oracle, not presently [4]
Set on their thrones with scepters in their fists.
But use your own detraction; [5] 'tis our pleasure    40
To give our cousin York for wife our kinswoman,
The Lady Katherine.  Instinct of sovereignty
Designs the honor, though her peevish father
Usurps our resolution.[6]

HUNT.                    O, 'tis well,
Exceeding well.  I never was ambitious
Of using congees to my daughter-queen—
A queen?  Perhaps a quean![7]  Forgive me, Daliell,
Thou honorable gentleman.  None here
Dare speak one word of comfort?

DAL.                    Cruel misery!

CRAW. The lady, gracious prince, maybe hath settled    50
Affection on some former choice.

DAL.                    Enforcement
Would prove but tyranny.

HUNT.                    I thank 'e heartily.
Let any yeoman of our nation challenge
An interest in the girl, then the king
May add a jointure of ascent in titles,
Worthy a free consent; now a pulls down
What old desert hath builded.

[1] Lacked.
[2] Lunatic.
[3] Fool.
[4] I.e., if not actually.
[5] I.e., speak to your own injury.
[6] Power of decision.    [7] Strumpet.

K. JA.                    Cease persuasions.
I violate no pawns of faiths, intrude not
On private loves.  That I have played the orator
For kingly York to virtuous Kate, her grant    60
Can justify, referring her contents
To our provision.[8]  The Welsh Harry[9] henceforth
Shall therefore know, and tremble to acknowledge,
That not the painted idol of his policy
Shall fright the lawful owner from a kingdom.
We are resolved.

HUNT.                    Some of thy subjects' hearts,
King James, will bleed for this.

K. JA.                    Then shall their bloods
Be nobly spent.  No more disputes; he is not
Our friend who contradicts us.

HUNT.                    Farewell, daughter!
My care by one is lessened: thank the king for 't.[10]    70
I and my griefs will dance now.—Look, lords, look;
Here's hand in hand already!

K. JA.                    Peace, old frenzy!—

*Enter Warbeck, leading Katherine, complimenting; Countess of Crawford, Jane, Frion, Major of Cork, Astley, Heron, and Sketon.*

How like a king a looks!  Lords, but observe
The confidence of his aspect.    Dross cannot
Cleave to so pure a metal.    Royal youth!
Plantagenet undoubted!

HUNT. [*Aside.*]                    Ho, brave lady!
But no Plantagenet, by'r Lady, yet,
By red rose or by white.

WAR.                    An union this way
Settles possession in a monarchy
Established rightly, as is my inheritance.    80
Acknowledge me but sovereign of this kingdom,

[8] Oversight.
[9] Henry VII's grandfather was a Welshman.
[10] Original has *Enter* in the margin.

Your heart, fair princess, and the hand
  of providence
Shall crown you queen of me and my
  best fortunes.
KATH. Where my obedience is, my lord, a
  duty,
Love owes true service.
WAR.          Shall I—
K. JA.          Cousin, yes,
  Enjoy her; from my hand accept your
    bride;        [He joins their hands.]
And may they live at enmity with com-
  fort
Who grieve at such an equal pledge of
  troths!
Y' are the prince's wife now.
KATH.          By your gift, sir.
WAR. Thus I take seizure of mine own.
KATH.          I miss yet  90
A father's blessing. Let me find it.
[Kneels.] Humbly
Upon my knees I seek it.
HUNT.          I am Huntley,
  Old Alexander Gordon, a plain subject,
Nor more nor less; and, lady, if you
  wish for
A blessing, you must bend your knees to
  heaven,
For heaven did give me you. Alas, alas,
What would you have me say? May all
  the happiness
My prayers ever sued to fall upon
  you
Preserve you in your virtues!—Prithee,
  Daliell,
Come with me, for I feel thy griefs as
  full          100
As mine.    Let's steal away and cry
  together.
DAL. My hopes are in their ruins.
         Exeunt Huntley and Daliell.
K. JA.          Good, kind Huntley
Is overjoyed. A fit solemnity
Shall perfit [1] these delights.—Crawford,
  attend
Our order for the preparation.
Exeunt.   Manent Frion, Major, Astley,
         Heron, et Sketon.
FRI. Now, worthy gentlemen, have I not
  followed
My undertakings with success? Here's
  entrance
Into a certainty above a hope.

[1] Perfect.

HER. Hopes are but hopes; I was ever
confident, when I traded but in rem-  [110
nants, that my stars had reserved me to
the title of a viscount at least. Honor is
honor, though cut out of any stuffs.
SKE. My brother Heron hath right
wisely delivered his opinion; for he that
threads his needle with the sharp eyes of
industry shall in time go through-stitch [2]
with the new suit of preferment.
AST. Spoken to the purpose, my fine-
witted brother Sketon; for as no in-  [120
denture but has its counterpawn,[3] no
noverint[4] but his[5] condition or defeasance;[6]
so no right but may have claim, no claim
but may have possession, any act of parliament to the contrary notwithstanding.
FRI. You are all read in mysteries of state,
  And quick of apprehension, deep in judg-
    ment,
Active in resolution; and 'tis pity
Such counsel should lie buried in obscurity.
But why, in such a time and cause of
  triumph,          130
Stands the judicious Major of Cork so
  silent?
Believe it, sir, as English Richard pros-
  pers,
You must not miss employment of high
  nature.
MAJ. If men may be credited in their
mortality, which I dare not peremptorily
aver but they may or not be, presumptions
by this marriage are then, in sooth, of
fruitful expectation. Or else I must not
justify other men's belief more than other
should rely on mine.          140
FRI. Pith of experience! Those that have
  borne office
Weigh every word before it can drop
  from them.
But, noble counselors, since now the
  present
Requires in point of honor—pray, mistake not—
Some service to our lord, 'tis fit the Scots
Should not engross all glory to themselves
At this so grand and eminent solemnity.

[2] Finish thoroughly.
[3] Indentures were torn in two, each person
keeping half.       [5] Its.
[4] Writ, deed, bond.   [6] Nullifying provisions.

SKE. The Scots? The motion is defied. I had rather, for my part, without trial of my country, suffer persecution under [150 the pressing iron of reproach, or let my skin be punched [1] full of oilet-holes [2] with the bodkin of derision.

AST. I will sooner lose both my ears on the pillory of forgery.

HER. Let me first live a bankrout, and die in the lousy Hole [3] of hunger, without compounding for sixpence in the pound.

MAJ. If men fail not in their expectations, there may be spirits also that [160 disgest [4] no rude affronts, Master Secretary Frion, or I am cozened—which is possible, I grant.

FRI. Resolved like men of knowledge! At this feast then,
In honor of the bride, the Scots, I know,
Will in some show, some masque, or some device
Prefer their duties. Now it were uncomely
That we be found less forward for our prince
Than they are for their lady; and by how much 169
We outshine them in persons of account,
By so much more will our endeavors meet with
A livelier applause. Great emperors
Have for their recreations undertook
Such kind of pastimes; as for the conceit, [5]
Refer it to my study. The performance
You all shall share a thanks in. 'Twill be grateful.

HER. The motion is allowed. I have stole to a dancing school when I was a prentice.

AST. There have been Irish hub- [180 bubs, [6] when I have made one too.

SKE. For fashioning of shapes and cutting a cross caper, [7] turn me off to my trade again.

MAJ. Surely there is, if I be not deceived, a kind of gravity in merriment, as there is, or perhaps ought to be, respect of persons in the quality of carriage, which is, as it is construed, either so or so.
[Demonstrates.]

FRI. Still you come home to me; upon occasion 190
I find you relish courtship [8] with discretion,
And such are fit for statesmen of your merits.
Pray 'e wait [9] the prince, and in his ear acquaint him
With this design. I'll follow and direct 'e.        Exeunt; mane[t] Frion.
O, the toil
Of humoring this abject scum of mankind,
Muddy-brained peasants! Princes feel a misery
Beyond impartial sufferance, whose extremes
Must yield to such abettors. Yet [10] our tide
Runs smoothly without adverse winds.
Run on! 200
Flow to a full sea! Time alone debates[11]
Quarrels forewritten in the book of fates.
Exit.

ACTUS TERTIUS. SCENA PRIMA.

[The presence chamber at Westminster.]

Enter King Henry, his gorget[12] on, his sword, plume of feathers, leading staff;[13] and Urswick.

KING. How runs the time of day?
URS.                    Past ten, my lord.
KING. A bloody hour will it prove to some,
Whose disobedience, like the sons o' th' Earth,[14]
Throw a defiance gainst the face of heaven.
Oxford, with Essex and stout De la Pole,
Have quieted the Londoners, I hope,
And set them safe from fear.
URS.                    They are all silent.
KING. From their own battlements they may behold
Saint George's Fields o'erspread with armed men,

---

[1] Suggested by Gifford-Dyce. Original reads *pincht*.        [2] Eyelet-holes.
[3] One of the worst cells in the Counter Prison.
[4] Digest.        [6] Celebrations.
[5] Idea.        [7] A movement in dancing.

[8] Court behavior.    [9] Await.    [10] Thus far.
[11] Argues out.
[12] A piece of armor for the throat.
[13] A baton borne by a commanding officer.
[14] *I.e.*, the Titans.

Amongst whom our own royal standard
   threatens                                      10
Confusion to opposers. We must learn
To practice war again in time of peace,
Or lay our crown before our subjects'
   feet—
Ha, Urswick, must we not?

URS.                            The powers who seated
King Henry on his lawful throne will ever
Rise up in his defense.

KING.                          Rage shall not fright
The bosom of our confidence. In Kent
Our Cornish rebels, cozened of their
   hopes,
Met brave resistance by that country's [1]
   earl,
George Abergeny,[2] Cobham, Poynings,
   Guilford,                                   20
And other loyal hearts; now, if Black-
   heath
Must be reserved the fatal tomb to
   swallow
Such stiff-necked abjects[3] as with weary
   marches
Have traveled from their homes, their
   wives and children,
To pay, instead of subsidies, their lives,
We may continue sovereign. Yet, Urs-
   wick,
We'll not abate one penny what in parlia-
   ment
Hath freely been contributed; we must
   not.
Money gives soul to action. Our competi-
   tor,
The Flemish counterfeit, with James of
   Scotland,                                   30
Will prove what courage need and want
   can nourish,
Without the food of fit supplies. But,
   Urswick,
I have a charm in secret that shall loose
The witchcraft wherewith young King
   James is bound,
And free it at my pleasure without blood-
   shed.

URS. Your majesty's a wise king, sent from
   heaven,
Protector of the just.

KING.                          Let dinner cheerfully
Be served in; this day of the week is
   ours,
Our day of providence; for Saturday

Yet never failed in all my undertak-
   ings                                        40
To yield me rest at night. (*A flourish.*)
What means this warning?
Good fate, speak peace to Henry!

*Enter Dawbney, Oxford, and Attendants.*

DAW.                            Live the king,
Triumphant in the ruin of his enemies!

OX. The head of strong rebellion is cut off,
The body hewed in pieces.

KING.                          Dawbney, Oxford,
Minions[4] to noblest fortunes, how yet
   stands
The comfort of your wishes?

DAW.                           Briefly thus!
The Cornish under Audley, disappointed
Of flattered expectation, from the Kent-
   ish
(Your majesty's right trusty liegemen)
   flew,                                       50
Feathered[5] by rage and heartened by
   presumption,
To take the field even at your palace
   gates,
And face you in your chamber royal.
   Arrogance
Improved their ignorance, for they, sup-
   posing,
Misled by rumor, that the day of battle
Should fall on Monday, rather braved
   your forces
Than doubted[6] any onset; yet this morn-
   ing,
When in the dawning I by your direc-
   tion
Strove to get Dartford Strand bridge,
   there I found
Such a resistance as might show what
   strength                                    60
Could make. Here arrows hailed in
   showers upon us
A full yard long at least, but we pre-
   vailed.
My Lord of Oxford, with his fellow peers
Environing the hill, fell fiercely on them
On the one side, I on the other, till, great
   sir
(Pardon the oversight), eager of doing
Some memorable act, I was engaged
Almost a prisoner, but was freed as soon
As sensible of danger. Now the fight

---

[1] County's.   [2] Abergavenny.   [3] Castaways.      [4] Favorites.   [5] Winged.   [6] Feared.

Began in heat, which, quenched in the blood of                                        70
Two thousand rebels, and as many more
Reserved to try your mercy, have returned
A victory with safety.

KING.                                Have we lost
An equal number with them?

Ox.                              In the total
Scarcely four hundred.  Audley, Flammock, Joseph,
The ringleaders of this commotion,
Railed [1] in ropes, fit ornaments for traitors,
Wait your determinations.

KING.                            We must pay
Our thanks where they are only due.  O, lords,                                     79
Here is no victory, nor shall our people
Conceive that we can triumph in their falls.
Alas, poor souls!  Let such as are escaped
Steal to the country back without pursuit.
There's not a drop of blood spilt but hath drawn
As much of mine.  Their swords could have wrought wonders
On their king's part, who faintly were unsheathed
Against their prince, but wounded their own breasts.
Lords, we are debtors to your care; our payment
Shall be both sure and fitting your deserts.

DAW. Sir, will you please to see those rebels, heads                              90
Of this wild monster-multitude?

KING.                            Dear friend,
My faithful Dawbney, no.  On them our justice
Must frown in terror; I will not vouchsafe
An eye of pity to them.  Let false Audley
Be drawn upon an hurdle from the Newgate
To Tower Hill in his own coat of arms,
Painted on paper, with the arms reversed,
Defaced, and torn; there let him lose his head.
The lawyer and the blacksmith shall be hanged,

Quartered, their quarters into Cornwall sent                                       100
Examples to the rest, whom we are pleased
To pardon and dismiss from further quest. [2]
My Lord of Oxford, see it done.

Ox.                                I shall, sir.

KING.  Urswick!

URS.       My lord?

KING.                    To Dinham, our high treasurer,
Say we command commissions be new granted
For the collection of our subsidies
Through all the west, and that speedily.
Lords, we acknowledge our engagements due
For your most constant services.

DAW.                          Your soldiers  109
Have manfully and faithfully acquitted
Their several duties.

KING.                    For it we will throw
A largess free amongst them, which shall hearten
And cherish up [3] their loyalties.  More yet
Remains of like employment; not a man
Can be dismissed till enemies abroad,
More dangerous than these at home, have felt
The puissance of our arms.  O happy kings
Whose thrones are raiséd in their subjects' hearts!            *Exeunt omnes.*

[SCENA SECUNDA.

*A room in the palace at Edinburgh.*]

*Enter Huntley and Daliell.*

HUNT. Now, sir, a modest [4] word with you, sad gentleman.
Is not this fine, I trow, [5] to see the gambolds, [6]
To hear the jigs, [7] observe the frisks, b' enchanted
With the rare discord of bells, pipes, and tabors,
Hotchpotch of Scotch and Irish twingletwangles,

---

[1] Tied in a row.

[2] Inquest, inquiry.                    [4] Quiet.
[3] Cheer, encourage.
[5] Here merely an expression of contempt.
[6] Gambols.          [7] Lively songs or ballads.

Like to so many quiristers [1] of Bedlam
Trolling a catch! [2] The feasts, the manly
   stomachs,
The healths in usquebaugh [3] and bonny-
   clabber, [4]
The ale in dishes never fetched from
   China,
The hundred thousand knacks [5] not to
   be spoken of—         10
And all this for King Oberon and Queen
   Mab—
Should put a soul int'e. Look 'e, good
   man,
How youthful I am grown. But, by
   your leave,
This new queen-bride must henceforth
   be no more
My daughter; no, bur [6] Lady, 'tis unfit.
And yet you see how I do bear this
   change,
Methinks courageously, then shake off
   care
In such a time of jollity.
DAL.                Alas, sir,
How can you cast a mist upon your
   griefs,
Which, howsoe'er you shadow, but pre-
   sent          20
To any judging eye the perfect sub-
   stance,
Of which mine are but counterfeits?
HUNT.            Foh, Daliell!
Thou interrupts the part I bear in
   music
To this rare bridal feast. Let us be
   merry,
Whilst flattering calms secure us against
   storms.
Tempests, when they begin to roar, put
   out
The light of peace, and cloud the sun's
   bright eye
In darkness of despair; yet we are safe.
DAL. I wish you could as easily forget
The justice of your sorrows as my
   hopes         30
Can yield to destiny.
HUNT.          Pish! Then I see
Thou dost not know the flexible condi-
   tion

---

Of my apt nature. I can laugh, laugh
   heartily,
When the gout cramps my joints; let
   but the stone
Stop in my bladder, I am straight a-
   singing;
The quartan-fever, shrinking every limb,
Sets me a-capering straight. Do but
   betray me,
And bind me a friend ever. What! I
   trust
The losing of a daughter, though I
   doted
On every hair that grew to trim her
   head,        40
Admits not any pain like one of these.
Come, th' art deceived in me. Give me
   a blow,.
A sound blow on the face, I'll thank thee
   for 't.
I love my wrongs. Still tb' art deceived
   in me.
DAL. Deceived? O, noble Huntley, my
   few years
Have learnt experience of too ripe an
   age
To forfeit fit credulity. Forgive
My rudeness; I am bold.
HUNT.            Forgive me first
A madness of ambition; by example
Teach me humility, for patience scorns
Lectures, which schoolmen use to read
   to boys       51
Uncapable of injuries. Though old,
I could grow tough in fury, and disclaim
Allegiance to my king, could fall at odds
With all my fellow peers that durst not
   stand
Defendants gainst the rape done on
   mine honor.
But kings are earthly gods; there is no
   meddling
With their anointed bodies; for their
   actions
They only are accountable to heaven.
Yet in the puzzle of my troubled brain
One antidote's reserved against the
   poison       61
Of my distractions; 'tis in thee t' apply
   it.
DAL. Name it; O, name it quickly, sir!
HUNT.             A pardon
For my most foolish slighting thy de-
   serts:

---

[1] Choristers.
[2] Singing a round song.
[4] Coagulated sour milk.
[5] Knickknacks, trifles.
[3] Whiskey.
[6] By our.

I have culled out this time to beg it. Prithee,
Be gentle.   Had I been so, thou hadst owned
A happy bride, but now a castaway,
And never child of mine more.

DAL.                     Say not so, sir;
It is not fault in her.

HUNT.                 The world would prate
How she was handsome; young I know she was,                                    70
Tender and sweet in her obedience—
But lost now.   What a bankrupt am I made
Of [1] a full stock of blessings!   Must I hope
A mercy from thy heart?

DAL.                     A love, a service,
A friendship to posterity.[2]

HUNT.                   Good angels
Reward thy charity!   I have no more
But prayers left me now.

DAL.               I'll lend you mirth, sir,
If you will be in consort.[3]

HUNT.                 Thank ye truly.
I must; yes, yes, I must.   Here's yet some ease,
A partner in affliction; look not angry. 80

DAL. Good, noble sir!         [Flourish.]

HUNT.        O, hark!   We may be quiet;
The king and all the others come, a meeting
Of gaudy sights.   This day's the last of revels;
Tomorrow sounds of war; then new exchange.
Fiddles must turn to swords.   Unhappy marriage!

Flourish.   Enter King James; Warbeck
   leading Katherine; Crawford, Countess,
   and Jane [, with other Ladies].   Huntley
   and Daliell fall among them.

K. JA. Cousin of York, you and your princely bride
Have liberally enjoyed such soft delights
As a new-married couple could forethink;
Nor has our bounty shortened [4] expectation.
But after all those pleasures of repose, 90

Or amorous safety, we must rouse the ease
Of dalliance with achievements of more glory
Than sloth and sleep can furnish.   Yet, for farewell,
Gladly we entertain a truce with time
To grace the joint endeavors of our servants.

WAR. My royal cousin, in your princely favor
The extent of bounty hath been so unlimited
As only an acknowledgment in words
Would breed suspicion in [5] our state and quality.
When we shall, in the fullness of our fate,                                    100
Whose minister, necessity, will perfit,[6]
Sit on our own throne; then our arms, laid open
To gratitude, in sacred memory
Of these large benefits, shall twine them close,
Even to our thoughts and heart, without distinction.
Then James and Richard, being in effect
One person, shall unite and rule one people,
Divisible in titles only.

K. JA.               Seat ye.
Are the presenters ready?

CRAW.                 All are entering.

HUNT. Dainty sport toward, Daliell! Sit; come, sit,                            110
Sit and be quiet.   Here are kingly bug's words! [7]

Enter at one door four Scotch Antics,[8] accordingly habited; enter at another
   four Wild Irish in trowses,[9] long-
   haired and accordingly habited.   Music.
   The Masquers dance.

K. JA. To all a general thanks!

WAR.                 In the next room
Take your own shapes again; you shall receive
Particular acknowledgment.
                          [Exeunt Masquers.]

[1] From.
[2] I.e., remembered by posterity.
[3] Harmony.          [4] Come short of.

[5] As to.
[6] I.e., bring our destiny to perfection.
[7] Words of a bug, or bogey; swaggering language.
[8] Burlesque performers.   [9] Close-fitting trousers.

K. JA.                                Enough
Of merriments.—Crawford, how far's
    our army
Upon the march?
CRAW.            At Hedonhall, great king;
Twelve thousand, well prepared.
K. JA.                      Crawford, tonight
Post thither. We in person with the
    prince
By four a-clock tomorrow after dinner
Will be w'e.[1] Speed away!
CRAW.            I fly, my lord. [Exit.] 120
K. JA. Our business grows to head now.
    Where's your secretary,
That he attends 'e not to serve?
WAR.                  With Marchmount,
Your herald.
K. JA.            Good! The proclamation's
    ready;
By that it will appear how the English
    stand
Affected to your title. Huntley, com-
    fort
Your daughter in her husband's ab-
    sence; fight
With prayers at home for us, who for
    your honors
Must toil in fight abroad.
HUNT.            Prayers are the weapons
Which men so near their graves as I
    do use.
I've little else to do.
K. JA.            To rest, young beauties! 130
We must be early stirring; quickly part.
"A kingdom's rescue craves both speed
    and art."
Cousins, good night.        Flourish.
WAR.            Rest to our cousin king.
KATH. Your blessing, sir.
HUNT. Fair blessings on your highness!
    Sure, you need 'em.
Exeunt omnes; manent Warb[eck, Jane,]
                        et Katherine.
WAR. Jane, set the lights down, and from
    us return
To those in the next room this little
    purse;
Say we'll deserve [2] their loves.
JANE.            It shall be done, sir. [Exit.]
WAR. Now, dearest, ere sweet sleep shall
    seal those eyes,
Love's precious tapers, give me leave to
    use                              140

A parting ceremony, for tomorrow
It would be sacrilege to intrude upon
The temple of thy peace. Swift as the
    morning
Must I break from the down of thy em-
    braces,
To put on steel, and trace the paths
    which lead
Through various hazards to a careful [3]
    throne.
KATH. My lord, I would fain go w'e;
    there's small fortune
In staying here behind.
WAR.                  The churlish brow
Of war, fair dearest, is a sight of horror
For ladies' entertainment.        If thou
    hear'st                          150
A truth of my sad ending by the hand
Of some unnatural subject, thou withal
Shalt hear how I died worthy of my
    right,
By falling like a king; and in the close,
Which my last breath shall sound, thy
    name, thou fairest,
Shall sing a requiem to my soul, unwill-
    ing
Only of greater glory, cause [4] divided
From such a heaven on earth as life
    with thee.
But these are chimes for funerals. My
    business
Attends on fortune of a sprightlier
    triumph,                        160
For love and majesty are reconciled,
And vow to crown thee empress of the
    west.
KATH. You have a noble language, sir;
    your right
In me is without question, and how-
    ever
Events of time may shorten my deserts
In others' pity, yet it shall not stagger
Or constancy or duty in a wife.
You must be king of me; and my poor
    heart
Is all I can call mine.
WAR.                  But we will live,
Live, beauteous virtue, by the lively
    test                            170
Of our own blood to let the "counter-
    feit"
Be known the world's contempt.
KATH.                  Pray, do not use

[1] With ye.        [2] Reward.
[3] Full of care.        [4] Because.

That word; it carries fate in 't. The first
    suit
I ever made, I trust your love will grant.

WAR. Without denial, dearest.

KATH.               That hereafter,
If you return with safety, no adventure
May sever us in tasting any fortune.
I ne'er can stay behind again.

WAR.             Y' are lady
Of your desires, and shall command
    your will;
Yet 'tis too hard a promise.

KATH.         What our destinies 180
Have ruled out in their books we must
    not search,
But kneel to.

WAR.         Then to fear when hope is
    fruitless,
Were to be desperately miserable,
Which poverty our greatness dares not
    dream of,
And much more scorns to stoop to.
    Some few minutes
Remain yet; let's be thrifty in our hopes.
                        *Exeunt.*

[SCENA TERTIA.

*The presence chamber in the palace at*
                  *Westminster.*]

*Enter King Henry, Hialas, and Urswick.*

KING. Your name is Pedro Hialas, a
    Spaniard?

HIAL. Sir, a Castilian born.

KING.            King Ferdinand,
With wise Queen Isabel, his royal con-
    sort,
Write 'e [1] a man of worthy trust and
    candor.
Princes are dear to heaven who meet
    with subjects
Sincere in their employments; such I
    find
Your commendation, sir. Let me de-
    liver
How joyful I repute the amity
With your most fortunate master, who
    almost
Comes near a miracle in his success  10
Against the Moors, who had devoured
    his country
Entire now to his scepter. We for our
    part

Will imitate his providence,[2] in hope
Of partage [3] in the use on 't. We
    repute
The privacy of his advisement to us
By you, intended an ambassador
To Scotland for a peace between our
    kingdoms,
A policy of love which well becomes
His wisdom and our care.

HIAL.            Your majesty
Doth understand him rightly.

KING.               Else 20
Your knowledge can instruct me;
    wherein, sir,
To fall on ceremony would seem use-
    less,
Which shall not need, for I will be as
    studious
Of your concealment in our conference
As any council shall advise.

HIAL.           Then, sir,
My chief request is that, on notice
    given,
At my despatch in Scotland you will
    send
Some learned man of power and ex-
    perience
To join entreaty with me.

KING.          I shall do it,
Being that way well provided by [4] a
    servant                30
Which may attend 'e ever.

HIAL.         If King James
By any indirection should perceive
My coming near your court, I doubt
    the issue
Of my employment.

KING.       Be not your own herald;
I learn sometimes without a teacher.

HIAL.           Good days
Guard all your princely thoughts!

KING.       Urswick, no further
Than the next open gallery attend him.
A hearty love go with you!

HIAL.         Your vowed beadsman.[5]
        *Ex[eunt] Ursw[ick] and Hialas.*

KING. King Ferdinand is not so much a
    fox
But that a cunning huntsman may in
    time                40
Fall on the scent. In honorable actions
Safe imitation best deserves a praise.—

[1] Report ye.

[2] Foresight.       [4] With.
[3] Share.          [5] Devoted servant.

*Enter Urswick.*

What, the Castilian's passed away?

URS.                                              He is,
And undiscovered.   The two hundred
    marks
Your majesty conveyed,[1]   a   gently
    pursed
With a right modest gravity.

KING.                              What was 't
A muttered in the earnest [2] of his wis-
    dom?
A spoke not to be heard.   'Twas
    about—

URS.                                        Warbeck:
How if King Henry were but sure of
    subjects,
Such a wild runagate[3] might soon be
    caged,                                        50
No great ado withstanding.

KING.                        Nay, nay; something
About my son Prince Arthur's match.

URS.                            Right, right, sir.
A hummed it out, how that King Ferdi-
    nand
Swore that the marriage twixt the Lady
    Katherine,
His daughter, and the Prince of Wales,
    your son,
Should never be consummated as
    long
As any Earl of Warwick lived in Eng-
    land,
Except by new creation.

KING.                              I remember
'Twas so, indeed.   The king his master
    swore it?

URS.  Directly, as he said.

KING.                    An Earl of Warwick!  60
Provide a messenger for letters in-
    stantly
To Bishop Fox.   Our news from Scot-
    land creeps,
It comes so slow.   We must have airy
    spirits;
Our time requires depatch.—[*Aside.*]
    The Earl of Warwick!
Let him be son to Clarence, younger
    brother
To Edward!   Edward's daughter is, I
    think,
Mother to our Prince Arthur.—Get a
    messenger.                            *Exeunt.*

---

[1] Sent.    [2] Soberness.    [3] Runaway, fugitive.

*Before the castle of Norham.*]

*Enter King James, Warbeck, Crawford,*
    *Daliell, Heron, Astley, Major, Sketon,*
                            *and Soldiers.*

K. JA.  We trifle time against these castle
    walls;
The English prelate will not yield.
    Once more
Give him a summons.              *Parley.*

*Enter above, Durham, armed, a truncheon*
                    *in his hand, and Soldiers.*

WAR.                        See, the jolly clerk[4]
Appears, trimmed[5] like a ruffian!

K. JA.                                Bishop, yet
Set ope the ports, and to your lawful
    sovereign,
Richard of York, surrender up this
    castle,
And he will take thee to his grace; else
    Tweed
Shall overflow his banks with English
    blood,
And wash the sand that cements those
    hard stones,
From their foundation.

DUR.          Warlike King of Scotland,  10
Vouchsafe a few words from a man en-
    forced
To lay his book aside and clap on arms
Unsuitable to my age or my profession.
Courageous prince, consider on what
    grounds
You rend the face of peace, and break a
    league
With a confederate king that courts
    your amity.
For whom too?   For a vagabond, a
    straggler,
Not noted in the world by birth or name,
An obscure peasant, by the rage of hell
Loosed from his chains to set great kings
    at strife.                                    20
What nobleman, what common man of
    note,
What ordinary subject hath come in,
Since first you footed on our territories,
To only feign a welcome?   Children
    laugh at
Your proclamations, and the wiser pity

---

[4] Ecclesiastic.                        [5] Armed.

So great a potentate's abuse by one
Who juggles merely with the fawns [1]
and youth
Of an instructed compliment.    Such
spoils,
Such slaughters as the rapine of your
soldiers
Already have committed, is enough    30
To show your zeal in a conceited jus-
tice.[2]
Yet, great king, wake not yet my mas-
ter's vengeance,
But shake that viper off which gnaws
your entrails.
I and my fellow subjects are resolved,
If you persist, to stand your utmost fury
Till our last blood drop from us.
WAR.                    O, sir, lend
Me ear to this seducer of my honor!—
What shall I call thee, thou gray-bearded
scandal,
That kick'st against the sovereignty to
which
Thou   owest   allegiance?—Treason   is
boldfaced                                40
And eloquent in mischief.  Sacred king,
Be deaf to his known malice.
DUR.                    Rather yield
Unto those holy motions which inspire
The sacred heart of an anointed body.
It is the surest policy in princes
To govern well their own than [3] seek en-
croachment
Upon another's right.
CRAW. [Aside.]    The king is serious,
Deep in his meditation[s]. [4]
DAL. [Aside.]            Lift them up
To heaven, his better genius!
WAR.                Can you study
While such a devil raves?  O, sir!
K. JA.            Well, bishop, 50
You'll not be drawn to mercy?
DUR.                Conster me
In like case by a subject of your own.
My resolution's fixed.  King James, be
counseled.
A greater fate waits on thee.
                Exit Durham cum suis.[5]
K. JA.                Forage through
The country; spare no prey of life or
goods.

WAR.  O, sir, then give me leave to yield
to nature;
I am most miserable.  Had I been
Born what this clergyman would by
defame [6]
Baffle belief with, I had never sought
The truth of mine inheritance with rapes
Of women  or  of infants murthered,
virgins                                61
Deflowered, old men butchered, dwell-
ings fired,
My land depopulated, and my people
Afflicted with a kingdom's devastation.
Show more remorse,[7] great king, or I
shall never
Endure to see such havoc with dry eyes.
Spare, spare my dear, dear England!
K. JA.            You fool [8] your piety,
Ridiculously careful of an interest
Another man possesseth.  Where's your
faction?[9]
Shrewdly the bishop guessed of your
adherents,                            70
When not a petty burgess of some town,
No, not a villager, hath yet appeared
In your assistance.  That should make
'e whine,
And not your country's sufferance,[10]
as you term it.
DAL. [Aside.]  The king is angry.
CRAW. [Aside.]            And the
passionate duke
Effeminately dolent.[11]
WAR.            The experience
In former trials, sir, both of mine own
Or other princes cast out of their thrones,
Have so acquainted me how misery
Is destitute of friends or of relief    80
That I can easily submit to taste
Lowest reproof without contempt or
words.

*Enter Frion.*

K. JA. An humble-minded man!—Now,
what intelligence
Speaks Master Secretary Frion?
FRI.                    Henry
Of England hath in open field o'erthrown
The armies who opposed him in the
right
Of this young prince.

---

[1] Fawnings.        [2] Imagined act of justice.
[3] Rather than.     [4] Added by Gifford-Dyce.
[5] With his men.

[6] Defamation.                    [9] Party.
[7] Pity.                          [10] Suffering.
[8] Make foolish.                  [11] Doleful.

K. JA.                His subsidies,[1] you mean.
    More, if you have it?
FRI.              Howard, Earl of Surrey,
    Backed by twelve earls and barons of
        the north,
    An hundred knights and gentlemen of
        name,                                    90
    And twenty thousand soldiers, is at
        hand
    To raise your siege.  Brooke, with a
        goodly navy,
    Is admiral at sea; and Dawbney follows
    With an unbroken army for a second.
WAR.  'Tis false!  They come to side with
        us.
K. JA.        Retreat!
    We snall not find them stones and walls
        to cope with.
    Yet, Duke of York, for such thou sayest
        thou art,
    I'll try thy fortune to the height.  To
        Surrey,
    By Marchmount, I will send a brave
        defiance
    For single combat.  Once [2] a king will
        venter [3]                              100
    His person to an earl, with condition
    Of spilling lesser blood.[4]  Surrey is bold,
    And James resolved.[5]
WAR.              O, rather, gracious sir,
    Create me [6] to this glory, since my cause
    Doth interest [7] this fair quarrel; valued
        least,
    I am his equal.
K. JA.            I will be the man.—
    March softly off.  "Where victory can
        reap
    A harvest crowned with triumph, toil is
        cheap."                        *Exeunt omnes.*

ACTUS QUARTUS.  SCENA PRIMA.

[*The English camp near Ayton, on the
                              border.*]

*Enter Surrey, Durham, Soldiers, with drums
                          and colors.*

SUR.  Are all our braving enemies shrunk
        back,
    Hid in the fogs of their distempered [8]
        climate,

[1] Auxiliaries.       [2] For once.      [3] Venture.
[4] With the intention of spilling less blood.
[5] Resolute.                   [7] Is concerned in.
[6] *I.e.*, advance me.        [8] Intemperate.

    Not daring to behold our colors wave
    In spite of this infected air?  Can they
    Look on the strength of Cundrestine
        defaced,
    The glory of Hedonhall devasted,[9] that
    Of Edington cast down, the pile of
        Fulden
    O'erthrown, and this the strongest of
        their forts,
    Old Ayton Castle, yielded and demol-
        ished,
    And yet not peep abroad?  The Scots
        are bold,                               10
    Hardy in battle; but it seems the cause
    They undertake, considered, appears
    Unjointed in the frame on 't.
DUR.                  Noble Surrey,
    Our royal master's wisdom is at all times
    His fortune's harbinger, for when he
        draws
    His sword to threaten war, his provi-
        dence
    Settles on peace, the crowning of an
        empire.                       *Trumpet.*
SUR.  Rank all in order; 'tis a herald's
        sound,
    Some message from King James.  Keep a
        fixed station.

*Enter Marchmount and another Herald in
                          their coats.*

MARCH.  From Scotland's awful majesty
        we come                                20
    Unto the English general.
SUR.                      To me?
    Say on.
MARCH.            Thus then: the waste and
        prodigal
    Effusion of so much guiltless blood
    As in two potent armies of necessity
    Must glut the earth's dry womb, his
        sweet compassion
    Hath studied to prevent, for which to
        thee,
    Great Earl of Surrey, in a single fight
    He offers his own royal person, fairly
    Proposing these conditions only, that,
    If victory conclude our master's right,  30
    The earl shall deliver for his ransom
    The town of Berwick to him, with the
        fishgarths; [10]
    If Surrey shall prevail, the king will pay

[9] Devastated.                    [10] Weirs.

A thousand pounds down present for his freedom,
And silence further arms.    So speaks King James.
SUR. So speaks King James!    So like a king a speaks.
Heralds, the English general returns
A sensible devotion from his heart,
His very soul, to this unfellowed [1] grace.
For let the king know, gentle heralds, truly,                                                    40
How his descent from his great throne to honor
A stranger subject with so high a title
As his compeer in arms, hath conquered more
Than any sword could do, for which— my loyalty
Respected—I will serve his virtues ever
In all humility.  But Berwick, say,
Is none of mine to part with. "In affairs
Of princes, subjects cannot traffic rights
Inherent to the crown." My life is mine;
That I dare freely hazard· and—with pardon                                              50
To some unbribed vainglory—if his majesty
Shall taste a change of fate, his liberty
Shall meet no articles.[2] If I fall, falling
So bravely, I refer me to his pleasure
Without condition; and for this dear favor,
Say, if not countermanded, I will cease
Hostility, unless provoked.
MARCH.                          This answer
We shall relate unpartially.
DUR.                              With favor,
Pray have a little patience.—[Aside to Surrey.]  Sir, you find
By these gay flourishes how wearied travail                                                60
Inclines to willing rest; here's but a prologue,
However confidently uttered, meant
For some ensuing acts of peace. Consider
The time of year, unseasonableness of weather,
Charge, barrenness of profit; and occasion
Presents itself for honorable treaty,
Which we may make good use of.  I will back,

As sent from you in point of noble gratitude,
Unto King James, with these his heralds. You
Shall shortly hear from me, my lord, for order                                            70
Of breathing or proceeding; and King Henry,
Doubt not, will thank the service.
SUR. [Aside to Durham.]          To your wisdom,
Lord Bishop, I refer it.
DUR. [Aside to Surrey.]      Be it so, then.
SUR. Heralds, accept this chain and these few crowns.
MARCH. Our duty, noble general.
DUR.                                In part
Of retribution [3] for such princely love,
My lord the general is pleased to show
The king your master his sincerest zeal,
By further treaty, by no common man.
I will myself return with you.
SUR.                        Y' oblige   80
My faithfullest affections t'e, Lord Bishop.
MARCH. All happiness attend your lordship!
SUR.            Come, friends
And fellow soldiers! We, I doubt, shall meet
No enemies but woods and hills to fight with.
Then 'twere as good to feed and sleep at home.
We may be free from danger, not secure.
                              Exeunt omnes.

[SCENA SECUNDA.

The Scottish camp.]

Enter Warbeck and Frion.

WAR. Frion, O Frion, all my hopes of glory
Are at a stand! The Scottish king grows dull,
Frosty, and wayward, since this Spanish agent
Hath mixed discourses with him.  They are private;
I am not called to council now.  Confusion
On all his crafty shrugs! I feel the fabric
Of my designs are tottering.

[1] Unique.
[2] I.e., no conditions shall be imposed.
[3] In partial payment.

FRI.                          Henry's policies
Stir with too many engines.[1]
WAR.                              Let his mines,
Shaped in the bowels of the earth, blow
    up
Works raised for my defense, yet can
    they never                              10
Toss into air the freedom of my birth,
Or disavow my blood Plantagenet's.
I am my father's son still. But, O, Frion,
When I bring into count with my dis-
    asters
My wife's compartnership,[2] my Kate's,
    my life's,
Then, then my frailty feels an earth-
    quake. Mischief
Damn Henry's plots! I will be England's
    king,
Or let my aunt of Burgundy report
My fall in the attempt deserved[3] our
    ancestors!
FRI. You grow too wild in passion. If you
    will                                    20
Appear a prince indeed, confine your
    will
To moderation.
WAR.                    What a saucy rudeness
Prompts this distrust! If? If I will
    appear?
Appear a prince? Death throttle such
    deceits
Even in their birth of utterance! Curséd
    cozenage
Of trust! Ye make me mad. 'Twere
    best, it seems,
That I should turn impostor to myself,
Be mine own counterfeit, belie the truth
Of my dear mother's womb, the sacred
    bed
Of a prince murthered and a living
    baffled.                                30
FRI. Nay, if you have no ears to hear, I
    have
No breath to spend in vain.
WAR.                        Sir, sir, take heed!
Gold and the promise of promotion
    rarely
Fail in temptation.
FRI.                    Why to me this?
WAR.                                Nothing.
Speak what you will; we are not sunk so
    low

But your advice may piece again the
    heart
Which many cares have broken. You
    were wont
In all extremities to talk of comfort;
Have ye none left now? I'll not interrupt
    ye.
Good, bear with my distractions. If
    King James                              40
Deny us dwelling here, next whither
    must I?
I prithee, be not angry.
FRI.                        Sir, I told ye
Of letters come from Ireland—how the
    Cornish
Stomach their last defeat, and humbly
    sue
That with such forces as you could par-
    take[4]
You would in person land in Cornwall,
    where
Thousands will entertain your title
    gladly.
WAR. Let me embrace thee, hug thee.
    Th'ast revived
My comforts; if my cousin king will fail,
Our cause will never.—Welcome, my tried
    friends!                                50

*Enter Major, Heron, Astley, Sketon.*

You keep your brains awake in our
    defense.
Frion, advise with them of these affairs,
In which be wondrous secret; I will listen
What else concerns us here. Be quick
    and wary.            *Ex[it] Warbeck.*
AST. Ah, sweet young prince!—Secretary, my fellow counselors and I have consulted, and jump[5] all in one opinion
directly: that, if this Scotch garboils[6] do
not fadge[7] to our minds, we will pell-mell
run amongst the Cornish choughs[8] [60
presently and in a trice.
SKE. 'Tis but going to sea and, leaping
ashore, cut ten or twelve thousand unnecessary throats, fire seven or eight
towns, take half a dozen cities, get into the
market place, crown him Richard the
Fourth, and the business is finished.
MAJ. I grant ye, quoth I, so far forth
as men may do, no more than men may

[1] Contrivances.        [3] Was worthy of.
[2] Copartnership.       [4] Bring together.   [6] Tumults.   [8] Crows.
                        [5] Agree.            [7] Succeed.

do. For it is good to consider when [70 consideration may be to the purpose; otherwise—still you shall pardon me— little said is soon amended.

FRI. Then you conclude the Cornish action surest?

HER. We do so, and doubt not but to thrive abundantly. Ho, my masters, had we known of the commotion when we set sail out of Ireland, the land had been ours ere this time.                                    80

SKE. Pish, pish! 'Tis but forbearing being an earl or a duke a month or two longer. I say, and say it again, if the work go not on apace, let me never see new fashion more. I warrant ye, I warrant ye; we will have it so, and so it shall be.

AST. This is but a cold, phlegmatic country, not stirring enough for men of spirit. Give me the heart of England for my money!                                    90

SKE. A man may batten there in a week only, with hot loaves and butter, and a lusty cup of muscadine[1] and sugar at breakfast, though he make never a meal all the month after.

MAJ. Surely, when I bore office, I found by experience that to be much troublesome was to be much wise and busy. I have observed how filching and bragging has been the best service in these last [100 wars, and therefore conclude peremptorily on the design in England. If things and things may fall out, as who can tell what or how—but the end will show it.

FRI. Resolved like men of judgment. Here to linger[2]
More time is but to lose it. Cheer the prince
And haste him on to this; on this depends
Fame in success, or glory in our ends.
                                    *Exeunt omnes.*


[SCENA TERTIA.

*Another part of the same.*]

*Enter King James, Durham, and Hialas on either side.*

HIAL. France, Spain, and Germany combine a league
Of amity with England. Nothing wants

For settling peace through Christendom but love
Between the British monarchs, James and Henry.

DUR. The English merchants, sir, have been received
With general procession into Antwerp;
The emperor confirms the combination.

HIAL. The King of Spain resolves a marriage
For Katherine his daughter with Prince Arthur.

DUR. France courts this holy contract.

HIAL.                    What can hinder    10
A quietness in England—

DUR.                    But your suffrage
To such a silly creature, mighty sir,
As is but in effect an apparition,
A shadow, a mere trifle?

HIAL.                    To this union
The good of both the church and commonwealth
Invite 'e—

DUR.            To this unity, a mystery
Of providence points out a greater blessing
For both these nations than our human reason
Can search into. King Henry hath a daughter,
The Princess Margaret; I need not urge    20
What honor, what felicity can follow
On such affinity twixt two Christian kings
Inleagued by ties of blood. But sure I am,
If you, sir, ratify the peace proposed,
I dare both motion[3] and effect this marriage
For weal of both the kingdoms.

K. JA.            Dar'st thou, Lord Bishop?

DUR. Put it to trial, royal James, by sending
Some noble personage to the English court
By way of embassy.

HIAL.                    Part of the business
Shall suit my mediation.

K. JA.                    Well; what heaven    30
Hath pointed out to be, must be. You two
Are ministers, I hope, of blessèd fate.

[1] A sweet wine.                    [2] Delay.

[3] Move, propose.

But herein only I will stand acquitted—
No blood of innocents shall buy my
  peace.
For Warbeck, as you nick [1] him, came to
  me
Commended by the states of Christen-
  dom,
A prince, though in distress. His fair
  demeanor,
Lovely behavior, unappalléd spirit,
Spoke him not base in blood, however
  clouded.
The brute beasts have both rocks and
  caves to fly to,                                        40
And men the altars of the church; to
  us
He came for refuge. "Kings come near
  in nature
Unto the gods in being touched with
  pity."
Yet, noble friends, his mixture with our
  blood,
Even with our own, shall no way inter-
  rupt
A general peace. Only I will dismiss
  him
From my protection, throughout my
  dominions
In safety, but not ever to return.

HIAL. You are a just king.

DUR.           Wise, and herein happy.

K. JA. Nor will we dally in affairs of
  weight.                                                  50
Huntley, lord bishop, shall with you to
  England
Ambassador from us. We will throw
  down
Our weapons. Peace on all sides now.
  Repair
Unto our council; we will soon be with
  you.

HIAL. Delay shall question no despatch;
  heaven crown it.

        *Exeunt Durham and Hialas.*

K. JA. A league with Ferdinand? A mar-
  riage
With English Margaret? A free re-
  lease
From restitution for the late affronts?
Cessation from hostility? And all
For Warbeck, not delivered, but dis-
  missed.                                                    60
We could not wish it better.—Daliell!

[1] Nickname.

*Enter Daliell.*

DAL.                        Here, sir.

K. JA. Are Huntley and his daughter sent
  for?

DAL.                       Sent for
And come, my lord.

K. JA.       Say to the English prince
We want his company.

DAL.              He is at hand, sir.

*Enter Warbeck, Katherine, Jane, Frion,*
    *Heron, Sketon, Major, Astley.*

K. JA. Cousin, our bounty, favors, gentle-
  ness,
Our benefits, the hazard of our person,
Our people's lives, our land hath evi-
  denced
How much we have engaged on your
  behalf.
How trivial and how dangerous our
  hopes
Appear, how fruitless our attempts in
  war,                                                     70
How windy, rather smoky, your assur-
  ance
Of party [2] shows, we might in vain
  repeat!
But now obedience to the mother church,
A father's care upon his country's weal,
The dignity of state, directs our wis-
  dom
To seal an oath of peace through Chris-
  tendom,
To which we are sworn already. 'Tis
  you
Must only seek new fortunes in the
  world,
And find an harbor elsewhere. As I
  promised                                                 79
On your arrival, you have met no usage
Deserves repentance in your being here;
But yet I must live master of mine own.
However, what is necessary for you
At your departure, I am well content
You be accommodated with, provided
Delay prove not my enemy.

WAR.                 It shall not,
Most glorious prince. The fame of my
  designs
Soars higher than report of ease and
  sloth
Can aim at. I acknowledge all your
  favors

[2] Support.

Boundless and singular, am only
wretched                    90
In words as well as means to thank the
grace
That flowed so liberally.  Two empires
firmly
You're lord of—Scotland and Duke
Richard's heart.
My claim to mine inheritance shall
sooner
Fail than my life to serve you, best of
kings.
And, witness Edward's blood in me, I am
More loath to part with such a great
example
Of virtue than all other mere respects.
But, sir, my last suit is, you will not
force
From me what you have given—this
chaste lady,               100
Resolved on all extremes.[1]

KATH.                    I am your wife;
No human power can or shall divorce
My faith from duty.

WAR.                    Such another treasure
The earth is bankrout of.

K. JA.                    I gave her, cousin,
And must avow the gift, will add withal
A furniture[2] becoming her high birth
And unsuspected[3] constancy, provide
For your attendance.  We will part good
friends.        *Exeunt[4] King and Daliell.*

WAR. The Tudor hath been cunning in
his plots.                109
His Fox of Durham would not fail at last.
But what! Our cause and courage are
our own.
Be men, my friends, and let our cousin
king
See how we follow fate as willingly
As malice follows us.  Y' are all resolved
For the west parts of England?

OMNES.                Cornwall, Cornwall!

FRI. The inhabitants expect you daily.

WAR.                    Cheerfully
Draw all our ships out of the harbor,
friends;
Our time of stay doth seem too long.
We must
Prevent intelligence.[5]  About it sud-
denly!

OMNES. A prince, a prince, a prince!    120
                    *Exeunt Counselors.*

WAR. Dearest, admit not into thy pure
thoughts
The least of scruples, which may charge
their softness
With burden of distrust.  Should I prove
wanting
To noblest courage now, here were the
trial.
But I am perfect, sweet; I fear no change
More than thy being partner in my
sufferance.

KATH. My fortunes, sir, have armed me
to encounter
What chance soe'er they meet with —
Jane, 'tis fit
Thou stay behind, for whither wilt thou
wander?

JANE. Never till death will I forsake my
mistress,                130
Nor then, in wishing to die with 'e
gladly.

KATH. Alas, good soul!

FRI.            Sir, to your aunt of Burgundy
I will relate your present undertakings.
From her expect on all occasions wel-
come.
You cannot find me idle in your services.

WAR. Go, Frion, go! Wise men know how
to soothe
Adversity, not serve it.    Thou hast
waited
Too long on expectation.  "Never yet
Was any nation read of so besotted
In reason as to adore the setting sun."
Fly to the archduke's court; say to the
duchess                141
Her nephew, with fair Katherine his
wife,
Are on their expectation to begin
The raising of an empire.  If they fail,
Yet the report will never.  Farewell,
Frion.—                *Exit Frion.*
This man, Kate, has been true, though
now of late
I fear too much familiar with the Fox.

*Enter Huntley and Daliell.*

HUNT. I come to take my leave.  You need
not doubt
My interest in this sometime child of
mine.

---

[1] Extremities.
[2] Portion.
[3] Not distrusted.
[4] Original reads *Exit.*
[5] Forestall disclosure.

She's all yours now, good sir. O, poor
  lost creature,                                 150
Heaven guard thee with much patience!
  If thou canst
Forget thy title to old Huntley's family,
As much of peace will settle in thy mind
As thou canst wish to taste but in thy
  grave.
Accept my tears yet, prithee; they are
  tokens
Of charity as true as of affection.

KATH. This is the cruel'st farewell!

HUNT.                    Love, young gentleman,
  This model of my griefs. She calls you
  husband.
Then be not jealous of a parting kiss:
It is a father's, not a lover's offering.   160
Take it, my last.—[Kisses her.] I am too
  much a child.
Exchange of passion is to little use;
So [1] I should grow too foolish. Goodness
  guide thee!              Exit Hunt[ley].

KATH. Most miserable daughter!—Have
  you aught
To add, sir, to our sorrows?

DAL.                            I resolve,
  Fair lady, with your leave, to wait on all
Your fortunes in my person, if your lord
Vouchsafe me entertainment.

WAR. We will be bosom friends, most
  noble Daliell,
For I accept this tender of your love   170
Beyond ability of thanks to speak it.
Clear thy drowned eyes, my fairest;
  time and industry
Will show us better days, or end the
  worst.              Exeunt omnes.

[SCENA QUARTA.

The presence chamber at Westminster.]

Enter Oxford and Dawbney.

OX. No news from Scotland yet, my lord?

DAW.                            Not any
  But what King Henry knows himself. I
  thought
Our armies should have marched that
  way; his mind,
It seems, is altered.

OX.                    Victory attends
  His standard everywhere.

DAW.                    Wise princes, Oxford,
  Fight not alone with forces. Providence

[1] Thus.

Directs and tutors strength; else ele-
  phants
And barbéd [2] horses might as well prevail
As the most subtile stratagems of war.

OX. The Scottish king showed more than
  common bravery                             10
In proffer of a combat hand to hand
With Surrey.

DAW.                    And but showed it. Northern bloods
Are gallant, being fired, but the cold
  climate,
Without good store of fuel, quickly
  freezeth
The glowing flames.

OX.                    Surrey, upon my life,
  Would not have shrunk an hair's
  breadth.

DAW.                    May a forfeit
  The honor of an English name and
  nature,
Who would not have embraced it with a
  greediness
As violent as hunger runs to food!    19
'Twas an addition [3] any worthy spirit
Would covet, next to immortality,
Above all joys of life. We all missed
  shares
In that great opportunity.

Enter King Henry and Urswick, whispering.

OX.                            The king!
  See, a comes smiling.

DAW.                    O, the game runs smooth
  On his side, then, believe it. Cards, well
  shuffled
And dealt with cunning, bring some
  gamester thrift,
But others must rise losers.

KING.                    The train [4] takes?

URS. Most prosperously.

KING.                    I knew it should not miss.
  He fondly [5] angles who will hurl his bait
Into the water cause the fish at first   30
Plays round about the line and dares not
  bite.
Lords, we may reign your king yet.
  Dawbney, Oxford,
Urswick, must Perkin wear the crown?

DAW.                            A slave!

OX. A vagabond!

[2] Barded, armored.          [4] Plot.
[3] Honor.                    [5] Foolishly

Urs.          A glowworm!

King.             Now, if Frion,
   His practiced politician, wear a brain
   Of proof, King Perkin will in progress ride
   Through all his large dominions. Let us
     meet him,
   And tender homage. Ha, sirs? Liegemen
     ought
   To pay their fealty.

Daw.         Would the rascal were,   39
   With all his rabble, within twenty miles
   Of London.

King.        Farther off is near enough
   To lodge him in his home. I'll wager odds
   Surrey and all his men are either idle
   Or hasting back. They have not work, I
     doubt,
   To keep them busy.

Daw.        'Tis a strange conceit, sir.

King. Such voluntary favors as our people
   In duty aid us with, we never scattered
   On cobweb parasites, or lavished out
   In riot or a needless hospitality.
   No undeserving favorite doth boast   50
   His issues [1] from our treasury; our charge
   Flows through all Europe, proving us but
     steward
   Of every contribution which provides
   Against the creeping canker of disturb-
     ance.
   Is it not rare, then, in this toil of state
   Wherein we are embarked, with breach
     of sleep,
   Cares, and the noise of trouble, that our
     mercy
   Returns nor thanks nor comfort? Still
     the west
   Murmur and threaten innovation,[2]
   Whisper our government tyrannical,   60
   Deny us what is ours, nay, spurn their
     lives,
   Of which they are but owners by our gift.
   It must not be.

Ox.         It must not, should not.

*Enter a Post.[3]*

King.           So then—
   To whom?

Post.       This packet to your sacred
     majesty.

King. Sirrah, attend without. [*Exit Post.*]

Ox. News from the north, upon my life.

Daw.           Wise Henry
   Divines aforehand of events; with him
   Attempts and execution are one act.

King. Urswick, thine ear: Frion is caught;
     the man
   Of cunning is outreached. We must be
     safe.                            70
   Should reverend Morton, our archbishop,
     move
   To a translation higher yet,[4] I tell thee
   My Durham owns a brain deserves that
     see.[5]
   He's nimble in his industry, and mount-
     ing.[6]
   Thou hear'st me?

Urs.      And conceive your highness fitly.

King. Dawbney and Oxford, since our
     army stands
   Entire, it were a weakness to admit
   The rust of laziness to eat amongst them.
   Set forward toward Salisbury; the plains
   Are most commodious for their exer-
     cise.                           80
   Ourself will take a muster of them there,
   And or disband them with reward or else
   Dispose as best concerns us.

Daw.            Salisbury?
   Sir, all is peace at Salisbury.

King.            Dear friend,
   The charge must be our own; we would a
     little
   Partake the pleasure with our subjects'
     ease.—
   Shall I entreat your loves?

Ox.          Command our lives.

King. Y' are men know how to do, not to
     forethink.
   My bishop is a jewel tried and perfect;
   A jewel, lords. The post who brought
     these letters                 90
   Must speed another to the Mayor of
     Exeter.
   Urswick, dismiss him not.

Urs.        He waits your pleasure.

King. Perkin a king? A king?

Urs.         My gracious lord.

King. Thoughts busied in the sphere of
     royalty
   Fix not on creeping worms,[7] without their
     stings

---

[1] Monetary grants.      [2] Revolution.
[3] This stage direction follows the King's speech in the original.

[4] *I.e.*, die.           [6] Ambitious.
[5] *I.e.*, of Canterbury.     [7] Snakes.

Mere excrements of earth.  The use of time

Is thriving safety and a wise prevention
Of ills expected.  W' are resolved for Salisbury.                    *Exe[unt] omnes.*

[SCENA QUINTA.

*The coast of Cornwall.*]

*A general shout within.  Enter Warbeck, Daliell, Katherine, and Jane.*

WAR.  After so many storms as wind and seas

Have threatened to our weather-beaten ships,
At last, sweet fairest, we are safe arrived
On our dear mother earth, ingrateful only
To heaven and us in yielding sustenance
To sly usurpers of our throne and right.
These general acclamations are an omen
Of happy process [1] to their welcome lord.
They flock in troops, and from all parts with wings                                    9
Of duty fly to lay their hearts before us.
Unequaled pattern of a matchless wife,
How fares my dearest yet?

KATH.                     Confirmed in health,
By which I may the better undergo
The roughest face of change; but I shall learn
Patience to hope, since silence courts affliction
For comforts, to this truly noble gentleman,
Rare unexampled pattern of a friend,
And my beloved Jane, the willing follower
Of all misfortunes.

DAL.                      Lady, I return           19
But barren crops of early protestations,
Frost-bitten in the spring of fruitless hopes.

JANE.  I wait but as the shadow to the body;
For, madam, without you, let me be nothing.

WAR.  None talk of sadness; we are on the way
Which leads to victory.  Keep cowards' thoughts
With desperate sullenness.  The lion faints not,

Locked in a grate,[2] but loose disdains all force
Which bars his prey—and we are lionhearted—
Or else no king of beasts. (*Another shout [within].*)  Hark, how they shout,
Triumphant in our cause!  Bold confidence                                          30
Marches on bravely, cannot quake at danger.

*Enter Sketon.*

SKE.  Save King Richard the Fourth! Save thee, king of hearts!  The Cornish blades are men of mettle, have proclaimed, through Bodnam and the whole county, my sweet prince monarch of England.  Four thousand tall yeomen, with bow and sword, already vow to live and die at the foot of King Richard.

*Enter Astley.*

AST.  The mayor, our fellow coun-  [40 selor, is servant for an emperor.  Exeter is appointed for the rendezvous, and nothing wants to victory but courage and resolution.  *Sigillatum et datum decimo Septembris, anno regni regis primo, et cætera; confirmatum est.*[3]  All's cocksure.[4]

WAR.  To Exeter!  To Exeter, march on! Commend us to our people.  We in person Will lend them double spirits; tell them so.

SKE. AND AST.  King Richard!  King Richard!                                        50

WAR.  A thousand blessings guard our lawful arms!
A thousand horrors pierce our enemies' souls!
Pale fear unedge their weapons' sharpest points
And, when they draw their arrows to the head,
Numbness shall strike their sinews!  Such advantage
Hath majesty in its pursuit of justice
That on the proppers-up of Truth's old throne
It both enlightens counsel and gives heart

---

[1] Progress.

[2] Cage.
[3] Sealed and dated on the tenth of September, in the first year of the king's reign, etc. Confirmed.                    [4] Perfectly safe.

To execution, whiles [1] the throats of
   traitors
Lie bare before our mercy.  O, divin-
   ity                                                    60
Of royal birth! How it strikes dumb the
   tongues
Whose prodigality of breath is bribed
By trains to greatness!  Princes are but
   men
Distinguished in the fineness of their
   frailty,
Yet not so gross in beauty of the mind,
For there's a fire more sacred purifies
The dross of mixture.  Herein stand the
   odds:
"Subjects are men on earth; kings, men
   and gods."         *Exeunt omnes.*

ACTUS QUINTUS.  SCENA PRIMA.

[*St. Michael's Mount, Cornwall.*]

*Enter Katherine and Jane in riding suits,*
              *with one Servant.*

KATH.  It is decreed; and we must yield to
   fate,
Whose angry justice, though it threaten
   ruin,
Contempt, and poverty, is all but trial
Of a weak woman's constancy in suffer-
   ing.
Here, in a stranger's and an enemy's
   land,
Forsaken and unfurnished of all hopes
But such as wait on misery, I range
To meet affliction wheresoe'er I tread.
My train and pomp of servants is reduced
To one kind gentlewoman and this
   groom.                                              10
Sweet Jane, now whither must we?
JANE.               To your ships,
Dear lady, and turn home.
KATH.          Home!  I have none.
Fly thou to Scotland; thou hast friends
   will weep
For joy to bid thee welcome.  But, O,
   Jane,
My Jane, my friends are desperate of
   comfort,
As I must be of them.  The common
   charity,
Good people's alms and prayers of the
   gentle,

Is the revenue must support my state.
As for my native country, since it once
Saw me a princess in the height of great-
   ness                                               20
My birth allowed me, here I make a vow
Scotland shall never see me, being fallen
Or lessened in my fortunes.  Never, Jane,
Never to Scotland more will I return.
Could I be England's queen—a glory,
   Jane,
I never fawned on—yet the king who
   gave me
Hath sent me with my husband from his
   presence,
Delivered us suspected to his [2] nation,
Rendered us spectacles to time and pity.
And is it fit I should return to such    30
As only listen after our descent
From happiness enjoyed, to misery
Expected, though uncertain?    Never,
   never!
Alas, why dost thou weep, and that poor
   creature
Wipe his wet cheeks too?  Let me feel
   alone
Extremities, who know [3] to give them
   harbor.
Nor thou nor he has cause.  You may
   live safely.
JANE.  There is no safety whiles your dan-
   gers, madam,
Are every way apparent.
SERV.             Pardon, lady
I cannot choose but show my honest
   heart—                                              40
You were ever my good lady.
KATH.            O, dear souls,
Your shares in grief are too-too much!

*Enter Daliell.*

DAL.                 I bring,
Fair princess, news of further sadness yet
Than your sweet youth hath been ac-
   quainted with.
KATH.  Not more, my lord, than I can
   welcome.  Speak it;
The worst, the worst I look for.
DAL.             All the Cornish
At Exeter were by the citizens
Repulsed, encountered by the Earl of
   Devonshire
And other worthy gentlemen of the coun-
   try.

---

[1] While.              [2] Perkin's.        [3] Know how.

Your husband marched to Taunton, and
   was there                                                 50
Affronted [1] by King Henry's chamber-
   lain,
The king himself in person with his army
Advancing nearer to renew the fight
On all occasions. But the night before
The battles [2] were to join, your husband
   privately,
Accompanied with some few horse, de-
   parted
From out the camp, and posted none
   knows whither.

KATH. Fled without battle given?

DAL.                              Fled, but followed
By Dawbney, all his parties [3] left to taste
King Henry's mercy—for to that they
   yielded—                                                 60
Victorious without bloodshed.

KATH.                              O, my sorrows!
If both our lives had proved the sacrifice
To Henry's tyranny, we had fallen like
   princes,
And robbed him of the glory of his pride.

DAL. Impute it not to faintness or to
   weakness
Of noble courage, lady, but foresight;
For by some secret friend he had in-
   telligence
Of being bought and sold by his base fol-
   lowers.
Worse yet remains untold.

KATH.                              No, no, it cannot.

DAL. I fear y' are betrayed: the Earl of
   Oxford                                                   70
Runs hot in your pursuit.

KATH.                              A shall not need;
We'll run as hot in resolution gladly
To make the earl our jailor.

JANE.                              Madam, madam,
They come, they come!

*Enter Oxford with Followers.*

DAL.     Keep back! Or he who dares
Rudely to violate the law of honor
Runs on my sword.

KATH.                    Most noble sir, forbear.
What reason draws you hither, gentle-
   men?
Whom seek 'e?

OX.     All stand off!—With favor, lady,
From Henry, England's king, I would
   present

Unto the beauteous princess, Katherine
   Gordon,                                                  80
The tender of a gracious entertainment.

KATH. We are that princess, whom your
   master king
Pursues with reaching arms to draw into
His power. Let him use his tyranny;
We shall not be his subjects.

OX.                              My commission
Extends no further, excellentest lady,
Than to a service; 'tis King Henry's
   pleasure
That you, and all that have relation t'e,
Be guarded as becomes your birth and
   greatness,
For, rest assured, sweet princess, that
   not aught                                              90
Of what you do call yours shall find dis-
   turbance,
Or any welcome other than what suits
Your high condition.

KATH.                    By what title, sir,
May I acknowledge you?

OX.                              Your servant, lady,
Descended from the line of Oxford's earls,
Inherits what his ancestors before him
Were owners of.

KATH.               Your king is herein royal,
That by a peer so ancient in desert
As well as blood commands us to his
   presence.

OX. Invites 'e, princess, not commands.

KATH.                              Pray, use   100
Your own phrase as you list. To your
   protection
Both I and mine submit.

OX.                    There's in your number
A nobleman whom fame hath bravely
   spoken.
To him the king my master bade me
   say
How willingly he courts his friendship;
   far
From an enforcement, more than what in
   terms
Of courtesy so great a prince may hope
   for.

DAL. My name is Daliell.

OX.                    'Tis a name hath won
Both thanks and wonder from report, my
   lord.
The court of England emulates your
   merit,                                                  110
And covets to embrace 'e.

[1] Confronted.          [2] Armies.          [3] Allies.

DAL.                                    I must wait on
The princess in her fortunes.
OX.                                    Will you please,
Great lady, to set forward?
KATH.                                    Being driven
By fate, it were in vain to strive with
    heaven.                            *Exeunt omnes.*

[SCENA SECUNDA.

*Salisbury.*]

*Enter King Henry, Surrey, Urswick, and a
    guard of Soldiers.*

KING. The counterfeit, King Perkin, is
    escaped—
Escape, so let him; he is hedged too fast
Within the circuit of our English pale[1]
To steal out of our ports, or leap the walls
Which guard our land.    The seas are
    rough and wider
Than his weak arms can tug with.—Sur-
    rey, henceforth
Your king may reign in quiet; turmoils
    past,
Like some unquiet dream, have rather
    busied
Our fancy than affrighted rest of state.
But, Surrey, why, in articling a peace    10
With James of Scotland, was not restitu-
    tion
Of losses which our subjects did sustain
By the Scotch inroads questioned?
SUR.                                    Both demanded
And urged, my lord, to which the king
    replied,
In modest merriment, but smiling ear-
    nest,
How that our master Henry was much
    abler
To bear the detriments than he repay
    them.
KING. The young man, I believe, spake
    honest truth;
A studies to be wise betimes.[2]—Has, Urs-
    wick,
Sir Rice ap Thomas and Lord Brooke our
    steward                              20
Returned the Western gentlemen full
    thanks
From us for their tried loyalties?
URS.[3]                                 They have—

[1] Fence, boundary.                    [2] Early.
[3] Suggested by Weber.    Original has *Sur.*

Which, as if health and life had reigned
    amongst 'em,
With open hearts they joyfully received.
KING. Young Buckingham is a fair-
    natured prince,
Lovely in hopes, and worthy of his
    father.
Attended by an hundred knights and
    squires
Of special name, he tendered humble
    service,
Which we must ne'er forget; and Devon-
    shire's wounds.
Though slight, shall find sound cure in
    our respect.[4]                     30

*Enter Dawbney with [a Guard, conducting]
    Warbeck, Heron, John a Water, Astley,
                                        Sketon.*

DAW. Life to the king, and safety fix his
    throne!
I here present you, royal sir, a shadow
Of majesty, but in effect a substance
Of pity—a young man, in nothing grown
To ripeness but th' ambition of your
    mercy,
Perkin, the Christian world's strange
    wonder.
KING.                                    Dawbney,
We observe no wonder.    I behold, 'tis
    true,
An ornament of nature, fine and polished,
A handsome youth indeed, but not ad-
    mire[5] him.
How came he to thy hands?
DAW.                                    From sanctuary   40
At Bewley, near Southampton, regis-
    tered,
With these few followers, for persons
    privileged.
KING. I must not thank you, sir; you were
    to blame
To infringe the liberty of houses sacred.
Dare we be irreligious?
DAW.                                    Gracious lord,
They voluntarily resigned themselves
Without compulsion.
KING.                                    So? 'Twas very well;
'Twas very, very well.—Turn now thine
    eyes,
Young man, upon thyself and thy past
    actions.

[4] In respect to us, at our hands.
[5] Wonder at.

What revels in combustion through our
    kingdom                          50
A frenzy of aspiring youth hath danced,
Till, wanting breath, thy feet of pride
    have slipped
To break thy neck!
WAR.          But not my heart; my heart
Will mount till every drop of blood be
    frozen
By death's perpetual winter. If the sun
Of majesty be darkened, let the sun
Of life be hid from me in an eclipse
Lasting and universal. Sir, remember
There was a shooting in of light when
    Richmond,
Not aiming at a crown, retired, and
    gladly,                         60
For comfort to the Duke of Britain's [1]
    court.
Richard, who swayed the scepter, was re-
    puted
A tyrant then; yet then a dawning glim-
    mered
To some few wandering remnants, prom-
    ising day
When first they ventured on a frightful
    shore
At Milford Haven—
DAW.        Whither speeds his boldness?
Check his rude tongue, great sir.
KING.           O, let him range.
The player's on the stage still; 'tis his part;
A does but act.—What followed?
WAR.             Bosworth Field,
Where, at an instant, to the world's
    amazement,                 70
A morn to Richmond and a night to
    Richard
Appeared at once. The tale is soon
    applied:
Fate, which crowned these attempts
    when least assured,
Might have befriended others like re-
    solved.
KING. A pretty gallant! Thus your aunt
    of Burgundy,
Your    duchess-aunt,    informed    her
    nephew; so
The lesson, prompted and well conned,
    was molded
Into familiar dialogue, oft rehearsed,
Till, learnt by heart, 'tis now received for
    truth.

[1] Bretagne's.

WAR. Truth, in her pure simplicity, wants
    art                              80
To put a feignéd blush on. Scorn wears
    only
Such fashion as commends to gazers' eyes
Sad ulcerated novelty, far beneath
The sphere of majesty. In such a court
Wisdom and gravity are proper robes,
By which the sovereign is best distin-
    guished
From zanies [2] to his greatness.
KING.               Sirrah, shift
Your antic [3] pageantry, and now appear
In your own nature, or you'll taste the
    danger
Of fooling out of season.
WAR.              I expect  90
No less than what severity calls justice,
And politicians safety. Let such beg
As feed on alms, but, if there can be
    mercy
In a protested enemy, then may it
Descend to these poor creatures, whose
    engagements,
To th' bettering of their fortunes, have
    incurred
A loss of all. To them if any charity
Flow from some noble orator, in death
I owe the fee of thankfulness.
KING.            So brave!
What a bold knave is this!—Which of
    these rebels                   100
Has been the Mayor of Cork?
DAW.          This wise formality.
Kneel to tne king, 'e rascals!
KING.            Canst thou hope
A pardon where thy guilt is so apparent?
MAYOR. Under your good favors, as men
are men, they may err; for I confess, re-
spectively, in taking great parts, the one
side prevailing, the other side must go
down. Herein the point is clear, if the
proverb hold, that hanging goes by destiny,
that it is to little purpose to say this  [110
thing or that shall be thus or thus; for, as
the Fates will have it, so it must be; and
who can help it?
DAW. O, blockhead! Thou a privy-coun-
    selor?
Beg life, and cry aloud, "Heaven save
    King Henry!"
MAYOR. Every man knows what is best,
as it happens; for my own part, I believe it

[2] Clownish imitators.       [3] Fanciful, theatrical.

is true, if I be not deceived, that kings must
be kings and subjects subjects; but which
is which, you shall pardon me for that. [120
Whether we speak or hold our peace, all are
mortal; no man knows his end.

KING. We trifle time with follies.

OMNES.                              Mercy, mercy!

KING. Urswick, command the dukeling
and these fellows

To Digby, the lieftenant [1] of the Tower;
With safety let them be conveyed to
London.

It is our pleasure no uncivil outrage,

Taunts, or abuse be suffered to their
persons;

They shall meet fairer law than they deserve.

Time may restore their wits, whom vain
ambition                                    130

Hath many years distracted.

WAR.                            Noble thoughts
Meet freedom in captivity. The Tower?
Our childhood's dreadful nursery!

KING.                              No more.

URS. Come, come, you shall have leisure
to bethink 'e.

*Exit Ursw[ick] with Perkin and his [Follow-
ers].*

KING. Was ever so much impudence in
forgery?

The custom, sure, of being styled a king
Hath fastened in his thought that he is
such;

But we shall teach the lad another language.

'Tis good we have him fast.

DAW.                    The hangman's physic
Will purge this saucy humor.

KING.                              Very likely;  140
Yet we could temper[2] mercy with extremity,

Being not too far provoked.


*Enter Oxford, Katherine in her richest attire,
[Daliell,] Jane, and Attendants.*

OX.                          Great sir, be pleased,
With your accustomed grace to enter-
tain

The Princess Katherine Gordon.

KING.                          Oxford, herein
We must beshrew[3] thy knowledge of our
nature.

[1] Lieutenant.    [2] Blend.    [3] Deprecate.

A lady of her birth and virtues could not
Have found us so unfurnished of good
manners

As not, on notice given, to have met her
Half way in point of love.—Excuse, fair
cousin,

The oversight. O, fie! You may not
kneel;                                    150

'Tis most unfitting. First, vouchsafe this
welcome,

A welcome to your own, for you shall
find us

But guardian to your fortune and your
honors.

KATH. My fortunes and mine honors are
weak champions,

As both are now befriended, sir. However,

Both bow before your clemency.

KING.                              Our arms
Shall circle them from malice.—A sweet
lady!

Beauty incomparable!—Here lives majesty

At league with love.

KATH.            O, sir, I have a husband.

KING. We'll prove your father, husband,
friend, and servant.                      160

Prove what you wish to grant us.—
Lords, be careful

A patent presently be drawn for issuing

A thousand pounds from our exchequer
yearly

During our cousin's life.—Our queen
shall be

Your chief companion, our own court
your home,

Our subjects all your servants.

KATH.                    But my husband?

KING. [*To Daliell.*] By all descriptions,
you are noble Daliell.

Whose generous truth hath famed a rare
observance.

We thank 'e; 'tis a goodness gives addition

To every title boasted from your ancestry,                                    170

In all most worthy.

DAL.            Worthier than your praises,
Right princely sir, I need not glory in.

KING. Embrace him, lords.—[*To Kath-
erine.*] Whoever calls you mistress
Is lifted in our charge. A goodlier beauty
Mine eyes yet ne'er encountered.

KATH.                              Cruel misery
  Of fate! What rests[1] to hope for?
KING.                            Forward, lords,
  To London.—Fair, ere long I shall pre-
    sent 'e
  With a glad object, peace, and Huntley's
    blessing.                    *Exeunt omnes.*

[SCENA TERTIA.

*The Tower Hill, London.*]

*Enter Constable and Officers; Warbeck,*
*Urswick, and Lambert Simnel like a*
*falconer [, followed by a Mob]. A pair*
                      *of stocks.*

  CONST. Make room there! Keep off,
I require 'e; and none come within twelve
foot of his majesty's new stocks, upon
pain of displeasure.—Bring forward the
malefactors.—Friend, you must to this
gear[2]—no remedy.—Open the hole, and
in with his legs, just in the middle hole;
there, that hole.—[*Warbeck is put in the*
*stocks.*] Keep off, or I'll commit you all.
Shall not a man in authority be [10
obeyed?—So, so, there; 'tis as it should be.
Put on the padlock, and give me the key.—
Off, I say, keep off!
URS. Yet, Warbeck, clear thy conscience.
  Thou hast tasted
King Henry's mercy liberally; the law
Has forfeited thy life; an equal[3] jury
Have doomed thee to the gallows, twice,
  most wickedly,
Most desperately, hast thou escaped
  the Tower,
Inveigling to thy party with thy witch-
  craft
Young Edward, Earl of Warwick, son
  to Clarence,                              20
Whose head must pay the price of that
  attempt.
Poor gentleman, unhappy in his fate,
And ruined by thy cunning! So a mon-
  grel
May pluck the true stag down. Yet,
  yet confess
Thy parentage; for yet the king has
  mercy.
LAM. You would be Dick the Fourth;
  very likely!
Your pedigree is published; you are
  known

For Osbeck's son of Tournay, a loose
  runagate,
A landloper;[4] your father was a Jew,
Turned Christian merely to repair his
  miseries.                                30
Where's now your kingship?
WAR.                          Baited to my death?
  Intolerable cruelty! I laugh at
The Duke of Richmond's practice on
  my fortunes.
"Possession of a crown ne'er wanted
  heralds."
LAM. You will not know who I am?
URS.                          Lambert Simnel,
  Your predecessor in a dangerous uproar,
But, on submission, not alone received
To grace, but by the king vouchsafed
  his service.
LAM. I would be Earl of Warwick, toiled
  and ruffled
Against my master, leaped to catch the
  moon,                                    40
Vaunted my name Plantagenet, as you
  do;
An earl, forsooth, whenas in truth I
  was,
As you are, a mere rascal! Yet his maj-
  esty,
A prince composed of sweetness—heaven
  protect him!—
Forgave me all my villainies, reprived[5]
The sentence of a shameful end, ad-
  mitted
My surety[6] of obedience to his service;
And I am now his falconer, live plen-
  teously,
Eat from the king's purse, and enjoy
  the sweetness
Of liberty and favor, sleep securely.   50
And is not this, now, better than to
  buffet
The hangman's clutches, or to brave
  the cordage
Of a tough halter which will break your
  neck?
So, then, the gallant totters!—Prithee,
  Perkin,
Let my example lead thee; be no longer
A counterfeit. Confess and hope for
  pardon.
WAR. For pardon?    Hold, my heart-
  strings, whiles contempt

---

[1] Remains.    [2] Business.    [3] Impartial.

[4] Vagabond.                    [6] Accepted my oath.
[5] Reprieved.

Of injuries, in scorn, may bid defiance
To this base man's foul language!—
     Thou poor vermin,
How dar'st thou creep so near me? Thou
     an earl?                                    60
Why, thou enjoy'st as much of happi-
     ness
As all the swinge [1] of slight ambition
     flew at.
A dunghill was thy cradle. So a puddle,
By virtue of the sunbeams, breathes
     a vapor
To infect the purer air, which drops
     again
Into the muddy womb that first ex-
     haled it.
Bread and a slavish ease, with some as-
     surance
From the base beadle's whip, crowned
     all thy hopes.
But, sirrah, ran there in thy veins one
     drop                                        69
Of such a royal blood as flows in mine,
Thou wouldst not change condition to
     be second
In England's state, without the crown
     itself.
Coarse creatures are incapable of ex-
     cellence.
But let the world, as all to whom I am
This day a spectacle, to time deliver, [2]
And by tradition fix [3] posterity,
Without another chronicle than truth,
How constantly my resolution suffered
A martyrdom of majesty.
LAM.                              He's past
Recovery; a Bedlam cannot cure him.  80
URS. Away, inform the king of his be-
     havior.
LAM. Perkin, beware the rope!   The
     hangman's coming.
URS. If yet thou hast no pity of thy
     body,
     Pity thy soul!              *Exit Simnel.*

*Enter Katherine, Jane, Daliell, and Ox-
                                    ford.*

JANE.            Dear lady!
OX.                        Whither will 'e,
     Without respect of shame?
KATH.                   Forbear me, [4] sir,

---

[1] Sway.
[2] Proclaim.

And trouble not the current of my
     duty.—
O, my loved lord!   Can any scorn be
     yours
In which I have no interest?—Some
     kind hand
Lend me assistance that I may partake
Th' infliction of this penance.—My
     life's dearest,                             90
Forgive me. I have stayed too long from
     tendering
Attendance on reproach; yet bid me
     welcome.
WAR. Great miracle of constancy!   My
     miseries
Were never bankrout of their confi-
     dence
In worst afflictions, till this. Now I feel
     them.
Report and thy deserts, thou best of
     creatures,
Might to eternity have stood a pattern
For every virtuous wife without this
     conquest.
Thou hast outdone belief; yet may
     their ruin
In after-marriages be never pitied,   100
To whom thy story shall appear a fable!
Why wouldst thou prove so much un-
     kind to greatness
To glorify thy vows by such a servitude?
I cannot weep; but trust me, dear, my
     heart
Is liberal of passion.—Harry Richmond,
A woman's faith hath robbed thy fame
     of triumph!
OX. Sirrah, leave off your juggling, and
     tie up
The devil that ranges in your tongue.
URS.                       Thus witches,
Possessed, even [to] [5] their deaths de-
     luded, say
They have been wolves and dogs, and
     sailed in eggshells                        110
Over the sea, and rid on fiery dragons,
Passed in the air more than a thousand
     miles
All in a night. The enemy of mankind
Is powerful, but false; and falsehood
     confident.
OX. Remember, lady, who you are; come
     from
That impudent impostor.

---

[3] Assure.
[4] Let me alone.
[5] Supplied by Gifford-Dyce.

KATH.                              You abuse us,
    For, when the holy churchman joined
        our hands,
    Our vows were real then; the ceremony
    Was not in apparition,[1] but in act.—
    Be what these people term thee, I am
        certain                                    120
    Thou art my husband; no divorce in
        heaven
    Has been sued out between us; 'tis in-
        justice
    For any earthly power to divide us.
    Or we will live or let us die together.
    There is a cruel mercy.
WAR.                              Spite of tyranny
    We reign in our affections, blessed
        woman!
    Read in my destiny the wrack of honor;
    Point out, in my contempt of death, to
        memory
    Some miserable happiness, since herein,
    Even when I fell, I stood enthroned a
        monarch                                    130
    Of one chaste wife's troth, pure and
        uncorrupted.
    Fair angel of perfection, immortality
    Shall raise thy name up to an adora-
        tion,
    Court every rich opinion of true merit,
    And saint it in the calendar of Virtue,
    When I am turned into the selfsame
        dust
    Of which I was first formed.
OX.                              The lord ambassador
    Huntley, your father, madam, should
        a look on
    Your strange subjection in a gaze so
        public,
    Would blush on your behalf, and wish
        his country                                140
    Unleft for entertainment to such sorrow.
KATH. Why art thou angry, Oxford? I
        must be
    More peremptory in my duty. Sir,
    Impute it not unto immodesty
    That I presume to press you to[2] a
        legacy
    Before we part forever.
WAR.                              Let it be, then,
    My heart, the rich remains of all my
        fortunes.
KATH. Confirm it with a kiss, pray.
WAR. [Kissing her.]              O, with that

I wish to breathe my last! Upon thy
    lips,
Those equal twins of comeliness, I
    seal                                           150
The testament of honorable vows.
Whoever be that man that shall un-
    kiss
This sacred print next, may he prove
    more thrifty
In this world's just applause, not more
    desertful!
KATH. By this sweet pledge of both our
        souls, I swear
    To die a faithful widow to thy bed,
    Not to be forced or won. O, never,
        never!

*Enter Surrey, Dawbney, Huntley, and
                              Crawford.*

DAW. Free the condemnéd person;
        quickly free him!
    What has a yet confessed?
        [*Warbeck is released from the stocks.*]
URS.                              Nothing to purpose;
    But still a will be king.
SUR.                              Prepare your journey  160
    To a new kingdom, then.—Unhappy
        madam,
    Willfully foolish!—See, my lord am-
        bassador,
    Your lady daughter will not leave the
        counterfeit
    In this disgrace of fate.
HUNT.                              I never pointed[3]
    Thy marriage, girl; but yet, being mar-
        ried,
    Enjoy thy duty to a husband freely.
    The griefs are mine. I glory in thy con-
        stancy,
    And must not say I wished that I had
        missed
    Some partage in these trials of a patience.
KATH. You will forgive me, noble sir?
HUNT.                              Yes, yes;  170
    In every duty of a wife and daughter
    I dare not disavow thee. To your hus-
        band—
    For such you are, sir—I impart a fare-
        well
    Of manly pity. What your life has
        passed through,
    The dangers of your end will make ap-
        parent.

<hr>

[1] Appearance.                    [2] For.

[3] Appointed.

And I can add, for comfort to your sufferance,
No cordial but the wonder of your
frailty,
Which keeps so firm a station. We are
parted.

WAR. We are. A crown of peace renew
thy age,
Most honorable Huntley.—Worthy
Crawford,                                    180
We may embrace; I never thought thee
injury.

CRAW. Nor was I ever guilty of neglect
Which might procure such thought. I
take my leave, sir.

WAR. To you, Lord Daliell—what? Accept a sigh;
'Tis hearty and in earnest.

DAL.                              I want utterance.
My silence is my farewell.

KATH.                    O, O!

JANE.                                    Sweet madam,
What do you mean?—[To Daliell.] My
lord, your hand.

DAL.                              Dear lady,
Be pleased that I may wait [1] 'e to your
lodging.
                Exeunt Daliell, Katherine, Jane.

Enter Sheriff and Officers, Sketon, Astley,
Heron, and Mayor, with halters about
                                    their necks.

OX. Look 'e; behold your followers, appointed
To wait on 'e in death!

WAR.              Why, peers of England,    190
We'll lead 'em on courageously. I read
A triumph over tyranny upon
Their several foreheads. Faint not in
the moment
Of victory! Our ends, and Warwick's
head,
Innocent Warwick's head—for we are
prologue
But to his tragedy—conclude the wonder
Of Henry's fears; and then the glorious
race
Of fourteen kings, Plantagenets, de-
termines [2]
In this last issue male. Heaven be obeyed!
Impoverish time of its amazement,
friends,                                    200

And we will prove as trusty in our pay-
ments
As prodigal to nature in our debts.
Death? Pish! 'Tis but a sound; a name
of air;
A minute's storm, or not so much. To
tumble
From bed to bed, be massacred alive
By some physicians for a month or two,
In hope of freedom from a fever's tor-
ments,
Might stagger manhood. Here the pain
is past
Ere sensibly 'tis felt. Be men of spirit!
Spurn coward passion! So illustrious
mention                                    210
Shall blaze our names, and style us
kings o'er death.

DAW. Away, impostor beyond president!
No chronicle records his fellow.
        Ex[eunt] all Officers and Prisoners.

HUNT.                              I have
Not thoughts left; 'tis sufficient in such
cases
Just laws ought to proceed.

Enter King Henry, Durham, and Hialas.

KING.                    We are resolved.
Your business, noble lords, shall find
success
Such as your king importunes.

HUNT.              You are gracious.

KING. Perkin, we are informed, is armed
to die;
In that we'll honor him. Our lords shall
follow
To see the execution; and from hence  220
We gather this fit use:[4] that "public
states,
As our particular bodies, taste most
good
In health when purgéd of corrupted
blood."                    Exeunt omnes.
        FINIS.

EPILOGUE

Here has appeared, though in a several [3]
fashion,
The threats of majesty, the strength of
passion,
Hopes of an empire, change of fortunes—
all

---

[1] Attend.                    [2] Terminates.

[3] Separate.    [4] Draw this proper application.

What can to theaters of greatness fall,
Proving their weak foundations. Who
   will please,
Amongst such several sights, to censure [1]
   these
No births abortive, nor a bastard brood

[1] Judge.

(Shame to a parentage or fosterhood),
May warrant,[2] by their loves, all just
   excuses,[3]                                   9
And often find a welcome to the Muses.

FINIS.

[2] Authorize, sanction. [3] Deserved defenses(?).

# JAMES SHIRLEY

James Shirley has been called "the last of the Elizabethans" partly because he was actually the last of the significant dramatists of his age to be born (in 1596, in London) and the last to die (in 1666, from exposure in the Great Fire). But even more, his work bears an extremely close and interesting relationship to that of his fellows, while at the same time—especially in comedy—it anticipates much of the material and characters of the Restoration. John Dryden, the greatest of the Restoration critics and Charles II's poet laureate, however, was as unfair to Shirley as he had been to Thomas Heywood when in his attempt to dispose of his enemy Thomas Shadwell, in the guise of "Mac-Flecknoe," he had written:

> Heywood and Shirley were but types of thee,
> Thou last great prophet of tautology.

Actually, tautology was not one of Shirley's greatest faults, though in some of his plays, such as *The Cardinal*, he did compose a good many tortured and often obscure sentences, because of his fondness for ellipses.

Since the publication of Arthur H. Nixon's *James Shirley, Dramatist/A Biographical and Critical Study* (Columbia University Press, 1915), superseding the introduction to Alexander Dyce's and William Gifford's edition of *The Dramatic Works and Poems* in 1833 and P. Nissen's *James Shirley* (Hamburg, 1901), many new facts in Shirley's biography have been discovered by various scholars.

He was born in or near the parish of St. Mary Woolchurch, London (later absorbed into the parish of St. Mary Woolnoth, Walbrook), probably on September 13, 1596. There have been various conjectures about his family—that he was descended from the Shirleys of Sussex or Warwickshire, and that he was the son of the very minor dramatist, Henry Shirley. Sir Adolphus W. Ward in the *Dictionary of National Biography* stated that he was not of "gentle blood," but on the title pages of many of his plays he claimed to be "James Shirley, Gent."

On October 4, 1608, he was enrolled in the famous Merchant Taylors' School, and in 1612 was mentioned in the records as a "monitor." From there he proceeded to St. John's College, Oxford, of which Dr. William Laud (later to become the notorious Archbishop Laud of the Star Chamber) had recently been appointed president. According to the story of Anthony à Wood, Shirley was planning at this time to enter the Anglican ministry, but Laud, who "had a very great affection for him, especially for the pregnant parts that were visible in him," nevertheless discouraged him from his intention, because the boy had a large mole on his left cheek, a deformity which Laud thought would disqualify him from becoming a successful clergyman. This story receives some confirmation from the fact that the two extant portraits of Shirley show this mole, and also depict him with a sparse mustache, long curls covered up with a skull cap, and a large, sharp nose. But even if Laud thought Shirley's physical appearance made him unfit to enter the church, the young man refused to take his advice, since not only did Wood state that he eventually took Holy Orders, but Albert C. Baugh has found a writ in legal Latin issued by Shirley on November 10, 1623, in which he describes and signs himself as a "presbyter." The records of the London bishopric, however, do not record his ordination there, and he never held a parish (Baugh, "Further

951

Facts about John Shirley," *RES*, 1931, supplementing "Some New Facts about Shirley," *MLR*, 1922).

Before this, and perhaps because of Laud's opposition, Shirley dropped out of college after a very short stay. In a Chancery suit in which he was a witness he deposed that for two of the two and three-quarters years in question (June 1612 to April 1615), a period which Gerald E. Bentley in *The Jacobean and Caroline Stage* had called "a puzzling gap" in our knowledge of Shirley's career, he was a "servant" to a London scrivener named Thomas Frith (J. P. Feil, "James Shirley's Years of Service," *RES*, 1957). When Shirley was ready to resume his education, he did so at Catharine Hall, Cambridge, where he proceeded B.A. before 1618 and soon after 1619 received his M.A.

Shirley started his professional career as a teacher in the St. Albans grammar school, and on June 1, 1618, as Baugh discovered in the marriage licenses of the town, married Elizabeth Gilmet, probably the daughter of Richard Gilmet, the mayor. He must have made good, either through his marriage or through his teaching ability (although the *Victoria History of the County of Hertfordshire* conjectured, without evidence, that he was "negligent and unworthy"), since on November 2 of the same year he was promised the mastership of the same school when a vacancy occurred, as it did in January 1621. But on July 1, 1624, he gave up his position because he did as Ben Jonson and other dramatists had done and, according to Wood, was converted to Roman Catholicism, a conversion confirmed by two recent scraps of evidence (A. M. Taylor, "John Shirley and 'Mr. Vincent Cane,' the Franciscan," *NQ*, 1960; Marvin Morillo, " 'Frier Shirley': John Shirley and *Mercurius Britannicus*," *ibid.*). Perhaps these religious views had something to do with his later appointment as one of the Valets of the Chamber and a "Servant of Her Majesty," the Roman Catholic Queen Henrietta Maria (Morillo, "Shirley's 'Preferment' and the Court of Charles I," *Studies in English Literature, 1500–1900*, 1961). But even before his resignation of his teaching position he had apparently moved his family to London, since on February 26, 1624, his son Mathias was christened at St. Giles's, Cripplegate.

About this time Shirley took up residence at Gray's Inn, where he absorbed some knowledge of the law, as shown in his plays, but where primarily it appears he intended to "set up for a playmaker," as Wood phrased it. He remained closely enough associated with Gray's Inn to compose and produce one of the most elaborate and expensive of all the masques given by the Inns of Court, *The Triumph of Peace*, in 1634. His first play, the imitative *Love Tricks, or The School of Compliment*, apparently acted in 1625 before the death of King James, was a composite of the comedy of manners, the tragicomedy, and the pastoral, and started him off on a prolific career as writer, first for the Queen's Men and then for the King's. He quickly found his forte in the comedy of manners, with successes like *The Wedding* (1626), *The Witty Fair One* (1628), three plays in the year 1632, *The Changes, or Love in a Maze, Hyde Park*, and *The Ball* (which got him into trouble because it introduced several well-known court figures, thinly disguised), and *The Gamester* (1633). *The Lady of Pleasure* (1635) is commonly regarded as the best of this genre. He also tried his hand a few times at tragedy, of which *The Traitor* (licensed 1631; printed 1635) and *The Cardinal* (licensed 1641; printed 1653) are the best examples. Usually, unlike so many of the playwrights of the time, Shirley worked alone, but in two or three instances he is supposed to have had the assistance of the septuagenarian George Chapman.

Besides his active role in the theater in England, Shirley played an important part in establishing the theater in Ireland. In 1635, while Thomas Wentworth, the Earl of Strafford, was Lord Deputy and maintained an almost regal court in Dublin, John Ogilby (the later translator of Homer and Virgil) was appointed his Master of the Revels, and together they opened the first Irish playhouse, in Werburgh Street. In 1636, when the London theaters were closed for many months on account of the plague, the Irish Earl of Kildare (one of Shirley's patrons) persuaded his friend to go to Ireland to write for the new theater and bring with him a company of actors and musicians enticed away from the London companies. At least four of Shirley's plays, including

*St. Patrick for Ireland,* were written there. Allan H. Stevenson and Albert H. Carter have followed his Irish activities and the dates of his arrival and permanent return to England without always quite agreeing on the details (Stevenson, "James Shirley and the Actors in the First Irish Theater," *MP,* 1942; "Shirley's Years in Ireland," *RES,* 1944; "Shirley's Dedications and the Date of His Return to England," *MLN,* 1946; Carter, "Shirley's Return to London in 1639–40," *MLN,* 1943).

While his headquarters remained in Dublin, Shirley recrossed the Irish Sea once or twice to keep in touch with his affairs in London, where his plays continued to be produced at the Blackfriars, and where he had various problems to solve with his publishers, Crooke and Cooke (Stevenson, "Shirley's Publishers: The Partnership of Crooke and Cooke," *Library,* 1945). But this relatively quiet situation lasted for only two years after his return in 1640, since in 1642 all the theaters were closed by Parliament on the outbreak of the civil war, which marked the end of his theatrical career. He entered the royal service and seems to have taken part in the unsuccessful campaigns of another of his patrons, William Cavendish, the Earl (later the Duke) of Newcastle, who had literary ambitions and some comic ability himself, and whom, according to Wood, Shirley had helped in writing his plays, published after Newcastle had withdrawn from the fighting and retired to the Continent. From 1644 to 1649 Shirley returned to his old profession of teaching, and kept a school in Whitefriars, for which he wrote a textbook on Latin and another on English grammar. He published a volume of his poems in 1646, and in the next year helped to bring out the first folio collection of the plays of Beaumont and Fletcher "& Co.," which he provided with his own preface. But he was nevertheless reduced to doing hack work for his old colleague John Ogilby, on his uninspired translations of Homer and Virgil. For a time he was also helped by the patronage of the wealthy classical scholar, Thomas Stanley.

When the theaters reopened in 1660, Shirley kept his resolve not to return actively to the stage, as expressed in the preface to his little privately produced play, *Honoria and Mammon,* in 1659. But several of his old plays were revived from time to time. He was living with his second wife, Francis, in a house near Fleet Street, in the parish of St. Giles's in the Fields, Middlesex, when the Great Fire destroyed most of London in 1666. Wood described the couple's end two months later with laconic pathos when he wrote "being in a manner overcome with affrightments, disconsolations, and other miseries occasion'd by that fire and their losses, they both died within the compass of a natural day: whereupon their bodies were buried in one grave in the yard belonging to the said Church of St. Giles's, on the 29th of Octob. in sixteen hundred sixty and six." Shirley's will mentions three surviving sons and two daughters, one a widow. One of these sons was butler of Furnival's Inn, a law school, in Wood's time, and another may have been the "Mr. Sherly" who, according to prompter Downes's *Roscius Anglicanus,* joined Killigrew's company after it had moved to Drury Lane in 1663.

Shirley seems to have been a modest and amiable man, who had no real enemies, and kindly praised the work of others as they praised his. He had sound moral principles of right and wrong, which he almost invariably applied in the endings of his plays. It was both an advantage and a handicap to him to have had before him the examples of his great predecessors; in fact, the playwright was so steeped in his study of these men that scarcely one of his scenes but has its parallels in plays which had gone before (see Robert S. Forsythe, *The Relations of Shirley's Plays to the Elizabethan Drama,* Columbia University Press, 1914). At the same time, however, so great was his ingenuity and dramatic sense that out of this material he was able to construct plays of considerable effectiveness and even originality—plays which in general read with naturalness and ease even though they fall very short in the usual Elizabethan poetry.

## THE LADY OF PLEASURE

*The Lady of Pleasure,* acted by the Queen's Men at the private theater in Drury Lane in 1635 and printed in 1637, is a first-rate example of these generalizations. Forsythe devotes some eight pages to examining its echoes, analogues, and parallels found in other plays, including Shirley's own. But at the same time it has no source as a whole. Very little has been written about it, perhaps because it presents no particular problems in the comic satire of its main plot on the socially ambitious wife who is cured of her follies by an understanding husband who outdoes her by pretending to follow similar courses. The underplot offers a picture of what Schelling, in his *Elizabethan Drama*, described as "the regeneration of a noble roué by the wit and charms of a virtuous woman." W. A. Neilson, in his chapter in the *Cambridge History of English Literature*, agreed with Schelling, but added: "The satire against rakish men about town is scathing enough; but, like many satirists, Shirley proves unable to touch pitch without defiling himself." Moody Prior, in *The Language of Tragedy*, after discussing Shirley's chief tragedy, *The Cardinal*, went somewhat out of his self-chosen path to show how serious comedies such as *The Lady of Pleasure* were beginning to supplant original tragedy in the popular taste. He remarked: "The play is in verse, but clearly verse remains as a survival of a tradition, for the diction, the idiom, the rhythms are those of everyday speech; no other treatment would have been suited to the exacting verisimilitude of the rest of the play;" and he ended by speculating, somewhat rashly: "Had not the closing of the theaters checked normal development in the drama, it is not unlikely that realistic social drama would have come into full flower some two centuries before it came into being as a new and vitalizing force in the theater during the closing years of the nineteenth century."

Surprisingly, *The Lady of Pleasure* seems to have had no stage history in its original form after its own day. However, as Forsythe points out, Mrs. Aphra Behn seems to to have borrowed from parts of it in *The Lucky Chance, or An Alderman's Bargain* (1687). William Taverner also borrowed more liberally from it in *The Artful Husband* (1717), which itself was revived in 1746 as a benefit for the popular Peg Woffington, and then itself was altered by the elder William Macready as *The Bank Note, or Lessons for Ladies* in 1795. This version became quite popular and was given in New York in 1797. *Masquerade*, by Charles Johnson, played at the Drury Lane in 1718, is also based on Shirley's play. But the Lady of Pleasure herself was unable to hold the stage in her own person.

The basis of the present text is a copy of the first quarto (1637) in the Newberry Library in Chicago.

# THE LADY OF PLEASURE[1]

## BY

## JAMES SHIRLEY

### PERSONS OF THE COMEDY

LORD.
SIR THOMAS BORNWELL.
SIR WILLIAM SCENTLOVE.
MR.[2] ALEX[ANDER] KICKSHAW.
MR. JOHN LITTLEWORTH.
MR. HAIRCUT [, a barber].
MR. FREDERICK [, Lady Bornwell's nephew].
STEWARD to the Lady Aretina.
STEWARD to the Lady Celestina.

SECRETARY [to Lord].
SERVANTS, etc.

ARETINA, Sir Thomas Bornwell's lady.
CELESTINA, a young widow.
ISABELLA [NOVICE] } [Kinswomen of Ce-
MARIANA [NOVICE] } lestina].
MADAM DECOY [, a procuress].
[GENTLEWOMAN.]

SCENE: The Strand.

[TIME: Contemporary.][3]

THE FIRST ACT. [SCENE i.

*A room in Bornwell's house.*]

*Enter Aretina and her Steward.*

STEW. Be patient, madam; you may have
    your pleasure.
ARE. 'Tis that I came to town for.  I
    would not
Endure again the country conversation,[4]
To be the lady of six shires!  The men,
So near the primitive making they re-
    tain
A sense of nothing but the earth, their
    brains
And barren heads standing as much in
    want
Of plowing as their ground!  To hear
    a fellow
Make himself merry and his horse, with
    whistling
"Sellinger's Round"![5]  To observe with
    what solemnity    10

They keep their wakes,[6] and throw for
    pewter candlesticks!
How they become the morris,[7] with
    whose bells
They ring all in to Whitsun ales,[8] and
    sweat
Through twenty scarfs and napkins,
    till the hobbyhorse
Tire, and the Maid Marian, dissolved
    to a jelly,
Be kept for spoon meat![9]
STEW. These, with your pardon, are no
    argument
To make the country life appear so
    hateful,
At least to your particular,[10] who en-
    joyed
A blessing in that calm, would you be
    pleased    20
To think so, and the pleasure of a kingdom.
While your own will commanded what
    should move
Delights, your husband's love and power
    joined

[1] The title continues: "A Comedy, As It Was Acted by Her Majesty's Servants at the Private House in Drury Lane."
[2] I.e., Master.
[3] Here follows a brief dedication to Richard, Lord Lovelace of Hurley.
[4] Association.
[5] An old-fashioned country dance tune.
[6] Annual parish festivals.
[7] A dance in which the hobbyhorse and Maid Marian were characters.
[8] Parish festivals held at Whitsuntide.
[9] Liquid food eaten with a spoon.
[10] In your case.

955

To give your life more harmony. You
  lived there
Secure and innocent, beloved of all,
Praised for your hospitality, and prayed
  for;
You might be envied, but malice knew
Not where you dwelt. I would not
  prophesy,
But leave to your own apprehension
What may succeed your change.
ARE.           You do imagine,  30
  No doubt, you have talked wisely, and
    confuted
  London past all defense. Your master
    should
  Do well to send you back into the coun-
    try,
  With title of superintendent-baily.[1]
STEW.            How, madam!
ARE. Even so, sir.
STEW.           I am a gentleman,
  Though now your servant.[2]
ARE.          A country gentleman,
  By your affection to converse with stub-
    ble.
  His tenants will advance your wit, and
    plump it so
  With beef and bag pudding!
STEW.    You may say your pleasure;
  It becomes not me dispute.
ARE.        Complain to the  40
  Lord of the soil, your master.
STEW.         Y' are a woman
  Of an ungoverned passion, and I pity
  you.

*Enter Sir Thomas Bornwell.*

BORN. How now![3] What's the matter?
STEW.         Nothing, sir. [*Exit.*]
BORN. Angry, sweetheart?
ARE.       I am angry with myself,
  To be so miserably restrained in things
  Wherein it doth concern your love and
    honor
  To see me satisfied.
BORN.         In what, Aretina?
  Dost thou accuse me? Have I not
    obeyed

All thy desires?   **Against** mine own
  opinion
Quitted the country, and removed the
  hope     50
Of our return, by sale of that fair lord-
  ship [4]
We lived in? Changed a calm and re-
  tire[d] life
For this wild town, composed of noise
  and charge? [5]
ARE. What charge more than is neces-
  sary for
A lady of my birth and education?
BORN. I am not ignorant how much no-
  bility
Flows in your blood—your kinsmen great
  and powerful
I' th' state; but with this lose not your
  memory
Of being my wife. I shall be studious,
Madam, to give the dignity of your
  birth     60
All the best ornaments which become
  my fortune,
But would not flatter it to ruin both,
And be the fable of the town, to teach
Other men loss of wit by mine, employed
To serve your vast expenses.
ARE.         Am I then
  Brought in the balance? So, sir!
BORN.      Though you weigh
  Me in a partial [6] scale, my heart is
    honest,
And must take liberty to think you have
Obeyed no modest counsel, to effect,[7]
Nay, study, ways of pride and costly
  ceremony:     70
Your change of gaudy furniture, and
  pictures
Of this Italian master and that Dutch-
  man's;
Your mighty looking-glasses, like ar-
  tillery,
Brought home [8] on engines; the super-
  fluous plate,
Antique and novel; vanities of tires; [9]
Fourscore-pound suppers for my lord,
  your kinsman,
Banquets for tother [10] lady aunt, and
  cousins,

---

[1] Bailiff.
[2] Here and in several other passages the line
division has been somewhat regularized, although
much of the original meter is rather rough.
[3] Gifford-Dyce's reading. Original reads *how.*

[4] Estate
[5] Expense.
[6] Prejudiced.
[7] Affect, desire.
[8] Gifford-Dyce's reading. Original reads *whom.*
[9] Headdresses.
[10] The other.

And perfumes that exceed all; train of servants
To stifle us at home and show abroad
More motley than the French or the Venetian,    80
About your coach, whose rude postillion
Must pester[1] every narrow lane, till passengers[2]
And tradesmen curse your choking up their stalls,
And common cries pursue your ladyship,
For hind'ring o' their market.
ARE.       Have you done, sir?
BORN. I could accuse the gaiety of your wardrobe
And prodigal embroideries,[3] under which
Rich satins, plushes, cloth of silver, dare
Not show their own complexions; your jewels,
Able to burn out the spectators' eyes,   90
And show like bonefires[4] on you by the tapers.
Something might here be spared, with safety[5] of
Your birth and honor, since the truest wealth
Shines from the soul, and draws up just admirers.
I could urge something more.
ARE.       Pray do; I like
Your homily of thrift.
BORN.       I could wish, madam,
You would not game so much.
ARE.       A gamester[6] too?
BORN. But are not come to that acquaintance[7] yet
Should teach you skill enough to raise your profit.
You look not through the subtilty of cards    100
And mysteries of dice, nor can you save
Charge with the box,[8] buy petticoats and pearls,
And keep your family by the precious income.

Nor do I wish you should. My poorest servant
Shall not upbraid my tables nor his hire,
Purchased beneath my honor. You make play
Not a pastime but a tyranny, and vex
Yourself and my estate by 't.
ARE.       Good! Proceed.
BORN. Another game you have, which consumes more
Your fame than purse—your revels in the night,    110
Your meetings called the "Ball,"[9] to which appear,
As to the Court of Pleasure, all your gallants
And ladies, thither bound by a subpœna
Of Venus, and small Cupid's high displeasure;
'Tis but the Family of Love[10] translated
Into more costly sin! There was a play on 't,
And, had the poet not been bribed to a modest
Expression of your antic gambols in 't,
Some darks[11] had been discovered, and the deeds too.
In time he may repent, and make some blush    120
To see the second part danced on the stage.
My thoughts acquit you for dishonoring me
By any foul act; but the virtuous know
'Tis not enough to clear ourselves, but the
Suspicions of our shame.
ARE.       Have you concluded
Your lecture?
BORN.       I ha' done; and, howsoever
My language may appear to you, it carries
No other than my fair and just intent
To your delights, without curb to their modest[12]
And noble freedom.
ARE.       I'll not be so tedious    130
In my reply, but, without art or elegance,

[1] Obstruct.
[2] Passers-by.
[3] Embroideries.
[4] Bonfires.
[5] Gifford-Dyce's reading. Original reads *which safely*.    [6] Shirley wrote a play on this subject.
[7] Emended by Gifford-Dyce. Original reads *repentance*.
[8] Dice box.
[9] The newly invented subscription dance, upon which Shirley wrote a play.
[10] A religious sect, object of scandalous charges; also the title of a play by Middleton.
[11] Secrets.    [12] Moderate.

Assure you I keep still my first opinion;
And, though you veil your avaricious
  meaning
With handsome names of modesty and
  thrift,
I find you would intrench and wound
  the liberty
I was born with. Were my desires un-
  privileged
By example, while my judgment thought
  'em fit,
You ought not to oppose; but, when
  the practice
And tract [1] of every honorable lady  139
Authorize me, I take it great injustice
To have my pleasures circumscribed
  and taught me.
A narrow-minded husband is a thief
To his own fame,[2] and his preferment
  too;
He shuts his parts and fortunes from
  the world,
While, from the popular vote and knowl-
  edge, men
Rise to employment in the state.
BORN.              I have
No great ambition to buy preferment
At so dear rate.
ARE.        Nor I to sell my honor
By living poor and sparingly. I was not
Bred in that ebb of fortune, and my
  fate                     150
Shall not compel me to 't.
BORN.           I know not,
Madam; but you pursue these ways—
ARE.           What ways?
BORN. In the strict sense of honesty,[3] I
  dare
Make oath they are innocent.
ARE.         Do not divert,
By busy troubling of your brain, those
  thoughts
That should preserve 'em.
BORN.     How was that?
ARE.          'Tis English.
BORN. But carries some unkind sense.

*Enter Madam Decoy.*

DEC. Good morrow, my sweet madam.
ARE.        Decoy, welcome!
This visit is a favor.
DEC.       Alas, sweet madam,
I cannot stay. I came but to present  160

My service to your ladyship; I could
  not
Pass by your door but I must take the
  boldness
To tender my respects.
ARE.      You oblige me, madam;
But I must not dispense so with your
  absence.
DEC. Alas, the coach, madam, stays for
  me at the door.
ARE. Thou sha't command mine; prithee,
  sweet Decoy—
DEC. I would wait on you, madam, but
  I have many
Visits to make this morning; I beseech—
ARE. So you will promise to dine with
  me.
DEC.             I shall
Present a guest.
ARE.      Why, then good morrow,
  madam.                170
DEC. A happy day shine on your ladyship!
                           *Exit.*

*Enter Steward.*

ARE. What's your news, sir?
STEW.      Madam, two gentlemen.
ARE. What gentlemen? Have they no
  names?
STEW.     They are
The gentleman with his own head of
  hair,
Whom you commended for his horse-
  ship
In Hyde Park, and becoming the saddle,
The tother day.
ARE.       What circumstance is this
To know him by?
STEW.    His name's at my tongue's end—
He liked the fashion of your pearl chain,
  madam,
And borrowed it for his jeweler to
  take                 180
A copy by it.
BORN. [*Aside.*]    What cheating gallant's
  this?
STEW. That never walks without a lady's
  busk,[4]
And plays with fans—Mr. Alexander
  Kickshaw—
I thought I should remember him.
ARE.        What's the other?
STEW. What an unlucky memory I have:

[1] Course of action.  [2] Reputation.  [3] Chastity.
[4] Corset.

The gallant that still [1] danceth in the street,
And wears a gross of ribbon in his hat;
That carries oringado [2] in his pocket,
And sugarplums to sweeten his discourse;                                    189
That studies compliment, defies all wit
On black, [3] and censures plays that are not bawdy—
Mr. John Littleworth.

ARE.                    They are welcome; but
Pray, entertain them a small time, lest I
Be unprovided.

BORN.                    Did they ask for me?
STEW. No, sir.

BORN.        It matters not; they must be welcome.

ARE. Fie! How's this hair disordered?
Here's a curl
Straddle[s] [4] most impiously. I must to my closet. [5]                    Exit.

BORN. Wait on 'em; my lady will return again.—                    [Exit Steward.]
I have to such a height fulfilled her humor,
All application's [6] dangerous. These gallants                    200
Must be received, or she will fall into
A tempest, and the house be shook with names
Of all her kindred. 'Tis a servitude
I may in time shake off.

Enter Alexander [Kickshaw] and Littleworth.

AL. }
LIT. }                    Save you, Sir Thomas!
BORN. Save you, gentlemen!
AL.                    I kiss your hand.
BORN. What day [7] is it abroad?
LIT. The morning rises from your lady's eye;
If she look clear, we take the happy omen
Of a fair day.
BORN.                    She'll instantly appear,
To the discredit of your compliment;    210
But you express your wit thus.
AL.                    And you, modesty,
Not to affect [8] the praises of your own.

[1] Always.        [2] Candied orange peel.
[3] In black, in print.
[4] Supplied by Gifford-Dyce.        [5] Chamber.
[6] I.e., all pleading to be reasonable is.
[7] Weather.        [8] Appear to be pleased with.

BORN. Leaving this subject, what game's now on foot?
What exercise carries the general vote? [9]
O' th' town now, nothing moves without your knowledge.
AL. The cocking [10] now has all the noise; I'll have
A hundred pieces of one battle. O,
These birds of Mars!
LIT.                    Venus is Mars his bird too.
AL. Why, and the pretty doves are Venus's,
To show that kisses draw the chariot. 220
LIT. I am for that skirmish.
BORN.                    When shall we have
More booths and bagpipes upon Banstead Downs?
No mighty race is expected?—But my lady
Returns!

Enter Aretina.

ARE.        Fair morning to you, gentlemen!
You went not late to bed by your early visit.
You do me honor.
AL.                    It becomes our service.
ARE. What news abroad? You hold precious intelligence.
LIT. All tongues are so much busy with your praise
They have not time to frame other discourse.
Will please you, madam, taste a sugarplum?                    230
BORN. What does the goldsmith think the pearl is worth
You borrowed of my lady?
AL.                    'Tis a rich one.
BORN. She has many other toys, whose fashion you
Will like extremely. You have no intention
To buy any of her jewels?
AL.                    Understand me—
BORN. You had rather sell, perhaps. But, leaving this,
I hope you'll dine with us.
AL.                    I came a-purpose.
ARE. And where were you last night?
AL.                    I, madam? Where
I slept not; it had been sin, where so much

[9] Approval.        [10] Cockfighting.

Delight and beauty was to keep me wak-
ing. 240
There is a lady, madam, will be worth
Your free society; my conversation
Ne'er knew so elegant and brave [1] a
soul,
With most incomparable flesh and blood,
So spirited, so courtly, speaks the lan-
guages,
Sings, dances, plays o' th' lute to ad-
miration,
Is fair and paints not, games too, keeps
a table,
And talks most witty satire, has a wit
Of a clean [2] Mercury—
LIT.  Is she married?
AL.  No. 249
ARE. A virgin?
AL.  Neither.
LIT.  What! A widow? Something
Of this wide commendation might have
been
Excused. This such a prodigy?
AL.  Repent,
Before I name her. She did never see
Yet full sixteen, an age, in the opinion
Of wise men, not contemptible. She
has
Mourned out her year, too, for the
honest knight
That had compassion of her youth, and
died
So timely. Such a widow is not com-
mon;
And now she shines more fresh and
tempting
Than any natural virgin.
ARE.  What's her name? 260
AL. She was christened Celestina; by her
husband,
The Lady Bellamour. This ring was
hers.
BORN. You borrowed it to copy out the
posy.[3]
AL. Are they not pretty rubies? 'Twas
a grace
She was pleased to show me, that I
might have one
Made of the same fashion, for I love
All pretty forms.
ARE.  And is she glorious?
AL. She is full of jewels, madam; but I am

[1] Fine.
[2] Veritable.
[3] Inscription in a ring.

Most taken with the bravery [4] of her
mind,
Although her garments have all grace
and ornament. 270
ARE. You have been high in praises.
AL.  I come short;
No flattery can reach her.
BORN. [Aside.]  Now my lady
Is troubled, as she feared to be eclipsed;
This news will cost me somewhat.
ARE.  You deserve
Her favor, for this noble character.
AL. And I possess it, by my star's benevo-
lence.
ARE. You must bring us acquainted.
BORN.  I pray, do, sir;
I long to see her too.—Madam, I have
Thought upon 't, and corrected my
opinion.
Pursue what ways of pleasure your
desires 280
Incline you to, not only with my state,
But with my person; I will follow
you.
I see the folly of my thrift, and will
Repent in sack and prodigality,
To your own heart's content.
ARE.  But do not mock.
BORN. Take me to your embraces, gen-
tlemen,
And tutor me.
LIT.  And will you kiss the ladies?
BORN. And sing and dance. I long to see
this beauty.
I would fain lose a hundred pounds at
dice now.
Thou sha't have another gown and petti-
coat 290
Tomorrow. Will you sell my running
horses?
We have no Greek wine in the house, I
think;
Pray, send one of our footmen to the
merchant,
And throw the hogsheads of March-
beer [5] into
The kennel,[6] to make room for sacks and
claret.
What think you to be drunk yet before
dinner?
We will have constant music, and maintain

[4] Finery, excellence.
[5] Bock beer.
[6] Channel, gutter.

Them and their fiddles in fantastic
liveries;
I'll tune my voice to catches. I must
have
My dining room enlarged, to invite am-
bassadors.                                        300
We'll feast the parish in the fields, and
teach
The military men new discipline,
Who shall charge all their new artillery
With oranges and lemonds,[1] boy, to play
All dinner upon our capons.
AL.                              He's exalted!
BORN. I will do anything to please my
lady—
Let that suffice—and kiss o' th' same
condition.
I am converted; do not you dispute,
But patiently allow the miracle.

*Enter Servant.*

ARE. I am glad to hear you, sir, in so good
tune.                                             310
SER. Madam, the painter.
ARE.                     I am to sit this morning.
BORN. Do, while I give new directions to
my steward.
AL. With your favor, we'll wait on you;
sitting's but
A melancholy exercise without
Some company to discourse.
ARE.                          It does conclude
A lady's morning work. We rise, make
fine,
Sit for our picture, and 'tis time to dine.
LIT. Praying's forgot.
AL.               'Tis out of fashion.  *Exeunt.*

[SCENE ii.

*A room in Celestina's house.*]

*Enter Celestina and her Steward.*

CEL. Fie, what an air this room has!
STEW.                        'Tis perfumed.
CEL. With some cheap stuff. Is it your
wisdom's thrift
To infect my nostrils thus? Or is 't to
favor
The gout in your worship's hand, you are
afraid
To exercise your pen in your account
book?

Or do you doubt my credit to discharge
Your bills?
STEW. Madam, I hope you have not
found
My duty, with the guilt of sloth or
jealousy,
Unapt to your command.
CEL.                    You can extenuate
Your faults with language, sir; but I
expect                                            10
To be obeyed. What hangings have we
here?
STEW. They are arras, madam.
CEL.                    Impudence! I know 't.
I will have fresher and more rich, not
wrought
With faces that may scandalize a Chris-
tian,
With Jewish stories stuffed with corn and
camels.
You had best wrap all my chambers in
wild Irish,
And make a nursery of monsters here,
To fright the ladies comes to visit me.
STEW. Madam, I hope—
CEL.            I say I will have other,  19
Good Master Steward, of a finer loom—
Some silk and silver, if your worship
please
To let me be at so much cost. I'll have
Stories to fit the seasons of the year,
And change as often as I please.
STEW.                    You shall, madam.
CEL. I am bound to your consent, for-
sooth! And is
My coach brought home?
STEW.            This morning I expect it.
CEL. The inside, as I gave direction,
Of crimson plush?
STEW.            Of crimson camel plush.
CEL. Ten thousand moths consume 't!
Shall I ride through
The streets in penance, wrapped up
round in haircloth?                               30
Sell 't to an alderman; 'twill serve his
wife
To go a-feasting to their country house,
Or fetch a merchant's nurse child, and
come home
Laden with fruit and cheesecakes. I
despise it!
STEW. The nails adorn it, madam, set in
method
And pretty forms.

CEL. But single gilt, I warrant.
STEW. No, madam.
CEL. Another solecism! O, fie!
This fellow will bring me to a consumption
With fretting at his ignorance. Some lady
Had rather never pray than go to church in 't. 40
The nails not double gilt? To market wo't? [1]
Twill hackney out to Mile End, or convey
Your city tumblers [2] to be drunk with cream
And prunes at Islington.
STEW. Good madam, hear me.
CEL. I'll rather be beholding [3] to my aunt,
The countess, for her mourning coach than be
Disparaged so. Shall any juggling tradesman
Be at charge to shoe his running horse with gold,
And shall my coach nails be but single gilt?
How dare these knaves abuse me so?
STEW. Vouchsafe 50
To hear me speak.
CEL. Is my sedan yet finished,
And liveries for my men-mules, [4] according
As I gave charge?
STEW. Yes, madam, it is finished,
But without tilting-plumes [5] at the four corners;
The scarlet's pure, but not embroidéred.
CEL. What mischief were it to your conscience
Were my coach lined with tissue, [6] and my harness
Covered with needlework? If my sedan
Had all the story of the prodigal
Embroidered with pearl?
STEW. Alas, good madam, 60
I know 'tis your own cost; I am but your steward,
And would discharge my duty the best way.
You have been pleased to hear me; 'tis not for

My profit that I manage your estate
And save expense, but for your honor, madam.
CEL. How, sir, my honor?
STEW. Though you hear it not,
Men's tongues are liberal [7] in your character,
Since you began to live thus high. I know
Your fame is precious to you.
CEL. I were best
Make you my governor, audacious varlet! 70
How dare you interpose your doting counsel?
Mind your affairs with more obedience,
Or I shall ease you of an office, sir.
Must I be limited to please your honor,
Or, for the vulgar breath, confine my pleasures?
I will pursue 'em in what shapes I fancy,
Here and abroad; my entertainments shall
Be oft'ner and more rich. Who shall control me?
I live i' th' Strand, whither few ladies come
To live, and purchase more than fame. I will 80
Be hospitable then, and spare no cost
That may engage all generous report
To trumpet forth my bounty and my bravery,
Till the court envy, and remove. I'll have
My house the academy of wits, who shall
Exalt [their genius] [8] with rich sack and sturgeon,
Write panegyrics of my feasts, and praise
The method of my witty superfluities.
The horses shall be taught, with frequent waiting 89
Upon my gates, to stop in their career
Toward Charing Cross, spite of the coachman's fury;
And not a tilter [9] but shall strike his plume
When he sails by my window; my balcony
Shall be the courtier's idol, and more gazed at
Than all the pageantry at Temple Bar
By country clients.

---

[1] With it.
[2] Prostitutes.
[3] Beholden.
[4] Chairmen.
[5] Plumes for a canopy.
[6] Fine silk cloth.
[7] Free-spoken.  [8] Supplied by Gifford-Dyce.
[9] One riding to the tilting grounds.

STEW.                    Sure, my lady's mad.

CEL. [*Striking him.*] Take that for your ill
manners.

STEW.                    Thank you, madam.
I would there were less quicksilver in
your fingers.                    *Exit.*

CEL. There's more than simple honesty in
a servant
Required to his full duty; none should
dare                                        100
But with a look, much less a saucy language,
Check at their mistress' pleasure. I'm
resolved
To pay for some delight; my estate will
bear it;
I'll rein it shorter when I please.

*Enter Steward.*

STEW.                    A gentleman
Desires to speak with your ladyship.

CEL.                    His name?

STEW. He says you know him not; he
seems to be
Of quality.

CEL.                    Admit him.—[*Exit Steward.*]

*Enter Haircut.*[1]

Sir, with me?

HAIR. Madam, I know not how you may
receive
This boldness from me; but my fair intents,                                    109
Known, will incline you to be charitable.

CEL. No doubt, sir.

HAIR.                    He must live obscurely, madam,
That hath not heard what virtues you
possess;
And I, a poor admirer of your fame,
Am come to kiss your hand.

CEL.                    That all your business?

HAIR. Though it were worth much travel,
I have more
In my ambition.

CEL.                    Speak it freely, sir.

HAIR. You are a widow.

CEL.                    So.

HAIR.                    And I a bachelor.

CEL. You come a-wooing, sir, and would
perhaps
Show me a way to reconcile these two.

[1] In the original this stage direction appears
at the end of Celestina's speech.

HAIR. And bless my stars for such a happiness.                                        120

CEL. I like you, sir, the better, that you do
not
Wander about, but shoot home to the
meaning;
'Tis a confidence will make a man
Know sooner what to trust to; but I
never
Saw you before, and I believe you come
not
With hope to find me desperate upon
marriage.
If maids, out of their ignorance of what
Men are, refuse these offers, widows may,
Out of their knowledge, be allowed some
coyness.
And yet I know not how much happi-
ness                                        130
A peremptory answer may deprive me of;
You may be some young lord, and,
though I see not
Your footmen and your groom, they may
not be
Far off, in conference with your horse.
Please you
To instruct me with your title, against
which
I would not willingly offend.

HAIR.                    I am
A gentleman; my name is Haircut,
madam.

CEL. Sweet Mr. Haircut, are you a courtier?

HAIR. Yes.

CEL.                    I did think so, by your confidence.
Not to detain you, sir, with circum-
stance,[2]                                    140
I was not so unhappy in my husband
But that 'tis possible I may be a wife
Again; but I must tell you he that wins
My affection shall deserve me.

HAIR.                    I will hope,
If you can love, I sha' not present,
madam,
An object to displease you in my person;
And, when time and your patience shall
possess you
With further knowledge of me, and the
truth
Of my devotion, you will not repent
The offer of my service.

CEL.                    You say well.    150

[2] Detailed narration.

How long do you imagine you can love,
sir?
Is it a quotidian,[1] or will it hold
But every other day?

HAIR. You are pleasant,[2] madam.

CEL. Does 't take you with a burning at
the first,
Or with a cold fit? For you gentlemen
Have both your summer and your winter
service.

HAIR. I am ignorant what you mean; but
I shall never
Be cold in my affection to such beauty.

CEL. And 'twill be somewhat long ere I be
warm in 't.

HAIR. If you vouchsafe me so much honor,
madam,                                         160
That I may wait on you sometimes, I sha'
not
Despair to see a change.

CEL. But now I know
Your mind, you shall not need to tell it
when
You come again; I shall remember it.

HAIR. You make me fortunate.

*Enter Steward.*

STEW. Madam, your kinswomen,
The Lady Novice and her sister, are
New lighted from their coach.

CEL. I did expect 'em;
They partly are my pupils. I'll attend
'em.                          [*Exit Steward.*]

HAIR. Madam, I have been too great a
trespasser                                     169
Upon your patience; I'll take my leave.
You have affairs, and I have some em-
ployment
Calls me to court; I shall present again
A servant [3] to you.       *Exit Ha[ircut].*

CEL. Sir, you may present,
But not give fire, I hope.—Now to the
ladies.
This recreation's past; the next must
be
To read to them some court philosophy.
                                   *Exit.[4]*

[1] Something of daily occurrence.
[2] Facetious.
[3] *I.e.*, present myself as a servant, with a pun
on the meaning *lover*.
[4] Original reads *Exeunt.*

THE SECOND ACT. [SCENE i.

*A room in Bornwell's house.*]

*Enter Sir Thomas Bornwell.*

[BORN.] 'Tis a strange humor I have under-
taken,
To dance, and play, and spend as fast as
she does;
But I am resolved. It may do good upon
her,
And fright her into thrift. Nay, I'll en-
deavor
To make her jealous too; if this do not
Allay her gamboling, she's past a woman,
And only a miracle must tame her.

*Enter Steward.*

STEW. 'Tis Mr. Frederick, my lady's
nephew.

BORN. What of him?

STEW. Is come from the university.

BORN. By whose directions?

STEW. It seems, my lady's.

BORN. Let me speak with him   10
Before he see his aunt.—[*Exit Steward.*]
I do not like it.—

*Enter [Steward, with] Mr. Frederick.*

Mr. Frederick, welcome! I expected not
So soon your presence. What's the hasty
cause?

FRED. These letters from my tutor will acquaint you. [*Gives Bornwell letters.*]

STEW. Welcome home, sweet Mr. Frederick!

FRED. Where's my aunt?

STEW. She's busy about her painting in
her closet;
The outlandish[5] man of art is copying
out
Her countenance.

FRED. She is sitting for her picture?

STEW. Yes, sir; and when 'tis drawn she
will be hanged
Next the French cardinal in the dining
room.                                          20
But, when she hears you're come, she
will dismiss
The Belgic gentleman, to entertain
Your worship.

FRED. Change of air has made you
witty.                          [*Exit Steward.*]

[5] Foreign.

BORN. Your tutor gives you a handsome character,
Frederick, and is sorry your aunt's pleasure
Commands you from your studies; but I hope
You have no quarrel to the liberal arts.
Learning is an addition [1] beyond
Nobility of birth. Honor of blood,
Without the ornament of knowledge, is                    30
A glorious [2] ignorance.
FRED. I never knew more sweet and happy hours
Than I employed upon my books.    I heard
A part of my philosophy, and was so
Delighted with the harmony of nature
I could have wasted my whole life upon 't.
BORN. [Aside.] 'Tis pity a rash indulgence should corrupt
So fair a genius!  She's here; I'll observe.

*Enter Aretina, Alexander, Littleworth, Steward.*

FRED. My most loved aunt!
ARE.                    Support me; I shall faint.
LIT. What ails your ladyship?
ARE.                    Is that Frederick,     40
In black?
AL.                    Yes, madam; but the doublet's satin.
ARE. The boy's undone!
FRED.                    Madam, you appear troubled.
ARE. Have I not cause? Was not I trusted with
Thy education, boy, and have they sent thee
Home like a very scholar?
AL.                    'Twas ill done,
Howe'er they used him in the university,
To send him to his friends thus.
FRED.                    Why, sir, black
(For 'tis the color that offends your eyesight)
Is not, within my reading, any blemish;
Sables are no disgrace in heraldry.     50
AL. 'Tis coming from the college thus that makes it
Dishonorable. While you ware [3] it for

Your father, it was commendable; or, were
Your aunt dead, you might mourn, and justify.
ARE. What luck [4] I did not send him into France!
They would have given him generous education,
Taught him another garb, to wear his lock
And shape as gaudy as the summer, how
To dance, and wag his feather *à la mode,*
To compliment and cringe,[5] to talk not modestly,                    60
Like, "ay, forsooth," and "no, forsooth," to blush,
And look so like a chaplain!  There he might
Have learned a brazen confidence, and observed
So well the custom of the country that
He might by this time have invented fashions
For us, and been a benefit to the kingdom,
Preserved our tailors in their wits, and saved
The charge of sending into foreign courts
For pride and antic fashions.  Observe
In what a posture he does hold his hat now!                    70
FRED. Madam, with your pardon, you have practiced
Another dialect than was taught me when
I was commended to your care and breeding.
I understand not this.  Latin or Greek
Are more familiar to my apprehension;
Logic was not so hard in my first lectures
As your strange language.
ARE.                    Some strong waters—O!
LIT. [Offering a box.] Comfits will be as comfortable to your stomach, madam.
ARE. I fear he's spoiled forever! He did name
Logic, and may, for aught I know, be gone                    80
So far to understand it.  I did always
Suspect they would corrupt him in the college.—
Will your Greek saws and sentences[6] discharge

<hr>

[1] Title, ornament.
[2] Vainglorious.                    [3] Wore.
[4] *I.e.,* bad luck.  [5] Bow.  [6] Proverbs and maxims.

The mercer? Or is Latin a fit language
To court a mistress in?—Mr. Alexander,
If you have any charity, let me
Commend him to your breeding. I sus-
    pect
I must employ my doctor first, to purge
The university that lies in 's head;
It alters his complexion.[1]

AL.                              If you dare   90
    Trust me to serve him—

ARE.                    Mr. Littleworth,
    Be you joined in commission.

LIT.                    I will teach him
    Postures and rudiments.

ARE.               I have no patience
    To see him in this shape; it turns my
        stomach.
    When he has cast his academic skin,
    He shall be yours. I am bound in con-
        science
    To see him bred; his own state shall
        maintain
    The charge, while he's my ward.—Come
        hither, sir.

FRED. What does my aunt mean to do
    with me?

STEW. To make you a fine gentleman, and
    translate you                          100
    Out of your learnéd language, sir, into
    The present Goth and Vandal, which is
        French.

BORN. [Aside.] Into what mischief will
    this humor ebb?
    She will undo the boy; I see him ruined.
    My patience is not manly, but I must
    Use stratagem to reduce her—open ways
    Give me no hope.               Exit.

STEW.          You shall be obeyed, madam.
    Exeunt [All but Frederick and Steward].

FRED. Mr. Steward, are you sure we do
    not dream?
    Was 't not my aunt you talked to?

STEW.               One that loves you
    Dear as her life. These clothes do not be-
        come you;                          110
    You must have better, sir—

FRED.               These are not old.

STEW. More suitable to the town and time;
    we keep
    No Lent here, nor is 't my lady's pleasure
        you
    Should fast from anything you have a
        mind to—

[1] Disposition.

Unless it be your learning, which she
    would have you
Forget with all convenient speed that
    may be,
For the credit of your noble family.
The case is altered since we lived i' th'
    country;
We do not invite the poor o' th' parish
To dinner, keep a table for the tenants;
Our kitchen does not smell of beef; the
    cellar                                 121
Defies the price of malt and hops; the
    footmen
And coachdrivers may be drunk like
    gentlemen
With wine, nor will three fiddlers upon
    holidays,
With aid of bagpipes, that called in the
    country
To dance and plow the hall up with their
    hobnails
Now make my lady merry. We do feed
Like princes, and feast nothing but
    princes;
And are these robes fit to be seen amongst
    'em?

FRED. My lady keeps a court then! Is Sir
    Thomas                                 130
    Affected with this state and cost?

STEW.               He was not,
    But is converted; and I hope you wo' not
    Persist in heresy, but take a course
    Of riot, to content your friends; you shall
    Want nothing, if you can be proud, and
        spend it
    For my lady's honor. Here are a hun-
        dred
    Pieces will serve you till you have new
        clothes;
    I will present you with a nag of mine,
    Poor tender of my service—please you
        accept.
    My lady's smile more than rewards me
        for it.                            140
    I must provide fit servants to attend you,
    Monsieurs, for horse and foot.

FRED.               I shall submit,
    If this be my aunt's pleasure, and be
        ruled;
    My eyes are opened with this purse al-
        ready,
    And sack will help to inspire me. I must
        spend it?

STEW. What else, sir?

FRED.　　　I'll begin with you. To encourage
　You to have still a special care of me,
　There is five pieces—not for your nag.
STEW. No, sir; I hope it is not.
FRED.　　　　　Buy a beaver [1]
　For thy own block; I shall be ruled. Who does　　　　　150
　Command the wine cellar?
STEW.　　　Who command but you, sir?
FRED. I'll try to drink a health or two, my aunt's,
　Or anybody's; and, if that foundation
　Stagger me not too much, I will commence
　In all the arts of London.
STEW.　　　　　If you find, sir,
　The operation of the wine exalt
　Your blood to the desire of any female
　Delight, I know your aunt wo' not deny
　Any of her chambermaids to practice on;
　She loves you but too well.
FRED.　　　I know not how　160
　I may be for that exercise.—Farewell, Aristotle!
　Prithee, commend me to the library
　At Westminster; my bones I bequeath thither,
　And to the learned worms that mean to visit 'em.
　I will compose myself; I begin to think
　I have lost time indeed.—Come, to the wine cellar.　　　Exit [with Steward].

[SCENE ii.

A room in Celestina's house.]

Enter Celestina, Mariana, Isabella.

MAR. But shall we not, madam, expose ourselves
　To censure for this freedom?
CEL.　　　　　Let them answer
　That dare mistake us. Shall we be so much
　Cowards, to be frighted from our pleasure,
　Because men have malicious tongues, and show
　What miserable souls they have? No, cousin,
　We hold our life and fortunes upon no
　Man's charity; if they dare show so little

[1] Beaver hat.

Discretion to traduce our fames, we will
　Be guilty of so much wit to laugh at 'em.
ISA. 'Tis a becoming fortitude.
CEL.　　　　　My stars　11
　Are yet kind to me; for, in a happy minute
　Be 't spoke, I'm not in love, and men shall never
　Make my heart lean with sighing, nor with tears
　Draw on my eyes the infamy of spectacles.
　'Tis the chief principle to keep your heart
　Under your own obedience; jest, but love not.
　I say my prayers, yet can wear good clothes,
　And only satisfy my tailor for 'em.
　I wo' not lose my privilege.　　　20
MAR. And yet they say your entertainments are—
　Give me your pardon, madam—to proclaim
　Yourself a widow, and to get a husband.
CEL. As if a lady of my years, some beauty,
　Left by her husband rich, that had mourned for him
　A twelvemonth too, could live so obscure i' th' town
　That gallants would not know her, and invite
　Themselves, without her chargeable [2] proclamations!
　Then we are worse than citizens.[3] No widow
　Left wealthy can be throughly warm in mourning,　　　30
　But some one noble blood or lusty kindred
　Claps in with his gilt coach and Flandrian trotters,
　And hurries her away to be a countess.
　Courtiers have spies, and great ones with large [4] titles,
　Cold in their own estates, would warm themselves
　At a rich city bonefire.
ISA.　　　　　Most true, madam.

[2] Expensive.
[3] Dwellers in the city, i.e., middle-class persons.
[4] Gifford-Dyce's reading. Original reads charge.

CEL. No matter for corruption of the
blood—
Some undone courtier made her husband
rich,
And this new lord receives it back again.
Admit it were my policy, and that    40
My entertainments pointed to acquaint
me
With many suitors, that I might be safe
And make the best election, could you
blame me?
MAR. Madam, 'tis wisdom.
CEL.                    But I should be
In my thoughts miserable, to be fond [1]
Of leaving the sweet freedom I possess,
And court myself into new marriage
fetters.
I now observe men's several wits and
windings,
And can laugh at their follies.
MAR.                    You have given
A most ingenious satisfaction.    50
CEL. One thing I'll tell you more, and this
I give you
Worthy your imitation, from my prac-
tice:
You see me merry, full of song and danc-
ing,
Pleasant in language, apt to all delights
That crown a public meeting; but you
cannot
Accuse me of being prodigal of my favors
To any of my guests. I do not summon,
By any wink, a gentleman to follow me
To my withdrawing chamber; I hear all
Their pleas in court, nor can they boast
abroad    60
(And do me justice [2]) after a salute
They have much conversation with my
lip.
I hold the kissing of my hand a courtesy,
And he that loves me must, upon the
strength
Of that, expect [3] till I renew his favor.
Some ladies are so expensive in their
graces
To those that honor 'em, and so prodigal,
That in a little time they have nothing
but
The naked sin left to reward their serv-
ants,

Whereas a thrift in our rewards will
keep    70
Men long in their devotion, and preserve
Ourselves in stock, to encourage those
that honor us.
ISA. This is an art worthy a lady's practice.
CEL. It takes not from the freedom of our
mirth,
But seems to advance it, when we can
possess
Our pleasures with security of our honor;
And, that preserved, I welcome all the
joys
My fancy can let in. In this I have given
The copy of my mind, nor do I blush
You understand it.

*Enter Celestina's Gentlewoman.*

ISA.                    You have honored us.    80
GEN. Madam, Sir William Scentlove's
come to wait on you.
CEL. There's one would be a client.—Make
excuse
For a few minutes.    [*Exit Gentlewoman.*]
MAR.                    One that comes a-wooing?
CEL. Such a thing he would seem, but in
his guiltiness
Of little land, his expectation is not
So valiant as it might be. He wears [rich] [4]
clothes,
And feeds with noblemen; to some, I
hear,
No better than a wanton emissary
Or scout for Venus' wild fowl, which
made tame,
He thinks no shame to stand court
sentinel,    90
In hope of the reversion.
MAR.                    I have heard
That some of them are often my lord's
tasters;
The first fruits they condition for and will
Exact as fees, for the promotion.
CEL. Let them agree; there's no account
shall lie
For me among their traffic.

*Enter Gentlewo[man].*

GEN.                    Mr. Haircut, madam,
Is new come in, to tender you his service.
CEL. Let him discourse a little with Sir
William.    *Exit [Gentlewoman].*

---

[1] Foolishly desirous.
[2] Gifford-Dyce's reading.    Original reads
*justifie.*
[3] Wait.
[4] Supplied by Gifford-Dyce.

MAR. What is this gentleman, Mr. Hair-
    cut, madam?
I note him very gallant, and much
    courted                                    100
By gentlemen of quality.
CEL.                            I know not,
    More than a trim, gay man; he has some
    great office,
    Sure, by his confident behavior.
    He would be entertained under the title
    Of servant to me, and I must confess
    He is the sweetest of all men that visit
    me.
ISA. How mean you, madam?
CEL.                    He is full of powder;
    He will save much in perfume for my
    chamber,
    Were he but constant here.—Give 'em
    access.

*Enter Sir Will[iam] Scentlove, Mr. Haircut.*

SCENT. Madam, the humblest of your
    servants is                                110
    Exalted to a happiness, if you smile
    Upon my visit.
HAIR.            I must beg your charity
    Upon my rudeness, madam; I shall
    give
    That day up lost to any happiness,
    When I forget to tender you my serv-
    ice.
CEL. You practice courtship, gentlemen.
SCENT.                    But cannot
    Find where with more desert to exercise
    it.—
    What lady's this, I pray?
CEL.                    A kinswoman
    Of mine, Sir William.
SCENT.        I am more her servant.
                *[Takes Mariana aside.]*
CEL. You came from court, now, I pre-
    sume.
HAIR.            'Tis, madam,            120
    The sphere I move in, and my destiny
    Was kind to place me there, where I
    enjoy
    All blessings that a mortal can possess,
    That lives not in your presence; and I
    should
    Fix my ambition, when you would vouch-
    safe
    Me so much honor to accept from me
    An humble entertainment there.

CEL.                            But by
    What name shall I be known? In what
    degree
    Shall I be of kinred [1] to you?
HAIR.            How mean you, madam?
CEL. Perhaps you'll call me sister—I shall
    take it                                    130
    A special preferment; or it may be
    I may pass under title of your mistress,
    If I seem rich and fair enough to engage
    Your confidence to own me.
HAIR.                    I would hope—
CEL. But 'tis not come to that yet; you
    will, sir,
    Excuse my mirth.
HAIR.            Sweet madam!
CEL.                    Shall I take
    Boldness to ask what place you hold in
    court?
    'Tis an uncivil curiosity,
    But you'll have mercy to a woman's
    question.
HAIR. My present condition, madam, car-
    ries                                       140
    Honor and profit, though not to be named
    With that employment I expect i' th'
    state,
    Which shall discharge the first maturity
    Upon your knowledge; until then, I beg
    You allow a modest silence.
CEL.                    I am charmed, sir;
    And, if you scape ambassador, you can-
    not
    Reach a preferment wherein I'm against
    you.
    But where's Sir William Scentlove?
HAIR.                    Give him leave
    To follow his nose, madam; while he
    hunts
    In view, he'll soon be at a fault. [2]
CEL.                    You know him?    150
HAIR. Know Scentlove? Not a page but
    can decipher him;
    The waiting-women know him to a
    scruple.
    He's called the blister-maker [3] of the town.
CEL. What's that?
HAIR. [4]            The laundry ladies can
    resolve [5] you,

---

[1] Kindred.
[2] *I.e.*, while now he can see the quarry, he'll
soon lose the scent.        [3] *I.e.*, whoremaster.
[4] Emended by Gifford-Dyce. Original reads
*Isa.*                            [5] Inform.

And you may guess—an arrant epicure
As this day lives, born to a pretty wit,
A knight, but no gentleman. I must
Be plain to you; your ladyship may have
Use of this knowledge, but conceal the
author.
SCENT. I kiss your fairest hand.
MAR.        You make a difference;   160
Pray reconcile 'em to an equal whiteness.
SCENT. You wound my meaning, lady.
CEL.            Nay, Sir William
Has the art of compliment.
SCENT.        Madam, you honor me
'Bove my desert of language.
CEL.            Will you please
To enrich me with your knowledge of
that gentleman?
SCENT. Do you not know him, madam?
CEL.            What is he?
SCENT. A camphire [1] ball. You shall know
more hereafter;
He shall tell you himself, and save my
character.
Till then—you see he's proud.
CEL.            One thing, gentlemen,
I observe in your behavior, which is
rare                        170
In two that court one mistress: you pre-
serve
A noble friendship.  There's no gum
within
Your hearts; you cannot fret,[2] or show an
envy
Of one another's hope.  Some would not
govern
Their passions with that temper!
SCENT.            The whole world
Sha' not divorce our friendship.—Mr.
Haircut!
Would I had lives to serve him! He is
lost
To goodness does not honor him.
HAIR.            My knight!
CEL. [Aside.] This is right playing at
court shuttlecock.

*Enter Gentlew[oman].*

GEN. Madam, there is a gentleman desires                        180
To speak wi'e, one Sir Thomas Bornwell.

[1] Camphor, which was supposed to induce
coldness.
[2] Gum was used to stiffen velvet, which
thereafter fretted easily.

CEL.            Bornwell?
GEN. He says he is a stranger to your lady-
ship.
SCENT. I know him.
HAIR.            Your neighbor, madam.
SCENT.            Husband to
The lady that so revels in the Strand.
HAIR. He has good parts, they say, but
cannot help
His lady's bias.
CEL.        They have both much fame
I' th' town, for several merits.  Pray, ad-
mit him.            [*Exit Gentlewoman.*]
HAIR. [Aside.] What comes he for?

*Enter Sir Thomas.*

BORN. Your pardon, noble lady, that I
have
Presumed, a stranger to your knowl-
edge—            [*Kisses Celestina.*]
CEL.        Sir,            190
Your worth was here before you, and
your person
Cannot be here ingrateful.
BORN.            'Tis the bounty
Of your sweet disposition, madam.—[*To
Isabella.*] Make me
Your servant, lady, by her fair example,
To favor me.—[*Offers to kiss Isabella, who
turns her cheek. Aside.*] I never knew
one turn
Her cheek to a gentleman that came to
kiss her,
But sh'ad a stinking breath.—Your serv-
ant, gentlemen.
Will Scentlove, how is 't?
CEL.            I am sorry, coz,
To accuse you; we in nothing more be-
tray                        199
Ourselves to censure of ridiculous pride
Than answering a fair salute too rudely.
O, it shows ill upon a gentlewoman
Not to return the modest lip, if she
Would have the world believe her breath
is not
Offensive.
BORN.        Madam, I have business
With you.        [*The Rest step aside.*]
SCENT. [Aside.] His looks are pleasant.
CEL.            With me, sir?
BORN. I hear you have an ex'llent wit,
madam:
I see you're fair.

CEL.                    The first is but report;
And do not trust your eyesight for the
    last,
Cause I presume y' are mortal, and may
    err.                                        210
HAIR. [*Aside.*] He is very gamesome.
BORN.                    Y'ave an ex'llent voice
(They say you catched it from a dying
    swan),
Which, joined to the sweet harmony of
    your lute,
You ravish all mankind.
CEL.                    Ravish mankind?
BORN. With their consent.
CEL.                    It were the stranger rape;
But there's the less indictment lies
    against it,
And there is hope your little honesties [1]
Cannot be much the worse, for men do
    rather
Believe they had a maidenhead than put
Themselves to th' rack of memory how
    long                                        220
'Tis since they left the burden of their
    innocence.
BORN. Why, you are bitter, madam!
CEL.                    So is physic;
I do not know your constitution.
BORN. You shall, if please you, madam.
CEL.                    Y' are too hasty;
I must examine what certificate
You have first, to prefer you.
BORN.                    Fine! Certificate?
CEL. Under your lady's hand and seal.
BORN.                    Go to.
I see you are a wag.
CEL.                    But take heed how
You trust to 't.
BORN.        I can love you in my wedlock
As well as that young gallant o' th' first
    hair                                        230
Or the knight bachelor, and can return
As amorous delight to thy soft bosom.
CEL. Your person and your language are
    both strangers.
BORN. But may be more familiar; I have
    those
That dare make affidavit for my body.
CEL. D'e mean your surgeon?
BORN.                    My surgeon, madam?
I know not how you value my abilities,
But I dare undertake as much, to express
My service to your ladyship, and with

[1] Chastities.

As fierce ambition fly to your commands
As the most valiant of these lay siege to
    you.                                        241
CEL. You dare not, sir.
BORN.                    How, madam?
CEL.                    I will justify 't.
You dare not marry me; and I imagine
Some here, should I consent, would
    fetch a priest
Out of the fire.
BORN.                    I have a wife indeed.
CEL. And there's a statute not repealed, I
    take it.
BORN. Y' are in the right; I must confess
    y'ave hit
And bled me in a master vein.
CEL.                    You think
I took you on the advantage; use your
    best
Skill at defense, I'll come up to your
    valor,                                      250
And show another work you dare not do:
You dare not, sir, be virtuous.
BORN.                    I dare,
By this fair hand I dare, and ask a par-
    don
If my rude words offend thy innocence,
Which, in a form so beautiful, would
    shine
To force a blush in them suspected it,
And from the rest draw wonder.
HAIR. [*Aside.*]                    I like not
Their secret parley; shall I interrupt 'em?
ISA. [*Aside.*] By no means, sir.
SCENT. [*Aside.*] Sir Thomas was not wont
To show so much a courtier.
MAR. [*Aside.*]                    He cannot   260
Be prejudicial to you. Suspect not
Your own deserts so much; he's married.
BORN. I have other business, madam.
    You keep music;
I came to try how you can dance.
CEL. You did?—[*Aside.*] I'll try his humor
    out of breath.—
Although I boast no cunning, sir, in
    revels,
If you desire to show your art that way,
I can wait on you.
BORN.                    You much honor me;
Nay, all must join to make a harmony.
                            *They dance.*
BORN. I have nothing now, madam, but
    to beseech,                                 270
After a pardon for my boldness, you

Would give occasion to pay my gratitude.
I have a house will be much honor[é]d,
If you vouchsafe your presence, and a wife
Desires to present herself your servant.
I came with the ambition to invite you;
Deny me not.   Your person you shall trust
On fair security.

CEL.                    Sir, although I use not
This freedom with a stranger, you shall have
No cause to hold me obstinate.

BORN.                    You grace me.   280
Sir William Scentlove—

HAIR.                    I must take my leave.
You will excuse me, madam; court attendances—

CEL.  By any means.

BORN.                    Ladies, you will vouchsafe
Your company?

ISA. }
MAR. }                    We wait upon you, sir.

                    *Exeunt.*

THE THIRD ACT. [SCENE i.

*A dressing room.*]

*Enter Lord, unready;* [1] *Haircut preparing
his periwig; table and looking-glass.*

LORD.  What hour is 't?

HAIR.                    'Bout three a-clock, my lord.

LORD.[2] 'Tis time to rise.

HAIR.                    Your lordship went but late
To bed last night.

LORD.                    'Twas early in the morning.

*Enter Secre[tary].*

SEC.  [*Calling back.*]  Expect[3] awhile.—My
lord is busy?

LORD.  What's the matter?

SEC.                    Here is a lady
Desires access to you upon some affairs
She says may specially concern your
lordship.

LORD.  A lady?  What her name?

SEC.                    Madam Decoy.

LORD.  Decoy?  Prithee, admit her.—

*Enter Decoy.*

                    Have you business, madam,   9
With me?

DEC.        And such, I hope, as will not be
Offensive to your lordship.

LORD.                    I pray, speak it.

DEC.  I would desire your lordship's ear
more private.

LORD.  [*To Secretary and Haircut.*]  Wait i'
th' next chamber till I call.—(*Exeunt
[Haircut and Secretary].*)  Now, madam.

DEC.  Although I am a stranger to your
lordship,
I would not lose a fair occasion offered
To show how much I honor and would
serve you.

LORD.  Please you to give me the particular,
That I may know the extent of my engagement.
I am ignorant by what desert you should
Be encouraged to have care of me.

DEC.                    My lord,   20
I will take boldness to be plain; beside
Your other excellent parts, you have
much fame
For your sweet inclination to our sex.

LORD.  How d'e mean, madam?

DEC.                    I' that way your lordship
Hath honorably practiced upon some
Not to be named, your noble constancy
To a mistress hath deserved our general
vote,
And I, a part of womankind, have
thought
How to express my duty.

LORD.                    In what, madam?

DEC.  Be not so strange, my lord.   I
know the beauty   30
And pleasures of your eyes—that handsome creature
With whose fair life all your delight took
leave,
And to whose memory you have paid
too much
Sad tribute.

LORD.        What's all this?

DEC.                    This: if your lo[rd]s[hip]
Accept my service, in pure zeal to cure
Your melancholy, I could point where
you might
Repair your loss.

LORD.                    Your ladyship, I conceive,
Doth traffic in flesh merchandise.

DEC.                    To men
Of honor, like yourself.  I am well known
To some in court, and come not with ambition   40
Now to supplant your officer.

---

[1] Partly dressed.        [3] Await.
[2] Original reads *Bor.*

LORD.                                    What is
The lady of pleasure you prefer?
DEC.                                        A lady
Of birth and fortune, one upon whose
    virtue
I may presume, the Lady Aretina.
LORD. Wife to Sir Thomas Bornwell?
DEC.                            The same, sir.
LORD. Have you prepared her?
DEC. Not for your lordship, till I have
    found your pulse.
I am acquainted with her disposition;
She has a very appliable [1] nature.
LORD. And, madam, when expect you to
    be whipped                            50
For doing these fine favors?
DEC.                            How, my lord?
Your lordship does but jest, I hope; you
    make
A difference between a lady that
Does honorable offices, and one
They call a bawd. Your lordship was not
    wont
To have such coarse opinion of our prac-
    tice.
LORD. The Lady Aretina is my kins-
    woman.
DEC. What if she be, my lord? The nearer
    blood,
The dearer sympathy.
LORD.                    I'll have thee carted. [2]
DEC. Your lordship wo' not so much stain
    your honor                            60
And education to use a woman
Of my quality—
LORD.                    'Tis possible you may
Be sent off with an honorable convoy
Of halberdiers.
DEC.                    O, my good lord!
LORD. Your ladyship [3] shall be no protec-
    tion,
If thou but stay'st three minutes.
DEC.                            I am gone.—
When next you find rebellion in your
    blood,
May all within ten mile o' th' court turn
    honest! [4]
                                        *Exit.*
LORD. I do not find that proneness, since
    the fair
Bella Maria died; my blood is cold,    70

Nor is there beauty enough surviving
To heighten me to wantonness.—Who
    waits?

*Enter Haircut.*

And what said my lady?
HAIR. The silent language of her face, my
    lord,
Was not so pleasant as it showed upon
Her entrance.
LORD.                    Would any man that meets
This lady take her for a bawd?
HAIR.                            She does
The trade an honor, credit to the pro-
    fession.
We may in time see baldness, quarter
    noses,
And rotten legs to take the wall of [5]
    footcloths. [6]
                                        80
LORD. I ha' thought better.—[*To Secretary
    within.*] Call the lady back.
I wo' not lose this opportunity.
Bid her not fear. The favor is not com-
    mon,
And I'll reward it.—I do wonder much
Will Scentlove was not here today.
HAIR. I heard him say this morning he
    would wait
Upon your lordship.—She is returned,
    sir.

*Enter Secre[tary] and Decoy.*

SEC. Madam, be confident; my lord's not
    angry.
LORD. You return welcome, madam; you
    are better
Read in your art, I hope, than to be
    frighted                            90
With any shape of anger, when you bring
Such news to gentlemen. Madam, you
    shall
Soon understand how I accept the office.
DEC. You are the first lord, since I studied
    carriage, [7]
That showed such infidelity and fury
Upon so kind a message. Every gentle-
    man
Will show some breeding, but if one right
    honorable
Should not have noble blood—

---

[1] Pliable, compliant.
[2] Bawds were punished by being whipped
through the streets at the tail of a cart.
[3] Station as a lady.            [4] Chaste.
[5] Take precedence over.
[6] The caparison of a horse.
[7] Acting as a go-between.

LORD.                    You shall return
My compliment in a letter to my Lady
Aretina.    Favor me with a little pa-
tience.—                                    100
Show her that chamber.
DEC.              I'll attend your lordship.
[*Exeunt Decoy and Haircut.  Secretary pre-
                        pares to write.*]
LORD. Write—"Madam, where your honor
is in danger,
My love must not be silent."—

*Enter Scentlove and Kickshaw.*

                    Scentlove and Kickshaw!
KICK. Your lordship's busy.
LORD. Writing a letter.—Nay, it sha' not
bar
Any discourse.
SEC.                        "—silent."
LORD. "Though I be no physician, I may
Prevent a fever in your blood."—And
where
Have you spent the morning's conversa-
tion?
SCENT. Where you would have given the
best Barbary                              110
In your stable to have met on honorable
terms.
LORD. What new beauty?  You acquaint
yourselves
With none but wonders.
SCENT.                'Tis too low—a miracle.
LORD. 'Twill require a strong faith.
SEC.                        "—your blood."
LORD. "If you be innocent, preserve your
fame, lest this Decoy,
Madam, betray it, to your repent-
ance."—
By what name is she known?
SCENT.                        Ask Alexander;
He knows her.
AL.              Whom?
SCENT.              The Lady Celestina.
LORD. He has a vast knowledge of ladies.
'Las, poor Alexander!
When dost thou mean thy body shall lie
fallow?                                    120
AL. When there is mercy in a petticoat.
I must turn pilgrim for some breath.
LORD.                        I think
'Twere cooler travel, if you examine it,
Upon the hoof through Spain.
SCENT.                Through Ethiopia.

LORD. Nay, less laborious to serve a pren-
ticeship
In Peru, and dig gold out of the mine,
Where all the year is dog days.
SEC.                "— to repentance."
LORD. "In brief, this lady, could you fall
from virtue,
Within my knowledge, will not blush to
be a bawd."
SCENT. But, hang 't, 'tis honorable journey-
work:                                    130
Thou art famous by 't, and thy name's
up.
AL.                            So, sir!
Let me ask you a question, my dear
knight:
Which is less servile, to bring up the
pheasant
And wait, or sit at table uncontrolled
And carve to my own appetite?
SCENT.                        No more;
Th' art witty, as I am.
SEC.              "— a bawd."
SCENT.                        How's that?
AL. O, you are famous by 't, and your
name's up, sir.
LORD. "Be wise, and reward my caution
with
Timely care of yourself, so I shall not
repent
To be known your loving kinsman and
servant"—                                140
Gentlemen, the Lady Celestina,
Is she so rare a thing?
AL.                    If you'll have my
Opinion, my lord, I never saw
So sweet, so fair, so rich a piece of nature.
LORD. I'll show thee a fairer presently, to
shame
Thy eyes and judgment; look o' that.—
[*Shows him a picture.*]  So, I'll sub-
scribe. [*Signs his name.*]
Seal it; I'll excuse your pen for the direc-
tion.
AL. Bella Maria's picture!  She was hand-
some.
SCENT. But not to be compared—
LORD. Your patience, gentlemen; I'll re-
turn instantly.            *Exit.*  150
AL. Whither is my lord gone?
SEC. To a lady i' th' next chamber.
SCENT.                    What is she?
SEC. You shall pardon me; I am his secre-
tary.

SCENT. I was wont to be of his counsel. A
    new officer,
And I not know 't? I am resolved to
    batter
All other with the praise of Celestina.
I must retain him.

*Enter Lord.*

LORD.                Has not that object—
    Convinced your erring judgments?
AL.             What, this picture?
LORD. Were but your thoughts as capable
    as mine                     159
Of your idea, you would wish no thought
That were not active in her praise, above
All worth and memory of her sex.
SCENT.              She was fair,
    I must confess; but, had your lordship
    looked
With eyes more narrow and some less
    affection
Upon her face—
AL.            I do not love the copies
Of any dead; they make me dream of
    goblins.
Give me a living mistress, with but half
The beauty of Celestina. Come, my lord,
'Tis pity that a lord of so much flesh
Should waste upon a ghost, when they
    are living                 170
Can give you a more honorable consump-
    tion.
SCENT. Why, do you mean, my lord, to
    live an infidel?
Do, and see what will come on 't; observe
    still
And dote upon your vigils; build a cham-
    ber
Within a rock, a tomb among the worms,
Not far off, where you may in proof
    apocryphal
Court 'em not devour the pretty pile
Of flesh your mistress carried to the
    grave.
There are no women in the world; all eyes
And tongue and lips are buried in her
    coffin!                   180
LORD. Why, do you think yourselves com-
    petent judges
Of beauty, gentlemen?
BOTH.          What should hinder us?
AL. I have seen and tried as many as an-
    other
With a mortal back.

LORD.             Your eyes are bribed,
And your hearts chained to some desires;
    you cannot
Enjoy the freedom of a sense.
AL.              Your lordship
Has a clear eyesight, and can judge and
    penetrate.
LORD. I can, and give a perfect censure[1] of
    Each line and point; distinguish beauty
    from
A thousand forms, which your corrupted
    optics                    190
Would pass for natural.
SCENT.          I desire no other
    Judge should determine[2] us, and, if your
    lordship
Dare venture but your eyes upon this
    lady,
I'll stand their justice, and be confident
You shall give Celestina victory
And triumph o'er all beauties past and
    living.
AL. I dare, my lord, venture a suit of
    clothes
You will be o'ercome.
LORD.      You do not know my fortitude.
SCENT. Nor frailty; you dare not trust
    yourself to see her.
LORD. Think you so, gentlemen? I dare
    see this creature            200
To make you know your errors, and the
    difference
Of her whose memory is my saint. Not
    trust
My senses? I dare see and speak with
    her.
Which holds the best acquaintance to
    prepare
My visit to her?
SCENT.          I will do 't, my lord.
AL. She is a lady free in entertainments.
LORD. I would give this advantage to your
    cause.
Bid her [3] appear in all the ornaments
Did ever wait on beauty, all the riches
Pride can put on, and teach her face more
    charm                  210
Than ever poet dressed up Venus in;
Bid her be all the Graces and the Queen
Of Love in one, I'll see her, Scentlove,
    and

---

[1] Judgment.                   [2] Decide for.
[3] Emended by Gifford-Dyce. Original reads
*him.*

Bring off my heart, armed but [with a] [1]
single thought
Of one that is dead, without a wound,
and, when
I have made your folly prisoner, I'll
laugh at you.

SCENT. She shall expect you; trust to me
for knowledge.

LORD. I'm for the present somewhere else
engaged;
Let me hear from you.        [*Exit.*]

SCENT.        So! I am glad he's yet
So near conversion.

AL.        I am for Aretina.    220

SCENT. No mention of my lord.

AL.        Prepare his lady;
'Tis time he were reduced [2] to the old
sport.
One lord like him more would undo the
court.        *Exit [with Scentlove].*

[SCENE ii.

*A room in Bornwell's house.*]

*Enter Aretina with a letter; Decoy.*

DEC. He is the ornament of your blood,
madam;
I am much bound to his lordship.

ARE.        He gives you
A noble character.

DEC.        'Tis his goodness, madam.

ARE. [*Aside.*] I wanted such an engine. [3]
My lord has
Done me a courtesy to disclose her na-
ture;
I now know one to trust, and will employ
her.—
Touching my lord, for reasons which I
shall
Offer to your ladyship hereafter, I
Desire you would be silent; but, to
show
How much I dare be confident in your
secrecy,    10
I pour my bosom forth. I love a gentle-
man,
On whom there wo' not need [4] much con-
juration
To meet.—Your ear.    [*Whispers to her.*]

DEC.        I apprehend you, and I shall
Be happy to be serviceable. I am sorry

Your ladyship did not know me before
now.
I have done offices, and not a few
Of the nobility but have done feats
Within my house, which is convenient
For situation and artful chambers
And pretty pictures to provoke the
fancy.    20

*Enter Littleworth.*

LIT. Madam, all pleasures languish in your
absence.

ARE. Your pardon a few minutes, sir.—
[*Walks aside with Decoy.*] You must
Contrive it thus.

LIT.        I attend, and shall account it
Honor to wait on your return.

ARE.        He must not
Have the least knowledge of my name or
person.

DEC. I have practiced that already for
some great ones,
And dare again, to satisfy you, madam;
I have a thousand ways to do sweet
offices.

LIT. [*To himself.*] If this Lady Aretina
should be honest,    29
I ha' lost time. She's free as air; I must
Have closer conference, and, if I have art,
Make her affect me in revenge.

DEC.        This evening?
Leave me to manage things.

ARE.        You will oblige me.

DEC. You shall commend my art, and
thank me after.        *Ex[it].*

ARE. I hope the revels are maintained
within.

LIT. By Sir Thomas and his mistress.

ARE.        How? His mistress?

LIT. The Lady Celestina; I ne'er saw
Eyes shoot more amorous interchange.

ARE.        Is 't so?

LIT. He wears her favor with o'er-pride [5] —

ARE.        Her favor?

LIT. A feather that he ravished from her
fan—    40
And is so full of courtship, which she
smiles on.

ARE. 'Tis well.

LIT.        And praises her beyond all poetry.

ARE. I'm glad he has so much wit.

LIT. [*Aside.*]        Not jealous!

---

[1] Supplied by Gifford-Dyce.
[2] Brought back.        [3] Device.
[4] Gifford-Dyce's reading. Original reads *meet*.
[5] Immense pride.

ARE. [*Aside.*] This secures me. What
　　would make other ladies pale
With jealousy, gives but a license to my
　　wand'rings.
Let him now tax me, if he dare; and
　　yet
Her beauty's worth my envy, and I wish
Revenge upon it, not because he loves,
But that it shines above my own.

*Enter Alex[ander].*

AL.　　　　　　　　　　　　Dear madam!
ARE. [*Aside.*] I have it.—You two gentle-
　　men profess　　　　　　　　　　50
Much service to me; if I have a way
To employ your wit and secrecy—
BOTH.　　　　　　　　You'll honor us.
ARE. You gave a high and worthy char-
　　acter
Of Celestina.
AL.　　　　　　　I remember, madam.
ARE. Do either of you love her?
AL.　　　　　　　　　Not I, madam.
LIT. I would not, if I might.
ARE.　　　　　　　　She's now my guest
And, by a trick, invited by my husband
To disgrace me. You, gentlemen, are
　　held
Wits of the town, the consuls that do
　　govern
The senate here, whose jeers are all
　　authentic.　　　　　　　　　　60
The taverns and the ordinaries are
Made academies, where you come, and
　　all
Your sins and surfeits made the time's
　　example.
Your very nods can quell a theater;
No speech or poem good without your
　　seal;
You can protect scurrility, and publish;
By your authority believed, no rapture
Ought to have honest meaning.
AL.　　　　　　　Leave our characters.
LIT. And name the employment.
ARE.　　　　　　　You must exercise
The strength of both your wits upon this
　　lady,　　　　　　　　　　　　70
And talk her into humbleness or anger,
Both which are equal, to my thought. If
　　you
Dare undertake this slight thing for my
　　sake,

My favor shall reward it; but be faith-
　　ful,
And seem to let all spring from your own
　　freedom.
AL. This all? We can defame her. If you
　　please,
My friend shall call her whore, or any-
　　thing,
And never be endangered to a duel.
ARE. How's that?
AL. He can endure a cudgeling, and no
　　man　　　　　　　　　　　　　80
Will fight after so fair a satisfaction.
But leave us to our art, and do not limit
　　us.
ARE. They are here; begin not till I whis-
　　per you.

*Enter Sir Thomas, Celestina, Mariana, Isa-
　　　　　　　　　　　　　bella.*

ARE.[1] *Je vous prie, madame, d'excuser
l'importunité de mes affaires, qui m'ont fait
offenser, par mon absence, une dame de
laquelle j'ai reçu tant d'obligation.*
CEL. *Pardonnez-moi, madame; vous me
faites trop d'honneur.*　　　　　　89
ARE. *C'est bien de la douceur de votre na-
turel, que vous tenez cette langage. Mais
j'espère que mon mari n'a pas manqué de
vous entretenir en mon absence.*
CEL. *En vérité, monsieur nous a fort
obligé.*
ARE. *Il eût trop failli, s'il n'eût taché de
tout son pouvoir à vous rendre toutes sortes de
services.*
CEL. *C'est de sa bonté qu'il nous a tant
favorisé.*　　　　　　　　　　100
ARE. *De la vôtre plutôt, madame, que
vous fait donner d'interprétation si bénigne
à ses efforts.*
CEL. *Je vois bien que la victoire sera tou-
jours à madame, et de langage et de la
courtesie.*
ARE. *Vraiment, madame, que jamais per-
sonne a plus désiré l'honneur de votre
compagnie que moi.*
CEL. *Laissons-en, je vous supplie,* [110
*des compliments, et permettez à votre servante
de vous baiser les mains.*

---

[1] The French as well as some of the English
which follows has been printed as prose, although in the original an unsuccessful attempt
at line division has been made.

Are. *Vous m'obligez trop.*[1]

Born. I have no more patience; let's be merry again

In our own language. Madam, our mirth cools.—

*Enter Frederick [, intoxicated, and Steward].*

Our nephew!

Are. Passion of my brain!

Fred. Save you, gentlemen! Save you, ladies!

Are. I am undone!　　　　　　　　120

Fred. I must salute, no matter at which end I begin.　　　　　*[Kisses Celestina.]*

Are. There's a compliment!

Cel. Is this your nephew, madam?

Are. *Je vous prie, madame, d'excuser les habits et le rude comportement de mon cousin. Il est tout fraîchement venu de l'université, où on l'a tout gâté.*

Cel. *Excusez-moi, madame; il est bien accompli.*[2]　　　　　　　　　　　130

Fred. This language should be French by the motions of your heads and the mirth of your faces.

[1] Are. I beg you, madam, to pardon the importunity of my affairs, which have made me offend, by my absence, a lady from whom I have received so much obligation.

Cel. Pardon me, madam; you do me too much honor.

Are. It is indeed from the kindness of your good nature that you use such language. But I hope that my husband has not failed to entertain you in my absence.

Cel. In truth, your husband has been very kind.

Are. He would have been too remiss if he hadn't tried with all his might to render you all kinds of services.

Cel. It is out of his good nature that he has been so good to us.

Are. It is your good nature rather that makes you give such a gracious interpretation to his efforts.

Cel. I see indeed that the victory will always be madam's both in language and in courtesy.

Are. Truly, madam, no one ever more desired the honor of your company than I.

Cel. Leave compliments, I pray you, and permit your servant to kiss your hand.

Are. You are too kind.

[2] Are. I beg you, madam, to excuse the dress and the rude behavior of my kinsman. He has but lately come from the university, where they completely corrupted him.

Cel. Excuse me, madam; he is indeed accomplished.

Are. I am dishonored.

Fred. 'Tis one of the finest tongues for ladies to show their teeth in. If you'll Latin, I am for you, or Greek it; my tailor has not put me into French yet. *Mille basia, basia mille.*[3]　　　　　　　　　　　139

Cel. *Je ne vous entends pas, monsieur*— I understand you not, sir.

Fred. Why, so?

You and I then shall be in charity,

For, though we should be abusive, we ha' the benefit

Not to understand one another. Where's my aunt?

I did hear music somewhere, and my brains,

Tuned with a bottle of your capering claret,

Made haste to show their dancing.

Lit. *[Offering sweetmeats to Celestina.]*
　　　　　　　　　　　Please you, madam,

They are very comfortable.[4]

Stew.　　　　　　　　　Alas, madam,

How would you have me help it? I did use　　　　　　　　　　　150

All means I could, after he heard the music,

To make him drunk, in hope so to contain him;

But the wine made him lighter, and his head

Flew hither, ere I missed his heels.

Al. Nay, he spoke Latin to the lady.

Are. O, most unpardonable! Get him off

Quickly, and discreetly; or, if I live—

Stew. 'Tis not in my power; he swears I am

An absurd, sober fellow, and, if you keep

A servant in his house to cross his humor,　　　　　　　　　　　160

When the rich sword and belt comes home, he'll kill him.

Are. What shall I do? Try your skill, Master Littleworth.

Lit. He has ne'er a sword.—Sweet Mr. Frederick—

Born. 'Tis pity, madam, such a scion should

Be lost. But you are clouded.

Cel.　　　　　　　　　Not I, sir;

I never found myself more clear at heart.

[3] A thousand kisses, kisses a thousand (Latin).
[4] Comforting.

BORN. I could play with a feather; your fan, lady.—

Gentlemen, Aretina, ta, ra, ra, ra! Come, madam.

FRED. Why, my good tutor in election? You might have been a scholar.

LIT.                              But I thank 170
My friends they brought me up a little better.

Give me the town wits, that deliver jests

Clean from the bow, that whistle in the air,

And cleave the pin at twelvescore! Ladies do

But laugh at a gentleman that has any learning;

'Tis sin enough to have your clothes suspected.

Leave us, and I will find a time to instruct you.

Come, here are sugarplums. 'Tis a good Frederick.

FRED. Why, is not this my aunt's house in the Strand?

The noble rendezvous? Who laughs at me?                              180

Go, I will root here if I list,[1] and talk

Of rhetoric, logic, Latin, Greek, or anything,

And understand 'em too. Who says the contrary?

Yet, in a fair way, I contemn all learning,

And will be as ignorant as he, or he,

Or any taffeta, satin, scarlet, plush,

Tissue, or cloth-a-bodkin[2] gentleman,

Whose manners are most gloriously infected.—

Did you laugh at me, lady?

CEL.                              Not I, sir;
But, if I did show mirth upon your question,                              190

I hope you would not beat me, little gentleman.

FRED. How, "little gentleman"? You dare not say

These words to my new clothes and fighting sword.

ARE. Nephew Frederick!

FRED.                    "Little gentleman"!
This an affront both to my blood and person!

[1] Please.
[2] Baudekin was a rich gold and silk cloth.

I am a gentleman of as tall[3] a birth

As any boast nobility; though my clothes

Smell o' the lamp, my coat[4] is honorable,

Right honorable, full of *or* and *argent*.—

A "little gentleman"!

BORN.          Coz, you must be patient;
My lady meant you no dishonor, and

You must remember she's a woman.   202

FRED. Is she a woman? That's another matter.—

D'e hear? My uncle tells me what you are.

CEL. So, sir.

FRED.      You called me "little gentleman."

CEL. I did, sir.

FRED. A little pink[5] has made a lusty ship

Strike her topsail. The *Crow*[6] may beard the *Elephant*;[6]

A whelp[7] may tame the *Tiger*,[6] spite of all

False decks[8] and murderers;[9] and a "little gentleman"                              210

Be hard enough to grapple with your ladyship,

Top and topgallant.—Will you go drink, uncle,

Tother enchanted bottle? You and I

Will tipple, and talk philosophy.

BORN.                    Come, nephew.—
You will excuse a minute's absence, madam.—

Wait you on us.

STEW.          My duty, sir.

*Ex[eunt] All but [Aretina and] Cel[estina] and Alex[ander] and Little[worth].*

ARE.                    Now, gentlemen.

AL. Madam, I had rather you accuse my language

For speaking truth than virtue suffer in

My further silence; and it is my wonder

That you, whose noble carriage hath deserved                              220

All honor and opinion, should now

Be guilty of ill manners.

CEL.                    What was that
You told me, sir?

LIT.          Do you not blush, madam,
To ask that question?

[3] High.                    [4] Coat of arms.
[5] A small coasting vessel.
[6] Probably the name of a ship of war.
[7] A small ship.
[8] Barricades raised against boarders.
[9] Cannon discharging grapeshot.

CEL.                    You amaze rather
My cheek to paleness.  What mean you
    by this?
I am not troubled with the hiccup, gen-
    tlemen,
[1] You should bestow this fright upon me.[2]
LIT.                              Then
Pride and ill memory go together.
CEL.                          How, sir?
AL.  The gentleman on whom you exercise
Your thin wit was a nephew to the lady
Whose guest you are, and, though her
    modesty                        231
Look calm on the abuse of one so near
Her blood, the affront was impious.
LIT.                    I am ashamed on 't.
You an ingenious lady, and well man-
    nered?
I'll teach a bear as much civility.
CEL.  You may be master of the college,
    sir,
For aught I know.
LIT.              What college?
CEL.[3]                    Of the bears.
Have you a plot upon me?  D'e possess
Your wits, or know me, gentlemen?

*Enter Bornwell [behind].*

BORN.                        How's this?
AL.  [*Aside.*]  Know you?  Yes, we do know
    you to an atom.                    240
LIT.  Madam, we know what stuff your
    soul is made on.
CEL.  But do not bark so like a mastive,[4]
    pray.—
[*Aside.*]  Sure they are mad.—Let your
    brains stand awhile
And settle, gentlemen.  You know not
    me.
What am I?
LIT.          Th' art a puppet, a thing made
Of clothes and painting, and not half so
    handsome
As that which played Susanna in the fair.
CEL.  I heard you visited those canvas
    tragedies,
One of their constant audience, and so
    taken

[1] Supply *so that.*
[2] A reference to the belief that fright cured
the hiccups.
[3] In the original this speech head appears at
the beginning of the next line.
[4] Mastiff.

With Susan that you wished yourself a
    rival                            250
With the two wicked elders.
AL.                        You think this
Is wit now.  Come, you are—
CEL.                What, I beseech you?
Your character will be full of salt and
    satire,
No doubt.  What am I?
AL.                Why, you are a woman—
CEL.  And that's at least a bow [5] wide of
    your knowledge.
AL.  Would be thought handsome, and
    might pass i' th' country
Upon a market day, but miserably
Forfeit to pride and fashions, that if
    heaven
Were a new gown, you'd not stay in 't a
    fortnight.
CEL.  It must be miserably out of fashion
    then.                            260
Have I no sin but pride?
AL.                    Hast any virtue,
Or but a good face, to excuse that want?
CEL.  You praised it yesterday.
AL.                That made you proud.
CEL.  More pride?
AL.        You need not to close up the
    praise;
I have seen a better countenance in a
    sybil.
CEL.  When you wore spectacles of sack,[6]
    mistook
The painted cloth,[7] and kissed it for your
    mistress.
AL.  Let me ask you a question: how much
Have you consumed in expectation
That I would love you?
CEL.            Why, I think as much  270
As you have paid away in honest debts
This seven year.  'Tis a pretty impu-
    dence,
But cannot make me angry.
LIT.                    Is there any
Man that will cast away his limbs upon
    her?
AL.  You do not sing so well as I im-
    agined,
Nor dance; you reel in your coranto,[8]
    and pinch

[5] Bowshot.
[6] *I.e.*, had drunk too much sack.
[7] Cheap wall hangings.
[8] A lively dance.

Your petticoat too hard; y'ave no good
    ear
To th' music, and incline too much one
    shoulder,
As you were dancing on the rope, and
    falling.                  279
You speak abominable French, and make
A curtsy like a dairymaid.—[*Aside.*] Not
    mad?
Lit. [*Aside.*] Do we not sting her hand-
    somely?
Born. [*Aside.*]            A conspiracy!
Al. Your state is not so much as 'tis re-
    ported.
When you confer [1] notes, all your hus-
    band's debts
And your own reconciled—but that's
    not it
Will so much spoil your marriage.
Cel.                   As what, sir?
Let me know all my faults.
Al.             Some men do whisper
You are not overhonest.
Cel.               All this shall not
Move me to more than laughter, and
    some pity,
Because you have the shapes of gentle-
    men,                        290
And, though you have been insolent
    upon me,
I will engage no friend to kick or cudgel
    you,
To spoil your living and your limbs to-
    gether.
I leave that to diseases that offend you,
And spare my curse, poor silken vermin,
    and
Hereafter shall distinguish men from
    monkeys.
Born. [*Coming forward.*] Brave soul!—
You brace of horseleeches!—I have
    heard
Their barbarous language, madam; y' are
    too merciful.
They shall be silent to your tongue; pray,
    punish 'em.
Cel. They are things not worth my char-
    acter,[2] nor mention          300
Of any clean breath, so lost in honesty
They cannot satisfy for wrongs enough,
Though they should steal out of the
    world at Tyburn.[3]

Lit. We are hanged already.
Cel. Yet I will talk a little to the pil-
    chards.[4] —
You two, that have not twixt you both
    the hundred
Part of a soul, coarse woolen-witted
    fellows,
Without a nap, with bodies made for
    burdens,
You, that are only stuffings for apparel,
As you were made but engines [5] for your
    tailors                      310
To frame their clothes upon, and get
    them custom,
Until men see you move, yet then you
    dare not,
Out of your guilt of being the ignobler
    beast,
But give a horse the wall, whom you excel
Only in dancing of the brawls,[6] because
The horse was not taught the French
    way! Your two faces,
One fat, like Christmas, tother lean, like
    Candlemas
And prologue to a Lent, both bound to-
    gether,
Would figure Janus, and do many cures
On agues and the green disease [7] by
    frighting;                  320
But neither can, with all the characters
And conjuring circles, charm a woman,
    though
Sh'ad fourscore years upon her and but
    one
Tooth in her head, to love or think well
    of you;
And I were miserable to be at cost
To court such a complexion [8] as your
    malice
Did impudently insinuate. But I waste
    time,
And stain my breath in talking to such
    tadpoles.
Go home and wash your tongues in bar-
    ley water,
Drink [9] clean tobacco, be not hot i' th'
    mouth,                   330
And you may scape the beadle; so I leave
    you

---

[1] Compare.              [2] Characterizing.
[3] Place of execution.

[4] A term of contempt, perhaps *sardines.*
[5] *I.e.,* manikins.
[6] A French dance like a cotillion.
[7] Greensickness, chlorosis (?).
[8] Disposition.
[9] Smoke.

To shame, and your own garters!¹ —
Sir, I must
Entreat you, for my honor, do not pen-
ance 'em—
They are not worth your anger. How I
shall
Acquit your lady's silence!

BORN. Madam, I
Am sorry to suspect, and dare revenge—

CEL. No cause of mine.

BORN. It must become me to attend you
home.

CEL. You are noble.—Farewell, mushrooms! [Exit with Bornwell.]

ARE. Is she gone?

LIT. I think we peppered her.

AL. I am glad 'tis over; 340
But I repent no service for you,
madam.—

Enter Servant, with a letter [and a jewel].

To me? From whence?—A jewel! A
good preface.
Be happy the conclusion.

ARE. Some love letter. He² smiles
upon 't.

LIT. He has a hundred mistresses. You
may
Be charitable, madam; I ha' none.
He surfeits, and I fall away i' th' kidneys.

AL. I'll meet.— [Exit Servant.
Aside.] 'Tis some great lady, questionless, that has
Taken notice, and would satisfy her
appetite.

ARE. Now, Mr. Alexander, you look bright
o' the sudden; 350
Another spirit's in your eye.

AL. Not mine, madam;
Only a summons to meet a friend.

ARE. What friend?

AL.³ By this jewel, I know her not.

ARE. 'Tis a she-friend. I'll follow, gentlemen;
We may have a game at sant⁴ before
you go.

AL. I shall attend you, madam.

LIT. 'Tis our duty.
[Exit with Alexander.]

ARE. I blush while I converse with my
own thoughts.

¹ I.e., for hanging themselves.
² I.e., Alexander. ³ Original reads Lit.
⁴ Cent, a game at cards.

Some strange fate governs me, but I must
on;
The ways are cast already, and we thrive
When our sin fears no eye nor perspec-
tive.⁵ Exit. 360

THE FOURTH ACT. [SCENE i.

A room in Decoy's house.]

Enter two Men leading Alexander, blinded,⁶
and go off suddenly.

AL. I am not hurt; my patience to obey
'em,
Not without fear to ha' my throat cut
else,
Did me a courtesy. Whither ha' they
brought me? [Pulls off bandage.]
'Tis devilish dark; the bottom of a well
At midnight, with but two stars on the
top,
Were broad day to this darkness. I but
think
How like a whirlwind these rogues caught
me up,
And smotheréd⁷ my eyesight. Let me
see.
These may be spirits, and, for aught I
know,
Have brought me hither over twenty
steeples. 10
Pray heaven they were not bailiffs (that's
more worth
My fear) and this a prison! All my debts
Reek in my nostril, and my bones begin
To ache with fear to be made dice; and
yet
This is too calm and quiet for a prison.
What if the riddle prove I am robbed?
And yet
I did not feel 'em search me. [Music
within.] How now? Music?

Enter Decoy, like an old woman, with a light.

And a light? What beldam's this? I
cannot pray.—
What art?

DEC. A friend. Fear not, young
man; I am
No spirit.

AL. Off!

DEC. Despise me not for age, 20
Or this coarse outside, which I wear not
out

⁵ Telescope. ⁶ Blindfolded. ⁷ Smothered.

Of poverty. Thy eyes be witness, 'tis
No cave or beggar's cell th' art brought
    to; let
That gold speak here's no want, which
    thou mayst spend,
And find a spring to tire even prodigality,
If thou beest wise. [*Gives him a purse.*]

AL.             The devil was a coiner
From the beginning; yet the gold looks
    current.

DEC. Th' art still in wonder. Know, I am
    mistress of
This house, and of a fortune that shall
    serve
And feed thee with delights. 'Twas I sent
    for thee;                    30
The jewel and the letter came from me.
It was my art thus to contrive our meet-
    ing,
Because I would not trust thee with my
    fame,
Until I found thee worth a woman's
    honor.

AL. [*Aside.*] Honor and fame? The devil
    means to have
A care on 's credit. Though she sent for
    me,
I hope she has another customer
To do the trick withal; I would not turn
Familiar [1] to a witch.

DEC.             What say'st? Canst thou
Dwell in my arms tonight? Shall we
    change kisses,                40
And entertain the silent hours with pleas-
    ure,
Such as old Time shall be delighted with,
And blame the too swift motion of his
    wings,
While we embrace?

AL. [*Aside.*]         Embrace? She has had no
    teeth
This twenty years, and the next violent
    cough
Brings up her tongue; it cannot possibly
Be sound at root. I do not think but one
Strong sneeze upon her, and well meant,
    would make
Her quarters fall away; one kick would
    blow
Her up like gunpowder, and loose all her
    limbs.                      50
She is so cold an incubus would not heat
    her;

[1] Familiar spirit.

Her phlegm would quench a furnace, and
    her breath
Would damp a musket bullet.

DEC.                Have you, sir,
Considered?

AL.         What?

DEC.              My proposition.
Canst love?

AL.      I could have done. Whom do you
    mean?
I know you are pleased but to make
    sport.

DEC.          Thou art not
So dull of soul as thou appear'st.

AL. [*Aside.*]             This is
But some device; my grannam has some
    trick in 't.—
Yes, I can love.

DEC.        But canst thou affect [2] me?

AL. Although to reverence so grave a ma-
    tron                       60
Were an ambitious word in me, yet
    since
You give me boldness, I do love you.

DEC.               Then
Thou art my own.

AL. [*Aside.*]       Has she no cloven foot?

DEC. And I am thine, and all that I com-
    mand
Thy servants; from this minute thou art
    happy,
And fate in thee will crown all my de-
    sires.
I grieved a proper [3] man should be com-
    pelled
To bring his body to the common mar-
    ket.
My wealth shall make thee glorious; and,
    the more
To encourage thee, howe'er this form
    may fright                 70
Thy youthful eyes, yet thou wo't find,
    by light
Of thy own sense, for other light is ban-
    ished
My chamber, when our arms tie lovers'
    knots,
And kisses seal the welcome of our lips,
I shall not there affright thee, nor seem
    old,
With riveled [4] veins; my skin is smooth
    and soft
As ermines, with a spirit to meet thine,

[2] Fancy, love.    [3] Handsome.    [4] Shriveled.

Active and equal to the Queen of Love's
When she did court Adonis.

AL. [*Aside.*]                This doth more
Confirm she is a devil, and I am        80
Within his own dominions. I must on,
Or else be torn a-pieces. I have heard
These succubae must not be crossed.

DEC.                        We trifle
Too precious time away; I'll show you a
    prospect
Of the next chamber, and then out the
    candle.

AL. Have you no sack i' th' house?  I
    would go armed
Upon this breach.

DEC.            It sha' not need.

AL.                        One word,
Mother—have not you been a cat in
    your days?

DEC. I am glad you are so merry, sir. You
    observe
That bed?                [*Opens a door.*]

AL.        A very brave one.

DEC.                    When you are  90
Disrobed, you can come thither in the
    dark.
You sha' not stay for me. Come, as you
    wish
For happiness.                *Exit.*

AL.            I am preferred, if I
Be modest and obey. She cannot have
The heart to do me harm, and [1] she were
    Hecate
Herself. I will have a strong faith, and
    think
I march upon a mistress, the less evil.
If I scape fire now, I defy the devil. *Exit.*

[SCENE ii.

*A room in Bornwell's house.*]

*Enter Fred[erick], Little[worth], Steward.*

FRED. And how d'e like me now?

STEW.                    Most excellent.

FRED. Your opinion, Mr. Littlewor[th].

LIT.                    Your French tailor
Has made you a perfect gentleman; I
    may
Converse now with you, and preserve my
    credit.
D'e find no alteration in your body
With these new clothes?

FRED.                My body altered? No.

LIT. You are not yet in fashion then. That
    must
Have a new motion, garb, and posture
    too,
Or all your pride is cast away; it is not
The cut of your apparel makes a gallant,
But the geometrical wearing of your
    clothes.                        11

STEW. Mr. Littleworth tells you right; you
    wear your hat
Too like a citizen.

LIT.                'Tis like a midwife.
Place it with best advantage of your hair.
Is half your feather molted?  This does
    make
No show; it should spread over, like a
    canopy.
Your hot-reined[2] monsieur wears it for a
    shade
And cooler to his back.  Your doublet
    must
Be more unbuttoned hereabouts; you'll
    not
Be a sloven else. A foul shirt is no blem-
    ish;                            20
You must be confident, and outface clean
    linen.
Your doublet and your breeches must be
    allowed
No private meeting here; your cloak's
    too long.
It reaches to your buttock, and doth
    smell
Too much of Spanish gravity; the
    fashion
Is to wear nothing but a cape; a coat
May be allowed a covering for one elbow,
And some, to avoid the trouble, choose
    to walk
In *quirpo*,[3] thus.

STEW. [*Aside.*]                Your coat and
    cloak's a-brushing
In Long Lane, Lumbard.[4]

FRED.            But what if it rain?  30

LIT. Your belt about your shoulder is suffi-
    cient
To keep off any storm; beside, a reed
But waved discreetly has so many pores
It sucks up all the rain that falls about
    one.

---

[1] If.   [2] The loins were once thought to be the
seat of the passions.

[3] *Cuérpo* (Span.); *i.e.*, in your shirt.
[4] The Lombard district was famous for pawn-
shops.

With this defense, when other men have
  been
Wet to the skin through all their cloaks,
  I have
Defied a tempest, and walked by the
  taverns
Dry as a bone.
STEW. [*Aside.*]      Because he had no
  money
To call for wine.
FRED.     Why, you do walk enchanted.
  Have you such pretty charms in town?
  But stay.                   40
Who must I have to attend me?
LIT.                Is not that
  Yet thought upon?
STEW.      I have laid out [1] for servants.
LIT. They are everywhere.
STEW.        I cannot yet be furnished
  With such as I would put into his
  hands.
FRED. Of what condition must they be,
  and how
  Many in number, sir?
LIT.          Beside your fencing,
  Your singing, dancing, riding, and
  French master,
  Two may serve domestic, to be constant
  waiters
  Upon a gentleman: a fool, a pimp.
STEW. For these two officers I have in-
  quired,                 50
  And I am promised a convenient
  whiskin.[2]
  I could save charges, and employ the pie-
  wench,
  That carries her intelligence in white-
  pots; [3]
  Or 'tis but taking order with the woman
  That holds the ballads—she could fit him
  with
  A concubine to any tune; but I
  Have a design to place a fellow with
  him
  That has read all Sir Pandarus' works, a
  Trojan [4]
  That lies concealed, and is acquainted
  with
  Both city and suburbian fripperies,[5]  60
  Can fetch 'em with a spell at midnight to
  him,

And warrant which are for his turn; can,
  for
  A need, supply the surgeon too.
FRED.                I like
  Thy providence; [6] such a one deserves a
  livery twice a year.
STEW. It sha' not need; a cast [7] suit of your
  worship's
  Will serve; he'll find a cloak to cover it,
  Out of his share with those he brings to
  bed to you.
FRED. But must I call this fellow pimp?
LIT.                   It is
  Not necessary—or [8] Jack or Harry,
  Or what he's known abroad by, will
  sound better,            70
  That men may think he is a Christian.
FRED. But hear you, Mr. Littleworth: is
  there not
  A method and degrees of title in
  Men of this art?
LIT.           According to the honor
  Of men that do employ 'em. An emperor
  May give this office to a duke; a king
  May have his viceroy to negotiate for
  him;
  A duke may use a lord; the lord a knight;
  A knight may trust a gentleman; and,
  when                79
  They are abroad and merry, gentlemen
  May pimp to one another.
FRED.        Good, good fellowship!
  But for the fool now, that should wait on
  me,
  And break me jests?
LIT.           A fool is necessary.
STEW. By any [9] means.
FRED.     But which of these two servants
  Must now take place? [10]
LIT.       That question, Mr. Frederick,
  The school of heraldry should conclude
  upon;
  But, if my judgment may be heard, the
  fool
  Is your first man; and it is known a
  point
  Of state to have a fool.
STEW.         But, sir, the other
  Is held the finer servant; his employ-
  ments                90
  Are full of trust, his person clean and
  nimble,

---

[1] Been on the lookout.
[2] Go-between.      [4] Sly rascal.
[3] Milkpuddings.     [5] Suburban prostitutes.

[6] Foresight.     [8] Either.
[7] Discarded.    [9] All.      [10] Precedence.

And none so soon can leap into preferment,
Where fools are poor.

LIT.        Not all; there's story for 't:
Princes have been no wiser than they
should be.
Would any nobleman, that were no fool,
Spend all in hope of the philosophers'
stone,
To buy new lordships in another coun-
try?
Would knights build colleges, or gentle-
men
Of good estates challenge the field, and
fight,
Because a whore wo' not be honest?
Come,        100
Fools are a family over all the world;
We do affect one naturally; indeed
The fool is lieger [1] with us.

STEW.        Then the pimp
Is extraordinary.

FRED.        Do not you fall out
About their places.—Here's my noble
aunt!

*Enter Aretina.*

LIT. How do you like your nephew, madam,
now?

ARE. Well!—Turn about, Frederick.—
Very well!

FRED.[2] Am I not now a proper gentleman?
The virtue of rich clothes! Now could I
take
The wall of Julius Cæsar, affront        110
Great Pompey's upper lip, and defy the
senate.
Nay, I can be as proud as your own heart,
madam;
You may take that for your comfort. I
put on
That virtue with my clothes, and I doubt
not
But in a little time I shall be impudent
As any page, or player's boy. I am
Beholding to this gentleman's good disci-
pline;
But I shall do him credit in my practice.
Your steward has some pretty notions,
too,
In moral mischief.

ARE.        Your desert in this   120
Exceeds all other service, and shall bind
me
Both to acknowledge and reward.

LIT.        Sweet madam,
Think me but worth your favor; I would
creep
Upon my knees to honor you, and, for
every
Minute you lend to my reward, I'll pay
A year of serviceable tribute.

ARE.        You
Can compliment.

LIT. [*Aside.*]        Thus still she puts me off;
Unless I speak the downright word, she'll
never
Understand me. A man would think that
creeping
Upon one's knees were English to a
lady.        130

*Enter Alex[ander].*

AL. How is 't, Jack?—Pleasures attend
you, madam!
How does my plant of honor?

ARE.        Who is this?

AL. 'Tis Alexander.

ARE.        Rich and glorious!

LIT. 'Tis Alexander the Great.

AL.        And my Bucephalus
Waits at the door.

ARE.        Your case is altered, sir.

AL. I cannot help these things. The Fates
will have it.
'Tis not my land does this.

LIT.        But thou hast a plow
That brings it in.

ARE.        Now he looks brave and lovely.

FRED. Welcome, my gallant Macedonian.

AL. Madam, you gave your nephew for my
pupil.        140
I read [3] but in a tavern; if you'll honor us,
The Bear at the bridge foot shall enter-
tain you.
A drawer [4] is my Ganymede; he shall
skink [5]
Brisk nectar to us. We will only have
A dozen partridge in a dish; as many
pheasants,
Quails, cocks, and godwits [6] shall come
marching up

---

[1] Ledger, resident, as an ordinary ambassador.
[2] Original reads *Are.*

[3] Lecture, teach.
[4] Waiter.

[5] Draw.
[6] Snipe.

Like the trained-band; [1] a fort of sturgeon
Shall give most bold defiance to an army,
And triumph o'er the table.
ARE.                    Sir, it will
But dull the appetite to hear more, and
mine                                      150
Must be excused.  Another time I may
Be your guest.
AL.                    'Tis grown in fashion
now with ladies.
When you please, I'll attend you.  Little-
worth!—
Come, Frederick.
FRED.        We'll have music; I love noise.
We will outroar the Thames, and shake
the bridge, boy.  Ex[it with Alexander].
LIT.  Madam, I kiss your hand; would you
would think
Of your poor servant.  Flesh and blood is
frail,
And troublesome to carry without help.
ARE.  A coach will easily convey it, or
You may take water at Strand Bridge.
LIT.                    But I  160
Have taken fire.
ARE.                    The Thames will cool—
LIT.  But never quench my heart; your
charity
Can only do that.
ARE.                    I will keep it cold
Of purpose.
LIT.        Now you bless me, and I dare
Be drunk in expectation.        [Exit.]
ARE.                    I am confident
He knows me not, and I were worse than
mad
To be my own betrayer.—Here's my
husband.

*Enter Born[well].*

BORN.  Why, how now, Aretina?  What!
Alone?
The mystery of this solitude?  My house
Turn desert o' the sudden?  All the game-
sters                                     170
Blown up?  Why is the music put to
silence?
Or ha' their instruments caught a cold,
since we
Gave 'em the last heat?  I must know thy
ground
Of melancholy.

[1] London militia.

ARE.                    You are merry, as
You came from kissing Celestina.
BORN.                              I
Feel her yet warm upon my lip; she is
Most excellent company.  I did not think
There was that sweetness in her sex.  I
must
Acknowledge 'twas thy cure to disen-
chant me                                  179
From a dull husband to an active lover.
With such a lady I could spend more
years
Than since my birth my glass hath run
soft minutes,
And yet be young.  Her presence has a
spell
To keep off age; she has an eye would
strike
Fire through an adamant.
ARE.                    I have heard as much
Bestowed upon a dull-faced chamber-
maid,
Whom love and wit would thus com-
mend.  True beauty
Is mocked when we compare thus, itself
being
Above what can be fetched to make it
lovely,
Or could our thoughts reach something
to declare                                190
The glories of a face, or body's elegance
(That touches but our sense), when
beauty spreads
Over the soul, and calls up understanding
To look what [2] thence is offered, and ad-
mire!
In both I must acknowledge Celestina
Most excellently fair, fair above all
The beauties I ha' seen, and one most
worthy
Man's love and wonder.
BORN.                    Do you speak, Aretina,
This with a pure sense to commend?  Or
is 't
The mockery of my praise?
ARE.                    Although it shame  200
Myself, I must be just, and give her all
The excellency of women; and, were I
A man—
BORN.        What then?
ARE.                    I know not with what loss
I should attempt her love.  She is a piece
So angelically moving, I should think

[2] Gifford-Dyce's reading.  Original reads *when.*

Frailty excused to dote upon her form,
And almost virtue to be wicked with her.
*Exit.*

BORN. What should this mean? This is no jealousy,
Or she believes I counterfeit. I feel
Something within me, like a heat, to give                                    210
Her cause, would Celestina but consent.
What a frail thing is man! It is not worth
Our glory to be chaste, while we deny
Mirth and converse with women. He is good
That dares the tempter, yet corrects his blood.                            *Exit.*

[SCENE iii.

*A room in Celestina's house.*

*Enter]* Celestina, Mariana, Isabella.

CEL. I have told you all my knowledge; since he is pleased
To invite himself, he shall be entertained,
And you shall be my witnesses.

MAR.                    Who comes with him?

CEL. Sir William Scentlove, that prepared me for
The honorable encounter. I expect
His lordship every minute.

*Enter Scentlove.*

SCENT.                    My lord is come.

*Enter Lord, Haircut.*

CEL. He has honored me.

SCENT.    My lord, your periwig is awry!

LORD. You, sir—

*While Haircut is busy about his hair, Scent-
love goes to Celestina.*

SCENT. You may guess at the gentleman that's with him.                    9
It is his barber, madam, d'e observe,
And your ladyship wants a shaver.

HAIR.                    She is here, sir.
I am betrayed.—Scentlove, your plot. I may
Have opportunity to be revenged. *Exit.*

SCENT. She in the midst.

LORD.            She's fair, I must confess;
But does she keep this distance out of state?

CEL. Though I am poor in language to express

How much your lordship honors me, my heart
Is rich and proud in such a guest. I shall
Be out of love with every air abroad,
And, for his grace done my unworthy house,                                20
Be a fond prisoner, become anchorite,
And spend my hours in prayer, to reward
The blessing and the bounty of this presence.

LORD. Though you could turn each place you move in, to
A temple, rather than a wall should hide
So rich a beauty from the world, it were
Less want to lose our piety and your prayer.
A throne were fitter to present you to
Our wonder, whence your eyes, more worth than all
They look on, should chain every heart a prisoner.                        30

SCENT. [*Aside.*] 'Twas pretty well come off.

LORD.    By your example
I shall know how to compliment; in this,
You more confirm my welcome.

CEL.                    I shall love
My lips the better, if their silent language
Persuade your lordship but to think so truly.

LORD. You make me smile, madam.

CEL.            I hope you came not
With fear that any sadness here should shake
One blossom from your eye. I should be miserable
To present any object should displease you.

LORD. You do not, madam.

CEL.        As I should account    40
It no less sorrow, if your lordship should
Lay too severe a censure on my freedom.
I wo' not court a prince against his justice,
Nor bribe him with a smile to think me honest.
Pardon, my lord, this boldness and the mirth
That may flow from me. I believe my father
Thought of no winding sheet when he begot me.

LORD. [*Aside.*] She has a merry soul.—It
  will become
  Me ask your pardon, madam, for my
    rude
  Approach, so much a stranger to your
    knowledge.               50
CEL. Not, my lord, so much stranger to
  my knowledge;
  Though I have but seen your person afar
    off,
  I am acquainted with your character,
  Which I have heard so often I can
    speak it.
LORD. You shall do me an honor.
CEL.               If your lordship will
  Be patient.
LORD.        And glad to hear my faults.
CEL. That, as your conscience can agree
  upon 'em.
  However, if your lordship give me privi-
    lege,
  I'll tell you what's the opinion of the
    world.
LORD. You cannot please me better.
CEL.             Y' are a lord  60
  Born with as much nobility as would,
  Divided, serve to make ten noblemen
  Without a herald, but with so much
    spirit
  And height of soul as well might furnish
    twenty.
  You are learnéd, a thing not compatible
    now
  With native honor, and are master of
  A language that doth chain all ears,[1]
    and charm
  All hearts, where you persuade; a wit so
    flowing,
  And prudence to correct it, that all men
  Believe they only meet in you, which,
    with                70
  A spacious memory, make up the full
    wonders.
  To these, you have known valor, and
    upon
  A noble cause know how to use a sword
  To honor's best advantage, though you
    wear none.
  You are as bountiful as the showers that
    fall
  Into the Spring's green bosom, as you
    were
  Created lord of Fortune, not her steward;

[1] Gifford-Dyce reading. Original reads *years.*

So constant to tne cause in which you
  make
Yourself an advocate, you dare all dan-
  gers;
And men had rather you should be their
  friend              80
Than justice or the bench bound up
  together.
LORD. But did you hear all this?
CEL.              And more, my lord.
LORD. Pray, let me have it, madam.
CEL. To all these virtues there is added
  one
  (Your lordship will remember, when I
    name it,
  I speak but what I gather from the voice
  Of others)—it is grown to a full fame [2]
  That you have loved a woman.
LORD.           But one, madam?
CEL. Yes, many. Give me leave to smile,
  my lord;
  I shall not need to interpret in what
    sense.             90
  But you have showed yourself right hon-
    orable,
  And, for your love to ladies, have de-
    served,
  If their vote might prevail, a marble
    statue.
  I make no comment on the people's text.
  My lord, I should be sorry to offend.
LORD. You cannot, madam; these are
  things we owe
  To nature for.
CEL.         And honest men will pay
  Their debts.
LORD.     If they be able, or compound.
CEL. She had a hard heart would be un-
  merciful,           99
  And not give day [3] to men so promising;
  But you owed women nothing.
LORD.             Yes, I am
  Still in their debt, and I must owe them
    love;
  It was part of my character.
CEL.          With your lordship's
  Pardon, I only said you had a fame
  For loving women; but of late men say
  You have, against the imperial laws of
    love,
  Restrained the active flowings of your
    blood,

[2] Report.

[3] "Good day," *i.e.*, notice, attention.

And with a mistress buried all that is
Hoped for in love's succession, as all
    beauty
Had died with her, and left the world be-
    nighted!                                  110
In this you more dishonor all our sex
Than you did grace a part, when every-
    where
Love tempts your eye to admire a glori-
    ous harvest,
And everywhere as full-blown ears sub-
    mit
Their golden heads, the laden trees bow
    down
Their willing fruit, and court your
    amorous tasting.
LORD. I see men would dissect me to a
    fiber.
But do you believe this?
CEL.                It is my wonder,
I must confess, a man of nobler earth
Than goes to vulgar composition    120
(Born and bred high, so unconfined, so
    rich
In fortunes, and so read in all that
    sum
Up human knowledge, to feed gloriously,
And live at court, the only sphere where-
    in
True beauty moves, nature's most
    wealthy garden,
Where every blossom is more worth than
    all
The Hesperian fruit by jealous dragon
    watched,
Where all delights do circle appetite,
And pleasures multiply by being tasted)
Should be so lost with thought of one,
    turn ashes.                              130
There's nothing left, my lord, that can
    excuse you,
Unless you plead what I am ashamed to
    prompt
Your wisdom to.
LORD          What's that?
CEL.               That you have played
The surgeon with yourself.
LORD.               And am made eunuch?
CEL. It were much pity.
LORD.               Trouble not yourself;
I could convince your fears with demon-
    stration
That I am man enough, but knew not
    where,

Until this meeting, beauty dwelt.  The
    court
You talked of must be where the Queen
    of Love is,
Which moves but with your person; in
    your eye                                  140
Her glory shines, and only at that flame
Her wanton boy doth light his quick'ning
    torch.
CEL. Nay, now you compliment; I would
    it did,
My lord, for your own sake.
LORD.                You would be kind,
And love me then?
CEL.               My lord, I should be loving
Where I found worth to invite it, and
    should cherish
A constant man.
LORD.         Then you should me, madam.
CEL. But is the ice about your heart fallen
    off?
Can you return to do what love com-
    mands?—                                  149
Cupid, thou shalt have instant sacrifice,
And I dare be the priest.
LORD.                Your hand, your lip.
                            [*Kisses her.*]
Now I am proof gainst all temptation.
CEL. Your meaning, my good lord?
LORD.                I, that have strength
Against thy voice and beauty, after
    this
May dare the charms of womankind.—
    Thou art,
Bella Maria, unprofanéd yet;
This magic has no power upon my
    blood.—
Farewell, madam!  If you durst be the
    example
Of chaste as well as fair, thou wert a
    brave one.
CEL. I hope your lordship means not this
    for earnest;                            160
Be pleased to grace a banquet.
LORD.                Pardon, madam.—
Will Scentlove, follow; I must laugh at
    you.
CEL. My lord, I must beseech you stay,
    for honor
For her whose memory you love best.
LORD.                Your pleasure.
CEL. And, by that virtue you have now
    professed,
I charge you to believe me too; I can

Now glory that you have been worth my
trial,

Which, I beseech you, pardon.  Had not
you

So valiantly recovered in this conflict,

You had been my triumph, without hope
of more                                          170

Than my just scorn upon your wanton
flame;

Nor will I think these noble thoughts
grew first

From melancholy for some female loss,

As the fantastic world believes, but from

Truth and your love of innocence, which
shine

So bright in the two royal luminaries

At court,[1] you cannot lose your way to
chastity.

Proceed, and speak of me as honor guides
you.                                *Exit Lord.*

I am almost tired.—Come, ladies, we'll
beguile

Dull time, and take the air another while.
                                        *Exeunt.*

THE FIFTH ACT.  [SCENE i.

*A room in Bornwell's house.*]

*Enter Aretina and Servant [with a purse].*

ARE.  But hath Sir Thomas lost five hundred pounds
Already?

SER.        And five hundred more he borrowed.

The dice are notable devourers, madam;

They make no more of pieces than of
pebbles,

But thrust their heaps together to engender.

"Two hundred more!" the caster[2] cries
this[3] gentleman.

"I am w'e.  I ha' that to nothing, sir."
The caster

Again: " 'Tis covered!"—and the table
too,

With sums that frighted me.  Here one
sneaks out,                                        9

And with a martyr's patience smiles upon

His money's executioner, the dice,

Commands a pipe of good tobacco, and

I' th' smoke on 't vanishes.  Another
makes

The bones vault o'er his head, swears
that ill-throwing

Has put his shoulder out of joint, calls for

A bonesetter, that looks to th' box, to bid

His master send him some more hundred
pounds,

Which lost, he takes tobacco, and is
quiet.

Here a strong arm throws in and in, with
which

He brusheth all the table,[4] pays the
rooks[5]                                           20

That went their smelts[6] apiece upon his
hand,

Yet swears he has not drawn a stake this
seven year.

But I was bid make haste; my master
may

Lose this five hundred pounds ere I come
thither.                                    *Exit.*

ARE.  If we both waste so fast, we shall
soon find

Our state is not immortal.  Something in

His other ways appear not well already.

*Enter Sir Thomas [with Servants].*

BORN.  Ye tortoises, why make you no
more haste?

Go pay to th' master of the house that
money,

And tell the noble gamesters I have another                                              30

Superfluous thousand pound; at night I'll
visit 'em.

D'e hear?

SER.        Yes, and please you.

BORN.        Do 't, ye drudges.—
                            [*Exeunt Servants.*]

Ta, ra, ra!—Aretina!

ARE.    You have a pleasant humor, sir.

BORN.  What, should a gentleman be sad?

ARE.                      You have lost—

BORN.  A transitory sum; as good that
way

As another.

ARE.        Do you not vex within for 't?

BORN.  I had rather lose a thousand more
than one

Sad thought come near my heart for 't.
Vex for trash?

Although it go from other men like drops

---

[1] Charles I and Queen Henrietta Maria.
[2] Thrower of dice.          [3] *I.e.*, to this.

[4] Wins all the stakes.
[5] Gulls, fools.        [6] Bet their half-guineas.

Of their life blood, we lose with the
alacrity   40
We drink a cup of sack, or kiss a mistress.
No money is considerable with a game-
ster;
They have souls more spacious than
kings. Did two
Gamesters divide the empire of the world,
They'd make one throw for 't all, and he
that lost
Be no more melancholy than to have
played for
A morning's draught. Vex a rich soul for
dirt,
The quiet of whose every thought is
worth
A province!

ARE.    But, when dice have consumed
all,
Your patience will not pawn for as much
more.   50

BORN. Hang pawning! Sell outright, and
the fear's over.

ARE. Say you so? I'll have another coach
tomorrow
If there be rich above ground.

BORN.      I forgot
To bid the fellow ask my jeweler
Whether the chain of diamonds be made
up;
I will present it to my Lady Bellamour,
Fair Celestina.

ARE.      This gown I have worn
Six days already; it looks dull. I'll give it
My waiting-woman, and have one of
cloth
Of gold embrodered; shoes and pant-
ables [1]   60
Will show well of the same.

BORN.      I have invited
A covey of ladies, and as many gentlemen
Tomorrow, to the Italian ordinary;
I shall have rarities and regalias [2]
To pay for, madam; music, wanton
songs,
And tunes of silken petticoats to dance
to.

ARE. And tomorrow have I invited half
the court
To dine here. What misfortune 'tis your
company
And ours should be divided! After dinner
I entertain 'em with a play.

[1] Slippers.      [2] Regalos, delicacies.

BORN.      By that time   70
Your play inclines to the epilogue, shall
we
Quit our Italian host, and whirl in
coaches
To the Dutch magazine of sauce,[3] the
Stillyard, [4]
Where deal,[5] and backrag,[6] and what
strange wine else
They dare but give a name to in the
reckoning,
Shall flow into our room, and drown
Westphalias,[7]
Tongues, and anchovies, like some little
town
Endangered by a sluice, through whose
fierce ebb
We wade, and wash ourselves into a boat,
And bid our coachmen drive their
leather tenements   80
By land, while we sail home with a fresh
tide
To some new rendezvous.

ARE.      If you have not
Pointed [8] the place, pray, bring your
ladies hither;
I mean to have a ball tomorrow night,
And a rich banquet for 'em, where we'll
dance
Till morning rise and blush to interrupt
us.

BORN. Have you no ladies i' th' next room
to advance
A present mirth? What a dull house you
govern!
Farewell! A wife's no company.—Aretina,
I've summed up my estate, and find we
may have   90
A month good yet.

ARE.      What mean you?

BORN.      And I'd rather
Be lord one month of pleasures, to the
height
And rapture of our senses, than be years
Consuming what we have in foolish tem-
perance,
Live in the dark, and no fame wait upon
us!

[3] Storehouse of sauce, tavern.
[4] The Steelyard, in the former German trading
district of the same name.
[5] An unidentified kind of German wine.
[6] Baccarach, a Rhenish wine.
[7] Westphalian hams.      [8] Appointed.

I will live so posterity shall stand
At gaze when I am mentioned.
ARE.                    A month good!
And what shall be done then?
BORN.                    I'll over sea,
And trail a pike. With watching, march-
ing, lying
In trenches, with enduring cold and
hunger,                              100
And, taking here and there a musket shot,
I can earn every week four shillings,
madam;
And, if the bullets favor me to snatch
Any superfluous limb, when I return
With good friends, I despair not to be
enrolled
Poor Knight of Windsor.[1] For your
course, madam,
No doubt you may do well; your friends
are great;
Or, if your poverty and their pride can-
not
Agree, you need not trouble much in-
vention
To find a trade to live by; there are cus-
tomers.                              110
Farewell; be frolic, madam! If I live,
I will feast all my senses, and not fall
Less than a Phaëton from my throne of
pleasure,
Though my estate flame like the world
about me.
ARE. 'Tis very pretty!—

*Enter Decoy.*

Madam Decoy! *Exit [Bornwell].*
DEC.                    What! Melancholy
After so sweet a night's work? Have
not I
Showed myself mistress of my art?
ARE.                              A lady.
DEC. That title makes the credit of the
act
A story higher. Y'ave not seen him yet?
I wonder what he'll say.
ARE.                    He's here.

*Enter Alexander and Frederick.*

AL.                    Bear up,  120
My little myrmidon;[2] does not Jack
Littleworth
Follow?

FRED.    Follow? He fell into the Thames
At landing.
AL.              The devil shall dive for him,
Ere I endanger my silk stockings for
him.
Let the watermen alone; they have drags
and engines.
When he has drunk his julep, I shall
laugh
To see him come in pickled the next tide.
FRED. He'll never sink, he has such a cork
brain.
AL. Let him be hanged or drowned, all's
one to me;                          128
Yet he deserves to die by water, cannot[3]
Bear his wine credibly.
FRED.              Is not this my aunt?
AL. And another handsome lady; I must
know her.        [*Takes Decoy aside.*]
FRED. [*Aside.*] My blood is rampant too;
I must court somebody—
As good my aunt as any other body.
ARE. Where have you been, cousin?
FRED.                    At the bridge
At the Bear's foot, where our first health
began
To the fair Aretina, whose sweet com-
pany
Was wished by all. We could not get a
lay,
A tumbler, a device, a *bona roba*,[4]
For any money; drawers were grown
dull.                                140
We wanted our true firks[5] and our
vagaries.—
When were you in drink, aunt?
ARE.                    How?
FRED.                    Do not ladies
Play the good fellows too? There's no
true mirth
Without 'em. I have now such tickling
fancies!
That doctor of the chair of wit has read
A precious lecture, how I should behave
Myself to ladies; as now, for example—
ARE. Would you practice upon me?
FRED.        I first salute you. [*Kisses her.*]
You have a soft hand, madam; are you so
All over?
ARE. Nephew!
FRED.        Nay, you should but smile.  150
                    [*Kisses her again.*]

---

[1] A pensioned knight who had quarters in
Windsor Castle.        [2] An obedient retainer.

[3] *I.e.,* who cannot.
[4] Four synonyms for *courtesan.*        [5] Tricks.

And then again I kiss you, and thus draw
Off your white glove, and start, to see your hand
More excellently white. I grace my own
Lip with this touch, and, turning gently thus,
Prepare you for my skill in palmistry,
Which, out of curiosity, no lady
But easily applies [1] to. The first line
I look [2] with most ambition to find out,
Is Venus' girdle, a fair semicircle,
Enclosing both the mount of Sol and Saturn;                                                          160
If that appear, she's for my turn—a lady
Whom nature has prepared for the career;
And, Cupid at my elbow, I put forward.
You have this very line, aunt.
ARE.                                    The boy's frantic!
FRED. You have a couch or pallet; I can shut
The chamber door. Enrich a stranger, when
Your nephew's coming into play!
ARE.                                    No more.
FRED. Are you so coy to your own flesh and blood?
AL. [*Coming forward.*] Here, take your playfellow; I talk of sport,
And she would have me marry her.        170
FRED. Here's Littleworth.—

*Enter Littleworth, wet.*

Why, how now, tutor?
LIT.                        I ha' been fishing.
FRED. And what ha' you caught?
LIT.                        My belly full of water.
AL. Ha, ha! Where's thy rapier?
LIT.                        My rapier is drowned,
And I am little better. I was up by th' heels,
And out came a tun of water, beside wine.
AL. 'T has made thee sober.
LIT.                        Would you have me drunk
With water?
ARE.    I hope your fire is quenched by this time.
FRED. It is not now, as when your worship "walked                                    179
By all the taverns, Jack, dry as a bone."

AL. You had store of fish under water, Jack.
LIT. It has made a poor John [3] of me.
FRED. I do not think but if we cast an angle
Into his belly, we might find some pilchards.
LIT. And boiled, by this time.—Dear madam, a bed.
AL. Carry but the water spaniel to a grass plot,
Where he may roll himself; let him but shake
His ears twice in the sun, and you may grind him
Into a posset. [4]
FRED.        Come, thou shalt to my bed,
Poor pickerel.
DEC.        Alas, sweet gentleman!    190
LIT. I have ill luck and I should smell by this time;
I am but new ta'en, I am sure.—Sweet gentlewoman!
DEC. Your servant.
LIT.        Pray, do not pluck off my skin;
It is so wet, unless you have good eyes,
You'll hardly know it from a shirt.
DEC.                        Fear nothing.
*Exeunt [All but Aretina and Alexander].* [5]
ARE. [*Aside.*] He has sack enough, and I may find his humor.
AL. And how is 't with your ladyship? You look
Without a sunshine in your face.
ARE.                        You are glorious
In mind and habit.
AL.                Ends of gold and silver!
ARE. Your other clothes were not so rich. Who was                                    200
Your tailor, sir?
AL.        They were made for me long since;
They have known but two bright days upon my back.
I had a humor, madam, to lay things by;
They will serve two days more. I think I ha' gold enough
To go to th' mercer. I'll now allow myself
A suit a week, as this, with necessary
Dependences, beaver, silk stockings, garters,
And roses, [6] in their due conformity;

[1] Yields.
[2] Emended by Gifford-Dyce. Original reads *look*.        [3] A poor John was a small dried fish.
[4] A spiced drink.
[5] This stage direction follows the next line in the original.        [6] Rosettes.

Boots are forbid a clean leg but to ride
in. 209
My linen every morning comes in new;
The old goes to great bellies.
ARE. You are charitable.
AL. I may dine w'e sometime, or at the
court,
To meet good company, not for the table.
My clerk o' th' kitchen's here, a witty
epicure,
A spirit, that, to please me with what's
rare,
Can fly a hundred mile a day to market,
And make me Lord of Fish and Fowl. I
shall
Forget there is a butcher; and to make
My footman nimble he shall feed on
nothing
But wings of wild fowl.
ARE. These ways are costly. 220
AL. Therefore I'll have it so; I ha' sprung
a mine.
ARE. You make me wonder, sir, to see
this change
Of fortune; your revenue was not late
So plentiful.
AL. Hang dirty land and lordships!
I wo' not change one lodging I ha' got
For the Chamber of London.
ARE. Strange, of such a sudden
To rise to this estate! No fortunate hand
At dice could lift you up so, for 'tis since
Last night; yesterday you were no such
monarch.
AL. There be more games than dice.
ARE. It cannot be 230
A mistress, though your person is worth
love;
None possibly are rich enough to feed
As you have cast the method of your
riots.
A princess, after all her jewels, must
Be forced to sell her provinces.
AL. [Showing a jewel.] Now you talk
Of jewels, what do you think of this?
ARE. A rich one.
AL. You'll honor me to wear 't. This
other toy
I had from you. This chain I borrowed
of you;
A friend had it in keeping. [Gives her the
jewelry.] If your ladyship
Want any sum, you know your friend,
and Alexander. 240

ARE. Dare you trust my security?
AL. There's gold;
I shall have more tomorrow.
ARE. You astonish me.
Who can supply these?
AL. A dear friend I have.
She promised we should meet again i' th'
morning.
ARE. Not that I wish to know
More of your happiness than I have a
ready
Heart to congratulate, be pleased to lay
My wonder.
AL. 'Tis a secret—
ARE. Which I'll die
Ere I'll betray.
AL. You have always wished me well;
But you shall swear not to reveal the
party. 250
ARE. I'll lose the benefit of my tongue.
AL. Nor be
Afraid at what I say. What think you
first
Of an old witch, a strange, ill-favored
hag,
That, for my company last night, has
wrought
This cure upon my fortune? I do sweat
To think upon her name.
ARE. How, sir, a witch?
AL. I would not fright your ladyship too
much
At first, but witches are akin to spirits.
The truth is—nay, if you look pale al-
ready, 259
I ha' done.
ARE. Sir, I beseech you.
AL. If you have
But courage then to know the truth, I'll
tell you
In one word: my chief friend is—the
devil!
ARE. What devil? How I tremble!
AL. Have a heart;
'Twas a she-devil too, a most insatiate,
Abominable devil, with a tail
Thus long.
ARE. Goodness defend me! Did you see
her?
AL. No, 'twas i' th' dark; but she appeared
first to me
I' th' likeness of a beldam,[1] and was
brought,

[1] Original reads bedlam.

I know not how nor whither, by two
   goblins,                                    269
More hooded than a hawk.
ARE.                    But would you venter [1]
   Upon a devil?
AL.                    Ay, for means.
ARE. [*Aside*.]                    How black
   An impudence is this!—But are you sure
   It was the devil you enjoyed?
AL.                    Say nothing;
   I did the best to please her; but, as
   sure
   As you live, 'twas a hell-cat.
ARE.                    D'e not quake?
AL. I found myself in the very room [2] i' th'
   morning,
   Where two of her familiars had left me.

*Enter Servant.*

SER. My lord is come to visit you.
AL.                    No words,
   As you respect my safety. I ha' told
   tales
   Out of the devil's school; if it be
   known,                                    280
   I lose a friend. 'Tis now about the
   time
   I promised her to meet again; at my
   Return I'll tell you wonders. Not a
   word!                                    *Exit.*
ARE. [*Looking in a mirror.*] 'Tis a false
   glass; sure I am more deformed.
   What have I done? My soul is miserable.

*Enter Lord.*

LORD. I sent you a letter, madam.
ARE.                    You expressed
   Your noble care of me, my lord.

*Enter Bornwell, Celestina.*

BORN.                    Your lordship
   Does me an honor.
LORD.                    Madam, I am glad
   To see you here; I meant to have kissed
   your hand                                 289
   Ere my return to court.
CEL.                    Sir Thomas has
   Prevailed to bring me, to his trouble,
   hither.
LORD. You do him grace.

BORN.                    Why, what's the matter,
   madam?
   Your eyes are tuning "Lachrimæ." [3]
ARE.                    As you
   Do hope for heaven, withdraw, and give
   me but
   The patience of ten minutes.
BORN.                    Wonderful!
   I wo' not hear you above that proportion.
   She talks of heaven.—Come, where must
   we to counsel?
ARE. You shall conclude [4] me when you
   please.                                    [*Exit.*]
BORN.          I follow.
LORD. [*Aside.*] What alteration is this? I,
   that so late                               299
   Stood the temptation of her eye and voice,
   Boasted a heart 'bove all licentious flame,
   At second view turn renegade, and think
   I was too superstitious, and full
   Of phlegm, not to reward her amorous
   courtship
   With manly freedom.
CEL.                    I obey you, sir.
BORN. I'll wait upon your lordship pres-
   ently.                                    [*Exit.*]
LORD. [*Aside.*] She could not want a cun-
   ning to seem honest
   When I neglected her. I am resolved.—
   You still look pleasant, madam.
CEL.                    I have cause,
   My lord, the rather for your presence,
   which                                      310
   Hath power to charm all trouble in my
   thoughts.
LORD. I must translate that compliment,
   and owe
   All that is cheerful in myself to these
   All-quick'ning smiles; and, rather than
   such bright
   Eyes should repent their influence upon
   me,
   I would release the aspects, and quit the
   bounty
   Of all the other stars. Did you not think
   me
   A strange and melancholy gentleman
   To use you so unkindly?
CEL.                    Me, my lord?
LORD. I hope you made no loud complaint;
   I would not                                320
   Be tried by a jury of ladies.

---

[1] Venture.
[2] Emended by Gifford-Dyce. Original reads
*the very same in.*

[3] *I.e.*, beginning to weep. "Lachrimæ," or
"Tears," was a melancholy song.          [4] Stop.

CEL.                              For what, my lord?

LORD.  I did not meet that noble entertainment
You were late pleased to show me.

CEL.                              I observed
No such defect in your lordship, but a brave
And noble fortitude.

LORD.                            A noble folly;
I bring repentance for 't.  I know you have,
Madam, a gentle faith, and wo' not ruin
What you have built to honor you.

CEL.                            What's that?

LORD.  If you can love, I'll tell your ladyship.                        329

CEL.  I have a stubborn soul else.

LORD.                          You are all
Composed of harmony.

CEL.                        What love d'e mean?

LORD.  That which doth perfect both.  Madam, you have heard
I can be constant, and, if you consent
To grace it so, there is a spacious dwelling
Prepared within my heart for such a mistress.

CEL.  Your mistress, my good lord?

LORD.                        Why, my good lady,
Your sex doth hold it no dishonor
To become mistress to a noble servant
In the now court Platonic way.  Consider
Who 'tis that pleads to you; my birth and present                    340
Value can be no stain to your embrace.
But these are shadows when my love appears,
Which shall in his first miracle return
Me in my bloom of youth, and thee a virgin,
When I, within some new Elysium,
Of purpose made and meant for us, shall be
In everything Adonis but in his
Contempt of love, and court thee from a Daphne
Hid in the cold rind of a bashful tree,
With such warm language and delight, till thou                      350
Leap from that bays into the Queen of Love,
And pay my conquest with composing garlands
Of thy own myrtle for me.

CEL.                        What's all this?

LORD.  Consent to be my mistress, Celestina,
And we will have it springtime all the year,
Upon whose invitations, when we walk,
The winds shall play soft descant [1] to our feet,
And breathe rich odors to re-pure the air;
Green bowers on every side shall tempt our stay,
And violets stoop to have us tread upon 'em.                        360
The red rose shall grow pale, being near thy cheek,
And the white blush, o'ercome with such a forehead.
Here laid, and measuring with ourselves some bank,
A thousand birds shall from the woods repair,
And place themselves so cunningly behind
The leaves of every tree that, while they pay
Us [2] tribute of their songs, thou sha't imagine
The very trees bear music, and sweet voices
Do grow in every arbor.  Here can we
Embrace and kiss, tell tales, and kiss again,                      370
And none but heaven our rival.

CEL.                          When we are
Weary of these, what if we shift our paradise,
And through a grove of tall and even pine
Descend into a valley, that shall shame
All the delights of Tempe, upon whose
Green plush the Graces shall be called to dance
To please us, and maintain their fairy revels
To the harmonious murmurs of a stream
That gently falls upon a rock of pearl.
Here doth the nymph, forsaken Echo, dwell,                          380
To whom we'll tell the story of our love,
Till at our surfeit and her want of joy
We break her heart with envy.  Not far off,
A grove shall call us to a wanton river
To see a dying swan give up the ghost,

[1] Melody.
[2] Gifford-Dyce's reading.  Original reads *As.*

The fishes shooting up their tears in bubbles

That they must lose the genius of their
waves—

And such love linsey-woolsey, to no purpose!

LORD. You chide me handsomely; pray,
tell me how                                    389

You like this language.

CEL.                     Good my lord, forbear.

LORD. You need not fly out of this circle,
madam;

These widows so are full of circumstance!
I'll undertake, in this time I ha' courted
Your ladyship for the toy, to ha' broken
ten,

Nay, twenty colts—virgins, I mean—and
taught 'em

The amble, or what pace I most affected.

CEL. Y' are not my lord again—the lord I
thought you;

And I must tell you now you do forget
Yourself and me.

LORD.          You'll not be angry, madam?

CEL. Nor rude (though gay men have a
privilege)                                      400

It shall appear. There is a man, my lord,
Within my acquaintance, rich in worldly
fortunes,

But cannot boast any descent of blood,
Would buy a coat of arms.

LORD.               He may, and legs
Booted and spurred, to ride into the
country.

CEL. But these will want antiquity, my
lord,

The seal of honor. What's a coat cut out
But yesterday, to make a man a gentle-
man?                                            408

Your family, as old as the first virtue
That merited an escutcheon, doth owe [1]
A glorious coat of arms; if you will sell now
All that your name doth challenge in that
ensign,

I'll help you to a chapman [2] that shall pay,
And pour down wealth enough for 't.

LORD.                     Sell my arms?

I cannot, madam.

CEL.                Give but your consent,
You know not how the state may be inclined

To dispensation; we may prevail
Upon the Herald's office afterward.

[1] Own.                              [2] Merchant.

LORD. I'll sooner give these arms to th'
hangman's ax,

My head, my heart, to twenty execu-
tions,                                          420

Than sell one atom from my name.

CEL.                          Change that,
And answer him would buy my honor
from me—

Honor, that is not worn upon a flag
Or pennon that without the owner's dangers

An enemy may ravish and bear from
me,

But that which grows and withers with
my soul,

Beside the body's stain. Think, think,
my lord,

To what you would unworthily betray
me,

If you would not, for price of gold or
pleasure

(If that be more your idol) lose the
glory                                          430

And painted honor of your house. I ha'
done.

LORD. Enough to rectify a satyr's blood.
Obscure my blushes here.

*Enter Scentlove and Haircut [behind].*

HAIR.                Or this or fight with me.
It shall be no exception that I wait
Upon my lord. I am a gentleman;
You may be less and be a knight. The
office

I do my lord is honest, sir. How many
Such you have been guilty of, heaven
knows.

SCENT. 'Tis no fear of your sword, but that
I would not

Break the good laws established against
duels.                                         440

HAIR. Off with your periwig, and stand
bare.          [*Scentlove removes his wig.*]

LORD.          From this
Minute I'll be a servant to thy goodness.
A mistress in the wanton sense is com-
mon;

I'll honor you with chaste thoughts, and
call you so.

CEL. I'll study to be worth your fair opinion.

LORD. Scentlove, your head was used to a
covering

Beside a hat; when went the hair away?

SCENT. I laid a wager, my lord, with Hair-
cut,
Who thinks I shall catch cold, that I'll
stand bare                                    449
This half hour.
HAIR.                    Pardon my ambition,
Madam. I told you truth; I am a gen-
tleman,
And cannot fear that name is drowned in
my
Relation to my lord.
CEL.                        I dare not think so.
HAIR. From henceforth call my service
duty, madam.
That pig's head, that betrayed me to
your mirth,
Is doing penance for 't.
SCENT.                        Why may not I,
My lord, begin a fashion of no hair?
CEL. Do you sweat, Sir William?
SCENT.        Not with store of nightcaps.

*Enter Aretina, Bornwell.*

ARE. Heaven has dissolved the clouds that
hung upon
My eyes, and, if you can with mercy
meet                                          460
A penitent, I throw my own will off,
And now in all things obey yours. My
nephew
Send back again to th' college, and my-
self
To what place you'll confine me.
BORN.                          Dearer now
Than ever to my bosom, thou sha't
please
Me best to live at thy own choice. I did
But fright thee with a noise of my
expenses;
The sums are safe, and we have wealth
enough,                                       468
If yet we use it nobly. My lord—madam,
Pray, honor [us] [1] tonight.
ARE.                    I beg your presence
And pardon.
BORN.            I know not how my Aretina
May be disposed tomorrow for the coun-
try.
CEL. You must not go before you both
have done
Me honor to accept an entertainment
Where I have power; on those terms I'm
your guest.

[1] Supplied by Gifford-Dyce.

BORN. You grace us, madam.
ARE. [*Aside.*] Already
I feel a cure upon my soul, and promise
My after-life to virtue. Pardon, heaven,
My shame, yet hid from the world's eye.

*Enter Decoy.* [2]

DEC.                        Sweet madam!  480
ARE. Not for the world be seen here! We
are lost.
I'll visit you at home.—[*Aside.*] But not
to practice
What she expects; my counsel may recover her.                        [*Exit Decoy.*]

*Enter Alexander.*

AL. Where's madam?—Pray, lend me a
little money;
My spirit has deceived me. Proserpine
Has broke her word.
ARE.                    Do you expect to find
The devil true to you?
AL.                        Not too loud!
ARE.                        I'll voice it
Louder, to all the world, your horrid sin,
Unless you promise me religiously
To purge your foul blood by repentance,
sir.                                          490
AL. Then I'm undone.
ARE.                Not while I have power
To encourage you to virtue. I'll endeavor
To find you out some nobler way at court
To thrive in.
AL.        Do 't, and I'll forsake the devil
And bring my flesh to obedience. You
shall steer me.—
My lord, your servant.
LORD.                    You are brave again.
AL. Madam, your pardon.
BORN.                    Your offense requires
Humility.
AL.        Low as my heart.—Sir Thomas,
I'll sup with you, a part of satisfaction.
BORN. Our pleasures cool. Music! And,
when our ladies                              500
Are tired with active motion, to give
Them rest, in some new rapture to ad-
vance
Full mirth, our souls shall leap into a
dance.                            *Exeunt.*

FINIS.

[2] This stage direction follows the next line in the
original.

# JAMES SHIRLEY

## THE CARDINAL

As *The Lady of Pleasure* is historically as well as intrinsically interesting because it anticipates the Restoration comedy of manners, so *The Cardinal* is both historically and intrinsically interesting because it is the last of the long line of the tragedies of blood, lust, and revenge of its age. It was licensed by Sir Henry Herbert for production at the Blackfriars by the King's Men on November 25, 1641. Charles R. Forker, in his valuable edition of the play (*Indiana University Humanities Series*, Bloomington, 1964), concludes that it was probably written in the summer or early fall of the same year because Shirley, after his return from Ireland in the spring of 1640, had succeeded Massinger as the mainstay of the writing staff of the King's Men and was providing them with about two plays a year, one for the spring season and one for the fall. It was entered for publication in the Stationers' Register on September 4, 1646, but was not printed till 1653, in an octavo collection of *Six New Plays* by James Shirley, none of the other five being of any importance. Although the acting of plays was forbidden during this unsettled period of Parliamentarian and Puritan dominance, certain enterprising booksellers dared to continue to appeal to the irrepressible human taste for drama, even though only in printed form. Some copies of this volume carry an engraved portrait of the playwright by the prolific illustrator, James Marshall, reprinted from the collection of Shirley's *Poems, &c.* published by Humphrey Moseley in 1646. The text is a careful one, probably seen through the press by the author himself, who according to Stevenson ("Shirley's Publishers: The Partnership of Crooke and Cooke") apparently kept control of the printing of his manuscripts in his own hands even before he went to Ireland.

The stage history of the play is somewhat longer than that of *The Lady of Pleasure*, though by no means so long as it deserves. It was performed more or less regularly during the seven months which passed between its premier and the closing of the theaters. For one of these performances, sometime after April 26, 1642, Shirley wrote an alternative prologue (Forker, Appendix B). It was not one of the first plays to be offered by Killigrew to the Restoration audience on the reopening of the theaters, but was given on July 23, 1662, and was listed by Herbert among the "plays acted by the King's Company at the Red Bull and the new house in Gibbon's Tennis Court near Clare Market." Downes also lists it among the old plays "Acted but now and then between 1663 and 1682" when the King's and the Duke's Companies underwent a temporary merger. Sam Pepys saw it three times, with improving reactions. In 1662 he recorded in his diary, ". . . nor is there any great matter in it." Five years later, however, he wrote, ". . . wherewith I am mightily pleased," and in 1668 called it definitely "a good play." Here its stage history seems to have ended, but Forsythe adds that on April 20, 1796, Sophia Lee produced a play entitled *Almeyda, Queen of Granada*, and admitted in her "Advertisement" that her tragedy, acted five times, was based in many respects on *The Cardinal*.

As might be expected from Shirley's general practice, no comprehensive source for *The Cardinal* has been discovered, but Forsythe has again listed five pages of resemblances. It has reminded many readers of *The Duchess of Malfi*, and perhaps contains some verbal echoes of *The White Devil*, but these similarities are only general. Karl Frölich attempted to find a Spanish source, *El Buen Vecino*, attributed to Lope de Vega (*Quellenstudien zu Einigen Dramen James Shirleys*, Herford, 1913), but Forker finds his evidence "less than convincing." And Fredson Bowers suggested that the Cardinal's ravishing the Duchess in revenge before murdering her might have been borrowed from

Samuel Harding's academic tragedy, *Sicily and Naples*, never acted, but published in 1640 (*The Elizabethan Revenge Tragedy*, Princeton, 1940). Forker mentions some other minor and incidental analogues and imitations.

Irving Ribner, in his *Jacobean Tragedy: The Search for Moral Order*, places the plays of Shirley along with those of Massinger as "no longer vehicles for profound self dis-covery and philosophical statement" and calls them "exploitations for the sake of an amusement-loving court of the theatricality learned from Beaumont and Fletcher." And he adds, "A play like *The Cardinal*, although brilliantly constructed and no doubt extremely effective upon the stage, is merely the shallow imitation of some external features of Webster's Italian tragedies." To Ribner, as to most critics, "The great age of English tragedy had come to a close with John Ford, some ten years before the closing of the theaters." Prior, too, in *The Language of Tragedy*, describes Ford as the last playwright to make "a serious attempt to adapt the traditions of Elizabethan tragedy to original ends," and regards *The Cardinal* as closing the books just before the closing of the theaters. Prior admitted, however, that Shirley could have taught Webster "a number of useful lessons in smooth and plausible play-building," and praised the dialogue as well-handled and the language as vivid. But in spite of the effectiveness of the play as an acting vehicle (which, after all, should be the first criterion of a good play), he found nothing really memorable in it. Strangely enough, in view of his general critical principles, William Archer does not even mention Shirley. Forker, however, after calling attention to the recognition of Shirley's "constructive power" by most critics, and refusing to claim any great depth for his characters, nevertheless maintained that "they are strongly and, in the main, consistently individualized." To Forker, the Cardinal is in some ways the most interesting character in the play and the mysteriousness of his motivation, which some critics have thought a blemish, was probably deliberate on Shirley's part, since he has planted clues all along. Conse-quently, his "character is not changed in the final episode so much as it is revealed." Francis Manley rather too ingeniously defends Shirley's handling of another somewhat ambiguous episode by suggesting, in "The Death of Hernando in Shirley's *Cardinal*" (*NQ*, 1965), that this death should not be regarded as suicide but as a case of a sporting offer to fight with his enemies ironically turning on himself.

The most original and valuable part of Forker's introduction deals with the historical background of the play and the identification of certain major figures in it. Pointing out that previous editors like Gifford and commentators like Frederick S. Boas and Tucker Brooke have been content to remark casually that the Cardinal was probably intended to represent Cardinal Richelieu, the chief minister of Louis XIII of France, whom most Englishmen detested and feared, Forker makes out a plausible case for identifying the Cardinal with Archbishop William Laud, and the King with Charles I. In fact, the prologue itself warns the audience that it should not let the mere title of the play transport it to France. After all, asks Forker, "What, moreover, would pacify the Puritans so well and yet remain so palatable and entertaining to a large non-Puritan audience as a play implicitly attacking Laud? His fall from power was still news, he was awaiting trial in the Tower, and he must have symbolized to Shirley and the whole theatrical profession that detested Court of High Commission whose restrictive policy had pinched before." Moreover, if Wood's story is to be trusted, Shirley had been pinched by Laud, who had tried to prevent him from entering the ministry many years earlier. Of course, this was many years before Laud's later career had developed in him "the deceit, cruelty, anger, ambition, hypocrisy, craft, and even lust" which his enemies attributed to him, and which are among the characteristics Shirley gives his Cardinal. On the other hand, it is also possible that Shirley was daringly implying to his audience that both England and France had high ecclesiastics in political power who were hardly honors to their churches and their countries.

The basis of the present text is that of the Library of Congress copy, dated 1652, of the 1653 collection of *Six New Plays*. Forker's collation of six copies of the volume showed that they vary only in slight and insignificant details, mostly punctuation.

# THE CARDINAL[1]

## BY

## JAMES SHIRLEY

### PERSONS

KING OF NAVARRE.
CARDINAL.
COLUMBO, *the cardinal's nephew.*
[COUNT D']ALVAREZ.
HERNANDO, *a colonel.*
ALPHONSO [, *a captain*].
LORDS.
[ANTONIO,] *secretary to the duchess.*
COLONELS.
ANTONELLI, *the cardinal's servant.*

SURGEON.
GUARD.
ATTENDANTS, *etc.*

DUCHESS ROSAURA.
VALERIA }
CELINDA } *ladies.*
PLACENTIA, *a lady that waits upon the duchess.*

SCENE: *Navarre.*

[TIME: *Contemporary.*]

## PROLOGUE[2]

*The Cardinal!* Cause[3] we express no scene,
We do believe most of you gentlemen
Are at this hour in France,[3] and busy there,
Though you vouchsafe to lend your bodies
   here;
But keep your fancy active, till you know,
By th' progress of our play, 'tis nothing so.
A poet's art is to lead on your thought
Through subtle paths and workings of a
   plot,
And, where your expectation does not
   thrive,     9
If things fall better, yet you may forgive.
I will say nothing positive; you may
Think what you please; we call it but a
   "play."
Whether the comic Muse, or ladies' love,
Romance, or direful tragedy it prove,
The bill determines not; and, would you be
Persuaded, I would have 't a comedy,

For all the purple in the name and state
Of him that owns it;[4] but 'tis left to fate.
Yet I will tell you, ere you see it played,
What the author—and he blushed too, when
   he said,     20
Comparing with his own (for 't had been
   pride,
He thought, to build his wit a pyramide
Upon another's wounded fame), this play
Might rival with his best, and dared to
   say—
Troth, I am out. He said no more. You,
   then,
When 'tis done, may say your pleasures,
   gentlemen.[5]

### ACT I. [SCENE i.

*A room in the king's palace.*]

*Enter two Lords at one door; Secretary at the other.*

1 Lo. Who is that?
2 Lo.            The duchess' secretary.
1 Lo. Signior!
SEC.          Your lordship's servant.
1 Lo. How does her grace since she left
   her mourning

[1] The title continues: "A Tragedy As It Was Acted at the Private House in Blackfriars." The unimportant dedication, "To My Worthily Honored Friend, G. B., Esq.," is omitted.
[2] The prologue appears before the cast in the original.
[3] Because we hang out no placard, "The Cardinal" recalls Richelieu in France.

[4] Alluding to the cardinal himself.
[5] Here follows a complimentary poem by Hall.

For the young Duke Mendoza, whose timeless [1] death
At sea left her a virgin and a widow?

2 Lo. She's now inclining to a second bride.[2] —
When is the day of mighty marriage
To our great cardinal's nephew, Don Columbo?

Sec. When they agree. They wo' not steal to church.
I guess the ceremonies will be loud and public.        10
Your lordships will excuse me.        *Exit.*

1 Lo. When they agree? Alas, poor lady, she
Dotes not upon Columbo when she thinks
Of the young Count d'Alvarez, divorced from her
By the king's power.

2 Lo. And counsel of the cardinal to advance
His nephew to the duchess' bed. 'Tis not well.

1 Lo. Take heed; the cardinal holds intelligence [3]
With every bird i' th' air.

2 Lo.        Death on his purple pride!
He governs all, and yet Columbo is        20
A gallant gentleman.

1 Lo. The darling of the war, whom victory
Hath often courted; a man of daring
And most exalted spirit. Pride in him
Dwells like an ornament, where so much honor
Secures his praise.

2 Lo.        This is no argument
He should usurp and wear Alvarez' title
To the fair duchess; men of coarser blood
Would not so tamely give this treasure up.

1 Lo. Although Columbo's name is great in war,        30
Whose glorious art and practice is above
The greatness of Alvarez, yet he cannot
Want soul, in whom alone survives the virtue
Of many noble ancestors, being the last
Of his great family.

2 Lo.        'Tis not safe, you'll say,
To wrastle with the king.[4]

1 Lo. More danger if the cardinal be displeased,
Who sits at helm of state. Count d'Alvarez
Is wiser to obey the stream than, by
Insisting on his privilege to her love,        40
Put both their fates upon a storm.

2 Lo. If wisdom, not inborn fear, make him compose,[5]
I like it. How does the duchess bear herself?

1 Lo. She moves by the rapture [6] of another wheel [7]
That must be obeyed, like some sad passenger,
That looks upon the coast his wishes fly to,
But is transported by an adverse wind,
Sometimes a churlish pilot.

2 Lo. She has a sweet and noble nature.

1 Lo.        That        49
Commends Alvarez; Hymen cannot tie
A knot of two more equal hearts and blood.

*Enter Alphonso.*

2 Lo. Alphonso!

Alph.        My good lord.

1 Lo.        What great affair
Hath brought you from the confines?[8]

Alph.        Such as will
Be worth your counsels, when the king hath read
My letters from the governor. The Aragonians,
Violating their confederate oath and league,
Are now in arms; they have not yet marched towards us,
But 'tis not safe to expect,[9] if we may timely
Prevent invasion.

2 Lo.        Dare they be so insolent?

1 Lo. This storm I did foresee.        60

2 Lo. What have they but the sweetness of the king
To make a crime?

[1] Untimely.
[2] Bridegroom.
[3] Communication.

[4] Here and in several other passages the line division has been regularized.
[5] Agree.        [6] Energy, force.
[7] *I.e.*, steering wheel.        [8] Border.        [9] Wait.

1 Lo.       But how appears the cardinal
At this news?
ALPH.                 Not pale, although
He knows they have no cause to think
   him innocent,
As by whose counsel they were once sur-
   prised.
1 Lo.  There is more
Than all our present art can fathom in
This story, and I fear I may conclude
This flame has breath at home to cherish
   it.
There's treason in some hearts, whose
   faces are                              70
Smooth to the state.
ALPH.            My lords, I take my leave.
2 Lo.  Your friends, good captain. *Exeunt.*

[SCENE ii.

*A room in the duchess' palace.*]

*Enter Duchess, Valeria, Celinda.*

VAL. Sweet madam, be less thoughtful;
   this obedience
To passion will destroy the noblest
   frame
Of beauty that this kingdom ever
   boasted.
CEL. This sadness might become your
   other habit
And ceremonies black for him that died.
The times of sorrow are expired; and all
The joys that wait upon the court, your
   birth,
And a new Hymen, that is coming to-
   wards you,
Invite a change.
DUCH.             Ladies, I thank you both.
I pray, excuse a little melancholy      10
That is behind; my year of mourning
   hath not
So cleared my account with sorrow but
   there may
Some dark thoughts stay, with sad re-
   flections,
Upon my heart for him I lost. Even this
New dress and smiling garment, meant
   to show
A peace concluded twixt my grief and
   me,
Is but a sad remembrance. But I resolve
To entertain more pleasing thoughts;
   and, if

You wish me heartily to smile, you
   must
Not mention grief, not in advice to
   leave it.                              20
Such counsels open but afresh the
   wounds
Ye would close up, and keep alive the
   cause,
Whose bleeding you would cure.  Let's
   talk of something
That may delight.  You two are read in
   all
The histories of our court.  Tell me,
   Valeria,
Who has thy vote for the most handsome
   man?—
[*Aside.*]  Thus I must counterfeit a peace,
   when all
Within me is at mutiny.
VAL.                    I have examined
All that are candidates for the praise of
   ladies,
But find—may I speak boldly to your
   grace?                                30
And will you not return it in your mirth
To make me blush?
DUCH.               No, no; speak freely.
VAL. I wo' not rack your patience,
   madam; but
Were I a princess, I should think Count
   d'Alvarez
Had sweetness to deserve[1] me from the
   world.
DUCH. [*Aside.*] Alvarez! She's a spy upon
   my heart.
VAL. He's young and active, and composed
   most sweetly.
DUCH. I have seen a face more tempting.
VAL.                        It had then
Too much of woman in 't. His eyes speak
   movingly,
Which may excuse his voice, and lead
   away                                  40
All female pride his captive; his hair,
   black,
Which, naturally falling into curls—
DUCH. Prithee, no more; thou art in love
   with him.—
The man in your esteem, Celinda, now?
CEL. Alvarez is, I must confess, a gentle-
   man
Of handsome composition; but with
His mind, the greater excellence, I think

[1] Be worthy of.

Another may delight a lady more,
If man be well considered. That's
     Columbo,
Now, madam, voted to be yours.
DUCH. [*Aside*.]          My torment! 50
VAL. [*Aside*.] She affects [1] him not.
CEL. He has person, and a bravery beyond
All men that I observe.
VAL.                    He is a soldier,
A rough-hewn man, and may show well
     at distance.
His talk will fright a lady; War and
     grim-
Faced Honor are his mistresses; he raves
To hear a lute; Love meant him not his
     priest.—
Again your pardon, madam. We may
     talk,
But you have art to choose, and crown
affection. [*Celinda and Valeria retire.*]
DUCH. What is it to be born above these
     ladies,                          60
And want their freedom! They are not
     constrained,
Nor slaved by their own greatness, or
     the king's,
But let their free hearts look abroad and
     choose
By their own eyes to love. I must repair
My poor afflicted bosom, and assume
The privilege I was born with, which now
     prompts me
To tell the king he hath no power nor art
To steer a lover's soul.—

*Enter Secretary.*

               What says Count d'Alvarez?
SEC. Madam, he'll attend you.
DUCH. Wait you, as I directed. When he
     comes,                          70
Acquaint me privately.
SEC.               Madam, I have news;
'Tis now arrived the court we shall have
     wars.
DUCH. [*Aside*.] I find an army here of
     killing thoughts.
SEC. The king has chosen Don Columbo
     general,
Who is immediately to take his leave.
DUCH. [*Aside*.] What flood is let into my
     heart!—How far
Is he to go?
[1] Likes.

SEC.               To Aragon.
DUCH.                    That's well
At first. He should not want a pilgrimage
To the unknown world, if my thoughts
     might convey him.                79
SEC. 'Tis not impossible he may go thither.
DUCH. How?
SEC. To the unknown other world. He
     goes to fight;
That's in his way. Such stories are in
     nature.
DUCH. Conceal this news.
SEC.               He wo' not be long absent;
The affair will make him swift to kiss
     your grace's hand.          [*Exit.*]
DUCH. He cannot fly
With too much wing to take his leave.—
[*To the Ladies.*] I must
Be admitted to your conference. Ye have
Enlarged my spirits; they shall droop no
     more.
CEL. We are happy if we may advance
     one thought                     90
To your grace's pleasure.
VAL. Your eye before was in eclipse; these
     smiles
Become you, madam.
DUCH. [*Aside*.] I have not skill to contain
     myself.

*Enter Placentia.*

PLA. The cardinal's nephew, madam, Don
     Columbo.
DUCH. Already? Attend him.
                    *Ex[it] Plac[entia].*
VAL.               Shall we take our leave?
DUCH. He shall not know, Celinda, [2] how
     you praised him.
CEL.[3] If he did, madam, I should have the
     confidence
To tell him my free thoughts.

*Enter Columbo.*

DUCH. My lord, while I'm in study to
     requite                         100
The favor you ha' done me, you increase
My debt to such a sum, still by a new
     honoring
Your servant, I despair of my own free-
     dom.

[2] Original reads *Valeria*, but *cf.* ll. 45ff. The
reversing of the two names here and later in the
scene was first suggested by Gifford. Forker
dissents.          [3] Original reads *Val.*

COL. Madam, he kisseth your white hand,
    that must
Not surfeit in this happiness—and, la-
    dies,
I take your smiles for my encouragement!
I have not long to practice these court
    tactics.                    [Kisses them.]
CEL. [Aside.] He has been taught to kiss.
DUCH.                    There's something, sir,
Upon your brow I did not read before.
COL. Does the character please you,
    madam?
DUCH.            More,                    110
Because it speaks you cheerful.
COL.                    'Tis for such
Access of honor as must make Columbo
Worth all your love; the king is pleased
    to think
Me fit to lead his army.
DUCH.                    How, an army?
COL. We must not use the priest, till I
    bring home
Another triumph that now stays for me
To reap it in the purple field of glory.
DUCH. But do you mean to leave me, and
    expose
Yourself to the devouring war?    No
    enemy
Should divide us; the king is not so
    cruel.                    120
COL. The king is honorable; and this grace
More answers my ambition than his gift
Of thee and all thy beauty, which I can
Love, as becomes thy soldier, and fight
                    She weeps.
To come again, a conqueror of thee.
Then I must chide this fondness.[1]

*Enter Secretary.*

SEC. Madam, the king and my Lord Car-
    dinal.                    [Exit.]

*Enter King, Cardinal, and Lords.*

KING. Madam, I come to call a servant[2]
    from you,
And strengthen his excuse; the public
    cause
Will plead for your consent.    At his
    return                    130
Your marriage shall receive triumphant
    ceremonies;
Till then you must dispense.
        [He walks aside with the Duchess.]

CAR. [Walking aside with Columbo.]    She
    appears sad
To part with him.—I like it fairly,
    nephew.
CEL.[3] Is not the general a gallant man?
What lady would deny him a small
    courtesy?
VAL. Thou hast converted me, and I begin
To wish it were no sin.
CEL. Leave that to narrow consciences.
VAL.                    You are pleasant.
CEL. But he would please one better.    Do
    such men
Lie with their pages?
VAL.        Wouldst thou make a shift?[4]    140
CEL. He is going to a bloody business;
'Tis pity he should die without some heir.
That lady were hard-hearted now that
    would
Not help posterity, for the mere good
O' th' king and commonwealth.
VAL. Thou art wild; we may be observed.
DUCH. Your will must guide me; happiness
    and conquest
Be ever waiting on his sword!
COL.                    Farewell.
*Ex[eunt] K[ing], Col[umbo], Card[inal], and
                    Lo[rds].*

DUCH. Pray, give leave to examine a few
    thoughts;                    149
Expect me in the garden.
LADIES.        We attend. *Ex[eunt] Ladies.*
DUCH. This is above all expectation
    happy.
Forgive me, Virtue, that I have dis-
    sembled,
And witness with me I have not a
    thought
To tempt or to betray him, but secure
The promise I first made to love and
    honor.

*Enter Secretary.*

SEC. The Count d'Alvarez, madam.
DUCH.                    Admit him,
And let none interrupt us.—[Exit Secre-
    tary.]    How shall I
Behave[5] my looks?    The guilt of my neg-
    lect,
Which had no seal from hence, will call
    up blood

---

[1] Foolishness.                    [2] Lover.

[3] The original reverses the names of *Cel.* and
*Val.* throughout this dialogue.
[4] *I.e.,* exchange places.        [5] Control.

To write upon my cheeks the shame and
   story                          160
In some red letter.

*Enter d'Alvarez.*

D'ALV.              Madam, I present
   One that was glad to obey your grace,
     and come
   To know what your commands are.
DUCH.             Where I once
   Did promise love, a love that had the
     power
   And office of a priest to chain my heart
   To yours, it were injustice to command.
D'ALV. But I can look upon you, madam,
     as
   Becomes a servant; with as much humil-
     ity,
   In tenderness of[1] your honor and great
     fortune,
   Give up, when you call back your bounty,
     all that                  170
   Was mine, as I had pride to think them
     favors.
DUCH. Hath love taught thee no more
     assurance in
   Our mutual vows thou canst suspect it
     possible
   I should revoke a promise made to
     heaven
   And thee so soon? This must arise from
     some
   Distrust of thy own faith.
D'ALV.         Your grace's pardon;
   To speak with freedom, I am not so old
   In cunning to betray, nor young in time,
   Not to see when and where I am at loss,
   And how to bear my fortune and my
     wounds,                  180
   Which, if I look for health, must still
     bleed inward,
   A hard and desperate condition.
   I am not ignorant your birth and great-
     ness
   Have placed you to grow up with the
     king's grace
   And jealousy, which to remove, his
     power
   Hath chosen a fit object for your beauty
   To shine upon, Columbo, his great favor-
     ite.
   I am a man on whom but late the king

[1] Regard for.

Has pleased to cast a beam, which was
   not meant               189
To make me proud, but wisely to direct
And light me to my safety. O, dear
   madam,
I will not call more witness of my love
(If you will let me still give it that name)
Than this, that I dare make myself a
   loser,
And to your will give all my blessings up.
Preserve your greatness, and forget a
   trifle
That shall at best, when you have drawn
   me up,
But hang about you like a cloud, and dim
The glories you are born to.
DUCH.               Misery
   Of birth and state! That I could shift
     into                    200
   A meaner blood, or find some art to purge
   That part which makes my veins un-
     equal! Yet
   Those nice distinctions have no place in
     us;
   There's but a shadow difference, a title.
   Thy stock partakes as much of noble sap
   As that which feeds the root of kings; and
     he
   That writes a lord hath all the essence of
     Nobility.
D'ALV.        'Tis not a name that makes
   Our separation; the king's displeasure
   Hangs a portent to fright us, and the
     matter                 210
   That feeds this exhalation[2] is the car-
     dinal's
   Plot to advance his nephew; then Co-
     lumbo,
   A man made up for some prodigious act,
   Is fit to be considered. In all three
   There is no character you fix upon
   But has a form of ruin to us both.
DUCH. Then you do look on these with
     fear?
D'ALV.       With eyes
   That should think tears a duty, to lament
   Your least unkind fate; but my youth
     dares boldly
   Meet all the tyranny o' th' stars, whose
     black                 220
   Malevolence but shoot my single tragedy.
   You are above the value of many worlds
   Peopled with such as I am.

[2] Meteor.

Duch.　　　　　　　What if Columbo,
　　Engaged to war, in his hot thirst of
　　　honor
　　Find out the way to death?
D'Alv.　　　　　　　　'Tis possible.
Duch. Or say (no matter by what art or
　　motive)
　　He gives his title up, and leave me to
　　My own election?
D'Alv.　　　　　If I then be happy
　　To have a name within your thought,
　　　there can
　　Be nothing left to crown me with new
　　　blessing.　　　　　　　　230
　　But I dream thus of heaven, and wake
　　　to find
　　My amorous soul a mockery. When the
　　　priest
　　Shall tie you to another, and the joys
　　Of marriage leave no thought at leisure to
　　Look back upon Alvarez, that must
　　　wither
　　For loss of you, yet then I cannot lose
　　So much of what I was once in your
　　　favor,
　　But in a sigh pray still you may live
　　　happy.　　　　　　　　　*Exit.*
Duch. My heart is in a mist; some good
　　star smile
　　Upon my resolution, and direct　　240
　　Two lovers in their chaste embrace to
　　meet!
　　Columbo's bed contains my winding
　　sheet.　　　　　　　　　　*Exit.*

### Act II. [Scene i.

*Columbo's tent outside the walls of a frontier
　　city.*]

*Enter General Columbo, Hernando, two Colo-
　　nels, Alphonso, two Captains, and other
　　Officers, as at a council of war.*

Col. I see no face in all this council that
　　Hath one pale fear upon 't, though we
　　　arrived not
　　So timely to secure the town, which gives
　　Our enemy such triumph.
1 Col.　　　　　　　'Twas betrayed.
Alph. The wealth of that one city
　　Will make the enemy glorious.[1]
1 Col.　　　　　　　They dare
　　Not plunder it.

　　　　[1] Boastful.

Alph.　　　　They give fair quarter yet;
　　They only seal up men's estates, and
　　　keep
　　Possession for the city's use; they take up
　　No wares without security, and he　　10
　　Whose single credit will not pass puts in
　　Two lean comrades, upon whose bonds
　　　'tis not
　　Religion to deny 'em.
Col.　　　　　　　To repair this
　　With honor, gentlemen?
Her.　　　　　　　My opinion is
　　To expect awhile.
Col.　　　　Your reason?
Her.　　　　　　Till their own
　　Surfeit betray 'em, for their soldier[s],
　　Bred up with coarse and common bread,
　　　will show
　　Such appetites on the rich cates they find,
　　They will spare our swords a victory,
　　　when their own
　　Riot and luxury destroys 'em.
1 Col.　　　　　　　That　20
　　Will show our patience too like a fear.
　　With favor of his excellence,[2] I think
　　The spoil of cities takes not off the cour-
　　　age,
　　But doubles it on soldiers; besides,
　　While we have tameness to expect, the
　　　noise
　　Of their success and plenty will increase
　　Their army.
Her.　　　　'Tis considerable; we do not
　　Exceed in foot or horse, our muster not
　　'Bove sixteen thousand both, and the
　　　infantry
　　Raw, and not disciplined to act.
Alph.　　　　　　Their hearts,　30
　　But with a brave thought of their coun-
　　　try's honor,
　　Will teach 'em how to fight, had they not
　　　seen
　　A sword. But we decline[3] our own too
　　　much;
　　The men are forward in their arms, and
　　　take
　　The use with avarice of fame.
　　　　　*They rise, and talk privately.*
Col.　　　　　　　　Colonel,
　　I do suspect you are a coward.
Her.　　　　　　　　Sir!
Col. Or else a traitor; take your choice.
　　No more.

　　　[2] Begging your pardon.　　[3] Undervalue.

I called you to a council, sir, of war;
Yet keep your place.
HER.                I have worn other names.
COL. Deserve 'em. Such                40
Another were enough to unsoul an army.
Ignobly talk of patience, till they drink
And reel to death? We came to fight, and
    force 'em
To mend their pace; thou hast no honor
    in thee,
Not enough noble blood to make a blush
For thy tame eloquence.
HER.                My lord, I know
My duty to a general; yet there are
Some that have known me here. Sir, I
    desire
To quit my regiment.
COL.                You shall have license.—
Ink and paper!                50

*Enter with paper and standish.*[1]

1 COL. The general's displeased.
2 COL.                How is 't, Hernando?
HER. The general has found out em-
    ployment for me;
He is writing letters back.
ALPH. }
1]CAP. }                To his mistress?
HER. Pray, do not trouble me; yet, prithee,
    speak,
And flatter not thy friend. Dost think I
    dare
Not draw my sword, and use it, when
    cause
With honor calls to action?
ALPH. }
[1]COL. } With the most valiant man alive.
HER. You'll do me some displeasure in
    your loves.
Pray, to your places.                60
COL. So; bear those letters to the king;
It speaks my resolution, before
Another sun decline, to charge the
    enemy.
HER. [*Aside.*] A pretty court way
Of dismissing an officer.—I obey; success
Attend your counsels!                *Exit.*
COL. If here be any dare not look on dan-
    ger,
And meet it like a man, with scorn of
    death,
I beg his absence; and a coward's fear
Consume him to a ghost!

[1] A stand for writing.

1 COL.                None such here.  70
COL. Or, if in all your regiments you find
One man that does not ask to bleed with
    honor,
Give him a double pay to leave the army;
There's service to be done will call the
    spirits
And aid of men.
1 COL.                You give us all new flame.
COL. I am confirmed, and you must lose no
    time;
The soldier that was took last night, to
    me
Discovered[2] their whole strength, and
    that we have
A party in the town, the river that   79
Opens the city to the west unguarded.
We must this night use art and resolu-
    tions.
We cannot fall ingloriously.
1 CAP. That voice is every man's.

*Enter Soldier and Secretary with a letter.*

COL. What now?
SOL. Letters.
COL. Whence?
SOL. From the duchess.
COL. They are welcome.—[*Takes the let-
    ter.*]
Meet at my tent again this evening;
Yet stay, some wine.—The duchess'
    health!                90
See it go round.                [*Opens the letter.*]
SEC.        It wo' not please his excellence.
1 COL. The duchess' health!        [*Drinks.*]
2 CAP. To me! More wine.
SEC. The clouds are gathering, and his eyes
    shoot fire;
Observe what thunder follows.
2 CAP. The general has but ill news.  I
    suspect
The duchess sick, or else the king.
1 CAP.                May be
The cardinal.
2 CAP.        His soul has long been looked
    for.
COL. [*Aside.*] She dares not be so insolent.
    It is
The duchess' hand. How am I shrunk in
    fame                100
To be thus played withal! She writes,
    and counsels,

[2] Revealed.

Under my hand, to send her back a free
Resign of all my interest to her person,
Promise, or love; that there's no other
    way,
With safety of my honor, to revisit her.
The woman is possessed with some bold
    devil,
And wants an exorcism; or I am grown
A cheap, dull, phlegmatic fool, a post
    that's carved
I' th' common street, and holding out my
    forehead
To every scurril wit to pin disgrace   110
And libels on 't.—Did you bring this to
    me, sir?
My thanks shall warm your heart.
                        *Draws a pistol.*
SEC.                Hold, hold, my lord!
I know not what provokes this tempest,
    but
Her grace ne'er showed more freedom
    from a storm
When I received this paper. If you have
A will to do an execution,
Your looks, without that engine, sir, may
    serve.
I did not like the employment.
COL.                    Ha! Had she
No symptom, in her eye or face, of anger,
When she gave this in charge?
SEC.                    Serene as I   120
Have seen the morning rise upon the
    spring;
No trouble in her breath, but such a wind
As came to kiss and fan the smiling
    flowers.
COL. No poetry.
SEC.        By all the truth in prose,
By honesty and your own honor, sir,
I never saw her look more calm and gentle.
COL. I am too passionate; you must for-
    give me.
I have found it out; the duchess loves me
    dearly.
She expressed a trouble in her when I
    took                     129
My leave, and chid me with a sullen eye.
'Tis a device to hasten my return;
Love has a thousand arts. I'll answer it
Beyond her expectation, and put
Her soul to a noble test.—Your patience,
    gentlemen;
The king's health will deserve a sacrifice
    of wine. [*Sits at the table and writes.*]

SEC. [*Aside.*] I am glad to see this change,
    and thank my wit
For my redemption.
1 COL. Sir, the soldier's curse on him loves
    not our master!
2 COL. And they curse loud enough to be
    heard.
2 CAP. Their curse has the nature of gun-
    powder.                    140
SEC. They do not pray with half the noise.
1 COL. Our general is not well mixed;
He has too great a portion of fire.
2 COL. His mistress cool him (her com-
    plexion [1]
Carries some phlegm) when they two
    meet in bed!
2 CAP. A third may follow.
1 CAP. 'Tis much pity
The young duke lived not to take the
    virgin off.
1 COL. 'Twas the king's act to match two
    rabbit-suckers. [2]
2 COL. A common trick of state;    150
The little great man marries, travels then
Till both grow up, and dies when he
    should do
The feat. These things are still unlucky
On the male side.
COL. This to the duchess' fair hand.
                [*Gives Secretary a letter.*]
SEC.                She will think
Time hath no wing, till I return. [*Exit.*]
COL.                    Gentlemen,
Now each man to his quarter, and en-
    courage
The soldier. I shall take a pride to know
Your diligence, when I visit all your
Several commands.
OMNES.        We shall expect.
2 COL.                    And move   160
By your directions.
COL.        Y' are all noble.    *Exeunt.*

[SCENE ii.

*A room in the duchess' palace.*]

*Enter Cardinal, Duchess, Placentia.*

CAR. I shall perform a visit daily, madam,
In th' absence of my nephew, and be
    happy
If you accept my care.
DUCH.        You have honored me
[1] Temperament.    [2] Sucking rabbits, children

And, if your entertainment have not been
Worthy your grace's person, 'tis because
Nothing can reach it in my power; but,
   where
There is no want of zeal, other defect
Is only a fault to exercise your mercy.
CAR. You are bounteous in all. I take my
   leave,
My fair niece, shortly, when Columbo
   has                                        10
Purchased more honors to prefer [1] his
   name
And value to your noble thoughts; mean-
   time,
Be confident you have a friend, whose
   office
And favor with the king shall be effectual
To serve your grace.
DUCH.        Your own good deeds reward
   you,
Till mine rise equal to deserve their bene-
   fit.—              *Exit Cardinal.*
Leave me awhile.—      *Exit Placen[tia].*
Do not I walk upon the teeth of serpents,
And, as I had a charm against their poi-
   son,
Play with their stings? The cardinal is
   subtle,                                    20
Whom 'tis not wisdom to incense, till I
Hear to what destiny Columbo leaves
   me.
May be the greatness of his soul will
   scorn
To own what comes with murmur, if he
   can
Interpret me so happily.—Art come?

*Enter Secretary with a letter.*

SEC. His excellence salutes your grace.
DUCH.                        Thou hast
A melancholy brow. How did he take my
   letter?
SEC. As he would take a blow; with so
   much sense
Of anger his whole soul boiled in his face,
And such prodigious flame in both his
   eyes                                       30
As they'd been th' only seat of fire, and at
Each look a salamander leaping forth,
Not able to endure the furnace.
DUCH.                Ha! Thou dost
Describe him with some horror.

[1] Advance.

SEC.                        Soon as he
Had read again, and understood your
   meaning,
His rage had shot me with a pistol, had
   not
I used some soft and penitential language
To charm the bullet.
DUCH.        Wait at some more distance.—
My soul doth bath itself in a cold dew.
Imagine I am opening of a tomb.       40
                    [*Opens the letter.*]
Thus I throw off the marble, to discover
What antic posture death presents in this
Pale monument to fright me. (*Reads.*)
   Ha!
My heart, that called my blood and
   spirits to
Defend it from the invasion of my fears,
Must keep a guard about it still, lest this
Strange and too mighty joy crush it to
   nothing.—
Antonio.
SEC.        Madam.
DUCH.                Bid my steward give thee
Two thousand ducats. Art sure I am
   awake?                                     49
SEC. I shall be able to resolve [2] you, madam,
When he has paid the money.
DUCH. Columbo now is noble.
                    *Exit Duch[ess].*
SEC.                    This is better
Than I expected—if my lady be
Not mad, and live to justify her bounty.
                                    *Exit.*

[SCENE iii.

*A room in the king's palace.*]

*Enter King, Alvarez, Hernando, Lords.*

KING. The war is left to him, but we must
   have
You reconciled, if that be all your dif-
   ference.
His rage flows like a torrent, when he
   meets
With opposition. Leave [3] to wrastle with
   him,
And his hot blood retreats into a calm,
And then he chides his passion. You shall
   back
With letters from us.
HER.                Your commands are not
To be disputed.

[2] Inform.                        [3] Cease.

KING.                    Alvarez. [*Takes him aside.*]
1 Lo.                                        Lose not
Yourself by cool submission; he will find
His error, and the want of such a soldier.
2 Lo.  Have you seen the cardinal?
HER.                                    Not yet.  11
1 Lo.  He wants no plot—
HER.                        The king I must obey;
But let the purple gownman place his
engines[1]
I' th' dark, that wounds me.
2 Lo.                              Be assured
Of what we can to friend you; and the
king
Cannot forget your service.
HER.                              I am sorry
For that poor gentleman.
D'ALV.                        I must confess, sir,
The duchess has been pleased to think
me worthy
Her favors, and in that degree of honor
That has obliged my life to make the
best                                              20
Return of service, which is not, with bold
Affiance in her love, to interpose
Against her happiness and your election.
I love so much her honor I have quitted
All my desires, yet would not shrink to
bleed
Out my warm stock of life, so the last
drop
Might benefit her wishes.
KING.                        I shall find
A compensation for this act, Alvarez;
It hath much pleased us.

*Enter Duchess with a letter; Gentleman Usher.*

DUCH.                    Sir, you are the king,
And in that sacred title it were sin      30
To doubt a justice. A'l that does concern
My essence in this world, and a great part
Of the other bliss, lives in your breath.
KING.  What intends the duchess?
DUCH.  That will instruct you, sir. —[*Gives
him the letter.*] Columbo has,
Upon some better choice or discontent,
Set my poor soul at freedom.
KING.        'Tis his character.[2]      *Reads.*[3]
"Madam, I easily discharge all my preten-
sions to your love and person; I leave you to
your own choice; and, in what you have  [40

<hr>

[1] Plots.                          [2] Handwriting.
[3] The letter is divided into lines of verse in the
original.

obliged yourself to me, resume a power to
cancel, if you please.
                              COLUMBO."
This is strange!
DUCH.                    Now do an act to make
Your chronicle beloved and read forever.
KING.  Express yourself.
DUCH.                    Since by divine infusion,
For 'tis no art could force the general to
This change, second this justice, and
bestow
The heart you would have given from
me, by
Your strict commands to love Columbo,
where                                            50
'Twas meant by heaven; and let your
breath return
Whom you divorced, Alvarez, mine.
LORDS.                                    This is
But justice, sir.
KING.                    It was decreed above;
And, since Columbo has released his
interest,
Which we had wrought him, not without
some force
Upon your will, I give you your own
wishes.
Receive your own Alvarez.  When you
please
To celebrate your nuptial, I invite
Myself your guest.
DUCH.        Eternal blessings crown you!
OMNES.  And every joy your marriage!  60
*Exit King, who meets the Cardinal; they confer.*
D'ALV.  I know not whether I shall wonder
most
Or joy to meet this happiness.
DUCH.                              Now the king
Hath planted us, methinks we grow
already,
And twist our loving souls, above the
wrath
Of thunder to divide us.
D'ALV.                    Ha! The cardinal
Has met the king! I do not like this con-
ference;
He looks with anger this way.  I expect
A tempest.
DUCH.        Take no notice of his presence;
Leave me to meet, and answer it.  If the
king
Be firm in 's royal word, I fear no light-
ning.                                              70
Expect me in the garden.

D'ALV.                              I obey,
But fear a shipwrack on the coast. *Exit.*
CAR.                              Madam.
DUCH. My lord.
CAR. The king speaks of a letter that has
   brought
A riddle in 't.
DUCH.              'Tis easy to interpret.
CAR. From my nephew? May I deserve
   the favor?
              [*Duchess hands him the letter.*]
DUCH. [*Aside.*] He looks as though his
   eyes would fire the paper.
They are a pair of burning glasses, and
His envious blood doth give 'em flame.
CAR. [*Aside.*] What lethargy could thus
   unspirit him?                          80
I am all wonder.—Do not believe,
   madam,
But that Columbo's love is yet more
   sacred
To honor and yourself than thus to for-
   feit
What I have heard him call the glorious
   wreath
To all his merits, given him by the king,
From whom he took you with more pride
   than ever
He came from victory. His kisses hang
Yet panting on your lips; and he but now
Exchanged religious farewell to return,
But with more triumph, to be yours.
DUCH.                          My lord,
You do believe your nephew's hand was
   not                                    91
Surprised or strained[1] to this?
CAR. Strange arts and windings in the
   world! Most dark
And subtle progresses! Who brought this
   letter?
DUCH. I inquired not his name; I thought
   it not
Considerable[2] to take such narrow
   knowledge.
CAR. Desert and honor urged it here, nor
   can
I blame you to be angry; yet his person
Obliged you should have given a nobler
   pause
Before you made your faith and change
   so violent                            100
From his known worth into the arms of
   one,

However fashioned to your amorous
   wish,
Not equal to his cheapest fame,[3] with all
The gloss of blood and merit.
DUCH.                    This comparison,
My good lord cardinal, I cannot think
Flows from an even justice; it betrays
You partial where your blood runs.
CAR.                        I fear, madam,
Your own takes too much license, and
   will soon
Fall to the censure of unruly tongues.
Because Alvarez has a softer cheek,   110
Can like a woman trim his wanton hair,
Spend half a day with looking in the
   glass
To find a posture to present himself,
And bring more effeminacy than man
Or honor to your bed, must he supplant
   him?
Take heed, the common murmur, when
   it catches
The scent of a lost fame—
DUCH.              My fame, Lord Cardinal?
It stands upon an innocence as clear
As the devotions you pay to heaven.
I shall not urge, my lord, your soft in-
   dulgence                               120
At my next shrift.
CAR.              You are a fine court lady!
DUCH. And you should be a reverend
   churchman.
CAR.              One
That, if you have not thrown off mod-
   esty,
Would counsel you to leave Alvarez.
DUCH.                              Cause
You dare do worse than marriage, must
   not I
Be admitted what the church and law
   allows me?
CAR. Insolent! Then you dare marry him?
DUCH.                              Dare?
Let your contracted flame and malice,
   with
Columbo's rage, higher than that, meet
   us
When we approach the holy place,
   clasped hand                          130
In hand we'll break through all your
   force, and fix
Our sacred vows together there.
CAR.                              I knew

_____
[1] Compelled.        [2] Weighty, important.        [3] Reputation.

When, with as chaste a brow, you
    promised fair
To another.  You are no dissembling
    lady!
Duch. Would all your actions had no
    falser lights
About 'em!
Car. Ha!
Duch. The people would not talk and
    curse so loud.
Car. I'll have you chid into a blush for
    this.
Duch. Begin at home, great man; there's
    cause enough.                              140
   You turn the wrong end of the perspec-
    tive [1]
   Upon your crimes, to drive them to a
    far
   And lesser sight; but let your eyes look
    right,
   What giants would your pride and surfeit
    seem!
   How gross your avarice, eating up whole
    families!
   How vast are your corruptions and abuse
   Of the king's ear, at which you hang a
    pendant,
   Not to adorn, but ulcerate, while the
    honest
   Nobility, like pictures in the arras,
   Serve only for court ornament.  If they
    speak,                                     150
   'Tis when you set their tongues, which
    you wind up
   Like clocks, to strike at the just[2] hour
    you please.
   Leave, leave, my lord, these usurpa-
    tions,
   And be what you were meant, a man to
    cure,
   Not let in, agues to religion.
   Look on the church's wounds.
Car.                          You dare presume,
   In your rude spleen to me, to abuse the
    church?
Duch. Alas, you give false aim, my lord;
    'tis your
   Ambition and scarlet sins that rob     159
   Her altar of the glory and leave wounds
   Upon her brow, which fetches grief and
    paleness
   Into her cheeks, making her troubled
    bosom

Pant with her groans, and shroud her
    holy blushes
Within your reverend purples.
Car.                    Will you now take breath?
Duch. In hope, my lord, you will behold
    yourself
In a true glass, and see those injust acts
That so deform you, and by timely cure
Prevent a shame, before the short-haired
    men [3]
Do crowd and call for justice.  I take
    leave.                                  *Exit.*
Car. This woman has a spirit that may
    rise                                       170
To tame the devil's.  There's no dealing
    with
Her angry tongue; 'tis action and revenge
Must calm her fury.  Were Columbo
    here,
I could resolve; but letters shall be sent
To th' army, which may wake him into
    sense
Of his rash folly, or direct his spirit
Some way to snatch his honor from this
    flame.
All great men know, "The soul of life is
    fame."                                  *Exit.*

### Act III. [Scene i.

*An apartment in the king's palace.*]

*Enter Valeria, Celinda.*

Val. I did not think, Celinda, when I
    praised
Alvarez to the duchess, that things thus
Would come about.  What does your
    ladyship
Think of Columbo now?  It staggers all
The court he should forsake his mis-
    tress; I
Am lost with wonder yet.
Cel.                        'Tis very strange,
Without a spell; but there's a fate in love.
I like him ne'er the worse.

*Enter two Lords.*

1 Lo. Nothing but marriages and triumph[4]
    now!
Val. What new access of joy makes you,
    my lord,                                   10
So pleasant?
1 Lo.          There's a packet come to court

---

[1] Telescope.          [2] Exact.
[3] Perhaps an allusion to the Puritans.
[4] Celebrations.

Makes the king merry; we are all con-
cerned in 't.
Columbo hath given the enemy a great
And glorious defeat, and is already
Preparing to march home.
CEL. He thrived the better for my prayers.
2 LO.                    You have been
His great admirer, madam.
1 LO.                    The king longs
To see him.
VAL.    This news exalts the cardinal.

*Enter Cardinal.*

1 LO. [*Aside.*]                    He's here.
He appears with discontent; the mar-
riage                          .          19
With Count d'Alvarez hath a bitter taste,
And not worn off his palate. But let us
leave him.
LADIES. [*Aside.*] We'll to the duchess.
                    *Exeunt. Manet* [1] *Car*[*dinal*].
CAR. He has not won so much upon the
Aragon
As he has lost at home; and his neglect
Of what my studies had contrived to add
More luster to our family by the access
Of the great duchess' fortune, cools his
triumph,
And makes me wild.

*Enter Hernando.*

HER.                    My good Lord Cardinal!
CAR. You made complaint to th' king
about your general.
HER. Not a complaint, my lord; I did but
satisfy                                    30
Some questions o' the king's.
CAR.                    You see he thrives
Without your personal valor or advice,
Most grave and learnéd in the wars.
HER.                    My lord,
I envy not his fortune.
CAR.                    'Tis above
Your malice, and your noise not worth
his anger;
'Tis barking gainst the moon.
HER.                    More temper would
Become that habit.
CAR. The military thing would show some
spleen.
I'll blow an army of such wasps about
The world. Go look [2] your sting you left
i' th' camp, sir.                            40

[1] Remains.                    [2] Look for.

*Enter King and Lords.*

HER. The king!—This may be one day
counted [3] for.                          *Exit.*
KING. All things conspire, my lord, to
make you fortunate.
Your nephew's glory—
CAR.                    'Twas your cause and justice
Made him victorious; had he been so
valiant
At home, he had had another conquest
to
Invite, and bid her welcome to new wars.
KING. You must be reconciled to provi-
dence, my lord.
I heard you had a controversy with
The duchess; I will have you friends.
CAR. I am not angry.
KING.                    For my sake, then,  50
You shall be pleased, and with me grace
the marriage.
A churchman must show charity, and
shine
With first example: she's a woman.
CAR. You shall prescribe in all things, sir.
You cannot
Accuse my love, if I still wish my
nephew
Had been so happy, to be constant to
Your own and my election; yet my brain
Cannot reach how this comes about; I
know
My nephew loved her with a near [4] affec-
tion.

*Enter Hernando.*

KING. He'll give you fair account at his
return.—                                    60
Colonel, your letters may be spared; the
general
Has finished, and is coming home. [*Exit.*]
HER. I am glad on 't, sir.—My good Lord
Cardinal,
'Tis not impossible but some man pro-
voked
May have a precious mind to cut your
throat.
CAR. You shall command me, noble col-
onel; [5]
I know you wo' not fail to be at th'
wedding.
HER. 'Tis not Columbo that is married,
sir.

[3] Accounted.        [4] Close.        [5] Trisyllabic.

Car. Go teach the postures of the pike and
   musket;                                          69
Then drill your myrmidons into a ditch,
Where starve,[1] and stink in pickle.—You
   shall find
Me reasonable. You see the king expects
   me.
Ier. So does the devil.
Some desperate hand may help you on
   your journey.                    *Exeunt.*

[Scene ii.

*A room in the duchess' palace.*]

*Enter Secretary and Servants.*

Sec. Here, this; ay, this will fit your
part: you shall wear the slashes, because
you are a soldier. Here's for the blue [2]
mute.
1 [Serv.] This doublet will never fit me;
pox on 't! [3] Are these breeches good
enough for a prince too? Pedro plays but a
lord, and he has two laces more in a seam.
Sec. You must consider Pedro is a foolish lord; he may wear what lace he    [10
please.
2 [Serv.] Does my beard fit my clothes
well, gentlemen?
Sec. Pox o' your beard!
3 [Serv.] That will fright away the hair.
1 [Serv.] This fellow plays but a mute,
and he is so troublesome, and talks.
3 [Serv.] Mr.[4] Secretary might have let
Jaques play the soldier; he has a black
patch already.                              20
2 [Serv.] By your favor, Mr. Secretary,
I was asked who writ this play for us.
Sec. For us? Why, art thou any more
than a blue mute?
2 [Serv.] And, by my troth, I said I
thought it was all your own.
Sec. Away, you coxcomb!
4 [Serv.] Dost think he has no more wit
than to write a comedy? My lady's chaplain made the play, though he is con-  [30
tent, for the honor and trouble of the business, to be seen in 't.

*Enter Fifth Servant.*

5 [Serv.] Did anybody see my head,[5]
gentlemen? 'Twas here but now. I shall
have never a head to play my part in.

Sec. Is thy head gone? 'Tis well thy
part was not in 't. Look, look about; has
not Jaques it?
4 [Serv.] I his head? 'T wo' not come
on upon my shoulders.                      40
Sec. Make haste, gentlemen; I'll see
whether the king has supped. Look every
man to his wardrope[6] and his part.
                    *Exit [with Fifth Servant[.*
2 [Serv.] Is he gone? In my mind, a
masque had been fitter for a marriage.
4 [Serv.] Why, mute? There was no
time for 't, and the scenes are troublesome.
2 [Serv.] Half a score deal tacked together in the clouds.[7] What's that? A
throne, to come down and dance; all  · [50
the properties have been paid forty times
over, and are in the court stock, but the
secretary must have a play to show his wit.
4 [Serv.] Did not I tell thee 'twas the
chaplain's? Hold your tongue, mute.
1 [Serv.] Under the rose,[8] and would
this cloth of silver doublet might never
come off again, if there be any more plot
than you see in the back of my hand.
2 [Serv.] You talk of a plot! I'll  [60
not give this for the best poet's plot in the
world, and if it be not well carried.[9]
4 [Serv.] Well said, mute.
3 [Serv.] Ha, ha! Pedro, since he put on
his doublet, has repeated but three lines,
and he has broke five buttons.
2 [Serv.] I know not; but, by this false
beard, and here's hair enough to hang a
reasonable honest man, I do not remember,
to say, a strong line indeed in the  [70
whole comedy but when the chambermaid
kisses the captain.
3 [Serv.] Excellent, mute!

*Enter another Servant.*

5 [Serv.] They have almost supped, and
I cannot find my head yet.
4 [Serv.] Play in thine own.
5 [Serv.] Thank you for that! So I may
have it made a property! If I have not a
head found me, let Mr. Secretary play my
part himself without it.                    80

*Enter Secretary.*

Sec. Are you all ready, my masters?
The king is coming through the gallery.

_____
[1] Die.                    [3] A plague on it!
[2] Color worn by servants.  [4] *I.e.*, Master.
[5] Headdress or wig.        [6] Wardrobe.
[7] Ten planks nailed together under the roof of
the stage.        [8] *Sub rosa*, confidentially.
[9] Probably Sucklings plot in 1641.

Are the women dressed?

1 [SERV.] Rogero wants a head.

SEC. Here, with a pox to you, take mine! You a player? You a puppy dog! Is the music ready?

*Enter Gentleman Usher.*

GENT. Gentlemen, it is my lady's pleasure that you expect till she call for you. There are a company of cavaliers in [90 gallant equipage, newly alighted, have offered to present their revels in honor of this Hymen; and 'tis her grace's command that you be silent till their entertainment be over.

1 [SERV.] Gentlemen?

2 [SERV.] Affronted?

5 [SERV.] Mr. Secretary, there's your head again; a man's a man. Have I broken my sleep to study fifteen lines for an [100 ambassador, and after that a constable, and is it come to this?

SEC. Patience, gentlemen, be not so hot; 'tis but deferred, and the play may do well enough cold.

4 [SERV.] If it be not presented, the chaplain will have the greatest loss; he loses his wits.    *Hautboys.*

·SEC. This music speaks the king upon entrance. Retire, retire, and grumble [110 not.    *Exeunt [All but Secretary].*

*Enter King, Cardinal, Alvarez, Duchess, Celinda, Valeria, Placentia, Lords, Hernando. They being set, enter Columbo and five more, in rich habits, vizarded; between every two a Torchbearer. They dance, and after beckon to Alvarez, as desirous to speak with him.*

D'ALV. With me!
    *They embrace and whisper.*

KING.    Do you know the masquers, madam?

DUCH.    Not I, sir.

CAR. There's one—but that my nephew is abroad,
And has more soul than thus to jig upon
Their hymeneal night, I should suspect
'Twere he.
    *The Masquers lead in[1] Alvarez.*

DUCH. Where's my Lord Alvarez?
    *Recorders.*

KING. Call in the bridegroom.

*Enter Columbo. Four Masquers bring in Alvarez dead, in one of their habits, and, having laid him down, exeunt [the four Masquers].*

DUCH.    What mystery is this?

CAR. We want the bridegroom still.

KING.    Where is Alvarez?    119

*Columbo points to the body; they unvizard it, and find Alvar[ez] bleeding.*

DUCH. O, 'tis my lord! He's murdered!

KING. Who durst commit this horrid act?

COL. [*Removing his mask.*]    I, sir.

KING. Columbo? Ha!

COL.    Yes; Columbo, that dares stay
To justify that act.

HER.    Most barbarous!

DUCH. O, my dearest lord!

KING. Our guard seize on them all. This sight doth shake
All that is man within me.—Poor Alvarez,
Is this thy wedding day?

*Enter Guard.*

DUCH. If you do think there is a heaven, or pains
To punish such black crimes i' th' other world,
Let me have swift and such exemplar[2] justice    130
As shall become this great assassinate.
You will take off our faith else, and, if here
Such innocence must bleed, and you look on,
Poor men, that call you gods on earth. will doubt
To obey your laws, nay, practice to be devils,
As fearing, if such monstrous sins go on,
The saints will not be safe in heaven.

KING.    You shall,
You shall have justice.

CAR. [*Aside.*]    Now to come off[3] were brave.[4]

*Enter Servant.*

SERV. The masquers, sir, are fled; their horse, prepared    139
At gate, expected to receive 'em, where

---

[1] *I.e.*, lead him off stage.    [3] Escape, get clear.
[2] Exemplary.    [4] Fine.

They quickly mounted.  Coming so like
    friends,
None could suspect their haste, which is
    secured
By advantage of the night.
Col. I answer for 'em all; 'tis stake
    enough
For many lives.  But, if that poniard
Had voice, it would convince they were
    but all
Spectators of my act.  And now, if you
Will give your judgments leave, though
    at the first
Face of this object your cool bloods were
    frighted,                                  149
I can excuse this deed, and call it justice,
An act your honors and your office, sir,
Is bound to build a law upon for others
To imitate.  I have but took his life,
And punished her with mercy, who had
    both
Conspired to kill the soul of all my fame.
Read there—and read an injury as deep
In my dishonor as the devil knew
A woman had capacity or malice
To execute.  Read there how you were
    cozened, sir,
       [*Gives the King the duchess' letter.*]
Your power affronted, and my faith; her
    smiles,                                    160
A juggling witchcraft to betray, and
    make
My love her horse to stalk withal, and
    catch
Her curléd minion.
Car.                              Is it possible
The duchess could dissemble so, and for-
    feit
Her modesty with you, and to us all?
Yet I must pity her.  My nephew has
Been too severe, though this affront
    would call
A dying man from prayers, and turn him
    tiger,
There being nothing dearer than our
    fame,
Which, if a common man, whose blood
    has no                                     170
Ingredient of honor, labor to
Preserve, a soldier (by his nearest tie
To glory) is, above all others, bound
To vindicate.  And yet it might have
    been less bloody.
Her. [*Aside.*]  Charitable devil!

King. (*Reads.*)  "I pray, my lord, release under your hand what you dare challenge in my love or person, as a just forfeit
to myself.  This act will speak you honorable to my thoughts, and, when you    [180
have conquered thus yourself, you may
proceed to many victories, and after, with
safety of your fame, visit again
             The lost Rosaura."
To this your answer was a free resign?
Col. Flattered with great opinion of her
    faith,
And my desert of her (with thought that
    she,
Who seemed to weep and chide my easy
    will
To part with her, could not be guilty of
A treason or apostasy so soon,           190
But rather meant this a device to make
Me expedite the affairs of war), I sent
That paper, which her wickedness, not
    justice,
Applied [1] (what I meant trial) her di-
    vorce.
I loved her so, I dare call heaven to wit-
    ness,
I knew not whether [2] I loved most, while
    she
With him whose crimson penitence I pro-
    voked [3]
Conspired my everlasting infamy.
Examine but the circumstance.
Car.                                        'Tis clear.
This match was made at home, before
    she sent                                   200
That cunning writ, in hope to take him
    off,
As knowing his impatient soul would
    scorn
To own a blessing came on crutches to
    him.
It was not well to raise his expectation
(Had you, sir, no affront?) to ruin him
With so much scandal and contempt.
King.                                We have
Too plentiful a circumstance to accuse
You, madam, as the cause of your own
    sorrows,
But not without an accessary more
Than young Alvarez.
Car.                         Any other instrument?  210
King.  Yes; I am guilty, with herself, and
    Don

[1] Considered as.      [2] Which.      [3] Caused.

Columbo, though our acts looked several
　　ways,
That thought a lover might so soon be
　　ransomed,
And did exceed the office of a king
To exercise dominion over hearts
That owe to the prerogative of heaven
Their choice or separation; you must,
　　therefore,
When you do kneel for justice and re-
　　venge,
Madam, consider me a lateral agent
In poor Alvarez' tragedy.　　　　　220
1 Lo. It was your love to Don Columbo,
　　sir.
HER. [Aside.] So, so! The king is charmed.
　　Do you observe
How, to acquit Columbo, he would draw
Himself into the plot. Heaven, is this
　　justice?
CAR. Your judgment is divine in this.
KING.　　　　　　　　　　And yet
Columbo cannot be secure, and we
Just in his pardon, that durst make so
　　great
And insolent a breach of law and duty.
2 Lo. [Aside.] Ha! Will he turn again?
KING.　　　　　　　　And should we leave
This guilt of blood to heaven, which cries,
　　and strikes　　　　　230
With loud appeals the palace of eternity?
Yet here is more to charge Columbo
　　than
Alvarez' blood, and bids me punish it,
Or be no king.
HER. [Aside.]　　　　　'Tis come about,
　　my lords.
KING. And, if I should forgive
His timeless death, I cannot the offense,
That with such boldness struck at me.
　　Has my
Indulgence to your merits, which are
　　great,
Made me so cheap your rage could meet
　　no time
Nor place for your revenge but where
　　my eyes　　　　　240
Must be affrighted, and affronted with
The bloody execution? This contempt
Of majesty transcends my power to par-
　　don,
And you shall feel my anger, sir.
HER. [Aside.] Thou shalt have one short
　　prayer more for that.

COL. Have I, i' th' progress of my life,
No actions to plead me up deserving
Against this ceremony?
CAR.　　　　　　　　Contain yourself.
COL. I must be dumb then. Where is
　　honor
And gratitude of kings, when they for-
　　get　　　　　250
Whose hand secured their greatness?
　　Take my head off;
Examine then which of your silken lords,
As I have done, will throw himself on
　　dangers;
Like to a floating island move in blood;
And, where your great defense calls him
　　to stand
A bulwark, upon his bold breast to
　　take
In death, that you may live. But soldiers
　　are
Your valiant fools, whom, when your
　　own securities
Are bleeding, you can cherish, but, when
　　once
Your state and nerves are knit, not think-
　　ing when　　　　　260
To use their surgery again, you cast
Them off, and let them hang in dusty
　　armories,
Or make it death to ask for pay.
KING.　　　　　　　　　　No more.
We thought to have put your victory
　　and merits
In balance with Alvarez' death, which,
　　while
Our mercy was to judge, had been your
　　safety;
But the affront to us, made greater by
This boldness to upbraid our royal
　　bounty,
Shall tame, or make you nothing.
[2] Lo. [Aside.]　　　　　　　Excellent!
HER. [Aside.] The cardinal is not pleased.
CAR.　　　　　　Humble yourself　270
To th' king.
COL.　　　And beg my life? Let cowards
　　do 't
That dare not die; I'll rather have no
　　head
Than owe it to his charity.
KING.　　　　　To th' Castle with him!—
　　　　[The Guard take Columbo away.]
Madam, I leave you to your grief, and
　　what

The king can recompense to your tears,
   or honor
Of your dead lord, expect.
DUCH.       This shows like justice. *Exeunt.*


ACT IV. [SCENE i.

*A room in the king's palace.*]

*Enter two Lords, Hernando.*

1 Lo. This is the age of wonders.
2 Lo.                    Wondrous mischiefs!
HER. Among those guards, which some
   call tutelar angels,
   Whose office is to govern provinces,
   Is there not one will undertake Navarre?
   Hath heaven forsook us quite?
1 [Lo.]                    Columbo at large!
2 [Lo.] And graced now more than ever.
1 [Lo.]                    He was not pardoned;
   That word was prejudicial to his fame.
HER. But, as the murder done had been a
   dream
   Vanished to memory, he's courted as
   Preserver of his country.  With what
   chains                                    10
   Of magic does this cardinal hold the
   king?
2 [Lo.] What will you say, my lord, if they
   enchant
   The duchess now and by some impudent
   art
   Advance a marriage to Columbo yet?
HER. Say!  I'll say no woman can be
   saved; nor is 't
   Fit, indeed, any should pretend to
   heaven
   After one such impiety in their sex.
   And yet my faith has been so staggered,
   since
   The king restored Columbo, I'll be now
   Of no religion.
1 [Lo.]                    'Tis not possible    20
   She can forgive the murder; I observed
   Her tears.
HER.                    Why, so did I, my lord;
   And, if they be not honest, 'tis to be
   Half damned to look upon a woman
   weeping.
   When do you think the cardinal said his
   prayers?
2 [Lo.] I know not.
HER.                    Heaven forgive my want of
   charity,

But, if I were to kill him, he should
   have
No time to pray; his life could be no
   sacrifice,
Unless his soul went too.
1 [Lo.]                    That were too much.
HER. When you mean to despatch him,
   you may give                              30
Time for confession.  They have injured
   me
After another rate.
2 [Lo]. You are too passionate, cousin.

*Enter Columbo, Colonels, Alphonso, Court-
   iers.  They pass over the stage.*

HER. How the gay men do flutter to con-
   gratulate
His goal [1] delivery!  There's one honest
   man.
What pity 'tis a gallant fellow should
Depend on knaves for his preferment!
1 [Lo.] Except this cruelty upon Alvarez,
Columbo has no mighty stain upon him;
But for his uncle—
HER.                    If I had a son    40
Of twelve years old that would not fight
   with him,
And stake his soul against his cardinal's
   cap,
I would disinherit him.  Time has took a
   lease
But for three lives, I hope; a fourth may
   see
Honesty walk without a crutch.
2 [Lo.]                              This is
But air and wildness.
HER.                    I'll see the duchess.
1 [Lo.][2] You may do well to comfort her;
We must attend the king.
HER.                    Your pleasures.
                              *Exit Her[nando].*

*Enter King and Cardinal.*

1 [Lo. *Aside.*] A man of a brave soul.
2 [Lo. *Aside.*]                    The less his safety.
The king and cardinal in consult!    50
KING. Commend us to the duchess, and
   employ
What language you think fit and powerful

[1] Gaol, jail.
[2] In the original this speech head introduces
the following line.

To reconcile her to some peace.—My
　　lords.
CAR. Sir, I possess all for your sacred uses.
　　　　　　　　　　　　　*Exeunt severally.*

[SCENE ii.

*A room in the duchess' palace.*]

*Enter Secretary and Celinda.*

SEC. Madam, you are the welcom'st lady
　　living.
CEL. To whom, Mr. Secretary?
SEC. 　　　　　　　　If you have mercy
　　To pardon so much boldness, I durst say,
　　To me—I am a gentleman.
CEL. 　　　　　　　　And handsome.
SEC. But my lady has much wanted you.
CEL. Why, Mr. Secretary?
SEC. You are the prettiest—
CEL. So!
SEC. The wittiest—
CEL. So! 　　　　　　　　　　　　　　10
SEC. The merriest lady i' th' court.
CEL. And I was wished[1] to make the duch-
　　ess pleasant?
SEC. She never had so deep a cause of sor-
　　row;
　　Her chamber's but a coffin of a larger
　　Volume, wherein she walks so like a
　　　ghost,
　　'Twould make you pale to see her.
CEL. 　　　　　　　　Tell her grace
　　I attend here.
SEC. 　　　　　　　I shall most willingly.—
　　[*Aside.*] A spirited lady! Would I had
　　　her in my closet!
　　She is excellent company among the
　　　lords.
　　Sure she has an admirable treble.—
　　Madam. 　　　　　　　　*Exit.*　20
CEL. I do suspect this fellow would be nib-
　　bling,
　　Like some whose narrow fortunes will not
　　　rise
　　To wear things when the invention's rare
　　and new,
　　But, treading on the heel of pride, they
　　hunt
　　The fashion when 'tis crippled, like fell
　　tyrants.
　　I hope I am not old yet. I had the honor
　　To be saluted by our cardinal's nephew
　　This morning. There's a man!

*Enter Secretary.*

SEC. 　　　　　　　　I have prevailed.
　　Sweet madam, use what eloquence you
　　can
　　Upon her, and, if ever I be useful 　　30
　　To your ladyship's service, your least
　　breath commands me. 　　　　[*Exit.*]

*Enter Duchess.*

DUCH. Madam, I come to ask you but one
　　question:
　　If you were in my state, my state of grief,
　　I mean an exile from all happiness
　　Of this world, and almost of heaven (for
　　my
　　Affliction is finding out despair),
　　What would you think of Don Columbo?
CEL. 　　　　　　　　　　Madam?
DUCH. Whose bloody hand wrought all
　　this misery.
　　Would you not weep as I do, and wish
　　rather 　　　　　　　　　　　　　39
　　An everlasting spring of tears to drown
　　Your sight than let your eyes be cursed
　　to see
　　The murderer again, and glorious?
　　So careless of his sin that he is made
　　Fit for new parricide, even while his soul
　　Is purpled o'er, and reeks with innocent
　　blood?
　　But do not, do not answer me; I know
　　You have so great a spirit (which I want,
　　The horror of his fact[2] surprising all
　　My faculties), you would not let him live.
　　But I, poor I, must suffer more. There's
　　not 　　　　　　　　　　　　　50
　　One little star in heaven will look on me,
　　Unless to choose me out the mark, on
　　whom
　　It may shoot down some angry influence.

*Enter Placentia.*

PLA. Madam, here's Don Columbo says
　　he must
　　Speak with your grace.
DUCH. 　　　But he must not, I charge you.—
　　　　　　　　　　　[*Exit Placentia.*]
　　None else wait?—Is this well done,
　　To triumph in his tyranny? Speak,
　　madam,
　　Speak but your conscience.

[1] Sent for. 　　　　　　　　　[2] Deed.

*Enter Columbo and Secretary.*

SEC.                    Sir, you must not see her.
COL. Not see her? Were she cabled up
    above
    The search of bullet or of fire, were
        she                                          60
    Within her grave, and that the toughest
        mine
    That ever nature teemed and groaned
        withal,
    I would force some way to see her.—[*Exit
        Secretary.*] Do not fear
    I come to court you, madam; y' are not
        worth
    The humblest of my kinder thoughts. I
        come
    To show the man you have provoked,
        and lost,
    And tell you what remains of my re-
        venge.
    Live, but never presume again to marry;
    I'll kill the next at th' altar, and quench
        all
    The smiling tapers with his blood. If,
        after,                                       70
    You dare provoke the priest and heaven
        so much
    To take another, in thy bed I'll cut him
        from
    Thy warm embrace, and throw his heart
        to ravens.
CEL. This will appear an unexampled
        cruelty.
COL. Your pardon, madam. Rage and my
        revenge,
    Not perfect, took away my eyes. You are
    A noble lady—this not worth your eye-
        beam—
    One of so slight a making and so thin
    An autumn leaf is of too great a value
    To play, which shall be soonest lost i' th'
        air.                                         80
    Be pleased to own me by some name in
        your
    Assurance; I despise to be received
    There. Let her witness that I call you
        mistress;
    Honor me to make these pearls your
        carcanet.          [*Gives her a necklace.*]
CEL. My lord, you are too humble in your
        thoughts.
COL. [*Aside.*] There's no vexation too
        great to punish her.                *Exit.*

*Enter Secretary.*

SEC. Now, madam?
CEL. Away, you saucy fellow!—Madam, I
    Must be excused, if I do think more hon-
        orably
    Than you have cause, of this great lord.
DUCH.                    Why, is not   90
    All womankind concerned to hate what's
        impious?
CEL. For my part—
DUCH.               Antonio, is this a woman?
SEC. I know not whether she be man or
        woman;
    I should be nimble to find out the experi-
        ment.
    She looked with less state when Columbo
        came.
DUCH. Let me entreat your absence.—
    [*Aside.*] I am cozened in her.—
    I took you for a modest, honest [1] lady.
CEL. Madam, I scorn any accuser; and,
    Deducting the great title of a duchess,
    I shall not need one grain of your dear
        honor                                       100
    To me make full weight. If your grace be
        jealous,
    I can remove.                            *Exit.*
SEC.               She is gone.
DUCH.                          Prithee, remove
    My fears of her return.—(*Ex[it] Sec-
        [retary].*) She is not worth
    Considering; my anger's mounted higher.
    He need not put in caution for my next
    Marriage. Alvarez, I must come to thee,
    Thy virgin, wife, and widow; but not till
    I ha' paid those tragic duties to thy
        hearse
    Become [2] my piety and love. But how?
    Who shall instruct a way?

*Enter Placentia.*

PLA.                    Madam, Don   110
    Hernando much desires to speak with
        you.
DUCH. Will not thy own discretion think I
        am
    Unfit for visit?
PLA.               Please your grace, he brings
    Something he says imports your ear, and
        love
    Of the dead Lord Alvarez.
DUCH.                    Then admit him.

_____
[1] Chaste.                    [2] *I.e.*, which become.

*Enter Hernando.*

HER. I would speak, madam, to yourself.

DUCH.        Your absence. [*Exit Placentia.*]

HER. I know not how your grace will censure so

Much boldness, when you know the affairs I come for.

DUCH. My servant has prepared me to receive it,

If it concern my dead lord.

HER.                Can you name 120

So much of your Alvarez in a breath,

Without one word of your revenge? O, madam,

I come to chide you, and repent my great

Opinion of your virtue, that can walk,

And spend so many hours in naked solitude,

As if you thought that no arrears were due

To his death, when you had paid his funeral charges,

Made your eyes red, and wept a handkercher.

I come to tell you that I saw him bleed;

I, that can challenge nothing in his name 130

And honor, saw his murdered body warm

And panting with the labor of his spirits,

Till my amazed soul shrunk and hid itself,

While barbarous Columbo, grinning, stood

And mocked the weeping wounds. It is too much

That you should keep your heart alive so long

After this spectacle, and not revenge it.

DUCH. You do not know the business of my heart,

That censure me so rashly; yet I thank you. 139

And, if you be Alvarez' friend, dare tell

Your confidence that I despise my life,

But know not how to use it in a service

To speak me his revenger. This will need

No other proof than that to you, who may

Be sent with cunning to betray me, I

Have made this bold confession. I so much

Desire to sacrifice to that hovering ghost

Columbo's life that I am not ambitious

To keep my own two minutes after it.

HER. If you will call me coward, which is equal 150

To think I am a traitor, I forgive it

For this brave resolution, which time

And all the destinies must aid. I beg

That I may kiss your hand for this, and may

The soul of angry honor guide it.

DUCH.                        Whither?

HER. To Don Columbo's heart.

DUCH. It is too weak, I fear, alone.

HER. Alone? Are you in earnest? Why, will it not 158

Be a dishonor to your justice, madam,

Another arm should interpose? But that

It were a saucy act to mingle with you,

I durst, nay, I am bound in the revenge

Of him that's dead (since the whole world has interest

In every good man's loss) to offer it.

Dare you command me, madam?

DUCH.                Not command;

But I should more than honor such a truth

In man, that durst, against so mighty odds,

Appear Alvarez' friend and mine. The cardinal—

HER. Is for the second course. Columbo must

Be first cut up; his ghost must lead the dance. 170

Let him die first.

DUCH. But how?

HER. How? With a sword; and, if I undertake it,

I wo' not lose so much of my own honor

To kill him basely.

DUCH.                How shall I reward

This infinite service? 'Tis not modesty

While now my husband groans beneath his tomb,

And calls me to his marble bed, to promise

What this great act might well deserve, myself, 179

If you survive the victor; but, if thus

Alvarez' ashes be appeased, it must

Deserve an honorable memory;

And, though Columbo (as he had all power,

And grasped the fates) has vowed to kill the man

That shall succeed Alvarez—

HER.                              Tyranny!
DUCH. Yet, if ever
  I entertain a thought of love hereafter,
  Hernando from the world shall challenge
    it,
  Till when, my prayers and fortune shall
    wait on you.
HER. This is too mighty recompense.
DUCH.                    'Tis all just.   190
HER. If I outlive Columbo, I must not
  Expect security at home.
DUCH.                    Thou canst
  Not fly where all my fortunes and my
    love
  Shall not attend to guard thee.
HER.                        If I die—
DUCH. Thy memory
  Shall have a shrine, the next within my
    heart,
  To my Alvarez.
HER.               Once again your hand.
  Your cause is so religious you need not
  Strengthen it with your prayers; trust it
    to me.

*Enter Placentia and Cardinal.*

PLA. Madam, the cardinal.
DUCH.               Will you appear?   200
HER. And [1] he had all the horror of the
    devil
  In 's face, I would not balk him.
    *He stares upon the Cardinal in his exit.*
CAR. [*Aside.*] What makes [2] Hernando
    here?  I do not like
  They should consult; I'll take no note.—
    The king
  Fairly salutes your grace, by whose com-
    mand
  I am to tell you, though his will and
    actions,
  Illimited, stoop not to satisfy
  The vulgar inquisition, he is
  Yet willing to retain a just opinion
  With those that are placed near him;
    and, although               210
  You look with nature's eye upon your-
    self,
  Which needs no perspective to reach, nor
    art
  Of any optic [3] to make greater what
  Your narrow sense applies [4] an injury

(Ourselves still nearest to ourselves),
  but there's
Another eye that looks abroad, and walks
In search of reason and the weight of
  things,
With which, if you look on him, you will
  find
His pardon to Columbo cannot be   219
So much against his justice as your erring
Faith would persuade your anger.
DUCH.               Good my lord,
  Your phrase has too much landshape,[5]
    and I cannot
  Distinguish at this distance; you present
  The figure perfect, but indeed my eyes
  May pray your lordship find excuse, for
    tears
  Have almost made them blind.
CAR.               Fair, peace restore 'em!
  To bring the object nearer, the king says
  He could not be severe to Don Columbo
  Without injustice to his other merits,
  Which call more loud for their reward
    and honor               230
  Than you for your revenge; the kingdom
    made
  Happy by those, you only, by the last,
  Unfortunate; nor was it rational
  (I speak the king's own language) he
    should die
  For taking one man's breath, without
    whose valor
  None now had been alive without dis-
    honor.
DUCH. In my poor understanding, 'tis the
    crown
  Of virtue to proceed in its own tract,[6]
  Not deviate from honor.  If you acquit
  A man of murder, cause he has done
    brave               240
  Things in the war, you will bring down
    his valor
  To a crime, nay, to a bawd, if it secure
  A rape, and but teach those that deserve
    well
  To sin with greater license.  But dispute
  Is now too late, my lord; 'tis done; and
    you,
  By the good king, in tender [7] of my sor-
    rows,
  Sent to persuade me 'tis unreasonable
  That justice should repair me.

[1] If.                    [3] Magnifying glass.
[2] Does.                  [4] Interprets as.

[5] Landscape.
[6] Track.                          [7] Consideration.

CAR. You mistake,
For, if Columbo's death could make Alvarez 249
Live, the king had given him up to law,
Your bleeding sacrifice, but, when his life
Was but another treasure thrown away
To obey a clamorous statute, it was wisdom
To himself, and common safety, to take off
This killing edge of law, and keep Columbo
To recompense the crime by noble acts
And sorrow, that in time might draw your pity.

DUCH. This is a greater tyranny than that
Columbo exercised; he killed my lord,
And you have not the charity to let 260
Me think it worth a punishment.

CAR. To that,
In my own name, I answer: I condemn
And urge the bloody guilt against my nephew;
'Twas violent and cruel, a black deed,
A deed whose memory doth make me shudder,
An act that did betray a tyrannous nature,
Which he took up in war, the school of vengeance,
And, though the king's compassion spare him here,
Unless his heart
Weep itself out in penitent tears hereafter— 270

DUCH. This sounds
As you were now a good man.

CAR. Does your grace
Think I have conscience to allow the murder?
Although, when it was done, I did obey
The stream of nature, as he was my kinsman,
To plead he might not pay his forfeit life,
Could I do less for one so near my blood?
Consider, madam, and be charitable;
Let not this wild injustice make me lose 279
The character I bear, and reverend habit.
To make you full acquainted with my innocence,
I challenge here my soul and heaven to witness.

If I had any thought or knowledge with
My nephew's plot, or person, when he came
Under the smooth pretense of friend to violate
Your hospitable laws, and do that act
Whose frequent mention draws this tear, a whirlwind
Snatch me to endless flames!

DUCH. I must believe,
And ask your grace's pardon. I confess
I ha' not loved you since Alvarez' death,
Though we were reconciled.

CAR. I do not blame 291
Your jealousy,[1] nor any zeal you had
To prosecute revenge against me, madam,
As I then stood suspected, nor can yet
Implore your mercy to Columbo. All
I have to say is, to retain my first
Opinion and credit with your grace,
Which you may think I urge not out of fear
Or ends[2] upon you (since, I thank the king, 299
I stand firm on the base of royal favor),
But for your own sake, and to show I have
Compassion of your sufferings.

DUCH. You have cleared
A doubt, my lord, and by this fair remonstrance
Given my sorrow so much truce, to think
That we may meet again and yet be friends.
But be not angry, if I still remember
By whom Alvarez died, and weep, and wake
Another justice with my prayers.

CAR. All thoughts
That may advance a better peace dwell with you! *Exit.*

DUCH. How would this cozening statesman bribe my faith 310
With flatteries to think him innocent!
No; if his nephew die, this cardinal must not
Be long-lived. All the prayers of a wronged widow
Make firm Hernando's sword, and my own hand
Shall have some glory in the next revenge.

[1] Mistrust.      [2] Designs.

I will pretend my brain with grief dis-
tracted;
It may gain easy credit, and, beside
The taking off examination
For great Columbo's death, it makes
what act                                                 319
I do, in that believed want of my reason,
Appear no crime, but my defense. Look
down,
Soul of my lord, from thy eternal shade,
And unto all thy blessed companions
boast
Thy duchess busy to revenge thy ghost!
                                                        *Exit.*

[SCENE iii.

*A lonely spot outside the city.*]

*Enter Columbo, Hernando, Alphonso, Colo-
nel.*

COL. Hernando, now I love thee, and do
half
    Repent the affront my passion threw
    upon thee.
HER. You wo' not be too prodigal o' your
    penitence.
COL. This makes good thy nobility of
birth;
    Thou mayst be worth my anger and my
    sword,
    If thou dost execute as daringly
    As thou provok'st a quarrel. I did think
    Thy soul a starve'ing, or asleep.
HER.                              You'll find it
    Active enough to keep your spirit wak-
    ing,
    Which, to exasperate, for yet I think    10
    It is not high enough to meet my rage—
    D'e smile?
COL.        This noise is worth it.—Gentle-
    men,
    I'm sorry this great soldier has engaged
    Your travail; all his business is to talk.
HER. A little of your lordship's patience.
    You shall have other sport, and swords
    that will
    Be as nimble 'bout your heart as you can
    wish.
    'Tis pity more than our two single lives
    Should be at stake.
COLONEL.          Make that no scruple, sir.
HER. To him then that survives, if fate
    allow                                             20

That difference, I speak, that he may tell
The world I came not hither on slight
anger,
But to revenge my honor, stained and
trampled on
By this proud man. When general, he
commanded
My absence from the field.
COL.                              I do remember,
    And I'll give your soul now a discharge.
HER.                                        I come
To meet it, if your courage be so fortu-
nate.
But there is more than my own injury
You must account for, sir, if my sword
prosper,
Whose point and every edge is made more
keen                                                   30
With young Alvarez' blood, in which I
had
A noble interest. Does not that sin be-
numb
Thy arteries, and turn the guilty flowings
To trembling jelly in thy veins? Canst
hear
Me name that murder, and thy spirits
not
Struck into air, as thou wert shot by
some
Engine from heaven?
COL.        You are the duchess' champion!
    Thou hast given me a quarrel now. I
    grieve
    It is determined all must fight, and I
    Shall lose much honor in his fall.
HER.                              That duchess    40
(Whom but to mention with thy breath
    is sacrilege),
An orphan of thy making, and con-
demned
By thee to eternal solitude, I come
To vindicate; and, while I am killing
thee,
By virtue of her prayers sent up for
justice,
At the same time in heaven I am par-
doned for 't.
COL. I cannot hear the bravo.
HER.                              Two words more,
    And take your chance. Before you all I
    must
    Pronounce that noble lady without
    knowledge                                         49
    Or thought of what I undertake for her.

Poor soul, she's now at her devotions,
Busy with heaven, and wearing out the earth
With her stiff knees, and bribing her good angel
With treasures of her eyes, to tell her lord
How much she longs to see him. My attempt
Needs no commission from her. Were I
A stranger in Navarre, the inborn right
Of every gentleman to Alvarez' loss
Is reason to engage their swords and lives    59
Against the common enemy of virtue.
COL. Now have you finished? I have an instrument
Shall cure this noise, and fly up to thy tongue
To murder all thy words.
HER.                                  One little knot
Of phlegm, that clogs my stomach, and I ha' done:
You have an uncle, called a cardinal.
Would he were lurking now about thy heart,
That the same wounds might reach you both, and send
Your reeling souls together! Now have at you!
ALPH. We must not, sir, be idle.
        *They fight; Columbo's Second slain.*
HER. What think you now of praying?
COL.                                  Time enough.  70
        *He kills Hernando's Second.*
Commend me to my friend; the scales are even.
I would be merciful, and give you time
Now to consider of the other world;
You'll find your soul benighted presently.
HER. I'll find my way i' th' dark.
*They fight, and close; Columbo gets both the swords, and Hernando takes up the Second's weapon.*
COL.                                  A stumble's dangerous.
Now ask thy life. Ha!
HER.                        I despise to wear it,
A gift from any but the first bestower.
COL. I scorn a base advantage. Ha!
*Columbo throws away one of the swords.*
        *They fight; Hernando wounds Columbo.*
HER.                                  I am now
Out of your debt.

COL.        Th'ast done 't and I forgive thee.
Give me thy hand. When shall we meet again?    80
HER. Never, I hope.
COL. I feel life ebb apace, yet I'll look upwards,
And show my face to heaven.        [*Dies.*]
HER.                                  The matter's done;
I must not stay to bury him.        *Exit.*


ACT V. [SCENE i.

*A garden.*]

*Enter two Lords.*

1 Lo. Columbo's death doth much afflict the king.
2 Lo. I thought the cardinal would have lost his wits
At first, for 's nephew; it drowns all the talk
Of the other that were slain.
1 [Lo.]                        We are friends.
I do suspect Hernando had some interest,
And knew how their wounds came.
2 [Lo.]                        His flight confirms it,
For whom the cardinal has spread his nets.
1 [Lo.] He is not so weak to trust himself at home
To his enemy's gripe.
2 [Lo.]        All strikes not me so much
As that the duchess, most oppresséd lady,    10
Should be distracted, and before Columbo
Was slain.
1 [Lo.]        But that the cardinal should be made
Her guardian is to me above that wonder.
2 [Lo.] So it pleased the king; and she, with that small stock
Of reason left her, is so kind and smooth
Upon him.
1 [Lo.]        She's turned a child again. A madness,
That would ha' made her brain and blood boil high,
In which distemper she might ha' wrought something—
2 [Lo.] Had been to purpose.
1 [Lo.] The cardinal is cunning, and, howe'er    20

His brow does smile, he does suspect
  Hernando
Took fire from her, and waits a time to
  punish it.
2 [Lo.] But what a subject of disgrace and
  mirth
Hath poor Celinda made herself by pride,
In her belief Columbo was her servant! [1]
Her head hath stooped much since he
  died, and she
Almost ridiculous at court.

*Enter Cardinal, Antonelli, Servant.*

1 [Lo.]                              The cardinal
Is come into the garden, now—
CAR.                Walk off.—[*Exeunt Lords.*]
  It troubles me the duchess by her loss
Of brain is now beneath my great re-
  venge.                                    30
She is not capable to feel my anger,
Which, like to unregarded thunder spent
In woods, and lightning aimed at sense-
  less trees,
Must idly fall, and hurt her not, not to
That sense her guilt deserves. A fatal
  stroke,
Without the knowledge for what crime,
  to fright her
When she takes leave, and make her tug
  with death,
Until her soul sweat, is a pigeon's tor-
  ment,
And she is sent a babe to the other world.
Columbo's death will not be satisfied, 40
And I but wound her with a two-edged
  feather.
I must do more. I have all opportunity
(She by the king now made my charge),
  but she's
So much a turtle [2] I shall lose by killing
  her,
Perhaps do her a pleasure and prefer-
  ment;
That must not be.

*Enter Celinda with a parchment.*

ANT. [*Stopping her.*] Is not this she that
  would be thought to have been
Columbo's mistress? Madam, his grace
  is private,
And would not be disturbed; you may
  displease him.

[1] Admirer.    [2] Turtledove.    [3] Rumor.

CEL. What will your worship wager that
  he shall                                   50
Be pleased again before we part?
ANT. I'll lay this diamond, madam, gainst
  a kiss,
And trust yourself to keep the stakes.
CEL.                              'Tis done.
               [*Approaches the Cardinal.*]
ANT. [*Aside.*] I have long had an appe-
  tite to this lady;
But the lords keep her up so high—this
  toy
May bring her on.
CAR. This interruption tastes not of good
  manners.
CEL. But where necessity, my lord, com-
  pels,
The boldness may meet pardon, and,
  when you
Have found my purpose, I may less ap-
  pear                                       60
Unmannerly.
CAR.            To th' business.
CEL.                        It did please
Your nephew, sir, before his death, to
  credit me
With so much honorable favor, I
Am come to tender to his near'st of blood,
Yourself, what does remain a debt to him.
Not to delay your grace with circum-
  stance,
That deed, if you accept, makes you my
  heir
Of no contemptible estate.    *He reads.*
  —[*Aside.*] This way
Is only left to tie up scurrile tongues
And saucy men, that since Columbo's
  death                                      70
Venture to libel on my pride and folly;
His greatness and this gift, which I enjoy
Still for my life (beyond which term a
  kingdom's
Nothing), will curb the giddy spleens of
  men
That live on impudent rhyme, and railing
  at
Each wandering fame[3] they catch.
CAR.                        Madam, this bounty
Will bind my gratitude and care to serve
  you.
CEL. I am your grace's servant.
CAR.                        Antonelli! *Whisper.*
And, when this noble lady visits me,
Let her not wait.                            80

CEL. [*Aside.*] What think you, my offi-
    cious sir? His grace
Is pleased, you may conjecture. I may
    keep
Your gem; the kiss was never yours.
ANT. [*Aside.*]                    Sweet madam—
CEL. [*Aside.*] Talk if you dare; you know
    I must not wait.
And so, farewell for this time.      [*Exit.*]
CAR. 'Tis in my brain already, and it forms
    Apace—good, excellent revenge, and
    pleasant!
She's now within my talons; 'tis too
    cheap
A satisfaction for Columbo's death,   89
Only to kill her by soft charm or force.
I'll rifle first her darling chastity;
'Twill be after time enough to poison her,
And she to th' world be thought her own
    destroyer.
As I will frame the circumstance, this
    night
All may be finished; for the colonel,
Her agent in my nephew's death (whom I
Disturbed at counsel with her), I may
    reach him
Hereafter, and be master of his fate.
*We starve our conscience when we thrive in*
    *state.*                         *Exeunt.*


[SCENE ii.

*A room in the duchess' palace.*]

*Enter Secretary and Placentia.*

SEC. Placentia, we two are only left
Of my lady's servants; let us be true
To her and one another, and be sure,
When we are at prayers, to curse the
    cardinal.
PLA. I pity my sweet lady.
SEC. I pity her too, but am a little angry;
She might have found another time to
    lose
Her wits.
PLA.       That I were a man!
SEC.               What wouldst thou do,
    Placentia?
PLA.               I would revenge my lady.
SEC. 'Tis better being a woman; thou
    mayst do                          10
Things that may prosper better, and the
    fruit
Be thy own another day.

PLA.                       Your wit still loves
To play the wanton.
SEC.               'Tis a sad time, Placentia
Some pleasure would do well. The truth
    is, I
Am weary of my life, and I would have
One fit of mirth before I leave the world.
PLA. Do not you blush to talk thus wildly?
SEC. 'Tis good manners
To be a little mad after my lady.       15
But I ha' done. Who is with her now?
PLA. Madam Valeria.
SEC. Not Celinda? There's a lady for my
    humor!
A pretty book of flesh and blood, and well
Bound up, in a fair letter too. Would I
Had her with all the errata!
PLA.                       She has not
An honorable fame.
SEC.               Her fame? That's nothing;
A little stain; her wealth will fetch again
The color, and bring honor into her
    cheeks
As fresh. If she were mine, and I had
    her
Exchequer, I know the way to make her
    honest—                          30
Honest to th' touch, the test, and the
    last trial.
PLA. How, prithee?
SEC. Why, first I would marry her—that's
    a verb material;
Then I would print her with an *index*
*Expurgatorius*, a table drawn
Of her court heresies; and, when she's
    read
*Cum privilegio*,[1] who dares call her whore?
PLA. I'll leave you, if you talk thus.
SEC.                       I ha' done.
Placentia, thou mayst be better com-
    pany
After another progress;[2] and now, tell
    me,                              40
Didst ever hear of such a patient mad-
    ness
As my lady is possessed with? She has
    raved
But twice; and she would fright the
    cardinal,
Or at a supper if she did but poison
    him,
It were a frenzy I could bear withal.
She calls him her dear governor—
———————————————————
[1] With license.          [2] Royal excursion.

*Enter Hernando disguised, having a letter.*

PLA.                                Who is this?
HER.  Her secretary!—Sir,
  Here is a letter, if it may have so
  Much happiness to kiss her grace's hand.
SEC.  From whom?
HER.            That's not in your commis-
    sion, sir,                                    50
  To ask, or mine to satisfy; she will
    want
  No understanding when she reads.
SEC.                                    Alas!
  Under your favor, sir, you are mistaken;
  Her grace did never more want under-
    standing.
HER.  How?
SEC.  Have you not heard?  Her skull is
    broken, sir,
  And many pieces taken out; she's mad.
HER.  The sad fame of her distraction
  Has too much truth, it seems.
PLA.                    If please you, sir,
  To expect awhile, I will present the
    letter.                                        60
HER.  Pray, do.—            *Exit Placen[tia].*
  How long has she been thus distempered,
    sir?
SEC.  Before the cardinal came to govern
    here,
  Who, for that reason, by the king was
    made
  Her guardian.  We are now at his devo-
    tion.[1]
HER.  A lamb given up to a tiger!  May
    diseases
  Soon eat him through his heart!
SEC.                        Your pardon, sir.
  I love that voice; I know it too a little.
  Are not you—be not angry, noble sir;
  I can with ease be ignorant again,       70
  And think you are another man; but, if
  You be that valiant gentleman they
    call—
HER.  Whom?  What?
SEC.  That killed—I would not name him,
    if I thought
  You were not pleased to be that very
    gentleman.
HER.  Am I betrayed?
SEC.        The devil sha' not
  Betray you here.  Kill me, and I will take
  My death you are the noble colonel.

We are all bound to you for the general's
    death,                                          80
  Valiant Hernando!  When my lady knows
  You are here, I hope 'twill fetch her
    wits again.
  But do not talk too loud; we are not all
  Honest[2] i' th' house; some are the car-
    dinal's creatures.
HER.  Thou wert faithful to thy lady.  I
    am glad
  'Tis night.  But tell me how the church-
    man uses
  The duchess.

*Enter Antonelli.*

SEC.  He carries angels in his tongue and
    face, but I
  Suspect his heart.  This is one of his
    spawns.—
  Signior Antonelli.
ANT.                    Honest Antonio!  90
SEC.  And how, and how—a friend of mine
    —where is
  The cardinal's grace?
HER.  [*Aside.*]      That will be never an-
    swered.
ANT.  He means to sup here with the duch-
    ess.
SEC.        Will he?
ANT.  We'll have the charming bottles at
    my chamber.
  Bring that gentleman; we'll be mighty
    merry.
HER.  [*Aside.*]  I may disturb your jollity.
ANT.                    Farewell, sweet—[*Exit.*]
SEC.  Dear Antonelli!—[*Aside.*]  A round[3]
    pox confound you!
  This is court rhetoric at the back stairs.

*Enter Placentia.*

PLA.  Do you know this gentleman?
SEC.                                Not I.
PLA.  My lady presently dismissed Va-
    leria,                                         100
  And bade me bring him to her bed-
    chamber.
SEC.  The gentleman has an honest face.
PLA.                            Her words
  Fell from her with some evenness and
    joy.—
  Her grace desired your presence.

---

[1] Power of disposal.               [2] Loyal.               [3] Thorough.

HER.                        I'll attend her.
                    *Exit* [*with Placentia*].
SEC. I would this soldier had the cardinal
Upon a promontory. With what a spring
The churchman would leap down! It
    were a spectacle
Most rare to see him topple from the
    precipice,
And souse in the salt water with a noise
To stun the fishes; and, if he fell into    110
A net, what wonder would the simple
    sea gulls
Have, to draw up the o'ergrown lobster,[1]
So ready boiled! He shall have my good
    wishes.
This colonel's coming may be lucky; I
Will be sure none shall interrupt 'em.

                *Enter Celinda.*

CEL.                                      Is
    Her grace at opportunity?
SEC.                        No, sweet madam;
    She is asleep, her gentlewoman says.
CEL. My business is but visit. I'll expect.
SEC. That must not be, although I like
    your company.                          119
CEL. You are grown rich, Mr. Secretary.
SEC. I, madam? Alas!
CEL. I hear you are upon another pur-
    chase.
SEC. I upon a purchase?
CEL.            If you want any sum—
SEC. If I could purchase your sweet favor,
    madam?
CEL. You shall command me, and my
    fortune, sir.
SEC. [*Aside.*] How's this?
CEL.        I have observed you, sir, a staid
    And prudent gentleman—and I shall
    want—
SEC. Not me?
CEL. (*Aside.*)  A father for some infant.
    He has credit
    I' th' world.  I am not the first cast
        lady                              130
    Has married a secretary.
SEC. Shall I wait upon you?
CEL.                        Whither?
SEC.                        Any whither.
CEL. I may chance lead you then—
SEC. I shall be honored to obey. My blood
    Is up, and in this humor I'm for any-
        thing.

[1] An allusion to the color of the cardinal's robes.

CEL. Well, sir, I'll try your manhood.
SEC.                        'Tis my happiness;
    You cannot please me better.
CEL. [*Aside.*]                This was struck
    I' th' opportunity.
SEC.                I am made forever.
                                [*Exeunt.*]

                [SCENE iii.

        *Another room in the same.*]

        *Enter Hernando and Duchess.*

HER. Dear madam, do not weep.
DUCH.                Y' are very welcome.
    I ha' done; I wo' not shed a tear more
    Till I meet Alvarez; then I'll weep for
        joy.
    He was a fine young gentleman, and sung
        sweetly;
    And you had heard him but the night
        before
    We were married, you would ha' sworn
        he had been
    A swan, and sung his own sad epitaph.
    But we'll talk o' the cardinal.
HER.                    Would his death
    Might ransom your fair sense! He should
        not live
    To triumph in the loss. Beshrow[2] my
        manhood,                          10
    But I begin to melt.
DUCH.                I pray, sir, tell me,
    For I can understand, although they say
    I have lost my wits; but they are safe
        enough,
    And I shall have 'em when the cardinal
        dies,
    Who had a letter from his nephew, too,
    Since he was slain.
HER.                From whence?
DUCH. I know not where he is. But in
        some bower
    Within a garden he is making chaplets,
    And means to send me one; but I'll not
        take it;
    I have flowers enough, I thank him,
        while I live.                     20
HER. But do you love your governor?
DUCH. Yes, but I'll never marry him; I am
        promised
    Already.
HER.        To whom, madam?

[2] Beshrew, curse.

Duch.                                Do not you
  Blush when you ask me that? Must not
    you be
  My husband? I know why, but that's a
    secret.
  Indeed, if you believe me, I do love
  No man alive so well as you. The cardi-
    nal
  Shall never know 't; he'll kill us both; and
    yet
  He says he loves me dearly, and has
    promised                                    29
  To make me well again. But I'm afraid
  One time or other he will give me poison.
Her. Prevent him, madam, and take
  nothing from him.
Duch. Why, do you think 'twill hurt me?
Her.                              It will kill you.
Duch. I shall but die, and meet my dear-
  loved lord,
  Whom, when I have kissed, I'll come
    again and work
  A bracelet of my hair for you to carry
    him,
  When you are going to heaven; the
    poesy [1] shall
  Be my own name, in little tears, that I
  Will weep next winter, which, congealed
    i' th' frost,
  Will show like seed pearl. You'll deliver
    it?                                          40
  I know he'll love and wear it for my sake.
Her. She is quite lost.
Duch.                    I pray, give me, sir, your
  pardon.
  I know I talk not wisely; but, if you
    had
  The burthen of my sorrow, you would
    miss
  Sometimes your better reason. Now I'm
    well.
  What will you do when the cardinal
    comes?
  He must not see you for the world.
Her                              He sha' not;
  I'll take my leave before he come.
Duch.                                Nay, stay;
  I shall have no friend left me when you
    go.
  He will but sup; he sha' not stay to lie
    wi' me.                                      50
  I have the picture of my lord abed;
  Three are too much this weather.

[1] Posy, inscription.

*Enter Placentia.*

Pla.                            Madam, the cardinal.
Her. He shall sup with the devil.
Duch.                            I dare not stay;
  The red cock [2] will be angry. I'll come
    again. *Exeunt [Duchess and Placentia].*
Her. This sorrow is no fable. Now I find
  My curiosity is sadly satisfied.—
  Ha! If the duchess in her straggled wits
  Let fall words to betray me to the car-
    dinal,
  The panther will not leap more fierce to
    meet
  His prey, when a long want of food hath
    parchèd                                      60
  His starvèd maw, than he to print his
    rage,
  And tear my heartstrings. Everything
    is fatal;
  And yet she talked sometimes with chain
    of sense,
  And said she loved me. Ha! They come
    not yet.
  I have a sword about me, and I left
  My own security to visit death.
  Yet I may pause a little, and consider
  Which way does lead me to 't most hon
    orably.
  Does not the chamber that I walk in
    tremble?                                     69
  What will become of her, and me, and all
  The world in one small hour? I do not
    think
  Ever to see the day again; the wings
  Of night spread o'er me like a sable
    hearsecloth;
  The stars are all close[3] mourners too; but I
  Must not alone to the cold, silent grave,
  I must not.—If thou canst, Alvarez, open
  That ebon curtain, and behold the man,
  When the world's justice fails, shall right
    thy ashes,
  And feed their thirst with blood! Thy
    duchess is                                   79
  Almost a ghost already, and doth wear
  Her body like a useless upper garment,
  The trim and fashion of it lost.—Ha!

*Enter Placentia.*

Pla. You need not doubt me, sir. My lady
  prays
  You would not think it long; she in my
    ear

[2] *I.e.*, the cardinal.          [3] Secret, silent.

Commanded me to tell you that, when last

She drank, she had happy wishes to your health.

HER. And did the cardinal pledge it?

PLA.            He was not

Invited to 't, nor must he know you are here.

HER. What do they talk of, prithee?

PLA. His grace is very pleasant    90

            *A lute is heard.*

And kind to her; but her returns [1] are after

The sad condition of her sense, sometimes Unjointed.

HER.        They have music.

PLA.            A lute only.

His grace prepared, they say, the best of Italy,

That waits upon my lord.

HER.           He thinks the duchess

Is stung with a tarantula.

PLA.           Your pardon;

My duty is expected.        *Exit.*

HER.           Gentle lady!—

A voice too?

            SONG *(within)*

STRE. Come, my Daphne, come away;
      We do waste the crystal day.    100
      'Tis Strephon calls.

DA.           What says my love?

STRE. Come, follow to the myrtle grove,
      Where Venus shall prepare
      New chaplets for thy hair.

DA.    Were I shut up within a tree,
      I'd rend my bark to follow thee.

STRE. My shepherdess, make haste;
      The minutes slide too fast.

DA.    In those cooler shades will I,
      Blind as Cupid, kiss thine eye.   110

STRE. In thy bosom then I'll stay;
      In such warm snow who would not
          lose his way?

CHOR. We'll laugh, and leave the world
          behind,
      And gods themselves that see,
      Shall envy thee and me,
      But never find
      Such joys, when they embrace a
          deity.

[HER.] If at this distance I distinguish, 'tis not

Church music; and the air's wanton, and no anthem

[1] *Replies.*

Sung to 't, but some strange ode of love and kisses.       120

What should this mean?—Ha, he is coming hither.

I am betrayed; he marches in her hand.

I'll trust a little more; mute as the arras,

My sword and I here.

     [*With drawn sword*] *he observes.*

*Enter Cardinal, Duchess, Antonelli, and*
                 *Attendants.*

CAR. Wait you in the first chamber, and let none

Presume to interrupt us.—

           *Ex[eunt] Serv[ants].*

         [*Aside.*] She is pleasant;

Now for some art to poison all her innocence.

DUCH. [*Aside.*] I do not like the cardinal's humor; he

Little suspects what guest is in my chamber.       129

CAR. Now, madam, you are safe.

           [*Embraces her.*]

DUCH.       How means your lordship?

CAR. Safe in my arms, sweet duchess.

DUCH.          Do not hurt me.

CAR. Not for the treasures of the world!
     You are

My pretty charge. Had I as many lives

As I have careful thoughts to do you service,

I should think all a happy forfeit to

Delight your grace one minute; 'tis a heaven

To see you smile.

DUCH.       What kindness call you this?

CAR. It cannot want a name while you preserve

So plentiful a sweetness; it is love.

DUCH. Of me? How shall I know 't, my lord?       140

CAR. By this, and this, swift messengers to whisper

Our hearts to one another.     *Kisses.*

DUCH. Pray, do you come a-wooing?

CAR.          Yes, sweet madam;

You cannot be so cruel to deny me.

DUCH. What, my lord?

CAR.          Another kiss.

DUCH.          Can you

Dispense with this, my lord?—(*Aside.*)
     Alas, I fear

Hernando is asleep, or vanished from me.

CAR. [*Aside.*] I have mocked my blood
　into a flame; and what
My angry soul had formed for my re-
　venge                                       149
Is now the object of my amorous sense.
I have took a strong enchantment from
　her lips,
And fear I shall forgive Columbo's death,
If she consent to my embrace.—Come,
　madam.
DUCH. Whither, my lord?
CAR.　　　　　But to your bed or couch,
Where, if you will be kind, and but
　allow
Yourself a knowledge, Love, whose shape
　and raptures
Wise poets have but glorified in dreams,
Shall make your chamber his eternal
　palace,
And with such active and essential
　streams
Of new delights glide o'er your bosom,
　you                                          160
Shall wonder to what unknown world you
　are
By some blessed change translated. Why
　d'e pause,
And look so wild? Will you deny your
　governor?
DUCH. How came you by that cloven foot?
CAR.　　　　　　　　Your fancy
Would turn a traitor to your happiness.
I am your friend; you must be kind.
DUCH.　　　　　　　Unhand me,
Or I'll cry out a rape.
CAR.　　　　　　You wo' not, sure?
DUCH. I have been cozened with Her-
　nando's shadow;
Here's none but heaven to hear me.—
　Help! A rape!
CAR. Are you so good at understanding?
　Then,                                        170
I must use other argument.
　*He forces her.* [*Hernando rushes forth.*]
HER. Go to, cardinal!
　　　*Strikes him. Ex[it] Duch[ess].*
CAR. Hernando? Murder! Treason!
　Help!
HER. An army sha' not rescue thee. Your
　blood
Is much inflamed; I have brought a
　lancet wi' me
Shall open your hot veins, and cool your
　fever.

To vex thy parting soul, it was the same
Engine that pinced[1] Columbo's heart.
CAR.　　　　　　　Help! Murder!
　　　　　　[*Hernando stabs him.*]

　　*Enter Antonelli and Servants.*
ANT. Some ring the bell; 'twill raise the
　court.                                       179
My lord is murdered! 'Tis Hernando!
　　　　　　　　*The bell rings.*
HER. I'll make you all some sport.—[*Stabs
　himself.*] So; now we are even.
Where is the duchess? I would take my
　leave
Of her, and then bequeath my curse
　among you.　　　*Her[nando] falls.*

*Enter King, Duchess, Valeria, Lords,
　　　　　　　　　　　Guard.*
KING. How come these bloody objects?
HER. With a trick my sword found out. I
　hope he's paid.
1 Lo. [*Aside.*] I hope so too.—A surgeon
　for my Lord Cardinal!
KING. Hernando?
DUCH. Justice! O, justice, sir, against a
　ravisher!
HER. Sir, I ha' done you service.
KING.　　　　　　A bloody service.
HER. 'Tis pure scarlet.                        190

　　　*Enter Surgeon.*
CAR. [*Aside.*] After such care to perfect
　my revenge,
Thus banded[2] out o' th' world by a
　woman's plot!
HER. I have preserved the duchess from a
　rape.
Good night to me and all the world
　forever.　　　　　　　*Dies.*
KING. So impious!
DUCH.　　　'Tis most true; Alvarez' blood
Is now revenged; I find my brain return,
And every straggling sense repairing
　home.
CAR. I have deserved you should turn from
　me, sir.
My life hath been prodigiously wicked;
My blood is now the kingdom's balm.
　O, sir,                                       200

[1] Pinched, wounded.
[2] Bandied.

I have abused your ear, your trust, your people,
And my own sacred office; my conscience
Feels now the sting. O, show your charity,
And with your pardon, like a cool, soft gale,
Fan my poor sweating soul, that wanders through
Unhabitable climes and parchéd deserts.
But I am lost, if the great world forgive me,
Unless I find your mercy for a crime
You know not, madam, yet, against your life,
I must confess, more than my black intents          210
Upon your honor; y' are already poisoned.

KING. By whom?
CAR. By me,
In the revenge I owed Columbo's loss.
With your last meat was mixed a poison that
By subtle and by sure degrees must let In death.
KING.          Look to the duchess, our physicians!
CAR. Stay! I will deserve her mercy, though I cannot
Call back the deed. In proof of my repentance,          219
If the last breath of a now dying man
May gain your charity and belief, receive
This ivory box; in it an antidote
'Bove that they boast the great magistral [1] medicine.
That powder, mixed with wine, by a most rare
And quick access to the heart, will fortify it
Against the rage of the most nimble poison.
I am not worthy to present her with it.
O, take it, and preserve her innocent life.
1 Lo. Strange, he should have a good thing in such readiness.
CAR. 'Tis that, which in my jealousy and state,          230
Trusting to false predictions of my birth,
That I should die by poison, I preserved

[1] Sovereign, effectual.

For my own safety. Wonder not I made
That my companion was to be my refuge.

*Enter Servant with a bowl of wine.*

1 Lo. Here's some touch of grace.
CAR. In greater proof of my pure thoughts, I take
This first, and with my dying breath confirm
My penitence; it may benefit her life,
But not my wounds. [*He drinks.*] O, hasten to preserve her;
And, though I merit not her pardon, let not          240
Her fair soul be divorced.
                              [*The Duchess drinks.*]
KING. This is some charity; may it prosper, madam!
VAL. How does your grace?
DUCH. And must I owe my life to him whose death
Was my ambition? Take this free acknowledgment;
I had intent this night with my own hand
To be Alvarez' justicer.
KING.                    You were mad,
And thought past apprehension of revenge.
DUCH. That shape I did usurp, great sir, to give
My art more freedom and defense; but, when          250
Hernando came to visit me, I thought
I might defer my execution,
Which his owe [2] rage supplied without my guilt,
And, when his lust grew high, met with his blood.
1 Lo. The cardinal smiles.
CAR.                    Now my revenge has met
With you, my nimble duchess! I have took
A shape [3] to give my act more freedom too,
And now I am sure she's poisoned with that dose
I gave her last.
KING.          Th' art not so horrid?
DUCH. Ha, some cordial!
CAR.          Alas, no preservative          260
Hath wings to overtake it. Were her heart

[2] Own.          [3] Disguise, trick.

Locked in a quarry, it would search and
     kill
Before the aids can reach it. I am sure
You sha' not now laugh at me.
KING. How came you by that poison?
CAR.                              I prepared it,
Resolving, when I had enjoyed her,
     which
The colonel prevented, by some art
To make her take it, and by death con-
     clude
My last revenge. You have the fatal
     story.
KING. This is so great a wickedness it
     will                                         270
Exceed belief.
CAR.              I knew I could not live.
SURG. Your wounds, sir, were not desper-
     ate.
CAR.        Not mortal?
Ha, were they not mortal?
SURG.               If I have skill in surgery.
CAR. Then I have caught myself in my
     own engine.
2 LO. It was your fate, you said, to die by
     poison.
CAR. That was my own prediction to
     abuse
Your faith. No human art can now re-
     sist it;
I feel it knocking at the seat of life;
It must come in. I have wracked all my
     own
To try your charities. Now it would be
     rare                                         280
If you but waft me with a little prayer;
My wings that flag may catch the wind,
     but 'tis
In vain; the mist is risen, and there's
     none
To steer my wand'ring bark.      *Dies.*
1 LO.                    He's dead.
KING.                       With him
Die all deceivéd trust.
2 LO. This was a strange impiety.
KING.                       When men
Of gifts and sacred function once de-
     cline
From virtue, their ill deeds transcend
     example.
DUCH. The minute's come that I must
     take my leave, too.
Your hand, great sir; and, though you
     be a king,                                   290

We may exchange forgiveness. Heaven
     forgive,
And all the world! I come, I come,
     Alvarez!                          *Dies.*
KING. Dispose their bodies for becoming
     funeral.
How much are kings abused by those
     they take
To royal grace, whom, when they cherish
     most
By nice[1] indulgence, they do often arm
Against themselves, from whence this
     maxim springs:
*None have more need of perspectives than*
     *kings.*                          *Exeunt.*

## EPILOGUE

[VOICE.] (*Within.*) Mr. Pollard! Where's
     Mr. Pollard, for the epilogue?
*He is thrust upon the stage, and falls.*
EPI. [*Rising.*] I am coming to you, gentle-
     men; the poet
Has helped me thus far on my way, but
     I'll
Be even with him: the play is a tragedy,
The first that ever he composed for us,
Wherein he thinks he has done prettily,

*Enter Servant.*

And I am sensible.[2]—I prithee, look.
Is nothing out of joint? Has he broke
     nothing?
SERV. No, sir, I hope.
EPI. Yes, he has broke his epilogue all to
     pieces.                                       10
Canst thou put it together again?
SERV.                       Not I, sir.
EPI. Nor I. Prithee, begone!—[*Exit Serv-*
     *ant.*] Hum!—Mr. Poet,
I have a teeming mind to be revenged.—
[*To audience.*] You may assist, and not
     be seen in 't now,
If you please, gentlemen, for I do know
He listens to the issue of his cause;
But blister not your hands in his ap-
     plause,
Your private smile, your nod, or hum,
     to tell
My fellows that you like the business
     well.                                         19
And, when without a clap you go away,

_____
[1] Foolish.                    [2] Satisfied.

I'll drink a small beer health to his
   second day,
And break his heart, or make him swear
   and rage
He'll write no more for the unhappy
   stage.

But that's too much; so we should lose.[1]
   Faith, shew it,
And, if you like his play, 't 's as well he
   knew it.

FINIS.

[1] *I.e.*, lose our livelihood.